W9-CRA-699

Italian Foreign Policy

GIOVANNI AGNELLI FOUNDATION SERIES
IN ITALIAN HISTORY

In recent decades Italian historians and social scientists have produced a broad range of profound and subtle works that merit wide reception among an English-speaking readership. The Giovanni Agnelli Foundation Series in Italian History was formed to ensure the wide distribution of these works in English translation. Together, the Giovanni Agnelli Foundation and Princeton University Press will publish a number of key works that illuminate Italian history and national development and serve as some of the best specimens of a rich historiographical and interpretive tradition. In so doing, the series will promote a more realistic, complete, and balanced understanding of Italian history, and hence modern Italian culture and society, in the English-speaking world.

Editorial Advisory Committee,
the Giovanni Agnelli Foundation Series in Italian History

Gabriele de Rosa, Professor of Modern History, University of Rome

Giuseppe Galasso, Professor of Medieval and Modern History, University of Naples

Adrian Lyttelton, Professor of History, University of Pisa

Charles S. Maier, Professor of History, Harvard University

Massimo Salvadori, Professor of History, University of Turin

Ideological Profile of Twentieth-Century Italy, by Norberto Bobbio; translated by Lydia G. Cochrane

Italian Foreign Policy: The Statecraft of the Founders, by Federico Chabod; translated by William McCuaig

Federico Chabod

Italian Foreign Policy

THE STATECRAFT OF THE FOUNDERS

• TRANSLATED BY WILLIAM McCUAIG •

GIOVANNI AGNELLI FOUNDATION
SERIES IN ITALIAN HISTORY

PRINCETON UNIVERSITY PRESS

PRINCETON, NEW JERSEY

Copyright © 1996 by Princeton University Press
Translated from *Storia della Politica Estera Italiana dal 1870 al 1896.* First published in 1951.
This translation is based on the following edition: Bari: editori Laterza, 1990; ISBN
88-420-3595-5.
Published by Princeton University Press, 41 William Street,
Princeton, New Jersey 08540
In the United Kingdom: Princeton University Press, Chichester, West Sussex
All Rights Reserved

Library of Congress Cataloging-in-Publication Data

Chabod, Federico.
[Storia della politica estera italiana dal 1870 al 1896. English]
Italian foreign policy : the statecraft of the founders /
Federico Chabod ; translated by William McCuaig.
p.   cm. — (Giovanni Agnelli Foundation series in Italian history)
Includes bibliographical references and index.
ISBN 0-691-04451-1 (cloth : alk. paper) — ISBN 0-691-04450-3 (pbk. : alk. paper)
1. Italy—Foreign relations—1870–1915.   I. Title.   II. Series.
DG564.C43   1995   327.45—dc20   95-489

This book has been composed in Times Roman.

Princeton University Press books are printed on acid-free paper
and meet the guidelines for permanence and durability of the
Committee on Production Guidelines for Book Longevity of the
Council on Library Resources

Printed in the United States of America

1   3   5   7   9   10   8   6   4   2

1   3   5   7   9   10   8   6   4   2

· *FOR JEANNE* ·

$\bullet \quad C \quad O \quad N \quad T \quad E \quad N \quad T \quad S \quad \bullet$

F O R E W O R D   T O
• T H E   S E R I E S   B Y •
C H A R L E S   S.   M A I E R

WHAT is the value of reading modern Italian history? What lessons might Americans, and an English-language public more generally, derive from Italy's national experience and its historians' interpretation of that experience? What approaches to historical study can their outstanding works propose that we might not have already learned from the *mentalités* analyzed by the French, the documentation of class and elite politics contributed by the British, or the earnest archival scrutiny and national reassessment on the part of the Germans? To be sure, these questions presuppose an *American* reader or at least a reader oriented in his or her own national narrative. But the point is that Americans, including the historians among us, have had comparatively little opportunity to read the landmark postwar works of modern Italian history. A few books have made their mark in recent decades, for example the superbly erudite studies of the late Franco Venturi on the Enlightenment era, which this press has already begun to publish in translation. Studies of popular culture during earlier epochs, preeminently those of Carlo Ginzburg, have become celebrated as part of an international historiography that has reevoked the world of rural Europe. But the Italians' interpretation of their own experience as a unified nation, or their vigorous study of long-term and recent economic development have remained largely unknown outside specialist circles. For most Americans, Italian history has been mediated through gorgeous films: Visconti's *Leopard,* Olmi's *Tree of Wooden Clogs,* Fellini's *Amarcord,* Bertolucci's *Conformist* or *1900.* Historical prose, though, deserves its own chance.

The conviction that the Italian tradition of history writing deserves a wider international and English-language public has prompted the Giovanni Agnelli Foundation of Turin, together with Princeton University Press, to translate and publish some key works of modern Italian historiography. The Agnelli Foundation has long nurtured programs to diffuse knowledge of Italian culture outside Italy, including "La Biblioteca Italiana," the distribution abroad of important works in Italian. Princeton University Press takes pride in its continuing publication of monographs in Italian history by American authors and a limited number of translations by important authors. They have combined efforts to select, translate, and publish other works that promise to be especially rewarding. A committee of historians, Italian- and English-speaking, convened to decide on priority of titles and, further, to plan some thematic anthologies of outstanding articles and key primary documents. The series starts with three diverse works, revealing the broad range of historical discussion, and will, it is hoped, continue with others that introduce the history of Catholic and Socialist political movements.

The initial translations include the intellectual sketch of twentieth-century Italian political currents by Italy's preeminent post-war political writer—perhaps better described as public moralist—Norberto Bobbio. Bobbio (b. 1909) has brought his encyclopaedic reading of Western political and legal theory to bear on the conditions of post-war politics, especially from the turbulence of the late 1960s to the recent sea change in Italian politics. The Press will also issue Emilio Sereni's historical survey of patterns of settlement in Italy since antiquity. Sereni's work is one of the most distinguished examples of the Marxian historiography that constituted a fundamental strand of Italian historical and political culture for over four decades after the Second World War. It also continues the notable tradition of Italian intellectuals' critical scrutiny of their rural society, which began in the Enlightenment and was carried on by conservative and democratic reformers after national unification. Finally this first "triptych" includes what may be the most luminous work in the Italian neo-historicist tradition: Federico Chabod's profound study of the aspirations and concepts of the founders of Italian statehood, preoccupied with establishing their fragile but ambitious new nation in the comity of rival great powers.

These works exemplify different disciplinary and ideological approaches to history. Bobbio began as a student of philosophy and law. In continental Europe that meant for his generation, who completed their studies between the wars, a far less technical education than American legal training suggests. Law faculties have sheltered the historians of public institutions and political theorists. History and political science departments have traditionally maintained specialists in the history of political doctrines and parties. Bobbio addresses those familiar with these diverse approaches as well as the general reader. He has focused increasingly on the long experiment in postwar Italian democracy of which he has been, simultaneously, a public critic and exponent.[1]

Emilio Sereni (1907–77), as R. Burr Litchfield's introduction to the *History of the Italian Landscape* points out, was one of the remarkable small, Italian Jewish intellectual elite, who have contributed so powerfully to culture, economy, and politics in the twentieth century.[2] Even more notably Sereni was trained in agriculture and concerned with the long history of the shaped environment in Italy over the millennia. His works exemplify the premises of Italian Marxism, which ever since the massive impact exerted by Community Party theorist Antonio Gramsci, has concentrated on the peculiar obstacles to Italian historical progress allegedly posed by the power of Southern landlords allied with Northern industrialists. Sereni, in fact, represents a longer tradition of critics, conservative as well as liberal or Marxist, who have confronted the agricultural problems of Italy as the major constraint on political justice and economic development. Despite Sereni's intense ideological commitment, his historical sensibility is not neatly

---

[1] In addition to Massimo Salvadori's introduction to the volume, see Perry Anderson's 1988 appreciation, "The Affinities of Norberto Bobbio," in Anderson, *A Zone of Engagement* (London: Verso, 1992), pp. 87–129.

[2] For an introduction to this milieu, see H. Stuart Hughes, *Prisoners of Hope: The Silver Age of the Italian Jews, 1924–1974* (Cambridge, Mass.: Harvard University Press, 1983).

contained in a political framework. Like Marc Bloch, the great French medieval-
ist two decades his senior, Sereni communicates an emotional attachment to the
shaped landscape—the interaction of dwellers on the land with the variable resources of soil and water, forest, plain, and uplands that they were given to
exploit. Perhaps, too, both historians' intense patriotism as assimilated Jews
strengthened the cathexis to their national terrains—an emotional pull that could,
displaced in objective, lead Sereni's Zionist brother to Palestine. And if Sereni
and Bloch might share conservatives' love of local countryside, as democrats and
historians they remained far more clearsighted about the continuing patterns of
social domination and hierarchy that organized settlement.

Finally the Agnelli series offers the principal modern work of Federico Chabod
(1901–60), who must rank, along with Franco Venturi (1914–94), as one of
Italy's preeminent academic historians of the twentieth century. Chabod produced important studies of Machiavelli and the Renaissance as well as the magisterial and original work of international history that we publish in this series.
Italian Foreign Policy was crafted not as a diplomatic narrative, but as an exploration of the agendas for state-building among the national founders. Chabod
focuses on their differing orientations toward potential allies, whether the conservative powers of Central Europe or liberal France and Britain, on their awareness
of national vulnerability, and their concern, as democrats, conservatives, or
would-be nationalist authoritarians, with the resources of civic culture and public
opinion. If Marc Bloch serves as a non-Italian pendant for Sereni, Chabod might
usefully be contrasted with the German historians of state-building, either
Friedrich Meinecke of an older generation, or the critical researchers of the
1960s such as Fritz Fischer or Hans-Ulrich Wehler. Like Meinecke—indeed as
an intellectual heir of German idealist historical culture—Chabod focuses on the
national project as an expression of powerful developing ideas. But he never
assigns the Italian nation-state a teleological role; neither does he grade his protagonists according to their national commitment; nor unlike the later Meinecke
does he propose a chronicle of *raison d'état* that fatalistically dictates national
Realpolitik. On the other hand, Chabod has little interest in exploring the economic and class variables that help to shape differing prescriptions for foreign
policy and which historians influenced by social democracy or orthodox Marxism would emphasize in the 1960s and after. As with all neo-historicist accounts
that seek to place the reader empathetically within the mind of the protagonists,
there is danger of mystification. The apparently serene and lofty mastery of written texts can obscure a welter of personal rivalries and material interests. Nonetheless, Chabod is hardly uncritical; he must ask why state-building led, at least
temporarily, to a fascist outcome; and his perspective remains so cosmopolitan
and encompassing that it reveals far more than it might obscure. Without self-
conscious rhetoric it renews international history with intellectual and cultural
analysis.

It is fitting that two of these writers should have Piedmontese roots, given the
Agnelli Foundation and the Fiat firm's own roots in Turin. Turin has long pro-

duced a rather proud community of intellectuals nurtured by the city's syncretic traditions. A dynamic industrial culture and a politically mobilized industrial labor force long allowed an interaction among market-oriented liberals and young democratic and Marxist intellectuals. But to what degree can these works be viewed as exemplifying a characteristically Italian national historiographical approach? Can one find categories to compare the historical output of the past half century in Italy with that, say, of France or Germany, Britain or the United States? It would be too facile to identify a single national tradition. The historians chosen here—who represent a generation that achieved its influence after the War but not in the most recent transformations—are less of a university-based cohort than some of the younger contributors. They present work less as a part of a group effort or enterprise than as monuments of a broader effort to define a national culture. How might we characterize their output, and that of related great scholars whose work is already translated, in comparison with scholars elsewhere?

For one thing, the works we have chosen are in effect in deep dialogue with key debates about the nature of Italian political society. Each of the writers in this first tranche of authors—Bobbio, Chabod, and Sereni—had to conceive his work in the aftermath of Italy's twenty-year acceptance, indeed invention, of fascism. No developmental trend might be discussed that did not pose the issue of what long-term vulnerability might afflict national politics, and conversely, what long-term strengths could be drawn upon. To be sure, German historians such as Hajo Holborn or Hans Rosenberg, who had migrated to the United States, or Theodore Schieder, posed similar questions with respect to Nazism. Historians and political commentators in both cultures had to ask to what degree the previous political cultures had been incompletely democratized and vulnerable to authoritarianism. But there were differences: unified Italy had been the creation of self-conscious liberals, some of whom admired Germany and others of whom feared its authoritarian tendencies. Most did not depart from a liberal or a conservative-liberal testimony of faith, whereas the exponents of German statehood had always been more explicitly divided between authoritarian and liberal currents. That is to say, the Italians could believe that Italian political society as created at the national level in the nineteenth century still had a positive, indeed redemptive agenda; this was harder for the Germans.

Of course, Italian historians and commentators—Massimo Salvadori cites Gaetano Salvemini in his foreword to the Bobbio volume—were sharply critical of Italy's insufficient democratization. And many historians, including the Englishman Denis Mack Smith, would develop a historiography of lost democratic opportunities. Conversely, conservative German historians would over the course of the last forty years endeavor to liberate the German national project from the retrospective shadow of having led up to Hitler. By and large, however, the Italians could suggest that national politics might play a positive role in overcoming backwardness, creating a civic community, and educating for citizenship. The framework of civic life was not so problematic from the outset as the Prussian-German tradition appeared to postwar historians of Germany. In a period when we have discovered again the pathologies of ethnic nationalism, the works offered here provide a revealing glimpse into how thoughtful, acutely responsible political historians envisaged a potential national society that might satisfy longings for community association without brutal chauvinism.

The historians represented in this initial series—like Venturi—were keenly aware that after fascism, the project of constructing an Italian national community must be built on a democratic basis. They differed to what degree Italy's Marxist tradition might play a constructive role in that endeavor. Bobbio has been preeminently concerned with drawing on liberalism and socialism and explaining the points of contact but confirming the differences. Sereni, of course, was a committed Marxist and never felt that his commitment must violate democratic norms. Chabod was less preoccupied by this issue although he too wrote a small volume about Italy's descent into fascism and was clearly pledged to a postwar liberal democratic order.

Each of these historians was old enough to be caught between the great division in Italian ideologies represented by Benedetto Croce on the one side, and Antonio Gramsci on the other. Although he lived long enough to participate in politics after fascism, Croce exemplified Italy's pre-fascist liberalism. In the steps of an even earlier generation of Neapolitan Hegelians, he helped implant into Italian culture the currents of German idealism and historicism. In this framework, history constituted a clash of ideas between the liberals who gradually opened the frontiers of a civic community to a mass citizenry, and two sorts of demagogues. On the Right were the elitists and later fascists, on the Left the collectivists who would endanger this democratic progress—a threat of interacting extremes that preoccupied Bobbio, too, in the 1970s. Chabod's scenario of state-building also exemplified this grand narrative line according to which national politics must ultimately represent a contest between emancipatory and reactionary or demagogic concepts.

On the other side, Gramsci, whose prison writings oriented a generation of intellectuals after fascism, criticized Crocean idealism as a conservative mystification that served to uphold the regime of landed and industrial property. What distinguished his analysis from Marxist critiques elsewhere was its grounding in the fundamental constraints of Italy's peculiar history. His dualist conclusions, confirmed by the fascist outcome of the 1920s, envisaged a backward Mezzogiorno, enmeshed in clientelism and feudal legacies, undermining critical intellectuals and frustrating the forces of modern technology and proletarian democracy based in the industrial North. Sereni suggests some of the same duality. A Marxist like Gramsci, he understood that capitalism penetrated the countryside—but only imperfectly and not without drawing on the political resources of pre-market hierarchies. It is his affection for this long agrarian history, however, that keeps his work from becoming just a schematic narrative and delightful exploration of how men lived with the country. History is presented as a story of constraint, but the constraint imposed by the soil and elements as much as by landlords.

It is fitting that the Princeton-Agnelli series begins with these three authors, for together they exemplify the grand narrative lines in which Italians conceived their national history from the Risorgimento through the long era of political and economic modernization that followed the fall of fascism and the institution of the postwar republic. These authors emphasize the conflict between liberating ideas and constraining hierarchies; they envisage Italian history as a great contest between projects for civic emancipation and habits of domination, between politics as ideas and politics as ancient constraints. In part because Italian intellectuals imported these grand narrative lines from abroad, they took on an exaggerated clarity, less polarizing than in Spain, but dramaturgic nonetheless. This simultaneous sensibility for the force of contending ideas and the tenacity of material structures endows Italian scholarly historiography with a sense of drama that British and American authors summon more readily from biography. We tend to personify the contests that the Italian scholars translated in this series could incorporate in collective narratives.

Will the reader find such monuments of synthesis today? Contemporary Italian historians, like their counterparts in this country and elsewhere in Europe, have become more preoccupied by multiple voices, fragmentation, and the dissolution of overarching "metanarratives." Even the great national drama of the Resistance to fascism and nazism, which for almost half a century helped to orient the alliances of national politics, has become less clear and more confused. Still, historians writing today have understood how to transform even the new ideological and methodological uncertainties into various reassembled histories. What Italian historians continue to furnish even as their narratives decompose is an acute self-awareness of political ideas. If they can no longer offer us a confident footing either as liberals or Marxists, they continue to provide sophisticated self-awareness. Like the residents of Italo Calvino's imaginary city of Ottavia who live suspended over an abyss into which they know they must ultimately fall, they provide structures all the more remarkable for their vulnerability. The writers of the successive postwar generations—first Sereni and Chabod, then later Bobbio, the interpreter of the ideological conflicts of the years of upheaval and terrorism in the late 1960s and 1970s—wrote with more certitude than we are likely to find today. Perhaps, too, with more power and penetration. The English-speaking reader now has a valuable chance to judge.

F E D E R I C O C H A B O D :
A B I O - B I B L I O G R A P H I C A L
P R O F I L E
B Y F R A N C E S C O T U C C A R I

ANYONE WHO SEEKS to comprehend the public figure, and the oeuvre, of Federico Chabod, even in their essential outlines, is bound to feel a sense of profound and extraordinary complexity, despite the passage of almost forty years since his death.

The events of his life and his intellectual evolution took place in parlous times: he was born in 1901 and died prematurely in 1960. Chabod was thus a member of the generation whose youth coincided with the First World War, and which then had to face the traumatic events and the radical transformations that left their indelible mark on the history of Italy and Europe in the twentieth century: the crisis of the immediate postwar period, the decline of liberal Italy, the seizure and consolidation of power by the fascist regime, the growing menace of Hitler's plans for expansion, the Second World War, the resistance, the foundation of the Italian republic, postwar reconstruction, the definitive loss of Europe's former centrality, the cold war.

Chabod's stance with regard to the politics and culture of his own times was complex, particularly during the years of Mussolini's dictatorship. His convictions were thoroughly liberal, but his predilection for the studious life of a professor overrode any vocation for active politics. In his own practice of what he called his "trade of historian" he felt no inclination to make his research serve ends dictated by political and ideological commitment, and thus was able to work, in a relatively untrammeled fashion, within two cultural institutions that were strategically important for the regime, and that, with the passage of time, were forced to become progressively more fascist: the *Enciclopedia Italiana,* organized and directed by Giovanni Gentile, and the universities of the kingdom of Italy, in which the oath of loyalty to fascism was made compulsory in October 1931. Yet Chabod's intellectual activity should not, despite these circumstances, be seen as in some way "disengaged." Many of the significant, recurring themes in his work—for example, the densely textured pages on the idea of the nation and of Europe—clearly derive from his restless and impassioned meditation on the great problems of the contemporary world. Even his university teaching, while shunning any sort of professorial "prophetizing," roused deep and lasting enthusiasm in those who had perforce to receive their education in the oppressive atmosphere of fascism. At one of the grimmest moments of the twenty years the regime lasted, and again in the period immediately after it collapsed, Chabod did not avoid the responsibilities of action: on the first occasion, during the crisis following the assassination of Matteotti, he helped Gaetano Salvemini (who recalls the occasion vividly in his *Memorie di un fuoruscito*) cross over into France; on the second, virtually two decades later, he assumed a leading role after 8

September 1943 in the resistance movement against Nazi-fascist oppression in his native Valle d'Aosta; and on the third, after Italy was liberated, he pursued a course of action consistent with the one he had already been following by waging a battle for the autonomy of his region, of which he became president from January to October 1946.

Finally, his work is complex in its extent, its methods, and its results. A pupil of the great contemporary masters of historiography, Italian and European, from Benedetto Croce to Friedrich Meinecke, from Gaetano Salvemini to Gioacchino Volpe, Chabod proved capable of reworking, in an original way, inspirations from very different historiographical traditions, and focused his research interests on a wide spectrum of major historical issues, including the crisis of communal government and the birth of the *signorie* in Italy from the fourteenth to the sixteenth centuries, the political thought of Machiavelli and Botero, the culture of the Renaissance, the age of the Counter Reformation, the birth of the modern state, the history of the duchy of Milan and the empire of Charles V, the Enlightenment, the idea of the nation, the idea of Europe, the history of Italian foreign policy during the last thirty years of the nineteenth century, and of Italy in the twentieth century. What is more, he tackled each of these subjects by combining (in a manner to which he was later to give a degree of theoretical consistency in his *Lezioni di metodo storico*) very disparate techniques and perspectives, traditional and otherwise: archival research, the biographical method, the history of mentalities, economic history, administrative history, diplomatic history, the history of political thought, and so on. In a number of cases Chabod's choice of these subjects, and approaches, was made for purely contingent reasons. And in a number of such cases, this choice resulted in extremely weighty, but nevertheless occasional, scholarly contributions, such as lectures, university courses, reviews, and encyclopedia entries. For that matter, Chabod himself, with his extraordinarily acute feeling for the problematic nature of history, continued to view as "provisional" even his most finished productions, the ones that make him an authoritative figure in modern Italian historiography. Hence he continued to revisit, always from a fresh point of view, areas he had explored and results he had arrived at throughout the course of his life. Hence too—and a perfect example of this is the work now brought before an English-language readership, the *Storia della Politica Estera Italiana dal 1870 al 1896, Le Premesse*—his tendency to dwell on the "premises," on the "material and moral bases," on the underlying causes that produce manifold effects, and that give back to what may have been depicted as a well-defined and circumscribed historical process the true inclusiveness of its development, and its implications.

The stimulus imparted by Chabod's oeuvre, and by his unflagging energy as teacher and organizer of historical studies, has given to the Italian historiography of the last fifty years a multiplicity of new directions in research, the evidence for which is to be found in a large volume, entitled *Federico Chabod e la 'nuova storiografia' italiana 1919–1950*, that appeared in the mid-eighties. It is likely that, in future retrospective, this influence will be the key factor when a new attempt is made to assess critically his personality and his accomplishment. For now a review of the main phases of his life, drawing attention to the enduring interests and the prevailing logic of his "trade as historian," will at any rate provide readers with an overview of the basic elements of his intellectual profile. (A brief bibliography of Chabod's principal works, and of the essential secondary literature dedicated to him and his oeuvre, will be found below. Thus, in what follows, references will be given summarily by title and year of publication.)

Federico Chabod was born in Aosta on 23 February 1901, the son of Laurent Chabod and Giuseppina Baratono. He completed secondary school in his native city, obtaining his degree from the *liceo* in the summer of 1918.

In November of the same year he enrolled in the Faculty of Letters and Philosophy at the University of Turin and began to cultivate his principal interests: literature, art, and above all history. Chabod became one of the favorite pupils of Pietro Egidi, who held the chair of modern history at Turin from 1915–16 and was, from 1923 to 1929, the director of *Rivista Storica Italiana*, the journal which from that time forward was destined to publish a large portion of Chabod's writings on history. Almost entirely isolated at first, and shaken by the death of his father in 1919, the young student remained more or less aloof, during his university years, from the group that was forming at Turin around the figure of Piero Gobetti. Mario Fubini, one of his fellow students, mentions this in a moving memorial of Chabod. By that time, he explains, an attitude that we have already remarked on in general terms was beginning to manifest itself: the tendency to translate moral, civic, and political commitment—at a time when Italian history was taking a dramatic turn—into an incentive to research rather than to direct action or ideological engagement. This "scholarly habit," this *medietas*, Fubini adds, revealed even then an "authentic vocation as a historian" (M. Fubini, "Federico Chabod studente di lettere," in *Rivista Storica Italiana* 72.4 [1960]: 630–31).

In any case, it was during these years that the first major nucleus of the young Chabod's historiographical interests began to take shape, consisting on the one hand of his research into the crisis of the communes and the arrival of the *signorie* in Italy from the fourteenth to the sixteenth centuries, but primarily of his studies on Machiavelli. These two fields of research were of course closely connected, as has often been noted, since both related to a concrete historical process—the transition from the commune to the *signoria*—and to the consciousness that contemporaries had of that process, especially the eminent personality who served as secretary of Florence. These studies, and especially his studies on Machiavelli, were to remain at the center of Chabod's historical reflection until 1927; even in the sequel they were to play a major part in the overall mosaic of his oeuvre. Once again it is Fubini, who discussed these matters almost daily with his young companion, who emphasizes two points of capital importance. Most notable was a revival of interest in Machiavelli at just that time, not only in Italy but internationally. In this connection it will be sufficient to recall, in addition to Croce's *Elementi di politica*, Meinecke's German edition of *Il Principe*, which appeared in 1923, and above all his *Die Idee der Staatsräson in der neueren Geschichte*, published in 1924, in which he traces the modern fortune of the idea of "reason of state" from its beginnings with Machiavelli. This was, if you like, a historiographically "lofty" revival, but as Fubini notes, Machiavelli also became a virtually obligatory point of reference in the rhetoric of the nascent regime at the start of the twenties. Mussolini himself, we may add, voiced the intention around 1924 of writing at length on Machiavelli and on the role of statesmen; in the same year he did in fact compose a very brief *Preludio al Machiavelli*, which Chabod later had occasion to cite (with a certain embarrassment, one imagines) in the bibliography for the entry he wrote on Machiavelli for volume 21 of the *Enciclopedia Italiana*, which appeared in 1934.

Still, the young Chabod practically stumbled upon Machiavelli, just as he was later to do with other areas of research that became central to his oeuvre. He turned to the Florentine secretary, interrupting studies that were already under way for his projected thesis on the passage from the commune to the *signoria*, because he undertook to edit and introduce, replacing Egidi, who had given up the task, the edition of *Il Principe* which the Turin publishing house UTET planned to include in the series "Classici italiani." This labor came to absorb all his energies and became the definitive focus of his thesis, which he prepared between 1923 and 1924 and defended in June 1924. This thesis supplied Chabod with the brief introduction to the UTET edition of *Il Principe*, published in 1924, as well as with the longer essay entitled "Del *Principe* di Niccolò Machiavelli," which appeared in *Nuova Rivista Storica* in 1925; it was republished the following year in a separate volume. Also in 1925 Chabod returned to the original subject of his thesis research, seen now in light of his studies on Machiavelli: the result was a close-knit and important historiographical review published in *Rivista Storica Italiana* and entitled "Di alcuni studi recenti sull'età comunale e signorile nell'Italia settentrionale," in which he brought out more clearly one of the leading ideas of his work on Machiavelli—the substantial "untimeliness" of the latter's faith in a "new Signore" against the background of the new equilibria that were emerging in the sixteenth century. This was a Machiavelli all the more unserviceable for those who were aping him in the twentieth century.

These first productions by the young historian immediately brought him favorable attention. The UTET introduction was well received by Benedetto Croce in 1924, and the essay "Del *Principe* di Niccolò Machiavelli" was enthusiastically reviewed by Ernesto Sestan in 1926. Chabod in the meantime was acquiring new and valuable experience. In 1924–25, years in which the construction of the total state was begun following the assassination of Matteotti, he took a postgraduate course at Florence with Gaetano Salvemini, in a university rocked almost daily by the violence of the blackshirts. It was here that he wrote his review of studies on the communal age and the age of the *signori*, and it was then, in August 1925, that he assisted Salvemini to escape into France over the little St. Bernard pass. In 1925–26 Chabod frequented the history seminar at the University of Berlin and came into contact with Friedrich Meinecke, with whom he engaged in a debate over the dating and composition of *Il Principe*. The experience of these years provided him with material for his next publications, both of which appeared in 1927: the first, entitled "Sulla composizione de *Il Principe* di Niccolò Machiavelli," was a longer version of a seminar paper given at the University of Berlin in May 1926 and was published in *Archivum Romanicum*, and the second, entitled "Uno storico tedesco contemporaneo: Federico Meinecke," appeared in *Nuova Rivista Storica*.

Many themes that emerged in this early phase of Chabod's research were to remain fundamental throughout the course of his life's work as a historian. To Machiavelli in particular he was to dedicate further important contributions, including the encyclopedia entry of 1934 mentioned above; his course of lectures for 1952–53, which was published in 1953 under the title *Niccolò Machiavelli, Il segretario fiorentino;* and a celebrated lecture given at Florence in 1952 and published three years later as "Metodo e stile di Machiavelli" in an edited collection entitled *Il Cinquecento*. Chabod's early studies also formed the matrix, from around 1927, of his further studies on the Renaissance, his essay on Giovanni Botero, and his wide-ranging investigation—taken up repeatedly from different perspectives—of the state of Milan and the Habsburg Empire of Charles V.

This new phase of his studies received strong impetus beginning in 1928 from his experience of doing research in Spain in the Archivo General de Simancas, research that continued, with few interruptions, until 1934, and that widened to include many other Italian and foreign archives. In this case as well, chance played a part in Chabod's choice of the path to follow, for the idea of exploiting the Spanish archive originated with his mentor in Turin, Pietro Egidi, and the mission of collecting and sifting the documents to be found there relating to the state of Milan was entrusted, in the first instance, to Vittorio Di Tocco. The latter, however, fell ill with typhoid soon after he had begun his work and died in Valladolid in October 1927. Egidi, who was to die prematurely himself in the summer of 1929, then invited Chabod to take up this research project, which in the end furnished the documentary basis for a series of works that rank among the most noteworthy he ever produced.

The experience of Simancas, where Chabod became acquainted with Fernand Braudel, was followed by other, equally influential encounters in the years immediately following. In 1928 he began to draft entries on modern history for Giovanni Gentile's *Enciclopedia Italiana*, in the pages of which many of his most important contributions, historiographically speaking, appeared. Then, in 1930, he joined the Scuola di Storia Moderna e Contemporanea in Rome, directed by Gioacchino Volpe, and remained with that institution until November 1934. Here Chabod formed a strong bond of friendship with Carlo Morandi (with whom he later directed the historical journal *Popoli* in 1941–42) and with Walter Maturi: together they were affectionately known to their friends as the "three musketeers." It was thanks to the support of Volpe and the Scuola di Storia Moderna e Contemporanea that Chabod found the means to continue the research he had launched at Simancas.

This, then, was the specific context in which the researches alluded to above first came to fruition—the vast body of his writings on the Renaissance and the epoch of the Counter Reformation, and his ample sequence of studies of the duchy of Milan and the empire of Charles V. But, once again, these topics continued to bear fruit, as he returned to them and reflected on them from different perspectives and on different occasions, for the rest of his life. Among his Renaissance and Counter Reformation studies may be mentioned the paper he gave at the Seventh International Congress of Historical Sciences at Warsaw in 1933, published that year as "Il Rinascimento nelle recenti interpretazioni" in the *Bulletin of the International Committee of Historical Sciences*; the entry "Rinascimento" published in 1936 in the *Enciclopedia Italiana*; the two essays "Il Rinascimento" and "Gli studi di storia del Rinascimento," which appeared in 1942 and 1950 respectively; the entry on Francesco Guicciardini published in the *Enciclopedia Italiana* in 1933; the important volume on Giovanni Botero that appeared in 1934 but was partly composed in 1931–32; the university lectures given by Chabod at the University of Rome in 1950–51 on "La politica di Paolo Sarpi"; and finally the conference paper "Alle origini dello stato moderno," from 1957.

Among his studies of Milan and the Habsburg Empire, pride of place belongs to three major works, *Lo stato di Milano nell'impero di Carlo V* (1934), *Per la storia religiosa dello stato di Milano durante il dominio di Carlo V* (1938), and the long section on *L'epoca di Carlo V* that appeared posthumously in 1961 in the *Storia di Milano* published by the Fondazione Treccani degli Alfieri. They are flanked by several important university courses, such as the ones given at the University of Rome in 1948–49 and 1954–55, and by three briefer but highly significant articles: "Milano o i Paesi Bassi? Le discussioni in Spagna sulla alternativa del 1544," "Stipendi nominali e busta paga effettiva dei funzionari dell'amministrazione milanese alla fine del Cinquecento," and "Usi e abusi nell'amministrazione dello stato di Milano a mezzo il Cinquecento," all published in 1958. Finally there was Chabod's review of Karl Brandi's *Kaiser Karl V*, followed by his preface to the Italian translation of the work by Leone Ginzburg and Ettore Bassan (1940, 1961).

Out of this network of studies, all of them based (it is worth noting once more) on an enormous amount of documentation and carried out in a way that demonstrates an exceptional capacity to conjoin the analysis of major shifts between epochs with microscopic research into the most apparently arid archival details, there emerge new interests and problematic concerns pregnant with significance. First, there is the progressive shift of Chabod's historiographical focus from the Renaissance to the age of the Counter Reformation. Second, there is the idea that the decadence of Italy was structural in nature, a point of view which, in the eyes of more than one competent scholar, constitutes a dominant theme in Chabod's entire oeuvre, from the studies on Machiavelli to the entry on Guicciardini, and from his *Botero* to his *Storia della Politica Estera Italiana*. Third, and this is particularly evident in his books on Milan and the Habsburg Empire, there is his increasing discernment with regard to the great themes of the origin, development, and structure of the modern national states. Fourth, the dimension of his analysis is ever more clearly "European." And lastly—although this list could be extended to a much greater length—there is his profound sensitivity to the his-

tory of mentalities: the ethos, modern or semifeudal, of the imperial functionaries; the inner conflicts of the emperor Charles V, with his dramatic sense of
death; and the large-scale manifestations of collective religious life.

In 1935, having left the Scuola di Storia Moderna in Rome, Chabod was
appointed to teach modern history in the Faculty of Political Science at the University of Perugia. In 1938 he obtained the chair of medieval and modern history
at the University of Milan, which remained his academic affiliation, in a formal
sense at least, until 1946.

Not long after he began to teach at Perugia, Chabod's field of research was
reoriented around a new and decisive coordinate, one that was hardly predictable. Once again, this took place for reasons that were, to a large extent, external, and on the initiative of one of his mentors, Gioacchino Volpe. Volpe made a
proposal to the Institute for the Study of International Politics to sponsor a massive research project on the history of Italian foreign policy from 1861 to 1914, a
project to be carried out by Carlo Morandi, Walter Maturi, Augusto Torre, and
Federico Chabod. The work was divided into chronological periods, and Chabod
assumed responsibility for the period from 20 September 1870 to March 1896.

The project was launched in 1936. From then until 1943 Chabod largely set
aside his studies on Italian and European history in the sixteenth and seventeenth
centuries, and gave himself over to a systematic exploration of the Historical
Archive of the Ministry for Foreign Affairs and of various other public and private archives, Italian and foreign. In 1946, following the dramatic climax of the
war and the resistance, Chabod was nominated for membership on the commission charged with organizing the publication of the *Documenti Diplomatici Italiani* from 1861 to 1943, and he himself edited the volume covering the period
from September to December 1870.

The results of Chabod's immense labor in the archives came before the public
only fifteen years later, in 1951. Once again, in Chabod's eyes at least, his results
were "definitive" only to a very limited degree. The *Storia della Politica Estera
Italiana dal 1870 al 1896* [the original title of the present work], in the form in
which it appeared from the presses of the Laterza firm, constituted, in terms of
the original project, no more than a volume of "Premises" and was meant to be
followed by another four volumes dedicated to diplomatic history in the narrow
sense.

Chabod's *Politica Estera*, which constitutes his true masterpiece in the judgment of many, is the subject of an essay by Walter Maturi translated for inclusion
in the present volume, and although for this reason we will not discuss the work
in detail, nor its significance in the development of Chabod's historiography, a
few salient points may be noted. One is the complex interplay of intellectual
influences at work in the book—from Croce to Volpe, from Meinecke to Ranke
and Burckhardt. Another point worth noting is that Chabod's profound feeling
for the complexity of history is very much in evidence here: he portrays a global
process, one that proves absolutely impossible to rigidify according to an abstract
division between domestic politics and foreign policy, much less to schematize
according to a supposed "primacy" of the first over the second, or vice versa.

Finally we may ponder the fact that Chabod actually did the writing in the aftermath of the period 1943–46—dramatic years in which he engaged in political action, years when he was cut off from his normal professorial routine, and his papers. It has been suggested that these particular years had some influence on the judgment that Chabod eventually formed on the political class of post-unification Italy, and indeed on contemporary Italy.

At the University of Milan in the academic year 1943–44, Chabod gave his celebrated course on "The Idea of Nationhood" and the "History of the Idea of Europe." He was to repeat this course several times between the late 1940s and the end of the 1950s, and the lectures were published by Laterza in two best-selling paperbacks in 1961. But after it was given in Milan for the first time, the darkest period of the war and the partisan conflict intervened, and Chabod was forced to abandon research of any kind, which meant setting aside such promising enterprises as the one begun in 1940, in collaboration with Gino Luzzatto and Ugo La Malfa, to edit an economic and social history of modern and contemporary Italy. Chabod went to his house in Dégioz in the Valle d'Aosta and there concealed the notes and drafts for the *Storia della Politica Estera*. Between 1944 and 1945 Chabod assumed the identity of "Professor Lazzaro" and took an active part in the operations of the partisan band led by his cousin Remo Chabod. From the summer of 1944 he played an important part in organizing the first free elections to be held for the communal council of the Valsavaranche, and in galvanizing the local response to the grave crisis provoked by France's intention to proceed with the annexation of Aosta and the surrounding territory. The annexation might have succeeded because there was genuine discontent among the people of the valleys, who had not forgotten the catastrophic experience of being forced to undergo compulsory Italianization at the hands of the fascist regime. The logical response to the danger was to obtain administrative autonomy for the region.

In this situation, rendered more hazardous by the fighting going on between the Nazi-fascist troops and the partisans, Chabod took determined action in two directions. He requested substantial local autonomy for the Valle d'Aosta while giving assurance that its loyalty to Italy was beyond question; more than that, he worked to put a general project for conceding broad administrative and cultural autonomy to *all* the frontier regions of Italy on the agenda of national politics. Chabod acted in the belief that by refounding the Italian state on the basis of a "system of extensive administrative decentralization" it would be possible to launch the reconstruction of a Europe that had been left in a state of prostration by the war. In the rebuilding of Europe, as he foresaw it, the border regions would cease to be the cause, or the object, of nationalistic appetites or the lust for power, but would instead transform themselves into "connecting links" between the various political and cultural areas of the old Europe, and would serve to contain, if not entirely to vanquish, the "arrogance of nations." The second direction in which Chabod moved, an offshoot of the first, was to take urgent political and diplomatic measures, incidentally displaying a considerable gift of practicality, when he learned in August 1944 that concrete discussions were taking place between French diplomats and large sections of the political class in the Valle d' Aosta with a view to annexation. Chabod gathered a small group of like-minded friends around him, and established contacts with the leaders of the resistance locally and nationally and with the parties in government, producing a large quantity of documents and memoranda on the critical situation in the region in order to create momentum for a solution based on local autonomy.

Representing the Party of Action on the Committee for National Liberation for the Valle d'Aosta, Chabod succeeded in obtaining solid assurances from the CLNAI and the government concerning the course to be followed after Italy was liberated. In November 1944, however, he was forced to flee into France (which entailed a risky mountain crossing) in order to escape the Nazi-fascist roundups and reprisals. At Grenoble, where he lived as a political refugee for a number of months, he reorganized the resistance groups of the Valle d'Aosta, of which he was named commandant in January 1945. He was expelled from eastern France in March and left Grenoble for Paris. Only in May 1945, with liberation achieved, was he able to return to Aosta. Here he encountered once more the ongoing problem of the French desire for annexation, a problem fueled by the deep-rooted distrust felt by the people of the valleys toward the new political authority in Italy, and their consequent willingness to consider seceding. Chabod's efforts were decisive in moving the Italian government in the direction of a solution based on local autonomy, a solution set out in September 1945 in two government decrees concerning the new regional constitution for the Valle d'Aosta, and enshrined in constitutional law on 26 February 1948. Chabod himself was elected president of the new region in January 1946 and remained in office until October of the same year, a difficult period of reconstruction in a situation that had not yet entirely settled back into peacetime routine. Only in the wake of his resignation from office was Chabod able to turn all his energies once more to the life of a scholar and professor.

He obtained the chair of modern history in the Faculty of Letters and Philosophy at the University of Rome and began to teach there in 1946–47. All the threads of his multifarious historical research were taken up again, and the rhythm of publication resumed with the appearance of the fundamental studies of Machiavelli, the Renaissance, Charles V, and the duchy of Milan mentioned above. Chabod came before the English-language public in 1958 with the book *Machiavelli and the Renaissance*, in which he collected, and in part revised, his principal writings on the subject. The *Storia della Politica Estera Italiana* came out in 1951 and the first volume of the *Documenti Diplomatici Italiani* in 1960. The courses on the idea of nationhood and of Europe were taken up and developed further. Of particular importance for understanding the deep roots of Chabod's approach to history are the two essays he wrote for *Rivista Storica Italiana* on the occasion of the deaths of Benedetto Croce and Friedrich Meinecke: the well-known "Croce storico" and the shorter but equally perspicacious "Friedrich Meinecke" (1952, 1955; reprinted in *Lezioni di metodo storico*, 1969). A new departure in terms of content, if not structure, came with Chabod's twelve lectures on contemporary Italy, delivered in January 1950 at the Institut d'Études Politiques at the University of Paris and published that year in French. The Italian translation, *L'Italia contemporanea (1918–1948)* appeared posthumously in 1961 and enjoyed extraordinary popularity; the English translation of 1963 was made from the Italian version and given a variant title, *A History of Italian Fascism*. In this book the author, adhering only in part to the Crocean model and achieving a profundity of his own, traces the main lines of Italian history from the post-World War I crisis, through fascism and the years of the resistance, down to the foundation of the republican state and the effort of reconstruction.

With *L'Italia contemporanea* we arrive at the conclusion of a historiographical career that indubitably constitutes a fundamental chapter in the history of Italian and European historical writing in this century. It is a career that, apart from displaying sheer technical competence and the capacity to adopt varying perspectives, embraced a truly enormous range in space and time, beginning with Italy in the age of the communes and the *signoria* and moving on to the Renaissance, Counter Reformation, and Baroque ages; and then, after a rapid, brilliant survey of the Enlightenment, to the later nineteenth century, and finally to twentieth-century Italy.

Nor is this the complete inventory of Chabod's legacy, for he was also a great mentor and organizer of scholarly undertakings, most obviously as a university professor but also as director of the series of historical works published by Sansoni (1939–43), by the Institute for the Study of International Politics (1940–42), by Edizioni Scientifiche Italiane (1951–60), and by Einaudi (1951–60). He was co-director of *Rivista Storica Italiana* from 1948 to 1958 and was active in the International Committee of Historical Sciences, becoming a member of the Bureau of that organization in 1950 and being chosen as its president in 1955 at the congress held that year in Rome. Most important, however, was his role in the Istituto italiano per gli studi storici [Italian Institute for Historical Studies], which was founded in Naples by Benedetto Croce in 1947. That same year Chabod was asked by Croce to become the director, following the untimely death of Adolfo Omodeo, and he continued in this position until 1960. He was thus one of the principal architects of the practical side of the institute—its system of study grants, its series of publications, its library, the design of the lectures—and at the same time its most prestigious teacher.

Federico Chabod remained at Palazzo Filomarino, the home of the institute, until close to the end of his days. He died in Rome on 14 July 1960.

WORKS BY FEDERICO CHABOD

"Introduzione" to Niccolò Machiavelli, *Il Principe* (Turin: UTET, 1924); now in *Scritti su Machiavelli* (Turin: Einaudi, 1964).

"Del *Principe* di Niccolò Machiavelli," in *Nuova Rivista Storica* 9 (1925): 35–71, 189–216, 437–73; republished separately in 1926 (Milan-Rome-Naples: Società Editrice Dante Alighieri); now in *Scritti su Machiavelli*.

"Di alcuni studi recenti sull'età comunale e signorile nell'Italia settentrionale," in *Rivista Storica Italiana* 42 (1925): 29–47.

"Sulla composizione de *Il Principe* di Niccolò Machiavelli," in *Archivum Romanicum* 11 (1927): 330–83; now in *Scritti su Machiavelli*.

"Uno storico tedesco contemporaneo: Federico Meinecke," in *Nuova Rivista Storica* 11 (1927): 592–603.

Art. "Borghesia," in *Enciclopedia Italiana* 7 (1930): 471–73.

Art. "Guicciardini, Francesco," in *Enciclopedia Italiana* 18 (1933): 244–48; now in *Scritti sul Rinascimento* (Turin: Einaudi, 1967).

Art. "Illuminismo," in *Enciclopedia Italiana* 18 (1933): 850–54.

"Il Rinascimento nelle recenti interpretazioni," in *Bulletin of the International Committee of Historical Sciences* 19 (1933): 215–29; now in *Scritti sul Rinascimento*.

Giovanni Botero. Rome: Anonima Romana Editoriale, 1934; now in *Scritti sul Rinascimento*.

Art. "Machiavelli, Niccolò," in *Enciclopedia Italiana* 21 (1934): 778–90; now in *Scritti su Machiavelli*.

Lo stato di Milano nell'impero di Carlo V. Rome: Tumminelli, 1934; now in *Lo stato e la vita religiosa a Milano nell'epoca di Carlo V* (Turin: Einaudi, 1971).

Art. "Rinascimento," in *Enciclopedia Italiana* 29 (1936): 346–54; now in *Scritti sul Rinascimento*.

Per la storia religiosa dello stato di Milano durante il dominio di Carlo V. Note e documenti. Bologna: Zanichelli, 1938; now in *Lo stato e la vita religiosa a Milano nell'epoca di Carlo V*.

"Carlo V nell'opera del Brandi," in *Studi Germanici* 4 (1940): 1–34; now in *Carlo V e il suo impero* (Turin: Einaudi, 1985).

"Il Rinascimento," in E. Rota, ed., *Problemi storici e orientamenti storiografici*, pp. 445–491. Como: Cavalleri, 1942; now in *Scritti sul Rinascimento*.

"Gli studi di storia del Rinascimento," in C. Antoni and R. Mattioli, eds., *Cinquant'anni di vita italiana 1896–1946. Scritti in onore di Benedetto Croce*. Naples: Edizioni Scientifiche Italiane, 1950; now in *Scritti sul Rinascimento*.

Storia della Politica Estera Italiana dal 1870 al 1896, Le Premesse. Bari: Laterza, 1951.

"Croce storico," in *Rivista Storica Italiana* 64 (1952): 473–530.

"Friedrich Meinecke," in *Rivista Storica Italiana* 67 (1955): 272–88.

"Metodo e stile di Machiavelli," in *Il Cinquecento*, pp. 1–21. Florence: Sansoni, 1955; now in *Scritti su Machiavelli*.

Machiavelli and the Renaissance. London: Bowes and Bowes, 1958.

"Milano o i Paesi Bassi? Le discussioni in Spagna sulla 'alternativa' del 1544," in *Rivista Storica Italiana* 70 (1958): 508–52; now in *Carlo V e il suo impero*.

"Stipendi nominali e busta paga effettiva dei funzionari dell'amministrazione milanese alla fine del Cinquecento," in *Miscellanea in onore di Roberto Cessi*, vol. 2, pp. 187–363. Rome: Edizioni di storia e letteratura, 1958; now in *Carlo V e il suo impero*.

"Usi e abusi nell'amministrazione dello stato di Milano a mezzo il Cinquecento," in *Studi storici in onore di Gioacchino Volpe per il suo ottantesimo compleanno*, pp. 93–194. Florence: Sansoni, 1958; now in *Carlo V e il suo impero*.

"Introduzione" to Karl Brandi, *Carlo V*, trans. by Leone Ginzburg and Ettore Bassan. Turin: Einaudi, 1961; now in *Carlo V e il suo impero*.

L'epoca di Carlo V (1535–1559), in *Storia di Milano*, vol. 9. Milan: Fondazione Treccani degli Alfieri, 1961. Republished as *Storia di Milano nell'epoca di Carlo V*. Turin: Einaudi, 1971.

Storia dell'idea di Europa. Bari: Laterza, 1961.

L'idea di nazione. Bari: Laterza, 1961.

L'Italia contemporanea (1918–1948). Turin: Einaudi, 1961. English translation: *A History of Italian Fascism*, trans. by Muriel Grindrod. London: Weidenfeld and Nicolson, 1963; reprinted: New York: Fertig, 1975.

Scritti su Machiavelli. Turin: Einaudi, 1964.

Scritti sul Rinascimento. Turin: Einaudi, 1967.

Lezioni di metodo storico. Bari: Laterza, 1969.

Lo stato e la vita religiosa a Milano nell'epoca di Carlo V. Turin: Einaudi, 1971.

Storia di Milano nell'epoca di Carlo V. Turin: Einaudi, 1971.

Carlo V e il suo impero. Turin: Einaudi, 1985.

WORKS ON FEDERICO CHABOD

Federico Chabod nella cultura e nella vita contemporanea. Special issue of *Rivista Storica Italiana* 72.4 (1960): 617–834. Writings by Fernand Braudel, Charles Webster, Mario Fubini, Arnaldo Momigliano, Giorgio Spini, Vittorio De Caprariis, Ernesto Sestan, Delio Cantimori, Giuseppe Galasso, Giorgio Falco, Walter Maturi, Armando Saitta, Leo Valiani, Alessandro and Ettore Passerin d'Entrèves, and Luigi Firpo.

G. Sasso. *Profilo di Federico Chabod*. Bari: Laterza, 1961.

R. Romeo. "Federico Chabod," in *Momenti e problemi di storia contemporanea*. Assisi-Rome: Beniamino Carucci Editore, 1971.

B. Vigezzi, ed. *Federico Chabod e la 'nuova storiografia' italiana 1919–1950*. Milan: Jaca Book, 1984.

S. Soave. *Federico Chabod politico*. Bologna: Il Mulino, 1989.

FEDERICO CHABOD: HISTORIAN OF ITALIAN FOREIGN POLICY
• BY WALTER MATURI •

I WAS STILL a university student when I became aware of Chabod through Benedetto Croce's admiring review of his edition, with introduction and notes, of Machiavelli's *Il Principe* for the Unione Tipografica Editrice Torinese.[1] Upon reading Chabod's introduction for myself I came to share Croce's verdict, and after I had gone on to read his long essays on Machiavelli and Meinecke, published by *Nuova Rivista Storica* in 1925 and 1927 respectively, and his publications in *Rivista Storica Italiana* from 1925 to 1929, I soon recognized him, almost by instinct I would say, as the finest historian of my generation. But my personal acquaintance with Chabod, and with Carlo Morandi—who was, however, exchanging correspondence with both of us from 1927 on—came only on the occasion of a philosophy conference held in Rome in the spring of 1929; our friendship dates from the same year and remained steadfast until the end.

Chabod was an extremely complex personality: it was as though a number of human strata had been overlaid to produce him, each clearly marked by the idiosyncrasy of his native region. The first impression he gave was that of a Piedmontese officer of the old school, the sort who would have known how to maintain the proper reserve toward superiors and inferiors, who would have felt himself on duty even when he was out of uniform, and whose greatest happiness would have consisted in fastening his piercing gaze on someone who was committing some blunder and giving him a severe and peremptory "dressing down."

But cast in certain roles and placed in certain circumstances, Chabod the Piedmontese officer transformed himself into the subtlest of diplomats, one able to win the approbation of competent observers, although he was never a professional diplomat himself. He gave the best proof of his talent for diplomacy in his approach to the problem of the Valle d'Aosta, both in his dealings with the British and the Americans and with the central government in Rome. The problem of the Valle d'Aosta was, however, one that went deeper than diplomacy for

This essay was written by Walter Maturi, one of the leading exponents of the historical study of the Italian Risorgimento, for an issue of the *Rivista Storica Italiana*, vol. 72.4 (December 1960), which appeared shortly after the death of Federico Chabod and was dedicated in its entirety to the figure, and to the work, of the great scholar. The intellectual portrait of Chabod which Maturi was moved to limn with deft, incisive strokes, and his penetrating analysis of the fundamental design and the methodological choices made by Chabod in his work on Italian foreign policy, are still, at a distance of more than thirty-five years, an enlightened, and enlightening, point of entry into the complexities of one of the most significant works—and authors—of the Italian historiography of this century. Maturi's essay, which has been lightly abridged and adapted for this translation, is published by courteous permission of Edizioni Scientifiche Italiane of Naples.

[1] *La Critica*, 20 September 1924, pp. 313–15.

Chabod, for he always felt the sturdy links that bound the Valle d'Aosta to Italy. During the facist period everyone knew the direction in which Chabod's political sympathies lay, but he was extremely prudent about this, in speech and in writing. The first time I ever saw him lash out, in the presence of others, against a measure taken by the fascist regime was when Mussolini had the unhappy idea of "nationalizing" the Valle d'Aosta his way. "In every one of Italy's wars," Chabod exploded, "the Valdostani always fought like the other Italians, in fact even better, so what does it matter if instead of crying *Viva il re* they prefer to cry *Vive le roi?*"

When Chabod did throw himself into the political arena he sided with the *partito d'azione*, and he viewed the problem of the Valle d'Aosta in the context of his larger dream of democratic renewal: a free Italy, its component parts well articulated, in a free Europe. But this phase, reminiscent of Mazzini and Cattaneo and indicative of the fundamental generosity of his nature, vanished immediately when the flame of his true vocation, that of historian, blazed up again: just as, if I may venture a comparison, the noble dreams of Burgundian chivalry of one of Chabod's favorite protagonists, Charles V, were smothered by his occupational duties as monarch.

In Chabod, the man and the scholarly discipline he had chosen formed a whole and cast a spell over those who attended his lectures: he succeeded in imparting a sense of high and solemn seriousness to the teaching of history, without ever indulging in histrionics of any kind. About the force of his teaching our strongest testimony comes from the students who followed his courses at the State University of Milan, including Vittorio Orilia, who wrote:

> Those who were twenty years old at the eve of the Second World War and who were enrolled in the Faculty of Letters at Milan realized immediately that Federico Chabod was a professor *different from the others*. He wasn't all that old himself, not yet forty, but the first two courses he gave at the university, which were on the passage from the ancient world to the middle ages, and from the middle ages to the modern era, seemed to those young people, who remembered the disgraceful way that history was taught in the secondary schools, to come from another world, because they revealed so many new factual aspects, and so many processes and connections. Most of them had had no inkling of these dimensions of history.[2]

I myself possess a set of mimeographed lecture notes of his course for 1943–44,[3] at the beginning of which one of these young Lombards, a woman, scribbled the following enthusiastic declaration: "Reader, if you know Chabod, you will be able to picture him rising from these pages waving his long, restless arms that remind you of the wings of an eagle in free flight through the free skies." And Raffaele Mattioli rightly notes: "It was precisely as a teacher that Chabod seemed to proclaim his true calling. Whenever he was giving a lecture or evaluating a student's research project, his face would lose the absorbed and slightly troubled

---

[2] "Chabod, maestro solitario," *Il Giorno* (Milan), 19 July 1960.
[3] Università statale di Milano, Corso di storia moderna, anno accademico 1943–1944.

expression it customarily wore, and which betrayed the disquiet, rising to peaks of angst, of a spirit committed with quasi-religious devotion to the study of mankind's search—yesterday, today, centuries ago, always—for understanding."[4]

A strong individual, one capable of swaying masses of people and equally capable of standing alone in proud solitude, Chabod was nevertheless truly content when he found himself in the company of a handful of close friends. Mattioli was equally perceptive in noting this characteristic, essential to the understanding of his personality:

> But in discussion, or in informal conversation with a handful of others, the joy of communication, the lively rush of thought flowing from the depths of the soul and igniting new ideas, new perceptions, even fresh doubts, in the soul of another—this was enough to relieve him of the profound melancholy of contemplation and allow him to unlock the core of tenderness in himself, his own chaste desire for spiritual companionship, and what I would call his transcendent faith in the virtue of activity and investigation. These things were the beating heart of his rugged, but not rough, personality."[5]

Chabod thus showed his true self in familiar colloquy, whether with masters and friends for whom he felt an elective affinity such as Pietro Egidi, Benedetto Croce, Friedrich Meinecke, and Ernesto Sestan, or with masters and friends whose mental orientation was different from his, but whose intercourse with him was no less deeply fruitful, such as Gaetano De Sanctis, Gaetano Salvemini, Gioacchino Volpe, Lucien Febvre, Fernand Braudel, and Delio Cantimori.

When in 1936 Gioacchino Volpe advised the Institute for the Study of International Politics of Milan to entrust to Chabod the task of analyzing Italian foreign policy from 1870 to 1896, for a general history, freshly based on primary sources, of our foreign policy from 1861 to 1914, Chabod was not new to the study of international relations. His book, *The Milanese State in the Empire of Charles V*,[6] was based on the monumental conflict between the ideal of universal empire, entirely medieval in origin, and the new idea of nationhood: this conflict occurred within the imperial framework itself in the case of the opposition between imperial interests and the purely Spanish interests that ultimately prevailed; it also occurred externally, for it motivated the victorious resistance of the French national monarchy to the empire. Then, with his introductory lecture at the University of Perugia in 1935, Chabod had transferred his attention to the study of the balance-of-power principle on which the European state system had been constructed and out of which there had flowered, in the early modern period, the consciousness of Europe as one and many at the same time. That introductory lecture was not published, but his review of W. Kienast, *Die Anfänge des*

---

[4] *Istituto italiano per gli studi storici, Napoli. Commemorazione di F. Chabod*, pp. 10–11 (Naples, 1960).

[5] Ibid., p. 11.

[6] *Lo stato di Milano nell'impero di Carlo V* (Rome, 1934).

Europäischen Staatensystems im späteren Mittelalter (Munich-Berlin, 1937),[7] conveyed its essential message. For Chabod the principle of the European balance of power was not merely an empirical guideline for diplomatic action; rather, it acquired "importance as the political symbol of the commonality of interests and traditions that continued to give Europe its own physiognomy even after the national states had grown to full practical and conceptual maturity. It is no accident that this principle was identified as a distinctively European trait at exactly the period—the eighteenth century that is—at which the contrast between the civilizations of other countries and the civilization of our continent began to emerge."[8]

Chabod thus arrived at the next stage, the history of the idea of Europe. He proceeded to analyze this subject fully in a course given at the University of Milan in 1943–44, in an essay entitled "L'idea d'Europa,"[9] and in several courses given at the University of Rome. His studies of the notion of the European balance of power, and of the idea of Europe, allowed Chabod to penetrate to the heart of the spiritual and political culture of the Italian Risorgimento, to see in Cavour and the men of the nineteenth-century Right the European ideal of the eighteenth and early nineteenth centuries, an ideal founded on the cultural and civil unity of Europe and the equilibrium of its political forces: the ideal that by and large governed the Italians in their choice of the unitary, moderate, liberal state during the Risorgimento. But his studies also enabled Chabod to see in Mazzini a new, more personal ethico-political European ideal, one destined to grow in importance.[10]

In 1946 the sponsorship of a history of Italian foreign policy from 1861 to 1914 by the Institute for the Study of International Politics of Milan was coupled with a project launched by the Italian Ministry of Foreign Affairs to publish the series of Italian diplomatic documents from 1861 to 1943. In fact the ministry was relaunching, and extending the basis of, an initiative it had first entrusted in 1927 to the care of Francesco Salata. Salata, however, although an enthusiastic hunter in the archives, became the hero/victim of a compulsion to make historiography relevant to current events. Not a single problem of foreign policy was raised by the convulsive activity of Mussolini for which he did not feel required to illustrate the historical precedents; not a single centenary of an event of the Risorgimento, or even one remotely connected to the Risorgimento like the death of the king of Rome, could he let pass without a publication. Thus he died without having brought forth even one volume of the Italian diplomatic documents. In the commission created in 1946 to resume this task Chabod played a leading role, for the basic scheme followed in preparing the publication of our

---

[7] In *Rivista Storica Italiana* (1936): fasc. 4, pp. 86–89.

[8] Ibid., p. 88.

[9] In *Rassegna d'Italia* (April 1947): 3–17; (May 1947): 25–37; now in F. Chabod, *Storia dell'idea di Europa* (Bari, 1961).

[10] "Il pensiero europeo della Destra di fronte alla guerra franco-prussiana," in *La comunità internazionale* 1 (1946): 3–77, 209–29.

diplomatic documents is his. Salata had modeled the Italian publication on the classic collection of German documents, *Die Grosse Politik der Europäischen Kabinette 1871–1914*, with the material divided into issues such as the Roman question, the question of Venetia, the question of the recognition of the kingdom of Italy, and so on. Chabod on the other hand supported the system used in the *Documents Diplomatiques Français 1871–1914*, with the documents appearing in chronological order, an arrangement that makes it possible to grasp the relations of interdependence among the issues, which is so essential to the full comprehension of episodes in diplomacy. What is more, Chabod gave the Italian collection a focus that differed from those of the great foreign diplomatic collections, which were organized around historical catastrophes such as the Franco-Prussian War of 1870–71 or the First and Second World Wars; he made it very clear that the Italian compilation, although concluding with the year 1943, was not to be seen as the chronicle of a fatal march toward disaster.

Chabod left behind, ready for the press, the first volume of the second series of Italian diplomatic documents, the ones for 1870–96 that had been entrusted to his general editorship. The volume covers the period from 21 September to 31 December 1870 and has been edited in a manner so exemplary that it deserves to become the beacon for the rest. The fact is that Chabod put all of himself into all the tasks of our trade, from the humblest, the tracking down and collating of documents, to the highest, the writing of historical prose.

Chabod, a formidable researcher in public and private archives, had gathered an immense quantity of material for his history of Italian foreign policy from 1870 to 1896, but he stood apart from the philologist-historians of preceding generations by refusing to concede an absolute primacy to archival sources vis-à-vis such sources as personal memoirs, periodicals, and contributions to public debate. He carefully scrutinized the documents for authenticity; in that connection, his doubts about the authenticity of the well-known memorandum supposedly sent by the Prussian chancellery in April 1868 to the Prussian envoy at Florence, Usedom, to be forwarded to Mazzini, ought to be examined and debated further.[11] While clearly distinguishing the subjective evaluations made by historical actors from the objective historical process that the historian verifies by comparing them with other sources, Chabod did not fail to point out the practical effect of those subjective evaluations on the course of events: the threat from the Italian republicans in 1880–82 was not as strong as it appeared to the Austro-Hungarian ambassador at Rome, Count Wimpffen, but that was his judgment, and it contributed to the concluding of the Triple Alliance.[12] Chabod never lost his bearings in methodological questions of this kind, because he possessed that gift of the historian that Guicciardini possessed to the highest degree, and that he called *discrezione*.

[11] See Chapter 4, n. 47, below; also cf. Chabod, "Questioni metodologiche," in Università di Roma, Corso di storia moderna, anno accademico 1955–1956, pp. 31–44.
[12] Ibid., pp. 65–66

And so I come to the work that was immediately seen by all to be a classic of historiography when it appeared in 1951, Chabod's *Storia della Politica Estera Italiana dal 1870 al 1896*, vol. 1: *Le Premesse* [the work here translated as *Italian Foreign Policy*].

In a review of Chabod's *Lo stato di Milano nell'impero di Carlo V*, Corrado Barbagallo had written:

> The text, while it meets the highest standards of historical writing, has a very easy narrative flow, since it has been relieved, as far as possible, of the burden of detail. The notes on the other hand are not used simply to supply references: they constitute another text, one filled with information and circumstance, a rich feast of learning to which the author seemingly welcomes his readers and fellow scholars. Now I must say that I would have preferred to have the text bolstered and enlivened by particular incidents, and a sparer set of notes.[13]

Chabod appears to have profited from this observation, for in his book on Italian foreign policy he abandons the two-layer design, thus making his composition more organic and concrete.

Fully alert to the modern problematic of historiography, Chabod nevertheless felt driven to practice the narrative art of history writing as it was practiced by the traditional historians, or rather by the historians of every age. As a result there arises an occasional unevenness, which Nino Valeri, whose point of view is different from my own, caught acutely:

> The tone of the judgments he makes on isolated events and personages is not constant, since at times he reconstructs them from the critical perspective of a man of today, and at other times with the *animus*, the tone and style, of nineteenth-century contemporaries. The reason for this is the necessity he felt to privilege retrospective judgment in some places, and re-create the atmosphere of those times in others.[14]

Chabod's book has rightly been deemed, in Italy and abroad, to be the most authoritative voice from this country to express dissatisfaction with pure diplomatic history. Indeed, in his preface Chabod renounces any attempt to erect a self-sufficient diplomatic history founded on geopolitics or the permanent interests of states, the so-called constant factors of foreign policy, and affirms the existence of a history "which is unacquainted with any abstract scheme clearly separating foreign policy from domestic politics, just as it is unacquainted with the 'primacy' of one or the other. History sees them both in close association, overlapping and interpenetrating, with more specifically internal factors sometimes having a greater bearing on the stance taken internationally, and vice versa international considerations shaping the contours of national politics, beginning with the contest among the political parties."[15]

Foreign policy and domestic politics are, for Chabod, two facets of the ethico-political consciousness of the governing class of a country, a conception to which

---

[13] *Nuova Rivista Storica* (1936): 152.
[14] *Nuova Rivista Storica* (1952): 278.
[15] From Chabod's preface below, p. xlii.

he was guided by Croce's *Storia d'Italia dal 1871 al 1915*; this influence Chabod himself hints at in his magisterial essay on Croce as historian:

> The chapter on Italian foreign policy from 1871 to 1887 (and foreign policy was, along with economic affairs, the practical activity most removed from Croce's thoughts and dominant concerns) bears a tone and an emphasis that highlight the theme; it has a heightened sense of the concreteness of things, and brings the history of diplomatic events fully within the bounds of ethico-political history, which is thereby shown to be truly capable of encompassing all the things that make up the complex weave of human history.[16]

Another disciple of Meinecke, Peter Rohden, had in fact already succeeded in interpreting diplomatic history as ethico-political history, demonstrating that while on the plane of international relations, the alignments and predicaments of politics may repeat themselves, what changes is the ethos that motivates the decision-making process.[17] Rohden thus surmounted *l'histoire diplomatique* in the sense in which it had been understood by Albert Sorel, but in substance he still remained within the bounds of diplomatic history. In Chabod, on the other hand, the history of international relations, which he also places in its ethico-political context, is no longer viewed apart but is located, as a manifestation of the ethico-political consciousness of the governing class, in the framework of general history or, better still, of history, period.

Individual leaders, and the governing class, are front and center in the work of Chabod. That "taste for the affairs of men" which our past masters of the Renaissance and Counter Reformation (Machiavelli, Guicciardini, Sarpi, the Venetian ambassadors) had, and which passed over to German historiography with Ranke, then to French historiography with Sorel and Vandal, and which seemed finally to have come to rest with the English historians Gooch, Temperley, and Webster, returns with Chabod to Italian historiography. His personal profiles of the diplomats have been admired universally, but from the group I would single out those of Emilio Visconti Venosta and Count di Robilant. We gain acquaintance with these individuals gradually, firmly, attribute by attribute: the technique is that of the mountain climber. Each man is identified with his role in politics and history. Other factors are barely mentioned. Among the papers of Costantino Nigra, now in the possession of the family de Vecchi di Val Cismon, Chabod found the most beautiful love letters from noble foreign ladies to Nigra, but he scrupulously refrained from making public the slightest extract from these.

Chabod was an unrivaled student of public opinion among the governing class, but of course a more basic level of public opinion exists in the form of attitudes among the mass of citizens who are outside active political life. Chabod has been accused of neglecting this level, but in fact he did deal with it to some extent when he described the "apathy" of the Italian population;[18] moreover, as Rosario Romeo has perceptively observed in his review of a book by an eminent Ameri-

---

[16] Chabod, "Croce storico," in *Rivista Storica Italiana* (1952): 515.
[17] *Die Klassische Diplomatie von Kaunitz bis Metternich* (Leipzig, 1939).
[18] See chapter 4 below.

can historian, M. Lynn Case: "the full weight and specificity of attitudes for or against a war, or a particular alliance, can only be understood in relation to the more complex and articulated point of view that politically adept persons are able to take of such matters."[19]

Nor does it seem to me that my friend Arnaldo Momigliano does justice to Chabod in stating that the latter retreated from a salient historical vantage point attained by Croce. [Maturi refers to A. Momigliano, "Appunti su F. Chabod storico," published in the same issue of *Rivista Storica Italiana* as the present article.—Trans.]. After Croce's *Storia d'Europa*, according to Momigliano, the problem faced by his successors was "to enfold the history of Italy in the history of Europe, and find a rhythm that would allow Italian events to keep their own distinctiveness within European history generally." It seems to me that Chabod's work, permeated as it is with Europe-wide resonance, found exactly that rhythm. Chabod went so far as to portray France and Germany as "the two poles on which depended peace and war for the Italian people."[20]

Momigliano's other criticism, arising out of the previous one, is similarly inexact: "There is the further reproof that Chabod failed to take economic factors into sufficient consideration, which perhaps goes back as well to the lack of a specifically European character in his history. The economic outlook would have yielded an entirely different evaluation of the place of Italy in Europe." The fact is that in the part of the work dedicated to the "objective" factors,[21] Chabod demonstrates precisely that Italy could not be a genuine great power in the period from 1870 to 1896 because it lagged behind its rivals from the economic and financial point of view, with a consequent military and naval lag as well.

It is true that this analysis was not taken to the limit because of a lack of research on several fundamental problems to which Renouvin drew attention in his review of the work.[22] What was the importance of the French and German markets for the export of Italian agricultural products? Where did international capital flow within Italy? What was the position of the Italian textile industry compared to the corresponding industries in France and Germany? Renouvin recognized, however, with scholarly fairness, that even had these subjects been investigated, Chabod's fundamental thesis would have remained valid: that at critical moments, collective sentiments have greater weight than the pure calculation of material interests. Chabod for his part acknowledged, in a certain sense, that the economic underpinning of his work needed to be reinforced, for he had assumed the task of directing the massive project of the Banca Commerciale for an economic history of Italy from 1700 to the present and of summarizing the results in a historical introduction.

On the other hand, Chabod, whose study of Max Weber had given him an extremely keen interest in the mentality and economic ideals of the Italian moderates (and created a divergence between himself and Croce), wrote perhaps the

---

[19] In *Rivista Storica Italiana* (1955): 109.
[20] See chapter 11 below, p. 384.
[21] See chapters 12–14 below.
[22] In *Revue Historique* (1954): 165–68.

most penetrating pages in our entire historiography on that subject. The validity he assigned to religious experience as such also divided Chabod from Croce and resulted in his remarkable study of one particular expression of the myth of Rome, the aspiration for a *Renovatio Ecclesiae*.

Finally, Chabod diverged from Croce in the importance he gave to the Paris Commune of 1871. Croce had already placed strong historical emphasis on the Franco-Prussian War and the Italian capture of Rome, and Chabod did not fail to expand both topics, but he also added a third: the Commune of 1871. The result was one of the most original sections of the book, the one subtitled "Order and Liberty."[23] Nor did he exaggerate the effects of the Commune. In Chabod's pages the objective historical situation of Italy in the years 1870–96 is clearly evident, a situation that may be summarized in these phrases taken from an unpublished letter of 4 September 1871 written by Michelangelo Castelli to Isacco Artom: "You are living between two fearsome threats, that of the papalists and that of the Communists (by which I mean the ultraradicals and the International). It is my belief that the first is a reality but that the others are specters, for now. They will be a problem for the grandsons of the present generation, but although they make us apprehensive because of the trials of Paris, they create no real danger."[24] But the pattern that escaped the notice of Castelli the political actor, because it had no immediate practical importance, did not escape Chabod the historian at the conclusion of his chapter 8. Having alluded to the germination of nationalism and socialism, he commented:

> Whether it was the nationalistic drive at work, or the drive to socialism, either way society was coming to be seen as divided into blocs. It lost the aspect of extreme mobility with which the classical liberalism of the early nineteenth century had endowed it. The two new forces of the contemporary world, inexorably spreading after 1870, and so much alike in contrasting the individual to a higher, inclusive entity—the homeland or a social class—began to deform the liberal world from the right and the left. Thus, when the Italian governing class asserted that its own realm was not exclusive, this did not prevent it from feeling that it reigned nonetheless, though its realm was not economic, but moral and political in character, not composed of a social structure but rather of civic functions. . . . Apart from polemics, and postures assumed in debate, the fact is that it was becoming evident that society was divided into different, in fact opposed, social strata.[25]

Into Chabod's work are interwoven themes that prolong the political and spiritual life of the past, the specific preoccupations of a given historical moment, and the first shoots destined to grow into the future. All things find their place in time. The present continues to illuminate the past—if not, those first shoots would obviously never have come forth—but the past does not simply mirror every feature of the present, despite that species of historical narcissism that constitutes the limit of too much of our historiography today. The past, in other

[23] See chapters 8–10 below.
[24] Artom archive (private).
[25] See chapter 8 below, pp. 291–92.

words, must not be understood *totally* as a function of the present, otherwise one is engaged in politics, not history. "Every age is immediate to God" was Ranke's great motto, one Chabod loved to repeat and one he followed as an ethical and religious imperative. And that, in my opinion, is his most precious bequest to anyone who wishes to be a historian above all else, and not a monk preaching inside the walls of his own monastery.

This preface was written for the first edition of Storia della Politica Estera Italiana dal 1870 al 1896, *published in 1951, at a time when the author intended to publish four further volumes on Italian foreign policy from 1870 to 1896, containing more specific and technical researches than those found in the present work, which in 1951 bore a subtitle that has since been dropped:* "Le Premesse" *or* "The Premises."

THE PRESENT WORK had its origin in what is by now the distant past. In 1936 the Institute for the Study of International Politics, on the initiative of Alberto Pirelli, its president, Pier Francesco Gaslini, the general secretary, and Gioacchino Volpe handed the task of writing a *History of Italian Foreign Policy from 1861 to 1914* to the late and lamented Carlo Morandi (to whose memory my thoughts turn), Walter Maturi, Augusto Torre, and myself. I assumed the portion of the work covering the period from 20 September 1870 to March 1896.

The Institute gave us precious assistance in every way, and I wish here to express my warm gratitude to Alberto Pirelli, Alessandro Casati, Gioacchino Volpe, Pier Francesco Gaslini, and Gerolamo Bassani, the present secretary of the Institute for the Study of International Politics. Above all it was this assistance that made it possible to obtain free access to the Historical Archive of the Ministry for Foreign Affairs, and to explore it fully, during the course of more than six years of research between 1936 and 1943. Thus one indispensable condition was guaranteed to our work from the outset: it was grounded on the primary documents. Without this access, the project would not have been conceived in the first place.

The documentary basis is not, however, limited to this archive alone. As the research progressed it became increasingly evident that we needed to round out the contents of the official papers with those private collections of personal correspondence that—in the case of Italian history no less than in that of other countries—are the essential complement to the official record; sometimes indeed they are the only source from which one can get a clear and precise idea of the development of a situation and the position of a government. There are some judgments, and some motives, that you will never find in any official correspondence. So we felt it was necessary to extend our research to other state archives that also contain correspondence and diaries, or at any rate documents that have an immediate relationship to Italian foreign policy. These included, for example, the Visconti Venosta and Depretis papers at the Central State Archive in Rome, but also, whenever possible, private archives. Here too I was favored by fortune, for in virtually every case the descendants or relatives of former ministers and ambassadors courteously and generously opened their archives to me. This material, gathered (I may say) during the patient research of many years, I also intend to include in the full published series of Italian Diplomatic Documents, the first volumes of which are now appearing. As a member of the commission in charge of this publication, it will be my task to edit the documents for the period 1870–1896, and I am confident that the inclusion of documents from private archives —something that has not yet been done in any of the other national collections— will go a long way toward providing the most complete portrayal possible, not only of the courses of action pursued but also of the understanding of events that impelled the men of the Italian government to make the choices they did at that time.

Let me therefore record with gratitude the names of the late Marchese Giovanni Visconti Venosta di Sostegno, who put the papers of Emilio Visconti Venosta at my disposition; and the late senator Francesco Salata, who permitted me to take advantage of his copies of bundles of documents from the archive at Vienna which I was unable to consult *in loco*. Let me also express my thanks to the head of the House of Savoy, who with great liberality allowed me to use documents from the personal archive of Vittorio Emanuele II. And I am grateful to the Marchesa Dora Daniele di Bagni for the Mancini papers; to Madame Maria Pansa for the diary of her husband Alberto; to Count Cesare Maria de Vecchi di Val Cismon for the Nigra papers.

Along with the Italian archives, public and private, it was necessary finally to use, to the extent possible, foreign ones. Even when the governments had already published their documents for the period 1871–1896, further research seemed appropriate: since in the great published collections it was impossible to include everything, it was obvious that much of the material directly relevant to Italy must still be lying unexplored in the archives. This conjecture was fully confirmed by my research in the archives of the Quai d'Orsay in Paris and the comparison between the materials I gathered there and the exiguous quantity actually published in the *Documents Diplomatiques Français* for the years from 1871 to 1896. It is hardly necessary to emphasize that in Germany's *Grosse Politik* the correspondence exchanged directly between Berlin and Rome goes unrecorded until the year 1880.

Although my attempt to get permission to consult the holdings of the German archives came to nothing, I was able to research exhaustively the period down to 1896 in the archive at Vienna. At the archive of the Quai d'Orsay, however, my time was limited by the rules currently in effect there. I hope to be able to review the English documents as I pursue my research, in relation to the specific problems that will be treated in it.

Let me close by offering my thanks to the officials of the various archives, especially those of the archive of the Ministry for Foreign Affairs in Rome, Ambassador Raffaelle Guariglia and Professor Ruggero Moscati, who sent me documents and information which I have used from the archive of Vittorio Emanuele II, and the colleagues and friends who gave me precious assistance during the research or during the checking of the proofs of printed documents and texts against the originals: Professor Maria Avetta and Professor Emilia Morelli, the hon. Professor Roberto Cessi, Professors Giorgio Cencetti, Luigi Bulferetti,

Carlo Cipolla, Armando Saitta, and Dr. Rosario Romeo and Dr. Giuseppe Giarrizzo, who also undertook together the burden of compiling the index to the present volume, the first in the history of Italian foreign policy which Laterza has courageously agreed to publish. Chapter 3 of the present text is a reworked and expanded version of the article "Il pensiero europeo della Destra di fronte alla guerra franco-prussiana," published in *La Comunità internazionale*, January-April 1946.

This first volume is not, and is not intended to be, dedicated to an analysis along chronological lines of specific problems, and of the various phases of Italian foreign policy, between 1870 and 1896. Certainly there are allusions to these problems, sometimes indeed more than just allusions, but in any case the points in question are destined to be taken up again and developed fully at the proper time, and they are mentioned here purely in order to clarify the fundamental direction, in fact the structure itself, of the project. An ample and sequential narrative will be built up in the course of a series of volumes (four are planned at present) to follow.

The reason is that, before setting out to weave the pattern of Italian foreign policy in detail, before immersing myself in the more specific, I might say more technical, part of my task, it seemed to me that I had an obligation to make plain to the reader the nature of the material and moral bases which necessarily acted as supports to the specific and technical part, to illustrate the complex of forces and feelings that surrounded the country's diplomatic initiative and constituted the environment within which it moved at that historical period. That is to say: passions and all forms of affect, ideas and ideologies, the situation of the country and of individuals—in a word everything that makes foreign policy a component or aspect of a much larger and more complex historical process that embraces the entire life of a nation, defies any separation into watertight compartments, and binds the field of foreign relations tightly and inseparably to its counterpart, the internal life of the nation in its moral, economic, social, and religious aspects.

The foreign policy of a state, whichever one it may be, cannot be summed up in diplomatic negotiations alone, in the official correspondence between the minister for foreign affairs and his ambassadors; likewise (and this is not a matter of debate but is taken for granted) domestic politics is not encapsulated in the correspondence between the interior minister and his prefects, or even in the contest among the political parties, if that contest is seen exclusively from the point of view of domestic problems, in isolation from the repercussions of international events and the vicissitudes of other parties in other countries. To presume to seal oneself inside one or the other of these two abstract compartments and, with the door firmly shut, to imagine that one can then grasp the significance and the importance of events, would be like trying to provide street lighting for a great modern metropolis with a few oil lamps.

Nevertheless, in the principal and most significant schools of modern historiography in Italy and elsewhere, one could (and indeed still can) observe a certain impatience, not to speak of distaste, for what is termed diplomatic history. The main reason is that the type of history that bears this label is practiced, not in all cases certainly (outstanding exceptions to the rule are not lacking) but still far too often, as the exercise of very highly honed technical skills—but with a corresponding narrowness of underlying vision. Even now in the middle of the twentieth century, and even in the best of cases, diplomatic history is always based on ideas about the relative importance of things that go back to the origins of modern historiography: to the purely political, diplomatic, and military criteria that were legitimate and indeed innovative when they first appeared in the writers of the sixteenth and seventeenth centuries.

This set of norms can be justified, it is true, by invoking what are called the "permanent interests" of a country; these are imagined as a sort of hidden divinity floating high above everything that constitutes the actual life of a people (political struggle, ideals and ideologies, passions in conflict) and forming both the precondition and the goal of foreign policy: a polar star on which to fix one's gaze in the course of a perilous voyage, disregarding everything else. To say that the interests of a state ought to be the central focus of the thoughts and the actions of the political actors of that state, an observation repeated for centuries in the theoretical tradition from the time of Machiavelli and the Duke of Rohan, is an obvious banality. If one then qualifies those interests as "permanent," one merely highlights the shackles one has imposed on oneself by attempting (in vain) to create a sphere of "foreign policy" independent of all the rest, set over above the sphere of so-called domestic politics. "Permanent interests" are a pure doctrinaire abstraction. No history of any country at any time has ever produced an example of such immutable and fixed interests, but all our history overflows with more or less sudden "reversals of alliances," sensational rearrangements of the relationship among the different powers, the collapse of what are called political systems and the creation of new ones, destined to vanish in their turn.

Long before the historian comes on the scene, the political actor has the difficult burden of evaluating exactly what the preponderant interests are at a given moment. And if he believes in the necessity and inevitability of certain enmities, he might, for example, find himself in the shoes of the statesmen of Wilhelmine Germany: they maintained that an accord between England and Russia was an impossibility, and they lived to see the way things actually turned out. Continual movement, a historical process ever evolving, and never measurable by the standards of the past—this absence of the permanent and the immutable is the condition of international relations too.

Yet in our time an attempt has been made to engineer a solid physical foundation for these supposedly everlasting interests. Geopolitics has been invented, cloaking things that were known to ordinary good sense with new and pompous names, and succeeding often enough in suffocating both good sense and the good old things that it knew under the weight of up-to-date nonsense. From the fundamentally important fact, as old as human thought, that the geographical position of a country has an influence on its interaction with its neighbors (something so obvious that one repeats a cliché in stating it), a new determinism on a geographic basis has been erected, a fatalistic mechanism through which nature shapes the history of a country. What importance to give to "location" was already well known to theorists and writers on politics centuries ago, and is discussed in detail, for example, by the writers of the Cinquecento, who nevertheless had the discernment to leave plenty of space for human *virtù*, which not even location can enslave. But our modern doctrinaires believed that they could do away with that free space, as they vainly pursued the revelation of fixed laws which they could impose on the course of events in a country. It did not occur to them that any state always has at least two different courses of action before it from which to choose, and that the hard part, both for the political actor in deciding and later for the historian in understanding, lies here and here alone: which to follow at that particular moment, in that precise situation. History abounds in examples, from the time of Charles VIII of France (nor is this the earliest case), at whose court there was *mainte disputation* between those who supported the invasion of Italy and the *gens saiges et experimentéz* who conversely found it *très deraisonnable* and wanted nothing to do with the *fumées et gloires d'Italie*; or from the time of the Emperor Charles V, when there were similar debates between the proponents and opponents of his Italian policy.

Heated contrasts of opinion of this kind then passed all too arbitrarily into the subsequent historiography, with the help of scholars who were convinced that the dominant political interests of the age in which they themselves were writing was an absolute, and who made their own political preoccupations the criterion for evaluating historically the remote past. These historians condemned the Italian policies of Charles VIII and Louis XII, for example, as futile, wasteful, and unnatural; for them (with an illegitimate shift of France's concerns in the nineteenth and twentieth centuries back into the world of the fifteenth) the only natural direction of French policy ought to have been toward the Rhine. Or another typical example: the extended polemic launched by German scholars from von Sybel to von Below (and beyond) against the *italienische Kaiserpolitik* of the Middle Ages. This policy was portrayed as another unnatural, deplorable waste of Germany's resources in the south, the cause of the dilapidation of the German crown and the loss of the opportunity to create a strong national German state, the obstacle to a more natural and fruitful *Ostpolitik*. Once again what they did was to transpose, improperly, Germany's worries and problems in the nineteenth and twentieth centuries to the period from the tenth to the thirteenth centuries. How easy it was for them to describe the interests and aspirations of the political situation in which they themselves were living as permanent and eternal!

The fact is that when the moment comes, in international affairs properly speaking, to make a decisive choice, then (at least since the time of the French Revolution) the whole life of a people, its ideal aspirations and political ideologies, its economic and social conditions, its material capacities, and the tensions among its various internal currents of feeling and interest, all have the greatest weight. And here pure diplomatic history, which gives a technical account of the relations among governments, shows its limitations. Those who care only for pure diplomacy, and are gripped by the spell of the *arcana imperii* of the *ancien régime*, can perfectly well register their dismay when forces that have nothing to do with diplomacy, especially political ideologies, intrude "inappropriately" into diplomatic calculation; they can perfectly well dream of a new state of Utopia where such contaminations will not occur: chimeras of this kind are regularly swept away by history, which is unacquainted with any abstract scheme clearly separating foreign policy from domestic politics, just as it is unacquainted with the "primacy" of one or the other. History sees them both in close association, overlapping and interpenetrating, with more specifically internal factors sometimes having a greater bearing on the stance taken internationally, and vice versa international considerations shaping the contours of national politics, beginning with the contest among the political parties. And if ever there was a classic example of this, it is the history of Italy in the period following unification.

In sum, no one who wishes to study Italian foreign policy can avoid coming to terms, before anything else, with just what this country was and became while realizing its own national unity, or fail to recognize the many elements that were fused at the moment of its birth. This heterogeneity was made clear—all too clear!—in the different directions and solutions that were variously proposed for its foreign policy. It is only against this background that international events can be placed in their just perspective.

Likewise it would be an advantage, if I may say so, if those who are conducting specific research on problems of so-called domestic politics did not forget that these problems are in their turn tightly bound to those of foreign policy, the influence of which makes itself felt in different ways. I wish they would bear this in mind: because all too often what happens is that one finds oneself reading historical reconstructions in which Italy appears to exist in some sort of lunar orbit, a world unto itself, perfectly isolated and able to control every aspect of its own life. In consequence one is forced to listen to reprimands about the way the events of the Risorgimento (for example) ought to have turned out, when naturally that's not the way they turned out at all, from people who never seem to feel a touch of doubt about whether or not, in Europe as it then was, or even in Italy taken by itself, certain outcomes would even have been possible. Such people never seem to remember 1848–49 and the general failure of the European revolution, which if nothing else might serve to alert them to the fact that it is necessary to keep in mind, when passing judgment on Italian history, what actually was feasible at that time in Europe.

Our task, then, is to arrive at an understanding of the intellectual and moral forces, of the interests and aspirations, of which the life of united Italy was composed: forces, interests, and aspirations that were to condition the conduct of diplomacy over time, just as attitudes, manifestations, and disturbances within Italy were to weigh, even more heavily perhaps than in other countries, on Italy's international position. The clamorous, violent explosion of discontent and protest in the summer of 1878, following the Congress of Berlin, or the heightened signs of anticlericalism in 1881—both of which were closely connected with traditions, emotions, and inclinations of the Italian character as it then was—signified something about the stance of Italy vis-à-vis Europe too, and the preoccupations of domestic politics played a much greater role than is often realized in the concluding of the Triple Alliance.

The point of this—that one ought to try to take in not only attitudes and facts but also impressions and states of mind, not only governmental action but people's opinions—is that it makes it possible in the end to understand more fully the reasons behind certain actions taken by government leaders, even though in retrospect those actions may appear to have been mistaken. It is all too easy for a historian to pass judgment fifty or sixty years after the fact, when he can learn the real intentions and the secret moves of the various players on the international stage—that is, of the various states; all too easy, if one fails to go further and ask oneself whether what was capable of being known at that time about the subjective viewpoint of another government, and the impressions people had, and majority opinion, did not in fact provide justification for an attitude that in the sequel was seen to be misguided. Not even the greatest among contemporary statesmen, not Cavour and not Bismarck, were immune from such errors, much less the others. In this connection it is enough to recall the gross distortion of political perspective that consisted, even after 1870, in attributing to Bismarck the constant secret desire to annex the German portion of Austria to the Reich: a gross distortion certainly, but one shared by many, Italians and foreigners, politicians and journalists. The extent to which this was believed must be kept in mind when one is pondering, for example, the phrase uttered by Crispi to Bismarck during their meeting of 17 September 1877.

Finally, in addition to everything else, there remains the task of learning to know the men who took decisions as personalities with their own thoughts and feelings; for history, at least down to now, has been made by men and not by automatons. Systems of thought and structures (so called), which in and of themselves amount to pure abstractions from the point of view of historiographical evaluation, attain the status of historical forces only when they are able to blaze into life in the minds of human individuals and human groups, when they become a faith, an interior religion capable ultimately of producing martyrs—in other words, when ideologies or social relations become moral facts, drawing to the platform of this or that political party, rallying behind this or that banner, the many who only then, through this sudden arousal of a new faith, perceive that that which they themselves in the past, or their forebears, had regarded as destiny, something to which they were resigned, or which they even accepted as a normal and obvious fact, is an injustice to be fought against, whether the injustice be manifested in the partition of Italy and its enslavement to outsiders, or in a given set of social and economic arrangements.

It is all the more necessary to make this effort to get through to the human personality when the matter at hand, as in the present case, is political history, especially the story of international political relations, because not only the personality of the single politician or diplomat, his ideas and his program generally, but also his style of action, is an important factor in events. The way in which a man plans and carries out a certain policy, the way in which he approaches and deals with different questions, the way in which he reacts, in a word his style, are at least as important as his formal programs in the case of men such as those we shall be observing, who were men of action and not theoreticians or scholars. Let me be even more definite about this: it is impossible in my opinion to distinguish, in a given political action, its substance from the way that substance is presented. As with artists, so it is with politicians, who are artists too, proceeding by intuition and not by abstract logic, and who are born to their role by the grace of God and not as the result of applied doctrine: the form and the content amount to the same thing. If you try to privilege the latter and neglect the former, you become a student of ideologies, not of political action. So we shall seek to convey the essential natures of the men who guided policy, or were in charge of carrying it out, and to take account of their diversity of styles, a diversity rich in practical consequences.

I am aware that much of modern historiography disdains the individual as such and, after confounding frivolous tattle with the portrayal of a moral and spiritual personality, shuns what it likes to call psychologism in order to go in pursuit of pure systems of ideas, of pure structures, or of the latest marvelous *trouvaille* of up-to-date historiography, statistical tables, percentages, averages, graphs—all of which are useful enough within certain limits, but which according to some contain the secret of history itself, hidden in diagrams and statistical averages. When I encounter this sort of thing I always think of that excellent general, Cartier de Chalmot, depicted by Anatole France in the midst of organizing his army with the aid of file cards: every *fiche* is a soldier, every *fiche* is a reality, and the excellent general maneuvers, disposes, commands, studies tactical plans, imperturbable in the conviction that reality lies before him in his *fiches*, never apprehensive for a single instant that on the ground true reality in the form of his flesh-and-blood soldiers might react to the orders given in some quite unforeseen way. Quite a few historical scholars today are so many generals Cartier de Chalmot, so we shall leave them to command their troops by shuffling their *fiches*.

That does not at all imply a wish to return, even in a study such as this, to the sixteenth-century *virtù* of the prince as the sole historical force. But it is a way of affirming that, in a given situation, the deeds of a single statesman always make a difference to the course of events. Either he is mediocre and in the end lets himself be swept along by them, or he has greatness, and succeeds instead in channeling them in a certain way, forcing them to develop with a certain rhythm rather than another, steering them in the direction of certain solutions rather than others, retarding or accelerating them, and in the last analysis creating a situation upon which those who succeed him will recognize that he left his own individual imprint. Greatness or inferiority—this is history's unending secret. Just as, given the geographical location of a state, the possibility of the *arbitrium indifferentiae* [choosing not to choose] does not exist, but only the choice of one thing or the other, and choice is made by man and so is free, likewise in a certain historical situation it is not permitted, even to the greatest of statesmen, to indulge in capricious action, for his point of departure will always be the reality facing him—but this reality always allows him to make choices and to pursue different courses. In this lies precisely the indestructible liberty of history, and its unknowable secret as it perpetually unfolds into the future.

ARCHIVAL SOURCES

Documents cited without specifying an archive are in every case to be found in the Archivio Storico del Ministero degli Affari Esteri in Rome, and belong to the ordinary series—that is, to the registers of incoming and outgoing telegrams, to the registers of dispatches, to the political correspondence (reports) of the various embassies and legations. Documents from the same archive contained in special series, on the other hand, are given a precise indication using the following archival abbreviations:

AE = Archivio Storico del Ministero degli Affari Esteri, followed by the indication of the specific series. Two of these series have the following abbreviations:

Ris. =   *riservato* (classified)
Cas. Verdi =   Cassette Verdi

It is to be noted that these indications are based on the organization of the archive as it was in the years 1936–1943 (the period, that is, in which the research was accomplished). In recent years the archive has been reorganized (in fact, this reorganization is taking place at the moment I write), and the distinct former series, such as "Riservato," have been replaced by a single general one under the name of *Archivio del Gabinetto e del Segretariato Generale* (1861–1887), comprising the special series as distinct from ordinary political correspondence, whether telegraphic or epistolary. But there are concordances that allow one to locate documents identified by the previous system of reference under the new system without difficulty, and for this reason I have maintained the archival references exactly as they were at the time of my research. In the Robilant papers (which have been kept as a separate series, distinct even from the *Archivio del Gabinetto*), the letters of Robilant to Corti are in typescript copies.

For other archives, the abbreviations are the following:

ACR =   Archivio Centrale dello Stato, Rome
AEP, *C.P.* =   Archives du Ministère des Affaires Etrangères, Paris, Correspondance Politique

I note that here again the references to volumes are given according to the classification in use until very recently, a classification in which the correspondence with the French representative to the king of Italy had a numeration that continued on from the preceding series *Sardaigne*. Very recently the series *Italie* has received its own numeration, number 1 being the volume for January 1861. Volumes 379–393, to which reference is made in the present work, are therefore presently volumes 29–43.

BCB =   Biblioteca Comunale di Bologna
MRP =   Museo del Risorgimento di Pavia
MRR =   Museo e Archivio del Risorgimento di Roma
MRT =   Museo e Archivio del Risorgimento di Torino
SAW, *P.A.* =   Haus-, Hof- und Staatsarchiv, Vienna, Politisches Archiv. For fascicles III/112, XI/76, and *rot* 459, I used the typescript copies of Senator Salata.

No abbreviations are employed for other archives.

PRINTED SOURCES

A.P. =   *Atti Parlamentari, Discussioni*
D.D.F. =   *Documents Diplomatiques Français (1871–1914)*
G.P. =   *Die Grosse Politik der Europäischen Kabinette, 1871–1914*
Libro Verde 17 =   Documenti Diplomatici relativi alla Questione Romana comunicati dal ministro degli Affari Esteri (Visconti Venosta) nella tornata del 19 dicembre 1870 [which is number 17 in the general printed list of the Green Books or Libri Verdi entitled *Documenti Diplomatici (Libro Verde) presentati al Parlamento Italiano dal 27 giugno 1861*, Biblioteca del Ministero degli Affari Esteri (Ufficio Intendenza)].

Except where otherwise indicated, words and phrases given in italics in quotations from manuscript documents or printed texts are always underlined in the originals, or appear in italics in the edition cited.

THE FIRST THING to point out is that the title given to this English translation of Chabod's work does not render the literal sense of the original. *Storia della Politica Estera Italiana dal 1870 al 1896 (History of Italian Foreign Policy from 1870 to 1896)* was the title of a projected series of volumes, of which Chabod's was the only one to appear, a circumstance which makes the title inappropriate to the contents of his book. When I was thinking about what to call it in English, Professor Charles S. Maier suggested something along the lines of *Italian Foreign Policy: The Statecraft of the Founders, 1870–1896*. I found I was unable to improve on this suggestion, and so it stands.

When the language of the sources upon which Chabod drew was French, which is very frequently the case (with German also appearing, and a few traces of Spanish, Latin, and the dialects of Piedmont and Lombardy), he kept the citation in the original language, but I have reduced all citations (or almost all) to English. On the other hand, he translated the infrequent English sources cited into Italian (except for a handful of literary citations), and in these cases I have located the published text of the original and used that.

Chabod structured the book in two parts, with four chapters in the first and two chapters in the second, each chapter containing a number of sections. The chapters were numbered separately in each part, and the sections were numbered separately in each chapter. However, I have designated those sections, the smallest units, as chapters and given them a continuous numeration throughout. In the original the footnotes were numbered separately on each page, but I have given them a continuous numeration in each chapter. The bibliography and index are by me; a short preface to the bibliography explains its character.

For consultation on the meaning of a number of passages, I am grateful to Michael Lettieri, Guido Pugliese, and G. P. Clivio. Via the Internet list "H-Italy" Franco Andreucci, Charles S. Maier, and others provided illuminating replies to my queries on historical questions. The meticulous copyeditor, Roy Thomas, contributed substantially to the improvement of the text.

PART ONE

Passions and Ideas

I. *The Franco-Prussian War and Italy*

What Prussia Had to Teach

Our Italian genius is going to take on its own new and original form of expression here. The endearing habits formed in exile, the attachments of the heart felt by the generation that is in its prime today for those who were its teachers in youth, the conceptions formed in a series of progressive stages by the nation during the last fifty years, Guelphism, Liberal Catholicism, the collaboration of Italy and the papacy in politics, the alliance of the Latin races, all these will be preserved as touching souvenirs and as proofs of our good faith and our good will in each of the situations through which we have passed—but let us break the hold they have on our ideas and our actions in the present. Germany, following in the steps of England and America, has gained such a lead on the rest of the world that we shall have to hurry our pace and pursue reality, leaving behind affections, dreams, and the sentimental ideal, and grasp hold vigorously of the only things that are solid and secure: positive science, productivity, and the force that comes from both of them. It pleases me to repeat to you these things that you yourself have been saying for a long time now, because here in Rome I sense a spirit and a setting which, although not endowed with any incontrovertible moral or intellectual superiority, ought to sustain, so it seems to me, a more serious and elevated standard for our political and social action than what we had in Florence, and a less exclusive one than what we found in Turin. This effect of sober enthusiasm, of ardor tempered with reflection, of confidence without boastfulness, of the honest desire to do much and do it well, all of which I observe here, are felt by everyone, all the Italians from the other parts of the country have felt it too. Let us endeavor to make sure that it is not an illusion. . . . Happy the one who shall find himself at the vital points in the magnificent dawn that is commencing for Italy.

WITH THESE HOPES for the future, the secretary general of the Ministry of Foreign Affairs, Alberto Blanc, then on a mission to Rome, finished a long letter of 12 October 1870 to Marco Minghetti, who at that moment was in Vienna.[1] Rome was now part of Italy and Prussia was supreme in Europe, and the two great events of the dramatic September of 1870, a month that would not be forgotten "until the distant revolution,"[2] were thus closely linked by Blanc: in both it was possible to glimpse the commencement of a *novus ordo*, and above all a radiant dawn for Italy, the "third Italy" that now had to stride resolutely toward the future, relying on the heritage and the genius of Rome and the powerful friendship of Germany, free of the trammels of the past.

---

[1] BCB, *Carte Minghetti*, cart. XV, fasc. 66.

[2] R. Bonghi (for the *Nuova Antologia*, 30 September 1870), in *Nove anni di storia di Europa nel commento di un italiano (1866–1874)*, ed. M. Sandirocco, vol. 2, p. 385 (= vol. 10 in *Opere* [Milan, 1942]).

And in fact Blanc seemed already to be working out a new subjective attitude, one entirely suited to the new political course he was propounding. A Savoyard raised under the direct political guidance of Cavour[3] and bound permanently to the men of the Right, cabinet chief to La Marmora and general secretary to Visconti Venosta, Blanc was overall a man who might well, as a result of this background and this professional experience, have continued to embrace as true and real the values of La Marmora, Lanza, or Visconti Venosta. Instead he chose to call them *souvenirs émouvants*. Blanc said a firm farewell to the *attaches du coeur*, to the tradition of the past, in order to set himself new goals, and goals with a moral dimension, not merely those of political success. Sentimental ideals were banished, and he welcomed the only things that were now "solid and secure": science, productivity, force—for the concept of *Realpolitik*, though not the term, was by this time widespread, in the sense that the only forces to be taken into account were the tangible and observable ones, using the empirical sensory apparatus and mathematical calculation to do so. There was an overriding sense that the meaning of life ought basically to be looked for in the economic realm, and in the further development of civilization through mechanical and industrial technology, and hence that the dominant moral and cultural concerns of the men of the period from 1820 to 1850 ought to recede into the background. It was on this basis that Blanc, in another letter to Minghetti, insisted that the influence of economic factors was increasing almost daily in international politics, so that it was imperative to permit the fundamental laws of economics to bring about their effects, unhindered by the deleterious "inclinations to sentimentality or to classicism that still have a grip on so many distinguished intellects among us,"[4] and that his injunction to "grasp hold vigorously of the only things that are solid and secure" was truly the expression of a new way of facing the problems of political life. It was not the case, certainly, that before this time a sense of the concrete, of the politically possible, of the driving forces, had been absent; on the contrary, it would be utterly ridiculous to speak of, or even to suppose, such an absence, if one recalls that Cavour had already come and gone. But the fact is that only now, in 1870, were the driving forces so nakedly and openly defined as technology, productivity, material capacity: politics as pure, quantitatively definable force. To repeat, concepts and ideas of a Prussian cast were already in the air, and the *realité* endorsed by the general secretary at the foreign ministry was being assimilated to the *Reelle* to which the Sergeant King had once brutally recalled the attention of his son Frederick, then still a dreamy youth.[5] There was an affinity between Blanc's *choses solides* and the *realité* which Frederick II, when he became king of Prussia, had based his actions on, and

---

[3] Blanc, in a letter to Mancini of 15 December 1882, recalls going to the house of Cavour at five in the morning, with Artom, in order to work under the guidance of the great nobleman (MRR, *Carte Mancini*, b. 638, no. 8/15).

[4] Letter of 10 September 1870 (BCB, *Carte Minghetti*, cart. XV, fasc. 66). Despite this expression of Blanc's views, Minghetti never saw positivistic science and force as the only "solid and secure" things. See below, pp. 200, 305, 312, 315.

[5] "Halte dich an das Reelle" (E. Lavisse, *La jeunesse du grand Frédéric* [Paris, 1891], p. 134).

which now manifested itself anew as the canon followed by Count Bismarck, the man of the hour. In fact, the new reality was even more physically embodied and massive, comprising not only well-drilled formations of armed soldiery, but also numerous smokestacks rising above roaring factories, and warehouses filled with bales of merchandise in vast quantities, and the diffusion of these phenomena throughout the world.[6]

Blanc's aspiration was thus not merely strategic—in other words, that Italy should have a more friendly political alignment with Prussia (many of the most obstinate Francophiles of 1870 would soon follow him in that)—but was rather a way of approaching political problems, the logical result of which was a distinct moral and intellectual leaning toward the new Germany. Such an approach was a fact of considerable significance since, quite apart from any single diplomatic episode, it lay at the root of the desire, which was destined to grow continually stronger in Italy, to join its own destiny to the future of the empire of central Europe. This desire was to be realized eleven years later, in the turmoil of the summer of 1881, when Blanc was to be among the earliest and most influential architects of the policy that steered Italy closer to Austria and Germany, and thus to the Triple Alliance.

For now, the word "alliance" remained unspoken. Blanc appeared rather to favor a policy of waiting until the outcome of events should have indicated what course to follow, whether that of a triple alliance of Austria, Italy, and France, if the new Germany revealed that its aims were primarily expansionistic, or that of an alliance with Germany, if it showed that it was sated with military conquest, and thus proved suitable to become "the continental base of operations for our future destiny in the Mediterranean, where France, and even Austria as regards the Adriatic, are our natural rivals."[7] Nevertheless, the emphasis he placed on the necessity to facilitate "the natural flows which ought to be established between Germany, the Italian ports, and the Orient," and vice versa his underlining the fact that, before it could even constitute a threat to Italy's frontiers, Germany would have had to swallow up Austria,[8] both showed clearly enough in what

---

[6] It should not be forgotten, however, that—as is well known—the "realism" of Bismarck had taken shape in opposition to legitimist ideology; see esp. the wonderful letters to Leopold von Gerlach from May 1857 in Bismarck, *Gesammelten Werke* 14¹:464 ff., esp. p. 470: "I too acknowledge as my own the principle of a struggle against revolution, but I . . . hold that it is not possible to implement this principle as such in politics"; to do so would amount to ignoring "die Realitäten" (p. 464). (Further, *Erinnerung und Gedanke*, in *Gesammelten Werke* 15:110 ff.) See also E. Marcks, *Otto von Bismarck* (Stuttgart, 1935), pp. 37–38; and E. Eyck, *Bismarck* 1:271 ff., who sets limits to the general importance of those letters, and rightly, inasmuch as Bismarck often allowed himself to be influenced by the forces of domestic politics—that is, by ideological forces. In general, see the acute observations of L. Salvatorelli, "Bismarck," in *Rivista Storica Italiana* 60 (1948): 56 ff., esp. p. 63.

On the other hand, O. Vossler, "Bismarcks Ethos," *Historische Zeitschrift* 171 (1951): 263 ff., is generally unconvincing because too far removed from the concrete problems of the period, from which the "principles" of Gerlach (or of others) and the "reality" of Bismarck derive their full significance. By this I mean: in the "realism" of Bismarck, in which only force is important, the genuinely political element always remains overwhelmingly, practically totally, dominant, while the economic element, so important in later "realism" (as for instance in Blanc himself), is to a great extent overshadowed.

[7] Letter of 10 September, cited at n. 4 above.

[8] Ibid.

direction Blanc's sympathies were turning. This was confirmed by the general tone of his public utterance, his repeated affirmation of the necessity of staying close to solid reality, and his polemic against the sentimental tendencies of the Italians—which were really only the so-called Francophile tendencies that had appeared to dominate Italian politics for over a decade.

His opposition to these, together with his awareness of the economic and military force of Prussia, drove him forward intellectually and spiritually, toward a new emotional outlook and new aspirations; Blanc openly declared as much. He did not join with his friends in regretting the fact that Italy had not intervened on the side of Napoleon III, because by maintaining its neutrality Italy had acquired the moral autonomy that the rest of Europe had previously refused it. Just as the death of Cavour not long before had proved that the existence of Italy did not depend on that of one individual, the fall of Napoleon now demonstrated that likewise the fate of the kingdom did not depend on a foreign dynasty.[9] The existence of a united Italy, in sum, had received its anointment from Sedan and from 4 September, not so much because they had made it possible to take the city of Rome, as because Italy had proved by its deeds that it was not a French protectorate, a vassal state. Finally it had a personality of its own, a personality which all could clearly see.

The same set of ideas, taken up by other men on the Right, inspired the campaign in favor of a decisive rapprochement with Germany that Civinini was conducting in the pages of the *Nazione* of Florence,[10] and reappeared with particular vividness in another of the diplomats who had an active part in Italian foreign policy. A Savoyard like Blanc, and as a result embittered (much more than Blanc) against France for having made him a foreigner in the land of his ancestors,[11] a man of immediate and impetuous reactions, Count Edoardo de Launay, the Italian ambassador at Berlin, had already gone a good deal farther than his colleague in the direction of friendship and alliance with Prussia.

It may be that the declarations of Cavour, which he himself had once been the first to read, still rang in his ears: "we march at the head of the great national party of Italy, just as the Prussian government has placed itself at the head of the

---

[9] Ibid.

[10] See the articles "La Pace" (24 October 1870) and esp. "All'estero" (19 February 1871). In the *Nuova Antologia* see the articles "L'antico e il nuovo impero in Germania" (no. 16: 807 ff., and no. 17: 34 ff.), and the (posthumous) letter "Agli elettori del collegio di Pistoia" (no. 19 [1872]: 435 ff.), in which Civinini declares that he is "neither Catholic nor Latin," that in his view the mission of Italy is to destroy the papacy, and that for the security and moral and intellectual progress of Italy a close alliance with Germany and a complete break with France are necessary. At the death of Civinini in January 1872, the ambassador of Prussia, Brassier de Saint Simon, sent Massari a letter (*La Nazione*, 27 January) of condolence, praising Civinini as "a friend who had come to understand the advantages of a rapprochement of the two nations [Germany and Italy], which know too little of each other," and announced his offer of 1,000 lire for a subscription begun in aid of Civinini's son. The Austrian ambassador Wimpffen saw this action as "assez charactéristique" (Wimpffen, report, 3 February 1872, no. 4; SAW, *P.A.*, XI/80). The gesture of Brassier de Saint Simon was noted by the English ambassador A. Paget as well (report, 29 January 1872, no. 24; *F.O.*, 45, 197).

[11] On the attachment of de Launay to his native soil, and his distress in 1860 at having to choose between his Savoy and his king, see in G. Greppi, "Lettres du comte Ed. de Launay . . . au comte J. Greppi," *Revue d'Italie* (December 1906): 738.

German national ideal."[12] In any case he was resolved, implacable, insistent to the point of monotony, in maintaining the necessity of the alliance with Prussia. The time had come to break with France once and for all, with exaggerated French claims to hegemony, with the presumption of tutelage emanating from Paris. He had expressed these opinions forcefully from the onset of the Franco-Prussian War, when Visconti Venosta had warned him, on 23 July, that it was his intention to try to limit the conflict and so remain neutral, but that it was his (Visconti Venosta's) duty to point out that, should it become impossible to maintain neutrality, Italy "would be unable, and I mean this in practically a material sense, to do anything but join with France."[13] This made the fervid Savoyard explode: "My national sentiments revolt at the idea that we cannot be who we are; that we are hitched to France's destiny; that if required to do so we should turn our backs on Germany, to whom the future belongs." For the good of Italy and its ruling dynasty it was now necessary to "make a break with the French claim that they are our protectors, and that we are tugged along in their wake." It was necessary to avoid "the worst sentimental policy of all, that of taking sides with the loser, weaker party as we are." Italy should not let itself be conditioned by a motive from the past, fear of the Germans, because the times of the Holy Roman Empire were distant now, and as for Pan-Germanism (and Pan-Slavism), "those are just big words, and like *feux follets* they recede when you chase after them."[14]

These ideas were in fact much like those of Blanc, but they were expressed more forcefully and peremptorily, and also more continuously from that time on. For years de Launay never ceased to hammer at the same points in the many reports and private letters he sent from Berlin to the ministry or to colleagues like Robilant: Italy ought to show France its claws and make it abandon the pretensions of superiority it still advanced.[15] Certain of the Prussian victory as early as

---

[12] Cavour to de Launay, ambassador at Berlin, 23 November 1858. For the motives that drove Cavour to make this statement to the Prussian government of the "new era," and for the attitude of the latter, see F. Valsecchi, "La politica di Cavour e la Prussia nel 1859," *Archivio Storico Italiano* 94, no. 1 (1936): 39 ff. See also the letter of Cavour to Manteuffel, 18 February 1858, in *Lettere*, ed. Chiala, vol. 6, p. 177; and L. Chiala, *Pagine di storia contemporanea* 1:14 and 28.

[13] AE, *Ris.*, cart. 10. Visconti Venosta expresses to de Launay ideas completely analogous to those that Lanza expresses to Stefano Jacini two weeks later (S. Jacini, *Un conservatore rurale della nuova Italia* 2:43). [*Translator's note:* The author of this work was the eponymous nephew of the statesman.]

[14] De Launay to Visconti Venosta, personal letter, 29 July 1870 (AE, *Ris.*, cart. 10). In the reference to the age, now remote, of the Holy Roman Empire, de Launay does nothing more than repeat as his own affirmation what Bismarck had said to him two days before: "you will have nothing to fear from a victorious Germany. It will not take its inspiration from the outdated traditions of the Holy Roman Empire" (private letter of de Launay to Visconti Venosta, 27 July 1870, AE, *Ris.*, 10). (Similar ideas were to be developed by German ideologues: see for example the article of W. Lang, "Deutsche und italienische Einheit," *Preussische Jahrbücher* 27 [1871]: 219 ff., later translated into Italian as *L'unità tedesca e l'unità italiana* [Rome, 1871].) De Launay's anger against the French ostentation of superiority was also cleverly fanned by the Prussian statesman: "However, you would have an opportunity, perhaps unique, to topple this French affectation of believing you to be their dependents" (same letter).

[15] See for example his private letter to Visconti Venosta, 26 March 1871: ". . . when France strutted about as the preponderant power, and took a great deal of care to let us feel it. It had to be got out of our way, since it was reducing our freedom of action" (AE, *Ris.*, cart. 10); and to the same, 20 July 1871, "it is a matter of regret to me that we do not take steps to make our neighbor understand that we treat with it on a footing of perfect reciprocity. . . . I am telling you as loudly as I can: *dare*"

July 1870,[16] convinced in addition—and he wasn't wrong—that Austria would sooner or later seek the friendship of Germany,[17] he felt free to give vent almost every week to his rancor against France with unusual passion and persuasive force. Though there was no doubt a substantial element of personal human resentment at work beneath the surface in this case, de Launay's private motives were nonetheless only a part of the texture of his more general urge to free Italy from subjection to France. It is a drive that brought de Launay and many others together to form a major stream of opinion running through the history of Italy during the entire nineteenth century.

If in Blanc the triumph of Prussia and the triumph of industrial civilization amounted to the same thing, and if economic considerations therefore came to the fore in his thought, so that his outlook was practically identical to that of a businessman, in de Launay these factors were not given due weight, whereas the much older antipathy to France that had colored so much of Italian thought at the time of the Risorgimento disgorged itself with all the more force. Just as a reaction against French *civilisation* and its claims to remake everything in its own image had been present during the rise of the German nation in the eighteenth century, from Justus Möser to Herder, along with the exaltation of the primitive Germans and the good old customs of the Saxons, similarly (and with undeniable parallelism) Gallophobia had been one of a number of swelling springs that had burst to the surface at the rise of the Italian nation. It was, as before, a means of defending the national personality and preventing it from being suffocated at birth by excessively faithful imitation of the culture of another people. Alfieri had said as much when he exalted not only the necessity of national "hatreds" in general but also the peculiar necessity for Italy of hatred against France, the indispensable preliminary to its political existence, whatever that was destined to be;[18] and the *Saggio Storico* of Cuoco had conveyed the same idea in a much

---

(ibid.). Against the French claims "to dominate and to talk down to Europe," see the earlier private letter of de Launay to Visconti Venosta, 5 January 1870 (ACR, *Carte Visconti Venosta*, pacco 4, fasc. 4).

[16] Letter cited at n. 14, 29 July; and see the report of de Launay, 27 February 1871, no. 788: "Your Excellency will recall that I have been saying the same thing since 1867 . . . concerning Prussia's and Germany's chances of victory, should there be an armed conflict with France."

[17] De Launay, report, 23 September 1870, no. 660: "Everything points to the conclusion that very soon relations between Vienna and Berlin will take a very friendly turn."

[18] *Il Misogallo*, prosa prima, *Opere* 4:124 (Turin ed., 1903). And see G. Gentile, *L'eredità di Vittorio Alfieri*, pp. 106 ff. Alfieri was followed by Foscolo, and by Leopardi: "Where there is no national hatred, there is no virtue" (*Zibaldone*, ed. Flora [Milan, 1937], vol. 1, p. 1165, and cf. 585 ff.). Leopardi insistently criticized French influence, because of which the character of Italian customs has become "utterly French" (ibid., 1:998). In composing "Sopra il monumento di Dante," the poet had written

> . . . la Francia scellerata e nera [France black and wicked]

subsequently modifying this to

> . . . la più recente e la più fera,
> Per cui presso alle soglie
> Vide la patria tua l'ultima sera.

> [But I will speak of] the most recent and fiercest [affliction],
> Because of which, approaching the threshold [of death]
> Your country [Italy] watched as the light faded.

more measured fashion. They had been followed by Mazzini, and Gioberti's *Primato*, and Pisacane.[19] The nature of this anti-French polemic had varied: at times the purely cultural inspiration so vivid in Leopardi predominated, and at others the purely political reasons for it were thrust into the foreground.

Even an insistence on the past glories of the Italian people had an evident anti-French purpose, revealing the same urge to preserve the national self and its own spiritual life by erecting defenses against a force that seemed to have a fatal grip on Europe—the imitation of French examples no matter whether they were good ones or not.[20] Various factors might have combined to smother this resentment against France: Cavour himself; the high regard in which French and English civilization were held as a result of their contribution to Italian liberal thought; above all, the events of 1859. But that is not how it was: the anti-French tradition, continually kept ablaze by Mazzini, had been fueled anew after 1860 for reasons having nothing to do with Mazzinian passions, and not entirely explainable either as a result of Mentana. Rather this came about because of the general complexion of events, for it seemed that the moral and political personality of the new kingdom was dominated, humiliated, and oppressed by that of France, an older nation, great and powerful. It was a case of protector and vassal. Hence Mazzini persisted in his aversion to France, and even a man of an utterly different cast of mind like Ricasoli considered French influence on Italy to be a source of great harm.

> France troubled and hurt us no matter what its form of government. Whether by means of its deliberate policies, or its revolutions, or its military expeditions, however fractiously it proceeded on its zig-zag course, its traces held in harness the political and social thought of the Italian people, making it eternally servile to France, even when it decried France most loudly. It is a damnable fate for us. This not knowing how to be Italian, this failure of our own national genius, this ceaseless wounding of our own true nature by things we do ourselves, for the sake of imitating like adolescents everything French, and the spirit of their sociopolitical structures, is a perennial source of weakness and discontent for us.[21]

Ricasoli, who was certainly not anti-French in the political sense,[22] and who

---

[19] On Gioberti's hatred of the French, cf. Gentile, *L'eredità*, pp. 127 ff. As for Pisacane, see his polemic against those Italians who make apologies for France (*Saggio su la Rivoluzione*, ed. G. Pintor, pp. 154 ff.).

[20] C. Balbo, *Della monarchia rappresentativa in Italia*, p. 93. Balbo was not, however, averse to imitation, different in this as in other things from Gioberti; see his critical observations on the "rage for originality" which is a sure sign of littleness of spirit (*Pensieri sulla storia d'Italia*, p. 295).

[21] Letter of 17 September 1870 to Francesco Borgatti (*Lettere e documenti del barone Bettino Ricasoli*, ed. Tabarrini-Gotti, vol. 10 [Florence, 1895], pp. 128–29). Again on 31 March 1871, faced with the uprising of the Commune of Paris, he repeated to Borgatti: "whoever doesn't wish to suffer the same ruin himself must cease to absorb from France that barren spirit of dissolution that guided its whole legislative and social program. Who will succeed, I ask myself, who will succeed in bringing Italy back to its own spirit, its own genius, and give it institutions fitting for this genius?" (ibid., 10:220).

[22] See his letter to Nigra of 30 August 1871 (*Lettere e documenti* 10:229); and his concern that Italy should show its gratitude to Napoleon III, posthumously at any rate, by erecting a monument to him at Milan (ibid., 10:275 ff.).

fully acknowledged the value of the emotions "sealed with the blood of 1859,"[23] nevertheless aimed to safeguard the personality of the Italian nation, the soul and the spirit of his own people, and was hostile to the imitation of imported modes[24] just as Alfieri and Leopardi had been, and all the Tuscan moderates from Capponi to Lambruschini. In fact, after 1870 he was to become alarmed by the prevalence of German doctrines in Italy, since they were even more remote from the Italian spirit than those of France.[25]

In this way, concern over Italian servility to France could at a given moment produce a coalition of tendencies that in other respects were quite at odds with one another, such as Mazzini's enthusiasm for revolution, which led him to deprecate the France of 1789 as merely the conclusion of a historical epoch, not the beginning of a new one, and the conservatism of a Ricasoli, who deplored the disappearance of religious faith and authority after the revolution in France, and who opposed the spirit of Jacobinism, expressing his disquiet over the "stupid excesses to which the principles of 1789 were carried."[26] And as we have seen, de Launay was part of this coalition too, though an extreme conservative, a lover of authority who despaired to observe the lack of it in his own time and was convinced with Guizot that "at present it is not *la liberté* that requires defenders, but *l'autorité*."[27]

His hostility to France was of a simple kind, denuded of cultural and moral values and limited exclusively to the most immediate and elementary problem, that of politics. The twelve years from Plombières to Sedan put heavy pressure, as far as he and many others were concerned, on the individuality of their new kingdom. You can hear, the moment a propitious occasion presented itself, their resentment finally breaking out against a state of affairs that was becoming increasingly difficult for them to tolerate, the resentment that hums through a phrase heard everywhere in August 1870: "It's a pleasure to see the French getting a good lesson; they needed knocking down."[28] This resentment, fed by further sources of grievance such as Tunis, economic competition, Aigues Mortes, continued to ferment in the hearts of many Italians, who never stopped suspecting that France was treating them like minors, became ever more bitter toward their "Latin sister," and were finally driven to hope for a chance not only to stand by while others gave France its "good lesson," but even to be in a position them-

---

[23] Letter, 3 September 1870, to Luigi Torelli (*Lettere e documenti* 10:124).

[24] See C. Morandi, *La sinistra al potere*, p. 40.

[25] Letter to Francesco Borgatti, 5 March 1876: "if before our schools were inoculated with French philosophy, today they are inoculated with German philosophy, both of which are ill-adapted to the Italian spirit; but the second even more so than the first, it seems to me" (*Lettere e documenti* 10:362). And even earlier he had written that German philosophy had been even more deleterious to the foundations of morality than socialist maxims and French ideas "with the difference that there is lacking in Germany the power and the influence of the Catholic clergy, which will be able to save France, and which makes the civil sword of Prussia a necessity for Germany" (*Carteggi*, ed. Nobili-Camerani, vol. 3 [Rome, 1945], p. 460; cf. G. Gentile, *Gino Capponi e la cultura toscana nel secolo decimonono*, pp. 76–77).

[26] Letter of 2 September 1870 to Francesco Borgatti (*Lettere e documenti* 10:117).

[27] Letter to Count Robilant, 7 March 1871 (AE, *Carte Robilant*).

[28] C. Bon Compagni, "Francia e Italia," letter 8, in *L'Opinione* for 27 November 1871.

selves to administer "a good thrashing to the French," as Queen Margherita (so dear to Carducci as an example of blond, meek womanhood) once expressed it.[29]

As with many Italians at this time, certainly with all of the patriots, de Launay was driven by another long-standing motive that had its roots in the past and is still with us, since it was tied to the events surrounding the formation of a united Italy. I mean the burning sense of hurt, of bitterness and rage, at the memory of the recent military defeats suffered at Custoza and Lissa, which, with Novara, were to remain a burden, and a heavy one, on the international reputation of the kingdom, since European public opinion seized upon them in a crude and often exaggerated fashion in order to deny any military capacity to the "lovable" Italians. In fact there were those prepared to state, with Hippolyte Taine, that Italian history had remained too Latin and too town-based to have known the Germanic loyalty of the feudal vassal to his lord and the sense of a soldier's honor that had formed the great modern states, and so lacked the military spirit.[30] Even the least ungenerous, like Treitschke, were willing at most to concede that Italy needed to fight hard to become a great power in actuality.[31]

But even Italy itself felt that it was "more lucky than heroic,"[32] that there are certain wounds that don't heal quickly, and that there are some defeats that those who have only recently been unified as a people can't accept without wishing to achieve military glory for themselves too, and thus to consecrate their existence as an emerging nation.[33] True, there were those like Jacini who thought that, even though it was natural enough to smart at the memory of 1866 and to hope for a chance some day to "offer the world irrefutable proof of Italian courage on the battlefield in the service of a just cause," there was no need to try to create such an opportunity at any cost, no need to "look for the right moment every time a fly buzzes past, as though it was our last hope of survival."[34] But on the other hand there were many who were tormented by the possibility of missing such a chance,[35] and who were ready, long before the vogue for the ideas of D'Annun-

---

[29] These were the words of the queen to Farini, president [i.e., speaker] of the Senate, at the court reception for the new year in 1894 (Farini, *Diario* 1:402). That Margherita was often of a combative frame of mind, and that her royal mildness and gentleness overlaid urges of a commoner kind to hand out a few smacks, is revealed by her expression in a letter to Minghetti: "it's enough to make you want to give a beating to those rascals"—that is, to the republicans of Forlì, who on 10 September 1883 had hurled stones at a few paper lanterns decorated with the arms of Savoy, and had then rioted (*Lettere fra la regina Margherita e Marco Minghetti*, ed. L. Lipparini, p. 99). It follows naturally that at the last she should warn Francesco Ruffini that the stick was indispensable: "the stick, my dear Ruffini, the stick was wanted" (B. Croce, "Incontri con Vittorio Emanuele III," in *Corriere della Sera*, 5 April 1949).

[30] So wrote Taine in 1864 (*Voyage en Italie* 1:407).

[31] *La Politica* (Italian translation: Bari, 1918), vol. 4, p. 186.

[32] Bon Compagni, "Francia e Italia," letter 7, *L'Opinione*, 20 November 1871.

[33] Speech of De Sanctis to the Chamber, 23 April 1874 (partially republished by Croce, "Dai *Discorsi politici* . . . di Francesco De Sanctis," in *La Critica* 11 (1913): 331–32).

[34] Stefano Francesco Jacini, *Pensieri sulla politica italiana*, p. 69

[35] Antonio Gallenga made the following acute observation: "there can be no doubt that underlying all the disquiet, the jealousy, the demanding irritability of the Italians in every question relating to their position in the European concert, there is hidden the memory, painful and nagging, of the defeats suffered at Custoza and Lissa. . . . The old accusation, cruel and in many ways unjustified, that "the Italians don't fight' still wounds their ears, and they feel that the baptism of blood, capable

zio, to look for a "heroic purification, a steaming bath of warm blood"[36] as the only way to make a country that was leaving behind centuries of slavery really great. They wanted a striking victory,[37] and in the meantime they felt burdened by a shameful memory, for as Nigra, who was far from being a warmonger, once had occasion to remark: "whatever we say and whatever we do, in Europe we still bear the mark of Custoza and Lissa. And, regrettably, this situation might last until Italy has had the good fortune to wipe away the errors of La Marmora and the faults of Persano on other fields of battle. In other words, ever since the time those events took place, Italy found itself, and still finds itself, faced with the alternative between bearing the disgrace of undeserved defeats and wishing to be swept up in a large-scale war in order to have the chance to demonstrate its military ability."[38] Palestro and San Martino, Calatafimi and the Volturno, Castelfidardo and the Tyrol, all these cannot obliterate the memory of our defeats, Francesco Crispi warned. The shining moments of Italian military history are fine episodes for a poem, but they are not a poem.[39] Even men who were generally known for their antimilitarism felt that something was missing in the new Italy, and that was glory won by the sword. They included Cavallotti, whose hymn was democracy, yet who took note of this feeling and exhorted his colleagues in parliament not to forget "that Italy's position in Europe is still suffering after fifteen years, still bitterly suffering the cost of failure in the clash of arms; and until failure one day turns to success in some bloody act of baptism it will never have a place worthy of its new destiny among the nations."[40]

Thus there were more than just a scattered few who believed that only "a crisis in Europe, leading to war, could rouse in our country the forces that revive and invigorate the life of nations,"[41] who believed that the longed-for vision of an integral state in which the Italians would embrace their common citizenship would come within reach "only on the day that a great new return of virility, a second trial of arms and blood, gives Italy back the vigor it now seems to lack, the capacity to feel itself whole and set a course, based on fundamental structures and vital reforms, toward its own bright future."[42] Oriani had not yet appeared with his call to war ("the inevitable form taken by the struggle for existence"),

---

of bringing about the real regeneration of a people, has not been sufficient in their case to remove all the tarnish that centuries of humiliation had left on their moral and social character. However much they may love peace, the Italians should be happy almost to be presented with a chance to fight simply for the sake of fighting" (*L'Italia presente e futura* [Florence, 1866], pp. 24–25). The same opinion in Guiccioli: "war is always a misfortune, but it would do a good deal for our national spirit. The Italian people has to acquire consciousness of its military ability" ("Diario," in *Nuova Antologia*, 16 July 1935, p. 224.)

[36] The words in July 1882 of Rocco de Zerbi in *Difendetevi!* p. 49.

[37] There is no doubt that this was the desire of Vittorio Emanuele II, even though there may be some doubt as to whether he intended to translate it into reality in the summer of 1887; see Crispi, *Politica estera* 1:9 and 683.

[38] Nigra to Robilant, private letter, 9 August 1886 (AE, *Carte Robilant*).

[39] "I doveri del Gabinetto del 25 marzo," in *Scritti e discorsi politici di Francesco Crispi*, pp. 381–82.

[40] Speech to the Chamber on 21 March 1881 (*Discorsi Parlamentari di F. Cavallotti* 1:273).

[41] Thus Domenico Farini (Diary, MRR, under 14 February 1897).

[42] P. Turiello, *Governo e governati in Italia* 2:337 (Bologna, 1882).

with his cry for blood ("the finest dew heralding grand ideas"), with his wish for a conflict that alone could guarantee Italy's future, giving it back its natural territorial limits and cementing through the tragedy of mortal peril the unity of national sentiment in the country.[43] Yet the notions of Oriani were already in the air.

Nor was this a totally new state of mind emerging in the aftermath of 1866, inasmuch as the war fought in that year had been deeply desired, and the Prussian alliance had been sought in the spring of the year of Custoza, in the compelling hope of finding an occasion "to affirm militarily the existence of the nation." The acquisition of Venetia merely through diplomatic accords "would have been greeted by Italy with resignation, not satisfaction."[44]

The necessity to create a warlike spirit—that is, to raise the tone of the moral life of a people dishonored for centuries—lay behind the frequent evocation, even before 1866, even earlier than 1859, of the ancient military glory of the Italians, the teachers of war to the world. It was a call to the nobler passions as a remedy for the softer ones, the moral diseases produced by centuries of servitude.[45] Pisacane had seen in the military problem the essential point of departure for the creation of an Italy capable of true and lasting revolution.[46] The recollection of the Italian troops who had served in Russia in 1812 had attained epic status, for in their case the ancient valor of Italy had come back to life, although in a distant northern land and in another's cause; there was satisfaction in repeating the saying of Napoleon that the Italians would one day be the finest soldiers on earth. To the galleries of paintings and statues found in the other regions of Italy, d'Azeglio had paralleled the "Gallery of Battles" of Piedmont, battles "sometimes won and sometimes lost, but in any case the only battles that were able to prevent foreign occupation of Italy, battles that, concluding with San Martino, have finally broken the chains that bound us all."[47] Cesare Balbo declared that he would give three or four Alfieris and Manzonis, even Dantes, or a similar number of Michelangelos and Raphaels, "for an officer capable of leading two hundred thousand Italians to victory—or even to defeat."[48] Yet recent experience had done too much to shatter such dreams: not just the events of Custoza and Lissa, but also the reduced eagerness for combat revealed in many areas, that widespread reluctance to serve in the military that was not the least of the internal problems afflicting the new kingdom.[49] Hence the haunting vision of a great

---

[43] Oriani, *Fino a Dogali*, p. 146.

[44] A. La Marmora, *Un po' più di luce sugli eventi politici e militari dell'anno 1866*, p. 312.

[45] Thus Foscolo in the dedication to General Caffarelli of his *Illustrazioni alle Opere di Raimondo Montecuccoli*.

[46] See for example the sixth and last *Lettera ai suoi antichi commilitoni*, 16 October 1855: "We Italians were and will be again the masters of war to the world. . . . We shall rouse our former boldness" (Pisacane, *Epistolario*, ed. A. Romano, pp. 237 ff.; see also p. 218).

[47] M. De Rubris, *Confidenze di Massimo d'Azeglio*, p. 305.

[48] *Lettere di politica e letteratura* (Florence, 1855), p. 439.

[49] D'Azeglio expressed his contempt for this attitude in 1848 (*Scritti e discorsi politici*, ed. M. De Rubris, vol. 2, p. 10 and note [Florence, 1936]). For the reluctance of Tuscans in 1859 to take part in the war on the fields of Lombardy see F. Martini, *Confessioni e ricordi, 1859–1892*, pp. 6 ff. When Villari requested that the students of the Scuola Normale of Pisa be given an exemption from

passage of arms, the necessary and long-awaited moral seal of the material unity of Italy, was all the more vivid and urgent.

That was not all: a man like Crispi could at least take comfort in examples of popular heroism, could recall the great and glorious days of mass initiative of the Risorgimento—the Five Days of Milan, Rome, Venice, Calatafimi, the Volturno. Such comfort was unavailable to the conservative monarchist de Launay, who was not even remotely able to give due acknowledgment to the part played by insurrectional and popular movements, to Mazzini and Garibaldi. The Risorgimento, as far as he was concerned, was no more than the political and military program of the house of Savoy; everything beyond that amounted to the sort of antinomian tendencies that merely harmed the principle of authority, and that ought to be repressed. Hence Italy united seemed to him to be even more barren of military glory. As a vassal state of France down to the present moment, and with no reputation in war, it had to exonerate itself in Europe's eyes from this long state of subjection and give irrefragable proof of its warrior virtue. So for de Launay the kingdom had only one road to follow, alignment with the powerful nation of the future, Germany, and estrangement from France to the point of active opposition.

Indeed: to the point of actively opposing France. The direction of the Savoyard statesman's thoughts was well summed up in a declaration that burst from his heart at the beginning of 1872: "Italy will never be truly fused into one, the prestige of Authority will never really be grounded on a solid basis, except through a great war against France."[50]

This was de Launay's intuition of what was needed: a great war that would subject the moral unity of the Italian people to the greatest stress, and thereby harden it. The future would show that to this extent he was right—but through channels and passages utterly different from the ones he dreamed of, in the course of a struggle far more distant than he imagined, and not against France but against Austria-Hungary and Germany itself: the story that had begun badly at the Mincio fifty-two years earlier would arrive at a final victorious conclusion at the Piave. But even as he identified a precise war aim for Italy, even as he called for battle against France, de Launay was far from eccentric. As in other cases, the words and the attitude of the ambassador of Vittorio Emanuele II in Berlin were, although he failed to realize this, no more than glimpses of a wider and more general current of thought, so much so that the outburst of this stubborn conservative, enemy of socialism that he was, can be heard to echo a similar utterance from the soul of Pisacane, the patriot who had been the outstanding evangelist of socialism in the Risorgimento, and who had declared that the nineteenth century would become famous in the annals of mankind "not by reason of the servile and cowardly crew of doctrinaires whom it produced, but because in

---

conscription, Amari as minister replied without mincing words: "I tell you that I will never back such a proposal. Conscription is the foundation of Italy, and I would be glad to exchange a pair of students from the Scuola Normale and a dozen secondary school teachers for a single footsoldier. Call me barbaric as much as you like" (*Carteggio di Michele Amari* 2:181; 5 May 1864).

[50] De Launay to Visconti Venosta, private letter, 24 January 1872 (AE, *Ris.* cart. 10.).

this epoch socialism went from being an aspiration to a living emotion, gave rise to a party, and shall be brought about."[51] Pisacane had in fact already come to the following conclusion in the course of an animated polemic against those who looked to France as the protector of Italy and preached the brotherhood of the two nations: "in order to realize our brotherhood with France, we will have to fight it and beat it; failing that, we shall at least have to excel it in a noble competition of feats of glory while fighting against a common enemy on an equal footing and with equal forces, on the same battlefield."[52]

If de Launay rejoiced that Italy had ceased to bow and scrape to France, it was certainly not because he wanted it to prostrate itself before Prussia. No matter how great his admiration for the sun that was rising in the east, he would never have wished deliberately to play the part of vassal to the king of Prussia; in fact he warned that if Germany should ever wish to exercise undue influence in Italy, he himself would be the first to counsel a certain stiffness, a raising of barriers against any such claim on the part of Germany or any other power: "With a character like Bismarck's, and that of statesmen trained in his likeness, you undermine yourself if you give way more than is just and reasonable."[53] *Chacun maître chez soi.*[54]

Later still he repeated that it would be better not to tie Italy to Germany by a formal treaty of alliance, since it was exceedingly dangerous to sail in convoy with a man like Bismarck, who notwithstanding his great qualities was so lacking in convictions that he was capable of suddenly changing the rules of the game and upsetting all calculations. De Launay admired the man a great deal, but without deluding himself about any putative predilection for Italy on Bismarck's part, and in this he showed himself to be much more acute and judicious than those on the Left, who instead were convinced that the Iron Chancellor's heart throbbed with affection for Italy.[55] For de Launay it was better to let things work themselves out and await whatever results the direction of events should bring. There was an alliance *in re*, it had an effective existence, and that was much more desirable than a treaty on parchment.

There is no doubt that he was sincere in affirming all this. But the difficult part, as always, is to set the boundaries of the "just and reasonable," and he was perhaps in danger of extending them far past what was precisely in Italy's best interest, drawn as he was by admiration for the new power, and above all driven

---

[51] *Saggio su la Rivoluzione*, p. 139.

[52] *Saggio su la Rivoluzione*, p. 156. On this anti-French reaction of Pisacane, which had something of the "lover betrayed" about it, see G. Falco, "Note e documenti intorno a Carlo Pisacane," *Rivista Storica Italiana* 44 (1927): 293.

[53] Report of de Launay, 27 February 1871, no. 788. Cf. below, ch. 17, n. 15.

[54] De Launay to Visconti Venosta, private letter, 5 January 1870; see also private letters of 6 and 12 January (ACR, *Carte Visconti Venosta*, pacco 4, fol. 4). Even at this point he was counseling a close understanding, not an alliance, with Germany.

[55] De Launay to Visconti Venosta, private letter, 19 March 1872 (ACR, *Carte Visconti Venosta*, pacco 5, fasc. 2). "Prince Bismarck is the most skeptical, the least scrupulous, of statesmen, but he is endowed with a rare understanding of his own political advantage. This is the best, I dare not say the sole, guarantee of his good faith in our regard." Private letter to Visconti Venosta, 22 September 1872 (ibid.).

by aversion to France.[56] Indeed, even at the point in February 1871 when relations between Berlin and Rome were chilly, de Launay showed not only that he did not believe in the possibility of any hegemonic tendencies, then much feared, on the part of the German chancellor, but that he did not even credit the threat of German interference in the internal politics of other states, in Napoleonic fashion.[57] This revealed a streak of sturdy optimism which the events of 1874 and 1875 were to put to a severe test.

So we see the same fundamental orientation as that of Blanc coming out in de Launay too; in fact we are struck much more emphatically by his satisfaction at the collapse of the French domination that had kept united Italy fettered, and at the moral independence that the latter thereby gained; and by his gratified admiration for the work of Bismarck, from which in his view the policies formulated in the cabinet of Vittorio Emanuele II ought to take their cue.[58]

It is only logical that we find in de Launay as well the unmistakable signs of a style of thought that tends to value ever more highly a solid and compelling "reality" as against any form of sentimentality. So he reports, as though imparting an exemplary lesson, Bismarck's decisions to seek "security" for the future not in the attitudes of the French people, but rather in specific material assurances, meaning possession of Alsace-Lorraine and the payment by France of crushing war indemnities.

De Launay too was a "realist" in politics.

Quintino Sella was a man of much stronger character than de Launay. But the same apprehension about the overpowering influence of France on Italy, although stripped of fervor and informed primarily by moral and cultural, as opposed to political, concerns, had also led him to adhere to the same general trend of

---

[56] For example, on 21 July 1874, irritated by the speech given by Nigra three days earlier at Vaucluse on the occasion of the festivities for the fifth centenary of the death of Petrarca, in which he discovered "an unending stream of clichés about our community of race, about our gratitude for the part played in the liberation of Italy," de Launay returned to his own fixed idea: "In order for this gratitude to become sincere and free of hidden reservations, it would be necessary first of all to reopen discussions on the cession of Savoy and Nice, a cession that was extorted from us by the right of the stronger party under a deceptive show of universal suffrage. There is a reparation to be made, and I for my part would be happy and proud to attach my name to it; I hope to live long enough to help to bring it about." De Launay to Visconti Venosta, private letter no. 2 (ACR, *Carte Visconti Venosta*, pacco 8, fol. 3).

It is significant that de Launay, in his disdain for the Petrarchan and Francophile paean of Nigra, found himself in complete agreement with the organs of the Left (cf. *Il Diritto* for 22, 23, 25, 28 July 1874). On the clear propensity of de Launay for Germany and his malevolence toward France, cf. also Greppi, "Lettres du comte Ed. de Launay," pp. 739 and 754 (de Launay's letter of 17 June 1867: ". . . considering the French character, its controlling mania of vainglory and its chauvinism").

[57] "If the cabinet in Berlin, as may be hoped in light of the perspicacity of Count Bismarck, does not fall into the same error as the emperor Napoleon and his maladroit counselors, who were too disposed to behave as regents of Europe . . ." (from de Launay's report of 27 February 1871, no. 788).

[58] De Launay, report of 4 March 1871, no. 789: "It is clear . . . that in view of the likelihood [of further complications] the option prevailed . . . of looking for sureties not in the dispositions of the French people, but in material guarantees." De Launay here repeats almost exactly the formula already used by Bismarck on 22 August 1870 in a colloquy with Moritz Busch: "Our protection against this evil lies not in fruitless efforts to awaken momentarily the sympathy of the French, but in the achievement of good solid frontiers" (Bismarck, *Gesammelten Werke* 7:321).

opinion even more squarely. He was not a diplomat like Blanc and de Launay but a man practiced in government, in fact a genuine example of a statesman, in whom the impulses of mere instinct and passion were pushed into the background of consciousness, and had no more than ephemeral influence on his judgment. Hence it was not so much sympathy, although he felt that strongly, for Germany and its tradition of learning[59] that inspired his political stance, but rather his foresight, which as everyone knows had been perfectly accurate in the case of the Franco-Prussian War, making him one of the few Italians to have seen in advance who the winner was going to be.[60] No, his sympathy for Germany had arisen out of a previous distrust of France, and on the basis of cold calculation. From the time of his postgraduate studies at the École des Mines in Paris, the belief that French influence was a danger to Italy had crystallized in his mind: a danger not only in terms of their political relationship but also and especially in terms of the moral and spiritual formation of the Italian people.[61]

Sella's opinion was only fortified by the spectacle of the events of 1848–49, when the French failed to keep their promises, and in fact "stabbed" the Roman Republic in the back. Nor perhaps was he entirely free of traces of the cultural repugnance toward France characteristic of Gioberti and Gioberti's circle. In any case it was an opinion that was to guide him in the future, despite the debt of gratitude that France was to earn in 1859 and that Sella, as a matter of honor, never repudiated.[62] Even as his term of years drew to a close, Quintino Sella's anti-French sentiment reappeared once more, fueled by the ongoing course of

[59] In his speech to the electors of Masserano on 13 November 1870, Sella recalls his youthful impressions when he studied in the center of learning that is Germany, and his impassioned discussions with German students: "In our juvenile ardor it appeared to us then that Italy and Germany were two sister nations, which could be free and whole not only without harm or danger but with a great deal of reciprocal gain. Now, as a government minister, I have found I am unable to fight against the aspirations of my younger self, and I have given my vote in favor of neutrality" (*L'Opinione*, 17 November 1870).

[60] Among these can be mentioned Oreste Baratieri, who at that time was writing in *Fanfulla* under the pseudonym of "Fucile" (Martini, *Confessioni e ricordi*, p. 87).

[61] "[F]rom now on an insuperable barrier will divide us from the French. The satisfaction I take in this is not because the fact is in harmony with the sentiments of my heart, but because I have always feared that Italy would find itself under French influence, and in that case, the Italians being still babies, and untrained, we would have clung to the French spirit for a long time, and our homeland would thus have followed the wrong road for a long time, leading once again to its ruin. . . . Here Italy is regarded as the natural auxiliary of France, destined to supply it with its men, its treasure, its fields. . . . [Y]ou will see why . . . I hold that French influence is one of the greatest evils that can threaten Italy." Quintino Sella to his brother, July 1849, in A. Guiccioli, *Quintino Sella* 1:24–25 and 26–27. Cf. G. Finali, *La vita politica di contemporanei illustri*, pp. 339–40. It was certainly as a result of Sella's influence (not Mazzini's!) that similar ideas were taken up by other moderates, as for instance Sella's biographer Guiccioli, for whom "French influence has been and will be our bane. I would wish to raise a Chinese wall between us and France" ("Diario," in *Nuova Antologia*, 16 July 1935, p. 242).

[62] In the Chamber on 16 March 1880, when replying to Cairoli, who had spoken severely of the policies of the Right in 1870, Sella was still willing to declare that he was proud to have remained faithful, within the limits of what was feasible, to the old friendship with France, with a government "to whom Italy has an infinite debt of gratitude" (*Discorsi Parlamentari di Quintino Sella* 1:195–96 [Rome, 1887]). Here the exigencies of debate have made Sella much more "faithful" to France than in reality he had been in 1870; yet it is still worth noting that he never tried (unlike Crispi, Cairoli, and also de Launay) to deny or diminish the services done by Napoleon III to Italy.

recent events but nourished by historical memory, not least by that of the Sicilian Vespers, and the resentment against the house of Anjou inspired by his cherished Malabayla Codex.[63] A sympathy for Germany reinforced by direct acquaintance with the country and its people did the rest, along with the enthusiasm for science that was so characteristic of the man, and that necessarily extended to the Germanic world as a great center of scientific research. Sella's resolute and widely known opposition to the intermittent desire of Vittorio Emanuele to come to the aid of France thus had its source in the past and, as in the case of de Launay but with a wider horizon in view, went far beyond any single moment or diplomatic episode. In Sella too we find that the polar notions are those of science, economics, industry, and progress; we encounter the sense that force "has to be reckoned with," and repugnance for the fantasizing and the sentimentality to which the Italians were prone. We see his admiration for "fateful men" and for those "fated peoples" whom nothing can halt.[64]

There was another Italian, neither a member of the government nor a diplomat, not even at the moment an active participant in politics but a military man dedicated to study, who was also seeking a way to go beyond the kaleidoscopic shifts of politics. He had an acute and refined mind which sought to ascend from knowledge of the episodic and the particular to knowledge of the universal, and to discover the laws of history as well as the guiding principles of political action. This was Nicola Marselli, not yet the famous author of *La scienza della storia* and *La guerra e la sua storia*,[65] not yet a parliamentary deputy, but simply a major in the army who taught at the Scuola superiore di guerra [the War College] and had written two volumes on the events of 1870–71 (*Gli avvenimenti del 1870–71*). In these the opinion of the "Prussophiles," as they were called, received its most thorough, rigorous, and unprejudiced formulation. Once he entered parliament, Marselli would join the Center, and like many another contemporary, would look for a way to build the great liberal-national party that they felt was lacking, a party of the Center containing progressive elements from the Right and moderate ones from the Left. In sum, Marselli was not, properly speaking, a man of the Right, and in fact was capable of criticizing it severely. But it was a clue to his character that he greatly admired Sella, whom he held in "a sort of veneration,"[66] and he fully agreed with Sella's judgment of France and Germany.

The basis of Marselli's reflections was also political: it had its source in his

---

63 Sella to Amari, 25 April 1882 (Amari, *Carteggio* 2:276).

64 Guiccioli, *Quintino Sella* 2:6. The fact that Sella was an admirer of Bismarck, contrasting in this with the typical feeling of the "Francophiles" of the Right such as Bonghi and Visconti Venosta, is another significant example of his own style of thought.

65 On Marselli as historian, see B. Croce, *Storia della storiografia italiana nel secolo decimonono* 2:172 ff.

66 Cf. Marselli, *La rivoluzione parlamentare del marzo 1876*, pp. 107 and 127 ff.; for his criticism of the Right, pp. 11–12, 53, 63, 75, 91. His own program was later fully laid out in the *Lettera agli elettori sulla situazione parlamentare*, published in 1880. See also his *La politica dello Stato italiano*, pp. 54 ff., and C. O. Pagani, "Per Nicola Marselli nel primo anniversario della sua morte," *Nuova Antologia*, 1 October 1900, p. 462.

hostile reaction to "the overbearing, conquering frame of mind of the French," which had held Italy in subjection in the decade after Cavour. The first conclusion he therefore drew was that Italy should form an alliance with Germany and Spain. But this was a reaction to the purely diplomatic and military aspects of the problem, which was also rapidly superseded. Marselli came to see that French predominance had to subside because France was too unsettled internally; its continual upheavals and revolutions were an incessant menace to European tranquillity, and "after having done a somnolent Europe the eminent service of shaking it to life, it now disturbs the rest of us with its commotion while we are trying to learn, to labor, to organize ourselves, and to make intelligent progress." The incendiary turmoil of the Commune, the last of a series of convulsions undergone by France since 1789, showed that the time had come for Europe to greet with elation the loss of French control: the former conductor of the European orchestra now must leave the podium and join the rest of the players.[67]

For Marselli it was no longer just a case of political hegemony passing from one nation to another, but something even more profound, something that could be called a change in the rhythm of European civilization: "if we do not succeed in applying a brake of German design to the wheels of a social wagon that has been designed in France, the wagon will be smashed to bits."[68] In other words, his aim was to abandon "the French ideal of chaotic progress, of plebeian democracy," in order to "work together with Germany for the triumph of *harmonic Democracy and orderly Progress.*"[69]

What exactly this harmonic, and above all Germanic, Democracy was to consist in, is never made entirely clear, and it may be doubted whether it was totally clear to the author himself, despite the historical and political premises that led him to assign, in accordance with a set of ideas that were very popular both then and later, essential characteristics to the two civilizations—the Latin, which in Rome had given expression to the sovereignty of the state, and the Germanic, which had contributed "the lordship of the autonomous Individual." Elsewhere we find him observing with satisfaction that, as a result of the blending of culture and the state, the strengths of the Hellenic and the Latin, with Germanic individualism and Christian orientalism, the other three molecules of the European compound had rendered individualism sociable, so that it had lost its rawness and its other shortcomings, transforming itself into a new, civic individualism, "the true modern masterpiece." The towering new central European empire issued "from the fusion of developed culture, a strengthened state, and restricted individualism," so as to represent harmony between the forces of preservation and of progress, between free inquiry and respect for the law,[70] and so would be in a

[67] Marselli, *Gli avvenimenti del 1870–71* 2:198, 200–201.

[68] *Avvenimenti del 1870–71* 2:202. Against the radical, typically French, tendency to want miracles, which has not aided France to advance a single step in training its people in the use of their liberty, and in favor of an entirely different approach, Marselli took up the cudgels again in 1876 (*La rivoluzione parlamentare*, pp. 84 ff.).

[69] *Avvenimenti del 1870–71* 2:208.

[70] Ibid., 2:204–208.

position to show Europe how to balance freedom of the individual and the authority of the law, the enlargement of freedom for science and freedom for living, unity at the center and the vitality of the individual members, military force and the prerequisites of agriculture, industry, and prosperity.[71]

Marselli foresaw the dawn of a new period in the history of civilization, in which ordered calm would take the place of the continuing violent oscillation between revolution and reaction provoked by French domination; seriousness would triumph over frivolity . . . Germanic seriousness, the true victor in the war that had just been fought, now finally arriving on the scene to restore order out of chaos.[72] Italy would be able to play a leading role in this new age, acting as a counterweight to the slightly overpitched conservatism of the German empire, which tended to advance with the somewhat ponderous gait one would expect from a serious individual. Germany needed a friend able to push it along, to speed things up, to constitute the necessary progressive element fully geared to the necessary conservative element: who better for this role than the Italian people? The time had come; the third civilization of Italy was arising, the third great historical period was opening for the peninsula, and it would see Italy and Germany proceeding together, opening up the roads of harmonic progress to the European peoples.[73] The mission of one was strictly bound to the mission of the other.

This was the prophetic voice of Nicola Marselli announcing a general vision of European civilization present and future, under the inspiration of the victory of Prussian arms, and at the moment at which he was preparing to take the vows of the new religion of positivism, though metaphysics clung to him like the robe of Nessus and he was never quite able to rip it off. So, like Quintino Sella, he combined his respect for science with respect for force. Doubtless his vision was replete with commonplaces, and he indulged to excess in antiquated formulas derived from Germany's intellectual tradition, such as the notion of German individualism;[74] a number of his guiding concepts were far from clear, and in fact were exceedingly nebulous; he was far too hasty in adopting old clichés and assuming a moralizing tone, as when he exalted Germanic seriousness over French frivolity, this being simply a renewed manifestation of an old notion utterly familiar from eighteenth-century polemics against French *politesse*, portrayed as a synonym for superficiality and corruption.[75] Marselli summoned up all the old ritual warnings against French corruption and the contrasting endorsements of the pure and innocent customs of the Germans, which were no longer those described by Tacitus, but which were here painted with many of the same virtuous colors that Tacitus had so generously applied to the descendants of Arminius in order to scourge the corruption of the imperial court of Rome.

The fact is that at this time such schematic contrasts were being revived every-

---

[71] Ibid., 2:86.

[72] Ibid., 2:202, n. 1.

[73] *Avvenimenti del 1870–71* 2:209–10.

[74] But it is to be noted that he openly combated the German racism that was already familiar, and the claim of German superiority (ibid., 2:205); he would never have wished that all the connotations of *chez nous* should be translated into *bei uns*.

[75] Cf. C. Antoni, *La lotta contro la ragione*, pp. 10 ff.

where for the purpose of furnishing a moralistic explanation of the collapse of the Second Empire, indeed of the nullity and impotence of France, which obviously owed the instability of its political constitution and its slide from revolution into despotism to its moral decay.[76] Paris, like Babylon of old, had for ages been displaying its painted charms to arouse the senses of its admirers,[77] while Berlin meant seriousness, morality, virtue. Puritan hatred of the corruption and immorality of Babylon had inspired the detestation felt by strict Queen Victoria for Napoleonic France.[78] Gino Capponi, old and moralistic as ever, was not unhappy to see the *demi-monde* of Paris be taught a lesson.[79] And another historian, no longer a student of Florence but rather of the mercenary companies, and the Savoyard monarchy, also discovered that the defeat of France had been caused by its moral vices, its "disordered style of life, crazy expenses, rash speculations, indulgence in sensual passion leading to concubinage and adultery and on to suicide and the duel, the calculated reduction of fertility, corrupt books and corrupt shows."[80]

This whole way of seeing the situation was of course pervaded with an awareness of military power, and therefore cloaked a certain authoritarian tendency, a certain aspiration toward a strong state which Marselli would later fully display in his criticisms of Italian politics. In fact, not long after, angered by the "sleepiness" affecting all Italians, he was to express a desire for the methods of Bismarck to be applied in Italy in order to cure the country of its ills—for Italy seemed to him to remain skeptical and unmoved even when faced with the gravest problems.[81]

But however adequate or inadequate it was, the general frame of mind we have described represented at least an attempt to comprehend the totality of things. De Launay confined himself to the purely political aspect. Blanc went beyond it to some extent with his admiration for the new forces, meaning economic power, and thus showed that he had a clear presentiment of new modes of life and thought. Sella viewed the problem of how to react to French influence on a wide front embracing Italian culture and politics. But Marselli was the only one explicitly to formulate the whole question in terms of European civilization, in terms of a new order for all; in the mind of this intelligent and cultured professional military officer, who had studied the armed maneuvers that had taken place between August 1870 and January 1871, there germinated a whole new political, cultural, and moral system. It was no longer simply a question of adjusting the

---

[76] See for example *La Nazione* for 9 September 1870; and 12 March, 27 March, 25 June 1871 ("Ammaestramenti," "Le condizioni della Francia," "Cose di Francia," "L'Avvenire").

[77] Cavour had written this in 1837, though he did not pose as a preacher and was perfectly content to find himself amid those "charms" (*Lettere* 5:69 and 266).

[78] Cf. B. Nolde, *L'Alleanza franco-russa* (Italian translation: Milan, 1940), p. 25.

[79] *Lettere di Gino Capponi e di altri a lui*, ed. Carraresi, vol. 4 (Florence, 1885), p. 260.

[80] E. Ricotti, *La libertà e il sapere* (Turin, 1871), p. 19.

[81] Marselli to Robilant, 7 January 1873 (AE, *Carte Robilant*). Marselli's presentiments are "dark, very dark." The same ideas appear in another letter of 25 March 1873: "I tremble at my own forebodings. I torment myself endlessly with the question whether we are an old people, or a young people with a great future ahead" (ibid.). Already in the *Avvenimenti del 1870–71* he had put the question "are we a young nation starting to move again, or an old one to which a couple of crutches were thrown?" (2:140).

political equilibrium of the old Europe, but of restructuring the whole edifice from the foundation up.

A scholar who was still outside the political fray and the struggle of opposing sides could of course adopt such a high tone. But to do so was much more difficult if one plunged into the world of the political parties, into the thick of the political battle, especially if one concentrated on the Left, where the trend of pro-Prussian thought had taken hold most strongly.

There is no doubt that in the Left's rejoicing at the fall of the empire of Napoleon III, and the persistent hatred for the beaten emperor, ideological and party motives were at work. That is, for a de Launay and also for a Blanc, French influence had been deleterious not because it was Bonapartist but because it was French, and it would have been so even if in place of Louis Napoleon there had been a "legitimate" sovereign or a president of a republic. Likewise, in Ricasoli's view France had been harmful to Italy under whatever form of government, with the democratic, republican, irreligious Jacobin mentality responsible for inflicting the worst calamities. But for those on the Left in general, not to speak of those in the party of action, hostility to France had been above all hostility to Bonapartism.

The fact that France had come between the national will of Italy and Rome had given offense to de Launay as much as to Crispi and Cairoli.[82] But the fact that this obstruction had been the work of the "tyrant" Napoleon III, the man of 2 December, the trampler of liberty, had exasperated only Crispi, Cairoli, and their companions. As far as they were concerned, it was even a matter of regret that Bonapartism had fallen under the blows of a foreign power, following a war, given that France ought to have been the one to liberate itself,[83] and they postulated a clear distinction between the French people and their hated tyrant, between the guilt of the imperial usurper and France, which was at least the heir of the principles of 1789.[84] Indeed they declared that "France is suffering, but democracy has won a great battle."[85]

[82] "Why was our aspiration for Rome the most vibrant symbol of Italian independence? Because our sentiments were rightly offended by the violent and oppressive action of foreign intervention; because France intended to interpose its sole will between Italy and Rome" (de Launay to Visconti Venosta, private letter, 2 May 1871; AE, *Ris.*, c. 10).

[83] "Il Bonapartismo," in *La Riforma* for 7 September 1870.

[84] From a speech by P. S. Mancini to the Chamber of Deputies, 19 August 1870: "[G]o into the piazze of the cities of Italy, go into the countryside, the workshops, and you will realize that, without obliterating the memory of the benefits that Italy has received from France, and without believing themselves discharged of the burden of gratitude for the sums lent, nonetheless the whole Italian nation felt [after Mentana] injured by a friend and protector, it felt mutilated, rendered impotent, calculatedly condemned to be eternally a vassal of the French empire. And in all Italian souls there arose spontaneously, and there spread, a singular alienation of Italian affections, I won't say for France, toward that generous nation to which we are bound by indissoluble ties, which inaugurated the principles of liberty and is a prolific disseminator of civilization in the world, but toward its government, which had decreed and carried out that odious intervention" (*Discorsi Parlamentari di P. S. Mancini* 3:350–51). De Launay on the other hand had gone so far as to fear that, given the innate defects of the French nation (meaning the claim to act as the boss of Europe), a regime of liberty might only encourage them even more (private letter to Visconti Venosta, 5 January 1870).

[85] "Il martirio della Francia," in *La Capitale*, 6 February 1871. Cf. the article "Parigi," in the issue of 2 February, stating that under the republican banner "France has been regenerated," a further demonstration "that servitude corrupts, while freedom heartens."

For them it was not just the power relations of France and Italy that mattered; it was a general ideological problem, a problem of party ideology. Bonapartism they took to mean not just the blocking of Italy's road to Rome but the imposition, first in France itself and then in an Italy enslaved to the Tuileries, of a "moral system," a whole complex of ideas and usages, a particular mode of judging, thinking, and feeling, in which Italy was schooled and whose product was the "slavish" soul of the party of the Italian moderates[86] with its servile policies toward foreigners, as Crispi put it in an outburst during a famous session of the Chamber of Deputies as late as 1891.[87]

Once again, although the animating spirit is very different, we find ourselves on the same terrain upon which Marselli had taken his stand: the talk is of moral and political systems, the incommensurable values of two different worlds oppose one another. Yet this point of view ought to have had an immediate and logical consequence: with the fall of Napoleon III and the collapse of Bonapartism, the cause of France was no longer identical with that of the loser of the battle of Sedan, so why remain hostile to the reborn republic, which Gambetta was stirring with his spectacular eloquence? How was it possible not to sympathize with France, given that if the junior Napoleon had not arrived with his usurping violence, it would since 1852 have peacefully rebuilt itself in liberty, gladdening and benefiting with its friendship the peoples of Europe?[88]

This was in fact the conclusion reached by Garibaldi and Carducci. Both of them, the simple and magnanimous man of action and the ever more impetuous poet, had descried, with the disappearance of the emperor, nothing less than the return of the France of 1789, regenerator of humankind, the sister nation. As early as July 1870, when the whole party of action was decidedly in favor of Prussia, and was even ready to collaborate with Bismarck and offer him precious aid in the form of revolts inside Italy should the government of Vittorio Emanuele II show any serious intention of intervening to help Napoleon III, even in July Garibaldi did not keep silent about what he called the "masked despotism" of the Berlin government.[89] Now, on 7 September, he turned to his friends and

---

[86] "L'educazione bonapartista," in *La Riforma*, 15 September 1870. Earlier, on 28 July, *La Riforma* had insisted that Bonapartism "corrodes everything vital and strong in Italian politics, and makes it weak and servile" and on 8 August had repeated that "our moral force therefore largely depends on the divorce of our cause from that of the Napoleonic empire." Cf. in the *Gazzettino Rosa* the insult to Visconti Venosta, "valet of all the powers," and against the Italian government, "domestic" of the "master" Napoleon III (in P. M. Arcari, *La Francia nell'opinione pubblica italiana dal '59 al '70*, p. 134).

The "servility" to France of the governments of the Right is a theme found even in the less intemperate politicians of the Left, such as Mancini in his speech to the Chamber of Deputies on 19 August 1870: "those men who have known no other policy but that of docile and servile clientage of the imperial government of France" (*Discorsi Parlamentari di P. S. Mancini* 3:375; cf. also p. 386).

[87] The celebrated words, which were uttered during the session of the Chamber of 31 January 1891 and which led to the resignation of Crispi's second ministry, have to be seen in the context of the overall judgment passed by the Left for the previous twenty years on the Right.

[88] "La Repubblica a Parigi," in *La Riforma* for 6 September 1870. Previously, *Il Popolo d'Italia*, a democratic and republican paper published in Naples, hostile since August to monarchic and feudal Prussia, had said "the Second Empire is not France" (no. 2, 19 August); on 5 September the headline was "Long Live the Republic in Paris."

[89] Garibaldi, *Scritti e discorsi politici e militari* 3 (National Edition, vol. 6: Bologna, 1937), p. 44.

asserted: "Yesterday I told you: all out war against Bonaparte. Today I say: support the French republic by any means."[90] And then he set off to uphold the "only system" capable of ensuring the peace and prosperity of the nations, to defend the imperiled homeland of the principles of 1789. When Napoleon was gone, it became "Italy's duty to fly to the aid of France."[91] With his instinctive and uncomplicated (and thus more deeply felt) sensitivity to the moral factors, the man of Caprera embraced without hesitation the logical consequences of his own earlier position.

The poet Carducci, who wished to hold aloft on the field of his art the banner of Rome and Marsala, of Aspromonte and Mentana,[92] and who would always recall the "sad" November of the "sad" year of 1870, when the Prussians surrounded Paris and he suffered the death of a child, switched fronts in exactly the same fashion.[93] His imprecations against the "brigand of France," the emperor Cain, his toast to the

> day that would stain . . .
> with trembling and ghastly pallor
> the obscene cheek[94]

were replaced by exultation for the seventy-eighth anniversary of the French Republic, 21 September 1870. And the royal government of Prussia became the tyrannical oppressor of France.

> But iron and bronze are in the tyrants' grasp
> And Kant sharpens with his *Pure Reason*
> the cold bayonet of the Prussian rifle,
> Körner draws the Bavarian cannon

A year and a half later, recalling Garibaldi's adventure on French soil, Carducci imposed the form of reasoned discourse on his impulses and poetic fantasies, contrasting the ancient feudal house of Brandenburg, greedy for conquest, with democracy, which could not forget 1789 nor ignore the fact that liberty and philosophy had spread over all of Europe from Paris, so that "wherever a French soldier is buried, even one who died for the sake of the violence of the moment, rather than for liberty . . . there the earth has brought forth revolution ever since."

And as he peered into the future the poet foresaw with certainty, as "a fact of nature," the confederation of the Latin peoples, a confederation perhaps only moral and ideal at the outset, but one based on the principles of democracy, among peoples who were sisters in their speech, their traditions, their institutions, and their art. Dreaming and hoping in this fashion, he saluted in Garibaldi,

---

[90] Ibid., 6:46.

[91] Ibid., 6:50–51 (to sympathizers in Greece, 4 October 1870).

[92] Carducci to Garibaldi, early May 1871 in *Lettere* (National Edition: Bologna, 1943), vol. 7, p. 4.

[93] To Adolfo Borgognoni, 21 February 1878 (Carducci, *Lettere* 11:256).

[94] Carducci, *Dopo Aspromonte*.

and in those who had followed him to Dijon, the *ver sacrum* of the Italian people.[95]

These two men, who in a sense belonged to no one party, and who were unquestionably beyond the formal discipline of any party, were joined by Giuseppe Ferrari, who was initially convinced that France would win the war,[96] and who felt himself age ten years in ten days during August of 1870.[97] There were others, less renowned but much more closely involved in the parliamentary tactics of the Left, who felt the same way. One was Riccardo Sineo, whose speech in favor of France, in the debate in the Chamber on 21 January 1871, was so partisan that another deputy of the Left, Luigi La Porta, was forced to point out that the things he had uttered were Sineo's personal opinions, not those of all his friends on the Left.[98] Agostino Bertani himself, who in the session of the Chamber of 20 August 1870 had referred to Germany as "the forerunner of civilization and progress,"[99] changed his mind when France became republican again, and in the end gave a shock to Mazzini by writing to him in January 1871 that "if there is a spark of hope for Italy, it comes from France."[100]

On account of the role it was to play in the future politics of Italy, the attitude of Felice Cavallotti, whose brother Giuseppe was a member of Garibaldi's expedition to France and died after being wounded on 23 January 1871, was the most important of all in this regard. His paper, *Il Lombardo*, set up a stark antithesis between generous France, the mother of civilization and freedom, and the usurper Napoleon III. The moderates, he charged, were in sympathy with imperial France, the France that had imposed a humiliating and opprobrious servitude on Italy, whereas he and his friends had fought against this France, this "handful of wretches who blacken its name and barter its blood."

"Yes, we waited for the true France to appear and make common cause with us; we thought that expiation and loss would make it pure and great. We waited for the time when its cause would be that of a nation and not of one man; of justice, not of conquest; of liberty, not of despotism. We waited until we could bless the arms of France, until they were the arms of a people and of a civilization."[101] Other lesser voices also bestowed their blessing on the arms of France

---

[95] Carducci, *Opere* 19:24–26, 29 (National Edition, 1943).

[96] Ferrari, *Scritti editi ed inediti*, vol. 1, *Carteggio inedito*, ed. A. Monti, p. 245.

[97] In his speech to the Chamber on 19 August 1870, now in *La disfatta della Francia*, ed. U. Guanda, p. 19.

[98] *A.P., Camera*, p. 259. Against the opinions expressed by Sineo *La Riforma* immediately took a stance in the article "Italia e Francia" on 23 January 1871. Sineo also sent a letter to the French ambassador, Rothan, on 15 February, to protest on behalf of a number of his colleagues as well as himself, against certain affirmations of *La Riforma* concerning the past and future relations between Italy, France, and Prussia. He considered Italy indissolubly bound to France by common interests as well as by gratitude (G. Rothan, *L'Allemagne et l'Italie, 1870–71*, vol. 2, *L'Italie*, p. 275, n. 1, and cf. p. 295).

[99] Bertani, *Discorsi Parlamentari*, p. 128.

[100] In Mazzini, *Epistolario*, vol. 57 (*Scritti*, National Edition, vol. 90), p. 241, and cf. p. 239. Naturally this caused Mazzini to erupt: "my whole spirit rebels against such an assertion coming from *you*. France is lost since 1815; it does not lead, it follows."

[101] From the article "Le nostre contraddizioni!" in the issue of 22 January 1871.

and the French republic, the representative of the rights and the liberties of peoples.[102]

In any case, all those who were part of the opposition had good reason to adopt a cooler attitude to Prussia after 4 September 1870, in part because they sincerely and profoundly felt that their reasons for hating France had ended with the fall of the Second Empire, and the spell the word "republic" cast over many of them transformed the Franco-Prussian War into a war of principles, republican liberty against the invading Prussian monarchy—an attitude deplored by Mazzini.[103] Or it may have been because, faced with the growing evidence of popular sympathy for France after Sedan, they saw that it would do their own political fortunes little good if they were seen to be locked rigidly and totally into prejudice against France. Finally, it may have been that when they saw how elated the supporters of the Bourbons and the clerical party were at the collapse of the European power that had supported the "usurping" Italian state, this indicated to them that "there must be something wrong if their enemies were that pleased."[104] It was not only in Italy that public opinion, favorable to Prussia at the outset, had undergone a rapid change.[105] In all of Europe the continuation of the war swayed public sympathy toward France. Partly this was because of the general conviction that the cause of the conflict was to be found exclusively in the ambition and arrogance of Napoleon III, so that with the fall of the main culprit, there was no more good reason to continue the bloody fray.[106] Partly it was because European public opinion was disconcerted to behold the absolutely novel hardness, the unrelenting will to achieve victory, of the Prussians. The bombardment of Strasbourg, and later that of Paris, appeared monstrous to a generation that had never experienced, nor found in historical memory, anything of the kind.[107] Certainly

[102] Thus in the address of the committee of Reggio Emilia of the International League of Peace and Liberty to Jules Favre, 18 September 1870 (AEP, *C.P., Italie*, t. 379, fol. 207).

[103] Mazzini, *La guerra franco-germanica* (*Scritti*, National Edition, vol. 92, p. 122). On the influence of the word "republic," see Ferrari, *La disfatta*, p. 58. *La Nazione* noted sarcastically that "hardly have a handful of Frenchmen succeeded in substituting the name of republic for the name of empire, when the judgment and the language of our wise and marvelous radicals about the present war has changed in an instant" ("Amenità radicali," 10 September 1870).

[104] Thus Bonghi, on 20 August in *La Perseveranza* (article "L'Opinione pubblica in Italia"), who harps on the theme that the enemies of France are the enemies of the monarchy, and therefore of the unity of Italy. (My attribution to Bonghi of unsigned editorials in *La Perseveranza* is based on the Bonghi files, which I was able to examine thanks to the courtesy of Signorina Maria Sandirocca, whom I warmly thank.)

[105] On 29 July Dina wrote to Castelli: "It seems to me that public opinion is improving. There is in general no affection for France, but people are beginning to understand that a Prussian victory would do us very serious harm" (*Carteggio politico di Michelangelo Castelli* 2:472). Later Visconti Venosta spoke of this great change of European public opinion to the French chargé d'affaires, De la Villestreux, who for his part signaled to his government the notable change of tone of the Italian press (report, 19 December 1870, AEP, *C.P., Italie*, t. 379, fols. 384–85).

[106] With Napoleon fallen, "God is no longer on the side of the Prussians." Republican France "represents at this moment the justice that previously made Europe favor Prussia" (*La Capitale*, 20 January 1871, article "La religione di re Guglielmo e il bombardamento di Parigi"). Cf. earlier, on 17 December 1870, the following opinion: in France there now streams "a sympathetic banner, among whose folds the code of liberty is religiously preserved" (article "Le tradizioni").

[107] See the articles in *Il Lombardo*, edited by Felice Cavallotti, for 16, 18, and 20 January 1871. A few of the expressions of this paper of the extreme Left might have been pronounced by the

the campaign of 1859, or the one of 1866, which finished so rapidly, could not have prepared contemporaries for a conflict pursued with such implacable, cold, logical perseverance, and all its attendant cruelties.

These were matters of sentiment. But there were also, indeed there preponderated, worries of a political nature among the great powers: Prussian force had now passed all desirable limits; Bismarck and his empire were going too far, becoming too potent. Europe was losing a mistress, according to an expression then current, but was gaining a master. The result was that public opinion quickly turned in favor of France, even in countries initially well disposed toward the Prussian crusade, such as Russia and England.[108]

In Italy, where the tendency of the great majority to prefer neutrality for themselves (a factor in Prussia's favor) had not hindered the growth of a movement of sympathy for France, the events that took place at Sedan increased the sense of horror at what was considered to be a pointless slaughter. At the idea that Paris itself might be bombed, private citizens, newspapers, and cultural organizations bestirred themselves.[109] In its meeting of 24 November 1870 the Institute of Sciences and Letters of Lombardy expressed the desire that during the fighting damage to the art treasures of the French capital should be avoided; and it was followed on 31 December by the Royal Society of Naples, which requested Visconti Venosta to use his good offices with Bismarck to the same end.[110] These resolutions and actions were of course destined to have no practical effect. The Academy of Dublin had passed a resolution similar to that of the Lombard Institute, but the University of Göttingen, when invited to adhere to it, had replied

---

moderate Bonghi, viz.: there is an implacable ferocity in the Prussians; our age has gone back many hundreds of years and now rivals the ferocity of the Middle Ages. And note the similar judgments in F. Engels, *Notes sur la guerre de 1870–71* (French translation: Paris, 1947), pp. 95 ff., 185 ff., and 225 (articles sent by Engels to the *Pall Mall Gazette*).

[108] For English public opinion, favorable to Germany until Sedan and then swinging to support of France, see K. Meine, *England und Deutschland in der Zeit des Überganges vom Manchestertum zum Imperialismus, 1871 bis 1876*, pp. 26, 28, 30–32, 39–41; further, J. Morley, *The Life of William Ewart Gladstone* (London, 1903), vol. 2, p. 357. The shift is underlined in *La Perseveranza* for 26 October (article "L'Opinione pubblica inglese"). On 17 January 1871 the ambassador in London, Carlo Cadorna, informed Visconti Venosta that English public opinion had changed noticeably since the beginning of the war, "when France was seen purely and simply as the nation that had provoked a war that was considered unjust." The main factor producing this change of opinion had been the bombardment of Paris (Cadorna, report, 17 January 1871, no. 187).

In Russia there was a parallel change of public opinion, brought about by political preoccupations over the excessive strength of Prussia, and by commiseration for the French. "Such an alteration in general opinion in the press, even in the *Russian Gazette* of Petersburg, which earlier stood for the German cause, is even more evident and alive among the citizenry and the people of Russia, and it would be impossible to overlook the manifestations of this in the everyday language of the merchants, peasants, and townspeople of this country" (Caracciolo, report, Petersburg, 1–13 February 1871, n. 217). For the Swiss press, cf. H. U. Rentsch, *Bismarck im Urteil der schweizerischen Presse, 1862–1898*, pp. 101 ff.

[109] The *Piccolo Corriere* of Bari, for example, was violent in attacking Kaiser Wilhelm of Prussia himself on 14 January: "We call Ferdinand of Bourbon *re Bomba* [King Bomb] . . . so ought we not today call Wilhelm of Prussia *re Bombone* [King Big Bomb]?" In result there was a protest from the vice-consul in Bari for the North German Confederation.

[110] The Ministry of Public Instruction to the Ministry of Foreign Affairs, 27 January 1871 (AE, *Rapp. Germania*).

through its vice-rector, Richard Dove, in such a brusque and yet triumphal manner that even the Prussian secretary for foreign affairs, von Thile, had to concede the excessive "harshness of its expression."[111]

The myth of the solidarity of men of learning, united across all political boundaries by the cult of the beautiful and the true, suffered some rude shocks in those winter months: harsh months indeed, both physically and also morally.[112] But however little fruit they bore, similar protests gave a clear sign of what most people were thinking and feeling in the face of the continuation of the war and the bombardment of cities, especially a city such as Paris.[113]

If only because of the political costs and benefits involved, or if one prefers, electoral costs and benefits, even those most hostile to France on the Left had to assume a moderate tone. So we see *La Riforma* arguing, from September 1870, that there was no longer any reason for the war to go on: on 16 July Germany had had sound reasons to mobilize and pour into France in order to prevent Napoleon from crossing the Rhine with his troops. That state of necessity had ended, "and any more blood spilled would amount to an insult to humanity."[114] Again, *La Riforma* hammers at the idea that Germany runs the risk of overstepping the just limits of its right to self-defense, and would be in the wrong if it sought to annihilate France, to drive it to a point of intolerable humiliation by taking Alsace-Lorraine away from it, instead of settling for the more equitable way out, which would be to make of Alsace-Lorraine a free state, independent and neutral.[115] This was a solution that Crispi had taken over from Cattaneo and had been proposing since the end of August.[116]

---

[111] Report of de Launay, 31 December 1870, n. 747. Dove's reply is in the *Staatsanzeiger* for 18 December and is summarized as "La risposta dell'Università di Gottinga" in *La Perseveranza* for 30 December. Note the following: "The German people, which in its intellectual aspirations strives always to follow the superb precept of Paracelsus: *English, French, Italians, follow me, not I you*, has been obliged to set aside its work" of peace by an aggression. But it is fighting for its national existence, its moral conscience, its honor, and also "for peace in the world and for human morality, inasmuch as these things would be lost if the idea of a vengeful Justice should be erased from the conscience of the peoples. If the world, however, retains faith in such justice, that is owing, after God, to the German people."

[112] M. Macchi, in *I dottrinarii d'Alemagna*, pp. 6 ff., spoke out against the "grim" efforts of the learned men of Germany, who, sooner than join in "the useful and mandatory apostolate of peace and liberty," employed their genius, learning, and authority to heighten antagonism.

[113] Another significant indication of the frame of mind of the majority was the initiative to aid the French growers by sending supplies of seed, or money, undertaken by an "Italian Committee" headed by Sen. Luigi Torelli, prefect of Venice, and by the "Agrarian Society" of Lombardy. See *La Perseveranza* for 11 February 1871.

[114] "La voce della Francia," in *La Riforma* for 9 September 1870. In an earlier article of 6 September, "La Repubblica a Parigi," one finds the following: "If the war continues it will become a war between races, and the outcome would be impossible to predict. It is time for hatreds to die down, and for the memories that fed them to fade."

[115] "Il conflitto franco-germanico," in *La Riforma* for 29 September 1870. The papers *Roma* and *Il Pungolo* of Naples also began very much to temper their anti-French attitude. When the peace talks begin, *La Riforma* observes that the conditions imposed by Germany constitute an enormous mistake, and although they may be allowed by the letter of the law, they are culpable failures of magnanimity and political prudence, leading to a peace that will breed and nurture war ("La Pace," 1 March 1871).

[116] "La neutralizzazione delle provincie renane," in *La Riforma* for 30 August 1870. Cf. Crispi, *Ultimi scritti e discorsi extraparlamentari (1891–1901)*, p. 394.

The article for 29 September voiced these ideas, together with an appeal to the generosity of the victor, and statements that might have come from the pen of the anti-Prussian Bonghi,[117] or of Dina at any rate. There was also a humanitarian entreaty in favor of France. But amid all this it was possible to detect other motifs with an entirely different burden, motifs that effectively blocked the possibility of a shift of emotional support in favor of France.

For one thing any sort of racial solidarity with France was dismissed by *La Riforma*. At this time in Europe an enormous amount of discussion about ethnic questions was going on, and there were many who were ready to interpret the events of the war as the expression of a fatal contrast between the Latin world and the Germanic one, while others went to the length of prophesying the inevitable decadence of the Latin peoples as they were overcome by the younger and more vigorous German and Slavic races.[118] In Italy Francesco Montefredini was already sounding ideas that would later appear in Guglielmo Ferrero,[119] and in France Flaubert was lamenting the twilight of the Latin world, the source of all that he loved.[120] Others propounded renewal, hopefully predicting the political alliance of the three great Latin nations. The idea of Latin brotherhood came back into vogue: warmly embraced by Carducci, it was taken up by Cesare Orsini as the basis of a projected alliance of Italy, France, and Spain,[121] while outside Italy it found an advocate full of pathos in Jules Favre, the man who had once defended Felice, the older brother of Cesare Orsini.[122] The notion of such a

---

[117] Bonghi wrote in *La Perseveranza* for 13 November ("L'Europa e la guerra"): "in fact it is true, though many who have become barbarians overnight forget it, that when a civil people has won, it has salvaged through victory all its legitimate interests; and it does not continue, for the purpose of inflicting crushing defeat, a war that it sees cannot be brought to a conclusion without failing in every duty of humanity, and without doing infinite and irreparable harm to itself."

[118] Even a statesman of the caliber of Andrássy believed in a "struggle, not yet exhausted, between the Latin and the German races [*Völkerstämmen*]" (in secret instructions to Beust on 1 April 1872 concerning a close accord with England; in F. Leidner, *Die Aussenpolitik Österreich-Ungarns vom deutsch-französischen Kriege bis zum deutsch-österreichischen Bündnis, 1870–1879*, p. 15). *La Perseveranza* for 29 July 1870 saw in the war a "race struggle" handed down for centuries from fathers to sons between the French and the Germans, for two thousand years between Latins and Teutons. For some there was a little consolation to be found in the fact that among the Latin nations it was Italy that was in the best position at this juncture (*L'Opinione* for 25 February 1871, article "La razza latina"); it was Italy, so it was said, who held high the Latin banner (P. Villari, *La guerra presente e l'Italia* [Florence, 1870], p. 23). Wholly pessimistic views are expressed, on the other hand, in C. Alfieri, "Considerazioni a proposito della guerra del 1870," in *L'Italia liberale*, p. 437 ff.

[119] Cf. B. Croce, *La letteratura della nuova Italia* 3:359 ff. (4th ed.; Bari, 1943). As for Ferrero, it is well known that in *L'Europa giovine* (1897) he contrasted the young Europe of the Germans and the Slavs to the aged Europe of the Latins.

[120] Flaubert, *Correspondance*, 4th ser., p. 44 and cf. p. 42.

[121] Orsini, *L'alliance latine* (Paris, 1871), esp. pp. 72 ff. In *La Perseveranza* for 18 October 1870 too there is talk of the utility of linking together Spain, Italy, and France, the Latin stocks that might one day oppose their 80 million men to the 60 million of German descent. And in the issue for 25 November the election of the duke of Aosta as king of Spain is greeted as "the beginning of a closer . . . union between the Spanish stock and the Italian in the common Latin name," that may give rise to a civilization "gentler, more substantial, truer" than that of Germany (the writer is Bonghi). Such ideas had found supporters even earlier; see for example G. De Simone, *La pace di Vienna e l'Italia* (Naples, 1866), p. 34, and *Del principio di nazionalità come fondamento delle nuove alleanze e dell'equilibrio europeo*, p. 46 (with Austria to join the alliance of the Latin nations).

[122] Favre, *Rome et la république française*, pp. 201 ff. and esp. 206.

kinship transpired in other comments made by men and by papers of the Left.[123] But Crispi's circle explicitly repudiated it as "a grave ethnographic and historical error, a prejudice flowing from the predominantly French education that has seeped into Italy since the last century."[124]

Much more important as an indication of underlying hostility was the reproof directed at republican France itself for not having had "the difficult courage to separate completely the cause of the empire from that of the nation," since in this way the door was opened to doubts about the effective validity of the distinction between Bonapartism and the French nation. Thus the position of those democrats who had become favorable to France was undercut by annulling the distinction and relegating the transitory phenomenon of Bonapartism to the background; France itself was left standing alone as the guilty party. With Napoleon's fall, Garibaldi and Carducci had saluted once again the France of 1789, the bearer of liberty to the human race, but Crispi and his friends no longer believed in France, and they treated hackneyed phrases about its being the mistress of civilization and liberty as little better than fairy tales.[125]

For them France was not the instructor of the nations in a new political faith, but rather "a vigorous affirmation, perhaps the most vigorous there has ever been, of national unity," and therefore a magnificent state organism, which was not only not necessarily the friend of Italy but might very well be its enemy, and not just on occasions. The anti-Bonapartist and democratic ideological motif vanishes, and in place of Carduccian fantasies of the emperor as Cain, or of the sansculottes of 1792, there appeared the vision of a France intent on weaving a history not for others but uniquely for itself. In this history there was no salvation for humanity, only conquest for France,[126] along with the necessary dosage of looting and savagery. It was a history written in the name of its own egoism, the egoism of a France hostile to Italy, and foe of Italian national unity, whatever government sat in Paris.[127] In fact, if anything, the revolting tyrant of 2 December had personally been the most favorable to Italy, or least unfavorable, of all the past and present leaders of France.[128]

---

[123] The *Gazzettino Rosa* had written on 28 July 1870: "I don't love the Prussians because they are of the German race, the eternal enemy of the Latin. I don't love the French because in general I hate those who want to throw their weight around in other people's houses, because of their *blague*, and for Mentana" (Arcari, *La Francia*, p. 131).

[124] The phrase quoted is from the article "Il conflitto franco-germanico," in *La Riforma* for 29 September 1870 (cited at n. 115 above). On 17 December 1871 *La Riforma* comes out openly ("L'alleanza latina") against the ideas of Orsini, which had been endorsed by *La Perseveranza* on 11 December ("L'alleanza latina"). For *La Riforma* the idea of a Latin empire, Napoleonic in origin, ought to be relegated to the land of dreams; Orsini's opuscule is "an aberration." It is a wretched mistake "to make the race principle the cogent reason for an alliance," all the more in that it is a mistake to speak of Latin races, as it is of Germanic races.

[125] "It is not even the case that we must fear the irreparable decline of civilization with the political decline of France . . . nor that with the fall of France the cause of liberty would be lost in the world: no, unhappily, liberty was not France's lesson for the nations, no matter what form of government it adopted, or aspired to."

[126] Crispi, *Pensieri e profezie*, p. 133.

[127] *La Riforma* for 21 February 1871 (article "Italia e Francia"). Crispi will repeat this idea: "France detests Italy, and all the French governments—Directory, Consulate, Empire, monarchical, or republican—have nourished hatred" (*Pensieri e profezie*, p. 123).

[128] See the declarations of Mancini to the Chamber on 19 August 1870 (cited at n. 158 below).

This conception seemingly grew out of the attitude of Mazzini, who had come out unequivocally against idolization of France much earlier than 1851. In fact from 1843 Mazzini was stubbornly demanding that other peoples, especially the Italians, seize the initiative which the French had let slip from their hands,[129] declaring explicitly that progress for the nations would mean emancipating themselves from France.[130] The suffocating influence of French culture and French ideologies had provoked, both on his part and that of Gioberti, an energetic refusal. It was Mazzini who took the position that 1789 was the summation of eighteen centuries of intellectual labor, not the onset of a new era; who had protested against the veneration of the French past; who had written in 1835: "The past is deadly for us. I declare I am convinced that the French Revolution is crushing us. It presses like an incubus on our hearts and almost makes them cease to beat. Dazzled by the splendor of its gigantic struggles, fascinated by its victorious gaze, we still remain prostrate today before it."[131]

This vigorous reaction was a way of assuring Italy's place in Europe, and by preventing it from gravitating like a simple satellite into France's orbit, saving the nation's individuality.[132] It was a reaction that went beyond contingent political events and passing forms of government and grappled with the problem of the existence of two different, sharply national individualities, each worthy of living its own life. But later Mazzini too had occasion to launch his own shafts against Bonapartism and made some acknowledgment of the distinction between the two Frances, good and bad—the pure republican France and the other, the breeding ground of tyranny and of deviant communistic sects.[133]

Mazzini's campaign against *timor reverentialis* of France, against adoration of an idol by now incapable of any new initiative, had for decades been so thorough, organic, and coherent that there was no real surprise when in 1870–71, even after Sedan, he continued to show diffidence toward the republic of 4 September and disrespect for the men who formed the new government of Paris-Tours-Bordeaux. Never before perhaps, or certainly very rarely, had Mazzini's irritation against the Italian "Francophiles" been so acute and been pitched in such heartfelt terms as those that pervade his letters and writings, especially the composition he dedicated specifically to the *Guerra Franco-Germanica*. He begs his friends not to be "too French," for the French do not deserve it;[134] he exhorts them to look no longer to France, for its force is spent;[135] as with the group around *La Riforma* and Cairoli, he expresses his regret that so many promising young men have been dragged off to die for France by the dreamer Garibaldi,

---

[129] Mazzini, *Dell'iniziativa rivoluzionaria in Europa*, in *Scritti* 4:163, 170–71. Cf. *Fede e avvenire*, ibid., 6:317; and, from 1871, *Sulla rivoluzione francese del 1789: Pensieri*, in *Scritti* 92:217 ff.

[130] *Dell'iniziativa rivoluzionaria in Europa*, in ibid., 4:178.

[131] Mazzini, *Fede e avvenire*, ibid., 6:339 (and cf. again *Sulla rivoluzione francese del 1789: Pensieri*, ibid., 92:218–19). Crispi picks this up almost verbatim in *Pensieri e profezie*, p. 130.

[132] Cf. A. Omodeo,"Primato francese e iniziativa italiana," in *Figure e passioni del Risorgimento*, pp. 51 ff.

[133] Mazzini, *Agli italiani* (1853), in *Scritti* 51:37–38.

[134] Mazzini, *Epistolario*, vol. 57 (*Scritti* 90), p. 162.

[135] Ibid., p. 264. But examples could be multiplied; see for example pp. 267, 300–301, 318, 321–22.

men who ought to have taken action only on Italian soil and for Italy.[136] Mazzini rebukes the sentimentalists who are concerned at the bombardment of Strasbourg and Paris, and who use "stupidly exaggerated" expressions about the new Huns, forgetting that every war is a duel of greater or less ferocity, and that until the reasons for war itself are vanquished through a republican confederation of peoples and an international institution of arbitration, "each of the combatants has the *duty*, in the name of his own Nation, to win": this was Mazzini's reaction to the events of the war.

It is not that he saw, as the group around *La Riforma* and many other Italians did, the actualization of his own ideals, even his ideal of nationhood, in the German ground swell. It is true that he had changed his views since the time when, on the eve of the war of 1866, he had found the alliance between Italy and Prussia "shameful and contrary to all our natural inclinations as a nation,"[137] believing that if the two had indeed joined forces, "such a guilty deed" ought to be kept a dark secret. "Italy ought not to contaminate any more than it has done the sanctity of its flag, and should not proclaim to Europe that it only looks for friends among those who represent despotism. Only three years ago the Prussian government, alone in Europe, was the federated satellite of the tsar against the insurrection in Poland. Not long after, it violated every principle of justice and right in the case of Denmark. In that piece of bloody work it broke all faith with its own treaties and lied brazenly to the European Powers, to the conquered populations, to the German Confederation. It recently infringed on the rights of Parliament and of Liberty, and it still does so on its own territory; in the issue of the moment it represents the worse part."[138] In the upshot, however, the events of the war of 1866, and the blow they dealt to the hated emperor of the French, had not only reduced Mazzini's hostility to Bismarck[139] but had even, in 1867–68, led the agitator from Genoa to make approaches to the Prussian government.

But not even in 1870 was there any real sympathy, any full conjunction of sentiments and ideas. On the contrary, as in 1867 when he turned to Bismarck, offering him an alliance with his own party of action so as to obtain in return money and arms, but with the proviso that he did not share Bismarck's political ideas but only desired to see German unity, so now he had no hesitation in accusing Bismarck of veneration of force and action, and in branding the approach taken by Germany in defense of its own nationality as "not good."[140]

---

[136] Ibid., p. 179; and vol. 58 (91), p. 176.

[137] Mazzini, *Epistolario*, vol. 51 (*Scritti* 82), pp. 157–58 (29 May 1866). Cf. as well F. Quintavalle, *La politica internazionale nel "Pensiero" e nella "Azione" di Giuseppe Mazzini* (Milan, 1938), pp. 208 and 210.

[138] *La Guerra*, in *Scritti* 83:243 (originally in *Il Dovere* for 14 May 1866).

[139] Cf. the valid observations of Menghini in the introduction to Mazzini, *Scritti* 86:xxi ff.

[140] "I do not share the political views of Count Bismarck; his method of unification does not have my sympathy. But I admire his tenacity, his energy, and his spirit of independence vis-à-vis the foreigner. I believe in the unity of Germany, and I desire it as I desire that of my own country. I abhor the Second Empire and the supremacy that France claims over Europe" (*Scritti* 86:107–108). In these lines Mazzini's attitude to Germany is made perfectly clear. Cf. his letter to Karl Blind on 1 August 1870: "We wish for German unity as for Italian; and we hate the Empire" (*Epistolario*, vol. 56 [*Scritti* 89], p. 337).

Above all, Mazzini—this time in perfect agreement with the moderates Dina and Bonghi—found the German takeover of Alsace-Lorraine "without the free vote of the citizens" to be "a wicked lesson in liberty for the people that commit the act," a choice of the road of "conquest," that would inevitably compel another war between the two nations in the short term. His final warning was severe: "Under the guidance of a greedy monarchy Germany has in its turn trespassed the boundaries of right which its inborn reverence for ideals should have taught it to respect, and has substituted a notion of vengeance that is sowing the seeds of future wars for the right of self-protection."[141]

But in Mazzini there was one firm conviction that stood above all these reservations, most of which would not in themselves have set him apart from the moderates: not only was France paying the penalty for its errors, the errors of an entire people and not purely of a dynasty or of one man,[142] but the moment had come for Italy to take the European initiative that had been vacant since 1815 and to begin its mission. Let there be insurrection in Italy, the proclamation of a republic; let the banner of liberty be raised triumphantly in a Rome redeemed from the papal yoke, just as the whole nation was now finally freed from subjection to France. Never before had the agitator dreamed as he did in those days of the summer of 1870 that the moment was near for the realization of his prophecy, and believed so strongly that the hour was nigh for Italy to come to the fore in a "European epic."[143]

In the sequel these hopes collapsed, his morale plunged, he saw his "twofold dream"[144] go up in smoke, and once again he felt himself isolated among the degenerate race of Italians. But even after this disillusionment, even when he saw Rome profaned by a monarchy and a mere semblance of a republic in France, without a republican soul,[145] even then Mazzini remained firm in his

---

[141] Mazzini, *La guerra franco-germanica*, in *Scritti* 92:124–25 and 139. And observe his reference to [Prussian] "militarism" as opposed to the "anarchy" and the "vacuum of ideas" [of the French] in the letter to Camillo Finocchiaro-Aprile on 5 April 1871 (*Epistolario*, vol. 58 [*Scritti* 91], p. 3); and in *Agli italiani* (1871): "Germany threatens to sterilize the vast potential for thought that is contained in it, entrusting the *action* that ought to be collective, and the creation of its own unity, to a military monarchy hostile to liberty" (*Scritti* 92:88).

[142] "The events that followed gave a further grave lesson to Europe, and that is that a people is, at least in part and when it tolerates it for a long time, responsible for the unjust and immoral policy of its government. By the law of things it has to suffer the consequences. The fall of that government is not enough to avoid these, when it is caused not by the faith and spontaneous sacrifice of the people, but by an error or a cowardly act of the government itself" (*Scritti* 92:130–31).

[143] *Epistolario*, vol. 56 (*Scritti* 89), p. 320.

[144] "My dear Nicolò, I am sunk in gloom . . . we allowed—perhaps by not very much—the first [republican] *initiative* to come from France, and we allowed profanation to be inflicted on Rome through the monarchy. My twofold dream has vanished" (letter to Nicolò Le Piane, 17 October 1870; *Epistolario*, vol. 57 [*Scritti* 90], p. 63). Cf. the letter to the workers of Genoa, 24 October 1870, ibid., pp. 81–82: "The republican *initiative*, which should have rebaptized Italy for its third mission, has sprung up (lasting or not) in France. And Rome, the home of my soul, is profaned by a monarchy." And in his letter to Giorgina Saffi of 6 November 1870, ibid., p. 111: "None of you could know my state of mind leaving Gaeta . . . the ideal of a lifetime gone up in smoke!"

[145] "It is a republic in name only" (*La guerra franco-germanica*, in *Scritti* 92:128 and cf. p. 123). Note as well in the *Epistolario*: "I do not believe that France can now incarnate the *principle* and the initiative in itself. If I thought differently, I would be . . . in France" (vol. 57 [*Scritti* 90], p. 132, and see also pp. 57–58).

convictions and continued to insist, as he had done for thirty-five years, on a handful of fixed ideas. One was that the French Revolution had represented not the beginning of a new era but a conclusion, albeit a miraculous one, the last product of an era that had ended;[146] another was that since 1815 France not only was no longer Europe's leader[147] but in fact had deviated from its own mission, letting itself be led astray by its tendency to dominate, and trampling the rights of its sister nations by claiming rights of autocratic primacy among them, so that its expiation was just, even though excessively severe.[148] And again Mazzini repeated that Italy now ought to take the leading role.

In sum he was opposed to France and not just to Bonapartism: opposed because he feared the deleterious consequences for the capacity to act, the will, the very purposes, of Europeans in general and the Italians in particular, that would flow from France's profound and lasting influence;[149] opposed because it was his unavoidable duty to be combative in order to save Italian individuality, to awaken in his people the will to act, by which he meant the self-awareness that the Italians seemed to him still utterly to lack.[150] So it was that after having preached to Bismarck in 1867 that it was urgent to combat Bonapartism, a permanent danger to Europe,[151] he now painted all of France guilty, accusing it of being too ready to look for a scapegoat and to heap on one man (in accordance with ancestral custom) the sins of all.[152]

Mazzini staked his position out clearly, therefore, with regard to France as a nation, not just the Second Empire of France. He would be just as ready to take a stance against Germany, when German influence came to seem as menacing as French influence had been, with the result that in August of 1871 he was deploring Italy's "eternally fluctuating obeisance" to German and French influence.[153] Carducci was in agreement in this respect, and not long after, in January 1872, attacked "the conventional bourgeoisie, which always admires force and success," which "dresses its children in the costume of uhlans, just as it dressed them in the costume of Zouaves a few years previously." Most Italians, he

---

[146] Thus in 1834 in *Dell'iniziativa rivoluzionaria in Europa* (*Scritti* 4:163 ff., and esp. p. 168 and n. 1). And thus in 1871: see esp. *Sulla rivoluzione francese del 1789: Pensieri*, in *Scritti* 92.

[147] Cf. the harsh judgment expressed on 5 June 1871 to Emilia Venturi (*Epistolario*, vol. 58 [*Scritti* 91], p. 74): "I was not really optimistic about France. But I would never have thought that it could fall so low." The last piece published by Mazzini in *Roma del Popolo* between 22 February and 7 March 1872 was to be his severe criticism of Ernest Renan's *Réforme intellectuelle et morale* (*Scritti* 93:229 ff.). For Mazzini, the belief that the French Revolution constituted the beginning of a new epoch, and that the initiative was still with France, were the two fundamental errors that "falsified the nature of the progressive movement and held it back in France and in Europe" (p. 232).

[148] *Scritti* 92:137–39.

[149] "I see today that the excessive sway exercised by France, and by the memories of its great revolution on the minds of our young people, is more alive and more potent than I thought" (*Sulla rivoluzione francese del 1789: Pensieri*, in *Scritti* 92:218).

[150] On this absence in the Italians of a consciousness of themselves, seen as the source of all that was wrong, Mazzini dwelt often in the period 1870–71; cf. the *Epistolario*, vol. 57 (*Scritti* 90), p. 88: "We have everything within us except the consciousness of our mission and our force"; p. 294: "Italy seems to be sunk in the sleep of the Seven Sleepers"; and in vol. 58 (91), pp. 3–4, 34, etc.

[151] *Scritti* 86:109–10.

[152] *Scritti* 93:231.

[153] *Epistolario*, vol. 58 (*Scritti* 91), p. 163.

claimed, behaved toward the French "like a slave newly fallen into servitude, exulting in the disgrace of the master he fears."[154]

But in the dichotomy between France and Italy that Crispi and his friends sought to impose, new themes that did not reecho those of Mazzini were now making their appearance. These were moral postulates much more than they were political ones in the strict sense of the term, advanced in connection with a program at whose summit there shone the ideal of *Humanity*, and which therefore required the harmonious cooperation of all,[155] in brotherhood, for the triumph of a principle, for the "new social goal of a European synthesis that might lift *initiative* up from the hearts of any *one* people and spread it over *all*, imparting to every man the activity that is missing today." The corollaries were also largely matters of principle, such as that development should be identical, and ideas and ends be common property, in the national movements of both Germany and Italy, which would therefore be bound together in a single destiny—with the obvious consequence that the future of Italy did not coincide with that of France.[156] But to a large extent these points of view were really derived from pure practical politics; they were the fruits of unambiguous interstate rivalry. From the dream of a Europe to come, Crispi and company came back to the narrower and more concrete Europe of today, with its self-evident interests in territorial, political, and economic power, in immediate embodied realities. In

---

[154] Carducci, *Giuseppe Garibaldi: Un anno dopo, 21 gennaio 1872*, in *Opere* 19:23–24. The identical thought is expressed in the poem *Canto dell'Italia che va in Campidoglio*:

> Sí, sí, portavo il sacco a gli zuavi
> E battevo le mani
> Ieri a Turcòs: oggi i miei bimbi gravi
> Si vestono da ulani
>
> Al cappellino, o a l'elmo, in ginocchione
> Sempre: ma lesta e scaltra
> Scoto la polve di un'adorazione
> Per cominciarne un'altra.
>
> (Yes, yes, I was carrying the packsack for the Zouaves
> And clapping my hands
> The day before at Turcòs. Today my grave children
> Are dressed as uhlans.
>
> Always on my knees before the cap or the helmet,
> Yet agile and shrewd,
> I shake off the dust of one adoration
> So as to commence another.)

[155] Mazzini, *Scritti* 6:318.

[156] Among the chief proponents of the parallel development of the principle of nationality in the two countries was always Mancini, who in his speech to the Chamber in support of the law of Guarantees on 28 January 1871 recalled the views expressed by Bismarck on the close affinity between the Italian and German questions, which constituted "a single question, or two aspects of the same question; it is not possible to separate them and to combat one without offending and renouncing the other as well." Mancini stated his own adherence to these views, "because of the naturally shared interests, and national designs, of Italy and Germany" (*Discorsi Parlamentari di P. S. Mancini* 3:426; cf. F. Ruffini, "Nel primo centenario della nascita di P. S. Mancini," in *Nuova Antologia*, 16 March 1917, p. 13, in the offprint seen). Six months earlier on 25 July 1870, another leader of the Left, Miceli, had affirmed that Italy, "obeying its principles," was drawn to Germany (*A.P., Camera*, p. 3681).

this descent from principles to practice, the substance of Mazzini's thought was abandoned. Crispi had already cast off his republicanism and made his accommodation with the monarchy, and he likewise passed from Mazzini's European program to the evaluation, normal for a politician or a diplomat, of the "necessary" clashes of interest between adjacent states. One further metamorphosis of this kind, the last in the arc of his career, still lay ahead for Crispi: the passage from his original emphasis on liberty (never abandoned in theory) to the practice of virtually authoritarian government in Italy.

The conception of the Crispians is virtually nationalistic: they see specific interests in conflict with one another and nothing else; they talk of strength and wish to make no further concessions to "sentimentalism"; as with Blanc they repudiate the "old principles" and the doctrines of the past.[157] This conception brings the Crispians and others of the Left as well, including even on occasions Mancini,[158] close to the conservative de Launay[159] without their consciously intending it, and distances them considerably from Garibaldi and Carducci.

The fall of the Second Empire and the advent of the Third Republic are no longer in themselves sufficient, therefore, to decide the question for or against France. Instead these men, proclaiming the necessity for a purely Italian policy,[160] in the sense of a policy uninfluenced by memories of the past, by preconceptions of race, religion, or history, a policy guided by nothing but Italian interests rationally weighed and ranked, men who assume the modish posture of devotees of *Realpolitik* in harmony with the general tone of the period, maintain an attitude full of reserve toward France, even after 4 September.

Germany may be described without hesitation as "the country that in many ways reveals its points of contact with Italy," but France is still on probation: "whenever it completely gives up its inclination to protect the papacy, and its presumptuous belief in its role as the dominant power in the Mediterranean and the tutelary power over Italy, when its form of government gives us some security against the danger of reaction, then it may become, exactly like Germany, an

---

[157] *La Riforma*, 16 January 1873 (article "Laboremus").

[158] If in his speech of 19 August 1870 Mancini had made the ritual distinction between France and Napoleon III (above, n. 84), a little later on the same occasion he began to reveal mistrust of France as such: the Convention of 7 September "inspires me with much less fear in the hands of the emperor Napoleon III than it does in the hand of any other government that might take his place in France, because having fought at Magenta and Solferino . . . he would always find that his own previous actions impeded him morally from undoing what he had done, and from going beyond certain limits, even when he wanted to give satisfaction to our enemies. But, gentlemen, let me tell you as a good Italian, a title of that nature and force [i.e., Convention] in the hands of any other French government, not excluding those of a republican government, would make me tremble" (Mancini, *Discorsi Parlamentari* 3:357). There is a profound contradiction between the two positions taken one after the other by the speaker, of which Mancini himself seems unaware. But this is precisely the crucial moment when we see the inadvertent shift from being anti-Bonaparte to being anti-French, from a primarily ideological stance to one deriving essentially from considerations of power.

[159] This was noted by G. Salvemini, "La politica estera della Destra (1871–1876)," *Rivista d'Italia* 27, no. 3 (1924): 362.

[160] Cf. the editorial in *La Riforma* for 28 July 1870; and esp. the two articles entitled "Le nostre alleanze" in the issues for 22 and 23 October 1870.

ally of ours, on whose concurrence in the development of liberal principles we shall be able to count." This last was a glittering mirage. And it was accompanied by so many cautious preambles, and so many ifs, ands, and buts, that a mirage was exactly what it appeared to be. Here we have the germ of the whole future attitude of the Left, for in the coming years the inclination of France to defend the papacy and the threat of reactionary movements on French soil were to reappear, at times with disquieting violence, and give depth to the shadowy fears that were sketched in the article of 22 October in *La Riforma*.

From here only one further step was needed to arrive at the idea of the "naturalness" of the German-Italian alliance, and conversely of the "natural" opposition between Italy and France. As for Bismarck, he might perfectly well state, and repeat, that Prussia was the "natural" and proven ally of Italy;[161] he was far too astute a politician to let himself be deluded into believing in the reality of a phrase that he uttered whenever it suited his purposes, and which he was always ready to discard when he had no further reason to win over the government in Rome. Perhaps the phrase contained a higher quotient of sincerity when spoken by Mommsen.[162] But whenever some Italians got it into their heads that there was a natural alliance between Germany and Italy, they asserted it with deep seriousness and warm conviction: the momentary concord of interests between Berlin and Rome would assume the perpetuity of natural fact, and correspondingly (with any remaining traces of specific anti-Bonapartism forgotten) a "natural" gulf would appear to open up between France and Italy. This was seen as a chasm decreed by fate, not to be spanned by the will of man. The development of Italian life foretold for the new kingdom "a greatness and a political potency in the south of Europe, which cannot come about without France feeling that its traditional ambition to dominate is under assault."[163]

This, then, is the sort of thing being said in Italy. And it was being said much more frequently in France itself, where the enemies of Italian unity had for a long

---

[161] *Die auswärtige Politik Preussens, 1858–1871* 9:774 (Bismarck to Usedom, 9 March 1868). The notion of Germany as a natural ally etc. reappears a month later in the well-known memorandum to Mazzini ([E. Diamilla-Muller], *Politica segreta italiana, 1863–1870*, pp. 346 ff.), the authorship of which seems to me, however, to be highly doubtful.

[162] "[D]o not forget the natural alliance with our nation" (Mommsen, in the first "Lettera agli Italiani" published in *La Perseveranza* for 10 August 1870). But when Mommsen went on to speak of "our cries of admiration for the combatants of Novara," and of the "outburst of enthusiasm [in Germany] when the Lombards threw off the chains of Austria," *La Perseveranza* was driven to note that in Mommsen's letter there prevailed "a particularly German bent for fantasy," and to recall instead the attitude of the Parliament of Frankfurt in 1848, and that of the Prussian government in 1859. (This confutation of Mommsen came from the pen of Bonghi.)

[163] *La Riforma* for 21 February 1871 (article "Italia e Francia"). Crispi took up this motif again in this passage (*Pensieri e profezie*, p. 128): "The alliances of the sort I would call natural are those between powers that have an identical interest to defend, an identical goal in mind. Are we in this position with France? Unfortunately there exist two questions that are enough by themselves to keep the two countries apart: the Mediterranean and the Pope." It will not be superfluous to note that when Cavour in 1858 and 1861 had spoken of Prussia as of a "natural ally" of Italy (cf. references given at n. 12 above), at a moment when tactical convenience was no less important to him than it was to Bismarck, he had certainly not made Prussia Italy's "only" natural ally and had not drawn a comparison (as Crispi and company were later to do) between this putative naturalness and an equally natural divergence between Italy and France.

time invoked in their turn the "naturalness" of the contrast between the two nations.[164] In fact proponents of the natural Italian-Prussian alliance had been in evidence since 1866, even before Mentana, and a by-product of this had been the discovery that the hearts of the two nations, Italy and Germany, destined to beat in unison in the future, had always done so in the past though the two peoples had failed to realize it, "because they had shared aspirations, desires, fears and hopes."[165]

No need for surprise, then, in light of this trend of opinion, if the Garibaldian expedition to France was looked at askance by many on the Left,[166] nor that, when the expedition turned out badly, with its leader being ill-received by the national assembly in Bordeaux, and the red-shirted expeditionaries suffering some tribulation after the armistice, the whole thing turned into one more reason to affirm that ungrateful France, haughty even amid its debacle, had shown its hatred (its, the entire nation's) for everything even remotely Italian. Thus the last enterprise of the great man of Caprera was converted, against his will, into an argument of anti-French propaganda.

The old association between France and liberty had sunk from view among the men of the Left; they no longer thought of it as the chosen nation that had merely been besmirched in passing by a tyrant. And so they generously conferred its former attributes on Germany instead, and Germany was proclaimed the defender of the principles of independence and national autonomy,[167] of civilization and European liberty,[168] even of true and sturdy democracy.[169]

[164] Readers are referred to the second volume of the present work for more on this. [*Translator's note:* The later volumes never appeared.]

[165] G. Raitti, *Le alleanze d'Italia* (2d ed.; Milan, 1866), p. 13 and cf. pp. 9, 19, 20 ff., 53 ff. Here the basic reason for the Italian-French clash is naturally their rivalry for domination in the Mediterranean. For the views of Blanc, see p. 7 above. In Turiello, a strong supporter of Italian colonial expansion and of the recovery of equilibrium in the Mediterranean, the same basic reason also leads to personal dislike of France (Turiello, *Governo e governati in Italia* 2:335 [Bologna, 1882]; he was even more firm and sharp about this in the second edition, vol. 2, p. 235 [Bologna, 1890]).

[166] Cf. the article "Le spedizioni di volontari in Francia," in *La Riforma* for 19 September 1870: the cause of liberty in the world now lies not in France but "in Italy: the assigned place for all who believe in liberty, in the duty of Italian patriots, is here." And note as well a letter of Benedetto Cairoli to Orazio Dogliotti of 9 November 1870: "I also told [Garibaldi] that I was convinced that his sacrifice would not only be useless but dangerous, because it would take away German sympathy for us without gaining us that of France, which continues to vaunt our debt to it in spite of its earlier, and more recent, misdeeds. I wish I was wrong . . . but I fear that Garibaldi will later bitterly regret his impetuous decision" (L. C. Bollea, "Documenti inediti della famiglia Cairoli," *Bollettino della Società Pavese di Storia Patria* 15 [1915]: 270). On the other hand, *Il Diritto* gave its approval to Garibaldi's decision (13 October: "Garibaldi e la quistione di Nizza").

[167] Thus *La Riforma* for 23 July 1870.

[168] Thus *Il Diritto* for 23 September 1870 ("Le condizioni della pace e la lettera di T. Mommsen"). Stimulated by Germany's *Kulturkampf*, this praise of the German mission was prolonged for a time: cf. *La Riforma* for 16 January 1873 ("Laboremus"), in which Germany is portrayed as "the torch and beacon of civilization and progress" as against "the tired principles and outmoded doctrines that are imputed to the Latin race."

[169] Cf. "All'Oriente" in *La Riforma* for 21 August 1871: "If there is . . . a nation constituted on a truly democratic basis, it is precisely Germany, where the armed forces are an integral part of the nation, and political representation rises up out of a widespread suffrage; where science and virtue constitute authority, where education is a common right and duty. There true liberty has a secure

For a number of those of the Left who took this view, Crispi at their head, there was no need even to wait for the revival of France's clerical-monarchic penchant. Long before it resurfaced openly in the assembly at Bordeaux, when France seemed to be incarnated in the eminently republican Gambetta, and the French envoy at Florence, Senard, was congratulating the king and his government on the occupation of Rome, the disposition of Crispi and his friends toward France had once again, after a brief moment of sunshine, become mistrustful and hostile.

This was not just a carryover of old doubts about the real capacity of a "free" France to resurrect itself. Doubts of that kind lived on even in the minds of a number who would have been pleased to see a strong republican France, and viewed the future of the newborn, and badly born, republic, with fear and uncertainty. For example, Cairoli exulted to see the Second Empire topple and the "shame of Europe, so long in decay" vanish in disrepute, and was happy for the partially recovered honor of France, the "true" France of the rights of man, whose resurrection he wished for. Still he remained very troubled about its future, and hence, despite all his good wishes, doubtful and fundamentally wary.[170]

No, it was not the existence of a solidly and reliably republican France that was at stake, but something else. On the same day that it called for an end to the war, which could be interpreted as taking up a position favorable to France, *La Riforma* touched on the question of Nice—or rather of the Italian city of Nizza.[171] This was not put forth as the last remaining unresolved issue in which the "national right" of Italy was involved. Nice was one among a number of claims advanced, but one that was destined to surface, according to the newspaper, every time the occasion presented itself, if the foresight of governments should fail to find a way to settle it. One of a number of claims: others included the Trentino, and Savoy itself, for which the paper did not in point of fact request reintegration into the kingdom but "neutralization," just as it had called for the neutralization of the Rhine provinces, for the purpose of separating France from Germany and Italy by means of a continuous strip of inviolable territory, and so creating a solid guarantee of European peace.

In this, apart from anything else, one is struck yet again by the analogy between the ideas of Crispi's group,[172] who in this case were quite out of line with

---

future: and this is quite another thing than the unceasing convulsions of a moral anarchy to which the prejudice of French education attributes the false name of liberty and democracy." And it will be recalled that Nicola Marselli had hoped for the triumph of "harmonic democracy" on the German model (above, p. 21).

[170] "The reawakening of France after so many years of lethargy makes me rejoice; but I cannot deceive myself. I wish with all my soul that the memory of 1792 might inspire the energy of faith in this titanic struggle. I wish, but I don't hope, and I don't close my eyes to the evidence. Even prodigies have their limits, and so I fear that a Republic whose revival is based on nothing more than the incapacity to strike back at a foreign invasion will be ephemeral" (Cairoli, letter to his cousin Fedelina, 6 September 1870, in M. Rosi, *I Cairoli* 2:266).

[171] *La Riforma* for 6 September, in a dispute with *L'Italie*.

[172] It will be well to remember that *La Riforma* was founded in 1867 by Crispi, Cairoli, Bertani, and others (Crispi, *Politica interna*, p. 32), that it was edited by Crispi and Oliva, and later also by Miceli and Lazzaro (J. White Mario, *Agostino Bertani e i suoi tempi* 2:333 and 337). After a brief

opinion in other areas of the Left,[173] and those of the conservative de Launay. The latter would also redraw the map of Europe to suit his own desires following the victory of which he dreamed, that of Italy and Germany over France, and in the course of this exercise he was later to observe that it would perhaps be better to neutralize Savoy by joining it to Switzerland.[174] The anti-French fervor displayed in each case brought them substantially close together on a question of foreign policy without their even realizing the fact and despite enormous differences between them on problems of domestic politics. It was their longing for Italy to achieve greatness, which for them meant demonstrating its military strength, that linked them. Such dreams and longings the ever alert Bismarck had sought to foster, encourage, and prompt, especially the claim to Nice in the summer of 1870.[175] Later on he would allude to these wish-dreams using veiled phrases in discussions with de Launay,[176] just as other important German leaders, including Moltke, were to continue to dangle the bait before the eyes of other influential Italians.[177] This undoubtedly had its effect on those who had forgotten Magenta and Solferino, and even a man like Mommsen, who had no

---

suspension of publication between 10 and 16 December 1872, it resumed with an editorial board composed of Colonna di Cesarò, Crispi, Nicotera, Oliva, and Seismit-Doda (*La Riforma*, 17 December 1872). Only once, on 26 April 1874, did Crispi have occasion to state openly, in a letter to the paper, his disagreement with it, and to state that this disagreement also applied to a few articles from the past "that did not exactly reflect my own position." The disagreement, however, concerned politics at the national level.

[173] See for example *Il Diritto* for 13 October 1870 ("Garibaldi e la quistione di Nizza"): Italy cannot "favor the agitation in Nice, which would make it guilty of treachery to France just at the moment when that country is being overwhelmed by its enemy, and would mean denying that plebiscitary right that is the basis of our own public law. Nor on the other hand can we oppose it, because this agitation is, in substance, a demonstration of affection."

[174] "Nice would open its arms to us, and as for Savoy, it would be in our interest to separate it from France, if not to incorporate it ourselves, then at any rate, in fact best of all perhaps, to establish it as a neutral state in a personal union with Switzerland" (de Launay to Visconti Venosta, personal letter, 24 January 1872, cited above at n. 50).

[175] On 27 July 1870, at a very critical moment in Italian-Prussian relations, Bismarck, after affirming that Germany, so far from being inspired by the traditions of the Holy Roman Empire, would derive great advantage from seeing Italy's power increased, insinuated: "Why shouldn't you send an observation corps toward Nice?" (de Launay to Visconti Venosta, private letter, 27 July 1870, cited above at n. 14). Further, Bismarck's intrigues with the Left, and Holstein's mission to Italy, both largely exploited the theme "Nice should be Italian." Artom spoke openly to Rothan about these German approaches: "we have received repeatedly . . . insinuations on the subject of Nice, and have always repulsed them with indignation" (Rothan, *L'Allemagne et l'Italie* 2:169, and cf. p. 277, but under the date 23 February, whereas report no. 44 dates from 21 February; AEP, *C.P.*, *Italie*, t. 380, fol. 266r-v). *La Perseveranza* for 30 October 1870 ("La stampa francese") dismissed with scorn such temptations: "no man of good sense and feeling in Italy thought that we should be kicking France because we were unable to assist it!" And cf. as well the issue for 19 December ("Siamo parziali?"). Both articles are by Bonghi.

[176] After a long meeting with Bismarck on 23 March 1871, de Launay reported that "he led me to understand that it was up to us alone to profit from this war by laying claim to Savoy and the county of Nice. A simple demonstration of our intent, backed up by 4,000 troops, would have been sufficient" (de Launay to Visconti Venosta, private letter, 24 March 1871, AE, *Ris.*, 10).

[177] In 1872, after observing the maneuvers of the Prussian Guard, Lt. Gen. Petitti di Roreto was told by Moltke himself: "I have never understood why you did not then [during the Franco-Prussian War] retake Nice. It was there if you wanted it, and by now the thing would be over and done." Petitti added that this viewpoint was very widespread in the German army (Petitti di Roreto, report to the war ministry, 20 October 1872, forwarded to the foreign ministry on 30 October). And note the

hesitation in using his authority as a scholar to support the policies of Bismarck in the summer of 1870, did not disdain to employ it.[178] Another of the learned, the Indianist Albert Weber, also tried intermittently to conjure up the mirage of Nice, when he was not reproving the Italians for their "ingratitude" to Prussia. Admittedly, Italy was also in moral debt to France for past benefits, which predated its obligations to Prussia, but in politics such sentiments don't count, "your shirt is closer to you than your outer garment is."[179]

With the question of Nice, which the group around Crispi would try to exploit in coming months in order to get a definitive solution in Italy's favor, new shoots of deep dissension, of rancor on the Italian side and mistrust on the part of the French, sprang up, though Bonapartism was dead and buried, and there were no more French troops in Rome.[180] Thus there continued to be an obstacle to real Italian-French accommodation, in the eyes of those close to La Riforma,[181] quite apart from ideological questions such as the usurpation of 2 December 1851 and the immorality of Bonapartism. It was a territorial question—but it emerged because in the restless spirit of the old conspirator Crispi there flickered those phantasms of strength and greatness which would later inspire his actions as head of the Italian government. "To take nationalism to its extreme degree of austerity, in everything and toward everyone: that is what we require and cannot dispense with, after having been subjected for so many years to policies dictated by a foreign power. It is the only way to regain full consciousness of our national personality, the only way to demonstrate to the world that Italy is, and should be, and desires to be, for the Italians."

This is the language of La Riforma for 23 October 1870,[182] and it was a cry from the heart, this call for nationalism: precisely the "mean jealous hostile nationalism" that Mazzini, a year later, in October 1871, prayed should not be confounded with the holy name of "nationality."[183] Greatness, strength, national

---

remarks of the Intendant General of the Prussian army, Stosch, to Robilant on 14 October 1870, in Salvemini, "La politica estera della Destra" (1924), p. 365 n. 2.

[178] "[Y]ou know as well that the cradle of your kings is now a French department, and your hero French by birth ex-post" (T. Mommsen, Agli italiani, p. 6). This passage is from his first letter to La Perseveranza (10 August 1870). Subsequently, Mommsen too came round to the view that "perhaps" it was "suitable and proper" not to take advantage of the occasion to lay claim to Italian territories that had passed to France (ibid., p. 26).

[179] [Literally, "la camicia ci sta più vicina del soprabito."] Macchi, I dottrinarii d'Alemagna, pp. 6 ff. and 24 ff., registers a firm protest against Weber.

[180] At a certain point there also appeared a Corsican irredentism: Mauro Macchi went to see Rothan to tell him that some Corsicans had arrived in Florence and, probably incited by Prussia, planned to meet with deputies of the extreme Left for the purpose of organizing a separatist committee similar to the one for Nice (Rothan, report, 4 March 1871, no. 56 [AEP, C.P., Italie, t. 381, fol. 103]; cf. Rothan, L'Allemagne et l'Italie 2:362, but under the date 25 March [sic!] and without mentioning Macchi's name). On these endeavors, see D. Spadoni, "Perchè la Corsica nel 1870–71 non tornò all'Italia," Archivio Storico di Corsica 14 (1938): 1–20; and cf. G. Volpe, Italia moderna 1:67–68. But the question had much less resonance than that of Nice.

[181] The question comes up again, although in more muted fashion, later on: cf. Il Diritto for 17 June 1872.

[182] Article "Le nostre Alleanze," part 2.

[183] Mazzini, Scritti 93:85. Yet again it is necessary to distinguish carefully between letter and spirit to understand the difference of position between Mazzini and Crispi's circle (Mazzini for his

dignity were the watchwords: and since it appeared that national dignity had been offended, or rather, to use the language of this group, prostituted, during a decade of French preponderance and interference, these proud sentiments were turned almost inevitably in France's direction.

It was all very well for Crispi to state in the Chamber that "my soul is torn and bleeds to see the dreadful blows that have befallen France."[184] The truth is that, however sincere and spontaneous this impulse of sympathy may have been, it signified nothing more than an ephemeral sentimental outburst, while his instinct, which outran even his political calculations, was steering him almost fatally into opposition to France. In his attitude and his thought in those dramatic months of 1870–71 there could already be found the nucleus of his attitude and his thought in the period 1887–1896: repeated and no doubt sincere declarations of friendship for France, but at bottom a line of conduct deeply distrustful of that country and therefore in the last analysis hostile to it. This hostility was admittedly greatly facilitated, in fact was very much elicited, by animosity and malice on the French side as well.

For now the focus was Nice. Later Italy's claims on the Alpine border would be set aside if not abandoned,[185] and the focus would shift to Biserta, Tripoli, and Mediterranean equilibrium. But in both cases the nation that had aided Italy's first steps, even propped it up, figures as the "natural" rival of the new kingdom.

The spell of the ideas of 1789, and of their homeland, would continue to diminish, and France would be clothed ever more markedly in the colors of cold calculation. Ideology evaporates, and after the process of distillation there remains only the pure analysis of the elements of power, of well-armed national entities driven only by their own self-interest and intent on fighting for hegemony

---

part had found Crispi's conduct in May of 1871 "miserable"; *Epistolario*, vol. 58 [*Scritti* 91], p. 44). Mazzini also wanted Nice: the two names of Nice and Rome are joined in the program he lays out in August 1870 and repeats obstinately ("We want Rome and Nice"; *Epistolario*, vol. 56 [*Scritti* 89], p. 337, 1 August 1870). But both cities are seen within the framework of a general republican revolution in Italy (in which Spain might join; cf. *Epistolario*, vol. 58 [*Scritti* 91], p. 141): they are part of a more thorough, profound, and general "redemption," moral and political. Hence, although he did not believe that an uprising in Nice was opportune, if one should occur "I think that it would be well to show a strong desire for its union with Italy, and appeal for this, in order to have a vantage point from which to strike at the government—which would refuse—in Italy" (letter to Luciano Mereu, 14 April 1871, ibid. p. 19). Later, when hope of a general, "organic" renovation had failed, the agitator could still write: "if Trent, Trieste, and Nice were ours, we would have the material support, the inert structure, of Italy: what is still missing is the life-giving breath of God, the soul of the Nation" (ibid. p. 162). In Mazzini the question of Nice is always indissolubly bound up with that of the general movement for a republic in Italy and a "general renovation" of Europe: it is not a pure territorial acquisition in and for itself (although it may amount to reclaiming formerly Italian regions), which is how it appeared to Crispi and the other instigators of the committee in Florence.

[184] 19 August 1870 (Crispi, *Discorsi Parlamentari* 2:78). On Crispi's "protests" of tenderness for France and the "crocodile tears" of *La Riforma* after 4 September, see the acute note of Bonghi ("Contraddizioni," in *La Perseveranza* for 12 September 1870).

[185] Adriano Lemmi, a strong defender of Crispi's policy, says in writing to Giovanni Bovio on 17 July 1889 for the purpose of preventing irredentist agitation for Trent and Trieste: "in the minds of the best men there is the conviction that the question of Trent and Trieste, *like that of Nice*, cannot be resolved at a stroke." Lemmi also criticized the agitators in a letter of 23 July to Aurelio Saffi: "They say nothing about Nice, you know—what do you think? It is not Italian territory" (MRR, *Carte Crispi*, b. 660, n. 7/7, and b. 664, n. 13/10).

in one area of the world or another. This was called realistic politics or Bismarckian politics, and Francesco Crispi was later to attempt to practice it too, much later, when he had taken command of the ship of Italy. It was a politics in which the weight given to principles, to so-called ideals, shrank continually, and that given to calculable and ponderable material force loomed ever larger.

That the value attached to principles was under threat in this first display of nationalistic austerity was demonstrable from *La Riforma* itself in the later months of 1870. The sovereignty of the nationalist idea became an insistent refrain in the pages of the paper; it was portrayed as the foundation stone upon which the whole of Italian policy ought to rest. The occupation of Rome at this time gave the matter urgency, and the principles of nationality and the self-determination of peoples, from which it followed that the breaching the Porta Pia and the occupation of Rome were legitimate acts, were exalted without restraint.

The nationalist idea, together with the idea of political liberty, had provided both the igniting spark and the fuel for the Risorgimento. It was a deep source of motivation for Italians and retained its power to rouse their hearts and their imaginations, as well as being necessary to legitimate a unified Italy in the face of world Catholicism.

So Crispi reaffirmed it before the Chamber of Deputies,[186] and *La Riforma* glorified it: according to one writer for the paper, the idea of nationality amounts to a "great and productive moral principle" even before it is a political one. It has an aura of the religious and the mystical, it takes on the character "of a true civic religion," it is the necessary precondition of the idea of humanity: without the notion of homeland, the notion of humanity would lack its primary foundation.[187] And nation means mission; every people is given one, but none is more lofty than that of the Italian nation, which the providence of history calls on to "affirm the principle of nationality on the rubble of theocracy, to glorify religious liberty and the rights of civilization in the land of the Syllabus of Errors and of dogma."[188]

Thus Mazzinian principles were revived yet again,[189] although in the act of linking the nation and humanity, the emphasis tended to shift to the first member of the pair, and the second was spoken of without the warmth and the faith which had surrounded it in the sermons of Mazzini.[190] It is another sign of the growth of

---

[186] 19 August 1870 (Crispi, *Discorsi Parlamentari* 2:78).

[187] "La moralità dell'idea nazionale," in *La Riforma* for 25 September 1870.

[188] "L'ora solenne," in *La Riforma* for 3 October 1870.

[189] See esp. the writings on *Nationalité* (*Scritti* 6:123 ff.), and *Dell'iniziativa rivoluzionaria in Europa* (ibid., 4:180). Cf. A. Levi, *La filosofia politica di G. Mazzini* (Bologna, 1917), pp. 217 ff.; G. Salvemini, *Mazzini*, pp. 43–44; L. Salvatorelli, *Il pensiero politico italiano dal 1700 al 1870*, pp. 235–36, 243, 246; O. Vossler, *Mazzinis politisches Denken und Wollen in den geistigen Strömungen seiner Zeit* (Munich-Berlin, 1927), p. 73, and *L'idea di nazione dal Rousseau al Ranke* (Italian translation: Florence, 1949), pp. 115–16; H. Kohn, *Profeti e popoli* (Italian translation: Milan, 1949), p. 97.

[190] "Universal brotherhoods and cosmopolitan democracies are fine things, but without the primordial idea of the homeland [*patria*], they are illogical and vacuous ideas" (*La Riforma*, 25 September 1870). Compare this with Mazzini's credo: ". . . the general law of humanity, source of all nationality" (in French in the original; Saffi's translation into Italian is less incisive: *Scritti* 6:134). It will be seen that in Crispi's *Riforma*, the relationship between the two terms, nation and humanity, has changed from what it is in Mazzini. And although in other cases Mazzini's ideas may be grounded more specifically on the term *patria*, its validity is always a function of humanity: there is

the kind of nationalism that, when fully matured, would scorn the "holy family of humanity" as a daydream of the fainthearted.

Unswerving in its view of nationalism as a great moral principle, *La Riforma* was just as decided in wanting to see it applied "in all of its logical consequences, without exception, without restrictions," in not admitting that it could ever be subordinated "to principles that deny it in any manner, wholly or in part, or that might block it, or modify the practice and the development of it,"[191] in the conviction that "as products ourselves of the principle of nationalism, we have the duty always to support with our sympathy and benevolence, and where required, with even stronger assistance, the oppressed nations that . . . are struggling to reach the same goal that we, more fortunate than they, have already gained."[192]

Consequently, after dragging nationalism into the question of Nice, the vehement left-wing journal attempted, in the summer of 1871, to have it applied in what was (along with the Ottoman empire), and would remain until its demise, the preferred theater of action for the advocates of oppressed peoples, or at any rate of peoples who had not obtained respect for their national personalities— that is to say, in the Habsburg empire. The double monarchy of Austria-Hungary was undergoing violent internal dissension (for and against federalism, for and against the policies of Hohenwart's government) and it provided easy fodder for the columns of Crispi and Oliva and their ilk.[193]

There was more going on here than simply fraternal love for the Italians of the Trentino,[194] or Trieste,[195] more than just the nascent voice of the movement later so well known under the name of irredentism. The love felt by *La Riforma* for the

---

no humanity without a *patria*. But both are equally sacred: the nation is the instrument through which one arrives at the ultimate goal, and *patria* "is the fulcrum of the lever that must operate to the benefit of humanity" (*La Santa Alleanza dei Popoli*, in *Scritti* 39:214). In the vision of *La Riforma*, there remains, on the contrary, only disdain for the "uncertain, ill-defined *cosmopolitanism*" of the second half of the eighteenth century, which Mazzini had also condemned because it lacked the idea of *patria*, a condemnation launched again with particular polemical vehemence in 1871 against the internationalists of all kinds (*Scritti* 93:85); but in Mazzini this "anticosmopolitanism" never attenuates his sense of humanity (cf. again his *Doveri dell'uomo*, ibid., 69:47–69).

"Without homeland [*Patria*] no ordered structure of humanity is possible" Mazzini declares in 1871; but he then repeats "humanity is the *end*, the *nation* is the means." For Crispi, Oliva, and the rest, humanity, even as an end, is fading away.

[191] *La Riforma*, 28 April 1871.

[192] "La politica italiana in Oriente," in *La Riforma* for 1 September 1872.

[193] See, in the wake of the article of 5 June 1871 on the Austrian situation, the series of articles in *La Riforma* from August to October 1871, beginning on 14 August, then following on with: "All'Oriente" (21 and 27 August); "Il problema austriaco" (7 September); "Il partito liberale austriaco" (19 September); "Il problema austriaco è sul tappeto" (21 September); "Il principio di nazionalità" (11 October); "La Dieta di Trieste e l'Austria" (18 October).

[194] Cf. "La questione del Trentino" (26 August 1871, and cf. 7 October): our brothers in the Trentino "must know that they are a cherished and integral part of the Italian family; that the doors to our common house lie amid their mountains; and that if fortune has not been propitious to us so far, that does not take away the fact that we ought to lay claim to them, and that one day they will be restored." It must be remembered that in the summer of 1871 the question of the Trentino had resurfaced in the Italian press (A. Sandonà, *L'irredentismo nelle lotte politiche e nelle contese diplomatiche italo-austriache* 1:95–96).

[195] "La dieta di Trieste e l'Austria" (18 October 1871): ". . . the affection that the Triestines feel for the stock to which they belong [the Italian] and their strong aspirations, for which fulfillment will come in the future."

principle of nationality embraced, in Mazzini's style, all peoples and especially the peoples of the Habsburg empire; it dwelt with satisfaction on the supposedly growing desire of the German empire to annex the German part of Austria, on the program for a "Greater Germany" which, with a foggy grasp of realities and a meager understanding of politics, the paper claimed was favored by Bismarck himself.[196] It poured out forecasts of world-shaking revolutions to come, culminating (*o sancta simplicitas!*) in the declaration that "self-interest and the logic of the politics of nationality must have inscribed in Germany's intentions the reconstruction of Polish nationality, independence for the Czech nation, and the entry of German Austria into the imperial fold."[197]

It really seemed that a messianic breeze had wafted through the hearts of the editors of *La Riforma*, who continued generously to confer upon Bismarck all of their own opinions and sentiments regarding liberty and nationalism—so messianic that they failed to see how ridiculous it was to infer favorable tendencies toward the Polish nation not only in the German patriots *en masse*, a number of whom had in fact been very explicit as early as 1848 and the Parliament of Frankfurt in stating repeatedly and roundly that when it came to the Poles, their position was "Germany above all,"[198] but even more in a man like Bismarck, who in April of 1848 had expressed his disdain for the romantic sentimentalism of the Berliners in favor of the Poles,[199] who in 1863 had fully supported Russian policy, and who always saw the pro-Polish attitude as one of the greatest threats to his own aims. They did not even notice, as they surveyed with pleasure the federalist movement in Austria, not just their own ridiculousness but the real harm that would have been done to Italy's position at that particular juncture by the eventual triumph of the German federalists in Austria.

As long as the Roman question was unresolved, France was dominated by a clerical-conservative majority in the National Assembly, and Belgium was cleri-

---

[196] These views on Austria in *La Riforma* help us to understand how, in 1877, during his famous meeting with Bismarck at Gastein, Crispi was able to make an attempt to entice the German chancellor by speaking to him of a German Austria and of the "unfinished" German unity, going so far as to say "Austrian territory attracts you" (Crispi, *Politica estera* 1:27). To get a better idea of the gross error of political perspective involved, one may note that even among the moderates in Italy there were those who feared the fatal and not far distant absorption of Austria into the Reich (Bonghi in *La Perseveranza* for 13 August 1870 and 15 January 1871); that in England too, then and in 1875, Bismarck's appetite for German Austria was credited; that among those who believed in it was the British ambassador in Berlin, Lord Odo Russell (cf. Meine, *England und Deutschland*, pp. 69, 164, 166, 176, 187). In 1878 still, after the Congress of Berlin, the general secretary at the foreign ministry, Maffei di Boglio, maintained that Bismarck's objective could only be that of "reclaiming every bit of German territory and so transferring the seat of the Austro-Hungarian edifice from Vienna to Pest" (Maffei to Robilant, personal letter, 9 September 1878; AE, *Carte Robilant*).

[197] "All'Oriente," part 2 (27 August 1871).

[198] Cf. V. Valentin, *Geschichte der deutschen Revolution von 1848–1849* 2:125 ff. (Berlin, 1931); L. B. Namier, "1848: The Revolution of the Intellectuals," *Proceedings of the British Academy* 30 (1944): 88.

[199] Bismarck in the *Magdeburgische Zeitung* for 20 April 1848: "I could understand how in the first outflow of German national force, Alsace would be demanded from France and the German banner planted on the cathedral of Strasbourg. But to play at games from the chivalric romances, to liberate and cheer on the Polish prisoners at Berlin [he alludes to the actions of 20 March], with the result that there is then a Polish insurgency against the Germans" (Bismarck, *Gesammelten Werke* 14¹:105–106). On the importance of this piece, cf. E. Marcks, *Bismarck und die deutsche Revolution, 1848–1851*, ed. W. Andreas (Stuttgart-Berlin, 1939), pp. 41 ff.

cal, a victory in Austria for clerical-feudal reaction, with all its clear and explicit tenor of papalism and anti-Italianism[200] (which was what, internationally, Austrian federalism stood for), would have been a real danger for Italy.

But Crispi and the others, dreaming of the speedy reunion with the motherland of the Italian portion of the Habsburg empire, and convinced that the return of its German part to the Reich was imminent,[201] no longer paid any attention to such quibbles and continued to highlight for their readers the ineluctability, the fatality, the imminence, of a profound transformation of the Habsburg empire.[202] They also continued to attack the government of the Right, of those moderates who now wanted to claim that the period of the great movements had come to a close, and who had replaced the poetry of the heroic period of 1859–1861, the source of "marvel after marvel, prodigy after prodigy, reality surpassing imagination," with "a bare, mean, chilly prose, a leaden cloak."[203]

But notwithstanding everything, these were still at least formally the principles of Mazzini. Those principles had been founded in their turn on the axiom of the nation as a moral fact, as the "will" to nationhood, as the expression of the free decision of the citizens. The theorem of the continuous plebiscite was to be formulated by Renan in 1882, but Mazzini had already coined its essence.[204] It could be glimpsed even in Mancini, where it was much more tied up in natural-law concepts.[205] The predominance of the factors of will, consciousness, spirit

---

[200] It is noteworthy that *La Riforma* reproved the Austrian liberal party: Viennese democracy, like Parisian, has a mania for centralism, and this is the self-contradiction in which it is trapped ("Il partito liberale austriaco," 19 September 1871).

[201] As early as 5 June 1871: "before too long the German and Italian parts of the empire will each have to be rejoined to its own family, with whom they are called to live by the irresistible voice of nature and their most vital interests."

[202] Even after the fall of the minister Hohenwart, *La Riforma* continued to believe in the imminence of a radical solution, either the collapse or else the profound territorial and political transformation of the Habsburg empire ("Le due crisi austriache").

[203] "Il sentimento nazionale" (25 June 1872).

[204] This is in fact the gist of Mazzini's affirmations on nationality. It is as clear in the writings cited from 1834 and 1835 as it is in the last ones, perhaps even more so. In 1859, "your homeland [*La Patria*] is your collective life, the life that ties together in a tradition of inclinations and shared affections all the generations that arose, labored, and passed away on your soil . . . the homeland is the *faith* in homeland" (*Ai Giovani d'Italia*: *Scritti* 64:165–66). In 1871, "the nation is not a territory to be strengthened by augmenting its size, not an agglomeration of people speaking the same language . . . but an organic whole through unity of *purpose* and of faculty. . . . Language, territory and race are only the connotations of *nationality*, and are weak when they are not bound together; and they require in any case confirmation from historical tradition, from the long unfolding of a collective life marked by the same characteristics" (*Nazionalismo e nazionalità*: *Scritti* 93:92–93). In *Doveri dell'uomo*, the reference to the "vote" is explicit (*Scritti* 69:67). This is not the place to discuss whether or not the doctrine of nationality as a moral fact (*un but commun*) ought to be claimed for Buchez and Saint-Simonism, as R. Treves does in *La dottrina sansimoniana nel pensiero italiano del Risorgimento*, pp. 71 ff. See rather, on the "spiritual and voluntary" nature of the nation, V. G. Galati, *Il concetto di nazionalità nel Risorgimento italiano*, pp. 50 ff., and G. Gentile *I profeti del Risorgimento italiano* (Florence, 1928), p. 39.

[205] "You can multiply as much as you like the material and exterior points of contact among the members of a human group; they will never become a nation without the moral unity of common thought, of a predominant idea that makes a society what it is because it is realized in it. The invisible power of such a principle of action is like the brand of Prometheus, that awakens clay to independent selfhood and life and so creates a people. It is the 'I think therefore I exist' of the philosophers applied to nationality" (*Della Nazionalità come fondamento del diritto delle genti*, in P. S. Mancini, *Diritto Internazionale: Prelezioni*, pp. 35–36). And in the summer of 1870 Mancini confirms his beliefs, in

was known to be characteristic of Italian thought on the nation, and in this it diverged from the German tradition, which was always characterized principally by the predominance of nature. This was the faith of the age, and of a people among whom social reformers had emphasized voluntarism and refused the concepts, held dear by Marxism, of the unfolding of necessary and inevitable economic laws and forces.[206] The recollection of history and of the glories of the past, of that which men had created, and not their ethnic stock, which was the creation of nature, had been the dominant motif in the highest appeals made for the reawakening of the Italian spirit.

But now, brusquely, this elevated conception, which, because it saw the inner spirit of man as the decisive factor, took a wider view of the human situation, was threatened by the onset in Crispi's circle of an utterly different way of thinking. According to this new point of view, the decisive element was not to be found in the moral field, in the inner life of man, but in the complex of external, putatively objective "facts," the givens of geography, ethnography, linguistics. These were thought of as existing prior to and as conditioning absolutely the human will.

In December 1870 an organ of the moderates, *L'Opinione*, aroused the ire of a pro-German writer for having contested Germany's right to annex Alsace and a part of Lorraine in defiance of "the vote of the peoples and the conscience of nations," purely and simply by right of conquest, and therefore contrary to the rights of nationality. Hence in its reply *L'Opinione*, which was joined by Ruggero Bonghi's paper *La Perseveranza*, attempted to neutralize the difference of opinion by clarifying the specifically "Italian" concepts of nation and nationality, which were founded on the free will of peoples.[207]

---

his speech of 19 August to the Chamber, recalling his preceding statements: "The same principle that in internal public law is called *national sovereignty*, and is realized through *universal suffrage*, is what in international law is called *principle of nationality*." This equation would in itself be enough to demonstrate the importance of the factor of will in the principle of nationality; but a little further on the thought is made even more explicit: "It was as a consequence of these premises that the magnificent formula 'Rome of the Romans' was applied, and when the Romans were ready, of Italy too" (Mancini, *Discorsi Parlamentari* 3:341 and 347. But see earlier the speech to the Chamber of 18 November 1864, ibid., 2:119. Here, in sum, the factor of will appears as decisive. Cf. F. Lopez de Oñate, preface to P. S. Mancini, *Saggi sulla nazionalità*, pp. xiv ff.). The thesis recently advanced by Curcio (*Nazione Europa Umanità* [Milan, 1950], pp. 154, 161, 189), that in Mancini the nation is above all a natural reality, is valuable inasmuch as it brings out the nonorganic nature of the principles of the "nationalitarian" theory, the admixture of heterogeneous elements in Mancini, and esp. the fact that nature and the natural-law theories have much more importance for him than they have for Mazzini (in fact in Mancini nature alternates with Providence, causing an oscillation between natural-law theory and mysticism). But Curcio in his turn has clearly undervalued the "consciousness" that Mancini, in his prolusion of 1872 in Rome, again speaks of as the "outstanding" element among those that constitute a nationality, as the "vivifying spirit" of it, etc. (*Diritto Internazionale*, pp. 189 and 203). It is the position of Crispi that is fully, totally based on natural law; not that of Mancini. [*Translator's note:* "nationalitarian" (and variants) renders the word *nazionalitario* (and variants) used repeatedly by Chabod in the Italian text.]

   206 Cf. P. E. Taviani, *Problemi economici nei riformatori sociali del Risorgimento Italiano*, pp. 239 ff.

   207 Cf. ch. 3 below, n. 70. On 28 September 1870, Bonghi in *La Perseveranza* had already maintained that before any decision was made the inhabitants of Alsace and Lorraine had the right to take part in a vote ("Le condizioni della pace").

La Riforma chose to enter this debate by denying that there was any value in the ideas expressed by the two moderate papers. Was this only an example of polemical furor for domestic consumption, within the party? Or was it the old hostility, in Mazzini's style, against the modern "plebiscite" of Bonapartist and dictatorial origin? Was it the concern, understandable at a moment when Rome had barely entered into the national sphere, that the theory of the plebiscite might in the future be used against the young kingdom,[208] or that it might be asserted on practical grounds that the vote that had occurred had not been "free," but had been extorted through intimidation and similar measures at a time when the "blacks" [papalists] were still a majority among the Romans?[209] Or was it simply the desire to support German policy against France, the eternal enemy? Certainly *La Riforma* upheld the belief, a singular one in the land of Mazzini and at a time when Mazzini himself was deploring the annexation of Alsace "without the free vote of the citizens," that the character of nationality is by its nature prior to and higher than any single or collective expression of will: that the principle of nationality is an *a priori*, a "natural" right embodied in every Italian, and that the will of the citizens ought to be consulted in regard to the form of the state, but nothing else, for it would be unjust and absurd to put to any part of the nation the question of whether or not it wished to be Italian, or German, or French.[210] This was the most forceful antithesis that one could imagine to the formula "Rome of the Romans," which had been so much in vogue since 1861.[211]

How then was it possible to recognize the different nationalities if not by exterior signs, meaning essentially geography, race, and language—by those signs to which Mazzini had denied any value in and of themselves? The *a priori* was determined by the nature, and of course by the history of a country, but in this fashion history itself became a purely objective datum, antecedent to the consciousness and the will of individuals and therefore completely naturalistic in

---

[208] This preoccupation is evident at the beginning and the end of the article: "If the doctrines advanced in *La Perseveranza* and *L'Opinione* should be applied, the consequence would be that the unity of our country would be at risk of foundering because of the schismatic desires of a few sections of the population. It is a possibility that may please the separatists, but which the *unitary* party has to oppose with all its might" ("Il principio di nazionalità," *La Riforma*, 20 December 1870).

[209] Mommsen had said as much on 17 September 1870: we hear that the large majority of the Romans are "black" [papalist] and prefer the shackles of the papacy and the cardinalate to Italian liberty. Even if that were true, the right of the Italians to have Rome as their capital remains intact, because the birth of Italy is anterior to any plebiscite (*Il Diritto* for 22 September 1870; and later in T. Mommsen, *Agli italiani*).

[210] "Il principio di nazionalità," *La Riforma*, 20 December 1870. In the issue for 30 August 1870 there are analogous ideas: "the unitarian principle . . . anterior and superior to any particular form of government. It is from this source that the Italian revolution draws its legitimacy." And *La Riforma* returns to the question of Alsace-Lorraine on 8 October 1872 (the article is also entitled "Il principio di nazionalità"), referring to the emigration to France of the French patriots in the two regions and continuing to maintain the same ideas on the "imprescriptible rights" of the nation, which always subsist "as long as the natural confines that separate one nation from another last, and even in the absence of these, as long as one race with one history and one language survives"; and on the idea of national unity "which exists by itself independently of any vote and any plebiscite."

[211] On 17 September 1870 the concept "Rome of the Romans" had been embraced again by *La Perseveranza* (article "L'andata a Roma") in order to assert that "the vote of the people is necessary to join the Roman territory to the others." It was just this position that roused Crispi to fury.

character. Sooner or later, ideas of this sort were bound to lead to the identification of the *a priori* with the race factor, which was to be transmuted into a categorical imperative despite its equivocal and dubious content. The lives of peoples and of individuals were to be subordinated to it, and the idea of nation would be submerged by the idea of racial stock.[212]

This principle was not only foreign to the thought and the feeling of Italians, it was pregnant with dangerous consequences, of the sort capable of legitimating all forms of conquest, or to use the term that later became current, of imperialism.

In truth *La Riforma* had occasion a few weeks later to change its tune. Upon receiving news of the results of the elections of February 1871 in France, which had produced a triumph for the Italian party in Nice, Crispi's organ announced that this new manifestation of popular choice had annulled the factitious plebiscite of 1860 and thus made a deciding criterion out of the will of individual citizens, which it had peremptorily expelled from consideration a month and a half before.

Such contradictions were comprehensible up to a point as products of controversial zeal, and as tactical responses to the swirling and evolving pressures of the political situation. But only up to a point, beyond which a substantial alteration of principle became evident. In the case at hand it really was a question of principles slowly but surely mutating in the direction of nationalistic conceptions profoundly different to those that had predominated in the period of the struggle for national redemption. This mutation was specific to the group around Crispi, not generalized among the circles on the Left, which continued firmly to demand self-determination for all peoples and were therefore averse to the Germanic notions of natural and unreflective nationality.[213]

For those who did choose to follow the new road, the example of Germany's victory, and the influence, already very much in evidence and soon to become widespread and dominant, of German ideas and systems of thought, gave a powerful impetus. In the Italy of the period 1830–1850, much of cultural and intellectual life was an offshoot of the civilization of the France of the Restoration and of the July monarchy, to the extent that the very posture of those who were anti-

---

[212] The point is well put in *La Perseveranza* for 23 August 1870 (article "Le condizioni della pace secondo i Tedeschi").

[213] The point comes out clearly in the polemic of September 1870 between *Il Diritto*, the other major organ of the Left, and Mommsen, concerning Alsace-Lorraine. *Il Diritto* makes an appeal to the "will" of the two regions, whose populations alone ought to resolve the question, and proclaims that the plebiscite is the basis of modern public law. It criticizes "certain other democratic journals" in Italy, whose tendency is "Jacobin democracy," and which deny these principles (12, 22, 23, 24, and 25 September 1870). Mancini took a middle position that was rather self-contradictory: on one hand he declared that "belonging to one nation rather than to another" did not depend on the will, and that a vote was no more than "an extrinsic indication" of unity and national identity—the position of Crispi and *La Riforma*—while on the other he defended the utility of plebiscites, expressing the wish that it should be "an obligatory canon of the Rights of Peoples to subject the legitimacy of any territorial incorporation to the approval, in a vote, of the population whose destiny is at stake"—the position of the moderates and of *Il Diritto* (Mancini, prolusion of 1872, in *Diritto Internazionale*, pp. 202–203). Mancini was, however, firm in maintaining the indispensability of the plebiscite in cases in which the existence of nationality was in doubt, something that not even *La Riforma* denied in the article of 20 December 1870.

French seemed like the impatience of adolescents toward their parents. But now there were those who were ready to adopt styles and forms of spiritual life from the new dominator of Europe, and the first sign of this could already be seen here, in what might be called the militant objectification of the principle of nationality, a principle that had nonetheless been the supreme ideological achievement of the century among Italians. What was happening was that it was being given *a priori* status, as if it were one of the categories of Kant, but a category that would allow, and indeed would call for, the politics of force. From being a thing of the spirit, of the soul, of faith, it was being made a thing of nature.

In a similar vein writers and political commentators in Germany upheld with virtual unanimity Germany's right to Alsace as German territory by race, language, and the traditions of old, even against the present desires of the inhabitants of the region. Treitschke warned that Alsace and Lorraine were German territory "by right of the sword, and we dispose of them in virtue of a superior right, the right of the German nation, which will not permit its lost sons to remain outside the German Empire. We Germans know Germany and France, and we know what is good for the inhabitants of Alsace better than do those unhappy victims themselves, who under the perverting influence of their ties to the French have remained strangers to the currents of feeling stirring in the new Germany. We shall make them come to their senses, even against their will."[214]

The superior right of the nation: how portentous it was that at that moment men like Mommsen, Treitschke, and Crispi shared the same views! And the minds of these Italians began to take on yet other notions, certainly not of purely Germanic origin,[215] but by now largely diffused from Germany. The belief that war is a necessity began to slither into the open. And so in the pages of *La Riforma* it was possible to read, what might have seemed virtually a novelty to many Italians at that time but which future generations were to hear repeated from many platforms, that war is part of the cycle, that it also fulfills "its cruel but indispensable role in the progress of the human spirit."[216] And since many were already disposed to accept that Italy especially needed a great victory, a victory belonging to it alone, one that would consolidate its prestige and its power, this theoretical suggestion fell on receptive ears.

It was the first step toward conceptions that were to dominate the age known as that of imperialism, with great political entities in permanent, though not open, conflict, for the prize of continental and maritime predominance, for the conquest of colonies and markets, accompanied by the hosannas of a new literature to which the invocations of liberty and humanity that had been dear to Romanticism were alien, which aspired instead to sing of dominion and of force, the literature of Kipling and D'Annunzio. In this new age nationalism was to transform completely the former sense and value of the idea of nationality, and was

---

[214] Cf. *La Perseveranza* for 1 November 1870 (article "Lo spirito crociato dei Tedeschi").

[215] One can find in De Maistre the justification of war as the origin of all greatness in art, science, etc.: "blood is the fertilizer of that plant that is called *genius*" (*Considérations sur la France*, ch. 3, pp. 41 ff.). And after 1870, there is Renan (see below, p. 79).

[216] "L'attività nazionale," in *La Riforma* for 28 December 1870.

eventually to give way in its turn to the full expression of naturalistic tendencies that triumphed with the emergence of the doctrine of race. In the latter, the objectification of the nation, the placing of it *a priori*, were to lead to a logical conclusion: for when the nation was dissociated from the free will of men, nothing remained but to look for the foundation of the nation, and its legitimacy, in the ethnic *a priori*, in blood. *Blut und Boden.*

At the time, of course, not even the men of *La Riforma* wanted to hear talk about race. It appeared to them an idea that led back to the Latin brotherhood that Crispi and his companions so detested, or it brought to mind the professorial hauteur of German science and the familiar claims about the innate superiority of the Germans—which were equally distasteful to the editors of Crispi's party paper.[217] But they themselves in cutting the tight bonds between the ideas of nation and the national will opened the door, without realizing it or wishing it, to the growth of the racist tendencies they abhorred.

This was not just a temporary lapse from convictions long held. That the positions being taken in *La Riforma*, and indeed being taken repeatedly,[218] were not fleeting wraiths in a war of words, but the expression of a new and different way of feeling, is proved by the heartfelt opinions of Francesco Crispi, the paper's guiding light. Both before and after 1870 he put forward the concept of the nation as *a priori*, independent of individual human wills, preconstituted, immutable over time, absolute, indestructible, eternal.

In his already famous letter of 18 March 1865 to Mazzini, the nation was depicted as a given, as an entity existing prior to any manifestation of the popular will: "the nation exists in the same way the individual does, and has no need for a people or a Parliament to proclaim the fact in order to exist. Hence I could not make the unity of Italy depend upon a *yes* or a *no*, upon the subtleties of the rhetors and the syllogisms of the jurists, for it is grounded in Italian geography, the Italian language, and in all of the other moral conditions known to everyone. . . . So it was my opinion that the people ought not to affirm national unity, nor constitute it, but simply declare that they desire it, after which assemblies would be held which would be bound by the terms of plebiscites and which would establish the balance of liberty and of constraint so that the popular will might become actual."[219]

As the years passed, the "naturalness" of the nation was asserted ever more bluntly. As prime minister, Crispi went so far as to say, in his speech in Palermo on 14 October 1889, that "if the plebiscite had been a requirement, it would have given the final sanction to the legitimacy [of the occupation of Rome]. But even without it, the right of the nation was proof against any protest. A nation exists by virtue of itself within the enclosure formed by its borders. Now, there is no

---

[217] Overall the article of 17 December 1870, "L'Alleanza latina" (above, n. 124), is firmly anti-racist.

[218] "It is not for nothing that we have always professed . . . the unity and indivisibility of the national sovereignty as a right anterior and superior to the actual suffrage of the diverse populations of Italy" ("Gli avvenimenti di Parigi," in *La Riforma* for 24 March 1871).

[219] *Scritti e discorsi politici di Francesco Crispi*, pp. 329–30.

nation in the world that has borders as well defined and as secure as those of Italy. *Natio quia nata.*"[220] The nation's *"virtù propria"* [innate potency] was seen as a natural and timeless force: "the existence and the independence of nations cannot be subject to the arbitration of plebiscites. Nations live by natural law, eternal and immutable, and neither by force of arms nor by the expressed will of a mass of common people can this right undergo any alteration."[221]

Natio quia nata: this expression applied natural-law principles to nations, discovering a natural, rational and eternal right, valid for all peoples as for individuals. In terms of the history of ideas, Crispi thus still belonged to the eighteenth century, if not to an even earlier period at which thinkers relied upon an appeal to God and divine creation; at a single bound he escaped from all normal rationalistic premises.[222] But this kind of insistence on the naturalness of the nation, and denial of the voluntaristic component in its existence, could not in the long run be maintained on the basis of an abstract right of nature or vaguely theistic suggestions. It was going to be necessary to find a more physical, solid, and massive underpinning by appealing to blood, in other words to the only element effectively capable of distinguishing one nation from another *ex initio*, before history —the work of man—could intervene and imprint different characters on the different nations. This process was in fact taking place in German thought, which as a result of having placed excessive emphasis on the naturalness of the nation was well on its inevitable way to finding its identifying and characteristic element in its own ethnic descent. In sum, Francesco Crispi's appeal to naturalness, to the eternity and immutability of the nation, carried a very different message from that articulated by Marco Minghetti and others, who also allowed that the plebiscites had not created a right but rather had recognized the existence of one, and who also appealed to geography—but no less to the will and the faith of men in the form of history, culture, and the blood of the national martyrs.[223]

When portrayed as a force of nature, antecedent to man's will, the nation was thereby also assigned a sort of ineluctable course, which was indeed the intention of those who were beginning to dream of increase and expansion as national goals. But when the being of the nation was split off from the national will, a gap was also opened between the nation and the idea of liberty, so that the formula

[220] Ibid., p. 723. The formula *Natio quia nata* ["a nation is because it is born such"] reappears in Crispi's letter to Primo Levi of 16 November 1891: "For the rest, I have said more than once that our nation exists *quia nata*; and had no need of plebiscites to exist"; and in another letter to Levi of 16 August 1892: "*Natio quia nata*: remember that" (*Carteggi politici inediti di Francesco Crispi (1860–1900)*, pp. 466, 471).

[221] Crispi to Raiberti, 14 November 1891; ibid., p. 461.

[222] "The existence of a nation or the denial of its existence cannot depend on the vote of a people. The nation is because God has made it. A plebiscite may constitute a juridical fact, but it cannot create a fact contrary to nature" (Crispi, *Pensieri e profezie*, p. 148). The concept expressed here also surfaces in a letter to Primo Levi of 4 November 1891: "plebiscites are null when they are against the right of nationality and against liberty. Just as suicide is forbidden to an individual, so it is to a nation" (Crispi, *Carteggi politici inediti*, p. 459). The position was one that Mancini had taken in the prolusion of 1872 (*Diritto Internazionale*, p. 203): it is impossible for a nation to deny the fact of its own nationality.

[223] Minghetti, *Discorsi Parlamentari* 8:124 (Rome, 1890).

natio quia nata, which was already well suited to act as the justification for political platforms purporting to make the country great, was also perfectly suited to the authoritarian tendencies in the country. The latter were to experience increasing frustration in coming years at the oppositional politics of the parliamentary parties, and to develop the aspiration to replace them with a strong man, someone commanding obedience internally so as to be able to fulfill the mission of greatness which the existence of the nation imposed, and which was also "natural" and "fatal."

Once again, this was a willful abandonment of the Italian tradition of the Risorgimento, which had held firm ever since Alfieri[224] to its insistence on the inseparable pairing of the ideas of nationality and liberty,[225] a pairing firmly grounded in the identification of the concept of nation with that of civilization as liberty. On this Mazzini and Cavour had been in accord; in fact, Cavour had at first been inspired by the impulse of liberalism and had taken a different route from Mazzini only later when he came to desire the independence of the nation, and ultimately also its unity.[226] Even if we leave out of consideration Pisacane, in whom the problem of liberty had already taken on a social content that was uncertain and contradictory in its formulation but certain and precise in its aspiration, even apart from Pisacane the large and various currents that flowed together to make the Risorgimento had been solidly in agreement on this point.

The entire moderate group was heir to this credo, and there was no doubt that Bonghi expressed their common position when on 3 February 1879 he declared before the Chamber that the different peoples, before they could bear the "pure and simple application of the principle of nationality, have to have undergone a thorough internal reworking of the raw human material, and be highly civilized. . . . [I]f these preconditions of civility are not met . . . the principle of nationality cannot be the basis of a vigorous reconstitution."[227]

Mancini stated that the principle of nationality in international law is equivalent to what is called national sovereignty, realized through universal suffrage, in domestic public law.[228] Or, in the words, and very apt ones indeed, of a less well-known politician, "it is nothing other than [the principle] of political liberty

---

[224] Cf. L. Russo, *Ritratti e disegni storici*, 1st ser., *Dall'Alfieri al Leopardi* (Bari, 1946), pp. 98–99.

[225] One may simply cite Mazzini's appeal *Ai Giovani d'Italia*, of 1859: "Adore liberty. Lay claim to it from the first moment, and keep it jealously intact. . . . Those who tell you that: *you must have first independence, then a homeland, then liberty*, are either fools, or else they think to betray you and give you neither liberty, nor a homeland, nor independence. Since independence means emancipation from foreign tyranny, and liberty . . . [means emancipation] from domestic tyranny, as long as you have tyranny of either kind, how can you have a homeland? A homeland is a dwelling for man, not for a slave" (*Scritti* 64:182–83). In the earlier manifesto *Giovine Italia* Mazzini had said explicitly: "the three inseparable foundations are independence, unity, liberty."

[226] Cf. L. Salvatorelli, *Pensiero e azione del Risorgimento*, p. 174.

[227] Bonghi, *Discorsi Parlamentari* 1:700 (= vol. 3 in *Opere*); and cf. Walter Maturi, "Ruggero Bonghi e i problemi di politica estera," *Belfagor* 1 (July 1946): 416.

[228] Mancini in his speech to the Chamber of 18 November 1864, and again on 19 August 1870 (*Discorsi Parlamentari* 2:119 and 3:341). On nationality as the outgrowth of the principle of liberty in Mancini, cf. F. Lopez de Oñate, preface to P. S. Mancini, *Saggi sulla nazionalità*, pp. liv ff. and lxiii ff.

applied to sections of territory; it is the successive phase of the public law of 1789, it is the referral of the great principles of the French Revolution to the relations between one people and another."[229] In consequence, no less a patriot than Francesco De Sanctis asserted before the Chamber on 10 December 1878, while minister of education, that if the unlucky day should come when he should have reason to fear that liberty of thought was in danger in Italy, on that day he would deny his country.[230]

For as long as the nation is sought in the will and the faith of men, and is continually replenished by the free vote of the peoples, there is an inescapable identity between nationality and liberty. When the nation, however, is no longer moored to the will of the citizens but is made into something existing *a priori* and independently of that will, the identity disappears, the pairing is abolished, and political liberty is no longer a necessary condition of the safe and strong life of the nation. In fact it can even be seen as an obstacle to the untrammeled exercise of the spirit of conquest, to which the "natural" nation is by nature summoned.

Nationalism and authoritarianism, acceptance of the providential benefits of war and an aversion to humanitarians: a little or a lot of each of these elements of the European and Italian political climate of the last seventy years is already seminally there in the public debates and comments of the partisans of Prussia.

The sense of Europe was also, fatally, overshadowed in their minds—that sense of a civil community that had been so strong in the eighteenth-century Enlightenment, and with the value of the political more clearly accentuated, in Romanticism too. In place of this central theme in writers such as Montesquieu, Voltaire, Sismondi, Mazzini, Adam Müller, and Heeren, "nationalitarian" tendencies [*tendenze nazionalitarie*], or to use an expression more familiar in our day, autarkic ones, grew vigorous again. They had already been darkly conveyed by the anti-European Rousseau when he insistently urged adherence to ancient usage and national custom, on the grounds that only thus do the citizens remain devoted to their own country, and are imbued with "a natural repugnance for mingling with foreigners."[231]

National hatreds, exalted at one time by Alfieri, reappeared;[232] those national hatreds that European thought between 1815 and 1848 had been at great pains to attenuate, indeed to abolish, by reconnecting the ideas of homeland and Europe: this trend had reached its highest expression in the preaching of Mazzini, in which love for one's country and at the same time love for the larger civil com-

---

[229] C. Caracciolo di Bella, *Dieci anni di politica estera*, p. 20. (This is the speech he gave in the Senate on 4 May 1878, *A.P., Senato*, p. 134).

[230] F. De Sanctis, *Scritti politici*, ed. Ferrarelli, p. 220. Cf. B. Croce, "La commemorazione di Francesco De Sanctis," now in *Pagine sparse* 2:362 (Naples, 1943).

[231] Rousseau, *Considérations sur le gouvernement de Pologne*, ch. 3, in *Oeuvres complètes*, p. 358.

[232] Carducci caught this moment perfectly: "in others the vicious national hatreds instilled by the historians and writers of the time of servitude or misfortune, sublimely impassioned, continued to ferment, now more chill and atrocious than ever, until they became political theories" (*Giuseppe Garibaldi: Un anno dopo, 21 gennaio 1872*, in *Opere* 19:24). Here the counterpoint between the passion of an earlier age (Alfieri) and the doctrinaire coldness of the present is very acute.

munity that was Europe are maintained and harmonized. For three decades, nation and Europe, like nation and liberty, had been indivisible terms. But the old centrifugal forces now regained momentum and capacity to influence. As in Europe, so in Italy, the great events of 1870 deepened and widened the fissures that in 1848 had been opened in the ideal world of pre-1848, making them solid and lasting. In result the triptych of nation-liberty-Europe, the new trinity of history prophesied with such fire by Mazzini, was shattered. This meant above all the lapsing of the link between the nation as an idea and Europe. It was "nationalitarism" [*nazionalitarismo*] above all that was breaking up the old chorality and giving the signal for the start of a new age.[233]

In drawing up the political balance for the year 1870, *La Riforma*, prompted by the famous phrase of Count von Beust "je ne vois plus d'Europe," did not mourn the presumed end of the old Europe; in fact, it gloated that this disappearance removed the barriers in the way of the forces being unleashed within "the powers that have a future," in the states in which there seethed "a ground swell of emancipation, personal emancipation so to speak, that tends to give maximum room for development to the initiative of national policies."[234] The single nation, the single state, launched toward the future, following the unique impulse of its own forces, and with no more thought for any limitations than those of its own interest and its own greatness: these were the new values that would assert themselves in the coming age.

At the same time, there began to reappear themes that recalled the Alfieri of the *Misogallo*. For many years Mazzini had preached reciprocal love among the peoples, and even Giusti, who was much less driven by conviction, felt himself touched by this love at the sight of Croat visitors to the basilica of Sant'Ambrogio. Now a much less significant figure, but a typical herald of the coming nationalism, was reiterating Alfieri's slogan of hatred. "Oh yes, it is hatred that makes the peoples great!" proclaimed Rocco de Zerbi to applause in the Castelli theater in Milan on 2 July 1882.[235]

Was there really any hope of replacing the old Europe of the governments with a new Europe of peoples, as Mazzini and Cattaneo had prognosticated? A general revolution, a profound upheaval of the international order, based on the full application of the principle of nationality?

Close to the end of his life, in fact in 1871, in what can be considered his political testament in regard to international relations, Mazzini restated the value

---

[233] L. Magagnato, *Nazione e rapporti internazionali nel pensiero di Mazzini* (Vicenza, 1943), pp. 25 ff., and Kohn, *Profeti e popoli*, pp. 87, 88, 101–102, have insisted on the danger of nationalism concealed in Mazzini's exaltation of the nation (and of the primacy of Rome). There is no doubt that in the Mazzinian glorification the later nationalism found an inspiration that it did not find in a Cattaneo, or even in the moderates. Still, it would be erroneous and unjust to condemn Mazzini excessively for events that took place after he was gone (which is perhaps what Kohn does) and to forget that in Mazzini the nation is always indissolubly bound up with humanity (i.e., Europe, however vaguely, and in political terms indistinctly, conceived) and with liberty, which together constitute its two limits. And for the infringement of those limits Mazzini is not responsible.

[234] "La eredità politica del 1870," *La Riforma*, 2–3 January 1871.

[235] De Zerbi, *Difendetevi!*, p. 55.

of the nation as "principle," as the means of making the ascent to humanity: consequently the mission of Italy, the guiding motive of its whole foreign policy, ought to be "the development of the principle of *nationality* as the supreme regulator of international relations and a secure pledge of peace in the future," the "reordering of the map of Europe," an alliance with the Slavic family so as to save it from the titanic Russian effort to turn Europe into a land of Cossacks, and also speed the death of the Turkish and Habsburg empires, which were irrevocably condemned to perish at the hands of the Slav populations. Let the Slavs receive this message from the Italians: "You who have risen up in the name of National Right, we also believe in your right, and we offer you our aid in winning it. But the final goal of our mission is a peaceful and permanent settlement in Europe. We cannot permit that Russian tsarism, a perpetual threat to liberty, should slip into the place now held by your masters. Every time an isolated uprising occurs, confined to one of the single Slav groups, unable to win, and incapable if it did win of erecting a strong barrier against the greed of the tsar, it only furthers his aim of aggrandizement. Unite among yourselves; forget the old rancors; join in a confederation, and let Constantinople be your Amphictyonic City, the city of your central powers, open to all, servant of none. You will have us with you."[236]

And it seemed that Crispi, the Crispi of 1871 and 1872, and *La Riforma*, and many others too on the Left, were continuing to follow this teaching; a few years later, at the height of the eastern crisis, their homage to the principle of free nations was renewed. Some of the appeals to the "holy" principle of nationality were indeed full of pathos;[237] it "forms our political religion, it is almost a God we bear within us, *agitante calescimus illo*."[238] There were frequent reminders that Italy "was the harbinger of the fruitful principle of the independence of peoples on the basis of national rights," and could not participate in talks about the fate of other peoples (meaning the Balkan peoples) unless it took a position "rigorously consistent with the foundations of its own existence, which are the principles of nationality and liberty that have enabled it to reawaken and take its seat at the banquet of the great nations."[239] But even at such times, even when the sacred sense of nationhood was apparently destined once again to set hearts afire—and the memory of Legnano, together with a longing to succor the Italians of the Trentino and Trieste groaning under the Habsburg yoke was combined with devotion to the Christians groaning under the Turkish yoke to produce an

---

[236] Mazzini, *Politica Internazionale* (1871), in *Scritti* 92:153 ff. and 164–65.

[237] The hon. Miceli to the Chamber on 8 April 1878 (*A.P., Camera*, p. 344).

[238] Caracciolo di Bella, *Dieci anni di politica estera*, p. 19. Caracciolo di Bella, who had previously been Italian ambassador at Constantinople and at Petersburg, later joined the Left as a senator, from May 1876. The phrase quoted in the text is from his speech to the Senate of 4 May 1878.

[239] Thus, in the Chamber on 18 December 1876, the hon. Miceli, one of the experts on the Left in debates on foreign policy—so much so that Bonghi called him "the Left's minister of foreign affairs" when the Left was still in opposition (*A.P., Camera*, pp. 407–408, and below, p. 444). Miceli was to make similar statements in the future, maintaining that the only solution worthy of the age was to constitute the Balkan nationalities, and that he expected "the greatest results" from a policy aimed at protecting the principle of nationality (8 and 9 April 1878, *A.P., Camera*, pp. 343, 346, 383).

expansive and revolutionary vision of Europe—even in these periods it was easy to see how the old ideals were being intrinsically transformed.

Of course the tones in which this transformation was voiced were softened, for the men of the Left were in power in the years we are speaking of now, and were responsible for the government. Depretis and Cairoli may have lacked the sense of Europe that Minghetti and Visconti Venosta had had, but the difficulties of the hour were enough to set prudent limits on their pronouncements and their actions. And if they had not held themselves back, Vittorio Emanuele II would have done so, for his old wish to govern in person was flaring up one last time.[240] A damper was put on patriotic hymns, and the actualization of the Italian national ideal was wisely postponed until better times; the general triumph (and specifically the triumph in the Balkans) of the principle of nationality sank to a secondary consideration in face of the necessity of not turning Europe upside down. Defense of "the interests of general order," the watchword of European diplomacy since the Restoration, wound up being proclaimed by the foreign ministers of the Left as well; in his first meeting as minister of foreign affairs with the Austrian ambassador, Mancini too made a distinction between the past and the present, of which the gravamen was: as professor of international law I upheld the principle of nationality, but I understand perfectly the difference between theory and practice, and I know that if one were to try to apply that principle to the relations between the different states, one would in the end make them impossible, and destroy them.[241]

Every so often the memory of the great notions once held would resurface,[242] and these recurrences, while merely verbal, provided ammunition to those who, mostly from abroad, accused the Italian government of duplicity, or at any rate of vacillation and lack of direction. The ancien régime sense of a European community was not deeply rooted in men like these, as it had been in the moderates, but amounted instead to a tactic employed in a political contingency (while the principles they had once professed lay in rubble). It was for this reason that, even when the words were the same, they had a different sound when uttered by Cairoli and Depretis than they had had when uttered by Visconti Venosta.[243]

In sum, the passwords in the government camp were prudence, peace, the European concert, to the extent that the most pointed reference to the rights of nationality would come from the lips of a minister, Corti, who was certainly not

---

[240] Cf. below, p. 555.

[241] Wimpffen, report, 10 June 1881, n. 27 A; SAW, *P.A.*, XI/91. In fact, Mancini had already sought to calm fears in his prolusion of 1872: the principle of nationality "will not impose the slightest obligation to launch new crusades and convulse the existing states by remaking the territorial map of Europe" (Mancini, *Diritto Internazionale*, p. 199).

[242] "The Italian government has not abandoned either the principles to which it owes its origin, or their consequences," said Depretis in the Chamber on 18 December 1876 (*A.P., Camera*, p. 414; not included in his *Discorsi Parlamentari*). In his speech to the Chamber of 23 April 1877, Depretis gave a summary of his ministerial program: "Italy must continue the pacific, prudent, dignified policy that up to now has won it the sympathy of the European powers." But this is qualified: "without renouncing its devotion to the great principles of civilization and humanity through excessive prudence" (ibid., p. 2716, likewise not included in his *Discorsi Parlamentari*).

[243] Wimpffen did not in fact attach much importance to the declarations of Mancini.

left-wing in his ideas and sentiments, and withal highly prudent and averse to risk.[244] Even then it was very vaguely worded and not at all compromising.

More telling is the fact that even outside the ranks of the government numerous spokesmen for the Left changed their tone quite markedly. One of the most faithful, devoted, and disciplined followers of Depretis, a deputy named Musolino, supported Turkey, declaring himself more Turkish than the sultan and asserting that in the eastern question nationality and liberty were not involved, only the ambitions of Russia.[245] In the spring of 1878 the hon. Musolino returned to this theme, proposing an alliance with Austria in the conviction that he was doing "a deed of real patriotism" and belittling as "utterly trivial, nothing at all" the little territorial differences between Rome and Vienna in comparison to "the great common cause that ought to bind us together."[246] And the next day it fell to the bard of democracy himself, Felice Cavallotti, to pronounce in the Chamber words that might have left a hearer gasping: in the eastern question the interests of Italy were identical with those of Austria—modern Austria, the defender of the Romanians and a place as different from the Austria of Metternich as the England of Disraeli, the defender of the Greeks, was from the England of Castlereagh. It was up to Italy to be a friend to Austria once the latter had made satisfaction to Italian national interests by handing over the "unredeemed" lands. "We are the friends of Austria": with this the ideals of Mazzini were left in shards; the problem was reduced to a specifically Italian question of limited proportions, and beyond that, let the double monarchy continue, let it descend the valley of the Danube, and let the way to the Balkans, and the east, be thrown open. Such an intention on the part of Austria was within reason, for the principle of nationality in relation to the Balkan peoples "cannot be discussed without certain restrictions and . . . certain reservations," being so often confused, uncertain, indistinct, too vague to give "vigor, solidity, and cohesion to each of those small agglomerations." Only Austria, opening to the east, is capable of opposing a stout barrier to the menacing expansion of Russia, against the danger of a tsarist unification of the Balkans, which would directly threaten Italy in the Mediterranean and the Adriatic.[247] Where was the shade of Carlo Cattaneo, who had foretold the rise of federations of free peoples upon the dissolution of the old and fortuitous empires of central Europe?[248] It was not the shade of Cattaneo or of Mazzini but that of Cesare Balbo that walked again. Cavallotti, the fiery Lombard democrat, followed in the footsteps of the Piedmontese count, a moderate par excellence, even taking up the warnings of Gioberti against the Russian peril and adopting the political agenda of the Right against which he had fought so

---

[244] In the session of the Chamber of 9 April 1878: "within the limits imposed by existing treaties and by the necessary regard for friendly powers, our diplomatic action will also be aimed at supporting, as effectively as possible, the interests of those nationalities for whom the Italians have, indeed, lively sympathy" (*A.P., Camera*, p. 383).

[245] Speech of 23 April 1877 (*A.P., Camera*, pp. 2693–94). The same tone is found in the speech of 8 April 1878 (*A.P., Camera*, pp. 374 ff.).

[246] Speech of 8 April 1878 (*A.P., Camera*, pp. 355–56).

[247] Speech in the Chamber of 9 April 1878 (*Discorsi Parlamentari di F. Cavallotti* 1:85 ff.).

[248] Carlo Cattaneo, *Dell'insurrezione di Milano nel 1848 e della successiva guerra*, p. 306.

long. Mazzini's message had been: the Balkan peoples are unable, each on its own, to withstand the encroachment of the tsar, so let them all join in a free confederation, built on the ruins of the Habsburg empire, which was a form of administration, not a state, and of the Turkish empire, an isolated foreign encampment on territory not its own. Now Cavallotti responded: not only each single small independent Slav state, but even a "so-called" confederation of all of them, would be impotent against Muscovite absorption; so let Austria go ahead and raise a staunch barricade to halt the Russian peril. In the wake of the peace of St. Stephen, dread of the Cossack advance had grown, and the fears of decades were honed by recent events. So the conclusion was: let us forget about the ideal of free peoples in brotherhood, and let us opt for the shelter of a military force already organized, let us opt for Austria-Hungary.

There was more. For Cavallotti the problems of international arrangements were at bottom entirely secondary. The words *liberty*, *democracy*, and especially *republic* were what really stirred his soul; but he did not rest his gaze upon Europe, nor even pretend to. He rested it upon France and Italy because in both nations the major domestic problems appeared to be identical, or nearly so, and because French radicalism served as his preceptor and guide. But Mazzini's sweeping view of the whole continent was gone; there were no more appeals to the new Europe of the peoples, because the ensemble of Europe meant little to Cavallotti. What mattered to him was the ideological problem, the party problem, and so he focused only on those countries like France in which the political situation appeared identical or very similar. So the revolutionary potency of the principle of nationality shrank to the question of Trent and Trieste, becoming simple irredentism, and not even general irredentism but one narrowly concentrated on those two areas, with the odd allusion to others thrown in.[249]

A man like Crispi did, on the contrary, try to take in the whole. He always had his eyes fixed on the large problems of the relations between states, and in the end, in antithesis to Cavallotti, domestic politics would be reduced for him to a simple function of foreign policy, and domestic matters concerning his party and his political ideology would be subordinated to his preoccupations about the greatness and the power of Italy. Of course Crispi and his allies no longer accepted the old Europe of the governments and were glad to see it subside. But did they still believe in a Mazzinian Europe of peoples? Or, distant as they were from the older European faith of the moderates, did they not in reality also jettison the new European faith of their master Mazzini? After all, nothing remained now but the forces surging up in the powers that were set to dominate the future, meaning the individual, single nations, each marching on its own.

If we were to take at face value the position of *La Riforma* in 1871, we would have to conclude that the torch of Mazzini was still ablaze, for there were predictions of the imminent transformation of the Habsburg empire and the annexation of the Germans to mother Germany, but also of the imminent fall of the Turkish

---

[249] In Cairoli's speech of 28 May 1876 at Milan the claim for Nice is advanced, as well as for Trent and Trieste (Sandonà, *L'irredentismo nelle lotte politiche* 1:124).

empire. Let the Turks withdraw into Asia, the paper said, and the populations of the east be set free. Napoleon III, the emblem of violence in western Europe, has fallen; the temporal power of the papacy has crumbled and the Pope-monarch, the negation of all civil reason, has vanished; the work of justice will be complete with the disappearance of the sultan, the emblem of the absurd. First there was Sedan, then came 20 September; after 20 September . . . we need another date to mark, another step forward. Let Greece become whole, let there be complete autonomy for the Albanians, the Bulgarians, the Serbs, the Romanians; let there be a confederation of these peoples linked together by a central government in Constantinople, and the eastern question will be settled.[250] This was how, in the most acute phase of the crisis caused by the Russian refusal of the stipulations regarding the Black Sea, Crispi's circle proposed to resolve matters. Their solution plainly still bore the stamp of Mazzini and virtually anticipated the message that was soon to follow from the apostle himself.

But *La Riforma* was also strongly in favor of Russia, and that in itself was an appreciable departure from Mazzini, who had been very apprehensive about the projected expansion of tsarism and had opposed anything that savored of Russian meddling in the Balkans—whereas *La Riforma* was ready to applaud. For instance, it declared that the Gorchakov circular, which had fluttered the dovecotes of the old-style diplomacy, had provided a clear example of "what a state has the *duty* to do to stake out and protect its own *right*."[251] In other words *La Riforma* was yet again exalting the rights of states full of youthful force, of states with a future: it was exactly the same response as the one elicited from the paper by the feats of arms of Bismarck's Prussia. And such was its enthrallment that questions of principle, such as the opposition between liberty and autocratic tsarism, simply dropped into oblivion.

The later development of the ideas of Francesco Crispi was to demonstrate that Mazzini's Europe of the peoples had indeed sunk from view. Of course Crispi continued to sing the praises of the free life of the "four distinct nationalities" of the Balkans in his public speeches,[252] and he always sought ways to further the concrete aspirations of Greece. At the end, with his time in power behind him, he returned to the old Mazzinian ideal, proclaiming anew the necessity of a Balkan confederation and the return of the Turk to Asia,[253] just as he sought to renew his link to Cattaneo by expressing the wish for a United States of Europe.[254] But

---

[250] "La questione d'Oriente," in *La Riforma* for 16 November 1870.

[251] "La eredità politica del 1870," in *La Riforma* for 2–3 January 1871.

[252] See the speech made at Turin on 25 October 1887, (*Scritti e discorsi politici*, pp. 709–10); and the speeches to the Chamber of 3 February 1879 (*Discorsi Parlamentari* 2:339); 15 March 1880 (ibid., 2:408), where the Mazzinian scheme for a confederation is taken up again; and 4 May 1894 (ibid., 3:746). And cf. Crispi, *Politica estera* 1:296 ff., and *Questioni internazionali*, pp. 231 ff., where his position is uniformly treated as being that of the old Mazzinian he had once been by Palamenghi-Crispi, the arranger of the *Diario* and other documents of Crispi, and the editor of these works.

[253] Crispi, *Questioni internazionali*, pp. 241 ff. (an interview with *Le Figaro* of February 1897).

[254] Crispi, *Pensieri e profezie* p. 6 (ed. of 1900). But when he was in government Crispi doubted the possibility of effecting international arbitration in Europe (*Discorsi Parlamentari* 3:589–90). And note his discussions with Demarest in September-October 1891, in which his recognition of the great advantages of European union gets lost amid discussions on Italian-French relations and the Triple

these were the late posturings and proclamations of one who had lost the political battle; they were not unlike the twilight liberalism of Bismarck, the fierce enemy of Germany's parliament when he himself was in power, and then, when he had been stripped of it, a sudden and fervent convert to the defense of liberty and parliamentarianism. In power Crispi had indeed given attention to the problem of Greece, but he had contaminated Mazzini's dreams for the freedom of the Balkan nationalities with something else, with the sort of scheming that was now habitual among the diplomats of the great European powers for the division of Turkish territory.[255] To speak plainly, Crispi tried to make sure of getting, somewhere or other, a slice of the Turkish empire, in conformity to the dictates of power politics.[256]

When faced with the "sick man of Europe," even ex-Mazzinians ended up as converts to the classic principles of governmental diplomacy: the fall of the Turkish empire might be inevitable, but there was no need to hurry it along and run the risk of exposure to grave dangers "that all the great powers have an equal interest in avoiding."[257] Prudence, alertness, and vigilance were in order so as not to be caught off guard by events; there was no call for the torches of revolution. This was said aloud by the likes of Cairoli and Zanardelli, and it was what Crispi thought as well.

The shift of ideas can be seen even more clearly when one turns from the Turkish monster to that other monster, and likewise target of Mazzini's imprecations: because Crispi followed Cavallotti, and on 15 March 1880, although he was only a deputy without governmental responsibility, affirmed in the Chamber the necessity of Austria's existence.[258] This would have been blasphemy for the Crispi of ten or twenty years earlier; he repeated it as prime minister on 4 May

---

Alliance, and polemics against the "present allies" of France, the Tsar and the Pope. To arrive at European union, France must join the Triple Alliance, which at this point is "the main node of European confederation" (!). His conclusions are very clear: "in practical politics you have to take the world as it is . . . and not waste time discussing hypotheses which it will require centuries to bring about. . . . [W]e leave it to our successors to crown the work of progress" (Crispi, *Ultimi scritti*, pp. 381–97).

[255] *G.P.* 9:54 ff. and 56 n. 1. Cf. H. Krausnick, *Holsteins Geheimpolitik in der Ära Bismarck, 1886–1890* (Hamburg, 1942), p. 73.

[256] Crispi's report of a meeting with Nigra, 25 January 1896: "It is our desire that the territorial status quo not change in the Balkan peninsula. But if change does start to happen, if the carve-up of the Turkish empire begins, we want Italy to get its share. Count Nigra is in agreement" (MRR, *Carte Crispi*, b. 668, n. 1/4). Italy's share was to be Tripoli (Crispi's meeting with vice-admiral Accinni and ship's captain Bettolo, 16 November 1895; MRR, *Carte Crispi*, b. 667, n. 35/10. In Crispi, *Questioni internazionali*, p. 253, this portion of the meeting goes unmentioned).

[257] *Il Diritto* for 9 February 1877 ("La Costituzione in Turchia").

[258] "The Austro-Hungarian empire is a necessity for us. That empire, and the Helvetic confederation, keep us at the right distance from other nations with whom we want to be amicable . . . but whose territory we do not want to see immediately contiguous with Italy's's" (Crispi, *Discorsi Parlamentari* 2:408. Crispi repeats this practically verbatim in *Pensieri e profezie*, p. 3, and the same chain of thought often appears in his preliminary notes for his speeches). It is no surprise to learn that he first proffered utterances about the "necessity" of Austria and its role as a civilizing element in regard to the east during his voyage to Vienna in October 1877, speaking to the editors of the Viennese papers (Crispi, *Politica estera* 1:63). It is worth noting that in his meetings with Bismarck a few weeks earlier there is no trace of such views (ibid., 1:25 ff. and 46). But ten years later, in another meeting with Bismarck on 2 October 1887, Crispi will fully acknowledge the necessity of Austria for European equilibrium (ibid., 1:290).

1894.[259] This amounted to complete acceptance of the position that in 1871 had been defended by the moderates of *La Perseveranza* and of *Italie* against the wish of *La Riforma*, that is of his own paper, to see the fated, felicitous, and imminent dismemberment of the empire of the Habsburgs.[260] If a state like Austria-Hungary did not exist it would be necessary to invent it.[261]

As prime minister, Crispi acted in the way that Count Robilant had recommended for so many years against anti-Austrian demonstrations; he dissolved the committee for Trieste and Trent, discharged the minister Seismit-Doda, his former editorial colleague on *La Riforma*, and publicly branded irredentism as "the most detrimental error in Italy."[262]

Rising above such specific questions as those posed by the Habsburg and Ottoman empires, the very principle of nationality was wrapped up in numerous reservations and counsels of prudence by the Sicilian statesman, inasmuch as "in its ultimate expression, it cannot in fact, whatever might be thought ideal, be the constant and exclusive measure of what is right in politics and diplomacy." How absurd it would be to embark on adventures in the name of that principle, and to destroy the unity of Italy by provoking European wars and powerful anti-Italian coalitions: a "mad" plunge to ruin. The principle of nationality required "a wise moderation" on the part of governments.[263] These were the same ideas, couched in more or less the same language, that had been advanced immediately following the events of 1870 by Visconti Venosta, Dina, and Bonghi. The holy principles of nationality were not renounced—but anyone could see that the world was now headed in a different direction.[264]

That the world had changed was true, just as it was true that the government leader had to think and to speak differently than had the conspirator of 1860 or the opposition deputy of 1870. European events were unfolding in a way that required increasing prudence and the relegation of old ideals to the attic. At the time when Crispi was prime minister, Italy was allied to Austria whereas relations between Russia and Italy were troubled; they were to grow increasingly so,

---

[259] If Austria should break up, he says, Italy would lose its buffer to the east. "Within the sphere of the Empire there is no nation among those that constitute it whose population and political situation gives it sufficient strength so that it would amount to a power capable of resisting the invasions that would come from the east or the west of the Austro-Hungarian empire. And so? Italy would be in direct contact with great powers which, when there was friction, could dominate it just as it was harshly dominated in past centuries" (Crispi, *Discorsi Parlamentari* 3:746).

[260] *La Perseveranza* for 17 June 1871 states that the journal *L'Italie* has said that if Austria did not exist it would be necessary to invent it, so necessary does such a state seem. Yet *L'Italie* also believes that the Austrian Germans will join with Germany. But, continues *La Perseveranza*, in that case Germany, "already too ponderous," would increase notably in size, and Austria, "too weak already," would fall to the rank of a secondary power. European equilibrium, already severely unbalanced in the recent war, would be completely toppled, and then Italy would find that it had for an Adriatic neighbor the young and vigorous Germany, with which either peaceful competition or open hostilities would both be much more arduous than with Austria. This is the reason that in the interests of all of Europe and especially of Italy the progressive weakening of Austrian power must be viewed with alarm.

[261] In the speech at Florence on 8 October 1890 (Crispi, *Scritti e discorsi politici*, p. 760).

[262] In the same speech (ibid., p. 750).

[263] Ibid., pp. 750–52.

[264] Speech to the Chamber, 4 May 1894 (Crispi, *Discorsi Parlamentari* 3:746).

and to a large extent because of the fears that he, Crispi, was prey to, fears of a great conspiracy against Italy on the part of the Vatican, France, and Russia. In these circumstances Austria became a protecting shield, and the collapse of the Ottoman empire a dangerous leap into the unknown.

But it was not just the prudence of a prime minister that tempered the passions of the man, for the restless and impulsive Crispi would never have accomplished such a transformation on his own if he were still attached in 1890 to the ideals he had held in 1860, nor would he ever have seen in Franz Joseph I the prince "whose mental and moral qualities outshine those of the other European princes."[265] No, something had changed in the inner man, whether as a result of experience, or of having practiced the art of government, or because the times now showed him a different lesson. The change was the abandonment of revolutionary principles and Mazzini's program. Crispi said as much when he told the Chamber that those who sat on the extreme Left were mistaken in continuing to speak the language of the Mazzini of 1854: "In forty years so much progress has been made that the questions that moved our souls and readied us for the great battle when we were young conspirators are dead issues today."[266]

Politics holds no absolutes; "man must adapt himself to changed circumstances over time, to varied conditions."[267] This is an unambiguous denial of the core of Mazzini's teaching, in which principles are always and everywhere to the fore. Crispi now accepts, in theory at least, the policy of the happy medium. In practical politics you have to take the world as it is and not lose time discussing hypotheses that will need centuries to come about.[268]

There was to be no more general revolution, no more Europe of the peoples of which Mazzini had dreamed. But neither was there in Crispi the sense of Europe characteristic of the moderates, the old Europe of Visconti Venosta and Bonghi. Letting go of the revolutionary principle did not mean becoming a conservative in his inmost heart. Crispi no longer believed in European revolution, but this did not transform him into a sincere and convinced proponent of Europe in its classic form. He could accept the existence of a "European system" in practice, as a matter of tactics; to make of it an ideal, as the moderates had done, was impossible for him under the weight of his years of experience, of thoughts and feelings contrary to such an ideal. So the universal ideal decayed and in its place there remained only the particular ideal of the greatness of one's own country. The

---

[265] Crispi's meeting with the Austrian ambassador, Pasetti, on 25 October 1896: Pasetti declares that the emperor has great esteem for Crispi. Crispi replies: "In truth I feel true devotion to your sovereign. When I recall the beginning of his reign, and the difficulties he was able to overcome, I view Franz Joseph as the prince whose mental and moral qualities outshine those of the other European princes. When I was at Vienna and Budapest I was able to see that he is loved by his peoples. And I said to myself, the emperor must have special qualities if his peoples, forgetting the severities of the government in 1848 and 1849, love him so" (Crispi, autograph notes, MRR, *Carte Crispi*, b. 668, n. 2/10).

[266] 4 May 1894 (Crispi, *Discorsi Parlamentari* 3:746). When in this speech he refers to humanity developing "with all the liberty and the vigor that could not be attained by the nationalities divided," it is a pure rhetorical ornament and has no link with the preceding analysis.

[267] MRR, *Carte Crispi*, b. 668, n. 14/6.

[268] Crispi, *Ultimi scritti*, p. 396.

project for a general renewal of Europe shrank to a project for Italian power; faith in concord, in the fraternal advancement of all the young nations endowed with vitality was lost, and hunger for the advancement of one's own young nation took its place. That Crispi was wholly in tune with the times is past doubt. He had the example of Europe's outstanding politician, Bismarck, who was hostile to a revolutionary Europe yet equally skeptical where European tradition was concerned, and who was convinced that there really ought to be only one ideal, the greatness of his own country.

So grand visions were trimmed back not simply out of governmental prudence but as an integral part of the growing nationalistic sentiment. Thus clipped, they gained a corposity, a precision, and a hardness of outline they had not had before. Irredentism itself, born of revolutionary Mazzinianism (nationality and liberty fused together in the messianic expectation of the great general resurgence of the peoples), was in the end abetted by a nationalism that cast off all hope for the general renovation of humanity and grounded itself solely in the power, prestige, and greatness of Italy alone.

The Lesson of "Reality" in France

WE HAVE SEEN that the establishment of a powerful empire in central Europe was in itself sufficient to bring about the reawakening everywhere on the continent of the spirit of force and the desire for greatness, and we have seen the detriment that this wrought to the spirit of liberty and peace. Even in the land of Cobden and Gladstone it had the power to stimulate a revival of national pride, so that one heard Disraeli appealing to "the dominating spirit of these islands."[1] But there was more. The triumphant demonstration of the art of military victory by Bismarck and Moltke had thrown conventional values into confusion, as the shock waves of the war spread from the political and military domain to the moral and spiritual one, from the isolated problems of international coexistence to the very way in which those problems were conceived. In Germany the lesson of force had already been learned: there the Prussianization of thought and feeling was rooted in the experience of 1848, which had shifted the focus of public opinion to conceptual horizons very different from those of the Romantic age, a process witnessed most strikingly in Droysen's evolution from the rich and complex moral content of his first period to the praise of politics as pure force of his later phase.[2] New modes of experience rippled outward from Germany, and not to Italy and the Italians alone. In France itself, the conquered nation, the events of the war reverberated in the consciousness of the people, and not just in the obvious sense that there was hurt and resentment, a reexamination of past events in an attempt to pin the blame for them on someone, but also in the sense that settled ideas and beliefs were plunged into turmoil. In result a large part of the older France was laid to rest and a new France was born—new in its political regime and institutional structure, new as well in spirit and creed. Morally and culturally the France of the Restoration and the July Monarchy had survived under the Second Empire, but its ideals and purposes did not withstand defeat in the war of 1870. German arms had inflicted on them a lesson in "reality."

First to disappear was the ideal of Franco-German collaboration, which had enriched French thought for more than half a century, from the time in fact when Madame de Staël had pointed to Germany as the heart of Europe and had affirmed that a supranational association of the continental countries would have its

---

[1] In his speech at the Crystal Palace in 1872 (W. Langer, *La diplomazia dell'imperialismo* [Italian translation: Milan, 1942], pp. 120–21).

[2] For this internal as well as external Prussianization of German national sentiment, see F. Meinecke, "Johann Gustav Droysen: Sein Briefwechsel und seine Geschichtsschreibung," *Historische Zeitschrift* 141 (1929): 249 ff.; and also Werner Kaegi, *Historische Meditationen* 1:290 ff. (Zurich, 1942). But most important is Felix Gilbert, *Johann Gustav Droysen und die preussisch-deutsche Frage*, pp. 120 ff.

only guarantee of independence in the existence of German independence.[3] Saint-Simon had followed, with his project for Anglo-Franco-German society as the necessary premise for the reconstruction of Europe, and had likewise saluted the Germans as the people destined to exercise the leading role in the continent as soon as they were united under a free government.[4] Following this there was an influx of German thought into France, with the principal representatives of French cultural life falling under the spell of Germany's teachers of the life of the spirit—Lessing, Herder, and Kant. One thinks of Victor Cousin and the *passion allemande* of Michelet,[5] of the hopes for close cultural and political collaboration between the two nations, and the desire that Germany be solidly liberal so that, with France, it might underpin a liberal and enlightened Europe, a Europe of science and progress.[6] And science was accompanied by liberty on this way of hope for the future. July 1830 fanned hope anew, lighting the fires of enthusiasm on either side of the Rhine, and a love for France in the young German liberals, for whom, as for the Italian liberals, the France of the *trois glorieuses* appeared once again as the bringer of deliverance to the oppressed peoples of Europe. Yet glaring discrepancies between nationality and the common ideal of freedom were soon revealed, and many German liberals began to perceive once again the menacing profile of a nation that had also produced Napoleon, and under him had imposed its hegemony on others while flaunting the name of liberty; while in France Edgar Quinet, who had at first been seduced like Michelet by the Germany of Herder, raised an early cry of alarm in denouncing the choleric German style of nationalism and the threat it posed to Alsace-Lorraine.[7] Above all, the grave diplomatic crisis of 1840 in Europe provoked by the eastern question had opened a gap, and a wide one; there were calls by the French nationalists for war on the Rhine, while on the other side German national consciousness was immediately galvanized, as a bond of shared national passion overrode all political ideologies.[8] Becker and De Musset had expressed in verse the inevitability of what was happening, the one extolling the German freedom of the Rhine, the other longing for the time when both banks of the Rhine had been French. An underlying layer of animosity, centuries-old, reemerged brusquely and brutally, one that not even a common political ideal was capable of blanketing over. Heine, for example, was a proponent of Franco-German friendship, but that did not prevent him from uttering the following: "M. Thiers with his clamorous

---

[3] *De l'Allemagne* (Paris, 1857), p. 6.

[4] *La riorganizzazione della società europea* (Italian translation: Rome, 1945), pp. 95 ff. and esp. p. 100.

[5] On Michelet and Germany, see W. Kaegi, *Michelet und Deutschland* (Basel, 1936), and also "Der junge Michelet," in *Historische Meditationen* 2:115 and 117 ff. (Zurich, 1946).

[6] On the whole problem, see J. M. Carré, *Les écrivains français et le mirage allemand*.

[7] Carré, *Les écrivains français*, pp. 63 ff.

[8] Cf. O. J. Hammen, "The Failure of an Attempted Franco-German Liberal Rapprochement, 1830–1840," *American Historical Review* 52, no. 1 (1946): 54 ff., and Carré, *Les écrivains français*, pp. 72 ff. It is indicative that in the Rhineland, where the French nationalists believed they had strong support, and where up to that point there actually had been strong sympathies for France, the European crisis of 1840 and the French attitude should provoke a violently anti-French and German-national reaction (cf. J. Droz, *Le libéralisme rhénan, 1815–1848* [Paris, 1940], pp. 208 ff.).

drumbeat woke our good Germany from its lethargic slumber and brought it into the great commotion of Europe's political life. So strongly did he sound the reveille that we were unable to go back to sleep, and since then we have stayed out of bed. If we one day become a people, M. Thiers will have every right to claim a share of the credit, and Germany history will render him his due for this service."[9]

Yet not even the crisis of 1840, however pregnant with distant consequences it may have been, had really been able to shatter the dream. Victor Cousin, a philosopher and a government minister at that very difficult time, had continued to speak with enthusiasm of German art and science, of German profundity of intellect and spirit, of the love of justice and humanity that was proper to Germany,[10] and when the crisis had passed the old alacrity had reappeared, primarily among French men of culture, who had not really grasped the deeper significance of the political episode, and whose passion for German science and scholarship remained intact. When he first read Goethe and Herder, Renan felt that he had entered a sanctum, and that henceforth everything which had seemed to him divinely inspired now took on the appearance of faded and crumpled paper flowers,[11] so that he proposed to dedicate his life to working for intellectual, moral, and political union between France and Germany.[12] His counterpart on the other side was Ludwig Börne, who declared in 1844 that he loved Germany more than he did France because Germany was unhappy, but that for the rest he felt himself to be as much a Frenchman as a German, and that he saw the liberty and the felicity of France inseparably bound to the liberty and the felicity of Germany. The pillars of France's liberty ought to be sunk, he asserted, not in the Place de la Bastille, but on the banks of the Elbe.[13]

Then came 1848. At the outset at least, it was like 1830 again and raised again the ferment of shared passions: for liberty and democracy, for a European revolution, for the peoples to be set free. These were the bywords that resounded in France, in Germany, in Italy, in Poland; only in Russia and England did they go unheard.[14] Marx had already fixed his attention principally on France and Germany, from the time of the ephemeral *Deutsch-französische Jahrbücher*, when he was carried away by the principle of Gallo-Germanism dear to Feuerbach: a French heart and a German head.[15] The Communist rallying cry this time was the

---

[9] Cited in F. Ruffini, *La giovinezza del conte di Cavour* 2:230 (Turin, 1912).

[10] Ibid., 2:229–30.

[11] "Lettre à M. Strauss," in the *Journal des Débats* for 16 September 1870, reprinted in Renan, *La réforme intellectuelle et morale* (cited hereafter as *La réforme*), p. 168. On Renan and Germany, see esp., as well as Carré, *Les écrivains français*, pp. 81 ff., H. Tronchon, *Ernest Renan et l'étranger* (Paris, 1928), pp. 155 ff.

[12] Renan, *Correspondance, 1846–1871*, p. 341.

[13] Börne, *Menzel der Franzosenfresser* (Bern, 1844), pp. 53 ff.; and in F. Federici, *Der deutsche Liberalismus*, pp. 170–71.

[14] Cf. Namier, "1848: The Revolution of the Intellectuals," p. 3. In the Parliament of Frankfurt those on the left always saw France as the France of 1789, thus reopening once again, as they had after 1830, an old quarrel with the right: see E. Sestan, *La Costituente di Francoforte (1848–1849)*, pp. 79 ff.

[15] Cf. A. Cornu, *Karl Marx: L'homme et l'oeuvre. De l'hégélianisme au matérialisme historique*

same one, though in a different key, that had been heard in the past from Saint-Simon, with Germany once again looming as the crucial arena in the struggle to shape a future[16]—a struggle based on an unending search for common themes and uniform ideals for the French and the German peoples. Herwegh and Bornstedt had called upon the French citizens to furnish arms to the German émigrés and democrats "who are marching to aid their brothers," and their aim had been to follow the proclamation of the republic in France with the proclamation of a republic in Germany.[17]

In sum, the aspiration for close cultural and political collaboration between the two peoples survived 1840. And it survived 1848 as well, which meant that it outlasted the swing of the pendulum between an initial hour of extravagant hope and the subsequent renewal of strident nationalism, and the clash between that nationalism and the spirit of liberty. In 1848 Poles and Czechs and Italians discovered that there was a great distance between them and the rigid and exclusive patriotism of the Germans, and the expedition to Rome set the French and the Italians starkly against one another. In 1848 national egoism triumphed over the shattered ideal of free peoples when the Parliament of Frankfurt was faced with the Italian question, and above all the Polish question, and when Wilhelm Jordan exclaimed, liberty for all, but the power and prosperity of the German homeland above everything.[18] Yet the aspiration survived, and an axiom of Tacitus which

---

(Paris, 1934), pp. 259 ff.; K. Vorlaender, *Karl Marx* (Italian translation: Rome, 1946), pp. 71 ff.; O. Maenchen-Helfen and B. Nicolajevski, *Karl Marx* (Italian translation: Turin, 1947), pp. 80 ff.; and, still, F. Mehring, *Karl Marx: Geschichte seines Lebens* (2d ed.; Leipzig, 1919), pp. 53 ff. None of these scholars, however, has observed how the Franco-German program of Marx in 1843 fits into the general atmosphere created by the liberals and the Saint-Simonians of harmonious Franco-German cooperation for the good of Europe. The ideology changes radically, but in Marx the general European framework inherited from the liberal era of the first part of the nineteenth century remains.

[16] The following passages, one from Saint-Simon and the other from the *Communist Manifesto*, may be contrasted: "the German nation . . . is destined to exercise the leading role in Europe as soon as it is reunited under a free government" (Saint-Simon, *La riorganizzazione della società europea*, p. 100). "Communists pay special attention to Germany. There are two reasons for this. First of all, Germany is on the eve of a bourgeois revolution. Secondly, this revolution will take place under comparatively advanced conditions as far as the general civilization of Europe is concerned, and when the German proletariat is much more highly developed than was the English proletariat in the seventeenth century and the French proletariat in the eighteenth. Consequently, in nineteenth-century Germany, the bourgeois revolution can only be the immediate precursor of a proletarian revolution" (*Manifesto del partito communista*, Italian translation by E. Cantimori Mezzomonti [Turin, 1948], vol. 4, p. 227). [*Translator's note:* The English translation is taken from *The Communist Manifesto of Karl Marx and Friedrich Engels*, ed. D. Ryazanoff (1930; rpt., New York, 1963), vol. 4, pp. 67–68.]

[17] Cf. primarily Maenchen-Helfen and Nicolajevski, *Karl Marx*, pp. 171 ff.; and Vorlaender, *Karl Marx*, pp. 155–56. It is well known that Marx was strongly opposed to such ventures, as being useless and harmful.

[18] Namier, "1848: The Revolution of the Intellectuals," p. 88. One may note further Bismarck's hostility to the Italian national movement, and his fear that infatuation with vain theories might cause the loss of territories that German arms had conquered in the course of centuries in Poland and Italy (Bismarck in the *Magdeburgische Zeitung* for 20 April 1848; *Die Gesammelten Werke* 14[1]:106, cited above at ch. 1, n. 199). For the hostility of the Parliament of Frankfurt to Italian national aspirations—with a few exceptions among those on the extreme left—cf. Sestan, *La Costituente di Francoforte*, pp. 82 ff.

had become a cliché, first in German political theory and literature from Hutten to Möser and Herder, then in the European literature of the Romantic age, was still widely credited. It spoke of the lofty qualities of the German nation, "the purest morality, a sincerity that never deceives, a probity that is proof against anything."[19] The German spirit was an affirmation of liberty, a liberty born in the forests as Montesquieu said, amid the rude German warriors, "our fathers."[20]

Love for Germany and German culture, for the Germans as a race, found new and strenuous champions in France, chief among them Ernest Renan, a pontiff who proclaimed that "the Gallic race needs to be impregnated from time to time by the German race, to be able to bring forth all it is capable of"; so that if the Restoration had laid the groundwork for the real intellectual development of France in the nineteenth century, it was because Germanism had flowed freely in, and had had more beneficial effects than, for example, the Italian cultural invasion of France in the sixteenth century, which had been primarily dictated by the will of the royal house.[21] It was this same Renan who found nothing "shocking" in the conquest by a superior race of a country of inferior racial stock, who in fact attributed the regeneration of bastardized and inferior races by the superior ones to the providential order of humanity. He considered European expansion in Asia and Africa a *ver sacrum*, with a people of soldiers and masters, the Europeans, encountering a people of laborers of the soil, the Africans, and a people of artisans, the Chinese.[22] This was to accept the most dangerous premises of Germanism, and Renan became an apostle of colonialism and imperialism. He never shook off the conventional belief in the profundity of German idealism,[23] and was convinced as late as 1866 of the necessity of the Franco-German alliance in culture and politics,[24] in which England would also be given membership and in which he saw "a force able to govern the world, that is to direct it on the road to liberal civilization, equally removed from the foolish blind impatience of democracy and from the puerile dreams of a return to a past that has died for good."[25]

The war of 1870 ripped away all the illusions; every dream vanished. Michelet

---

[19] Saint-Simon, *La riorganizzazione della società europea*, p. 95. For the judgment of Cousin, see above p. 69; and for the remote origins of the tradition, E. Hölzle, *Die Idee einer altgermanischen Freiheit vor Montesquieu* (Munich-Berlin, 1925), and Antoni, *La lotta contro la ragione*, pp. 80 ff. and 172.

[20] Montesquieu, *Esprit des Lois* 28.27. The idea comes up again in Renan ("Philosophie de l'histoire contemporaine," *Revue des Deux Mondes*, 1 July 1859; now in *Oeuvres complètes* 1:34 ff. [Paris, 1947]) and in Montalembert (letter to Renan, 9 August 1859, in Renan, *Correspondance, 1846–1871*, p. 382).

[21] Cf. G. Sorel, "Germanesimo et storicismo di Ernesto Renan," *La Critica* 29 (1931): 200.

[22] Renan, *La réforme*, pp. 93–94.

[23] E. Renan and M. Berthelot, *Correspondance, 1847–1892*, p. 56 (for the contrast between the profound German soul and the brilliant plastic superficiality of the Italians); and Renan, *Correspondance, 1846–1871*, p. 276 (Germany is "so superior in matters of the spirit").

[24] *Correspondance, 1846–1871*, p. 276 and cf. p. 285.

[25] Renan, *La réforme*, p. v and cf. p. 42. On this triple alliance of the English, French, and Germans as the requisite basis for the moral and intellectual greatness of Europe, see as well the article "La guerre entre la France et l'Allemagne," *Revue des Deux Mondes* 15 (September 1870), later republished in *La réforme*, pp. 123 ff.

felt that his prolonged romantic and democratic love for Germany had been erased by triumphant Prussian militarism, and he fell into the pessimism that pervades his *Origines du XIX siècle*;[26] he died not long after, morally and spiritually slain by the events of 1870.[27] Taine, no less filled with admiration for Germany before the war, emerged from the catastrophe as though jolted from dreaming into "wakefulness."[28] As for Renan, he declared that he himself had followed a chimera, but that it had now vanished forever, and that an abyss had opened between the two nations that not even centuries would be enough to close. The myth of the German as an individual entirely composed of purity, idealism, moral rigidity, now vanished, its place taken by the Prussian in military uniform, a soldier like every soldier in history, like the marauding bands of Wallenstein: evil, thieving, a drunk and a vandal. The soaring conception of reason and humanity that had once inspired love of Germany existed no longer, and Germany was now only a nation, the strongest one at the moment, but no more.[29] The universal mission that had given the Germany of Kant and Goethe, of Lessing and Herder, its greatness, was over, and a time of politics was now beginning under the direction of Bismarck. It was no longer German *Geist* that ruled, but Prussian force.[30] Jacob Burckhardt thought so: one evening in December 1870 after he had been reading the works of Mörike, he laid the book aside and said that such things would no longer be possible in Germany, for it is not given to a people to aim for ascendancy in the arts of civilization at the same time that it aims for ascendancy in politics. Germany has now chosen to be guided by politics, he said, and must suffer the consequences.[31]

For Renan, the war was sowing a violent hatred between the two parts of Europe whose union was most necessary to the progress of the human spirit, and thus rupturing humanity's intellectual, moral, and political accord; it was introducing a harshness and dissonance into the concert of Europe that would last for centuries; it was breaking the triple alliance of England, France, and Germany, Europe's only possible shield against the United States of America, and even more against the unbridled appetites of Russia and its barbaric Asian hinterland.[32] Still he was unable to cease yearning, even now, for his old dream. He

---

[26] D. Halévy, *La fin des notables*, p. 68.

[27] M. Reclus, *L'avènement de la 3 république*, p. 138.

[28] Cf. V. Giraud, *Essai sur Taine, son oeuvre et son influence*, pp. 85 ff.

[29] *La réforme*, pp. vi ff. Cf. the judgment of Taine: "the war has revealed the bad and crude side of their character, which was covered by a skin of civilization. The German animal is brutal at bottom, hard, despotic, barbarous . . . all this has now come to light, and it causes horror" (*Hippolyte Taine: Sa vie et sa correspondance* 3:49 [Paris, 1906]; cited hereafter as Taine, *Correspondance*); and of Flaubert: "what use is learning, since this people full of scholars commits abominations worthy of the Huns, and worse, since the Germans are systematic, cold, determined, and have neither passion nor hunger as an excuse?" (Flaubert, *Correspondance*, 4th ser., p. 42 and cf. p. 46).

[30] The contrast between Germany on the one hand, with its generous, poetic, and philosophical spirit, and Prussia on the other, a military and political machine, is in fact an obligatory note to be sounded by French writers, including Michelet in *La France devant l'Europe*, pp. x and 91 ff., and also Renan, "Lettre à M. Strauss" (September 1870), reprinted in *La réforme*, pp. 171 ff.

[31] Cited in Kaegi, *Historische Meditationen* 1:313.

[32] "La réforme intellectuelle et morale de la France," in *La réforme*, p. 42; and "La guerre entre la France et l'Allemagne," ibid., pp. 124–25. [*Translator's note:* The essay "La réforme intellec-

had solicited the German sense of moderation, asking for a just peace that would not deepen the abyss between the two peoples. He had uttered a prophetic *vae victoribus!* and had turned to a much-admired fellow scholar, David Strauss,[33] to deplore the excesses of patriotism. In the end Renan, the proponent of Franco-German friendship, had to pronounce a disconsolate *nunc dimitte* as he withdrew into silence, unable any longer to urge his compatriots to love and unwilling to urge them to hate.[34] "Even those who are philosophers before they are patriots cannot remain unmoved by the cries of the two million people whom we have been forced to cast adrift in order to save the other survivors of the shipwreck, though they were a part of us in life and in death."[35]

And yet, and yet . . . much remained in him, if not of the old European ideal, at any rate of the old feeling for things German. In fact this feeling came out of the war involuntarily strengthened by the terrible trial, strengthened in the sense that German doctrines and forms now exercised even more power of suggestion over the Breton with the unassuming countenance. The proof of this is "La réforme intellectuelle et morale de la France," which in its conclusion looked once more for a model to the German spirit, and extolled the militarism, Germanic in origin, of which France had unhappily deprived itself through the Enlightenment and the Revolution by putting a philosophical and egalitarian ideology in its place.[36] And proof of this is also found in the racism already alluded to,[37] a racism that only hardened views Renan had already held in the past,[38] and carried him completely outside the ambit of the great French liberal tradition, the tradition of Tocqueville.[39] The

---

tuelle et morale de la France" appeared in book form in 1871 as the first part of the collection entitled *La réforme intellectuelle et morale.*]

[33] *Correspondance, 1846–1871*, pp. 317 and 320.

[34] "Nouvelle lettre à M. Strauss," 15 September 1871, published in *La réforme*, p. 209.

[35] *La réforme*, p. 59.

[36] *La réforme*, pp. 24 ff.

[37] The selection of the governing class by birth is declared preferable to the method of holding elections in *La réforme*, p. 45. "A society is only strong to the extent that it recognizes natural superiorities, which are fundamentally reducible to superiority of birth, inasmuch as intellectual and moral superiority is no more than the superiority of a germ of life that blossoms in particularly favorable conditions" (ibid., p. 49).

[38] On 19 August 1854 we can find Renan accepting the basic thesis of Gobineau but expressing reservations about how to apply it. On 26 June 1856 he accentuates these reservations, asserting that the race factor is immensely important at the outset, but that it continually loses incidence over time, until it has none left, as in France (the last theme is taken up again in 1882 in *Qu'est-ce qu'une nation*, in *Oeuvres complètes* 1:895 and 898). His conclusion was that, leaving aside the genuinely inferior races, whose admixture with the great races would only be to poison humankind, the future prospect for humanity was a homogeneity, in which all memory of specific origin would be lost (*Correspondance, 1846–1871*, pp. 84 and 120–21). Further evidence of Renan's tendency to interpret events in ethnic terms can be found in 1859, when he claimed that the French Revolution, which he found ever more repugnant, was the victory of the "Roman" element over the "Germanic" (G. Strauss, *La politique de Renan*, p. 157). In 1890 he stated that "the inequality of races is established" (in the preface to *L'Avenir de la Science*).

[39] It was characteristic of Tocqueville that he informed Gobineau directly of his own unshakable opposition to the "principles" enunciated in the latter's *Essai sur l'inégalité des races humaines* (*Correspondance entre Alexis de Tocqueville et Arthur de Gobineau, 1843–1859*, pp. 253–54 and 287).

proof of this is his continued admiration, whether direct or indirect, for the political, military, and social organization of Prussia.[40]

But overall, a flame of attraction that had burned brightly for fifty years was now flickering feebly to extinction, and a strong new voice was raised against the idols: not only against Bismarck's Germany but against the Germanic myth itself, against the "blind" enthusiasm for the world beyond the Rhine that had washed over most Frenchmen between 1815 and 1870 thanks to the repulsion aroused in the liberal age by Napoleon I and the consequent predilection for his enemies. Among these idols was the traditional image of the pure and honest Germans, and of German science and scholarship, which were now seen not in the light of a chaste and disinterested pursuit of truth, but rather as the utilitarian promotion of the national advantage. The voice was that of Fustel de Coulanges, whose lectures in the city of Strasbourg before its recent capture still seemed to reverberate in the air, just as a whole structure of myth, past and present, seemed to shiver and collapse first with his attack on German historiography in 1872,[41] then with his battle against the glorification of the Germans from ancient times in his *Histoire des institutions politiques de l'ancienne France*, the greatest of his three great historical works, the one in which the gyre of ideas and affects brought about by the war found its fullest expression.[42] The author of *La cité antique* was now moved by the pathos of events, by a rending love for his suffering country, by his drive to unmask the malignant errors propagated by German

[40] Fully to comprehend "La réforme intellectuelle et morale de la France," one must remember that, as Sorel observed ("Germanesimo et storicismo di Ernesto Renan," p. 362), Renan was always very subtle and careful not to affront public opinion head-on. He therefore employed (*La réforme*, pp. 64–84) two imaginary personages to put forward two contrasting points of view, leaving himself free, if challenged, to opt for the one or the other as his own position. And in fact, when faced with the vigorous criticism of Mazzini (*Scritti* 93:229 ff.), Renan affirmed that neither of the interlocutors represented his own thought. He had introduced them so as better to depict the various aspects of the question, the various ways, that is, in which one might envision the reform of France (letter of 7 April 1874 to M. Yung, editor of the *Revue politique et littéraire*, published in his *Correspondance, 1872–1892*, pp. 53–54).

[41] His article "De la manière d'écrire l'histoire en France et en Allemagne depuis cinquante ans," which appeared in the *Revue des Deux Mondes* for 1 September 1872, and was republished in his *Questions Historiques* (Paris, 1893), has now appeared in an Italian translation together with other writings related to the events of 1870, in a volume entitled *La guerra franco-prussiana*, pp. 59 ff.

[42] G. Monod, in reviewing the lectures given by Fustel de Coulanges at Strasbourg between 1861 and 1868, found that his well-known theory about the Roman character of the Merovingian monarchy was already fully formed before 1870; and he therefore does not believe that Fustel's undeniable political hostility to Germany, or his scant appreciation for the "erudite scholars" of that country, had any influence on the concepts expressed in the *Histoire* (Monod, *Portraits et souvenirs* [Paris, 1897], pp. 148 ff.). But there cannot be any doubt that his tone and his contentiousness were profoundly influenced by the events of 1870. Before then he would not have written words like these: ". . . today we live in an epoch of war. It is almost out of the question that the historical sciences should retain the serenity of the past. All about us, and against us, is struggle; it is inevitable that scholarship too should take up sword and shield. For fifty years the ranks of the erudite have made France the target of their assaults. Is it to blame if it takes thought for its defense against these blows?" ("Del modo di scrivere la storia," in *La guerra franco-prussiana*, p. 74). And cf., for confirmation of the views put forward here, G. Hanotaux, *Sur les chemins de l'histoire* 2:236 ff. (Paris, 1924). In any case the decade spent in Strasbourg, on the frontier, was bound to give rise to some disquiet in the historian and to suggest certain ideas to him: this has been acutely noted by A. Sorel, *Notes et portraits* (Paris, 1909), pp. 13–14.

scholarship, to impugn the Germanizing interpretations of the decline of the ancient world that had been dominant for over a century, and to demolish the myths of original Germanic purity, of primitive Germanic liberty, and of mankind's salvation at the hands of the invading hordes.

The magnificent dream of moral and spiritual cooperation between the two peoples divided by the Rhine evaporated, and so did the idea of an Anglo-Franco-German alliance as a broad base upon which to found a European civilization and a future of progress. The latter was an idea that Mazzini had sought to bend to his own advantage ever since 1832, proposing instead an Italo-Franco-German moral alliance as the nucleus of a grand brotherhood and eventual Alliance among the Peoples. Mazzini had tried to make Italy the pioneer in this movement, but he had never really succeeded in making any deep impact on European thought. Now there was nothing left. Instead of moving closer together and intertwining, French and German culture were drifting apart, as the political rivalry between the two countries overflowed into a much more somber and profound struggle between opposing spiritual tendencies, with the result that the purely political rivalry between them wound up as rivalry between different forms of civilization. The rallying cries and the polemics that were later to be heard in the Great War of 1914–1918 would prove it.

Instead of love and kindly courtesy, it was hatred among peoples that was preached after 1870. All graciousness, wrote Flaubert at the time of the invasion, is lost to us now and for a long time; a new world has commenced; children will be taught to hate the Prussian.[43] The case of Paul Déroulède, the champion of *revanche* and a father of French nationalism, is emblematic: he only assumed this guise following the severe moral shock the war gave him, for before 1870 he had been by his own admission a "cosmopolitan," disdainful of arms and a fervent devotee of the arts, incapable of understanding the *grandeur militaire* of De Vigny. In 1872 he intoned his *Chants du soldat*, lauding the hatred that presently existed and the use of force that would soon come about, and foretelling

> la revanche . . . lente peut-être,
> mais en tout cas fatale, et terrible à coup sûr.[44]

In 1814 the reaction to the collapse of the First Empire had also been a reaction against the spirit of conquest, or to put the matter in our terms, against militarism; but now the reaction was just the opposite. *Grandeur militaire* became the dominating motive for all parties, including Gambetta and the radicals. The urge to recover Sedan and Metz gnawed at the French soul continuously from the time of their loss, and the torment was even sharper and more penetrating than the urge to redeem Lissa and Custoza, which stung the soul of Italy.

---

[43] Flaubert, *Correspondance* 4:37. Later, in July 1871, he resumes the thought: "We begin to hate Prussia in a natural manner, in other words we are returning to French tradition. The praises of its civilization are no longer uttered" (ibid., p. 67).

[44] Cf. H. Fisher, "French Nationalism," in *Studies in History and Politics*, pp. 149 ff.; G. P. Gooch, "Franco-German Relations, 1871–1914," in *Studies in Diplomacy and Statecraft* (4th ed.; London, 1948), pp. 3–4. The lines cited are from *Vive la France!*

There is no more eloquent sign of this visceral transformation than the changing public posture of a man like Renan, who in 1849 had inveighed against the tendency to exclusive nationalism as the negation of the ideal of humanity,[45] who still rose up publicly against extreme patriotism and the nationalist frame of mind as late as 1870, with the war in progress,[46] and who in his heart never forgot his old ideal, characterizing the new patriotism as a trend destined to last fifty years and leave Europe bloody, after which it would no longer even be understood.[47] But publicly he was not above turning with the popular wind and assuming the pose of patriot and abettor of Déroulède.[48]

The question of Alsace-Lorraine was to be the sticking point in international relations among the European states. But the fate of the two provinces also weighed down the European nations in the cultural domain as it did in politics, like a curse from which they could find no release.

"We were deluded," wrote Michele Amari when the cannon fire had barely fallen silent, "in hoping that learning and civilization had tamed mankind, or at least the Christian portion of it, enough to make wars less frequent, less easy, less unjust, and less cruel." Far from it! "The nations still live in a state of nature, if not like that of the savages of Oceania, then certainly like that of the tribesmen of Arabia."[49] And even before, when the cannon fire had only just begun, Flaubert had condensed into a single heartfelt exclamation all the dismay and the disillusionment of being brutally torn from a rosy dream: "Ah, we men of letters! Humanity is far from our ideal, and it is a towering error, a dreadful error, on our part to imagine that it is as we are, and to want to treat it accordingly."[50]

Thus Germany now appeared to lie on the far side of a deep chasm. But for all that, the lesson of things as they are, the weight of defeat, the shame of seeing France invaded—how much these things influenced the ideas and ideals of the French writers and politicians, forcing them to come to grips with the Prussian victor's own standards and codes of conduct, even if only to fling them back in his teeth!

The new men like Gambetta and Ferry, the architects of republican France, did indeed take a stand against Germanism, against the notion of force and in favor of liberty. In the years after 1870 French radicalism was really the channel through which the most fruitful impulses of French political life in the nineteenth century passed on to safety, progress, and development. The real import of Gambetta's defense of Latinity, of the Latin ideas as the only "generous" one, in

---

[45] Renan and Berthelot, *Correspondance*, p. 39.

[46] Renan, "La guerre entre la France et l'Allemagne," in *La réforme*, pp. 139, 152, 164.

[47] Renan and Berthelot, *Correspondance*, p. 467 (from 1878). Cf. as well the preface to *L'Avenir de la Science*, published in 1890.

[48] In 1879 Renan thought the *Chants du soldat* ought to be given a prize by the Académie, thus putting Déroulède ahead of other candidates notoriously superior to him as poets: "but . . . we simply demonstrate our patriotic support for sentiments that ought to be promoted" (*Correspondance, 1872–1892*, p. 181). Conversely, in 1888 he protested at the award of an Académie prize to a French translation of von Sybel: "I believe that the Académie française has some obligation to be patriotic" (*Correspondance, 1872–1892*, p. 325).

[49] Amari, *Carteggio* 2:198 (in a letter dated 13 March 1871).

[50] Flaubert, *Correspondance* 4:29 (the letter is dated 3 August 1870).

opposition to the Germanic idea,[51] was this: it was a forceful reaction against the pernicious influence of German-style "realism." Fustel de Coulanges took a stand as well, protesting in sublime language against the right of invasion and the spirit of conquest, against the purely material evaluation of actions, and vindicating the interior life, the morality and spirituality of nations; he was sagacious in foreseeing the woe that Bismarckism was to bring upon Germany.[52] The voice of Edgar Quinet was not still, and in his mind's eye the old fighter for liberty also beheld the cathedral of Strasbourg.[53] Aged but not enfeebled, he saluted the revival of liberty and was almost the only distinguished intellectual to defend radicalism—which was the incarnation of liberty that required at that juncture to be defended in France.[54] Far from falling back on the prescriptions of force and "authority," far from conceding anything to the conservatives, he vehemently assailed their outlook and their notions, contradicting virtually point for point the ideas of men such as Renan.[55]

And yet withal, what a loss of faith there was, what a dispersal of hope and relinquishment of idealistic intensity, all sacrificed to the putatively real and positive forces! The icy tide of "realism" was rising, and it encouraged the repudiation of old principles, begot pessimism, and froze into postures of force men of lofty sentiment and refined culture. Realism and force: how ridiculous to cling to the wisps of the ideal when faced with these! But how saddening to behold Ernest Renan saying so. Even though the war was in progress, when his friends gathered at the ritual dinners at Brébant he foolishly repeated his belief in the superiority of the Germanic race and became so excited that he (the historian of the life of Jesus) endorsed the slogan of force over right as if it were an eternal law.[56]

---

[51] J. Adam, *Nos amitiés politiques avant l'abandon de la Revanche* (Paris, 1908), p. 213.

[52] Fustel de Coulanges, *La guerra franco-prussia*, esp. pp. 15, 17, 21 ff., 38 ff., 47 ff. Of course Fustel was by no means free of the general uneasiness provoked by the advance of democracy; cf. G. Guiraud, *Fustel de Coulanges* (Paris, 1896). pp. 84–85.

[53] *L'Esprit Nouveau* (Paris, 1875), p. 125.

[54] Ibid., p. 120 and cf. p. 127.

[55] "This hatred of the people, of the proletariat, in other words of the fourth estate, who are condemned like a plague; universal suffrage derided; the rich given full prerogative to speak, the artisan one tenth of that; the nobility and the haute bourgeoisie as lords and master; the monarchy our only hope" (*L'Esprit Nouveau*, p. 114 and cf. pp. 132 ff.).

[56] *Journal des Goncourt* 4:25–28 and 235 (Paris, 1903). And see the preface to vol. 5, in which Goncourt replies to Renan, who had accused him of falsifying the truth completely. It is certainly the case that the contents of the *Journal* have been much debated; but it is also the case that Taine, for example, who was likewise drawn into this debate, and was likewise very irritated, protested not so much against misunderstandings concerning historical and philosophical matters ("once or twice he has me saying the opposite of what I thought and think . . . because it was beyond him") as against the indiscretion committed: "to speak in his [Goncourt's] presence is to risk discovering in a book or a newspaper words that one had not spoken for public consumption" (Taine, *Correspondance* 4:254–57). In the case at issue, the substance of the words attributed to Renan by Goncourt corresponds overall to what Renan was saying publicly in *La réforme*, and in his private letters to his friends (cf. Strauss, *La politique de Renan*, p. 197). It is evident that, given Renan's characteristic avidity for popularity, Goncourt's publication must have been maddening to him, coming as it did at the height of French nationalism (cf. Renan, *Correspondance, 1872–1892*, pp. 347–48).

On the issue of Renan in 1870, see now two opposing works: one by H. Psichari, *Renan et la guerre de '70* (Paris, 1947), who rightly points to an internal drama being played out within Renan (cf. esp. pp. 42, 46, 57), but who is naturally too quick to spring to his defense; and by canon L. Vié,

Ideas such as these only honed Renan's condemnation of democracy, toward which he was already ill-disposed.[57] Democracy was at fault for French decadence, for rampant materialism, and for *la platitude bourgeoise*;[58] and universal suffrage was condemned for having made the peasantry, the inferior component of civilization, masters of public life.[59] The outcome of this current of ideas was "La réforme intellectuelle et morale de la France." In it the French Revolution, the republic, democracy, and universal suffrage are all put on trial in the name of realism and the will to power.[60] It is a deplorable work. Mazzini perceived at once its rotten core: the unconscionable regress to the glorification of military force, in the manner that Prussia had made its own,[61] and the exhortation to France to reconstitute itself on the Prussian model, vigorous and feudal, with a strong monarchy and a strong nobility—provided that France was still able, and not yet moribund.[62]

Sedan and Metz and the capitulation of Paris inspired Renan's final judgment on the evils afflicting France: the essence of modern democracy is a lack of abnegation and an asperity in demanding individual rights, and war is its polar opposite. The democratic spirit makes war an impossibility. Democracy is the most potent solvent of military organization, and the German victory was the victory of the disciplined individual over the undisciplined one. It was both a victory for science and reason, and a victory for the ancien régime, for the principle that denies the sovereignty of the people and the right of human populations to decide their own destiny. That sovereignty and this right, far from strengthening a race, disarm it and render it unfit for any military undertaking, and to make

---

Renan: La guerre de '70 et la "Réforme' de la France (Paris, 1949), who vice versa highlights in a nationalistic spirit and with evident partiality everything that can possibly damage Renan, and sometimes hits his mark (so for example at pp. 315 ff. on *La réforme*). Cf. my review in *Rivista Storica Italiana* 61 (1949): 446 ff., in which I also touch on the Goncourt question.

[57] From 1852: the reason for the tired somnolence of France is, he says, democracy; "until now the world belonged to thought, to action, to the class that under one form or another lived most fully; the head used to govern, now the stomach is taking over, and the stomach loves repose" (*Correspondance, 1846–1871*, pp. 57–58 and cf. p. 66). Note also the preface to the *Essais de morale et de critique* (dated 28 April 1859), now in *Oeuvres complètes* 2:16 ff.

[58] *La réforme*, pp. 25 ff., 31 ff., 47, 49, 115. At p. 43: "a democratic country cannot be well governed, well administered, well commanded."

[59] *Journal des Goncourt* 4:28: I prefer peasants as they are in Germany where they get kicked in the behind, says Renan, to peasants like ours, whom the universal suffrage has turned into our masters. Peasants are "the inferior element of civilization, imposed on us by . . . this government [Second Empire]." Here again Goncourt's account is confirmed by Renan's own words: "the superior morality of the German people comes from the fact that down to our time they have been very ill-treated" (*La réforme*, p. 40). And cf. p. 15: the universal suffrage of 1848 only served the interests of five million peasants, strangers to any liberal notion; and p. 68: "the people properly so called, and the peasants, today the masters of the house, are really only intruders in it, drones who have taken over a hive they never built."

[60] Cf. Reclus, *L'avènement de la 3 république*, p. 137; Halévy, *La fin des notables*, p. 71; A. Bellessort, *Les intellectuels et l'avènement de la troisième République*, pp. 135 ff.

[61] For Renan, only the Prussians and the Russians are refusing to follow "this way of materialism, of vulgar republicanism towards which the whole modern world . . . seems to be turning" (*La réforme*, p. 82).

[62] When Déroulède asked him to join the *Ligue des Patriotes*, Renan replied: "Young man, France is dying, don't disturb its death throes" (Fisher, "French Nationalism," p. 151).

things worse they do not prevent it from putting itself in the hands of a government that makes it commit the stupidest blunders.[63] Civilization is the work of aristocracies, of a small number. The soul of a nation is purely aristocratic. Universal suffrage is a heap of sand, not a nation.[64] Hence the final corollary: war is a necessity, the only means to avoid the debasement of the human race. War is the precondition of progress, the lash that keeps a nation from drowsing off into slumber, and if all of humanity should one day become an enormous and pacific Roman empire, with no external enemies, on that day morality and intelligence would be in the gravest jeopardy.[65]

As with the disciple Peter and his Lord, the historian of the life of Jesus now denied in this manner fifty years of European thought, of his own thought, renouncing the dream of peaceful progress through the collaborative effort of the nations, above all the collaborative effort of France and Germany. He wasn't alone. Taine as well had been prey for some time to *des idées grises* concerning France, and now he saw the gray turning to black,[66] as he lost faith in all political systems founded on the best in human nature and became just as haughtily antidemocratic as Renan,[67] while absorbing nothing of the latter's persistent Germanism. Taine too was averse to the idolatry of the greatest number and was persuaded that after eighty years France had still not found a suitable political system.[68] Convinced that it was everyone's duty to make a contribution to politics, and his own duty in particular to make it in the form of history,[69] Taine began his *Origines de la France contemporaine*, a solemn summary of the prosecution case against the French Revolution, which was here stripped of the poetic and mystic aura in which it had been wrapped, and was in the last analysis accused of guilt for the disasters of 1870.[70]

---

[63] *La réforme*, pp. 54–55 and cf. pp. 66, 76 (with pointed shafts against the *francs tireurs*, meaning volunteers like Gambetta).

[64] Renan and Berthelot, *Correspondance*, p. 395 (26 February 1871); cf. *La réforme*, p. 47.

[65] *La réforme*, p. 111.

[66] Taine, *Correspondance* 3:55.

[67] Taine, *Correspondance* 3:172, 225, 284, 326 ff., 348 ff. Cf. his opuscule on *Suffrage universel* (Paris, 1871).

[68] Taine, *Les Origines de la France contemporaine* 1, preface.

[69] Taine, *Correspondance* 3:48, 90, 115, 175 (the decision to write *Les Origines* is made between April and May 1871). Cf. Giraud, *Essai sur Taine*, pp. 90 ff. and 190 ff.

[70] Taine's reprise of Burkean antirevolutionary ideas, noted by Omodeo (*La cultura francese nell'età della Restaurazione*, pp. 235 and 249, n. 3; also Giraud, *Essai sur Taine*, p. 95), and in any case asserted by the author himself (Taine, *Correspondance* 4:122), derives from his basic point of view, and also from his state of mind. For him the Revolution had been "an insurrection against humans by mules and horses, led by 'apes with the larynxes of parrots'" (Taine, *Correspondance* 3:266; and cf. G. Hanotaux, *Mon temps* 2:164–65 [Paris, 1938]).

But far from being confined to Taine, this state of mind was common to virtually all French intellectuals after 1870 (cf. R. Stadelmann, "Hippolyte Taine und die politische Gedankenwelt des französischen Bürgertums," in *Deutschland und Westeuropa* [Schloss Laupheim, 1948], pp. 61 ff.). In September 1847 Renan had been willing to defend the "sublime" aspect of the French Revolution against his friend Berthelot (Renan and Berthelot, *Correspondance*, pp. 31–32), and at the beginning of 1851 to state that he held "the normal French bias" where the Revolution was concerned (*Essais de morale et de critique*, in *Oeuvres complètes* 2:16). But over the course of the Second Empire, and because of it, Renan revised his earlier opinions (*Correspondance, 1846–1871*, pp. 50 and 154, and *Essais de morale*, loc. cit.) and concluded that for France the nineteenth century was "an expiation

Flaubert, irascible, tormented, and gloomy, was more violent still, a total enemy of democracy[71] who had no more illusions and doubted the very possibility
of progress, of civilization, of a role for literature;[72] who was convinced that the
prime remedy for the state of things would be to do away with universal suffrage,
"the shame of the human spirirt,"[73] and that the great Revolution had been an
"abortion."[74] He had no taste for 4 September, for the war, for the Commune, for
the Republic, it all disgusted him,[75] and he had the sensation that after paganism
and Christianity, the third great phase of human evolution was now dawning—
the epoch of what he called *boorism*.[76]

And there were others who felt the same, like the bewildered, antidemocratic,
and antirepublican Edmond de Goncourt;[77] faced with the overwhelming victories of the Prussian armed forces, they now wondered what value to attribute to
ideas as a factor in history. The situation was one of moral deflation, of disorientation even among the leading figures of French thought,[78] and it would only be
worsened by the Commune,[79] which had the lasting effect of pushing those men
of letters and thinkers into the camp of pure conservatism, into phobic fear of
revolution and democracy, into acknowledgment of the God of the army and the
police forces, the only guarantor of victory on the battlefield and order in the
streets of the city.

Once before, following the dictatorship of Napoleon I, French thought had
revolted against the theories of popular sovereignty and universal suffrage that
had in practice led to the Napoleonic pseudo-plebiscites, and to the dissolution of
democratic sovereignty into despotism.[80] But then, at least there had been *la*

---

for our Revolution" ("La monarchie constitutionelle en France," written in 1869 and reprinted in *La
réforme*, pp. 237 ff.).

[71] "I hate democracy." Democratic egalitarianism seems to Flaubert to be an element of death in
the world (*Correspondance* 4:55 and 232). The faith of Gambetta's party in universal suffrage drove
Flaubert wild (J. Adam, *Mes angoisses et nos luttes, 1871–73* [Paris, 1907], p. 384), whereas
Renan's *La réforme* seemed to him "very good, his ideas are similar to mine" (*Correspondance*
4:87). See further, in general, Reclus, *L'avènement de la 3 république*, p. 139; Halévy, *La fin des
notables*, p. 72; Bellessort, *Les intellectuels*, pp. 34 ff.

[72] *Correspondance* 4:42 and cf. p. 46: "I never took myself for a progressive and a humanitarian,
of course. Still, I had illusions! But what barbarism! What a regression! I have it in for my
contemporaries for having given me the feelings of a brute of the twelfth century! *I am suffocating in
bile!*" He concludes that one must believe in nothing: "it is the beginning of wisdom" (ibid., p. 55).

[73] *Correspondance* 4:74 and cf. also pp. 29, 79, and 82.

[74] "We are wallowing in the afterbirth of the Revolution, which was an abortion, a failed
enterprise, a flop, 'whatever they say'" (ibid., p. 73). There must be an end of the French Revolution
as a dogma, and it must reenter the domain of exact knowledge, like everything else human (ibid.,
p. 48). This is precisely Taine's position.

[75] "Oh how sick I am of ignoble workers, inept bourgeois, stupid peasants, and odious clerics!"
(ibid., p. 71).

[76] Ibid., p. 44. [*Translator's note:* "boorism" renders Flaubert's *muflisme*].

[77] *Journal des Goncourt* 4, passim (for example, pp. 150–51).

[78] Bellessort, *Les intellectuels*, stresses this, but his analysis is very tendentiously
antidemocratic.

[79] One may note the "dry despair" and the mute anger of Taine at the Commune (*Correspondance*
3:77). Théophile Gautier repeated "je crève de la Commune" ["the Commune disgusts me to death"],
and according to Flaubert, he died from "la charognerie moderne" ["the putridity of modern life"]
(Flaubert, *Correspondance* 4:123).

[80] Cf. Omodeo, *La cultura francese*, p. 47.

gloire, which not even 1814 and Waterloo could tarnish, because 1814 and Waterloo were felt as defeats for Napoleon, not for France, and at Vienna France had not been humiliated; however much the political commentators of the Restoration might hate military glory and reject its seductions,[81] it remained dear to a large part of the people as the visible legacy of the First Empire, still engraved in the hearts of the masses and destined before long to be proudly displayed and extolled once again. But now it was different; not just the renewal of internal dictatorship but an external catastrophe never seen before in the illustrious history of France; not only despotism flowing from plebiscites and popular sovereignty but a climax of ignominious defeat, with France overrun and trampled, Metz and Strasbourg lost. And this time it was not a defeat for the usurper alone, for after Sedan the loser was no longer Napoleon III but France itself, the France of Gambetta and Jules Favre and Thiers; France whose capital, Paris, was besieged, bombarded, forced to capitulate and to watch the Prussian soldiers marching down the Champs Elysées; France forced to sue for peace and to accept it in the harsh and humiliating form imposed by the enemy.

Reform was necessary. Renan offered a prescription and thereby became the spokesman for the same attitudes that, on the concrete political plane, found expression in the electoral triumph of the conservative and monarchist forces, with their nostalgia for a historical pageant of kingship, nobility, and warfare. What a trick of fate, to ally at this juncture the writer who detested clericalism, and was detested by it, with that same clericalism, so closely allied to monarchism, the nobility, and the army! At least in Flaubert's case, the writer dreamed of a legitimate aristocracy of "mandarins," meaning men of learning and culture, able to govern that eternal adolescent, the people:[82] though the degree of unreality involved was much greater, the illusion was much more conformable to the mind and spirit of a member of the clerisy of intellectuals.

Differently than in Italy, therefore, the "lesson of things" in France led not only to appreciation for force and detachment from the old Europeanist dreams but also to a shaply antidemocratic and even antiliberal polemic. Differently than in Italy, where it was mainly men of the Left and old revolutionaries like Crispi who proclaimed themselves realists, political realism in France grew up mainly among conservatives and appeared at this stage to convey nostalgia for a certain version of the past. In parallel with this the rift between the old upper classes and the *nouvelles couches sociales* was widening, finding political expression in the struggle over radicalism and marking the early phase of the Third Republic. In the course of this dispute the radicals were destined to be the winners on the specifically political and parliamentary terrain. But something survived of that

---

[81] Ibid., p. 48, n. 1. This is the burden of Benjamin Constant's *De l'esprit de conquête et d'usurpation* (in his *Cours de politique constitutionnelle*, ed. Laboulaye).

[82] Flaubert, *Correspondance* 4:55–56 and cf. p. 73. Renan too had at one time imagined that perhaps in the future France would have an institution analogous to the "lettrés chinois" [the mandarins of China], with government becoming the appanage of the "competent," that is of a sort of academy of moral and political sciences (cf. H. Jaspar, *Ernest Renan et sa république* [Paris, 1934], p. 65). But now he had recovered from the dreams and illusions of his youth, as he said in 1890 in the preface to *L'Avenir de la Science*.

mentality of crisis into which such a large part of the higher French intelligentsia had plunged as a result of Sedan and Metz: it was a need for force, meaning no longer the force of ideas, but rather the force of arms and men; it was the invocation of a politics of realism, capable of detaching itself from the desires and preferences of the masses and (on the Prussian example, whether silently or explicitly) directing the ship of state with a firm hand while ignoring empty ideological rhetoric in favor of concrete and well-defined interests. It was a powerful stimulus to the formation of nationalistic doctrines.

There was another tendency of very different origin which also stood out clearly after 1870, and which ultimately led to the same result. The sudden collapse of the second Napoleonic empire endowed those who had tenaciously opposed the foreign policy of that empire with new legitimacy, and appeared to verify completely their critique of the principle of nationality. To obey the principle of nationality had been the capital mistake of Napoleon III, leading him astray to the detriment of France and the benefit of Italy and even of Prussia: France's true interest had been sacrificed to that "absurd" principle.[83] Thus the old hostility of the opponents of the Second Empire, from Thiers to Broglie, found easy justification in the disaster of Sedan, and also in the failure of Italy to send assistance—Italy, the creature of Napoleon III, Italy which at the moment of truth had deserted its benefactor and demonstrated that the politics of sentimentality was the stupidest politics of all. Only a dreamer like Napoleon III could have fooled himself into thinking differently: a dreamer who was also a dilettante, a man without expertise. It took Napoleonic ignorance of the political traditions of France to get caught that badly in a trap like the principle of nationality. Taine stripped the Revolution of its mystic aura; Albert Sorel removed the halo with which Mazzini and Michelet had surrounded the principle of nationality, presenting it not as an ideal but simply as a tactical weapon in the hands of governments, an instrument equally apt in the service of grand designs and noble initiatives, and in that of gross appetite for power. Force—ineluctable— remained the sovereign reason of kings and nations.[84]

But it needs to be applied properly, and for that a long immersion in the world of the past is required, a sound knowledge of the diplomatic and political traditions of a country, which alone can provide a sure feel for its real interests and give the stateman the proper context in which to frame his actions. The practitioners of politics in the Second Empire had brought France to catastrophe because they lacked such sound knowledge.[85] This charge, made on all sides by legitimists and republicans, nobles and plebeians,[86] had been aired on 5 Septem-

---

[83] Duc de Broglie, *Mémoires* 3:16 (Paris, 1941). For de Broglie's criticism of the principle of nationality in 1863 and 1868, cf. G. Fagniez, *Le duc de Broglie, 1821–1901* (Paris, 1902), pp. 64 ff.

[84] A. Sorel, *Histoire diplomatique de la guerre franco-allemande* 1:372–73 (Paris, 1875).

[85] So thought both Sorel and Taine (Hanotaux, *Mon temps* 2:155, and cf. Sorel's preface to the *Histoire diplomatique*). It was the view of de Broglie as well that Napoleon III had overturned all the traditions of French politics (cf. n. 83). As for Thiers, his opinion was that in foreign policy Napoleon III understood nothing: "he was a dreamer who had absurd ideas about European affairs, and knew nothing" (E. L. G. de Marcère, *L'assemblée nationale de 1871*, vol. 2, *La présidence du maréchal de Mac-Mahon* [Paris, 1907], p. 43; a direct statement of Thiers to the author).

[86] Nolde, *L'Alleanza franco-russa*, p. 20.

ber 1870 by the first Republican minister for foreign affairs, Jules Favre, who was neither a reactionary nor a nationalist: "France embarked on this war isolated in the midst of a hostile Europe. The government that senselessly flung us into this formidable gamble had failed to think of any alliance, offer any treaty, foresee any alignment." It was necessary to revive this forgotten wisdom in order to get France back on its feet. The result was a massive effort in the postwar years, when all persons of distinction desired to assist the reconstruction of their beaten and dejected country, and the younger and more energetic ones apportioned the various tasks among themselves, some in historiography, others in fiction or in poetry.[87] So it was that while Taine renounced his purely speculative studies and began the *Origines* for the purpose of instructing his countrymen, Sorel set himself the goal of recalling France to its luminous traditions in foreign policy, and began *L'Europe et la Révolution française*, the other great work in which the French historiography of the late nineteenth century subjected all that had been said and thought concerning the revolutionary event to a process of revision.[88] Thirty years before, spurred by the preoccupations of liberal thought in the early nineteeth century, Tocqueville had looked for continuity between the periods preceding and following the Revolution in the internal structure of the country. Sorel now looked to the area of international relations and became the preceptor of the diplomats of the Quai d'Orsay.

The hard, firsthand experience of seeing right trampled by force and military power (which is how every Frenchman interpreted without hesitation the peace of Frankfurt and the loss of Alsace-Lorraine), and the consequent return to the past, produced a natural result: a fresh regard for the old criteria, for policies of equilibrium and alliance that aimed at creating a French "system" in Europe against potential rivals. In place of the foolish and woolly principle of nationality, the cause of so much grief, in whose name Alsace-Lorraine had in the end been carved off from France,[89] it was finally time to restore the principle of European equilibrium, the diplomatic gospel of the past and, so it was hoped, of the future.[90] This was the old axiom of centuries of French history, a history of power, prestige, and *grandeur* capable of beguiling the understanding of those who immersed themselves in it looking for prescriptions for the present.[91] No more love for all the different homelands, as Michelet, who looked to "his" Germany, "his" Italy, and "his" Poland, had said,[92] only love for one's proper homeland, for France and France alone.

So it was that gradually the desire to stick close to reality, not to lose oneself in

---

[87] This general frame of mind is well portrayed in Hanotaux, *Mon temps* 1:249–50 (Paris, 1933).

[88] This intention is already evident in the preface to *Histoire diplomatique de la guerre franco-allemande*, vol. 1. For Sorel this really became his life's mission, to which he sacrificed everything, including the chance to take a direct part in politics; cf. Hanotaux, *Mon temps* 1:330–31, and 2:154 ff., and also his *Sur les chemins de l'histoire* 2:213–14 and 218.

[89] Cf. Charles Gavard, *Un diplomate à Londres: Lettres et notes, 1871–1877*, p. 9

[90] Duc de Broglie, *Mémoires* 1:330 (Paris, 1938).

[91] This comes out very clearly in the case of Hanotaux, who began to fall under the spell of Henri IV and Richelieu and ended as an enthusiast, while foreign minister, for the policy of colonial expansion (*Mon temps* 1:315–17, and 2:34–37).

[92] Michelet's notes from 1854; G. Monod, *Jules Michelet*, pp. 33 and 35.

the fumes of idealism but rather to reach back across the vacuous intermezzo of
the Second Empire and reconnect with the prudent guidance of the past, led once
more to velleities of power politics based on the old maxims of spheres of influence and vassal states, a politics full of sacred egoism and free of sentimental
"mistakes."[93] And, here as elsewhere, the incipient spirit of nationalism received
continual and subtle nourishment from this turn. It took its antidemocratic animus from Taine; and from Sorel, the ideal mentor of France's diplomats for half
a century, the taste of grandeur, the drive for power, the feeling for "positive"
results and lasting edifices,[94] and the firm belief, typically German, in the "primacy" of foreign policy. *Fin de siècle* nationalism drew on many different
sources.[95]

An enhanced appreciation for realism and force, and skepticism about large
idealistic notions (though they did have their tactical uses)—these were the upshot of the Prussian victories of 1870. Ideals declined, including the ideal of
liberty, which in light of the Paris Commune was treated with a much cooler sort
of affection. Reality ruled;[96] *Comprendre et apprendre pour agir* was the new
watchword, signifying that the ultimate goal was action and that all the rest, even
culture, served only as the means.[97] On one hand, as Alberto Blanc had said,
there was positive science, meaning science applied to industry, and the astonish-
ing progress it was making, the productivity and the force of technology.[98] On
the other there was politics as a like science of solid and secure things, with
affects and ideals banished and principles set aside: politics as numerically calculable power and force.

The two things—technical progress, gigantic industrial development, implacable rationality in the conduct of business, and in political life evolution toward
a type of state ever more quantitatively forceful in terms of wealth, arms, organization, extension, and colonies—helped each other along. The small artisanal
business enterprise declined, as did the ideal of the small state cherished by the
Enlightenment and Romanticism, by Montesquieu, Rousseau, Sismondi, Adam

[93] Thus Chaudordy, who in the winter of 1870–71 directed from Tours the foreign policy of the
government of National Defense (*La France à la suite de la guerre de 1870–1871* [2d ed.; Paris,
1887], p. 95).

[94] Hanotaux, *Sur les chemins de l'histoire* 2:211–12.

[95] For the influence of Taine on Barrès, cf. P. H. Petitbon, *Taine, Renan, Barrès: Étude
d'influence* (Paris, n.d. but 1935), pp. 98 ff.

[96] "The era of positivism in politics is going to commence," Flaubert, *Correspondance* 4:67; "so
many crimes have been committed by the ideal in politics that it will be necessary for some time to do
nothing but 'administer our assets'" (ibid., p. 77 and cf. p. 79). This is a leitmotife of the dark and
despondent Flaubert, who had the feeling of slipping over a precipice into a period of human
degradation: "I am convinced that we are entering a hideous world in which people like us will have
no more reason to exist. We will all be utilitarian, military, economic, small, poor, abject" (ibid.,
pp. 34, 39, 41, 46). Hence he is irritated by the enthusiasm of others: "your enthusiasm for the
Republic deeply annoys me. At a time when we are dominated by the most unambiguous positivism,
how can you still believe in phantoms?" (from a letter to Georges Sand, ibid., p. 32).

[97] Reclus, *L'avènement de la 3 république*, p. 143.

[98] It is worth noting that a scientist of the caliber of Berthelot deplored, in 1873, this triumph of
applied science and industrialism; and that he deplored it in relation to Italy, which he had hoped to
see revive the spiritual élan of the Italian Renaissance following its unification; whereas he was now
forced ruefully to acknowledge that Italy was doing no more than imitate the example of the United
States by attending to the applications of science (*Journal des Goncourt* 5:95).

Müller, its place taken now by states on a grand scale.[99] Both of these phenomena in turn are only aspects of a single historical process, in which quantity tended ever increasingly to prevail over quality, big industry over craftsmanship, big states over small ones, masses of voters over personal values, numerical weight over the refinements of culture and intelligence.

But Benjamin Constant had erred in predicting that an age of commerce would replace an age of war,[100] anticipating Cobden's optimism about the new commercial spirit and its capacity to spread peace and prosperity in the world. Commerce would be the ally of war. The peoples strong in manufacturing and commerce, contrary to the belief of the young Minghetti,[101] would not refrain from spilling blood, and wars would gain in terrible destructiveness what they lost in length of time in comparison with the protracted warfare of the Middle Ages. The triumph of commerce had been interpreted by those earlier optimists as the triumph of the spirit of peace and the relinquishment of the appetite for military conquest, together with disdain for the glory of war. But military glory kept its allure, and indeed the spirit of conquest looked to considerations of economic utility for justification and pretext (and often enough found genuine motivation) to outstrip rivals and crush dangerous competition. The old abhorrent political spirit of conquest was not absorbed into, but rather absorbed into itself, the economic outlook of business. So it was that in a world that bound its different parts to one another more tightly every day by ties of economic interdependence, and in which it seemed that petty and antiquated frontier questions in Europe would be reduced to irrelevance, Europe's frontier questions continued to be the decisive factor capable of toppling all of humanity into conflicts never seen before. The "nationalitarian" spirit erupted into history and unleashed the peoples against each other; as Mirabeau had discerned,[102] the wars of the ancien régime seemed child's play compared to the modern ones. Commerce joined with liberty had been the message of the Manchester school: but the triumph of protectionism would reveal before long that dreams of universal harmony were finished.

This was the essence of the new reality, a reality comprising many elements that were becoming more pressing as the pace of change modern life picked up. In all of its aspects the relative importance of the numerical was growing. Even Bismarck's *Realpolitik* ended up being no more than a manifestation of the same general spirit, a spirit destined to rule the world of the next generations, and the Prussian chancellor became the political incarnation of a historical trend that swept all the various forms of life along with it.[103] Marco Minghetti in old age,

---

[99] Cf. W. Kaegi, "Der Kleinstaat im europäischen Denken," in *Historische Meditationen* 1:251 ff., and my own "L'idea di Europa," *Rassegna d'Italia* 2, no. 5 (May 1947): 33 ff.

[100] *De l'esprit de conquête et d'usurpation*, in *Cours de politique constitutionnelle* 2:140–41 and 179.

[101] Minghetti, *Della economia pubblica e delle sue attinenze colla morale e col diritto*, pp. 494–95.

[102] Cf. P. R. Rohden, *Die klassische Diplomatie von Kaunitz bis Metternich*, pp. 35–36.

[103] On the dawn of a new era in all fields, intellectual, economic, and political, cf. the acute observations in R. C. Binkley, *Realism and Nationalism, 1852–1871* (vol. 16 of *The Rise of Modern Europe*, ed. W. L. Langer), p. 306.

tired and discouraged, took cognizance of it: "we believed in justice and liberty; today they believe in force and in number."[104]

Force: and in place of Mazzini's sermons in the name of humanity, and Cattaneo's appeals for a United States of Europe, and Balbo's and d'Azeglio's equation of public and private morality, one heard Droysen's warning that the political world is ruled by the laws of power as the physical world is by the laws of gravity,[105] of Treitschke's that the state is force, and its duty the preservation of power; those insufficiently virile to face this fact should take up other pursuits than politics. [106] Force: if it provoked feelings of revulsion, that made no difference, as long as it gave its possessor material security. *Oderint dum metuant* became, more than ever, an axiom of politics with Bismarck as its exemplar, as when he declared that in dealing with the French the best thing was to have one's frontiers well fortified. Even his ill-concealed contempt for men in general was part of the paradigm. He was truly called a "club of a man" destined to be "a source of amazement and terror for all, but not in the next world."[107] His lieutenants were cast in the same mold, among them Schweinitz, the ambassador at Vienna, who in 1872, when he observed the animosity, the envy, fear, and hatred directed from all sides against Germany, drew the conclusion that, though moderate and accommodating, the Germans had no choice but to become stronger.

There was another factor, this time an intellectual system, that played a role in augmenting the desire for power and making competition the ideal of life for the upcoming generations, in rendering men habitually indifferent to principles so that they might better be trained in the hardness of attitude that the times required: this was Darwinian evolutionism, accompanied by the evolutionary sociology of Spencer.[108] It exercised a tremendous power of attraction, as though the struggle for existence, the necessity of adaptation to the environment, and things of this sort, amounted to precise scientific equations for what was going on in the real world, where the dominant states were practicing the politics of force, and huge industrial and commercial complexes were engaged in merciless competition. This novel idiom soon found proselytes in Italy, and as they spoke the Risorgimento died away and a new age was born. Here is Pasquale Turiello in 1882:

> The grand leagues of brotherhood that Italian and French philosophers dreamed of, and Napoleon III tried to bring about, are vanishing along with the other ideals of

---

[104] From a letter to Luigi Torelli of 21 October 1886 (not 1887!), in A. Monti, *Il conte Luigi Torelli, 1810–1887*, p. 322. Similarly, from a letter to Queen Margherita of 22 September 1886: "the moral sentiment has lost ground in politics, and is losing more every day, making way for force and force alone" (Minghetti, *Lettere fra la regina Margherita e Marco Minghetti*, p. 268).

[105] Droysen, *Historik*, ed. Hübner, p. 352.

[106] Treitschke, *La Politica* 1:87, 99. Cf. F. Meinecke, *Die Idee der Staatsräson in der neueren Geschichte* (Munich-Berlin, 1924), pp. 508–509.

[107] From a letter of the Countess Alessandrina Tolstoi to General von Schweinitz, February 1871 (*Briefwechsel des Botschafters General von Schweinitz* [Berlin, 1928], p. 72).

[108] See the brilliant analysis of Langer, *La diplomazia dell'imperialismo* 1:145 ff.; and R. Hofstadter, *Social Darwinism in American Thought* (Philadelphia, 1945), p. 147. (I was unable to see C. J. H. Hayes, *A Generation of Materialism, 1871–1900* [New York, 1941]).

the century, which has already become an age of iron through economic rivalry, through heightened mutual suspicion, through zeal for arms. Now the same virile exigency that in the past made every Greek and Roman citizen a soldier has returned and is spreading from a few citites out over vast nations. Each of them fixes its gaze on possible enemies. Every one of the great states is hurrying to grab as much, and as fast as it can, of the territories around the Mediterranean that are still without a strong master. All the others, even France, knew what they wanted and got it, whether in Tunis or Egypt. But Italy knows that what it wants is insignificant, or that it doesn't want anything. While others grin it attempts to dress up its irresolution as pudor, betraying its future generations. It pretends to be the guardian of right and peace, the impartial judge of the other nations, but it has not bolstered its own authority, and the sanctions it proposes are limp.[109]

Turiell often rehearsed his favorite themes: there was the theme of the struggle for existence among the nations, and there was the notion that certain peoples were fated to fall behind in the vital contest while those "better adapted to the new arrangements" surged ahead. Indeed he often indulged in prophecies about the "imminent danger of a worldwide struggle for survival."[110] Not coincidentally, Turiello was to become, not long after, the first self-aware and systematic Italian imperialist.[111]

Four years later, Novikov contended that "international politics is the art of carrying on the struggle for existence between social organisms,"[112] and Oriani joined in this fashionable evolutionism, adopting its slogans about the struggle for life, which among peoples signifies making war.[113]

Crispi protested at this, as he had protested against racist ideas. Though at heart a nationalist and therefore perfectly attuned to the new epoch, his conceptual world was still that of the first half of the nineteenth century.[114] So once again he was undercut by the internal logic of the situation and was unable to

---

[109] Turiello, *Governo e governati in Italia* 2:311–12 (with a few alterations in the second edition, vol. 2, pp. 215–16).

[110] Ibid., 2:313, 320, 326. Turiello applies the same Darwinian and Spencerian terminology in discussing the "organic institutions that maximally adapt capacities to the limit." The allusion to these ideas in E. Tagliacozzo, *Voci di realismo politico dopo il 1870* (Bari, 1937), p. 59, is insufficiently elaborated. See instead the accurate observations of C. Curcio in the introduction to P. Turiello, *Il secolo XIX ed altri scritti di politica internazionale e coloniale* (Bologna, 1947), pp. xix ff. Nor is Turiello alone: there were those who proclaimed themselves not conservative, not radical, not monarchist, not republican, but "evolutionarian" (Di Cagno-Politi, *Saggi di politica positiva* [Naples, 1881], p. 7); and others investigated the consequences of evolutionism on politics (A. Valdamini, *Dottrina dell'evoluzione e sue principali conseguenze teoriche e pratiche* [Florence, 1882]).

[111] Curcio, loc. cit., pp. 20 ff.

[112] Langer, *La diplomazia dell'imperialismo* 1:147.

[113] Oriani, *Fino a Dogali*, p. 146.

[114] "Certainly the predominance of philosophical and atomistic theories in anthropology and history, legitimating the struggle for existence and explaining how the most highly endowed and strongest animal races must of necessity take the place of the weaker races, has in the end created a saturnine philosophy, according to which, if the fathers do not devour their children, the children will devour the fathers. These things have been said, repeated, and confuted many times thanks to that other philosophy which recognizes a creative force in human instincts that does not submit to the brutality of physical nature" (Crispi, *Scritti e discorsi politici*, p. 674).

grasp that overbearing national pride was really a contributing factor, or rather the principal factor, in this harsh struggle for existence among the peoples—the factor that, more than any other, risked letting loose on mankind the brutality of the physical world, as though to corroborate the bleak aphorism of Grillparzer: "from humanity, through nationality, to bestiality.[115]

---

[115] *Sprüche und Epigramme, Zeitgemässes (Der ewige Grillparzer* [Linz, 1947], p. 591).

Against the "Realism" of Bismarck

MOST ITALIAN POLITICIANS of the Right, in contrast to many of the figures examined in the preceding chapter, were much more strongly disposed to withstand the onslaught of the new ideas on the intellectual and moral code to which they adhered; this was true of those then in government, and those who supported the government in parliament, or the newspapers, or in some other area of public life.

Though they curtly denied the charge of servility,[1] these men were not blind to the unquestionable fact that Italian policy had operated in the shadow of French policy, even in 1866, so that the new kingdom had had its liberty of action cramped to a great extent, and its personality diminished. Visconti Venosta very clearly acknowledged this in a long letter to de Launay of early March 1871 in which he analyzed Italian-German relations: "the Roman question was the fetter that reduced our freedom of action, and made our policy dependent for a long time on that of the French. Now this fetter is broken, and it is in everybody's interest that it not be reforged. The resolution of the Roman question, and the neutrality we maintained during the recent war, have given independence to Italy's political situation."[2]

Artom, a firm supporter of neutrality, had already said as much, on the grounds that if Italy should commit "the grave error of throwing in its lot with that of France on this occasion, the result would be that our assistance would not keep France from suffering defeat, but the kingdom of Italy would be seen by Europe as a mere appendage of the Napoleonic structure, destined to disappear along with the Second Empire."[3] France's claims on Rome were "the symbol of the vassalage to France that all of Europe accuses us of."[4] Considerations of this order, along with a concern that the war not become generalized, dragging in

---

[1] Cf. Bonghi, "La monarchia italiana e l'Impero francese," in *La Perseveranza* for 11 August 1870, a polemic against *La Riforma*: France is not the lord or Italy the vassal, despite what the Left says. Rather, "although there are . . . conflicting views and differences between us, which resulted from our reciprocal independence, and sealed it, the close understanding and alliance between our two governments that underlay the formation of Italy remains unshaken."

[2] Visconti Venosta, private letter to de Launay of 7 March 1871 (ACR, *Carte Visconti Venosta*, pacco 5, fasc. 2). The foreign minister insists on the same points at other places in the letter: "[by remaining neutral] Italy . . . showed . . . that it is a morally autonomous power, independent of the European concert." Analogous ideas are found in another private letter of Visconti Venosta to de Launay of 18 October 1870 (in the Visconti Venosta archive); and in Minghetti, who in writing to Visconti Venosta on 22 October 1870, observed: "the disappearance of the Emperor (and what a miserable disappearance!) has left us much freer to act" (ibid.).

[3] Artom, private letter to Visconti Venosta from Vienna, 17 August 1870 (Visconti Venosta archive). On 24 February 1871, Artom professed these views again to Nigra: "for Italy the direct brunt of the events . . . of last year, would have cost it both unity and life. Our inertia was blameless, and we have preserved our existence" (AE, *Carte Nigra*).

[4] Artom to Visconti Venosta, from Vienna, 30 July 1870 (Visconti Venosta archive).

Austria and therefore Russia, and fomenting a European conflict whose outcome might have threatened the very existence of the Kingdom of Italy, had in fact inspired the policies of Visconti Venosta, who thanks largely to Sella had succeeded in playing for time and had thus been able to come out of an extremely difficult situation without damage.[5] Neutrality during the Franco-Prussian War and the establishment of Rome as Italy's capital therefore constituted proof in the eyes of everyone, including the moderates, that united Italy was not just an ephemeral Napoleonic creation.

Furthermore, there were moderates like Stefano Jacini, not to speak of Ricasoli, who complained as much as those on the Left about the passion for following after France and taking it faithfully for a model.[6] It was even generally conceded that France had done much to cause the war to erupt. Nigra himself, for whom such a concession came at a high price, did not hesitate to affirm: "the war was begun by France unjustly, and against the principles of its own policy. And when I say France I mean not only the Emperor Napoleon and the French Government, but the country, since the Legislature, with the exception of a few members of the Left, the Senate, the press, the public meetings, were all unanimous, or almost unanimous, in wanting and approving the conflict."[7]

But such an admission did not conduce, as in the case of de Launay and Crispi, to an attitude of hostility to France and open sympathy for Prussia. Men like Visconti Venosta, Nigra, Lanza, Dina, and Bonghi could perfectly well own this and more; they could perfectly well agree with Blanc, de Launay, and Crispi that the Franco-Prussian War and its aftermath brought an era of history to a close and opened a new one for all of Europe.[8] They could call to mind the words of Virgil, *novus ab incepto saeclorum nascitur ordo.*[9] But instead of greeting with joy the rising of a new sun over Europe, they viewed it with consternation.

Sentimentally they were still bound to France, the great teacher of civilization that had so deeply influenced the formation of Italian thought in general, and specifically that of the moderates, between 1830 and 1848; and to the loser of Sedan, Napoleon III, the man to whom, in spite of all, the Italians owed Magenta and Solferino, that is the first decisive step in their campaign of liberation, the step that had made all those that followed possible, and without which everything that came after would not even have been thinkable. "Sons of Magenta and Solferino": later on the phrase would sound like a crude piece of rhetoric, and sig-

---

[5] Guiccioli, *Quintino Sella* 1:263 ff.

[6] Stefano Francesco Jacini, *Sulle condizioni della cosa pubblica in Italia dopo il 1866*, p. 82. For Ricasoli, see above pp. 11–12.

[7] Nigra, report, 30 January 1871, no. 1386. Similar ideas are found in Ricasoli (*Lettere e documenti* 10:123) and in Amari, though the latter retained many personal ties to France (*Carteggio* 2:198).

[8] For example, personal letters of Visconti Venosta to de Launay, 7 March 1871 (cited above, n. 2), and Visconti Venosta to Nigra, 27 February 1871: "until now everything else was drowned out by the blare of the French catastrophe. Now that we have calm again in Europe, and the smoke of battle is dissipating, every government is looking about it to gauge this new Europe and the shape in which it finds itself in the situation following such shattering events" (Visconti Venosta archive).

[9] Nigra, private letter to Visconti Venosta, 6 March 1871 (ibid.; the quote is reproduced verbatim from Nigra's letter).

nify nothing, especially when it was drummed into generations who were born into an Italy already fully formed and were unable to relive the time of anxiety, hope, and fear, or the enthusiasm of the day when freedom was finally recovered, and so, as always happens with children and grandchildren, felt that their elders had been excessively grateful for the help received. In fact its validity was already being contested by those on the Left, who either found that the debt of gratitude had been generously paid off with Nice and Savoy,[10] not to mention Mentana, which had destroyed any sentimental bonds,[11] or else denied, following Mazzini, that there had ever been any debt of gratitude at all.

The customary terms for these two positions were *filofrancese* and *antifrancese* [pro- and anti-French], and the dissension between them was to a degree rooted in party politics, because the beaten emperor was recognized by both sides as the supporter, protector, even author of the fortune of the moderates,[12] and was either loved or hated for it, according to one's affiliation. But more than that, there was a fundamental and broader difference of opinion at work. Gratitude to Napoleon III came naturally to those by whom the Italian Risorgimento was seen as the work of the house of Savoy, a governmental creation that had been able to succeed because at a certain point the king of Sardinia and Piedmont had found a potent ally in the emperor of the French. There was no such gratitude on the part of those who saw the Risorgimento as the creation of revolutionary forces, the reward of passion and of a long effort of propaganda that had triumphed despite the repeated attempts of Napoleon III to impede the process, first at Villafranca, then at Aspromonte and finally at Mentana. The forces that made the Risorgi-

---

[10] For an example, see the proclamation of the party of action, published on 21 July 1870 in the *Gazzettino Rosa*, and signed by, among others, Cavallotti and Marcora: "considering that the services rendered by the Second Empire to Italy in a just cause . . . impose no obligation on Italy to show solidarity with it in an unjust cause; the more so in that those services were only a delayed repayment for all the Italian blood that was spilled for the First Empire, and were in any case repaid with interest after that at the cost of further blood, and money, and territory" (Arcari, *La Francia*, p. 135).

[11] From Crispi's speech to the Chamber of 3 February 1871: "Mentana . . . liberated our people from a moral servitude in which we had become entrapped" (*Discorsi Parlamentari* 2:88). The same attitude is seen in Rattazzi (M. L. Rattazzi, *Rattazzi et son temps* 2:339 [Paris, 1881]), and in De Sanctis (E. Cione, *Francesco De Sanctis*, pp. 194–95).

[12] On behalf of the Right, Bonghi acknowledges this as early as 31 July 1870: "Not only has the Emperor had a primary role in the formation of Italy as a nation and an independent state, but the nature and the strength of his government in France have been the principal reason that the political movement in Italy never turned into a real revolution. It is not he who has governed Italy; but if the moderate party in Italy has in the end remained in control, that is owing to the fact that in France he has firmly repressed all the evil humors, and hence reduced the level of poisonous acrimony that was spreading among us here. Even when his actions, as in the question of Rome, sometimes turned out to be galling and regrettable to the moderate party itself, in reality he was helping to reinforce the power it held. Because, if we want to be frank, we must admit that although the French flag flying in Rome was an irritant, yet it acted as a brake on the very people it irritated, and finally forced both the radicals and the moderates to shun the paths and the methods of revolution in the one Italian question that was most likely to turn heated and violent, if we had abandoned patient compromise and the use of moral suasion" (*Nove anni* 2:356–57). From the Left, *La Riforma* gives the same assessment at the death of Napoleon III: the moderate party owed its power to the late sovereign, without whose support it would not have lasted even for a year. Napoleon III was the real founder, the strong backbone of the moderate party in Italy ("Una difesa precoce" and "Mazzini e Napoleone III," 25 January and 2 February 1873).

mento, the royal initiative and the revolutionary initiative as they were called, were profoundly heterogeneous in a way whose consequences would soon be seen in debates on the problems of foreign policy, and which made the Italian national movement something utterly different to the German national movement, which was well and truly compacted around the monarch and the government. This heterogeneity emerged clearly in the problem at hand, for each side took up its preordained position, and neither was able to comprehend the point of view of the other.

Crispi had, it is true, come over to the side of the monarchy. But his soul (he himself liked to say) was still that of an old conspirator, convinced that Italy had been made by Mazzini, Garibaldi,[13] and even a little bit by himself—with a deep bow, a sincere one at the close of his years, to Vittorio Emanuele II. The egoistic intervention of Napoleon III had complicated more than it had furthered the cause; the decisive moment for unity had been, not 1859, but 1860 and the expedition of the Thousand. Cavour's contribution was scarcely appreciated by Crispi, and as prime minister he did not even pronounce the name of Cavour when on 20 September 1895 he unveiled the monument to Garibaldi on the Janiculum and spoke of the fathers of national unity;[14] this provoked a degree of outraged comment. The scant esteem for Cavour shown on this and other occasions by Crispi[15] as well as by his friends[16] was a meaningful indication of a way of seeing the Risorgimento that was the complete antithesis of the way it was seen by the moderates. In the crisis summer of 1870, *La Riforma* naturally took the opportunity to recall the "flaw" in Cavour's policy, meaning his accord with Napoleon III, and to portray the Italian "Revolution" as the key to national unification.[17] A few months later the paper claimed for itself and its adherents the

[13] He said this directly to Queen Margherita on 2 January 1897: "unity would not have been accomplished in Italy if Garibaldi and Mazzini had not placed themselves at the head of the movement, and if Vittorio Emanuele had not adhered to it, and acted as its captain" (*Politica estera* 1:281 n. 1).

[14] Vittorio Emanuele, Garibaldi, Mazzini (*Ultimi scritti*, p. 219).

[15] One day, after he had affirmed that the three great men to whom Italy owed its highest recognition were Vittorio Emanuele, Garibaldi, and above all Mazzini, Martini asked him, "And Cavour?" Crispi replied with a shrug of his shoulders: "Cavour? What did Cavour do? Nothing except *diplomatize* the revolution" (Martini, *Confessioni e ricordi*, p. 151). This judgment is implicit in the speech made by Crispi on the Janiculum. It reappears, much attenuated, in his speech to the Chamber of 18 May 1883, where the fact that they "diplomatized" the revolution is depicted as meritorious on the part of Cavour and Minghetti, "the bridlers of our impatience, who perhaps prevented Italy from plunging over a precipice because of our audacious and hasty actions" (*Discorsi Parlamentari* 2:647). But the reason for this statement was mainly Crispi's personal regard for Minghetti, who was present and whom he represents as the equal partner of Cavour. For Crispi, Cavour's great fault was always that of not having been "a supporter of unity before the fact."

[16] Cavour, "if he has no other true accomplishment that impartial history can record," will certainly have as titles of honor his belief in science and his support for the construction of the Cenisio tunnel! ("L'attività nazionale," in *La Riforma* for 28 December 1870). Occasionally the paper of the Left concedes a little more to the Piedmontese statesman, "who although weighed down by traditions, habits, and the party to which he fatally belonged, did not lack the vigor of the divine spark" (*La Riforma*, 25 June 1872, "Il sentimento nazionale"). Again on 29 October 1872 the paper recognizes that Cavour was able "to rise at times to being equal to events" and that although loyal to Napoleon III, he was never servile like his successors Visconti Venosta and Nigra.

[17] "Italia e Germania," in *La Riforma* for 8 August 1870: "until the time came when the thrust of

burden of serving as guardians of the unitary idea against the moderates, no less.[18] In both cases it emphasized the thesis that the revolutionary idea had been the first, the indispensable, in fact the only true forge of national liberation.

Certainly Visconti Venosta, Lanza, Nigra, Dina, Bonghi, and their sympathizers saw the matter in a different light. Since the Risorgimento for them was the accomplishment of the house of Savoy, albeit with the help initially of the moral groundwork laid by Mazzini,[19] and later of the revolutionary impulses incarnated in Garibaldi, which had been of use to the degree that they had been exploitable, or had voluntarily placed themselves in the service of Piedmontese policy,[20] the undertaking appeared to have been possible only thanks to the assistance of France. Hence their gratitude for Magenta and Solferino was not at all rhetorical or banal, and unlike the Left they did not feel that Mentana had extinguished their obligation.[21]

A man like Crispi, whose style of thought and past life showed that he was unrestrained by sentimental bonds, could even envision seizing the chance to grab Nice back from France; a man like Visconti Venosta drew back in disdain before such an idea, as though affronted by something that injured the honor of the Italian government. The question of Nice did not exist and could not exist for the Italian government: Nice had been ceded to France in virtue of a treaty sanctioned by a plebiscite, and there was no going back on it.[22] He wrote the following only in 1877, but his views were the same seven years earlier, in 1870: "if Germany were to attack France for some deliberate purpose, and we were to promise to join it in order to get Nice or Savoy, we would be following a policy directly contrary to that of Cavour, one that would plant an evil seed in our country. I don't even speak of the odious side there would be to our conduct, we who are the sons of Magenta and Solferino, if we took part in such an irony of fate not in order to defend ourselves from aggression, or the threat of it, but

---

the anti-Napoleonic national policy threw off all disguise and revealed itself in its full glory in the expedition of Quarto and the proclamation of unity."

[18] "Il principio di nazionalità," in *La Riforma* for 20 December 1870.

[19] Cf. *L'Opinione* for 12 March 1872: "the name of Giuseppe Mazzini is indissolubly joined to the national cause. . . . How many of those who now sit on the highest councils of the nation first learned from his writings to stammer out the sacred name of Italy! He had the merit of putting an end to the eunuch's rhetoric and of summoning the youth to worship the grand idea of the homeland. . . . He fought for the principle of Italian unity at a time when it seemed far off, and its liberation a difficult enterprise." These words were written by Dina; the basis of the attribution to Dina personally of unsigned editorials in *L'Opinione* is L. Chiala, *Giacomo Dina e l'opera sua nelle vicende del Risorgimento italiano* 3 (1903). Chiala does not of course give an exhaustive list of Dina's contributions; cf. his p. 348.

[20] Note the judgment of Visconti Venosta: "but it is also the case that if Garibaldi represented the impulse toward a revolution in Italy, yet he lacked the qualities necessary to reduce this revolution to any sort of order and make it produce any viable or lasting result" (from a letter to his brother Giovanni, 28 June 1882; Visconti Venosta archive).

[21] Thus Massarani in *Cesare Correnti nella vita e nelle opere* (Rome, 1890), p. 277, who conveys the sentiments of virtually all the moderates.

[22] Statements of Visconti Venosta to the French ambassador Rothan (Rothan, *L'Allemagne et l'Italie* 2:277; but see above, ch. 1, n. 175: Rothan's report no. 44, in which the statements of Visconti Venosta are reported, is dated 21 February, not 23).

solely to recover, with the help of a stronger party, the price we freely paid in return for the blood that was shed in our cause."[23]

For all those who were similarly disposed, the news from France produced an appalling and unnerving effect. From August 1870 to January 1871, from Weissenburg and Wörth to the armistice, the great majority of the moderates, including Visconti Venosta, Lanza, and Bonghi, felt even their joy over Rome turn to gall at the reports. News of Sedan produced consternation,[24] and some months after they were still in a frame of mind that made the festivities for the king in Rome seem inappropriate "when the French are in mourning."[25]

Political calculation had persuaded most people that it would be impossible for Italy to enter the conflict on the side of Napoleon III; but the pain of forced inaction ate at La Marmora, who as a general and a politician had counseled against intervention, while laying claim to the honor of leading a detachment across the frontier immediately to fight with the French, whenever the government should decide to enter the fray. "To think that France, without whom we would have been unable to constitute ourselves as a nation, is threatened with dismemberment without receiving the slightest aid from us, and that the Emperor risks losing his crown, perhaps in part for having compromised his own plans in 1866 in order that we should have Venetia—such a combination of circumstances is deeply painful to anyone with a sense of decency and gratitude."[26] Cialdini would have chosen to intervene directly alongside Napoleon III, and La Marmora had warned of the cost: but these two men, so unlike one another, and so unfriendly, shared exactly the same feelings about the matter.

As with the two leading military men, so with the men of the government, Quintino Sella excepted. Lanza felt that it broke his heart to live through the "rending" spectacle of France's ruin, could not restrain his tears at the news of Sedan,[27] and was incensed by Europe's impassivity during the bombardment of

---

[23] Visconti Venosta, personal letter to Minghetti, 13 October 1877 (BCB, *Carte Minghetti,* cart. XX, fasc. 93. Published by Walter Maturi, "Un buon europeo: Emilio Visconti Venosta," in *La Nuova Europa* 2, no. 34 [1945]: 9). The expressions used here reecho those of Cavour in his speech to the Chamber of 2 October 1860 (*Discorsi Parlamentari* 11:240 [Rome, 1872].

[24] Thus Visconti Venosta (cf. Bülow, *Memorie* 4:170 [Italian translation: Milan, 1931]).

[25] La Marmora to Lanza, 3 December 1870 (*Le carte di Giovanni Lanza* 6:306 [Turin, 1938]).

[26] La Marmora to Achille Arese, 1 September 1870 (in G. Massari, *Il generale Alfonso La Marmora* [Florence, 1880], pp. 410–11); for La Marmora's attitude to the war: ibid., p. 409; Chiala, *Pagine di storia contemporanea* 1:54; S. Castagnola, *Da Firenze a Roma: Diario storico-politico del 1870–71,* p. 6, n.; Guiccioli, *Quintino Sella* 1:287. In the "Commemorazione" of Alfonso La Marmora by Verax (5 January 1879; first published in *Fanfulla* and later enlarged and published as a separate volume, *Alfonso La Marmora: Commemorazione* [Florence, 1879]), the emphasis is placed on the general's desire to aid France; this is based on things La Marmora said later on, when he too magnified the degree to which he had been pro-French in the summer of 1870, though he claimed to have taken this position only after the "first disasters" (*I segreti di Stato nel governo costituzionale* [2d ed.; Florence, 1877], p. 32).

[27] L. Luzzatti, *Memorie* 1:307 (Bologna, 1931). Lanza's tears, the reason for which was misinterpreted, led Crispi to make an ironic remark in the Chamber in 1880, and newspaper polemics followed (cf. E. Tavallini, *La vita e i tempi di Giovanni Lanza* 2:179 ff. [Turin, 1887]; A. Colombo in *Il Risorgimento Italiano* 22 (1929): 132 ff.).

Paris.[28] Visconti Venosta felt the same way, and so did Minghetti, though he was the least biased toward the French of all of them and was not overly surprised by the catastrophe of the Second Empire.[29] Though skeptical about the future of a "profoundly corrupt" country,[30] Minghetti was "very strongly" moved by the words of Thiers when the latter passed through Vienna to entreat (in vain there too) Austrian aid, and he deplored as inhuman the inertia of the neutral powers,[31] to the point that he was willing to entertain the theoretical possibility of an armed intervention in aid of France, provided that it could be an effective one.[32]

Around these leaders there were the lesser figures, some of whom were lesser only in official terms and were able to exercise continual and substantial influence on public affairs. One was Giacomo Dina, the perspicacious and much-heeded editorial director of *L'Opinione*, who was favorable to Napoleon at the outset and was in due course left prostrate at the thought of "such an immense downfall," though he was forced to acknowledge the recklessness of the French.[33] There was Michelangelo Castelli, the influential private counselor not only of Vittorio Emanuele II but also of the leaders of the Right, who was unable to choke back his urge to join in on France's side.[34] There was Ruggero Bonghi, who more than anyone else poured onto the printed page his dismay and took a resolutely anti-Prussian line both in his fortnightly columns in the *Nuova Antologia* and in the Milanese paper *La Perseveranza*. There was Michele Amari, whose rejoicing at

---

[28] Lanza to La Marmora, 8 December 1870 and 13 January 1871 (Lanza, *Le carte* 6:314, 7:34).

[29] "The great catastrophe of the empire is understandable for anyone who had reflected on the condition of France during recent years" wrote Minghetti to Lord Acton on 23 September 1870 (BCB, *Carte Minghetti*, cart. XV, fasc. 107).

[30] *Carteggio tra M. Minghetti e G. Pasolini* 4:196 (Turin, 1930).

[31] Minghetti, report from Vienna, 10 October 1870, no. 16, *ris.*

[32] "I grieve for France's situation, and I say that if we could be certain of deciding the question by putting our sword in the balance like Camillus, I might be ready to say, *let us go*. But to get ourselves thrashed by the Prussians without giving any real relief to France, and to have to deal internally with all the furies that Prussia would rouse, would seem to me an utterly imprudent policy . . . however I advise, and request, that you use the greatest regard with Thiers, and show him the greatest sympathy" (Minghetti, personal letter to Visconti Venosta, 9 October 1870; Visconti Venosta archive). Platonic sympathy, of course: in fact on 20 October Minghetti says that he is reassured by the outcome of Thiers's mission, "not that in the present state of affairs I feared we would launch an armed intervention; but we had to show good will without taking action, to keep from alienating Thiers, but not commit ourselves" (ibid.) And on 22 October, the echo of Thiers's moving words having faded, Minghetti was yet more forthright: he was just as sorry for France, but had never believed "that we had to demonstrate our solidarity" (ibid.).

[33] Dina to Castelli, 15 July, 14 September, and 17 October 1870 (Castelli, *Carteggio politico* 2:471, 484, 487). The editorials in *L'Opinione* are the most eloquent record of the views of Dina, who desired the mediation of the neutral powers. Later on, some strong language on his part with regard to Germany drew down on him a reproof from Sella: "what the devil do you mean by goading and offending Bismarck, the most vindictive man in the world?" (Chiala, *Giacomo Dina* 3:288–89). That *L'Opinione* could, within certain limits, be considered the only semiofficial newspaper, was admitted even by the very cautious Visconti Venosta, although he added a "perhaps" (in a private letter to Nigra, 30 May 1871; Visconti Venosta archive). There were differences between Dina and the government, but they arose mainly in the area of finance and in relation to the projects of Sella (cf. Chiala, *Giacomo Dina* 3:311 ff.). See further in Chiala, pp. 240 and 316, for the relations between Visconti Venosta and Dina, and pp. 293–94 for Lanza and Dina.

[34] *Ricordi di Michelangelo Castelli*, p. 192 and cf. p. 185.

the conquest of the Capitol was overshadowed by the French disasters.[35] And there was Count Guido Borromeo, Minghetti's close friend.[36]

Among the diplomats, Nigra naturally felt anguish and trepidation for the fate of the country in which he had acquired fame and contracted strong and lasting friendships. In 1868 he had expressed a wish to leave his post in Paris and transfer to London, because he saw affairs in France continually worsening and it was "painful to be present at the ruin of this great edifice, the French empire, with which all of our policies to this day have been coordinated."[37] As late as 7 August 1870, even after Weissenburg and Wörth, he had telegraphed to Visconti Venosta to try to get him to intervene immediately in aid of the emperor.[38]

Naturally, commiseration for France grew as its calamity swelled. Artom, another of the principal advisers who had opted firmly for neutrality,[39] said that the memory of Solferino and Magenta became more vivid following Sedan.[40] At a time when even *La Riforma* voiced an appeal for an end to the "pointless slaughter," despair at the collapse of France continued to grow among the moderates, and the expression of it in their party organs reached a high point in the burning articles in which Bonghi deprecated the obstinate ferocity of the victors.

We have already seen the manner in which Carducci was moved to sympathy for France; now the voice of another great artist arose to express impetuously what in many had been reluctantly held back by the voice of practical reason. Giuseppe Verdi, who as a friend of the moderates and of Visconti Venosta[41] was politically far distant from Carducci and yet on this occasion so much resembled him, lamented the French disaster and the ruin, consequent on it, of modern civilization, and did not hesitate to say that for Italy it would have been better to

---

[35] Amari, *Carteggio* 3:288.

[36] If Cavour were still alive, "Italy would not have let its hands be tied by the neutrals, and we would not have been forced to assist impassively at the excruciating agony of the nation that alone won respect for the Latin race" (Borromeo to Minghetti, 17 November 1870; BCB, *Carte Minghetti*, cart. XV, fasc. 69). And in another letter of 26 February 1871 he said: "Would you feel able to justify, if not the facts themselves [meaning the occupation of Rome and the acceptance by the Duke of Aosta of the Spanish crown], at any rate the morality of the time and place we chose to resolve two questions of the greatest importance for France? Do you feel able to maintain that it was up to us, who had twice signed the Convention, to profit from the agony of France in order to advance our own position, and even give the Pyrenees to one who already has the Alps?" (ibid., cart. XVI, fasc. 4).

[37] Nigra to Artom, 19 January 1868 (AE, *Carte Nigra*).

[38] "France's partial setbacks have not changed my opinion. In addition to the other good reasons for it, there is now the added one of maintaining Europe's threatened equilibrium. By sending immediate aid to France we risk nothing, and we make Italy play a great and generous role, worthy of it and favorable to its interests" (AE, *Ris.*, 48). And cf. his preceding telegram, also of 7 August, in which he refers to the request advanced by Napoleon III to the Italian government for assistance in the form of 60,000 men: "I add nothing to what I have already said. You know my feelings" (Castelli, *Ricordi* , p. 185; but the precise text, and date, are given in Tavallini, *La vita e i tempi di Giovanni Lanza* 1:509).

[39] See above, p. 89.

[40] Artom to Nigra, 29 September 1870 (AE, *Carte Nigra*).

[41] Cf. the *Carteggi Verdiani* 3:121 (Rome, 1947). And further R. Barbiera, *Il salotto della Contessa Maffei*, p. 380.

go down to defeat with France than to continue in the inertia to which it had been reduced.[42]

Yet it would be superficial to see these men as doing no more than venting their unhappiness; that would mean confining their political vision within the narrow limits of the timeless human emotions. That they were gripped by strong emotions is past doubt: sorrow was the first impulse, the immediate reaction to the bad news; it constituted the ground from which sprang subsequent thoughts and considerations. But that is the point. Without their thoughts and their ideas the men of the Right would never have emerged to prominence on the political scene, or even put in an appearance on it. These were persons, if ever there were such, accustomed by mental habit and training to ponder, sometimes even to an excessive degree, before acting, and a typical example of the breed was the minister for foreign affairs, the very reflective and cautious Emilio Visconti Venosta, eternally weighing the pros and the cons.

Their quasi-official spokesmen affirmed the necessity for a major state to have an ideal, lacking which there would be no positive policy, but merely diplomatic empiricism from day to day. But they also spoke out forcefully against any form of "sentimental" policy-making.[43] A year earlier Milan's *La Perseveranza* had stated exactly that, adding that it was not sympathies that should lay down a line of conduct for a people, "but rather self-interest, interest properly understood, foresighted interest that does not take into account only what has already happened, and does not stop at planning only the combinations possible at the moment, but seeks out the eventualities of tomorrow, and the day after tomorrow."[44]

If this was the publicly announced doctrine, how much more attentive to reality was the man who was actually in power. Visconti Venosta became impatient when things were addressed in sentimental terms: "'Italy loves France, Italy doesn't love France'—this type of discussion belongs to lovers' quarrels rather than to policy."[45] He was already of the view that the time of intimacy between Italy and France had passed long since, and he therefore did not let himself go in sentimental effusions, but based his conduct on a precise political evaluation— his conviction that "on the day that an ineluctable and permanent cause of hostil-

---

[42] "I would have liked a more generous policy, one *that paid our debt of gratitude*. One hundred thousand of our men could perhaps have saved France, and us. In any case I would have preferred peace following defeat in company with France, to this inertia that will make us despised one day." From a letter of 30 September 1870 in A. Luzio, *Profili biografici e bozzetti storici* 2:528–29 (Milan, 1927). And cf. a letter of 10 August 1870 (*Carteggi Verdiani* 1:122 [Rome, 1935]; and A. Luzio, *Garibaldi, Cavour, Verdi*, p. 33). Verdi reproached the French for their *morgue*, the insolence that made them unbearable: "but anyone who thinks seriously, and feels himself a true Italian, ought to be above such points of amour propre" and ought to regret the Prussian victory, which carried many dangers for Italy. Cf. as well the letter of Giuseppina Strepponi, 2 September 1870, in *Carteggi Verdiani* 1:122–23.

[43] "La politica francese," in *L'Opinione* for 9 August 1871.

[44] *La Perseveranza* for 30 July 1870.

[45] Visconti Venosta, private letter to Nigra, 22 May 1871 (Visconti Venosta archive).

ity between the two countries should be created, a large question mark would hang over our future."[46]

The supporters of a change of direction in policy leading to a close alignment with Germany spoke of their own realism in contrast to the sentimentalism of others, meaning the moderates. But there was no more real contrast here between realism and sentimentalism than there had been in France under the Second Empire, whose French critics charged it with a policy dictated exclusively by sentimentalism, as though Napoleon III had not also tried to serve his own interests and those of the French people, however accurate or mistaken his calculations may have been.

A sense of reality, an appreciation of reality: the whole moderate tradition spoke this language, right back to the time of the founders of the moderate movement, Balbo, d'Azeglio, and Durando, who had insisted so much on the requirement for solid political realism, for a practical sense of reality, for good sense![47] And the dénouement of the Risorgimento, willed and attained by the moderates —what else had that been if not the triumph of the spirit of reality, of the policy of the golden mean, over against the myth derived from 1848 of a universal democratic revolution? What had Mazzini, the apostle of the latter idea, reproached his adversaries with if not precisely their compromise, the adjustment to reality that extinguished the idealistic flame?

To feel sympathy for the Second Empire, to defend the cause of Napoleon III, did these things not in fact grossly compromise the principle of liberty, so energetically defended at home but no longer defended abroad, against the dictator of France? It was a compromise, dictated by the conviction that the best bulwark of the Italian cause in Europe was still, out of sheer necessity and self-interest, that very dictator; and which therefore put Italian national interest decisively ahead of an ideological principle. Never mind sentimentalism and the love of abstract principles!

If anything, we might within limits say of Cavour's lieutenants what was said of Cavour himself, to wit that his gaze never passed beyond the confines of the real, but that for a man of his genius the horizon of the real was much vaster than it was for other men.[48] That genius was no more. The precise feeling for the possible, moment by moment, the nose for politics, the ability to maneuver, might not even be possessed to an exceptional degree by these generals of Alexander; and at this point individual values, the various personalities of the political actors, came into play. And it was precisely here that a statesman like Bismarck towered above his Italian, English, Austrian, French, and Russian counterparts. But the criterion of action was always the same, attention to reality, in every case. The reality of the moderates, however, embraced more elements, and presented a more complex image, than that of the neorealists. For a Bismarck and for his lesser imitators, political calculation, the weighing only of forces that

---

[46] Visconti Venosta, private letter to Nigra, 26 April 1885 (Visconti Venosta archive).

[47] Cf. Salvatorelli, *Il pensiero politico italiano*, p. 263.

[48] Thus Artom (in his introduction to I. Artom and A. Blanc, *Il conte di Cavour in Parlamento* [Florence, 1868], p. xiii).

could be applied in political terms, meaning in terms of power, was everything. For the moderates, reality was made up not only of materially describable and quantifiable forces but also of those found in the moral domain, so called: movements of ideas and affects, the attitudes expressed in public opinion, and similar phenomena. Government action, for them, was to be based on consensus, not on fear, and so they took account of many elements that politicians of Bismarck's stamp left to one side, or depreciated. The result, apart from the greater or less capacities of individuals, was slower and more cautious action, and much less tendency to force situations. These things were the necessary consequence of the repudiation of authoritarianism and the search for consensus.

Cavour had already shown, at least in his attitude to the religious problem and the church, that realism in his case was augmented by aspects not usually found in the politicians who like to call themselves realists. The difference came clearly to light not long after 1870, with the actions and language of Bismarck during the *Kulturkampf*. In the heirs of Cavour, who were much less mentally nimble than he, much less instinctively politicians, much more tormented by moral preoccupations in the style of d'Azeglio, the importance given to the moral component in the assessment of events grew. In sum, the realism of the moderates was something different from the realism preached by the advocates of the new way. But not even the most rigid and moralistic of the epigones of Alexander ever intended to practice a doctrinaire or sentimental politics; and the solution of the Roman question provided reliable witness of this, since until early September 1870 their intention was to achieve it by the use of moral force alone, and the swift decision to resort to arms was only made when the European situation plunged into turmoil, and the polemical temperature rose in Italy, bringing the danger of serious internal disturbances.

They believed in gratitude, and morality in political action, but at the same time kept an eye on reality, a very attentive eye on concrete interests. They pursued the policy of the golden mean, an old ideal handed down from the time of the July Monarchy which meant not only equidistance from the two extreme poles represented by the reds and the blacks—in other words, the Jacobins and the reactionary ultras—but also equidistance between pure doctrinairism and pure empiricism, between the policy of trying to superimpose the preconceived schemes of an abstract body of doctrine on the flow of events, and the policy of treating each case in isolation, meaning pure tactics, with no strategic purpose except that of aggrandizing the state.

If the moderates of whom we are speaking, who were mostly men of solid intellectual and moral worth, had grave doubts and severe reservations where Prussia and the policies of Bismarck were concerned, therefore, it was not just because of the memory of Magenta and Solferino, and the ties of gratitude between their new kingdom and the French empire. Perhaps only Vittorio Emanuele II would have charged off into the fray, in obedience to the imperatives of personal and dynastic sentiment; and it may even be permitted to wonder whether the king himself did not experience at least some of the doubts, the realistic doubts so to speak, that tormented his counselors.

These doubts were political in nature. There was a fear of altering the European balance of power too much, of a displacement of force to the advantage of a power, Prussia, that had been our ally four years earlier, but whose ultimate aims and purposes were difficult to grasp fully. Or rather: it seemed that a glimpse of them could indeed be had, and it was not reassuring to behold the outline of a distinct hegemonic ambition.

The notion of lost European equilibrium is amply and precisely formulated in a letter of Visconti Venosta to de Launay: "Before the Prussian victories one would have said that [in Italy] the government was French and the country was Prussian. Now, in contrast, opinion in the country has changed enormously. It is uneasy, it feels itself committed to a certain solidarity of the Latin races, it sees the rupture of European equilibrium; it fears that the Prussian victories may contain the nucleus of future perils for Italy and bring back the tradition of the Germanic invasions of antiquity; it fears one day seeing the Holy Roman Empire in Trent and Trieste, it believes that the Mincio has been declared a German stream. . . . Italy . . . along with the rest of Europe would feel itself at risk if victory were abused."[49]

Germany had not arrived at the banks of the Mincio, but many feared it would soon be in Trent and Trieste, since on all sides there was talk of the inevitable and not far distant annexation of German Austria to the German empire. In Crispi's circle this development was even welcomed, though Crispi himself later changed his mind and adopted the view that his beloved Germany was better kept at a distance. But the moderates, with much more acute political sense, drew back horrified at the idea of Bismarck in a position to dispatch orders to some governor residing in the castle of Buonconsiglio in Trent.

But there was worse. Prussia was the friend and ally of Russia, and the unchallenged position of the first meant the dominance of the other in Europe too. Indeed, the Gorchakov circular, in which Russia repudiated the clauses of the treaty of Paris of 1856 that had tied its hands in the Black Sea, appeared in the wake of the Prussian victories on French soil. What better proof that Europe was going to pieces, making way for a Russian-German hegemony, a formidable combination of forces able to crush the other states?

Michelet's voice rang out: the Franco-German conflict was opening the gates to the tsar, who was greedily waiting, and it signified the future victory of Russia over Europe and the world; all of Germany's doggedness in destroying

---

[49] Visconti Venosta to de Launay, 11 August 1870 (Visconti Venosta archive). It will be seen that Visconti Venosta had not been completely convinced by the statements made by Bismarck to de Launay, and by the optimism of the latter (above, ch. 1, p. 9 and n. 14). For more on similar worries about the rebirth of the old German empire, cf. *La Perseveranza* for 23 July 1870 (Bonghi), and the letter of Vittorio Imbriani to De Meis in August of 1870 (in B. Croce, "Dal carteggio inedito di Angelo Camillo De Meis," in *Atti dell'Accademia Pontaniana*, 1915, p. 31 in the offprint seen). Artom on the other hand did not share them, and did not see why Italy ought to be any more alarmed by German unity than Austria, "which is threatened with the loss of eight million Germans" (private letter to Visconti Venosta, from Vienna, 17 August 1870, cited above at n. 3). Artom sympathized with German unity (private letter to Visconti Venosta, 7 August 1870, from Vienna; Visconti Venosta archive).

France was smoothing the road westward for the Russian-Tartar armies. *Vae victoribus!* and let Germany watch out, since in Prussianizing itself it was opening up an abyss into which in due course it would be plunged at the hands of the Cossacks![50]

Previous, less apocalyptic writers had also perceived, looming behind the clustering of the Germanic tribe, the shape of the Slavic race gathering itself together, and had seen in either or both of these phenomena the end of any political possibility for Italy: "in such enormous agglomerations, which could only be managed by absolutist governments, what space would be left for the individual geniuses of the historic nations, as for example the Italian nation? Would it not be reborn just in time to find itself dwarfed by these new groupings of peoples to an even greater degree than the formerly independent states of the Italian peninsula once were by the other nations in the old European order?"[51]

Only the fantasies of political commentators? Not at all. The specter of the Russian-Prussian alliance disturbed the repose of the minister of foreign affairs himself; and a Europe in which the west belonged to Germany and the east to Russia was no more soothing, given that Italy "is one of those countries that cannot make a place for themselves and shape their own future except in a Europe in which there exists a certain equilibrium of forces."[52] So preoccupied was Visconti Venosta that Italian policy on the Black Sea question between November 1870 and March 1871 was oriented toward the fundamental goal of preventing the creation of a true formal alliance between Prussia and Russia.[53]

So Bonghi, the political commentator, was expressing concepts that underlay Italian foreign policy when he spoke repeatedly of his preoccupations about the menacing emergence of colossal empires all too similar to the universal monarchies combated centuries before by Europe in the name of liberty: "because of the errors of some and the negligence of others a state of things has come about in which Prussia, with Germany in tow, is becoming the master of western Europe, and Russia master of the east. The close links between the two, in existence for

---

[50] Michelet, *La France devant l'Europe*, pp. iii ff., 94 ff., and the entire chapter entitled "Ce que c'est la Russie," pp. 99 ff. It was only after the defeat of France and the worries it brought for the future that Michelet began to think, like Thiers and many others, of Russia as a desirable collaborator against Germany. In a note of 4 May 1871 in his *Journal* he says that he had a dream vision of where France's salvation could come from: "It was just the opposite of what I had hitherto thought. Salvation will come from an alliance with Russia" (in J. M. Carré, *Michelet et son temps* [Paris, 1926], p. 232).

[51] "Le condizioni della pace secondo i Tedeschi," in *La Perseveranza* for 23 August 1870. The territorial diminution of France would constitute, it is said, the onset of this new and detrimental change in the European situation.

[52] Visconti Venosta, letter to Robilant, 1 July 1875, in Salvemini, "La politica estera della Destra" (1925), p. 194.

[53] Visconti Venosta's instructions to Cadorna, the Italian envoy in London, regarding the conference on the Black Sea, 28 December 1870: "it is a piece of great good luck for Europe that an offensive and defensive alliance between Prussia and Russia does not yet actually exist. It is in Europe's urgent interest to block its formation" (AE, *Missioni all'Estero*, cart. 2). That a Russian-German alliance, the greatest peril for Europe, might come about, was a source of worry for other governments too, especially the one in Vienna: see Andrássy's analysis in 1872, in F. Leidner, *Die Aussenpolitik österreich-Ungarns*, p. 17.

some years now, provide each of them with the opportunity for a scheme that will need a number of years to be realized, but whose first foundation can now be laid in a fashion that will make it impossible to stop them from continuing in the future.[54] Is this consummation desirable for any powers other than Russia and Prussia? For England, Italy, Austria, Spain, or any other? To us it appears detrimental to all of them in every respect, not because they gain from preventing German unity, or think it possible to prop up the Turkish empire forever; but because united Germany for its own good and that of others must not become huge, and the Ottoman empire must not be replaced by Russia but by a state which ought to be able to develop independently of Russia and be able to survive and hold its place. If the statesmen who guide Italy, Austria, and England are aware of this, let them note that with every passing day, as the prostration of France increases, the difficulty of opposing the ambitions of Prussia and Russia in the future also grows."[55]

Even if one chose to leave aside forecasts for the future, or to leave Russia out of consideration, one thing was certain: the European political situation was entirely up in the air. The support that Italian policy had enjoyed for a decade was no longer in place, and the continent was at the mercy of Bismarck and Moltke. And there were more specific dangers facing Italy, for in France the clerical party was no longer held in check by Napoleon III, and as for Germany. . . until the spring of 1871 it was not at all clear, whatever the Left might say, which side of the Roman question Germany would come down on.

It was an uncertainty that caused some to be more apprehensive than others. Lodovico Frapolli feared "this new inundation of barbarians" that was devastating France today and would pour over the other nations tomorrow.[56] Bonghi spoke of the Germans as a "numberless gathering of vandals, who with sword and fire leave the mark of their passing wherever they go."[57] But even men whose reflexes were more controlled and who refused to believe in a new era of barbarism in Europe[58] were worried at seeing French power plummet, leaving behind a vacuum where until a few months ago had stood one of the major forces of European politics. They were worried at seeing a single powerful empire in the center of Europe whose march appeared irresistible and to whose good graces the tranquillity of the other states was therefore entrusted. Even Minghetti, who

---

[54] To Bonghi the only "union" that looks solid in Europe at the end of December 1870 is the one between Russia and Prussia, which is too strong to be "cajoled into relaxing or dissolving itself by any promise" (Bonghi, *Nove anni* 2:439, at the end of December 1870).

[55] Bonghi, "La risposta del Beust," in *La Perseveranza* for 28 November 1870.

[56] Frapolli, personal letter to Visconti Venosta from Angoulême, 24 September 1870 (Visconti Venosta archive).

[57] "La pace," in *La Perseveranza* for 17 January 1871 (Bonghi).

[58] Minghetti, personal letter to Visconti Venosta, 22 October 1870: ". . . nor am I one of those who fear the irruption of barbarism into Europe" (Visconti Venosta archive). He takes the same position in his letter of the same date to Pasolini: "But then I don't share the fear of our friends who see the flood of barbarism in the triumph of Prussia" (Minghetti, *Carteggio Minghetti-Pasolini* 4:196). Neither did Nigra share "the vulgar error that France has fallen so far that it will not be able to raise itself back up within a few years, or the other of believing that a unified Germany will bring slavery and barbarism to Europe" (report, 30 January 1871, no. 1386, cited at n. 7 above).

was not one of those who trembled at a pending revival of barbarism, and who was one of the least favorable to France among the bosses of the Right, even Minghetti maintained that the absence of a vigorous and well-ordered France might create considerable dangers for Europe.[59] That blessed France, said Gino Capponi; it was like the pound of flesh of the merchant of Venice, you couldn't extract it without causing loss of blood.[60]

There was no one at that moment who could foresee that France would be able to recover from defeat with such miraculous speed, and that within a few years it would once again be a vital presence in the European concert—that it would begin anew to weave the strands of a national and indeed imperial policy of overseas expansion, and that it would once again be a source of constant worry to Bismarck. Concerning Bismarck himself there was a parallel failure of prognostication, since none foresaw that when German unification had been completed he would forget about any dreams of further expansion or fresh conquest and would devote himself only to preserving the status quo and maintaining peace in Europe; a peace that satisfied all his desires because it was the peace of a triumphant Germany.

For now there was no inkling of these developments. From September 1870 to the spring of 1871, Bismarck's peace conditions caused growing uneasiness.[61] If one cared to go back to the treaties of 1814–15 one would find nothing comparable to the current German demand for Alsace-Lorraine,[62] no similar attempt to wreak harm on a great power in defeat, which is what France had been at that earlier time as well. For in regard to the exchanges of territory, and the annexations inflicted on the smaller countries in the interests of general European equilibrium—in other words, in regard to the territorial arrangements imposed in Italy and Germany—the transactions that took place in Vienna had fitted perfectly into the mentality and the moral climate of the period and had not stunned anyone in Europe.[63]

Only in the sequel, with the full flowering of the idea of nationality, would the work of the diplomats at Vienna be resented as unjust and oppressive in some parts of Europe, where patriots would spring into action to reverse the injustice

---

[59] Minghetti, personal letter to Beust, 14 April 1871 (BCB, *Carte Minghetti*, cart. XVI, fasc. 22). Minghetti had expressed the same views to Luzzatti on 30 September 1870: "I think it is bad for Europe that France should remain crushed and humiliated" (Luzzatti, *Memorie* 1:309).

[60] Capponi to Reumont, 12 October 1870 (*Lettere* 4:260).

[61] The only hope Michele Amari had in October 1870 was to be able "to persuade the German substitute for Lady Providence to make peace like a moderate barbarian" (*Carteggio* 3:290 and cf. 2:199). How little expectation there was of a policy of prudence and preservation of the status quo on Germany's part is confirmed by Marselli in 1872: "Let's admit it frankly . . . we didn't think that Germany would be that composed and inoffensive after its clamorous victories, because the case was pretty much without precedent in history. And yet it is so" ("Francia, Italia, e Germania," in *Nuova Antologia* 20 [July 1872]: 541).

[62] It is singularly instructive in relation to the point I wish to make that in 1871 a man like Bonghi, who was certainly not suspect of being reactionary, antipatriotic etc., was able to speak of the "mildness" and the "prudence" shown by the European states in 1815, except for Prussia (*Nove anni* 2:453). Here we see how the Franco-Prussian War and the peace that followed it seemed to be something novel, something whose only precedent was the conquests of Napoleon I.

[63] On this see Rohden, *Die klassische Diplomatie von Kaunitz bis Metternich*, pp. 117–18.

committed. But while they had combated Metternich and his system for decades, and had tried to set the powder magazine alight in Italy and Hungary and Poland, they had always legitimized their action on the basis of the principle of nationality and the self-determination of peoples, so that in their eyes they were making no "conquest" in the imperialistic sense of the word, but were destroying the unjust conquests of the past and restoring rights to those from whom they had been stolen in the past by violence. This interpretation prevailed to the point that when the Italian national movement was crowned with success, and Lombardy and Venetia were pried from the grasp of one of the great European powers, these were not regarded as "conquests" by even the most stubborn opponents of the idea of Italian unity. The deed might be deplored, as the reactionaries and clericals of the whole of Europe deplored it, and it might be seen as the victory of a principle extremely dangerous to the general tranquillity, that of internal revolt against the constituted order: no one could say, and nobody did say, because it would have been utterly ridiculous, that Cavour, Mazzini, and Garibaldi represented a return of the spirit of "conquest," or that the old aspiration for hegemony over the continent was flickering up again in Italy.

The Italian Risorgimento seemed dangerous as a revolutionary force, a leaven that risked not only altering the territorial state of play in Italy but also spilling over the Alps and changing the whole European social order in ways of which Metternich had darkly warned: that is, by shifting the old and still reactionary continent in a liberal direction, converting the principle of nationality into liberalism.[64] But the Italian national movement in itself was not a threat to European equilibrium and the general peace; the relative forces were out of proportion. A threat to general stability could only ensue if an external power should try to exploit the Italian movement for its own ends, driving Austria out of the peninsula and replacing it with a new hegemony of its own: this is what London and Berlin,[65] no less than Vienna, had feared from the French-Piedmontese alliance. But Villafranca and the events that followed, especially the Roman question that had opened a gulf between Italian aspirations and Napoleon III's policies, had salvaged Europe's peace of mind. The serious dangers for European equilibrium were not to come from the valley of the Po.[66]

---

[64] Cf. A. Omodeo, *L'opera politica del Conte di Cavour* 1:246 (2d ed.; Florence, 1941).

[65] On Prussian fears concerning France's policy of expansion in Italy, cf. F. Valsecchi, "La politica di Cavour e la Prussia," pp. 41 ff., "Il 1859 in Germania: la stampa e i partiti," in *Studi Germanici* 1 (1935): 98, and "Il 1859 in Germania: idee e problemi," in *Archivio Storico Italiano* 93, no. 1 (1935): 273 ff. It is worth noting that in Switzerland too Napoleon III's intervention chilled enthusiasm for the Italian cause, raising alarm for European order (M. Bauer, *Die italienische Einigung im Spiegel der schweizerischen Oeffentlichkeit* [Basel, 1944], pp. 20–21, 25, 124, 183–84).

[66] This is the point made by *La Riforma* in a polemic against Cialdini, who in his famous speech to the Senate of 3 August 1870 had affirmed that Germany was hostile to Italian unity: Germany, he said, was alarmed because it saw Italy falling prey to Napoleonic imperialism, its national movement the instrument of others' ambitions. *La Riforma* replied in the article "Italia e Germania" on 8 August 1870: "it sufficed that the Italian revolution declare without equivocation, frankly and outspokenly, that it intended to be and remain Italian, and not serve French ambitions, in order that the old antagonism, the inveterate political antipathy of Germany toward us cease." Here the writer hits the mark in recognizing that Prussia, and with it the other states, England in the forefront, had perceived

Looked at on its own, quite apart from the alliance of the Piedmontese government with Napoleonic France, the Italian national movement had roused alarm because of its revolutionary origins, origins of which Cavour had availed himself in order to compel the great powers to back him in bringing "order." The dangerous aspects of the movement were its appeal to the self-determination of peoples, and thus to constituent assemblies, and even, through the machinations of the house of Savoy, to plebiscites. It was not, nor did it ever appear as, a genuine menace to the whole of Europe.

The general peace of the continent was not felt to be at risk even after 1859. Bismarck's moderation had been demonstrated in 1866, for in that year a war that had been fought very hard from the military point of view had been concluded with a peace that was truly unusual for the lack of harshness of its conditions.[67] Then there was 1867 and the question of Luxembourg, and Prussia's renunciation of force; all were examples of temperate political calculation.

Now suddenly the picture changed totally. Italian newspapers and politicians were far from being the only ones to request, after Sedan and the disappearance of the cause of the war (as many ingenuously supposed), that there be an end to a conflict that seemed gigantic in its proportions. Nor were they the only ones to be concerned by Prussia's unlimited appetite. But concerned they were, for this was no longer defensive but offensive war; no longer, as in 1859, a struggle to affirm the principle of nationality, but a struggle for conquest, a return to the hegemonic drive of Napoleon I.

And at this point something emerged, a very deep-seated feeling that passed beyond the concrete particulars of the moment (peace conditions, war ferocity) to attain the status of an overall appraisal of the German national movement compared to its Italian counterpart. Because, after all, it would have been possible to say to those who were not the friends of Prussia in Italy that at bottom they were not in a position to blame in the Germans what they themselves had approved and continued to approve in Piedmont one day and in united Italy the next. Bismarck was doing what Cavour had done; Prussia was completing the process of German unification just as Piedmont had done in Italy. And in fact this is largely what the friends of Prussia did say, whether they came from the left or the right, and what the German papers said in their polemical exchanges with *L'Opinione* and *La Perseveranza*.[68] The same logic has been taken up in another form by historians who have asserted that Italian and German history underwent an identical development in the nineteenth century, underlining the substantial affinities between the Italian Risorgimento and German unification.

Back came the reply from Dina and Bonghi: this professed affinity was purely

---

a menace to European equilibrium in the Napoleonic intervention, not in the Italian movement as such.

[67] Cf. "Le basi della pace," in *L'Opinione* for 5 February 1871: the European wars from Crimea to 1866 appeared to have been terminated in a spirit of moderation, whereas all was now changing, and Germany's peace conditions were filling hearts with consternation.

[68] See for example the debates between H. Homberger and *La Perseveranza* (for 12, 25, and 26 August 1870); or *La Riforma* as late as 7 July 1873 (article "Sadowa"); or *La Nazione* for 11 September 1873 (article "Il viaggio del Re a Berlino e il presente momento storico").

imaginary, limited at most to the particular and the epiphenomenal. There remained a chasm of substantial diversity between the two cases. One of the two movements, the Italian one, went by the name of "liberty," while the German movement took the appellation of "force."[69] The first had made its appeal, and continued to do so, to the free expression of the popular will; proof of this was the plebiscite of Rome on 2 October, while the second fiercely refused to hear the voices of the populations that it intended to fit into the iron framework of the new *Reich* whether they desired it or not. The first had proceeded virtually without loss of blood, amid the exulting population,[70] the other bombarded Strasbourg and Paris and conducted a war past the point at which its legitimate aims had been reached with a single-mindedness worthy of the most savage tribe in Africa.[71] The first opened wide the doors of the future, the other represented a brutal return to the right of the strongest, to the pristine notion of "conquest," in accordance with the character of the German people, "slow but unrelenting in invading other peoples."[72]

The two movements had different foundations and different modes of realization. Italy began with a unified tradition, history, and language, precise territorial boundaries, and a group of states of a certain nature. To these had been added

> the actual feeling, the real consciousness of the nation to which we all belong, a feeling and a consciousness that popular suffrages have attested to. . . . [T]he voting in the plebiscites was the basis and the reason of the constitution of Italy.

> To add to these four real and concrete elements the lone, abstract, uncertain, vague, and ancient element of language once again converts a political question into

---

[69] "La guerra," in *L'Opinione* for 28 December 1870.

[70] We Italians who "have become a nation . . . amid feasts and songs of universal joy, cannot understand how Prussia can wish to round off its boundaries with cannonades, and bring the lost sheep back into the bosom of the motherland by storms of slaughter." This violent article, which appeared in *L'Opinione* for 2 October 1870, provoked bitter resentment in Germany (de Launay, personal letter, 17 October 1870; AE, *Ris.*, 10) and a reply from the *Augsburger Allgemeine Zeitung*, according to which the spontaneity of the Italian movement was owing to intrigue, corruption, and "the assassin's dagger," said to have been one of the instruments employed by Cavour. These were habitual courtesies for the *Augsburger Zeitung*, which had already been described in 1847 as an enemy of the very name of Italy (Ricasoli, *Carteggi* 2:298), had denigrated in 1848 the Italian national movement, which it depicted as a ruse practiced by a handful of nobles, a few individuals of the white race who were bleeding the darker-skinned race of peasants dry (Cattaneo, *Dell'insurrezione di Milano*, p. iv), and in 1859 was openly hostile to the Italian cause, to the free Italy said to have been founded "through assassinations, and with French assistance" (Valsecchi, "Il 1859 in Germania: la stampa e i partiti," p. 109). Even the historian Reuchlin, irritated by the language of *L'Opinione*, spoke of the dishonorable means thanks to which Italy had achieved its unity: cf. Greppi, "Une coulisse du théâtre de la guerre (1870)," in *Revue d'Italie* (May 1906): 367. A fresh polemic between *L'Opinione* and "a German" was provoked by Dina's article "Il diritto della forza" (9 December 1870) and led to another article, "Conquista e nazionalità" (15 December), and a note published on 20 December. The theme is always that Germany confuses the right of the nation with the right of force.

Once again on 31 July 1871 *L'Opinione* reiterated the character of the Italian uprising: "we are the country of the plebiscite par excellence, because our political life is a continuous plebiscite. . . . This is the character of our national movement. . . . There is no mourning in our family, no city or village that angrily bites at the halter imposed on it" ("Il Re a Roma").

[71] Bonghi, *Nove anni* 2:440 (31 December 1870).

[72] Bonghi, ibid., 2:354 (31 July 1870). Cf. the polemic in *La Perseveranza* for 12 August 1870.

archaeological and philological speculation, and consigns Europe to the passions that smolder beneath its surface. The Germans believe they can make up for the fact that linguistic unity lacks firmness as a foundation . . . with the firmest of all arguments, that of force. But if this is the instrument, we depart from all the norms and logic of modern law, and go back to the right of conquest, at which we had thought that our modern civilization by now must blush with shame. If this is right of conquest, then we must accept it in all its nakedness, and not strive to cover it up with a false veil of primordial blood-relationship, which does nothing to reduce the harm done and the shame inflicted on the peoples on whom it is exercised, at the moment when the foreign and hostile hand of force falls upon them, since they themselves are ignorant of the past age when that hand presumably belonged to brothers and blood-relations.

In Italy, the plebiscite. In Germany, the refusal of a plebiscite to Schleswig. Doubtless Bismarck would not be any happier to put the question to the Polish population of Poznań, who are not saved by the fact they speak a Slavic language,

since the interests of the Prussian state prevent it from taking any notice of linguistic diversity in this case, just as they do require it, on the contrary, to consider nothing else but the linguistic unity of Alsace and Lorraine, which it wants to grab from France.

Here we really find the principal, substantial difference between the way the Italian nation has been formed and that in which, according to the zeal of German erudition, the German nation must be formed. The Italian nation has looked to the actual, existing feeling, emerging from the consciousness of the peoples, about where its own frontiers lie. The German nation is not satisfied with this, does not find its principal warrant in this, but reverts to periods and criteria of the past that favor its expansion on all sides, clashing with and hurting more than one European state. The result of this divergence is that, just as the Italian nation has been able to state categorically that it brought an augury of peace and concord in Europe, so the German nation, if it does not halt or is not halted, will have to admit that it brings an augury of war and lasting turmoil.

And in this diverse orientation, Italy had demonstrated

that it possesses a great deal more of that intelligence and that sense of what is real in the world and will be so in the future, which is the fruit of the riper cultures, cultures that have attained repose and distilled themselves over time into the soul of the people.[73]

La Riforma, under the influence of Crispi's circle, was starting to accept an idea of nationhood extraneous to the common Italian tradition, and was already modeling itself on ideas and notions of Germanic stamp. The organs of the Right reacted with extreme energy, and sometimes even—as with the impetuous Bonghi—with a singular violence of language, in order to point the forceful

---

[73] "Il diritto delle nazioni" (the author is Bonghi) in *La Perseveranza* for 31 August 1870.

contrast between the Italian idea of nation and national rights, and the German approach to these topics.

They emphasized spontaneity and an essential "will" to be united, so that as ever, as in Mazzini, there was absolute primacy of the moral and spiritual factors. We Italians, said Bonghi, are friends of the principle of nationality, we are appalled to see what a false conception the Germans have of it. For us the members of a nation are "all the peoples who in their consciousness feel that they do belong to it," and we consider it an injustice to want to force peoples "who do not believe, do not feel intimately, that they are linked by a national bond" to be united by force to a state. The Germans, in contrast, seek the frontiers of a nation in past history and in future destinies; but everyone looks for what is most flattering to his own ambitions in the past; and everyone settles on whatever assemblages of territory he thinks will bring him the greatest political and economic advantage in the future. In result, the principle of nationality will become the source of prolonged and ruthless war among the peoples, where it was meant to be the gage of a settled and peaceful order.[74] This was the essence of Italian doctrine, common to the revolutionaries and the moderates. An exception was Durando and his theory of geostrategic nationality, that is of nationality dependent on the nature of the terrain;[75] and it is also strange that Mancini, the codifier in Italy of the rights of nationality, remained blind to the profound difference between Italian doctrine and German, in which the combination "nationality-nature" took ever-increasing precedence over the combination "nationality-will."

The debate flamed up in all its asperity over the question of Alsace: for the moderates it had a French soul, and therefore was no repast for Bismarck and the Prussian General Staff, while for the apologists for Germany it was German by race and language, and therefore German politically as well, whether the inhabitants of Strasbourg and Mulhouse liked it or not—in a good example of that imperative *a priori* of nationality that was advocated so brilliantly in Italy by *La Riforma*. The "intimate" character of the two regions was completely German, Gervinus assured Gregorovius,[76] who for his part was convinced of the naturalness of Alsace's Germanness. For the great Mommsen, this was not a conquest but a revendication, an action projected backward into the past. He was prepared to concede, certainly, that "every conquest is a crime that wounds nationality, and whoever tramples one people underfoot offends all peoples," that in the case at hand the process of transition would be "long and hard," and that during this process the Alsatians would be Germans more in name than in reality . . . that is, he conceded that the soul of these racial and linguistic Germans was not exactly German.[77] And that was precisely why this was a conquest, said Bonghi in

---

[74] "Siamo parziali?" in *La Perseveranza* for 17 December 1870, and cf. also the issue for 19 December. The article takes issue, not for the first time, with the Florentine correspondent of the *Augsburger Zeitung*.

[75] G. Durando, *Della nazionalità italiana*, pp. 58 ff.

[76] F. Gregorovius, *Diari Romani* (Italian translation: Milan, 1895), pp. 452 and 454.

[77] Mommsen, *Agli italiani*, pp. 22–23. *L'Opinione* for 4 October 1870 takes issue with Mommsen.

response, there was no respect for the desires of the population; and to try to disguise the right of force as an idea of nationality was, if anything, a sad indication of the decline of the moral sense the war had caused among the Germans.[78] There were rights of nationality, but they were in favor of France, not of Germany.[79]

At least David Strauss, another great scholar, was more frank. Forgetting about the Gospels and the life of Jesus, and reviving instead the figure of Arminius, so dear to his new hero Ulrich von Hutten, Strauss too pronounced on the political situation of the moment, declaring loudly and clearly that Germany ought to keep Alsace and Lorraine for itself, having won the war, for its own "security." The thesis of his illustrious, and French, colleague, Renan, on the advantages for Germany itself and for Europe of a peace that would leave the two provinces in French hands, and on the dangers of forcing through an annexation, was refuted by the German professor, who had already had occasion to jest at the pacifists' notions around 1866, and had come out with a comparison between war and a storm: both are necessary because they cleanse the atmosphere.[80] Now he was insisting that there was no advantage to Germany in accommodating France, and much advantage in dictating peace terms as the victor, so as to be able firmly to command the portal of Germany, which lay between Basel and Luxembourg.[81]

The same opinion was held by a third illustrious historian, the national-liberal von Sybel, who in the pages of the *Kölnische Zeitung* also admitted that it was not easy to turn the Alsatians back into Germans, given their feelings, but still demanded that Alsace and Lorraine should be German, along with Metz and its surrounding territory, rebutting the views of those outside Germany who proposed that Germany make a disinterested peace so as to win over the French people and thus lay the foundation of a lasting peace; "it would be worse than frivolous for us to ground our future security on France's gratitude, and not uniquely and exclusively on our own strength."[82]

The minister responsible for Italian foreign policy could not of course wade into this fray in a bold and straightforward fashion, but Visconti Venosta too, albeit in a prudent and impersonal form, and making direct reference only to the Roman question, repeated the essential thought that guided the commentators of the Right in the debate concerning the peace and Franco-German relations, when in his speech at Milan on 9 November 1870 he insisted on the importance of the "moral forces."[83] Against those who believed that the highest degree of liberal-

---

[78] Bonghi, *Nove anni* 2:407.

[79] Letter of C. Guerrieri Gonzaga in *La Perseveranza* for 28 August 1870.

[80] J. Ter Meulen, *Der Gedanke der Internationalen Organisation in seiner Entwicklung*, vol. 2, part 2 (The Hague, 1940), pp. 44–45.

[81] The first and second letters of Strauss to Renan were published in translation in *Il Diritto* for 26 August and 16 and 17 October 1870. Strauss's reasoning was perfectly identical to that of Bismarck (above, ch. 1, n. 58), and was fully shared by other learned Germans, as for example Albert Weber in a letter to De Gubernatis, published in *Il Diritto* for 18 November 1870.

[82] Von Sybel's article was published in translation in *La Perseveranza* for 24 September 1870.

[83] The text was published in *La Perseveranza* for 11 November, and *L'Opinione* for 12 and 13 November 1870.

ism in foreign policy consisted in ignoring European opinion, the statesman from the Valtellina appealed to the great example of Cavour, one of whose merits, and not the least, was undoubtedly that of having given our Risorgimento a tradition, sincerely liberal, of policy that always aimed to gain the adhesion of the great moral currents of opinion. Certainly it was possible to break "the bond of this moral factor" by appealing to pure and simple force, thus cutting through a number of knotty questions in international relations: but with what result? The Italian tradition of taking into account the moral forces thus received public reaffirmation from the lips of Visconti Venosta, a diplomat whose style was all indirection and finesse, but a man of solid moral temper, unshakable in his faith in liberty and hence unpleasing to Bismarck, at a time when Europe was witnessing the insolent triumph of armed forces.

Bonghi wrote a famous essay on Bismarckism a few months later, continuing the theme: the Italian idea, founded on "inquiry into the actual conscience of the people," announced a dawn of peace and justice in Europe. And if the idea of force, which for fifty years Europe had tried to subject to the idea of right, now suddenly rose up once more with a smile of mockery on its face for those who had been so deluded, if the new system took iron and fire for its name, this was the work of Count Bismarck, the man who toyed with principles; and of his people too, a litigious people, more stubborn and intrusive than any other, a people that reads more and reads better than others do, but in whom no light descends to the soul from the peaks of intellect.[84]

Stripped of its polemical fervor, which was overly drastic and drew schematically crude and simplistic comparisons, inasmuch as the Italian movement had not been without its demonstrations of pure force and the German one had not lacked reinforcement from idealism even in its Bismarckian phase, the core of the thesis of Bonghi, Dina, and Bon Compagni, to which the foreign minister also adhered, was true. It conveyed a much clearer grasp of the underlying state of affairs than the subsequent efforts of historians who have toiled to reveal affinities between the two great European national movements of the nineteenth century have done.

How right these Italians were in predicting that a treaty like the one imposed on France could never lead to real peace but only to a truce, an armed interlude destined to prepare a new and more tremendous conflict.[85] In viewing the incorporation of Alsace-Lorraine into the new empire as a dreadful error,[86] one whose

---

[84] In Bonghi, *Ritratti e profili di contemporanei* 3:147, 150, 157, 159, 161 (= vol. 6 in *Opere* [Florence, 1935]. De Simone had referred to Bismarck in 1867 with the phrase "I am *iron and fire*" (*Del principio di nazionalità*, p. 38). Both Bonghi and De Simone have in mind Bismarck's expression of September 1862 "durch Blut und Eisen," ["with blood and iron"], which had raised such a sensation but which in any case echoed the Latin expression he had used in 1859, "ferro ignique" (cf. Eyck, *Bismarck* 1:429, and the characteristic defense of A. O. Meyer, *Bismarck*, pp. 185–86).

[85] Bonghi, *Nove anni* 2:448–49, 453–54, 460. Cf. as well Amari, *Carteggio* 2:199.

[86] *L'Opinione* hammers at this point for many months, as does Bonghi, who writes very acutely at one point that Alsace and Lorraine "will be as much of a lesion on the body of the new Germany as Lombardy and Venetia were on the body of the old Austria. In fact they will be a much more malignant and dangerous sore. In Italy there was not a strong nation already constituted on the borders of Lombardy and Venetia, as France is on the borders of Alsace and Lorraine" ("E Parigi?" in

first consequence for Europe would be a continuous mistrustful armed watch, followed by its tearing itself apart in a tragic conflagration, how perspicacious they were—and a historian of today can only corroborate the views they espoused as they fought their own combat.[87] Likewise their belief in the objective disparity between the Italian Risorgimento and its German counterpart, as the two movements worked themselves out, was unerring.

From the outset the problems of nationhood and of "national mission" had been approached in two clearly divergent ways: On the one hand, the tendency to shift the defining component of nationality outside the sphere of human will and locate it in a naturalistic *a priori*, from which the idea that race conditions the life of a people from its origins would later fatally be derived, grew steadily stronger.[88] On the other hand, from the time of Foscolo and Cuoco, there was the opposing tendency to insist on the factor of will, hence education: dominant themes of Mazzini's message. In the sequel this ideological differentiation was fleshed out in the diversity of forms and modes through which the two tendencies advanced toward their climaxes. The former was completely bound up with the initiatives of state and monarchy: this was a result of the total failure of the revolution of 1848, which seemed to have passed away without leaving behind any residue capable of producing action. In fact, the "mistakes" made then seemed to legitimize the appeal to pure force. Blood and iron, Bismarck had said, contrasting these to the speeches and the resolutions carried by majorities in the style of 1848: Germany does not turn to Prussia because it is liberal but because it is strong.[89] Unity has to be created not by liberty, not by national decisions, but by the power of a state set against that of other states. Droysen had pointed to unity as a problem of foreign policy, having undergone a considerable change of heart and shed the ideals he had held in 1848.[90] In Italy the national movement was divided from the outset into two very different forces, which to a

---

La Perseveranza for 26 November 1870). Another writer also observes that as a result of the peace too much pressure is being brought to bear on the loser by the winner, and says that France will remain at the heart of Europe, "hurting and feverish, until the day comes when it believes that the hour of its revenge has arrived and seizes its chance" (*La Perseveranza* for 30 January 1871).

[87] H. A. L. Fisher, *Storia d'Europa* 3:226 (Italian translation: Bari, 1937). It was Bonghi who said so repeatedly at the time: "The peace will certainly suspend hostilities, whatever the terms may be. But a peace that takes two provinces away from France has no more hope of lasting than the one Napoleon imposed on Prussia after the campaign of 1806. This is what is in store for France and for all of Europe: we have escaped the immediate danger of war by leaving it to hang over our heads for many years to come. This will be the first of the penalties to be paid by the states that have for the present displayed their serene avoidance of any risk" ("Un amaro consiglio," in *La Perseveranza* for 10 December 1870).

[88] From F. Schlegel's *Philosophische Vorlesungen aus dem Jahren 1804 bis 1806*: "the more ancient and pure the racial stock, the more ancient and pure are the customs; and the more the customs are so, . . . the greater will be the Nation" (cited in F. Meinecke, *Cosmopolitismo e Stato nazionale* 1:81 [Italian translation: Perugia-Venice, 1930]). Cf. the acute observations (in relation to Herder) of Antoni, *La lotta contro la ragione*, p. 179, on the German idea of the nation, which was not the idea of a national will but that of a national "nature," antecedent to human will. In Herder factors that are naturalistic in the biological sense already make their appearance (Antoni, ibid., p. 160; a different opinion in H. Kohn, *The Idea of Nationalism* [4th ed.; New York, 1948], p. 430).

[89] Eyck, *Bismarck* 1:429, cited at n. 84 above.

[90] Gilbert, *Johann Gustav Droysen*, pp. 120 ff., cited at ch. 2, n. 2 above.

large extent never subsequently merged: the revolutionary initiative and the royal one; Mazzinian republicanism and Cavour's allegiance to the house of Savoy. The second carried the day, having cleverly made use of the first, but not to the point of burying all signs of the two different points of departure. In fact it was forced to take on board many of the ideas and sentiments of the revolutionaries. The state of Piedmont and its ruling house of Savoy had been able to assume and retain leadership only by accepting, within certain limits and with certain reserves, the ideals that Mazzini's propaganda had planted in the hearts of Italians, especially the ideals of independence and unity. Bismarck's Prussia took on board nothing at all from the "agitators" and underwent no interior mutation as Piedmont had done from Carlo Alberto to Vittorio Emanuele II. The Prussia of Wilhelm I carried out its mission between 1864 and 1870 while denying any connection with the men of 1848. The Piedmont of Vittorio Emanuele II had carried out its between 1859 and 1861, shaping a parliamentary system out of the Statuto, seeking and obtaining the collaboration of Garibaldi, all under the guidance of a prime minister, Cavour, who had made the necessity of political liberty his credo before and after 1848 and never deviated from it, even when he had naturally to resort to diplomatic maneuvers and use force to cut through certain impasses.

Admittedly, this line of conduct had been imposed on him because of the much weaker military and political power of Piedmont, which when fighting alone had been beaten at Novara. Prussia on the other hand had won victories from the beginning. In consequence Piedmont had largely fallen back on the sort of moral armaments that Prussia usually chose to dismiss out of hand, and had appealed to public opinion to a degree that was never dreamed of in Prussia. The very diversity between the physical and moral beings of the two leaders—Cavour short, rotund, and vivacious; Bismarck tall, stocky, hard, and irritable—could almost symbolize the diversity between their methods of action and the spirit that guided it in each case. For the profoundly liberal Cavour, the plebiscite had been indispensable. Bismarck was disposed to make use of the ideas and energies of liberalism only as long as they served his purposes and contingent political calculations. He made his way forward with shattering military victories, compelling the surrender of entire enemy armies. One side used force, which from being a means turned into a self-sufficient ideal, as usually happens, while the other repudiated force for its own sake, as being that which for far too long had suffocated the free expression of the national life.[91]

The identification of nationhood and liberty brought about by the Risorgimento, and the Italian idea of the nation as a thing of the spirit, produced the consequence that the principle of nationality had a universal import for the Ital-

---

[91] On this fundamental diversity between Italian and German unity, cf. B. Croce, *Storia d'Europa nel secolo decimonono*, pp. 247 ff., and E. Sestan in *Primato* for 15 December 1942. Novikov had already insisted on this in *La missione dell'Italia*, pp. 292 ff. On the continual struggle between liberalism and nationalism in the German movement, and the noticeable tendency to veer toward the second, cf. Sestan, *La Costituente di Francoforte*, pp. 11 ff.

ians, not one limited to their own land. Nationality applied in every portion of the earth on which oppressed peoples were groaning—though this became a passion mainly in the case of Mazzini, who had made himself the prophet of this kind of universality, and had drawn upon it in turn for the revolutionary impact he made. But even those who were not Mazzinians and revolutionaries nonetheless showed his influence when they professed their belief that nations should be free wherever they were found—though in point of fact they had no intention of putting themselves in jeopardy for the sake of others. The Italian national movement could thus easily form ties with other analogous movements and tendencies, and Mazzini was not the only one to try to bring Italians, Hungarians, South Slavs, and Poles together; in fact, royal diplomacy sometimes did the same, borrowing once again ideas and concepts from Mazzini and pruning them down for tactical use in its campaign. As an offshoot, the act of volunteering to fight for the cause of others became a typically magnanimous expression of the Risorgimento, and many, some well known and others not, went off to fight and die for liberty and independence in other countries, keeping faith with the Mazzinian precept to love one's own homeland because one loved all the homelands. This was truly noble. It gives a warm human glow to the accomplishments of the Risorgimento, and the soul of the people rightly recognized and honored it in the person of Garibaldi when they called him the hero of two worlds.

The Germans form a striking contrast. They were dynamic and tenacious in securing the ideal of German nationhood, but the great majority of them remained indifferent, when not hostile, to the national movements of others. The Italians were to find this out in 1848, when in the Parliament of Frankfurt it was pronounced necessary that the Confederation hold the line of the Mincio in the interests of its own self-defense.[92] Ten years later, in December of 1858, the same de Launay who was to be the great friend of Germany in 1870 had been forced to recognize this: "The Prussians are passionate proponents of the principle of nationality only at home. . . . One recalls the position of the Parliament of Frankfurt in 1848–49, when it loudly proclaimed the rights of nationality while being careful not to apply them to the Poles or the Bohemians, and hadn't a word to say about the Italian independence movement, choosing instead to endorse the theory of military enclosure and the necessity of the line of the Mincio for the defense of the Confederation."[93] The year 1859 had seen, it is true, a few cases of German sympathy for the Italian cause, especially from Lassalle, who was of

[92] The position taken in 1848 becomes easier to understand if one recalls the mistrust of German public opinion in the preceding years toward any alteration in the territorial status quo in Italy; cf. S. Bortolotti, "La stampa germanica nei riguardi del movimento nazionale italiano negli anni 1841–1847," *Rassegna Storica del Risorgimento* 25 (1938): 519 ff. On the sudden evaporation in 1848 of the "warm sympathies" of the court of Berlin for the kingdom of Sardinia, cf. F. Cataluccio, "Piemonte e Prussia nel 1848–49," *Archivio Storico Italiano* 106 (1948): 62 ff. On the mission of Arese to Munich and its immediate end, cf. R. Bonfadini, *Vita di Francesco Arese* (Turin-Rome, 1894), pp. 78 ff.

[93] De Launay to Cavour, 25 December 1858 (cited in Valsecchi, "La politica di Cavour e la Prussia," p. 45).

course a revolutionary. But in the press and among political commentators hostility was much more frequent.[94]

There were no young men from the much more populous and bellicose Germany volunteering to fight for the liberty and independence of foreign regions. Those who fell did so in their own cause, not that of others, and the nation that produced Moltke had no Garibaldi. What would Jeanne d'Arc have been, outside France? asked Treitschke, a typical representative of this German patriotism. A silly fool. The case was the same with Garibaldi, one of those men "with large hearts and empty heads" whose force derives from their fidelity to the idea that devours them: without faith in their ideal, they appear weak and fatuous.[95] Treitschke had not the remotest suspicion that it was out of fidelity to his idea that Garibaldi fought on French soil. Powerful but closed in on itself, the life of the Germanic idea of nationhood was confined to Germany, to the point that it seemed in the end to the Italian moderates to be bound up with the reborn spirit of conquest.

But it was not only the idea of nationality as it was understood in Italy that came into conflict with the postulates and the manifestations, political and ideological, of Germany in its hour of victory. The preoccupations of Dina, Bonghi, Bon Compagni, and in the circle of those with political responsibility, of Visconti Venosta and Nigra, were not in fact exclusively those of Italians struck by the wide gap between their own ideology and that of others. They were the preoccupations of Europeans who saw that the basis of the harmony and civilization of the continent was cracking. The right of force and the principle of conquest, as they were being put into practice by the armies of Moltke and the policies of Bismarck, were a direct blow to European equilibrium, to European society, to the community of states without which it was impossible to imagine an orderly conduct of life among the nations, and without which there was a risk of returning to the age of the invasions, of universal convulsions.

The Franco-Prussian War left "the structure of all of Europe shaken, half in ruins";[96] conditions were bad and the evil had been greatly aggravated, or rather created in the first place, by the spinelessness of the great powers and their inability to make themselves heard in the midst of a conflict to which none could remain indifferent, since it involved the entire "political body of Europe," and which ought to have been halted and reconciled in time through collective intervention.[97] But nothing had worked. The principles of humanity and political

[94] Cf. Valsecchi, "Il 1859 in Germania: la stampa e i partiti," pp. 97 ff., 231 ff., and "Il 1859 in Germania: idee e problemi," pp. 268 ff.

[95] H. von Treitschke, *Briefe* 3:300 (Leipzig, 1920). It was entirely understandable that Treitschke should oppose Garibaldi at that moment, but the important point is the way he goes beyond the moment and the specific question. The citation of Jeanne d'Arc is also significant: it implies that each person must fight for his own country, and for it alone.

[96] Bonghi, *Nove anni* 2:433. And cf. p. 440: "we see all of Europe appalled by [Germany's] excessive use of force; the moral consortium of all the nations has been shattered by the harsh self-interest of each" (31 December 1870).

[97] Bonghi referred to "the fearfulness and cowardice" of Europe (*Nove anni* 2:448 and cf. pp. 411–13 and 453). See as well *La Perseveranza* for 23 August 1870 ("Le condizioni della pace secondo i Tedeschi"). Another writer remarked that it was painful "to see Europe reduced to an

generosity were nowhere to be seen, and the European concert, that modern version of the ancient Greek Amphictyony built up over half a century from the Congress of Vienna, had miserably failed the test.[98] Europe had given proof of thoughtless egoism when faced with the events of a war in which its vital interests were nevertheless implicated.[99]

Much of the blame lay with England. Forgetting the glorious traditions of Palmerston, it was now immured with Gladstone in its splendid isolation, insensible as it seemed to the rapid decline in its influence in international life and satisfied with domestic prosperity, manufacturing and commerce, domestic freedom.[100] England was committed to a policy "half mystical and half mercantile," which in the long run would strip the English character of its vigor and the English name of all its prestige. The "effacement of England," which a number of British writers and politicians were themselves lamenting,[101] was the primary cause of the "effacement of Europe." The other powers were to blame as well,

---

impotence that assumes the appearance of timidity and fear." If the neutral powers do not take action, "we cannot imagine any longer what European society will be reduced to. We will have a state of dissolution that will loosen every bond of solidarity among the peoples and threaten us with a permanent state of war" ("La politica estera," in *L'Opinione* for 21 January 1871). *L'Opinione* had already been calling for action by the neutral powers, given that the problem of France "is a problem for all of Europe" (*L'Opinione* for 7 October 1870; and much more cautiously on 3 November). Journalists were not the only ones to express these preoccupations: on 13 January 1871, as noted above at n. 28, Lanza as prime minister wrote to La Marmora: "There is nothing notable to report here except the horror aroused by the bombardment of Paris! But Europe remains unmoved, as though it were a fireworks display! The consequences might however be fatal for future generations too" (Lanza, *Le carte* 7:34).

[98] C. Bon Compagni, "Francia e Italia," letter 9, in *L'Opinione* for 2 December 1871.

[99] "Le condizioni della pace secondo i Tedeschi," in *La Perseveranza* for 24 September 1870. And cf. the articles in the numbers for 28 September, 4 and 20 October, and 13 November; all except the one on 4 October are by Bonghi.

[100] Bonghi, *Nove anni* 2:412, 436–37; *La Perseveranza* for 2, 20, and 21 October 1870 (Bonghi), 1 January, 21 February (Bonghi), 1 March 1871 (Bonghi); *L'Opinione* for 19 November 1870 (article "L'attitudine dell'Inghilterra"), 8 December 1870 ("La rassegnazione dell'Inghilterra"), 8 January 1871 ("La politica inglese"), 11 March 1871 ("La politica dell'Inghilterra"). On 15 January 1871 the bombardment of Paris inspired the observation that in England it was finally beginning to be understood "that in order to fulfill its true mission it is not enough to be a great manufacturer; it is necessary as well to be a great nation and have a great policy"—meaning the policy that Gladstone and Granville had been incapable of pursuing and realizing. What Dina thought about England generally in that period is revealed in the naturally cruder language of a private letter to Castelli of 19 November 1870: "England makes a fuss about the eastern business but in the end it will drop its breeches [= submit, give in]. It has allowed France to be dismembered and is threatening war. Against whom? I have never seen a more miserable policy" (Castelli, *Carteggio politico* 2:492). He was not alone in this: Visconti Venosta had observed to de Launay as early as 23 July 1870: "I fear that England, which ought to be in the forefront of situations like this one, after having done little to prevent the war, will do equally little to bring about the second result [of limiting the war]" (AE, *Ris.*, cart. 10). Minghetti uttered similar judgments (Luzzatti, *Memorie* 1:309). It was not only the men of the Right who viewed English policy with astonishment and regret; Mazzini, with his accustomed intransigence, was much more severe, finding that England had deliberately surrendered the *initiative* by "embarking under the name of *nonintervention* on a policy of local *interest*" (*Agli italiani* [1871], in *Scritti* 92:88); and cf. *Politica internazionale* (1871), ibid., 92:144 and 149: the theory of nonintervention propounded by England is "the negation of all the principles intellectually acquired by Humanity down to our day . . . atheism carried over into international life, or if you like the deification of Egoism."

[101] Meine, *England und Deutschland*, p. 56.

including Italy, for their indolence and incapacity, which local conditions might partially excuse but not completely justify.

Mixed with these worries there was disdain for the arrogance of the victors and the passive complicity of others, sentiments that found an outlet in projects to involve the neutral powers for the purpose of putting an end to the war, and in the requests for a more energetic policy. A request in this sense was addressed by Nigra to Visconti Venosta from Tours on 1 October 1870; "I cannot refrain from communicating to you the grave preoccupations aroused in me by the present state of affairs in France and Europe. My view is that it is time the neutral powers got together to try seriously to put an end to this wretched, murderous war. France bears much of the blame for breaking the peace; it is equally guilty of letting itself be beaten. No one denies that it must pay the price for both transgressions. But *est modus in rebus*, and even victory has its limits. Prussia has every right to obtain guarantees against future attacks. But is it really necessary to take Alsace and Lorraine in order to obtain that? Is it necessary or useful for Prussia itself and for Europe to create a new problem of nationality on the left bank of the Rhine and on the Moselle? Wouldn't it be sufficient guarantee for Germany, by now united and formidably prepared for war, to have the fortresses in eastern France dismantled? It seems to me that Europe is not using foresight, and that it is preparing for itself a future full of danger and turbulence through its indifference. Nor do I find it in the least acceptable that Prussia should say to the neutral powers: 'You did not take part in the war, you therefore have no right to take part in the peace.' This maxim is contrary to the interests of European equilibrium, contrary to humanity, contrary to the principle of localizing and limiting wars. And it tends to favor the formation of armed coalitions."[102]

Months later Anselmo Guerrieri Gonzaga wrote in a similar vein to the minister for foreign affairs: "All the forecasts proved inadequate. The *tutelary conditions* of *European equilibrium* which the league of neutrals was supposed to protect—where are they? It was these, along with the principles of nationality and liberty, that we were supposed to maintain together with England. . . . Wouldn't the right thing to do at this point be to disavow the famous obligation we have assumed with England, and let each resume his own liberty of action? At least then we wouldn't have the air of being accomplices in a policy for which I have not yet been able to find a suitable epithet, assuming there is one. The days of Paris are ringing terribly in my ears."[103]

In these and similar ideas there certainly inhered an element of practical purpose. The friends of France intended to rouse the governments out of their torpor by painting a turbid portrait of what lay in the future. When they cried that Europe was in danger, it is evident they were more or less consciously heeding the call of their own affections, the feelings and memories that welled up from the depths of their souls; in sum, they were heeding sentimental impulses, and the inclinations of the party to which they belonged. When French propaganda

---

[102] Visconti Venosta archive.
[103] February 1871; Visconti Venosta archive.

was able to raise its voice above a feeble whisper, it availed itself of arguments of the same kind. The reasoning of French writers and the French government in their desperate effort to attract assistance for their devastated country was perfectly analogous.[104]

Italian concern for Europe's shaken equilibrium obviously derived from the fact that the current fearful spasm was judged to be harmful to Italy.[105] Italian foreign policy had turned on a pivot for the last twelve years that, despite Mentana, had brought great advantages for the kingdom. Now it had been dislodged, and Italy was faced with a man, Bismarck, whose policy between September 1870 and March 1871 was anything but reassuring on the most pressing question for Italy, that of Rome. Meanwhile the clericals and circles close to the Vatican raised a clamor and appeared at times to be hailing a savior in the person of the Protestant Wilhelm I, a new protector against the usurpation of Savoy. So it is not surprising that in the government and among those close to the government the alteration of European equilibrium seemed full of menace for Italy. As well there was something of the sense of disorientation of those who see their whole environment, in which they know how to maneuver with ease, changing completely, and must now invent a new line of conduct, different from the customary one. The disorientation was worse for the moderates because it meant they could no longer follow guidelines laid down by Cavour; his paradigm no longer functioned in the changed circumstances. The teachings of the great nobleman had been a fifth gospel for the moderates, their staff and their comfort in all the major questions, whether those of foreign policy, or making a capital of Rome, or a free church in a free state. Now they were forced to create policy for themselves, assume positions, find their way without being able to turn any longer to their ancestral genius for counsel.[106]

So there were purely emotive and instinctual drives at work, and immediate worries on Italy's account, but that was not all. In these men there was a part of

---

[104] "Europe has an overriding interest in not having either of the two nations too victorious, or too thoroughly beaten. . . . Peace can only be established and maintained by the common interest of Europe, or to put it another way, by having the league of neutral powers assume a threatening position" (E. Renan, "La guerre entre la France et l'Allemagne," in *Revue des Deux Mondes*, 15 September 1870, later republished in *La réforme*, pp. 152 and 156). And cf. the Chaudordy circular of 15 January 1871: does Europe intend to sign its own abdication and abandon itself to whatever fate Prussia assigns it? "European society is on the way to dissolving itself, that is the situation!" (*Archives diplomatiques*, 11–12 [1871–72], t. 4, n. 1112, p. 1515).

[105] This worry is expressed on 29 July 1870 by Dina to Castelli: "a Prussian victory would do us serious harm" (Castelli, *Carteggio politico* 2:472). It reappears on 25 August 1870 in the words of Ercole Oldofredi to Dina: "With European equilibrium broken . . . we will feel the burden falling on us more than on any other state" (Chiala, *Giacomo Dina* 3:248–49; Cavour's old friend goes on to express his regret for Italy's impotence). Another who expressed worry was Cialdini, who feared that reactionism was rising with the rise of Prussia and Russia (Castelli, *Carteggio politico* 2:481). Finally, R. Bonfadini wrote to his friend Visconti Venosta on 15 November 1870: "Prussia's overwhelming superiority is very threatening for Europe's future. It seems to me that England is destined to be the first to feel the effects of the vacuum left by France. But I fear that we will be the second. I hope you will do your best to keep us immune from maladies that are predictable, and have been predicted" (Visconti Venosta archive).

[106] This sense of disorientation is evident, for example, in the letter of Oldofredi to Dina, cited in the previous note.

their own mode of being and thinking, a whole political and ideological commitment, that was shocked and hurt by the act of "conquest." It was the "European" consciousness of the moderates. No matter how strong the national idea was, it was not sufficiently so to stifle all other thought, to suffocate the aspiration toward a wider community in which the single nations, while clearly retaining their own political and moral physiognomy intact, would nevertheless live a common life on the basis of a few general principles, and not only theoretical principles but a certain uniformity in general criteria of action. These men appealed to an idea of nationhood that did not go far enough to be called nationalism; which had not overflowed all bounds to make a desert all about it. It did not propound and glorify struggle for its own sake. It did not offer conquest for the sake of conquest as the supreme ideal. The notion of a "European consortium" was a corollary of the idea of nationhood, and not just among Italians who were pro-French, and adherents of the Right, but also in those whose views were different. The chief example is Marselli, a man of the center and strongly sympathetic to Germany, yet for whom "the principle of nationality has to be joined to that of equilibrium," the latter being understood as a law of general preservation. For Marselli the right to nationhood could only be defended by harmonizing it with the right that came from being European, from being human, so that events had to be judged by Italians as Italians, but also as Europeans.[107] Europe's interests could and should eventually impose limits on the interests of a single nation. The principle of nationality had to be affirmed; and with it the principle of equilibrium also returned, not "in its former dress, but renewed by being wedded" to the rights of the nations: this was the way to escape from the licentious tyranny of the very principle thus affirmed.

Faced with the problems raised by German unification, wrote the moderates, "we who are constant proponents of the principle of nationality are reduced to perplexity by this exaggeration of it, and we think that just as in private life no one is allowed to increase what is his by causing loss to others, all the more should it be illicit in the concert of nations for one of them to win an increase in size that prejudices the security of the others. It is necessary in order to maintain an equilibrium of forces and reduce the opportunities for war, that each nation be in a condition to survive and keep what belongs to it."[108] This was all the more necessary with Germany, which, as soon as it became powerful, had always set about infringing on others, without recognizing frontiers. Its doctrines about natural nationhood were for now confined to the language factor, and it preached that the homeland embraced all the countries where the German tongue sounded,

---

[107] Marselli, *Avvenimenti del 1870–71* 2:118 ff., esp. p. 126. And cf. an article that appeared in the course of a debate between Marselli and Bon Compagni in 1872: "Francia, Italia, e Germania," in *Nuova Antologia* 20 (July 1872): 551–52 (cited above at n. 61). In terms of intellectual history, Marselli's ideas might be traced back to Mazzini (the emphasis on the nation and on Europe as the equivalent of humanity), except for the fact that in Marselli the Mazzinian presuppositions, and the revolutionary aim, are entirely absent.

[108] In a reply to the German Homberger in *La Perseveranza* for 26 August 1870 it is stated that German unity ought to be made dependent upon changes of frontier to the advantage of France and Italy.

but soon it would reach the linguistic frontier and would then be driven to look for another sort of frontier: the "natural" sort. On that basis German unity might well threaten the liberty of Holland and Denmark, the security of Austria, and the independence of Italy.[109]

Even if one looked past the specific and most serious case, that of Germany, it was still necessary to set fixed limits to the application of the principle of nationality, which like every other human principle brought with it good effects but also a number of deleterious ones, and in certain cases was capable of exciting "desires, presumptions, and prejudices that raise an insuperable barrier to any kind of peaceful and permanent ordering of life."[110]

Gino Capponi was also perplexed and disturbed by the peace conditions of Bismarck and recited a *mea culpa* for himself and the other liberals: by decrying the wars made in the cabinet rooms of the ancien régime, he said, look what we have done, we have given birth to wars made by nations—the worst of all.[111] Thus he resumed with hindsight a theme that Mirabeau had been the first to intuit, before the fact. Even Sella, so blunt in maintaining the rights of nationhood, so Italian in his actions, even Sella openly acknowledged that there are "questions superior to those of homeland and nationality, which like the commune, the family, the individual, are only parts of humanity."[112]

There was Luzzatti, readier with sentimental effusions but a no less faithful patriot, who when faced a few years later with the spectacle of the Congress of Berlin, which was conducted amid the "dark deceits" of diplomacy and the reign of force and cunning, nostalgically recalled the Middle Ages, "more generous, more magnanimous . . . with their unreflective enthusiasms," and their Christian outlook, an outlook totally lost in the nineteenth century. He lamented the fact that the narrow idea of nationality should prevail over the idea, both human and sublime, of Christianity,[113] returning to the dreams that in 1799, while wars were raging, had inspired in Friedrich Novalis a hymn to medieval Christianity, and a prophecy of a new Christianity.

This was a path characteristically taken by those who wished to find a way around the myth that nationality was the exclusive principle to be followed in international relations. It was the attitude that would open the way, in practical terms, to agreements with Austria and the renunciation, temporarily at least, of irredentism: in other words, it was the attitude that would make the Triple Alliance, and the development of Italian foreign policy from 1882 to 1914, possible. The example of Marselli confirms this, for in 1871 he was already tending to set limits on the universality of the rights of nationhood, and in 1881, when backing the alliance with Austria and Germany, he declared that for Italy the Habsburg

---

[109] *La Perseveranza* for 9 and 29 August 1870 (Bonghi); the danger is felt to be a potential one at the moment, not a certainty.

[110] Thus Bonghi, referring to the national struggles in eastern Europe ("Rassegna politica," 30 September 1871, in *Nuova Antologia* 18: 452).

[111] Capponi, *Lettere* 4:260.

[112] In a letter to Luzzatti of 16 June 1874 (Luzzatti, *Memorie* 1:496).

[113] Luzzatti, *Memorie* 2:96 (Bologna, 1935).

empire provided valuable frontline protection against the possibility of a German empire in the Alps and in Trieste, a breastwork that had to be shored up, a state that might well be a contradiction of the principle of nationality, but one that had its advantages for the cause of humanity, since it prevented "the sort of immediate contact between huge, electrically charged, masses that produces history's worst shocks."[114]

The moderates did not give up the faith they had held in their youth, and continued to acknowledge its moral imperatives, even when they announced that the making of Italy had been completed, and so laid aside, for the moment, any further designs on regions that were Italian by language and descent but not by government. Visconti Venosta himself, a constant and sincere defender of the "general interests" of Europe, speaking in the Chamber at a time when there was once again a great deal of talk and debate about the rights of the nations, reaffirmed the respect (if no longer exactly the passion) of the moderates for the principle of nationality.[115]

But the truth is that for them the revolutionary period was over; the era in which "Italy sought in the complications of Europe a suitable opportunity to crown the edifice of its independence and its unity"[116] was finished. A new era had commenced, in which it was necessary above all to defend "the interests of general order,"[117] to use the classic formula of the diplomatic tradition from Metternich onward, and to follow criteria that were European in nature, not purely national.[118] In this way the advantage and the usefulness for Europe of Italy's presence in the concert of the great powers would be underlined.[119] When concrete decisions had to be made they would try to avoid violent shocks to the system, eruptions of armed conflict, and to facilitate instead the gradual development of the individual national movements, a development that they hoped could be brought to a happy conclusion without turning the continent upside down, thus reconciling the twin principles of nationality and European order.[120]

---

[114] "Politica estera e Difesa nazionale," in *Nuova Antologia* 58 (1881): 142.

[115] "[W]e knew, gentlemen, that the course of history cannot be halted. From the time it was represented by Piedmont, Italy always showed itself to be a benevolent protector of the populations and nationalities of the east. This is a tradition we cannot abandon because, I hasten to say, I believe it would be a black day for our country if we were to set ourselves against the great liberal and moral principles that are the honor of our epoch" (9 April 1878; *A.P., Camera*, p. 363).

[116] Visconti Venosta in his speech to the Chamber of 23 April 1877 (*A.P., Camera*, p. 2687).

[117] Jacini, *Pensieri sulla politica italiana*, p. 65.

[118] Jacini reproves "a considerable phalanx of the governing class" for not having done so (ibid., p. 66).

[119] Visconti Venosta in the speech of 23 April 1877, cited at n. 116 above.

[120] Visconti Venosta offers the following definition in the speech of 9 April 1878 (cited at n. 115 above): "This policy was not in the least disruptive. It proceeded with respect for treaties, but when occasions were offered and it was possible to get Europe's agreement, it helped to promote, through social evolution and the progress of the populations involved, the future of the nationalities that were called upon to furnish the elements of a new equilibrium with which the interests of Europe could have been accommodated, of an equilibrium destined to replace the old one when the components of the latter had ceased to exist" (*A.P., Camera*, pp. 363–64). There could not be clearer, more precise testimony to the aspirations of the moderates to combine Europe and nationality. Naturally it was a very elevated conception, one requiring exceptionally balanced judgment and a high level of culture. So one is not surprised at the interruption of the hon. Mazzarella: "This is too subtle a policy."

Until 20 September 1870, when Italian troops entered Rome, their policies had been revolutionary; now they had moved to the style of policy generically known as reformist. To put it another way, they now recommended in the case of other parts of Europe which did not yet enjoy free nationhood the application of the same reforming, gradualist program—first the railroads, the infant asylums, the savings and credit banks, then political liberty, and perhaps also independence, but everything done gently, without smashing down the doors and breaking the windows—that foreigners had recommended for Italy itself thirty years earlier,[121] that the Italian moderates themselves had endorsed, and that the firestorm of 1848, with its popular insurrections, had scattered to the winds, forcing the moderates and the house of Savoy to take the road of direct action.

The principle of nationality was thus contained, its universal revolutionary impact drained off. It remained a high ideal, but one not always susceptible of practical, immediate application; a principle of great moral value but one not always or everywhere valid politically. It assumed the specific form of "irredentism," a word widely used after 1876 which took the place of the previous term, "European revolution," and which in fact signified the substitution of a precise and well-defined territorial problem for the general appeal that had formerly been broadcast far and wide. The ideal took on a more solid and definite, but more restricted, aspect and became a question much more easily manageable by governments. Italian official policy was well aware of this, and as late as 1915, in fact even later, drew upon this remote premise to define its war aim in the 1914–1918 conflict: not the undoing of the Habsburg empire, which the heirs of Mazzini still hoped for, but merely the liberation of Trent and Trieste. Thus the momentous disappearance of the empire on the Danube caught the majority of the Italian governing class unprepared and disoriented.

In the foregoing pages we have been examining currents of thought among the moderates of the Right that looked out from Italy to Europe and even to humanity in general. It may be asked at this point: to what extent were they influenced by Mazzini, who had postulated such close connections between the single nation and wider humanity (which still essentially meant Europe for him), the Mazzini of *Giovine Italia* and *Giovine Europa*? To bring Italy back into Europe had been the dream of Mazzini from his youth, the dream of his essay *D'una letteratura europea*.[122] To push Europe ahead, the new young Europe that was to take the place of the moribund older one, to make it recover the "initiative" lost in 1814 and inaugurate a new, social epoch bearing the banner *God and humanity*,[123] these were the ideas that inspired his apostolate in the period of its greatest

---

[121] When Cattaneo was in Paris in the late summer of 1848, these things were preached to him by many "as they might have been to an Egyptian" (Cattaneo, *Dell'insurrezione di Milano*, p. iv).

[122] Cf. Salvatorelli, *Il pensiero politico italiano*, pp. 224 ff., and his *Pensiero e azione del Risorgimento*, p. 115.

[123] Mazzini, *Dell'iniziativa rivoluzionaria in Europa*, in *Scritti* 4:155, 163, 167, 176 ff. Cf. C. Morandi, *L'idea dell'unità politica d'Europa nel XIX e XX secolo*, pp. 51 ff.

intensity and force.[124] We might logically expect to find the influence of the greatest intellectual agitator that the Italian Risorgimento had produced, indeed the only personality of European stature in the field of ideology, as Cavour had been in the field of action.

Not a bit of it. The invocation of Europe by the men of the Right did not retain even the faintest trace of the revolutionary ferment that underlay Mazzini's appeal. They were not reaching toward a future Europe, bearing in its ample bosom the new peoples joined in brotherhood by the general political and moral revolution. Instead their gaze never left Europe as it had been molded by its august past, by its age-long tradition in culture, religion, and politics, and by eighteenth- and early nineteenth-century thought.

This is the Europeanism of the old school of moderates, of Balbo and Durando, and of Cavour himself: a cultural and political Europeanism of wide horizons, fed by learning and by personal experiences of travel and friendship; a Europeanism informed by a strong sense of liberty, but without the revolutionary impulse.

Mazzini's aim had been not just to rejoin Italy and Europe but also to revolutionize Europe, since in its existing form it was utterly unequal to its task, a mere relic of the past, not a forerunner of the future, as the Italy of the Renaissance princes had been. For the moderates and Cavour the aim had been to raise Italy to the level of the great peoples of the west, meaning essentially France and England,[125] certainly not to alter the foundations on which European civilization still rested. Those foundations appeared quite secure and utterly necessary. For Mazzini the present Europe had to die, while for the moderates it represented the highest flowering of civilization, the standard to which the spirit and the life of the new Italy had to be raised. Mazzini had cried out "revolutionize Italy and Europe"; the moderates had replied "let us modify Italy," by bringing it to the level of the great European powers. Mazzini's Europe was a Europe emerging from revolution, while the Europe of the others was a Europe of the "juste milieu," the judicious avoidance of extremism in matters of opinion so dear to the moderates of Italy and France.[126]

The two languages were profoundly different; the two tribes were not meant to communicate with each other. Mazzini dreamed of a universal renovation of the human stock, a redemption of mankind that was to begin with revolution in Italy and spread outward from there.[127] The moderates wanted only to solve the Italian problem. When independence and unity were attained, when Venetia and Rome

---

[124] Cf. also G. O. Griffith, *Mazzini profeta di una nuova Europa* (Italian translation: Bari, 1935), pp. 108–109.

[125] Salvatorelli, *Il pensiero politico italiano*, pp. 299–300, and *Pensiero e azione del Risorgimento*, pp. 122 ff.

[126] On the *juste milieu* as one of the fundamental political concepts of western Europe after 1830, cf., for Cavour, D. Zanichelli, *Cavour*, pp. 40 ff; Ruffini, *La giovinezza del conte di Cavour* 1:162 ff. and 247, and 2:297; Omodeo, *L'opera politica del Conte di Cavour* 1:13; Salvatorelli, *Il pensiero politico italiano*, pp. 292 ff.

[127] "The creation of Italy is an aim that, when reached, must alter the fate of Europe and of Humanity" (Mazzini, *La situazione* [1857], in *Scritti* 59:121).

were incorporated into Italy, the Europeanism of these cultivated Italians became a pacific Europeanism of conservatives and friends of the status quo. They had no wish to throw the European house into disorder. Once they had arranged things to their liking in their own quarters, they took the view that the edifice as a whole, in its present condition, did not require demolition and was in fact still handsome and solid and worth living in. Even before Balbo wrote, the idea that Italian independence should be promoted because it would strengthen the European fabric had been canvassed: broken up as it was, the country served no purpose, whereas if it were independent it would serve as a counterweight between France and Austria, and to the east between Russia and Austria.[128]

Alessandro Manzoni has a place in this pattern. He too extolled the "animated yet peaceful prevalence, the virtual unanimity, of free wills" in the Italian Risorgimento as opposed to the French Revolution, and when it was accomplished he wrote: "the other powers that forty-five years ago came to an agreement to stitch together a division of Italy which they supposed in their wisdom would be one of the fundamental conditions of a stable European order, later came to see that the destruction of their fine work in this peninsula, far from subverting true order, had done nothing but remove a source of recurring warfare, of fleeting advantages and costly disillusionments for some, and nagging anxiety for others. They found themselves, without realizing it, nearer to that ideal equilibrium of which they so often prated."[129]

What little there had been of general revolutionary ferment in the Europeanism of the moderates during the years of struggle was in any case destined to vanish like mist in the sunshine as soon as their final aspirations were realized. The taking of Rome closed, in effect, the cycle, placated their desires, and caused them to wish that the status quo should henceforth prevail.[130] They feared that a general European upheaval might have serious and unforeseeable repercussions for the newly constituted Italy, but they also had an instinctive conservatism, a temperamental reluctance to upset the apple cart and provoke general confusion. It was in their character. Having gotten exactly what they had known they wanted, they willingly assumed the role of *beati possidentes* and could no longer understand, if they ever had done, the restlessness and the discontent of a

---

[128] In 1826 the Piedmontese exile G. B. Marochetti, who had been involved in the uprisings of 1821, printed a volume entitled *L'Indépendance de l'Italie; moyen de l'établir dans l'intérêt général de l'Europe, considéré specialement sous le point de vue de l'équilibre politique* (2d ed., revised and corrected, 1830). Cf. M. Petrocchi, "Equilibrio politico ed indipendenza d'Italia," in *Archivio Storico Italiano* 98, no. 2 (1940): 131 ff. It is well known that Balbo too appealed to the interests of Europe and Christianity in order to support his ideas on the turning to the east of Austria and Italian independence; in addition to his *Speranze d'Italia*, cf. as well *Meditazioni storiche* (3d ed.; Florence, 1855), pp. 534 ff.

[129] See the introduction to *La Rivoluzione Francese del 1789 e la Rivoluzione Italiana del 1859* in *Tutte le opere di A. Manzoni*, ed. Lesca (Florence, 1923), pp. 994 and 998.

[130] In his report of 2 October 1860 to the Chamber, Cavour had asserted that the resolution of the Italian question would end forever the era of wars and revolutions in the south of Europe (*Discorsi Parlamentari* 11:240 [Rome, 1872]). Nor was this a mere tactical expedient; it corresponded to his sincere conviction and desire.

Mazzini, who never seemed to be satisfied and so appeared dangerous and "subversive," now more than ever.

The principle of nationality was, for the moderates, likewise "a great conservative principle," albeit of enlightened conservatism, according to a maxim of Cavour.[131] They interpreted it as domestic opposition to revolutionary agitation, and externally as the preservation of a European order, of a "European community." One of the major reproaches addressed to France by those friendly to it in Italy concerned its too frequent changes of government, the unstable humor of its people, its not knowing how to slacken its tension and be content at a certain point with the results it had achieved, all of which made it a cause of general instability. The idea of Europe constantly defended by the moderates was the Europe Mazzini had described as old and decrepit, a refrain taken up in Mazzinian tones by Carducci, who condemned it as rotten to the core: *putrescat et resurgat.*[132]

"European unity as the past understood it is dissolved; it lies in the tomb of Napoleon," wrote Mazzini.[133] But Bonghi, Dina, Visconti Venosta, and Nigra were thinking no longer of the unity, but of what could more correctly be defined as a society, or as they called it, a "consortium," of Europe. Theirs was the "governmental Europe" regarded as degenerate by Mazzini, against which he had always violently fought.[134] The consortium had codified its practice as the doctrine of equilibrium and the concert of the great powers, two principles that were meant to save Europe from imperialistic adventures and hegemonic attempts like that of Napoleon I: in other words, from enterprises that, by suffocating the single states and the individual ways of life of the different peoples, would have signified the death of European civilization, a fruit into which the sap of many different nations had to flow for it to ripen. If one peered into the distance one could make out a *deus ex machina* looming behind the ideas of these men of the Right, a remote figure in whose vicinity they would certainly not, at one time, have imagined finding themselves. It was the figure of Klemens Wenzel Lothar, Prince of Metternich.

In recognizing the mildness of the peace treaties of 1815 in contrast to what Bismarck intended to impose on France,[135] and finding in those distant pacts "a homogeneous basis" that was missing from the current ones,[136] the leading political commentators of the Right revealed a typical characteristic of the conservative mentality of the Italian governing party, as regards European affairs. But the remote Metternichian origins of the political Europeanism propagated in *L'Opinione*, *La Perseveranza*, and the *Nuova Antologia* were fully revealed, at the end of 1871, by Carlo Bon Compagni, one of the most eminent men of the Right and

---

[131] In the speech to the Senate on the annexation of the Mezzogiorno, on 16 October 1860 (*Discorsi Parlamentari* 11:277).

[132] Carducci to Giuseppe Chiarini, 26 July 1877 (*Lettere* 11:161).

[133] Mazzini, *Dell'iniziativa rivoluzionaria in Europa*, in *Scritti* 4:177.

[134] Ibid., 4:155–56.

[135] Bonghi, *Nove anni* 2:453.

[136] "La pace," in *L'Opinione* for 12 April 1871.

one of Cavour's most faithful collaborators,[137] the man who on 27 March 1861, with Cavour's full agreement, had presented in the very recently created Italian parliament the order of the day that proclaimed Rome as the capital of Italy. This was not a reactionary, therefore, not a one-time partisan of Austria. And yet it was he who pronounced a eulogy, from a Europeanist point of view, of the system of Metternich.

The recent war, he observed in the ninth of his letters published under the title *Francia e Italia*,[138] has altered the conditions of the whole European consortium. What is this consortium? "The peoples of modern Europe take part in the same political system, just as all the heavenly bodies that orbit round the sun take part in the same planetary system." The real difference between the Middle Ages and the modern period lies in the existence, ever since the sixteenth century, of such a system; for it was then that we find "the origins of a *political equilibrium* aimed at limiting the power of any sovereign who showed an intention to overwhelm the other states. These days the system of political equilibrium is regarded as an old relic by quite a few badly mistaken people. The concept of political equilibrium derives from a circumstance that unfortunately always obtains, which is that those who are overpowerful become overweening."

Admittedly, the victors of 1815 had stabbed Italy in the back and entered into an association to suppress liberty. "This is the story of the Holy Alliance as we were taught it in our youth, and unfortunately the story is true. But it is a story that is not yet over." The victors left to formerly Napoleonic France all the territory that had made it a great power under the old monarchy, giving proof of a moderation "if not unique, certainly very unusual in history. As a result of this moderation, the abolition of the right of conquest, promulgated by the Constituent Assembly with solemn declarations that turned out to be empty words, became a reality." And there was another benefit from the Holy Alliance: "the recognition that in all questions of international law, the interests of the single states must be reconciled with the general interests of Europe." The five great powers have, since that time, constituted a "European Amphictyony," whose intervention was for the most part beneficial, when it ceased to present itself as the implacable enemy of all forms of liberty. In result Europe has been able to enjoy one of its longest and most beneficial periods of peace.

European equilibrium as the political system characterizing the modern era, the pentarchy of the great powers: how these concepts take us back to the atmosphere of 1814–15, to the world of Metternich and Castlereagh and Friedrich von Gentz! When he referred to the "European system," Bon Compagni was expressly citing Ancillon, and Heeren, the author of the *Handbuch der Geschichte des europäischen Staatensystems und seiner Kolonien*, the chief formulator of the idea of the European system,[139] revered by Göttingen. The German statesmen of

---

[137] Omodeo, *L'opera politica del Conte di Cavour* 1:171.

[138] In *L'Opinione* for 2 December 1871. These letters, with the addition of two more to Marselli published in the *Nuova Antologia* were subsequently collected in the volume *Francia e Italia* (Turin, 1873).

[139] Antoni, *La lotta contro la ragione*, pp. 114 ff.; Kaegi, *Historische Meditationen* 1:283–85.

the Napoleonic age and the Restoration, including Hardenberg, received their intellectual formation from Heeren, as did Metternich himself, through Koch at Strasbourg. Bon Compagni was deliberately accepting the idea of Europe cherished by every conservative. It should not be surprising to find that, without realizing it, Bon Compagni sketched out ideas and used expressions almost identical to those that we come upon when we open the *Mémoires* of Metternich: ". . . there are no more isolated states; . . . one must never lose sight of the *society* of states; . . . what characterizes the modern world and distinguishes it essentially from the ancient one is the tendency of states to draw closer to one another and to form a sort of *corps social*. . . . Modern society . . . reveals to us the application of the principles of solidarity and equilibrium among states, and presents us with the spectacle of a number of states joining their efforts to oppose the preponderance of any single one."[140] Metternich too, the chancellor devoted to the idea of order, had had to take up arms against those who denied the principle of equilibrium: "The idea of *political equilibrium* has often been attacked since the general peace (1814–15), and the imperial cabinet itself has been reproached for promoting such a folly. Nonetheless, when the idea is rightly understood, it is the only correct approach. Peace without equilibrium is a chimera."[141]

Other voices from the past also reechoed as Bon Compagni expatiated on the European Amphictyony: for instance, the observations of Castlereagh, the friend and colleague of Metternich, on the union of the great powers as the indispensable prerequisite to European peace, the secure safeguard of the liberty and tranquillity of the "Commonwealth of Europe";[142] and indeed everything that the first half of the European nineteenth century had said and written on the function of the great powers, from the essay of Ranke which applied the new term[143] to the past and made the concept of a "great power" a key to the interpretation of history,[144] to the notes of Thouvenel, French minister of foreign affairs, who in

---

[140] Metternich, *Mémoires* 1:30–31 (in the Italian translation [Turin, 1943], pp. 38–39). On the "European" ideas of the Austrian chancellor, see H. von Srbik, *Metternich* 1:350 ff. (Munich, 1925); Rohden, *Die klassische Diplomatie von Kaunitz bis Metternich*, passim and esp. pp. 138–39.

[141] Metternich, *Mémoires* 1:127, n. 1 (in the Italian translation, p. 143, n. 1).

[142] Cf. for example Castlereagh to Liverpool (1818): ". . . and it gives the efficacy and virtually the simplicity of the resolutions of a single state to the councils of the great powers," in C. K. Webster, "Castlereagh et le système des congrès (1814–1822)," *Revue des études napoléoniennes* (1919): 79 and cf. p. 80, and Webster, *The Foreign Policy of Castlereagh* 1:427 ff. (London, 1931). And see above all *British Diplomacy, 1813–1815: Select Documents Dealing with the Reconstruction of Europe*, ed. C. K. Webster (London, 1921), pp. 93, 101, 116, 126, 141, 194–95, 218, 233, 238–39, 256, 270, 275, 397, etc.

[143] The term "great power" [*grande puissance*] is in fact very rarely found even in the second half of the eighteenth century; the scheme then in use was still that of a struggle between a *puissance dominante* and a *puissance rivale*, two powers of the first order, flanked by those *de second ordre*. But in Mably there is already a contrast between *grandes puissances* and *puissances subalternes* (*Oeuvres complètes* 5:19 [Lyon, 1796]). Certainly in 1815 at Vienna the representative of Holland, Hans von Gagern, observed that "he did not know the precise meaning nor the intention of this newly invented term, *grandes puissances*." Cf. Ch. Downer Hazen, "Le congrès de Vienne (1814–15)," *Revue des études napoléoniennes* (1919): 69; and also M. H. Weil, *Le dessous du Congrès de Vienne* 1:219, 276 (Paris, 1917).

[144] The celebrated work *Die grossen Mächte* appeared in 1833.

1860 detailed with bureaucratic exactness the tasks, prerogatives, and duties of the great powers.[145]

Bon Compagni was not alone. Others who felt more or less the same way expressed their regret for the end of the old European consortium which had arisen out of the tempest of the Napoleonic era. No doubt it had had its drawbacks. But now Europe had arrived at a harmful (and total) "dissociation" among the states: "the perpetual coordination of their views and interests by a group of powers was a despotism, so in reaction we denied it any authority at all, any possibility of being exercised. Now the solitary and warlike domination of the most powerful single state has replaced the calm and united domination of the group."[146] Nicola Marselli also came forward, eleven years later, with very similar considerations. He declared that the principles of *laisser faire* and *laisser passer* could not be applied even to the nationalities when their evolution into autonomous empires, ultrapowerful and ambitious, became a menace for the other states that were necessary components of the "general European organism," and he posited that if there was a distinction to be made between European politics in the second half of the nineteenth century and the politics of the century and a half before that, it was not because the principle of intervention was to be replaced by its complete opposite, "indifference on the part of the nations," but because "the rules governing intervention" ought to be tightened up and to some degree changed. This perceptive historian and theorist of military institutions in their connection with the entire life of the people then turned back to the Metternichian system as well. He cited at length the celebrated pages of the *Mémoires*, published only recently, in which Metternich had expounded his theory about the necessity for the European system, seen as characteristically modern in comparison to the medieval world. Marselli admitted that Metternich's "practice" did not correspond to the "Christian love" that was found in his theory, that Metternich had in fact recognized "rights deriving from *totally successful conquest*." The conclusion drawn by Marselli was that "there should be a gulf between international politics in our time and the methods of chancellor Metternich"—only to assert, immediately after, his adhesion to the European principles of Metternich: "ought we also to say that there should be a gulf between our politics and the principle of solidarity among states, the united efforts of a number of states to oppose the preponderance of a single one, to halt the advance of its supremacy? If that were the

[145] Cf. *Fontes iuris gentium*, ed. V. Bruns (Berlin, 1932), ser. B, sec. 1, t. 1, part 1, fasc. 2, pp. 971–74. This is the clearest and most complete exposition of what was meant by "great power" in the nineteenth century. On the import of the terms "balance of power" and "European concert" at the middle of the nineteenth century, see the penetrating observations of Binkley, *Realism and Nationalism, 1852–1871*, pp. 157 ff. On the end of the idea of a "federative" policy in 1870–71, see ibid., pp. 299 ff.

[146] "Il 1871," in *La Perseveranza* for 1 January 1871. Reflections in the same vein appeared in an anonymous work published at Bologna in 1870, *La nazionalità e l'equilibrio europeo*, in which the possibility and necessity of an accord between the two principles of nationality and equilibrium, so as to avoid the two extremes of excessive agglomeration of peoples on one hand, and the excessive splitting up of them on the other, is maintained (pp. 16 ff. and 29).

case, there would be no more reason to speak of a practical international politics, and Europe really would become a mere geographic expression."

As for Bon Compagni, so also for Marselli, the fault of the Quadruple Alliance of 1814–15 had been to oppose the free government of peoples. Today international solidarity concedes "that every nation has the freedom to constitute itself and govern itself in its own way; but on the condition that it not become a disruptive element of the social whole, an element that threatens the peace, liberty, and independence of the other nations. When this occurs, it is legally possible to set a limit to the constitution of a national Empire."[147]

With this trend of thought we find ourselves in a world congenial to European conservatives and professional diplomats, a world whose roots went back to the lengthy discussions of the sixteenth and seventeenth centuries on European equilibrium, which even at that time was considered a species of "constitution" of Europe,[148] but which had really only emerged into its own after the Napoleonic tempest, as something precise, complete, with every part well honed, and above all with the aim of general peace, in the form of the system of Metternich.

It was a curious destiny that, in a certain sense, took men whose mission had been to overthrow the Habsburg domination in Italy and positioned them in the tradition of the chancellor of Franz I of Austria! Curious, if not for the fact that Metternich had been the major exponent and most eminent advocate of a general mode of dealing with the problem of European politics in the aftermath of Napoleon, and that after him it had become the common formula, the collective property almost, of the diplomats of Europe and the commentators on international relations. It was a formula from which it was no doubt possible to break free, but doing so would mean making revolution on a European scale, a revolution that would overflow national boundaries and pervade all the nations.

Only if that should occur could one forget about all the equations of equilibrium and refuse (in obedience to the moral and juridical principle of the parity among all the nations, great and small, because all were equally God's creatures) the concept typical of international conservatism, that of "great power." Mazzini, who had coupled Young Italy and Young Europe, might do so; for him the new "equilibrium" that would be established among the nations associated for a common end was not meant to preserve any trace of the old equilibrium among governments.[149]

But not the moderates! For them the Risorgimento had been and remained an affair of Italy and Italy alone, not Italy and Europe together. With business taken care of internally, they wanted to assume their place with a good conscience at

---

[147] Marselli, *La politica dello Stato italiano*, pp. 374–80; Marselli was concerned specifically with Pan-Slavism.

[148] Cf. Ter Meulen, *Der Gedanke der Internationalen Organisation* 1:42 (The Hague, 1917). Note that for Mazzini, in contrast, these attempts at European equilibrium "were lies without permanence" (*Nazionalismo e nazionalità*, in *Scritti* 93:95—the work was composed in 1871), and that the French Revolution changed nothing, being unable to eradicate that "miserable and unworthy policy." Once again, a total opposition of views.

[149] On "equilibrium" in Mazzini, acute considerations are found in Salvatorelli, "Mazzini e gli Stati Uniti d'Europa," *Rassegna storica del Risorgimento* 37 (1950): 457–58.

the "banquet of the nations,"[150] enter the so-called concert of the great powers: the last to arrive and the least important, but withal members of the Areopagus. And no remorse for the fact that they had never been touched by fervor for a "Holy Alliance of the Peoples" would ever afflict them. It was Mazzini who preached a Europe of the peoples. Theirs was, culturally, a Europe of all intelligent people, but politically it was still a Europe of governments. Nor would they ever have dreamed of revolutionizing the "European mind," which to them appeared very well contrived as it was, whereas to Mazzini it seemed "destitute of any common faith, of any notion of a common goal capable of bringing about union among the nations and assigning to each its task for the good of all; destitute, too, of any unity of law fit to direct its moral, political, and economic life."[151]

It is certainly not my purpose here to reproach the men of the Right for not having been Mazzinians, for not having wanted a general revolution of morals and politics, or for having been too ready to take their place in the ranks of the countries that stood for order and the status quo, as soon as their job was done in Italy. They carried out their mission and it was a great mission; more than this it was a miracle that they were able to fight for their own country without turning into zealots and forgetting about everything else, without locking themselves into an egoistical and limited vision of pure national interest; that on the contrary they never forgot how to see and appreciate and love the great European civil collectivity. Mazzini's ideal too had been characteristic of the times,[152] much more so in fact than that of the moderates, for theirs had deeper roots in the old traditions of political equilibrium. Mazzini's had flowered in the fullness of the Romantic age, around 1830, and he had lifted it from the purely literary plane of Romantic dishevelment, to which it was often confined,[153] making it a political will and a political faith—the faith of the Romantic left, adoring its own country but wanting to love all countries. Now this faith, which Michelet had shared, was declining, and only the adoration of one's own country remained.

My purpose is merely to demonstrate that the Europeanism of the moderates was not innovatory but conservative, that it grew up out of the rich humus of the political philosophy of the European Restoration and eighteenth-century rationalism,[154] and that the Italian Risorgimento, in the form in which it came to fruition, meaning that of a liberal-monarchic state, had contained its energies, and its impulse to destroy and rebuild, within the frontiers of Italy itself, leaving Europe as a whole undisturbed.

Mazzini had accused Cavour of the opportunistic surrender of "principles,"

---

[150] The expression is Cavour's, in a speech of 16 October 1860 in the Senate (*Discorsi Parlamentari* 11:277).

[151] Griffith, *Mazzini profeta di una nuova Europa*, p. 468.

[152] Valid observations are made in H. G. Keller, *Das "Junge Europa," 1834–1836* (Zurich-Leipzig, 1938), p. 80.

[153] Cf. F. Baldensperger, "Le grand schisme de 1830: 'Romantisme' et 'Jeune Europe,'" *Revue de littérature comparée* 10 (1930): 6 ff.

[154] On the rationalistic origins, generally speaking, of the moderate tradition, cf. Salvatorelli, *Il pensiero politico italiano*, p. 261.

and these had indeed declined as components of policy. This diminution had been imposed and continued to be imposed by objective reality, and it led perforce to the splitting, at a certain point, of foreign policy and domestic politics, to avoid the risk of creating pandemonium.[155] Commitment to liberty remained unshaken, over that no compromise was possible; but commitment to nationality as a principle was diluted, since to pursue it to the limit would have meant putting Italy in the role of the great permanent revolutionary, sending it off into adventures whose outcomes were liable to be extremely dangerous. The possibilities for applying it in practice were limited so as to make possible collaboration on the international stage even with states like the Habsburg and Ottoman empires, which constituted, to use an expression of Mazzini, the living negation of the principle of nationality.

The split was seen in the great maneuver of the strongly liberal Cavour, who had decided to seek the support of the Napoleonic dictatorship in order to rebuild Italy. In different situations, and in other guises, it had been the line of conduct of his epigones, faithful to his precept and instinctively much more inclined than he to "conserve," very much disposed to bring the period of the revolutions and the grand gestures to a close, and permit united Italy to live and to attend, in peace, to its internal reordering and consolidation. Visconti Venosta said as much repeatedly, and with extreme clarity and sincerity, as when in his speech to the Senate of 22 April 1871 concerning the law of Guarantees, he affirmed that the Italian national movement had had a profoundly civil aim: "to be considered a step forward for the general cause of order and liberty in Europe," and that it had transformed a turbulent and rebellious people into "one of the calmest and most conservative of Europe."[156] And on 27 November 1872 he insisted on the community of interests between Italy and Europe: "Today in Europe the outstanding need, the one most strongly felt and articulated, is the preservation of peace. Europe is and wishes to be liberal. . . . And . . . since for Italy peace is and always will be one of our great lasting interests, . . . our own cause is part of the cause of liberty in Europe . . . and there is not . . . any country in a better position to associate its own particular interests with those that today are the general interests of Europe, which is to say with the preservation of peace, liberal progress, and social conservatism."[157]

Still later, in a campaign speech delivered at Tirano on 25 October 1874, he returned to the same themes, asserting that the aim of Italian foreign policy after 1870 had been to "speed the arrival of the day when Italy would finally succeed in not being talked about. What this meant was bringing Italy to the much-needed point at which, feeling secure and untroubled by more pressing problems, it would have the leisure, the peace, and the time necessary to occupy itself with domestic questions."[158] And finally, no longer minister but speaking now from

---

[155] On the decline of the "policy of principles" in Europe, see the acute observations of Omodeo, *L'opera politica del Conte di Cavour* 1:244–45.

[156] *A.P., Senato*, p. 776.

[157] *A.P., Camera*, pp. 3388–89. And cf. the speech of 14 May 1872 (p. 2121).

[158] Published in *L'Opinione* for 30 October 1874.

the opposition benches, he summarized once more his political credo on 23 April 1877: "When . . . our period of nation-building was not yet complete, Italy sought in European complications an opportune occasion to finish the edifice of its independence and its unity. Now Italy is made, is a constituted state, and I believe that the only policy that we should follow is one of prudence and reliability, untainted by any spirit of adventure, and such as to make others see the advantage and the utility for European interests in the presence and the moral action of this young state in the concert of the great powers."[159] This was not only the political credo of Visconti Venosta, but that of all those of the Right: of Dina, quick to declare an end to the time "of agitation";[160] of Minghetti, convinced as well that it was important to alter the program of the government with respect to Italy so as to make it become "conservative";[161] of Bonghi, who felt it was necessary to "surround Italy with peace";[162] of Count Guido Borromeo, who issued an invitation to "proceed on tiptoe so as not to make a lot of noise";[163] of Jacini, who lucidly summarized all these ideas much later on, reproving those who, in the period after unification, had not "adopted European criteria," taking instead their own desires for their only guide and thus giving birth to political megalomania.[164]

Unshakable faith in the principle of liberty, the central spring of spiritual and moral life, was the great difference between the Europeanism of the moderates and reactionary Europeanism in the manner of Metternich. None was a more forthright and decisive spokesman for this strong attachment to the great liberal principles than the minister for foreign affairs, Emilio Visconti Venosta, who in 1871 expressed the hope that France would renew its liberal tradition and not set itself against "the living forces of our time."[165] In November 1873, when the Chamber was discussing Mancini's motion on international arbitration, he stated his conviction that "a staunch guarantee of peace is found in free institutions" and that "the sincere and open practice of free institutions favors the sentiment of justice."[166] And when he was no longer minister he restated his and his party's credo in the Chamber, maintaining that "it would be a black day for our country if it should take a position against the great liberal and moral principles that are the honor of our time."[167]

What other minister of foreign affairs who was not a member of one of Gladstone's cabinets would ever have been heard to make declarations in which the liberal credo was embraced with the frankness and sincerity shown by Visconti Venosta in the Chamber on 27 November 1872? "Today in Europe the outstand-

[159] *A.P., Camera*, p. 2687.

[160] Article "I partiti parlamentari," in *L'Opinione* for 20 July 1871.

[161] Minghetti, *Carteggio Minghetti-Pasolini* 4:195 (22 October 1870).

[162] In a speech given at Naples on 29 October 1874 (published in the supplement to *L'Opinione* for 7 November, and separately at Rome in 1874, p. 9).

[163] G. Borromeo to Minghetti, 3 March 1871 (BCB, *Carte Minghetti*, cart. XVI, fasc. 4).

[164] Jacini, *Pensieri sulla politica italiana*, pp. 66 ff.

[165] Visconti Venosta, private letter to Nigra, 5 August 1871 (Visconti Venosta archive).

[166] *A.P., Camera*, p. 34. On the same day Boselli sang the same praises of liberty (pp. 35–36).

[167] In the speech of 9 April 1878 (*A.P., Camera*, p. 363).

ing requirement, the one felt and expressed most strongly, is that of preserving peace. Europe is and wants to be liberal. It does not want to throw itself into the arms of reaction; but it abhors demagogy. Peace is and always will be one of the great and permanent interests of Europe. By the very nature of the questions we are called upon to confront, linked as they are to our national existence, our cause is one with that of liberty in Europe. Liberal opinion knows that our victories are its victories, just as any defeat for us would be a defeat for it."[168]

In this the religion of liberty celebrated its real triumph. It had given poetry to the great days of the Risorgimento and it remained the poetry of the latter days, in which life appeared more modest and subdued, and was not stirred by summons to combat and the chanting of hymns in the streets of insurgent or newly liberated cities, but was nonetheless usefully employed in the peaceful and ongoing creation of a solid basis for the future of the unified homeland. Liberty, the spontaneous wish of the peoples, was not cast away but was melded with the sense of Europe, reinforcing its foundation. Bonghi noted that the practice of holding plebiscites was "entirely suited to serve as a brake on any violent territorial changes in the future. It is a safeguard that all of Europe must see that it has an interest in maintaining, since if depreciating and abandoning it serves Prussia's interests today, and harms only France, it will harm others tomorrow, and in any case it causes public law to sink back to the level of the pure right of force, a stage that we had thought had been surpassed."[169]

The ideal of liberty remained firmly in place, but for the rest the trend was to attenuate, blur, relegate to the background anything that might lead to international clashes. This meant in the first instance attenuating and blurring the principle of nationality and accepting, in this area, the cherished principles of the diplomatic brand of Europeanism characteristic of the Restoration. There was a good example of this in the winter of 1870–71, when on top of the Franco-Prussian War there materialized once again the eastern question in the form of the Russian renunciation of the clauses regarding the neutralization of the Black Sea: while the group around Crispi kept faith with their Mazzinian legacy by supporting the abolition of the sultanate (the "absurdity" of international life as they called it) and demanded that Greece be reunited, and the Albanians, Bulgarians, Serbs, and Romanians be given autonomy while joining in a confederation with its seat at Constantinople,[170] the Italian government was quite rightly worried only about avoiding at any cost the new international crisis that Russia's gesture might well have provoked, and saving the peace even at the cost of compromises that would leave the "sick man of Europe" tottering but still erect.

The era in which policy was driven by the vehement emotional experience of principles sharply and rigidly contrasted, the time of Metternich and Mazzini, had ended after the failure of the general European revolution in 1848.[171] Before

[168] *A.P., Camera*, p. 3888. And cf. above, p. 130.

[169] "Il Thiers in Firenze," in *La Perseveranza* for 14 October 1870.

[170] Cf. above, p. 62.

[171] On the profound change in European politics after 1848, see Salvatorelli, *Storia d'Europa dal 1871 al 1914* 1:34–35 (Milan, 1941).

that, to utter the word "liberty" meant opting for a new Europe, and the diplomatic Europeanism of Metternich was entirely identified with reaction. Then, every nation appeared to have seen that the liberty of others was the necessary condition of its own, to have understood that this mutual recognition was the secret of its own being.[172] But after 1848 it was possible to remain perfectly steadfast in one's liberal faith while willingly accepting one's role in the old diplomatic Europe and tasting the delights of the concert of the great powers, of equilibrium, and other practical accommodations that for Mazzini had been immoral and absurd.

It was an inevitable adaptation to the times and the circumstances, one that took place throughout Europe, for the man who now exercised a dominant influence on the European continent was Bismarck, no avatar of Metternich, but instead a man who spurned "principles" and paid attention to nothing but practical convenience, case by case. The end of the era of principles was connected to a visceral urge for the kind of "realism" of which the triumphant Prussians had given an example.[173] Realism in this sense meant the repudiation of any policy based on abstract principles.

In Italy *La Nazione* of Florence had crudely embraced this philosophy at the outset, even before it became the heartfelt friend of Prussia. Why get worked up over France and Prussia, as though either one represented some great principle? "It is impossible to talk of principles when interests, in their grossest and most brutal form, dominate." It was a question of utility, of balancing the books, and if Italy were constrained to relinquish neutrality it ought to have no scruples or remorse about "choosing the side that is most to our benefit, the one from which we have the most to gain, or the least to lose," now that Bismarck and Benedetti "have happily freed us from the patriotic effusions and sentimental displays of the admirers of liberal Prussia and the worshipers of humanitarian France."[174]

This anticipated the sacred egoism that lay ahead; realism was fully fledged. Bismarck for his part still had more examples of the latter to show the world, and so did others, especially Disraeli, another prototype of a world very different from that of Mancunian and Gladstonian liberalism, in fact a true champion of the imperialism that was showing its head. The century would close with an alliance between republican France and the tsarist empire, to the horror, naturally, of all who preferred to keep faith forever with principles, and refused to contaminate themselves with any sort of compromise. And considering the overall trend, the Italian moderates were still very much attached to principles, as the difficult events of 1874 and 1875 would show, when Visconti Venosta and his colleagues preferred to face a period of coolness, in fact of real tension in their relations with the all-powerful Germany of Bismarck, rather than be dragged into an Italian version of the *Kulturkampf* and thus be forced to disown their liberal soul.

---

[172] These are the expressions of Cattaneo in the program for *Il Cisalpino*, 17 March 1848 (*Scritti politici ed epistolario*, ed. G. Rosa and J. White Mario, vol. 1 [Florence, 1892], p. 123).

[173] Cf. Croce, *Storia d'Europa nel secolo decimonono*, pp. 254 ff.

[174] *La Nazione* for 6 August 1870 ("La nostra politica").

Nor would the adaptation of principles to reality be confined to international relations. It entered perforce into the domestic politics of the various European countries, in which the struggle among the political parties in the last decades of the century and beyond no longer had that atmosphere of absolute intransigence and excessive obedience to logic that had characterized the political climate of the Restoration,[175] and even subsequently had set liberals and reactionaries at each others' throats. The reactionaries continued for some time to be irreducible in their fanatical opposition to "revolution"; whether they were French legitimists or Spanish Carlists or Italian clericals, they continued to see in liberalism the mortal sin of humanity, and in France it was only when the policy of *ralliement* began to take hold that the officially sanctioned movement not just of individuals but of entire groups away from reactionism began to take place. And for that matter the anticlericals as well continued in the intransigence of their forefathers for some time. But in purely political terms, the Italian Right was perhaps the last remaining example of an attachment—overall a firm attachment—to its own principles, at the cost of risking popularity and electoral favor. This attachment admittedly rigidified and fixed in place once and for all a position that Cavour had originally taken as a result of a tactical compromise. Then the Left came to power. What was so often portrayed in their case as diminished moral stature was in fact simply their greater ability at tactical compromise and practical facility at coming to terms with reality even in contradiction to their own ideas. And finally there arrived "transformism," to signify the triumph of the new method of conducting the political struggle under the parliamentary system.

Bonghi, the pessimist, loudly bemoaned the tendency: today, he alleged, it seems "that the very parties that claim to be most *progressive* do not demonstrate *principles* except to create the opportunity to abandon and renounce them whenever it suits them, or a gust of sympathy moves them. The goal of each is different from the principles he professes, and these are valid or not to the extent that they help to reach the goal, and serve it. Whenever they appear detrimental or superfluous they are thrown on the rubbish heap, where they can be found another time if the occasion presents itself."[176] Of course this judgment was excessive, and like many another uttered by Bonghi, was distorted by the unending polemical animus against contemporaries and their doings that beset the mind of this brilliant journalist. But, as always with his judgments, there was a sediment of truth in his exaggeration, acutely expressed: for truly those who were disposed to repeat the experience of Lambruschini in 1849, standing alone in purity, wisdom, and foresight, never descending to any transaction with the opposing "sects," not even to achieve a particular, shared goal, were becoming ever more rare.[177]

To a large extent this was a result of the new way of understanding life and its values in the post-Romantic climate of Europe: the triumph of the capitalist econ-

---

175 Omodeo, *La cultura francese*, pp. 53 ff. and 63.
176 "Il Thiers in Firenze," in *La Perseveranza* for 14 October 1870.
177 Lambruschini to Ricasoli, 9 May 1849 (Ricasoli, *Carteggi* 3:388).

omy, of technical expertise, of business, of a world in which principles give way to practical convenience in each individual case, in which bargaining leading to compromise is the main scenario, and it is essential to be flexible rather than rigid. Romantic ideals and modes of life faded, and very different ones took on color and depth instead, with an indubitable lowering of the moral and cultural tone, but with equally indubitable quantitative impact. The sphere of state activity expanded, and it intruded increasingly into questions that had once been low on its agenda, primarily economic questions; it was becoming Leviathan, and the fatal corollary of this was reduced concern for intellectual doctrines and greater consideration for the case at hand, for the individual question, whatever it was. This was all the more true in that the problems posed were often ones that the old systems of principle had not contemplated, and around which no doctrine had evolved.

Experience too had taught a lesson, which was that the men of principle of the first half of the century had reposed too much confidence in moral forces and taken too little account of material force: hence the disappointments of 1848 and 1849, the shattering of the dream of European revolution. In the case of Italy the ground swell in favor of national unity came to fruition thanks to the combinations of European politics, in which the factor of power had had a preponderant role—the so-called diplomatization of the Italian revolution, that is its acceptance of the forces of royal armies and imperial allies alongside the forces of moral rectitude. Even before the Risorgimento was over a monarchical constitution had been adopted for Italy, and this in itself had amounted to a compromise in the eyes of the doctrinaires, one crowned by the conversion of old Mazzinians and republicans to the monarchical faith. Mazzini might cry betrayal, but these were much more than simply personal choices; they were the result of the lesson of reality, the lesson of "things as they are," and they signified the advent of an age of less craggy and steep principles.

The tendency then was toward the acknowledgment of a politics without principles, and that had become sufficiently clear after 1848. But the impressive spectacle of might, and the manner in which force had triumphed in the achievement of German unity, put the seal definitively on what had already been learned in twenty years of history. The only remaining question was how far it was possible to go with compromises and adaptations, and Bismarck was on his way to finding out, with his well-calculated but also very sudden changes of front when they were called for by circumstances. In 1870 he switched from hints of wanting to support the pope to the *Kulturkampf*, following which he established friendly relations with Leo XIII. He first accepted an alliance with the German liberals and then broke it. In the international field there were first the proposals to Austria made at Schönbrunn against Italy in 1864, then the alliance with Italy against Austria in 1866. There were hostilities against France until 1878, then blandishments to France until 1885, then once again hostilities. There were insults to Italy in 1879 and 1880, followed by an alliance with Italy. It really can be said that Bismarck expressed and incarnated, as no one else, the new spirit of the new Europe.

The idea of nationality had separated the Italian moderates from the moderates of other countries, but the idea of Europe, which took on "the value of a home-land,"[178] joined them in concord, just as it joined members of the French right and English liberals.[179] Likewise, at the moment of the famous spring crisis of 1875 the Marquis de Noailles, French ambassador at Rome, and Visconti Venosta, a typical Italian moderate, found themselves in agreement, despite the latter's distant Mazzinian roots, in the view that one of the major reasons for the dangerous European situation "was the absence of what used to be called 'one Europe.'"[180]

Examples might be multiplied. In deploring the lack of European spirit and the dissolution of the old politico-diplomatic sense of a *corps de l'Europe*, in the tragic summer of 1870 the likes of Visconti Venosta, Bonghi, and Bon Compagni[181] found themselves in full agreement with the Saxon chancellor of the Austro-Hungarian empire, Count Friedrich von Beust, who included in an official dispatch, published in the Austrian *Red Book*, his celebrated dictum, "je ne vois plus d'Europe," and subsequently came back to this notion, firmly convinced that it contained the explanation for many of the evils that had occurred.[182] Later it fell to his Hungarian successor, Count Julius von Andrássy, a very different sort of man but one who also belonged to the good old European diplomatic tradition, to declare that his aim had been "to find Europe again," to "reconstitute a European sentiment."[183]

They might be Italians, Austrians, or French, men of the most varied origin; but when Europe was in question their sentiment was the same, and when the Italians were members of the moderate party, they shared it with the diplomats of the old Habsburg school or those of the Quai d'Orsay. The abdication of Europe in the face of Prussian might was as discouraging and disgusting for a man like

---

[178] Metternich to Wellington in 1824: "The fact is that for a long time Europe has taken on the value of a homeland for me" (in Srbik, *Metternich* 1:320).

[179] Charles Gavard noted from England: "Everyone here is horror-struck by the news. . . . There is no more Europe, no more society of peoples, if we let force be carried to the limit in this manner" (Gavard, *Un diplomate à Londres*, p. 6).

[180] Noailles to Decazes, 11 May 1875 (*D.D.F.*, 1st ser., vol. 1, no. 411, p. 448): "It is time to start thinking about reconstituting [Europe], but one can only pursue this with the maximum caution."

[181] Marselli shared their preoccupation: "This reasoning is founded on the belief that a Europe still exists. If this is an illusion, if England really continues to hesitate, the Latins to decline, and Austria to tremble, then two powers will constitute Europe: Germany and Russia" (*Avvenimenti del 1870–71* 2:121, n. 1).

[182] Beust, *Trois quarts de Siècle, Mémoires* 2:392 and 414 (French translation: Paris, 1888). *La Perseveranza* for 3 October 1870 also wrote: "Europe! Who can say any more whether it exists politically?"

[183] Declarations of Andrássy to the French ambassador in Vienna, de Vogüé, on 29 April 1878 (*D.D.F.*, 1st ser., vol. 2, p. 307). For the persistence of such a belief in "European society" in diplomatic circles during later decades see for example the report of the French ambassador to Constantinople, Bompard, of 3 October 1912: "The Congress of Paris [1856] had . . . in principle brought Turkey into the society of European nations . . . but in fact the assimilation had always fallen a long way short of realization, and Turkey continued in actuality to be considered by Europe as a state of a particular genre, against which the Powers had common interests to defend" (*D.D.F.*, 3d ser,, vol. 4, p. 35).

Bonghi as it was for one of the typical representatives of the old European caste system and traditional diplomacy, Prince Richard von Metternich.[184]

In fact the feeling for Europe and its moral unity was not limited to the diplomats of the various chancelleries and the members of the moderate parties. Even men who in domestic politics passed for radicals, for demagogues, for promoters of novelty revealed a fidelity to traditional conceptions when they spoke of the European consortium. On this topic a Gambetta became just as conservative as the diplomats trained in the school of the Quai d'Orsay and dispatched abroad by the duc de Broglie,[185] and the "European homeland" composed of suffering, exile, and emigration that Michelet had extolled in Mazzinian style,[186] was replaced, within France, by a Europe of political equilibrium, great powers, order, and constituted governments.

In their slow swirl, ideas take a long time to bring forth all their effects in history. The idea of nationality as most people conceived it was not seen as a force that would leave all the old baggage of Restoration political and diplomatic ideology strewn in disorder. There was an exception, a man who resolutely broke the bonds of the past and, as a *Realpolitiker* and a scorner of principles, disdained what he called mere words, refusing to recognize any surviving substance in the myth of Europe as a moral unity, as a *corps politique*: this of course was Bismarck, who was accused by a large section of European opinion in the winter of 1870–71 of having destroyed the sense of Europe, and who a few years later in the midst of the eastern crisis, did in fact express, clearly and briskly, his incredulity about so-called Europe. He did so at first in his marginal annotations to the letter of 2 November 1876 from Gorchakov to him; then in the *Diktat* of Varzin, dated 9 November, the great chancellor gave free reign to his skepticism.[187]

Where lies Europe? "Who speaks of Europe is in error. A geographical notion." A fiction, a word that Bismarck had been accustomed to hear pronounced by politicians desirous of obtaining something, but lacking the courage to ask for it in their own name, without circumlocution. A fiction wielded more than once against Germany, as in 1870, or used to make Germany serve the interests of somebody else. The hypothetical duty to be "Europeans!" Carrying it out won

---

[184] Cf. his letter to Beust of 26 September 1870 in H. Salomon, *L'ambassade de Richard de Metternich à Paris*, p. 276.

[185] In a letter of 27 January 1877 to Juliette Adam, Gambetta in fact observes that "as long as there is no Europe," there will be no security against aggression on Bismarck's part. And Europe for him means a "European concert" against Germany (that is, the old sixteenth- and seventeenth-century idea of the powers united against the aspirant to hegemony, in order to protect the "liberty" of the single states), it means reconstructing "the former equilibrium of the powers, the European equilibrium," the basis of the "common security" altered by Prussia which has imposed its supremacy and left "the old public law in tatters." We seem to hear Metternich speaking, but the writer is the founder of the secular and democratic French republic, Gambetta! (*Lettres de Gambetta, 1868–82*, ed. D. Halévy and É. Pillias, no. 300). Gambetta never ceased to be a tenacious defender of European equilibrium in the form in which the diplomats of the end of the eighteenth century had conceived it (P. Deschanel, *Gambetta* [Italian translation: Milan, 1935], p. 253).

[186] In a note of 4 April 1854, published by Monod, *Jules Michelet*, p. 35 and cf. p. 33.

[187] *G.P.* 2:87–88 and cf. also p. 98. And note the irony with which Bismarck refers to the celebrated remark of Beust on Europe in *Erinnerung und Gedanke*, in *Gesammelten Werke* 15:317. There is a perceptive comment in Eyck, *Bismarck* 3:242–45.

gratitude from nobody. If Germany was to make a commitment to something other than its own interests, it ought to do so not in fulfillment of such hypothetical Europeanist obligations, but in order to please a friendly power, by whom it might legitimately expect the favor to be returned.

Europe, a fiction: although even Bismarck, in his circular of 16 September 1870, had for once made an appeal to the interests of Europe, on whose behalf he claimed that Prussia was laboring in its struggle with France, the disturber of the peace and therefore of Europe.[188] But perhaps it was just because this had been nothing but a tactical feint, employed in a struggle in which it was necessary to use any weapon, that Bismarck, on the basis of this personal experience, did not believe in the European sincerity of others. In the case of Gorchakov he was right, as it happens. But it was symptomatic that from the specific example he derived an unconditional general statement of principle, a denial that the idea in itself had any validity.

Bismarck's was a political credo that truly constituted the harsh antithesis of half a century of European tradition, and it marked a turning point. Fifty years before, Prince Metternich had treated Italy—that is, the idea of the nation—as a purely geographic term. But the great Rhenish statesman had had an ideal, that of a *corps politique d'Europe*, and it was this that was now in turn being dismissed as a geographic notion, in whose place there would remain only the idea of the single state, of the strongly individualized nation, with its particular needs and its specific interests. Metternich had refused the rights of nationality, that is of individuality, in the name of his principle of the preservation of the European order, of the collectivity. Now Bismarck was denying the consortium of Europe and affirming the contrary, the single state, rugged and harsh in its solitary outline, destined to become an absolute. The perspective had been totally reversed in little more than half a century.

This was a real revolution, the antithesis of the Mazzinian ideal: a revolution that sought to place a tombstone on the politics of principles, recognizing nothing more than practical convenience, moment by moment and case by case, and sweeping away any attempt to create even the appearance of a moral and civil unity overshadowing the single state organisms. Also liquidated were any traces of the old ideal of a *corpus christianum*, which had implied a necessary solidarity of principles and sentiments among the European peoples. It was the end of Europeanism and the onset of the various nationalisms and imperialisms, of Pan-Germanism and Pan-Slavism. And it was launched (through his style of thought and his excessive adherence to the material reality of the facts) by a man who for the rest of his political life feared French chauvinism and Pan-Slavism as the greatest dangers imaginable for the German homeland,[189] and who was certainly not even a Pan-Germanist himself.

And it was against Bismarck the man that liberals and conservatives in Italy

---

[188] Bismarck, *Gesammelten Werke* 6b:501.

[189] On Bismarck's hostility to Pan-Slavism, cf. also S. A. Kaehler, "Bemerkungen zu einem Marginal Bismarcks von 1887," *Historische Zeitschrift* 167 (1942): 106.

and England and France and Austria who retained a European sense rose up in the winter of 1870–71, rightly anticipating the danger. By 1876, however, Bismarck was no longer the only one openly rebuffing all considerations that went beyond the short term, not the only one scornful of all "bloated words," like the duties of Europeans, or Christians, or anything else of the sort. In 1870 the "humanitarianism" and "sentimentality" of Gladstone, scoffed at by Bismarck, had dominated England. Now from across the channel there advanced to meet him, *similia similibus*, the new artificer of Britain's imperial fortunes, Disraeli, who in respect of indifference to principles and exclusive appreciation for "power and glory," had nothing to learn, even from Bismarck. Disraeli had sounded the fanfare of imperialism first in 1872, and had also offended the ideas of the moderates, especially Bonghi, who saw in the British statesman another sign that the new epoch of naked power was approaching and his own familiar world sinking into twilight.[190]

From this point of view Visconti Venosta, Bonghi, Dina, Minghetti, Lanza, and their ilk were spiritually much closer to the European moderates, and even to the conservatives, than they were to Crispi and company, for whom, as we have seen, the putative sunset of the old Europe was a reason for rejoicing, not for regret, since it meant the end of "diplomatic" Europe, with its ephemeral compromises and absurd treaties, and removed the barriers in the way of the forces emerging in "the powers that have a future," in which there seethed "a ground swell of emancipation, personal emancipation it can be called, that tends to give maximum room for development to the initiative of national policies."[191]

With this *La Riforma* heralds the new age of heightened nationalism. We have seen the connection between this and the crystallization of the principle of nationality into a metaphysical *a priori*; and we see a striking similarity here between Bismarck, a politician whose approach was almost entirely made up of reason and calculation, and the impetuous Crispi, who was breaking free not only from the Europeanism of the Restoration but also from the Mazzinian conception of the Europe to come, toppling the ideals of a common mission, of humanity so that only the ideal of the nation was left standing, magnified and exasperated, an end in itself, no longer, as with Mazzini, a means.

This is the reason the Italian moderates did not see the display of German power against France as a further manifestation of the principle of nationality for which they themselves had fought, suffered, and won, but rather a new incarnation of the spirit of conquest, the first since the time of Napoleon I. With Bismarck and Moltke, the black beast that Europe had managed to keep at a distance

---

[190] Cf. the essay on Disraeli in Bonghi, *Ritratti e profili di contemporanei* 2:255–56 (Florence, 1935), and esp. 272 ff. And cf. Maturi, "Ruggero Bonghi e i problemi di politica estera," p. 419 n. 1.

[191] Cf. above, ch. 1, p. 57 and n. 234. In *La Nazione* of Florence, a moderate paper but with leanings toward Prussia, there is open disdain for the "usual grand and profound theories on European equilibrium," which might entail the sacrifice of Italy's real interests. "A fine success for us, if with European equilibrium assured and the Latin primacy asserted as usual through French prevalence, European equilibrium and Latin primacy wind up driving us out of Rome!" ("La pace," 24 October 1870).

for fifty years was returning; the peace imposed by Germany was a blow to the principles that had prevailed in the public law of Europe during that time.[192] Conservative as it was, the political Europeanism of which we are speaking abhorred one thing above all: attempts at continental hegemony or, as Metternich had already called it, "the system of conquest."[193] It had been abhorrent in Napoleon I, and it was the menacing shade of the great Corsican who appeared in the eyes of the moderates to be the true prefiguration of the new German empire.[194]

In response, the old but recurrent idea of European equilibrium, the sole guarantee of the peace and civilization that were threatened by the ambitions and the drive for conquest of one country, was revived. Once before it had animated the offensive against Napoleon I; but now it flickered feebly. The Europe of 1870–71 was discordant and unfocused, and not even a new Metternich would have succeeded in the kind of maneuvers that succeeded in 1814–15. And for that matter Bismarck would soon take it on himself to muffle the threat, and calm the fears he had aroused, by adopting conservative policies; we have seen how they made a rapid and favorable impression on the Italians. The specter of conquest appeared to recede, and only ulterior events and changed circumstances, decades in the future, would summon it up again, wearing a different countenance. So the partisans of the European system, the "good Europeans" who belonged to the various aggregations of the right in Italy, drew a sigh of relief, as did their confrères abroad, for the state of alarm caused by the shattering Prussian successes, and the trepidation on behalf of equilibrium and the concert of the powers, had been just as great in other countries.[195] This is further proof of the true nature of the political Europeanism of the Italian moderates.

The instinctive resort to political and ideological notions from the time of the struggle against Napoleon was the characteristic European way of acknowledging the basic contrast between equilibrium and hegemony in international life. Down the road, further and greater trials lay in wait, in a future that the men of 1870 perhaps feared but were not of course able to descry. Their approach reflected the organic structure of the thing called Europe itself: clearly differentiated state

---

[192] *La Perseveranza*, 28 February 1871.

[193] Metternich, *Mémoires* 1:200–201 (Italian trans., p. 219).

[194] "L'azione dei neutri," in *L'Opinione* for 3 November 1870: the nascent German empire menaces European equilibrium as Napoleon I had done; but a league like the one formed against Napoleon is no longer possible. Suspicion of France was long-standing in Europe, but the powerful German empire is a recent phenomenon. No one can run ahead of the times: we are in 1870, not in 1900.

Taine's judgment was analogous: Wilhelm I and Bismarck are playing the part of Napoleon at this moment, a detestable part which may also lead them to a similar final catastrophe (*Correspondance* 3:15 and also p. 125). For the Swiss press, see Rentsch, *Bismarck im Urteil der schweizerischen Presse*, p. 103. For contrary opinions, see Meyer, *Bismarck*, p. 668.

[195] See for example the speech of Kuranda to the Austrian Delegation ["*Delegazione Cisleitana*"] in Pest on 17 January 1871: here again we find evoked the pentarchy of the great powers that had directed European life for the last 30–40 years, and fear for the present, given that England is egoistically thinking only of itself and has no interest in continental affairs, while France is out of the game. These preoccupations, it will be seen, are very much the same ones as those of Bonghi, Dina, etc. (The speech is in the *Wiener Abendpost* for 18 January 1871).

entities, in concord among themselves on the negative aim of preventing "universal monarchies" and impeding the excessive growth of any single power, if necessary by shifting power to other parties in compensation. Above all it was fear of the spirit of conquest, of the predominance of brute force, that made the liberals want to hobble the principle of nationality, for left to itself it was capable of overturning the Europe they knew.

The new German expansion contrasted, in its origins, with the animating spirit of the Risorgimento as the Italian moderates conceived it, opposing the rights of force to the "spontaneous vote of the peoples," and it also contrasted with their Europeanism. In fact the second contrast was seen as a fatal consequence of the first. Wherever there was recourse to pure force, there was danger for Europe. The right to nationhood had been actuated in the Italian peninsula without creating turmoil in European life. But the right of conquest, as well as harming the principle of nationality itself, threatened to smash up Europe,[196] subverting the system that made it possible for nations to live together.

"The recognition of the right of nations to constitute themselves as states," wrote Bonghi, "seemed to be a result of the progress of the social spirit, because it seemed to be the most secure bond, the strongest basis, of a tranquil and lasting consortium among the civil societies of Europe. For it to be able to fulfill this promise, its application has to be accompanied by a high degree of equity. No nation can claim to assume a form that threatens the other nations. Otherwise . . . it is not peace and concord that the right of nationhood will bring to the world, but rather jealousy and discord, both of them indomitable."[197]

The antithesis of ideas and methods is total. Bonghi was taking aim at the Prussians in his great speech of 31 January 1871 to the Chamber concerning the law of Guarantees, when he proclaimed: "All our lives we have been laying a precise claim to our own rights and scrupulously respecting those of all the other nations. We arrived in the world with a promise of peace and justice. As we rose up we threw off a flash of light, but we did not follow it with the cannon's sorrowful thunder, the fire of advancing troops, the cavalry charge, and the sword's deadly glitter. We did not preach the doctrine of iron and fire. We asked Europe to give us the place that belongs to us, and we took it without infringing the rights of others. We declared that we wished to have it without infringing even the conscience or the moral interests of any nation in Europe."[198]

Years later, when the race for power was in full course among the great European nations, and the "armed peace" was showing more alarming cracks with every passing day, the old moderate, busying himself with far too many things but tenacious as ever in his ideas, repeated once again the views of his comrades and himself: "We constituted the nations so that they might be the natural mem-

---

[196] "Never before has history given us the example of Europe watching unmoved its own undoing, for that is what the collapse of our old allies means. The right of the strongest is on the march again, for Prussian science is not Latin civilization." E. Oldofredi to Dina, 7 November 1870 (in Chiala, *Giacomo Dina* 3:275).

[197] From the article "Il diritto delle nazioni," in *La Perseveranza* for 31 August 1870.

[198] Bonghi, *Discorsi Parlamentari* 1:236.

bers of the human race and operate as such. The intention to give a national basis
to the states, which was to a large extent carried out during this century, which
was indeed its greatest accomplishment, was the intention to bring concord and
peace. The newly erected nations were not meant, in the eyes of our generation,
to face each other in arms, hostile and challenging, but to live as friends, having
received their portion of justice, and compete in doing good, in effecting the
highest degree of felicity and virtue that man is capable of. Perhaps our ideal was
too lofty, and perhaps we believed it was nearer than it was. But it does no good
to reduce the stature of one's ideals, or to push them too far into the future. There
may be younger men to whom ours will appear an ideal of old men: but they are
decrepit in their youth. Our ideal deserves to be erected once more. There must
be, and there is, cooperation, slow but sure, between the popular conscience on
one hand and superior intelligences on the other. If statesmen are only capable of
stumbling around in the gloom of their own prejudices and the pale reminis-
cences of their past, so much the worse for them. It won't be the first time in
history that the light shone into their eyes from the quarter where they least
expected it, and they followed it for no other reason than to stay on top."[199]

The Germans, in contrast, of all the peoples have the least aptitude for "separating what is just from what is unjust in their own desires."[200] They are carrying the world back to an age of "trial by sword and fire,"[201] and indeed the great
teacher, Cavour, had presaged and warned against the perils of Germanism as
early as 1848.[202] To allow France to be crushed, as Bismarck wished, would
amount to making Germany the boss of Europe, since the system of equilibrium
functioned in such a way that the sudden failure of one of the main components
threw the whole mechanism out of kilter. The situation was made worse by the
fact that as a result of its near total defeat France was now incapable of pulling
itself together internally, and was oscillating dangerously between reaction and
anarchy, between the legitimism of Henri V and the incendiaries of the Paris
Commune. To rip Alsace and Lorraine away from France would signify creating
a permanent and powerful motive of conflict in Europe, transforming peace into
a mere armed truce. This was also the judgment of Karl Marx, a man otherwise
far distant from the Italian moderates but equally convinced that the annexation
of Alsace and Lorraine would be the most certain means of transforming the
Franco-Prussian War into a permanent condition.[203]

[199] "La situazione europea e la pace," in *Nuova Antologia* for 16 September 1891, pp. 225–26.
[200] Bonghi, *Nove anni* 2:409.
[201] Ibid., 2:448.
[202] Cavour's speech to the Chamber of 20 October 1848: "Germanism is hardly born and already
it threatens to disturb the European balance, already it shows tendencies to predominance and
usurpation" (*Discorsi Parlamentari* 1:64, ed. A. Omodeo [Florence, 1932]).
[203] In a letter to the Committee of the Social Democratic party, shortly after the onset of the war
(*Histoire de la diplomatie* 1:529, ed. V. Potiemkine [French translation: Paris, 1946]). And cf. a
piece probably belonging to the period 1887–88, entitled (in translation) "Violence et économie dans
l'établissement du nouvel empire allemand," in F. Engels, *Le rôle de la violence dans l'histoire*
(Paris, 1946), pp. 77 ff. For the protests of the German Social Democrats against the annexation, and
the arrest of the Brunswick Five and of Johann Jacoby at Königsberg, see F. Mehring, *Geschichte der
deutschen Sozialdemokratie* 2:297 ff. (Stuttgart, 1898).

The normal functioning of Europe's economic life was also at risk from the triumph of Germany. Bismarck was requesting an enormous war indemnity, an astronomical sum for that time, and this brought fear of serious financial difficulties and disturbance in the markets that would have had adverse consequences for all the states. As before, the preoccupation was not felt in Italy alone. In fact the British government was the first to voice it, even before the peace preliminaries had been signed in February,[204] and the Austro-Hungarian chancellor, Count von Beust, picked this up, as did Visconti Venosta,[205] while *L'Opinione* conveyed it in print.[206]

Once again the difference of principles is seen over and above the specific instance: on one side, the doctrine of economic freedom endorsed by the moderates, sometimes even to the point where they dreamed of a customs union among the nations as a warrant of political peace; on the other side the closure of national markets in defense of self-interest, which Bismarck was already threatening, and which was indeed to lead to the triumph of protectionism.[207]

Thus the violent anti-Prussian polemics that burst out in Italy, and the general attitude of many men of the Right, signified their opposition both to principles

---

[204] Cf. V. Valentin, *Bismarcks Reichsgründung im Urteil englischer Diplomaten* (Amsterdam, 1937), p. 453.

[205] Visconti Venosta, dispatch to Cadorna in London, 13 March 1871: "he [Beust] believes that the general condition of the financial markets will be so unsettled by the enormous sum of the indemnity that it will increase the financial difficulties in the future for every state that has recourse to public credit. Hence Count Beust believes that it would be helpful in the common interest of Europe to take steps to try to have the figure reduced, or else to find a way, during the negotiations for the definitive peace treaty, not to oppress France too heavily with burdens that its economic resources would not be equal to. . . . The economic considerations set forth by Count Beust in his dispatch to Count Apponyi [in London; Visconti Venosta received them through Kübeck, the Austro-Hungarian envoy at Florence] are absolutely correct, and both Italy and Austria are obliged to heed them. Paris during the last twenty years was the principal money market of the continent. The commercial interests of France and Italy are highly interdependent; any threat of financial disaster in France would have a deleterious influence on the Italian exchanges, and it is certainly our strong desire that France . . . not be drained of all its economic strength, and that the sources of its public and private wealth not be destroyed." He adds that England, whose interests are not dissimilar to Italy's, ought to try to find a way to reduce the onus on the loser of paying the indemnity. Beust's dispatch to Kübeck of 10 March 1871 is in SAW, *P.A.*, XI/79. Kübeck's reply of 18 March is in SAW, *P.A.*, XI/77, no. 21 B. Rothan, the French ambassador, had called Visconti Venosta's attention on 2 March to the "utterly regrettable repercussions" for Italy of the financial stipulations of the peace; and the article in *L'Opinione* [see following note] was, according to him, the outcome of his talk with the foreign minister. Quintino Sella also lamented the "harmful repercussions" of the peace, from the financial point of view (Rothan, telegram of 2 March and reports of 3 March, no. 53, 16 March no. 68; AEP, *C.P., Italie*, t. 381, fols. 32v, 191v. And cf. E. Rothan, *L'Allemagne et l'Italie* 2:296–97).

[206] "Il credito pubblico," in *L'Opinione* for 3 March 1871. On 14 October the paper took note of the first effects of the economic disturbance caused by the war and the enormous indemnity: a rise in the Bank of England's discount rate, etc. ("Il mercato pecuniario d'Europa"). Two years later the paper noted the unfortunately very real effects of the huge war indemnity: in order to handle the war loans, the French market dumped foreign instruments, including those of Italy; and since there was no other market in a position to absorb them, the Italian instruments migrated back to Italy. The *rendita* [*rente*, government bond] fell, the *aggio* [the premium on gold and silver coin over paper money] grew, there was difficulty in discounting, and credit shortages occurred; these were the effects in Italy of the international crisis caused by the payment of five billions to Germany ("La crisi finanziaria," in *L'Opinione* for 26 October 1873).

[207] Cf. Bonghi, *Ritratti e profili di contemporanei* 3:165; and Maturi, "Ruggero Bonghi e i problemi di politica estera," p. 419.

and to methods which they abhorred, though no doubt this was also the result of sentimental affection for France.

Engels was right when he said that the Franco-Prussian War was real war, war between nations, something of which Europe had lost the memory over two generations. The war in the Crimea, the war for Italian unity, the Austro-Prussian War, had been wars purely to resolve questions concerning covenants and pacts among governments, and they brought the fighting to a halt as soon as their military machine broke down or began to fray.[208] But not now; this was a war between peoples for the first time since the epoch of the French Revolution and Napoleon, it was "the" war that swept away the illusions, dreams, and myths of half a century.

The Franco-Prussian conflict appeared laden with consequences for all the countries, including the neutrals. Hence Ricasoli, stunned, shaken, and angry, saw the war from the outset as an "apple of European discord,"[209] and Bonghi, who sixteen years later would have occasion to define 1870 as a fatal year for peace, civilization, and unity in Europe,[210] did not hesitate at the time to state (what might have seemed blasphemy when spoken by an Italian) that amid such a difficult and complicated state of affairs as that in which Europe found itself under the threat of Prussia's excessive increase in power, "the Roman question, the only thing on which the Italians seem to be fixing their gaze and their attention, appears to us, if I dare say so, to be of secondary importance."[211]

---

[208] F. Engels, *Notes sur la guerre de 1870–71*, p. 219.

[209] Ricasoli, *Lettere e Documenti* 10:123 (3 September 1870).

[210] *Nuova Antologia* 89 (16 September 1886): 298–99 and 305.

[211] Bonghi, *Nove anni* 2:382 (1 September 1870). And note the opinion of Gregorovius: "In other circumstances this event [the entry of the Italian troops into Rome] would have riveted the world, today it is no more than a small episode in the great universal drama" (*Diari Romani*, p. 451).

II. *The Idea of Rome*

The "Mission" of Rome

NONE THE LESS, what profound and lasting consequences flowed from the transfer of Italy's capital to Rome!

Some of them were obvious to everyone, including the man in the street: for one thing, the process of national unification was thereby completed, but this of course exacerbated the conflict with the Roman curia to the point where the most extreme consequences were to be feared, meaning the departure of the pope from the city of St. Peter. These things constituted the immediate, public effect of the entry into Rome by Italian troops on 20 September, and Italian policy-making concentrated on them in the immediate aftermath. The Roman question was at the center of Italian policy both before and after 20 September in any case; it was the *porro unum* [the most important thing] in the life of the nation. Hence, just as foreign policy would for many years be dominated almost exclusively by the Roman question, which put friendships and enmities to the acid test, the overriding problem domestically, perhaps second only to the critical financial situation, would continue for many years to be that of relations with the Catholic church— or, to use an expression adopted at the time not only by the fieriest tribunes on the left but also by men of the greatest calm and composure on the Right, the problem of the clerical threat.

There were other obvious consequences of the move to Rome that could not escape the notice of any reasonably alert observer. There was the jubilation expressed in organs of opinion and by politicians from southern Italy,[1] with their outspoken proposals for ending the Piedmontese hegemony that continued in the civil service, although it no longer obtained in the government[2]—and in contrast,

---

[1] On 24 September 1870 *La Riforma* (in the article "L'impenitenza") proclaims that there must finally be installed at Rome "a civil service that is completely Italian," so as to bring about "the true fusion that up till now has been a wish rather than a reality." The journal *Roma* of Naples weighed in on 10 November in a much more explicit fashion: it is a matter of employment, of jobs. The prevalence of Piedmontese in the bureaucracy has to be abolished, and the way to do that is to elect opposition deputies, take power, and then establish an equal distribution of jobs (this among other things explains the electoral successes of the Left in the Mezzogiorno). Later, on 24 January 1871, in a debate in the Senate on moving the capital to Rome, Antonio Scialoja stated that there was a benefit to be derived from moving the national capital closer to the southern provinces, which had hitherto not been sufficiently active in public life; this distinguished speaker also felt that having Rome as the capital "will help to redress the balance of influences in the direction of the public administration" (*A.P., Senato*, p. 141). Finally, Minghetti, after a meeting with Pisanelli while on a visit to Naples, noted the incipient desire to create "a Neapolitan party capable of deciding parliamentary majorities, in imitation of the center parties and the Piedmontese in the most recent Chamber. . . . In any case they see that their importance is going to increase with the transfer of the capital, and they wish to profit from this" (Minghetti to Visconti Venosta, 11 January 1871; Visconti Venosta archive).

[2] In the session of the Chamber of 22 December 1870, the hon. Toscanelli asserted that the hegemony of the Piedmontese, which he considered advantageous, was a reality both in the civil

the vexation, the regret, the dark forebodings of a number of politicians from the north who looked with misgivings on the decline of their own region's predominance because they were convinced that the other regions of Italy were too much lacking in the kind of moral and political development required to produce good state administrators.[3] The latter was not the least of the reasons advanced by those who opposed transferring the capital to Rome, and it provided one more justification for those who wanted large-scale administrative decentralization.[4]

The outcome of this north-south contrast was to be an important interior transformation of the life of the kingdom, one with repercussions both wide and deep, although on the surface they were not immediately striking: for within a few decades the membership of the civil service would no longer be Piedmontese, or be cast in a Piedmontese mold, but would instead be recruited in large part from the south. With the passage of time the corollary of this process would become ever more strongly accentuated, as northerners correspondingly withdrew from civil service careers and turned instead to participation in industrial and commercial enterprise, which was expanding in the north in those decades at a rate

---

service and in the government: eight of the general secretaries were members of the "hegemony," and on the question of Rome, those who held the key positions were Piedmontese: the count of San Martino, General Cadorna, La Marmora (*A.P., Camera*, p. 176). Again in 1875 the hon. Mazzoleni declared that the presidency of the Chamber was an exclusive domain of the Piedmontese (Mazzoleni, *L'XI Legislatura: Memorie di un defunto*, p. 103 n. 1).

Roma for 10 November 1870 (in the article "Gl'interessi meridionali davanti all'urna," by G. Lazzaro) observed that only one of the directors-general of a ministry (that of telegraph communications) was a southerner, and that of seventy prefects only eight were from the south. And cf. further articles, also by Lazzaro, in *Roma* for 14 November ("Fatti e non ipotesi") and 21 November ("All'*Opinione* di Firenze: Predica a braccia").

[3] Count Guido Borromeo was the one who complained the most: "the *mezzogiorno* will unfortunately become more powerful at Rome, perhaps too powerful!" He saw this as one of the greatest banes awaiting the northerners in Rome, where "the *mezzogiorno* will triumph, incited by the Roman element" (letters to Minghetti, 12 June and 14 September 1871; BCB, *Carte Minghetti*, cart. XVI, fasc. 4). Bon Compagni was apprehensive as well, taking the view that Neapolitan and Sicilian ministers had worsened the condition of the state "relative to the distribution of jobs." In the Ministry of Justice employees from the south abounded, "which makes it difficult for a minister who is from the same region himself to escape from their influence." The government should take the opportunity offered by the resignation of Raeli not to appoint to that department in future "a minister who is a native of the provinces in which the idea of legality is weakest" (letter to Lanza, 20 February 1871, in Lanza, *Le carte* 7:60). Note that Borromeo, who was a Lombard and a follower of Minghetti, was himself hostile to Piedmontese predominance (cf. his letter to Minghetti of 31 July 1871; BCB, *Carte Minghetti*, cart. XVI, fasc. 4) and feared the rise of the south to the detriment of the north in general, not of Piedmont alone. Rattazzi held dark forebodings (Rattazzi, *Rattazzi et son temps* 2:374, 426, 428–29). Another is Carutti di Cantogno, the historian of the house of Savoy, who was also preoccupied by the shift in the political center of gravity that would result from the transfer of the capital to Rome (*A.P., Camera*, 21 December 1870, p. 127). Jacini deplored the inevitable diminution of Piedmontese influence "because the tenacity of that people will be needed by Italy for many years (*A.P., Senato*, p. 122). Rothan, the French envoy at Florence, noted on 10 January 1871 the discontent of the northerners who feared that the public service would become meridionalized at Rome (*L'Allemagne et l'Italie* 2:193).

[4] For example Pasolini (*Carteggio Minghetti-Pasolini* 4:193). Minghetti agreed (ibid., 4:195), and wrote as much to Visconti Venosta on 27 October 1870 (Visconti Venosta archive): "it is certain that we shall have to shift the least possible amount of administrative work to Rome and leave as much of it as possible in the hands of local authorities." In fact there was a great deal of talk and debate in the aftermath of 1870, even in papers of the Left, about administrative decentralization (cf. *La Riforma* for 11 July and 30 November 1871).

consonant with modernization elsewhere, and was able to offer young men more alluring prospects financially, as well as the chance to engage in the unfettered play of individual capacity and will through the exercise of free personal initiative. A gap was opened up, a deep one whose existence was not always admitted, between the "productive" Italy and the bureaucracy, or as it was sometimes called, the "unproductive" Italy. There was an analogous distinction, less grave certainly but not without its own dangers, between the country as a legal entity and the "real Italy," about which a lot was said and written after 1870. The result was to promote regional rivalry, accompanied by reciprocal accusations and polemics between the north (always ready to boast of its productivity, its factories, and commercial establishments, the billions deposited in its banks or invested in new construction and in business dealing of all kinds) and the south (which was accused of being content with a desk in a government office, of willingness to lead a scant and ill-paid life, but one with the advantage of being untroubled by haste or initiative—to which the reply was that the already impoverished agrarian economy of the south had to carry the burden of the protectionist government policies that favored the industries and the commerce of the north).

It became a commonplace that individual initiative had found its home in the north, while in the south the source of most people's expectations was the state, which, as Turiello noted, was considered the sole source of public welfare.[5] This was an old mental habit that survived from the Bourbon period, and it made it all the easier for the sons of the bourgeoisie of the former Kingdom of the Two Sicilies to aim for the *cursus honorum* of the state bureaucracy.

Above the sphere of the civil service, in the realm of politics in the full sense of the word, the shift of Italy's center of gravity was to have long-term repercussions, since the fixing of the capital at Rome and the rise to greater significance of the south were to give overriding importance to questions such as those connected with the Mediterranean, questions that were less pressing in the valley of the Po. There the highest degree of attention would always be reserved for continental matters, for properly European concerns. The north of Italy had been the battlefield for centuries of the great powers as they contended for hegemony in Europe; it had achieved liberty in large measure by taking advantage of a favorable international moment, by becoming the principal element in certain strategic calculations being made in Europe. It could not fail to remain essentially continental in its way of putting and solving political questions. In Lombardy, despite all that took place between 1870 and 1914, despite economic emulation of Germany and the frequent friendly contacts with German merchants, bankers, industrialists, and journalists, the memory of the Five Days of 1848 and of the "German" overlords of the time of Radetzky remained vivid, since no one in fact made a distinction between Austrians and Germans. Likewise the north generally would exhibit a continental mentality in facing foreign policy problems, and would look for the core of any question in the dynamic relations among the various states of Europe.

[5] Turiello, *Governo e governati in Italia* 1:379, 383 (1882).

In contrast, the south overall had little feeling for these relations and was much quicker to feel the importance and the fascination of the Mediterranean problem. It brought to the political life of the new kingdom an awareness of Africa, and specifically an aspiration to obtain Tunis—if for no other reason because the great majority of the Italians who had settled there were from the south, and there were ties of interest, affection, and memory binding North Africa to the lands of southern Italy.

The increased importance of the south with the capital at Rome, and its greater and more active participation in public life, therefore implied a tendency, latent perhaps but in the long run discernible enough, toward a greater attention to Mediterranean and colonial problems. It is not a matter of pure chance that it was a Neapolitan, Mancini, who launched Italy's colonial policy by going to Massaua, or that its Mediterranean aspirations were incarnated in the Sicilian Crispi.

All of these developments would in themselves have been significant enough to make the year 1870 a decisive turning point in Italian history, quite apart from the great European conflict then taking place. But they were not isolated developments. The entry into Rome, the city in which "there breathes an air that turns one's head,"[6] eventually brought about other and weightier consequences that revealed themselves only after working slowly and at length in the depths of the Italian spirit. An event of this magnitude spreads its influence beyond limited questions, beyond this or that object of political debate. Having Rome as their capital city influenced the very manner of being and thinking of the Italians and signified the birth not of a problem with well-defined historical and political contours but the advent of a new mental world in which individual problems were seen in a different light, and in which the ruling impulses were not those of the generations of the past. With Rome as the capital, large strata of the population were led in the long term to evaluate moral and political situations differently: this was the major and lasting consequence of the breach of the Porta Pia.

Not that the air of Rome turned the heads of all the Italians who breathed it in the first moments. Not all of them found there the milieu that had made such a favorable impression on Blanc. When the first surge of jubilation had passed, and with it the moment in which the phrase "Rome is ours" ran like "an electric spark from one end of Italy to the other, exciting profound enthusiasm,"[7] there came a phase of doubt, perplexity, and recrimination concerning the suitability of transferring, and transferring immediately, the capital from Florence to the Eternal City, and the advantages that the acquisition of Rome was going to bring to the country. These doubts and recriminations beset the same men who had opted for the solution of the forced entry of 20 September, or who had at least shared in and approved of the government's policy and continued to do so. As for the clericals, it would be superfluous even to mention the effect produced on them by the sight of the soldiers of Vittorio Emanuele II in Rome, or to recall the lamenta-

---

[6] Bonghi, *Nove anni* 2:417.
[7] Sella to Minghetti, 21 September 1870 (BCB, *Carte Minghetti*, cart. XV, fasc. 127).

tions and invectives, and the prophecies of disaster worse than anything in the Bible, with which they filled the air.

There were the initial and inevitable difficulties of a practical, material nature at the outset. There was also, among those who were the earliest to arrive, the contrast between dream and reality, and the shadow of disappointment that usually haunts the fulfillment of a desire that has long been close to one's heart. In the present case, this came when they saw that a large part of the population of Rome was still intimately papalist, that it was a population more appalled and annoyed than delighted by a change that was likely to disturb profoundly the habits and attitudes to which it had grown accustomed over centuries, that it wished no disturbance of its placid, indifferent, and skeptical way of life, a life of sunshine, feasts, and processions against a backdrop of priests, women, and foreigners.[8] The Roman upper class, the so-called black aristocracy, was connected by too many ties of interest and sentiment to the pontifical government not to lash out in rancor against the "usurpers." And the rest, those of the Romans who were actually Italian patriots, soon greeted the newly arrived representatives of the government with claims, requests, signs of impatience,[9] a certain haughti-

---

[8] Diomede Pantaleoni was the author of a long memorandum of 10 May 1871 entitled "On Present Conditions in Rome, and on the Present State of Relations with the Papacy and with Foreign Powers, as They Appear from Rome" (Visconti Venosta archive). Pantaleoni was described by a contemporary as a man unable to "leave off the habit of giving advice" (Artom to Nigra, 19 June 1871; AE, *Carte Nigra*), and had been judged by his master, Cavour, to be rather fatuous and loquacious (*La questione romana negli anni 1860–61: Carteggio del Conte di Cavour con D. Pantaleoni, C. Passaglia, O. Vimercati* 2:187, 199, 201 [Bologna, 1929]). Pantaleoni described the Roman bourgeoisie to Visconti Venosta in these terms: "the land-owning bourgeoisie in Rome does not exist, except for the ownership of a few vineyards . . . and a few blocks of apartments . . . ; there is no trace of factories or industries. The only bourgeoisie that has any power is the very restricted group of merchants active in the rural hinterland and large-scale renters of rural holdings. All the rest of the bourgeoisie has remained poor and has had to dedicate itself to the arts, the sciences, and the liberal professions. And since they all depend on the rich and people of property for their employment, it is a bourgeoisie that has not had the slightest independence and has become servile, false, invidious, and withal needy because of the fierce competition in every field of employment." Pantaleoni goes on to speak of the "arrogant servility" of the middle class as compared to the proud ways and independence of thought of the lower class. He concludes that the state of things would be extremely serious "except that the influx of a new and select population from all the provinces of Italy offers a guarantee that it will soon be . . . altered." Nicomede Bianchi expressed an analogous wish, saying that it was necessary to bring "the industriousness of subalpine life to the dead land of Lazio, whose former inhabitants are destined to make way for the true sons of modern Italy" (Castelli, *Carteggio politico* 2:498). Castelli for his part lamented the inertia of the municipality and the absence of initiative in the population, unaccustomed to "anything but the *government*" (ibid., 2:497). A discouraging view of Rome and the Romans is also found in G. Raimondi, *Roma tre mesi dopo l'occupazione* (Milan, 1871), pp. 9 ff.

[9] ". . . instead of giving thanks to God that, with no effort on their part, they have got out of a situation intolerable for any people that has any sense of self-worth, the Romans are continually in the piazza, ready to agitate and get agitated, and though they are the last to join our great family, ready to impose themselves with their displays of impatience and their childish behavior. Is there then some sort of fatality in this city of Rome, that it has to make itself damnable for Italy?" (Ricasoli to Luigi Torelli, 20 November 1870: in Monti, *Il conte Luigi Torelli*, p. 297; in the text published in Ricasoli, *Lettere e Documenti* 10:169, these phrases are omitted). The same sentence is passed in *La Perseveranza* for 20 November on the impatience of the Romans, who are said to have no other concept of a civil, liberal, and secular state than "that of a state in which any group of persons that mounts a disturbance in the streets calls itself *the people*, and the *Government* gives in immediately to any sort of *pressure* or *cry* or *demand* from this *people*."

ness of demeanor seemingly calculated to offend those who came to Rome bearing the memory of the years of struggle undergone—and not by the Romans—in
order to get there.[10] It was as though the modern Quirites were stooping low to
welcome Italy and the house of Savoy inside their walls, and were claiming all
the credit for the arrival to boot.[11]

If these were the recriminations uttered against the Romans, the Romans responded with their own complaints: they were offended by the excessively military
and peremptory bearing of the newcomers, by the air of being conquistadores
that royal officials, soldiers, bureaucrats, and politicians assumed.[12] These were
the least suitable airs to put on when coming into contact with a skeptical but
intelligent population substantially lacking in political energy except for the un-
sophisticated but proud class of popular republicans of Trastevere, but very sensitive to formal dignity and easily wounded in its own self-regard. The Romans
were both highly susceptible and also (with the experience of a race that over the
centuries had seen it all) very ready to perceive the ridiculous side of men and
things, especially when the men in question had the pedantic seriousness of certain bureaucrats of the pure Piedmontese strain. Added to this was the damage

---

[10] "If the Romans themselves had been the makers of Italy, instead of having been liberated by
the Italians, they still wouldn't have the right to make so many demands and impose themselves so
proudly on the other provinces. By dint of screaming that without Rome as the capital Italy would not
exist, these gentlemen have come to believe it themselves. But it would not surprise me if their
exorbitant demands provoked a reaction against Rome" (La Marmora to Lanza, 19 November 1870;
Lanza, *Le carte* 6:271). In an opuscule entitled *Dal Reno al Tevere* by "a Roman citizen" (Naples,
1870, but dated from Rome, 10 August 1870), we can already find the attitude that in future would be
so jarring: "Come [to Rome, O Italians], but remember that Rome from the beginning announces the
universe, because it announces a people that is the people of peoples" (p. 27 and cf. p. 26).

[11] Offended by the electoral manifesto of the Roman liberals, who in November 1870 offered the
candidacy to Quintino Sella as the only zealous proponent inside the government of the national
program, and as a sign of protest against the cabinet, which, with the exception of Sella, did not wish
the immediate transfer of the king to Rome, a writer in *La Perseveranza* spoke out roundly: "No one
had more desire for Rome than we did; no one venerates it more; no one is more inclined to want it as
the head of the peninsula. But on one condition, that it feel itself to be a member of the peninsula, and
not presume to be the whole substance of it, simply because it has had less of a struggle than any
other member to find its place; and on condition that the head be full of brains, not virtually empty of
them, as it seems to be right now. Italy is the mistress of Rome, not Rome of Italy. Let us be frank: if
Rome becomes the capital of Italy without demonstrating that sobriety of public spirit that so
marvelously distinguished Turin down to the last fatal hour, and that always made, and still makes,
Florence admirable, it will be a sad and melancholy day when the seat of government migrates for a
third time!" ("Il Sella e i Romani," in *La Perseveranza* for 21 November 1870; and cf. as well *La
Nazione* for 17 and 22 November 1870). Years later Guiccioli made the same observation: "These old
Romans are curious. They think they have done Italy and the house of Savoy a great honor by
accepting them into their city" ("Diario," in *Nuova Antologia* for 1 August 1935, p. 433).

[12] "The very severe, curt, and peremptory conduct of a few of the first government officials
roused a good deal of discontent. But much more was produced in some circles when they saw that
the university chairs and other eminent positions were being filled by individuals from the rest of Italy
instead of from Rome. This is still an open wound, especially among the middle class, which is the
most numerous of all and the most indigent; its members are often highly intelligent, but rarely
dignified to an equal degree. There were claims that Rome had been invaded and conquered; the
municipal opposition got a lot of support. . . . There is opposition of the same sort at work inside the
Provincial Deputation" (Pantaleoni, memorandum cited at n. 8 above). Cf. as well La Marmora to
Lanza, 9 December 1870; Vigliani to Lanza, 14 December; Lanza to La Marmora, 15 December
(Lanza, *Le carte* 6:315, 321, 323).

done to their interests,[13] the same local interests that had already been bruised in Naples, by the nomination to important public offices of non-Romans, nominations that created a pretext (a just pretext in some cases) for claiming that this was conquest. And there was the burden of new and heavier taxes to pay,[14] a shirt of Nessus that the various populations of Italy had had to wriggle into one after the other upon unification, and which in Rome as in other places naturally brought grist to the mill of those who preferred to praise the good old days.[15] In sum, there were economic costs, which the allies of the pope and the representatives of foreign powers were happy to stress in order to highlight the mistake committed by the Italian government on 20 September.[16]

On one side there was a sort of bitter amazement at finding that the promised land was anything but a paradise,[17] that the Romans were less enthusiastic than they were expected to be. There was loud wailing at the degree of corruption which, it was claimed, was rooted more deeply than anyone had dared to suppose,[18] and harsh judgment was passed, especially by the many anti-Roman

---

[13] Pantaleoni (memorandum cited at n. 8 above) stated that the only real opposition to be feared was that based on interests: "Opposition based on opinion in Rome counts for very little, because convictions are feeble and the level of feeling is low." For this reason, the discontent of those in Rome who had favored the new order in hopes of getting some personal advantage from it, and had been disappointed, was much more "noteworthy" than the discontent of those who had lost out when the papal power vanished.

[14] "[A] notable discontent has grown up over the new taxes, which are a lot heavier than the old ones, and have fallen on the people and the bourgeoisie before economic development and the resulting increased incomes have had a chance to make them bearable, and even to produce net gains" (Pantaleoni, memorandum cited at n. 8 above).

[15] Gadda, the government commissioner in Rome, found that in the space of a few months "we have been unable to gain ground in Rome, and in fact we are losing it. We were able to win over very few persons whose influence counts, or perhaps none at all, from the clerical party. And of those who supported us, we have rendered lukewarm all who hoped for great things for the country, since we have been able to do nothing except impose taxes. Those opposed to the government include all the people who wanted jobs, incomes, and similar graces that we do not have for anyone, and which our opponents show them glimpses of and make them hope for. The result is that a new class of malcontents has been formed among the former pontifical employees who lost their posts. They have an extensive network of supporters who spread their protest everywhere. This is a serious problem. The government couldn't find a dog in the streets to defend it here. The worst of it is that the Vatican trawls among these people, and lures them by giving them money and promising to make up the salary differential they have lost" (Gadda to Visconti Venosta, 8 February 1871; Visconti Venosta archive).

[16] For example, the French chargé d'affaires at the Holy See, Lefebvre de Béhaine, insisted on the economic advantages that the papal army, which spent a good deal more freely than the Italian one, brought to the city (reports of 4 January and 29 March 1871, nn. 1 and 58; AEP, *C.P., Rome*, t. 1049, fol. 7, and t. 1050, fol. 168v. On the economic harm caused by the end of the temporal power, reports of 11 January and 8 April, nn. 5 and 67, t. 1049, fol. 46v, t. 1050, fol. 236 ff.).

[17] "Unhappily, I fear that the Roman question had many deceptions wrapped up in it that are now coming to light" (La Marmora to Lanza, 14 November 1870; Lanza, *Le carte* 6:248). And cf. the harsh judgment of Rattazzi (*Rattazzi et son temps* 2:429).

[18] ". . . profound corruption that is rooted in this *promised land*" (Lanza to La Marmora, 16 January 1871; Lanza, *Le carte* 7:36). Lanza was also uneasy about the costs: "some people have lost their heads to the point where they believe that with Rome we have acquired some kind of California. They will find out when the accounts are drawn up" (letter to La Marmora, 8 December 1870; ibid., 6:313). A little later, Guido Borromeo opined that Rome had not yet produced a single individual worth anything to Italian public life. "Sadly it seems to me that the promised land in which we have arrived has not produced to this point a *featherless biped* who is worth any more than one of the

Florentines, on the indolence of the Romans and their aversion to work, which surpassed any conceivable limit.[19] On the other side, there was complaint and irony about the *buzzurri*, the "outsiders," meaning northerners in general and Piedmontese in particular. It was a perfectly understandable state of affairs, in which each side, as in the literary world of Manzoni, was a little bit right and a little bit wrong. But all in all, even if the tension in Rome was capable of inflecting the correspondence of the king's lieutenant there, the rigid La Marmora, with pessimism,[20] and was not exactly transitory (since the chronicles would continue to be full of complaints about the Romans and about bureaucratic and ministerial Rome), at any rate it was not a matter of the utmost gravity: it was still only the little world of citizen life in Rome, narrow and fertile in anecdotal evidence like that of every other city.

But at Rome, above everyday life with its miseries and its frictions, there was something else, there was the idea of Rome: an idea that caused men of the profoundest sentiments to await the moment of their entry into it, after many years of hope and desire, with their souls in tumult,[21] and to give way to the rush of emotion[22] after having passed trembling and almost adoring through the Porta del Popolo,[23] struck with reverence before the palpitating power "of the immense, eternal life of Rome beneath the artificial surface which the priests and courtesans had spread like a winding sheet over the vast sleeper."[24]

This idea had already manifested itself at other crucial moments in the history of Italy. The medieval German emperors had employed it for its connotations of

---

feathered bipeds. When I reflect that two of the great men here are Doria and Pallavicini, I ask myself whether it wouldn't be worthwhile to secularize a number of the cardinals and the monsignors" (Borromeo, letter to Minghetti of 12 June 1871, cited above at n. 3; BCB, *Carte Minghetti*, cart. XVI, fasc. 4). Foreigners continued to see the Romans this way for years. The French chargé d'affaires in 1874 said that what passes for a bourgeoisie in Rome has shown nothing but mediocrity in city government for four years (Tiby, report, 21 September 1874, n. 66; AEP, *C.P., Italie*, t. 390, fol. 160). Only Sella remained firm in his "Romanism." "The Romans are a population worthy of a capital city," he wrote on 28 July 1871 to Castelli (Castelli, *Carteggio politico* 2:512).

[19] See "Lettere Romane" in *La Nazione* for 21 April 1871: "Of all the peoples that have a history, the Roman people is the only one I know of that has never borne the universal condemnation of the human race to live by the sweat of its brow. It has never worked, either for others or for itself."

[20] La Marmora himself, in the tradition of d'Azeglio, did not favor making Rome the capital of Italy (Verax, *Alfonso La Marmora* [5 January 1879], p. 130; Castelli, *Carteggio politico* 2:484). Cf. the letter to Torelli in G. Paladino, *Roma: Storia d'Italia dal 1866 al 1871 con particulare riguardo alla Questione Romana*, p. 202. Even when he was in Rome, he did not hide the fact that he had been opposed to the action of 20 September (Lefebvre de Béhaine, report, 15 November 1870, n. 106; AEP, *C.P., Rome*, t. 1048, fol. 166v).

[21] "So tomorrow evening I will be in Rome. I still cannot believe it. Certainly, when this desire has been satisfied, what will be left to wish for?" And the shout of triumph followed: "Yes, finally I have arrived in the capital of the world!" (Goethe, *Viaggio in Italia*, 28 October and 1 November 1786; cited from the translation of Zaniboni [Florence, n.d.], vol. 1, pp. 144–45).

[22] "My temper is not very susceptible of enthusiasm. . . . But at the distance of twenty-five years I can neither forget nor express the strong emotions which agitated my mind as I first approached and entered the *Eternal City.* . . . [S]everal days of intoxication were lost or enjoyed before I could descend to a cool and minute investigation" (Edward Gibbon, *Memoirs of My Life*, ed. Georges A. Bonnard [London, 1966], p. 134). [*Translator's note:* Chabod cites Gibbon in an Italian translation, *Memorie* (Milan, 1825), pp. 144–45.]

[23] Mazzini, *Note autobiografiche* (*Scritti* 77:341).

[24] Ibid., 77:346.

empire and political power; and later it had been invoked, this time by men of Italian origin and spirit, as the supreme expression of civic life. After the Renaissance had come the interlude of the baroque age, followed by the eighteenth century; but during the course of the latter there began to be heard ever more frequent and forceful references to the greatness, to the mission in fact, of Rome, which even then was seen as the only imaginable center for a union of all the Italians.[25]

Now the idea rose up again, as it had in the Renaissance, superimposed upon the contingent, the poor and miserable, aspects of the life of the city and its inhabitants, which thereby disappeared, leaving the moral, religious, political, and cultural significance of the millennial tradition standing alone. The spirited demand that the ebullient Mommsen addressed to Quintino Sella one evening in 1871 signified nothing less than a summons to heed the necessity and the fatality of the idea of Rome: "But what do you intend doing in Rome? This is what makes the rest of us uneasy. One does not remain in Rome without some cosmopolitan purpose. What do you intend to do?"[26]

The double aspect of Rome, its existence as a universal idea over and above its existence as an Italian city, was as evident to other foreigners as it was to Mommsen. There was another German also enamored of Rome who successfully conjured up the aura that still hung over the ancient world city, much as Mommsen had. This was Gregorovius, who had been a good friend to the Italian national movement,[27] and had greeted with joy the "liberation" of humanity from the papal yoke as the collapse of a second nightmare of megalomania after the collapse of the first in the shape of the Napoleonic empire.[28] Nevertheless he grew melancholy at seeing the city descend from being the moral center of humanity, the republic of all the world, to being the capital of a kingdom of average stature,[29] a capital erected by German luck and German victories, but weak at heart and unequal to the gifts of fortune.[30] A little later, in 1877, there was another great writer of very different origin and outlook, Dostoevsky, who also pressed this point in the pages of his *Diary*. He too was unconvinced that a united Italy would accomplish much, and also sought for the "grand Roman idea of the peoples united," the universal idea of which the Italian people was the depositary

---

[25] Denina is an example, and so is Bettinelli, though he wanted only literary and scientific union (C. Calcaterra, *Il nostro imminente Risorgimento*, pp. 159–60).

[26] Sella, *Discorsi Parlamentari* 1:292; Guiccioli, *Quintino Sella* 1:353.

[27] Gregorovius, *Diari Romani*, pp. 75, 105, 129, 140. In 1859 he tried to win over the editors of the *Augsburger Allgemeine Zeitung*, who till then had been hostile, to the Italian cause (p. 117).

[28] Gregorovius, *Diari Romani*, p. 442 and cf. p. 450: "I would have been so glad to see with my own eyes the fall of the papacy." The papal state he called a "mummy" (p. 66).

[29] Ibid., pp. 460 and 462. Similar thoughts had come to Gregorovius in 1861 while awaiting the "destiny" of Rome (pp. 157–58). It was for the purpose of salvaging the cosmopolitical character of Rome while at the same time satisfying the Italian national sentiment that Gregorovius (like many another) had excogitated a weird combination, in which the city and its surrounding territory would be left to the pope, while the Romans would be given Italian citizenship (p. 262).

[30] The notion that Italian unity was a gift of fortune, and to a large extent the result of Prussian success (in the cases of Venetia and Rome), recurs throughout Gregorovius's *Diari Romani* (pp. 460, 463, 478–79).

and which certainly was not being actualized by the actual "little second-rate kingdom . . . without ambition, gentrified."[31]

Renan was kinder. But in his case as well the "modest and honorable" rebirth of Italy as a nation was a piece of good fortune for humanity, since by ending the temporal power of the papacy it was bound to bring an end to the unity of the Catholic world, which meant unity round the figure of the pope, the lamentable condition that had caused the principal woes of Catholicism ever since the time of the Council of Trent.[32] For Renan too the unification of Italy, a negligible event in itself, could assume general importance only through its non-Italian repercussions.[33]

Foreigners were accustomed to think of Rome as the center of Catholicism, that is of a universal idea, and the purely national problem of Italy left them unmoved. If Italy was to be the political power in Rome, it had to find a supranational purpose or else it would remain tiny and trivial in foreign eyes compared to the Vatican. And few of them would have been satisfied simply by the project for land reclamation in the Agro Romano that Wilhelm I of Germany pointed out to King Vittorio in 1875 in Milan as the best way to "justify the presence of your government in Rome."[34] Some kind of international self-justification was necessary; it was inescapably true that in a city full of so many and such illustrious memories, a place intertwined with universal history, indeed with the Vatican itself still present as a living piece of universal history, the king, parliament, and government of Italy appeared very small indeed, incapable of counterbalancing by themselves so many centuries of glory. The papacy was there, alive and powerful and universal; and no one could quite get rid of the nightmarish feeling of not being equal to the Vatican. The new government had to find appropriate official buildings [*palazzi*], and all of them, as Gino Capponi said, were "lower" than the Vatican.[35]

There was another compelling reason for the resurgence of the idea of Rome: it might almost have been designed to satisfy an ideal that had been unknown to the Renaissance but lay at the heart of the Romanticism of the nineteenth century— the ideal of a different "mission" for each of the various peoples. This conception came into the world as a virtual twin of the idea of the nation itself. Traces of it can be found on all sides between the end of the eighteenth century and the first decades of the nineteenth, but it first sprang into life with particular intensity in Germany, where Humboldt, Schiller, and Schlegel had proclaimed a German

---

[31] Dostoevsky, *Diario di uno scrittore* (Italian translation: Milan, 1943), p. 645.

[32] Renan, *Correspondance, 1872–1892*, pp. 26–27.

[33] Renan had already written as much in 1850: "An assembly sitting on the Capitol and deliberating on the little local concerns of Italian municipalism would forever be ridiculous" (Renan and Berthelot, *Correspondance*, p. 116).

[34] The anecdote is recounted by Finali, who was present at the meeting (*La vita politica di contemporanei illustri*, p. 223). Von Schweinitz had said to Minghetti in 1871: "And so? What have you done to reclaim the Roman *campagna*? . . . I will be waiting for you there to see what you can do" (Minghetti, letter to L. Torelli, 21 January 1883, in Monti, *Il conte Luigi Torelli*, p. 485).

[35] In his speech to the Senate of 29 December 1870 on the Roman plebiscite (G. Capponi, *Scritti editi e inediti* 1:461, ed. M. Tabarrini [Florence, 1877]).

mission to the world, that of being humanity's purest mirror, of living in contact with the world spirit, of living in a day the harvest of all the other days lived by mankind.[36] But it was very strong in the France of the Revolution and the Restoration as well, from de Maistre, theorist of the French "magistracy" over Europe,[37] to Guizot and Michelet[38] and the Saint-Simonians,[39] and strong too in England, whose mission, from being divine in Cromwell's time, had become a human vocation for imperial dominion that was soon to be extolled by Tennyson, Froude, and Seeley.[40]

It was as though, at the very moment at which the new driving idea of modern times, that of national individuality, was emerging to sweep away forever every last remnant of the old *respublica christiana*, it required a moral justification of universal stature that would legitimate its inception. The first phase of this process had come about in the field of international politics from the second half of the seventeenth century onward, when the practice of European equilibrium was elevated to the status of a theory, to the dignity of a principle. Such a new theoretical emphasis had represented an attempt to maintain a unified general framework over and above the multiplicity of the individual states by substituting a conspicuously articulated unity for the previous idea of unity as a homogeneous block. In the ages of Enlightenment and Romanticism, European life evolved still further toward differentiated forms in culture and morality. And as before the reaction was to seek for a common motive, a principle able to hold together a Europe in which the confessional division had subsided, making the national individualities stand out all the more clearly. Something was needed that could function as a bridge between the isolated nations and the civilization they shared, whose greatness, strength, and dignity were exalted as never before.

Hence the idea of the national mission was in certain respects a residue of the cosmopolitanism of the eighteenth century, a fortunate legacy of the powerful ideological development that had brought the values of man, and of humanity, to the center of European life. Yet it was forged in Romanticism, which, following Rousseau and Herder, had taken to its heart the individuality of the nations. So it had a twofold, and diverse, origin: the sense of the particular and the aspiration to a general communion of destinies mingled together, sometimes in happy accord, sometimes colliding and canceling one another out reciprocally. Because of this the idea of mission became in turn the forerunner, on the one hand, of humanitarianism, and on the other of modern nationalism. In the first case there was a tendency to put the emphasis increasingly on the "duty" to carry out the mission of the nation, and therefore to emphasize, as Mazzini would say, the purpose, by which he meant humanity, with the nation limited to the role of

---

[36] Meinecke, *Cosmopolitismo e Stato nazionale* 1:54–55.

[37] De Maistre, *Considérations sur la France*, ch. 2, p. 9: "Each nation, like each individual, has received a mission that it must carry out. France exercises a veritable magistracy over Europe." And cf. p. 29: "Providence . . . has given exactly two instruments to the French nation . . . with which it acts on the world, its language and the spirit of proselytism that forms the essence of its character."

[38] Cf. Omodeo,"Primato francese e iniziativa italiana," pp. 27 ff.

[39] Cf. Treves, *La dottrina sansimoniana*, p. 75.

[40] Cf. Langer, *La diplomazia dell'imperialismo* 1:119 ff.

"means." This would be shown in the sequel by the careers of a number of individuals originally nourished on Mazzinian ideas who then passed over to preaching one type or another of humanitarianism and pacifism, or transformed themselves into apostles of the Internationals. When they did, they felt the ire of their master, who was always concerned to preserve both terms of the dichotomy, with no sacrifice of humanity—but even less with any sacrifice of the nation, for it was the nation that always remained the central, the most clear-cut and lucid, impulse of his thought. In the second case, there was a tendency to accentuate the "right" that went with the mission, and thus gradually to place the end before the means, the homeland above humanity, and hence to arrive ultimately at full-blown nationalism.

The latter development was facilitated by the fact that, very early on, there was considerable readiness to transform the word "mission" into another word: *primato* [supremacy, preeminence, primacy]. Indeed, why should any people be considered to have a particular mission, unless it had demonstrated attitudes and capacities, and vaunted traditions, superior to those of the other peoples, at least in a given field? As early as Schiller and Schlegel the idea of the German mission was linked to the idea of German superiority, with a certain disdain for the other peoples as a natural offshoot.[41] Germany's consciousness of itself was intensified, but so was the feeling that the modern world was Germany's creation and in some sense belonged to it.[42] And it was all too easy for this idea of superiority to seek an apparently objective basis, something continuous and lasting, in ethnic factors, in racial criteria. We see this beginning to happen in Schlegel.

Italy was not exempt, and there had been a series of ostentatious, if rather scholastic, claims made for Italian supremacy of one kind or another long before Mazzini and his idea of mission, beginning with the Bolognese abbot Pietro Tosini, who as early as 1718–1720 averred that Italy had always been the leading country in the world, and that the Italians had dominated the other nations. He was followed by Algarotti, Genovese, Bettinelli, and Verri,[43] and Italian preeminence in particular fields was claimed by Denina and Galeani Napione.[44] Some devoted their efforts to illustrating this ancient supremacy, following in the footsteps of Vico, who extolled the *antiquissima Italorum sapientia*; to this line belongs Cuoco and his *Platone in Italia*. Others limited themselves to maintaining with Alfieri that from Italian soil there sprang individuals of more robust

[41] In Schiller cf. especially the preparatory fragment for a lyric—*Deutsche Grösse*—written probably in 1801: "The other peoples will prove to be flowers that wilt, this [German] people will be the lasting golden fruit. The English are avid for treasure, the French for splendor; to the lot of the Germans has fallen the highest destiny; 'to live in contact with the world spirit. . . . Every people has its day in history; the day of the Germans will be the harvest of all the other days'" (Meinecke, *Cosmopolitismo e Stato nazionale* 1:55).

[42] The expressions are those of De Sanctis in his speech to the Chamber of 22 November 1862 (*La Critica* 11 [1913]: 75).

[43] Cf. the various passages assembled by E. Rota, *Il problema italiano dal 1700 al 1815* (Milan, 1938), pp. 42, 47, and Rota, *Le origini del Risorgimento italiano (1700–1800)* 1:140 ff., 532, 540, 583 (Milan, 1938). Further, G. Natali, "L'idea del primato italiano prima di Vincenzo Gioberti," *Nuova Antologia* (16 July 1917), pp. 126 ff.

[44] Cf. Calcaterra, *Il nostro imminente Risorgimento*, pp. 282, 412.

constitution, fit to accomplish great things. In either case the old idea of an original Italian primacy in civilization, of the Italian peninsula as the mistress of the outlying provinces and instructress of the other peoples, had become a tired cliché by the time the abbot Gioberti seized on it as a counterweight to be set against the idea of French primacy. Gioberti carried the notion to the limit and gave it a resonance and a celebrity that it had never previously had.

With this the emphasis has clearly shifted to the second of the two possibilities contained in the idea of mission—the nationalistic one. Contemporaneously, Mazzini was emphasizing the first theme, that of duty, pointing out to Italy and the other enslaved nations the European task that awaited them, and speaking of an initiative of one for the benefit of all. Later on Mazzini too, in reaction against the neocosmopolitanism of the hated "Internationals," would play up the theme of right.[45] And when that occurred it was possible to detect in the mission that he outlined for Italy an indubitably particularistic note: even in Mazzini the accent shifted toward a politics of power, in accordance with the dictates of the European governmental praxis that he had so often execrated. Even this man, the European citizen of a Europe of much wider spirit and more open comprehension than the Europe of Metternich, the apostle of humanity as an end in itself, even Mazzini did not always recoil before the temptation to see national problems from the perspectives of diplomatic and military power. And just as he was seduced by the old notion of an Italic civilization anterior to that of Greece,[46] likewise he fixed his hopes not only on an Italy that might open the way to modern civilization, and initiate a new epoch of human history, but also on an Italy that, after reaching its true national frontiers, would then go on to acquire colonial dominions and, with a foothold in Tunis, rule the Mediterranean once more,[47] as the Roman eagle had done in the past.

[45] In the work of 1871, *Nazionalismo e nazionalità* (*Scritti* 93:85 ff.). The polemical intention is declared very openly.

[46] Cf. among other writings the *Note autobiografiche* (*Scritti* 77:32).

[47] Mazzini, *Politica Internazionale* (1871), in *Scritti* 92:143 ff. Here, after having insisted once more on the common purpose of the nations (humanity, the progressive discovery of the moral law, and the embodiment of that law in real situations), and after speaking of the third mission of Italy in the world (Rome of the people, etc.), the purpose of which is a peaceful and permanent settlement in Europe, Mazzini does indeed point to participation in a "Slavic-Hellenic-Dacian-Roman initiative" as the fundamental drive of Italian foreign policy—but then goes on to speak of opening up to Italy the roads that lead to the Asiatic world, even by means of a colonizing invasion of Tunis: "as Morocco belongs to the Iberian peninsula, and Algeria to France, Tunis, the key to the central Mediterranean, . . . belongs visibly to Italy. Tunis, Tripoli, and Cyrenaica form part . . . of the zone of Africa that really belongs to the European system as far as the Atlantic. And it was on the peaks of the Atlantic that the banner of Rome fluttered when, with Carthage overthrown, the Mediterranean was called *Mare nostrum*. We were the masters of that whole region until the fifth century A.D. Today the French are eying it, and before long they will have it if we do not" (ibid., 92:167–68). Here the references to the banner of Rome and to "our sea" would suffice, even without the explicit reference to the aims of France, to reveal a tendency to put the problem in the same terms in which one of the nationalists that Mazzini so execrated would have put it (cf. Kohn, *Profeti e popoli*, pp. 87–88, 101–102, but bearing in mind the reservations expressed above—pp. 56–57—concerning the thought of Mazzini in general).

These pages offer an opportunity to those who make it their business to hunt for "precursors" to see in Mazzini "the prophet of the times in which we are living" (E. Passamonti, *L'idea coloniale nel Risorgimento italiano* [Turin, 1934], p. 15; first published in *Rivista delle Colonie Italiane* [June–

In sum, whether it took on the color of a humanitarian impulse or that of a nationalistic drive, the idea of mission had been and remained an idea with a very strong grip on men's minds. After 1870 it was instilled, so to speak, with the concrete and precise value, virtually tangible and visible, of the name and the history of Rome. The old Renaissance attachment to Rome the mother, which in Renaissance Italy was joined with scorn for the "barbarians" from north of the Alps, was now interwoven, to the point of making a seamless whole, with the Romantic concept of mission, which in its highest manifestations sought to transform the sense of national force and dignity into an initiative for the good of all, to make the gifts and the glories of the different groups serve the common cause.

In this nineteenth-century reprise of the idea of Rome, the precept of imitation that had been prized by the writers and artists of the Quattrocento was missing. Nor could it be otherwise, seeing that men were now dominated by faith in human progress, and so were no longer able to persuade themselves that the True and the Beautiful had been revealed once and for all in the ancient world, making it a paradigm to which the eyes of humanity ought to be forever turned, so as to draw from it guidance and comfort.[48] There was in addition a sense of shared labor for the good of all humanity, something to which certainly neither Ghiberti and Alberti, nor Valla and Politian, had given a great deal of thought. The reason for this is obvious: the sense that all men shared a common nature and destiny had been impressed deeply on men's minds by eighteenth-century thought, as indeed it had been many centuries before by the Christian evangel, though in its renewal the tone was no longer religious but secular.

Mazzini's was to be a third Rome, a Rome of the people in succession to the Rome of the Caesars and the Rome of the popes: a universal Rome, since Italy's historical tradition had taught it, in a way not given to the other peoples, the "mission to universalize its own life." Thus the life of the peninsula had always been, in its great epochs, the life of Europe: "from Rome, from the Capitol, and from the Vatican, the story of mankind's unification unfolds through history."[49]

The vision of this imminent third life for Italy spurred the wandering apostle of its unification, one who nurtured in himself "the cult of Rome,"[50] who had made of Rome the "religion of his soul,"[51] to compose one of those passages full of religious and prophetic passion that retain their potency even though the stylistic overload diminishes the effect:

Halt your step and peer toward the southward horizon, turning to the Mediterranean.

In the midst of the immensity you will see, rising to meet your gaze like a beacon in

---

July 1932]). It is to be noted, however, that Passamonti makes the mistake of attributing to Mazzini, as if it had been written for Bismarck, the well-known memorandum that is thought instead to have been directed by the Prussian chancellery (?) to Usedom in April 1868 ([Diamilla-Muller], *Politica segreta italiana*, pp. 346 ff.; Mazzini, *Scritti* 86:xxxi ff.; cf. ch. 1 above, n. 161), thus reversing the positions.

[48] On this I refer to my article "Rinascimento," in *Problemi storici e orientamenti storiografici* (Como, 1942), pp. 462–63 and 477 ff.

[49] *Agli italiani* (1853), in *Scritti* 51:55.

[50] *Note autobiografiche* (*Scritti* 77:32).

[51] Ibid., 77:341.

the ocean an isolated point, a sign of distant grandeur. Bend your knee and adore: there beats the heart of Italy; there rests the eternal solemnity of Rome.

And that salient peak is the Capitol of the Christian World. And not far distant from it there stands the Capitol of the Pagan World. And those two prostrate worlds await a third World more vast and sublime than the other two, one that is struggling into existence amid their ruins.

And this is the Trinity of History whose Word lies in Rome.[52]

Rome: a mission of greatness in the future as in the past, when Europe had been semibarbarian and the Roman eagles flew from triumph to triumph, instructing "the conquered peoples in the wisdom of laws that is still revered, the comforts of civil life, and that drive toward Unity that prepared the world for Jesus." And a second time, with Europe "wrapped in the shadows of feudal servitude . . . you came once again to life, and affirmed the republican liberty of man and citizen in your Communes; you disseminated to the uttermost regions the benefits of civilization, of letters and of commerce."[53]

In the stormy soul of Mazzini all the themes of the Italian tradition, of Rome, and of preeminence were fused, and then reshaped and sublimated by him into the lofty concept of a European mission. Still, the strongly national subthemes, and even the complaints against others for their ingratitude (which later became more frequent), were never abolished and emerged into the light from time to time.[54]

In him it was a driving idea, a potent flame of action, lived and felt with the religiosity of all great things. And all of Mazzini's devotees felt it no less vividly, even though in their case as well the rhetorical emphasis may seem to undercut the seriousness of the utterance. For example, there is Mameli, the Tyrtaeus of Italy, who in May 1846, a year and more before composing his famous hymn, had envisioned the resurgence of the Mistress of the Latins:

> Fuor del feretro armata s'affacia,
> Ha trovato il valore primiero,
> Ritrovò la sua lucida traccia
> Della gloria nel noto sentiero,
> Non ne spenser mille anni le impronte,
> L'elmo antico s'adatta alla fronte,
> Roma è sorta, dinanzi ci sta.

> She steps forth in arms from her tomb
> She has found her pristine valor
> She has found the shining traces
> Of glory in her familiar path
> A thousand years did not cancel their imprint

---

[52] *Ai giovani d'Italia* (1859), in *Scritti* 64:180.

[53] Ibid. 64:157.

[54] "And when ungrateful Europe threw you down and divided up your spoils, the genius of Italy, before veiling itself for a time, threw down from its cross, as a token of that which it might one day be capable of, a new world for Europe" (ibid.).

She fits the ancient helmet once more to her brow
Roma has arisen, before us she stands.[55]

The myth also retained its grip on those who had acquired their first ideological baggage from Mazzini, but had then drifted away from him, without letting go of the inspiration that a few of the fundamental components of his message had given them. So it was for Crispi and his friends on *La Riforma*, who as we have seen were prone to force Mazzinian nationality into a nationalistic key, and were thus only too ready to accept from him the myth of Rome, for it could easily be turned to use in kindling the fires of nationalism. In this light it is hardly surprising to find *La Riforma* proclaiming that those who now legislate from the city that was once the teacher of civic wisdom have by virtue of this an appointed mission;[56] that Italy has a mission in the world of nations.

"In the current revolutions that are changing the political world, no people has been given a higher calling of civilization by the providence of history than the Italian people. To affirm the principle of nationality on the rubble of theocracy, to

[55] It is true that around the end of 1846 or in May 1847 (for discussion of the dating, see G. Mameli, *La vita e gli scritti*, ed. A. Codignola, centenary edition [Venice: n.d. but 1927], vol. 2, p. 40) Mameli appears to dismiss the ancient glories in the poem *Roma*:

> Ad altri le memorie
> I secoli che fûro

> For others the memories
> The centuries that were

(and Calosso, *Colloqui col Manzoni*, pp. 34–35, insists on this). But in fact his prophecy of a new Rome, the third Rome of Mazzini

> Ove nel mondo i Cesari
> Ebbero un dí l'impero,
> E i sacerdoti tennero
> Schiavo l'uman pensiero . . .
> Ondeggerà fiammante
> L'insegna dell'Amore . . .
> Città delle memorie
> Città della Speranza
> Le cento suore Italiche
> Chiama e a pugnar ti avanza

> Where the Caesars at one time had
> Empire over the world
> And the priesthood held
> Human thought enslaved . . .
> The standard of love
> Will undulate in flames . . .
> Summon the hundred sisters of Italy
> City of memories
> City of hope
> And you will have more than enough to fight

is still an appeal to Rome, which therefore must still be the forerunner. And cf. also the composition *Roma ritorna al Campidoglio*: "The light is shining out from the Capitol. It will spread over all of Italy, because with the fall of Rome and its pontiff kings, Rome will become once more the Rome of the people!" (Mameli, *La vita e gli scritti* 2:308–309).

[56] "L'Italia e Roma," in *La Riforma* for 22 September 1870.

glorify religious liberty and the rights of civilization on the very dogmatic soil from which sprouted the Syllabus: this is a mission worthy of a great people, one that history by means of its miraculous workings has reserved for Italy. . . . When it occupied Rome with its arms it made a formal undertaking before the civilized world to resolve the problem in a way corresponding to the interests and the will of universal civilization."[57] The plebiscite of 2 October was a solemn moment in the life of Italy and of all humanity: "the Middle Ages crumble, the modern age shines over the ruins of theocracy."

This was rhetorical phrase-making, often enough. Yet it would be a mistake to deny on that account that it was also a living and sincere expression of faith, a faith that had grown all the stronger because, as the writer for the paper correctly noted, "we have seen proof that our previous convictions about the power of the idea of Rome in the minds and the consciousness of the Italians was not far from the truth. We have seen the degree of moral force this idea possesses in every part of the nation, in every social class, amongst every category of persons. It seems to have an extraordinary vigor, it has summoned up from the depths of the national consciousness those grandiose manifestations that attest the essential laws of life: it is the life of the nation itself."[58]

He was quite correct. The spell of the idea of Rome-as-mother extended far beyond the circles directly influenced by Mazzini. It extended far enough to touch even a man like Carlo Cattaneo, so averse to swelling rhetoric and so solidly anchored in the practical, variegated reality of the regions of Italy. Even he, in 1848 and in the aftermath of 1849, was impelled to link Rome and Italy and to exalt the resurgence of free Italy in Rome. The splendor and power of these two names in combination[59] were widely felt even in the unlikely milieu of the neo-Guelphs.

Though Mazzini with his impassioned preaching had been for a long time the greatest apostle of the idea and the mission of Rome, there were certainly many others who felt the same way about Rome, although the political doctrines of Mazzinianism were repugnant to them. Mazzini's message had a parallel, for instance, in the legacy of Gioberti, the Piedmontese abbot who had claimed for the Italians a primacy that was founded essentially on pagan Rome and the glories of Christian Rome, not on the pre-Roman Italic peoples.[60] His appeal to the Capitol, eternal citadel of the nations, and his warning that without Rome west-

---

[57] "L'ora solenne," in *La Riforma* for 3 October 1870.

[58] Ibid.

[59] Cattaneo, *Dell'insurrezione di Milano*, pp. 298, 300–301. The epigram of the Italian preface is *Italia e Roma!* Cf. *Per la Sicilia* (1848): "I agree with all you say about Sicily, and I still respond with the words of Torquato Tasso: *Italia e Roma*." Sicily, he says, "must join all of Italy in Rome" (*Scritti politici ed epistolario*, pp. 141–42). And cf. as well Cattaneo, *Epistolario*, ed. Caddeo, vol. 1, p. 356 ("The remedy is *Italia e Roma*") and cf. p. 346.

[60] I allude, clearly, to the Gioberti of the *Primato*, not the Gioberti of the *Rinnovamento*, in which the myth of Italian primacy fades away and the French initiative is emphasized instead (cf. A. Omodeo, *Vincenzo Gioberti e la sua evoluzione politica* [Turin, 1941], p. 104). But it was the *Primato* that had an influence on Italian history, because from the time the *Rinnovamento* was published until Omodeo, the points in it that attracted attention were the polemics concerning the events of 1848, and its "Piedmontese" program. For Gioberti's exaltation of Rome, cf. A. Bruers, *Roma nel pensiero di Gioberti* (Rome, 1937), pp. 11 ff.

ern and southern Europe would be thrown open to an inrushing tide of new barbarians, had survived the failure of his political aims and exercised a good deal of influence. The result was that those who deplored the "unreasonable pride" that had grown up in the Italian mind, the "grievous passion" that had precipitated Italy "into the conceit and the folly of believing in its own natural, and recoverable, superiority over the other European nations," laid the blame not at the door of Mazzini but at that of Gioberti, whose fatal word "escaped from the author's control and was taken in the widest, most extreme and most detrimental sense."[61]

Rome was at the heart of both of the two major ideological currents of the full-blown Risorgimento: it was the point of contact between Giobertians and Mazzinians, despite all their differences on the interpretation of the past and all their disputes concerning the solutions for the future. Between them, these two movements had succeeded in imposing their view of Rome on Italian public opinion.

An anti-Roman like Cesare Balbo might well cry "No more primacies, no more superb airs, no more dreams, for the love of God and of our country."[62] Italy had had enough of the greatness of its Roman ancestors; enough idolatry of the antique mixed up with gilded dreams for a distant future; enough of thinking that the endless trickle of the past was somehow going to renew the present. Giacomo Durando had declared that the history of the failure of Italian nationality to recover from its setbacks was the history of a continual reflowering of the idols of antiquity—that is, a history of artistic genius overlaying political genius—to the detriment of the country.[63] The worship of antiquity led good sense astray.

But these views were too much compounded of, precisely, good sense, and too little of imagination, too much of reality and too little of passion, at a moment when good sense was no longer sufficient, when fantasy and passion were needed. Hence the prescriptions of good sense, repeated by moderates like Balbo, Durando, and d'Azeglio, were outrun by the fantasy and the passion that animated Mazzini's much more heated diatribes, and even by the more seductive discourse of Gioberti.

Not even Cavour was completely immune: Cavour, who was at the antipodes both of Mazzinian influence and of the turgid oratory of Gioberti; who was so indifferent to classical memories,[64] and so little inclined to fantasticate about resurrections, primacies, third ages; whose anxiety to show himself unlettered was such that he was willing to make a kind of teasing charade of it,[65] to the

---

[61] Balbo, *Della monarchia rappresentativa*, p. 148.

[62] Ibid., p. 173. And cf. N. Valeri, "La "boria romana' nel pensiero di Cesare Balbo," in *Bollettino Storico Bibliografico Subalpino* 45 (1947): 91 ff.

[63] Durando, *Della nazionalità italiana*, pp. 10 ff.

[64] "I do not attach great importance to the memory of the classical period in itself" (from a letter of 1830 published in Ruffini, *La giovinezza del conte di Cavour* 1:95).

[65] For Cavour's repeated declarations to the effect that he was indifferent to the arts and had scant literary culture, cf. *Lettere* 5:42 and 93–94; H. d'Ideville, *Journal d'un diplomate en Italie . . . Turin, 1859–1862*, pp. 176 and 218. But Cavour exaggerated, presenting himself as much less cultured than he in fact was (Ruffini, *La giovinezza del conte di Cavour* 1:xiii and 29, n. 1, and

point of risking a confession to the full Chamber of the distress that he personally would feel at having to transfer to Rome.[66] Even for Cavour, at the last, the idea of Rome had started to bulk on his mental horizon, not longer just in its inevitable connection with Italian unity but also on account of its suggestion of universal mission, which imposed a heavy onus on Italy in the world's eyes. It was imperative to put an end to the battle between civilization and the church, between liberty and authority, and Cavour felt certain of reaching that goal. He dreamed of the day on which he would sign, on the heights of the Capitol, a "new religious peace, a treaty that will have much greater impact on the future direction of human society than the peace of Westphalia did!" This dream spurred him on to fresh enthusiasms, and in private conversations his train of thought came close to the poetic; Artom, who witnessed this, was dumbstruck "at seeing that economist, that clever politician, that practical mind, express himself with such warmth on the possible alliance, in fact the imminent alliance, between Catholicism and liberty."[67]

The artistic heritage is killing us, Durando had exclaimed.[68] Balbo had discerned the decadence of Italy in the prevalence of culture and pure form over virtue, of literature over the moral life, of art over the social conscience. Cavour was habitually of the same opinion,[69] but when he confronted Rome he leaped over the bounds of reason so important to the Piedmontese moderates, into the world of passion and poetry. Meanwhile the voices of Durando and Balbo continued to resound in that of d'Azeglio, who despite being a painter and a writer was in this case much more heedful, in the moderate style, of rational considerations.

In the period following the death of Cavour, one of the men who played a leading role in Italian politics was Quintino Sella. An alliance between Catholicism and liberty was certainly not what he was aiming for, but Rome spoke to his heart and his mind with equal strength of conviction and seriousness of intent. He was very far from sharing the pathos of Mazzini and Gioberti, and indeed was not subject to sudden, facile, and ephemeral bursts of enthusiasm of any kind. Rather he was a man of deliberation, clear ideas, systematic vision, and steady

---

Ultimi studi sul Conte di Cavour, p. 146). Cavour's reserve was similar to that demonstrated later by Giolitti, whose lack of cultural refinement was much talked of: in fact he had firm and precise tastes in culture. But, like Cavour, he did not wish to mix literature and politics (cf. F. Crispolti, *Politici guerrieri, poeti* [Milan, 1938], p. 63; G. Natale *Giolitti e gli Italiani*, pp. 72–75; G. Ansaldo, *Il ministro della buonavita* [Milan, 1949], pp. 49, 308–309. And cf. as well the interesting episode narrated by Count Sforza in *Les batisseurs de l'Europe moderne* [Paris, 1931]. p. 225).

[66] "Yes, gentlemen, as far as I am concerned personally, it is with some distress that I go to Rome. Having little artistic inclination, I am convinced that amid the most splendid monuments of ancient and modern Rome I will be nostalgic for the severe and unpoetic streets of my place of birth" (Cavour, *Discorsi Parlamentari* 11:318; 25 March 1861).

[67] E. Artom, *L'opera politica del senatore I. Artom nel Risorgimento Italiano* 1:333 ff. (Bologna, 1906). And cf. A. Omodeo, "Il conte di Cavour e la questione romana," *La Nuova Italia* 1, no. 10 (20 October 1930): 409–11.

[68] Durando, *Della nazionalità italiana*, p. 11.

[69] It is evident that rhetoricians of the caliber of Guerrazzi and Brofferio could comprehend nothing of all this; hence their literary disdain for the "prosiness" of Cavour (cf. F. Valsecchi, "Interpretazione di Cavour," *Quaderni dell'Almo Collegio Borromeo* [July 1946]: 2 ff. in the offprint seen; and Valsecchi, *Il Risorgimento e l'Europa: L'Alleanza di Crimea*, pp. 134 ff.).

will; his style was dry and plain, as the style of Cavour had been and the style of Giolitti would be, a style that had nothing in common with the oratory traditional in Italy.[70] Nevertheless, the man from Biella was one of those who found that, as Rome had been the great example of patriotism,[71] its name was still great and terrible, a name that bound the nation for the future. *"Noblesse oblige*; and in Rome there is a formidable heritage of nobility. I am unable to express what I feel at the sound of this name. . . . We did not come to Rome just to plant a colony of office workers. . . . I am certain that in the depth of our souls there are much more elevated thoughts."[72]

What these elevated thoughts were, Sella himself gave an indication in referring to the mission, or as he said, the cosmopolitan purpose of science.[73] He had been very insistent in supporting the view that Italy should push on to Rome, and stubborn he remained, between October and November 1870, in wishing the immediate transfer of the capital, and the king's residence, to Rome. This was reprovingly called "Romanizing" by the moderates who felt differently, especially the Florentine moderates.[74] But as Sella wrote to Minghetti, Rome for him was an example of *fata trahunt*.[75] He believed that Italy ought to show itself equal to this fate in the future, in recognition of the position it assumed vis-à-vis the civilized world from the moment it was installed at Rome.[76] The capital of the kingdom had to correspond "to the high office to which history, the virtually unanimous desire of the nations, and the supreme logic of progress, that of our people and I daresay of all humanity, fatefully called it."[77]

When in 1870 he had employed every effort to have Italy advance to Rome and then transfer its capital there, he had always thought "not only of giving to Italy its eternal capital but also of the effects that would follow from the abolition of the temporal power [of the papacy] and the creation in Rome of a center of science, in the interest of the nation and of humanity."[78] Hence he was tireless in promoting the cult of science, the new mission for Rome. The principal vehicle of this promotion was the activity of the Accademia dei Lincei, which he virtually brought back to life, and which thanks to him flourished once more, rising

---

[70] Sella was an efficacious speaker, but a labored one not given to adornment (Martini, *Confessioni e ricordi*, p. 130).

[71] "Who then has made us what we are, who teaches us to desire a homeland? Rome, nothing other than Rome . . . everything that we know and think and feel in the way of patriotism, we owe to ancient Rome. The consequence is that when we older men come here to Rome, which was our teacher, we feel a reverence which it is difficult to give you an idea of. . . . But do not forget . . . that we are Italians by virtue of Rome, because if it were not for the sacred name of Rome, the numerous setbacks and the frequent hostility that Italy had to confront would have broken it, annulled it. It was Rome that kept Italy alive" (Sella, *Discorsi Parlamentari* 1:308 and 310–11).

[72] Ibid., 1:229–30 (21 June 1876).

[73] Sella, letter to Minghetti, 21 September 1870, cited above at n. 7; Sella, *Discorsi Parlamentari* 1:292.

[74] For example, *La Nazione* for 20 November 1870.

[75] Sella, letter to Minghetti, 21 September 1870, cited above at nn. 7 and 73.

[76] Sella, *Discorsi Parlamentari* 1:292.

[77] From Sella's *Relazione* [report] to the Chamber on the bill providing for the state to tender for the construction of new buildings and the expansion of Rome (Sella, *Discorsi Parlamentari* 1:233).

[78] From a speech to the Chamber of 14 March 1881 (Ibid., 1:304).

to the level of the major scientific bodies of Europe and doing renowned work of lasting value. Sella, normally the most tight-fisted politician in Italy, pressed and fought[79] to obtain indispensable financial support,[80] and pressured his scientist friends as well to get them to collaborate sedulously in the work of the Lincei, as a patriotic duty.[81] "The fight for truth, and against ignorance, prejudice, and error makes us unanimous, just as when we have to fight for the defense of our country."[82]

With this the essential purpose of Italy's mission in Rome changed from being one of alliance between Catholicism and liberty, as Cavour had wished; for what Quintino Sella was asserting was the impossibility of such an alliance in the wake of the Syllabus, and consequently the necessity of waging a struggle against clericalism in the name of science. This in turn signaled a change of epoch, a passage from the climate of the Risorgimento to that of positivism in Italy and in Europe.

The reason for this is that Sella's faith in the mission of science as the teaching and practice of free experimental inquiry, in contrast to dogma,[83] was nourished from the same subsoil as that which, among individuals affiliated to the Left, and their organs of opinion, produced the cry that Italy's mission in Rome was to open new roads to human civilization by destroying the last remains of medieval theocracy. The common ground in both cases was the rationalistic heritage of the eighteenth century, but in the latter case the upshot was styles and attitudes of a positivistic stamp, amid which the last traces of the vague religiosity of Mazzini, a relic of the first half of the nineteenth century, would simply evaporate, and ideas associated with the name of Voltaire would take on greater density and weight, acquiring the precision and refinement of experience in the writings of Comte and Littré, and later of Darwin and Spencer. Between Quintino Sella and

---

[79] "The hon. Sella, who has so often spoken to us about [scrutinizing expenditures with] a miser's magnifying glass, uses a prodigal's magnifying glass when it comes to the Lincei," remarked the hon. Toscanelli in the session of 9 March 1881 (*A.P. Camera*, p. 4223).

[80] On 30 April 1878 he writes to Cairoli, the prime minister: "At some time or other you are going to have to take some thought for science in Rome. It is a matter that is going to have a very great bearing on our future" (MRP, *Carte Cairoli*, pacco 20). And again in his speech to the Chamber on 14 March 1881 he states: "I took the view that there was no higher duty to which I ought to devote myself than the development of science in Rome" (Sella, *Discorsi Parlamentari* 1:304). Even in a speech to the voters on the eve of the elections, he referred—*vox rarissima!*—to science, to the Accademia dei Lincei, etc. (Sella, *Discorso nel banchetto offertogli il 15 ottobre 1876 dagli elettori . . . di Cossato*, pp. 45–46).

[81] "[Y]ou simply must assist the scientific movement in the capital of the kingdom. The interests of *science* and of the *country* demand it" (Sella to Luzzatti, 29 July 1875; Luzzatti, *Memorie* 2:8). Sella was able to exert considerable influence in various circles; cf. Guiccioli's enthusiasm for the new scientific institutes in the universities, "the best way to take possession of Rome" ("Diario," in *Nuova Antologia* [16 July 1935], p. 238).

[82] Thus Sella, amid loud applause, in a speech he gave at the royal session of the Accademia dei Lincei on 19 December 1880 (Sella, *Discorsi Parlamentari* 1:836).

[83] Cf. Finali, *La vita politica di contemporanei illustri*, pp. 223 and 347–48. And cf. the statements of Sella to the Chamber on 21 June 1876: "I believe that the best counterweight to the papacy is simply science as such . . . if there is a necessity at Rome, it is that of a scientific counterweight to the papacy" (Sella, *Discorsi Parlamentari* 1:229). See as well his speech to the Constitutional Association of Romagna on 10 March 1879 (ibid., 1:818).

the positivism of the Left the difference in tone is notable. Sella was always extremely precise and serious in what he said and meant, whereas in the left-leaning press the tonal color is all too often that of emphatic populism with no solid foundation in objective reality. There was the further difference that on the Left the anticlerical accent became absolutely predominant, with the result that science, from being a self-sufficient ideal, was turned into a weapon with which to confound their opponents.

Not that the anticlerical undertone was absent in Sella: for him science constituted one of the supreme responsibilities of the Italian state in Rome, and this at a moment at which science was advancing with great rapidity along one path, while Catholicism, ever since the end of the eighteenth century, and especially since the Syllabus of Errors, was proceeding down one diametrically opposed. "Light the torches! Better still, light the electric lamps. Because we are dealing with people who deliberately close their eyes and block their ears. We are dealing with people who want to get hold of children from the time they are infants, then steer them into their own secondary schools, and finally hand over to them the highest offices any human being can hold: the control of conscience and the education of youth."[84] Rome as a center of science would mean a secular Rome able to stand solidly against the Vatican and the church's tradition. This was so keenly felt that Sella's proposals for an edifice to house the Academy of Sciences in Rome sometimes turned the debate in the Palazzo di Montecitorio into a debate for and against the faith, for and against science and human reason.[85] The voice of Cairoli joined with that of Sella, warning that "here at the very center of the church's dogmatic teaching, of its insistence on faith alone, science has to be protected as it advances toward perfectibility under the impress of reason."[86] And this was followed by the voice of Oliva, who in the posture of a tribune of the plebs urged that the ascertained truths of science be promulgated in Rome as part of the legal statute, in opposition to the Syllabus.[87]

What distinguishes Sella is that he always made one great exception: the God of religion had perforce to withdraw as the sciences of observation advanced, but

---

[84] Speech to the Chamber, 14 March 1881 (Sella, *Discorsi Parlamentari* 1:303 and cf. pp. 299 ff.). The *Osservatore Romano* for 14 September 1878, in the article "Le soldatesche e l'internazionalismo," called him a "master of materialism."

[85] *A.P., Camera*, 8–18 March 1881, pp. 4175–4469 (state tenders for the construction of new buildings in Rome).

[86] *A.P., Camera*, p. 4302 (12 March 1881).

[87] "[D]o you not see that, faced with an assembly of thinkers who are able year after year to promulgate an index of ascertained truths, the Vatican grows pale? The world will look to Rome as to a beacon of civilization, and in the face of such a beacon the dying spark of the Vatican will vanish, and vanish quickly" (*A.P., Camera*, p. 4245; 10 March 1881). For Alberto Mario as well, Italy's task at Rome had to be that of "sweeping away the dust of Catholicism and cleaning up the site for a congress of learned men from the secular world [*mondo civile*] at which all the intellectual conquests made from the time of Luther to the present would be confirmed" (cited by Zanichelli in *Monarchia e Papato in Italia*, p. 178, n. 1). Cf. the letter from Salvatore Morelli to Mazzini published in the *Popolo d'Italia* of Naples for 27 September 1865, with its appeal to Mazzini to convoke "a great council of all the world's free thinkers" and formulate a "new gospel, a civil gospel, the gospel of science," in A. Romano, *Storia del movimento socialista in Italia* 1:142. And for Ricciardi's project for an *anti-council* of free thinkers in Naples see ibid., 1:309.

certainly not to disappear, since "the infinite, the beginning and the end of things, God, the concept of God, does not fall within the observed realm of natural science. It is certain that the liberty we feel within us, if it corresponds to a continuation of responsibility even after this life, in other words if the soul is immortal, cannot be measured by any goniometer or dynamometer or microscope or telescope. . . . [So] it is clear that the concept of God and that of the immortality of the soul do not belong to the domain of the positive sciences," which in truth cannot destroy these concepts, and which therefore cannot in themselves destroy the concept of religion.[88] On the other hand, the anticlericals and the professional nonreligionists [*laici di professione*] disregarded this significant stipulation, claiming that religion was finished with the advance of science and preparing, with Guyau, to salute "the irreligion of the future."

But with that difference made quite clear, it remains true that in the confrontation between science and the church Sella was spiritually closer to the exponents of the Left than he was to many of his own colleagues on the Right, old moderates such as Jacini and Alfieri di Sostegno who simply dug in their heels when progress was dogmatically identified with the name and the power of science to the exclusion of any religious component, and reaffirmed the necessity of Catholic dogma, especially for peoples such as the Latins, who "choose to give a very large role to authority and precept from on high, in politics as much as in religion."[89]

This was the attitude of the moderates from Lombardy and Piedmont, not that of Sella, who was much closer to Neapolitans like Spaventa. Men of this latter sort were unaffected by the influences of Rosmini and Lambruschini, and in general by the European current of liberal Catholicism. Instead they were guided by their own long-standing anticurial tradition, which the influence of German idealism was transforming into a secular attitude to life. For Spaventa, remaking the Italians meant "casting off the old skin and making modern men out of us," men whose minds were furnished with solid and extensive scientific knowledge, men able to provide intellectual leadership in a great and free state.[90] If the liberal Catholics had, in their day, participated in a Europe-wide movement, Sella in turn was moving with the great European current of his own time, a new and different one in comparison to what had gone before. It was another case of consonance between an individual, Quintino Sella, and the times: for the truth is that his declaration about the mission of Rome in the field of science, which thirty years earlier would have brought a smile to the lips of Gioberti and Balbo as they extolled the Christian essence of Rome, and which would have brought a smile as well to those who fifty years later were to espouse *Realpolitik* and ap-

---

[88] Sella, *Discorsi Parlamentari* 1:299. And note his declarations that he does not wish to exaggerate his positivism to the point of denaturing its character and falling into a new metaphysic, or to destroy the religious sentiment or diminish the preoccupation felt by the religiously inclined at the rush to "pure material enjoyment" which follows from the absolute negation of any religious spirit (ibid., 1:810–11 and 300–301). Sella distinguishes between religion and the religious "tyranny" and "violence" that have atrophied scientific progress (ibid., 1:827 ff.).

[89] C. Alfieri, *L'Italia liberale*, p. 217.

[90] S. Spaventa, *La politica della Destra*, p. 302

praise nothing but the missions of force and conquest, was taken perfectly seriously at the time by the Italians who heard it, and even by Mommsen, who took
it seriously as well, though he was a man of extremely caustic and supercilious
character.[91]

The political instinct which said that Rome must ineluctably be the capital of
Italy was enhanced by the mystic attraction of the Eternal City, the need to believe in the mission recently given it by Mazzini and Gioberti. Even men who
were all too aware of what it was going to cost to make Rome the capital were
swept along by this combination of sentiments. Hence Michele Amari, who
could see clearly the trouble that was in store,[92] referred, in the course of a
debate in the Senate with Stefano Jacini, to the greatness of Rome's name, which
had inflamed and aroused all of the now elderly and white-haired senators in their
hot youth, and even to declare roundly that the name of the Urbs was just as
capable of bringing about these magical effects in the present. Jacini, a moderate
from Lombardy, was told by Amari that the tradition of Rome was no "idle
amusement for scholars and antiquarians," but an indissoluble part of Italian life,
the source of national renovation.[93]

The faith that flowed from submission to the sway of Rome was staunch,
generous, and serious. Rome was a driving idea, a necessary stimulus to action,
an indispensable support for the affirmation of the national identity of the Italians
as they faced other peoples long since constituted as nation-states. Such were the
happier consequences of the myth: a few select memories of the classical world,
certain enthusiasms felt by archaeologists and men of letters, formed one of the
ties that bound the various parts of Italy tightly to one another at a time when the
country was still divided by so many other issues.[94]

In this respect the spiritual life of Italy after unification was considerably different to what it had been in the first half of the nineteenth century, when it still
waited for redemption to come; then Rome had been relegated to the background, and enthusiasm and emotional attachment had fixed instead upon medieval Italy, the Italy of the communes, of Pontida, of the Lombard League and
Legnano, the Italy of Gregory VII and Alexander III; or even earlier, on the Italy

[91] This is well known; even so, it will not be otiose to recall that the great historian of ancient
Rome was personally disagreeable to most people because of his arrogance (Guiccioli, "Diario," in
the *Nuova Antologia* for 1 August 1935, p. 431; and cf. the anecdote narrated by Croce in "Intorno al
giudizio del Mommsen su Cicerone," *Quaderni della Critica* 6 [November 1946]: 68). Bülow also
narrates an anecdote that shows how mordant he could be, without cause, even to his own compatriots, even to a man like Gregorovius (Bülow, *Memorie* 4:333–34). No one at the time could
imagine the Mommsen revealed in the codicil to his will (G. Pasquali, "Il testamento di Teodoro
Mommsen," *Rivista Storica Italiana* 61 [1949]: 337 ff.).

[92] "From what I can gather, we are about to rush to the city of Rome, if the devil decides to open
its gates to us. And this is likely. We will rush in, closing our eyes to the enormous expense, the
future risks, the numerous disorders both physical and moral that we shall encounter on the seven
hills. Be that as it may, to go to Rome is today an ineluctable necessity" (Amari, letter to the Marquis
De Gregorio, 14 September 1870; *Carteggio* 2:197).

[93] *A.P., Senato*, pp. 125–26. More or less the same arguments appear in the speech of Antonio
Scialoja, which also attacks Jacini (ibid., p. 141).

[94] Guiccioli rightly notes this ("Diario," in *Nuova Antologia*, 16 July 1935, p. 222).

of Arduino when the nation was just beginning to form.[95] In the earlier nineteenth century it was to Florence, the cradle of Italian civilization in the Middle Ages, that gazes turned. Foscolo had sung not of the fated seven hills but of Santa Croce and its glories. The leading spirits of that age had congregated in Florence, first among them Manzoni, there to draw from the deepest springs of the spiritual life of the nation.

The resurrection of Rome, for which Mazzini and Gioberti had, each in his own way, fought, had been sanctioned by the events of 1848 and 1849. The Roman republic, and the epic Garibaldian defense of the city by the young men who flocked there from all parts of Italy, had brought Rome back into the hearts of Italians, placing it at the summit of the Risorgimento[96] and making it the sanctuary of liberty.[97] On the other hand, the practical failure of the earliest wars of independence, by demonstrating the insufficiency of the revolutionary impulse of the people and revealing the emptiness of the hopes that had been placed in an agreement among the Italian princes, did indeed open the way to an unhampered initiative on the part of the house of Savoy, but also forced it to propose, sooner or later, a final purpose larger than the simple hegemony of the city of Turin— nothing less than the unity of Italy with Rome as its capital. Put another way, this meant leaving behind projects for a confederation and embracing the thesis that Italy should be a unitary national state. Rome had spoken first to Mazzini's heart because Mazzini had been the apostle of unity, while the medieval communes and the small city-states had appealed to the hearts of those who shied at the idea of Italian unification. Both inside Italy and beyond its frontiers, in Cattaneo and Sismondi and Heeren, the tiny but glorious medieval states had been exalted while at the same time repugnance was voiced for the great unitary centralized states: Cattaneo fought against the Mazzinian idea of an Italy unified in the manner of France, and Heeren had forecast the end of German civilization and liberty in Europe on the day that Germany became united into a single state.[98]

On this one essential feature of his message, Mazzini had won out. Though it was far from matching his ideals and his predictions in so many other respects, the Italy that had sprung into being was, in this regard, his Italy indeed: one Italy, bound into a single organism, not articulated in a federation. Victory in this was Mazzini's. The proclamation of the kingdom in the hall of the Piedmontese Parliament on 17 March 1861 had been at the same time the burial of the mirage he

---

[95] Cf. Croce, *Storia della storiografia italiana* 1:113 ff.

[96] This very happy expression is Salvatorelli's, in *Pensiero e azione del Risorgimento*, p. 156. Cf. as well L. Ginzburg, "La tradizione del Risorgimento," *Aretusa* 2, no. 8 (1945): 16; and esp. A. M. Ghisalberti, "Popolo e politica nel '49 romano," in *Giuseppe Mazzini e la Repubblica romana* (Rome, 1949), esp. pp. 11 ff. in the offprint seen. Ghisalberti portrays very clearly the shift effected by Mazzini from the purely local Roman problem to the ideal goal of Rome as the center of a new Italy, in fact of a new humanity.

[97] The expression is Cattaneo's (*Dell'insurrezione di Milano*, per n. 59 above) and is the most significant proof of the full revival of the idea of Rome thanks to 1848. And cf. Carducci: "the heroic democratic youth of forty-eight and forty-nine, which took in its hands the honor and the future of Italy, and clutched them to its heart in Rome and in Venice" (*A commemorazione di Goffredo Mameli*, in *Opere* 7:349).

[98] Cf. Kaegi, *Historische Meditationen* 1:273 ff. and 284–85.

had pursued, and the triumph of a different, and for him even more substantial, idea. And unity brought with it, as though they were connected by an invisible thread, the idea of Rome, because the governing class "was able to discover the concept of Italian unity with Rome as the capital city only in the classical Roman tradition."[99]

The connection was one that Cavour had clearly perceived, and after he was gone Italian life came to be centered even more on Rome, not just through Garibaldi's "Rome or death" but also through the "Permanente" of the Piedmontese. After 1848 Rome came to occupy a place in the hearts of Italians it had not held during the first decades of the Risorgimento. The myth grew radiant once more.

[99] The very accurate observation is Zanichelli's, in *Studi politici e storici*, p. 500.

Science or *Renovatio Ecclesiae*?

ROME THEREFORE was a mission, a universal idea, a world city. The notions of mission, of primacy, of the world's third age were too closely interwoven with the history of the city ever to be divorced from it, so that the towering shadows of its past continued to loom over Rome's seven hills when it became Italy's capital.

In later years the spirits invoked would be those of Scipio and Caesar. But in the period immediately after 1870, it was the ghost of St. Peter that hovered in the thoughts of everyone, for the glory and the power of St. Peter represented an unbroken continuum over the centuries from the ancient past to the present, and it was for this reason that while one party strove to maintain them, the opposing side was stubbornly committed to seeing them finally brought low, to reducing St. Peter to a bloodless apparition. For in 1870 it was Christian Rome, the emblem of eternal faith, and not pagan and imperial Rome, that was fully and actively alive. It was Christian Rome that the Italian state now had to confront: at the moment it forced the walls of Rome, it found itself face to face with the papacy—in other words, with a universal idea. What possible counterpoise could it find, to prevent itself from being morally dominated, and finally crushed?

For Quintino Sella, the answer was science. But for the governing ministry, and for many of the leading personalities of the Right in general, the answer had already been given by Cavour: it was religious liberty, the separation of church and state. In 1870 and after, this was the goal of the majority of the leaders of the Right: the imposition in Italy itself, the seat of the papacy, of the principle that the problem of religion was one for the free conscience of the citizens. There was a corollary: "the coexistence of a free church alongside a free state is to be based not on a treaty of *reconciliation* between the two, but rather on the nature of the law of the state itself. The law should be such as to render possible the foundation, without impediment, of any *moral entity* or *religious association*." Thus the state should not interfere in the church's concerns. The only steps the state should take were those of reducing the church's means of suasion exclusively to the moral one, freely accepted by the faithful, and likewise that of depriving the church of its age-old power to extract revenue from the population by force.[1] To bring about this state of affairs, so easy to conceive and yet so formidably set about with obstacles to realization, seemed a task genuinely worthy of Italy and Rome, one that pointed the best way to mankind's moral and religious fulfillment.[2]

The men of the Right held fast to their conviction that Cavour's old ideal was the correct one, in spite of changing circumstances, in spite of the Syllabus of Errors and the Vatican Council, and the instrument with which they pursued it led

---

[1] *La Perseveranza* for 15 October 1870, and also 27 September.
[2] "La caduta del potere temporale," ibid., 18 September 1870.

to its successful achievement. This was the law of Guarantees. Notwithstanding all of the deficiencies and contradictions that could be mentioned in this legislation, it was a policy that permitted the idea of a nonconfessional state to grow in the consciousness of the Italian people, and to survive tempestuous moments of peril, so that, together with national unity and the sense of liberty, it constituted the true legacy left by nineteenth-century Italy to its twentieth-century heirs. But for other eminent thinkers, especially Bertrando Spaventa, Cavour's formula of religious liberty appeared insufficient and provisory, for they desired, in the place of the defunct religious state, to erect a state that was its own religion—what they later came to call an ethical state.[3] The response from the Right was that this would mean overstepping the bounds of liberty in the opposite direction and replacing the old theologically based government operating in a secular capacity with a secular government illegitimately draped in surrogate religious charisma,[4] bringing eventual downfall for both state and church by impeding not only the formation of a real and solid political consciousness but also the rebirth of religious feeling (which they always saw as the necessary premise of any morally sound national life).

The fact is that for most of the moderates, and this included men who were uninterested in the religious reform and the triumph of "pure" Catholicism desired for instance by Ricasoli, a healthy and robust national life still appeared to be an impossibility if it was backed only by the state's constitution. For them the political structure needed the support of a strong sense of inner life in order to survive, and such a sense of inner life could only be provided by religion. Once again this was a belief that had its source in the earlier nineteenth century, in the Romantic age, which had sought the origin and the basis of collective life *in interiore homine*, and which, unsatisfied with the politicizing tendency of Montesquieu, for whom even the morality and the substance of the inner life of the citizens could be seen as depending on the form of government and the system of public law, had wished like Rousseau to make the law live in men's hearts.[5] It was a current of belief shared by men of the most heterogeneous tendencies: this faith in the inner life, this driving force, was appealed to equally by Mazzini and by those who, far from calling for an end to the papacy as he did, continued to believe in a mission in the world for Catholicism. In both cases the ultimate purpose was to find a way to educate mankind, to prepare their souls for the great undertakings of collective life, although these undertakings were differently conceived in the two cases, and different were the forms of education envisioned. The moderates had always looked to religion to meet this need; Cavour himself had been cool to Voltaire while admiring Rousseau and had demonstrated an early and lively interest in the religious movement in Europe and in religious ideas, "le grand mystère du siècle." His only reservation then had been the hope that religion should not ally itself with political reaction.[6] It was only later, when

---

[3] Cf. L. Russo, *Francesco De Sanctis e la cultura napoletana (1860–1885)*, pp. 302 ff.

[4] *La Perseveranza* for 27 September 1870.

[5] Cf. my article "L'idea di Europa," *La Rassegna d'Italia* 2, no. 4 (April 1947): 11 ff.

[6] Cf. Cavour's letter to the duke of Dino, 16 April 1851, in *Lettere* 5:230; and Ruffini, *Ultimi studi*, pp. 22–23 and 54–55.

under the impetus of political rationality he was forced to face the problem in his public capacity, that Cavour pronounced his famous endorsement of religious liberty. And as formulated, that endorsement clearly conveyed the hope, indeed the certainty, that under the regime of full liberty religion would flower again, and the church remain a powerful force, albeit confined to its proper field. His epigones continued to trust in the same outcome.[7]

Hence the leaders of moderate opinion rejected the notion of the ethical state, but they did seek to reinvigorate the state as such, in the hope that a corresponding reinvigoration of religious feeling would spontaneously follow, without any direct political intervention from outside, and the belief that the state itself would derive immediate and considerable advantage from the moral temper this would give to the Italians' sense of themselves as citizens. What they sought was a nonconflictual separation of church and state, and their idea of separation did not allow (or at least this was the view of most) for a reconciliation of the kind characteristic of European governments in the past—a concordat. The common people also of course wanted reconciliation, although the picture they formed of it would have been similar to the image that appeared in a lithograph extremely popular after the events of 20 September 1870 entitled *Vaticinio*, in which Pius IX, in the act of imparting a blessing, offers his arm to Vittorio Emanuele II, who is leaning on the hilt of his sword.[8] The iconography implied that there was to be a precise and detailed agreement between the two powers; but the leaders of the political class foresaw a reconciliation of a much less simplistic and rather more complex kind. "When we speak of reconciliation, therefore," said Visconti Venosta in the Chamber, "we are certainly not speaking of the sort of pact that mixes up politics and religion, and compromises both the one and the other equally. We will follow just one road to reconciliation, the road of liberty; liberty not as the spirit of intolerance or revolutionary violence, but liberty inspired by respect for all rights, and therefore respect for the one most sacred among them and least subject to coercion, that pertaining to the religious conscience." The policy goal of the Italian government was thus "to make possible at some future point a peace agreement between the papacy and the Italian government, and their peaceful coexistence in Rome." As for the means to this end, there was to be no accord binding on both parties, but neither was there to be any use of coercive force by the Italian government, of the kind employed during the *Kulturkampf* by Bismarck in a manner which the Left in Italy would have been quite ready to emulate. For Visconti Venosta such use of force would merely have procured for Italy "the felicity of permanent religious conflict," just as the abandonment of liberal principles in favor of authoritarian methods would have rendered an eventual state of pacification much more difficult to obtain.[9] When he was reproved by Prince Jérôme Napoleon, an anticlerical, for being too moderate

---

[7] De Sanctis very acutely noted this in his speech to the Chamber on 1 July 1864 (*La Critica* 11 [1913]: 147). In consequence he declared himself opposed to the formula "liberty for the Church," as being the program of the conservatives (speech of 8 July 1867, ibid., pp. 311 ff.).

[8] U. Pesci, *I primi anni di Roma capitale, 1870–1878*, p. 506.

[9] Speech to the Chamber, 14 May 1872 (*A.P., Camera*, pp. 2118–19); and cf. *L'Opinione* for 17 September 1874 ("La Conciliazione").

on the Roman question, and was urged by the prince to "expel the pope from Rome" on the grounds that such a rival was less dangerous outside the fold than inside it, Visconti Venosta replied that such was not his policy, and that he would make every effort to prepare the grounds for an understanding between the papacy and the monarchy in Rome, the establishment of a modus vivendi acceptable to all.[10] Later, at a particularly difficult moment in the relationship between Italy and Germany, when the air was thick with talk of the protests directed at the Italian government, and the pressure applied to it—and to the Belgian government as well—by Bismarck, who imputed to both an excessively deferential posture with regard to the papacy, Visconti Venosta had a discussion with the French envoy; during this colloquium, while he avoided answering the latter's specific questions about the matter, Visconti Venosta affirmed his deep horror of religious conflicts; indeed he went so far as to summon forth the specter of the wars of religion of the sixteenth century.[11]

In fact the government of the Right and its leaders are above all entitled to the very highest praise for this, that they refused to follow Prussia down the road of force between 1873 and 1875, when the *Kulturkampf* was at its height, notwithstanding the violent attack on them launched from the Left, and what was worse, Bismarck's ill will: for in doing so they showed themselves prepared to risk their chances of a formal and substantial agreement with Germany at a time when the latter appeared to be the only reliable ally against the possibility of an impulsive action against Italy on the part of the reactionaries of France. Yet the majority on the Right (not to speak of the Left) refused to take into serious consideration then or later, even on a theoretical plane, reconciliation with the papacy through a concordat. Indeed there were those on the Right whose sentiment was so clearly anticlerical as to make them indistinguishable from the representatives of the extreme Left, as when they expressed the fear that a pope of benign character might be elected, one capable of drawing the nobility into his toils, and with it a part of the bourgeoisie, and hence of dominating the Italian state through moral pressures.[12] But the conviction that guided the greatest number was, to repeat, that state and church had to go their own separate ways in order that each should find a way to gain new vigor and therefore assist the other in doing the same. In religious life, as in economic life, there was to be no state intervention; it was an instance of the same fundamentally optimistic stricture to *laisser faire, laisser passer* that had emerged in western liberalism in the first half of the nineteenth century.

---

[10] Visconti Venosta stated this to the French chargé d'affaires, de Sayve (report of de Sayve, 5 March 1872, n. 27; AEP, *C.P., Italie*, t. 384, fols. 217r-v).

[11] Report of Noailles, 9 March 1875, no. 18; AEP, *C.P., Italie*, t. 391, fols. 253 ff.

[12] Amari to Renan, 23 April, 1873 (*Carteggio* 2:212). And cf. the reply of Renan, who agreed that a pope in the tradition of Benedict XIV would be the worst possible outcome, and reconciliation the ultimate piece of bad luck (ibid., p. 213). Amari offered a similar analysis to Hartwig in 1878, after the election of Leo XIII: ". . . the so-called reconciliation is impossible; and I would be appalled if I thought that it weren't" (ibid., p. 236). And again, in 1887, he expressed his pleasure at the failure of the negotiations of padre Tosti (ibid., p. 305): let the pretended successor of St. Peter stay where he is "until civilization removes this fetter from the national churches," and separates the religious idea "from every sort of magic spell, ancient and modern."

Views similar to those expressed by Visconti Venosta had already been aired shortly after 20 September by Bonghi, who spoke even then of a reconciliation to be arrived at naturally, not through diplomatic negotiations.[13] They were joined by Massari, who expounded to his fellow deputies assembled in the Chamber his preference that reconciliation not be codified in a concordat: "I long for the day on which love of one's country and love of one's religion will be able to meld together into a single unified sentiment. It is just because I wish, and wish sincerely, for this reconciliation, that I do not want efforts to be made and steps to be taken in the hope of speeding up the process; they would only prolong it. I believe . . . that the reconciliation of church and state ought not to be the artificial fruit of negotiation and bargaining, of legislative measures, but that it ought to be the spontaneous result of an enlightened and liberal policy. The passage of time, aided by our tact and our industrious patience, must be the agent of this resolution."[14]

There would be one or two who would waver over the course of time. Bonghi would be one, in the year 1887, when for a moment he would let go of the old principle of natural reconciliation in order to embrace the formal, legally codified variety. But others, less easily swayed by the flow of events than he, remained firm and unmoved to the last: Silvio Spaventa, in his last great speech, given at Bergamo on 20 September 1886, reaffirmed the fundamental points of the liberal doctrine that, in the person of Camillo di Cavour, had proclaimed an end to the era of the concordats.[15]

Of all the difficult problems that any political actor might find himself called upon to resolve, none was more delicate than the one in question. Visconti Venosta approached it in the same spirit in which he approached all the problems of foreign policy: in a spirit, that is, of measure, of calm, of balance; the foreign minister maintained a strong faith in the beneficial effects of the passage of time,[16] and of the self-regulating operations of a regime of liberty. These were of course the same criteria that guided the Right throughout the period in which it governed Italy after 1870, criteria that produced policies of slow deliberate prudence that looked to the future and ignored the fleeting moment; policies characterized by discretion, finesse, a sense of inherent limits; policies that required a great deal of wisdom and inner equilibrium. The foreign policy of Visconti Venosta was in fact once described in the Chamber as too subtle and long-term to provide any satisfaction for those impatient and avid for immediate and striking successes.

---

[13] Cf. W. Maturi, preface to Bonghi, *Stato e Chiesa* 1:xxv (= vol. 12 in *Opere* [Milan, 1942]). And cf. Bonghi's speech to the Chamber on 29 April 1872 (Bonghi, *Discorsi Parlamentari* 1:392).

[14] Speech of 13 March 1872 (*A.P., Camera*, pp. 1183). On a spontaneous state of concord between church and state as the prospective result of the liberty of the church, see also Minghetti's speech to the Chamber on 30 January 1871 (Minghetti, *Discorsi Parlamentari* 5:146).

[15] Spaventa, *La politica della Destra*, pp. 183 ff.; and cf. P. Romano (pseudonym of P. Alatri), *Silvio Spaventa*, pp. 261 ff. For Cavour's statements on the end of the era of concordats, cf. his instructions to Passaglia and Pantaleoni, 21 February 1861 (Cavour, *La questione romana* 1:313); and cf. Omodeo, "Cavour e la questione romana," p. 406.

[16] Visconti Venosta repeated this to De Laveleye during a discussion in the autumn of 1883 (De Laveleye, *Nouvelles lettres d'Italie*, p. 146).

No doubt this was true. And it was equally true that this line of conduct was dictated not only by profoundly held convictions but also, and very considerably, by considerations that had everything to do with the contingent circumstances in which Italy found itself and very little indeed to do with the abstract realm of ideals. The fact is that, with the exception of Sella and Spaventa, the leaders of the Right were a little bit scared by what they themselves had perpetrated on 20 September. All were Catholics of course, and the visible head of the Catholic church inevitably held a certain sway over their consciences; the clearest example of this was the king himself, filled as he was with timorous remorse. Apart from that, as a group charged with the government of the nation, they had every reason to fear that as soon as the Franco-Prussian War was over, the entire Catholic world might join together to demand that Italy pay for its affront to the supreme pontiff. Take the case of Marco Minghetti, who had once been a cabinet minister for the papal state under Pius IX: he had been a strong supporter of the action that culminated on 20 September, yet when news of it reached his ears his first mental impulse was one he dared not express even to his very close friend Visconti Venosta: it was "that the king should rush without delay to the Holy Father and throw himself down at his feet (to use the Roman expression)."[17] In other words, his impulse was to perform an act of contrition following the use of force against the pope, something that Spaventa for example, not to speak of Sella, would never have dreamed of doing. Minghetti was spurred to react in this way by the traditions of neo-Guelphism to which he was heir.[18]

The decision to avoid any act that might appear to constitute interference in the internal affairs of the church, while inspired by principle, was also the most suitable one at that particular juncture, when further violent shocks were to be shunned. The action of 20 September itself had been determined by a switch, at

[17] Minghetti only put this thought down on paper on 9 October, writing from Vienna to Visconti Venosta, and adding: "At this point it would no longer be opportune, even though it might be possible, by maneuvering skillfully inside the papal court, to arrange for the pope to receive the king, on the understanding that there would be no substantive discussions; he would be there purely as a Catholic prince. In that case it would be necessary to hold this ceremony in advance of the king's solemn entry into the city. But take note that in the long run it is inevitable. We have to face this difficulty and prepare ourselves to resolve it" (Visconti Venosta archive). Minghetti based his opinion on "the known character of the pope."

In the course of his mission to Rome after 20 September, Blanc made some attempt to find out how the ground lay within the Holy See; he told Cardinal Antonelli that the king had refrained out of tact from sending a designated personage to the pope, but that if the cardinal thought that Pius IX would not be unwilling to receive a royal envoy, Vittorio Emanuele would immediately send one of his ministers, "since it was his strong desire to do everything possible to render the situation less painful for His Holiness." Antonelli replied that it would be better not to, "since the sending of a representative or some other expressly designated personage would only increase the difficulties at the moment" (Blanc, report, 26 September 1870; AE, *Libro Verde*, riservato, *Roma, Settembre-ottobre 1870, Documenti* [Rome: Gabinetto del Ministero degli Esteri, 1895], no. 3, p. 9). Indeed, neither the marchese Spinola nor, later, in June of 1871, Gen. Bertolè Viale, were received (Monti, *Vittorio Emanuele II* , pp. 390–91).

[18] La Marmora also declared (to Vittorio Emanuele II) that "the king of Italy cannot, especially after what has taken place, go and kneel before the pontiff." But since he also maintained that "even less" could the king enter Rome "like a conquistador dealing haughtily with the head of Catholicism," he did not advise transferring the capital to Rome, at least while Pius IX was alive (in Paladino, *Roma: Storia d'Italia dal 1866 al 1871*, p. 202).

the last moment, from a policy of "moral suasion" to one of force, and it was only with great reluctance that Visconti Venosta had finally given up on the gradual approach (which he was still endorsing as late as 19 August) in favor of the abrupt one.[19] And the jolt had been severe, despite all the attenuating circumstances, which included the increasingly turbulent European situation, the appearance of the republic in France, uncertainty as to what the future (which hardly appeared bright in any case) might hold, and the risk of troubles in Italy if the Roman question, out of which the Left continued to make political capital, were not resolved by the government once again taking charge of the Italian revolution. In sum, it was a step that had had to be taken, and now that it was *fait accompli* there was one further effort required to bring an end to the anomaly and return the situation to normality: this was the law of Guarantees. With that in place it would be possible to resume once again the use of the tools of moral suasion, to avoid further upsets, to make sure that Italian policy would "not furnish the clerical party with any sort of plausible pretext, of the kind that hitherto we have had the good sense not to offer them; the point is to keep them from being able to speak in the name of the legitimate interests of religion. . . . It is necessary that the question not become a religious one; let us make sure that it remains . . . a purely political matter. Soon you will see that the raging passions of today . . . will rouse no echo, and in time you will see that they will have nothing left to feed on."[20]

Liberty, the liberty of Cavour—the government was perfectly willing to keep faith with this tenet of policy since it meant taking no further violent steps after 20 September, but rather waiting and watching while events took their course without placing any further burden of doubt and remorse on consciences. In this as in so may other things the moderates were guided by the testament of their historic leader, which as far as they were concerned amounted to a sort of fifth gospel. There were those who attempted to use their own faith against them, declaring that Cavour's offer of total liberty to the church had been made so as to bring Pius IX to surrender the temporal power spontaneously; but now, in the wake of the Syllabus and infallibility, and in the face of papal excommunications and similar insidious tactics, with the clergy waging a struggle against Italy, would even Cavour have laid down all of the state's arms?[21] The moderates responded with a literal interpretation of Cavour's gospel, free of any gloss or commentary.

It was understandable that this approach gave rise to feelings of uncertainty and trepidation, as though Italian policy were oscillating one way and another as it tried to keep two different balls in the air at the same time, rousing as much discontent on the Left as it did among Catholics like Tommaseo and Capponi,

---

[19] Declaration to the Chamber of 19 August 1870: "it may be . . . that the course we are following in our policy [gradualism] is a long one; it remains to be seen whether there is a shorter one, or whether there are only ones that can be called shorter simply because after a short distance they lead to an abyss" (*A.P., Camera*, p. 4027).

[20] Statements of Visconti Venosta to the Chamber, 9 May 1873 (*A.P., Camera*, p. 6196).

[21] Zanichelli also notes this in *Monarchia e Papato in Italia*, pp. 99 and 197.

and provoking the irony of Toscanelli, who took these lines from Giusti and applied them to the government's maneuvers:

> Quell'occhio dal ti vedo e non ti vedo,
> Quel tentennìo, non so se tu m'intenda,
> Che dice sì e no, credo e non credo.

> That look that says I see you no I don't
> That quivering (do I make my meaning clear?)
> That says yes I believe oh no I don't.[22]

This chorus of criticism would later be joined by the severe sentence of eminent historians.[23]

One thing is certain, quite apart from any judgment on the practical steps taken by the government from day to day, and that is that the line of conduct it was taking did absolutely nothing to deal with the feeling that the city of Rome embodied a mission. While this line had the disadvantage of alienating a portion of the governing party itself—the portion angered and perturbed in its intimate conscience by the breach of Porta Pia on 20 September[24] and resolutely opposed to the transfer of the capital to Rome, which it saw as a project that would create a hindrance to the eventual solution of the Roman question and put a continuous severe strain on the nation by setting pope and king, Vatican and Quirinal, Statuto and Syllabus against one another[25]—it gave no satisfaction to those, whether Catholic or anti-Catholic, who dreamed of a new mission for Rome. For after all, what was the best possible outcome of present policy? Welcome harmony between the Italian state and the church; the healing of an internal split; the consolidation of the state; the triumph in Italy of the spirit of liberty as both means and end—in other words, a purely national solution, Italian, honorable, but modest. And which of the two would be the real winner under that state of affairs? As before it would be the church and the papacy that would tower over the city. Rome as the capital of Italy would not add one whit to the stature of the old pontifical Rome. Italy would have no mission to the world.

The policy of leaving the church alone had other consequences: it meant allow-

---

[22] *Discorso* [di Giuseppe Toscanelli] *alla Camera . . . 23 gennaio 1871 . . . contro il progetto di legge [sulle Guarentigie]*, p. 40:

[23] Ruffini put it this way: "a species of ecclesiastical confusion, into which the Right plunged after it had made the great leap of the law of Guarantees, and which I can find no other way of characterizing except to say that it resembled the sense of fearful bewilderment of someone who, to use the vernacular, feels that he has really done it this time" ("L'elezione popolare dei parroci," in *Scritti giuridici minori* 1:341).

The sense that they had really done it this time was indeed felt. But Ruffini's judgment is too severe and depends too much on the diatribes of Mancini, whom he greatly admired, concerning the *exequatur* (for evidence of this see Ruffini's other study, "L'Exequatur alla nomina dei vescovi," in ibid., 1:329 ff.). As for Falco, while he observes the contradictions, uncertainties, and errors of the policy of the moderates on the ecclesiastical question, and states that it failed in its task, he also recognizes the "excellence" of the political idea by which it was guided (*La politica ecclesiastica della Destra*, pp. 33–34).

[24] Thus Gino Capponi, *Lettere* 4:259–60 (and cf. pp. 264, 266, 272).

[25] Thus Jacini in the Senate on 23 January 1871 (*A.P., Senato*, pp. 119–20). Similar ideas are found in the speech of Toscanelli to the Chamber on the same subject.

ing it to continue to tread the path on which it had entered with the Syllabus and infallibility, and the fact is that there were many among the Catholics who, without bearing the slightest trace of anticlericalism of the Jacobin or positivistic kind, had no wish to see the church continue in that direction, without any interior renewal. Lanza and Visconti Venosta, not to speak of Capponi, Jacini, Alfieri,[26] accepted the church substantially as it was, provided it abandoned its politically reactionary tendencies—while Ricasoli fought for a vision of the church as it might become following a vast movement of internal reform that would bring it back to "pure and true Catholicism." Thus he was another of those to whom the fine line being walked by the government in keeping the state aloof from the affairs of the church seemed to be a manifestation of exhaustion, weakness, pavidity. For Ricasoli, it was the duty of the Italian state to take part in a reform of the church.

Thus one political camp contained two totally antithetical points of view. Between Visconti Venosta, Lanza, and Massari on the one hand and Jacini, Alfieri di Sostegno, and Casati on the other, the difference was primarily about how to proceed rather than about the goal to be reached, a matter of tactics, not strategy, inasmuch as all were united in wanting to see the church left to its own devices. But between these men as a group and Ricasoli the point at issue was the ultimate goal itself, the actual substance of the situation.

The urgent drive to reform the church from within as opposed to launching an assault on it from without,[27] to which "the hermit of Chianti" (as Ricasoli once referred to himself)[28] was dedicated, had been inspired by Raffaello Lambruschini, the "hermit of San Cerbone,"[29] and it remained tenaciously alive in 1870 and after. Ricasoli had once written to Giorgini that he felt "that we are on the eve of a great revolution in Roman Catholicism, one that will lead us to true Catholicism; it is something I ardently desire and hope to see before I die. More than that, I am doing all I can to set the match to the fuse, but I do not know exactly where the fuse is." Under the stimulus of this passion he had in 1865

[26] The stance of Minghetti is characteristic: he followed closely the development of the Old Catholic movement in Germany but held that the chance of its having a positive effect was "to say the least problematic," while its negative effects were "grave . . . since it will detach many other spirits from Rome, and will make the cultivated classes even more hostile to the pontificate" (*Carteggio Minghetti-Pasolini* 4:200).

[27] Both Lambruschini and Ricasoli, unlike Piero Guicciardini, were in fact opposed to Protestant propaganda in Italy and to "conversions"; cf. A. Gambaro, *Riforma religiosa nel carteggio inedito di Raffaello Lambruschini* 1:clxxviii–clxxix, cccxvii, and 2:242; *Carteggi di Bettino Ricasoli* 3:461, and 4:83–84 (Rome, 1947).

[28] This is how Ricasoli described himself (*Carteggi* 2:15 [Bologna, 1940]). For the hermit of San Cerbone see 1:120 (Bologna, 1939).

[29] How decisive the influence of Lambruschini on Ricasoli was is now very plainly evidenced in the complete edition of Ricasoli's *Carteggi*: until 1837, that is until they became acquainted (with the friendship becoming close between October and November 1838, when they began calling each other *tu* instead of *voi*; *Carteggi* 1:137–39 and 266), Ricasoli's cultural interests are essentially confined to agriculture and the natural and technical sciences, and also of course general culture and politics, with an increasing interest in the problems of education as his little daughter Bettina grows; this is shown by the books he orders (ibid., 1:8, 11, 16, 19, 21, 40, 59–60, 66, 71, 74). After 1837 his interest in religious problems begins, rapidly swelling to a full diapason; and orders for books that treat religious problems begin to appear as well (ibid., 1:278, 374–75).

directed the work of the parliamentary commission that had led to the revolutionary project of Corsi,[30] and now that Rome was part of Italy he saw not so much a
shift in the location of the nation's capital as "the future transformation of the
papacy, which can only, I hope, work to the benefit of true religious feeling,
which today is compromised by indifferentism and immobility."[31]

"The soul of a new future for human society"[32] was there in waiting, if only
the right steps were taken under the guidance of wisdom. And for Ricasoli wisdom dictated that the banner of liberty for the church be unfurled, that there be a
complete and absolute separation of church and state that would lay the groundwork for a great politico-social revolution, a historical fact that, after the foundation of Christianity itself, "would be the second most beneficial and splendid
event."[33] But for Ricasoli and Lambruschini, liberty for the church, the separation of church and state, had a significance quite different to what they had had in
the mind of Cavour as interpreted by the moderate governing party.[34] They
wished to hand the church the means of reforming itself and then help it to do so,
intervening with measures that would lead the church to become once again a
community of the faithful uniting the clergy and the laity. The great question of
the church's temporal possessions offered an immediate and ready way to accomplish this; the state was not to stand by and observe the life of the church, but
rather to help it to transform itself. Such aspirations had occupied the mind of
Ricasoli for many years, from the time when he had read and expounded the
gospels to his little Betta,[35] or had given instructions to the canon Parronchi as to
how he should celebrate the Lenten cycle at Brolio in such a way as to open the
hearts and minds of the peasants to delectable truths of which they had no inkling;[36] or when, after coming to the city from the countryside and finding the
populace there morally adrift, he had begun to assemble the peasants in his house
on Sundays and regale them with religious parables, from which he extracted as
many relevant moral lessons as possible.[37]

So Rome was a religious problem for him. The mission of Rome was a religious mission, and the revolution in politics was to be followed by a revolution in

---

[30] Cf. Falco, *La politica ecclesiastica della Destra*, p. 14. But for the overall attitude of Ricasoli,
see esp. A. C. Jemolo, *Chiesa e Stato in Italia negli ultimi cento anni*, pp. 272 ff. See too the letter of
15 June 1865 to F. Della Valle di Casanova: "Rome and its Syllabus, papal Rome . . . is moving with
increasing speed down its own slope. We are slowly, and laboriously as yet, but steadfastly,
ascending a different gradient, that will lead us to our goal . . . whereas papal Rome . . . must in the
end plunge into the abyss that it has gouged out beneath itself" (in B. Ceva, "Un carteggio inedito di
Bettino Ricasoli," in *Nuova Rivista Storica* 24 [1940]: 6–7 in the offprint seen).

[31] *Lettere e documenti* 10:139 (to Giuseppe Pasolini, 4 October 1870).

[32] Ibid., 10:147 (to Francesco Borgatti, 2 November 1870).

[33] Ibid., 10:130 (to Francesco Borgatti, 17 September 1870).

[34] Cf. Lambruschini's interpretation of the formula of a free church in a free state in Gambaro,
Riforma religiosa 1:cdxiv–cdxv.

[35] Lambruschini to Ricasoli, 3 November 1842 (Ricasoli, *Carteggi* 1:307).

[36] The letter of Ricasoli to the canon Parronchi, in *Carteggi* 1:321 ff., is of great interest.

[37] Cf. the letter cited in the previous note; and Gentile, "Bettino Ricasoli e i rapporti fra Stato e
Chiesa," in his *Gino Capponi*, pp. 61 ff.; and A. Gotti, *Vita del barone Bettino Ricasoli* (Florence,
1895), pp. 22, 27 ff, 36, 38 ff.

religion,[38] for only when the latter had been brought about could the former be said to have completed its work. Rome as such, as a political center, as simply the capital of the kingdom of Italy, meant almost nothing to Ricasoli (he was quite unaware that this put him in the same objective category as Mommsen, Gregorovius, and Dostoevsky). "We desired Rome because it belonged to us, and because not having it was more detrimental to us than having it. If we make it our capital, that is a choice dictated by our own domestic political convenience, not because *Rome* signified anything more than the center of government of a nation, a nation which for that matter is uniformly hostile to political centralization, to seeing itself swallowed up by its own capital."[39] There was no secular mission attached to Rome, it was no beacon of light in the world by virtue of being the capital of Italy, and Ricasoli was so far from recognizing any cosmopolitan role for the nation's principal city that he fought against Sella's project to make it a great center of culture and science. In his frankly expressed diffidence toward Rome as the focus of a tendency to centralization, we can detect the contemporary anti-Romanism of the Tuscan moderates, as well as the old mistrust of Ricasoli, Salvagnoli, and their friends for any excessive centralization of public life and complexity in the machinery of government.[40]

But a mission for Rome there was in his eyes: a mission for Christian, Catholic Rome, to which the political episode of Italy's entry into the city should serve as stimulus and motive, the occasion for a triumphal new effort in the world. For Ricasoli there was no better proof of the low moral level to which the Italians had sunk than the fact that most saw the events surrounding Rome as purely material facts and had no presentiment "that the soul of a new future for human society is buried there."[41] Thus his spirit soared beyond the reality of the present, searching for the future. Cutting loose from the purely political problem of what attitude to adopt toward the papacy, his imagination sailed to breathless heights, descrying the renewal of the church from within, the reappearance of pure Christianity (meaning of course "pure Catholicism"), and the spectacle of humanity surrendering itself once more to the saving word of the Lord and setting forth on the road to more sublime forms of moral life. The sordid materialism of the century would at last be defeated.

This was not the dream of the Italian Catholics alone, for abroad there were heard similar voices, ones similarly inspired with reforming zeal. Amongst them was that of one of the most renowned prelates in the world of European Catholicism, Josip Juraj Strossmayer, the bishop of Djakovo, a leader of the Slav nationalist movement and, in addition, one of the firmest opponents of the dogma of

---

[38] He took this view from 1860 on; letter to Borgatti, 19 December 1870 (*Lettere e documenti* 10:203).

[39] Letter to Celestino Bianchi, 23 January 1873 (*Lettere e documenti* 10:277).

[40] "Among the things they are talking so much about wanting to do, I have my doubts that this *great university* of Rome ought to be numbered. The government is throwing itself into the project, spending vast sums of money and prejudicing the other universities of the kingdom. If any university was to be suppressed, it was the one in Rome" (letter to Bianchi, cited in the previous note). He speaks against the process of centralization in *Carteggi* 3:402, 417–20, and 4:33–34.

[41] *Lettere e documenti* 10:147 (to Francesco Borgatti, 2 November 1870), cited in n. 32 above.

papal infallibility. Strossmayer was bound to Minghetti by personal friendship,[42] as he was to Visconti Venosta, and when the law of Guarantees was under discussion his influence was sufficient to assure that a memorandum from his pen was discussed by the Italian cabinet.[43] He was quite willing to serve as an intermediary between Italy and France on the issues concerning papal Rome, and even more ready to prepare the ground for a possible conclave.[44] In international politics he worked for collaboration between the Latin and Slavic peoples,[45] while in religious affairs he fought for the internal reform of the church. Strossmayer

[42] Minghetti for his part esteemed him highly, to the point of ranking him with Bismarck as an exceptional personality. Cf. R. W. Seton-Watson, *Die südslavische Frage im Habsburger Reiche* (German translation: Berlin, 1913), p. 136 (ibid., p. 144, on the European friendships of Strossmayer, and pp. 589–630 for his correspondence with Gladstone between 1876 and 1886). And cf. Strossmayer's letter of 22 September 1873 (to princess Trouberzkoï, but intended for Thiers), which contains expressions of favor to Italy, in D. Halévy, *Le courrier de M. Thiers*, pp. 485 ff.

[43] Castagnola, *Da Firenze a Roma*, p. 133 (23 January 1871). The memorandum maintained that Italy ought not to give up all interference in the nomination of bishops, but ought to assign it "to the cathedral chapters, the parish priests, and the most upright members of the laity." The idea "is very acceptable to the majority of the cabinet." According to Castagnola, the memorandum was from Strossmayer's "secretary": in fact, it must have been presented by Monsignor Vorsak (on whom see below) in Strossmayer's name. It explains how Wickham Steed, who knew Visconti Venosta very well, was able to affirm that in the elaboration of the law of Guarantees the Italian foreign minister had requested Strossmayer's opinion (Wickham Steed, *Mes souvenirs, 1892–1914* 1:106 [French translation: Paris, 1926]).

[44] Monsignor Strossmayer, Minghetti, and Visconti Venosta encountered each other at Rome when the bishop was there, as in the winter of 1871–72, and Minghetti went to visit him at Graz on 25 June 1872. At other times Monsignor Vorsak, who lived in Rome at no. 108 via Ripetta, functioned as intermediary. Now, on 12 May [1872] Strossmayer asks Vorsak to tell Minghetti and Visconti Venosta, but only them, that he, Strossmayer, must go to Paris where Thiers and Rémusat wish to see him, and that he is prepared to act in Paris and at Versailles "in the manner that was decided upon by us at Rome, since I am ever more persuaded that it is a matter of immense importance in today's conditions that the future pontiff should be a moderate man and a friend of peace." In his discussion with Minghetti at Graz the question of the future conclave is amply discussed: Minghetti says that the bishop must insist, in his discussions with the French politicians, on "these principal points, i.e., that Rome offers the sole suitable location in which to hold the conclave . . . and that the Italian government is perfectly able to guarantee its security and liberty." However, before leaving Rome to accompany Strossmayer to Paris, Monsignor Vorsak will call on Visconti Venosta, who will give him whatever final communications he feels are required. Minghetti subsequently discusses the question at Munich with Döllinger, who is in contact with Lord Acton; Acton at this time has been asked by the British government to give his opinion on the outcome of an eventual conclave and has turned to Döllinger to gain insight into the situation. The question was a subject of discussion among the various governments at this time, and it was on this account that Minghetti had gone to Vienna, on a "confidential mission" from Visconti Venosta, to confer with Andrássy, before making his (secret) visit to Strossmayer (private letters of Minghetti to Visconti Venosta, 29 June and 9 July 1872, BCB, *Carte Minghetti*, cart. 83, fasc. b, letters 3 and 6).

[45] Strossmayer to Monsignor Vorsak, in the letter of 12 May [1872], cited in the previous note: "I think it is desirable and necessary for the most important European interests, that the Latin element should gradually come to an understanding with the Slav element, since what is required is to impede decisively the German element from reaching the Adriatic and Black Seas, which can only be done by reinforcing and encouraging the Slav element, freeing it from the yoke that oppresses a large part of it. Otherwise Europe . . . will have to bow its neck under . . . German supremacy." Vorsak was to relay these ideas to Minghetti and Visconti Venosta (BCB, *Carte Minghetti*, cart. 84, fasc. III, c). And cf. as well Vorsak's letter to Visconti Venosta of 4 May 1872, communicating to him the contents of a letter from Strossmayer of 29 April, in which the bishop confirms his long-standing opinion "that we and the Italians can and should finally become neighbors and friends, since we will have to cooperate to defend our independence against a third party" (ACR, *Carte Visconti Venosta*, pacco 5, fasc. 4).

believed that Italy as a political nation was called on to take part in this effort, favoring it and spurring it on. By occupying Rome and putting an end to the temporal power, the Italian government had, he said, carried out an action that was salutary in itself, "but equally beneficial to the church and to all humanity. The fact is that the temporal dominion had distanced the papacy from its divine purpose, converting it into a purely political institution. If the papacy has failed to maintain its universal character, if we see that it is hostile to all the most wise, correct, and generous intentions of Italy, it is the fault of the temporal dominion. This means that by occupying Rome, Italy has done no more than take the first step in its great mission, and there remains much to be done. This task, this mission, which I do not hesitate to describe as providential, cannot be neglected by Italy without great dishonor, and even peril. It is to steer the papacy back toward its own primary and eternal goal, so that after a reconciliation with Italy, and through it with all of civil society, it may strive successfully to purify and sanctify, in accordance with the precepts of divine law, the changes that have been wrought. It is to see that, when once the papacy has come to acknowledge frankly and fully that the independence and the liberty of the primate of all the Catholics are sufficiently grounded and guaranteed by the free institutions of the kingdom of Italy, it then becomes a leading component of the nation's moral greatness, instead of a deadly root of weakness and decay. Divine providence appointed Rome to be the seat of the papacy and in doing so imposed on Italy the obligation to act as guardian of the liberty of the church, as the protector of the papacy; Italy was thereby constituted as the natural mediator between the papacy and civil society."[46]

Strossmayer thus had no hesitation in approving fully of the law of Guarantees, in which he found that the Italian government had erred on just one point, and on the side of caution at that: it had left to the pope and the Roman curia the nomination of bishops, whereas it would have been better to restore the old prerogatives of "clergy and people," leaving the pope to exercise merely a right of confirmation. Italy, he said, must take the initiative on this fundamental point as well; it was in its own interest, and in the interest of the whole world, that the future he envisioned should come to pass—that the papacy should cease to be an exclusively Italian institution, as the curia still desired it should be, in order to become once more a Catholic and universal one.[47]

On a less exalted level, the opinion was commonly expressed at this time, especially in parliamentary debate, that the loss of the temporal power would help rather than hurt the papacy, separating it from the dross of earthly concerns

---

[46] Memorandum of Strossmayer for Minghetti, Rome, 20 January 1872 (BCB, *Carte Minghetti*, cart. 84, fasc. III, g).

[47] Excerpt from a letter of Strossmayer [to Monsignor Vorsak], received at Rome on 15 July [1871], and communicated to Visconti Venosta, with whom Strossmayer proposes to confer, when he comes to Rome during the following winter (Visconti Venosta archive). On the fixed idea of Strossmayer to make of Catholicism once more a "universal church" and put an end to the Italian predominance, cf. in general Seton-Watson, *Die südslavische Frage im Habsburger Reiche*, p. 144; and Loiseau, "La politique de Strossmayer," *Le Monde Slave*, n.s. 4 (1927): 394.

and leaving it free to occupy itself entirely with lofty spiritual ones.[48] Lanza, Visconti Venosta, Minghetti, and Bonghi were in agreement. But for most the matter stopped there: Italy's task had been the purely negative one of freeing the papacy of the burden that held it down. The regime of liberty would do the rest, operating in the manner of efficacious grace. The church could regulate its own internal life by itself, without the state taking a hand. This was the cardinal principle codified in the second clause of the law of Guarantees.

But for those who thought as Ricasoli did, the matter did not in the least stop there. The mission was only beginning at this point, in the minds of those who in 1870 were still under the spell of ideas and feelings that had flourished in Europe in the early nineteenth century, in a climate pregnant with the sense of religion, with messianic expectations of a new triumph of the faith. In this climate Lamennais, and the Italians Rosmini and Lambruschini, had propounded an accord between science and faith, between the church and liberty, between the church and modern thought. And the tradition of Rosmini, Manzoni, and Lambruschini was upheld by the latter's disciple, Ricasoli, who believed that it had to become a working faith even for the laity, and not remain the purely contemplative faith predicated by the government.

This was Romantic Catholicism, a heritage of ideas and sentiments from the world before 1848. But times had changed. Now the appetite for scientific knowledge characteristic of the age of positivism was growing ever stronger and displacing the Romantic urge for religious reform. The rapid decline of the Old Catholic movement in Germany, and the shift elsewhere of the attention that in 1871 was briefly focused throughout Europe on the figure of Döllinger, would soon reveal this change. In result the voices of the now aged Lambruschini, and of Ricasoli, who seemed a relic of the past, roused very little response, and it was the mission of Rome as understood by Sella that prevailed.

Sella led a chorus that included many of his own political companions on the Right, but the voices that really prevailed in it were those that chimed in from the Left, in a hymn to Rome as the capital of the kingdom, as the onset of a new epoch in human history. For them Italy would have no good reason to exist if it failed to meet the responsibility assigned to it by destiny. Mancini put it this way:

---

[48] Blanc even said so to Cardinal Antonelli, in a meeting on 3 October 1870. The cardinal observed that the pontiff could not forget that he had been despoiled of his domains; Blanc responded by agreeing "that the inevitable transformation of the status of a sovereign power was a very delicate circumstance, in fact an unavoidably painful one, even when this transformation may inaugurate a new era of greatness. I recalled that when King Carlo Alberto handed over to his people a part of the prerogatives of his ancient sovereignty, there were many who viewed this as a loss much more serious than the loss of a piece of territory, since it restricted the exercise of the very essence of supreme power. None the less, by restoring to its people the exercise of their own rights, the house of Savoy rendered itself able to fulfill the different destiny to which divine providence called it. At this time the papacy is in a position to make an equally auspicious surrender of the administration of territories which, since they divide Italy and keep alive a dire antagonism between the church and the people, have kept the supreme spiritual power from being exercised with the fullness and splendor and universal consensus that is due it. . . . His eminence answered that although he appreciated the sentiments I was expressing, yet he could not accept the parallel between a change in the internal constitution of a state, and the forced seizure of power from a prince" (Blanc, report, 3 October 1870; *Libro Verde*, riservato, *Roma*, cited in n. 17 above, no. 9, p. 15).

"Italy cannot refuse the mission, which I would call world-historical, given it by providence and now awaiting it. Italy presents itself before the other civilized nations of the world with an outstanding claim to their recognition and respect: it swept away the temporal power of the pope and thereby emancipated the spiritual power of that office, restoring it to a position of authority and veneration. The papacy must be set free from a disfiguring burden of political sovereignty; after centuries of conflict this ill-omened union must be dissolved. As it stands it is detrimental to us and to the great general interests of civilization and liberty in the world."[49]

This orotund declaration belongs to the period preceding the events of 20 September and contains conventional phrases, politically accommodating courtesies, which were certainly not shared by all, and perhaps not even by the speaker himself. His expressed wish to make the spiritual power of the pope more authoritative and venerable—this was nothing more than a tactical maneuver, an empty formula pronounced during a parliamentary debate. The real opinion of those whom we are now considering was that whatever had been accomplished to date was not enough: to sweep away the temporal power was not an end in itself but a means. As with Ricasoli, but for entirely different reasons, they felt that the kingdom of Italy ought not to "stand there watching," but go to work on the church. And it was to be a work of destruction, for the new Italy and the old Catholicism could no longer coexist, and the nation that had created the papacy must now destroy it, must divest itself of the papacy.[50] As with other currents of opinion, this one was articulated both in Italy and abroad; in France it was proclaimed that Italy had an obligation to dismantle Roman Catholicism in order to make reparation for all the ills inflicted on humanity by the Counter Reformation of the sixteenth and seventeenth centuries.[51]

Rather than a revival of the church, a rebirth of religious fervor in the collective human heart, they wanted just the opposite: an end to "superstition" (by which was meant the very idea of religion), the collapse of the spiritual power of the papacy following the collapse of its temporal power, the end of the "old cancer" that for centuries had gnawed at the healthy vitals of Italy,[52] and the triumph of free human thought. Eighteenth-century rationalism and Jacobinism, clothed in the up-to-date scientific mantle of the reigning positivism, replaced the religious messianism of the Romantic age and liberal Catholicism. Faith in an accord between religion and science, between the church and liberty, were replaced by a conviction that the church and liberty were utterly irreconcilable, that there was no common ground between the papacy and modern thought.

[49] Speech to the Chamber, 19 August 1870 (Mancini, *Discorsi Parlamentari* 3:373–74).

[50] Settembrini, *Epistolario*, pp. 260, 261, 283. What Settembrini meant by "reforming" Christianity (an expression that on the surface might appear similar to that used by Ricasoli) is seen in his affirmation that the new idea, the new religion in preparation in Italy, will show the world "that the great book is not the Bible, but reason."

[51] Thus Renan to Amari, from 1865 (Amari, *Carteggio* 2:187–88; and cf. as well Renan, *Correspondance, 1872–1892*, p. 27).

[52] The expression "old cancer" is also used by Amari, who in politics was an ally of the Right (Amari, *Carteggio* 2:232–33).

Dogma must end, and science hold sway. Science was the bringer of light, the vanquisher of clerical obscurantism, the guardian of truths capable of incubating a new morality. For a man like Quintino Sella, science in and of itself was a supreme purpose, even when it served at the same time as an instrument in the struggle against the reactionary and anti-Italian papacy, while for others its primary value was its instrumentality in the battle against the church. In this battle the name of science functioned as a watchword: it was pronounced by persons hostile to the papacy who in truth possessed extremely nebulous notions as to what exactly it meant and, unlike Sella, did not have the slightest intention of cultivating it seriously. A conspicuous badge that often failed to conceal a slight acquaintance with the art of thinking, it was exhibited most frequently in journalistic polemics and in parliamentary debate. To make Rome the capital of the modern spirit and thus the crown of civilization for the third time: clearly that meant something much more profound and substantial for a man like De Sanctis[53] than it did for the editors of the *Gazzettino Rosa*. But regardless of the degree of profundity and substance involved, science was at this juncture a clarion call that had the power to galvanize large numbers, just as other ideas such as the cry for religion to flower again in humanity's breast had had the power to do fifty years before. The combination of circumstances that gave it such deep and penetrating resonance can be summarized as, first, the Syllabus of Errors and the decree on infallibility, which had set the governments of half of Europe against the papacy, even that of prevalently Catholic Austria; and second, the Prussian triumph in the war, which appeared as the triumph of science applied in battle. Even death was present at the fête of scientific progress.[54]

The religion of progress in place of religion based on dogma: not long after, this theme would be sounded in unison by Bismarck's publicists too, and among the voices from the choir stall that of Treitschke was especially shrill, insisting that Germany, the great homeland of liberty of thought, was fighting not to elevate the power of the state but for a freer conception of Christianity, for freedom in thought and in science, for a new Germanic spiritual life that would flow out to humanity.[55] But in the months between September 1870 and the summer of 1871, before Bismarck took up the weapon that destiny proffered and launched the call to war "nach aussen wie nach innen,"[56] and then in the all-out *Kulturkampf* that followed, with Germans and Italians seeking to outdo each other in the role of liberators of the human race from spiritual enslavement to priests,[57]

---

[53] De Sanctis affirmed these hopes as early as 1864 (Cione, *Francesco De Sanctis*, p. 195).

[54] An allusion to this is in Michelet, *La France devant l'Europe*, p. 47.

[55] Cf. the article by Treitschke, "Libera Chiesa in libero Stato," in the *Preussische Jahrbücher* 36 (1875): 236–37, and even earlier his speech to the Reichstag on 23 November 1871 (in Federici, *Der deutsche Liberalismus*, pp. 342–43). Further, O. Hartwig, "Italien und Rom," *Preussische Jahrbücher* 29 (1872): 194, and the "Politische Correspondenz" for February 1872, in the same volume, p. 247.

[56] Article in the *Kreuz-zeitung* for 19 June 1871 (cf. K. Bachem, *Vorgeschichte, Geschichte, und Politik der deutschen Zentrumspartei* 3:218 (Cologne, 1927); Eyck, *Bismarck* 3:87.

[57] "Italy today has in common with Germany the glory of representing civilization in its struggle with the papacy" (Marselli, *La rivoluzione parlamentare*, p. 118). Marselli was a stubborn adversary of any sort of accord with Catholicism; on the contrary, it was necessary, he thought, "to find the

Italian free thinkers laid a strong claim to first place. Of all the tasks that were attached to Rome in its new role as the Italian capital, this was the one that was talked of most widely and animatedly, and in celebratory verse the goddess Roma drew the attention of Italy to

> . . . the columns and the arches;

> the arches that await new triumphs
> not of ancient kings or Caesars
> with no chains binding human limbs
> to ivory chariots

> but your triumph, O people of Italy
> over the dark age, the barbarous age.[58]

Science was embodied in the institutes of advanced study, in the Accademia dei Lincei and in the university, forming a bulwark of modern thought against the theocratic tradition. Scientific meetings and open debate, taking place in the ancient capital of orthodox doctrine (meaning false doctrine), would constitute momentous events in the history of the human spirit,[59] and human thought would acquire the concrete form of science—the only concrete form that the idea of a nonreligious renewal of humanity could assume.

Science as critical discussion, no longer as the blind acceptance of dogma, was the cry raised to the heavens on both sides of the Alps. *Entrer dans la science, dans l'examen*, thundered the irate Flaubert, though he was a great artist and as such had a predisposition to deplore the dawn of a utilitarian and positivistic age. But on the other hand the novelist was also a consummate anticlerical, enraged by the very existence of church dogma, and hence an apostle of science, of critical debate, of a new mandarin regime based on superior intelligence.[60] Then there was Taine, who asked: is not Reason, as it was called in 1789, or Science as it is called in 1878, the legitimate queen of the world and mistress of its future?[61] And there was Renan; he was intoning once more the themes of progress and reason, of science in short, just as he had done in 1848 in *L'avenir de la science*

---

strength either to overcome the papacy, and force it to change itself, or else to rid ourselves of it, and force it to emigrate" (ibid., pp. 103–104 and 125–27).

[58] "Nell'annuale della fondazione di Roma," composed in April 1877:

> . . . le colonne e gli archi:

> gli archi che nuovi trionfi aspettano
> non più di regi, non più di cesari
> e non di catene attorcenti
> braccia umane su gli eburnei carri;

> ma il tuo trionfo, popol d'Italia
> su l'età nera, su l'età barbara.

[59] Renan to Amari in 1873 (Renan, *Correspondance, 1872–1892*, p. 46; also, in curtailed form, in Amari, *Carteggio* 2:214).

[60] Flaubert, *Correspondance* 4:48, 55 ff.

[61] Ibid., 4:47.

and again with great optimism in 1869 on the eve of the war.[62] Like a modern
Ecclesiastes he declared that all was vanity except for science, to the point where
art itself came to seem a little hollow to him,[63] and forgetting the more judicious
views he had expressed in November 1849 concerning the naturally Catholic
character of the Italian people,[64] he proclaimed that the end of the temporal
power would bring about a schism similar to the Great Schism that had occurred
in the fourteenth century, and with it the end of Catholic unity.[65] For this reason
the "modest and honorable" rebirth of Italy as a nation was received by Renan as
a happy event for humanity,[66] and in 1881 he entrusted to the Roman anticlericals
the resolution of the great problem of the nineteenth century: total religious liberty, with the state agnostic in matters of faith. What he desired to see was the
expulsion from the world of the last vestiges of a regime that was opposed to the
basic principles of modern civilization, and a pledge of impunity for the rights,
which he viewed as sacrosanct, of the human conscience, of the human spirit, of
science.[67]

Renan often lacked faith in his own country, and for that matter was prey from
time to time to somber visions of the destiny of all humanity, as he was to a series
of inner conflicts, especially the one between his nostalgia for the aristocratic
past and his devotion to science, which brought with it industrial society, democracy, and nationalism. As he wavered indecisively between his personal artistic
and religious ideals on one hand, and the scientific ideal that was the common
property of his contemporaries on the other, the only train of thought that was
sure to make his spirits rise was the contemplation of the future triumph of science and the end of spiritual unity within the Roman church. This attitude was
reinforced by his voyage to Sicily in the summer of 1875, during which the ship
that was carrying this new apostle to the gentiles was surrounded, in the waters
off Selinunte, by a swarm of boats full of Sicilians crying "Viva la Scienza!" In
the days that followed, the plump and beaming Renan traversed the island like a
conqueror receiving the ovation of the entire populace, despite the modest demeanor he affected. He flattered himself that since the time of Empedocles no
other individual, with the exception of Garibaldi, had received a similar acco-

---

[62] In the lecture "Les services que la science rend au peuple" (in *Mélanges religieux et historiques*, p. 149). Science would improve the world, would make it a kingdom of the spirit, the kingdom
of free men.

[63] Renan and Berthelot, *Correspondance*, p. 467.

[64] Renan to Berthelot, from Rome, 9 November 1849: "I had not before understood what a
popular religion is, one held very naively and uncritically by a people; I had not comprehended a
people continuously creating in religion, accepting its dogmas in a living and true fashion. Let us not
delude ourselves, this people is as Catholic as the Arabs in their mosque are Muslims. Its religion is
the religion; to speak against its religion is to speak to it against an interest that it feels inside itself,
just as much a reality as any other of nature's needs" (Renan and Berthelot, *Correspondance*, p. 43
and cf. p. 54: "Catholicism is the very soul of this country; Catholicism is just as necessary to this
country as liberty and democracy . . . are to ours").

[65] Renan, *Correspondance, 1872–1892*, pp. 15, 24, 27, 131. And cf. Amari, *Carteggio* 2:213.

[66] Renan, *Correspondance, 1872–1892*, p. 26 (1872), and cf. p. 141: "as I love Italy very much,
both for itself and for the services of the first order that it renders to the human spirit" (1878). The
unity of Italy and the good of civilization seem to him to be indissoluble (ibid., p. 130).

[67] Ibid., pp. 215 ff.

lade, and it appeared that, after Hungary, Sicily was the territory closest to breaking the chains that bound it to papal Rome and initiating a religious reform[68]

Rome as a center of science and of secular inquiry capable of changing the world continued to receive the choral homage of many,[69] a homage that never died down in the decades following 1870, and in parliament the demand that the state secularize itself vis-à-vis the church was heard from illustrious deputies and from those who were less so. As Prime Minister Crispi stated, it was necessary for the third Italy to make its mark in the world of science so as to be able to face the Vatican and to combat the prejudices of the past.[70] Giordano Bruno was commemorated in Campo de' Fiori. And as late as 1913, when the Senate had occasion to discuss the chair of philosophy of history in the University of Rome, it was maintained that this particular university bore a special burden of responsibility, since it was "the true symbol of the emancipated modern spirit, as opposed to the age-old reign of theocracy."[71]

Renan was not alone among foreign observers in believing this. At the beginning of the twentieth century Novikov extolled the intellectual mission of Italy, which he saw as destined to become not only the "intellectual and moral sanatorium of the world," a harmonious asylum for refined spirits, but also, as in the past, the great teacher of science to humankind, the mother of the sciences and of the arts.[72]

It is understandable that in this vast swelling consensus of publicists and politicians, principally of the Left, and of professional free thinkers, the scientific ideal should gradually shade off into much vaguer pronouncements in which the positivistic commendation of hard science was mixed with fragments of Mazzinian sermonizing, characterized by their indefinite messianic hopes, their oratorical heat, their longing for a nebulous religion of the True and the Good. Quintino Sella was a man of his time, the later nineteenth century, and his own personal clarity and precision were fully in harmony with his program; the others who shared it with him were spiritually stranded between the first and second halves of the nineteenth century, between Mazzinian preaching and positivism in the

[68] See the picturesque account of Renan to Berthelot, in Renan and Berthelot, *Correspondance*, pp. 450–51. Cf. *Vingt jours en Sicile*, in *Oeuvres complètes* 2:383–84.

[69] Cf. too the publication by two illustrious professors of the universities of Palermo and Rome, P. Blaserna and C. Tommasi Crudeli, *L'Università di Roma: Pensieri di alcuni direttori di stabilimenti scientifici italiani* (Rome, 1871), pp. 17–18.

[70] For the statements by Crispi (who draws explicitly on Sella) in the Senate on 17 July 1890, see Crispi, *Discorsi Parlamentari* 3:584. In the case of the Accademia dei Lincei, Crispi also took his lead from Sella; and Sella thanked him in February 1878 for the benevolence he had shown to the academy as interior minister, and for the advice given by him and by Coppino, and followed by Umberto I, "to favor the sciences, letters, and arts," on which basis the first act, or one of the first acts, of the new sovereign had been the institution of the Premio Reale (Royal Prize) (Crispi, *Carteggi politici inediti*, pp. 355–56).

[71] Thus the rapporteur [*relatore*], Arcoleo, in defense of the bill, which had been vigorously attacked by Senators Croce, Garofalo, Lanciani, Comparetti, and Del Giudice (session of 30 May 1913, *A.P., Senato*, p. 11238). And cf. the previous statement of Arcoleo supporting the bill, p. 6: science "has the exalted duty to combat, and to take the place of, dogma" (*Documenti*, no. 879 A). In both cases, Arcoleo mentions Sella.

[72] Novikov, *La missione dell'Italia*, pp. 281 ff.

style of Littré, between a confused theism and atheism. A further influence on many, including those from southern Italy generally and Mancini in particular, was the old-fashioned jurisdictionalism of the eighteenth century. Others, principally Crispi, responded to Masonic doctrines, to the word of the great architect of the universe. All of these men were vessels of the Jacobin ethos, which was revived with peculiar energy at this time in connection with the problem of relations between Italy and the church.

Hence the fiery tones, the apostrophes and invocations that were heard in parliamentary oratory and in the political press, where the drier, more composed eloquence of Sella was followed by accents of Mazzinian pathos, grandiloquent images, and invectives against the pope.

The journal *Riforma* was energetic in its campaign to push Italy into conflict with its own internal enemy and the cancer of all humanity, the papacy. This was a battle against theocracy, a battle to erect an edifice based on morality and science over the ashes of the papal throne, a temple worthy of humanity.[73] If the Catholic religion were not reduced to "the original modest principles that gave it birth," liberal Europe would never have a moment's peace.[74] Every so often the paper's attention was briefly caught by the problems of Nice or Trent or the Orient, but for the most part it was mesmerized by the papacy and in consequence indignant at the intrigues of the French reactionaries, while it fully approved of the titan who was defying the papacy and protecting the liberty of Europe, Prince Otto von Bismarck.

Years before the decisive step was taken, Crispi had asserted that the nation had to set its sights on Rome because it was "necessary for our people as the true capital of Italy, and necessary for humanity as the logical culmination on which the conquest of liberty of conscience depends."[75] Likewise it was the emancipatory mission of Rome to break the tyranny of the priests, the enemies of the nation and of civilization that gave impetus to the *Appello alla Democrazia*, which Garibaldi and Cairoli launched on 1 August 1872.[76] The "hero of two worlds" was relentless, expressing his regret at not obtaining a decree from the government and the majority in the Chamber by which Italy would be liberated even from the spiritual influence of the papacy,[77] or addressing, from Frascati, an invitation to the people to commence the third phase of the civilizing process in Rome by substituting for all the religions based on revelation and falsehood "the religion of the true, a religion without priests founded on reason and science."[78] Lesser folk followed the lead of these august fathers of irreligion, convinced that the revolution had come to Rome for the purpose of combating Catholicism at close quarters and that the death knell of the papacy had sounded,[79] and conse-

---

[73] *La Riforma* for 20 September 1871 ("Il 20 settembre").

[74] *La Riforma* for 26 July 1872 ("Ancora dell'attentato di Spagna").

[75] Election campaign speech of 14 October 1865 (Crispi, *Scritti e discorsi politici*, p. 458).

[76] Garibaldi, *Scritti e discorsi politici e militari* 3:99 ff. The appeal was written by Cairoli (Rosi, *I Cairoli* 1:245).

[77] Letter to K. Blind, 28 March 1875 (Garibaldi, *Epistolario* 2:102, ed. Ximenes [Milan, 1885]).

[78] 14 June 1875 (Garibaldi, *Scritti e discorsi politici e militari* 3:153–54).

[79] Thus [L. G.], *Le prisonnier du Vatican, l'Italie, la France et la Prusse* (Rome, 1872), p. 106.

quently eager, having taken possession of the papal city, to act accordingly, for the deed had not signified a sterile fulfillment but the onset of a new era.[80] Furthermore, they often revealed a distinctive tendency to manifest their point of view through public displays that created a disturbance at best, and not infrequently sank into the improper and the ridiculous,[81] as when for example the last Thursday of Carnival was parodied down the Roman Corso in the "Catholic crusade of 1871,"[82] or at a public banquet held at Pisa on Good Friday,[83] or when the wedding ceremony of an ex-priest was transformed into a festival of "progress."[84] The warnings of those who were patriots and Catholics at the same time to the effect that the pope should be treated respectfully, especially in the public prints, in order to calm his fears and remove a pretext for all the world's Catholics to protest against the Italian nation, produced no result,[85] just as no heed was paid to those who had opined even earlier that the priests were certainly to be restrained when they gave provocation, but that priest-haters were for the most part even worse, and had done a lot of harm in Italy.[86]

Anticlericalism, with its Unions of free thinkers and their ambitious and optimistic projects,[87] spread. The forms it took were an obvious reaction to the

[80] Thus the hon. Mellana, in the session of the Chamber of 15 May 1872 (*A.P., Camera*, p. 2131).

[81] Tommaseo was right when he observed that "even if it were the moral course of action to alter the conscience of the Italian people, the notion of being able to alter it by uttering insults from the Capitol against the cardinals, or something of the sort, is not a necessary consequence of this morality" (*Roma e l'Italia nel 1850 e nel 1870 e le nuove elezioni: Presagi di N. T. avverati, e perché più non si avverino*, p. 81).

[82] P. Vigo, *Annali d'Italia: Storia degli ultimi trent'anni del secolo XIX* 1:40 ff. (Milan, 1908). For other excesses on the part of the anticlericals, cf. Pesci, *I primi anni di Roma capitale*, pp. 500–501. The *Gazzetta d'Italia* for 19 February 1871 protested against the masquerade; but the major protest came from Cardinal Antonelli in a circular to the nuncios, and Beust called for the Italian government to take seriously demonstrations of this "highly regrettable" kind (Beust, dispatch to Kübeck, 10 March 1871; and Kübeck, report to Beust, 14 March, no. 20; SAW, *P.A.*, XI/235). Cf. as well the report of the French chargé d'affaires at the Holy See, Lefebvre de Béhaine, 22 February, no. 33; AEP, *C.P., Rome*, t. 1049, fols. 261v ff. For other demonstrations by the anticlericals, which were answered by clerical demonstrations no less vulgar, cf. Gorresio, "Papalini e liberali dopo il '70," in *Il Mondo*, 23 July–27 August 1949.

[83] The banquet, organized by the free thinkers of Pisa, elicited a request to the minister of justice from Monsignor Ghilardi, the bishop of Mondoví, that it be prohibited; and subsequently there were acts of expiation (the via crucis) staged by Catholic associations in Turin, Milan, and other cities. Cf. the article by Bonghi, who strongly deplores the free thinkers' action, although without approving the request of Monsignor Ghilardi ("Fenomeni nuovi e vizii vecchi," in *La Perseveranza* for 11 April 1871).

[84] At Girgenti, on the occasion of the wedding of an ex-canon, a numerous crowd of "liberals" gathered at the city hall: the mayor praised the step being taken by the couple, expressed hopes for progress, and also the hope that the example offered by the man and his wife would be imitated by others (G. Arrò Carroccio, *Il cattolicismo ed il liberalismo*, p. 6, n. 1).

[85] Ricasoli to Torelli, 9 November 1870 (in Monti, *Il conte Luigi Torelli*, p. 295).

[86] Bon Compagni to Torelli, 27 July 1869 (ibid., p. 288).

[87] Cf. the *Statuto della unione dei liberi pensatori già società di mutua onoranza funebre tra i volontari* (Florence, 1871), p. 3, art. 1: "The aim of the society is . . . to remove through education all the prejudices and beliefs diffused by the revealed religions, as being harmful phenomena, contrary to civilization and liberty of conscience and thought"; art. 3: "They [members of the society] believe that human activity moves forward in endless progress." And see also, from 1869, the *Catechismo del razionalista* of Luigi Stefanoni (in E. Conti, *Le origini del socialismo a Firenze (1860–1880)*, pp. 251 ff.).

political stance taken by the Roman curia, the higher clergy, and the Jesuits against Italian unity, and this reaction was thus connected to a specifically Italian situation, so much so that it laid claim to remote and glorious origins in the distant past, and presented itself as a new Ghibellinism, with the Ghibelline Dante, who was thus transformed into a great hero of secularism,[88] as its patron and counterpart to the Vatican.[89] But anticlericalism was also the expression of a belief in the inevitable and imminent metamorphosis of the moral life of humanity, its rise from the debris of religious belief to the cultivation of science and progress. As such it was interwoven, indeed fused, with European anticlericalism, especially of the French variety, which had the same cultural stamp and the same roots in the Enlightenment, in positivism, and in Freemasonry. Together they celebrated, in 1878, the centenary of the death of Voltaire, the preacher of war against fanaticism, superstition, and religion.[90]

The fact is that there were many who believed sincerely that the hour of doom had come for the Rome that had been "built . . . on the rock of Christ by Peter and Paul,"[91] and Aleardi, in his fury against the "deceitful obscenity" that reigned in the Vatican, seriously imagined that the sway of the cross over consciences was at an end, and that, following "this spiritual upheaval," the peoples would perhaps no longer desire to see the cross "even on their graves."[92]

In sum, it was a period in which the life of the imagination lost none of its power. Hopes were still fervid, the expectation of the coming age was still tinged with the messianic. The last decades of the nineteenth century were a harder age, yet they still retained something of the atmosphere with which the century had opened, an atmosphere vibrant with faith in the future, in liberty, in concord among the nations, in the rebirth of religious feeling and the possibility of the perfection of human life; the objects of faith were now called science and progress. In the interval, the furies had been unleashed, including the clergy, the International, emperors and ex-emperors; nonetheless, the nineteenth century

---

[88] Dante's aims had been the liberation of the laity and the unity of Italy, according to F. De Sanctis, ("Il pensiero di Dante" [1865], in *Scritti politici*, pp. 32 ff.). And see the curious letter of the anticlerical Settembrini to Tulelli, 22 July 1870, concerning a painting by Angelo Mazzia in which Dante, descending from the light of Paradise, observes Rome immersed in darkness, crows wheeling about the Colosseum, a black cloud overhead, and the Vatican entirely overshadowed. Settembrini remarks: "The idea behind the painting is true for the time of Dante, and it is true for our time." The great Dante, a member of the laity, signifies the modern age in contrast to the Middle Ages; there is now no more reason for the clerics to command obedience, rather they must now obey, and the world is indifferent to them (Settembrini, *Epistolario*, p. 247).

[89] Giovanni Bovio intended the chair of Dante studies, created at Rome in 1887, to stand as a contrast to "the chair of St. Peter" (Crispi, *Carteggi politici inediti*, p. 409). How important this was considered in anticlerical circles is revealed by the letter that the grand master of the masons, Adriano Lemmi, wrote to his friend Crispi when the latter was prime minister, recommending that, in order to get Carducci to accept the chair, he should be offered an additional university assignment (for example, teaching medieval literature), which would allow him to earn a higher salary (letter of 24 September 1887, MRR, *carte Crispi*, b. 660, 6/11).

[90] Vigo, *Annali d'Italia* 2:283–85.

[91] "hedificata . . . super Christum petram per Petrum et Paulum": the words of Cardinal Umberto da Silva Candida, in the fragmentary *De sancta Romana ecclesia*, datable circa 1053 (P. E. Schramm, *Kaiser, Rom, und Renovatio* 2:129 [Leipzig-Berlin, 1929]).

[92] Letter of 2 March 1873 (Aleardi, *Epistolario*, p. 315).

had triumphed.[93] In the words of Michele Amari, we men of science must simply continue to work for the satisfaction of our spirit, for truth, for humanity,[94] while Francesco De Sanctis put it this way: today the ideal is not the province of the priest or the philosopher, but of the scientist: "we will have a scientific ideal, and the nineteenth century, *le siècle d'enfantement*, is carrying it in its womb. The ideal is dead; long live the ideal!"[95]

The truth is that understanding of the idea of a nonconfessional state founded on a nonreligious school system, which was taking shape in the minds of the moderates in their own typical intellectual style, was receiving nourishment and strength, along with a certain amount of intemperate excess, from other sources as well in the current atmosphere. The same process, involving the political passions of the moment and the battle against reactionary clericalism, was taking place, and to a greater degree, in France, where anticlerical passion was growing sharper and positivism becoming ever more antireligious,[96] with the secular state definitively establishing its own status through the education bills of Jules Ferry.

In Italy the law on compulsory elementary schooling passed by the Left in 1877 had exactly the same significance, and the earlier abolition of the faculties of theology in 1872 sounded a clear affirmation of the religious neutrality of the state,[97] so clear that Bonghi, under the influence of renewed hopes, Rosminian in origin, for an internal reform of the church, was averse to it. In this of course he was at odds with his own position, Cavourean and Tocquevillean in origin, on the rights of the modern state.[98] Bon Compagni was opposed to the measure as well, for he harked back to the neo-Guelphism of Pius IX in 1846 and 1847, the period in which Catholicism, liberty, and nationality had seemingly been fused into a whole—a whole that was certainly not the secular state in its post-1848 form, in Piedmont and then in united Italy.[99]

Overall, the evolution that was occurring was allied to the organization and consolidation of the Italian state in other fields, from public finance to public consciousness, a slow and arduous struggle amid grave difficulties of every kind. It was part of the progressive general ascent of Italian life to the level of western civilization in Europe, not just in the existence of free political institutions and the parliamentary regime but also in the processes of the economy and the experience of spiritual and moral life: western civilization was secular. The moderates and their opponents each contributed in their own fashion to this process of evolution, despite the intermittent fierce polemics between them, which were

---

[93] Thus Amari to Michelet, 6 July 1871 (Amari, *Carteggio* 3:297).

[94] Amari to Renan, 2 August 1871 (ibid.).

[95] F. De Sanctis, "Il realismo moderno" (1877), in *Scritti politici*, p. 143.

[96] Cf. G. Weill, *Storia dell'idea laica in Francia nel secolo XIX* (Italian translation: Bari, 1937), pp. 173 ff.

[97] Messedaglia said as much in the session of 25 April 1872: "We have laid down the principle of the separation of the state from the church . . . so let us be logical; let the church give instruction in the field that properly belongs to it, and let us attend to the responsibility that is ours. The state by its nature, in the manner we wish to understand it, is secular and cannot have any kind of teaching other than secular" (*A.P., Camera*, p. 1721).

[98] Cf. W. Maturi, preface to Bonghi, *Stato e Chiesa* 1:xx–xxi.

[99] Speech of Bon Compagni, 25 April 1872 (*A.P., Camera*, pp. 1715–16).

sharpened by the tone that prevailed on the Left, a tone that was not just anticlerical but anti-Catholic and was therefore simply alien to the majority of the moderates. In fact this was the principal point of ideological friction between the two
camps. With the conversion of virtually all the formerly republican politicians to
allegiance to the monarchy, the original disagreement about institutional forms
had disappeared, and in the period after 1870 in which Crispi and Cairoli were on
the verge of becoming the king's ministers, and indeed prime ministers, the main
ideological difference was over relations between church and state; proof of this
lay in the events of the period 1871–1876, and the totally divergent attitude with
which the two groups regarded the *Kulturkampf* in Germany and its possible
extension to Italy. All the rest—heated debate about Sella's tax schemes, contrasting domestic policies, and even contrasting ideas about foreign policy—
amounted in comparison to disputes about practical politics, and often enough to
no more than parliamentary and electoral in-fighting. But church and state, that
was a matter of principle, ideas were at stake.

Throughout the period of the Risorgimento and after, moderates such as Minghetti, Visconti Venosta, and Bonghi, not to speak of Ricasoli and Capponi, felt
that religious sentiment had, and could not lose, a fundamental importance in the
social life of mankind:[100] religion was the same thing as the moral life of a
people. Almost all of them agreed on this except for the group from Naples
around the Spaventa brothers and a few others like the vehement Amari, who
were exceptions to the rule and, although in parliamentary politics they stood
with the Right, could not be considered—and in effect were not considered—
moderates, or at any rate, not moderates of the classic type. For those on the
Left, and in this they were met halfway by Sella and joined whole-heartedly by
Amari, such views were mere harmful delusions; the Italian state would be truly
and strongly established only when reverential subjection to the church had dissipated for good.

To repeat, the existence of such views in Italy was closely connected to their
diffusion throughout Europe, and especially France. But the point is that they
were a new phenomenon in Italy, where until recently there had prevailed universal dreams, the expectation of a new embodiment in Rome of the revitalizing
message of human civilization. As the years slipped by, however, the fallacy of
believing in such hopes and anticipations became ever more apparent. The passing dream of a national Italian church in the context of a Europe divided up into
national churches rapidly proved ephemeral,[101] and so did the more deeply

---

[100] See the fine pages of G. Barzellotti, "L'idea religiosa negli uomini di Stato del Risorgimento," in *Dal Rinascimento al Risorgimento* (2d ed.; Palermo, 1909), pp. 145 ff. Visconti Venosta
asserted to the French envoy in 1875 that he believed in the influence and the development of
Catholicism in the future (Noailles, report of 9 March 1875, no. 18, cited above n. 11; AEP, *C.P.,
Italie*, t. 391, fol. 255.

[101] There were allusions to the necessity of national churches in 1870–71: cf. the speech of the
hon. Toscanelli, who was very much opposed to the idea, in the Chamber on 23 January 1871,
Discorso . . . contro il progetto di legge [sulle Guarentigie], p. 30; and *Guarentigie papali: Lettera
di Nicolò Tommaseo al deputato Giovanni Bortolucci e risposta al medesimo* (Florence, 1871),
p. 10. Crispi hoped they would come into being (Crispi, *Pensieri e profezie*, p. 87, and Zanichelli,

rooted vision of an internal reform of the church, the great myth of what might be called the left wing of Romantic Catholicism. In fact it was already no more than a faint memory on the day the Italian troops smashed through the walls of Rome, for in the interval there had been the Syllabus and the decree on infallibility, the two main responses which the apostles of renewal had received from the church. Now there was nothing left to hope for, no option except resolutely to leave the church and oppose it from without, following the example of Piero Guicciardini,[102] for gradual measures and compromise solutions reached within the fold were no longer possible. It was time for Italian life to become truly "progressive," not as the result of a profound reform capable of restoring religious feeling (Sismondi's formula),[103] but exclusively by virtue of the secular impulse, of secular forces; and when the Catholics did eventually decide to resume their participation in public life *qua* Catholics, and to contribute their ideas and their labor, a contribution destined to grow in weight and importance, they themselves would be doing so on a different basis than that of the Syllabus, accepting united Italy with Rome as its capital, and also the idea of liberty: in other words, they would enter into an intellectual legacy given to Italy by those Italians who believed in circumscribing the bounds of religious life. In Italy the vision of Rosmini, of Lambruschini, evaporated, just as in Germany the vision of the Old Catholics and Döllinger rapidly faded away, a vision that to some had seemed a secure promise of things to come.[104]

There was an old saying to the effect that the Italians were fundamentally indifferent to religious problems, and it was given a new twist by those who observed that the opposition between Italy and the Vatican was a purely political matter, warning against any illusion that there could be any movement in Italy similar to that led by Döllinger.[105] On the other hand, even those who were unable to give up their illusions about an imminent, inevitable, profound transformation of the church, and who did not share the assumption that the Italians were "naturally" indifferent to religion, were now driven to combine these illu-

---

Monarchia e Papato in Italia, pp. 207–209.) For Pannelli and Prota Giorleo, cf. S. Jacini, *Il tramonto del potere temporale nelle relazioni degli ambasciatori austriaci a Rome (1860–1870)*, p. 75.

[102] Cf. S. Jacini, *Un riformatore toscano dell'epoca del Risorgimento: Il conte Piero Guicciardini (1808–1886)* (Florence, 1940). Note that Protestant propaganda in Italy constituted another motive for the hostility of the Roman curia against the Italian government. Thus for example "L'Italia officiale protestante," in *L'Osservatore Romano* for 6 September 1878, reports the protest of the bishop of Tivoli (25 August) at the fact that the former priory of San Nicola at Tivoli, which had been declared state property, had then been leased to an evangelical minister who had come there to spread "the damnable tares of error and seduction."

[103] To Lambruschini, 9 July 1833 (Gambaro, *Riforma religiosa* 2:131 ff.)

[104] In addition to the well-known "Address by the professors of the University of Rome" ("Indirizzo dei professori della Università di Roma," 10 April 1871), which caused a tremendous stir, cf. the letter to Döllinger which prefaces the work by the Roman advocate C. Lozzi, *La questione pontificia delineata nella vita e nelle opere di Eusebio Reali* (Civitavecchia, 1871).

[105] Should a country like Italy, "in which one can count more people who are fanatical, or indifferent, than one can true and active believers, aim to have a religious reform, and a serious discussion about whether the gospel of Saint Luke 22:32 contains or doesn't contain the doctrine of papal infallibility?" (*L'Opinione* for 26 September 1874: "I vecchi cattolici in Italia").

sions with a much stronger hostility to the papacy and the official church, from which there was nothing more to be hoped. This happened for instance to Ricasoli, who in the aftermath of the Syllabus and infallibility remained convinced that he was living in one of those historical periods in which one epoch is in decline while another is taking shape, and whose mind was haunted despite himself by images that derived from the rhetorical excesses of the anticlericals and the free thinkers whom he detested. So it was that, looking out over Rome from the heights of the Janiculum, from which his gaze took in the Vatican, the Quirinal, and the Colosseum, he acknowledged as "perfectly admissible the notion of comparing the ruins of pagan Rome to the ruins of papal Rome. A day will come, though I could not in the least calculate the time of its arrival, when the Vatican will appear to us in a light that, compared to the light in which we view it at present, will lead us to make the same sort of remark concerning it that we make about the other ancient monuments, the soul of which lives on only in memories and in the pages of history."[106] In the end therefore, convinced of the impossibility of the papacy coming to understand the nineteenth century and adapting itself accordingly, convinced of the "hostility of the curate toward civil society,"[107] Ricasoli turned away from his former hope of a universal religious renewal and, for the time being, settled for the hope that Rome would become a center of the human arts and sciences, though he still permitted his imagination to wander freely in the realm of the distant future. Papal Rome had come to an end; the city was now the capital of Italy and nothing more: "but in this aspect it will in fact be much more than it was, and has been, and presently is, because it will be the seat of a nation that lives in liberty and independence, and thus there will still be a sacred flame in Rome: not the one tended by the Vestal virgins, but the sacred flame of civil progress."[108] Unlike the free thinkers, he certainly had no intention of barring the church from the sacred flame of progress, but as things stood he was compelled to admit that "the day on which this beautiful picture of the papacy as a positive element of civil life will be a reality is still far off."[109]

The debacle of the larger hopes of a religious palingenesis put an end to the more concrete and limited projects that were to have constituted the practical commencement of the grander plan. Lambruschini's "precious innovations" in the internal government of the church were not to be. The church was not to know a system of representation, with the bishops elected by the clergy and the people as Rosmini had desired, or by deputies elected in the parishes and the dioceses, according to a plan conceived by Lambruschini, or in any case elected with an element of popular participation rather than being imposed from above, as Cavour himself had agreed to propose (although with considerable hesitation) at the urging of Minghetti.[110] There was to be no active participation of the laity

---

[106] Letter to Naville, 10 March 1874 (Ricasoli, *Lettere e documenti* 10:304–305).

[107] Ricasoli, *Lettere e documenti* 10:299.

[108] Ibid., 10:212.

[109] For his faith in the future revival of the religious sentiment, cf. as well the letter to Bonghi of 27 March 1871, published by Maturi, preface to Bonghi, *Stato e Chiesa* 1:xix–xx.

[110] Minghetti, "the only adviser I have on this matter," according to Cavour (*La questione*

in the life of the church, as many had dreamed that there might be down to the very eve of the Vatican Council.[111]

Such desires for reform did, it is true, produce a few dying echoes in the period after 1870. While the law of Guarantees was under discussion the fear had been openly expressed that, if the state should renounce totally any interference in the life of the church at a moment when the church was increasingly rigidifying itself into an organism dominated from the top, the rights of ordinary practicing Catholics might suffer. Similarly, Bonghi adduced the hypothetical example of a turbulent priest who might be forcibly installed in a rural church, displacing one who was causing no trouble.[112] He was successful in using similar arguments to keep the *exequatur* and the *placet* in force, for he remained firm in his conviction that, transformed by the magic aura of liberty, the pope himself would soon restore to the clergy and people their original rights of election, and the church emend itself spontaneously, without the dire necessity of external coercion. The counterproposal of Peruzzi, backed by Minghetti and Ricasoli, to entrust the administration of the church's property to diocesan and parochial assemblies composed of clerics and laymen, was rejected.[113] Minghetti harked back to the idea in 1875: beginning with the administration of church assets, the laity would have gained participation "in something more, with the passage of time," as in European history the parliaments, which "began by getting hold of the purse strings and went on from there to claim extensive political prerogatives," had done.[114] In plain terms, they would have attained the participation of

---

romana 1:279), had at first proposed an idea of Rosminian origin, the "presentation" of the bishops to the clergy and people (project of 1 February 1861; ibid., 1:254). Cavour, according to Pantaleoni, wanted such matters reserved to the clergy alone (D. Pantaleoni, "Del presente e dell'avvenire del Cattolicismo: A proposito del concilio ecumenico" [Florence, 1969], offprint from the *Nuova Antologia*, December 1869, p. 42). After he had reviewed it, the final wording of the proposal for an agreement was left extremely vague: "the appointment of the bishops will be done through an elective system in a manner to be decided" (*La questione romana* 1:315). However, it results from the *Avvertenze* (ibid., 1:318) that the government aimed to create a system "in which the clergy itself in each diocese will take part in the appointment of the bishop through elections. The exact method would remain to be agreed subsequently." There would be no further intervention by the laity; but the system would be elective. Cf. as well the project of Artom (ibid., 1:308, n. 2 and p. 328).

[111] Cf. Pantaleoni, article cited in the previous note, pp. 42 ff. Also in December 1869, *L'Emancipatore cattolico* of Naples, which, even more than *L'Esaminatore* of Florence, was the organ of the Catholic-reformist groups, published (no. 50, 11 December) a "Memorandum dei cattolici italiani membri della Società Nazionale Emancipatrice e di Mutuo Soccorso del Sacerdozio Italiano in Napoli," by Prota Giorleo. This memorandum, addressed to the bishops gathered in Rome for the Vatican Council, promoted, among other things, a return to the election of bishops by clergy and people, in accordance with the practice of the apostles (p. 6 of the offprint). Such ideas were also floated by a well-known figure in France, Père Hyacinthe (H. Loyson, *Programme de la réforme catholique* [Paris, 1879], pp. 7–8).

[112] "Della libertà della Chiesa," in *La Perseveranza* for 7 January 1871.

[113] Cf. Maturi, preface to Bonghi, *Stato e Chiesa* 1:xv ff.; Falco, *La politica ecclesiastica della Destra*, p. 28, and esp. Falco, *Il riordinamento della proprietà ecclesiastica*, pp. 33 ff. The counterproject of Peruzzi (see esp. articles 27 and 28) is republished in F. Scaduto, *Guarentigie pontificie e relazioni fra Stato e Chiesa*, pp. 257–58.

[114] The idea of keeping control of the temporal institution in order to influence the spiritual institution also guided the men of the government in maintaining the *exequatur*. Cf. the statements of the keeper of the seals, Vigliani, on 4 May 1875, to the Chamber: "we hold the mensal property and will continue to hold it until the bishops who are in office without having been properly appointed

the laity in the government of the church,[115] mixed elections, the triumph of the representative system even within the ecclesiastical polity.[116] All this would have constituted a peaceful revolution, and a conclusive defeat for the reactionary faction, as Serra Gropelli, another strong supporter of the system of parochial and diocesan assemblies of laymen, had observed in 1865.[117] Minghetti, preoccupied as always by the religious problem, mindful of the teaching of Rosmini,[118] and attentive to the Old Catholic movement, as he was to all the symptoms of religious fervor in Europe, wished to salvage whatever possibility remained of bringing about the religious revival for which he hoped—though not with the surging passion of Bettino Ricasoli, and above all without admitting any intervention whatsoever by the political power in the life of the church, for he remained faithful to the principle of absolute separation between church and state.[119]

Those who were indifferent to the prospect of eventual reform from within the Catholic church were nevertheless agreed that it was imperative not simply to let the pope alone, because that would mean leaving him free to maintain his despotic position vis-à-vis clergy and laity. In that case, the lower clergy and the common people would find themselves ground down by the process of papal centralization and by the bishops, and in consequence a law liberal in intention would produce the utterly illiberal result of restoring the "tyranny of the priests over the laity," "the most intolerable of all despotisms."[120] Naturally this was the

---

grow tired and are constrained to make an act of submission and regularize their appointments" (*A.P., Camera*, p. 2901). Lanza saw the situation this way too (Tavallini, *La vita e i tempi di Giovanni Lanza* 2:93 ff).

[115] Minghetti's speech to the Chamber of 7 May 1875 (Minghetti, *Discorsi Parlamentari* 6:551). The same concepts are found in Minghetti, *Stato e Chiesa*, pp. 178–81: to introduce the elective principle in the ecclesiastical structure, and through the administration of property, put the laity in a position to compel the ecclesiastical hierarchy to listen to their claims and also their proposals for reform. Another proponent of the lay administration of the ecclesiastical patrimony, but one who favored a much more direct intrusion of the state into the intimate life of the church (which Minghetti refused), was Piola, *La libertà della Chiesa*, pp. 234 ff. and 247 ff.

[116] In October 1870 Minghetti, who always remained faithful to his ideas of 1861, made this proposal to Visconti Venosta: "I would recommend as well, with regard to the appointment of bishops, that His Majesty the king should declare right now that he is ready to renounce his entire prerogative in this matter, whenever the Holy See shall decide to bring back an elective system. Until that time the appointment of the bishops will be carried out by arrangement between the supreme pontiff and the king. In this case, the king would be the sole representative of the electors" (letter of 4 October). In a later letter of 12 October Minghetti is more precise: "whenever the Holy See decides to bring back the system in which the clergy and the people elect the bishops, His Majesty undertakes etc." (Visconti Venosta archive). This is the system promoted by Rosmini.

[117] E. Serra Gropelli, *Parrocchia e Diocesi: Piano di guerra contro la fazione episcopale* (1864), pp. 21 ff. The same ideas are found in his later publication *Le cinque piaghe del Regno d'Italia* (1870), pp. 59 ff., 69 ff.

[118] On the strong impression produced on the young Minghetti by Rosmini, cf. Minghetti, *Ricordi* 1:81.

[119] Cf. as well a letter of Minghetti to Nigra, 15 September 1872: "As for me, I wish we would move to higher ground and resolve all the questions with a single law separating church and state. But I fear that public opinion is not mature enough for that; what is more, it would require great calm— but the Vatican doesn't miss a chance to stir resentment in people's minds" (Visconti Venosta archive).

[120] Thus Carlo Cadorna, then Italian ambassador to London and later president of the Council of

position of the Left, and especially of Mancini, who was anxious that liberty for the church should not signify the predominance and exclusive power of a particular caste, meaning the higher clergy, and should not lead to a papal dictatorship, to "an autocratic concentration of power in the hands of the pope, such as has never yet been equaled in the history of the church." Mancini supported the free election of the bishops by the clergy and people, or at the very least the nomination of three candidates to a shortlist for the post in a free vote to be held in each cathedral chapter.[121]

In the law of Guarantees the *exequatur* and the *placet* were retained, but there was no mention of diocesan and parochial assemblies; only section 2, article 18 left open the possibility, which was never followed up, of a subsequent reform of the administration of church property which might have led to the realization of Peruzzi's project. Within a few years the problem was to be raised one last time in several small parishes in the region of Mantua, where it was given a radical solution: but this was to be the last flicker, before the flame died down for good.

The reason it died is to be sought in the strict intransigence of the Holy See toward the Italian state, which it saw as the usurper of its temporal power, and also, in fact principally, as the secular state that inherited the laws of Siccardi and perpetuated the hated ecclesiastical legislation passed in Piedmont in the period after 1850;[122] thus the political and national question, and the question of the relations between church and state, were closely intertwined, with the second

---

State, in a letter to Visconti Venosta of 16 February 1871 (Visconti Venosta archive). Cadorna denies the validity of the principle underlying the law of Guarantees, "that the priests alone are the church; and that the hierarchical church (meaning the priests) is *a power* in relation to the state." For him the church is the priests and the laity. The law of Guarantees, since it maintains the corporations associated with ecclesiastical benefices, and numerous other ecclesiastical institutions having a basis in civil law, takes from the laity its liberty where the temporal goods of the church are concerned. "Giving complete liberty to the priests, and leaving in place an arrangement that takes away liberty from all the other citizens, is one of the ways in which the state is still involving itself in religious affairs." Instead all the temporal goods of the church ought to be entrusted to elective assemblies at the diocesan and parochial levels. Cadorna later sought to give these ideas firmer shape in 1887, in his project for dealing with the church property taken over by the state (Scaduto, *Guarentigie pontificie*, pp. 602 ff.; Falco, *Il riordinamento*, pp. 36 ff.).

[121] In his speech to the Chamber of 13 March 1871 (Mancini, *Discorsi Parlamentari* 3, esp. pp. 644 ff.). Cf. as well the speech of 28 January, ibid., 3:462 ff., and that of 3 May 1875, ibid., 5:39. Article 19 of Mancini's counterproposal is in Scaduto, *Guarentigie pontificie*, p. 255. Crispi too hammers at the same point in his speech of 13 March 1871: what the government proposes is not liberty for the church but a despotism of the church's head (Crispi, *Discorsi Parlamentari* 2:115 ff.).

[122] Cf. the thesis of A. Binchy, *Church and State in Fascist Italy* (Oxford, 1941), pp. 19 ff., who insists on just this conjunction of religious and political questions; cf. also G. Salvemini and G. La Piana, "Chiesa e Stato nell'Italia del dopoguerra," *Nuovi quaderni di Giustizia e Libertà* 2–3 (July–October 1944), pp. 43–44. And this view certainly contains a large measure of truth, but it has to be rounded out in the sense that Piedmont had "had to" embark on the passage of ecclesiastical legislation. The abandonment by the Holy See of a pro-national policy after 1848, and its return to close ties with Austria and the absolutist states of the peninsula, forced the Italian liberals to adopt an anticlerical policy in the only state in which they were dominant, Piedmont, whereas before 1848 Piedmont had preoccupied them because of its very clericalism. Thus ecclesiastical policy was inseparable from Italian and liberal policy: cf. G. Salvemini, "L'Italia politica nel secolo XIX," in *L'Europa nel secolo XIX*, p. 356, but esp. the very fine pages of Jemolo, *Chiesa e Stato in Italia*, pp. 182 ff., who has illuminated the issue perfectly. Of course in the subsequent period the Roman curia took an even more rigidly hostile attitude, and antagonism became fiercer.

making the resolution of the first much more difficult.[123] This harsh attitude resulted in a drive to insert trusted and intransigent individuals into the ecclesiastical hierarchy at the higher and lower levels. If the priest was a good patriot, if the curate was a loyal citizen, they would have to be removed and their places taken by bishops and priests who were turned in on their own world, hostile to the civil hierarchy, and ready to spread propaganda against the state rather than for it.[124]

The tone of Italian life had undergone a major shift between mid-century and the later decades. Then there had been a considerable number of priests, especially in the northern and central regions, who were outspokenly patriotic and gave a lot of support to the national movement; some had even accepted martyrdom in the name of liberty and Italian nationality. But now such clerics were altogether exceptional and it was a notable thing to encounter men in holy orders who openly professed their civic and patriotic spirit, a padre Tosti who did not abandon the enthusiasms of 1846 and 1847, or a new adherent like Bonomelli. In that earlier phase Cavour, albeit with heightened rhetorical emphasis for tactical reasons,[125] had declared that he saw the distinctive character of the Risorgimento, in comparison to the English, French, and Spanish revolutions, in the support and cooperation that were given to it by the great majority of the clergy, "sincerely religious and frank in their allegiance to liberty."[126] In the enemy camp, Radetzky had warned his military commanders to make sure that the Austrian soldiers turned to their regimental chaplains for the performance of their duties as good Catholics, and not in any case to Italian priests, almost all of whom were "among the most declared and dangerous enemies" of Austria.[127] And the seminary students of Milan and Monza had immediately asked to be allowed to fight against the Austrians, because the place of the cross was on the battlefield; and fight they did.[128]

---

[123] There is proof of this also in the meeting between Cardinal Antonelli and Blanc, the general secretary of the foreign ministry, on 7 October 1870. To Blanc's assurances concerning postal and telegraphic communications between the pontiff and the Catholic world, Antonelli replied that he had confidence in the present ministers of the king, but that there was no guarantee of continuity; and, moving the discussion to a more general theme, he added: "In the Statuto . . . it is also established that the Catholic religion is the religion of the state, and yet we see the condition to which the church in Italy is reduced, and we know too the further steps that are in preparation in Rome. . . . It would be better if the church were separated from the state, as in Belgium and elsewhere; then everyone would have to attend to his own affairs; but you continue to impede appointments to the episcopal sees, you hinder the exercise of the ecclesiastical authority" (Blanc, report, 7 October 1870, *Libro Verde*, riservato, *Roma*, cited above n. 17, no. 10, pp. 17–18). For the background cf. also the meeting between Pius IX and Minghetti on 20 July 1857, in which Pius IX already foreshadows Antonelli's position in 1870 (Minghetti, *Ricordi* 3:179).

[124] Oriani had reason to describe don Giovanni Verità as "the last revolutionary priest" (*Fino a Dogali*, p. 2).

[125] Cavour himself says so in a letter to Matilde de la Rive of 13 February 1848, ten days, that is, after having composed his article for *Il Risorgimento* (following note): "I am treating the clergy with much consideration . . . ; if it turned to radicalism, we would be lost. If it stays with us, we have nothing to fear. But while treating it with consideration, I do not blind myself where it is concerned, and I keep close watch on all of its movements" (Cavour, *Lettere* 5:172).

[126] In the celebrated article published in *Il Risorgimento* for 4 February 1848.

[127] A. Luzio, *La Massoneria e il Risorgimento italiano* 1:273; and cf. Luzio, *I Martiri di Belfiore e il loro processo*, pp. 191 ff.

[128] Cf. A. Marazza, *Il clero lombardo nella Rivoluzione del '48* (Milan, 1948), pp. 68 ff.

But the oration of Pius IX and the vanishing of the myth of neo-Guelphism had inflicted decisive reversals on the optimism of the first months of 1848. Later, with the laws of Siccardi, the subsequent legislation of Castelfidardo on ecclesiastical matters, and now finally the action of 20 September, that earlier optimism and collaboration had simply disappeared from the scene. Only memories remained of the time when priests published declarations in favor of the independence and liberty of their Italian homeland[129] and padre Passaglia succeeded in gathering nine thousand signatures of members of the clergy begging Pius IX to ordain a state of peace between Italy and the papacy, between Rome the metropolis of the new kingdom and Christian Rome.[130]

Now recruitment to the ecclesiastical hierarchy took place from among individuals of a quite different type. The shift was felt in the first place at the level of the bishops, most of whom were nominated directly by the Holy See after the law of Guarantees, in every case from the extreme wing of the "black" faction.[131] The bishops for their part exerted strong pressure on the lower clergy, banishing ecclesiastics who were suspected of patriotism and liberalism, no matter how attached to them the local population might be, and installing reliable men in their places, regardless of whether or not they were acceptable to the parishioners. A new generation of fanatical young priests was bred in this way, declared enemies of the Italian government who busied themselves with great zeal "in introducing and spreading modern practices of devotion, in the belief that in doing so they are aiding the resurgence and the longed-for triumph of the Roman Catholic Church in the most effective way, and hastening the confusion and destruction of modern impiety."[132] Older clergy of the kind that either collaborated

---

[129] Cf. for example the "Dichiarazione del clero italiano" published by the journal *L'Amico* of Genoa in 1860, in which 568 priests of Genoa and Liguria, Emilia, Tuscany, and Lombardy, with a few from Piedmont, address Vittorio Emanuele II proclaiming "that they as Italian citizens love their country and wish for its external independence and the internal liberty that is assured by the Statuto that governs us: that in their role as priests they disapprove of those who, claiming to speak for the clergy, maintain theories or express desires contrary to Italian nationality, either invoking or justifying foreign oppression, or showing an exclusive preference for absolutist governments."

[130] *Petizione di novemila sacerdoti italiani a S. S. Pio Papa IX ed ai Vescovi Cattolici con esso uniti* (Turin, 1862). The signatures gathered were 8,943; others were announced, which would have made the number rise to 10,000. Passaglia's address, certainly orthodox, was against the temporal power ("deserving of suppression" it was called by Mollat, *La questione romaine de Pie VI à Pie IX* [Paris, 1932], p. 340); cf. Passaglia's preface to the *Petizione*, pp. 11–12, 15–16, 17 ff; and the address itself, urging the pope to announce a reconciliation between the expression "of religion, of Catholic piety: *Viva il Papa*" and the expression "of patriotism and . . . of national independence, *Viva Roma Metropoli del nuovo Regno.*"

[131] Between May 1871 and May 1875, 135 bishops and 15 coadjutor bishops with the right of succession were nominated by the Holy See: of these, only 94 requested the *exequatur*, of which the government conceded 28 and denied 65, with one still under examination on 7 May 1875 (Minghetti, speech to the Chamber, 7 May 1865, *Discorsi Parlamentari* 6:546. And cf. as well Mancini's speech of 3 May, *Discorsi Parlamentari* 5:41).

[132] See the portrait of the rural clergy of upper Lombardy drawn by E. Ferrario, *Qual'è la moralità de' campagnuoli e come possa migliorarsi*, pp. 62 ff. This work won the "Fondazione Ciani" competition held by the Istituto Lombardo di Scienze e Lettere, the judges for which were Cantù, Cantoni, and Piola. The name of Cantù by itself is enough to guarantee that Ferrario was not culpable of anticlerical tendencies, and that his description must have been well anchored in reality. Ferrario indeed hopes for an accord between church and state, since he subscribes to the conviction of Lambruschini that the moral improvement of the peasants must be brought about principally through the work of the clergy.

with the state or were not radically hostile to it were supplanted, as Guerrieri Gonzaga noted, by the "neophytes of Jesuitism," a clergy that lived in complete segregation from civil society.[133] The era that had witnessed collaboration between the Catholic clergy and Italian patriotism ended; now there was punishment for priests who gave blessing to the Italian armed forces; retractions were demanded from, and the last comforts of religion refused to, accomplices of "the usurpation;"[134] for a time entry into the churches was barred to the tricolor flag borne by the workers' societies.[135]

No doubt there were still priests who in their hearts remained patriotic, having come to maturity in the hopeful climate of the Risorgimento, and would even have welcomed the chance to acknowledge the fact. But how were they to do so in the face of the ongoing severe pressure exerted on them by the bishops, and vice versa the indifference of the government, which stuck firmly to its policy of not getting involved in the affairs of the church? Even worse was the indifference, or hostility, manifested by a considerable number of liberal patriots, who were convinced by this time that the clergy were the enemy and were actively working against Italy. The two conflicting attitudes simply reinforced each other: the stiffening of the Roman curia and the upper reaches of the ecclesiastical hierarchy on the one hand, and the hardening of anticlerical convictions in a large section of public opinion on the other. The sort of priest who had played a role in the events of 1848 became a rarity. Antireligiosity grew, with Freemasonry regaining power and prestige in Italy and in France, where, in a similar process, the ideas of Lamennais receded into memory while the reactionary ultramontanism of men such as Veuillot triumphed, and those who opposed it in the name of liberty were now the radicals, a party that brought to the struggle an anticlerical thrust foreign to the liberals of the July monarchy. In Italy the lower clergy, or at least that part of it that still felt some impulse to resist, sensed its own isolation, under pressure from the upper levels of its own hierarchy but lacking support from the population. It breathed an atmosphere heavy with dismay, as the theologian Clemente Tacchini, a Rosminian, noted; "a target of disdain and mistrust on every side," the humble priest saw an abyss opening up beneath his feet while overhead were heard the voices of his own superiors and the politicians "contending for power and wealth. And while he seeks in astonishment for the causes of this raging contest, the abject fellow feels the blows they are aiming at one another falling on him instead, so thick and heavy that he

---

[133] Guerrieri Gonzaga, "Cenni sulla tregua accordata al Vaticano," a preface to the Italian translation (Rome, 1876) of E. De Laveleye, *L'avvenire dei popoli cattolici*, p. 11; and cf. as well the speech of the hon. Tommasi Crudeli on 5 May 1875, *A.P., Camera*, p. 2934.

[134] The parish priest of Santa Maria del Carmine at Porta Portese, don Nicola Cafiero, was suspended *a divinis* for having celebrated a mass for new military recruits at Easter 1871 (Pesci, *I primi anni di Roma capitale*, p. 504). Funeral rites, and even burial in the Camposanto of Messina, were refused to the hon. Giuseppe Natoli, a former cabinet minister, for having refused to retract his actions as minister and legislator. Funeral rites and burial were likewise denied to the hon. Gaetano Caruso, who had also resisted pressure to make a retraction (Mancini, speech to the Chamber, 3 May 1875; *Discorsi Parlamentari* 5:58–59).

[135] A bishop nominated following the law of Guarantees, a pious and charitable individual but a "blind tool of the Jesuits" according to Sella (*Epistolario inedito*, p. 275), did this initially at Biella.

stands there bruised and naked, an object of scorn for the people, as though he himself were responsible for causing this horrendous battle."[136] "If the parish priest used to have one leg tied and the other partly free," wrote a country priest, "now he will have both legs bound."[137]

How could one demand that the minor clergy show resistance, much less revolt against the bishops on its own, without any support, Serra Gropelli had exclaimed in 1864.[138] How could a poor priest be expected to display patriotism when at any moment he might be thrown out on the street by his superiors, when the government and the country had demonstrated such indifference for the liberal clergy?[139] No priest dares to utter words of calm and peace any more, it was observed, for the omnipotence of the pope and the bishops on one side and the indifference of the laity on the other, combine to impose silence.[140] Many ecclesiastics who had been favorable to Italy and its government in the past, said Bishop Strossmayer, are now turning against the government, since "they see that by the law of Guarantees every church matter, including even their own futures and material interests, is being handed over to the absolute power of the pope and the bishops."[141]

A few years later, having concluded an inquiry based on a questionnaire that had produced more than four hundred responses, Leone Carpi summed up the condition of the lower clergy. In his view it was irresistibly bound, willingly or not, to the policies of the Vatican, since it found itself neglected and abandoned by the government, and opposed by the liberals; in most parts of Italy the priests were poor, prey to material hardship and to cruel moral torment. Only the most intolerant individuals were chosen to fill bishoprics and parishes, even if that meant passing over men of the cloth who were learned and morally exemplary, and the episcopate used an iron fist in constraining the lower clergy to carry out rigorously the instructions given by the Roman curia. How, given this situation, could anyone expect to find any love for liberal institutions among the impoverished clergy in the parishes? The lower clergy was being made the sacrificial goat for the high-handedness of the Vatican and the claims of the state, and there was no reason to be surprised if it was now drifting away from the patriotism it

---

[136] C. Tacchini, *La voce del sacerdote italiano sopra gli avvenimenti politico-religiosi compiuti nel 1870* (Rome, 1871), p. xi. On the reaction against the clergy after 1860, cf. also V. Gorresio, "Il processo al clero dopo il '60," in *Il Mondo*, 30 April–28 May 1949.

[137] In P. Mongini, *Il nuovo Sinodo di monsignor Gastaldi arcivescovo di Torino indetto per i giorni 25, 26, e 27 giugno 1873 e le libertà del clero* (Turin, 1873), p. 24, and cf. also p. 35. Mongini, formerly a parish priest, who had latterly been excommunicated (cf. Jacini, *Il tramonto del potere temporale*, p. 73), was a follower of Passaglia. He fought for the rights of the laity in the church, not only in the case of elections but also in synods, at which he believed the laity ought to participate.

[138] Serra Gropelli, *Parrocchia e Diocesi*, p. 47.

[139] Italicus, *Le condizioni presenti ed il prossimo avvenire della Chiesa* (Rome, 1874; an offprint from the paper *Libertà*, January–February 1874), p. 31. The author maintains that for these reasons the accusation of antipatriotism made against the clergy is largely unjust. The remedy is the usual one: the reform of the church, with the laity summoned to participate in its government (pp. 75 ff.).

[140] "Il clero e l'inondazione di Roma," in *La Perseveranza* for 4 January 1871.

[141] Strossmayer, memorandum for Minghetti, 20 January 1872, cited above n. 46.

had shown in the wars of independence to a degree equal to that of the laity, in most of Italy.[142]

This naturally meant triumph for the "ultras," the Catholics who hoped to see Italy punished by the ultramontane legitimists and clericals, French and Spanish, Henri V and Don Carlos. It meant triumph for the reactionaries, who were ready to see general devastation if it meant that the old regimes could be rebuilt out of the ruins of Italy.

> Then I beheld
> An assembly of the retrograde
> Swelling in ecstasy
> In rapture
> Dreaming of the approach
> The imminence
> Of a catastrophe
> An incident,
> In which the devil
> Will send home to their old places
> All the rascals
> Of the peninsula.[143]

Patriotic priests were forced to keep silent, and a whole section of the clergy, animated by civic spirit and love of country, but without great energy, disillusioned, disoriented, and anxious to dodge the impact of either side, put their faith in providence without perhaps doing all they might have to deserve its help.

---

[142] L. Carpi, *L'incameramento dei beni parrochiali, l'esercizio delle ferrovie dello Stato e l'ammortamento del corso forzoso* (Rome, 1877), pp. 51 ff., 55, 58, 73, 79. This study had been published in *Il Popolo Romano*, the organ by this time of Depretis. Cf. also Mazzoleni, *L'XI Legislatura*, p. 144, portraying the impoverished lower clergy as reduced to extreme indigence. And note how as early as 1861 Pantaleoni, who had been sent on a mission to Naples by Minghetti, pointed out that it was necessary to win over the lower clergy and blamed the government, even at this early date, for its policy of inertia (F. Della Paruta, "Contributo alla storia della questione meridionale: Cinque lettere inedite di Diomede Pantaleoni (1861)," in *Società* 6 [1950]: 79 and 89).

[143]

> Poi di retrogradi
> vidi un concilio
> che vanno in estasi
> in visibilio
> Sognando prossima,
> anzi imminente
> una catastrofe
> un incidente,
> Che a casa il diavolo
> manderà tutti
> della Peninsola
> i farabutti.

These are the verses of a priest, don Guido Piccardi, chaplain of Cavriglia in Valdarno Superiore, an antireactionary in whom the spirit of the patriotic and anti-abstensionist clergy of the Risorgimento lived on ("Un viaggetto a Roma uscente il novembre 1876," in *Le astensioni politiche dei 5 e 12 novembre 1876 celebrate in prosa ed in versi*, p. 64).

This abandonment of the lower clergy gave grounds, then and later, for severe criticism of the ecclesiastical policies of the Right, criticism to the effect that the lower clergy was a part of the common people too, which the senior levels of the church had been allowed to enslave because of the government's culpable neglect of "the first duty of any Italian statesman." Instead it had strengthened, "with false and specious theories about liberty," the arms of papal tyranny and the Jesuits' campaign of antinational sedition and propaganda. If any blame attached to the actions of the government since 1870, or really since the death of Cavour, it was this.[144]

By leaving to its own devices the very clergy that deserved its greatest solicitude, the clergy that was not factious, that was driven by civic spirit, the government had achieved a notable result: now even priests whose patriotism had held out against the counsel of the reactionaries were at length going over to the other side in droves, frightened and hurt by their undeserved abandonment. At this rate the gradual disappearance within a few years of the present generation of priests would mean that the memory of the common experience of suffering and the joy of priesthood and laity when they had struggled together to win a country of their own would be lost.[145]

Correspondingly, the voice of liberal lay Catholicism grew very faint, as it was branded a reprehensible sink of iniquity by the Vatican clergy.[146] In consequence the generous impulses and the religious fervor that had so enriched the liberal Catholic conscience of the first half of the nineteenth century were absent in its closing decades, and all the running was made by the reactionaries on the right, whose tactic was to create "a frightful image of the *liberal Catholic* as something worse than a heretic, or a Turk, or the devil, and then apply this etiquette with marvelous facility to anyone who dares to think differently from them. The offshoot is that every Christian who has the slightest reputation to lose prefers to evade such a label, and the wave of confusion and sometimes scandal it brings, by keeping quiet, while the *reactionaries* take advantage of this silence to endow their own fantasy with the force of *Catholic sentiment*."[147] These were the regret-

---

[144] Speech of Sidney Sonnino in the Chamber, 30 March 1881 (Sonnino, *Discorsi Parlamentari* 1:33). Cf. a not dissimilar judgment in Zanichelli, *Monarchia e Papato in Italia*, p. 200.

[145] Thus the hon. Tommasi Crudeli to the Chamber, 5 May 1875 (*A.P., Camera*, p. 2934). Given that Tommasi Crudeli was one of the most resolute opponents of the policy of the Vatican, his statements about the patriotism of the older clergy are significant.

[146] Pius IX uttered harsh words against the liberal Catholics (referring to Döllinger also) when he received the ambassador of France, d'Harcourt, on 19 June 1871, and also at a reception on 3 July for 2,500 former pontifical employees, declaring that the representatives of the *juste-milieu* were the worst of all (Harcourt, reports of 21 June and 5 July, nos. 21 and 25; AEP, *C.P., Rome*, t. 1051, fol. 174v and t. 1052, fol. 14v). In order to combat the liberal Catholics, an appeal was also made to the "greatness" of the nation, exploiting themes that were themselves quasi-nationalistic: thus on 15 October 1874 *L'Osservatore Romano* deplored the withdrawal of the *Orénoque* from Civitavecchia, an event that demonstrated, it said, "how in liberal Catholicism the spirit of dignity and national independence is lower than it is in Voltaireanism, or even in demagogy; and it shows how these two are more capable of protecting the greatness and honor of the nation than liberal Catholicism is."

[147] Thus don Guido Piccardi (in *Le astensioni politiche dei 5 e 12 novembre 1876*, pp. 37–38). The last target of a campaign of this kind against the "liberal Catholic" had been Eugenio Albéri, at Florence. The abbot Arrò Carroccio, *Il cattolicismo ed il liberalismo*, p. 13, notes (in 1872) that "the

ful words of a priest, and they were answered from the extreme right by the voice of another priest, a Lombard now rather than a Tuscan, who believed passionately in the battle against liberalism and the Italian government, and exulted in the death of liberal Catholicism,[148] just as the participants in the Catholic congress of Florence of September 1875 exuberantly acclaimed the severe declaration of Pius IX against the false brethren, meaning the liberal Catholics who were coming to terms with error.[149]

We may take the case of Mantua, the native soil of don Tazzoli, a diocese which until 1868 had been guided by a liberal Catholic, Monsignor Corti, who was made a senator of the kingdom of Italy,[150] and after that, in the quality of capitular vicar, by Monsignor Luigi Martini. The latter, well known to belong to the ranks of the liberal and patriotic priesthood, had been the "angelic" comforter of the martyrs of Belfiore (among them Pier Fortunato Calvi),[151] and was hated by the Roman curia precisely on account of his *Confortatorio*. As soon as the Italian state had left the field of action clear by refusing to assume the duty of nominating Italian bishops, the Holy See had moved to install a totally intransigent one, Monsignor Rota, formerly of Guastalla, in Mantua. As in other cases, the task of the new prelate of Mantua was to rule with iron authority in a diocese badly infected with liberal and national sentiment, and to teach a good lesson to the mischief makers. The predicament of a reactionary bishop surrounded by liberal clergy seemed an odd one to an American visitor, William Chauncy Langdon.[152] But the contrast did not last for long because, in the absence of *exequatur*, and after having been convicted on 2 May 1874 by the Court of Assizes

---

label of liberal Catholic, which many . . . used to fling as an insult at their political adversaries, is by now dead and buried." As a lover of liberty he does not view this outcome with disfavor, because for him religion has to maintain itself above political parties and trends, and therefore can be neither liberal nor illiberal, monarchical nor republican. We might say that he represents the opinion of the center, while Piccardi belongs to the Catholic left, and Nicora to the right.

[148] Don Luigi Nicora, *Sull'intervento del clero nella politica* (Milan, 1873; an offprint from the periodical *La Scuola Cattolica*, ed. Monsignor Parocchi, the bishop of Pavia), pp. 16 ff. and 40. Nicora, who later became bishop of Como, still stood for a line of complete intransigence at the Catholic congress of Bergamo in 1877: at the local elections there were to be no pacts with liberals, whether they were progressives, moderates, or liberal Catholics (F. Olgiati, *La storia dell'azione cattolica in Italia (1865–1904)* [Milan, 1922], p. 91).

[149] Noted by the French chargé d'affaires, Tiby (report, 6 October 1875, no. 85; AEP, *C.P., Italie*, t. 393, fol. 148v).

[150] Named to the senate on 5 November 1899, Monsignor Giovanni Corti was one of the three bishops to be so enrolled after the Siccardi laws (cf. *I Senatori del Regno: Nomina-convalidazione . . . etc.*, edited by the general secretariat of the Senate [Rome, 1935], vol. 1, p. 82).

[151] Cf. Luzio, *I Martiri di Belfiore*, pp. 246, 280, 292, 450 ff., and passim (pp. 196–206 on Corti); and Luzio, *Profili biografici* 2:393 ff. And see, by Martini himself, *Il Confortatorio di Mantova negli anni 1851, 52, 53 and 55*, published at Mantua in 1870, in the prologue to which he states: "I too confess to being an Italian, but at the same time I confess to being Catholic, to holding it my glory to profess the faith of the Catholic church," just as the martyrs were sincerely Catholic and sincerely Italian, Catholics and liberals at the same time, friends of Italy without being enemies of the church (vol. 2, p. 331). On the help given to Calvi see vol. 2, pp. 287 ff., and further *Memorie politiche di Felice Orsini*, ed. Ghisalberti (Rome, 1946), p. 269.

[152] On the situation in the dioceses of Mantua and Pavia after 1870, and the hunt for liberal priests conducted by the bishops, cf. the speech of Anselmo Guerrieri Gonzaga to the Chamber, 5 May 1875 (*A.P., Camera*, p. 2940). And further, Ruffini, cited below, n. 155.

of Mantua of an abuse in the exercise of his functions for having read a homily to the faithful in the cathedral at Epiphany in 1873 in which he censured the law that annexed Rome to the kingdom of Italy,[153] the intransigent bishop began to remove ecclesiastics whom he suspected, even when they were beloved by their flocks, and to replace them with men he trusted, whether the parishioners liked it or not.

This occurred in the parish of S. Giovanni del Dosso, where the vicar, don Lonardi, was well liked by the local population; Monsignor Rota nominated a priest to replace him who was not, and did the same again in the parish of Frassine, where his nominee was equally disliked by the parishioners. The response of the faithful was prompt and unhesitating: they held a perfectly calm and procedurally correct public meeting in the presence of a notary and elected their own parish priests, with don Lonardi being chosen for S. Giovanni del Dosso.[154] That was in the autumn of 1873. On 14 January 1874 at Palidano, where the elderly don Carlo Pavesi, a good priest and a good citizen who had always been devoted to Italy, had died, the parishioners followed the example and elected, solemnly and formally, a new priest, in defiance of the wishes of Monsignor Rota.[155]

Their cause was taken up by Carlo Guerrieri Gonzaga, who in 1848 had been a militant Garibaldian in the Medici company alongside Visconti Venosta, and who had then like Visconti Venosta turned resolutely away, with his brother Anselmo, from the Mazzinian faith and become a follower of Cavour. He was another example of the rural nobleman dedicated to improving his fields and rationalizing the practice of agriculture, and also to raising the living conditions of his peasants to a higher level, but at the same time preoccupied with the problem of religion, with raising the moral level of the people. Hence Guerrieri Gonzaga was a parliamentary supporter of the governing ministry on financial questions, but agreed with the opposition on the ecclesiastical problem, since the government of the moderates seemed to him in this respect to have failed and to continue to fail to meet the standards of decorum, dignity, and moral duty to which the state was obligated;[156] he was the Bettino Ricasoli of the province of

---

[153] Cf. A. Caucino, "I frutti della legge sulle Guarentigie," in *L'Unità Cattolica*, 23 July–4 August 1876, pp. 19–20 in the offprint.

[154] At S. Giovanni del Dosso the number of voters was 207, at Frassine 203.

[155] On these events cf. C. Guerrieri Gonzaga, *I parroci eletti e la questione ecclesiastica* and his articles in *Il Diritto* for 30 June and 15 August 1875; *L'Opinione* for 3 December 1873 ("I Parrocchiani di Frassine"); *La Perseveranza* for 7 December 1873 ("I parroci popolarmente eletti"); the debate in the Chamber of Deputies on 4 December 1873 (*A.P., Camera*, pp. 290 ff.); and the continuation of the discussion on 1, 4, 5, 6, 7 May 1875 (ibid., pp. 2834, 2842, 2906, 2940, 2994, 3013), esp. the speech in which Mancini also alludes to similar elections in several parishes in Sicily and other regions (Mancini, *Discorsi Parlamentari* 5:61 ff.); Scaduto, *Guarentigie pontificie*, pp. 450 n. and 452 ff.; Ruffini, "L'elezione popolare dei parroci," in *Scritti giuridici minori* 1:337 ff.; A. Della Torre, "Il cristianesimo in Italia dai filosofisti ai modernisti," an appendix to the translation of S. Reinach, *Orpheus* 2:874 ff. (Palermo, 1912).

[156] Cf. Luzio's preface to C. Guerrieri Gonzaga, "Memorie e lettere di Carlo Guerrieri Gonzaga," in *Rassegna Storica del Risorgimento* 2 (January–February 1915): 3 ff. in the offprint (also in his *Profili biografici* 2:473 ff.); and the statements of Guerrieri Gonzaga himself in *I parroci eletti*, pp. 6 ff., 61 ff., 70.

Mantua. Guerrieri Gonzaga addressed a parliamentary question to the government and did everything possible to aid a movement which he personally had not brought into being but in which he saw a hopeful promise for the future of Italy, since it meant a reawakening of the will of the laity in religious matters. Lonardi and his parishioners, who had been haled into court by the bishop's allies, found the great official champion of liberty of conscience, P. S. Mancini, coming to their defense as well; and Vigliani, the Keeper of the Seals [minister of justice], expressed his personal satisfaction in the chamber for this revival of honest religious feeling, which might be the occasion "of a great effect from a small cause," and a sign that the epoch was not far distant in which it would become possible to entrust the temporal business of the church to the people, impel the clergy into contact with the laity and force it to deal with them, constrain it to become a national institution and so finally attain a state of peace between civil society and religious society. Even Gladstone, who in 1871 had expressed his preoccupation for the excessive room given to the bishops by the law of Guarantees,[157] and now that he was no longer the prime minister of Her Britannic Majesty was free to indulge his predilection for pondering religious problems, took the matter up; he expressed his cordial sympathy for those "poor courageous peasants," for their resistance to the "system of despotism, deriving from the court of Rome, which is imposed on the clergy of Italy and which is waging war to the death on liberty in all its aspects."[158] From Germany there naturally arrived the voice of the combative Treitschke in support of Guerrieri Gonzaga.[159]

But the flame sputtered and died, even though the court of Mantua in the first place, and then the appeal court at Brescia, found for don Lonardi in the case brought against him and his deputy, don Seleuco Coelli, by forty-seven peasants who were dependents of two large landholders, representatives of orthodox Catholicism.[160] Not all the liberals supported the action of Guerrieri Gonzaga, though he had the sympathy of Bonghi, who was forcefully reminded of his own Rosminian roots.[161] Dina had, unofficially, serious reservations about following

---

[157] Cadorna, personal letter to Visconti Venosta, 16 February 1871, cited above, n. 120.

[158] Gladstone, *L'Italia e la sua Chiesa* (Italian translation: Rome, 1875), pp. 39 ff. Other examples of the popular election of parish priests are the following: at Pignano, near Cividale in summer 1875 (ibid., pp. 44–45); at Ricaldone (in the province of Acqui) in 1879, on which see F. Battaglia, "Lettere di Angelo Camillo De Meis a Donato Jaia," *Memorie dell'Accademia delle Scienze di Bologna*, 4th ser., 9 (1950): 128; and on the election there and at San Quirino (near Udine), also in 1879, see Della Torre,"Il cristianesimo in Italia," p. 927.

[159] Treitschke, "Libera Chiesa in libero Stato," pp. 238–39.

[160] The court's judgment recognized the right of the parishioners to hold a meeting and elect their pastor, just as the minority could also choose the priest it wanted; and it rejected the request of the plaintiffs that Lonardi should be prohibited from performing any spiritual functions in the parish (in *Il Diritto* for 5 July 1875). The only person in a position to do so would be the bishop of Mantua: but Monsignor Rota, who lacked the *exequatur*, was not the bishop of Mantua for the purposes of the civil law (cf. also Caucino, "I frutti della legge sulle Guarentigie," pp. 14 ff.).

[161] In addition to the article in *La Perseveranza* cited in n. 155 above, cf. as well, in order fully to grasp Bonghi's thought, his preceding speech to the Chamber on 29 April 1872 (*Discorsi Parlamentari* 1:387). His view is that there will be no internal movement in the church until the benefice and the fabric are replaced by associations of church members in the parishes and the dioceses as the juridical personalities holding ecclesiastical property. "Today the citizens have no rights except to leave the church naked, to be driven out, without the state doing anything more to defend them, or they themselves having any way to defend their rights."

a course of action that might bring back to life one of the hated memories of French Jacobinism, the civil constitution of the clergy, and thus break with the moderate policies followed to that point.[162] And in the end the government, which had no desire to change its political parameters, did indeed adopt the role of Pontius Pilate; more than that, it was substantially hostile, since it quite correctly saw very little possibility of a widespread movement developing along the lines of what was taking place in the province of Mantua.[163] The prefect of Mantua first enjoined the editor of the *Gazzetta di Mantova*, Cognetti De Martiis, who was taking the side of the parishioners, to cease doing so, and to let drop this "unthinkingly raised question." He also gave a warning to the mayor of Gonzaga, who was guilty of having made a speech at a banquet in honor of the priest elected at Palidano. As for Vigliani, having expressed his warm personal endorsement of this reawakening of the religious conscience, he changed his tune as Keeper of the Seals, stating that the government could only take negative action against members of the clergy who were opposed to the Italian state, but that it had no capacity to recognize those elected by the people and could offer only temporary financial assistance, except in cases in which the priest had already been invested with the office of spiritual steward of the parish.

As for the notion of imposing the principle of popular election from outside, Guerrieri Gonzaga himself, who defended the election of priests in cases where the people had decided that that was what they wished, was against any such idea.[164] To recognize parish priests where they had been elected—that was a far cry from using the power of the state to intrude into the life of the church, in defiance of the ecclesiastical hierarchy. Even those, like Minghetti, who had looked forward to the popular election of the clergy and the administration of church property by mixed assemblies, would have seen this as a mortal offense to the principle of liberty. Popular elections were a very good thing, a highly desirable reform, as long as the faithful expressed a desire for them in a spontaneous,

---

[162] A few of the major jurisconsults of Italy, such as Cassani and Padelletti, also expressed their doubts and reservations.

[163] Minghetti's statement to the Chamber on 7 May 1875: "I hope that the religious sentiment will reawaken in my country, and that what has occurred in one or two parishes will also take place, out of true and profound conviction in many cities. But as long as the affair is restricted to such small-scale manifestations I cannot believe that that tiny spark will produce a large flame. In any case . . . even if there are those who, observing the religious sentiment reawaken, desire to see it continue and assume the forms to which the hon. Guerrieri Gonzaga alluded, I nevertheless believe that the government ought to abstain completely from interfering in such matters. The state . . . [ought] never to come forward as the proponent and instigator of religious reforms" (*Discorsi Parlamentari* 6:556). Cf. too Artom's letter to von Treitschke in 1875, on the law of Guarantees, in E. Artom, *L'opera politica* 1:199: he holds no illusions about the "microscopic proportions" of the movement in Mantua. Similarly Pansa, then a young functionary at the foreign ministry, noted in his *Diario*: "it seems to me that the importance of the Mantua movement is exaggerated" (under the date 6 November 1875).

[164] He believed it was necessary to be very cautious about confronting the pitfalls and perils that would accompany a general disturbance in the ecclesiastical structure. The bishops and priests ought to be forced to respect the civil and political constitution of the kingdom through special laws; ecclesiastical abuses ought to be halted; the clergy should be educated in state schools; in sum, the revitalization of the religious sensibility should be promoted in Italy, and the internal reform of the church would follow from that: but nothing should be imposed from outside. For this reason he was against the setting up of assemblies of the laity to control ecclesiastical property (Guerrieri Gonzaga, "Cenni sulla tregua accordata al Vaticano," pp. 15 ff.).

general, and effective movement, and as long as both the higher and lower clergy were parties to a formal agreement within the church to hold them.[165] They were not to be imposed, nor even encouraged or favored, from outside the church by the political power.

And as a purely practical matter, apart from the theoretical aspect, what a heap of troubles would have been caused by getting involved in the sticky question of the popular election of parish priests at just that time! One *Kulturkampf* in Europe was enough; the Italian government had so far avoided getting caught up in it, despite the vexation this caused Bismarck, and had not the slightest intention of bringing fresh storms of controversy between itself and the papacy down on its head.[166]

Thus, when the elected priests, relying on the verbal assurances given by the Keeper of the Seals to Guerrieri Gonzaga, assumed their posts in the spring of 1874, they ran into trouble. It was only with great difficulty, and after months of waiting, that their meager stipend was paid by the substeward. In the long run it became impossible to carry on, and the Mantuan episode remained merely an episode. Internal renewal of the church at the hands of the laity survived only as a memory, and the church moved ever more strongly toward an internal, centralized organizational structure dominated from above.

Article eighteen of the law of Guarantees was never applied. It was often invoked;[167] a parliamentary commission went to work studying the means of applying it,[168] but the matter ended there, amid speeches and preparatory com-

[165] It will be remembered that in 1861 and 1870 Minghetti proposed that the question of popular elections in the church be submitted to the Holy See for its approval (above, nn. 110, 116).

[166] The political climate of 1874–75, with the *Kulturkampf* going on in Germany and the Left in Italy demanding a much more anticlerical policy, should be kept in mind in passing judgment on the actions of the government, and in particular the statements made in the Chamber by Minghetti as prime minister. He opposed the program of the Left, which he said would have boiled down to "more toughness and more persecution" (and he was right). In consequence he insisted that it was necessary for the state to keep its distance, and he watered down, to the point of seeming to abandon, several personal convictions that in fact he continued strongly to hold, before and after 1875 (cf. for example his statements on the counterproposal of himself and Peruzzi in 1871 in Minghetti, *Discorsi Parlamentari* 6:551 ff.). But he never wavered in his opposition to any sort of civil constitution of the clergy (cf. his speech of 17 March 1871, *Discorsi Parlamentari* 5:163 ff.) and to any sort of intervention by the state in the internal life of the Church (see the speech of 11 March 1871, ibid., pp. 154–55, and Minghetti, *Stato e Chiesa*, p. 180).

[167] Cf. the debate of 1 May 1875 in the Chamber (*A.P., Camera*, pp. 2834, 2841, 2847). In 1876 Marselli called for its enforcement (*La rivoluzione parlamentare*, pp. 66–67 and 124); and De Cesare took up the question again in the *Nuova Antologia* for 15 January 1895. In May 1909 the Keeper of the Seals, V. E. Orlando, made further reference to it in the Chamber (Cf. Falco, *Il riordinamento*, pp. vi ff.).

[168] The commission, created by a decree of 22 November 1871, appointed the parliamentarians Bonghi, De Filippo, and Mauri to draw up an initial scheme. The hon. Mauri presented one, in twenty-one articles, that included diocesan deputations of seven members (the bishop, a canon of the cathedral, a parish priest from the city, a priest of a rural parish, and three members of the laity to be designated by councils in each province), and parochial deputations of five or three members, according to whether the parish had more than ten thousand members, or less (the text is in B. De Rinaldis, *Dei rapporti fra la Chiesa e lo Stato e del riordinamento dell'asse ecclesiastico a norma dell' art. 18 della Legge sulle guarentigie della S. Sede*, pp. 118–20). There was another commission in 1885, and the scheme of Cadorna in 1887, both of which advanced proposals based on parochial and diocesan assemblies, but ones made up of members of the laity only (cf. Scaduto, *Guarentigie pontificie*, pp. 602 ff.; and Falco, *Il riordinamento*, pp. 36 ff.).

missions. It was easy to say that the administration of ecclesiastical property ought to be handed over to mixed assemblies: what if the church imposed a veto on the participation of Catholics in them? Or what if most of the laity showed no great interest and allowed itself to be guided in a docile fashion by the clergy when the parochial and diocesan assemblies were held?[169] When the lay members of the church had been grouped into a system of assemblies, the priests would swallow them up all the more easily, Giorgini had written in 1867, and others said the same thing later on.[170]

In any case the liberals continued to believe that in this domain external coercion served no purpose, and that the religious problem had to be left to the inner voice of conscience. And apart from anything else there was the practical but unavoidable consideration of how the parliament would react, at a time when there was no subject of debate more likely to raise its temperature than a bill dealing with religious matters. Visconti Venosta openly said as much in the Chamber: "as things stand, there would be no more secure and effective way to create confusion in the Chamber, cause rifts in the parties, dissolve the majority, and be forced to endure scenes of regretful parting of the ways, than to introduce in this arena a law dealing with ecclesiastical matters."[171]

More than twenty years later, when article eighteen was again in discussion, Visconti Venosta summed up the preoccupations of the moderates in the period after 1870: "for my part, if the church were able to agree to these congregations, I would have no objection. But if the pope prohibited Catholics from taking part, making it a violation of the rights of the church to do so, where would the members of the assemblies come from? It would create a source of numerous conflicts, and of a religious turmoil that might seep down to the parishes and the villages this time, into the lives of our tranquil population. This would be the opposite outcome to what we had intended. And that is the reason I would be fearful of seeing, given the still immature state of the question, a bill put to parliament that would be a cause of division in our own party. I recall the exhausting debate about the law of Guarantees on this subject. Italy faces so many

---

[169] Borgatti, for one, pointed out the danger of indifference on the part of the laity, in *Della libertà della Chiesa cattolica nel Regno e delle sue necessarie attinenze alle altre libertà* (Florence, 1870), p. 32.

[170] See *La Perseveranza* for 10 July 1867. Pacifici-Mazzoni, *La quistione romana nella seconda fase e la sua soluzione* (Florence, 1870), pp. 43–44, insists on the difficulties of setting up mixed institutions of clerics and laity able to guarantee a sound and regular administration. De Rinaldis, *Dei rapporti fra la Chiesa e lo Stato*, pp. 5–6, 11–12, 117, emphasizes most forcefully the dangers of the sort of reform contained in the project of Mauri: such an arrangement would only reinforce the clergy at the expense of the nation. The laity would be overpowered and absorbed by the very element that it was meant to modernize. De Rinaldis, who came from the tradition of Giannone and Tanucci, had already warned that the clergy would dominate the assemblies if they were set up, in *Sull'emendamento dell onor. Peruzzi al titolo II della legge sulle relazioni della Chiesa con lo Stato firmato da altri 76 Deputati* (Naples, 1871), pp. 49 ff. Marselli too is opposed to the creation of communities of the laity, for in his eyes it is the state that should administer ecclesiastical property (*La rivoluzione parlamentare*, p. 123). De Meis, on the other hand, is in favor, and he further hopes to see the popular election of parish priests and bishops (Battaglia, "Lettere di Angelo Camillo De Meis a Donato Jaia," pp. 127–28).

[171] *A.P., Camera*, p. 6190 (speech of 9 May 1873).

difficulties and problems that the question of how to transform ecclesiastical benefices doesn't seem to me the most urgent."[172]

Nor did the failure to renew the church in the fashion that Ricasoli and Guerrieri Gonzaga had wished to see it renewed signify the decadence of Catholicism which they had feared would result. There was no decline of religious sentiment, no unconditional triumph of indifference and unbelief. The church recovered from the long crisis that had wracked it for more than half a century; repelling the assaults of the innovators, it resumed its journey; it regained lost strength and in fact acquired new force. Its universal prestige, authority, and greatness returned, and it became an important world power once again. The structure of the church did not give the vote to its believers, and yet they followed. In fact they followed, in a revived and vigorous close formation, with the battalions of Azione Cattolica supplying a devoted and submissive base of lay adherents, not the recalcitrant one typified by Ricasoli. The clergy was held rigidly in check by the central power in order to prevent it from lurching as it had in recent decades, and was subjected to an iron discipline that flowed from the dogma of infallibility. The laity was from the outset summoned to channel its influence into those Catholic associations which the journal *Civiltà Cattolica* hastened to endorse and which spread rapidly throughout the kingdom, beginning with the Society for Catholic Interests founded at Rome and honored with a brief by Pius IX in February 1871.[173] From 1868 young people had their own organization, Catholic Youth. The "Opera dei Congressi" was the most potent arm of the organized laity.[174] These were the robust pillars of the church: defeated in the temporal realm, it

---

[172] Visconti Venosta, letter to De Cesare, no date but written in the early months of 1895 (Visconti Venosta archive). In November 1875, following Minghetti's speech at Cologna Veneta in which he made a renewed commitment to the law on ecclesiastical property, the French ambassador observed that such a law would be a source of serious turmoil, and that since the Italian politicians were well aware of this, they would try (according to what he had been told) to pass the least onerous law possible and above all to drag the business out as long as possible—which they did (Noailles, report, 9 November 1875, no. 92; AEP, *C.P., Italie*, t. 393, fols. 208 ff.). Cf. as well Minghetti, *Discorsi Parlamentari* 6:551–52.

[173] Cf. Vigo, *Annali d'Italia* 1:39. On the spread of these associations, through which the clericals "wish to fight against Italy with the arms that Italy itself gives them" by getting onto the communal and provincial councils, taking over the running of the charitable institutions, and from this base launching an attack on the country's political institutions "without having to enter Parliament and pass under the Caudine forks of the requirement to take the oath," see the article "Agitazioni religiose" in *La Perseveranza* for 15 May 1871.

[174] Cf. E. Vercesi, *Il movimento cattolico in Italia (1870–1922)* (Florence, 1923), pp. 12 ff. For the history of the Catholic movement in Italy, see esp. the perceptive observations of F. Fonzi, "I "cattolici transigenti' italiani dell'ultimo Ottocento," *Convivium* (1949): 955 ff., and "Per una storia del movimento cattolico italiano (1861–1919)," *Rassegna Storica del Risorgimento* 37 (1950): 140 ff. I would observe, however, that although it may be true that the intransigent Catholics of the later period arrived at a political and (above all) social stance much more radical than that of the transigents, so that they can't simply be called "conservatives," still it is true that for a considerable time after 1870 the intransigents were avowedly reactionaries, in the sense that they opposed the unification of Italy with Rome as its capital. This is how their actions were interpreted both in and outside Italy and influenced developments in the kingdom. To overlook this would be to stand historical reality on its head. As for the appeals launched to the people by the "intransigent" press after 1860, in a style that sounded almost socialistic, it must be remembered that the intransigents were using this as a tactic in their struggle against the Italian state (cf. below, pp. 333 ff.).

took up the struggle on spiritual terrain, as if to vindicate those who had foreseen that the loss of the temporal power would not diminish the church but instead would expand its energy, in the field that properly belonged to it.

A warning voice had been raised in 1870: those who thought that the church's power had been sapped forever, and the religious sentiment of the masses attenuated, were making a mistake.[175] The course of events revealed just how acute this opinion was, and how misguided the expectations of those who believed that they had buried the papacy for good with the breach of the Porta Pia.

In fact there were numerous observers, both before and after 1870, who deluded themselves that the Italian monarchy would drive the papacy out of Rome, or even do away with it altogether,[176] among them the visionary Renan,[177] and nobody was granted any premonition of the distant day in June on which the population of Rome, at the conclusion of one of the darkest and most tormented periods of its age-long history, would gather in the piazza of St. Peter's to receive the pope's blessing and acclaim him as a new *defensor urbis*, the protector and savior of the capital after it had been abandoned by the monarchy. Nobody foresaw, then or for some time to come, that the Romans would be forced to turn their anguished gaze in the direction of the sacred Christian basilicas, as their ancestors had done at the time of the collapse of the Roman empire, surrounded by the barbarian hordes, when "the shrines of the martyrs and the basilicas of the apostles . . . gave shelter amid the devastation of the city to all, Roman or foreigner, who fled to them . . . so that none was taken into captivity and led away by the cruel foe."[178] But ten years after Porta Pia, a few doubts concerning the comparative durability of the monarchy and the papacy began to creep into the minds of even the fiercest anticlericals; and Michele Amari, no longer under the spell of the myth of continuous progress, and pessimistic about humanity, which appeared to him eternally destined to be divided into foolish believers and intelligent unbelievers,[179] asked himself which of the two torches would be ex-

[175] "Il Papa va o resta?" in *La Perseveranza* for 17 October 1870. Cf. as well the issue of 18 September.

[176] Settembrini, for example: "the monarchy, firm and strong, with a respected prince, the monarchy settled in Rome, will necessarily and inevitably destroy the papacy, and whether this happens a little sooner or a little later doesn't matter" (*Epistolario*, p. 283).

[177] Renan, *Correspondance, 1872–1892*, pp. 15, 27, 29, 43, 131. And cf. also "La crise religieuse en Europe" (1874), in *Mélanges religieux et historiques*, p. 15, stating the view that papal conclaves will be impossible in a free Rome; the Pope will have to abandon the city. A certain French artist, who in 1867 advised Massari that Italy should not go to Rome, took a different view: "are you thinking of . . . placing a cradle inside a burial vault?" (Massari, speech to the Chamber, 13 March 1872, *A.P., Camera*, p. 1183).

[178] Augustine, *De civitate Dei* 1.1 and 1.7 (ed. Dombart [Leipzig, 1863]).

[179] Note how Amari attributes the entire responsibility for the Angevin oppression in Sicily to the papacy; and how, at age eighty-one, thinking again of "the intrigues of the popes with Pippin and Charlemagne . . . the base adulation, the fraudulent proposals, the superstitious insinuations," he felt "the rage I felt at age eighteen or twenty" (Amari, *Carteggio* 2:258, 304). As for his judgment on the papacy of the nineteenth century, cf. ibid., 3:291 (and ibid., 2:305): "Oh how I wish I had the spirit of Muhammad, to convert the Italians to some other religion than the Catholic Apostolic Roman!" On his early education, which was completely irreligious, cf. the *Elogio* of D'Ancona (*Carteggio* 2:321–22 and 368 n. 6); and on his disenchantment, his failure to believe any more in the "spiral" of progress, *Carteggio* 2:252.

tinguished first, the Vatican or the Quirinal. He feared that within one or two centuries the monarchy might well collapse, but that there would always be a vile multitude of the rich and the poor ready to run and kiss the feet of the pretended successor of the apostles.[180]

A few foreign statesmen had taken the view that the fate of the Italian monarchy was henceforth indissolubly tied to that of the papacy, in Rome: if the former fell, the latter would find itself in an untenable position, since both together represented the principle of authority in the face of republican revolution.[181] But there were other, more perspicacious, politicians who noted—long before the ecclesiastical authority in France ordered a *ralliement* of Catholics to republican France—that it might not work out that way, that the papacy could survive the fall of the monarchy and find some modus vivendi with a republic, or even with something more extreme than a republic.[182]

The many who believed that the end of the papal state meant the end of the political authority of the papacy measured the strength of the Roman curia by the same criteria that they applied to any other political organism—territory, population size, armaments—and forgot to apply to the modern world Machiavelli's old warning concerning ecclesiastical principates, which are "underpinned by long-standing religious traditions, which have proved to be so powerful and well suited to securing the state of the prince who incarnates them, no matter what he does or how he lives." Soon they were disabused, and as early as the period of Leo XIII they saw what a few acute observers had already predicted,[183] that the political power of the church not only held firm but even increased, and that the day would never come (as even the cautious *Opinione* had once thought that it might)[184] on which foreign governments would no longer send permanent diplomatic representatives to the Vatican, but would contact it through their delegations to the Quirinal, or through special officers for ecclesiastical matters attached to those delegations.

According to another current of opinion, the reason for the decadence of the Latin peoples in comparison to the Anglo-Saxons and the Germans lay not in their racial heritage, as was generally thought, but in the Catholic faith, for having suffocated their energies where the reformed religions had stimulated human activity, favoring nationhood and liberty. In anticipation of Max Weber, the industrial superiority of the Protestants and their more marked predilection for practical activity in comparison to the Catholics, who were absorbed in classicist traditionalism, was adduced as concrete proof of this.[185]

---

[180] To Renan, 30 March 1883 (Amari, *Carteggio* 2:282 and cf. p. 290).

[181] One was Kálnoky, at the outset of the negotiations that led to the Triple Alliance, and following him, Baron Hübner (*G.P.* 3:194; F. Salata, *Per la storia diplomatica della questione romana* 1:169). Cf. my note "Kulturkampf e Triplice Alleanza . . ." in *Rivista Storica Italiana* 62 (1950): 261–62 and 275.

[182] Bismarck was one (*G.P.* 3:197).

[183] Among them Anselmo Guerrieri Gonzaga, brother of Carlo: cf. *Discorso dell'on. A. Guerrieri Gonzaga agli elettori del collegio di Mantova*, 19 October 1876 (Mantua, 1876), p. 24.

[184] "La diplomazia in Roma," in *L'Opinione* for 2 March 1872.

[185] This is De Laveleye's thesis in *L'avvenire dei popoli cattolici*, pp. 25 ff. In 1872 Serra

But, decadence or not, it is certain that Catholic sentiment did not diminish; and Villari uttered a warning against dismissing too lightly the forces of the clergy, which were enormous, recommending alertness in preparation for the great battle that was coming, since the priests were already gaining control of the schools and would then strike back in the field of politics.[186] Sella maintained in 1881 that, too-easy assertions about the decline of the theocratic spirit of Catholicism notwithstanding, "the pope's influence is in reality greater in the world today than it was when he still had his temporal power."[187]

The pope was something more than a simple cathedral canon, which is what many imagined he had been reduced to,[188] nor was it possible to make of him a "respectable citizen" like anyone else.[189] Even the deist Crispi,[190] the great defender of the prerogatives of reason, the heir of the eighteenth century and of the Jacobins, was sometimes visited by an intuition of the failure of his life's dream, by the realization that the redemption of Rome from the temporal power did not yet mean the longed-for redemption of the human race from the spiritual power of the pope. Old, exhausted, and embittered, he registered the symptoms of the church's recovery with growing apprehension in his last years, discerning the movement "that has been developing in its favor in the world for some time," and once more he began to speak of the omnipotence of the curia and of the efforts of the diabolical league of Jesuits to shackle the human spirit yet again.[191] If the Italian bourgeoisie had a fault, it was not their aversion to the plebeian social class of which the socialists complained, but rather the fact that they had abandoned the plebeians to the clutches of sects and priests, without taking thought for their moral education.[192] Adriano Lemmi, a grand master of the Freemasons, expressed a similar frustration to his friend Crispi at the spread of pestilent clericalism, contaminating everything it touched, at the cocksureness of the "blacks" now that they had obtained virtually complete control of the education of the young; the point had been reached, he said, where if measures were not taken we

Gropelli published in *Il Diritto*, and then separately, thoughts on *L'Italia Nera* (2d ed.; Rome, 1873), maintaining (p. 5) that the peoples who adhered to the papal religion were either dead or dying. Marselli also believed that Catholicism was a potent cause of ruin for the Latin nations (*La rivoluzione parlamentare*, p. 103).

[186] Villari, speech to the Chamber, 6 May 1875 (*A.P., Camera*, pp. 2977–78). Vignoli also insisted in 1876 that the papacy was not an enemy to be taken lightly, and that believing in the approaching end of Catholicism was a dire mistake, a blunder common to many and a cause of continuous setbacks for the liberals. The papacy was, on the contrary, a power to be feared, he said (Villari, *Delle condizioni morali e civili d'Italia* [Milan, 1876], pp. 71 ff.).

[187] Sella, speech to the Chamber, 14 March 1881 (*Discorsi Parlamentari* 1:301).

[188] Visconti Venosta to Minghetti, 8 July 1874: "our friends in the Chamber and in journalism are wrong to imagine, as they read the papers, that the pope has been transformed overnight into something less significant than a canon of a cathedral" (BCB, *Carte Minghetti*, cart. 35 a). In an article of 22 November 1870, "La politica a Roma," *La Nazione* advised the impatient Romans to bear in mind "that the pope . . . cannot be treated with such disdainful self-assurance."

[189] This was what Giuseppe Ferrari was demanding in December 1870 (*Scritti*, vol. 1, *Carteggio inedito*, p. 253). Cf. Lanza, *Le carte* 6:323.

[190] Crispi himself affirmed in a speech to the Chamber of 28 November 1895 that he was not an atheist but a deist (*Discorsi Parlamentari* 3:860–61).

[191] Ibid., 3:859, and cf. *Pensieri e profezie*, pp. 80 and 92.

[192] Crispi, *Discorsi Parlamentari* 3:686.

would no longer have a population of citizens but one of clerics, and the prefects were partly to blame, since instead of trying to stem the tide they were assisting the clericals in combating Freemasonry.[193]

It remains true that, from Leo XIII onward, the church had to alter its tone considerably and to adapt itself in part to the *mariage de raison* with *l'esprit du siècle* which Amari had foreseen, but in a different sense.[194] While remaining inexorable where infallibility was concerned, it gradually allowed a good part of the Syllabus of Errors to lapse in practical application, it accepted liberty and progress, it gave up its rigid support for "the venerable majesty and imperium of kings" to which it had still appeared to be so indissolubly wedded between 1870 and 1880,[195] and it came to terms with the republic, urging French Catholics to a *ralliement* when it realized the sterility of their irrational attachment to the monarchical form of government.[196] Instead of mounting a conservative opposition to every social movement, the church itself began to speak about social questions. Concordats were reached with free governments, and some less than free. Finally, and this was decisive, the church showed a welcoming face not only to political liberty but also to science, seeking and finding, in its ageless wisdom, formulas of accord—thus forgetting that the final erroneous opinion condemned in the Syllabus, the eightieth, had been the opinion of those who maintained that "the Roman Pontiff can and should reconcile himself, and come to an agreement, with progress, with liberalism, and with modern civilization." Though between 1870 and 1880 the church had said, or had allowed its most faithful adherents to say, counterrevolution or nothing, we spit on the Revolution, with no distinction made between 1789 and 1793,[197] it eventually accepted 1789: the policy of Leo XIII toward France was the visible proof of this.

The church will destroy the Revolution, the Revolution will destroy the church: these were the emphatic claims made on either side. But if one stands at a distance from such polemics, one sees that the papacy was certainly not destroyed by the Revolution, but no more was the papacy capable of arresting and

---

[193] Letter, 24 August 1894 (MRR, *Carte Crispi*, b. 660, no. 8/4); and cf. also the letter of 6 November 1887 (ibid., b. 660, no. 6/12).

[194] Amari, *Carteggio* 2:215–16. But Amari did not foresee (nor desire!) this marriage taking place between the church and the secular world, but between the secular world "and the social utility of Christianity," a "reform," that is, which certainly would have left very little of the Roman church intact.

[195] Leo XIII in the encyclical *Quod Apostolici muneris*, 28 December 1878 (the Italian version is in I. Giordani, ed., *Le encicliche sociali dei Papi* [2d ed.; Rome, 1944], p. 25).

[196] I take the expression from Giordani, *Le encicliche*, p. 13. The church's theoretical indifference toward "the principate of one or of many, provided it be just and aim at the common good," is already affirmed, of course, in the *Diuturnum* (29 June 1881) and in the *Immortale Dei* (1 November 1885; ibid., pp. 57, 69, 81. Cf. E. Soderini, *Leone XIII* 1:322–23 [Milan, 1932].

[197] In France, on the eve of the policy of Leo XIII, the "ultras" continued to take the express position of the Syllabus: "present society is incurable, it was born full-fledged in 1789, we do not distinguish 1789 from 1793, we fight with the same ardor against both the cause and the effect." A Catholic, they said, had to choose counterrevolution or nothing; and he had to "spit" on the Revolution, whether it bore the inscription 1789 or 1793. A polemic against these excesses appears in the work of a firm Catholic, De Falloux, *La controrivoluzione* (Italian translation: Florence, 1879), pp. 12 and 27.

banishing liberalism, progress, modern civilization. *Caute et prudenter*, as was its way, the Roman church in the end accepted the lesson of the times. It did carry out an internal reform, not in the manner desired by Rosmini, Lambruschini, and Ricasoli, but thoroughly nevertheless, to the point that it not only recognized the unity of Italy with Rome as its capital, and thus ratified the "usurpation," but also accepted the existence of an Italian state that was no longer the confessional state of Carlo Felice and Carlo Alberto. Extremism was frustrated, as usual, on one side and on the other; instead each of the parties, even the church, had to face certain facts and treat with its opposite.[198]

Science, which had once appeared irreconcilable with religious faith, came instead to an ample understanding with it, and the church at times found an ally in the formidable progress being made in research. Scientists were opening up new worlds and climbing to dizzying heights, rapt by the unstoppable succession of their own experiments, whose final outcome increasingly escaped rational calculation, as did the future direction of research. They looked ever deeper into the secrets of nature, but then, as though overcome, asked of God the reason for those secrets. Hence it was that, as the century drew to a close, Pasteur, a mild individual and a great scientist, serenely opposed his own strong religious faith to the positivism of Taine, and the two men no longer understood one another, the latter still the heir of the mid-century mentality according to which science was free thought, loosed from its ties with the ineffable of religion, or rather an enemy of religion, and the former exemplifying a new type of scientist, daring in his technical conceptions but no longer a free thinker, in fact solidly anchored in the faith of his fathers. Taine still believed he could find in science the solution of man's eternal problems and employ it to resolve the great question of the immortality of the soul; to which Pasteur's smiling reply was "ah! Monsieur, à cette question vous ne trouverez pas une solution dans nos cornues."[199]

Faith in the triumphs of science as being the triumphs of a conception of the world in which there was no place for religion also faded slowly away, very slowly but no less certainly, between the end of the nineteenth and the beginning of the twentieth centuries, until the moment when the great catastrophes of the war arrived to fasten the grip of God's word definitively on man's spirit once again, and the consolation of the cross regained all its old fascination. So it was that, far from standing by while the papacy and the church tottered, tipped, and fell over like an ancient ruin, the proponents of science and free thought, who had believed that time was on their side with the incessant progress of the natural sciences and historical criticism,[200] watched as the church and the papacy grew

---

[198] On this coming to terms of Catholicism with the modern world, after the Syllabus and despite the Syllabus, cf. the penetrating observations in G. Pepe, *Il Sillabo e la politica dei cattolici* (Rome, 1945), pp. 7–8, 34. And cf. as well Jemolo, *Chiesa e Stato in Italia*, p. 191, on the many cases in which *La Civiltà Cattolica* condemned institutions, and proclaimed that situations were unacceptable, only to change its position later.

[199] The delectable episode of Taine's encounter with Pasteur is narrated in Hanotaux, *Mon temps* 2:165–67. One thinks as well of the "conversion" of Brunetière, and his announcement of the "failure of science."

[200] Thus Amari in 1878 (*Carteggio* 2:236).

ever more vigorous. Science did not destroy faith, nor did it become "the only religion, the only faith, the only consoler of mankind," carrying out these offices "much more fully, efficaciously, and constantly than all the positive religions of the world have been able to do to date," as Giovanni Maria Bertin had anticipated in 1874.[201]

The counteroffensive launched by the church was not the only thing, nor the most important thing, to sap the strength of the myth of science: within the community of the learned itself there could be detected hesitations, doubts, remorse, and with them the first cracks in the temple, which offered a token of the certain success of the church's counteroffensive. Culture and science had been offered as substitutes for faith; and culture entailed an effort to educate the common people, who had to be put in a position to understand, to discern the true from the false, to refuse superstitious beliefs. It was their illiteracy that had to be combated: Depretis was a man who usually avoided emotive language, but even he referred to the schools as "the church of modern times."[202] Education appeared to be the only effective weapon against the influence the church had over the masses,[203] and it was the government of the Left that finally passed, in 1877, a law making elementary instruction free and compulsory. The Left of course belonged to the most strongly anticlerical part of the spectrum, and this was its first major piece of reforming legislation, preceding by four years its reform of the law governing national elections. With the law of 1877, religious instruction in the schools became purely optional, after Benedetto Cairoli had declared in the Chamber that every good father ought to keep his children from even reading the catechism.[204]

Education seemed to be the remedy for every ill, and the "fearful specter of seventeen million illiterates" was flaunted as the specter of Italian shame, not only in the debates of the upper classes but even, or perhaps especially, among the workers themselves.[205] From as early as October 1856, the date of the congress of the Workers' Associations at Vigevano, they had requested that elementary schooling be made compulsory, a request that was repeated at the congress of Rome in April 1872.[206]

But it was not long before numbers of people began to think that the wider diffusion of culture, the education of the people, also meant handing over to the lower classes an arm they could use in their struggle against the continuing predominance of the middle and upper classes, that it meant giving nourishment to

---

[201] Cf. P. Gobetti, *Risorgimento senza eroi* (Turin, 1926), p. 313.

[202] Speech to the Chamber of 5 May 1881 (*Discorsi Parlamentari di A. Depretis* 7:681; and cf. as well M. Coppino, *Commemorazione di A. Depretis*, read at Stradella on 4 October 1888 [Turin, 1888], p. 38).

[203] Thus Spaventa, *La Politica della Destra*, p. 199.

[204] In the session of 9 March 1877 (*A.P., Camera*, p. 1922).

[205] *Congresso generale delle Società Operaie Italiane tenuto in Roma nell'aprile del 1872*, pp. 149 ff.; in general, G. Manacorda, "Il movimento operaio italiano attraverso i congressi operai e socialisti," supplement to *Rinascita* 8–9 (1949): 4.

[206] The congress of Rome approved Arbib's agenda recommending compulsory school attendance, with sanctions for those who did not comply (*Congresso generale delle Società Operaie Italiane*, p. 160–61).

socialism, anarchism, and similar movements of revolt against the bourgeois world. Unbelief might lead to the collapse of the church, but also to the collapse of the present state of society, as the Jesuit fathers of *Civiltà Cattolica* had been asserting for some time. In inducing the masses to lose their faith in God, one ran the risk of no longer being able to confine them, even outside the church, to their traditional way of life. Elementary schooling was necessarily connected, sooner or later, with universal suffrage and democracy: Flaubert had understood this from the outset, being an enemy of the latter two and consequently also an enemy of the former, convinced as he was of the necessity of a class of "mandarins." It mattered little to Flaubert if many of the peasants learned to read and no longer heeded the parish priest, but it was important to him that numbers of men like Renan and Littré should have a livelihood, and an audience.[207] And even Renan, though he continued to delude himself that rationalism, understood aright, was far from leading to democracy, deplored the fact that the French schools had become hotbeds of an unreflective democratic spirit, and of an unbelief that translated into fatuous popular propaganda.[208] And this enemy of the papacy saw the way to salvation in an accommodation with the church, on the basis of degrees of truth: the parish priests would educate the peasants in schools run by the church, while the learned would enjoy full and absolute liberty of thought. The priests could keep control of their flocks, and serve them up the catechism along with the school primer, as long as they left the elite to study in peace.[209] Was this mere cultural aristocratism on the part of the two French writers, disdain for the crowd, a feeling that the refined values of culture are for the select few? Yes, certainly.[210] But this attitude was reinforced by other kinds of disquiet, the sense that political democracy was insufferable, the fear that agitation from below

[207] Flaubert, *Correspondance* 4:29–30, 56.

[208] Renan, *La réforme*, p. 103. Naturally he extols the German universities, which are centers of liberal thought but not of indiscreet proselytism.

[209] "Let the church recognize two categories of believers, those who adhere to the letter, and those who cleave to the spirit. For most people who attain a certain degree of rational culture, belief in the supernatural becomes an impossibility; do not force them to wear a cope of lead. Do not interfere with what we teach, with what we write, and we will not contend with you for the people. Do not contest our place in the university and the academy, and we will hand the schools of the countryside unreservedly over to you. The human spirit is a scale in which each grade is necessary; what is good at one level is not so at a different one; what is deadly for one person is not so for another. Preserve religious education for the people; but leave us in liberty" (*La réforme*, pp. 98–99). It is difficult to think of a clearer example of a style of thought in which social-political preoccupations of a conservative kind and cultural aristocratism overlap and influence each other. Note as well the mutation of the Renan of 1871 with respect to the Renan of 1848–49, who had asserted exactly the opposite, that is the necessity to educate the people. Then he had thought that it was not enough for the progress of the human spirit for a few isolated thinkers to achieve great discoveries; a result has not been won until it has entered into circulation on a vast scale (*L'avenir de la science*, pp. 325, 335, 364). In writing the preface for the edition of 1890 he continues in the tone of 1871: the conquests of science have no relation to the spread of popular education; rather, to vulgarize science means to dilute it, and thus to weaken it (cf. Strauss, *La politique de Renan*, p. 75). Sorel's assumption ("Germanesimo et storicismo di Ernesto Renan," pp. 432–34) that the statements Renan makes in *La réforme* must have been inspired by Le Play and even by Proudhon seems to me not only unproved but not even necessary: the problem of the education of the people in the hands of the parish priest was one that dated from 1848–49 in France.

[210] Cf. Strauss, *La politique de Renan*, p. 230.

might disturb the peace and dispel the tranquillity of the man of learning, interrupting him as he communed serenely with his own ideas. Renan was a legitimist
by nature and hated revolutions, which had made his task so much more difficult.[211] As a conservative he was averse to universal suffrage and to the brute
masses of the peasantry, who were better off receiving a kick in the behind than
the right to vote. So let the dangerous beasts remain with their parish priest, the
only one who could keep them in line.

A century previously the men of the Enlightenment, with Voltaire in the lead,
had also spoken of the necessity that the light of understanding be shed gradually.
They also felt that the intellectual lights of the lower classes would never be
anything more than dim, which was just as well, as it was well that the revelation
of the truth should be reserved to the good bourgeois alone, to the *honnêtes
hommes*.[212] The epigones of the Enlightenment in the second half of the nineteenth century held fast to that principle, though the motives for holding it varied:
Voltaire had feared that peasants who received an education would become
theologians—in other words, he feared education through the seminary. Renan
feared that peasants and workers might find, in the "half-learning" of the secular
elementary schools, an incentive to become adepts of socialism and of the
International.

Nor was Renan's attitude something absolutely novel, if one recalls the cry of
"come, let us throw ourselves into the arms of the bishops; only they can save us
now" that was ascribed, after the Paris revolution of 1848, to Victor Cousin, the
official high pontiff of French university philosophy, an ex-carbonaro and liberal
who in truth had become very prudent indeed, even before 1848 when his custom
had been to advise his students, when they left to teach in the provinces, to stay
on good terms with the bishop, in fact to pay Monsignor a visit on their arrival
and assure him that philosophy would never have any influence except on the
learned, whereas religion was necessary for the people. After 1848 he became so
prudent that he abandoned his pupils to the vendetta of the clergy.[213] Much more
important was the decisive help given in 1849–50 by Thiers in getting the Falloux law passed, a Catholic law which by establishing liberty of instruction gave
the clergy large opportunities to influence the training of the future French governing classes once again.[214] The man who in 1845 had defended the monopoly

---

[211] Ibid., pp. 260 ff.

[212] Classic formulations of this thought are in Voltaire's letters of 1, 13 and 28 April 1766
(*Oeuvres complètes* 40:387, 392, 397 [Paris, 1911]).

[213] G. Weill, *Histoire de l'enseignement secondaire en France (1802–1920)*, pp. 102, 108, 126;
P. de la Gorce, *Histoire de la seconde République française* 2:274 (9th ed.; Paris, 1925); E. Beau de
Loménie, *Le responsabilità delle dinastie borghesi* (Italian translation: Milan, 1946), p. 150. Cousin
also recommended great prudence to his Italian friends, saying that Piedmont ought to keep very
quiet, and not remind the world that it was a free country, if it did not want to bring destruction on
itself (A. Malvezzi, ed., *Il Risorgimento Italiano in un carteggio di patrioti lombardi, 1821–1860*,
p. 503).

[214] It is interesting to note the position taken by Cavour in regard to the Falloux law, in his debate
in the subalpine Chamber with the hon. Valerio, on 21 November 1851. Cavour's faith in liberty,
and consequently in freedom of instruction, is set against Valerio's fear that freedom of instruction
may be converted into church power, a fear he justifies by the example of France (Cavour, *Discorsi*

of the secular university against the church and had been, with Dupin, the authoritative interpreter of French anticlericalism and anti-Jesuitism, switched fronts
totally four years later, driven by his terror of the "reds" and excited by a "sort of
mad rage," which had gripped him when faced with the upheaval of June
1848,[215] and which was to grip him again in 1871 when faced with the Paris
Commune. To the consternation of his admirers abroad[216] he embraced the
clergy, urging that they even be given the monopoly of elementary education,
something that went far beyond the hopes of the clergy itself and of his somewhat
wiser friend, the abbot Dupanloup, who was forced to rein in the excess of zeal
displayed by the new convert.[217]

Thiers, the vivacious and agile "Tamerlane with spectacles" of 1871,[218] frankly
admitted changing his mind, not because of a revolution in his convictions but
because of a revolution in the social condition of the country. "Today, when every
social ideal has been perverted, and they want to put a Jacobin school teacher in
every village, I consider the parish priest an indispensable corrector of the ideas
of the people. He at any rate will teach them in the name of Christ that there is
necessarily pain in every social condition, that this is a fact of life, and that when
the poor have a fever it is not because the rich gave it to them. . . . When the
university represented the good and wise French bourgeoisie, educated our sons
according to the methods of Rollin, placed tried-and-true classical studies ahead
of physics and the other purely material disciplines of the professional educa-
tionalists, oh I was happy then to sacrifice liberty of instruction to it! Today my
opinion is different. Why? Because nothing is as it was. The University has fallen
into the hands of materialists and Jacobins, and makes a claim to teach our sons a
little mathematics, physics, and moral science, and a lot of demagogy. . . . I am
what I was, and all I am doing is directing my hatred and my power to resist where
the enemy lies. The enemy is demagogy, and I will not hand the last remaining
piece of the social order, Catholic education, over to it." The result was that there
would be no free and compulsory education, for that would be to apply the

---

Parlamentari 4:511 ff. [Florence, 1934]). It is past doubt, however, that the Falloux law signified the
triumph of clerical tendencies in France and the onset of a harsh reaction in the area of teaching,
whose victims included Michelet and Taine. On Cavour's attitude, see my observations in *Convegno
di scienze morali storiche e filologiche, 4–10 ottobre 1948: Il 1848 nella storia d'Europa*, pp. 347–
49 (henceforth, *Convegno . . . 1848*).

[215] Halévy, *Le courrier de M. Thiers*, p. 240 and cf. also p. 230; H. Malo, *Thiers*, pp. 387 ff.
For the reaction of the French middle class against the "montagnards" of June 1848 and in favor of a
republic "des honnêtes gens" see de la Gorce, *Histoire de la seconde République française* 1:406 ff.

[216] ". . . can you explain to me the conduct of Thiers? Has he got so old that he is losing the train
of his own thoughts? What does he want? What is he hoping for?" Costanza Arconati to Jules Mohl, 7
January 1850 (Malvezzi, *Il Risorgimento Italiano*, p. 437).

[217] Halévy, *Le courrier de M. Thiers*, pp. 256 ff.; de la Gorce, *Histoire de la seconde République française* 2:274 ff.; Malo, *Thiers*, pp. 400 ff.; Beau de Loménie, *Le responsabilità delle dinastie
borghesi*, pp. 150–51; G. Cogniot, *La question scolaire en 1848 et la loi Falloux* (Paris, 1948),
pp. 183 ff.; G. Bourgin, "La question scolaire en 1848 et la loi Falloux," in *Convegno . . . 1848*,
pp. 329 ff. The judgment pronounced immediately by Marx was accurate (K. Marx and F. Engels, *Il
1848 in Germania e in Francia* [Rome, 1946], pp. 226 and 301–302).

[218] This is one of the monikers under which he was known to the communards (R. Dreyfus, *M.
Thiers contre l'empire, la guerre, la commune, 1869–1871*, p. 334 n. 2).

"communist system." In addition Thiers violently attacked the school teachers, "real antipriests in the communes, parish priests of atheism and socialism."

And so fear of socialism guided the bourgeois Thiers in the direction of new sympathies and political alliances. When it came to the secondary schools, however, the institutions attended by the sons of the bourgeois *honnêtes hommes*, where there was no danger, or so at least it was thought, of subversive tendencies,[219] he regained his old spirit and, anticipating Renan, demanded liberty of philosophical discussion and sought to limit the influence of the same clergy whose aid he had summoned against the lower classes; and Dupanloup had to remind him once more that religion is good for the rich as much as it is for the poor.

The fear of subversion, which had been soothed for a while in the lull of the Second Empire, had a recrudescence in the spring of 1871, when the Commune showed that the fire was still smoldering in the basement of the building. Taine, who in 1851–52 had been a victim of the clerical reaction, was perceptive in fearing that, faced with the spread of democracy, the upper and middle classes would tilt to the right, become clerical, and look for a *gendarmerie* where they were sure they could find it, in Catholicism, and that they would not hesitate, under pressure, to flee to the shelter of Bonapartism once again, the shelter of dictatorship.[220] Yet he himself, in the twilight of his busy life as a keeper of the temple of science, grew skeptical about the efficacy of the cult he had professed for so long and came to see anti-Christianism as a potent auxiliary of egalitarian socialism, a substance that had lodged in the bloodstream of France like alcohol in the veins of an alcoholic, or morphine in the veins of a morphine addict. In this disconsolate frame of mind he affirmed: "our books are of use to history, and science; but our influence on practical life is infinitely small."[221]

The common opinion came to be that by extinguishing the religious sentiment, and with it resignation in the face of suffering, the only thing one brought about was to unleash the bitterness and the violence of the hungry crowds, no longer restrained by reverence for the arcane decrees of God, no longer uplifted by the sweetness of their hope of eternal life amid the suffering of their life on earth.[222] If one reflected on the miserable and aggrieved peasants who did not rebel against their hard fate, but accepted it as the punishment of God and flocked to the church to pray with unshaken faith, one understood how mistaken Proudhon had been to proclaim the inutility of God.[223]

---

[219] Others however were nervous about what was being taught in the superior schools as well; studies of classical language and literature were accused of promoting socialism, by Bastiat for example, and the result of these worries was the program of study passed into statute by the government on 30 August 1852, which gave much more space to the sciences and modern languages, but which tended to lower the intellectual level, for fear of arousing too much ambition and too many dreams among the young (Weill, *Histoire de l'enseignement secondaire en France*, pp. 134 ff.)

[220] Taine, *Correspondance* 3:276 (9 September 1875).

[221] Ibid., 4:204 (25 June 1885).

[222] See the considerations of De Laveleye, *Nouvelles lettres d'Italie*, p. 57.

[223] Visconti Venosta expressed exactly this opinion, referring to the peasants of the Valtellina, in a letter of 1856 to the countess Clara Maffei (C. Olmo, "Lettere giovanili di Emilio Visconti Venosta," in *Nuova Antologia* 262 (1 July 1915): 8–9.

Similar thoughts gradually forced their way into the minds of many Italians, even free thinkers, as the internal conditions of the kingdom grew more complicated because of the unrest rising from below. Here too optimism had already begun to erode after 1848: perhaps there were those who recalled what Lambruschini had said in the Accademia dei Georgofili on 4 August 1850, basing his discourse on the "unforeseen and lamentable fact" that had arrived to put new weapons in the hands of those who opposed schooling for the people. This new development was "the propagation of subversive doctrines recently carried on in France by a certain number . . . of primary school teachers who have become evangelists of socialism." The result was that ancient animosities and doubts were augmented by new animosities and hesitations, "and a few of those who formerly fought on our side have begun to lose faith." They have been led to fear "that education is less able to infuse the people with respect for religion and law, to teach them the fulfillment of their own obligations to family, city, and church, to train them better in the practice of their trades, than it is apt to make them disenchanted with the simple and tranquil life of the countryside, the small shop, the household, to swell them with a vain conceit of wisdom, to trouble them with excessive desires, and to produce those blind and servile crowds that perturb the state under one flag or another, and violate the social hierarchy itself." But Lambruschini called such fears the trepidation of men of little faith, and for his part did not forswear his creed, nor let these new phantasms prevail and leave him daunted.[224] The phantasms did not, however, disappear, and after the Commune and the increasing signs of social unrest that followed, without sparing Italy, they haunted the minds of many more than before. Correspondingly, the number of those who lost their faith grew, and some of them were men of authority.

In 1871 Ruggero Bonghi protested against the association of university students of Pisa, guilty in his eyes of having praised the deeds of the communards of Paris and of confounding the minds of the youth in the universities with an evil unhealthy vicious spirit that turned them into an instrument of the International. He protested against the association formed by the secondary school students of Jesi, which he also suspected of alarming tendencies, and claimed that the heads of families were not obliged to tolerate "their sons coming back home and presuming to have the right, before they have had any experience of life, to teach private individuals how to run their business, and others how to govern the public business."[225] And yet the universities and secondary schools were the apple of

---

[224] Now in Lambruschini, *Scritti politici e di istruzione pubblica*, ed. A. Gambaro, pp. 465–66. Vittorio Emanuele II also shared the preoccupations of the men "of little faith," writing to Pius IX on 21 September 1849: "We must recognize that the present calamities have their sole origin in the lack of that faith which, by promising a reward for the sufferings of this life, induces and persuades man to suffer. The schools that take hope for the future away from him and teach him to do nothing but enjoy, drive him to search for his own advantage at any cost; in this way they undermine society. The principal office of the clergy is to prevent the people from drinking in such perverse doctrines" (in P. Pirri, S.J., *Pio IX e Vittorio Emanuele II dal loro carteggio privato* 1:41 [Rome, 1944]).

[225] Parliamentary interrogation by Bonghi, 13 June 1871, concerning the planned congress of university students at Florence etc. (*A.P., Camera*, pp. 2858 ff., not included in his collected

the eye of the bourgeoisie! If one descended from that level to the primary schools, which were in contact primarily with the lower classes, there was still more to brood over.

These conflicts emerged clearly in the debates on the bill to make primary schooling compulsory: in 1874 the hon. Lioy raised a cry of alarm against those who turned to teaching for lack of anything better, and who were "the apostles of those subversive notions by means of which the corrupt members of society hope to overthrow the civil association." The hon. Castiglia insisted on the damage that would be done by the bill, whose effect would be felt by the poor, and which would lead "the children of misery" merely to read funny papers—and other papers too, "in which is found the kind of knowledge that leads to socialism, and from socialism immerses you in the material world, in a materiality that leads on to the most reckless skepticism."[226] In 1877 Coppino as minister had to do battle, in presenting the bill, against those who were too much afraid that "half-learning" would create a discontented and unquiet proletariat; he affirmed that for his part he did not see the teaching of the alphabet as such a frightful enemy of order and social peace.[227] Two other deputies, Incagnoli and Fambri, joined him in maintaining that the dangers of merely rudimentary education, seen as good for nothing except to make people unsettled and unhappy, were exaggerated.[228] It was customary to hear, especially in the company of rural reactionaries, that since schooling was a source of socialism, much was gained when the people did not know how to read and write.[229] As time went on, the figure of the primary school teacher came to appear more and more worrisome in the eyes of right-thinking people: a figure soberly dressed but aflame in his soul, the sort of

---

Discorsi). Cf. as well *La Perseveranza* for 15, 19, and 20 June, which criticizes *Il Diritto* for defending the cause of the university associations. See further the debate in the Chamber on 13 and 19 December 1885 on the Coppino decree, which forbade political associations in the universities: some feared the Catholic groups, others feared the radical ones—the usual apprehension about the two perils, red and black (*A.P., Camera*, pp. 15697 ff, 15887 ff., and esp. 15889).

[226] Session of 20 January 1874 (*A.P., Camera*, pp. 770 and 784). Similar themes are found in Ferrario: peasants who get some education are the least hard-working or else become eager readers of "certain bad journals and booklets." Such "lettered villagers," meddlers and intriguers, hold forth in taverns and other dark holes, and in the piazze, becoming "masters of doctrines that smooth the way marvelously for the followers of the International" (Ferrario, *Qual'è la moralità de' campagnuoli*, p. 110). The same horror at the diffusion of "red" journals is found in Taine, *Correspondance* 3:181 (1872).

[227] *Relazione del ministro Coppino al progetto di legge sull'obbligo dell'istruzione elementare, 16 dicembre 1876* (*A.P., Camera, Documenti*, no. 42, p. 5). As a minister in 1874, Scialoja had already found the fears of the hon. Lioy to be exaggerated (*A.P., Camera*, p. 799).

[228] Session of 6 March 1877 (*A.P., Camera*, pp. 1818 and 1831). Renan had said that the half-literate were to be considered useless apes, full of demands (Strauss, *La politique de Renan*, p. 230).

[229] The hon. Luigi Ferrari spoke for the Left in the Chamber on 26 February 1883 against entrusting elementary education to the communes, precisely because in many of them, in which the democratic spirit had not yet penetrated and the atmosphere was still almost medieval, the conservatives would have done nothing to advance seriously the education of the people (*A.P., Camera*, p. 1513). Indeed, in 1894 the landed proprietors of Sicily, meeting in the sala Aragona in Palermo, proposed to cut the funds earmarked for elementary education from the obligatory expenditures of the communes; religious instruction was to be made compulsory in the schools that nonetheless survived (S. F. Romano, *Storia della questione meridionale* [Palermo, 1945], p. 189. And cf. *Avanti* for 9 April 1897: I owe the reference to the courtesy of Prof. Romano).

teacher among whom, in effect, socialism did reap a large crop of novices, propagandists, and cadres. Socialist Milan was indeed, at one point, a city of numerous, well-organized, and active elementary school teachers; and after the attempted assassination of Umberto I by Giuseppe Passanante, when the whole of conservative Italy rose up against the policy advocated by Cairoli and Zanardelli of detecting and punishing crime, but not taking prior measures to suppress it, Bonghi directed his attacks against, among others, professors who proclaimed the wildest doctrines from the lecture platform, and elementary school teachers holding extreme opinions, who were naturally mixed up with all the other subversives in the country.[230]

Education was not enough: proper upbringing was needed, a very different thing, and not to be confused with the first.[231] To make a fetish of basic literacy meant putting the state "into the hands of its plebeian citizens, the most discontented element, the most presumptuous because of its half-learning, the most deranged and subversive in our society."[232] Half-learning was the most dangerous social leaven,[233] and the crass ignorance of the multitudes was better than the presumption of those who remained at the threshold of the temple of science while believing themselves already deep inside it.[234] This blind confidence in schooling and in primary school readers, the rosy illusions of superficial pedagogues and antiquated rhetors, the superstition of our century, all lead to this— thundered out the hon. Lioy, a doughty stalwart of the Right, speaking in the Chamber against the electoral bill of 1881: you end by conceding the vote to the debased crowds that inhabit the cities, the idle and violent drones of the social beehive, just because they have been to school and know how to bellow nonsensical religious, political, and social doctrines in the taverns, while at the same time you deny it to the uncorrupted and healthy democracy of the fields, which represents the steadfast and useful workers in the hive. You give the vote to the seditious and deny it to those, like soldiers, whom you charge with guarding the seditious. Away with these fetishisms and superstitions of the nineteenth century! Science is not a fit diet for the plebs; the anarchic proletariat of science accepts only those scientific conclusions that provide confirmation of terrible negations and brutal demolitions. Science is eminently aristocratic.[235] The pro-

---

[230] Speech to the Chamber of 3 December 1878 (Bonghi, *Discorsi Parlamentari* 1:680).

[231] On these distinctions between upbringing and education, cf. the speech of De Sanctis to the Chamber of 6 May 1878 (*La Critica* 11: 337–38). [*Translator's note:* Italian *istruzione* = English "education, schooling"; Italian *educazione* = English "proper upbringing, good breeding, sound formation of character, training in manners and morals."]

[232] Thus Sonnino, in his speech to the Chamber of 30 March 1881 (Sonnino, *Discorsi Parlamentari* 1:36).

[233] Cf. also, during the debate on the electoral law of 1881, the attacks on incomplete education, on education disjoined from moral upbringing, of the deputies Di Rudinì, Brunetti, Pandolfi, Saladini speaking in the Chamber on 25, 28, 31 March and 4 April (*A.P., Camera*, pp. 4705, 4773, 4874 ff., 5034; also, the hon. Maurigi, p. 4695).

[234] T. Martello, *Storia della Internazionale dalla sua origine al congresso dell'Aja*, p. 399. Partial and superficial science, divorced from public moral standards [*pubblica educazione*] is much more fatal to the social order than ignorance, according to the hon. Brunetti in the Chamber on 28 March 1881 (*A.P., Camera*, p. 4773).

[235] 1 April 1881 (*A.P., Camera*, pp. 4923 ff., 4927).

gress of civilization is entrusted to the cultured classes, and it is only their education that has any importance for the human race: the theory of a "mandarin"
class, dear to Flaubert, recruited followers in Italy too,[236] not the least of whom
was Carducci, officially a democrat in those years and a friend of Cavallotti, but
for all that hostile to compulsory schooling, which he called "forced labor in
order to be able to read a little more than one actually needs to." Carducci de-
claimed against "this stupid, voluntary, material and moral degradation and torture of the century," against the alphabet, "the most hypocritical instrument of
corruption and crime that man, that eminently false animal, has invented."[237]

For a long time, certainly, the particular situation of Italy, in which the papacy
and a part of the clergy, especially the higher clergy, was opposed to national
unity, kept many from fleeing to the bishops for safety and surrendering the
schools to the parish priests, since their victory would have meant the end of Italy
once again. In Italy the danger posed by clericalism was much greater than it was
in France, and for many years appeared to be more serious than the danger of
socialism; or as Sella put it, the "black" International presented a much more
menacing countenance than the red one.

Both were a threat to the public institutions, but since the social problem was
much less acute in Italy, and the nature of the conflict with the church was different, Italy perforce felt the danger of a "black" reaction much more than France
did, though even in France it played a leading role in the history of the Third
Republic. The parliamentary battle to make primary schooling compulsory was
led by the Left in the name of free thought against theocracy, and it was a great
political battle against the curia.

Correnti, sponsoring the bill in 1874, declared that the heart of the question lay
here, in the choice between nonreligious schooling and clerical schooling; two
centuries were in arms against each other.[238] Coppino, speaking as minister in
1877, defined the question as that of whether or not Italy was to be a truly and
fully modern state, or continue to live in vacillation between the old and the new,
in the most contradictory and perilous of situations. "[B]y cultivating the old and
the new at the same time, the first out of habit, the second because we are
constrained to do so by the movement of the entire civilization that surrounds us
and invades us, we generate antagonism, opposition, and contradiction in the
country. A part of the population lives with its head in one century, and another
part in another, and in the last analysis the only arbiter able to come between
them will be violence. . . . Where, by the force of tenacious traditions, the religious conscience evolves tardily and unwillingly, schooling is the only means left
to raise people up to the level of liberal institutions, and to drive into the thought

---

[236] For example, Colonel A. Ricci, *Appunti sulla difesa dell'Italia in generale e della sua
frontiera nord-ovest in particolare* (Turin, 1872), p. 110, who protests against the notion that basic
literacy works miracles and maintains the necessity of raising a cultured class, the great characteristic
of civilization.

[237] To Lidia, 21 March 1877 (Carducci, *Lettere* 11:58. For his political attitude at this time see
ibid., 11:57, 63–64, 172).

[238] Session of 22 January 1874 (*A.P., Camera*, p. 822).

patterns and into the minds of everyone the basis of reforms that, without such a basis, do not sink into people's daily lives and remain on the surface, like plants without roots."[239]

At Rome we will stay, declared Benedetto Cairoli, "despite patent conspiracies and the possibility of aggression, not only with the moral force of right but by progressively demolishing prejudice through education."[240] The law on compulsory schooling, continued an ardent tribune of the Left, the hon. Michelini, is a measure of public order and of public safety: let us save the country, and draw a veil over the image of constitutional right which the new obligation offends. Our enemy is the enemy of liberty and of the civilizing process, it is the church; against it we must deploy the weapon of education, the only one to which it is vulnerable.[241] We inherited Catholics, concluded Petruccelli della Gattina, let us in turn leave free thinkers and free men to our heirs. "A Catholic is neither a citizen nor a man." Let us carry out in the moral domain what we have already accomplished in the political one, and having got rid of the temporal theocracy, let us topple the spiritual theocracy and deprive the church of its authority through secular schools.[242] The hon. Mazzoleni proposed on 28 January 1874 the compilation of a "civil catechism," to teach the maxims of justice and social morality; he too shared the conviction that it was necessary to set science against dogma.[243] In sum, schooling had to be compulsory. There must be no liberty of instruction, which was a fine thing in theory but could not be allowed to turn itself into liberty to poison souls.[244]

Fear of clericalism prevailed for a long time over fear of the reds. Faith in science was practically a corollary of faith in the country, and for many people amounted to the same thing as national feeling. Yet in a slow, steady, continuous process, the horror of "superstition" lost its force, and its grip on people's minds weakened. They were gripped instead by fear of demonstrations in the piazza staged by the lower classes. Between 1874 and 1877 voices were raised in opposition to the very principle of making elementary schooling obligatory, which was seen as a source of social danger. In 1881 it was said that the replacement of faith by science was the program of the Russian nihilists.[245] In 1883 a request was advanced in parliament for the government to take steps to improve the con-

---

[239] *Relazione del ministro Coppino al progetto di legge sull'obbligo dell'istruzione elementare* (cited above, n. 227), p. 15.

[240] Session of 20 January 1874 (*A.P., Camera*, p. 779).

[241] Session of 21 January 1874 (*A.P., Camera*, pp. 805–806).

[242] Session of 5 March 1877 (*A.P., Camera*, pp. 1810–11).

[243] Mazzoleni, *L'XI Legislatura*, pp. 430 ff., 445.

[244] Thus Amari in 1879 (*Carteggio* 2:244). Amari wrote this to Renan to express his opposition to the possibility that seminary students might be allowed to take the examinations for the secondary school diploma [*licenza liceale*] without having completed a single year of nonreligious studies.

In 1875 the Italian press, even the moderate part, had censured the freedom of higher education sanctioned by the French National Assembly as perilous, since it put the ultramontanes in a dominant position (cf. *La Perseveranza* for 18 June 1875; *La Nazione* for 19 June 1875). The French chargé d'affaires, Tiby, observes that in Italy this freedom is held to be a surrender of long-standing French traditions, and a gain for ultramontanism (Tiby, report, 8 September 1875, no. 78; AEP, *C.P., Italie*, t. 393, fol. 105r-v).

[245] The hon. Faldella, in the session of 16 March 1881 (*A.P., Camera*, p. 4406).

dition of the clergy, those "poor workingmen of the spirit . . . who . . . in the tiny rural communes are the only ones to provide a word of comfort for the abandoned population, and raise them to the point of receiving some inkling of moral sentiment, which they would never find elsewhere."[246]

For what, after all, were the fruits of the new schooling? What was its capacity to impart proper upbringing, what did it do to mold good, moral men, good citizens that is, devoted to the existing order? Was education enough? Or did truth not rather lie with those who had been insisting that it was indispensable to make religious belief the basis of instruction, to banish the message of materialism and atheism from the schoolroom as something that bred corruption and disorder, the downfall of the individual and of the collectivity? Social, or civil, or independent—in other words secular—morality was not "the morality of sacrifice, of the voluntary submission of man to an end that lies beyond him." It did not render the individual capable of great actions, and the state could not rest content with citizens educated in such a school. "To make morality independent of religious belief is no more comprehensible to us than making a building independent of its foundations." Hence, in the words of the jurist Giuseppe Piola, we should bar the position of teacher in the primary and secondary schools "to the atheist, the materialist, the skeptic, and even to the simple deist. He who has castrated from his own soul the religious idea and religious feeling, must be kept at a distance from the holy mission of the teacher. We should not entrust the moral and intellectual education of our children to such eunuchs."[247]

The difficulty common to all the liberal parties of Europe, especially in the Catholic countries, was posed in these terms: they tend to dissolve the system of discipline, doctrine, and sanctions that are proper to the Catholic church, a system that may be open to a good deal of objection, but which is considered real and consolatory for the classes that believe in it. And what do they put in its place? Nothing. They offer no moral doctrine to compensate for religious doctrine.[248] It is all very well to open schools, and savings and loan societies, but the terrible malady from which Europe is suffering is not curable by either of these, or by any similar means. Such remedies will have the same effect as throwing water on an oil fire. The lower classes who gave such a terrible example in Paris are not the least cultivated of their sort, but the most cultivated. A profound inner moral renewal, from top to bottom, is required, but where are we to find a source of moral education other than in religion? Where can the state find such a source, if it refuses the aid of any church? Only when religious influence and intellectual influence are united will the education of the poorer classes provide solace for society; otherwise it will gnaw at it like a worm.[249]

As a member of the cabinet in 1874, Bonghi lamented "this moral tragedy . . . of the human spirit," as the conscience of simple people was torn between civil

---

[246] The hon. Fusco, in the session of 22 February (*A.P., Camera*, p. 1425). Cf. too the hon. Indelli and Merzario on 23 February (ibid., pp. 1433 and 1442).

[247] Piola, *La libertà della Chiesa*, pp. 198, 203.

[248] "Il problema sociale e morale in Italia," in *La Perseveranza* for 30 May 1871.

[249] *La Perseveranza* for 2 June 1871 ("La voce de' fatti"; the author is Bonghi) and 7 June 1871 ("La donna a Parigi").

education and religious education.[250] In February 1882 he deplored the skepticism of the young, not in regard to the certainty of science but in regard to the beyond, the eternal problems about which science had nothing to say, "and when it does affirm or deny something about the beyond, it does so off the record, so to speak; when called to order it swallows its words," and the young find themselves abandoned and alone.[251]

On 1 March 1883 in the Chamber he provided a glimpse of the grave moral conditions obtaining in elementary education, which was producing obstreperous and ill-behaved students. Bonghi returned to his favorite theme: the friction between schooling and religious faith was a disaster in a country "in which all the members of the lower class you intend to send to these schools are religious." There was no attempt to make up for the lack of religious instruction by supplying youth with the moral notions once furnished by religion. Bonghi complained that elementary and secondary school teachers too often dedicated their time to politics and to political parties, instead of to educating the young, holding discussions of materialism here and of atheism there, leading demonstrations in the piazza, inducing skepticism in their pupils and moral and social disorder among the masses. Sooner or later the government would be forced to put on the brakes and steer the educators of the populace back onto the right track.[252] Free research, even when it overstepped the bounds of religion, was all right in the universities, but in the other schools, let anyone who harmed religion watch out. This was perfectly in the spirit of Thiers and Renan.

Doubt and remorse of this kind filtered into the minds of many other figures on the Right. Giovanni Lanza, who always held tenaciously to the principle of the separation of church and state, nevertheless expressed his perplexity about what education actually accomplished when he was no longer a minister, and warned that the divergence, and even worse the antagonism of religion and science, might prove fatal to modern society.[253] With the gospel absent from the schools, there were others who proposed educating young people on Epictetus and Marcus Aurelius and the proud morality of the ancient Stoics.[254] But the shared feeling on all sides was fear of the moral vacuum that the schools were leaving in their students. Even if one spoke in the name of science, there was a strong contradiction between wanting to cultivate it, and at the same time surrendering political power through universal suffrage to the classes that were furthest removed from science, to those herds of bipeds still sunk in the darkness of the stone age![255]

[250] Bonghi, *Discorsi Parlamentari* 1:487 (19 December).

[251] Bonghi, *Studi e discorsi intorno alla Pubblica Istruzione* (= vol. 8 in *Opere* [Florence, 1937]), p. 124.

[252] Bonghi, *Discorsi Parlamentari* 2:287 ff. In the debate Bonghi stipulated that he had not said that in the schools it was by now forbidden to pronounce the name of God, but that the country was on the way to reaching that state of affairs before long (*A.P., Camera*, p. 1626). In his complaints about the teachers etc., Bonghi had relayed the protests of a retired elementary schoolteacher, reading portions of his letter in the Chamber.

[253] Lanza, *Le carte* 10:106.

[254] Thus De Laveleye (in agreement with Luzzatti), *Nouvelles lettres d'Italie*, pp. 33–34.

[255] Thus Diomede Pantaleoni in a letter to De Laveleye, in 1882 (De Laveleye, *Nouvelles lettres d'Italie*, p. 103).

Even Crispi in his last years, embittered and pessimistic, said that reason ought to be stronger than faith, but that it wasn't,[256] and he regretted that the governments had neglected the moral training of the people, increasing the number of schools without seeing to it that in them the duties of man and citizen were thoroughly inculcated, the heart cultivated, the mind nourished with moral principles capable of giving a purpose to life: this was the cause of the skepticism and incredulity of the young,[257] this was the reason that tired and discouraged plebeians were embracing the old religion of the priests in some parts of the kingdom.[258] Though he was a consummate anticlerical, in the turbid period at the end of the century Crispi came round to saying: better the clericals than the socialists,[259] calling in his speech at Naples in September 1894 for the union of the civil and religious powers, with God and King for the country and against the infamous sect that had wriggled forth from the blackest fissures of the earth.[260]

Men of the Right and men of the Left, liberal Catholics and Freemasons, vented these griefs and fears in unison, and it fell to one of the younger generation, Ferdinando Martini, an individual certainly not suspected of "black" sympathies, to express them with complete clarity. The law of 1877, he said, has removed the catechism from the list of subjects examined in the schools; and it did well. But, he continued, as spokesman for the executive committee for the public education budget, it had also been recommended to the minister that he provide for religious instruction to be given to all the students whose parents requested it, through a regulation. This has not been done, and it remains in the power of the municipalities to have religious instruction given or not. This confusion must be resolved. "If certain ideals seem to you to be out of date, if you are able to replace them with others, if you think it is within your power, then make haste to effect this substitution. It is certain . . . that without ideals there is no statesman, however expert he may be, who can govern in the long run; there is no people, however docile it may be, that will let itself be governed in the long run. Nations do not prosper without high ideals, and civilizations do not flourish." Now, what is the Italian school system giving to the country after the law of 1877? Very little, much less than what had been hoped for as far as Martini was concerned, who was fully in agreement with other colleagues that the school system had been reduced to a factory of bad voters.[261] And the fault was in the system. "If you do not form the citizen in the schools, you can fill the arsenals with all the arms you want; they will be of no use if you do not put them into hands guided by strong and generous hearts that feel deeply the love of country." Bovio has said that until the social question is resolved, there will not be a good school system for the people: "I invert the terms . . . and I say that until there is a good school system for the people, the social question will be insoluble, and

256 Crispi, *Pensieri e profezie*, p. 177.
257 Ibid., pp. 163–64.
258 Notes of December 1896 (MRR, *Carte Crispi*, busta 668, no. 3/18).
259 In a talk with Farini, 12 March 1895 (Farini, *Diario* 1:663).
260 See the reactions of the irreducible anticlericals, and Crispi's firm statements opposing anarchy, which he depicts "advancing with dynamite and dagger" (Crispi, *Carteggi politici inediti*, pp. 519–20; Farini, *Diario* 1:577–78).
261 The hon. Rosano in the session of 2 March 1883 (*A.P.*, *Camera*, p. 1605).

however much you are ready to concede with your laws for social reform, they will only want more, because in the individual who is supposed to benefit there will be lacking sufficient moral training to appreciate the benefit. Until you have taught individuals to distinguish the austere aspect of truth from the alluring veneer of utopia, until you have provided good schooling for the people, the social question will be nothing more than the alternation of fruitless speculations on one side and blind violence on the other."[262]

The Voltaireans were fearful that Voltaireanism would beguile the people, the *populace* abhorred by the master; they were alarmed as they saw the eighteenth century being appropriated by the crowd instead of being the privilege of an elite band of the intelligent and enlightened. Villari, not a papalist certainly, had already expressed in 1875 his fear that they were raising a people of Voltaireans and clericals.[263] With much greater clarity of language and with the source of his concern in much clearer focus, Martini unburdened himself, at the murky close of the century, to a friend who was equally above suspicion of clericalism, Carducci. Neither you nor Crispi will accomplish anything, he said. "Take note that you are preaching to the converted: I am convinced, and have been for some time, of what Quinet says with great verbal force and demonstrates with very impressive examples: that political revolutions which are not accompanied by a religious renewal lose sight of their origin and their earliest aims, and finish up by releasing all the worst instincts in the plebs. But after the evil that *we*, all of us, dear Giosuè, have done, are we in a position to provide the remedy? To whom should we preach? We, bourgeois Voltaireans, are the ones that have brought into being the unbelievers, while the pope took care of the bad believers. Now, when the plebeians cry out for chicken in the pot, because they no longer believe in the *beyond*, shall we go forth and speak to them about God, whom yesterday we denied? They will not believe us: I speak of the lower classes in the cities and the villages; those of the countryside do not know what to make of a God without a church, without rites, without priests. The tomb is an insufficient reward for all the evil we (not you and I, we as a class) have done in our thoughtless pride. We chose to tear down without knowing how to build up anything. According to the chatter of the pedagogues, the school was supposed to substitute for the church. A fine substitution! I commend it to you."[264]

What had become of the ideal of science in Rome proclaimed by Quintino Sella? What had become of faith in secular schooling as the only road to knowledge of the finer feelings, the matrix of a people renewed in its mores and in its soul?

The skepticism of Martini was not shared by everyone, for by nature he had little inclination to nurse profound faith in anything. Others were more optimistic and believed it impossible that Noah's flood was going to return and wipe out civilization; they had little time for dark prognoses of a new universal upheaval caused by barbarians coming not from the north but from out of the bowels of

[262] Speech to the Chamber, 2 March 1883 (*A.P., Camera*, pp. 1616 ff.). For Bovio's speech on 26 February see ibid., p. 1518.
[263] Speech to the Chamber, 6 May 1875 (*A.P., Camera*, p. 2978).
[264] Martini to Carducci, 16 October 1894 (Martini, *Lettere (1860–1928)*, pp. 291–92).

society itself, against which the church was the only barrier.[265] But in either case there was little advance beyond positions previously arrived at; themes already familiar to European culture were reechoed, instead of new ones being created. In fact the intellectual period that came after was historicist in Italy, and so alien to the myth, which had been dear to the prophets of the period 1850–1900, of science as the liberator of the human race. The advances made by Italian culture came through historicism, which meant a refinement of the historical sense, but rendered the previous fanaticism for reason and science impossible.

While this was happening in the purely intellectual realm, there was a parallel development in daily life, where the mirage toward which increasing numbers of people directed their gaze was not that of learning as the source of freedom, but that of a socialist society, in which science and culture were seen as quite secondary components. Although socialism was also anticlerical and appeared to have the style and the tone of the old free thinkers, the truth is that its target was no longer just papal Rome but a whole world, of which the Vatican was merely a part. The aim was no longer to set up the religion of truth over against the religion of the priests, but proletarian society over against bourgeois society. The struggle took in a wider sphere, its center shifted; the attack on revealed religion lost strength while the attack on the established social order gained in intensity. On one hand the fear of socialism ended up inducing a more accommodating attitude to the Vatican in many formerly free thinkers, and made them love the Truth a little less, and social tranquillity a little more; this showed that in Italy, even more than in France, anticlericalism was not instinctive for the bourgeoisie but tactical, a matter of contingency more than of principle.[266] On the other hand, the growth of socialism in the end rendered the assault on the world of "'black' superstition and barbarism" in the name of the world of light and reason less direct and continuous. For the socialists, that world of light and reason, when all was said and done, was still "bourgeois."

In the first half of the century, there had been an opposition of principle, with liberty and nationality ranged against legitimism and the European order. Everywhere after 1870 it was replaced, even in the realm of ideas, by a more tangible conflict involving interests such as commercial expansion and colonial power and prestige. The old antithesis between religion and faith, truth and obscurantism, succumbed to the more palpable antithesis between the social classes, to the struggle for social justice.

In these conditions the universal mission of Rome as a center of science rapidly vanished. The illusion would have been shattered in any case by the evident disproportion between the dream and its capacities for realization, in an Italy that had embarked on an arduous struggle merely to reach the level of the other nations in the fields of study and of scientific progress, much less to overtake them.

[265] Thus Minghetti, *Stato e Chiesa*, pp. 227 ff.
[266] Cf. for France, Ch. Morazé, *La France bourgeoise* (Paris, 1946), p. 122.

The Shadow of Caesar

NEITHER *renovatio Ecclesiae* in the name of the church, nor *renovatio Romae* in the name of Science: only two mirages that vanished one after the other.

What then? Face up to a more modest reality with equanimity, acknowledge limits, abandon universal missions, and simply resolve to carry out as well as possible the duty of constructing the new state on a sound basis and transforming Italy into a great modern country: wouldn't this be the true fulfillment of a mission? Wouldn't this be a practical contribution to human existence? It would mean recognizing, as Bonghi had been insisting since September 1870, that the real meaning of Rome was the task of creating the moral fiber of the Italians, awakening their capacity for intellectual accomplishment, reviving their consciousness of their rights and their sense of their duty.[1] It would mean seeing, as Silvio Spaventa saw, that the taking of Rome could not and should not make Italians think they had some claim to exercise their rule beyond Italy's frontiers: a foreign dominion had to be justified, in reason and in practicality, by present needs and necessities and by the possession of the vital forces able to satisfy them—not by memories of the past.[2] One would have to forget the past, as Bonghi hoped the Italians would, and live entirely for the present—which might indeed appear less glorious when viewed at close range. Indeed it could bruise and depress one, whereas one read about the past in historical works that stripped away all of the human frailties that had attended its making.[3] In sum, the Italians would have to accept on the ideal plane what they were actually doing in practice, and be satisfied with putting their own house in good order.

Clearly, many did. Even those who, from beyond its frontiers, had been urging the third Italy to follow the vision of a grandiose religious revolution, to eject the papacy and enlarge the horizon of science, shifted their ground as these hopes evaporated, and envisioned Italy instead as a second-class power, happy enough with being average. None said this more clearly than the mercurial Renan, who shifted from trying to rouse the Italians against the papacy to expressing a very unflattering view of them.[4]

But it was hard, indeed impossible, for all the Italians to resign themselves. There had been too much talk, for too many decades, and on all sides, of the

---

[1] "Considerazioni malinconiche," in *La Perseveranza* for 11 September 1870.

[2] Spaventa, *La politica della Destra*, pp. 201–202.

[3] Speech to the Chamber on 1 March 1883 (Bonghi, *Discorsi Parlamentari* 2:284). Bonghi attacks the intention of the minister, Baccelli, to bring back Roman history and the ancient Roman style of education.

[4] "Italy will never be with anyone, it will always forsake them, until the time comes when, having rid itself of its politicians and journalists, it will resign itself to being a state of the second order, and very happy in its own way." (Renan and Berthelot, *Correspondance*, p. 504). Renan wrote this in 1881, after Tunis.

third Italy, of universal renewal;[5] too much emphasis had been placed on the immense task awaiting Italy when it had arrived in Rome for the Italians suddenly to settle down and attend to purely administrative and economic business. Rome was seen in every quarter as something much more grand than a normal capital; the trumpet blasts that sounded on the Left were answered, in a different key and for different purposes, certainly, by the voice of the pontiff extolling in his turn the universal mission of the city and appealing "to this our beloved city, the seat of the pontificate, which derived such singular benefit from the presence [of the popes] that it became not only the impregnable citadel of the faith but also the refuge of the fine arts, the domicile of wisdom, the marvel and envy of the world."[6] We may even wonder whether it was not their own militant irritation against Catholic Rome that goaded the "naturalists and rationalists" who were condemned in the papal encyclicals to search elsewhere for an indication as to what the new mission of the city should be.

So Rome dominated the mental world of contemporaries, who recalled the recent epoch of national redemption as a time of audacious undertakings, of unforeseen and miraculous events, of poetry. Were they now to content themselves with prosaic worries such as balancing income and outlay, or planning public works? Only high ideals and strong passions had made the Risorgimento possible; were they now to drop from the heavens back down to earth at the moment when Italy, newly emerged from inferno into the light of day, had to give the world proof of its resurrection?[7]

Such were the sentiments that stirred the elevated, unquiet spirit of a Carducci or a Crispi. These feelings touched others who held more temperate opinions, whose thoughts stayed closer to the ground, but who feared that their country, united at last, might have to play the role of Cinderella among the nations. The profound urge to set high political aims for Italy is surely revealed by the debate about the Franco-Prussian War, and the satisfaction felt at the fall of France and the end of Italy's vassalage to the dark figure of Louis Napoleon.

These particular concerns were entirely intrinsic to Italy. But beyond the Alps there was a general scene of roiling passions, of enthusiasm and hope being kindled for the greatness and the mission of each country. The thirst for power was felt ever more strongly. Imperialism of a doctrinaire kind trained its gaze toward the west and the east. The basis of international life was force, and attention was constantly focused on prestige. Each of the great nations backed up its concrete political actions by laying claim to an illustrious heritage, to special qualities of excellence. In Germany, France, and England, much earlier than in Italy, the belief that each of these countries had in its own moral and civic mission changed into the idea that its mission was political. Where Humboldt and Schiller had once hoped that the reign of the spirit would come about through the effort of the Germans, the Pan-Germanists now aimed to create a purely terri-

[5] Cf. as well the speech of Massari to the Chamber on 13 March 1872 (*A.P., Camera*, p. 1183).

[6] Leo XIII, in the encyclical *Inscrutabili Deo consilio*, 21 April 1878 (cf. the Italian text in Giordani, ed., *Le encicliche*, p. 17).

[7] C. Correnti to Michelet, 20 February 1871 (Monod, *Jules Michelet*, p. 59).

torial kingdom. Where men such as de Maistre and Guizot had once seen France in the role of teacher and guide, others now saw it donning a general's uniform covered with golden braids. The idea of mission lost its universal civilizing character everywhere, and the mission became one of lordship by one people over others. In England, the land from which the doctrines of Manchester had spread to the world, Disraeli in 1872 began invoking "the dominating spirit of these islands." Tennyson, an imperialist since 1870, reworked *Hands All Round* in 1882, making it a hymn to British imperial greatness; Froude and Seeley provided historiographical underpinning for the doctrines of imperialism; and spectacular events like the colonial exposition of 1886 and the Jubilee of Queen Victoria in 1887 sparked the enthusiasm of the crowds.[8] Finally, Kipling encapsulated the whole former and present imperial spirit of Britain, over which the Lord God presided at home and abroad:

> Fair is our lot—o goodly is our heritage!
> (Humble ye, my people, and be fearful in your mirth!)
> For the Lord our God Most High
> He hath made the deep as dry,
> He hath smote for us a pathway to the ends of all
> the Earth![9]

Holy Russia, the protector of brother Slavs and Christians in the Balkans, loomed in the distance: Russia destined with her virgin, untouched energies to renew the world—in the manifestos of the Pan-Slavists at least.

Whatever the mission, the great events and heroic figures of the past were summoned to justify it, a past that lay close at hand for the losers of the battle of Sedan, before whose gaze the figures of Richelieu and the French empire builders rose in splendor,[10] a past remote in time, vanishing in fact into the mist of prehistory, for the Germans, who followed Ulrich von Hutten and an age-old tradition of public ideology in looking to Arminius the savior, but now with a new sense of pride.

In Italy Alfredo Oriani wanted the monument to Vittorio Emanuele II placed on the Capitol: the first king of Italy should occupy the pedestal of Marcus Aurelius, to demonstrate to the world that every historical epoch came to realization nowhere else but on the Capitol; not even the Christian ideal had dared to displace the civic ideal that that hill embodied. Oriani was annoyed that no one else had thought of this, that no one else had perceived that it was necessary to connect Italy's history to ancient history, keeping alive the great Roman tradition

---

[8] Cf. C. A. Bodelsen, *Studies in Mid-Victorian Imperialism* (Copenhagen-Christiania-London-Berlin, 1924), pp. 124 ff., 147 ff., 174 ff.; D. C. Somervell, *English Thought in the Nineteenth Century* (London, 1929), pp. 182 ff., 188–89; R. H. Murray, *Studies in the English Social and Political Thinkers of the Nineteenth Century* 2:185 ff., 207–208 (Cambridge, 1929); and in general F. Brie, "Imperialistiche Strömungen in der Englischen Literatur," *Anglia* (1916): fasc. 1, pp. 110–84.

[9] Kipling, "A Song of the English (The Seven Seas)."

[10] It is symptomatic that Hanotaux, a prominent colonialist, dedicated his labors as a historian to a *Histoire du cardinal de Richelieu*.

that was the source of all of modern life.[11] Yet on 16 August 1875 forty thousand Germans had acclaimed the monument to Arminius on the Grotenburg with roaring enthusiasm, on the spot where, in the distant past, the proud Germans had rescued humanity and liberty from the Roman yoke: Arminius the savior, the herald of the German greatness that Wilhelm I, the new savior who had triumphed over Latin duplicity, had now brought into being. The statue of Arminius stood fifty-five feet in height and brandished in its right hand a colossal sword; below it appeared the profile of the king of Prussia and emperor of Germany: past and present joined in a single apotheosis of power and military glory.[12]

This was the panorama of Europe at the end of the nineteenth century, and Italy was a part of Europe. And so, between the memories and hopes associated with the Risorgimento, still so recent in memory, and the stimuli coming from the present reality of Europe, it was all the more difficult to accept the advice that Italy was receiving from more than one direction, advice that was often proffered in a friendly spirit, not out of disrespect or disdain: to content itself with a position like that of Switzerland and Belgium, the position most favorable to the security and prosperity of a nation.[13] Italy was counseled to renounce any greatpower policy, to busy itself making life in its own closed shell as comfortable as possible. Advice of this sort one day brought the response from Minghetti that "a great country cannot concentrate all its activity within itself in this fashion. Youth feels the urge for expansion, and if no vast prospects open up before it, it turns sour and finds its outlet in corruption and discontent. A distinguished member of the English parliament, Courtney, recently said that the Egyptians would just have to be left to stew in their own juices. I confess that such a future for my country does not appeal to me: the stew might get scorched." This answer, witticism included, was an appropriate one.

Since united Italy had no coal deposits, to ask it to content itself with the role of a Belgium meant, above all, asking it to confine itself to remaining an agricultural state in the midst of an industrialized world.[14] This was seen as simple ingenuousness, even by those Italians who did not feel the lure of the phantasms that dwelt in the pages of Livy, or on the Capitol.[15]

---

[11] Oriani, *Quartetto*, pp. 44–45.

[12] There was a certain amount of irritation in Italy on account of the inscriptions on the monument to Arminius: cf. R. De Zerbi, "Il trionfatore della doppiezza latina," in *Scritti Politici* (Naples, 1876), pp. 401 ff.; and Tiby, report, 8 September 1875, no. 78; AEP, *C.P., Italie*, t. 393, fol. 106).

[13] De Laveleye, *Nouvelles lettres d'Italie*, pp. 67 ff., 99–100. The Belgian writer had already urged Italy in 1871 to content itself with being a state of the second rank, rather than aspire to the role of a great power (De Laveleye, *Causes de la guerre en Europe* [Brussels, 1871], p. 122); and cf. *Lettres d'Italie*, p. 365: "the deplorable ambition to play a role in the complications of European politics." Berthelot, on the other hand, thought in 1872 that the Italians had comprehended "that happiness lies in mediocrity" (Renan and Berthelot, *Correspondance*, p. 425).

[14] In fact De Laveleye lamented the fact that Italy, lacking deposits of coal and iron ore, wanted to industrialize, and suggested that it dedicate itself to agriculture instead (*Nouvelles lettres d'Italie*, pp. 16 ff., 75).

[15] Note how Nigra too reacted as Minghetti had to the idea that Italy ought to confine itself to being "a bigger Belgium, minus its industries" (personal letter to Crispi, 7 August 1890, in Crispi, *Questioni internazionali*, p. 132, republished in C. M. De Vecchi di Val Cismon, "Lo scioglimento

The memory of past greatness and the expectation of greatness in the future had constituted the driving force of the Risorgimento, from Foscolo to Mazzini: to suggest now that Italy should settle for the position of a neutral state would have meant suggesting that it fling away the primary idea that had allowed it to gather the scattered fragments of the Italian homeland into a unit—even if this were possible for a country that found itself implicated in the major conflicts of European policy in any case because of its struggle with the papacy and the "black" international. The antipatriots who had derided the idealism and the self-less gestures of the conspirators as ludicrous would have been proved right in their exhortation to all the Italians to stay at home and pay attention to their own business, and not let their heads be turned by the illusion of an absurd and detrimental unification, since they could continue to live with such ease and tranquillity in the old states of the peninsula.

In sum, it was out of the question to demand that Italy withdraw from international politics and renounce any aspiration to play a role, even in the future. The task of wiser heads would be that of not letting themselves be swayed too much by the heritage of the past, of damping down tumult and vanity; it could not be that of renouncing *tout court* any active role in European affairs. But the point is that all of Europe was then setting off down the road to its own destruction, joining unanimously in the chant of power and glory: that chant reverberated in Italy, where the voice of ancient Rome seemed to answer it.[16] So it was that, while dreams of the final triumph of science faded away and a new European reality made up increasingly of greatness, force, and prestige took shape, the image of ancient Rome as the mistress of subject provinces began to replace the image of Rome as the teacher of truth. The narrow aim of building the country's political greatness overlaid the universal mission of culture and civilization.

Rome as the city of empire rematerialized. It did not scorn the book, nor refuse its homage to science, but joined the book and the sword, science and military force, spiritual greatness and earthly power. There would be education, but the schools would inculcate deep patriotic sentiment and form courageous soldiers.

The eloquent Guido Baccelli was among the first, as public speaker, deputy, and minister, to sketch the new task entrusted to the public education system. At this point it was no longer a novelty but a commonplace that schooling was a necessary premise to all greatness, including the political and military kind. Germany was extravagantly admired for its victories at Sadowa and Sedan, victories that were ascribed even more to the virtues of its elementary school teachers than to the virtues of its generals; learned Germany had been the creator of powerful Germany. Francesco De Sanctis had already called this to the attention of the Chamber, adding that the same compelling reasons for reforming Italy's army and navy were behind the drive to undertake the reform of education: scholastic

---

della "Pro Patria' di Trento nel carteggio Crispi-Nigra," *Rassegna Storica del Risorgimento* 21 [1934]: 17).

[16] On the influence that international events and the spread of imperialism later had on the formation of Italian nationalism, cf. the fine pages of Volpe, *Italia moderna* 2:341 ff.

conscription went with military conscription.[17] As minister he had already propounded, never failing to cite the example of Germany and Moltke, physical
training in the schools as the necessary foundation of physical and moral courage, the training of the will, the origin of the military virtues.[18]

The conjunction of schooling and life under arms, the inseparability of instruction and military service, arose out of the course of events, the evolution of
international politics. At the height of the Tunisian crisis, stung by Italy's moral
defeat and the "hard lesson inflicted on us by France with Europe's backing"
because of Italy's weakness, a man such as Cesare Correnti, who as minister of
public education had earlier sought to establish the principle that primary schooling should be compulsory, in obedience to the democratic credo,[19] also began to
think that Italy had to be strong and feared. To attain that goal, it had to find
strength in its own shame and disgrace, as Prussia had done following Jena. "The
generation, which is now in its twilight, of those who liberated Italy, grew up
with the experience of being beaten by the Croats. The generation that is now
ripening will be formed by the experience of France's insults. Schooling, arms,
prudence and concord . . . schools for the people and intelligence in arms. Let
the schools furnish voters, and let the schools be military, civic, and Christian.
Have no fear, my dear Cairoli. Christianity is the democratic form of religious
thought: the cult of the humble, of the poor, of those who seek life only for the
loftiest things, of those who do not fear death. Remember what Guerrazzi said to
Cavour one day in my presence, with his cynical turn of phrase. *The priest is a
dog you can poison with a mouthful of Gospel.* Cavour smiled without understanding these words. You however are capable of grasping the sense."[20]

But only in Baccelli, the Roman professor of medicine, was the shared credo
illuminated by the vision of ancient Rome admonishing her remote offspring. He
too desired to greet the triumph of science in Rome and, aflame with the spirit of
prophecy, foresaw the day when Rome's Policlinico [the medical center] would
be the first of its kind in the world, an object of noble envy for Italy.[21] But
knowledge had to be allied with the sword. Science and arms should find Italy
and Germany united on the sacred road leading to prosperity and national
honor.[22] The school must be the forge of character, must prepare brave soldiers
ready to offer the supreme sacrifice for the homeland; it must be the place in
which the citizen and the soldier are molded. In order to accomplish this, it must
be continually inspired by the great memories of the *alma mater*, the time when

---

[17] Session of 23 January 1874 in the Chamber (*La Critica* 11:324).

[18] Sessions of 30 May and 17 June 1878 (ibid., 11:398 ff. and 405 ff.).

[19] Cf. Morandi, *La sinistra al potere*, p. 86.

[20] Correnti to Cairoli, 28 April 1881 (MRP, *Carte Cairoli*, pacco 19). The day before, Correnti
had also said the same thing to Crispi. [*Translator's note:* Guerrazzi said, "Il prete è un cane che si
può avvelenare col boccone Vangelo."]

[21] Baccelli, speeches to the Chamber on 16 March 1881 (Rome, 1881, p. 16), and to the Senate
on 12 May (Rome, 1881, pp. 10 and 13), concerning the Policlinico and the Palazzo delle Scienze in
Rome. For his image of Rome gathering the rays of wisdom and light from the hundred cities of Italy
like a mirror, see too his speech on the Capitol on 8 October 1882, on the occasion of the prize-giving
ceremony for the contest among the best students of the secondary schools, in G. Gorrini, *Guido
Baccelli* (Turin, 1916), p. 50 n. 1

[22] Speeches to the Chamber of 17 and 18 December 1881 (Rome, 1882, p. 23).

"this city was admired by the world for the way it trained the citizen and the soldier." Let us return to the tradition of our fathers, said Baccelli, and we will be the leaders in moral training in the world; let us bring back to life the virtues of our homeland, "which gave it greatness in antiquity, and which indicate to it amid the shadows of the future the certain path to a new greatness." Why not return "to that soldierly material that conquered the world, leaving a trace on our history that is still deep, an immortal page of glory and magnanimous precedent"? To hear some people discourse, it might seem that the Roman period is virtually a prehistoric epoch, whereas we are much closer to it than might appear to be the case. So why not make the perfect type of ancient Roman live again, a man who "had to have the arm of a gladiator and the head of a jurisconsult"? We complain about the scant sense of discipline among the young, of their vacillating patriotism, of the subversive doctrines and the refusal to heed the law that are stealing into their minds, in place of feelings of devotion to the country's institutions; and we do nothing to oppose the wicked elements that are gaining control of their enthusiastic heads.

As a government minister, Baccelli determined to take measures. He presented a project for popular, or complementary, education that would put young people between sixteen and nineteen years old through a course of civic training, principally by means of "generalized military gymnastics," entrusted ideally to army officers. The government's responsibility in the field of education was to prepare citizens for the day when they would have to do their duty for their country. Thus it had to follow the model of the Roman legion, so that when the time came to face up to danger the soldiers would be aware that the greatest glory is to die for one's country. The religion of the homeland had to be a universal religion, it had to be inculcated in the young from the earliest years of school. The ideal of the century is that of the citizen soldier; the model is ancient Rome; the object of training is to arrive at the age when "the threshold of strength necessary for pure survival is crossed, and [the individual] exuberantly joins the contributors to society."[23]

Schooling was no longer guided by the ultimate aim of battling ignorance for the improvement of the life of the lower classes, its stated goal a decade earlier; now the ultimate end was a possible future battle against an external enemy. The army became "*a university providing training for the people*" and arms took the place of the alphabet in forming them,[24] to the point that a good soldier who was illiterate came to be thought preferable to an educated citizen without military capacity.[25]

---

[23] In addition to the speeches already cited, cf. Baccelli's speech to the Chamber on 28 February 1883, on the occasion of the debate on the education budget for 1883 [*A.P., Camera*, pp. 1554 ff.); his lecture at Genoa, 1 September 1881, on "La Scuola popolare: L'autonomia delle università," published in the *Giornale della Società di lettere e conversazioni scientifiche di Genova* (1881; esp. pp. 8 ff.); and further, the lecture given at Rome in 1897, "Educazione nazionale ed esercito." Cf. Bonghi's speech to the Chamber (*Discorsi Parlamentari* 2:283 ff.) against the Rome-centered outlook ("romanità") of Baccelli. Candeloro is perfectly correct in stating that while for Bonghi Rome represented a historical and cultural set of values, for Baccelli it was a political and national ideal (Candeloro, preface to Bonghi, *Studi e discorsi intorno alla Pubblica Istruzione*, p. xv).

[24] Baccelli, "Educazione nazionale ed esercito" (cited in previous note), pp. 12 ff.

[25] Ibid., p. 20.

As soon as the ideal of science for its own sake, or the myth of science as an instrument in the struggle against religion, was abandoned, and science was proposed instead as an instrument serving the political greatness of the country, the glorious deeds of ancient Rome were immediately appealed to, and thrust forward to be imitated. Of course these partisans of ancient Rome, no matter how ardent, protested that their goal was greatness in civil life for Italy, not the resurrection, impossible in any case, of the Roman empire: once the ghosts had been conjured up they refused to disappear, and they spoke of military and political glory even though they were left to themselves to roam the ruins of the Palatine and the Forum. The day might come when, with the right combination of general circumstances in Italy and Europe, the summoning of those ghosts would regain all its old spellbinding power, and its precise meaning.

The triumph of patriotic science entailed the triumph of the feeling for force, for force militarily organized: "the political dynamometer of a people measures its force much more exactly than population size; and its force lies in the tempered spirit of the citizens, and in the sound and sturdy organization of its military corps. The sciences ennoble, the fine arts embellish, agriculture and industry enrich a people; but a noble, embellished and rich people could be enslaved. Conversely a people less noble . . . but strong as a result of its training and its arms is able to fight victoriously for its independence."[26] The reply might have been: only for independence, only in the holy cause of self-defense? Or was it not also in the service of the "dynamic exuberance" for which the Roman physician hoped? For Baccelli was using unaccustomed language to express ideas that were different to the call to arms sounded in the Risorgimento, from Foscolo to d'Azeglio to Cattaneo—but very much akin to the exaltation of the youthful erupting forces, the vital forces rich with a future, promoted by *La Riforma* and Crispi.

Thus it was not mere haphazard when the voice of Guido Baccelli was joined by another of much greater weight and underlying intellectual force, the voice of Crispi. It is not enough to be materially in Rome, Crispi said in the Collegio Romano on 23 March 1884; nor does science suffice. "[T]he new mission of Italy begins here, and though we have taken over the city, abolished the temporal principate of the pontiffs and proclaimed the freedom of religion and of conscience, our work is incomplete until the time when we shall have demonstrated to foreigners with our scholarship, with our arms, with science and with force, that we are equal to our forefathers."[27] A few days later, speaking at the Circolo Universitario in Palermo, he pressed the point home, exhorting the young men present to remember the Germans and their victories, which they owed above all to science: science, which not only develops and reinforces the mind but makes the arm strike more forcefully, so that "by enlarging with the patrimony of science the areas of learning in which each of us is competent, you can make your contribution to the scientific power of our country, and by making yourselves useful as men of science, you can be useful at the same time as men of the sword."[28]

[26] Ibid., p. 28.
[27] Crispi, *Scritti e discorsi politici*, p. 441.
[28] Ibid., p. 449.

The adepts of science had not been dreaming of the Germany of Bismarck when they put their faith in a Rome that, "to make amends for armed oppression in antiquity and for the evil arts of recent times," would promote "the just freedom of endeavor and the unlimited freedom of thought" in the world.[29] But the glory of arms, even glory won at the cost of oppression, was becoming once more the goddess of fin-de-siècle Europe, and all the rest a memory of lost illusions. A new Rome, powerful and magnificent, sprang up in Crispi's imagination, splendid with the pomp of new monuments: "whoever enters that great city finds there the synthesis of two great epics, each rivaling the other in the realm of the marvelous. The monuments that celebrate these epics are the pride of the world; for the Italians they are a pungent reminder of their duty. . . . Rome must be restored and we too must erect monuments of civilization there, so that our descendants will be able to say that we were great, as our fathers were."[30]

The image of Rome had always remained vivid in the minds of foreigners, and for this reason, said Crispi, they feared the resurgence of Italy "as signifying, perhaps, its return to a greatness and a power that had left a deep mark on the world."[31] The antithesis between Italy and the foreigners to which Crispi here adverts is in itself sufficient to reveal how he was exceeding the bounds of a purely civilizing mission for Italy and passing over into a vision of political greatness, in terms of which the marked distinction between what belonged to oneself and what belonged to others was perfectly fitting. It is true that Crispi continued to repeat clichés about Italy's civilizing mission, and to state that he did not wish Rome to rule an empire, since the last one had cost the Italians dear over the centuries; it is also true that such affirmations came to be mingled with others, more heartfelt, about the lofty destiny of the homeland and the government's unique duty to advance "the development of national life, a higher standard of living for the masses, the enlargement of the power of the state." To be loved by the rest of the world was no longer enough, the country had to be feared.[32] Crispi was a man still conceptually anchored to the past in many respects, a creature of the first half of the nineteenth century as far as his mental structures went: yet his heart belonged entirely to the new age, and in him nature and impulse and imagination counted for more than intellectual doctrines. Consequently, the images of ancient Rome naturally drew from him these calls for Italy, newly risen, to gain power, and political and military greatness. His insistence on Rome, his desire to bring about a state of affairs in which an Italian citizen "could utter the words *civis Romanus sum* before the other peoples, and be taken seriously," his repeated assertion that the past had to live again in the national consciousness by reason of its glorious deeds and the virtues of the forefathers who gained us our fame, that it was up to us to make the past live

---

[29] The words of Amari at the conclusion of his *Storia dei Musulmani in Sicilia*, which appeared in 1872 (vol. 3, p. 895; now edited by Nallino, vol. 3, part 3 [Catania, 1939], p. 922).

[30] Crispi, *Scritti e discorsi politici*, p. 496. And cf. his speech to the Chamber on 10 March 1881 in favor of the bill for state participation in construction projects and in the expansion of the capital (Crispi, *Discorsi Parlamentari* 2:480 ff.).

[31] Crispi, *Scritti e discorsi politici*, p. 669 (his commemoration of Marco Minghetti, 1887).

[32] Ibid., pp. 544, 712.

again by making Italy great,[33] all helped to create a new atmosphere, charged with a sense of potency, in which the myth of Rome itself took on a new significance. It was not felt as a decorative motif or a rhetorical embellishment applied for the sake of ornamental luster, but rather as something welling up from deep inside, almost a natural instinct that coincided totally with the personality of a man like Crispi, a man of priestlike zeal, sincere and tireless, for the unity and greatness of Italy.

The exhortation of Ugo Foscolo that the Italians should turn to history to create for themselves a national consciousness, and Crispi's insistence on the same thing,[34] signified the amalgamation of the past and the present: it meant grounding the present in the glories of the past, glories which in turn signaled the duties to be fulfilled in the future; patriotism was the same thing as reverence for the wondrous memories of olden times. Foscolo had gazed with admiration on the glories of the Italian race—Machiavelli, Michelangelo, and Galileo—but now it was ancient Rome, the Rome of the Scipios and of Caesar, that surged into being again.

The old attraction felt in the Risorgimento for the age of the free communes was certainly not extinct, and the Italy of the twelfth and thirteenth centuries remained a constant presence for patriotic Italians in the years between 1870 and 1880; for some it was recalled as a maritime power and mistress of colonies, while others remembered the battles of the communes against German overlords, and accordingly Mediterranean aspirations in the 1870s were nourished by the recollection of the Fourth Crusade while irredentism sounded the trumpet of the battle of Legnano.[35] But it was the tendency to exalt the medieval expansion of the maritime republics in the Orient that increasingly prevailed among the proponents of Italic greatness, rather than the struggles against the medieval German emperors. Venice and Genoa counted for more as examples to emulate than did Milan, their ships more than the *carroccio* [the war wagon of the commune]. The traditions of ancient seagoing splendor[36] began to serve as a stimulus for tomor-

---

[33] Ibid., pp. 737 and 759. It is quite true that in the first of these texts (a speech of 14 October 1889 at Palermo), Crispi declares that he does not wish for "the Roman empire," which has burdened Italy for too many centuries: he is in favor of respect for all the peoples. On the other hand, this is the speech in which Crispi defends himself against the accusation of megalomania, of wanting to conduct an imperial policy (ibid., p. 735). Above all, as has been noted and will be again (see below, pp. 445 ff.), though it would certainly be absurd to make Crispi out to be a doctrinaire imperialist, even of the specifically late nineteenth-century kind, it is equally true that his appeals to Rome, to the power of Rome etc., end sooner or later by expressing—ineluctably—the lust for power.

[34] Crispi, *Scritti e discorsi politici*, pp. 593 and 603, and *Pensieri e profezie*, pp. 21 and 173 (the cult of the great heritage).

[35] The outburst of irredentism in 1876 began at Milan with the celebration of the seventh centenary of the battle of Legnano (Sandonà, *L'irredentismo nelle lotte politiche* 1:123 ff.). It must be remembered that the reigning interpretation of Italian communal history at this time was that of a struggle for liberty and independence against the German emperors (as in Carducci's "Canzone di Legnano"); only at the end of the century would this interpretation give way to a different mode of evaluating and understanding the nation's history.

[36] "La politica italiana in Oriente," in *La Riforma* for 1 September 1872; and note the glorification of Venice etc., as well as of Rome, in L. Campo Fregoso, *Del primato italiano sul Mediterraneo*, pp. 4, 9, 52 ff., 64 ff. P. L. Barzellotti, though he stops short of lofty flights into the realm of the imagination and is satisfied that Italy should have a "substantial share" of eastern trade without

row, and the ghosts of such clans as the Dandolo and the Spinola reappeared, indeed had already reappeared, reminding Italy of the time when

> . . . Italy fresh and young appeared
> rejuvenated for the third time: . . .
> and though it had lost the ancestral scepter
> made of its oars a scepter, and was feared.[37]

This was the historical reference adduced most frequently in the years between 1870 and 1880, the one that did most to excite national pride and cause the fierce disappointment of 1878 and the wave of recriminations and abuse directed against the work of the Italian plenipotentiaries at the Congress of Berlin.[38] It cropped up everywhere—in commercial evaluations of the ports of Marseilles and Genoa,[39] and in political analyses of the conduct of the Italian government vis-à-vis England and Russia, France and Austria. It inspired laments for the decadence of the kingdom of Italy in comparison not only to Venetian greatness in the Middle Ages but also in comparison to the more modest Italian regional states of the first half of the nineteenth century, which—it was said—had been capable of holding their own in the Orient and the Mediterranean better than the government of united Italy was capable of doing.

This is not the place to examine such accusations in detail. It will be enough to observe that the comparison does not stand up, since it was much more difficult for a great nation, an object of suspicion and opposition, to compete with the greatest European powers in the Mediterranean after the opening of the Suez Canal had given back to the internal sea all of its old importance, than it had been for the kingdoms of the Two Sicilies and Sardinia, second-class powers which posed no political threat, to retain a satisfactory position in the Mediterranean before 1859, a position of much less importance in international trade and consequently less subject to contention and scrutiny.[40] The purpose here is merely to point out how much currency this historical recollection still had after 1870: for the moderates it was validated in Cesare Balbo's eulogy of the second primacy of Italy—that is, the feat of medieval Venice, Genoa, and Pisa in making the Mediterranean an Italian lake once again[41]—while for others validation of it came

---

being number one, also summons up the glorious traditions of the maritime republics (*La questione commerciale d'Oriente: L'Italia e il Canale di Suez* [Florence, 1869], pp. 63 ff., 234, 237–38).

[37]
> . . . l'itala vergine apparìa
> ringiovanita per la terza volta: . . .
> e se lo scettro avito avea perduto,
> fe del remo uno scettro, e fu temuto.

"Le città italiane marinare e commercianti," in *Canti di Aleardo Aleardi*, p. 176.

[38] Acutely pointed out by Marselli, *Raccogliamoci!* (3d ed.; Rome, 1878), p. 5.

[39] A. Fagiuoli, *La Francia repubblicana* (Verona, 1879), p. 67.

[40] Cf. the very penetrating and valid considerations advanced by Jacini, *Pensieri sulla politica italiana*, pp. 73–75.

[41] Balbo, *Sommario della storia d'Italia*, vol. 6, part 15 (Florence, 1856), pp. 190–93.

from the predictions of Mazzini, in other words from the part of the apostle's thought most susceptible of nationalistic interpretations.

But the point is that the heritage of the medieval communes was no longer set up in opposition to the recollection of ancient Rome. In the early decades of the nineteenth century the two had often been seen as antithetical, and that was no longer the case. Then admiration of the free communes had meant admiration for new, fresh, original forces; the vision was that of Italy springing into existence after an extended interval of darkness in which any historical continuity with distant Rome had been ruptured. But now, with the great reprise of the myth of Rome after 1848, the two themes were conjoined. The medieval civilization of Italy appeared as the second great offshoot from the robust and ample trunk on which Latin civilization had previously sprouted, and historians attempted to find the connection between the two by discovering the secret sap they shared.[42] The roots of modern history twisted deep down into the lowest strata of primitive ages, the history of Italy was one and continuous, it began with Italy itself.[43] The early Risorgimento, down to Mazzini, had left ancient Rome alone, being reluctant to accept an excessively onerous legacy of military glory and political power; but now, with national unity achieved, and with Europe abandoning itself to the pursuit of the mirage of power abroad, it again became possible to accommodate ancient Rome and the medieval communes, the clan of the Scipios and that of the Dandolo, in one outlook. Rome and Venice together composed a splendid remembrance of Mediterranean glory that acted as a spur to new glory. "What Italian, knowing of this magnificent heritage of memories and facing such a proud future, does not feel himself moved and agitated by a febrile desire for activity?"[44]

The belief in an Italian primacy at certain periods of more recent history gained force from the profound recollection of the ancient primacy of the Romans, which had constituted the apogee of glory for a race whose later generations showed themselves not unworthy of such eminent forebears. Underlying every notion of Italic primacy there stood the primacy of ancient Rome, which had been condoned by God on account of the civic virtues of the Romans "qui causa honoris laudis et gloriae consuluerunt patriae"[45] and was the precondition on earth of the second and loftier primacy, that of Christian Rome. The point of departure was always the initial worldly glory and earthly felicity of the Urbs;

---

[42] One thinks, in fact, of all the labor dedicated, in the last decades of the nineteenth century and the first decades of the twentieth, to showing the "continuity" of the tradition of Rome in the Middle Ages and, in particular, to recovering the Roman element as compared to the Germanic one, even in the early Middle Ages: for example by finding links between medieval corporations and the associations of tradesmen in ancient Rome. On these general tendencies in Italian legal history, cf. L. Bulferetti, preface to Federico Patetta, *Storia del diritto italiano* (Turin, 1946), pp. xiii ff.; and esp. G. P. Bognetti, "L'opera storico-giuridica di Arrigo Solmi," *Rivista di storia del Diritto Italiano* (1947): 173 ff.

[43] Cattaneo, *La città considerata come principio ideale delle istorie italiane*, ed. Belloni, p. 102. This essay appeared in 1858, following the revival, growing out of the events of 1848, of the idea of Rome.

[44] Campo Fregoso, *Del primato italiano sul Mediterraneo*, p. 7.

[45] ". . . who gave their effort to their country, inspired by honor, praise, and glory." Augustine, *De civitate Dei* 5.13 and cf. 5.12 and 5.15.

this had been true even for St. Augustine, and many centuries later it held true for Mazzini, as it had for Dante. It was the bedrock on which Italian national sentiment had erected its dwelling, beginning with the exaltation of the Roman name and proceeding to search out traces of the Roman virtues down through the centuries of Italian history. Ancient Rome was never absent, even when the deeds of Genoa were hymned, in whose song there recurred perennially the cry "faithful to Rome: to the Rome of the Caesars, to the Rome of Christ, to the new Rome of Italy."[46]

The mentality that took shape in this way was an idiosyncratic one. Italian national sentiment had been the creation of thinkers and writers and for a long time had lacked the support of a concrete political reality, as opposed to the case in France and England. Thus it had had to feed almost exclusively on historical memory, and to base its claims principally on moral and spiritual bonds, that is on obligations created by history,[47] which in the last analysis all went back to pagan and Christian Rome. Turning to the past had been the only way to sustain hope for the future for such a long time; and Foscolo's appeal to history had merged with devotion to the hallowed homeland.[48]

It was a mentality impregnated with literature, and had all the advantages and shortcomings of literature: on one hand spiritual élan, and an appeal to higher forms such as thought, art, and culture, not to inferior ones such as race, blood, and territory; but on the other (and frequently), vanity, pride deriving from the past and disproportionate to the present—miserable pride, Manzoni had exclaimed. The consequences were a lack of the sense of limit and measure, and the predominance of historical phantasms over acquaintance with, and attentive evaluation of, the effectual reality of things. "A leftover idolatry of the antique mixed with gilded dreams for the distant future; but never actuality, never the present," in the words of Durando, who thought that art had been elevated to the point where it tyrannized Italy, and doomed the Italians.[49] Art and literature had been the beginning of great things: and they could also be the beginning of disastrous fantasies. They had given life, and they could kill.

And at the origin, Rome, always Rome, ever the cement of Rome later invoked by D'Annunzio.[50] If the memory of the Quirites, the citizens of ancient Rome, was not evoked so frequently and intensely in the immediate aftermath of 20 September as it would be later, pride in the high name nevertheless vibrated through the other evocations of Italian greatness: 20 September began to exercise a sway over men's minds even in the celebration of the seaborne glories of the Dandolo and the Morosini. The leaven of Rome, meaning the leaven of national

---

[46] Thus Gabotto in the speech inaugurating the academic year, *La gloria di Genova* (Genoa, 1907), p. 4.

[47] Vossler has observed that to use spiritual, moral, and apolitical means to patriotic ends is a characteristic Italian tradition (Vossler, *L'idea di nazione*, p. 108).

[48] In Mazzini too we find the appeal to history (cf. A. Codignola, *I fratelli Ruffini*, part 2 [Genoa, 1931], pp. lxxi–lxxii). Cf. in general Volpe, *Italia moderna* 1:38–39.

[49] Volpe, *Italia moderna* 1:10–11, 13, 16 (introduction).

[50] D'Annunzio, *Per l'Italia degli Italiani* (Milan, 1923), p. 14.

pride, fermented below the surface even when the theme was Venetian expansion in the Cyclades, or Genoa's role in the first crusade.

Such themes were better suited to what Italy could hope for in this phase, connoting as they did commercial expansion. Later, when Italy's power grew, aspirations would grow as well, and the dominion of ancient Rome would be the example explicitly cited. And yet even when that occurred, with military glory at full stretch, Venice and Genoa still fed the nationalistic flame: they were no longer depicted as mercantile cities but as warrior ones. The Genoa of Guglielmo Embriaco and the Venice of Enrico Dandolo were the continuators and heirs of the Roman Duilius, equally serviceable at need:

> Italy, to redemption, to redemption
> Sing again the song of overseas
> As you know how, with all your strength
> As when there rose above the sea
> Through blood and fire a single savage cry
> "Arremba! Arremba!" that made the ocean tremble.[51]

Blood and fire were summoned up out of the past as an augury for the blood and fire of the future, on the day when Italy should view

> . . . the Latin sea covered
> with slaughter in your war[52]

and the survivors, riding the seas, would offer myrrh and blood to God, on an altar bearing a rostrum.[53]

The tradition of Venice, Genoa, Pisa, and Amalfi was transmuted into a war cry, and that in itself showed how much the Italian spirit had changed from the days when it was a tradition honored for the peaceful glory of trade.

Both themes, the Roman one and that of the free communes, were intertwined. They provided inspiration from that moment on for D'Annunzio, the bard of the third Italy, who carried on the spirit of the Risorgimento, celebrating the rustic virtues of the communes and their hero, Alberto da Giussano—in other words, their internal liberty and their struggle against the Germans—but who also saluted in rapture the Goddess Roma and repeated Horace's *Nihil visere maius*.

---

[51]
> Italia, alla riscossa, alla riscossa!
> Ricanta la canzone d'oltremare
> come tu sai, con tutta la tua possa,
> come quando sorgeva sopra il mare
> in sangue e in fuoco un sol clamor selvaggio
> "Arremba! arremba!" e ne tremava il mare.

D'Annunzio, "La canzone d'oltremare."
[52]
> . . . il mare latino coprirsi
> di strage alla tua guerra

D'Annunzio, "Canto augurale per la nazione eletta (Elettra)," from 1899.
[53] D'Annunzio, "All'Adriatico (La Nave)."

D'Annunzio linked ancient Rome with medieval Genoa and Venice in an augury for the future, amid the raucous cries of joy of the Roman eagle, returning to spread its wingspan from the sea to the mountains, over a Mediterranean now for the third time Italian.[54] Crispi discovered the names of heroes in our history, and when the medieval and modern periods failed to supply them he sought names and examples from ancient, inexhaustible Rome.[55] He too bound the various epochs of the unique Italian spirit to one another, *civis Romanus sum* and the great age of colonial Venice expressing the same sense of pride.[56] For Alfredo Oriani there was an ideal continuity as the Italian flag returned to fly over seas that had almost forgotten it, rippling with menace atop the standard of the ancient Roman eagles as it pursued their former course. "From the time when the Roman eagles were slain by the swarm of Nordic sparrowhawks, the world had seen no others, and yet ever recalling their flight had eternally sought for them atop all the pennants and all the standards that passed over it in triumph. . . . All the efforts of Italy through the ages to rise to nationhood, the spilt blood of its heroes and the tragedies of its genius, aimed only for the day on which it would step into history again, an immortal actress, and after having been circumscribed within the confines of its own right, would sail the seas once more, bearing a new civilization. The people felt it, there is no doubt, at the great moment when they thronged the port, shivering with inexpressible emotion and saluting the soldiers returning to Africa with epic pride. Yes, they were returning to Africa, because the struggle between Africa and Italy had lasted for three thousand years, and Italy had already defeated Hannibal there, imprisoned Jugurtha, subjugated the Ptolemies, beaten the Saracens, scattered the Barbary pirates; because Italy, once again the synthesis of the whole of Europe and the prophet of its future, had combated the entire force of the Orient there and had won."[57] This is why the medieval maritime republics and free communes were adored in the shelter of the spreading wings of the Goddess Roma at the end of the century.

Though it remained the papal city, Rome still lacked true magnificence: "the king of Sardinia is too small a figure against the background of Rome. Rome is the capital of the world and it must either be the seat of a great monarchy, or of the pontificate."[58] Thoughts therefore turned to the establishment of a great monarchy at Rome.

There was no more forthright interpreter of this evolution of ideals than Alfredo Oriani. In his intense feeling that there must be a mission for Italy, he too was the heir of the Risorgimento: a third Italy without some ideal significance in the world would be the most absurd miracle of modern history, a resurrection without life, the fleeting reappearance of mere phantasms. But when he recorded

---

[54] "Per la morte di Giuseppe Garibaldi," D'Annunzio, *Opere* 7:456.

[55] This was in connection with the name of Ruggero di Lauria given to a warship—wrongly as far as Crispi was concerned, because Ruggero was a traitor and a pirate (Crispi, *Carteggi politici inediti*, p. 397).

[56] Crispi, *Scritti e discorsi politici*, pp. 737–38.

[57] Oriani, *Fino a Dogali*, pp. 311–12.

[58] Crispi, *Pensieri e profezie*, p. 111.

the unshakable greatness of papal Rome, and when he assigned a very different role to Italy than that of carrying out a religious reform or creating a cult of science, then his was the voice of the coming age, a presage of the future. Italy was Catholic: and Oriani, no longer a Voltairean, ripped away the veil of illusion and spoke the truth when he wrote:

Hatred for priests and scorn for religion are as yet very superficial. The masses still feel that only ecclesiastical matrimony is true matrimony, and that Catholicism is the one religion. Almost all infants are baptized and entrusted to the clergy for their earliest education, and pass through all the stages of religion. There is mistrust of lay colleges, but a fondness for convents that have been transformed into girls' boarding schools. All the Madonnas and the miracle-working saints are more alive than ever in the illusion of the people. There is an unspoken split in their consciousness: they want liberty in public life, but they still believe in servitude in spiritual life. Science is uncertain in its methods, dubious in its results, contradictory in its affirmations; it remains above them, transmitted and cultivated by a few. Philosophy is almost unknown. Literature, having been deserted by the forces of idealism for an unreflective passion for science, is no more than a superficial picture. The revolution began and grew instinctively; it has not yet developed into a mature, considered attitude. The majority of its supporters abjure it as they are dying, giving the priests reason to boast that its claim to truth does not hold firm in the face of death.

The dream expounded by a few, but longed for by almost everyone, is that of a reconciliation that would align religious conscience and political conscience, and bring back the state of calm that other centuries knew.[59]

The papacy was still something great, the ultimate imperial form in Italy; it had certainly cost the nation its enslavement to foreign nations and impeded its unification, but it still remained Italy's only source of pride in comparison to the leading foreign nations. If Rome were deprived of the papacy it would be nothing but a large and insignificant provincial city; instead its proud and noble front still looks down on the world. "What would the kings of the house of Savoy signify if they were alone in Rome? Highlanders who find themselves in the midst of the Pantheon and St. Peter's, the Colosseum and the Vatican, their fortune has merely a provisional significance: they are too ancient as counts of Savoy, too recent as monarchs of Italy, too much extraneous to the great national tradition to be able really to give Rome an indelible imprint of modernity."

And yet the times assigned a function and a primacy to Mediterranean Italy. It had to lift its gaze to distant horizons. It had to be strong in order to become great: "to expand, to conquer spiritually, materially, with emigration, with treaties, with commerce, with industry, with science, with art, with religion, with war. To withdraw from the contest is impossible: so we have to win it. The future will belong to those who have not been afraid of it; fortune and history are women, and they only love those who are strong, who are capable of using them violently, who accept the risks of adventure to arrive at the domination of

[59] Oriani, *Fino a Dogali*, pp. 134–35.

love. . . . Only weak people deride imperialism as a dream, only those incapable of commanding treat it as a vice. Our last heroes were all great adventurers, and our recent voyagers all saw in adventure an outline of Italian empire."[60]

For Oriani the struggle of the state against the church passed from politics to science after 20 September, "since the right of the nation, invincible by now on the Capitol, would respect, and impose respect for, the right of religion." Italy's task lay elsewhere, in Africa, on which Europe was exerting pressure now that Europe itself was no longer a sufficient field for European endeavor. History had not granted a third Italic resurrection in the interest of the Italians alone: "if Italy has again become a nation, the secret of this historical phenomenon lies in the need that world history might have for its contribution, and in the ability of our people to make it." The mission of Europe, and therefore principally of Italy, was to aim toward Africa and Asia, bringing the inferior races to its own civilized state, condemning those that did not respond, destroying those that resisted.[61] The *mare nostrum* thus became the object of a large-scale Italian foreign policy; the thirst for power diverted attention from the Alps and turned it toward the sea.

Along with this there went a polemic against the vile and egoistic bourgeoisie, seen as incapable of great deeds. It was a polemic that diverged completely from that of the socialists, since it branded the bourgeois not as the accumulator of property and exploiter of the proletariat, but as the mean-souled individual unable to rise to ideals of glory and power and afraid of arms and war. The wealthy bourgeois was not an object of scorn, it was the bourgeois as "philistine" lover of peace and avoider of risks, the man unable to comprehend the heroic, that was scorned. Even before Oriani the booming voice of Carducci had been raised, reviling the bourgeoisie for its cowardice, as had the much less resonant one of Pietro Ellero, with his imprecations against bourgeois tyranny, against the plutocracy, but at the same time against socialism and the delirium of the "reds" who were menacing the whole of Europe. He denounced "assets" [*averi*] for no other reason than that they had usurped the place of the moral and civil forces and extinguished the cult of the grand virtues and the sense of the heroic: bourgeois meanness had to be excised if humanity were to regain the royal road and Italy to regain its ancient splendor. There had to be a passage "from an Italy dishonored by middlemen and assassinated by publicans, to the Italy foretold by prophets and blessed by martyrs, from a bastard Italy . . . to the legitimate and holy Italy, from the present false Italy to the future true Italy." It was necessary to heighten national pride, national prejudice in fact; it was necessary to recall the primacy of Italy and Rome.[62]

While the myth of a scientific and anti-Catholic Rome gradually faded away, the new myth of a warrior Rome, no longer hostile to the church but rather desirous of its support, welled up.[63] Between 1870 and 1890 the fieriest patriotic orators had

[60] Oriani, *La rivolta ideale* (Napoli, 1908), pp. 282–85.

[61] Oriani, *Fino a Dogali*, pp. 313 ff., 319.

[62] P. Ellero, *La tirannide borghese* (2d ed.; Bologna, 1879), pp. 5, 14–17, 587 ff., 660, and *La questione sociale* (3d ed.; Bologna, 1889), pp. 414 ff.

[63] Turiello, for example, lamented the fact that the Italian state had not prepared "a number of

had for their motto the words "war on the Priest—raise high Italy's right and Italy's name!"[64] Conversely, the later doctrinaire nationalism loudly proclaimed itself not only prowar but Catholic, Apostolic, and Roman, and expressed its desire to have the pope collaborate in building Italy's political greatness. In this it was taking up and developing, unconsciously, ideas that had already glimmered around 1870 in the minds of a few of the liberal Catholics. They had glimmered in the mind of Ricasoli, who thought that Rome as the combined capital of both the pontiff and the king would have beneficial effects "thanks to the institutions connected with the papacy, which are in a position to give our nation great influence. Take for example the *Propaganda fide*, which carries the name of Italy to the most remote countries by means of its missionaries, and establishes connections and relationships that open the way to commercial exchange with the most distant regions."[65] They had glimmered in the vivid imagination of Diomede Pantaleoni, who wanted, so it was said, to get this process started and had wasted no time in going straight to the *Propaganda fide* right after 20 September to invite it to dispense with the protection of France, now finished as a nation, and accept instead the protection of Italy in the Orient, since the latter now represented Latin influence in the eastern Mediterranean.[66] One may recall that Proudhon had explained his strong opposition since 1861 to the unity of Italy partly as a reaction to the hopes of the Italian patriots for a pontifical and imperial Italy, which would make use of the papacy so as to gain for the kingdom a protectorate over the Catholic world;[67] and that French diplomats had been very alarmed right after 20 September, fearing the claim to sovereignty advanced by the Italians, who according to them would want

---

new Italies overseas for the destitute, providing an infrastructure and protection for numerous emigrants, opening up new habitations for them by force of arms in our dominions, and cultivating the moral bonds among them; sending the curate and the schoolmaster with them. But for that the schoolmaster here at home would first have to be transformed into a figure venerated and loved by families, in order to remain one abroad; and the country curate here at home would first have to feel for some time that he enjoyed the state's protection" (Turiello, *Governo e governati in Italia* 2:222, in the second edition of 1890. As in other cases, the second edition is more emphatic here than in the 1882 edition, which reads "opening up habitations in our overseas dominions" [2:322], without mentioning the use of armed force and omitting entirely the final reference to the country curate). Additionally, note here how the schools—and the schoolmasters—are appreciated for their political contribution to the drive for expansion.

[64] A. Lemmi to Crispi, 17 July 1892: "all your music is also written along this stave" (MRR, *Carte Crispi*, busta 660, n. 7/20).

[65] Ricasoli to his brother Vincenzo, 5 October 1870 (*Lettere e documenti* 10:140). E. G. Tancredi, *La vocazione d'Italia: Programma* (Genoa, 1867), p. 12, had also declared that Italy ought to share the protectorate over the Catholics in the east with France.

[66] The source is not entirely reliable, being the gossipy d'Ideville, *Les piémontais à Rome*, pp. 244–45. But in France there was in fact talk of the *promesses les plus séduisantes* being made by the Italian government to the *Propaganda fide*, and of the intrigues of the Italian government to supplant the French in the role of protector of the Catholics in the east, talk that might have been caused by Pantaleoni's initiative; he would, however, have been acting quite on his own (L. Valfrey, *Histoire de la diplomatie du gouvernement de la Défense Nationale* 2:145 [Paris, 1872]). Even earlier, in 1861, Pantaleoni had let himself "be carried away by his imagination" (in Cavour's words) to the point of deciding what part of the spoils of the east would eventually fall to Italy (Cavour, *La questione romana* 2:233). And cf. Lanza, *Le carte* 6:295.

[67] Proudhon, *La Fédération et l'Unité en Italie* (Paris, 1862), p. 47.

to make the church into a docile instrument of their overweening ambition, especially in the east.[68]

These were all distant and obscure ramifications of the idea of Rome: they were obscure because the urge to act tended to ignore the circumstances and the condition of the country; it became simply a yearning for adventure. To achieve domination one had to accept the risks, said Oriani: but the very comparison with the act of raping a woman, which so aroused both him and D'Annunzio, clearly showed how clarity of political thought could be clouded by dangerous states of inebriation.

The danger had been pointed out as early as 1865 by the Italian moderates, heirs of d'Azeglio, and also by the Genevan Rodolfo Rey: "Rome and the historical memories attached to it could overwhelm any government in Europe, all the more so the government of a new state, barely formed and obliged to use all kinds of circumspection. Rome is an onerous legacy, a magnificent name but too heavy to bear."[69]

But not even this was the most worrying aspect. A policy of expansion and conquest might at least have the virtues of solid substance and hard practicality. But when the dream of grandeur shrank to nothing more than the external forms of grandeur, to fatuous appearance, loud clamor, and the blaring of trumpets! When the recollection of a stupendous past stimulated not pride but vanity! When the memory of their forebears only had the effect, which Foscolo had already deplored, of rendering the Italians "entirely similar to the Israelites, who were satisfied boastfully to recall *that they were the descendants of Abraham*"[70]—as the Italians were of the Romans!

This was the greatest danger that the mission of Rome carried with it. An idea of powerful suggestiveness in a refined spirit, it was capable of being transmuted, in mediocre persons, into a tiresome rhetorical device. In fact it could affect the same person variously, in the case of individuals with less than an absolutely firm character: a beneficent force at one moment, a sort of saltpeter at another, causing the individual to switch from serious undertakings to histrionic attitudes, from sincere faith to propagandistic bluff.

Once in the past the myth of Rome had produced an alternation of this kind, for it lay behind the appeal of Cola di Rienzo to the cities of Italy on 7 June 1347,

---

[68] This problem will receive further study in the later volumes of the present work. For now, it will be enough to indicate that Italy's supposed intention to make use of the church, especially in the east, to undermine France (something of which Visconti Venosta never dreamed!), was a source of apprehension (reports of Lefebvre de Béhaine, 11 January, 1 and 15 February 1871, nos. 4, 22, 30. AEP, *C.P.*, *Rome*, t. 1049. fols. 38 ff., 167 ff., 227 ff.; report of d'Harcourt, 6 June, unnumbered, ibid., t. 1051, fol. 133, with attached memorandum from Monsignor Simeoni of the *Propaganda fide*, who requests that the foreign governments protect the *Propaganda* from Italian interference, fols. 134–39). And cf. *D.D.F.*, 1st ser., 1:22–23; Halévy, *Le courrier de M. Thiers*, p. 477; S. W. Halperin, *Italy and the Vatican at War*, pp. 205–206.

[69] Cited in S. Negro, *Seconda Roma, 1850–1870*, pp. 219–20. Rey was not French, however, but Genevan (Ruffini, *La giovinezza del conte di Cavour* 2:278). The fact that his opuscule was a "political gesture" in support of the stance of Napoleon III does not make the observation cited less interesting, and in any case it agrees perfectly with the views of a whole sector of the Italian moderates.

[70] Foscolo, letter of 15 October 1814 (*Epistolario* 2:69 [Florence, 1854]).

and his decree of 1 August on the sovereignty of the Roman people and the reordering of the empire. But then it had led to the ceremonies in which the tribune was consecrated a cavalier amid a riot of buffoons, "some sounding trumpets, some bagpipes, some *ceramelle*, some psalteries," with "trumpets of silver," and Cola proclaiming emphatically to the people "know that this night I must make myself a cavalier; tomorrow you will return, and will learn things that will please God in heaven and men on earth."[71] His immersion in the baptismal font of Constantine had followed, and then on 15 August his coronation with six crowns—all of this inspired by his own classical nostalgia, his desire to renew "the ancient titles of the Roman offices with the ancient rites."[72]

Now in the nineteenth century the perilous fascination with formal celebrations reappeared, obtruding itself on the notice of observers only a few weeks after the entry of the Italian troops into the city. The troops had entered, but not as yet the king. As this event—so it was hoped—drew nearer, the Roman commission for the preservation of monuments, libraries, and archives adopted the proposal of C. Rusconi that Vittorio Emanuele II should arrive at the Capitol along the Via Sacra, traversing the Roman forum and passing by the Colosseum and the arches of Constantine, Titus, and Septimius Severus. In overthrowing the temporal power of the popes, had he not earned a triumph compared to which the triumphs of the ancients were paltry things? Were the people not already calling for "the king on the Capitol," by which they meant "that this marriage of the marvels of time past and those of our time is already embedded in the very concept of the nation"? Away with considerations "worthy of a merchant," with philistinism: "in Rome everything must have an imprint of greatness."

On the surface this might have been the language of Quintino Sella. But in fact greatness was here turned into theatricality, spectacle, booming mortars and dazzling firecrackers, with horsemen performing sensational maneuvers, Vittorio Emanuele II with his flowing whiskers and twin-plumed commander's helmet and his generals galloping behind him, perhaps even the prime minister and the foreign minister, the utterly bourgeois Lanza and Visconti Venosta, mounted on mettlesome stamping chargers. To men like Lanza, Visconti Venosta, and Sella, this sort of thing had to seem pure folly. And in fact *L'Opinione*, the mouthpiece of the government, immediately adopted a position contrary to the proposal. "A laughable anachronism" is how the project of the Roman committee was described; the king ought to enter Rome as "a citizen king and not like a Roman conqueror;" Italy should not be proceeding toward the future on the roads of the past and should refrain from the attempt to resuscitate a bygone age, for every civilization had to have its distinctive symbols. Finally, the paper noted that the Via Sacra, though it may have been the route followed by generals in triumph, was also, in Horace's time, the strolling place of idlers and do-nothings.[73]

---

[71] *La vita di Cola di Rienzo*, ed. Ghisalberti (Florence-Rome-Geneva, 1928), p. 55. [*Translator's note:* The fourteenth-century text is quoted in the original dialect by Chabod and mentions *cornamuse* and *ceramelle*; these words designate two different types of bagpipe.]

[72] P. Piur, *Cola di Rienzo* (Italian translation: Milan, 1934), pp. 107 ff.

[73] Cf., in *L'Opinione* for 24 and 26 October 1870, the first article ("Il Re a Roma"), the letter of

A citizen king: the new reality was captured very well in this phrase. It was a reality that rendered impossible, or ought to have done, anachronistic exhumations of the past, even if there had not been reasons of a contingent but very palpable kind to abstain: the need, that is, to keep from pointlessly exasperating the pope and bringing unforeseeable consequences.[74]

The truth is that in this unimportant episode, two mentalities at opposite poles to each other were clashing: the mentality of the new type of Italian, raised amid a harsh experience of struggle and sacrifice, culturally and morally prepared for the weighty new tasks that history was settling on his country, accustomed, whatever his political party,[75] to see matters in a European context and convinced that the age of the village festivals was over; and the mentality of the type of Italian who had not changed for the last two or three centuries, an Italian to whom liberty and unity had come too rapidly and with too much assistance from fortune, an Italian having too little political preparation but a head full of literature and schoolroom memories of the helmet of Scipio and the Capitol, an Italian who breathed a false and corrupt atmosphere.

The propensity for festivals, for choreographic extravaganza, was already indomitably rooted in many Italians, and notably in the Romans, a people that in the early years of national unity left new arrivals to the city amazed and scandalized by their readiness for any bacchanal,[76] for seizing the slightest pretext to have a good time and spend money profusely.[77] This propensity was reinforced

---

Rusconi, and the reply. On this plan for the entry, cf. as well U. Pesci, *Come siamo entrati in Rome* (new ed.; Milan, 1911), p. 245.

[74] *L'Opinione* insisted that, with Europe in a seriously troubled phase, and with two nations that were friends of Italy fighting one another with savage determination, it was not the right time to be thinking of festivals and triumphal honors in Italy, which also belonged to the "great European family." This was a characteristic expression of the Europeanism of the moderates, to which considerable space has been devoted above.

[75] It is worth noting that *Il Diritto*, the organ—at that period—of Depretis, also took a view very similar to that of *L'Opinione*: "the entry of the king [into Rome], is not so much a dynastic triumph as a national one; it is a new and stirring reality despite its modest external trappings, in a country like this one, whose history, whose thoroughfares, whose imposing ruins bear the eternal traces of hundreds and hundreds of triumphs celebrated with dazzling ostentation and splendor. The consuls and the emperors, Caesar after Marius and Titus after Caesar, may have come into the city along the triumphal way amid a cheering crowd of enthusiastic slaves and courtesans claiming with presumptuous arrogance *civis Romanus sum*. But tomorrow Vittorio Emanuele will pass through the ranks of a population of free men, citizens of a country that does not aspire either to re-create the edifice of Catholicism, or the apotheosis of Caesarism" ("A Roma!" a despatch from Rome in *Il Diritto* for 3 July 1871).

La Nazione had already expressed opinions in this vein on 10 October 1870: "We are the heirs, in Rome, neither of the ancient aristocratic republic, nor of the military empire, nor of the papacy. In Rome we are the founders of modern right [*diritto*]. . . . It is not the Roman republic that is reborn; it died forever at Philippi. It is not the empire of the Caesars, from which the providential sword of the barbarian freed the human race, and whose last surviving remnant is vanishing today, since the vote of the Roman people has removed the regal diadem from the head of Pius IX . . . our triumph is the triumph of right [*diritto*] and of modern ideas over the antique" ("Roma italiana"). [*Translator's note:* The Italian word *diritto* bears the same range of meaning as French *droit*, German *Recht*.]

[76] Guiccioli, "Diario," in *Nuova Antologia* (1 July 1935), p. 86.

[77] In *L'Opinione* this point is made repeatedly: there is an excessive desire to holiday, to seize any chance to stop work and spend money. In August 1871 there was a debate about how to celebrate 20 September, which caused Dina to warn that "Italy did not choose Rome for its capital so as to take

and seemingly dignified by the changes taking place, by the solemn anniversaries of the national redemption, which had to be celebrated. In addition to the simple traditional festivities, there were now patriotic occasions, on most if not all of which allusions were made to the Roman citizens of the ancient past: what an incitement to pluck from the dictionary the most resounding epithets, to bring out from the storehouse of historical memory all the gaudiest and most baroque fixtures one could find! Perhaps the limit was reached in the hyperbole of those who had no hesitation in designating the Italians as "the leading soldiers in the world" for the breach of Porta Pia, at a time when, from Weissenburg to Sedan, the armies of Prussia and France were engaging in rather more serious battles.[78]

And how easy it was to talk of heroes and grandeur, and rouse the phantasms of the past into a sort of fury against the voices of intelligence and moderation and good sense, as Antonio Stefanucci Ala, the "defender" of the Romans, had done in 1865 against the anti-Roman tendencies typified by Giorgini, invoking formal greatness, exalting Italian national superiority, and belittling the other peoples.[79] Similarly, there was Francesco Coccapieller in 1883: though they

---

part in endless celebrations and anniversaries," and to state that absolutist powers have reason to distract their subjects with festivities, whereas a free state should be taking steps to involve the citizens in public affairs ("Le Feste," in *L'Opinione* for 23 August 1871). On another occasion the paper returns to this senseless urge for display, typical of 1848 ("Le dimostrazioni," in *L'Opinione* for 30 September 1873), having previously observed that in Rome carnival time lasted too long: ten days of work stoppage are excessive and would appear to signify that there exists in Rome very little desire to work ("Il Carnevale," in *L'Opinione* for 26 February 1873; the carnival in 1873 was in fact unusually splendid, cf. U. Pesci, *I primi anni di Roma capitale*, pp. 73 and 301 ff.).

Finally, the Roman citizenry took part in a very lively debate for a number of days in 1876 over whether or not to revive the race of the Barbary horses down the Corso. This debate inspired another sensible note in *L'Opinione* concerning such frivolous differences of opinion ("Questioni munici-pali," in *L'Opinione* for 15 January 1876, and also "Il Carnevale," in the issue for 26 January). *La Nazione*, for its part, had had harsh words on 17 November 1870 ("L'ingresso del Re a Roma") regarding the demonstrations of the Romans demanding the king's entry: "it appears . . . that up till now they have taken seriously the liberty brought to them under the Italian flag only to the extent of taking the chance to "demonstrate' at every hour of the day." Italy, says *La Nazione*, is beginning to get bored with "Roman demonstrations." And see too the issue for 31 October 1870 ("'A Roma"). The moderates were not the only ones to reprove the holiday-making proclivity of the Romans (and of the Italians in general); the papers on the left expressed ideas entirely similar to those of *L'Opinione*. An article in *La Riforma* for 15 February 1872 entitled "Il carnevale di Roma" expresses the same views as those of the article in *L'Opinione* for 23 August 1871: despotism needs noisy occasions, *panem et circenses*; but now "we may be allowed to enquire whether a free people, a people called to a high destiny, ought to surrender itself to idleness for ten days straight." *Il Diritto* also dwelt on the matter more than once, never failing to warn that proposals for holidays should be dismissed ("Non più feste!" 11 October 1870; "Gaudeamus," 19 February 1871; "Il Re e la capitale a Roma," 29 June 1871; "Nuove feste," 13 August 1871), and concluding in the end that the [London] *Times* was right, Italy was really the carnival nation.

[78] *Il Diritto*, one of the two leading papers of the left, protested very judiciously against this sort of "declamation" ("La retorica a Roma," 25 September 1870). Gregorovius, who had returned to the city from a visit to the battlefields of France, was "disgusted" by the "bragging" about Porta Pia (*Diari Romani*, p. 460).

[79] "[O]nly Rome breeds a people that goes forward and acts in the infinite. Every family there has a hero, in fact a pleiad of heroes. Every stone recalls a hero, and every sepulcher contains one. Oh how the other races shrivel and become pathetic when compared to a people that alone gave to the world men who were whole! . . . A people like the Romans, if it continues to live, must also continue to be great. Its condition is that it must be great because it is alive, or nothing because it is dead. If Rome exists, the deep causes of an immense existence must be present in it. The same reasons that gave rise to its past greatness are still there, strong and active, ready to give rise to its

called him deranged for the way he raved about Roman greatness, he was not a lone lunatic, for there was a distant rumble of sentiments widely shared by others in his mad declarations.[80]

The worst of it is that sometimes even men of spiritual refinement were unable to resist the force of rhetoric mantled in the Roman senatorial toga. After all, if the Roman commission for the preservation of monuments, libraries, and archives dreamed up the glorious idea of having Vittorio Emanuele enter Rome on horseback along the Via Sacra, there was little harm in it. Nor was there great harm if authors of occasional verse, even when they held the stage of the Argentina civic theater, summoned visions of the unconquerable Latin eagle in its lofty flight, or admonished the deputies arriving at Montecitorio to employ soaring language worthy of Cicero, Papirius, Cato, Regulus, and Fabricius, the great and terrible Latin souls risen with the laurel on their brow to judge the contestants in the new agon.[81] But from Bologna a very different voice echoed these feeble Roman efforts.

Giosuè Carducci, no less, was soon to enter the lists, hurling his invectives at official Italy for having conducted the king to his capital in an ignominious manner, for having given Italy a Byzantium when what it had asked for was Rome. Hush hush, softly softly, his verse made Lanza and Visconti Venosta seem to say:

> Geese of the Capitol, hush! I am
> Italy great and united.
>
> I come by night because Doctor Lanza
> Fears a sunstroke . . .
> Give over, my geese, making so much noise;
> Don't let Cardinal Antonelli hear you.[82]

---

future greatness." This passage is found in a booklet entitled *Roma ed i Romani nel loro passato, nel present, e nell'avvenire*, quoted in Negro, *Seconda Roma*, pp. 226–28.

[80] See for example his letter to Queen Margherita, with its reference to the Eternal City which should be "the most glorious capital metropolis of all, but instead is afflicted with a slow consumption," and which has to be made to rise to its former greatness (in Vigo, *Annali d'Italia* 4:40–41). The same theme—Rome as the first city of the modern world, as it was of the ancient world—is found in the work of the ex-Garibaldian V. Noghera, *L'avvenire di Roma Capitale* (Rome, 1871), p. 49.

[81] V. Ghinassi, *Canti* (Rome, 1871), and "Il 27 novembre [1871]. Canzone. Al Parlamento Italiano in Roma." Naturally occasional verse sprouted everywhere, for example G. Righi, *Una corona a Roma inaugurata capitale d'Italia nel luglio del 1871* (Ferrara, 1871), a collection of twenty sonnets with the inevitable references to primordial fate, resurrection, the soul of Mutius transfused into his descendants, etc.

[82]
> Oche del Campidoglio, zitte! Io sono
> L'Italia grande e una.
>
> Vengo di notte perché il dottor Lanza
> Teme i colpi di sole . . .
> Deh, non fate, oche mie, tanto rumore
> Che non senta Antonelli.

Carducci, "Canto dell'Italia che va in Campidoglio," which is from 12 November 1871. A similar spirit animates Oriani, who complains of the time and the manner of the king's entry into Rome (Oriani, *La lotta politica in Italia* 3:284 and 295 [5th ed.; Florence, 1921]).

The great poet, like others, did not always escape the fascination of rhetoric, and often, as he poetized, he succumbed completely to archaeological reminiscence of Rome. All passion and political furor,[83] but no political thinker, Carducci too wished there had been a different entry, something more triumphal, a loud blast of trumpets at least, if not exactly the Via Sacra. It meant nothing to him that the entry of the king had had to be simple and restrained, without useless parade, in order not to put more stress on Italy's already very delicate relations with the papacy and thereby with the European powers[84]; that the great merit of the government, notwithstanding all its uncertainties, moments of doubt, and oscillations, had been its success in entering Rome in a sober fashion, thus reducing the fall of the temporal power to an event of the same proportions as the Franco-Prussian War,[85] and gaining in permanence and security of possession what it lost in splendor and pomp of conquest; that this evidence of composure and tact not only did not cost Italy any of its dignity in the eyes of the other nations but earned it increased consideration.[86] The furious poet instead turned his fierce glare on himself and on Italy, which he damned along with the pope, the king, and the democrats.[87] In his temptation to paint the whole world black, he saw nothing in his own country but Custoza, Lissa, and all of its other little failings.[88]

---

[83] B. Croce, *Giosuè Carducci*, pp. 42 ff.

[84] It was to avoid numerous difficulties, to "provide an outlet through charitable aid for a throng of emotions," avoiding "clamor and celebration," that Visconti Venosta had insisted strongly that Vittorio Emanuele should seize the occasion of the flooding of the Tiber to make his first voyage to Rome (Visconti Venosta, letter to his brother Giovanni, 30 December 1870, Visconti Venosta archive).

[85] Thus, and quite rightly, Zanichelli, in *Studi politici e storici*, pp. 490–91.

[86] The *Times*, the principal organ of European opinion, noted on 6 July 1871, p. 9, that if the delay in the king's entry into Rome had been rightly considered blameworthy, nevertheless the affair was perhaps ending with an advantage for the Italian government, because it demonstrated "that the overthrow of the Papacy was not only practicable, but a very safe and easy enterprise—to be achieved, not by surprise, but calmly and deliberately, looking the world steadily in the face, compelling its acquiescence, if not its assent and encouragement." The calm and measured approach taken by Lanza was therefore—and the reason is evident—anything but discreditable for Italy.

[87] Cf. Carducci's letter to Chiarini, 23 December 1870: "everything deserves scorn, above all this ridiculous and cowardly Italy, with its pope, its king, and its democrats" (*Lettere* 6:262). On Carducci's negative mood, cf. as well P. M. Arcari, *Le elaborazioni della dottrina politica nazionale fra l'unità e l'intervento (1870–1914)* 1:151 ff.

[88] "Io triumphe!" (July 1871). And see as well "Per il trasporto delle reliquie di Ugo Foscolo in Santa Croce" (24 June 1871):

> Co 'l bello italo regno
> non crebber l'alme . . .
> . . . Ahi, ahi; mal con le impronte
> De le catene a i polsi e piú nel core,
> Mal con la mente da l'ignavia doma,
> Mal si risale il Campidoglio e Roma!

> The souls [of the Italians] did not grow
> With the fine Italian kingdom . . .
> . . . Alas, alas; with the mark
> Of chains on one's wrists, even more in one's heart,
> With a mind ruled by sloth,
> One does ill to ascend the Capitol and Rome!

Other outbursts from Carducci were directed against the substance of the new Italy, the shabbiness into which the life of the nation had descended according to the poet: outbursts that came from deep inside him, however much or little they were justified. But in the poem featuring the Capitoline geese, and "Doctor" Lanza, and Cardinal Antonelli, the poet alas fell victim to the same impressions and aspirations that had earlier given rise to the proposal advanced by the more modest and less tempestuous Rusconi: the poet too felt that some sort of crashing external effect should accompany the royal entry.

It was a bad sign, because Carducci was one of those in whom the idea of Rome was profound and sincere and often acted as a source of inspiration. He too held strongly to the myth of Rome as a mission, of the city as a goddess:

> . . . madre de i popoli
> che desti il tuo spirito al mondo,
> che Italia improntasti di tua gloria.

> . . . mother of peoples
> who gave your spirit to the world
> who stamped Italy with your glory.

In Mameli's hymn the voice of Rome had sounded in purity and freshness, stripping the helmet of Scipio of its rhetorical sheen for once and making it into an image of immediate naturalness and spontaneity; in Carducci that voice also attained the loftier ranges of real poetry; but not infrequently it coarsened into rhetorical exclamation and ugly verse.

More unpleasant than the ugliness of the verse, for those of us who are not critics of poetry, is the fact that notwithstanding the man's sincerity and his intellectual force, the images that poured out revealed all too plainly his taste for the theatrical. It is perfectly true that in Carducci this felt need for the antique, even for such external forms as pagan triumphs and processions, came as a reaction against papal Rome: "a mendicant plebs . . . a bourgeoisie of landlords, rosary-vendors, antique dealers, ready to sell anything and everything: conscience, sanctity, erudition, phony relics of martyrs, phony relics of the Scipios—and women in the flesh. A caste of monsignors and abbots in capes and hoods of every color that also buys and sells and laughs at everything. An aristocracy of gatekeepers. A society that actually lives, from top to bottom, in things sacred and profane, in the temple and in the tribunal, in the family and in the school, the way it is sketched in the satires of Settano and Belli—the most impudently skeptical, the most exquisitely immoral society, the most serenely incredulous and insensible of everything sublime, noble, virtuous, and human that other races are capable of believing, desiring, adoring, or dreaming."[89] It is also true that his fantasies of Roman triumphs and chariots and legionary eagles burst out of him as a spontaneous and virtually inevitable reaction to modern Rome, which seemed to him a slight and trivial city for anyone not willing to rest his gaze on St. Peter's, or more precisely for anyone who scorned and hated that symbol of

---

[89] Carducci, "XX Settembre" (from 1895), in *Opere* 19:60.

obscurantism. The poet dreamed of great things; the present seemed to him detestable, and hence the evocation not only of the spirit of the ancient world but also of the ancient rites.

All of this is true. But it is not the less true that in Carducci as well the idea of Rome emerged with that twin character of which we have spoken: Janus with two faces, one composed of illumination, idealism, substance, and the other darkened by the fumes of incense, and hollow within. Carducci's powerful national feeling was not the same thing as the petty brand of nationalism that later made its appearance, and he, this man of the Risorgimento, saw Italy in the context of the rest of the world, not against it, for he also loved the heroes and the deeds of glory of the other nations, especially those of the France of 1789. For him, as for the generation of the Risorgimento, the greatness of Italy was principally the deep civic sensibility of its citizens.[90] But the densely corporeal images of *Romanitas* created by Carducci did not belong to the Risorgimento. They signaled the first step away from Mazzini's mystic Romanism toward the hard-edged political Romanism embraced by a later epoch. The frequently ostentatious character of the latter sometimes meant that, for those who came after Carducci and had been raised with different ideals, his appeals to the glory and potency of Italy ensconced in Rome acted as an inducement to turn the country in on itself, and served nationalistic ends.

It came to seem as if there was an essential connection between external flamboyance and inner greatness: Rome as the parent of all great undertakings and source of all higher thoughts was felt to require that curial robes be donned and a solemn tone employed. Even some men who were moderates in the full political and moral sense of the term, and thus normally impervious to the enchantment of the fine gesture and the ornate phrase, men who were anything but devotees of the sacred bardic flame, believed this to be true. An example might be the Lombard friend of Marco Minghetti, Count Guido Borromeo, who was unquestionably a contrary fellow, always murmuring and muttering about this and that, and generally viewing the world in a rather dim light, who was rather hard on Lanza and the government in general, certainly not a man of excessively literary tendencies likely to be captivated by an imposing procession. And yet even he, who had never hid his low opinion of the Romans, and in fact clearly expressed the fear that if Rome were the capital, this would have the undesirable effect of increasing the influence of the Mezzogiorno in Italian political life, even this anti-Roman felt a sour taste in his mouth at the way matters were handled in Rome. He felt it was "a painful thing to see Italy complete her task in a fashion so little worthy of her, entering Rome with so little dignity, indeed with no dignity at all.

"After the breach was opened with cannon fire, it pains me to observe us taking possession as though we were virtually being forced into it by the Left,

---

[90] Cf. Croce, *Giosuè Carducci*, pp. 45 ff. And see as well L. Russo, "La fede politica e il nazionalismo letterario del Carducci," in *Belfagor* 5 (1950): 12.

with a king who will go there reluctantly for perhaps twenty-four hours, and a Chamber of Deputies at less than its full complement."[91]

It was a sign that the air of Rome really could produce inebriation, even at a distance.

[91] Borromeo to Minghetti, letter of 12 June 1871 (BCB, *Carte Minghetti*, cart XVI, fasc. 4, cited above, ch. 4, nn. 3 and 18). On 31 July Borromeo restates to Minghetti his displeasure at the "almost shamefaced manner" of Italy's going to Rome, and its remaining there. And on 14 September he continues: "We are in Rome as if we were staying at a hotel" (ibid.).

The Anti-Romans

THE DANGERS OF ROME were evident, therefore. And the subtle Lombard spirit of Stefano Jacini was fully alert to them. In his celebrated speech of 23 January 1871 in the Senate, against the plan to transfer the capital from Florence to Rome, the fundamental theme was undoubtedly his preoccupation that the "pedestal" of the eminent religious power, whose influence was still so potent all over the world, might be destroyed—a power with its seat in Rome, in the heart of the land of Italy. In his eyes the Roman question had ended on 20 September, and now he feared that a threatening "papal question" might be about to develop. This was the preoccupation of a practicing Catholic, but the man who held it was also a politician who as such viewed the proposed step as harmful and extremely perilous, a view shared by men like Menabrea and Alfieri di Sostegno.[1]

But, in the course of his argument, Jacini made a very determined and severe attack on the "myth" of Rome.[2] All the rest, including his discussion of the pros and cons of the city's geographical position, its climate, its military security, was merely ancillary to his main point; in fact it is surprising to see a man like Jacini, engaged in a debate concerning a problem as important as the choice of the nation's capital, proposing objections of little importance, ones that were quickly and easily refuted. Indeed, Cavour had already refuted them in advance a decade earlier: on the basis of climatic, topographic, and military criteria, London would certainly not be the capital of England, and neither perhaps would Paris be the capital of France.[3] The "most formidable" of the reasons adopted in favor of Rome as the capital was a quite different one: public opinion, in other words the "dogma" that it was necessary to locate the national government on the Tiber. And it was against this dogma that the liberal Catholic from Lombardy turned his trenchant logic, displaying all the aggressiveness that was part of his character.[4]

It was the literary idea of Rome that he impugned, an idea that he drained of its content and presented from one side only—the negative one, naturally. He described it as a concept dear to "antiquarians," a memento of a time that had passed away and that ought never to return: "a product of rhetoric, of that rhetoric whose influence should be the first thing we get rid of, now that Italy has come into existence, if we really desire to take our place among the modern civilized nations . . . the affectation of a decrepit Italy whose time has passed,

---

[1] On Jacini's position and in general on the debates surrounding the issue of Rome as the capital of Italy, cf. Jacini, *Un conservatore rurale* 2:44 ff., and *La crisi religiosa del Risorgimento: La politica ecclesiastica italiana da Villafranca a Porta Pia*, pp. 380 ff. [*Translator's note:* The author of these works was the statesman's nephew.]

[2] *A.P., Senato*, pp. 120 and 123.

[3] Cavour, *Discorsi Parlamentari* 11:317 (speech of 25 March 1861).

[4] Jacini, *Un conservatore rurale* 2:247.

not the ornament of the Italy for which we hope, an Italy called upon to travel the roads of liberty and progress if it wants to take its place on an equal footing with the most civilized nations of the world." The conception of Rome that the Risorgimento at its height had embraced, despite its diverse political tendencies, and which was still unanimously upheld in the 1870s by men of both the Right and the Left, men like Sella and men like Crispi, journals like *L'Opinione* and ones like *La Riforma* and *Il Diritto*, was very roughly handled indeed by the Lombard senator in his accusatory speech.

His words reechoed an anti-Roman frame of mind that had perhaps been most crudely expressed, before 1848, by Durando,[5] and that had been sounded in harsh terms only a few years earlier by d'Azeglio, for Jacini's speech of 23 January 1871 descended in a direct line from the *Questioni Urgenti*, the work in which the gallant Massimo had taken a firm stand ten years earlier against the plan to make Rome the capital of Italy. D'Azeglio had denied that the atmosphere of the Urbs, "impregnated with the miasma of 2,500 years of material violence, and moral pressure, exercised by its successive governments on the world," was suited to a young Italy, a new country that ought not to have anything more to do with the heritage of the ancient Roman world.[6] In Jacini's speech the underlying notion and the images were identical; even the objections he offered on hygienic and strategic grounds derived from the work of the Piedmontese statesman.[7] From that work—and also the speech that d'Azeglio, old and tired but still "stubborn as a toad," bitter, disrespectful, and polemical as ever against Cavour even after the latter's death,[8] had had read in the Senate on 3 December 1864[9]—there had flowed a current of opinion in which others joined, firmly convinced, like Gian Battista Giorgini, that Rome was alien to all the ideas on which modern society was founded, and that it was therefore beyond the pale of modern civilization.[10] They declared without ambiguity, as the marquis Carlo Alfieri made clear in 1870 and 1871, that it was a deadly mistake to transfer the capital to Rome, inasmuch as all the themes of Roman glory were "memories of the past, a past that modern liberty is unable to make any use of, and of which in fact it has

---

[5] Durando, *Della nazionalità italiana*, pp. 10 ff. (introduction).

[6] D'Azeglio, *Scritti e discorsi politici* 3:372ff., ed. De Rubris (Florence, 1938); and cf. as well De Rubris, *Confidenze di Massimo d'Azeglio*, pp. 296, 302, 309. Excited protests were raised in Rome against d'Azeglio's work: cf. *Sulle Questioni Urgenti di Massimo d'Azeglio: Esame e confutazione di un romano* (Turin, 1861); likewise an anti-Roman work by Giorgini raised a protest from Duke Sforza-Cesarini, *Che cosa è Roma? Osservazioni su l'ultimo opusculo del deputato Giorgini* (Turin, 1865). Recently E. Flori has taken it on himself to attack the "ridiculous rumor" that d'Azeglio did not want Rome to be the capital of Italy ("Massimo d'Azeglio e Roma capitale," *Nuova Antologia* [October 1950]: 143 ff.), but his argument rests on a misunderstanding: he confuses the desire to have Rome as part of Italy, which d'Azeglio, Giorgini, and later Jacini certainly shared, and the intention that it should be the Italian capital, which for them was a quite different matter, something that both d'Azeglio and later Jacini in his speech to the Senate make perfectly clear.

[7] D'Azeglio, *Scritti e discorsi politici* 3:378. On the advantages of Florence over Rome from both points of view see p. 383.

[8] Cf. Ruffini, *La giovinezza del conte di Cavour* 1:221–22; N. Vaccalluzzo, *Massimo d'Azeglio*, pp. 255 ff.; P. E. Santangelo, *Massimo d'Azeglio politico e moralista*, pp. 277 ff.

[9] D'Azeglio, *Scritti e discorsi politici* 3:425 ff.

[10] Negro, *Seconda Roma*, pp. 220 ff.

the honor and the duty to show itself the perennial and confident adversary."[11] Rome, he said, was the least Italian city in the peninsula because of its traditional cosmopolitanism, the least fitted to be the capital of a newborn nation. Only the Piedmontese, a people whose peculiar characteristic was that they never understood anything about the history of Italy, could have concluded that Rome must necessarily be its capital.[12]

Nor were the followers of d'Azeglio an isolated group. Others, whose political orientation was very different, aimed their fire at the dogma of Rome, none in a more violent style than Francesco Montefredini, who discovered a fresh example of the irremediable decadence of the Latin nations in the obstinate attachment to Rome. The fault was Mazzini's: "driven by his hallucinations, by those marvelous politico-religious beliefs of his, by his great hope of being able to preach his new evangel to the peoples (who have better things to do than listen to it) like a new apostle and pontifex maximus from Rome." Rome would very certainly be the ruin of the whole nation, just as it had been the burial ground of Italy as an integral country in the past.[13]

Montefredini's anticlerical odium toward Rome was something entirely different to Jacini's Catholic reverence for it; what they had in common was their animus against classical education and the Livian rhetorical reflex. Others joined in, some to the point of wishing to create an Italian Washington, a capital constructed from scratch, from the ground up—in the central basin of Umbria, for example, below Assisi, where it would have a central, secure, handsome, and healthful site. In this way the nucleus of the Italian state would be relieved of all the burden of the traditions and influences of past ages. As for Rome, Italy should plant its flag there, station a garrison, install a prefect, and leave it alone as a museum of antiquities and art, a reservoir of ancient memories and the Catholic metropolis.[14]

Rome, the rhetorical capital of the Italians: in this phrase of Massimo d'Azeglio, taken up by Jacini, there was contained a whole subjective approach to the problem of politics, an ample tradition of moderate political thought, which in parliament openly contested the dominant Roman trend.[15] And it can't

---

[11] The various writings and speeches of Alfieri on the problem of Rome are collected in *L'Italia liberale*, pp. 211 ff. and esp. pp. 225–26. Believing that it was useless to oppose the virtually irresistible current that was tugging the government in the direction of Rome, Alfieri wanted decentralization at least, to reduce the weight of the capital: for him, liberty had nothing to gain from Rome as the capital, so he proposed to ensure that at any rate it suffered no detriment. Similar themes recurred later and served the clerical press as a pretext with which to goad the "noble indignation" of the Romans (as in "Roma e i suoi conquistatori," in *L'Osservatore Romano* for 20 November 1874, against the *Gazzetta d'Italia* of Florence, which objected to concentrating all power in the capital).

[12] "Lettere romane," by K. in *La Nazione* for 21 April 1871.

[13] Montefredini, *Roma ci è fatale* (Florence, 1870), esp. pp. 12, 18–19, 27–28, 30, 35, 47.

[14] Rueful desires of this kind were expressed as late as 1896 by G. Corsi, *Italia, 1870–1895* (Turin, 1896), p. 20.

[15] Sen. Gabrio Casati, in the same session of 23 January 1871, endorsed Jacini's observations and passed up the chance to speak himself in order not to repeat what his friend and fellow Lombard had already said (*A.P., Senato*, pp. 126–27). Note as well the positions taken by Alfieri di Sostegno, Menabrea, and a few others (Jacini, *Un conservatore rurale* 2:47, and *La crisi religiosa del Risorgimento*, pp. 384 ff., *A.P., Senato*, 24 and 25 January 1871, pp. 133 and 153).

be denied that in the apprehensions of these men, their fear of Rome,[16] their anxious and at the same time contemptuous query "whether the Capitol is supposed to last to all eternity,"[17] there were a few well-grounded reasons. But they were fighting a desperate battle, one they were sure to lose, and their occasional outbursts of intemperate hostility to Rome did nothing to brighten their prospects. Jacini's speech was an example, with its evident one-sidedness and captiousness. What strikes us above all in his dryness of tone, a dryness fully in harmony with the face he presented to the world,[18] was the excessively rationalistic, and at the same time pragmatic, intellectual attitude he took.

To say, in a debate of this kind, that the problem of the capital was "so utterly practical, so utterly positive, so exclusively the competence of reflection, reasonability, and careful analysis," meant cutting off at the root not only the rhetoric of Rome but also that passionate, emotive, almost lyrical impulse that had given birth to the whole massive national movement. Without that impulse the Risorgimento would not have come about, or it would have been something completely different. To reduce the idea of Rome to pure rhetoric was to forget that in Rome the Italians had found a watchword common to all of them, at a time when a common principle was what they needed. Jacini himself had acknowledged this eight years before, accepting without reserve the judgment of Cavour and writing that for generations the idea of Rome as Italy's capital made the heart of every Italian vibrate, giving it the power to act in history simply by being spoken of, long before it became reality. Rome, he had said then, was the only Italian city whose traditions went beyond the municipal, which was associated with all the traditions of the country, with the education of the youth of the Risorgimento.[19]

Indeed, other observers had admitted that one could find a hundred good reasons to object to Rome as the capital: it was not central either geographically or intellectually or economically, it probably had the worst moral atmosphere of any city in Italy, it formed an outsized backdrop that dwarfed the average men destined to appear on its stage. And yet, despite all this, the general sentiment affirmed the necessity of going to Rome, seeing it as the ultimate and definitive sanction of the Risorgimento, the seal of a united, independent, and free Italy. For better or worse, the necessity of transferring the capital to Rome was politically unavoidable.[20]

It was significant that at the decisive moment it should be a Lombard who stated the strongest case against Rome as the nation's capital: one of those myste-

---

[16] *La Nazione* once expressed itself in these terms: "Rome makes us fearful."

[17] D'Azeglio, in the *Questioni Urgenti* (*Scritti e discorsi politici* 3:376).

[18] Jacini, *Un conservatore rurale* 2:249.

[19] Jacini, *La questione di Roma al principio del 1863* (Turin, 1863), pp. 8, 14 ff.

[20] *La Perseveranza* for 20 September 1870 ("Roma capitale"), and 28 January 1871, commenting on Jacini's speech. An unnamed deputy expressed exactly the same feelings in September 1874 to Tiby, the French chargé d'affaires: of all the cities of Italy, Rome is the worst as capital. There they don't believe in Italy. And yet it is just as necessary to us as the royal house of Savoy in order to guarantee our work of national unity (Tiby, report, 21 September 1874, no. 66; AEP, *C.P., Italie*, t. 390, fols. 161v–162).

rious prefigurations of history's pattern that are seen for what they are only in retrospect, affording a glimpse of the coming antagonism between the political capital and the "moral capital." Milan was ill-disposed to succumb in the present, just as it had once been ill-disposed in the past to give up the Ambrosian church at the insistence of the church of Rome.[21] It was quite ready to counter Montecitorio and the Capitol with its factories, its banks, the current accounts of its citizens, and was ever ready to take up the age-old contest for primacy with all the assurance of a long-established state,[22] and all the modern pride of its dynamic productivity.

A Lombard: one's thoughts turn inevitably to the total lack of fascination that Rome had held for another and much greater Lombard, Alessandro Manzoni, a Catholic who never in his life visited the seat of the successor of St. Peter, though he traveled often to the city on the Seine.[23] Manzoni had been politically favorable to Rome as the capital, even though this brought him into conflict with his son-in-law, d'Azeglio, and had not hesitated to accept honorary Roman citizenship in 1872,[24] but spiritually he was impervious to the great heritage of Rome and indeed found classical Rome not to his taste.[25] Or again, one thinks of the lack of influence that the Capitol had had, until 1848, on the robust political thought of another great Lombard, Carlo Cattaneo, different in this, as in so much else, from Mazzini.

Jacini was here giving voice to a lasting regional tradition, one that threw the overall tradition of the moderates, of which he was an heir, into sharper relief, and gave it a more acerbic flavor. He belonged to the moderate tradition not only in his refusal of rhetoric, and of the myth of Rome, but more generally in his appeal to the concrete aspect of things, to the "exclusive" competence of reflection and careful analysis, and in his readiness to spoil the party by banishing the emotive and passionate elements from public life, just as that *folle du logis*, the imagination, had been banished by the eighteenth-century rationalism that lived on in the mentality of the moderates in general, and that of the Catholic Jacini in particular. Concreteness, ratiocination, analysis: almost as if the life of nations could be governed by the pure calculus of reason, like an ingenious machine.

The difference between such an approach and the approach of a truly great politician, one careful not to let himself be led astray by fantasies and facile myths, but sensitive nonetheless to the voices of imagination and the imponder-

---

[21] One recalls the words of Arnolfo: "perhaps you will say: Rome is to be venerated in its Apostle. Indeed it is; but Milan gains glory from Ambrose" (*Historia Mediolanensis*, in *Rerum Italicarum Scriptores* 4:29. And this is in the eleventh century!).

[22] The expression is Cattaneo's, in *La città considerata come principio ideale*, p. 101 and cf. p. 111.

[23] Negro correctly notes this in *Seconda Roma*, p. 10.

[24] In 1864 Manzoni wished to go to Turin to vote his approval, in the Senate, of the September Convention (the first step, in his view, toward making Rome the capital), though d'Azeglio did everything possible to dissuade him (Ruffini, *La giovinezza del conte di Cavour* 1:222; Vaccalluzzo, *Massimo d'Azeglio*, pp. 274–75). This qualified him in the eyes of the Jesuits as *ce déplorable Manzoni* (F. Ghisalberti, preface to Manzoni, *Dell'Independenza dell'Italia* [Milan, 1947], p. xlviii). On Manzoni's "fixation on Rome," which was stronger than ever in 1864, cf. as well Flori, "Massimo d'Azeglio e Roma capitale," p. 151.

[25] On Manzoni's anti-Romanism, cf. Calosso, *Colloqui col Manzoni*, pp. 24 ff.

ables of history, becomes clear if one compares the speech of Jacini with the speech made by Cavour ten years earlier. Cavour was not in the least a slave to the ideas of the antiquarians and was ready to acknowledge, indeed took some pleasure in so doing, his personal indifference to the artistic fascination of Rome. But he was just as ready to acknowledge the force of "great moral reasons," and consequently the inevitability of Rome as Italy's capital. Jacini spoke of pure reflection; and Cavour had answered him in advance that it must be the sentiment of the people to decide such questions as that of the choice of the capital.[26] They held two antithetical conceptions concerning the very way in which political questions were posed. Jacini would claim that Cavour's attitude was nothing but a clever political tactic, aimed at stifling any last aspirations to federalism in Italy, not a serious intention to transfer the capital to Rome. The claim will not wash,[27] and this sort of argument was pointless in any case since it was free-floating, built on more or less arbitrary hypotheses, with Jacini's interpretation running counter to the completely opposite interpretations of many other friends, disciples, and collaborators of Cavour. Above and beyond controversy at this level, it remained the case that there was an abyss between Cavour's manner of seeing the situation, his appeal to spiritual and moral factors, to imagination and to feeling, and the concreteness of Jacini. It was an abyss that divided a great politician, receptive to every voice, capable of intuiting the positive value even in things that did not correspond to common sense, from a man of notable intelligence but locked into an excessively rigid framework, a man of too much analysis and too little intuition. Jacini's courageous, but overly harsh and one-sided, polemic against the idea of Rome, "the affectation of a decrepit Italy," left out everything fruitful that the patriots had found in it and neglected, or rather offended, living ideals profoundly felt by men above suspicion either of rhetoric or of the antiquarian's infatuation.

Jacini's speech caused a sensation in the Senate. But when it was over, his battle against the rhetoric of Rome, a battle that aimed a fierce blow at one of the greatest dangers facing the new Italy, produced no result. By presenting the idea of Rome as an antiquarian's delight, all he did was provoke a reaction in the opposite sense, so that no attention was paid even to the useful part of what he

[26] This Cavourian theme is naturally taken up as well by the politicians of 1870; see the *Relazione* of the Central Office of the Senate (the *relatore* [rapporteur] is Scialoja) on the bill for the transfer of the capital: "Primacy among cities, as among men, is largely a matter of opinion. It is more felt than thought out; and there were a hundred reasons keeping the cult of Rome alive in men's hearts, maintaining their deep admiration for its greatness and power, which were not always beneficial, but were always glorious, or preponderant, in the unfolding of history" (*Senato, Documenti*, eleventh legislature, session of 1870–71, no. 23 A, p. 2).

[27] It is well known that Cavour's exegetes diverged among themselves concerning the Roman question. Jacini dissented from the *communis opinio* regarding Cavour's theorem "Rome the capital," in which he was joined by Alfieri di Sostegno, an authoritative interpreter, indeed a relative, of the Count of Cavour (Jacini, *La crisi religiosa del Risorgimento*, p. 384), while Padelletti dissented on the Cavourian theorem "a free church in a free state" ("Libera Chiesa in Libero Stato," *Nuova Antologia* [July 1875]: 690–91). Both Jacini and Padelletti maintained that these were instances of Cavour's "opportunism." But on 2 April 1861 Cavour had written to Count de Circourt, in sending him his speeches on Rome: "I spoke without reticence, and without mental reservation," *Cavour e L'Inghilterra: Carteggio con V. E. d'Azeglio* 2:293 (Bologna, 1933). On Cavour's overall attitude, cf. the acute analysis of Jemolo, *Chiesa e Stato in Italia*, pp. 165 ff.

had to say. An exaggerated diatribe merely tended to inspire relentless hosannas in praise of the notional target—even if, for the moment, these hosannas were perforce confined to innocuous proposals for holidays, triumphal parades, imaginary projects, magniloquence; at most, they were capable of rising to the dignity of literature, in the pages of Carducci.

Such then was the aftermath of 20 September 1870. In the embryonic history of united Italy, a new force materialized when Rome became the capital, a force capable of good and evil. It was a potent stimulant, a standard round which to rally, a sign of national individuality in the days before the country was unified, never failing to inspire high ideals in whoever chose to accept it in the guise of a moral commandment that a great tradition imposed on the new Italy. It was also capable of exerting a sinister influence on the destiny of the country, in the case of those who let themselves be blinded and swollen with conceit, and who dreamed of impossible revivals.

All were ideas that could only arise with Rome materially in the possession of Italy. It was inane to believe that the feeling for Rome could thrive in some other city, that Milan could be a second Rome. There was absurdity in the plea of the imaginative De Zerbi that Rome should somehow be, at Milan or anywhere else—provided only that it be: "since faith in the lance of the Roman citizen, and the high unfailing destiny of the fatherland, pride in our own race and our own citizenship, impatience at narrow confines, the force of expansion that always looks beyond, always farther beyond, always always higher, always higher, and the indomitable persistence in desiring above all else the majesty of the Roman people—this, which is Rome—this is not yet in existence in any place in Italy!"[28]

Inane and absurd: because only in the very domicile of ancient glory, amid the remains of former magnificence, could dreams of Roman greatness really flourish again, and continue to flourish. Only amid the monuments that celebrated the great epics of the past, and that were "a pungent reminder of their duty"[29] for the Italians, was there born the aspiration to be great as their ancient forefathers had been.

The expansion of which De Zerbi, a nationalist ahead of his time, dreamed, would have had an entirely different character with Milan as its point of departure, would have employed very different means than the ones employed in the expansion which was later undertaken from Rome. Only at Rome was it possible to hold the phantasms of antiquity in one's mind in a serious and prolonged fashion; elsewhere they would rapidly have lost force and efficacy. In order to make Goethe's invocation of the stones of the city and its looming palazzi live again, in order to receive their inspiring message, it was necessary before all else to move among those palazzi, tread those stones. Now the political class to which the destiny of united Italy was entrusted was about to settle permanently among the ancient stones.

[28] De Zerbi, *Difendetevi!*, pp. 50–51.
[29] Thus Crispi, in 1881 (*Scritti e discorsi politici*, p. 496).

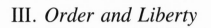

III. *Order and Liberty*

The Conservative Program

STILL, FOR THE MOMENT, it was the seat of St. Peter that continued to rouse passions, whether hostile or defensive. The arches and the columns of Rome did not yet speak convincingly of military force.

Anyway, compared to other cities in Italy, for a number of years Rome was simply engaged in a struggle to absorb the impact of its status as the capital. The condition of the public offices made the Urbs seem like a rooming house,[1] a provisional encampment lacking the order or the appearance of a capital.[2] From the strictly political point of view, observers often had the impression that the real center of the country was still somewhere else. Perhaps, said *Il Diritto*,[3] it was in the railway carriages in which government ministers were continually traveling northward or southward. Policy speeches by the party leaders were all delivered somewhere else, at Turin or Legnago or Cologna Veneta or Stradella or Cossato. Important international negotiations were conducted elsewhere, not in the capital.[4] The deputies were frequently seen departing, anxious to get back home as soon as possible and dissatisfied with the climate and the unhealthy environment of the region surrounding Rome.[5] The king's absences from the Eternal City were extremely lengthy,[6] since Vittorio Emanuele did not care for the climate either,[7] and his Catholic conscience was troubled with remorse,[8] with moral uneasiness every time he contemplated St. Peter's and the Vatican from the

---

[1] Thus Crispi, in his speech to the Chamber on 10 March 1881 (*Discorsi Parlamentari* 2:480).

[2] "Rassegna Politica," *Nuova Antologia* 56 (1881): 367.

[3] "Il partito moderato e la capitale d'Italia," in *Il Diritto* for 22 September 1875.

[4] On 29 August 1875 *L'Opinione* ("I rappresentanti di Roma") laments the "lack of life and political authority" of the capital and blames the government for handling important matters away from Rome. The negotiations between Luzzatti and Ozenne for the Italo-French commercial treaty were taking place at Bellagio.

[5] Luzzatti, *Memorie* 1:354; Aleardi, *Epistolario*, p. 400. Complaints of this kind roused the ire of the Romans, who asserted that the city was perfectly healthy and that there was malaria only in the countryside (F. Gori, *Sullo splendido avvenire di Roma capitale d'Italia e del mondo cattolico e sul modo di migliorare l'interno della città e l'aria delle campagne* [Rome, 1870]). On the rumors and clichés and prejudices concerning Rome, see A. Gabelli, *Roma e i Romani*, ed. Vinciguerra (Florence, 1949), pp. 31–33. But the anxiety about hygiene at any rate was felt equally among foreigners; and the French envoy, Fournier, observed that "there are times when the new capital of Italy inspires one with a single idea, which is to flee from it, so many serious and sudden risks does one's health run there" (Fournier, report, 1 July 1872, no. 31; AEP, *C.P., Italie*, t. 385, fol. 188).

[6] *La Riforma* for 22 August 1873 ("L'Italia senza governo") alluded in very harsh terms to the frequent and prolonged absences of the king from Rome, and their twofold motive: "MacMahon does not fear the muggy atmosphere of Versailles, nor does he fly in terror from the censures of the internationalists of Paris. He does not attempt to *scontare un breve fallo di gloria* by hunting chamois in the mountains or chasing with senile lustfulness after ballerinas and other women for hire."

[7] On 9 April 1875 the king telegraphed to Minghetti from Naples: "I inform you that until May I do not desire to go to the Eternal City because having just barely got over the fever I caught there, I have no wish to return and catch another" (BCB, *Carte Minghetti*, cart 35, b).

[8] Cf. below, pp. 542–43.

height of the Quirinal.[9] In those years observers often had the impression that Rome was the capital *pro forma*, but that the real political center was somewhere else.[10] Rome was not yet the great capital city of more recent times, nor during their years in power did the moderates, with the exception of Sella, wish it to become one, since they were all more or less fearful that a capital city of the French sort might suck in too much of the life of the nation: an outsized head compared to the body on which it sat.

Even without this slow transformation of Rome into a genuine capital, there were other factors at work reducing the impulse to brandish the spear of the ancient Quirites. One was the European situation, which by itself would have been more than enough, and another was the desire of the population and the intention of the men in the government to concentrate all their efforts on the immense and arduous domestic problems facing Italy, and to conduct an entirely

[9] That the king did not like living in the Quirinal is explicitly stated by Castagnola, *Da Firenze a Roma*, p. 86. The announcement by Berti that the king came to Rome "in a perfectly tranquil frame of mind" was made for patriotic and apologetic reasons and is completely unfounded (D. Berti, "L'educazione di Vittorio Emanuele ed il suo matrimonio," *Nuova Antologia* 57 [1881]: 217). A scholar who was also sympathetic to the king, but more exact, acknowledged the "pain" it caused him: Monti, *Vittorio Emanuele II*, pp. 387–88 and cf. p. 376. Castelli, one of the king's intimates, wrote on 13 July to Dina: "The king was very happy to have the thorn of his going to Rome removed. . . . [M]any believe that he was uneasy on account of the pope's threat to leave the city, but they are mistaken. He would prefer to be alone in Rome, free of those personal conflicts and that counteraltar" (Castelli, *Carteggio politico* 2:510–11 and cf. p. 509). This confirms the hesitations, the doubt, and the displeasure of Vittorio Emanuele at finding himself facing the pope at close range. Castelli's opinion is confirmed by the French chargé d'affaires, de Sayve, who corroborates the authenticity of what Vittorio Emanuele reportedly said to the queen of the Netherlands when she passed through Florence in November: that he wished the pope would leave Rome, because he could not look out the windows of the Quirinal without seeing the Vatican before him, and that it always seemed to him that Pius IX and he were both prisoners (report, 14 November 1871, no. 136; AEP, *C.P., Italie*, t. 383, fols. 201v–202r). An analogous expression used by the king on another occasion to his field adjutant is recorded in A. Lumbroso, "Vittorio Emanuele II e Pio IX: Il loro carteggio inedito dal 1870 al 1878," in *La Tribuna* for 11 September 1911.

As for the famous phrase that Vittorio Emanuele is supposed to have used to La Marmora upon arriving at Rome on 31 December 1870, "ci siamo e ci resteremo" ("here we are and here we shall remain"), it too appears to be an apologetic amplification. Oriani, then a young man who was present at the scene, states that the phrase, which was pronounced in Piedmontese dialect with the air of a traveler weary from his voyage, was "finalment i suma," "here we are at last" (*La lotta politica in Italia* 3:285 and n. 1). The presence of Pius IX in the Vatican certainly brought Vittorio Emanuele no pleasure: this is confirmed by an expressive comment he made in July 1871, recorded by Menabrea, in connection with his refusal to cross the river to Trastevere: "Il papa lí a doi pass a sentirà. I l'hai già faine abastansa a coul pover veii" ["The pope resides nearby, and he would feel it. I have already done enough to the poor old man"] (Lumbroso in *La Tribuna* for 6 September 1911). The words "ci resteremo" or *hic manebimus optime* came from Sella originally, not from the king, who said "ci resteremo" on 2 July 1871, at a reception for the mayors: this was the moment of the "historic phrase, which had the force and value almost of an oath, and was a source of great satisfaction to the liberals, who went about repeating it from one end of the peninsula to the other" (Vigo, *Annali d'Italia* 1:71).

[10] Naturally it was mostly the opposition papers who complained that Rome was not truly becoming the capital, because of the bad government of the moderates: in addition to *Il Diritto* and *La Riforma*, cf. *Il Popolo Romano* for 5 September 1875 ("La Capitale"), criticizing the itinerant, leisurely ministers, and the absence of the king and the princes. In 1893 Guido Baccelli could still declare angrily: "The Vatican stays here all year round; the court leaves, along with everyone else" (Farini, *Diario* 1:333). The deputies themselves felt they were present in a capital that was not the center of the country's public opinion and public spirit (Fournier, report, 23 April 1873, no. 114; AEP, *C.P., Italie*, t. 387, fol. 282v).

peaceful foreign policy. Even for the most excitable politicians of this period, the ones most easily inflamed by the recollection of the great heritage, the present moment was not the right one for a resurrection of the Rome of Scipio and Caesar, it was the moment for a struggle against Italy's internal enemy, and the cancer of all humanity: the papacy. As for the men of the Right, the watchword became: entrenchment. After a dozen years of unforeseen, unhoped-for gains, it was time to make sure they were retained, to transform Italy from the agent of revolutionary ferment in Europe into an element of order and peace. This was the new ideal, sincerely felt, loudly proclaimed, with direct appeals to the deeds and the thoughts of Cavour.[11]

The revolution was over. Now it was time to put the house in order,[12] restore "many principles, many ideas, many attachments that in the course of the revolution we have necessarily had to disregard, or injure,"[13] in fact to strengthen the principle of authority,[14] and so to put an end to the spirit of Jacobinism. Minghetti was saying this to the trusted Pasolini from Vienna as early as 22 October 1870,[15] and was even advising that the reform of the Statuto be addressed right away, with the goal of finally consolidating the institutions and thus interring once and for all any idea of holding a Constituent Assembly. He justified this by the necessity of resolving the position of the pope in Rome, proposing to introduce an apposite clause in the Statuto to deal with this, not a separate law.[16] A few months later, in the debate in the Senate on the law of Guarantees, Visconti Venosta again expressed officially and unequivocally his view and that of his colleagues in the government, stating that the Italian cause was indeed the cause of liberty for all of Europe, but also the cause of tranquillity and equilibrium; that the Italian national movement had had "the highly civilized ambition to be considered a step forward for the general cause of order and liberty in Europe"; and that the Italian people could be considered one of the most peaceful and conservative in Europe. The minister declared that the political task of the Italian revolution was over,[17] certain of being able to count on the consensus not only of the

---

[11] Jacini, in his speech to the Senate of 21 January 1871, developing his views on the general character of Italian foreign policy, "eminently conservative of peace and order in Europe," cited personal statements of Cavour, whose tenor was: "allow us to attain our goal, that is our national independence, and you will see what a guarantor of European order Italy will become" (*A.P., Senato*, p. 1110. As is well known, these are the underlying ideas of Jacini's *Pensieri sulla politica italiana*, in which cf. esp. pp. 65–67). Cf. as well the statements of Artom, *A.P., Senato*, p. 1112.

[12] C. Bon Compagni to Minghetti, 28 October 1870 (BCB, *Carte Minghetti*, cart. XV, fasc. 67).

[13] Thus Bonfadini to the Chamber on 21 March 1872 (*A.P., Camera*, p. 1383).

[14] Thus Castelli, the confidant of the king, to Dina (Castelli, *Carteggio politico* 2:511). Castelli believes that in Rome "the influence of the king can have a much more definite effect, and be exercised with real benefit to the constitutional cause," because Rome, more than other cities, enhances the title of king.

[15] "[T]he government's program must change as regards Italy. Politically it must become conservative, and administratively it should decentralize" (Minghetti, *Carteggio Minghetti-Pasolini* 4:195). In the session of 20 March 1872, Minghetti repeats to the Chamber his credo: "we have always said and believed that, having gained Rome, the period of the revolution is over, and Italy must have an essentially peaceful policy in its foreign relations, and an essentially conservative one in its internal conduct" (Minghetti, *Discorsi Parlamentari* 5:253).

[16] Minghetti to Visconti Venosta, 12 October 1870 (Visconti Venosta archive).

[17] *A.P., Senato*, pp. 776–77 (22 April 1871).

parliament but also of virtually unanimous public opinion, since there was no real opposition to what he was saying even from the leaders of the Left—Depretis, Rattazzi, Zanardelli, Cairoli. Visconti Venosta's words were sealed by the speech from the throne at the inauguration of the eleventh legislature on 5 December 1870, in which a free and undivided Italy was portrayed as an element of order, liberty, and peace for Europe.[18]

Order, peace, stability: Italy was to take its place like a well-behaved person in the European family and the concert of powers, no longer the disruptive individual it had been for so long. But order and stability in European life presupposed order and stability in the internal life of the individual countries, hence in that of Italy as well. Conservatism in foreign policy amounted to the same thing as the desire for conservatism and stability in domestic politics, and declaring for one meant declaring for the other. Just as the Italian political class wanted the European situation to remain undisturbed for as long as possible, so they wanted to avoid any sort of turmoil or innovation at home. What they wanted was to arrest the situation at the point it had reached, in their relations with the other states externally, and in relations among the various parties and social strata internally: and so these new Joshuas proceeded to entrench, falling back on clearly conservative positions. The interests of Italy, identical to those of Europe, were "the preservation of peace, liberal progress, and social conservatism," affirmed Visconti Venosta once again in the Chamber on 27 November 1871:[19] conservatism, in sum, in the domestic arena as well as in the international one.

The views expressed by La Marmora to Fournier, the French envoy at Florence in March 1872 were shared by numerous men of authority: it was possible to regret the "manner" in which Italy had made itself into a great nation, and indeed the Italian leaders did so; that manner, those "methods . . . are embarrassing for those in government, and who wish to be, must be, conservatives, after having made use of the revolution to get where we are: but what is done is done. We will employ time, wisdom, prudence, adjustments, force if necessary against those who . . . would continue to be revolutionaries . . . and will consolidate little by little our political and social condition."[20]

The theme of order, protected by the initiative of the house of Savoy, was familiar. It went back to 1848.[21] To wave the specter of revolution before the eyes of Europe had become a constant practice, almost a daily formula, especially from the moment when Cavour had made clever use of the alarm that Mazzinian propaganda inspired in the chancelleries of Europe to proclaim him-

---

[18] And again in the speech from the throne of 27 November 1871: "having made our revolution in the name of liberty, we must search for the secret of strength and reconciliation in liberty and in order."

[19] *A.P., Camera*, p. 3389.

[20] Fournier, report, 28 March 1872, no. 3; AEP, *C.P., Italie*, t. 384, fol. 280r-v.

[21] Cf. R. Moscati, *La diplomazia europea e il problema italiano nel 1848*, p. 8; Pareto's dispatch to the marchese Carrega, 23 March 1848, in *La diplomazia del regno di Sardegna durante la prima guerra d'indipendenza*, vol. 1, *Relazioni con il Granducato di Toscana (marzo 1848-aprile 1849)*, ed. C. Pischedda (Turin, 1949), p. 3, and Pischedda's acute remarks in the introduction, pp. xvi and lxxxvi–lxxxvii.

self the guardian of order in Italy, and demand a freedom of action that, if it were denied to him, would be used for very different purposes by the Genovese agitator. Cavour had successfully sought to reduce the conservative powers to silence, even when faced with his most revolutionary actions. He had stated, and his envoys had repeated, "that there was no way for us to act otherwise without letting ourselves be overrun by the real revolutionaries, and without putting the general order and security of Italy internally, and even those of her neighbors, at risk."[22] Either they allowed Cavour to act, or there would be republican anarchy in the peninsula, and that would put the torch to the whole continent. Visconti Venosta gave an example of the use of the technique in September 1870 when he sought to legitimize what the government had done by presenting it as a measure to preserve order at a very dangerous moment;[23] this brought criticism both from conservatives like Gino Capponi,[24] and especially from those on the Left, who rose to deny that there had been any danger,[25] but the minister was perfectly in tune with other representatives of public opinion.[26] The king himself had stated directly to Pius IX that he was acting to maintain order against the dark designs of the party of cosmopolitan revolution.[27] And later still, straining continually to

[22] Thus La Marmora, on 1 February 1861, to the Prussian minister of foreign affairs, von Schleinitz, attempting to justify the invasion of the papal state (La Marmora, *Un po' più di luce*, p. 15). Cavour unfailingly played the same card in dealing with Berlin (Valsecchi, "La politica di Cavour e la Prussia," pp. 49, 54–56, 59). Analogously, when on a mission to Paris after Villafranca, Peruzzi pointed to the threat of a republic in Tuscany, then in Italy, and perhaps even north of the Alps, if the annexation to Piedmont were not consented to (Zanichelli, *Studi politici e storici*, p. 451).

[23] Cf. the two great circulars to the Italian representatives abroad, 29 August and 7 September 1870, *Libro Verde 17*, nos. 2 and 3, pp. 11 and 13. And see further Minghetti's dispatch of 21 September, ibid., no. 24, p. 36. In fact, in the *Libro Verde*, perhaps to avert even stronger criticism from the Left, a whole sentence of the original text has been suppressed, in which Visconti Venosta musters the specter of revolution even more strongly. After the words *nécessités supérieures* (p. 36, line 13), the dispatch continued thus: "It was in effect necessary to take steps to prevent all notion of authority from being swept into a whirlpool of disorder, and to keep from suddenly finding ourselves no longer able to preserve the monarchical principle and the spiritual independence of the Holy See." And note the further reference to the principle of authority having been reinforced by Italy's action in the circular of 18 October (*Libro Verde*, no. 56, p. 71).

[24] The government says it has occupied Rome to defend it from the incursions of the Garibaldians and Mazzinians: but, says Capponi, "I don't really know what danger there was from Mazzini. . . . [I] believe that the surveillance maintained over Garibaldi was more than sufficient" (from a speech in the Senate on 29 December 1870; Capponi, *Scritti editi e inediti* 1:459).

[25] *La Riforma* for 25 September 1870 ("La moralità dell'idea nazionale") takes a stand against the "facetious pretexts" of the government, and in favor of an open and frank procedure. In the Chamber on 30 January 1871, the hon. Oliva, editor of *La Riforma*, on the other hand accused the government of having invaded the territory of Rome for reasons of public security, "driven by the necessity of preserving itself" (*A.P., Camera*, p. 432).

[26] From 7 September *La Nazione* of Florence ("La Francia repubblicana") had expressed ideas in the same vein as those of Visconti Venosta: "this deed [going to Rome] is so grave that we cannot justify it except by showing, what is true, that it conforms to the interests, and the necessity, of the European public order. By carrying out this deed, which is revolutionary in form, all we are really doing is revealing our force, affirming our existence, as an essentially conservative government."

[27] In the well-known letter of 8 September entrusted to Count Ponza di San Martino. The same themes are found in Lanza's instructions to Ponza di San Martino: we could always wait until agitation produces serious disorders etc. Blanc later assured Cardinal Antonelli that General Cadorna had taken Rome only to prevent the proclamation of a republic by Cernuschi, with the encouragement of Paris (report of the French chargé d'affaires, Lefebvre de Béhaine, 28 December 1870, no. 130; AEP, *C.P., Rome*, t. 1048, fols. 398 ff. Naturally, for Lefebvre, all these dangers were imaginary and invented).

block any new offensive by the ultramontanes of various countries, the foreign minister constantly availed himself of the old theme: the Italian government at Rome was a sure guarantee of order and tranquillity against anarchy.[28]

The same argument was used, whether it was believed or not, by foreign commentators favorable to the new order of things[29] and even, as in 1848,[30] by the foreign governments that had assumed a friendly attitude to Italy, and which sought in this fashion to mollify the Catholics, or indeed to prevent Italy's use of armed force against Rome from serving as a pretext for other disturbances of the international status quo. So for example in November 1870, when Russia had declared itself absolved from the clauses of the treaty of Paris relative to the Black Sea, and the ambassador of the tsar at Vienna attempted to justify the action of his government by adducing the example of 20 September—that is, of another putative violation of international undertakings—Beust and Andrássy replied even before Minghetti, pointing out that Italy's action, "occasioned by very compelling and urgent domestic motives . . . also had a special purpose connected with public order, and although it destroyed the temporal power of the pope, nonetheless maintained in the eyes of Europe a conservative character."[31]

---

[28] On 18 October 1870, instructing de Launay to include the question of Rome in his discussions with Bismarck, Visconti Venosta observes that this issue, as well as having reduced the freedom of action of Italian policy by tying it to French policy, was "one of those slogans that we could not let the revolutionary parties monopolize, because they really express a true and profound national feeling in the country. In the interest of the monarchical and conservative principle, the government itself had to grasp hold of this question with a resolute initiative, so as not to leave it in the grip of the revolutionary movement, which would have been prepared to resolve it with its own forces and on its own terms. The revolutionary party was completely disconcerted by our initiative, it was reduced to impotence, and the proof of this is the sterile and useless adventure that Garibaldi went looking for in France." He states that even the formula of Rome as a free city, proposed by Count von Arnim, has its perils: "Rome as a free city would inevitably become the Roman republic" (Visconti Venosta archive). The same ideas are found in two dispatches to Cadorna (in London), of 30 March and 12 April 1871 (AE, *Ris.*, 51): if the taking of Rome "has placed Italy in a difficult situation internationally, still it has produced security and tranquillity inside Italy. The extremist parties were deprived of any source of agitation; the elections turned out well; the country is deaf to any external solicitations; the government is master of the situation, and Italy asks nothing better than to be able to attend in security to its own peaceful progress. One is obliged to ask whether such would be the state of affairs if the national sentiment had not been satisfied in a definitive manner, if the question of Rome had remained open, furnishing a slogan for the revolutionaries. . . . [R]ather than Italy being one of the calmest and most tranquil countries in Europe, how would things stand now if, at the moment of the revolution in France, Rome had been an open arena for the Garibaldians?" (30 March). And on 12 April he insisted: "As for us, we have to think above all of maintaining internal tranquillity, of avoiding the backwash of events in Paris. It is better to have a certain amount of diplomatic friction than anarchy."

[29] Cf. the anonymous opuscule *Pro populo italico* (Berlin, 1871; Italian translation: *Difesa della nazione italica* [Rome, 1872], p. 21), which was written to counter the assertions of A. von Reumont in *Pro Romano pontifice* (Bonn, 1870). The reasoning employed by Visconti Venosta (that Rome was occupied to maintain order) was not in the least "the Italian government's own satire on itself," as Reumont claimed, but a genuine motive: Mazzini and Garibaldi would not have rested content with the destruction of the temporal power.

[30] The position taken by Piedmont in 1848 (that it was preventing Lombardy from becoming the center of a republican movement in Italy) had been adopted by the English government (Moscati, *La diplomazia europea*, p. 8).

[31] Minghetti, report from Vienna, 19 November 1870, no. 27. Analogously, Jules Favre accepted Nigra's contention that if the Italian government had taken no action, everything would have been lost: the demagogic parties would have seized Rome "and the tempest that swept the papacy

It was all the more necessary to insist on order, tranquillity, and respect for constituted authority, and to assume the role of the trusty guardian in the eyes of Europe, since the Italian government was accused by the ultramontanes, French, Belgian, Austrian, German, Irish, and Spanish, of sapping at their root the sacred principles of order and authority. They accused it of paving the way, with its acts of violence, to deleterious convulsions of the moral, political, and social order, and of harming (in the words of Monsignor Ledóchowski) the monarchical principle itself, "in such wise that it will be difficult to inspire in people respect for what is sacred and honorable, when in Rome the Italians are trampling it underfoot with impunity."[32]

Timid and backward-looking as far as the Left was concerned, the Italian government appeared a monster of impiety, abominable and subversive, in the eyes of the reactionaries of Europe. Now, just as in Cavour's lifetime, its lot was to maintain the tension between two extreme and antithetical impulses, one principally domestic and the other primarily external, seeking advantage by making use of each against the other in turn: it floated the specter of Mazzinian revolution abroad to defend the occupation of Rome on the diplomatic front, and it held up the scarecrow of a European intervention to extract guarantees for the pope from the Italian parliament, against the opposition of those who would have wished to reduce the pope to the status of a bishop like any other.[33]

Still, it was not the tactical requirement of pure politics that made the men of the Right tend to embrace conservatism internally and externally, nor was their conservatism a trap of their own making: they had not adopted principles and programs in order to win support, and then gradually convinced themselves of the truth and sanctity of affirmations initially meant to convince others. Cavour's aversion for creating revolution and turmoil, his reluctance to sweep away the structure of old institutions headed by the monarchy, had been anything but mere diplomatic pretense. For his successors the desire to stabilize the situation was naturally even stronger, since they considered that all the aims of the national movement had now been attained: unity, independence, liberty. They were sincere in asserting their desire for peace, their will to become a force contributing

---

away would have exposed us to the gravest disorders." And he concluded: "I believe, like you, that if you do not go there, Rome will fall under the sway of dangerous agitators. I prefer to see you there"; though he refused to express any formal approval (Favre, *Rome et la république française*, pp. 5–7). Rothan, on the other hand, observed that for many years Italy had succeeded "in duping us about its internal situation, in the interests of its own policy. It passed, in effect, for a hotbed of trouble in Europe as long as it was under foreign domination. At this time its statesmen were conspiring with Mazzini and Garibaldi for the independence of the peninsula" (Rothan, report, 27 March 1871, no. 77; AEP, *C.P., Italie*, t. 381, fol. 240r-v; cf. Rothan, *L'Allemagne et l'Italie* 2:348, under the date 21 March). The skeptical Decazes is said to have written on 22 December 1873: "I believe that the Italian government is more the master in its own house than one supposes. Indeed I am prepared to hazard that it doesn't so much endure democratic fervor as it exploits it" (in G. Hanotaux, *Histoire de la France contemporaine* 2:394 n. 2).

[32] In the address presented to King Wilhelm I of Prussia (*Libro Verde 17*, p. 110).

[33] In his speech to the Chamber on 21 December 1870, the hon. Toscanelli criticized the government for this policy of fear: the government's domestic policy, he said, was to be fearful of the Left, and its foreign policy to be fearful of the Right (*A.P., Camera*, p. 138). But the Tuscan deputy failed to see how successful the government was overall in exploiting this position.

to order in Europe. They were no less sincere when they claimed that they constituted the only valid safeguard of tranquillity within Italy against the fearsome eruption of extremist doctrines.

This real and profound fear of widespread subversion lay behind the government's strategy: it was necessary to seize control of the ideology of the revolution, lead it in order to bridle it, make use of it up to a point, but keep it from going beyond that point and getting out of hand.[34] And this of course was the difficulty, to grasp the moment when the revolutionary impulse would yield the maximum advantage and offer the least risk; there would be a price to pay for acting too soon, or too late. The instinct and the eye of a great captain were needed, and it is no surprise if more than once Alexander's generals failed to display the instinct and the eye that Alexander (Cavour) had possessed in supreme measure. Thus the policy of the moderates ran aground on reefs that bore the names of Aspromonte and Mentana, and still in 1870 gave the impression of being indecisive, oscillating, nerveless. Likewise it is not surprising that such conduct, such perpetual switching back and forth between reaction and revolution, should excite, in 1870 and later, the disdain of men like Crispi, Carducci, and Oriani, who were all for revolution and perceived as cowardice what was an ongoing difficult search for equilibrium between the opposing forces. But despite all the errors, hesitations, and uncertainties, the search succeeded: the Italy that went to Rome was a monarchy, Europe accepted the fait accompli, former republicans prepared to become ministers in the cabinet of the king of Italy.

For the fact is that the main form of threatening extremism was still republicanism. The shift to stability had to begin by defending the monarchy strongly against all forms of Mazzinian propaganda and, from 4 September 1870, propaganda of French origin. It was an old theme that went back to the past, to 1848 at least, and the current polemic produced nothing new on the ideological plane, but continued to hark back to the epoch of the great debates between the adherents of the government and the conspirators. The aversion of the monarchists for Mazzini, whose name was never pronounced except before an insult or after an injurious epithet,[35] was not now so fierce as the ire that had been capable, between 1848 and 1849, of exciting even Cavour to propose the immediate execution by firing squad of every seditious person.[36] But something new came on the

---

[34] Only in this sense is Gramsci accurate in asserting that historically the party of action was piloted by the moderates (Gramsci, *Il Risorgimento* [Turin, 1949], pp. 70 ff.): in the sense, that is, that the moderates from Cavour on were able, to an extent that varied in different cases and with different individuals, to bring about the concrete solutions that they themselves favored. But in their turn the moderates felt the pressure of the party of action, especially after Cavour, and to a large extent took the measures they did because they were being pressured. It is enough to reflect on the events of September 1870 when, if not for the Left and the menace of the party of action, the moderates would certainly not have gone to Rome in the manner they did. Sella could carry the day because behind him there loomed the Left. On the other hand it is quite true, and also understandable, that after 1870 the Left loses all its revolutionary spirit and assimilates instead the spirit, and the methods, of the moderates.

[35] Martini, *Confessioni e ricordi*, p. 71.

[36] "The indispensable thing is, above all, to repress energetically the slightest sign of a republican movement in Lombardy. Go ahead and shoot the first Lombard who utters a seditious cry, without

scene with September 1870 to rekindle uneasiness on the monarchical side, and also to reinforce with new arguments the now hoary precept that monarchy unites where a republic divides.

For one thing, a republic came into existence in France. It was a conservative one—indeed from February 1871 the majority in the Assembly was reactionary; still, it was a republic and, endowed with the glamour of French ideas, it was not something to ignore. Mazzini's death occurred shortly after. But north of the Alps there was now an example, and perhaps there would also be incitement and support for republicanism, more dangerous even than the message of the great unarmed agitator. Hence as early as 7 September 1870, three days after the events of Paris, *La Nazione* of Florence launched a cry of alarm, proclaiming that "from today" Italy was an essentially conservative nation, that being conservative meant saving the unity and independence of Italy, saving the Italian homeland and Italian society from the menace of those who desired once again to color Italy French in the name of republicanism. The paper added that the drive to republicanism, which had hitherto been combated in the name of party ideals, was now to be resisted in the name of the independence of the nation, so that anyone who raised the cry for a republic in Italy was to be regarded as a traitor who wanted to turn Italy into an instrument of the policies of a foreign nation.[37] It is not a coincidence that the Florentine paper became strongly pro-Prussian at this time, expressing support for the country in which public life was firmly anchored in monarchy. But *La Nazione* was not alone in fearing the reverberations of French republicanism in Italy; and neither was Milan's *La Perseveranza* alone in declaring, on 7 September, that the time for hesitation was past, and that now was the moment to go to Rome. In fact, the decision to commit to Rome was taken on 5 September by the king and by Lanza and was brought to pass in large part by the collapse of Napoleon III, which canceled Italy's obligations to the emperor. An even more important factor was their fear of what might happen in Italy if the government stood pat, and revolutionaries inspired by the events of 4 September took action.[38]

The events of February 1848 in Paris, with their European and Italian repercussions, did not belong to prehistory, after all, and the king and his ministers had them vividly in mind. The bare prose of the minutes of the meeting of the cabinet on 5 September said it all and spontaneously made the connection between the developments that were occurring:

---

worrying about what Brofferio and Valerio have to say": Cavour to the duke of Dino, 14 March 1849 (*Lettere* 5:193). Again in 1857, referring to Mazzini, "I would give I don't know what to have him arrested," and if it were discovered that he was behind the plot to assassinate Napoleon III, "we would string him up, to the great satisfaction of respectable people in every country" (*Carteggio Cavour-Salmour*, p. 129). He would not really have done so; but still . . .

[37] "La Francia repubblicana."

[38] Cf. above, n. 28, the letters of Visconti Venosta, esp. the one of 12 April 1871 to Cadorna which expresses fully what the preoccupations of the government were after 4 September (and cf., for the immediate repercussions of 4 September in Paris, the reports of the prefects of Bologna, Grosseto, and Caserta, in Lanza, *Le carte* 6:57–58, 65–66, 68, and 77). And for more on Visconti Venosta, see below, ch. 15, n. 20.

The cabinet decides to nominate Baron Ricasoli envoy extraordinary to Paris, and to send Count Ponza di San Martino on a special mission to Rome to inform the pontiff of the resolution of the Italian government to occupy Rome and the pontifical territory, offering all possible guarantees for his security and for the free exercise of the spiritual power.

The cabinet decides to order our envoy in Paris to recognize the Republic.

The cabinet further decides to give the prime minister the faculty to take all the steps necessary to prepare and facilitate the ingress of our troops into pontifical territory.

The cabinet decides as well to call to arms a levy of the second category.[39]

Once resolved on going to Rome, Italy needed its king more than ever. Faced with the pope, only a king could defend victorious Italy. Many years later Domenico Zanichelli stated this very clearly, though his views had long been those commonly held, however clearly or hazily.

"We firmly believe that Italy, if it had become a republic, might perhaps have been able, at the cost of many setbacks and dangers, to drive out the foreigners and the tyrants among us. But on the other hand we are convinced that in the struggle against the papacy a republican Italy would certainly have been the loser. We owe immense gratitude to king Vittorio Emanuele for the assistance he gave to the Risorgimento of Italy; but it is not just gratitude, it is also necessity that binds us closely to that institution which he merged with Italy, and the dynasty that personifies it. Woe to our country if it abandons the monarchy; it would be an act of suicide because the country that rose up after so many centuries would return to the grave, and later generations would say that the Italians were unable to preserve the precious inheritance of their fathers.

"In our view Italy will have a solid hope of winning the struggle with the papacy only if it remains monarchical."

He continued: the monarchy and the papacy are both types of political organization that tend fatally to hegemonize, that can exist only by occupying the first place; hence the contest between them is a natural one. In Italy the contest was direct and more serious than in any other country. Hence the monarchy here could never be brought to accept an accord that took away its supremacy, it would continue to combat the papacy, at least as long as the claims of the latter had any political and social importance.

"Let us suppose that a clerical-Catholic reaction prevailed in Italy, whether for general European reasons or specifically Italian ones. Let us suppose that this

---

[39] ACR, *Verbali delle deliberazioni del Consiglio dei Ministri* 2:69, published in Lanza, *Le carte* 6:404–405. And cf. Castagnola, *Da Firenze a Roma*, p. 32. It is noteworthy that, perhaps because of the excitement of the moment, "resolution of the pontifical government" was written instead of "Italian government." This was later corrected in blue pencil by another hand. Cf. as well Guiccioli, *Quintino Sella* 1:300–301, who however predates it to 3 September, when the news of Sedan was received; in fact the cabinet was still strongly divided between 3 and 4 September (Castagnola, *Da Firenze a Roma*, pp. 30–31); and now Halperin, *Italy and the Vatican at War*, pp. 42–43. Oriani saw perfectly clearly how matters stood: "either an immediate march to Rome, or preparation for a civil war against the revolutionaries" (*La lotta politica in Italia* 3:277–78).

force gained control of the electorate and filled the Chamber of Deputies with a majority ready to make an accord with the Vatican and desirous of giving it what it asks. Anyone can see that on this hypothesis there would be no authority or legal force able to save the secular and national state except for the monarchy, which, being naturally opposed to the political claims of the church for the reasons given, would summon from within itself sufficient energy to withstand the clerical current.

"Now, if it should be the duty of the Italians, and there is no doubt that it should, to erect strong and invulnerable defenses against possible attack from the Vatican, it is certain that they will have to reinforce the monarchy and refrain from weakening it, because in moments of necessity they will always find it their guide in battle, an inviolable fortress under whose protection they will be able to fight confidently, regroup if dispersed, take heart if they should suffer a temporary defeat, or if a moment of panic fear, or some deception, should shatter their morale."

The spell cast by the monarchy on the popular imagination also had to be taken into account: compared to the papacy, the most imposing institution in the world, what kind of figure would the president of a republic cut?

"A republic may be the desire of many, but all must admit that an assembly and a president in Rome, in the vicinity of the pope, would make a poor figure in comparison, and that the pontiff would appear immensely greater in the eyes and the understanding of the multitude than the representative of the political power. A president, however elected, would still be a man like other men, a simple delegate of the nation, without intrinsic force, without traditions, destined to return to the anonymity from which he emerged; he would be talked about, supported, opposed; how could he match the august authority that dominates the earth, claiming heaven's investiture, that surpasses the limits of mere states and relies on the force of a two thousand years' tradition and of the dominant religion in Italy?

"Imagine them side by side: the pope arrayed in white with the triple tiara on his head and sitting on the gestatorial chair, surrounded by his court, the most magnificent in the world; and a president dressed in the dark suit of a bourgeois, surrounded by ministers and senior functionaries. Imagine this spectacle and you will see at once that, whatever the reality of the situation, the president will appear inferior to the pope.

"Nor in the matter of display alone, but also in the inner nature of the institutions, would the pontiff always seem to dwarf the head of the government of Italy, and so win the obedience of the people by winning their reverence. What does the president of a republic represent? Nothing except the will of those who, more or less expressly, more or less freely, have elected him. His power has no other basis than consensus; when that fails him, either in appearance or in reality, he is left with nothing. Thus, in Italy he would be not an *authority* in himself, but simply the holder of a mandate, whose office would depend, from one moment to the next, on the will of the mandator. He might have effective power, but would lack any moral power.

"In order for such a man to be thought equal to the pontiff, the Italian people would have to forget its entire history, change its nature utterly. The people would have to join directly to his person the idea of the majesty of their country, which means they would have to be capable of an abstraction within the reach of cultivated and unfettered minds, but certainly not attainable by the people. The people do not understand sovereignty unless it is incarnated, and shown to them with its external attributes; so for them, if there were no king, no sovereign dynasty of Italy, respected and revered as such, there would be nothing left but the pope."[40]

Renan, who with time had become a republican where France was concerned while remaining an unwavering supporter of the monarchical cause in Italy, had already stated the same thing.[41] Not long after, Crispi, a former republican, did so too, deprecating the manner in which the dynasty was becoming bourgeois and the king losing stature, with a consequent rise in the stature of the pope.[42]

Zanichelli's analysis was certainly correct, at this historical juncture. The monarchy had formal prestige, which the attraction felt by many for the exemplary Queen Margherita strengthened, and a monarchical regime was necessary to face up successfully, inside Italy and abroad, to the offensive that the clerical party conducted against Italy for decades on the international stage. A republican Italy, in the wake of all that had happened between 1860 and 1870, would never have been tolerated by monarchical and conservative Europe; the fact that the thesis of Cavour and his successors was accepted was clear proof of the impossibility, at that time, of a revolutionary, Mazzinian solution to the Italian problem. The monarchy truly was the citadel and protector of the liberty, independence, and unity of the country, and the day on which that institution proved no longer equal to the task assigned it by history was also a disastrous day for Italy; and when it disappeared, the papal tiara shone forth even more splendidly.

Now, in 1870, it might have seemed that the danger of republicanism had been eclipsed. Mazzini and a few diehards were isolated and in decline. All the rest, the leading politicians who had once been republicans, or verged on being so, the most eminent among the old conspirators, from Crispi to Cairoli, had been won over to the monarchical cause. Soon they would be His Majesty's ministers. Garibaldi, despite his frequent spells of discontent and verbal outbursts of a republican, and indeed socialistic, tone, was not a serious threat.

But clouds were gathering abroad, with a republic in France; its figureheads might indeed be Thiers and the dukes, but behind them stood Gambetta and the radicals. There were menacing republican disturbances in Spain. In sum, there was sufficient fodder abroad for propaganda at home, and the embers of Mazzini's doctrines glowed once more.

Nor was that all. Behind the political struggle for and against the monarchy as an institution there began to take shape the outline of another struggle, this time

[40] Zanichelli, *Monarchia e Papato in Italia*, pp. 213–22.
[41] Renan, *Correspondance, 1872–1892*, p. 141.
[42] Crispi, *Pensieri e profezie*, pp. 96–98.

directed against the whole social hierarchy. Behind the republicans appeared the shadow of the International. Paris's 4 September was followed by the Paris spring of 1871, and republican extremism paled before a much more radical extremism that would have overthrown the whole social hierarchy. This new and more dangerous extremism saw the whole Italian political leadership, all the different sectors of the Right and the Left, finally in agreement and lined up together for the battle—as though to bear witness to Cavour's belief that if the social order were under threat, the first to join the conservative ranks would be the *frondeurs* and the republicans.[43]

In such men the cult of liberty was a true and profound religion. But they focused their gaze on the summit of liberty, its moral and juridical aspects, and often did not descend to a consideration of what material basis was necessary for the freedom of thought and action really to be within the reach of everyone. The liberty of the human personality was sacred—but how to guarantee circumstances such that every human could actually become a personality? For the most part this question was not faced.

Instead the recollection of 1848 loomed up continually, a frightening apparition of social revolution sounding a warning against the claims of the crowd, making many people look askance at the lower social strata: after all, they had actually linked the cry of battle against political reactionism and foreign influence to the cry of battle against their social superiors, against their masters. The year 1848 was a fatal year, destined to remain famous in history "both for the greatness of its initial impulse in favor of all the national struggles for independence, and also for the follies of exaggerated liberty that got mixed up with it, and diminished it everywhere."[44] The very fact that that date remained a vernacular synonym of disorder and anarchy, and that "fare un quarantotto" (make a forty-eight) was a demotic expression to designate an enormous upheaval, with the crowd filling the squares and houses being looted, is sufficient proof of what a deep impression had been made.

The French experience of 1848 had been decisive in turning liberal thought in Italy and in Europe in a strongly conservative direction, from the social point of view.[45] It had made Thiers favor the presidency of Louis Napoleon, because of his "fear"—of socialism, of street demonstrations.[46] It had made even Cavour, though he was disposed to recognize the gravity and importance of the social question,[47] stiffen when faced with the danger of worker extremism, to the point

---

[43] Cf. G. Falco, "Spunti sociali nel pensiero e nell'opera di Cavour fino al '48," in *Convegno . . . 1848*, p. 377.

[44] Balbo, *Della monarchia rappresentativa*, p. 322.

[45] Cf. G. Perticone, *Gruppi e partiti politici nella vita pubblica italiana*, pp. 13 ff.

[46] He himself admitted this many years later to De Marcère (De Marcère, *L'assemblée nationale de 1871*, vol. 2, *La présidence du maréchal de Mac-Mahon*, pp. 7–8). On his return from Paris, Arrivabene opined at Turin "that all these old liberals have no more faith in their own principles, and so will not have the energy to defend them" (Malvezzi, ed., *Il Risorgimento Italiano*, p. 449; May 1850).

[47] Cavour, *Diario*, ed. Salvatorelli (Milan-Rome, 1941), p. 199. Cf. as well R. De Mattei, "La prima coscienza in Italia d'una 'questione sociale,'" *Storia e politica internazionale* (March 1943): 98.

of greeting the repression in Paris in June 1848 as the salvation of modern civilization from a new invasion of the barbarians.[48] Cavour was able to save his liberal soul, to bear his faith in liberty intact, even through the fear and anger of 1848 and 1849. But many another emerged from that tormented phase with his convictions very much weakened. Massimo d'Azeglio wrote frankly: "all property owners, no matter how much they love liberty and hate despotism, no matter how much breath they expend talking, or even crying out, in favor of the former and against the latter, love liberty a little less, and hate despotism a little less, after the apparition of a socialist republic. If one could somehow gather the secret confidences, the pillow talk, of all the liberals of Europe, one would probably obtain a statistical profile showing that liberalism's stock had declined noticeably."[49] D'Azeglio continued to believe firmly in liberty and feared a conservative reaction, though even he opined that "if it is a question of who is to be the boss, better the well-dressed man with a full stomach than the naked and hungry man who must improve his situation at my expense."[50] Cavour could recall seeing, in the winter of 1848, men leaving Turin "who claimed to be much more liberal than I, and seeing them return infinitely more conservative than I am."[51] The existence of mistrust and fear of this kind was soon confirmed by the attitude of the majority to the coup d'état of 2 December, an arbitrary act that nevertheless prevented anarchy,[52] and a current of sympathy among the Italian moderates for the Napoleonic dictatorship and its capacity to hold at bay the "evil humors" of France would continue to testify to it.[53]

The vast majority had no wish to deny the theoretical importance of the problem, or simply to call out the carabinieri against the masses, even though there began to be heard calls for greater submission to the principle of authority, which the lower classes were now supposed to start regarding with humble devotion.[54] The marquis Carlo Alfieri di Sostegno, a liberal certainly but not of the left, said that those who thought only of force, and wanted "a formidable apparatus of pitiless repression," exemplified the ferocious wing of the empirical school, whereas the soft-hearted "if they saw themselves on the point of being overcome, or felt *in extremis* a certain repugnance to see blood shed, especially their own, would concede something, sacrifice some part of the rights of property, not of

---

[48] See his article in *Il Risorgimento* for 30 June 1848; and also his letter to Corio of 27 June (*Cavour agricoltore: Lettere inedite . . . a G. Corio*, ed. E. Visconti, p. 230). And cf. Salvatorelli, *Pensiero e azione del Risorgimento*, p. 165.

[49] "Timori e speranze" [October 1848], in d'Azeglio, *Scritti e discorsi politici* 2:83.

[50] D'Azeglio, ibid., 2:133 ("Ai suoi elettori," January 1849).

[51] In his speech to the Chamber of 30 January 1851 (Cavour, *Discorsi Parlamentari* 2:449). And see in general G. Salvemini, "La paura del socialismo fra il 1847 e il 1860," appendix C to his *Mazzini*, pp. 201 ff.

[52] Margherita Collegno to Antonio Trotti, 12 December 1851 (Malvezzi, ed., *Il Risorgimento Italiano*, p. 487). This is the opinion of the "great majority." Collegno herself shares the view of some others that "the arbitrary rule of the sword is a certain evil, the rule of demagogy was not."

[53] Cf. above, ch. 3, n. 12.

[54] Thus G. E. Garelli, *Del principio di autorità* (Turin, 1874; an address inaugurating the academic year in the university of Turin), pp. 43–44 and cf. pp. 8 and 17. Cf. as well R. Corniani, *Il principio d'autorità in Italia ed il partito conservatore*, pp. 35–36, 151–52, 217.

course to satiate but simply to propitiate for a while the defiant proletariat."[55] The latter erred as much as the former, said Alfieri di Sostegno: it was important to seek out ways to prevent the renewal of social war. Or take the case of Sonnino, who was then at the outset of his political career and was still open to the emerging voices of history, not yet closed in on himself and detached from the world, clinging stubbornly to fixed notions: he was one of the very few who did not bask in the generic and pervasive optimism which said that in Italy there was no flammable material because there was no industry, yet he firmly deprecated repression of the kind exercised by Thiers since it pushed those on whom it fell to greater extremes, created martyrs, transformed an initial passion into a faith. To answer riots with gunfire resolved nothing.[56]

So the remedy was to improve the lot of the disadvantaged classes: it was a formula on which all could basically agree, even the conservative de Launay. There were public debates as early as the spring of 1871, and the *Giornale di Modena* was the locus of a debate among its editor, Pietro Sbarbaro, Alfieri di Sostegno, Alessandro Rossi, a wool manufacturer, and Cesare Cantù. But in the event this remedy led mainly to larger and more general appeals to beneficence and charity,[57] in other words to the application of the same sticking plaster with which the upper classes had tried, and would continue to try for a long time, to cure social ills, deluding themselves that they were healing a sore which only festered on the supposed medication, producing a more determined moral revolt against the idea of alms-giving.

It is true that the belief that laws were needed to protect the working man was spreading, and that there were initiatives for social insurance and workers' protection coming from the Right, especially from Luzzatti, the economist from Padua who sought to impress on the Italian governing class that these were real problems.[58] But this and similar initiatives and debates only served to make it clear that the attitude of the great majority of right-thinking people still amounted to virtually complete ignorance of what the terms of the problem actually were.[59]

Paternalism, philanthropy, beneficence: it was the most the men of the governing class could conceive of, and even then they were impelled not by purely humanitarian reasons but also, indeed largely, by the conviction that that was what an enlightened conservative approach called for, in order to render the anarchic and subversive parties impotent.[60] Some took the view that it was necessary to improve wages and living conditions for the workers; and others, like Minghetti, who had for a long time been preoccupied by the dangers inherent in

---

[55] Alfieri di Sostegno, *L'Italia liberale*, pp. 477–78.

[56] Sonnino, *Del governo rappresentativo in Italia*, pp. 32 ff.

[57] This has already been shown in the case of Bonghi by Benedetto Croce, in *La letteratura della nuova Italia* 3:274–75 (5th ed.; Bari, 1949).

[58] Luzzatti, *Memorie* 1:287 ff. and 411, and 2:30 ff.

[59] Cf. N. Rosselli, *Mazzini e Bakounine*, pp. 42 ff. Many of the observations made by Pisacane concerning the moderates of 1848 (Pisacane, *Guerra combattuta in Italia negli anni 1848–1849*, p. 355) can be applied to the moderates of 1870 and after.

[60] Thus a typical moderate like Finali, in his eulogy of Minghetti (*La vita politica di contemporanei illustri*, p. 376).

capitalist development and believed that the ultimate purpose of the century had to be the redemption of the lower classes,[61] fully realized the misery of large masses of peasants[62] and grasped that poverty had become a grave political problem.[63] De Sanctis too observed that the social question was the greatest problem facing the Italian governing class, the only issue whose resolution would make it possible to go beyond the formal and juridical boundaries of liberty and create a living and harmonious political organism, triumphing over the indifference and apathy that dominated public life in the face of the persistence of parties and programs that by now were empty of content.[64]

But if there were a few who were beginning to open their eyes, there were others who had no hesitation in affirming that in Italy wealth was not unjustly distributed, and that it was vain to look for oppressors and oppressed in a country whose general conditions were fortunate "in regard to the fertility of the soil, the mildness of the climate, the sobriety of the inhabitants, and the good fortune of being neither centralized nor split up."[65] Luzzatti could maintain adamantly that a law for the protection of minors and women in factories and mines was required, but Alessandro Rossi denied emphatically that in the factories of Italy the workers were suffering under inhuman regulations or excessively long hours of work, and the editorial board of the *Nuova Antologia*, then so representative of the average opinion of the Italian intelligentsia, supported the position of the wool manufacturer from Schio, while the Italian industrialists aimed their fire at Luzzatti, who was asked by the editor of *Il Sole* not to write about the question any more, to avoid trouble.[66]

That of Rossi and the industrialists was an extreme position. But even after the great inquiries of Jacini and Franchetti-Sonnino had revealed the actual agrarian condition in Italy, especially the desolation of the Mezzogiorno, and after the inadequate nutrition of the lower classes and their primitive living conditions had been painfully and too frequently confirmed by concrete examples, even then, faced with crude factual reality, Italian politicians would always hold that it was possible to solve the problem by means of palliatives: philanthropy and beneficence.

Right and Left, almost to a man, were still attached to the ideal of charity. Tocqueville had written of charity as social duty, political imperative, and public virtue, seeing it as the most noteworthy innovation of modern times in the field of morality, the new form assumed by the ideas that Christianity had once

[61] L. Lipparini, *Minghetti* 1:11; D. Petrini, *Motivi del Risorgimento*, p. 73.

[62] Upon returning from an excursion in the territory bounded by the Po, the Panaro, and the Secchia, Minghetti wrote on 5 January 1872 to a friend in Bergamo, "I witnessed there great poverty, and need of every sort, and danger for the future" (BCB, *Carte Minghetti*, cart. XVI, fasc. 57).

[63] I take this happy expression from Bacchelli, *Il Mulino del Po* 3:148.

[64] Cf. Cione, *Francesco De Sanctis*, pp. 269 ff.

[65] The words of Sen. Alessandro Rossi, the eminent wool manufacturer of Schio and certainly a contributor to the development of industry in Italy ("Di una proposta di legge sul lavoro dei fanciulli e delle donne nelle fabbriche," *Nuova Antologia* 31 [1876]: 170–71 and 185). The opposing view is put in Luzzatti, "La tutela del lavoro nelle fabbriche," ibid., pp. 397 ff.). For his own workers, Rossi did a lot (day-care centers, schools, houses, pensions, etc.), but in discussing social welfare in general terms, he clashed very strongly with Luzzatti (cf. Luzzatti, *Memorie* 2:30 ff.)

[66] Luzzatti, *Memorie* 2:36.

preached.[67] Balbo and Gino Capponi had echoed him: charity was not only a private duty but a public one for the Christian nations; the first goal of humanity was the introduction of charity in the economy, in politics, in the legal code.[68] Cavour too had looked on legal charity as the only bond capable of uniting the different classes, the only system able to save society from the dangers that loomed.[69] His social legislation had amounted to nothing more than a law against pauperism, derived from England's.

That the problem was by now very different, and that simple crumbs from the banquet table of the rich would no longer cure it; that the situation called for a complete revision of all the current ideas and prejudices on the relations between capital and labor; that charity, as Mazzini had observed, was "the virtue of an epoch that has now passed, one morally inferior to our own";[70] all these things it fell to the socialist movement to say and to demonstrate, just as it eventually fell to Giolitti to abandon the repressive use of the carabinieri and the regular army, as well as the emergency measures act, instruments on which Crispi and Rudinì were still relying at the end of the century.

Giuseppe Ferrari's wish to enlist the government and the conservatives in order to bring about socialism[71] was thus a foretaste of the Giolitti era, but for now it fell on deaf ears. It was as though liberal thought no longer had the freshness, the force, the capacity to take the long view that it had had in the first half of the century, and that all it could do was hold on to what it had gained, without forging ahead.[72]

To this point we have focused on the moderates, as being the party on which rested the responsibility for government in the period under consideration. It is not, however, the case that opinion varied greatly among those who belonged to the Left. On the contrary, most of them were fundamentally conservative from the social point of view; few shared the protest of Agostino Bertani against bourgeois egoism, the warning that in Italy as elsewhere there had developed two races of men, "the one that eats white bread, and the one whose bread is dark."[73] Above all, Left and Right agreed in proposing remedies: all these men were the ideological offspring of the first half of the nineteenth century and were ranged together in defense of the existing social structure. If Balbo and Capponi recom-

---

[67] Tocqueville, letter of 5 September 1843 to Gobineau (*Correspondance entre A. de Tocqueville et A. de Gobineau*, pp. 8–9).

[68] Balbo, *Della monarchia rappresentativa*, pp. 182–83; Capponi, letter to Lambruschini, 14–18 August 1834, in Gambaro, *Riforma religiosa* 2:107. On the "science of charity," cf. also Lambruschini, *Scritti di varia filosofia e di religione*, pp. 209 and 222 ff.

[69] Cf. Cavour's letter to de Sellon, March 1836 (in Ruffini, *La giovinezza del conte di Cavour* 2:33–34 and 50), and his article in *Il Risorgimento* for 17 March 1848. Cf. the penetrating observations of Falco, "Spunti sociali," pp. 378 ff. On the attitude of the Italian liberals in general before 1848, cf. N. Rodolico in the same volume, pp. 362, 391, and also A. C. Jemolo, ibid., pp. 389–90.

[70] Mazzini, "De la nationalité: Au 'Propagador,'" in *Scritti* 7:339.

[71] Ferrari, *La disfatta*, p. 132.

[72] An observation made by Bonghi in 1872 (cf. P. Alatri, "Bonghi e la vita politica italiana," *Nuova Antologia* [October 1946]: 177).

[73] Rosselli, *Mazzini e Bakounine*, p. 13 n. 2 and p. 16. Naturally, the hon. Fanelli and the hon. Friscia, who were linked to the International, are a case apart (Rosselli passim, and M. Nettlau, *Bakunin e l'Internazionale in Italia dal 1864 al 1872*, passim).

mended charity, Crispi was not after all so far distant from the same remedy, for he too invoked beneficence and cited the methods used by the priests to ingratiate themselves with the populace: they accumulated great riches by means of church offerings and then used them to propagate their ideas.[74]

Divided on so many other questions, Right and Left united when it came to the defense of society as presently constituted. The Right used a crisper tone and more determined expressions, while the Left employed a more conciliatory style, but both agreed that property was sacred and the bourgeoisie a pillar of social and political life.[75]

It was *Il Diritto*, one of the two leading organs of the Left, rather than one of the moderate journals, that in fact sang the praises of the bourgeoisie at the end of March 1871, and it did so in the course of a polemic against the International and the Paris Commune, drawing attention to "the cohesion, the legitimate and merited influence of the bourgeois proprietor class" and emphasizing the entire legitimacy of such influence, inasmuch as no revolution was ever "identified with the bourgeoisie, the *third estate*, to the same extent as the one that has unfolded in Italy from 1848 to today: this class of citizens has paid, and lavishly, its debt to the country, conspiring, studying, combating on its behalf." Furthermore, the Italian bourgeoisie had not separated itself from the rest of the country, forming a distinct caste, but rather had opened up to the working and rural classes the road to complete emancipation.[76]

The fact is that the bourgeoisie said, and believed in good faith, that its regime was not exclusive but rather was open to whoever worked hard and intelligently. The clear-cut vision of social class, of the segregation of the world into two groups, had always been repugnant to liberal thought and continued to be so. Bourgeoisie? The bourgeoisie does not exist any more after 1789, it belongs to paleontology, Saint-Marc Girardin had written in 1831. Civic equality, sanctioned in 1789, means that every sort of person can enjoy the benefits of society: everyone creates his own destiny with his own good or bad conduct, in combination with the course of events. *Tout le monde est peuple, et tout le peuple est bourgeois.* "People" as opposed to "bourgeoisie"—it was a case of two old names no longer signifying anything, passwords of which everyone makes use according to different circumstances. In reality there are only two classes—those who work and those who want to take it easy, men who tend to their business and professional revolutionaries. From top to bottom in social life there is continual movement, arrival and departure, some on the rise while others descend: the rising man is intelligent, active, attentive to income and outgo; he ignores turbulent factions and declarations of principle and is more familiar with the street where the savings bank is than the street where the tavern lies. All possibilities

[74] Crispi, *Scritti e discorsi politici*, p. 472. Crispi approved the ideas of Minghetti (ibid., pp. 673–74).

[75] The accusations of Anelli against the social policies of the moderates are misleading in this regard (Anelli, *I sedici anni del governo dei moderati 1860–1876* [Como, 1929], pp. 85 ff.).

[76] "Il 'Terzo stato' in Italia," in *Il Diritto* for 31 March 1871. On the "effort" made by the upper classes in favor of the lower, note too Bonfadini in 1870, cited in L. Bulferetti, *Socialismo risorgimentale*, p. 250.

are open to the workers, those barbarians whose task is to harden the temper of modern society with their raw energy and their courage: except that possibilities open up to single individuals only, because the social stratum does not exist, and individuals can be admitted to society only after they have passed through the novitiate of property, because only then will they have an interest in supporting the social order.[77]

So the problem was seen not as that of one bloc against another, but of individuals facing other individuals. It was a matter, so to speak, of filtering them one by one, screening their personal conduct, their good will, their capacities, and their savings.[78] Not even at this late hour, in the aftermath of the French experience in 1848 and 1871, with the International in existence and Marx and Bakunin preaching to the masses, did the liberals give up this point of view. *Il Diritto* said, and many repeated, that the realm of property ownership was open to all men of good will, that it was all a matter of inculcating the classic virtues of the so-called bourgeois in the plebeian. A problem of pedagogy, in other words; and indeed valid examples of men of the people who had become proprietors and risen high on the social ladder thanks to their virtues were sought out. At around this time, between 1860 and 1880, the old Italian tradition that made of the country gentleman an exemplary figure, a mirror of the elevated moral life for his dependents, had something new grafted onto it: the Anglo-Saxon eulogy of the self-made man, who was in contrast a man of the town. Hence the good bourgeois figure of Benjamin Franklin was set before Italian working men, so that they would strive to get where he had got by hard work, honesty, and putting money by. Work hard, make your fortune; where there is a will there is a way; knowledge is power: these ringing slogans were propounded to the working class as the sole and secure mode of resolving the great social problem, without shocks and collisions, in the best of possible worlds. In instructional literature admirable examples of poor laborers who had risen to become employers through work, education, saving, and perseverance, abounded,[79] and generous reconciliations

---

[77] Cf. the articles published in the *Journal des Débats* on 22 June 1831, 18 April 1832, and 17 May 1853, collected in Saint-Marc Girardin, *Souvenirs et réflexions politiques d'un journaliste* (2d ed.; Paris, 1873), pp. 114 ff., 122 ff., 132 ff., 157–58. It should be remembered that, for Cavour too, property "was not, in Italy, thanks be to God, the exclusive privilege of any one class" (Falco, "Spunti sociali," p. 377). Cf. as well *Il Diritto* for 30 March 1871 ("La Francia").

[78] Similar tendencies appeared before 1848, in Piedmont, for example: cf. Bulferetti, *Socialismo risorgimentale*, p. 149.

[79] Cf. G. Martelli, *Ammonimenti morali agli artigiani* (Turin, 1871), pp. 49–50 and 74; I. Scarabelli, *I padroni, gli operai, e l'Internazionale: Libro di lettura popolare e di premio dedicato agli operai italiani* (Milan, 1872), pp. 7 ff.; C. Revel. *Il libro dell'operaio* (4th ed.; Turin, 1874), pp. 19 ff., 41–42, etc.; C. Faccio, *Della possibile azione della società operaia nell'educazione civile e sociale delle classi minori* (Vercelli, 1875), pp. 13–14, 20–21; A. Ravà, *Consigli agli operai* (Milan, 1878), pp. 7–8, 25 ff., etc.; also E. Strini, *Catechismo dell'operaio* (Turin, 1873), pp. 7 ff., who believes that the best book to give to the workers would be an unpretentious manual of political economy. For the influence of Franklin, see principally G. Decastro, *La morale dell'operaio desunta dalla vita e dai pensieri di Beniamino Franklin: Libro di lettura e di premio per le scuole popolari* (Turin, 1874). Samuel Smiles had a tremendous vogue: *Il carattere* roused "a degree of fanaticism" and was reprinted three times in a year (7,000 copies—at that period!); cf. G. Barbèra, *Memorie di un editore*, p. 388. Against the excesses of this self-help literature, cf. G. Boccardo, *Prediche di un laico*, pp. v–vi.

The German bourgeoisie was equally ready to recommend self-help to the workers (J. Ziekursch,

following conflict between workers and bosses were featured—friends and brothers at last.[80]

The lead of Samuel Smiles, the most popular of the foreign promoters of intelligent and persevering labor as the force capable of carrying men born in poverty and raised amid straitened circumstances and obstacles of every sort to conspicuous social success was followed by a number of Italians, the best known of whom was Michele Lessona, who had the benefit, even before his enormous success, of support from a high source: Menabrea, the foreign minister. The latter wished to see a book of the Smiles variety produced in Italy, with examples drawn exclusively from the lives of Italian citizens, and so urged his consuls abroad to gather biographical information "about Italians who gained honest riches in those countries, with special attention to the obstacles of their early lives, and the effort and ingenuity they utilized to overcome them."[81]

At bottom there was still a trace of the old condemnation of poverty as the general result of vice, and specifically of the lack of initiative and capacity, which had surfaced openly in Guizot, and earlier still, at the height of the Revolution.[82] These were the precepts of classical liberalism: the refusal to acknowledge the division of society into rigidly differentiated strata, and a belief in the ongoing process of recirculation. But there began slowly to emerge very novel ideas, which insisted instead on the existence of such rigidly differentiated strata, and whether they called them classes or "estates" (the latter term emptied now of its ancien régime juridical significance), conceptualized them in frankly economic terms. These ideas came to light and imposed themselves on the notice of many who were still decidedly reluctant to accept socialism, Marxism, or anything similar. In result, Italian liberal thought, which continued to follow, with some delay, the lead of western liberal thought, especially the French variety, began to descry (though it always fluctuated about this) the existence of a society composed of strata alongside the society of individuals. This meant an acceptance of new positions, and of a different set of premises for political debate, a process that the budding nationalism powerfully assisted, since it too tended to identify the bourgeoisie as being constituted by possessions and by a lust for possessions that amounted to baseness of soul and a failure of duty to the homeland. Many years after that paean to the bourgeoisie in *Il Diritto*, Crispi, a figure

---

Politische Geschichte des neuen deutschen Kaiserreiches 2:328 [Frankfurt-am-Main, 1927]). For the attitude of the industrialists in favor of moral training for the workers etc., G. Wittrock, *Die Kathedersozialisten bis zur Eisenacher Versammlung 1872* (Berlin, 1939), p. 186. "Rely on yourself," concentrating your own moral and spiritual forces, was the message of a deputy, Braun of Wiesbaden (cited in H. von Poschinger, ed., *Aktenstücke zur Wirtschaftspolitik des Fürsten Bismarck* 1:166 n. 1 [Berlin, 1890]).

[80] For example, cf. A. Alberti, *Memorie d'un maestro di scuola: Libro di lettura pel popolo* (Ferrara, 1877).

[81] Menabrea's circular to the consuls, dated 17 December 1867, is in M. Lessona, *Volere è potere* (14th ed.; Florence, 1889), pp. ix–x. Around 20,000 copies of this work were printed in eight years—a number similar to the number of copies printed of the *Ricordi* of Massimo d'Azeglio (Barbèra, *Memorie di un editore*, pp. 360–61).

[82] Cf. C. F. Volney, *La loi naturelle ou catéchisme du citoyen français*, ed. Gaston-Martin (Paris, 1934), p. 136 and the editor's note 1. For Mantegazza, see L. Bulferetti, *Le ideologie socialistiche in Italia nell'età del positivismo evoluzionistico (1870–1892)*, p. 106.

of the old Left convinced as ever that private property was sacred,[83] once again sang the praises of the bourgeoisie, to which he said the Italians owed everything that had been done to give the status of citizens to the dispossessed; to which they owed their political institutions, the independence of the country, the liberty of the citizens.[84] But he reproved the bourgeoisie, not for its class egoism vis-à-vis the lower classes but for materialistic egoism in relation to the high ideals of the homeland: not for social conservatism but for timid nationalism. The bourgeoisie thought of its stomach, not of honor, and was similar in this to the plebeians, who were also afflicted with concern for their stomachs, not the concerns of the spirit.[85]

Whether it was the nationalistic drive at work, or the drive to socialism, either way society was coming to be seen as divided into blocs. It lost the aspect of extreme mobility with which the classical liberalism of the early nineteenth century had endowed it. The two new forces of the contemporary world, inexorably spreading after 1870, and so much alike in contrasting the individual to a higher, inclusive entity—the homeland or a social class—began to deform the liberal world from the right and the left. Thus, when the Italian governing class asserted that its own realm was not exclusive, this did not prevent it from feeling that it reigned nonetheless, though its realm was not economic but moral and political in character, not composed of a social structure but rather of civic functions. In this light, the word *borghesia* [bourgeoisie] was to be understood not in the French sense but in the Italian one: "an assemblage of all men in whom the individual conscience is united to a marked political conscience, strong enough to render them fit not only to make judgments in relation to the state but also to shape it, to guide it, to inspire it in a direct and perfectly self-aware fashion."[86]

That such a reign might also be unjust was stated by a few of the men of order themselves. Opinions were uttered in which the stern pronouncement of Pisacane seemed to recur: "the word democracy, of which they made use, connoted for them the rule of the bourgeoisie, which reigned, even though it was oppressed politically, because of the way society was structured." Hence, notwithstanding the "noble victims" that the middle class had given to the cause of national redemption, there had been no substantial advancement on the "sterile doctrines" that had triumphed in the French Revolution. These had constituted France as a highly unequal society, a new tyranny, in which the middle class "which had carried out the revolution, gaining powerful understanding and powerful resources, oppressed the people, who had nothing."[87] Opinions of this kind were heard once more, from those who proclaimed that the Italians had made the

---

[83] Crispi, *Pensieri e profezie*, p. 62 The same idea, expressed in the same words, occurred in his speech to the Chamber of 28 February 1894 (*Discorsi Parlamentari* 3:686). Note the affinity with the attitude of Saint-Marc Girardin.

[84] Crispi, *Pensieri e profezie*, pp. 53 and 56; and speech to the Chamber of 28 February 1894 (cited in the previous note).

[85] Ibid., pp. 12, 51, and 54. Cf. above, p. 251.

[86] Zanichelli, *Studi politici e storici*, p. 499.

[87] In the *Prefazione* to *Guerra combattuta in Italia*, pp. 7 ff.). And see the final *Considerazioni*, p. 352, on the bourgeoisie, which in Italy possesses land and capital and monopolizes commerce, science, industry, employment, etc.

political revolution for a very well-defined economic purpose, the improvement of their own standard of living. In the absence of such improvement, it was ridiculous to discourse about morality, education, civic virtues.[88] Others declared publicly that up till now it was principally the well-off classes who had enjoyed liberty, and that in some provinces of Italy they had used it to maintain and increase their dominion over the ignorant and impoverished plebeians. In most areas, it was said, the people know the government only as an exactor of men, and of money; in many places the wealth of the most favored classes has grown, while the people have profited little or nothing.[89] Sonnino pressed the point home in the Chamber: "today the property owners often adduce the impoverished condition of the peasants for the purpose of turning it to their own advantage; they use it to shield themselves from the pressure of the collective interest, to create pity for their own lot, for the tax burden that weighs on landed property. But when they themselves are face to face with the peasants as a class, in the context of local administration or in that of myriad private contacts, then, gentlemen, that feeling of solidarity vanishes without leaving a trace. Whether in the south or in the north, proof lies in the famished hordes of peasants who are emigrating, and the hundred thousand sufferers from pellagra in the most fertile and best-cultivated region of Italy, and the hatred of the *cafoni* ["boors"] for the class known as *galantuomini* ["men of honor"], and the squalid hovels, and the physically and morally pitiable living conditions of the *paisani* [country people] of the lower valley of the Po."[90] Benedetto Cairoli expressed a wish to defend the bourgeoisie against Sonnino's onslaught, to recall its "displays of farsighted, spontaneous, untiring philanthropy," to extol its most recent generous proof of abnegation, the extension of voting rights, which was a sacrifice similar to that made by the nobility on 4 August 1789.[91] Apart from polemics, and postures assumed in debate, the fact is that it was becoming evident that society was divided into different, in fact opposed, social strata. To show worthy individuals the open doorway to self-improvement was no longer enough: it was becoming a problem of social classes. The Italian bourgeoisie had had its 1830;[92] now the recriminations over 1830 naturally commenced.

---

[88] R. De Cesare, *Le classi operaie in Italia*, pp. 2 ff., 11 ff.

[89] *Discorso dell'on. Corrado Tommasi Crudeli agli elettori politici del Collegio di Cortona* (Florence, 1876; a speech delivered at Foiano on 10 September 1876), p. 28. Tommasi Crudeli was allied with Sella—in other words he was not a subversive. The fact that he said these things in an electoral speech is not a reason to view them as simply *captatio benevolentiae*; in fact, given the composition of the body of citizens with the vote at this time, such a reproach might, if anything, have disaffected them. In another speech given at Lucignano on 29 October 1876, Tommasi Crudeli spoke again of "avaricious and tyrannical proprietors" (Florence, 1876: p. 18). On a voyage in Italy in October 1871, Renan observed that in Lombardy, among the lower classes, there was a certain nostalgic regret for Austria: "the new bourgeoisie is penny-pinching, sparing, it does nothing for the people, whereas, they say, 'the Germans spent freely,'" (Renan and Berthelot, *Correspondance*, p. 413, under the erroneous date 1872).

[90] Speech to the Chamber on 30 March 1881 (Sonnino, *Discorsi Parlamentari* 1:28). On Villari, see Bulferetti, *Le ideologie socialistiche in Italia*, pp. 86 ff.

[91] Speech to the Chamber on 13 May 1881 (*A.P., Camera*, p. 5687).

[92] The observation is Renan's (Renan and Berthelot, *Correspondance*, p. 413).

Among the Elite

THE MAIN THING blocking a mental shift from beneficence and public charity, the remedies best suited to a world of individuals, to drastic reforms of the organization of work itself, the necessary remedy when social strata were in question, was the attachment to hereditary or acquired goods—in other words, the sense of property. It was a sense deeply rooted in the hearts of those who constituted the governing class, a millenary tradition; even the French revolutionaries had reaffirmed it in article 17 of the Declaration of Rights of 1789, and still later, with the full-scale Jacobinism of 1793, they had repeated that property is one of the rights of man, and that each is free to dispose as he sees fit of his own fortune. This was the uncrossable limit that Thiers had once more postulated, in September 1848, in a work that was well received by the leaders of Italian opinion.[1] Even those most disposed to take measures in favor of the indigent rebelled as soon as they perceived the least infringement of their rights as proprietors. We know Ricasoli's sincere solicitude for the welfare of his peasants, his agonizing preoccupation about their fate, his frequent surrender to impulses of human compassion and understanding which overcame even the dictates of self-interest.[2] But whenever there was the least hesitant attempt to change customary relationships, with the peasants hinting at the existence of wishes diverging from those of their master, Ricasoli reacted swiftly, conveying to his factor at Brolio one of his brusque commands to straighten the matter out immediately, to make it clear to all that he was the master, that the property was his, that he alone could decide how to manage it, and the first peasant that dared to speak ill of him would be dismissed.[3]

When the situation became dire, and in the turbulence of February 1849 there were rumors that Brolio would be searched, the iron baron did not rest content

---

[1] "Adolphe Thiers, in his book *On Property*, which, although less splendid than some of his others, is perhaps the most exact of them all" (Balbo, *Della monarchia rappresentativa*, p. 121).

[2] Cf., for example, his letter to the factor at Brolio of 7 August 1849, after a ruinous hail storm: "a strong faith in God is needed to resign ourselves to such a bitter disappointment, especially for me, as my first thought is for the peasants, and it would displease me less if I learned that ten casks had been smashed and I had lost all the wine" (Ricasoli, *Carteggi* 3:424).

[3] Especially revealing in this respect are the letters to the factor of Brolio, Ferdinando Batistini, of 7 and 21 January 1852 (Ricasoli, *Carteggi* 4:198 ff. and 207–208): "I do not take it amiss that the peasants say that I want everything that is mine; I do want everything . . . yes, tell them I look out for every tiniest bit, because a fire is made with twigs after all, and I repeat that I absolutely and rigorously want all that belongs to me, and I want to make a profit from all of it. You can tell them that it is not you, but I myself that desire it so, and that I am right, and the peasants are wrong; nor do they see their own detriment, because in this manner they annoy me, for which someone will pay. . . . I see to it that all the peasants are as well-off as possible; but I desire to be the master and dispose of what is mine, which is my right." Hence "I will dismiss any peasant who takes the liberty of speaking ill of me . . . I will exact the payment of everything that I have right to be paid, every last thing that materially belongs to me."

with half measures: he ordered that if the public authorities armed with a valid warrant appeared, the gates should be opened, but that if any should present themselves without legal authorization, force should be used. Arms were to be got ready, and if "brigands" came they were to be fired upon, without scruple. Brolio was private property, no one could take measures against it, and if the authorities charged with protecting society were unable to carry out their duty, "we will have to defend our person and our possessions ourselves."[4]

To raise the standard of living of the social strata less favored by their birth, to improve them materially and morally: this was the first duty of those who had property, and over a long period of time Lambruschini, Ricasoli, and Minghetti said so in many different ways. But they had no intention of losing their grip on the reins, or permitting the preachers of iniquity, the evil brood "risen from inferno to wreck all that they touch, or speak of,"[5] to use their nefarious skills of incitement to stir up the masses, toppling civil life into a state of collapse and bringing a new barbarism.

It would have meant the domination of the lower orders, the peasants, and especially the workers. The latter were worthy of respect as human beings, and their worth was enhanced by their labor, through which life was rendered easier and more comfortable.[6] But taken together, as a social stratum, the only things they obeyed in politics were "their passions and instincts, when what is required is calm, tradition, and also a little prudence."[7] The upbringing received by the workers did not yet appear to have advanced far enough "to bring about a fusion of classes;"[8] their moral sense was not yet sufficiently reliable because of these deficiencies of upbringing.[9]

The lack of preparation of the masses, their incapacity to collaborate on the political plane with the higher orders: these were fixed convictions on which all were agreed;[10] nothing had changed from the time when Cesare Balbo had asserted that the only social stratum that counted was that of the persons who had been raised properly[11] One could trace the sentiment back to the disdain of the enlightened for the *populace* in the eighteenth century. "It seems to me essential that there should be ignorant beggars," Voltaire had written;[12] now there were those who hoped, and sometimes said openly, that the *gueux* of Voltaire ought to

---

[4] Ricasoli, letters to his factor, 14 and 28 February 1849 and, for another occasion, 11 April 1852 (*Carteggi* 3:313 and 322, and 4:214).

[5] The language is that of Lambruschini (Ricasoli, *Carteggi* 3:385).

[6] Sen. Alessandro Rossi, in "Di una proposta di legge sul lavoro," p. 166.

[7] "Versailles-Parigi," in *L'Opinione* for 14 March 1871. A related example of these beliefs is the attempt made by the moderates between 1850 and 1860 to keep the workers' associations restricted to the ambit of mutual aid: the workers can take part in politics as particular citizens, individually, outside their associations, but there can be no politics in the associations (cf. G. Manacorda, "Sulle origini del movimento operaio in Italia," *Società* 3 [1947]: 49). In 1861 and 1862 *La Nazione* of Florence was enjoining the people to abstain from politics (cf. Conti, *Le origini del socialismo a Firenze (1860–1880)*, p. 37).

[8] Rossi, "Di una proposta di legge sul lavoro," p. 166.

[9] Crispi, *Scritti e discorsi politici*, p. 726 (1889).

[10] Perticone, *Gruppi e partiti politici*, p. 21.

[11] Balbo, *Delle speranze d'Italia*, ch. 8, pp. 86–87).

[12] Voltaire, letter of 1 April 1766 (*Oeuvres complètes* 40:387).

remain ignorant.[13] And even those who hoped and wished for the elevation of the plebeians continued to maintain that for the moment at least the gap in moral and cultural preparation was still too wide for the two strata to be fused.

The workers felt this, felt that they were receiving no consideration even after the French Revolution, though they were the basis of the whole social structure. "We work perpetually, and are still sore at heart" today as were the workers in the ancient world and the feudal age. The working class had to attain dignity from the knowledge that it was indispensable.[14]

Education, free and obligatory, was what the workers' societies called for. Not even simple education is enough, replied a number of their social superiors: moral training is needed. This was a favorite refrain, one on which Mazzini and d'Azeglio, Lambruschini and Ricasoli, had insisted for decades, with differing accents and for different ends. But some, with Mazzini, viewed this training as being linked to the development of consciousness and to revolutionary events, while the others wanted it to be the conclusion of a slow, gradual process of evolution, without jarring shocks. In their view, the lower orders were to content themselves for now with receiving measured donations from the wise and far-sighted; they were to entrust themselves to the sage and prudent guidance of their betters, and proceed step by step under this tutelage, like the youngsters whom the hand of the teacher leads without haste from the alphabet to the simple story, and from the knowledge of numbers to arithmetical operations. The people are children, crying and fussing when their mother washes their face, and then beaming at her after they are bathed, said that old conspirator Settembrini, who was alarmed by the way the winds of change were now blowing.[15] But even Balbo had once admitted that you couldn't make a comparison between preparation for political life and raising a family,[16] and that the wise criterion of one thing at a time was not fully applicable in politics—though such an observation would have been ignored in any case. Just as the attempt to dole out liberty bit by bit had not succeeded, and it had had to be conceded whole and entire, under pressure from the crowd, so it was difficult to see how this further liberty could be acquired step by step, with no commotion. Above all, it was difficult to see how it could be made dependent on the completion of a course in good behavior for the people, which is what the leaders of the politically dominant class were

---

[13] Cf. above, p. 226.

[14] Declarations of Tavassi (from Naples) to the General Congress of the Workers' Societies in Rome, 18 April 1872 (*Congresso generale delle Società Operaie Italiane*, pp. 64–65). It is significant that the first theme of the congress was "What is the worker in the eyes of civil society?" (p. 15). And cf. the democrats in Florence in the period after 1860, in Conti, *Le origini del socialismo a Firenze (1860–1880)*, pp. 33–34. On the concerns of the French workers, who toward the end of the Second Empire were becoming ever more interested in "general" education, and less in the purely professional type, cf. G. Duveau, *La pensée ouvrière sur l'éducation pendant la seconde République et le second Empire* (Paris, 1948), p. 103 and cf. pp. 9, 41, 111.

[15] Settembrini, *Epistolario*, pp. 283 and 285.

[16] Balbo, *Della monarchia rappresentativa*, pp. 33–34. Similar ideas are found in the marquis Alfieri di Sostegno when, in defending the principle of electoral reform in the Senate on 12 December 1881, he asked whether they seriously intended to be "the pedagogues and tutors forever" of democracy (*A.P., Senato*, p. 2015).

saying, since it is unlikely that they would have announced that the people had graduated and were ready within any foreseeable span of time.

Certainly the theme of the people's immaturity sounded constantly. The lower classes were called the future hope, the future resource, of the country—but these sprouts had to be left to grow naturally, not overburdened and impaired by entrusting them with social roles to which they were not yet equal.[17] It was a theme that crossed inevitably from the social field into the political one and inspired aversion, for universal suffrage of course (which the Italian conservatives, like their French exemplars, loudly branded the delirium of the century),[18] but even for a simple extension of the suffrage beyond certain very narrow limits. Did one really wish blindly to entrust the fate of the country to the very imperfect training of the workers, unprepared as they were for public life, or badly prepared by the most detestable journals, an easy mark for red intriguers, ready to transform themselves "into close-ranked companies and battalions of voters, who will be at the disposal of whoever wants to lead them, and knows how"?[19] The workers were showing themselves more litigious every day, they were keeping bad company, their language and their attitude were foul, and cities once famous for their refinement were now debased by the obscene and provocative language of an unbridled plebs[20] Lowering the age limit from twenty-five to twenty-one years of age only meant increasing the clientele of the subversive parties, of the "reds."[21]

Democracy was a fine word, but often it meant no more than "dislodging the old insolence of the feudal barons from the upper layer of society and relocating it at the bottom." Having freed itself of the insolence of the aristocracy, society was now forced to tolerate the insolence of the crowd.[22] Beware, therefore, of letting the inexperienced multitude hold the reins of government: "the political excitation of the lower classes, their tumultuous intrusion into the government of the state" would always tend to become "egoistic" and assume the character of a social struggle.[23] This would cause the spread of class conflict on economic

[17] Pantaleoni, speech to the Senate, 10 December 1881 (*A.P., Senato*, p. 1959).

[18] Thus Senator Zini in the debate in the Senate on the bill for reform of the national elections, on 9 December 1881 (*A.P., Senato*, p. 1922). The next day Diomede Pantaleoni also thundered against "that leprosy of universal suffrage" (ibid., p. 1962).

[19] Zini, speech cited in the previous note (ibid., pp. 1927–29; cf. pp. 1923–24). Analogous ideas appear in the speech of Senator Tirelli (ibid., p. 1937).

[20] Senator Zini lamented that the lower classes had become accustomed to hold religion and the priesthood in low esteem, and thus had learned to scorn the principle of authority and deride its representatives: "today, when he encounters the parish priest, the urchin makes a grimace at him instead of raising his cap," he laughs at the mayor and the municipal guards and the police. Tomorrow this urchin will be "the recalcitrant worker, who not only will resist authority but will provoke the policeman and even the representatives of the law; and I use the words *will provoke* seriously: for the pleasure of provocation" (*A.P., Senato*, pp. 1926–27). Similar complaints are made in a report of the police official of S. Spirito in Florence in 1875 (in Conti, *Le origini del socialismo a Firenze (1860–1880)*, p. 220 n. 1).

[21] Thus Senators Zini and Tirelli (*A.P., Senato*, pp. 1922, 1928, 1937).

[22] Zini, speech cited above, n. 18 (*A.P., Senato*, p. 1932).

[23] Zanichelli, *Studi politici e storici*, p. 499.

grounds, something hitherto unknown in Italy. To concede universal suffrage would mean loosing on Italy the social question of which, for the moment, there was still no trace in the peninsula, thank God—said the loquacious Diomede Pantaleoni. "Property follows the ballot": let the masses have the vote, and sooner or later property will pass into the hands of the indigent.[24]

In this statement, or in that made in the course of a report in the Senate by Lampertico that the cause of property and social order amounted in the end to the cause of liberty itself,[25] or in the statement in the Chamber by Codronchi that the interests of property, which were so neglected as to be forgotten in Italy, should not be trampled,[26] the fear of the proprietors comes out into the open. In other opponents of the extension of the suffrage, fear of this kind was certainly less immediate and less pressing. They had their own reasons for opposition, such as the apparent threat to the solidity of the political institutions of the country, its liberty and unity, should the predominance of the masses come about. These other reasons were not simply a cover for naked fear derived from greed, nor was concern for ideals a pure pretense advanced to conceal threatened interests. If some feared the masses of workers becoming the obedient tools of factious "reds," and so a menace to social order and private property, others feared the mass of the rural population becoming the obedient tools of factious "blacks," and thus the enemies not of private property but of the freedom and unity of the nation.

As in the past, the Italian governing class found itself facing an extremism of the left, and an extremism of the right, the red international and the black international, Carlo Cafiero and Don Margotti; some considered one of these the principal danger, others the other. The conservatives of the Right preferred to emphasize the red peril, and in fact urged that Catholics be given the vote, since "by reason of their place in society, their interests, and their culture they are the natural allies of an established government,"[27] while the less conservative members of the Right, and naturally all who belonged to the Left, insisted on the black peril. So on one hand the peasants were extolled. In the past Lambruschini had seen them as a necessary counterweight to the effrontery of the "demented" city dwellers,[28] and now they were mustered once more in support of society as constituted, as a bulwark against the subversives.[29] In line with this, the perils of the cities were

---

[24] Pantaleoni, speech cited above, n. 17 (*A.P., Senato*, p. 1963). Pantaleoni opined that moneyed wealth was the most democratic of all the electoral principles in the world, given that "the true, the prime factor of progress and of humanity . . . lies in accumulating the fruits of labor, and thus of accumulating what is called capital" (*A.P., Senato*, p. 1944).

[25] *A.P., Senato*, p. 2190 (18 December 1881).

[26] *A.P., Camera*, p. 4653 (24 March 1881). And note as well the praise of wealth by the hon. Tenani (*A.P., Camera*, p. 4731, 26 March).

[27] Tirelli, speech cited at n. 19 above (*A.P., Senato*, p. 1937). It is to be noted that Tirelli opens with the statement that the Risorgimento was conducted from above by the aristocracy of intelligence, birth, and wealth, and believes it should continue in this fashion.

[28] Ricasoli, *Carteggi* 3:381 (2 May 1849).

[29] Cannizzaro, speech to the Senate of 13 December 1881 (*A.P., Senato*, p. 2037, adducing the example of the French rural classes). Similar statements had been appearing in *La Civiltà Cattolica* for some time (cf. Bulferetti, *Le ideologie socialistiche in Italia*, p. 302).

denounced. They were lively places, ready for progress, but also easy victims of all that was novel, even when it was "not good."[30] Electoral rights should rather be given to the numerous small rural lease-holders and persons like them, men "who were as well-affected to the social order as they were to the savings they had accumulated with long hours of toil, and which they do not wish to see scattered by the passing breezes."[31] Hence it was maintained that the electoral bill was unjust, because it would have assured that the turbulent inhabitants of the cities prevailed over the rural population, dividing the country instead of uniting it.[32] And there was the opposite point of view, the insistence on the perils accompanying the predominance of the rustic population—ignorant, superstitious, putty in the hands of the clericals and the priests who spoke ill of Italy, of all who wished for the restoration of the old order of things out of the destruction of Italian unity.[33] The supporters of one side adduced the harsh verdict passed by Taine on the rural dwellers of France, and the others appealed to Vacherot's quite opposite portrait of the peasants as the element of order and stability through the tormented vicissitudes of France.[34]

Often enough these contrasting viewpoints were overridden by the combined fear of both extremes and the grave danger they posed to the nation,[35] all the more in that they might even be capable of reinforcing each other, the reds being made use of in practice by the cleverly calculating blacks, socialism a tool wielded by the papacy.[36] Even without that, what a day it would be when Don Margotti unleashed his followers in the rural communes of Italy to make sure the urns were filled with black ballots, while simultaneously streetcorner orators and venal hack journalists were at work in the city to make sure that the electoral

---

[30] Thus Lampertico in the Senate on 18 December, in his capacity as rapporteur [*relatore*] (*A.P., Senato*, p. 2188). For the hon. Saladini, speaking in the Chamber on 4 April 1881, it is in the countryside that good sound customs are found (*A.P., Camera*, p. 5034).

[31] Thus Lampertico, in defending an amendment put forward by the Senate's Central Office, which proposed that the 19.80 lire in taxes which constituted the threshold for electoral rights should also include provincial surtaxes paid (*A.P., Senato*, pp. 2186–87). The amendment was approved with 109 in favor and 92 against.

[32] The hon. Codronchi to the Chamber on 24 March 1881 (*A.P., Camera*, pp. 4651–52). Giustino Fortunato also believed "that the agricultural class will surely be totally sacrificed to the industrial class" (*A.P., Camera*, pp. 4678 and 4688; 25 March). For this reason, and also because of the "harsh conditions" created in the Mezzogiorno, he was for universal suffrage, as were various other opponents of the law, for example the hon. Brunetti, who denied the clerical peril (*A.P., Camera*, p. 4774; 28 March).

[33] Thus Zanardelli, a member of the cabinet, on 18 December 1881 in the Senate (*A.P., Senato*, p. 2183). He had been preceded by Senator Griffini on 12 December (*A.P., Senato*, pp. 2009 ff.). Finali himself, who was so alarmed by left-wing influence, warned that "if, instead of the cry "neither elected nor electors,' the Vatican took a different line, perhaps the universal suffrage would be feared" (*A.P., Senato*, p. 2003). In the Chamber, the hon. Parenzo had painted a dark picture of rural dwellers: virtual brutes, they still speak "of the coming of the Italians, as if speaking of a change of overlords" (2 April 1881; *A.P., Camera*, p. 4963). Cf. too the speech of Faldella to the Chamber on 16 March 1881 (ibid., p. 4407).

[34] Pessina (*A.P., Senato*, p. 2171) and Zanardelli cite Taine; Lampertico cites Vacherot.

[35] The twofold fear was expressed in the Chamber by the hon. Arbib (28 March 1881; *A.P., Camera*, pp. 4783 ff.); and in the Senate by Senators Pantaleoni, Finali, Ricotti.

[36] Thus Senators Griffini and Ricotti (*A.P., Senato*, pp. 2012 and 2046). Griffini asks, what would happen if, other methods for reconstituting the temporal power having proved ineffective, the papacy should assume the leadership of socialism, appealing to the Gospel?

result would be red! What a spectacle would follow: "the opening of parliament in Montecitorio with three hundred deputies subscribing to *L'Unità Cattolica* and two hundred others working for certain filthy rags which I don't read and shan't name!"[37]

The point is that fear of the masses was a mixture of elements that were not always, or easily, distinguishable from one another, a mixture containing the love of liberty and the instinct of property, the love of country and the devotion to established institutions, especially the threatened monarchy, for universal suffrage was seen as leading directly and rapidly to a republic.[38] At one moment there came to the surface the instinct of true social conservatism, at another purely political concern. Only those bent on simplifying history could identify these two anxieties with one another, or make the second an offshoot of the first, because in those who feared the clericals personal greed played little part, while theoretical motives were all-important. Now it is the case that fear of clericalism still prevailed over fear of socialism for many years after 1870.[39] In 1872 Crispi was warning that it was necessary to make a stand against the common enemy, which was the papacy,[40] and two years later Quintino Sella pressed the point: the black international might appear more benign, but underneath it was much more of a threat, since for the sake of attaining its parricidal aim by bringing low the liberty and unity of Italy it had no hesitation in arming foreign elements against the country, meanwhile doing all it could internally to prepare the ground for its victory.[41] Rather than deplore the abstention from voting of the Catholics, Visconti Venosta expressed satisfaction in 1871 for the fact that Pius IX spurned democracy: otherwise the Quirinal would have had to come to terms with the Vatican.[42]

That the clericals provoked much more apprehension was logical in light of the

---

[37] *Il suffragio universale in Italia: Noterelle di un ex Deputato* (Turin, 1873), p. 17. From the dedication to Dina, which is signed E. Di S. (in the copy in the Biblioteca Nazionale of Rome; the printed letter of dedication is also signed with the initials D. S.), and other clues (cf. pp. 3–5), I would argue that the author was Ernesto di Sambuy, a deputy in the tenth legislature until 1870 who was not a member of the eleventh, but was reelected to the twelfth and from then on until the fifteenth. "Di S." is naturally against universal suffrage, which would have the consequences described above.

[38] That universal suffrage leads sooner or later to a republic is clearly stated by Senators Pantaleoni and Vitelleschi (*A.P., Senato*, pp. 1961 and 1985): universal suffrage and constitutional monarchy are irreconcilable, and the first implies an elected president, not a monarch. Finali too sees the widening of the suffrage as the demand of the parties hostile to the monarchy (*A.P., Senato*, pp. 2003–2004). Sonnino on the other hand declared that under current conditions universal suffrage would favor the monarchy, and that only if it were denied might it then become red or black in sentiment (Sonnino, *Discorsi Parlamentari* 1:42).

[39] According to A. Gualdo, *La riforma elettorale* (Venice, 1879), the moderates themselves, though fearful of the reds, were against universal suffrage principally because they feared that with an enlarged electoral body the clericals might emerge victorious (pp. 12 and 14).

[40] Crispi, *Scritti e discorsi politici*, p. 464.

[41] In a speech at Biolio, on 18 October 1874 (Sella, *Discorsi Parlamentari* 5:880). He had already written to Döllinger on 20 September 1872: Germany and Italy are closely linked by shared dangers, "since every day we observe an increase in the audacity of those who, with religion as the pretext for their parricidal actions, declare they will stop at nothing to keep us from ever enjoying what we have won, which we are barely able to defend, though the blood of many was shed for it, and it has very widespread support. So . . . we have a common battle to fight" (ibid., 1:804).

[42] Rothan, *L'Allemagne et l'Italie* 2:344.

international array of reactionary forces, which were potent in France and Austria and were on the point of becoming dominant in Spain between 1873 and 1874 with the violent reprise of Carlism. In these years the socialists were entirely without public international support, a minority of heretics; but the clericals had the wherewithal to influence official policy toward Italy in a number of countries. There was also a widespread conviction that Italy lacked the kind of kindling needed to start red fires because there were no large agglomerations of workers, a conviction validated by Crispi in his accustomed style with a peremptory "never,"[43] and which he continued for many years to maintain, refusing to credit socialism as anything more than a phantom. Only at the end did he discover that there was indeed combustible material in Italy, and that the fire had been crackling for some time. In the Senate, Jacini stated that the multitude in Italy were excellent persons, not to be confused with the sort of rascals who demonstrate in the piazza; and he even supported indirect universal suffrage.[44] Zanardelli, a resolute optimist who was sure that in this country there did not exist the sort of profound antagonism, the rancor and class hatred that plagued the other leading European nations, heard the dark forecasts of some fellow senators with impatience and demanded "whether the graves had opened up, and spirits dormant for centuries had issued forth."[45] Clear proof of the contemporary optimism of the progressives was their choice of an elementary education as the most appropriate requirement for being granted the vote: faith in science, which took the concrete form of popular faith in schooling, and faith in a peaceful, progressive, and harmonious development of society, without upheaval or tumult, were united.[46]

Should the clericals regain strength, the result would not be an attack on property, in principle at least,[47] but solely an attack on the national homeland. Hence it was nationalist sentiment that responded, even when the sensibilities of the property owner were not involved. In such cases the rural masses were feared because they might turn, not into the incendiaries of the Paris Commune, but into zealots for the holy faith.

Not that the incendiaries did not also threaten Italy's nationhood as well as private property. The very name "International" signified, at this juncture, the

---

[43] In a speech to the Chamber of 25 January 1875 (Crispi, *Discorsi Parlamentari* 2:208).

[44] 11 December 1881 (*A.P., Senato*, p. 1976). Identical statements are found in the speeches of Griffini, Deodati, and Rossi (ibid., pp. 2011, 2058, 2190–91).

[45] In a speech to the Senate of 15 December 1881 (*A.P., Senato*, p. 2094).

[46] The endorsement of education as an excellent criterion for deciding who is worthy of the vote and who is not occurs especially in the speech of Zanardelli to the Senate cited in the previous note (*A.P., Senato*, p. 2093). But see too the speech of Allievi to the Senate on 11 December 1881 (*A.P., Senato*, pp. 1992 ff.).

[47] There was, however, the question of ecclesiastical property, of which, by 31 December 1877, 124,551 lots for a total of 535,297 hectares had been sold (G. C. Bertozzi, "Notizie storiche e statistiche sul riordinamento dell'asse ecclesiastico nel regno d'Italia," *Annali di Statistica*, 2d ser., 4 [1879]: 200). But apart from the question of how many proprietors there would be who, because of such alienations, "had an interest" in defending the new order of things (for the territory round Rome, they would have been very few, cf. A. Caracciolo, "Le origini della lotta di classe nell'agro romano [1870–1915]," *Società* 5 [1949]: 610), the fact remains that the experience of the French Revolution had shown concretely that, in this respect, restorations were not after all much of a threat.

negation of the ideals in the name of which the battle had been fought and won, and with this we touch on one of the most central difficulties of Italy's existence. What the patriots had offered to the masses was their country, one and sovereign, and with this they were quite certain of having fulfilled the highest ideals of the people. But it sometimes seemed that this great political accomplishment received scant appreciation from the lower classes; indeed it was often derided as a trick used by their masters to keep the rebellious herd quiet.[48]

The advantages of unification seemed to be reserved for the property-owning stratum, and the donkey, meaning the people, was expected to continue to carry the same load as before, or perhaps a heavier one.[49] There were peasants who had raised the shout of *viva la libertà!* and hoped for the coming of a time when the poor could also have a better life and work less hard; but they had been left crestfallen: "liberty and equality—but he who doesn't have them is left scratching his stomach."[50] The Italian homeland and its liberty were fine things indeed, but not enough for those who were hungry. An anonymous person from Lodi said to Carducci in 1881, "enough talk of liberty! It is time now to start talking about poverty."[51]

Here again there was a gap between the governing class and the masses. In the past Giuseppe Mazzini had clearly seen the divergence that was occurring between ideologues and doctrinaires on one hand, and the people on the other, in Italy and in France. In response he had made it the foundation of his apostolate to raise the cultural level of the people and had even, albeit very vaguely, perceived the social problem underlying the political one.[52] After him, Andrea Luigi Mazzini, influenced by Saint-Simon and French and Belgian socialist circles, had pointed out much more forcefully that the Italian revolution would have to be to a large extent a social one,[53] while Pisacane had hoped for a revolution made not "to change ministers or convoke a chamber of deputies . . . but to eradicate from society the idle rich and the poor who have no bread, to bring it about that every citizen can enjoy the fruit of his own labor without being enslaved to others, and that no longer will anyone live at ease in a sumptuous palace on the blood of the poor people who work."[54]

But the Risorgimento had been accomplished in a different way and with dif-

---

[48] On the indifference of the masses to the political ideal of the Risorgimento—liberty, independence, unity—see the suggestive portrait painted by R. Bacchelli, even if one does not always agree with his particular views, in *Il Diavolo al Pontelungo* (fifth reprint), pp. 258 ff., and *Il Mulino del Po* 2:334, 534, and vol. 3, esp. pp. 144 ff., 211, 257 ff.

[49] Cf. N. Rosselli, *Saggi sul Risorgimento e altri scritti*, p. 262.

[50] Thus Ferrario, *Qual' è la moralità de' campagnuoli*, p. 43, referring to the peasants of northern Lombardy.

[51] Cited in Arcari, *Le elaborazioni della dottrina politica nazionale* 1:152–53.

[52] Cf. the fine pages of Omodeo in *La cultura francese*, pp. 74 ff.

[53] Cf. A. Saitta, "Sull'opera di Andrea Luigi Mazzini," *De l'Italie dans ses rapports avec la liberté et la civilisation moderne*," in *Annali della R. Scuola Normale Superiore di Pisa*, 2d ser., 10 (1941): 109; D. Cantimori, *Utopisti e riformatori italiani, 1794–1847* (Florence, 1943), pp. 177 ff.

[54] Pisacane, *Epistolario*, p. 144; and cf. too *Saggio su la Rivoluzione*, p. 108. But on the characteristics of Pisacane's socialism, cf. (in addition to G. Pintor's preface to *Saggio su la Rivoluzione*, p. 11) Falco, "Note e documenti intorno a Carlo Pisacane," p. 292; Taviani, *Problemi economici*, pp. 227 ff. And naturally, N. Rosselli, *Carlo Pisacane nel Risorgimento italiano*.

ferent results, according to the possibilities inherent in nineteenth-century history, which was ineluctably different from the history of the twentieth century,
and after it was completed the gulf separating the governing class and the masses
tended to grow wider. Social disruption and disorder, which the news chronicles
now began to record, only made the ruling class more diffident and fearful and
drove it to see social disturbance as a menace to liberty and to the nation. Liberty
and nationhood risked finding themselves in antithesis to social aspirations: if the
lower classes gained the upper hand, it would lead to egalitarianism and despotism; there would be social revolution and social leveling, with the final result a
dictatorship backed up by easy plebiscites: the plebeians would renounce political liberty if servitude would give them a better life. The dominion of the vile
mob, then anarchy, military dictatorship, despotism: it was the abhorrent sequence of events which the liberal historiography of the earlier nineteenth century had already condemned in the French Revolution, contrasting 1789 and
1793 as light and darkness. Opposition to socialism arose of necessity from these
premises of nineteenth-century liberal thought; and among the Italian liberals
the theoretical standpoint was backed up not only by the example of the two
Napoleonic dictatorships in France but also by that of the "socialism" of the
pontifical government, which in its last years had sought to make the population
oblivious of what Pius IX called "government concerns," meaning political concerns, by satisfying local concerns as much as possible, through public works
and largess in favor of the less well-off strata.[55]

So the liberals felt that political liberty was at risk, and Italy, the homeland,
under attack from the internationalism of the social movements, from the polemical stance that the innovators assumed toward what was holy writ for the governing class. Socialism now was not the patriotic and national socialism of a
Pisacane,[56] it was internationalism, an appeal to the classes against the nations.
Patriotism against internationalism: it was this that had split Mazzini off from the
nascent movement, and that was destined for decades to create an abyss between
the socialist parties and the patriots, with the note of exclusive nationalism gradually sharpening into polemical fury on one side, and the other side adopting
useless, indeed harmful, attitudes that wounded the deepest feelings of the patriots. The consequences were momentous: a large part of Italian history from the
end of the nineteenth century to 1922 revolves around this fierce dispute.

Yet another attitude nourished mistrust of the masses, in any case. Again it
was a question of breeding and education—but now, in place of any urge to open
these portals wider and let the outsiders in, the outsiders were barred and
scorned. This was the disdain of the man of intelligence for the foolish multitude,
the amorphous instinctual mass devoid of reason. "We must remain *we*, *we* pure,
we wise, *we* farsighted," Lambruschini had cried in 1849,[57] and in his cry there
was contained everything that raised an invisible but formidable barrier between
two worlds. It was not even something that could be encapsulated in a clear-cut

---

[55] On this, see the penetrating observations of Petrini, *Motivi del Risorgimento*, pp. 66 ff., 71 ff.
[56] Rosselli, *Carlo Pisacane*, pp. 213–14; V. Mazzei, *Il socialismo nazionale di Carlo Pisacane*
1:209–10.
[57] Ricasoli, *Carteggi* 3:388.

formula, it went beyond the unalloyed sensibility of the property owner or the patriot. There was an elite of intelligent people and there was the mob, or to use the language of Guicciardini, the "crazies" [*i pazzi*].[58] Even a writer less hostile than Guicciardini had said that the mob must always be fed "on what it can see, the outcome of the process,"[59] and Guicciardini in his aversion had also described it as "a crazed animal, full of a thousand errors and confusions, lacking taste, lacking discernment, lacking stability."[60] The mob was "that wild beast with numberless heads,"[61] the animal without thought, the animal in need of restraint,[62] which was constantly viewed with suspicion by the European cultural tradition, or more precisely, by the European tradition of political thought. It was the same *vile populace* which Voltaire had regarded with contempt in the eighteenth century, and which the elite of the nineteenth still regarded with contempt, alarmed as they were by the recent, unforeseen, and bloody outbursts of plebeian anger: the plebs "feels the affliction of the stomach, not the affliction of the spirit."[63]

Even before socialism and communism were attacked, mistrust and hostility were directed in the first instance against democracy. Democracy meant the law of numbers; quantity against quality; the raw weight of the mass against intelligence and learning; passion, fanaticism, and instinct against rationality. Fears of this kind nourished the antidemocratic attitude of Flaubert and Renan; and this was the case among writers and other members of the moderate party in Italy too, each of whom saw a grim future if democracy should prevail: the great mass state, militarized, adventurous, flattening everything with its bulk. They saw the masses marching in formation, a precisely controlled dosage of *Misère mit Avancement und in Uniform*, the drumbeat synchronizing every movement of the militarized collectivity.[64] They saw philistinism, ignorance, and indifference to moral and spiritual problems, with the sole remaining concern being the individual's own material welfare. They felt they were journeying "through the twilight hour."[65]

The present century tends to promote material interests: variations of this

---

[58] See, for example, Zini's speech to the Senate, 9 December 1881, on the electoral law, stating that it is necessary to keep "the unthinking many from overriding the wise" (*A.P., Senato*, p. 1921), or that of Vitelleschi, stating that a system based on majorities is progressive when it is understood that those participating in the vote are fit to do so, but that it is absurd if applied purely on the basis of numbers. In that case "it is the imposition of foolishness on wisdom, disorder on order, ignorance on culture" (ibid., p. 1981; 11 December 1881).

[59] Machiavelli, *Il Principe*, ch. 18.

[60] Guicciardini, *Scritti politici e Ricordi*, ed. Palmarocchi (Bari, 1933), p. 315.

[61] Thus in one of the classic texts of the Huguenot polemic against monarchical absolutism from the second half of the sixteenth century (Du Plessis Mornay, *Vindiciae contra tyrannos* 2:36–37 [Frankfurt, 1622]). And cf. the following from the *Francogallia* of François Hotman: "the naive crowd of the vulgar, whose characteristic is to know nothing" (Frankfurt, 1665), p. 147.

[62] Scipione Ammirato, cited in R. De Mattei, "L'idea democratica e contrattualista negli scrittori politici italiani del Seicento," *Rivista Storica Italiana* 60 (1948): 7 n. 1.

[63] Crispi, *Pensieri e profezie*, p. 51.

[64] This is the outline sketched in a letter of Jacob Burckhardt, dated 28 April 1872 (in Kaegi, *Historische Meditationen* 1:313).

[65] F. Schnabel, *Storia religiosa della Germania nell'Ottocento* (Italian translation: Brescia, 1944), pp. 163 ff.

charge were repeated for decades on both sides of the Alps by those who, in politics, embraced moderatism. People's souls are overwhelmingly occupied with economic welfare, they complained; egoism and greed, the love of pleasure and luxury dominate the contemporary world, and even in the councils of state the interests of commerce and industry are given pride of place "in preference to dignity and honor": this was written by the young Minghetti,[66] who laid at the door of the July Monarchy the great fault of having made France materialistic, and who urged upon Pius IX, at a time when the pope was convinced that he had to favor "material interests" in order to cure the ills of the papal state, the necessity not to do so at the expense of "more elevated ideas."[67] Minghetti was one of many who were worried that eating well, drinking well, and dressing well were becoming the supreme ends of humanity.[68] Even in Sella, so alien to all forms of Romanticism, the excessive devotion to material interests of the rising generations sometimes elicited a certain regret for the uprisings of 1848.[69] On the other hand, Luigi Blanch was driven to protest that this criticism was too severe,[70] and Francesco De Sanctis in 1869 gave his blessing to the new generation as it employed in the fields of industry, commerce, and the applied arts the energy that its elders had devoted to conspiracies and to theoretical studies.[71] The conviction that the century was materialistic enjoyed great success, indeed became a facile stereotype—except when the scorn of a Flaubert gave it blistering force. The age of commerce had been optimistically announced by Benjamin Constant; but others maintained that commerce signified, along with riches, the debasement of human sensibility, the brutalization of feelings and ideas.

The magnificent and progressive lot

of humanity left the author of the *Palinodia*, and others, skeptical. Leopardi thought that this virile age

> . . . turning to severe
> economic studies, and furrowing its brow
> over public affairs . . .

was fleeing from the exploration of its own soul and looking outside itself for what it could no longer find within.

---

[66] Minghetti, *Della tendenza agli interessi materiali che è nel secolo presente* (1841), the conclusion of which appears as an appendix to *La legislazione sociale*, pp. 53 ff.; and in a second opuscule, *Nuove osservazioni intorno alla tendenza agli interessi materiali che è nel secolo presente; lettera al signor A. P.* (also 1841, and also partially reprinted in *La legislazione sociale*, pp. 64 ff.); and *Della economia pubblica*, p. 52. For the consensus that greeted Minghetti's ideas, cf. Lipparini, *Minghetti* 1:262.

[67] Meeting with Pius IX, 6 August 1857; Minghetti, *Ricordi* 3:191–92.

[68] Among others, Gobineau writing to Tocqueville on 15 January 1856 (*Correspondance entre A. de Tocqueville et A. de Gobineau*, pp. 274 and cf. 279).

[69] Sella to Amari, 25 April 1882 (Amari, *Carteggio* 2:276 and cf. D'Ancona's note 1).

[70] *Di un' opinione sul carattere del secolo* (1845), in Blanch, *Scritti storici* 3:343 ff., ed. Croce (Bari, 1945). Cf. as well a composition of 1846, *Una disposizione dominante del nostro tempo: la noia* (in ibid., 3:349 ff.).

[71] Cf. Cione, *Francesco De Sanctis*, pp. 250–51.

From the time of the July Monarchy there arose the question of whether technical progress was not outstripping moral progress, thus creating great danger for the future. It became the subject of endless debate; there were disputes over how to make the two proceed at an equal pace, and in particular, how to bring the public economy back into close coordination with, in fact subordination to, moral principles.[72] In the course of these polemics Luigi Luzzatti, candid soul, attempted to refute the assertions of Buckle, which were then in great vogue and had already been combated with much more intellectual force by Droysen.[73] He sought, that is, to prove that morality and virtue were the necessary bases of all progress, so much so that, in their absence, the advance of science and technology itself could lead to unfortunate results.[74] Minghetti too sought the union of technical progress and moral progress, and sketched out a conjunction of the public economy and the morality of right, attempting to turn even cupidity, the vice of the age, to a useful purpose and emphasizing the need for industry to be guided by moral principles, if it were to be lasting and strong.[75]

The social question cropped up in all these debates. It was asked whether man was more content today than in the past, and if the reply was negative, it was then asked how the needs of the impoverished classes were to be met. Minghetti and others affirmed the necessity of social legislation, something midway between the theory of liberty as something entirely self-sufficient, a theory no longer fully sustainable, and the opposing theory of direct and continual state intervention. Once more it was a search for compromise, the just economic and social mean following the just mean in politics. There occasionally transpired a residuum of pre-1848, pre-Marxist optimism, based on the virtues of the good example: "when the people see a respectable man, honored by his family and by society, who attends to them and studies their needs, who is inspired by love of their class, I believe that they have a keen intuition, and that if they do encounter such a man, they will turn to him and shove the agitators away, back to the shadows from which they never should have come forth."[76] It was the old story

---

[72] On the necessity for intellectual development to proceed at an equal pace with the development of the economic forces, cf. the interesting letter of Salvagnoli to Ridolfi, dated November 1842 (in R. Ciampini, *Due campagnoli dell'800: Lambruschini e Ridolfi* [Florence, 1947], p. 107).

[73] In *Erhebung der Geschichte zum Rang einer Wissenschaft*, in Droysen, *Historik*, pp. 386 ff.

[74] Luigi Luzzatti, *La legge di evoluzione nella scienza e nella morale* (Venice, 1876); *L'Elemento morale nel progresso secondo la dottrina di Buckle* (Venice, 1876). Luzzatti's ideas are seconded in P. Sbarbaro, *Sulle condizioni dell'umano progresso* (Macerata, 1877), pp. 10–11, 18 ff.

[75] In addition to the work *Della economia pubblica*, cf. as well *La legislazione sociale*, esp. p. 48. The Bolognese statesman wrote about the relations between technical progress and moral progress to Queen Margherita (Minghetti, *Lettere fra la regina Margherita e Marco Minghetti*, pp. 42–43 and 53). Toniolo was following a similar line of thought: cf. a prolusion he gave at Padua on 5 December 1873, *Dell'elemento etico quale fattore intrinseco delle leggi economiche* (Padua, 1874).

[76] Minghetti, *La legislazione sociale*, p. 44. Hope that "sane and beneficial influence" may cure social ills is expressed by *La Perseveranza* as well ("Il problema sociale e morale in Italia," 30 May 1873). Analogous considerations on the example that the proprietors are called on to give are in Ferrario, *Qual'è la moralità de' campagnuoli*, pp. 73 ff. and 116 ff. And these were themes that Cavour had already broached (Falco, "Spunti sociali," pp. 379–80).

Vice versa, we find the bad examples given by many of the rich, who are busy promoting— unintentionally—the advent of the International "much more efficiently than the Committee of

of the power of example, in the manner of Lambruschini and Ricasoli: the gentleman ought to retain his former power in the state, but in a different manner, guiding the people by example, obtaining through the wisdom and authority of an uncorrupted life what before he had obtained through money, and through his clientele.[77] The altruistic man would resolve with his moral virtue the major problems of the age. Less eminent writers pointed the workers to the example of the self-made man, while Lambruschini, Ricasoli, and Minghetti continued to draw the attention of the governing class, especially the country gentlemen, to the classic example of the master who was a father to those beneath him. The myth of the hero, in its extreme form at any rate, had temporarily been driven out of the political arena, but it recurred in the discussion of social problems, just as enlightened absolutism, repudiated in politics and replaced by the will of the nation, maintained its old grip on the relations between the classes—between proprietors and dependents, that is.[78] Bonghi reveals this trend when he finds that one of the causes of the Paris Commune was the lowered intellectual and moral caliber of the upper classes, which diminished the cohesion that had once bound them to the urban and rural lower classes, and so their healthy and sound influence over them: the power of example was losing its force.[79]

Amid the pervasive anxiety for the announced decline of the moral sense and the triumph of egoism, the decline of the spirit and the advance of materialism, the end of the ideal and the victory of profit, the political and social debate as such actually opened up a good deal, bringing to light the uneasiness of a conspicuous part of the Italian governing class not just before set problems, but before modern civilization in general. The fact is that in wishing for an increase in wealth while fearing its effects, and so taking refuge in tired bromides against luxury and corruption, and in promoting what was then called public economy while at the same time fearing development that was not crowned by equal progress in morality and culture, there was at bottom a sort of mistrust and fear of the rapid and formidable development of modern society. In politics this was expressed in the moderates' unanimous disapproval of the reborn spirit of conquest, which they saw incarnated in Bismarckism, while in economics they deplored unbounded competition, the production and circulation of wealth, the vertiginous and disorienting rhythm of trade. In both cases, they perceived power and force, numerical preponderance, becoming the unique ideal; it was more or less what the democrats were aiming for in national politics when they tried to

---

London and the demagogues of all the capitals of Europe" deprecated by Boccardo (*Prediche di un laico*, pp. 193–94). Here too it would be possible to find antecedents for the value placed on example—for instance, in Voltaire's letter of 13 April 1766 (*Oeuvres complètes* 40:392): the lower orders have to be taught by the example of the leading citizens.

[77] See Lambruschini's very interesting letter to Ricasoli, 10 June 1847, in which the hermit of San Cerbone exhorts the baron to write an article on this theme for the first number of *La Patria* (Ricasoli, *Carteggi* 2:230).

[78] This "late flowering of enlightened absolutism among private country gentlemen" has been acutely delineated by E. Sestan in "Gino Capponi storico," *Nuova Rivista Storica* 27 (1945): 9, in the offprint seen.

[79] In the article "Parigi e l'Europa," in *La Perseveranza* for 26 March 1871.

make the mass of the voters prevail: quantity over quality. The moderates were disturbed and perplexed by the enlargement of economic questions, their profound encroachment on the political realm. The undeniable dominance of industry in Europe, its way of absorbing attention and forcing other, more familiar and better loved, forms of production into the background, perturbed them. This sense of dismay was not often voiced explicitly, but it found its way into their paeans to agriculture, the ancient provider of nourishment to the people, to which age-old tradition had always assigned the highest value, conferring on it a dignity and an esteem that industry and commerce had never enjoyed—notwithstanding the medieval communes and the trading ventures of the Italians in the most splendid period of their history.

The praise of country life, urging that the human hand and mind should be devoted to working the land, was familiar; but clearly a new element was creeping into it. There was a drive to bring technical improvements to production, to modernize methods and systems, to place Italy on the same plane as France and England. Agrarian science revived, with fervent discussion in journals, associations, and congresses; this was one of the principal signs of the rebirth of Italy, its new life.[80] On this subject, men as different as Cattaneo, Cavour, Ridolfi, Capponi, and Lambruschini shared the same views, and while some set about procuring merino sheep at Villach or raising English breeds of pigs, or setting up rice-threshing machines,[81] others, ashamed to be left behind, traveled through the vineyards and cellars of Burgundy and Médoc, sampling the wines, establishing comparative standards and learning lessons to be applied to the wines of Chianti.[82] But their agreement on technical questions concealed substantial differences of outlook.

For Cavour and Cattaneo, there was no antithesis between agriculture and modern industry, commerce and finance, but rather perfect synchronism of effort, with agriculture seen essentially as an economic domain, seen through the eyes of the economist, the producer, the technician. There was no bucolic aura, and even when they did acknowledge the ultimate educative and moral purpose of agriculture,[83] or claim for it the role of the great, unique educator of the people, there was nothing essential in this; above all, there was no exaltation of it as the sole basis of the political structure of the country.

Cavour's career proves it. He began his involvement with agriculture *par raison* and was then of course seduced by the fascination of the soil, drawn into and caught up by the continuous mental application required by agricultural enterprise; hence he became an agriculturalist *par goût*.[84] But never to the point of not keeping an eye open and his mind alert for industrial opportunities and the prob-

---

[80] Cf. R. K. Greenfield, *Economia e liberalismo nel Risorgimento* (Italian translation: Bari, 1940), passim.

[81] Cavour, *Lettere* 1:337, 350, 355, 360, and 5:86; *Diario*, pp. 234 ff.

[82] Ricasoli, *Carteggi* 4:158, 160, 163, 167–68, 178. For Ridolfi's interest in industrialized agriculture based on science and capital investment, cf. *La Mezzadria negli scritti dei Georgofili (1833–1872)*, pp. 156 ff.; and for the same interests in de Cambray-Digny, ibid., p. 217.

[83] Which Cavour sometimes did (Falco, "Spunti sociali," pp. 379–80).

[84] Cavour, *Lettere* 5:46, 61–62, 66 (cf. as well *Cavour agricoltore*, p. 13).

lems of high finance. He was driven by necessity to create a position for himself, to get rich, to gain independence and freedom from the thankless role of younger son,[85] constrained to give vent to his "ardent and tormented"[86] will in a different field to the one he had first chosen, in a country in which industry was regarded with suspicion by the government, as a handmaiden of liberalism. Hence, under Carlo Alberto, there was nothing for Cavour but to plant cabbage and cultivate vines.[87] For him agriculture was thus a temporary surrogate for politics, indeed almost a refuge for the politically battered. Lacking any idyllic appreciation of the divine and verdant peace of the countryside,[88] Cavour saw the fields as a productive resource, and agriculture as an industry, even an occasion for financial speculation by taking advantage of price differences in various European markets. The country gentleman of the ancien régime type attended, at most, to exploiting his fields with care: but his economic horizon was bounded by those same fields. Cavour saw his fields, but in the distance he also saw the Odessa market and the French market; he followed price fluctuations from the Baltic Sea to the Black Sea, taking positions as buyer or seller according to the situation.[89]

For him there was an end of preconceived notions, of the "primogenital pretensions of agriculture," tied in with the old and now crumbling political order, and in general linked to the millenary tradition which had made of the *paterna rura*, the ancestral earth, the foundation of civil life. The superiority of agriculture was an illusion; it had been a "harmful error, a fatal one to many," having in the past induced men risen to riches through commerce and industry to invest their capital immediately in land instead of reinvesting it to enlarge their workshops and extend their traffic, "as if this quality [of landholder] conferred on them a greater dignity, elevated them in the social scale." In Cavour all this vanishes and he recognizes that "all the industrial arts, the daughters of labor, have an equal claim on the government's attention and the sympathies of the country." They all contribute equally to the public good and are all equally worthy, he continued, thus turning upside down the old noble-rural mentality as well as the axioms of Italian politics.[90] The first effect of the new public life, of liberty, ought to be a powerful industry, since in order to develop, industry "has

---

[85] Cavour, *Lettere* 1:305, and 5:50: "My aim is to extract the largest possible sum from the land . . . I am trying to procure the greatest possible number of *écus*."

[86] Cavour, *Diario*, p. 122.

[87] Cavour, *Diario*, p. 155; *Lettere* 5:62 and 79.

[88] Cf. acute remarks in L. Ambrosini, "Cavour agricoltore," in *Cronache del Risorgimento* (Milan-Rome, 1931), pp. 125–26 and 130–31; also Zanichelli, *Cavour*, p. 47; P. Matter, *Cavour et l'unité italienne* 1:188 (Paris, 1922). In a famous letter of 18 October 1840, his father wrote to Cavour: "ne parle pas constamment de la campagne pour rester en ville" (Ruffini, *La giovinezza del conte di Cavour* 2:218).

[89] Cf. Cavour, *Nouvelles lettres inédites*, published by A. Bert (Turin, 1889), pp. 15 ff., 24–25, 80 ff. And on the businessman's mentality in Cavour, cf. Valsecchi's trenchant remarks in his *Il Risorgimento e l'Europa*, pp. 133–34.

[90] From a speech at a banquet held by the merchants of Turin on 29 December 1847 (the text of which is now printed in G. Falco, *Lo Statuto Albertino e la sua preparazione* [Rome, no year but 1946], pp. 72–74). Cavour and Cattaneo were certainly not the only ones to combat the "prejudice" about the land: cf. L. Bulferetti, "Sul progressismo sociale della borghesia nel Risorgimento— Antonio Scialoja," in *Miscellanea del centenario* (Turin, 1949), p. 10.

such need of liberty that we do not hesitate to affirm that its progress will be more universal and more rapid in a state where there is some agitation, but where liberty is strong, than it will be in a tranquil one living under the burden of a system of constraint and backwardness."[91]

But Cavour was a revolutionary, in deed if not in word. For many other Italian leaders, the quality of landed proprietor really was the thing that conferred eminent dignity in the social order, and agriculture had, and ought to keep, the privileges of primogeniture. Thus spoke the tradition of centuries, which went back to the agrarian state of ancient Rome and had been strongly renewed in the sixteenth and seventeenth centuries, when the resort to landed property and the title to nobility that it conveyed had subtracted financial and human capital from industrial and commercial activity, in Italy and in France—with the proviso that in Italy there was missing the corrective factor of groups of religious dissenters ready to take the burden of industry and commerce on their shoulders.[92] Salvagnoli had reason in 1834 to lament that in Tuscany real property was "prized so idiotically that the word *proprietor* is used by itself to mean the possessor of a piece of land," and to deride the "fine Castilian traditions" that the Tuscans of the nineteenth century perpetuated.[93] In Lombardy in 1837, Cattaneo observed that "very many merchants have themselves practically no esteem for a merchant except to the extent that he is not one"—to the extent, that is, that he owned land or houses: it was a deep-rooted prejudice, and it meant that advance credit was given only to those who had something tangible of this kind.[94] Again in 1855, one of the advocates of economic renewal, Frattini, had to acknowledge that the spirit of the landed proprietor, with his prudence and caution, still held sway, and he too, like Salvagnoli, detected in this one of the sources of "that species of opprobrium in which for a number of centuries Castilian ignorance held those who engaged in commercial operations."[95] Further proof lies in the mistrust and malicious gossip directed in Piedmont at Cavour himself, a businessman and a market speculator, hence a man who had failed to live up to the traditions of his social stratum.

Certainly, for someone like Ricasoli, agriculture was anything but a forced surrogate for politics. In fact, when forced to engage in political life, he endured

---

[91] From an article in *Il Risorgimento* for 15 December 1847.

[92] On this, see my own *Lo Stato di Milano nell'impero di Carlo V* 1:197 ff. (Rome, 1934); N. Rodolico, "Il ritorno alla terra nella storia degli Italiani," *Atti della R. Accademia dei Georgofili di Firenze* (1933): 329–30; G. Barbieri, *Ideali economici degli Italiani all'inizio dell'età moderna* (Milan, 1940), pp. 462 ff., 471 ff., 490–91. There is a substantial diversity of purpose, mentality, and result between the rush to acquire landed property in the sixteenth century, and the investment in land by merchants in the thirteenth and fourteenth centuries to undergird the system of credit (well depicted in A. Sapori, "I mutui dei mercanti fiorentini del Trecento e l'incremento della proprietà fondiaria," in *Studi di storia economica medievale* [Florence, 1940], pp. 43 ff.).

[93] In the *Memoria* now republished in *La Mezzadria negli scritti dei Georgofili*, pp. 35–36 and cf. also p. 42. Gino Capponi also observed that "any capital investment except land is considered good for nothing except to waste, or jealously conceal" (ibid., p. 70).

[94] Greenfield, *Economia e liberalismo*, pp. 208–209.

[95] Ibid., p. 203. Greenfield offers consistently sagacious observations, not only on the predominance of the agrarian sector but also on the agrarian mentality in Lombardy throughout the first half of the nineteenth century.

this onus with distaste, unlike Cavour,[96] and he dreamed in his heart of Brolio, with its plantations of vines, and those solitary and inhospitable regions "with which my mind immediately finds a full correspondence of thought and feeling, so that I leave my attentive beast to pick out the path, and commune with myself in the infinite space of memory and imagination, until after four or five hours of long spiritual voyage, my physical journey finds its limit and end at the door of the house which was my destination."[97] If one then passes to the other moderates, especially the ones from Tuscany, the difference between them and Cavour is truly striking.[98] Among Gino Capponi and his friends, the "Church of the Capponi,"[99] there was an exclusive passion for the land which tended to oppose agriculture to industry, marking well the gigantic projects and the vast plants of industry, but also the high costs and the risks it entailed, which were principally of a moral and social character. Too rapid mechanical progress, industrial progress, had a convulsive effect, bringing disorder and anxiety, creating poverty. Constantly moved by moral concerns, Gino Capponi saw the worker as a simple machine, muscle power without a mind, whereas in the agricultural laborer mind and muscle were joined. The first labored blindly, the second always intelligently. And he extended the comparison, recalling to his friends the "pitiable scenes of desperation in which a large number of manufacturers find themselves in those countries because of rapid change, where the gigantic projects and the vast plants . . . are monopolized by a few," recalling "hands raised to the sky," hands raised against their brothers. He saw the industrial world, like a new creation, struggling to find its equilibrium, struggling to create "a society similar to the society created in ancient times between the proprietor and the agricultural worker by agriculture, an art born with the birth of human civilization."[100] The "servitude of the loom" generated slave war, it erupted in the cry of passion, in the "rumble of the approaching storm" which all Europe now feared. Sharecropping, in which agriculture took great pride, was a means to extinguish hatred when it was on the point of turning into furor.[101]

Machinery meant a trail of human misery;[102] "great and terrible, immense in

---

[96] Cavour: "I am far from complaining of the fate that has forced me to leave the peaceful agricultural retreat in which I was ensconced, and to launch myself on the stormy seas of political struggle" (1 January 1849; Cavour, *Lettere* 5:186).

[97] Ricasoli, *Lettere e documenti* 10:323.

[98] On the conservatism of the Tuscans, including the economic conservatism that kept them insulated from the idea of the modern economic revolution, cf. N. Quilici, *La borghesia italiana*, pp. 242 ff. But for the worry that industrialization caused in Piedmont as well, cf. the report of Jacquemond and the study of Massino-Turina (A. Fossati, *Il pensiero e la politica sociale di Camillo Cavour* [Turin, 1932], pp. 13 ff.); and on the general sense of unease around 1830 at the collapse of the traditional (agrarian) system, R. Morandi *Storia della grande industria in Italia* (Bari, 1931), pp. 78–79.

[99] This is what Salvagnoli called them (Ricasoli, *Carteggi* 2:216).

[100] *La Mezzadria negli scritti dei Georgofili*, pp. 62–64.

[101] Thus Lambruschini in September 1871 (*La Mezzadria negli scritti dei Georgofili*, pp. 253–54; cf. also pp. 175–76). On these problems, see now the perceptive remarks of E. Passerin, "L'anticapitalismo del Sismondi e i 'campagnoli' toscani del Risorgimento," in *Belfagor* 4 (1949): esp. pp. 402 ff.

[102] Cf. also Greenfield, *Economia e liberalismo*, pp. 182–83 and 186.

its good and evil aspects,"[103] it characterized the century. It brought outward and material progress which brutalized the soul rather than raising it to God, in the way the open countryside did. Leopardi's sarcastic apostrophes to iron-shod roads and manifold commerce and machines rivaling heaven's power were echoed even by those who did not share his cosmic pessimism and chose instead to seek refuge in renewed religious and moral devotion.[104] What was this new education, equal for all, calculated to produce a generation of engineers? asked Gino Capponi.[105] That the people might become a machine: this was the highest wish of those politicians, the bent of those philosophers, who were called most progressive: "was this really the liberty that our fathers desired, for which they fought?" Industry was the study, the glory, the arm of the times, "the priestly calling of a century whose divinity is money." In Capponi the customary accusations of materialism and baseness of soul against the men of the nineteenth century were aimed higher, at the machine and at technical progress. The word mechanical meant soulless and was a term of disparagement.[106]

Increased production, the powerful motor of industrial development, refused to be satisfied with the traditional demands of the market, but tried instead to stimulate new demands and create new markets. Even the modern industrial world had its note of poetry, which had already induced Cattaneo to speak of an art for civil life,[107] and in a still distant future would find its apotheosis in the figure of Henry Ford. But some were unnerved: "the only thing sought and desired today is production; but at current levels it already exceeds demand, especially in England and France, and is thus already a thing contrary to the very nature of industry and the arts."[108]

The response was to recommend that there be technical innovation in agriculture, but that agriculture retain its primacy; the indigenous tradition, which was mostly rural and in which manufacturing had little place, was to be preserved. This, it was thought, would be the only way to serve the cause of civility, of morality, of the nation's standard of living: as though sharecropping were a heritage of enduring tradition, a source of moderate but general ease, a token of Christian charity and civil progress, almost an innate and inseparable part of the national character.[109] Agriculture "improved."[110] From being social and eco-

---

[103] Thus Michelet, very much the romantic, who sees in the machine an instrument of extermination (*La France devant l'Europe*, p. 43).

[104] Cf. R. Ciampini, "La 'Palinodia' di Leopardi e il 'sistema' di Gino Capponi," *Nuova Antologia* (June 1948): 136 ff. and esp. 142.

[105] *Pensieri sull'educazione*, in Capponi, *Scritti editi e inediti* 1:304.

[106] For the elderly Capponi, in November 1873, politics itself was by now "in mechanics" (Capponi, *Lettere* 4:326); he thought Bismarck "an utterly mechanical man" (p. 311).

[107] Greenfield, *Economia e liberalismo*, p. 292.

[108] S. Betti to the countess Pepoli-Serpieri, 24 September 1841 (in Lipparini, *Minghetti* 1:262). Cf. Minghetti, *Nuove osservazioni intorno alla tendenza agli interessi materiali che è nel secolo presente* in *La legislazione sociale*, p. 62.

[109] E. Rubieri, *Dottrine economiche e industriali* (1856), now in *La Mezzadria negli scritti dei Georgofili*, pp. 139 and 144.

[110] As Ridolfi said; another typical agriculturalist, Giuseppe Pasolini, who fully shared the point of view of the Tuscans, believed the same thing (Pasolini, *Memorie* 2:90 ff., 137 ff., 141 [Turin, 1915]).

nomic, the problem became political and moral; economic conservatism fused with political conservatism, and fear of industry became fear of the working masses.

The degree to which men who were unanimous in supporting technical improvements and greater productivity in agriculture could nevertheless be profoundly at odds on the overall question was shown by the debates of the Tuscan Georgofili between 1833 and 1834. These pitted Gino Capponi, a great admirer of the Grand Duke Pietro Leopoldo and his agrarian reforms, a man convinced of the primacy of agriculture, against Salvagnoli, who instead went beyond the specific problem of sharecropping and wanted to concentrate on the relationship of landed property to industry and commerce. Salvagnoli lamented that Tuscany, once a manufacturing and commercial region, had subsequently prostrated itself to the soil as if before an idol, sacrificing to the land all its capital and industrial activity; "and when one finally shakes off superstitious reverence for the land, one finds that there is no more mobile capital, no more manufacturing, no more commerce; one comes to the world market bearing meager ears of corn or a few olives, while our competitors are bringing to it products of every sort."[111]

The celebration of agriculture as the great moral educator, of the earth as the matrix of the familiar civic virtues, the sole reliable pledge of peaceful and ordered progress, grew out of the conservative worldview. This was a different world to the world of Cavour and Cattaneo, and while the younger generation might welcome the machine, their elders (and not only they) for the most part were still bound to traditional ideals of life. They believed that nature conducted man toward God, whereas the workshop made him an atheist, and it is not a coincidence that the great advocates of agriculture were also the ones advocating a revival of religious sentiment. In them, nature and God, work in the fields, faith, education, and the morality of the people were all joined in a single outlook on life. Even Minghetti was an agriculturalist, and in him as well the agriculturalist merged with the religious believer, though with less pathos than in the case of Ricasoli; just as he desired to see the public economy ruled by morality and right, likewise he desired to see industry ruled "by good laws, good institutions, education, proper upbringing, religion."[112] Cavour might admire Bentham and his utilitarianism; Minghetti repudiated it.[113]

If what Lambruschini said was true, that those who inhabited the cities were not of sound mind and that rural wisdom was needed to keep them in their place, then surely it followed that the mechanical arts turned the mind toward evil, whereas the land held it fast to the sane precepts of the Christian life. The ex-

---

[111] The extremely interesting debate can now be followed in *La Mezzadria negli scritti dei Georgofili*, esp. at pp. 16, 25 ff., 33 ff., 49, 57, 62, 70–71, 74 ff., 84.

[112] Said in the course of his meeting with Pius IX on 6 August 1857 (Minghetti, *Ricordi* 3:192). Minghetti's ideas are very clearly influenced by Rosmini, who also subordinated economics to morality and combated utilitarianism (cf. L. Bulferetti, *Antonio Rosmini nella Restaurazione* [Florence, 1942], pp. 172 ff. and 179 n. 1).

[113] Ruffini, *La giovinezza del conte di Cavour* 1:81 ff., 92; Minghetti, *Ricordi* 1:57, and 3:200 ff. On the moral value of agriculture for Minghetti, cf. G. Maioli, *Marco Minghetti*, pp. 315 ff.

tended debate on the relationship between economy and morality, technical progress and spiritual progress, came fully into focus in the discussion of agriculture and its ability to mold character, versus the contraction of morality that came with industry. Whether the first or the second of these two aspects was emphasized, it came to the same thing, for each expressed an identical stance in the face of the great questions posed by modern civilization, questions in which much more was at stake than just politics.

The humanist cultural tradition had a part to play in corroborating the general outlook of the conservatives, since it still dominated Italy in the nineteenth century, still spoke the language of ancient wisdom, the wisdom of the classical world, in which mechanical invention had been devalued in favor of the artist's creations and the beauties of nature. From Virgil's *Georgics* onward, praise of rustic existence had held the field, whereas the toil of the merchant, struggling with his wares over long distances, had never attained the status of an exemplary way of life, not even when the Italian cities lived on commerce and manufacture. Even in the Florence of the Quattrocento, Leon Battista Alberti had made the speakers in his dialogue, Gianozzo and Lionardo, extol life in a country villa, "surrounded by crystal-clear air, the delightful landscape, where all is grateful to the eye . . . everything pure and healthy," at a Horatian distance from the travail of other business, "the worry of purchasing, the fear of transporting, the danger of storing, the strain of selling, the suspicion of extending credit, the fatigue of collecting accounts, the cheating of the money changers." Only in one's villa was life "knowing, gracious, trusty, true,"[114] the work of "men of real goodness, of faithful stewards"; it was delectation and serenity; there there was no envy, no hatred, no malice. These notions were intoned again and again. To the proud Ricasoli the quiet of the country seemed "a vigorous and elevated peace, because it is the effect of the sublimation of one's spirit, as though it were recovering from a species of prostration in which it had lain till that moment. There so many things become indifferent to us, or pass entirely out of our thoughts, that in the city oppress and anger us!"[115]

In the still-dominant cultural tradition, the high walls of Rome, the ancient arches, the mythical heroes alternated with vignettes of rural life. Manzoni, the writer who believed in social economy as the foundation of all other studies, had freed himself from this tradition.[116] But Carducci had reclaimed it, in the period of which we speak. He reached the highest peaks of poetry not in his great historical frescoes but in his songs of abandonment to the voice of nature. Once again, peace and joy flowed into his soul from the green silence of the plain, the tawny fields of corn, the red clover on the sloping meadows. The glare of the foundry flashing in the night did not awaken his muse, as it did that of Walt Whitman, and in those of his poems that were most striking for the audacity of their content, their apparent break with the classical style, the highest degree of

[114] Alberti, *Della Famiglia*, ed. Pellegrini (Florence, 1913), part 3, pp. 379, 388–89, 392, 394.
[115] Ricasoli, *Carteggi* 3:299.
[116] Cf. in this connection Capponi's very interesting letter to Lambertico, in Capponi, *Lettere* 4:417–18.

modernity was the plaintive whistle of the steam engine, acute and strident, the somber carriages, the dark train, the "monster," the wicked monster with the metallic soul. Still it was an extraordinary thing (the literal meaning of the Latin word *monstrum*), and one that brought pain to Carducci, carrying his Lidia away from him, or bearing him far from the cypresses of Bòlgheri. The poet was even capable of saluting the beautiful and horrible monster as a kind of great Satan;[117] the power of steam, promising the coming of new industries to green Umbria, could suggest to him the resurgence of the human spirit after the dark spell of the dissolution of Christianity. But these were rapid and fleeting visions; above all they were simply a vehicle for the celebration of an eighteenth-century idea: the triumphant strength of reason. In Carducci there was none of the exaltation of dynamism found in Whitman, whose breast swelled with pride at the spectacle of steam power, the long and rapid rail lines, the gas, the kerosene, the surface of the earth transformed into a network criss-crossed with tracks of iron; Whitman, who called on the muses to abandon Greece, Italy, Europe, to search out a new and better world, a busier world, and to let go the fables of Troy and medieval castles in order to sing of industry, the deafening roar of its gears and wheels, its aqueducts, gasometers, artificial fertilizers. Two poets and two different worlds, one the rhapsode of an industrial civilization caught up in onrushing development, the other singing of a world still tied to earth, the mother of tawny harvests and nurse of familiar virtues.[118]

But to the conservatives even Carducci passed almost for a heretic, and gave rise to scandal! Really to be free and open to all the voices of the modern world, one would have to be like Cavour, cut off from the Italian cultural tradition. At times he might regret not having had a finished literary education, as Guicciardini regretted not having mastered the art of dancing, but in general he was indifferent to, and even disdainful of, literati and literature, unconcerned with the attention to detail required of a finished stylist. Cavour's interests were limited to economics and politics, and he believed himself fitted to discuss only what he could reason about.[119] To the Italian humanistic tradition, Cavour was a heretic. What else could you call a man who, when he visited the tomb of Romeo and Juliet, described it as "a drinking trough for oxen to which a pompous name has been given," or refrained from making notes of his impressions of Venice, since "the most summary guidebook will be enough to make me recall the things I saw in this city," or said that he did not attach much importance to the classical heritage as such.[120]

The eclectic Minghetti, though strongly aware of the problems of his time and capable of admiring the novelties of science and industry, still held to the old traditions. He had tastes formed by humanism, he wrote about art, he was a

[117] In the *Inno a Satana*, too, the only note of modernity, in the midst of classical citations and allusions to Wycliffe and Luther, is the reference to the railway, "beautiful, horrible monster."

[118] On this feeling for the earth and agriculture in Carducci, cf. Croce, *Giosuè Carducci*, pp. 50–51.

[119] Cavour, *Lettere* 1:299 and 330, and 5:42 and 93–94. Cf. above, p. 164; and G. Torelli, *Ricordi politici* (Milan, 1873), pp. 199–200 and also 306.

[120] Cavour, *Diario*, pp. 238 and 243; Ruffini, *La giovinezza del conte di Cavour* 1:95.

polished orator, and unlike Cavour he never cast off his reverence for the classical—and classical meant the land, not machinery. Minghetti never entirely surrendered to the enthusiasm for feverish modern activity, as Cavour had done and Sella was doing,[121] nor to the enthusiasm for science as a new divinity; rather he pointedly emphasized its limitations, and like Lambruschini and Capponi, set against science the necessity for man to have an inner life, which meant religious feeling.[122]

Positivism was at the gates and was about to burst onto the Italian cultural scene and expand its horizons, bringing a fresh breeze and dispersing antiquated notions, despite its theoretical weakness. Before many years had passed, it would be possible for an observer to remark that, just as it had once been impossible to listen to a speech without meeting Penelope at her weaving, or the sword of Damocles, or the boulder of Sisyphus, now it was impossible to avoid stumbling over evolution, natural selection, the struggle for life.[123] If a referendum were to be held on literary preferences, one would have found Spencer and Darwin displacing almost all the ancient glories from the literary Olympus, ceding first place only to the immense authority of Dante, the Bible, and Shakespeare.[124] But though it was in decline, the old culture fought on.

The cult of "ideal beauty" and "moral beauty" was contrasted to industrialism and materialism, the past with its human virtues and cultural refinement to a present of rising vulgarity and crudity,[125] discriminating style to the brutality of uncontrolled appetite. In the debates that ensued, the theme of the relationship between technical progress and moral progress assumed another guise: the defense of literary beauty as a counterweight to the materialistic tendencies of the century. Literary beauty rescued moral beauty from the threat of extinction.[126] "Beauty is the highest reach of nature and the human intellect, and I find in it the strongest argument against everything that tends to interpret things in material terms."[127] There were lively, ongoing polemics about education between those who demanded more practical, modern, schooling, with less classicism,[128] and those who insisted instead on the absolute necessity of keeping faith with the

---

[121] It is significant that Minghetti admired Capponi, who was a typical classically educated conservative (Minghetti, *Lettere fra la regina Margherita e Marco Minghetti*, pp. 157–58).

[122] Ibid., pp. 53 and 167 (and cf. Minghetti, *Ricordi* 3:79).

[123] The hon. Lioy in the Chamber, on 1 April 1881 (*A.P., Camera*, p. 4922).

[124] A. Baldini, "Lettere per Robinson," in *Il Corriere della Sera* for 10 August 1948.

[125] Something that d'Azeglio loved to talk about, even in private conversation (Minghetti, *Ricordi* 3:55).

[126] Cf. for example the prolusion delivered at the University of Genoa on 22 November 1860 by P. Giuria, *Lettere e industrialismo* (Genoa, 1860), esp. pp. 9 ff., 15–16; and G. Berio, *Preminenza delle lettere e dell'idealismo sulle scienze positive in ordine alla cultura dell'individuo, all'incremento delle arti e degli studi scientifici, alla potenza ed al decoro della nazione* (Oneglia, 1874).

[127] Minghetti, *Lettere fra la regina Margherita e Marco Minghetti*, p. 212. One of the arguments for denying that the International had any chance of catching on in Italy, according to Martello, was the feeling for beauty so widespread in Italy, and the bond of union and respect among the citizens (Martello, *Storia della Internazionale*, p. 381.

[128] Cf. for example P. Selvatico, *Educhiamo il capitale alle industrie* (Bergamo, 1871), pp. 21 ff., 28 ff. The hon. B. Castiglia, *Dell'istruzione e del libro vivente* (Rome, 1874), p. 5 in the preface and pp. 19 ff., takes a stand against "antiques" and in favor of the sort of education "necessary for a productive work ethic."

humanistic tradition, the superior "moral merit" of literature and the arts.[129] These debates were reverberations of a general battle of cultures, with the old world and the new everywhere opposed to one another. For the conservatives of Italy and Europe, love of classical culture, love of the beautiful as it was understood by tradition, the dream of the artist as a being removed from miserable earthly struggles, which he heals with his poetic imagery, all this was bound up with their refusal of modern, rational, industrial civilization, the civilization of the masses, not of individuals.[130]

Just as in the age of Burke and Cuoco, the love of tradition provided a platform for conservatism, which in exalting the traditions, meaning the characteristics, of the different countries, repudiated the revolutionary metaphysic: for the ideal of politics was not a generic abstraction but a given set of institutions that were fitted to a given place and time. This was, in our period, the view of Minghetti, who stated that the all-encompassing and generic declarations of the old revolutionary metaphysic, such as popular sovereignty, the complete equality, political as well as civic, of everyone, and the infallibility of the weight of numbers, had all been completely discredited.[131]

Tradition now required staunch defenders, if they were to protect it from the rising menace of the "corrupt and violent" plebs, who were not of course identical with the true, peaceful people.[132] Class struggle, the rights of the proletariat: these were slogans of war, which gave mass, and weight, and form to generic fears. They focused conservative reaction, not against the former fickle sentimentality of social romanticism,[133] but against precise movements—Marxism with its hard and stringent polemic, or the perpetual revolutionism of Bakunin. The mob was afoot, and other scenes of crowds demonstrating in squares leapt to mind, a memory odious to the moderates ever since 1848 had shown them that, when the fuse was lit, it was no longer possible to tell where and with what force the explosion would arrive. Even when he was traveling outside Italy, Ricasoli's blood would boil with anger at the sight of demonstrations, which reminded him "of what they led us Italians to, those demonstrations, which began spontaneously and then became the tool of iniquity."[134] The corrupted plebs meant the

---

[129] Balbo had already said as much in *Pensieri sulla storia d'Italia*, p. 290.

[130] It was Berthelot's opinion that "Renan . . . had less taste [than I] for democracy, for the French Revolution, and especially for that transformation at once rational, industrial, and socialistic, in which modern civilization is engaged. The older manner of envisaging protection of the sciences, the letters, and the arts by a superior and autocratic power had more attraction for him; he never made a mystery of this" (Renan and Berthelot, *Correspondance*, p. 2). Cf. in fact the very telling article "La poésie de l'exposition," in which Renan, in 1855, brands it an "error" to give too much importance to industry, expresses regret for the blurring of the distinction between the "liberal" arts and those that are not liberal, of which industry is one, and so on (now in *Oeuvres complètes* 2:239 ff.). Fundamentally, this is the same point of view as that of Capponi, Minghetti, and their fellows.

[131] Speech to the Chamber of 5 May 1881 (Minghetti, *Discorsi Parlamentari* 8:123).

[132] Ricasoli, *Carteggi* 3:333. For a rejection of the current attempt to give the sense of "the inferior and less well-bred part of the nation" to the word "people," cf. Balbo, *Della monarchia rappresentativa*, pp. 181–82.

[133] There are good remarks about this in G. Berti, "Appunti sull'epoca romantica," *Società* 2 (1946): 587 ff.

[134] Ricasoli, *Carteggi* 3:444.

communist crew, who had already decided on how they would reapportion private property even before they had seized it.[135] The people in the square was "always a bad thing."[136] One recalled the assassination of Pellegrino Rossi,[137] or at any rate Lambruschini at San Cerbone surrounded by the inhabitants of Livorno and forced to evacuate his house while "those robbers" swarmed over the wall of the garden,[138] or the grove of Marco Minghetti at Settefonti, cut down and carried off.[139] It was Jacobinism, demagogy, the overpowering of those capable of thought by those capable of making a racket, the abandonment of legal methods, whereas liberty meant, above all, respect for legality. It was to mistake every plebeian outburst for the will of the people, and to call by the name of people every throng that rumbled down the street and overwhelmed the legitimate powers; it was everything repugnant to liberal thought, as repugnant as one-man rule.[140]

Mob ferocity, spurred by hatred and rancor, flung itself against liberty like a black tempest.[141] Amid tumult and violence, the principles of the moderates could never triumph, for they were principles of reason. They allowed for the peaceful evolution of reform, but never revolution; this had always been, and it was still, the program of the moderates.[142] But now it was no longer unique to them, for with the conquest of unity and Rome as the capital, the Left too wanted to hear no more talk of revolution, and considered the phase of direct action closed.

Thus it was understandable that there was reluctance to concede electoral rights to the masses. The men of the Right truly considered themselves the pure and the wise, and in their hostility to the arrival in public life of large new groups of voters, there was not just the characteristic worry of any political party—the fear that is of being thrown out of their seats and having to give way, in the electoral arena, to parties not worn down by power, parties with fresh energies and more popularity. There was party allegiance, but there was also something more: there was the fear of the unknown, of meeting a huge and shadowy danger

[135] G. Bardi to Ricasoli, informing him of the discovery of a communist association at Ponte al Serchio, near Pisa, in November 1846 (Ricasoli, *Carteggi* 2:179). On this episode, see G. Andriani, *Socialismo e comunismo in Toscana tra il 1846 e il 1849* (Milan-Rome-Naples, 1921), pp. 4 ff.

[136] Lambruschini, "Ricordi di fatti posteriori all'8 febbraio 1849," in his *Scritti politici e di istruzione pubblica*, p. 417.

[137] What the opinion of the moderates, and of Minghetti in particular, was about the assassination of Pellegrino Rossi, is well known; cf. in addition Lipparini, *Minghetti* 1:73 ff.

[138] Ricasoli, *Carteggi* 3:339–40; Lambruschini, "Ricordi" (cited at n. 136 above), p. 419.

[139] Minghetti, *Ricordi* 2:143.

[140] This point of view is given characteristic expression by Bonghi in the pages of *La Perseveranza*: on 8 September 1870 against the proclamation of the republic in France through a sudden action of the people, without legal sanction; on 20 November 1870 against the impatience of the Romans for the delayed arrival of the king; on 26 March 1871 against the Paris Commune.

[141] Thus Domenico Carutti, the historian of the house of Savoy, in the ode *Liberi Voti* (Rome, 1878), lines 33–36.

[142] Cf. as well *Traccia per un programma dell'opinione nazionale moderata italiana nel 1856* by Diomede Pantaleoni, who in 1881 opposed the extension of the suffrage, seeing in it a stimulus to the two extreme parties, the reds and the blacks, to go all out, and hence the prelude to a tremendous final struggle between them (in Lipparini, *Minghetti* 1:288 ff.).

without being able even to measure its extent. "In the anxious prevision of future ills" their spirit grew pale and took refuge once more in the cry of "God protect Italy," as though there were no longer anything to hope for from men.[143] Even the more optimistic among them saw the future in bleak terms. Minghetti, like all the European moderates, viewed universal suffrage as an evil and defended mon-eyed wealth as an electoral criterion, since it represented not only property "but hard work, saving, industriousness, farsightedness," and felt "very scared" of the effects of the electoral law, dreading evil days for the country, threatened as it was by disorder, confusion, immorality, and debasement.[144] Visconti Venosta for his part perceived the electoral law of 1881 as an "enormous hazard."[145] No better expression could be found to define the state of mind of these men, and it connoted something more than mere fright, though that they acknowledged, at the prospect of a radical triumph at the next elections. Sella too had called the policy of universal suffrage a policy of risk many years before,[146] and now he deplored the fact that, under no other compulsion "than that of a crazy race to display liberalism," the country was being hurled into the unknown by widening the suffrage at a stroke.[147]

A crazy race to display liberalism. Pasquale Villari deplored it too, angered that at the last minute some of the moderates, in order not to be defeated too thoroughly, had gone so far as to propose universal suffrage, though neither Depretis nor Zanardelli desired it. They had resigned themselves "to handing the country over to the multitudes before raising them up out of their brutal state and soothing their hatreds." Thus the liberals were dying, he said, "like reactionaries . . . [trying to] swing to the hard left in hopes of staying alive."[148]

Were the Right conservatives? Yes; but the fear of seeing things fall apart as a result of the widening of the suffrage seeped into the minds of the Left as well,

---

[143] Thus Finali concludes his speech to the Senate on the electoral bill, on 12 December 1881 (*A.P., Senato*, p. 2006).

[144] Speech to the Chamber on 5 May 1881 (Minghetti, *Discorsi Parlamentari* 8:116 and 132). Minghetti also speaks of the "very fearful" effects of the electoral bill in a letter of 1 January 1882 to Visconti Venosta (Visconti Venosta archive).

[145] From a letter to his brother Giovanni, 7 February 1882 (Visconti Venosta archive).

[146] Sella, *Discorso nel banchetto offertogli il 15 ottobre 1876 dagli elettori . . . di Cossato*, pp. 26 ff.

[147] Amari, *Carteggio* 2:277. Amari too was against the law (ibid., 2:264–65). In 1894 Guiccioli repeated "it was a fatal error to widen the suffrage in 1882" (Farini, *Diario* 1:615).

For Sella and his allies, the extension of the vote meant "that the workers' associations would be masters of everything," and so they wished to have nothing to do with it (Sella to La Marmora, 27 October 1876, in *Epistolario inedito*, p. 76). When in 1881 some from the Right showed themselves much more radical even than the Cairoli-Depretis ministry, and proposed the universal suffrage, they did it in large part "out of desperation," according to Depretis in the Chamber (speech of 5 May 1881; Depretis, *Discorsi Parlamentari* 7:675). By this he meant that they wanted, if nothing else, to counterbalance the vote of the workers with the vote of the rural masses, to keep the state from falling into the grasp of the urban lower class (Sonnino, 30 March 1881; *Discorsi Parlamentari* 1:36). Even Minghetti preferred the "lesser evil" of universal suffrage to suffrage limited to those with elementary education, "since the former includes many conservative elements, which the latter excludes" (Minghetti, letter of 1 January 1882 to Visconti Venosta, cited at n. 144; and cf. his *Discorsi Parlamentari* 8:128).

[148] Villari, letter to Minghetti, 5 March 1881 (BCB, *Carte Minghetti*, cart. XXIII, fasc. 14).

though they themselves were putting forward the bill, and even Depretis, as Minghetti had shrewdly told him he would, took fright at the consequences, fearing that the participation of "new social strata" would have the logical result of overturning the country's institutions. According to those who were close to him, he therefore began to take steps to control the damage, erecting strong barriers against the floodtide.[149] The result was *trasformismo*, the search for a centrist parliamentary majority, obtained by subverting the parties as such, maneuvering with individuals and through individuals, substituting the ever-changing problem of tactics for the opposition of principles. And since the floodtide appalled Minghetti as much as it did Depretis, the Bolognese statesman proffered assistance to the man from Stradella in raising the dikes against "the invasion of democracy,"[150] doing more than the prejudices of many of the old Right would have allowed in order to meet the incumbent peril.[151] The only road to salvation, the only way not to be swept under by the republican or socialist current, appeared to be the union of all those well-affected to the established institutions.[152] The result was *trasformismo*, and with it Depretis succeeded in translating smoothly into practice what others, adherents of the Right, had conceived of and attempted—since the efforts of Sella to create a cabinet with Nicotera and the moderate Left, between June and July of 1879, and again in April of 1881, certainly signified *trasformismo* before the letter,[153] an attempt to create in Cavourian style a base at the center by overcoming the classic dichotomy of Right and Left.[154]

[149] Martini, *Confessioni e ricordi*, pp. 194–95.

[150] Minghetti to Luzzatti, 29 August 1881 (Luzzatti, *Memorie* 2:180); and esp. his speech to the Chamber on 12 May 1883, with its defense of *trasformismo*, "the general law of living things" (Minghetti, *Discorsi Parlamentari* 8:253 ff., 271 ff., 276–77).

[151] Visconti Venosta, for example, was "a little reluctant to go down the road that he [Minghetti] is taking. If the opposition that we have mounted in the last six years was serious, that was because we had moral reasons. Until we receive guarantees that diminish these reasons, I believe that we ought to continue to act as the opposition, not intransigent, not factious, but the opposition" (Visconti Venosta to his brother, 17 October 1882; Visconti Venosta archive).

[152] Minghetti said as much to De Laveleye; cf. the latter's *Nouvelles lettres d'Italie*, pp. 96–97.

[153] Sella had never been an orthodox follower of the doctrinaire constitutionalism that was fixed on the idea of two opposing parties. His speech to the Chamber on 19 May 1871 (in which, responding to La Marmora's demand to know whether the Lanza cabinet belonged to the Right or the Left, he replied that it was "independent of the parties") caused a sensation, throwing "the ideas of all the doctors of constitutional scholasticism" into a terrible muddle (G. Guerzoni, *Partiti vecchi e nuovi nel Parlamento italiano: Lettera ad Antonio Mordini* [Florence, 1872], p. 68). Cf. R. De Mattei, *Dal "trasformismo" al socialismo* (Florence, 1940).

[154] On this occasion, Visconti Venosta by contrast had been favorable (obviously, given that the linchpin of the combination was Sella, who was of the Right). Indeed he wrote to his brother Giovanni on 4 July 1879: "In fact an agreement was close, although not sealed, between Sella and Nicotera, to form a cabinet together. But on the last day I was at Rome the combination fell apart, because Sella wanted to be able to say that he had made it with the consensus of his political allies, and this was strongly opposed by Lanza and Spaventa. Sella himself spoke to me at length about it. In itself, the thing arouses all the repugnance that you can well imagine. But I was of the opinion that it was better not to assume the responsibility of dissuading Sella and holding him back, because with elections inevitable, this was perhaps the only possible way . . . to keep our party afloat, with the strong and necessary aid of the government, especially in the Mezzogiorno" (Visconti Venosta archive; and cf. Visconti Venosta to Minghetti, 8 July 1879, BCB, *Carte Minghetti*, cart. XXI, fasc. 129). And on 8 April 1881 Visconti Venosta wrote: "As for Sella, he would be disposed to form a

In the sequel, faced with the full flowering of socialism, other men of the Left who had tenaciously supported the electoral law of 1881 and opposed *trasformismo*, had occasion to ask themselves if they too did not regret "having enlarged the popular suffrage before having prepared the lower classes. We put a dangerous weapon in the hands of people who do not know how to use it, we laid the ground for moral disorder and corruption."[155]

Fear of the masses, strong reluctance to accept a separation of society into opposing blocs, the appeal to the individual, the single person, as a way of getting round rigid oppositions, all these characterized the political action of the governing class. There was all the more reason to take the same approach in social relations: because in this domain, if one accepted that the problem was structural and admitted that society was divided into classes, one would perforce have to embrace the intervention of the state. And if the state intervened in economic and social relations, legislating, limiting, constraining, was this not a flagrant, total contradiction of the liberty of individuals, of the basic principle of liberty? The state was supposed to be the guarantor of order, tranquillity, security for all and each, but not the coercer of the wills and interests of all and each. At the heart of the nineteenth-century idea of liberty there was always the individualism that Benjamin Constant had strongly emphasized, to the point of denying the old myth, dear to Montesquieu, of the liberty of the ancient Greeks.[156] Now there was a sense of alarm over the growing intrusiveness of the state, the multiplication of its functions, its creeping penetration into the private enclosures of humanity's various activities. Mistrust had already been awakened by the "statolatry," of which their party allies, and even more their adversaries, often accused Spaventa and Sella.[157]

The profound dislike of state regulation took many forms. It was seen when the assumption of railroad debts, and the running of the railways, by the state, which appeared to be the negation of liberal principles, caused a parliamentary crisis within the ranks of the Right. The creation of the postal savings banks was called misdirected interference by the state in the economic field, a new proof of the baneful progress of ideas leading to ever more government intervention in areas where liberty should have reigned supreme.[158] Voices were raised in pro-

---

cabinet by going some way to meet the Center and the moderate Left. He spoke to me yesterday to find out what I thought. I strongly encouraged him, because I do not see any other way to stop our downward slide, to begin to realign ourselves with moderate ideas, and to keep our heads above water in the coming elections" (Visconti Venosta archive). Cf. as well Guiccioli, *Quintino Sella* 2:265–66 and 338 ff.

[155] Crispi, *Pensieri e profezie*, p. 50.

[156] Constant, *De la liberté des anciens comparée a celle des modernes* (1819), in *Cours de politique constitutionnelle* 2:539 ff. For the ancients, the individual, sovereign as a member of the public assembly, was a slave in private; among the moderns, the sovereignty of the individual is limited, a matter of appearance, but the individual as a private person is free and independent in an absolute manner.

[157] Sella is the man, *Il Diritto* wrote, "who in an excess of authoritarian zeal has brought into existence a school of state-worshipers in Italy, who aim to concentrate in the state all the moral, political, and economic force of the nation" ("Il capo dell'opposizione," 7 May 1876).

[158] This measure was in fact combated forcefully in the Chamber by Francesco Ferrara and by Majorana Calatabiano; cf. the debates in the Chamber on 19 and 20 April 1875 (*A.P., Camera*, pp. 2493, 2520 ff.)

test against compulsory primary schooling, claiming for fathers the freedom to decide whether to send their own children to school or not.[159] That the liberty of the individual could have limits set to it by the interests of society was a monstrosity of the "innovators," for no one had ever dreamed previously that society could say to a landowner that he must leave a piece of his land uncultivated, could say "you must cultivate those borders, empty that ditch, channel those waters, so that a part of the national wealth does not deteriorate, and if not, you will be subject to financial penalties, and if necessary to imprisonment."[160] Liberty meant the right for everyone, always, "to speak his own opinion, to choose his own trade and follow it, to dispose of his property and even to abuse it; to come and go without asking permission and without having to account for his private reasons and private undertakings."[161] Cavour as always furnished an example, having been extremely hostile to any public intervention in economic life, to the point of opposing the creation of model farms.[162] The Subalpine Agrarian Society, the stage on which the libertarian spirit had perhaps enjoyed its greatest triumphs in Italy, was far from forgotten.[163]

Now the state was being asked to intervene in economic and social life, with protective laws, laws for social assistance, and similar measures, which were the greatest possible infringement of the principles of individual liberty and the sacred rights of property. Where was it all headed? It was headed straight for socialism and communism, with the takeover of enterprises by the state as the mere prelude.

The state should remain what it had been in the Declaration of Rights of 27 August 1789, and not exceed its competence, which was that of defense and the safeguarding of the juridical system.[164] A barracks there must be for the troops defending the country, and another for the carabinieri who supervised public order: but woe if everything should become one big barracks! State intervention, replacing private initiative, was "the coming slavery," Spencer had said, and the Italian moderates, even if they were not positivists, thought the same way: "what is this talk of augmenting the intrusion of the state? Does the state, limited to its

---

[159] This thesis was upheld by the hon. Merzario in the Chamber on 20 January 1874 (*A.P., Camera*, p. 763). The hon. Lioy was also opposed (ibid., p. 722), and Cairoli had to defend the planned measure, declaring that "the interest of society justifies a limit to liberty, a limit which emancipates the conscience" (ibid., p. 779). Also opposed to compulsory schooling was Francesco Ferrara, in "Il Germanismo economico in Italia," *Nuova Antologia* 26 (August 1874): 1012.

[160] Thus the hon. Merzario in the speech cited in the previous note, p. 763.

[161] Constant, *De la liberté des anciens comparée a celle des modernes*, in *Cours de politique constitutionelle* 2:541.

[162] *Cavour agricoltore*, pp. 64–66; G. Prato, *Fatti e dottrine economiche alla vigilia del 1848: L'Associazione agraria subalpina e Camillo Cavour*, pp. 58 ff. Ferrara, "Il Germanismo economico in Italia," appeals to the example of Cavour, against compulsory schooling.

[163] Prato, *Fatti e dottrine economiche alla vigilia del 1848*, pp. 181 ff.

[164] The state "has the duty to maintain and guarantee the security of persons and goods, order and public tranquillity; to repress offenses to right and liberty; to punish infractions of the laws of protection and general interest, frauds, criminal associations, interference with free competition. . . . And the state is indeed the first agent, and the first of all the economic forces of the nation, inasmuch as it produces security, and maintains liberty and right" (A. Magliani, "L'azione economica dello stato," *Nuova Antologia* 28 [January 1875]: 193–94). These are quite simply the beliefs of the drafters of the Declaration of Rights.

legitimate office of regulating *genuine* public services, not already have an immense and complex task to carry out? . . . The further competences that have been given, and the ones that some want to give, to the state, outside the reasons for its existence, are deleterious for the state itself, and for the individual citizens."[165]

Consequently, the intervention of the state in social questions, even in forms that may seem innocuous today, produced fierce and stubborn resistance. The German empire, which by reason of its social legislation could in fact be branded the socialist empire, appeared to many of the moderates not the prototype of liberty which the Left had proclaimed it in 1870, but a prototype of the authoritarianism of contemporary Europe, an authoritarianism that tended to compensate the people for the loss of their liberty with imperial alms-giving, with welfare.[166] The disciples who had received their faith from Cavour saw ranged against them "a species of Bismarckian *statolatry*, now taking the form of state socialism, now that of state tyranny over the church."[167] Their political mistrust of Bismarck's "spirit of conquest" and his antiparliamentary methods shows itself for what it really is, one element of a more complex and radical opposition between two worlds. In the course of a tirade against university socialists—the German professors and their earliest Italian followers—Francesco Ferrara exclaimed: "the sense of liberty has died in Italy; you could say it was buried with the corpse of Cavour, who had so egregiously awakened and nurtured it, and left it to his heirs as a sacred trust to keep."[168] In comparison Minghetti was already halfway to being a socialist when he recommended at least a "theoretical middle way," like Romagnosi: preserve individual initiative but pass social legislation, especially for women and minors in the workplace, which would be the real, the sole way for the state to intervene, to fulfill its duty of protection and relief.[169]

---

[165] Ricasoli to Borgatti, 10 February 1875 (Ricasoli, *Lettere e documenti* 10:338–39). And cf. his letter to the same, 5 March 1876: "Ten errors deriving from the use of liberty are not as bad as a single error attributable to government interference. Indeed, I would say more: ten errors deriving from liberty redound to the benefit of the nation, and a well-executed government action, if it was of the sort that private persons could have carried out, in the end produces an ill effect" (ibid., 10:361). For Luigi Ridolfi in October 1871, the primary prerequisite "for any effective improvement of the social state" is to remove the causes of the disturbances in industry, "by limiting government interference" (*La Mezzadria negli scritti dei Georgofili*, p. 263).

[166] Senator Alfieri, in the Senate, 12 December 1881 (*A.P., Senato*, pp. 2014–15).

[167] Artom to Minghetti, 21 May 1884 (BCB, *Carte Minghetti*, cart. XXIV, fasc. 65).

[168] Ferrara, "Il Germanismo economico in Italia," p. 1011. For Ferrara, those who believe that morality and the economy must be in harmony have already been converted to Germanism and professorial socialism: hence his polemic even against Toniolo (p. 1010). For the debates between the classical school and the positive or Germanic school, cf. S. Majorana Calatabiano, *La scuola germanica e la scuola Adamo Smith in economia pubblica* (Catania, 1875); Luzzatti, *Il centenario della pubblicazione dell'opera di A. Smith* (Rome, 1876), pp. 13–14 (offprint from the *Atti dell'Accademia del Lincei*). For Ricasoli too, the economic school "which they are trying to impose on us today" is ruinous for the economic, civil, and political future of Italy (Ricasoli, *Lettere e documenti* 10:362). On these debates, see now Bulferetti, "Sul progressismo sociale della borghesia nel Risorgimento—Antonio Scialoja," pp. 31–32.

[169] Minghetti, *La legislazione sociale*, pp. 11 ff., 30 ff. Cf. too Minghetti, *Ricordi* 3:207 ff., where Minghetti declares that he still holds to the middle position he had already assumed in the work *Dell'economia pubblica*, between the orthodox economic school and socialism, "however it is called, professorial socialism or popular socialism." See ibid., 3:208, for his opposition to Bismarckian

No, the chief and natural remedy for social ills still appeared to be individual action, the beneficence, the charity, the example supplied by the high-born person who extended the hand of pity to the poor and helped them morally and materially to emerge from their agony. It was still the philanthropic institutions typical of the Piedmont of Carlo Alberto, it was the marquise of Barolo, the canon Cottolengo, Don Giovanni Bosco;[170] it was, with renewed fervor, the work of social assistance inaugurated and disseminated by the Counter-Reformation, San Filippo Neri and San Camillo de Lellis, the Houses of Misericord, the hospices, the orphanages, the Institutions for Reformed Prostitutes, the rules about caring for the sick, and "motherly love for our neighbor, so as to be able to use him with every charity, of the soul and of the body."[171] It could even happen that, in the search for ways to counter the terrible red menace, with charity naturally being the answer, some suggested that it be channeled if possible through the clergy "so that the people will recognize them not only as spiritual consolers but also as their material benefactors."[172]

Cesare Balbo had called charity a sacred name, divine, indisputable, incorruptible, a force theoretically uniting all Christians: the finest book that could possibly be written would be a *History of Charity*.[173] "Charity, with Christianity" was now triumphing once more over the wreckage of those other names, philanthropy, socialism, social feeling, humanitarianism, all of which had tried to impose themselves as surrogates for Christian charity.[174]

The only fresh note sounded by the progressives of the time, a secular note typical of the period, one that went beyond the call for beneficence, was the appeal for schooling, "the finest and most effective way to civilize and give training to the needy plebs, raise them up, provide them with bread and with respectability," and also of course to warm one's own heart with noble sentiments.[175] The same faith in education that gave rise to deep disdain and proud utterances against the Vatican also inspired the conviction that out of books would come the right remedy to the social question: literacy would be the victo-

---

social legislation. Analogous conceptions on the indirect and cooperative action of the state are in Magliani, "L'azione economica dello stato."

[170] On charity in Piedmont, cf. N. Rodolico, *Carlo Alberto negli anni di regno, 1831–1843* (Florence, 1936), pp. 345 ff. Along these lines are proposals like those of Count Achille Laderchi of Bologna for an association among well-off persons willing to occupy themselves with the economic and moral improvement of the people (*La lega del bene* [Bologna, 1874]). In France too, traditionalism in charity persisted after 1870 (H. Rollet, *L'action sociale des catholiques en France, 1871–1901* [Paris, 1947], p. 8), notwithstanding the efforts of the nascent school of "social Catholicism" (J.-B. Duroselle, *Les débuts du catholicisme social en France (1822–1870)* [Paris, 1951], esp. pp. 699 ff., but also, for the traditionalism of the higher clergy in the field of charity, 689 ff.).

[171] *Le regole per ben servire gli infermi*, para. 26 (in M. Vanti, *S. Giacomo degli incurabili di Roma nel Cinquecento* [Rome, 1938], p. 132).

[172] Corniani, *Il principio d'autorità in Italia*, p. 216.

[173] Balbo, third appendix to *Delle speranze d'Italia*, pp. 320–21. There are very summary notes for a history of this sort in *Pensieri ed esempi*, pp. 337–40.

[174] Balbo, *Pensieri ed esempi*, p. 340. And cf. *Delle speranze d'Italia*, ch. 11, p. 189: "As a public work, charity is perhaps the final solution of those great economic problems . . . of a virtual agrarian law of the Christian world."

[175] Vignoli, *Delle condizioni morali e civili d'Italia*, pp. 98 and 104 ff. Vignoli, a democrat, relies on schooling in the struggle against the papacy (pp. 80 ff.)

rious conqueror of the red menace and the black peril. Nor was it always of much use when some pointed out that the economic conditions of the people ought first to be improved before speaking of education, since it was difficult to expect the virtue of regular school attendance from people who were struggling to keep themselves fed.[176]

Such, then, was the complex of attitudes held by the governing class in Italy. The slogans of those who rebelled against it were: class struggle, the rights of the proletariat, war against society as presently constituted.

[176] De Cesare, *Le classi operaie in Italia*, pp. 2 ff.

Liberty and Law

SO THE SUBVERSIVES were seen as the spawn of iniquity. Until around 1870 the term "subversive" had served to denote the Mazzinians, and sometimes even their opposite extreme, the legitimists and clericals:[1] all those who intended, that is, to overturn the established political order. But now it began to be used to designate this new sect as well, which wanted, as it seemed, to subvert the social order too. Republican propaganda was still a source of concern, but now there was also concern about red propaganda, which was seeking a toehold in the army,[2] and occasionally even in the loyal corps of royal carabinieri.[3] The Barsanti case in March 1870 had sounded a shrill alarm for the high command,[4] and that was still a case of republican activity. But in subsequent years, it was Andrea Costa, Errico Malatesta, Carlo Cafiero, and Tito Zanardelli who kept the politi-

---

[1] Cf. for example Lanza's circular to the prefects in 1870, in Lanza, *Le carte* 6:362.

[2] Cf., in the Archivio storico del corpo di stato maggiore in Rome, *Carteggio Confidenziale del Ministro*, cart. 75, fasc. 1 (1874), concerning disciplinary measures against Cpl. Odoardo Zirardini of Ravenna and his brother Giovanni, a private soldier, for being affiliated to the International and being in correspondence with Andrea Costa; and also against another soldier from Ravenna, Venturelli. On 26 April 1876, there was a circular from the war ministry to the general commands of Milan and Turin, ordering them to maintain surveillance of the propaganda which the Committee for Social Revolution, based in Locarno, was trying to spread in the army (ibid., cart. 75). Another classified circular of 16 December 1876 (ibid., cart. 80), refers to the same subject, following information received from the foreign and interior ministries, which is based on a report from the consul in Geneva. On 13 September 1878 another classified circular follows, from the war ministry to the commanders of army corps concerning propaganda and the diffusion of secret manifestos of the International (ibid., cart. 81). On this propaganda of the "social republican" party among the troops, "who are already partly infected," cf. as well the relation of an anonymous informer to Visconti Venosta, 27 November 1872 (ACR, *carte Visconti Venosta*, pacco 5, fasc. 4). And see the article "Le soldatesche e l'internazionalismo" in *L'Osservatore Romano* for 14 September 1878: "with God expelled from the barracks, it is natural that internationalism should enter." In 1870 around three hundred members of the armed forces, many of them noncommissioned officers, were affiliated to the International (A. Romano, *Storia del movimento socialista in Italia* 1:317).

[3] The minister of justice, Vigliani, to the minister of war, 23 November 1874 (Archivio storico del corpo di stato maggiore, *Carteggio Confidenziale del Ministro*, cart. 75).

[4] In this regard, the energetic General Pianell, the commander of the Second Army Corps in Verona, addressed a letter to the war minister on 16 April 1870, warning him not to be lulled into a false sense of security, not to "continue to dissimulate, and to rest content with a surveillance whose efficacy, in the end, we have no way to measure," but to work out a plan that would at least make it possible to expel from the army those noncommissioned officers whom there are strong reasons to consider guilty of treason. Previously, on 27 March, he had urged the general commanding the division at Milan to exercise alert vigilance, stating that it was necessary that generals, colonels, and all commanding officers "should not tolerate the sort of enervation that seems to have got an unshakable grip on the officers" (Archivio storico, cited in n. 2 above, cart. 59). It is to be noted that on 18 August 1870 Barsanti's appeal for clemency from his death sentence was rejected by the cabinet in a split decision taken by secret ballot, "taking into consideration the information received on the consequences for army discipline" (ACR, *Verbali delle deliberazioni del Consiglio dei Ministri* 2:67, published in Lanza, *Le carte* 6:403).

cal and military authorities on the alert, and writing sedulously to one another to identify those who were suspect.[5]

The factor that made them take these individuals seriously as a more dangerous type of subversive was, once again, contemporary events in France. Though manifestations of popular discontent had been frequent in Italy since 1860, with a peasant revolt lasting from the end of December 1868 into January 1869, such explosions had been caused by wretched living conditions, or by specific measures, especially the grist tax.[6] In fact, the revolt against the grist tax had been fomented by the extreme right, the clergy, rather than by the extreme left.

Apprehension was already in the air, certainly, even before the war broke out. In the tumults that took place at Milan on 24 July, and at Genoa on 3 and 4 August 1870, tumults which had alarmed the conservatives and caused them to criticize the government's weakness and inertia, a "strange coalition" of political and social elements had been noted: it had been a republican plot, but also an attack on property.[7] At Naples the government had become aware of the fact that at the beginning of 1870 the local section of the International comprised a fairly large membership, for it had faced a strike in the leather trade, which was openly supported by the international socialist organizations, and had had to carry out searches and seizures, and make arrests.[8] Another sign of the government's apprehension was its request to Nigra, in the period preceding the outbreak of the Franco-Prussian War, to forward the transcript of the trial taking place before the correctional tribunal in Paris against a large group of members of the International.[9] But when the war began, their fears resumed a form more consistent, one might say, with long-standing traditions.

What the moderates feared from the outset was that events in France might produce unwelcome repercussions in Italy. The authorities had foreseen this and taken preventive measures.[10] But the only thing that had caused this concern was the possibility of republican trouble-making, to which Bismarck would not have been above lending a hand.[11] "If the empire of Napoleon is weakened, or ex-

[5] In 1874 the interior minister repeatedly signals the penetration of internationalists, as well as republicans, into the army: Errico Malatesta on 12 February; and others on 6 and 15 March, and 17 and 18 April (Archivio storico, cited in n. 2 above, cart. 75).

[6] Rosselli, *Mazzini e Bakounine*, pp. 229 ff.

[7] *La Perseveranza* for 26, 28, 31 July, and 6 and 8 August. In fact we know that these were republican uprisings, which provided Mazzini with his last illusions about a general insurrection (cf. A. Codignola, *Mazzini* [Turin, 1946], pp. 359 ff.).

[8] Rosselli, *Mazzini e Bakounine*, pp. 268 ff.; Nettlau, *Bakunin e l'Internazionale in Italia*, pp. 165 ff.; R. Michels, *Storia critica del movimento socialista italiano* (Florence, 1926), pp. 26 ff. and 63 ff.

[9] Nigra, report, 16 May 1871, no. 1539. On this trial, which ended on 8 July, see E. Villetard, *Histoire de l'Internationale*, pp. 228 ff., 311 ff.

[10] Thus on 10 August 1870 the war ministry addressed a highly classified circular to the commanders of divisions on the "Subdivision of the continental territory of the kingdom for military service in aid of public order," a circular which predicted disorders "fomented by parties opposed to the actual political status of Italy" (Archivio storico, cited in n. 2 above, cart. 69, prat. 6). In fact, at Milan General Ricotti feared republican disorders in the wake of the severe turmoil in France, though he believed he could handle the situation (ibid., cart. 69, prat. 6).

[11] Lanza, *Le carte* 5:207–208 (personal letter to the prefect of Bologna, 19 July 1870). And note Lanza's reprimand on 12 August to the prefect of Genoa, who had asked him "on what grounds and with what warrant" he should arrest Mazzini (ibid., 5:233). For the maneuvers of Bismarck in Italy—through

hausted, the party that caused the military revolts at Pavia and Piacenza, the disturbance at Milan, and the barricades at Genoa, will raise up its head, and repeat in a serious key the *opera* that up till now has been an *opera buffa*. . . . The *republican* bands will multiply . . . . The Italian monarchy has relied on the French empire more than people think or admit, and although it would not be in fatal danger if the empire were indeed starting to wobble, it would certainly have to watch out for itself."[12] In sum, these were the fears that induced the king and Lanza to hesitate no longer after 4 September in Paris and to order Italian troops to march on Rome. And now, when they might have thought the worst was over, there arrived the news of the Paris Commune in the spring of 1871.

With hindsight it has become clear enough that the insurrection which broke out on 18 March 1871 in the French capital was not, in reality, a social movement properly speaking, at least in its initial phase, and it has been possible to identify the manifold causes, general and particular, lasting and brief, that set it off. Primarily it was the national, and republican, sentiment of the Parisians, exacerbated by defeat and by the deprivation undergone during the siege, that rebelled. They were offended by the arrogant march of the Prussian troops down the Champs Elysées,[13] irritated by the choice of Versailles as the seat of the Assembly, and (perhaps especially important) were stubbornly hostile to the monarchical tendencies of the same Assembly. But the impression that almost all contemporaries had of these events[14] was that they were essentially, in fact exclusively, a social revolution.[15] The French government itself encouraged this belief, as though to justify the unflinching savagery with which the Commune was put down, and to prepare the way for repressive legislation.[16]

The inner circles of the Italian government must have been deeply impressed by the compelling manner in which Nigra, their trusted collaborator and a man not generally given to excessively drastic pronouncements, commented on events as they unfolded. On 21 March he recorded the prevalent opinion at Paris, that the driving force behind the sedition was the International,[17] and the next day he stated, in categorical terms that were not habitual with him: "I have heard

---

Holstein—to prevent an Italian-French alliance, cf. G. P. Gooch, "Holstein: Oracle of the Wilhelmstrasse," in *Studies in German History*, pp. 395–96; Chiala, *Pagine di storia contemporanea* 1:84 n. 1

[12] *La Perseveranza* for 8 August 1870; and cf. the number for 11 August ("La Monarchia italiana e l'impero francese"). Both articles are by Bonghi. The envoy of the United States at Florence, Marsh, had expressed the opinion on 28 August that if the empire crumbled in France and a republic were established, there would be a serious republican danger in Italy (H. R. Marraro, "Unpublished American Documents on Italy's Occupation of Rome," *Journal of Modern History* 13 [1941]: 51 ff.).

[13] Thiers himself, who cannot be suspected of wanting to downplay the danger from the left, pointed to the entry of the Germans into Paris as one of the principal reasons for the revolt, in his deposition of 24 August to the commission of inquiry. This can be confirmed by examining the circumstances of the first demonstrations of 26 and 27 February (Dreyfus, *M. Thiers contre l'empire, la guerre, la commune*, pp. 286–87).

[14] Renan, for example, noted the extreme complexity of the events and said that they could not all be explained by the International (*Correspondance, 1846–1871*, p. 355).

[15] Rosselli, *Mazzini e Bakounine*, pp. 280 ff. Marx and the General Council of the International naturally took the view that the revolt was a "proletarian revolution" of the workers (K. Marx and F. Engels, *Il partito e l'Internazionale*, trans. Togliatti [Rome, 1948], pp. 169, 181, 207–208).

[16] It is enough to review the circular of Jules Favre to his agents abroad, 6 June 1871 (*Staatsarchiv*, 21 [1871], no. 4453).

[17] Report, 21 March, no. 1448.

it said that the insurrection in Paris is the work of this or that political party. This is possible, and it is also probable that the political parties may try to exploit the terrible events we are witnessing for their own benefit. But I am in no doubt that the insurrection in Paris is exclusively the work of the International, and that its most pronounced character, in fact its determining character, is social and communist, and nothing else."[18] On other occasions he expressed himself in less black-and-white terms, and what had been "exclusive" became "prevalent." But the diplomat from Piedmont kept returning insistently to the dark designs of the sect, with its hopes for world revolution and the shattering of the existing political and social order of things.[19]

It is true that Nigra declared that he had no wish to induce the Italian government to start exercising blunt police pressure at home; in fact he forwarded the *Notice Historique* and similar sources of information in order to suggest that it carry out "those spontaneous improvements, and possibly concessions, of which the king's government shows itself so sensible on every occasion," since there was more honor in prevention than in detection and punishment. In sum, he assumed a very different attitude and tone than did the conservative de Launay, who from Berlin thundered against the "heroes of the fusillade and assassination"[20] who held Paris in the grip of terror, making it "the rendezvous of universal demagogy."[21] This violent language revealed clearly the abhorrence with which, like a true Savoyard noble, de Launay viewed the peril of social chaos.

Even so, Nigra too believed that the doctrines of the International, triumphant at that moment in Paris, might penetrate with more or less force into other regions; and he was, after all, a man who stood for order and had produced a scholastic defense of the rights of property when he wrote the essay on political economy in the competition to enter the diplomatic service.[22] He saw particular danger, "beyond that of ordinary propaganda, in the return to their home countries of men who, after imbibing these doctrines, had been present and taken part when they were put into practice."[23]

Such assessments appeared to gain a great deal of credibility from the figures supplied by de Launay, according to whom the International already counted

---

[18] Nigra, report, 22 March, unnumbered (autograph note).

[19] Thus on 31 March he says: "Central Committee or Commune, the power that controls Paris since 18 March, the firstborn son of the 'International,' is making no secret of its hope of a rapid and extensive contagion of the ideas it represents, in the proximate outbreak of other revolutions and the establishment of other republics, and finally in the foundation of the universal republic" (report no. 1467; the report of 24 March, no. 1454, is less categorical). On 16 May, after having recalled "the rapid progress made . . . by the Society [the International], its recent appearance on the scene of active politics, the formidable proportions of the revolution of which it was and is the soul," he sent, for the information of the government, a *Notice Historique sur l'Association Internationale des Travailleurs*, compiled on 6 June 1870 at the order of E. Ollivier and communicated to several foreign governments (Nigra, report, no. 1539). This historical summary was forwarded by the foreign ministry to the interior ministry on 1 June.

[20] Report, 2 April 1871, no. 805.

[21] Report, 3 May 1871, no. 819. That Paris had become "the rendezvous of all the world's perversities" was stated by Jules Favre in the circular of 6 June, cited at n. 16 above.

[22] Cf. R. Moscati, "Costantino Nigra anticommunista," in *Risorgimento Liberale*, 24 December 1947.

[23] Nigra, report, 16 May 1871, no. 1539.

1,200,000 adherents in England and 800,000 in France, without taking account of the substantial numbers in other countries, including Germany.[24] They certainly received exceptionally strong and authoritative support in the Reichstag on 2 May from Bismarck. Though the chancellor was ready to grasp the Commune's rational motivation, its *vernünftige Kern*, in the struggle between the push for centralization and the desire for local autonomy, nevertheless he came out strongly, in speaking of the events in Paris, against the *repris de justice* [habitual criminals], malefactors, and international partisans of republicanism in Europe who had come together in the French capital and had swung the revolt in a direction "perilous for civilization."[25]

If Lanza and Visconti Venosta turned from the reports of their diplomats to the organs of public opinion, once again they were exposed to keen lamentations and cries of indignation: Paris was proof of a "terrifying moral disorder"[26] provoked by the International, which was threatening a barbarism without equal at any period of history,[27] caused not by poverty but by hatred against the upper classes, at a time when the latter were displaying compassionate alacrity "to rescue the poor man from his genuine misery" through institutions of charity and providence.[28] This was a danger from which no country was exempt any longer,[29] and which ought to give food for serious reflection about their own lack of foresight to those who in 1848 had treated the red menace as a joke—whereas in fact those who had set Paris ablaze were continuing the insurrection of June 1848.[30] Perhaps the danger was temporarily quieted by the victory of Versailles, but it was a suspension of hostilities, not peace. Let there be no illusions: we are now in a state of truce, but social war in the future is far from impossible. The torrent threatens to overrun modern civilization.[31] These views appeared in *L'Opinione*, the principal voice of government circles, in whose columns Giacomo Dina sometimes communicated the viewpoint of his friends Lanza and Sella, but which he also sometimes used to spur on Lanza and the rest—a paper, therefore, which in part expressed the frame of mind of the governing moderates and in part contributed to its formation.[32]

La Perseveranza joined in from Milan, with an invective on 26 March 1871 against the "rabble . . . unmindful of any love of country, crazed with rage,

[24] Nigra, report, 22 April 1871, no. 815. The way in which frightened imaginations multiplied the figures can be seen in the data furnished later by Martello, who made the adherents of the International in Europe number at least 1,000,000, while an "international" friend of his spoke to him of 2,594,000, and the [London] *Times* in June 1871 referred to 2,500,000 (Martello, *Storia della Internazionale*, pp. 464–65). Forni, the former *questore* [head of the police] of Naples spoke of 1,864,000 affiliates in Europe alone, and more than two million south of the equator (*L'Internazionale e lo Stato*, pp. 49 ff.).

[25] Bismarck, *Gesammelten Werke* 11:168.

[26] "La Francia," in *L'Opinione* for 3 April 1871.

[27] "La guerra sociale in Parigi," in *L'Opinione* for 30 May 1871. And cf. the issue for 13 April ("La repubblica sociale").

[28] "Parigi," in *L'Opinione* for 26 May 1871.

[29] Ibid.

[30] "La guerra sociale in Parigi," in *L'Opinione* for 30 May 1871.

[31] "L'Internazionale," in *L'Opinione* for 25 June 1871.

[32] What the moderates thought emerges as well in a letter of 13 June 1871 from Castelli to Dina: "Before there is a repetition of the Parisian drama, I will be someplace far from the politics of this world; but those who are still young should not consign it to oblivion" (Castelli, *Carteggio politico* 2:505).

greedy for gain, intolerant of restraint, invidious, perverted."[33] From Florence *La Nazione* warned that the crucial moment had come for the new barbarism with which the new Bagaudes were threatening Europe; the nations must now close ranks around the great principles of conservatism and civilization, rejecting French ideas under any form and pretext, indeed becoming anti-French in order to stay civilized.[34] In a column in the *Nuova Antologia*, Ruggero Bonghi gave further vent to the revulsion of all right-thinking people at the attempt by the working class of Paris to break up the natural hierarchy of all the social classes: they were subverting "not only the present [order] but the essential and perpetual order of human society."[35]

The organs of the Left did not contradict these views. *La Riforma*, anticipating Bismarck, acknowledged that excessive centralization and the lack of freedom for the municipalities lay at the root of the insurrection in Paris,[36] and so it also found that there was a kernel of reason in the program of the Commune, or as it later had occasion to put it, "elements worthy of the highest consideration."[37] But in the end it concurred with Mazzini in condemning the insurrection on account of its cosmopolitanism, and simultaneously rejecting its social doctrines.[38] *Il Diritto*, much more decisive, inveighed against anarchy,[39] against the most sinister form of internal strife, which was social struggle: "yes, social struggle; the rebellion of Paris can have no other significance . . . ; it is the emancipation of the proletariat, it is the fourth estate that is entering the field of combat." But this emancipation, in the form in which it was taking place, constituted a "menace to society,"[40] a "dreadful anomaly."[41]

The discomfort of the republican papers was revealing as they found themselves, very unwillingly, forced to take a position close to that of the conservatives.[42] Most telling of all in the eyes of the moderates was the fact that Mazzini himself, the subversive of yesterday, condemned the Commune and its doc-

[33] Cf. too the articles of 2 and 7 June ("La voce de' fatti," and "La donna a Parigi"). The articles of 26 March and 2 June are by Bonghi.

[34] "Parigi," in *La Nazione* for 26 May 1871. And cf. as well "L'anarchia francese e noi" (31 March), "Lezioni" (18 April), "I Giacobini" (21 May).

[35] Bonghi, *Nove anni* 2:469, 481, 492.

[36] "Gli avvenimenti di Parigi," in *La Riforma* for 24 March 1871.

[37] *La Riforma* for 10 May 1871.

[38] "Gli Internazionalisti," in *La Riforma* for 24 August 1871 states that the International Association of Workers has "the fundamental fault of being incompatible with the exigencies and logical necessities of the principle of nationality." It would be superfluous to condemn its social theories, "a refried mixture of juridical and economic errors." The "patriotic" standpoint that shapes the attitude of *La Riforma* reappears a little later, in November, in the debate between Giorgio Pallavicino, an anti-internationalist, and Garibaldi, whose sympathies at that time were of course strongly pro-communard and pro-internationalist (cf. *Su le quistioni del giorno: Alcune lettere di Giorgio Pallavicino*, ed. B. E. Maineri [Milan, 1874], pp. 47 ff. and cf. p. 79). It is worth noting that Pallavicino, who was generally a fierce opponent of the Right, came out with expressions entirely similar to those of the moderates he hated when faced with the peril of the International: phrases such as "the new irruption of the barbarians, with which we are threatened by the savage doctrines of the Commune" which he used to Guerrazzi in 1873 (ibid., p. 96), immediately call to mind the "new barbarism" anathematized by *L'Opinione* since March 1871.

[39] "Anarchia e reazione," in *Il Diritto* for 21 March 1871.

[40] "La Francia," in *Il Diritto* for 30 March 1871.

[41] "Il Diritto di estradizione," in *Il Diritto* for 29 May 1871.

[42] Rosselli, *Mazzini e Bakounine*, p. 283.

trines.[43] It was a sign that the latter must be something really abominable. In sum, there was wailing and gnashing of teeth. So it is no wonder that the Italian government, like others, grew worried and alert, all the more in that the revolt in Paris was not the sole symptom of subversive activity. Indeed it was only the most clamorous of a number of episodes, in which Italians, and Italian associations, were taking part.

In France itself, the events in Paris were accompanied, in March 1871, by similar ones in Lyon, Saint-Etienne, Toulouse, Narbonne, Limoges, and especially Marseilles; and in addition to the alarming reports of Nigra, the foreign minister was able to consult those of the Italian consuls (including the consul in Chambéry, who had been informing the ministry since September 1870 that the International was hard at work)[44] and the consul in Marseilles.[45]

Outside France there had been disturbances in Zurich on 9, 10, and 14 March 1871, even before the Paris outbreak, which were also attributed to the International.[46] Disorder had occurred in Spain, and there too it was said that agents of the red association were mixed up in intrigues with the republicans, who were accused of the assassination of Prim.[47] As for Italy, the government received confidential information on 11 March that a Garibaldian legion had been secretly organized in Paris, and that it had already joined with the International for the purpose of proclaiming a republic in Italy and Spain, and then linking up with France to take revenge on Germany.[48]

In light of all this, news of the Commune was highly alarming for Italian government ministers, and the self-possessed man from the Valtellina who headed the foreign ministry was among the most worried. Though he may never have heard it for himself, he was doubtless familiar from the stories of his brother and his mother with the refrain sung by the peasants of the Brianza in 1848: the Germans will return no more to Marian and Cantù [localities in Lombardy]; death to all *signori*.[49] The cry of death to all gentlemen had made a deep impres-

---

[43] On the reasons for Mazzini's attitude, cf. Rosselli, *Mazzini e Bakounine*, pp. 284 ff. Giuseppe Ferrari also condemned the madness of the movement at this time (*La disfatta*, esp. pp. 119 ff., and *Carteggio inedito* 1:257). And note too Giuseppe Petroni, the editor of the Mazzinian *Roma del popolo*, to Garibaldi (G. Fonterossi,"Garibaldi e l'Internazionale," *La Stirpe* 11 [1933]: 10–11).

[44] Basso, report, 1 October, no. 25.

[45] Cf. the report of the consul general, A. Strambio, 11 March 1871, no. 51 (concerning strikes etc.).

[46] "La lega Internazionale," in *L'Opinione* for 16 March 1871.

[47] Cf. ibid. and another, much more optimistic article, on 13 May, in the same paper ("L'Internazionale in Ispagna"), which notes with satisfaction that in Spain the sect is having little success.

[48] "Memoria" [memorandum] of the consul Cerruti. It contains numerous particulars: the organizational headquarters are at 3 rue des Couronnes in Paris; the cities designated for the commencement of the action are Nice and Genoa; among the Italian members (the legion also contained French and Polish members, and other nationalities) were the advocate Semenza of Milan, Biffi, also a Milanese, and Miele, of Naples (AE, *Rapp. Francia*, appended to the report of Nigra, 12 March 1871, no. 1436). The problem of the Garibaldians in France and of their return to Italy gave rise to serious concern in the government about internal order.

[49]

> Né a Marian né a Cantù
> I tedesch ghe tornen più
> E crepa i sciori.

G. Visconti Venosta, *Ricordi di gioventù*, pp. 150–51.

sion on the moderate party of the time,[50] just as it must have done on Visconti Venosta, who was then still a Mazzinian, but who later split from the master and became a typical moderate himself, meaning that he considered even the radicals as "reds," in other words asses and charlatans.[51]

It is certain that in the spring of 1871 he was very unsettled indeed by the turn events were taking at Paris, sufficiently preoccupied despite his natural prudence and caution to put the matter in grave terms to the Austro-Hungarian chargé d'affaires in Florence, Count Zaluski.[52] *Très alarmé*, Visconti Venosta saw in the capacity to resist being shown by the revolutionaries of Paris "a real danger for Europe. In spreading out from their source, the subversive principles embraced by the Commune might cause serious disturbances abroad. Italy is particularly at risk because of its proximity and also because of the numerous socialist elements it contains." Europe faced a general danger; hence "in the presence of a common enemy, the Powers must . . . come to an understanding on the means of reducing and disarming it. The security of the nations as well as the progress of civilization are at stake. The wave of impiety that has extinguished all moral sense and all sense of honor among these masses, and has fatally driven a great city toward collapse and desolation, will roll over other countries, if we do not erect sufficiently strong barriers against it."

The minister's unease was "very widely shared," and it was being heightened at that time by the particularly pessimistic information he was receiving: an officer of the Italian general staff who had been in Paris, and Baron Adolf Rothschild, who was passing through Florence, both asserted that the German troops would almost certainly intervene, given the inability of the government in Versailles to control the situation.

It was a moment of particular pessimism for Visconti Venosta. But his views as recorded in this private conversation ended there and did not lead to a formal proposal for an agreement among the governments. Nevertheless, they were a sufficient indication of the dismay the Paris Commune caused for the moderates. That a man like Visconti Venosta, normally so measured and careful in choosing his words, could consider even for a moment the possibility of an international agreement, a Holy Alliance in defense of the social order, is enough to reveal how serious his concern was.

Fortunately, neither Visconti Venosta nor his colleagues could bring themselves to launch in all seriousness a coordinated European policy of reaction.

---

[50] Cf. Salvemini, *Mazzini*, pp. 202–203, and also *I partiti politici milanesi nel secolo XIX*, under the pseudonym "Rerum scriptor" (Milan, 1899), pp. 60–62, 102–106. Cf. as well S. Canzio, "La reazione e la paura del socialismo nel 1848," in *Atti e Memorie del XXVII Congresso Nazionale dell'Istituto per la storia del Risorgimento italiano* (Milan, 1948), pp. 157 ff., and "Lotta di classe nel 1848 in Lombardia," in *Il 1848*, quaderni di *Rinascita* 1:77 ff. (Rome, no year but 1949); D. Demarco, "Le rivoluzioni italiane del 1848," *Società* 5 (1949): 201 ff., 218–19.

[51] Visconti Venosta to his friend Minghetti, referring to the "reds," meaning the radicals, in his electoral district of Tirano (letter, 31 August 1876, BCB, *Carte Minghetti*, cart. XX, fasc. 18).

[52] The conversation, personal and not official in nature, is recounted by Zaluski in his report to Beust of 21 April 1871 (SAW, *P.A.*, XI/77, no. 29 B, *riservato*). I have published a complete translation in the journal *Popoli*, 15 June 1941.

Whatever their fears, their love of liberty was stronger: liberty meant not only respect for legality, for juridical limitations, but also, and principally, an awareness that the power of ideas could never be suffocated in the long run by any use of force. Referring as they constantly did to the example of Cavour, they could not forget what he had said about the socialists; even in June 1848 he had stated that the arms of Cavaignac would not be enough to put an end totally to the social question, and when the immediate panic of 1848 had passed, he recovered all his old trust in liberty as the only certain cure for social ailments. The sole means to combat the socialist movement threatening to engulf Europe "is to oppose its principles with other principles. Whether in economics or politics or religion, ideas can be met effectively only with other ideas, principles only with other principles. Physical repression has little effect. Clearly cannons and bayonets can hold theories at bay for a time, they can maintain the material status quo. But if these theories gain ground in people's minds, believe me . . . sooner or later such theories and ideas will take effect, and will win victory in the political and social realms."[53] His followers had too much political flair not to see the danger lying in wait for the cause of liberty if they overreacted to the red menace.

In fact, fear inspired by the events of Paris was immediately exploited by the reactionaries in every country, who grasped this favorable opportunity to go beyond the question of the International and launch a broader attack on the whole nineteenth century and its fundamental conquests. This meant above all an attack on the idea of liberty, but also, though less frontally, on the principle of nationality, the two revolutionary forces that had been the motor of European history in the previous fifty years. To them was imputed all the blame for the excesses of the International, which was portrayed as the logical, albeit unintended, consequence of liberalism and national patriotism: you, the members of the bourgeoisie, desired the free expression of the national will, deliberative assemblies, parliamentary debates, responsible ministers; you undermined the sacred principle of authority, on which society had reposed peacefully for centuries; so now you can take pleasure in the deeds of the incendiaries of Paris, and look forward with delight to the redistribution of private property.

The clerical press played up this notion in Italy. It was an old ploy, after all: following the example of the French *ultras* of the Restoration, who had consistently depicted the third estate as the exploiter of the people and insisted that the chimeras of the Revolution had profited only the middle class,[54] the reactionaries in Italy had for some time been attempting to exploit, or rather to arouse, class resentment for the sake of combating the liberals and the patriots. Ever since 1848 they had flaunted the specter of communism, in order, said Brofferio, to transform it into a "symbol of fraternal discord, and to conjure up a deathlike apparition capable of driving society back into the past by making it fear the future."[55] The rural masses had been the preferred target of this campaign, both

---

[53] In his speech to the Chamber on 15 April 1851 (Cavour, *Discorsi Parlamentari* 3:268–69, ed. Omodeo-Russo). Cf. too Castelli, *Ricordi*, p. 121.

[54] Cf. Omodeo, *La cultura francese*, p. 88.

[55] Cited in Mazzei, *Il socialismo nazionale di Carlo Pisacane* 1:111. And cf. as well L. Dal

in the case of Metternich before 1848 and in that of the clericals. The purpose was to prod them into opposing the "signori," the gentlemen, who were liberals and patriots. The maneuver had enjoyed a certain success, enough to cause people like Aleardi to rail in anger against the rustic boor and his perennial, degenerate seed.[56] To claim that patriotism was only a manipulative tactic of the "signori" had been a principal theme of the opposition to the national movement: this was true of Metternich and Schwarzenberg, of the period before 1848 and after,[57] of Austrians and clericals.[58] In the sequel, it had served to create difficulties for the government of united Italy, as when clerical propaganda, making a political gambit out of a question of poverty, helped to create the atmosphere that made the revolt of the peasants against the grist tax possible.[59] This was clerical demagogy; Veuillot was also using it in France. Indeed a number of people at this time believed that there was a secret accord between the blacks and the reds, between the Vatican and the International, for the purpose of overturning the current order. A few even imagined that there might be clerics trying to stir up the workers against the bosses and provoke strikes;[60] and anyone could see that there was a significant resemblance between polemical opposition in the anarchist or socialist journals to the new order in Italy, and the opposition being mounted in the clerical papers.

The clerical press thus had plenty of material to work with. It was always quick to pounce on any chance offered by the hesitation of the liberals, and bring up the problem of the origin of present ills.[61] It urged that the works of Voltaire

Pane, "Il socialismo e le questioni sociali nella prima annata della *Civiltà Cattolica*," in *Studi in onore di Gino Luzzatto* 3:126 ff. (Milan, 1950).

[56] "Per un giuoco di palla nella valle di Fumane," 5 December 1857 (Aleardi, *Canti*, p. 292, but cf. p. 322 n. 3. And cf. Croce, *La letteratura della nuova Italia* 1:85 (5th ed.; Bari, 1947).

[57] On Schwarzenberg, cf. Moscati, *La diplomazia europea*, p. 80.

[58] Cf. in general A. Gori, *Gli albori del socialismo (1755–1848)* (Florence, 1909), pp. 123, 328 ff.; C. Spellanzon, *Storia del Risorgimento e dell'unità d'Italia* 3:389 and 430 (Milan, 1936). And cf. Palmerston's protest in November 1848 against Austria for perpetrating "communism" and rousing the lower classes against their social superiors, in Valsecchi, *Il Risorgimento e l'Europa*, p. 47.

[59] Rosselli, *Mazzini e Bakounine*, p. 241, and cf. *Saggi sul Risorgimento*, pp. 263 ff. and 273; Morandi, *La sinistra al potere*, p. 50. For Rosselli, "the first dissemination of class sentiment among the masses" in Italy was "black in color" (*Saggi sul Risorgimento*, p. 273). Again on 25 June 1877, Domenico Farini wrote to Depretis—warning him not to deliberately avert his gaze—that at Saluggia, on the day of the Statuto, there had been public illuminations inscribed to "Pius IX, the triumphator," and paeans to the pope-king. "To those who responded 'long live V. E. [Vittorio Emanuele]!' the papists replied, and I quote them verbatim, *V. E. slaps a tax on grist, Pius IX saves our souls*" (ACR, Carte Depretis, s. I, b. 22, fasc. 69).

These were some of the themes on which the clerical press enlarged: Rome is the capital of Italy, but poverty is growing, and the liberals can find no other remedy than police measures against the demands of the working class; Italy was once the garden of the world, a country envied for its ease of life, but twenty years of liberal domination have brought it the plague of pauperism; pauperism and corruption are the only fruits of liberty (cf. "Confronto di date," in *L'Osservatore Romano* for 28 September 1878; "Del pauperismo in Italia," in *Civiltà Cattolica*, 10th ser., 9:129 ff. (18 January 1879). On this undoubtedly efficacious clerical propaganda, and the myth of the "Risorgimento betrayed," cf. Conti, *Le origini del socialismo a Firenze (1860–1880)*, pp. 10, 26 ff., 133 ff.

[60] For example, the figure of Don Asdrubale in A. Ravà, *Gli operai* (Milan, 1872), a "social comedy" in five acts which was awarded a prize in the competition for popular drama instituted by Alessandro Rossi, the wool-manufacturer and senator from Schio.

[61] Thus on 28 March 1871 *L'Unità Cattolica* exploits an article in *La Perseveranza* for 26 March

be read again, and the principles of 1789, the source of all the trouble, be re-thought, in the frightening glare of the flames that leapt from the blazing Tuile-ries.[62] Socialism, the anarchism of the Paris Commune, and Italian liberalism all revealed the same origin and flowed from the same principles of rebellion against the moral authority of the church. They were connected with the Protestant Ref-ormation and eighteenth-century rationalism,[63] and each ran its course in a simi-lar concrete fashion,[64] exciting the people here in Italy to rebel against their legitimate governments, and in Paris exciting them to rebel against the assembly of Versailles.[65] The outcome was the absence of peace and order, a wild whirling tumult, the instability of governments, and the periodic convulsions that after 1789 had troubled not only France, the matrix of the evil, but also the part of Europe that had let itself be senselessly dragged along in France's wake. These convulsions would continue to afflict the nations until "the salutary and inviol-able norms of Catholicism and all that is right and proper"[66] had been restored.

The setbacks in foreign policy, the invasions and the collapse of regimes, were seen as the fruit of hollow principles: from the time when the Marseillaise had taken the place of religious hymns, France, once unconquerable, had been in-vaded by foreigners three times;[67] and what a contrast between Paris today, filled as it was with confusion, dismay, and horror, and Berlin, a city that gave every semblance of gaiety, unity, concord, and faith in the future![68] The Italian liberals were stupid and blind if they thought that their vacuous declarations about the infernal disorders in Paris would have the power to ward off similar tragedies in Italy.[69] Italy was already plunging headlong down the slope into the abyss, a Roman Commune was not only possible but probable, and the day might yet come when the basilica of St. Peter would meet the fate, or risk meeting the fate, of the column in the Place Vendôme.[70] The Italian communists would be dancing in triumph amid the ruins of St. Peter's, in the glow of the flames. It was all the fault of the Italian government, which was the primary, the most formidable enemy of its own country, since it was responsible for having sought to destroy

---

against the rabble, warning that what is happening now in France will happen tomorrow in Italy ("Oggi in Francia e domani in Italia").

[62] "L'incendio di Parigi," in *L'Unità Cattolica* for 26 May 1871.

[63] This motif, which goes back to the atmosphere of the Catholic reaction of the end of the eighteenth and beginning of the nineteenth centuries, in particular to Novalis and de Maistre, is taken up and developed by Pope Leo XIII as well in the encyclical of 28 December 1878, "Quod Apostolici Muneris" (Giordani, *Le encicliche*, p. 25), and again in "Diuturnum" and "Immortale Dei" (1881 and 1885; ibid., pp. 64 and 77).

[64] All these themes had been sounded in 1848, when communists, socialists, democrats, Free-masons, and liberals had been lumped together into a single depraved entity (Mazzei, *Il socialismo nazionale di Carlo Pisacane*). Cf. as well Padre Curci, *Sopra l'Internazionale, nuova forma del vecchio dissidio tra i ricchi ed i poveri* (Florence, 1871), pp. 103–104; G. Montaldini, *Uno sguardo al passato, al presente, e all'avvenire dell'Europa*, pp. 87 ff., 124 ff.

[65] "I veri comunisti d'Italia," in *L'Osservatore Romano* for 25 May 1871.

[66] "Parigi," in *L'Osservatore Romano* for 1 June 1871. Similar ideas appeared in the weekly political review in the issues of 28 May, 4 June, 2 July.

[67] The weekly political review in *L'Osservatore Romano* for 28 May 1871.

[68] The political review in *L'Osservatore Romano* for 31 March 1871.

[69] "Medici ignoranti," in *L'Osservatore Romano* for 23 April 1871.

[70] "La repubblica e la guerra sul collo del Regno d'Italia," in *L'Unità Cattolica* for 4 May 1871; and "La colonna Vendôme a Parigi e la Basilica di S. Pietro a Roma" on 20 May.

faith and reverence for the supreme head of the Catholic religion, and for its priesthood, in the hearts of the people;[71] by usurping the power of the popes it had undermined the sense of authority and dutiful submission.

On 6 May 1871 La Civiltà Cattolica had its own moment of triumph, as it gave a lesson to those who were criticizing the communards "for being too dialectical in applying what they had learned, and too active in imitating the example of their liberal and conservative masters." The gist was that the clericals, who had always said that the choice was between being Catholic with the pope, or barbarian with the socialists, were now the only ones who had the right to judge and condemn Paris without abruptly shifting their ground. The paper trumpeted the view that the infernal socialist system was the legitimate offspring of liberalism, the necessary consequence of the twin principles of separation of church and state, and popular sovereignty. For the organ of the Jesuits, it was "dazzlingly" evident that liberalism constituted "the natural family and school of communism," and that liberalism and socialism were no more than two different moments, successive stages, of the same concept.[72]

It was thus a piteous thing to see the liberals trying to distance themselves from the communists: far better to cleanse society of the germs of liberalism and its pestiferous influence, if one really wished to prevent the coming of a new iron age, brought on not by barbarians breaking in from outside but ones surging up from within the core of society itself, like worms out of a rotting carcass.[73] Still, if universal ruin were in store, let it come: only the eternal Church would survive, while the International, armed with its torches and kerosene, would be the servant of the wrath of God, the instrument with which the governors and the governed, the princes and the peoples, would be punished.[74] The choice between the pope and the International: this was the dilemma that the clerical papers set forth.

Within a few years, the voice of the pontiff himself, Leo XIII, would be raised in admonition against those who went about "under various and barbarous names," the socialists, communists, and nihilists who were "spreading through the whole world and joining among themselves in leagues of iniquitous conspiracy. They no longer even seek the safety of their shadowy secret conventicles, but come out openly into the light of day and set about executing the details of a master plan conceived long ago to shatter the very basis of civil society." The pope exhorted the princes and the peoples to "welcome and heed the church as a mistress, one that has served the public prosperity of the kingdoms well; and to

[71] "Medici ignoranti," in L'Osservatore Romano for 23 April 1871.

[72] To this question Civiltà Cattolica dedicates three articles that constitute the most significant testimony of the attempt by the clericals to turn the events of Paris to the advantage of the antiliberal reaction: "I liberali italiani ed i comunisti francesi"; "Il liberalismo generatore del socialismo" (8th ser., 2:257 [6 May 1871]; ibid., 2:524 ff. [3 June 1871]); "La progenie dei comunisti" (8th ser., 3:16 ff. [1 July 1871]). That liberalism is the "begetter and preceptor of this monstrosity" (socialism etc.), and thus the main source of all evil, remains a standard theme in the future: cf. for example Civiltà Cattolica, 10th ser., 9:336 (1 February 1879); and "Il socialismo," in L'Osservatore Romano for 18 September 1878.

[73] It was against such prophecies of doom that in 1878 Minghetti made a show of optimism, doubting that "this universal flood is about to drown civilization" (Stato e Chiesa, pp. 227–28).

[74] "L'Internazionale e la circolare del ministro Favre," in Civiltà Cattolica, 8th ser., 3:284.

persuade themselves that the reasons of religion and of imperium are so closely allied that when the former suffers detriment, the obedience of subjects and the majesty of command suffers just as much. Let them know that the church of Christ possesses more power to combat the plague of socialism than human laws can have, or the injunctions of magistrates, or the arms of soldiers; and let them restore to the church that condition of liberty in which it can efficaciously apply its beneficent influence in favor of human society."[75]

There were many among the laity who were convinced that the church did have this power, that they had to choose between the pope and the International. In a repetition of what had happened between 1848 and 1850, when Victor Cousin and Thiers had sought the aid of the bishops, while men of lesser renown in Italy were also turning to the clergy as the only barrier against socialism,[76] those who now saw the universal deluge as imminent began to preach in favor of an accord with the church. Even some government members, or men who had been members of the government until very recently, and who certainly had no intention of sacrificing the unity of Italy, made their anxiety known and maintained that it was high time to lay aside mistrust of the clergy and the papacy and instead seek an alliance with these solid pillars of order against the red peril. Collaboration with the church was required not only to soothe troubled consciences but also to build a strong buffer against the threat from the lower classes: this was the opinion of Luigi Federico Menabrea, an eminent personage and former prime minister who was still very close to the king, for whom he was a sort of Rattazzi of the right.[77] In his speech to the Senate of 25 April 1871 on the law of Guarantees, Menabrea advanced all the familiar polemical arguments against the degenerate age, venting the anxiety he shared with many others at the unsettled state of the times: it was an age of immorality and materialism, even in the schools, and these presaged grave consequences; it was an age that seemed to bring the convulsive final period of the Roman republic back to life. Then the doctrines of Epicurus had triumphed with Lucretius and his poem *De rerum natura*, and also with the conspiracy of Catilina; now the ancient system of Epicurus was reborn, while at the same time we were witnessing the growth of brutal appetites, the spread of immorality, and the rebellion of the workers.[78]

---

[75] The encyclical "Quod Apostolici Muneris" (Giordani, *Le encicliche*, pp. 24, 30–31). Analogous ideas are found in the pope's letter to Cardinal Nina, 27 August 1878: the violation of the most sacrosanct reasons of the Holy See "is also fatal to the welfare and the tranquillity of the peoples, in whom the ideas of duty and justice are profoundly shaken when they see the most ancient and sacred rights violated with impunity in the very person of the vicar of Christ; respect for the law falls away, and the point is reached where the very bases of common civil life are overturned" (*Leonis XIII . . . Acta* 1:107 [Rome, 1881]; *L'Osservatore Romano*, 27 September 1878). *Civiltà Cattolica* picks this up: "when hatred is sowed against the Holy See, what is reaped is a whirlwind against the state" ("La libertà del Papa e l'Italia," in 10th ser., 10:139 [19 April 1879]).

[76] Palluel, as a deputy in the Piedmontese Parliament in 1850, opposed the abolition of the ecclesiastical courts because he wanted to keep the support of the clergy against socialism. Cf. Salvemini, *Mazzini*, pp. 203 ff.

[77] This is how the French envoy, Fournier, described him (report, 26 June 1873, no. 142; AEP, *C.P., Italie*, t. 388, fol. 98).

[78] These analogies between the present times and the times of Caesar and Clodius had already been advanced by a Catholic, Count Paolo Campello, who was in contact with Menabrea, in an article entitled "I demagoghi nel tempo di Cesare," in the *Rivista universale* (January–February

France, which was the cradle of reborn materialism, was the first to pay, with the Commune, for its errors; but even Italy ought not to suppose that it was immune from the wicked designs of the International, which was well organized and only waiting for the right moment. We, said Menabrea, are debating whether the government should encroach on the life of the church, and acting like the Byzantines in 1453: "instead of continuing our war against a group that no longer poses a danger [the clergy], let us unite to repel the common enemy and give peace back to our people, who ask for nothing better than to live in security and tranquillity under the protection of the law."[79]

Though he was not the figure from the age of the Borgia that Garibaldi made him out to be, nor even the fierce reactionary attacked by the press of the Left,[80] Menabrea was well known as a firm conservative, one who in 1850 had voted against the Siccardi laws; but this did not lessen the impact of his words, which were greeted—according to the parliamentary record—with signs of the liveliest approval. It may well be that he had added a lurid hue to this picture simply in order to heighten the force of his opposition to the government's bill.[81] But in what he said there was a genuine felt preoccupation rising from the situation created by the Paris Commune, and many other patriots shared it. Ricasoli for example asked whether, faced with "this terrible flash of lightning from hell," the nation ought to persist in following the road "which, with such exaggeration, and such deficiency of practical sense, the absolutist democratic visionaries of 1789–1793 opened up before us, and down which we ourselves set off with unexampled recklessness, and with ever more baleful misfortune."[82] Was the French Revolution really on trial, in Italy as well as in France and Germany, in a hunt for the historical responsibility for present ills?[83] Certainly this was a part of it: a few years later Carducci protested against the habit of belittling and dismissing the Revolution, affirming that September 1792 remained the supreme epic moment of modern history.[84]

But whether or not 1789 was explicitly being put on trial, there was a growing number who, in defense of the status quo, invoked the "cordial wedding of the principle of authority with religious sentiment; this principle and this sentiment must be, and are, by their essence, in harmonious alignment in every civil society."[85] As time passed, the Catholics were increasingly urged to take part in the national elections, so as to create, together with the moderates, a solid wall against the enemies of social order, against the revolutionaries who were fighting

---

1870). Even today, he says, the party of Clodius (the "sectaries") wishes to gain power for its seditious elements (pp. 184–86, 287–89).

[79] *A.P., Senato*, pp. 825–27.

[80] Cf. Jacini, *La crisi religiosa del Risorgimento*, pp. 267 ff.

[81] Ibid., p. 478.

[82] To Francesco Borgatti, 31 March 1871 (Ricasoli, *Lettere e Documenti* 10:219–20).

[83] Cf. too Bonghi's article "Che sarà della Francia?" in *La Perseveranza* for 12 May 1871. In Germany, cf. von Treitschke's article, "Parteien und Fractionen," in *Preussische Jahrbücher* 27 (1871): 178–79 (the crumbling of the cult of the Revolution etc.).

[84] In the note to "Ça ira" (Carducci, *Poesie* [Bologna, 1902], p. 737).

[85] Thus the hon. Broglio in the Chamber on 14 May 1872 (*A.P., Camera*, p. 2115).

not only the Italian state but also the church and religion.[86] Appeals were made to the archconservatives, the men who had once ministered to the deposed princes, and who, having by now salvaged their personal dignity, were called on to defend the interest they had in common with their former enemies, meaning the integrity of the whole social fabric.[87] There were recommendations to do something about the press, which was thought to be a little too free in matters of religion: "take care, because that is the road that leads to *kerosene*."[88] There were even some police officials who expressed regret at the discord between church and state, and the end of the "sweet yoke of the Gospel," for these things were opening the way to the theories of socialism, against which the law was impotent.[89]

Many of the moderates now really appeared to share the opinion volunteered in 1859 by the stern Tommaseo, "that it is no joke to play at conspiracies, and those who try to use others as instruments make themselves into less than tools."[90] The Left had some reason to fear that an attempt was afoot to bind the throne to the altar,[91] or as it was put later on, that the priest was being summoned to exorcise the international demon.[92]

Fear was the dominant mood, and if in Paris in April 1871 too many people had been ready to turn to the Prussians, provided they would tame the "monster" that had been unleashed, had been ready in other words to betray their country in spirit for the sake of their bellies,[93] in France and Italy many members of the middle class turned their anguished gaze to the church of Rome, which was looked to as a kind of moral gendarme capable of saving persons and property, just as Taine had predicted.[94] He was echoed by Sonnino in the Chamber on 30 March 1881, in this harsh judgment on the clericalism of the bourgeoisie and the class of the comfortably well-off: "although themselves skeptical unbelievers,

---

[86] Cf. for example the opuscule *Concorso o astensione? Considerazioni proposte al clero italiano in occasione delle prossime elezioni politiche per C. S. F.* (Turin, 1874), pp. 33 ff.; C. Vanciano, *Come possa formarsi un partito conservatore* (Naples, 1879), pp. 8 ff., 18 ff., proposing an alliance between the Catholics and the moderates who respect religion; and Corniani, *Il principio d'autorità in Italia*, p. 213. Naturally the answer from the Catholic side is negative, for example the position taken by *Civiltà Cattolica* in the article "Il disegno d'un partito conservatore in Italia," 10th ser., 9:276 ff. (1 February 1879), and also 10th ser., 10:5 ff.

[87] Thus Pietro Sbarbaro in *La Perseveranza* for 13 June 1871.

[88] Thus Padre Tosti, on 2 June 1871 (in F. Quintavalle, *La Conciliazione fra l'Italia ed il Papato nelle letter del p. Luigi Tosti e del sen. Gabrio Casati*, p. 336).

[89] Conti, *Le origini del socialismo a Firenze (1860–1880)*, pp. 220–21.

[90] Tommaseo, letter to Capponi, 9 August 1859 (N. Tommaseo and G. Capponi, *Carteggio inedito dal 1833 al 1874*, ed. I. Del Lungo and P. Prunas, vol. 4, part 2 [Bologna, 1932], p. 165).

[91] Crispi, in the debate on art. 7 of the law of Guarantees, 13 February 1871 (*Discorsi Parlamentari* 2:110; the same doubt visits Crispi on other occasions: *Pensieri e profezie*, p. 103).

[92] Michele Amari to T. Massarani, in 1878 (Amari, *Carteggio* 2:240). Amari, who in parliament sat with the Right, feared the "strong temptation" of the moderates to "summon this dangerous coterie to their aid" (i.e., the clericals; ibid., 2:228). Identical fears are seen in Renan (ibid., 2:239, and Renan, *Correspondance, 1872–1892*, p. 131). Cf. too Ferrari, *La disfatta*, pp. 131–32.

[93] Though untouched by any tender feelings for the communards, "ces misérables," Flaubert is nevertheless fed up with the bourgeois: "'Ah! Thank god, the Prussians have arrived!' is the universal shout from the bourgeois. I put *messieurs les ouvriers* in the same bag, and I would like to see the whole lot chucked into the river" (*Correspondance* 4:55 and cf. 47 and 49).

[94] Taine, *Voyage en Italie* 1:385.

they consider religion a tool of government, desiring it and supporting it not for themselves but for the people. They see in the organization and secular authority of the church a powerful ally of their own class interests, one that allows them to be secure and at ease in their own petty individualism. They hope that as a result of the church's preaching the most unhappy class of society will be convinced that its suffering, which is caused by their [the bourgeoisie's] completely unchecked operations, comes from God; in other words, that they will resign themselves not only to the inevitable evil that befalls all humanity by a law of nature but also to the avoidable ills that derive from the partiality of the laws and our institutions, and from the blind and pitiless egoism of class."[95]

For the clericals, this was exactly the nature of bourgeois liberalism: "the fat bourgeois does not want any discomfort, he wants it both ways, and if the priest bothers him with the voice of conscience, reminding him of the name of God, he ignores him, only to call him back and ask his pardon when he feels his property, and his peace and quiet, menaced by the kerosene."[96] But it has to be said, of course, that it was the clericals themselves who led the comfortable classes to expect such a state of affairs by alternately deprecating the condition of the poor peasants oppressed by the Italian government and uttering phrases more reassuring for the bourgeoisie, as when they affirmed that universal suffrage, "revolutionary by its nature," became innocuous at least, if not beneficent, when the people were profoundly imbued with religious principles, since "religion, by imprinting on their souls the holy fear of God, restraining in them the unlimited appetite for material enjoyment, making them love virtue, and comforting them with the hope of eternal goods, makes mankind content with their own lot, and induces them to act always in accordance with the dictates of honesty, and respect scrupulously the rights of others."[97] This of course was exactly what Vittorio Emanuele II had expected the preaching of the clergy to perform between 1848 and 1850.

The feeling of fear had to be overcome. For the fact is that the solution for which Menabrea hoped would have worked entirely to the advantage of the reactionary forces: if he deluded himself that he could obtain the collaboration of the clergy against the International while holding onto what Italy had gained at the expense of the temporal power of the church, it has to be said that he was no politician. Such a collaboration would have meant subordination to the church, with Menabrea under the sway of the *Civiltà Cattolica*, which once already had addressed itself to him personally, with the statement that it was vain to hope to have Rome for Italy while keeping the friendship of the church.[98]

Such an attempt to forge a conservative coalition would have been all the more

---

[95] Sonnino, *Discorsi Parlamentari* 1:33.

[96] "Povera Francia!" in *L'Osservatore Romano* for 27 September 1878.

[97] "Gli ultimi avvenimenti della Francia," *Civiltà Cattolica*, 10th ser., 9:518 (1 March 1879).

[98] After his speeches in December 1867, *Civiltà Cattolica* had written: "even Menabrea, once so generous in refusing to infringe on the rights of the church, now boasts that he wants to despoil the pope utterly, and complete the assassination begun by Garibaldi!" (cited in Jacini, *La crisi religiosa del Risorgimento*, p. 271 n. 1).

dangerous at a time when the general atmosphere of Europe was turning conservative, in the wake of the Prussian victories and the triumph of Bismarck.[99] This conservative turn also gave rise to impressions and expectations about the future which often enough outstripped the actual course of events; still, even when they were not fulfilled, these impressions and expectations played a role. Long before the Commune occurred, they had lulled the conservatives of the Latin nations into dreaming rosy dreams, creating the illusory hope that the example of the Prussian monarchy and its faithful nobility might help them to recover much of the ground they had lost in their own countries. Thus, conservative prognostications had instilled in many bourgeois a faith in a serene and well-ordered future, guaranteed by the Prussian Junkers.[100]

Reactionism was already growing stronger in France, in the National Assembly against which Paris had risen. And in France, reactionism was most likely to lead to a legitimist monarchy, which would be hostile to Italy's occupation of Rome and would wage a struggle against the very principles of Italian unity and independence. Italy's cause was still, as always, the cause of liberty, and the triumph of reactionary tendencies in Europe was a danger incomparably greater than the danger of a revolt of the lower classes. Visconti Venosta, despite his alarm at the thought of what the Paris Commune might lead to, nevertheless acknowledged this unequivocally: "a period marked by strongly conservative tendencies is probably beginning for all of Europe. Italy, which wants to concentrate on its own domestic affairs, could survive such a period in reasonable security. But as long as the Roman question remains open, Italy has to remember that it is exposed to the consequences of it."[101]

Circumstances rather resembled those after 1848–49: victorious Prussia, a military and monarchical power with a strong nobility, now played the same role in the imagination of many as Austria, likewise military, monarchical, and noble, had then in its phase of postrevolutionary recovery. Both cases demonstrated that the dynamic of Italian history was profoundly different to that of the Germanic nations. Bismarck's Prussia may have been much less backward-looking in many respects than the Austria of Franz Joseph, but on the other hand the Paris Commune was a much more severe crisis than that of June 1848, so the parallel between the two situations held. And the experience of that earlier period, which

---

[99] Cialdini noted this as early as 11 September 1870: "I see Europe remaining in the absolute power of Prussia and Russia, in other words of an ineluctable reaction" (Castelli, *Carteggio politico* 2:481). And on 30 September, Minghetti wrote to Luzzatti: "It should not be forgotten that Prussian predominance will give Europe a period in which the conservative element will be strengthened. If you could only hear how these Prussians speak about republics, and even to some extent about parliamentary governments! And to think that the reds in Italy used to be Prussian sympathizers!" (Luzzatti, *Memorie* 1:309).

[100] "L'Europa e la guerra," and "Due principati nuovi" in *La Perseveranza* for 13 November and 12 December 1870. Both articles are by Bonghi, an acute observer.

[101] Visconti Venosta, personal letter to Cadorna in London, 5 June 1871 (Visconti Venosta archive). From the beginning of the Commune, Visconti Venosta was wary of a "white terror" in France and its inevitable international consequences (Rothan, *L'Allemagne et l'Italie* 2:373). Fear of a clerical reaction was also strong, for example in Hungary: cf. an interesting report of the consul general at Budapest, Luigi Salvini, 29 May 1871, no. 23.

many of the political leaders of 1871 could still vividly remember, proved how easily reactionism could win out by exploiting fear, and the residue of fear. Those who were faithful to Cavour had only to recall his warning that there was just one fundamental issue, to which everything else was secondary: the defense of liberty against the clerical and reactionary faction.[102]

Cavour was no longer with them, but his followers did not deviate from his teaching. Hence, within a short time, they would refuse to launch a *Kulturkampf* in Italy, and so would keep faith with liberty despite the fact that the papacy at that moment was their foremost enemy. Similarly, when faced with the red peril, they were able to dominate their fears. In both cases they gave a noble demonstration of what the spirit of liberty really meant. The result was that the Left and those who were anticlericals by conviction were not left isolated in their resistance to attempts to tie the throne to the altar. Members of the government, and the moderate leaders, did not want the events in Paris to serve as a pretext for a swing to the right. They wanted to keep the International from being used as a decoy to conceal the more dangerous "papalist conspiracy,"[103] and the result was that the journals of both the right and the left busied themselves calming down the Italians.

The moderate papers, attacking the clerical sheets, denied that there was any kinship or affinity between communism and the "great national movement" of the Risorgimento, or that the horrors of the present could be said to grow out of the history of modern thought, that series of titanic efforts made by the human intellect, from the Reformation to the French Revolution, to escape from the darkness of the Middle Ages. They revealed their moderatism forcefully when they asserted that the liberals had waged war on the thrones of the minor sovereigns that dotted the Italian landscape, never on the principle of authority itself: it had been a case of "forced expropriation, indispensable for the creation of Italy, and nothing more."[104] This of course was in full conformity with their overall point of view: there was no more need for the revolutionary spirit now that the job was done; there was no need to embark on new adventures—but no need to reverse direction either. Hence, they concluded, what we have to do is oppose the predictable rebirth in Europe of conservative tendencies because of the victories of Prussia, and the Commune, by sincerely cultivating liberal ideas as they are understood in England, Switzerland, and America.[105]

The papers of the Left were more vigorous, of course, in warning against unjustified and excessive alarmism,[106] but for the rest were in agreement with the moderate press in maintaining that ultramontanism and Jesuitism were not less dangerous, and that the force representing itself as the counterweight to the ex-

---

[102] Cavour, letter to La Marmora, 27 July 1852 (Cavour, *Lettere* 1:524). And cf. Omodeo, *L'opera politica del Conte di Cavour* 1:89 ff., 127 ff.

[103] Castelli, *Carteggio politico* 2:518. In France too, the liberals, although they abhorred the Commune, did not want to play into the hands of the reactionaries, nor allow liberty to be curtailed; cf. *Journal des Débats* for 18 June 1871.

[104] "La progenie dei comunisti," in *L'Opinione* for 1 June 1871.

[105] "La festa nazionale," in *L'Opinione* for 9 June 1871.

[106] "Ipotesi," in *Il Diritto* for 9 April 1871.

cesses of the Commune was itself no less capable of horrible crimes.[107] Left and Right were united in presenting the issue as that of the equal threat posed to the principles of nationality and liberty by the red and black sects, the internationalists and the Jesuits, each ready to give the other a hand to combat liberalism and nationality while preparing for an eventual confrontation between themselves—a confrontation in which the clericals would certainly not be the losers.[108]

This ulterior prophecy was often repeated in the next few years, with much speculation about secret understandings between the ultraclericals and the reds,[109] and reinforced by diplomatic communications from foreign governments alluding to what the Vatican hoped eventually to gain out of a state of general anarchy.[110] Rumors apart, the intransigents did publicly display their pleasure every time the Italian government appeared to be put in a bind by the opposition —which was the Left after all! The blacks would have been overjoyed if a general convulsion had allowed them to hoist the papal banner triumphantly aloft once more over the roiling seas of a civil war.[111]

Some of the foreign diplomats resident in Rome denounced "certain players" who made no mystery of their game, and whose motto was "back to the Syllabus

---

[107] "L'Internazionale e gli Ultramontani," in *Il Diritto* for 2 July 1871.

[108] "Un dilemma," in *L'Opinione* for 24 September 1871.

[109] Martello also accused the higher Catholic clergy of being temporary allies of the International (Martello, *Storia della Internazionale*, pp. 440 ff.).

[110] In February 1872, Visconti Venosta received from the Italian envoy in Lisbon, Oldoini, this report of statements made by Pius IX in an intimate conversation with the Portuguese envoy to the Holy See, and Oldoini's comments: " 'we are living in impossible circumstances. This state of affairs has to end in one way or another. It will be the International that will arrive first, to destroy everything. In the sequel there will be great reaction, which will experience much difficulty, but which will reconstitute society and reestablish religion.' The foreign minister and Count Thomar [Portuguese envoy to the Holy See] perceive in these words the entire present and future program of Vatican policy, and also the alliance of the faction that has inspired it with the International" (Oldoini, report, 5 February 1872, no. 165, appendix). It is to be remembered that the Savoy and Portuguese dynasties were blood relations, and that the latter sought to assist the former in dealing with the Holy See. In fact, Oldoini had been told by the government to "make Portugal . . . the intermediary between us and the Holy See" ("Mio ritorno in Portogallo," diary notes by Oldoini, AE, *Carte Oldoini*, cart. 6, fasc. IX). The apprehensions of Pius IX were confirmed by the pope himself to the Dutch envoy to the Holy See, du Chastel, in his final audience of the latter on 4 May 1872: "The Holy Father dwelt at length on the actual situation in Europe, on the dangerous principles that predominate in it, and that must necessarily lead society to its destruction if providence does not come to our aid" (Chastel, report, 5 May 1872; MRR, *Archivio della Legazione dei Paesi Bassi*, kindly communicated to me by Professor A. M. Ghisalberti).

[111] A characteristic example occurred in 1874, when intransigent Catholic circles rejoiced at the notable success of the opposition in the general elections of 9 and 15 November: this defeat for the government appeared to them to be the prelude to a more decided swing to the left, meaning (as they hoped) toward revolution, and through revolution, to the papal restoration for which they longed. Pius IX, who had more sense, was far from believing that the triumph of the radical party would advance the interests of the church. Cf. the personal letter of Wimpffen to Andrássy, 28 November 1874, SAW, *P.A.*, XI/82, published by me in translation in the journal *Popoli*, 15 April 1941, p. 27. Certainly in these elections the clericals backed the Left, just as, in the local elections of 1877, they sometimes joined with the republicans, and sometimes even with the socialists, against the liberals (Amari, *Carteggio* 2:234). As early as 1861 for that matter, according to Diomede Pantaleoni, Cardinal Antonelli had invited bishops, clergy, and Catholic laity to favor the republicans in the elections, so as to bring about a republic in Italy within a few months (Pantaleoni, private letter to Cavour, 7 January 1861, in Cavour, *La questione romana* 1:179).

by way of the commune."[112] Others, who were accredited to the Holy See and had no hesitation in describing as calumnies the rumors about an understanding between the Vatican and the republicans, nevertheless noted that there were two very unpleasant phenomena that could be cleverly exploited by the enemies of the papacy to give some appearance of substance to the rumors. The first was that the clergy and the clericals had been crying loud and long, for two years, that the full and complete restoration of the papacy would come about only after a revolution and an ephemeral red republic. The second was the tone taken by the clerical press in Italy, which rendered very bad service to the cause that it promoted, as when in November 1872, in view of the long-expected assembly at the Colosseum, it repeatedly predicted that on that day there would be a great catastrophe, an outbreak of revolution in Rome and the proclamation of a red republic. This sort of thing merely furnished arguments which allowed the press on the other side to accuse the Vatican of plotting with the extremists.[113]

This desperate, destructive attitude, which looked for salvation out of the excess of evil, was viewed with contempt by faithful Catholics like Tommaseo,[114] and was certainly unwelcome to Pius IX himself, who never totally forgot the experience of 1847. The pope was ready to protest to his last breath against the usurpation of his rights, but he also admitted that, at bottom, he would be very perplexed if his territories were returned to him: "it would be like finding myself in a palazzo without doors or windows, and I would not know what to do with it."[115] Despite all, the negative attitude was one to which many clung, then and

---

[112] This was said by Wimpffen, the Austrian envoy, to his French colleague, Fournier, shortly before the abdication of King Amedeo of Spain (Fournier, report, 11 February 1873, no. 97; AEP, C.P., Italie, t. 387, fol. 107r-v). Fournier for his part, on the occasion of the assembly at the Colosseum in November 1872, had already reported the rumors against the clergy, which was accused, "not without reason, as it seems," of using the International to promote social breakdown (Fournier, report, 20 November 1872, no. 68; ibid., t. 386, fol. 145).

[113] Report of Palomba, the chargé d'affaires, 30 November 1872, no. 12 (SAW, P.A., XI/229): he naturally excludes the possibility that the high ecclesiastical hierarchy and the intelligent clericals might have a hand in intrigues of this sort: they have a true horror of any revolutionary outcome and of bloodshed, even if it should later turn out entirely in favor of their cause. Cardinal Antonelli, however, was persuaded that the outcome of the present situation would be a revolution. Pius IX, who was convinced that Italy would not long remain in Rome, thought rather that its leaving would be the work of providence, and hoped that Rome would forever be spared bloody scenes. But occasionally, when making extempore speeches, Pius IX said things that, especially when interpreted malevolently, could be twisted to mean something analogous to the aspirations of the ultra-clericals (this observation of Palomba can usefully be set alongside the report of Oldoini, cited at n. 110 above).

[114] Tommaseo was in fact protesting as early as 1870 against the abstentionist tactic in the elections. What were the abstentionists hoping for? They were hoping "that disorder will increase, that there will be heaps of ruins, that the justice of God will come to give them their revenge." They were appealing to St. Michael, the avenging angel. These were desperate hopes, without faith or charity (Roma e l'Italia nel 1850 e nel 1870 e le nuove elezioni, p. 8). Wimpffen, in the personal letter to Andrássy of 28 November 1874, cited at n. 111 above, speaking of the clericals who in the Mezzogiorno had voted for the Left, added that, by acting in this fashion, the clericals were complying with instructions that came not from the pontiff but from a faction around the pontiff, "and which today more than ever follows the maxim of seeking for salvation in the excess of evil."

[115] Wimpffen, in the letter cited in the previous note and at n. 111. And cf. the pope's request merely for a "little plot of ground," abandoning his claims to his former dominions, in his discussion with d'Harcourt in April 1871 (Archives diplomatiques 2:224 (1874); and the comment of J. Favre, ibid., 2:227).

for some years to come. When the Catholics were invited to take part in Italy's public life, in the common interest, their answer would be that "the papacy is the center not only of our religious life but also of our political life too,"[116] and that all the rest meant nothing. When the intransigents sensed that this invitation was becoming a "desperate plea"[117] to the Catholics from the Revolution, by which they meant the entire national movement, Right included, they were exultant. The moderates were saying, we stand for order and legality, so help us to fight off the reds; and the answer was, you are the parents of the monster and must answer for the deeds of your offspring, which were possible only because you yourselves undermined the sacred foundations of human society.

In Italy and in Germany the liberals continued to accuse the reds and the blacks of working in concert to destroy society, with the former serving the purposes of the much shrewder clericals: the clerical party was using the others as a cat's paw to get the chestnut out of the fire, in the certainty that no one would be able to make a cat's paw out of it.[118] These accusations were fired back by the clericals, who depicted the liberals as the natural allies of the reds, the precursors of social disorder,[119] and claimed that the Gospel was totally refractory to communism.[120] The fires of polemic were stoked up, in Germany at least, by the first appearance of Christian socialism, of Ketteler, the *Christlich-Soziale Blätter*, and the "Christian social societies," which many thought to be camouflaging very different political and ecclesiastical purposes. It came to the point where it was not just von Sybel who was accusing the clericals, those virtuosi of demagogy, of using all the arts of radicalism and socialism: Bismarck personally denounced, to the Vatican and in parliament, the pact between the reds and the blacks.[121] In France accusations of socialism were still being flung at La Tour du Pin and the other proponents of social Catholicism as late as 1885.[122]

Around the events of the Commune, during its existence and after its demise, there thus took place a struggle between the old spirit of social conservatism and the new spirit of revolutionary social progress, with the revolutionaries taking the

[116] Thus the Catholic paper *Unione* of Bologna on 3 January 1879, cited in G. Zocchi, *Alle urne politiche si va? o non si va?* (Bologna, 1879), p. 49.

[117] A. Baschirotto, *La vita politica dei cattolici in Italia* (Padua, 1879), p. 15.

[118] Von Sybel, *Klerikale Politik im 19. Jahrhundert, Kleine Historische Schriften* 3:454 and cf. 377, 448 ff. (Stuttgart, 1880).

[119] L. Friedleb, *Die rothe und die schwarze Internationale oder Verhältniss der social-demokratischen Arbeiterbewegung zur Religion* (Munich, 1874), rebuts the accusation that the clergy is working for the revolution and socialism. Cf. E. Naujoks, *Die katholische Arbeiterbewegung und der Sozialismus in den ersten Jahren des Bismarckschen Reiches*, Giessen dissertation (*Neuen Deutschen Forschungen* 228:14 ff.).

[120] Monsignor P. E. Tiboni, *Il Comunismo e il Vangelo* (Brescia, 1872), a speech read to the Athenaeum of Brescia on 7 January 1872.

[121] Bismarck, *Gesammelten Werke* 6c: 9, 16, 22, and esp. 32, and 11:228, 241–42, 298, a speech to the Chamber of Lords, 24 April 1873: the state is threatened by two international parties, both enemies of the nation. This is the same theme enunciated by Sella in his speech at Biolio of 18 October 1874, against the red international and the black international (Sella, *Discorsi Parlamentari* 5:880). See further, in Bismarck, *Gesammelten Werke* 14²:894; Naujoks, *Die katholische Arbeiterbewegung*, pp. 20 ff.

[122] Cf. G. Hoog, *Histoire du catholicisme sociale en France, 1871–1931* (new ed.; Paris, 1946), pp. 24–25.

auspices from the blood of the slain.[123] But there was also reenacted once more the great conflict of ideas of the earlier nineteenth century, between liberty and political reaction; and once more the leaders of Italian liberalism, despite their fears, remained firm in defense of their ideal.

Thus polemical necessity, the desire to neutralize the reactionary backlash in advance, caused liberal editorialists, whether they belonged to the right or the left, to stake out another position: they claimed that the International did not amount to a serious danger for Italy. The left papers took this line from the outset; those on the right adopted it only after raising an initial outcry against the International, but after a certain point, for almost all the organs of liberal opinion, the danger, horrible and monstrous as it might be, did not concern Italy.[124] Here there was not even the trace of a revolt like the one in Paris, because overall, Italy's internal situation was fairly good: this was the judgment of *L'Opinione* in the issue for 1 June 1871, once the Commune had been suppressed.[125] One of the two major organs of the Left, *Il Diritto*, had already been taking this optimistic tone for some time, attempting on 31 March to counter the anxieties of "timorous souls," by observing that there was no reason to fear a menacing explosion of the social question in Italy. Italy was free of the great burden afflicting France and England, the existence of a proletariat; here there was not an oversupply of work, there was an undersupply of workers.[126] In *Il Diritto*'s optimism (in the statement about the labor shortage at any rate), one observes a determination to view the world through rose-colored glasses.

From the spring and summer of 1871, through 1872, this was the tactic repeatedly used and elaborated on: the insistence that in Italy the danger did not exist, in order to block a reaction which would not only have struck a blow at the International, but in the end would have damaged the principles of liberty and nationality themselves. If the French foreign minister, Jules Favre, drew all the world's attention to the Napoleonic government and the International as the causes of the Commune, he was answered with a more wide-ranging diagnosis, in which the root of the evil was located "in the violence of the parties, in the indifference to the means used to reach ends, in the preference for brutal force over liberty, in the substitution of the sudden maneuver for the popular vote, in the revolutionary spirit that justifies every coup d'état."[127] If the Spanish and French governments tried to promote international accords against the socialist

[123] Cf. A. Schiavi, "La formazione del pensiero politico di Andrea Costa," *Nuova Antologia* (May 1948): 12–13.

[124] *La Perseveranza* is an exception, believing that the danger exists and that measures must be taken to counter it: there is no point in saying that Italy lacks large concentrations of industrial workers: if the country is to progress, soon it will have them. Further, in many provinces of Italy those who work the land are much more resentful of the proprietors than the same class is in France, where it constitutes an important conservative force ("Il problema sociale e morale in Italia," 30 May 1871).

[125] "La progenie dei comunisti." Note that this article, which is a polemic against the clericals and reactionaries, asserts that the International presents little danger to Italy.

[126] "Il 'terzo stato' in Italia."

[127] "La circolare del signor Favre," in *L'Opinione* for 13 June 1871.

sect,[128] the response was that the influence of ideas could not be hindered by force, but only other, sounder, ideas; the wisest system was always that of liberty.[129] The essence of the social question lay exclusively in the fulfillment, on everyone's part, of his own duty, and in greater enthusiasm in individual initiative, the only true remedy for the greater part of the political, economic, and social ills with which Italy was still afflicted.[130]

For a year and a half, this song was sung in unison. Only after the strikes of the summer of 1872, the first strikes on a large scale in modern Italy,[131] did some apprehension begin to manifest itself again, for the first time since the Commune. The liberal papers continued to demonstrate confident assurance that nothing grave would happen,[132] all the more since they were trying to keep the fearful predictions of *L'Osservatore Romano* from gaining credence. On 20 August the Vatican paper had heralded the imminent coming of the time of dissolution, the day of God's vengeance, of slaughter, hastened by guilty governments. In the "code of the International" and its excesses, it saw the instrument through which divine justice would smite the peoples who had rebelled against God.[133] But the fact that the reds had made some progress in Italy could no longer be denied.[134] There was some connection between the strikes in Italy and those in Belgium, France, Berlin, and Trieste.[135] Italy might have less to fear than other

---

[128] "L'Internazionale" (the author is Dina), in *L'Opinione* for 31 October 1871, opposes the tendency of the Cortes of Madrid to pass special legislation against the International. In Italy, it says, the International has had less success than elsewhere; and "a few excessively vociferous cries make us suspect the existence of a desire for reaction that would go too far." When the Spanish government later sent out its circular of 9 February 1872 to promote a common defense by the various European governments against a common enemy, *Il Diritto* took a strongly contrary position: "the idea of forming a defensive league against the International appears to us to be one of those utopias comparable only to that other utopia of the peace league that has its headquarters at Geneva" ("La lega dei governi contro l'Internazionale," 26 February 1872). *L'Opinione* for 17 March 1872 ("L'Internazionale") agrees, rejecting any idea of forming a reactionary league and advising against "legislative arrogance." On 19 April another article on the subject ("L'Internazionale nella Camera dei Comuni") in *Il Diritto* repeats the customary refrain that in Italy the perils deriving from the International "are very far off" as yet.

[129] "Il Congresso dell'Aja," in *L'Opinione* for 2 September 1872.

[130] "L'Internazionale in Italia e la quistione sociale," in *Il Diritto* for 28 October 1871.

[131] Cf. "Padroni e operai," in *Il Diritto* for 8 August 1872: "a crowd of laborers is stopping work and showing Italy the first painful example of widespread strikes."

[132] "Gli operai e le autorità," in *L'Opinione* for 12 August 1872, and "Gli scioperi," on 20 August. The strikes are not seen as being a great danger for public order, given that the strikers have nowhere assumed a hostile attitude toward authority; Italy is not a country of strikers.

[133] "I Governi, l'Internazionale, e la Chiesa." Cf. "Gli scioperi" in the issue for 9 August, "I Sovrani a Berlino e l'Internazionale," on 21 August, and the political review in the issue for 22 August.

[134] "L'Internazionale e gli scioperi," in *Il Diritto* for 29 July 1872. But even at this point the principal organ of the Left is asserting that the first signs of the appearance of the International in Italy should not scare anyone, nor provoke any rigorous measures: "We should not transform a few obscure adherents of the International into sectaries, because engaging them in a struggle would give them the cohesion and vitality that they do not naturally have. It is not new, more severe laws that ought to be invoked; the ones that we already have ought to be severely applied."

[135] *Il Diritto* for 14 August 1872 ("Un'ultima parola a proposito dei recenti scioperi") is, however, optimistic once more: we are seeing the difference between our strikes, which are soon resolved, and the much more serious sort that occur elsewhere.

countries, but that did not mean it could go to sleep: "if we are less at risk, still we are not out of all danger."[136]

The truth is that there was now evidence of something to worry about: the spread of the International in Italy was palpable, being documented apart from anything else in many papers and other minuscule periodicals pullulating everywhere, with titles well calculated to make right-thinking people shudder.[137] In Spain the International came into the open, making new offensives in the southern and western part of the country in the summer of 1873.[138] Finally, there were the occurrences in Romagna in the summer of 1874, which easily led to confusion between subversion in the old sense of Mazzinian republicanism, and the new subversion of the followers of Bakunin and their ilk.[139] All these things made it impossible to believe any longer that the Paris Commune had been no more than an episode, serious but isolated. On the contrary, yesterday's optimism was replaced by the fear that Italy might become an easy target for the machinations of the reds.[140]

In the press, or the moderate press at least, there began to appear signs of a willingness to accept some forms of intervention by the public authorities: not of course to interfere in any way with political liberty, which none of the liberals would have wished to see diminished for any reason,[141] but to impose some initial restrictions on the absolute economic liberty of Manchesterian tradition. *L'Opinione* took the opportunity for comment offered by the Congress of Eisenach, in October 1872, at which many of the most illustrious German economists met to discuss the social question and the best way of forestalling the dangers it posed. The paper declared that the state could not remain indifferent in the face of the large questions of labor relations between workers and bosses, and that the old principle of laisser faire was running up against limitations in the social

---

[136] "L'Internazionale," in *L'Opinione* for 29 July 1872.

[137] For example, *Il Petrolio* ["*Kerosene*"], which appeared at Ferrara at the beginning of 1874. On the "surprising" spread of the International from the second half of 1871, cf. Rosselli, *Mazzini e Bakounine*, pp. 299 ff. The expression of surprise came from the General Council of the International itself (ibid., p. 316).

[138] Cf. "L'Internazionale in Ispagna," in *L'Opinione* for 18 August 1873.

[139] The confusion is evident in *L'Opinione* ("La polizia internazionale," 22 August 1874), which repeats that Italy is indeed not yet ripe for the International, since it still lacks large industries, but warns that it must be vigilant after the painful surprise it has had. "The country has woken up, as if from a bad dream."

[140] This happens with Bonghi, who is led by the case of Villa Ruffi, and the disorders in Romagna and Tuscany, to assert that in Italy the International "is much more widespread than we thought," and that "although in the economic conditions of Italian society the International finds less flammable material than it does elsewhere, perhaps it finds readier instruments in the turbulent inclinations and secret combinations among some classes," that is, in the sectarian spirit, an ancient and deleterious Italian practice. Thus he is led to fear that the next target of the attempts of the International may be Italy, "more than one of whose sons is already contemplating putting the torch to the monuments inherited from our forefathers, and overthrowing all the more stable social relations" (from the political review in the *Nuova Antologia* 27 [31 August 1874]: 225–26).

[141] "Le conferenze di Berlino," in *L'Opinione* for 17 November 1872: "We put all our trust in the healthy effects of liberty. . . . [Harmony between capital and labor] cannot be imposed autocratically; only when legislation keeps pace with economic progress can the process by enhanced."

field.[142] Almost a year later the congress of dissidents from the International at Geneva gave *L'Opinione* a chance to take up its polemic against the absolute libertarians, with their conviction that the state should simply stand aside; it was timely and necessary for the state to intervene in social questions, study them, and prepare solutions.[143] These views were, clearly, harbingers of the earliest forms of labor protection, of the legislation on social welfare and regulation of the work done by women and minors which Luzzatti was so tenaciously propounding. It is significant that before long he was to become the leading figure on *L'Opinione*.[144]

But things didn't stop there. Along with advice to the state to intervene to protect the workers, there cropped up advice, or rather expressions of opinion, which regarded more directly the work of the police. When the International was the subject under discussion, the optimism that had been in vogue between June 1871 and the summer of 1872 gave way to a renewed and ill-concealed anxiety. The state was urged to act, on the assumption that "it would be folly" to think that states could fail to take cognizance of societies like the International, which was engaged in a struggle "against intelligence." When extremely heavy sentences were imposed on a few internationalists accused of conspiracy against Italy's internal security, a few papers, including the very authoritative *Opinione*, had no hesitation in approving the rigor of the sentence, in the belief that "the more frequent the warnings such as the one given by the Assize Court of Rome, the more rarely will occasions arise to invoke those [criminal] laws, which create salutary dread in the enemies of the state."[145]

Labor protection laws on hygiene and insurance, but also a strong arm against the "sectaries": these were the two remedies offered; and in the latter there lay concealed a danger, which was that the use of strong-arm methods would, perhaps inadvertently, go farther than what had originally been intended. Proposals for reciprocal contact and exchange of information between the police forces of the various countries[146] ran the risk of creating a sort of new Holy Alliance. It was a danger that grew as fear of a European triumph of clericalism subsided: the less grave appeared the menace from the ultramontanes, Henri V, Don Carlos, and the Jesuits, and the less beset the unity of Italy with Rome as its capital, the more worrying the subversives came to seem. Stendhal's two dark colors, the red and the black, still formed the background of a picture in which the red, white, and green of unity and liberty shone forth.

As in the press, so among the members of the government, a series of emotions succeeded one another in those years: fear of the Commune, optimism that was sincere but also ostentatious for tactical reasons, and then a new disquiet.

---

[142] "Il Congresso d'Eisenach," in *L'Opinione* for 21 October 1872.

[143] "Il Congresso dell'Internazionale," in *L'Opinione* for 14 September 1873.

[144] Chiala, *Giacomo Dina* 3:389 and 426–27; Luzzatti, *Memorie* 1:392–93.

[145] "Un processo politico," in *L'Opinione* for 19 May 1875. The reference is to a trial held in the Assize Court of Rome; further details at n. 226 below.

[146] This was urged by *L'Opinione* on 22 August 1874 (in the article "La polizia internazionale" cited at n. 139 above). The police forces of the various countries, it said, must keep in daily contact, exchange information with one another, and lend each other assistance.

Formal assurances that the peril was absent in Italy began to alternate with secret and gradually increasing preoccupations that were never entirely laid to rest.

Among the private statements of Visconti Venosta to the Austrian chargé d'affaires there appeared the affirmation that the Italian government, in its vigilance, believed itself capable of repressing any subversive movement. The minister repeated this to Count de Launay, assuring him that in Italy, as in Germany, the vigilance of the government had hitherto been sufficient "to render impotent the intrigues of the agitators, to foil their plots, and guard the country from such grave perils."[147] And yet, despite all, at this time the foreign minister did not hide the fact that the danger existed for Italy, and that it was serious; to Zaluski he had spoken of the "numerous socialist elements" that the country contained.

Two and a half months later he was sounding a different note. Italy was an agricultural country with few industrial centers and there were only traces, practically insignificant, of the International, so the danger to it was neither grave nor imminent: this was Visconti Venosta's reply to Bismarck's invitation to act in combination against the adherents of the sect.[148] Real danger might come to pass only if all the adversaries of the regime, principally the Mazzinians, the "few sectaries among us who are still dreaming of overturning the present government,"[149] were to group themselves around the cells of the International. But even this was only a relative danger, because the tranquillity that Italy was enjoying, the natural consequence of the satisfactory solution of the great national questions that had been achieved, and the attachment of the people to the dynasty, would condemn any attempts by the Mazzinians and socialists to failure. At most there was anxiety about a possible alliance between the Mazzinian groups and the International, an anxiety that was ever-present among the men of the government, notwithstanding the very public dissension between Mazzini and the followers of Bakunin and Marx.[150]

This confidence suited admirably the government's old tactic: to present Italy as peaceful only in consequence of the royal government's ability to apply its program. How propitious it was to draw Europe's attention to the fact that Italy, the hotbed of the revolutionary spirit it had once feared so much, the terror of its *bien pensants* a decade previously, was a country of order and tranquillity, whereas other great nations, France and Spain in the lead, were fluctuating between anarchy and reaction! What better argument to back up the official declarations of the king and his ministers, who were attempting in every way to present the kingdom as an ordered and, by now, a mollified and serene member of the European concert!

[147] Visconti Venosta, dispatch to de Launay, 29 April 1871, no. 207.
[148] Visconti Venosta, dispatch to de Launay, 10 July 1871, no. 216. There was a similar dispatch on the same date to Nigra, no. 322.
[149] From the same dispatch to Nigra.
[150] It is to be noted that this anxiety had been suggested, in a manner of speaking, to Visconti Venosta by Lanza, who on 21 April had instructed him to have investigations carried out in London to verify whether or not the "International republican committee" of London, which included Marx and others, was in "active correspondence with the leaders of the party of action in Italy," and was supplying them with the means to carry out their subversive plans (AE, *Rapp. Inghilterra*, no. 1527).

Yet it was a sincere optimism, based on the inquiries and the information collected by the Ministry of the Interior. In his conversation with Zaluski, Visconti Venosta had given the impression of being weighed down by "detailed information of a disturbing kind," but not long after he received intelligence from his colleague in the interior ministry which restored his tranquillity. Just as news was reaching him from France that addresses and messages had been sent by associations in Italy to the Commune,[151] the interior minister informed him on 22 May that repeated investigations" had convinced that department that the attempts made to implant the International in Italy had been fruitless.[152] Not long after, the interior minister, while requesting the foreign minister to pursue the pertinent inquiries in London, told him that the prefect of Milan had concluded that 2,540 signatures on what claimed to be an address from the Milanese section of the International to the central committee in London were false.[153] And on 18 November Giovanni Lanza assured Visconti Venosta that in Italy the sect had only "a few scattered adherents of little influence."[154] As it happens, the excessively

---

[151] Nigra, report, 28 April 1871, no. 1519. The address in question was to the "Citizens of the Commune of Paris," and was sent on 14 April by the "International Democratic Society" of Florence, and published, as well as in *Il Dovere* of Genoa, in *L'Ami du Peuple* for 27 April and the *Journal Officiel* for 28 April. This society, which was neither a section of the International, nor a socialist group, was dissolved for having sent another address to the "Survivors of the Commune." Cf. Rosselli, *Mazzini e Bakounine*, pp. 303–305; Conti, *Le origini del socialismo a Firenze (1860–1880)*, pp. 100, 116–17, 247–49.

[152] The interior ministry to the foreign ministry, 22 May 1871, no. 1938 (AE, *Rapp. Francia*). After observing correctly that the "International Democratic Society" of Florence was not a section of the real International, the dispatch continues: "In recent years, and especially at the end of 1868 and the beginning of 1869, this ministry received information from abroad of the departure for Italy of agents of the International charged with finding ways of establishing it in Italy. They were meant to do this in the principal centers such as Turin, Milan, Naples, and Palermo, but from investigations carried out in the meantime, we have not been able to ascertain definitely that these agents arrived. In any case, if they came, their work must have been unavailing. Nor were this ministry's investigations limited to this, but it extended them to all the workers' strikes which have taken place in recent years, including the ones recently at Oggiono (near Como) and at Milan, for the purpose of establishing precisely whether or not the International had anything to do with them. However these investigations lead to the opposite conclusion, and further to the conclusion that the political parties had nothing to do with them either. In any case, the political parties at the moment are showing very little desire to bestir themselves, except perhaps in the Romagna, while the rest of Italy is entirely tranquil."

[153] Lanza to Visconti Venosta, 2 July 1871, no. 2590 (AE, *Rapp. Inghilterra*). The address was published in Paris by the *Paris-Journal* and the *Opinion Nationale* and bore the signatures of Maldini, Giovacchini, and Léon Dupont. Bonghi referred to it in *La Perseveranza*, declaring that not only had the events of Paris not made the members of the International any wiser but that the greatness of the battle they had fought had filled them with a sense of their own strength. He restated his views on the gravity of the situation ("L'impressione de' fatti," 28 June 1871). Visconti Venosta refers again to the falsity of this address (which is reprinted in Villetard, *Histoire de l'Internationale*, pp. 265–66), in the dispatch to de Launay, 10 July 1871 (cited above at n. 148).

[154] AE, *Rapp. Inghilterra*, no. 4623. Again at the end of May 1872, Lanza told the French envoy, Fournier, that he was fully informed about the activities of the International in Italy, but that he was also quite untroubled about its present ability to carry on propaganda on a large scale. He maintained that the number of its adherents in the whole kingdom did not exceed three or four thousand, that internationalists and Mazzinians were at odds, and that Garibaldi, who wished to unite them, did not have the requisite abilities as an organizer. "He is no more than a name and a flag, whose role has come to an end in Italy." The only danger, a relatively remote one, would be that the International and the Freemasons might start to cooperate (Fournier, report, 31 May 1872, no. 23; AEP, *C.P., Italie*, t. 385, fols. 128 ff.). The background of this statement was contacts that had

enthusiastic Riggio was assuring Engels contemporaneously that another year and "the destiny of the peninsula will be in our hands."[155]

These government communications may cause some surprise if one recalls that, in Naples at least, the police had already had to occupy themselves seriously with the local section of the International, arresting its leaders in February 1870,[156] and that it was still very worried about the best known and most active of them, the advocate Carlo Gambuzzi, seeking to trail him step by step on his voyages abroad, where he figured as one of the chieftains of the movement in Italy.[157] They were also assiduously following Carlo Cafiero,[158] the noble from Barletta who from that time forth would often be the cause of tiresome and vexatious bureaucratic paperwork for Italian diplomats abroad. London was the great center for subversive leaders, and Italians were being spotted more frequently there;[159] indeed the government began to think it might be necessary to hire a private detective expressly to keep track of Gambuzzi, La Cecilia, Cafiero, Zanardelli, and their companions. This proposal originated, logically, from the Italian legation in London, which had little talent, or appetite, for getting involved in police work, and which was placed in a difficult position by the fact that, contrary to what the legation in Paris could expect from a prefect of police generally willing to supply his Italian colleagues with secret information on this or that personage, the English police totally refused such collaboration and left foreigners alone, at least until they had broken the law of the land.[160] The pro-

taken place between Bakunin and the Freemasons in 1864–65 (cf. Nettlau, *Bakunin e l'Internazionale in Italia*, pp. 22–24, 46–47, and 58).

[155] 16 October 1871, in Marx and Engels, "Carteggio da e per l'Italia (1871–1895)," ed. G. Bosio, in *Movimento Operaio* 2, nos. 3–4 (December 1949–January 1950): 87.

[156] Cf. Rosselli, *Mazzini e Bakounine*, pp. 268–69; Nettlau, *Bakunin e l'Internazionale in Italia*, pp. 167 ff. On similar groups more or less throughout the Mezzogiorno, esp. in Puglia, see A. Lucarelli, *Carlo Cafiero*, p. 19. Clear signs of official optimism are still found in Forni, *L'Internazionale e lo Stato*, p. 50, who calculates the number of persons affiliated to the International in Italy at not more than two thousand, compared to almost two million such affiliated persons in Europe. And Forni had been *questore* in Naples for four years (cf. n. 24 above).

[157] Interior ministry to the foreign ministry, 7 September and 2 October 1871 (nos. 3413 and 3762). Gambuzzi was supposed to represent the Naples section at a meeting in London on 17 September (AE, *Rapp. Inghilterra*: this information came from a letter confiscated from Cafiero). The meeting took place "in a tavern situated at no. 17 Percy Street" with the participation of an Italian, probably Gambuzzi; cf. Maffei, report, 25 September (no. 248). On the activity of Gambuzzi, see also Marx and Engels, "Carteggio da e per l'Italia," in *Movimento Operaio* 1, no. 1 (October 1949): 8; no. 2 (November 1949): 47 ff.; vol. 2, nos. 3–4 (December 1949–January 1950): 90 ff. On the new steps taken against the internationalists of Naples in August 1871, ibid., no. 2, p. 51, and nos. 3–4, pp. 92–93; Nettlau, *Bakunin e l'Internazionale in Italia*, pp. 225 ff.

[158] Interior ministry to the foreign ministry, 7 September 1871 (no. 3413).

[159] "[A]t the moment there is an unusual degree of movement and coming and going by communists between the continent and this country [Britain] . . . and the number of Italian revolutionaries in London is also greater than usual" (Maffei, report, 25 September, no. 248). But on 31 August (no. 239) he had already written: "I know from a number of sources that members of the International have a very active center here at this moment, and from a private informant . . . I have learned that the infamous Félix Pyat and La Cecilia recently succeeded in taking refuge in London."

[160] The necessity of having a salaried special agent in London, it being "impossible to obtain here the assistance of the police in affairs of this nature," is emphasized by the ambassador, Carlo Cadorna, on 5 May 1871 (report no. 215). This is a response to Lanza's request of 21 April (n. 150 above) for information on presumed contacts between the leaders of the International in London and

posal was accepted by the interior ministry and was put into action at the end of 1871, and subsequently there were further proposals for the creation of a genuine Italian secret service in the British capital.[161]

But it is clear that, despite their attention to individual cases such as these, overall the government still viewed the efforts of the reds as not being dangerous; or rather it continued to concentrate primarily on the party of action and on Mazzini, who was always a source of concern, even in death, so much so that he inspired the government to take steps of very doubtful legality.[162] Gambuzzi and Cafiero and their like were mostly seen as possible or probable allies of the much older and more deeply rooted Mazzinian movement. The "subversive" enterprises of May 1871 were still, for Giovanni Lanza, those of the party of action;[163] the word still retained its pristine significance, and the time had not yet come when the minister of the interior would see, swelling up behind the customary "subversionism" of the republicans, the more dangerous "subversionism" of the reds, for the latter were still evaluated on a modest scale, as the auxiliary troops of the former.

This is the explanation for Visconti Venosta's optimism, which was rapidly followed by the gloom of April. His optimism was increased by the fact that fears about the return from France of the Garibaldians, who were viewed with suspicion as red agitators by the governments of France and Italy, proved groundless as their return went smoothly.[164] The result was that, far from supporting interna-

---

the leaders of the party of action in Italy. Following further requests from the interior ministry, Cadorna repeated that it was necessary to have a private agent (report no. 225, 10 July). There was a new exchange of notes between the foreign ministry and the interior ministry (a dispatch from the latter of 5 August); and another report of Maffei on 31 August (no. 239), in which he returns to the fact that the authorities in England do indeed maintain surveillance of the doings of the International, "but in accordance with the customs and principles of the British constitution, the results of their investigations are kept strictly secret." And on 2 October (and again on 18 November), the interior minister agreed that an agent might be hired for some months, under the immediate orders of the London legation. The agent's first report was forwarded from Cadorna to Rome on 22 January 1872 (no. 266). But the results were not, according to Cadorna, satisfactory, and the agent asked for, and received, a higher remuneration (Cadorna, report, 29 July, no. 322).

[161] This was also a suggestion of Cadorna (report, 13 November 1872, no. 365): if Rome wants the Italian legation in London to be informed of what the International is doing, and of its contacts with Italy, it is necessary to organize a police service, with an experienced person in charge, and a number of employees to carry out the research. Such an organization would cost £240 sterling annually, or 6,000 lire. There is no record of any steps having been taken to create such a service.

[162] On 21 March 1872 the cabinet decided "to annul the deliberations of municipalities that have proposed to commemorate Mazzini by erecting monuments or giving his name to piazze and streets, since they have gone beyond the bounds of municipal administration and infringed on political matters." Less than a year later, on 26 January 1873, the same cabinet decided "that there is no reason to consider subscriptions by municipalities for the monument to Napoleon III a political matter, and therefore no reason to forbid them" (ACR, *Verbali delle deliberazioni del Consiglio dei Ministri* 2:112 and 132; Lanza, *Le carte* 8:667 and 681).

[163] Thus in the dispatch of 21 April 1871 to the foreign ministry (n. 150 above).

[164] Lanza stated to Choiseul, the French envoy at Florence, that it was past doubt that Garibaldi and his two sons were affiliated to the International (Choiseul, report, 5 June 1871, no. 104; AEP, *C.P., Italie*, t. 382, fol. 111). On Garibaldi's attitude to the International see Rosselli, *Mazzini e Bakounine*, passim and esp. pp. 205 ff., 317 ff., and 386 ff.; Nettlau, *Bakunin e l'Internazionale in Italia*, passim and esp. pp. 214 ff. and 244; Fonterossi, "Garibaldi e l'Internazionale," pp. 9 ff. and 65 ff. On the relations between Marx and Engels and Ricciotti Garibaldi, who went to London to visit

tional agreements against the sect, the foreign minister of Vittorio Emanuele confined himself, in the following months, to giving his assent to proposals that arrived from Berlin in July regarding several measures that the different governments ought to take (that is, to share with one another the data they gathered on the International and its agents, which later in effect happened), and to declaring that as a general principle he concurred with the view that attempts on life and property of the sort that had taken place in Paris fell into the category of common delinquency, not that of political crime, and so were subject to extradition.[165]

In truth Visconti Venosta did not insist that a declaration of general principle should be made about this second point. He merely observed that he had already informed France that he was prepared to apply the extradition treaty to those who had committed homicide or incendiary acts at Paris, and that he was also prepared to repeat the same procedure in the case of Germany or any other power.[166] By confining himself to this specific event, the devastation of Paris, he avoided having to compromise himself with a general declaration of principle, which would in any case have exceeded his competence and passed over into the competence of parliament. It was a fine point, of course, but a fine point that gave the exact measure of the shift to optimism in the outlook of the foreign minister, and perhaps especially of his substantial reluctance (and with him, that of the governing moderates) to move to a reactionary policy.

Analogously, he informed the French government of the "firm intention" of the Italian government to cooperate with it in the defense of the social order, prevent-

---

Marx, cf. Marx and Engels, "Carteggio da e per l'Italia," in *Movimento Operaio* 2, nos. 3–4 (December 1949–January 1950): 89–90.

[165] The German proposal was communicated to Visconti Venosta by Count Brassier de Saint Simon on 10 July 1871. In the communication it is said that the action of the International has been manifested in Italy "in the riot at Pavia in March 1870, in the brigandage in Calabria, and the agitations in Sicily. Furthermore, after 18 March past, a great number of the Garibaldians who had taken up arms in France against the German troops drew notice as open partisans of the Paris Commune. It is evident that the return of these individuals to France will only redouble their activity" (AE, *Rapp. Germania*). It was partly to counter such largely mistaken assessments that Visconti Venosta sounded an optimistic note in his dispatch to de Launay, also of 10 July (see following note).

[166] Visconti Venosta, dispatch to de Launay, 10 July 1871, no. 216. The tenor of Bismarck's request was "to adopt as a preliminary the principle that attempts on life and property, of the kind that took place in Paris, belong to the category of common crime and not political crime." The Italian reply was in full agreement on the reciprocal exchange of information: "we warmly accept the proposition of His Highness Prince Bismarck concerning the reciprocal exchange of information regarding the organization and the plans of the International." On the second point, this was the tenor of the Italian reply: "As for the declaration to be made on the subject of the crimes and felonies of which it would be the pretext, I have only to remind you . . . that we were the first to declare to France that we were disposed to apply the conventions on extradition to the authors of the homicides and burnings of which Paris was the theater. We are prepared to repeat this declaration vis-à-vis Germany, or any other power. In my opinion that ought to suffice to attain the end proposed by the Prince Chancellor." The declaration to France to which he refers had been made on 31 May, in the form of a note of Visconti Venosta to Count Choiseul (AEP, *C.P., Italie*, t. 382, fols. 100, 101, 109. For other steps taken to increase vigilance at the borders, and the thanks of Jules Favre see ibid., fols. 83 and 88. Cf. *A.P., Senato*, 2 June 1871, p. 1010. For Bismarck's thinking see *Gesammelten Werke* 6c:7–8 (in Vienna, 7 June).

ing "the diffusion of the pernicious doctrines that are threatening Europe with a new barbarism." But the measures taken had to be "compatible with our institutions and our customs,"[167] and since the institutions, and even more than the institutions, the customs and the spirit in which the institutions were understood, were frankly and committedly liberal, it was clear that the king's government would not go too far in repression.

At that juncture, then, Visconti Venosta assumed a much more liberal attitude generally than the French (who were obviously influenced by the nightmare of the burnings and massacres in Paris), but also than the Russians and Germans. Bismarck's proposal had been the result of discussions that had taken place in Berlin between the chancellor and Prince Gorchakov, both of whom were animated by a holy zeal against international banditism,[168] to which Berlin and St. Petersburg both attributed an excessive diffusion and potency,[169] a conviction in which they were supported by their respective sovereigns and by other Prussian statesmen, one of whom, Count Eulenburg, the secretary of state for the interior ministry, declared his belief that the danger of a general revolt had only been postponed, and that the day would come "when we shall have to give battle to this social vermin."[170] Bismarck's proposal was derived from the ideas of the

---

[167] Visconti Venosta, dispatch to Nigra, 10 July 1871, no. 322, concerning the invitation of Jules Favre to the other powers to take common action (cf. M. Reclus, *Jules Favre* [Paris, 1912], pp. 493–94). The French chargé d'affaires, de la Villestreux, informed Favre of the "complete support" of the Italian minister for his ideas; in fact it was not complete (cf. his report of 12 July, no. 109; AEP, *C.P., Italie*, t. 382, fol. 215). In his dispatches to Nigra and de Launay on this date, Visconti Venosta recalls the precautions already taken by the Italian government, "the preventive measures that were compatible with our institutions." He recalls the recent legislative dispositions on the protection of persons and property, which give the government "a greater latitude for the defense of order." Rémusat, who succeeded Favre at the end of July, made efforts to attenuate, formally, the extent of the French requests (saying he had no intention of conjuring up a species of Holy Alliance against the International). Hence he stated that he viewed as sufficient the reciprocal exchange of information promised by the Italian government (Ressmann, report, 18 August, no. 1614). But in Berlin, on the other hand, he let it be known, even later on, that he viewed anticipatory measures as appropriate, meaning that the sole fact of belonging to the International should be considered a crime: thus he showed himself more "repressive" than he had done to the Italian government (Tosi, report, 28 September 1871, no. 878).

[168] On the anxiety felt by King Wilhelm, Bismarck, and in general by the government elite in Berlin because of the International, there is much information in de Gabriac, *Souvenirs diplomatiques de Russie et d'Allemagne (1870–1872)* (Paris, 1896), pp. 233 ff., esp. 238, 242 ff. Cf. as well L. Schneider, *L'empereur Guillaume: Souvenirs intimes* 3:279–80 (French translation: Paris, 1888).

[169] Two million followers! (de Launay, report, 12 June 1871, no. 832).

[170] Statements of Gorchakov and Count Eulenburg to de Launay (de Launay, report, 5 June 1871, no. 825). That the initiative came from Gorchakov is explicitly affirmed by the prince himself to de Launay: "The cabinet in St. Petersburg has ordered its different legations to compile reports in this regard [the International], to follow closely the intrigues of these dangerous associations. Prince Gorchakov proposed to speak of it to the emperor of Germany, and had no doubt that His Majesty would take the same view that all the governments should join together to guard ourselves against international banditism." After the failure of his initiative, Gorchakov said, in the course of fresh discussions with de Launay in the autumn, that he did not believe "in the possibility of formulating an accord on this important matter among the different countries. The diversity of their legislations would be one of the principal obstacles; but nothing would prevent each government from taking energetic measures at home in order better to protect itself against this worm gnawing at Europe" (de Launay, report, 2 November 1871, no. 897). Wilhelm I of Germany complained of this refusal by the

Russian chancellor on the importance of the solidarity of all the governments against the sect.[171]

Visconti Venosta, in contrast, remained much closer to the attitude, frankly and forthrightly liberal, of the English government, which, through its spokesman Granville, consented in general terms "to take part through an exchange of views in a process of mutual enlightenment on the intrigues and the means for action of the international association." The English government, however, declined the proposal to consider the crimes of the members of the International as ordinary felonies, viewing it as a very delicate question that fell under the competence of the courts rather than that of the government,[172] and reaffirming instead the right of asylum and English "liberty." Berlin viewed this as "a formal refusal,"[173] and the attitude of the Austrian chancellor, Beust, led to practically

---

Russian chancellor to take the necessary measures (*Occupation et libération du territoire, 1871–1873, Correspondances* 1:155 [Paris, 1900]). It is highly significant that Eulenburg attributed a large part of the responsibility for the Commune "to the Utopians and the nefarious liberals who, without foreseeing the consequences, have helped for years to sustain and revive the revolutionary spirit," since in declarations of this kind there emerges clearly the attitude not only anti-international but also antiliberal that characterized the polemic of the clericals in Italy against the events of Paris.

[171] De Launay, report, 12 June 1871, no. 832. Bismarck has informed the Italian envoy of the importance attributed by the Russian government, and by the Tsar personally, "to ensuring that the different powers show their solidarity in maintaining surveillance over, and combating, the tendencies of an association that counted more than two million adepts. His Highness did not doubt that we would share, as the cabinet of Berlin does, these views on the necessity of opposing a barrier to these doctrines, which are the negation of all social order. The Imperial Chancellor said he had no need to give us advice. But he believed that we would be acting wisely if we ordered our mission in Russia to let them see a dispatch establishing that our government abundantly shares these views. By doing so, we would produce the best effect on the spirit of the Tsar. It is an opportunity that it would be a good idea for us not to overlook." At the same time the German chancellor informed de Launay of the request that Brassier de Saint Simon had been ordered to put to Visconti Venosta, on which see n. 165 above.

[172] Cf. H. Rothfels, *Bismarcks englische Bündnispolitik* (Berlin-Leipzig, 1924), p. 13, and also Meine, *England und Deutschland*, p. 77. These two authors accentuate the "foreign policy" element in Bismarck's request, in the sense that, by proposing the creation of a common front against the International, Bismarck was seeking principally to draw England closer to himself. But the Italian documents, especially the reports of de Launay, run counter to this interpretation. The initiative came from Russia first, and for reasons of internal politics and ideology. The invitation was extended not only to England (as Rothfels, who only knew the Bismarck-Bernstorff correspondence, had supposed) but also to Italy, Austria, and even France. There is therefore no reason to imagine ulterior purposes in regard to England, to speak of "first tentative soundings" (N. Japikse, *Europa und Bismarcks Friedenspolitik: Die Internationalen Beziehungen von 1871 bis 1890* [Berlin, 1927], p. 21). Furthermore Bismarck, who knew very well the tendencies of the English in general, and the Gladstone cabinet in particular, where domestic "liberties" were concerned, would have given proof of a singular lack of political sense if he had tried to create closer ties with the United Kingdom by proposing to it an unwelcome accord, and reproaching it for the "moral responsibility" that it was assuming by harboring the adherents of the International (in his dispatch to Bernstorff of 14 June 1871). In his anger at the International, Bismarck was evidently sincere in that moment: the proof is that two months later, in discussions at Gastein, he took the matter up again with Beust, to persuade him to join in the repression of the International. And Bismarck's sovereign, Wilhelm I, was insisting on the same thing too, both to Beust and to Franz Joseph himself (Beust, *Trois quarts de Siècle, Mémoires* 2:491–92, 499; and cf. below p. 366). Cf. too the discussion with Gorchakov in April 1873, in Goriaïnov, *La question d'Orient à la veille du traité de Berlin (1870–1876)* (Paris, 1948), p. 51.

[173] Thus the secretary at the Ministry of Foreign Affairs, von Thile (de Launay, report, 15 July 1871, no. 848).

the same conclusion. Beust had formally welcomed the proposal, but had asked for more information on the sect, its organization, and the number of its adherents, and once in possession of this data no longer spoke of the matter to the German ambassador, Schweinitz. Later, at the meeting at Gastein in August, faced with Bismarck's insistence on the danger posed by the International, Austria proposed a working plan, but one based more on social improvements than on repression. The combined approach of the Russians and Germans was met by a liberal front, with England in the avant-garde but with Italy and even Austria substantially aligned.[174]

Equally, it is worth noting that the English minister, like his Italian opposite number, also had recourse to the argument that the International posed only a slight danger in order to justify his response.[175] This was still the prevalent opinion in the United Kingdom,[176] where there was a robust and, where England was concerned, well-founded optimism about the future.

The Italian government continued in the sequel to maintain the same, indeed an even more salient, attitude of fundamental liberalism, not just where unimportant incidents were concerned[177] but also when the question of extradition was put on the table once more in the early months of 1872 by the governments of France and Spain, the two nations that appeared to have the most reason to fear the activities of the reds—France because of the memory of the Commune, Spain because of the anarcho-revolutionary plots that alternated with the plots of the Carlists. On 9 February 1872 the Madrid government sent a circular to its legations abroad directing them to inform the various European powers that Madrid felt it was necessary that they all agree to examine and decide on the best measures with which to combat the International, suggesting that the case of persons belonging to the association be included in the extradition treaties, or in

---

[174] As for France, which was already promoting diplomatic action against the International, it understandably assumed an attitude of reserve toward the German proposal. "M. Thiers told the count of Waldersee that such a question merited serious examination, and that he would give him a reply in due course" (de Launay, report, 15 July 1871, no. 848).

[175] "For the rest, Lord Granville did not appear to attribute a very great size to the International, or think its propaganda dangerous, at least where England was concerned" (de Launay, report, 15 July 1871, no. 848).

[176] "In England the opinion prevails that the 'International' society does not exercise much sway over the working classes, which are united in associations based, of course, on democratic-radical principles, but which are not communist in the same manner as the affiliations that mostly exist among the working classes on the continent. It is believed, therefore, that even if the 'International' has been able to attract a certain number of imprudent persons into it, when the English masses realize the perversity and the negation of every social principle that animates this sect, they will hastily cut all their ties to it" (Maffei, report, 31 October 1871, no. 255).

[177] Thus, when in July 1871 the French government asked permission to send two police agents to Italy for the purpose of aiding the local authorities in the hunt for individuals who had participated in the Commune, Lanza, the interior minister, considered it preferable "that the two agents be allowed entry into the kingdom like any other foreigners in order to carry out their researches, but without taking any actions that might have the appearance of public functions through a direct or indirect coordination with our authorities. Naturally they would retain the right to advance, through their nation's representative, all the requests permitted by national interests and by the treaties in effect" (to the foreign ministry, 25 July 1871; AE, *Rapp. Francia*). This was very clearly a *fin de non recevoir* [a rebuff].

special accords.[178] Not long after, on 13–14 March 1872, the National Assembly in France debated and passed a law—which had been promoted since August 1871, but which was presented only now by the parliamentary committee— against the International. The law was followed, in April 1872, by a new request to the government in Rome, and to the others, that after so much discussion they should allow the extradition of all who were discovered to belong to the association.[179]

The French and Spanish initiatives both came to the same conclusion. They encountered a very different reception from the German, Russian, and Austrian courts on one hand, and the British government on the other. The German government was not disposed to accept the extradition of those affiliated to the International for that reason alone, but it did accept extradition for the authors of crimes committed "in consequence" of such affiliation.[180] The Russian government, the most reactionary, was always ready for rigorous measures,[181] and the

---

[178] AE, *Rapp. Spagna*; cf. the dispatch of Visconti Venosta to Robilant, 27 February 1872, no. 25 (and similar dispatches to other legations). The circular expresses the desire that one of the great powers should assume the burden of firming up the bases of the accord. De Launay, in a report of 26 February (no. 953), speaks of the idea of a treaty, or at least of a special accord for extradition, as being contained in the Spanish circular. On the actions of the minister Sagasta against the International, which was outlawed, cf. J. Guillaume, *L'Internationale. Documents et souvenirs (1864–1878)* 2:273.

[179] It was communicated to Visconti Venosta by Fournier, the French envoy, on 16 April 1872 (and also by Rémusat to Nigra on 22 April). The proposal is to complete the Franco-Italian convention on extradition by signing an extra article that would extend its application to include crimes mentioned in the French law of 14 March 1872. It is important to note that in this law the sole fact of being affiliated to the International, or to any other association professing the same doctrines and having the same ends, is considered a crime. The bill as originally presented in the summer of 1871 had contained a second part, which was omitted in the final text of the law, against citizens suspected of separatist intrigues (according to Nigra's report of 22 February 1872, no. 1803, this part was aimed at intrigues taking place in Nice and Savoy). On this law and the exchanges of views that took place with other governments, Hanotaux, *Histoire de la France contemporaine* 1:403, is very summary. Note that when in May Lanza proposed a continuous exchange of information between the French and Italian governments on the International (below, n. 198, with references there), Rémusat insisted again on the idea of completing the extradition treaty—but without result: the Italian government let the matter drop.

[180] Thile's declarations to de Launay: the German government is prepared to conclude, on this basis, a treaty of extradition with Spain. But it will still have to examine "whether the present laws of the empire governing the right of association could be modified in this sense," something that de Launay doubted (de Launay, report, 2 March 1872, no. 956). Subsequently, there was another exchange of views among Berlin, Vienna, and St. Petersburg (de Launay, report, 22 April, no. 996). The French law of 14 March did not displease Berlin, which found that it contained principles and dispositions "which it might be possible to adopt in Germany as well, in order to provide protection against such a dangerous association" (Thile, declarations to de Launay, in de Launay's report of 25 March, no. 979). But, it was noted in St. Petersburg, the difficulty of establishing an accord was great, especially with Germany, "in light of the tenor of the Prussian legislation, which did not encompass preventive measures against such a highly dangerous association, though its political aims were not a mystery, while its ostensible, purely economic and social aims, were in themselves of such a kind as not to give rise to legal sanction" (statements of the emperor Alexander II to the Spanish envoy; Caracciolo, letter from St. Petersburg, 7/19 March 1872).

[181] Gorchakov, however, observed that "the Spanish document appeared to him to have been conceived and expressed in too general and indeterminate a form, and it would be necessary, before entering negotiations on a committed basis, to define exactly what cases would be taken into consideration, and the specifically criminal acts of the affiliates [of the International] subject to the sanction of the treaty" (Caracciolo, letter cited in the previous note). Gorchakov foresaw a "special extradition aimed at the International."

Austrian one, with Andrássy replacing the liberal Beust, was quite willing to approve the Spanish proposal,[182] to the extent that Berlin did so too. But the British government once more declined the invitation from Madrid.[183]

Once again the government in Rome revealed that it was substantially inclined to follow the English approach of laisser faire, of taking no action, as opposed to rigorous general measures of prevention. First the minister of the interior, Lanza,[184] and then the minister of justice, De Falco,[185] informed their colleague, the foreign minister, of the impossibility of acceding to the French and Spanish demands.

It is true that from the purely formal standpoint, as Lanza noted "with satisfaction," the Italian position was not dissimilar to that of the Germans, at least where the Spanish request was concerned, since both refused to accept extradition for the simple fact of belonging to the sect. But in their hearts the politicians

---

[182] "Count Andrássy then said to me: 'yes, this is a question in which it seems to me we should coordinate our policies, inasmuch as the idea put forward by Spain seems to me a fairly practical and efficacious one: to extend, by an international action, the extradition permitted for common crimes to persons charged with actions deriving from their affiliation to the International. It would not seem to me difficult to achieve, if Austria, Italy, and Germany could agree on it'" (Robilant, report, 15 March 1872, no. 64).

[183] De Launay, report, 22 April, no. 996. De Launay naturally finds the British refusal "highly regrettable," given that anticipatory or reactive measures on the continent would lose their effectiveness as long as England granted asylum to members of the International. But Thile tells him that the English reply will not deter the German government "from devoting all its efforts to combating cosmopolitan intrigues, and facilitating, if possible, an understanding with the states that believe, as it does, that the system of *laisser faire* is inappropriate in such a case."

[184] Lanza to Visconti Venosta, 2 March 1872, no. 1231, ris. (AE, *Rapp. Spagna*) and 8 April 1872, no. 2282, ris. As things stand, there is lacking "adequate grounds and legal basis for an extension of the current extradition treaties that would embrace cases of affiliation and membership in the association. . . . There is no need to remind you of the liberal interpretation that prevailed where the right of association is concerned, both in the debates and proceedings of parliament, and in the Council of State; or of the breadth of philosophic, political, and religious discussion allowed by our press laws. As long as an association is formed around an economic and political program, even one inspired by the most absurd sophisms of the socialist school, the executive power cannot apply penal repression if it does not perceive any breach of the law or any positive threat of destruction of the existing order." Furthermore, there is no advantage in beginning trials that in most cases only succeed in making the association one is trying to combat better known. A crime commences only when "from the area of vague aspirations for a new order of things . . . a person passes to the deed, or the direct preparation for one through agreements and attempts to commit an offense against property or persons. In such circumstances the dispositions of our penal code, and the list of crimes for which we concede extradition . . . provide for the most relevant cases." The International, especially in Italy, is in any case "in a very rudimentary stage of formation"; and in such conditions "it is at present difficult to determine the cases which ought to be covered by penal dispositions, and thus it is also more difficult to decide what new crimes ought to be added to the list of those for which extraction [*sic*, i.e., extradition] is contemplated." The substance of this note by Lanza of 8 April (AE, *Rapp. Germania*) was then communicated on 12 April by Artom to de Launay (dispatch no. 244).

[185] The French proposal is discussed in a communication of De Falco to Visconti Venosta, 26 April 1872. The conclusion is: "if, however, the deeds imputable to persons affiliated to the International constitute one of the crimes enumerated in article 2 [of the Italo-French convention of extradition of 12 May 1870], or even a crime not enumerated there but recognized by Italian law, extradition should be and can be granted according to the extant norms. But beyond such cases, the king's government, with the best will in the world, would find itself unable to consent to requests that were made, because the simple fact of being affiliated to the International is not included among the crimes or felonies in the Italian penal code. And so, as long as the present state of the legislation is not changed, it would be pointless or superfluous to stipulate an accord in the sense proposed by the French government" (AE, *Rapp. Francia*).

of Rome were much closer to the attitude of Granville and Gladstone, an attitude unalloyedly and profoundly liberal, entirely imbued with what, in the realm of domestic policy, could be considered the informing principle of English liberalism, and thus of European liberalism: this was the principle of reacting to crime, not taking anticipatory measures against it. This principle would later be endorsed by two exponents of the Left, Cairoli[186] and, especially, Zanardelli;[187] in doing so they would be opposing Crispi, who was already promoting the necessity of anticipatory measures and was destined to become a zealot for strong government.[188] In any case, it was the same principle that guided the Right in 1871–72. The nucleus of an important speech to the Chamber on 10 December 1878, in which Francesco De Sanctis maintained the absolute indispensability of liberty of thought and expression,[189] could already be found in Lanza's communication to Visconti Venosta. Every association was free to adhere to an economic and political program, "even one inspired by the most absurd sophisms of the socialist school." As always, the liberals were convinced that the state could only make use of "those moral forces that constitute the health of the nation,"[190] and "respect legality and justice."

We suffered so much from arbitrariness—one of the Italian statesmen told the French envoy, Fournier, in the summer of 1872—when we had to obey the caprices of a throng of governments, that we want to believe in legality now that we feel ourselves strong enough to be a nation, united and free. And we have sufficient foresight not to believe in liberty except in the law. Fournier commented that there was no reason to fear that Italy would take special measures against the Jesuits similar to the violent policy of Bismarck; the Jesuits, like the International,[191] against which the Italian government had refused to pass special legislation, would be dealt with under the general statutes. The Italians, he went on,

---

[186] Cf. Cairoli, *Discorso pronunciato in Pavia . . . il 15 ottobre 1878* (Rome, 1878), p. 6: "The government authorities should be watchful that the public order is not disturbed; they should be inexorable in reacting, not arbitrary in forestalling."

[187] In the election speech at Iseo, 3 November 1878, and in a speech to the Chamber on 5 December (*A.P., Camera*, pp. 3077, 3081; and cf. as well 6 December, pp. 3085, 3089).

[188] "The political authority has the right to take anticipatory measures, just as the judicial authority has the right to react when crimes are committed." And anticipatory measures "consist in a complex of acts of prudence; in many cautious, secure, and moral provisions through which the government upholds the public peace without falling into arbitrariness. To exercise them is difficult. Those who do so must have not only foresight but also a strong sentiment of justice and a very strong morality" (Crispi, *Discorsi Parlamentari* 2:313 (5 December 1878). Here the extremely fuzzy criteria to be used in taking anticipatory measures, which in the last analysis are entrusted to the perspicacity of those in power, foreshadow the tendency to entrust government to the able individual, something for which Crispi expresses a wish in the same speech (though always with ringing praise for liberty, which is "our idol, our life").

[189] De Sanctis, *Scritti politici*, pp. 220 ff.

[190] The expression is Bonghi's; he was very much opposed to the International, but also opposed to the French law, and in general to any use of exceptional measures. Cf. the political review in *Nuova Antologia* 19 (30 March 1872): 921, and the review for 31 August in vol. 21 (1872), p. 222. The following phrase quoted in the text is from Lanza's note of 2 March 1872, no. 1231, cited at n. 184.

[191] This parallel between the Jesuits and the International, made by Fournier, who was certainly persona non grata to the clericals, and who had to leave Rome after the fall of Thiers, caused someone in the offices of the Quai d'Orsay to add an "!" in the margin of his report.

have too much experience of secret societies, and the propaganda advantage they gain from violent and exceptional laws, to wish to create martyrs; their statesmen have a strong belief that time and legal process will resolve even the most apparently compromising and complicated situations. In the parliament and in the country, it is the spirit of legality that reigns.[192]

This was certainly proof of the deep seriousness and solidity of the liberal convictions of the moderates. For the truth is that this reaffirmation of the right of free association was no longer due to the soothing feeling that nothing was amiss. Lanza might well repeat in the spring of 1872 that the "international association, in Italy especially, is anyhow in a very rudimentary state of formation, and is still grappling laboriously with the problem of deciding how to contrive a line of conduct and take concrete action." He might assure the French envoy to the Quirinal that, being very precisely informed on the activities of the International in Italy, he was not worried at all, and did not fear its capacity to propagandize, since it only had three or four thousand affiliates and there was dissension between the internationalists and the Mazzinians—and Garibaldi, who wanted to bring them together, lacked the necessary gifts of organization; the only danger on the horizon, not a grave one, was that the International might link up with the Masonic lodges, which had lost their former conspiratorial reason for existence.[193] Yet the minister himself was not perhaps as much at ease as he had appeared to be in the summer and autumn of the previous year.

More was happening than just the arrival of news from abroad that confirmed the diffusion of the International in other countries, or the links between its sections abroad and the Italian ones.[194] From January 1872 the Ministry of the Interior had noted an unusual level of activity among the Mazzinians and internationalists, aimed at a combined, and imminent, revolutionary action, to be synchronized with an analogous movement in France.[195] The date announced for this event, 24 February, passed without incident, north or south of the Alps. Still Lanza continued to receive alarming notices, some of them the usual fantasies.[196] The French and Austrian authorities reported frequent trips by known or

[192] Fournier, report, 12 August 1872, no. 46; AEP, *C.P., Italie*, t. 385, fol. 295 r-v.

[193] Fournier, report, 31 May 1872, no. 23, cited above at n. 154; AEP, *C.P., Italie*, t. 385, fols. 128 ff.

[194] The Vienna section was said to be entering into contact "with a few individuals of the demagogic party" in Italy (interior ministry to foreign ministry, 4 December 1871, no. 5063; AE, *Rapp. Austria*).

[195] Interior ministry to foreign ministry, 27 January 1872, no. 553 (AE, *Rapp. Francia*): the contents were communicated by Artom to Nigra on 28 January, and by Nigra to the French foreign minister, Rémusat. The French government had already been informed that on 24 February there would be an attempt to hold a demonstration in a French city, and had taken the required measures (Nigra, report, 8 February, no. 1793). On 22 February there was a new communication from the interior ministry to the foreign ministry, which mentions the possibility of a revolutionary action in Spain (no. 1055). Cf. the article in the *Journal des Débats* in December 1871 (Rosselli, *Mazzini e Bakounine*, p. 396, n. 2).

[196] On 8 March 1872, Lanza forwarded to Visconti Venosta (no. 1393) two highly secret circulars from the "Comitato Generale del Risorgimento Sociale" ("General Committee of the Social Uprising"; but called simply "Comitato Generale" in the second), of London, dated 24 September 1871 [written "1872"] and 5 February 1872. They are signed, respectively, E. Woordel [*sic*?] and

presumed agents of the sect,[197] and there resulted an increased exchange of communications about police matters between the ministries of the interior and foreign affairs, and between the latter and its diplomatic representatives abroad, who were perhaps not terribly pleased to be stuck with a new and unwelcome task.[198]

Engels and concern talks with Napoleon III. At first the Committee had made a commitment to the emperor's camp adjutant, Viscount Baute de Liverny "to give potent assistance toward the return of the house of Bonaparte to the throne of France, certain that if we succeed, we shall have made a great step toward our goal of uprising and social emancipation." (About this the interior ministry had already transmitted to the foreign ministry on 17 October 1871 [no. 4039] two circulars signed by Woordel of 4 and 8 October 1871; AE, *Rapp. Francia.*) When Napoleon III failed to live up "to several parts of our contract," the Committee decided on 3 February 1872 to "try a double movement in France and in Spain, and seize power at a stroke." In a further dispatch to the foreign ministry on the same date (no. 1421), Lanza stated that, in conformity with these orders, the general inspectorate of the Social Uprising in Rome "is telling the Italian sections of the International to hold themselves in readiness for an insurrectional movement, which they believe will be favored by present conditions in Europe" (AE, *Rapp. Inghilterra*). This project was a fantasy, of course, even though it is certain that there were contacts between Bonapartist circles and former communard elements (cf. R. Schnerb, *Rouher et le Second Empire* [Paris, 1949], pp. 296–98); probably there is some connection with the curious but real enterprise in 1870–71 of two "internationalists" of Lyon, Albert Richard and Gaspard Blanc, who had made concrete offers to Napoleon III, and published, in January 1872, an appeal in favor of the emperor; for this they had been condemned as traitors by Marx and the International (Guillaume, *L'Internationale* 2:256–57 and 260–61; and Nettlau, *Bakunin e l'Internazionale in Italia*, pp. 338–39.

[197] In February and March 1872 there was correspondence between the interior ministry and the foreign ministry, and between the foreign ministry and Nigra and the French government, concerning a certain Antonio Rocher, a Frenchman affiliated with the International who had participated in the insurrection of Lyon in 1871 and was now propagandizing in Naples, until he was expelled in March. His expulsion gave rise to a parliamentary question by the hon. Friscia in the Chamber (*A.P., Camera*, p. 1239, 19 March 1972). Another agitator in Naples was a Frenchman of Italian origin, Giuseppe Polio, who apparently had been Félix Pyat's secretary, and on whom reports arrived from the Parisian prefect of police (Nigra, reports of 25 April and 11 May, nos. 1842 and 1850). And on 14 June Fournier signaled to Visconti Venosta the departure from Geneva for Turin of a certain Gaillard, an agent of the International.

[198] Between April and August 1872, Nigra, in Paris, was required to try to trace a few individuals from Perugia, all reputed to belong to the "radical party," who had set out for France and caused the interior ministry in Rome to become alarmed (interior ministry to foreign ministry, 3 April). In vain the Italian diplomat assured Rome, as early as 7 May and again on 14 May, that according to the French police their trip had no political motivation. When these suspect persons had not returned to Italy by 25 June, the interior ministry asked for further information; and from Paris the reply was to exclude once again political motives (Nigra, report, 27 August, no. 1908). In September the French foreign minister, Rémusat, reported the departure for Italy of Mario Casaï, Marco Héridier, and Guyot, accompanied by ten other persons: according to Rémusat, this trip by these members of the International had greater importance than one might think at first, since their aim was to reach Rome and prepare for a general insurrection there (Nigra, reports, 3 and 8 September 1872, nos. 1910 and 1914). In December there was a fruitless investigation at Marseilles, with the cordial collaboration of the French authorities, of presumed shipments of arms and bombs to Italy, following the discovery of bombs near Livorno (interior ministry to foreign ministry, 28 November, and report of the consul general at Marseilles, Strambio, on 20 December, no. 78).

After the French envoy to the Quirinal had sent further information to Visconti Venosta, who forwarded it to Lanza (a report of the French consul at Genoa on the doings of the International and Garibaldi; Lanza responded to Visconti Venosta pointing out the inexactness of this information and reaffirming that the International had few followers and no resources: Fournier, report, 28 May 1872, no. 20, with an attached letter of Lanza to Visconti Venosta in translation; AEP, *C.P., Italie*, t. 385, fols. 111–12), a regular exchange of information between Italy and France was decided on, following a proposal made to Fournier by Lanza. The French interior minister did point out that the information from France would not always be complete, because the International was against the law there (which it was not in Italy) and conducted clandestine activities that were not easy to check

In the summer of 1872 there came the strikes: thirty-one of them, in twenty-five different localities, almost all in northern Italy, from the beginning of July to the end of August. Of these the most important were the ones that exploded contemporaneously on 24 July in Verona (the workers in the rail yards, for five days) and Turin (a general strike of nine days' duration), and the one in Milan (also a general strike), which began on 5 August. The government remained faithful to its tactic of displaying calm and composure in order not to play into the hands of its adversaries.[199] In appearance it continued to believe, like many Italians, that the issue posed by the workers did not entail the same dangers in the peninsula as it did elsewhere, and it did not wish to have the air of attributing excessive importance to what was happening in the industrial centers.[200] But the truth is that almost from the start it was concerned at the possible linkage between the strikes in Italy and those that were taking place at the same time in France: had they both been triggered by a single command given from the same control center?[201] The conclusion reached by the interior ministry after its investigation was that, in the case of the principal strikes, although there were no grounds to assert that the International alone had planned them, yet there was sufficient proof that it had promoted and favored them, and also to assert that, after the congress held by the Italian federation of the International at Rimini on 4, 5, and 6 August, the sect had made efforts to organize fresh strikes. In the cases of Turin, Milan, and Verona, its influence was past doubt.[202]

Hence it was no longer possible to make a show of absolute optimism, as it

---

on (Fournier, reports, 31 May 1872, no. 23, 10 July 1872, unnumbered, and an attached letter from Lanza of 3 July; Rémusat, dispatch to Fournier, 15 June 1872, no. 25; Rémusat to the French interior minister, 15 July; the French interior minister to Rémusat, 24 July: AEP, *C.P., Italie*, t. 385, fols. 128 ff., 151r-v, 206–208, 225r-v, 254, 274).

[199] It will be remembered that the *Osservatore Romano* concluded that the strikes were a sign of God's imminent vengeance (above, n. 133).

[200] The Austro-Hungarian chargé d'affaires, Herbert, observes this in a report of 10 August to Andrássy (SAW, *P.A.*, XI/80, no. 25 D). But for his own part Herbert already believed at this time in the existence of a precise, unified plan, with orders being given by more or less secret organizations. In any case, given the interesting aspects of the question, he asked for information from the Italian government; and on 19 October he forwarded to Vienna (ibid., at no. 35 C) a memorandum sent him by Tornielli which emphasized the role of the International. The Russian representative at the Quirinal also requested information on the strikes (foreign ministry to interior ministry, 19 August). Finally, de Sayve compiled an ample memorandum on "Workers' associations, political associations, and the International in Italy," which the envoy Fournier sent to Paris on 7 February 1873 (appendix to report no. 94; AEP, *C.P., Italie*, t. 387, fols. 70–77). On the strikes, cf. L. Valiani, "Le prime grandi agitazioni operaie a Milano e a Torino," *Movimento Operaio* 2 (October–November 1950): 365 ff.

[201] Peiroleri, dispatch to Nigra, 27 July, no. 402. Rémusat's reply was "that the French government had no positive proof that there was a visible and material link between the strikes in the two countries. But he appeared to me to be convinced that a moral connection existed, produced in part by identical causes and in part by example" (Nigra, report, 12 August, no. 1901).

[202] Interior ministry to foreign ministry, 2 September (with data on the strikes). Artom made similar declarations to the French envoy, Fournier, stating that it was the International that had sought to arouse the working populations of the principal cities of northern Italy. It was believed that these strikes were tied to the attempt in Spain on the life of King Amedeo (18 July), since they had spread, as if by a command, over parts of France, Italy, and Spain (Fournier, report, 16 August 1872, no. 48; AEP, *C.P., Italie*, t. 385, fol. 315). When King Amedeo abdicated, there was suspicion once again that a secret understanding existed among the extremist parties in Italy, Spain, and France (Fournier, report, 11 February 1873, no. 97; ibid., t. 387, fol. 107r-v).

had been the year before; though there was deep dissension between the Italian sections and the General Council in London,[203] which culminated in the former splitting off from the latter at the same congress in Rimini, still the International had now gained a foothold in Italy[204] and was starting to take action in an unequivocal manner, action that was having an effect.

Then in November 1872 the great meeting scheduled for the 24th at the Colosseum—not a meeting of the International!—roused the most vivid panic. It appeared to be a genuine revolutionary enterprise, aimed at altering the fundamental institutions of the state.[205] Many non-Romans fled the city, fearing that a bloody conflict would erupt; unnerving rumors spread, as always, not the least of which (reported in fact by the French envoy to the Quirinal) said that the clergy hoped, by raising the level of emotional tension, to provoke an open conflict and thus an act of force by the government, and new hatred against it in consequence. The alarm was great, the name of the International was on everyone's lips, and peaceful citizens trembled to meet here and there in the streets "the sort of figures who only emerge into the light at times when mischief is afoot."[206]

More strikes followed a year later, and among the members of the government there grew ever stronger "the grave suspicion that the strikes of the working class were promoted by subversive factions, and especially the International association. Thus suspicion is now reinforced . . . by the new disorders that have happened in several provinces, and information subsequently received."[207] Finally, the year 1874 saw the conspiracy of villa Ruffi, and the attempted insurrection of Andrea Costa, Cafiero, and Malatesta.

Optimism began to be replaced by a certain disquiet, among the members of the government and in the press. It was time to start looking for an answer. There was no more reason to hope for, or fear, combined initiatives by the powers; they carried many risks in any case, and if actually put into effect would have placed

---

[203] The interior ministry was aware of this dissension; it is referred to in a note from Lanza to Visconti Venosta of 1 May 1872 (no. 2994; AE, *Rapp. Inghilterra*). On this, cf. Rosselli, *Mazzini e Bakounine*, pp. 433 ff.

[204] In 1874 there were 155 sections of the International, with 32,450 members (F. Della Peruta, "La consistenza numerica dell'Internazionale in Italia nel 1874," *Movimento Operaio* 2, nos. 3–4 [December 1949–January 1950], pp. 104–106). Conti, *Le origini del socialismo a Firenze (1860–1880)*, p. 146, sticks to the lower official figure. But in 1874 the ten federations of the International believed that they could rely firmly on 33,000 followers ready to take up arms when the general insurrection came (Lucarelli, *Carlo Cafiero*, pp. 39 and 81). The event gave them a rude awakening.

[205] This is stated in Gadda's decree (19 November) prohibiting the meeting.

[206] Fournier, report, 20 November 1872, no. 68; AEP, *C.P., Italie*, t. 386, fols. 143 ff. And cf. too the reports of 23 and 26 November, nos. 70 and 71, ibid., fols. 154 and 160 ff. Cf. articles by Dina in *L'Opinione* for 19 and 21 November; Vigo, *Annali d'Italia* 1:208 ff.; G. Spadolini, "I radicali dell'Ottocento," in *Il Mondo* for 10 February 1951; and for the debate in the Chamber on 25 November, S. Cilibrizzi, *Storia parlamentare politica e diplomatica d'Italia da Novara a Vittorio Veneto* 2:51 (Milan-Rome-Naples, 1925). On the other hand, in the Vatican there was serious worry that, if there were disturbances in the city, there might be a direct attack on the Vatican itself; precautionary measures were taken, but Cardinal Antonelli was intensely anxious (Palomba, report, 30 November 1872, no. 12).

[207] Thus in circulars of the interior minister, Cantelli, on 5 July and 20 August 1873 (see *L'Opinione* for 30 August; on 1 September the paper returns to the subject on its own account with the article "L'Internazionale e li scioperi").

Lanza and his colleagues in conflict once again with their own vivid sense of liberty. The time had passed when a part of the press, and even the Swiss envoy in Rome, could fear that France, Germany, and Italy would attempt in concert to occupy the Swiss cantons on their borders with military force, and so put an end to the concentration of the internationalists on Helvetic soil.[208]

The Spanish proposal of February 1872 had come to nothing. The fact that it emanated from a second-class power which was then enduring a full-blown crisis and lacked the authority required to be taken seriously at the outset by the cabinets of Europe; the opposition to it from England; plus the difficulty of harmonizing legislation that varied widely from country to country—all these factors had caused it to fail, just as they had the French proposal of the previous year and, again, the renewed French proposal in the spring of 1872. From the outset of the discussion of the Spanish proposal, an underlying skepticism among some of the heads of government concerning the practical possibility of reaching a general European accord had surfaced.[209] The government in Madrid was itself well aware of the initial weakness of its proposal and expressed the desire that one of the great powers should adopt it and thus give it more weight, assuming the task of realizing the basis of the accord.[210]

Bismarck, the only statesman who would have had sufficient prestige to force the continental powers at least into an accord, was now no longer in the same frame of mind that had inspired the steps he proposed to the European powers in June 1871: now the *Kulturkampf* was beginning, and instead of the red International he was haunted by the black International, by ultramontanism. The recollection of the Commune paled, while the phantasm of the Vatican stood rooted before his gaze: instead of the red incendiaries of Paris, the black vestments of the priests. Not only would he no longer seriously consider international accords with his Russian and Austrian colleagues, even at their famous meeting in Berlin, though it was a spectacular display of European conservatism,[211] but even

---

[208] Report of the French chargé d'affaires, de Sayve, 25 January 1872, no. 10; AEP, *C.P., Italie*, t. 384, fols. 84 ff. Rémusat replied on 31 January (no. 4, ibid., fol. 94) that he did not understand how the Swiss envoy could give any credence to such rumors. The French government might regret that the fomenters of disorder had abused Swiss hospitality in order to centralize their efforts and ensure impunity for their guilty maneuvers, but it had not the slightest intention of resorting to such measures!

[209] Thus Andrássy (Robilant, report, 11 March 1872, no. 62).

[210] Thus in the circular of 9 February (cited at n. 128; and a dispatch of Visconti Venosta to Robilant, 27 February, no. 25, cited at n. 178). A year later the Portuguese foreign minister, very worried by the progress of the International, said to Oldoini: "if I were the minister of a great country . . . I would try to organize a European concert [against the International]" (Oldoini, report, 8 May 1873, no. 197, confidential; and report, 4 September 1872, no. 182, appendix—on the efforts of the Lisbon government to convince some great power to assume the initiative of a European congress against the International).

[211] The Italian government had foreseen that the International would be discussed at Berlin. "It is known that discussions are ongoing between Austria and Prussia to study the remedies to be used against the tendencies and the enterprises of the 'International.' The cabinet in St. Petersburg has often made known that it was very worried by the gains that this association was making in Europe. Therefore there are grounds to suppose that, just as last year at Salzburg and Gastein, so this year at Berlin, the situation created for the states by the aforementioned association will be one of the topics of the conversations of the sovereigns and their prime ministers. We should therefore consider

internal measures lost all priority. The laws of May would take precedence over the *Sozialistengesetz*, and not until 1878, and two consecutive attempts on the person of the emperor Wilhelm, would the latter come into force.

Nor for the moment was there any concrete result from the preparatory work of the German and Austrian commissions that had tried to elaborate plans to resolve the social question, in an effort to go beyond reactive measures and apply preventive ones. They had been the result of discussions between Bismarck and Beust in their meetings at Gastein and Salzburg in August and September 1871, with the German chancellor in agreement that reactive measures against the International would not be enough to resolve the social question, of which the former was mainly a symptom,[212] and Beust more than convinced that reaction by itself was insufficient, and that it was necessary to organize a "counterinternational" that would operate independently of the governments,[213] and "study the best means to set up a wall of conservative interests against the passions of those who want to destroy all governmental order." What was needed was to "favor and protect the demands of the workers, within the limits of justice; promote the associations that give them real and lasting advantages; in sum, pluck from the hands of the subversives the weapon they employ to maintain and exploit the discontent born of multiple causes during the modern development of enterprises and industries."[214] On this basis, which Bismarck accepted, the work of the

whether it would not be a good idea for the Italian envoy at Berlin to have exact information concerning the disturbances that have taken place among the Italian workers, so that, if he should be called upon to comment on this matter, he may do so with the necessary background on the case" (foreign ministry, signed by Artom, to the interior ministry, 19 August, cited in n. 200 above). On 25 August, in a private letter from Artom to de Launay, Artom says that if a practical idea, of the sort that a constitutional government could accept, should issue from the meetings in Berlin, Italy would be glad to be associated with it (Visconti Venosta archive).

At Berlin, Andrássy and Gorchakov spoke about the International with de Launay (de Launay, reports, 9 and 12 September, nos. 1061 and 1062); Gorchakov spoke with Gontaut-Biron (*D.D.F.*, 1st ser., vol. 1, no. 156, p. 186) and with Lord Odo Russell (cf. Russell to Granville, 12 September 1872, in W. Taffs, "Conversations between Lord Odo Russell and Andrássy, Bismarck, and Gorchakov in September 1872," *Slavonic Review* 8 (1929–1930): 705). The person at the meeting who took the initiative in discussing the International, and urging strongly reactionary measures against it, was Andrássy (cf. Gorchakov, report to Alexander II, 9 September 1872, in A. Meyendorff, "Conversations of Gorchakov with Andrássy and Bismarck in 1872," *Slavonic Review* 8, pp. 405 ff.) Cf. Gontaut-Biron, *Mon ambassade en Allemagne (1872–1873)* (Paris, 1906), pp. 157 and 166; E. von Wertheimer, *Graf Julius Andrássy* 2:74–75 (Stuttgart, 1913).

[212] Bismarck's thinking about this is clearly expressed on 21 October and 17 November 1871 (Poschinger, *Aktenstücke zur Wirtschaftspolitik des Fürsten Bismarck* 1:160–61, 164 ff.), and also on 19 June 1872 (cf. Bismarck, *Gesammelten Werke* 6c:10–11 and 22). According to Beust, however, in meetings of summer 1871 Bismarck was adopting a more repressive line, and it was the Austrian envoy himself who put the case for the preventive aspects of policy (so says Tosi as well, in report no. 878, cited below at n. 214). Certainly, in his reply to Itzenplitz on 17 November, Bismarck also emphasized the lively interest of Franz Joseph in the question, which thus became "a necessary part of our foreign policy."

[213] Thus Beust in his *Mémoires* 2:491–92.

[214] Report of Tosi, the chargé d'affaires at Berlin, 28 September 1871, no. 878 (and references in previous reports, 5 and 10 September, nos. 872 and 873). After the meetings, Beust sent to Berlin two memoranda in succession in which he insisted "on the insufficiency of repression" and expressed the wish "that the international commission should openly set as its agenda the aim of improving the condition of the suffering classes of society, and of satisfying, after a mature examination, their demands, which at present appear so perilous. Repression would be a corollary of this program and

German and Austrian commissions was supposed to be carried out, in preparation for a genuine international commission that would be proposed to the other
governments. In actuality, the two memoranda of Beust produced no immediate
outcome.[215] Only in the spring of 1872, after the Spanish proposal, were practical steps taken with the creation of two commissions, a German one and an
Austrian one, which were meant to come together in a conference at Berlin after
holding separate preliminary sessions.[216] The conference took place from 7 to 29
November at Berlin and decided, in effect, for anticipatory measures against
crime rather than reactive ones.[217] But it all ended there, without leaving any
immediate trace even in the domestic legislation of the two countries, and naturally without the question ever being raised of gathering the representatives of the
other great powers around the same table.[218]

---

would thus not appear so odious to the popular classes." Beust's extensive program of social
improvements met the approval of the new French foreign minister, Rémusat, who however insisted
at the same time on the necessity of repression (the sole fact of belonging to the International should
be a criminal offense).

[215] Robilant, report, 11 March 1872, no. 62, cited above at n. 209. Andrássy's declarations: the
only result of the discussions between Beust and Bismarck had been "the compilation of memoranda
by each of the two sides which contained nothing practical and nothing that corresponded in an
effective manner to the aim that the two governments had set themselves. After that nothing was
done, and the question was once more laid to rest." Andrássy equivocates here: there were not two
memoranda originating from the two different sides, but two memoranda from Beust alone (Tosi,
report, cited above at n. 214). The opinion of the Magyar count on the "negativity" of the memoranda
confirms that he did not share the views of his predecessor on prevention but was more disposed to
opt for repression; this was already apparent in the different attitude each took to the French and
Spanish proposals. The fact is that at Berlin a commission was appointed to undertake the preparatory
work (Poschinger, *Aktenstücke zur Wirtschaftspolitik des Fürsten Bismarck* 1:161 and 167 n. 2), but
its work went ahead very slowly in the winter of 1871–1872 (de Launay, report, 26 February 1872,
no. 953, cited above at n. 178).

[216] Robilant, report, 11 June 1872, no. 86. The conference in Berlin had "a very wide mandate,
but one limited to examining the question, and at most proposing modifications to be made to the
penal codes of the two states, so that the law would strike at the International through those affiliated
to it, or through the criminal misdeeds committed by it." This was stated to the Italian envoy at the
Ballhaus. In reality, the conference dealt principally with the social question as such, from the
standpoint of prevention. In any case there was already a divergence of views about this among the
delegates of the Austro-Hungarian empire themselves, for according to Robilant the two Hungarian
delegates were apparently prepared to introduce into their legislation penal sanctions arising from the
sole fact of affiliation to the International, while the Austrians seemed "little disposed to assume a
standpoint which, as the *Neue Freie Presse* said a few days ago, seems to herald a regression of
liberal ideas back to the principles of 1815." Once again we see the opposition between the liberal
attitude of Beust, and the more reactionary position of Andrássy. For the convocation of the conference, cf. H. Schultess, *Europäischer Geschichtskalendar*, vol. 13 (1872), p. 17, under the date 10
June.

[217] The Prussian commission had concluded its own work with statements on many points
(education of the working class, protection of workers against capitalists, improvement of the
material and moral conditions of the working classes, peaceful resolution of conflicts), but also with
the firm pronouncement that "as for the agitation of the socialists, the state ought not to adopt any
repressive measures" (de Launay, in an ample report of 10 November 1872, no. 685). That the work
of the plenary Austro-German conference also concluded with recommendations for preventive
measures rather than repressive ones is stated in the report of de Launay, 9 December, no. 704. Cf. as
well Robilant's report, 7 December, no. 119.

[218] When de Launay asked to be given details about the results of the conference, the secretary of
state, Balan, replied "'if the work of the Austro-German delegates was really of such a nature as to be
brought to the attention of the other cabinets, we [Italy] would be the first to be informed about it'"

Thus, no need either to hope for, or to fear, any general concerted European action. Each nation had to sort itself out, as the Italian government was doing when it proceeded, especially at the end of 1872, to dissolve republican and socialist circles and associations in the Marche, at Genoa, and notably in Tuscany.

In addition to the strikes, in addition to the information from abroad that hinted at severe dangers for Italy,[219] tension was raised by other events, or news of them, particularly apt to make an impression on government members of sincere and ardent monarchical faith: assassination attempts on sovereigns. Late in the evening of 18 July 1872 (just when the strikes in Italy were about to reach their high point), the king of Spain, a member of the house of Savoy, escaped by a miracle from a volley of gunfire aimed at him by five individuals. And just as the inquiries following the strikes came to the conclusion that the International had undoubtedly had a hand in them, in the case of the attempted assassination, the news came from London a few days later that it had been planned in the British capital, beyond doubt by the International, which wished through this regicide to provoke a revolt in the Iberian peninsula.[220]

This was a fact, a reality, which added force to the other frequent rumors about assassinations being planned against this or that sovereign.[221] No wonder that, at the end of 1872 and the beginning of 1873, news from London of an imminent attempt on Vittorio Emanuele II was taken very seriously at Rome, and the maximum surveillance of all subversives was ordered—even of the movements of Ricciotti Garibaldi, who was then in England and under ongoing suspicion of plotting with the International.[222]

(de Launay, report, 9 December, no. 704). After that, there was silence. In January 1873 Bismarck sent an ample report on the work of the conference to Vienna only, with a letter to the ambassador, von Schweinitz, in which he merely expanded on the links between ultramontanism and the International, between the reds and the blacks, which are already mentioned in the report (*Gesammelten Werke* 6c:32–33).

On this initiative of 1871–72, which had no concrete outcome, but which, as Poschinger, *Aktenstücke zur Wirtschaftspolitik des Fürsten Bismarck* 1:165 n. 1, had already noted, offered the *Grundzüge* of Bismarck's later social policy, cf. B. Seeberg, "Bismarck und die Soziale Frage," *Zeitschrift für Kirchengeschichte* 59 (1940): 388 ff. There is a reference in O. Quandt, *Die Anfänge der Bismarckschen Sozialgesetzgebung und die Haltung der Parteien: Das Unfallversicherungsgesetz, 1881–1884* (Berlin, 1938), p. 9.

[219] For example the Portuguese foreign minister, Andrade Corvo (and readers will remember the links between the Savoy and Portuguese dynasties, which meant that King Luis had turned directly to Vittorio Emanuele for information on the trial held at Rome against the International; Patella, report, 8 August 1873, appendix no. 201) said to the Italian chargé d'affaires, Patella, that he had no doubt "'that his [Italian] majesty's government is aware of what is happening in Italy, where, according to information reaching here, the International association is directing its major efforts . . . '"; numerous colleagues have said exactly the same thing to me, since their information appears to coincide perfectly with that of signor de Andrade Corvo" (Patella, report, 17 November 1873, no. 206).

[220] Cadorna, report, 28 July 1872, no. 320. Cadorna had been warned some time before that the assassination attempt would take place, and had informed the Spanish legation. The chargé d'affaires, Maffei, returns to the matter on 2 September, reporting the story of Carlo De Dominicis on the events of the attempt (report no. 340).

[221] The English envoy in Rome, A. Paget, gives information about an assassination attempt in preparation against the tsar of Russia, in a note of 26 April 1872 to Visconti Venosta.

[222] Cadorna, reports of 31 December 1872, no. 373; 24 and 31 January, 10 and 17 February

Fears thrived, and confidence alternated with anxiety, optimism with gnawing doubt. Italian politics henceforth had to navigate between two poles: the strong sense of liberty on one hand, and on the other apprehension in the face of the dark forces that were stirring in the depths; fear at one moment, succeeded the next by optimistic reasoning about the lack of flammable material in Italy.[223] So did foreign policy, to the extent at least that the major domestic problems exerted an influence on it. As the preoccupation expressed in the papers over the International grew, many members of the Italian governing class could no longer banish from their minds a wariness about what might erupt next from out of the deep.[224] To the aged epigones of Romanticism, to whom colorful language came naturally, the hand of the International appeared at intervals on the walls of modern society, like the tragic hand at the banquet of Belshazzar,[225] and when workers guilty of "conspiracy" were arrested and tried after the attempted insurrections of 1874, the courts came down hard on them, and the public prosecutor spoke of them as "social slime."[226] The files of government ministries swelled with correspondence in which the names of the great agitators figured, and sometimes the names of presumed great revolutionaries as well; these were signaled by Palazzo Braschi to the Consulta, and by the Consulta to the foreign legations, especially London: names of persons who were to be watched and followed so that Rome could feel secure. Today those who have occasion to consult the files of ordinary correspondence between Rome and London are struck, indeed are dumbstruck initially, by the fact that often a not insignificant part, quantitatively speaking, of the dispatches and reports does not deal with the major problems of international

---

1873, nos. 379, 380, 388, 392; and interior ministry to foreign ministry, 9 January 1873.

[223] These emotions were alternating within the same persons, who lashed out at communism while declaring at the same time that they did not fear it in Italy. Cf., for example, E. Musatti, *La proprietà* (Padua, 1878; a paper originally presented to the Reale Accademia di Scienze, Lettere ed Arti of Padua), who on one hand thunders against communism, and on the other affirms that he does not fear it in Italy, where property-holdings are continually being subdivided (pp. 29 ff.). The notion of the "lack of danger" is naturally developed by the advocates for the defense in the trials of the internationalists: cf. for example the summation of the advocate F. Sarri in the trial at Trani in 1875 (*La internazionale innanzi alla sezione d'accusa di Trani* [Barletta, 1875], p. 15).

[224] Vignoli, a former collaborator of the *Politecnico*, wrote in 1876: "Every day one hears, from persons of every order and stratum, including the wealthiest, grief and lamentation about the dangers that threaten us from universal demagogy. There is fear, trembling, imprecation, the end of the world is prophesied." But these people do nothing about it; they are waiting to be rescued by the sword of an archangel (*Delle condizioni morali e civili d'Italia*, p. 96). Renan too, in September 1874, found more reason for worry in Italy than he had expected, after the disturbances in Romagna. "The situation is not as good as it was two years ago, and if the king should die, Italy would be at some risk" (Renan and Berthelot, *Correspondance*, p. 441).

[225] For example Aleardi, who harbored dark forebodings: "Europe, sooner or later, will have to undergo a social war which will be less noble and more cruel than the slave war that Rome underwent. At least Spartacus did not have kerosene" (*Epistolario*, p. 309, 20 February 1872).

[226] In the trial at Rome in May 1875 for conspiracy etc., out of ten defendants five were condemned to ten years of hard labor, and the others to ten years of incarceration (*L'Opinione*, 9 May). Before sentence was passed, the defendant Giuseppe Bertolani spoke out: the prosecutor "has called us *ragged beggars* and *social slime*. We are poor and honest workers, and very proud to be so." The insult "cannot touch us" (F. Colacito, *L'Internazionale a Roma* [Rome, 1875], pp. 125–26). On the Roman section of the International, cf. F. Della Peruta, "Nuovi documenti sull'Internazionale in Roma," *Movimento Operaio* 1, no. 2 (November 1949): 38 ff.

politics, and neglects the names of Gladstone and Granville to analyze instead the comings and goings, between London-Paris-Geneva or London-Brussels or London-Milan, of one of these wandering apostles of the proletarian faith.

Thus there was the danger that, without in the least passing over into the reactionary camp, or repudiating the principles of liberty, in fact while reaffirming them confidently, the foreign policy of the young kingdom was nonetheless being subjected to pressures of mistrust and suspicion and a vague but real unease, which were working together to incline the members of the government to feel a greater sympathy for the so-called powers of order, reliable guarantors of the preservation of the political and social (meaning monarchical and bourgeois) status quo of Europe. The conservatism desired by Minghetti insensibly became a reality: one more reason to draw closer to imperial Germany and distance the country from France.

France was clearly very conservative, in fact the majority in the National Assembly elected in February 1871 was reactionary; it was a conservative and reactionary country in its rural social strata, in its nobility, and in a part of the bourgeoisie, so much so that it had to appear menacing to Italy in the years immediately following 1870 as the center of Catholic reaction, in other words as a threat to the unity of Italy. But even if France appeared conservative in general terms in those years, there was always the sinister shadow of the Commune in the background. And then in rapid succession, there was Gambetta, there was the appeal to the *nouvelles couches sociales*, there was the republic of 1876, there was the triumphant emergence of radicalism, which the Italian moderates saw as a close relative, much much closer than in reality it was, of socialism and subversion. Almost immediately there sprang up again the image of France as the nation that shifted, with sudden spasms, from reaction to anarchism, from red terror to white terror, a nation prone to any extreme, unquiet and unstable, capable of lighting a new revolutionary conflagration in the near future. At once *fille aînée de l'Église et mère de la Révolution*,[227] France alarmed all the Italian parties without exception in its clerical-reactionary guise. In its other, radical guise it certainly alarmed the men of the Right, the moderates[228] who felt themselves

---

[227] This mordant aphorism of Count Roger du Nord is reported by Bülow, *Memorie* 4:476. But its essence is already implicit in the opinion columns of the Italian press in 1871–72. "On one hand anarchic furor, on the other reactionary frenzy: that is France" ("Anarchia e reazione," in *Il Diritto* for 21 March 1871). And cf. the same journal on 23 March ("La Francia giudicata da G. G. Gervinus") and 30 March ("La Francia," portraying a fearful dilemma in French history between anarchy and reaction). For *La Riforma*, France has been turning in a vicious circle between insurrection and despotism for eighty years (8 July 1871, and cf. 2 July, 31 August, and again 13 July 1873). *L'Opinione* for 3 January 1873 ("La libertà del pensiero in Francia") observes that no other country provides an example of as many contrasts as France: one moment the adoration of liberty, the next scorn for it; one moment limitless tolerance, the next the most irrational despotism. It swings from one extreme to the other. Identical judgments appear in other papers of various ideological colors; cf. *La Nazione* for 8 September 1870 ("La repubblica e la libertà"). Likewise Ferrari: "the French nation is shifting, restless, and capricious, following a pattern of jolting reversals that render it flourishing today and desolate tomorrow" (Ferrari, *La disfatta*, p. 67). Minghetti takes a similar view in October 1870: "France . . . will stagger on between despotism and anarchy" (Minghetti, *Carteggio Minghetti-Pasolini* 4:196).

[228] It is to be remembered that in the early years especially the radicalism of Gambetta unnerved

more reassured, from the point of view of order and domestic tranquillity, when they gazed in the direction of Berlin and Vienna.

Symptomatically, the most ferocious anti-internationalist among the Italian diplomats was also the most adamant supporter of an alliance with Prussia. Count de Launay never concealed his point of view from Visconti Venosta. It was a very resolute one, and perfectly analogous to that of the French envoy to St. Petersburg, General Le Flô, who had been the minister of war in the Versailles government during the Commune.[229] Both men believed in acting and acting forcefully. Never mind about committees of technical experts and university professors and jurists holding sessions to find the solution when something was wrong![230] Given the times and the customs, the only salutary thing was to *sévir avec énergie*,[231] use the iron fist.

It was a perfectly logical position for a man like de Launay, who, let alone opposing the International, deplored the superfluous debates in the Italian Chamber of Deputies, in which "such an impractical spirit" reigned, and who prophesied a dim future for the parliamentary system and those who relied on it.[232] This was a man who endorsed Guizot's opinion that "at present it is not *la liberté* that requires defenders, but *l'autorité*." Authoritarian and antisocialist, de Launay demonstrated by personal example how those who feared an authoritarian reflux as a result of the Commune were not wide of the mark.

Not one of the men who held power in Italy, certainly, and none from among the other group of moderates who were to inherit their legacy in 1873, not Lanza or Minghetti or Visconti Venosta, not to speak of Sella, would ever have seconded the authoritarianism of the Savoyard: only another Savoyard, Menabrea, would have been able to subscribe to expressions of this kind, and both would have been certain of finding their ideas in full agreement with those of their king, who had been afraid that Thiers would let himself be carried along by

---

the moderates (cf. *L'Opinione* for 1 and 7 October 1872). Gambetta's appeal to the *nouvelles couches sociales* in his speech at Grenoble was greeted coolly by Nigra (report, 5 October 1872, no. 1924).

[229] Le Flô, in conversation with the Italian chargé d'affaires at St. Petersburg, showed continual preoccupation about the social question, and stated his strong belief in summary repression (Marochetti, report, 6 August–25 July 1871, no. 249).

[230] "[W]e see once again how difficult it is for these high functionaries, these jurisconsults, to decide on anything practical and salutary in the way of measures to be adopted, whether of the anticipatory kind or the reactive kind. I fear that they will produce never-ending commentaries on legality, on the theories of political economy, on the rights and duties of employers and employees, and meanwhile the International will be putting the time to good use by extending its organization. Yet we can still hope that the governments will depart from their traditional routine, and will launch open war against an association that aims at nothing less than overturning society, the family, and property, using every revolutionary means" (de Launay, report, 26 February 1872, no. 953, cited above at nn. 178 and 215).

[231] Speaking once more of the work of the German committee, de Launay comments on 23 June (no. 1027): "So we are still a long way off from the end in view. There is even cause to doubt that real progress is being made toward the solution of the problem. Until the level of public morality is raised, the best guarantee will still be to punish energetically the abuses that are committed by the workers, as well as by the employers."

[232] "The parliamentary system, which I do not confuse with veritable and proper constitutionalism, will be the end of us if we do not set up a barrier against it." This and the other expressions cited in the text are from a personal letter to Robilant, 7 March 1871 (AE, *Carte Robilant*).

the tendency to reconciliation, by some regard for the "bands" of Paris. "We have . . . thirty or forty thousand of these *misérables* in Italy, and I take the view that we have to be very forceful in dealing with them."[233]

But what really matters is something else, something that did not occur: no tincture of conservatism crept into Italian policy, and even in foreign policy, an area in which conservatism might easily have cloaked itself in other motivations and been reinforced by reasons of diplomatic convenience, and therefore have finished up being accepted, in perfect good faith, by men who were sincerely devoted to the liberal idea, and liberal institutions, it did not find a place. It is all the more noteworthy in that those who were beginning to make propaganda out of the social question among the masses were also making an issue out of the institutional question, with the monarchy being depicted as a bulwark of the interests of the so-called privileged classes, and a republic as a prerequisite of the victory of the workers and the realization of the new order. Thus the specter of a republic was never laid to rest. Even if it was the Mazzinians who raised it, it still meant revolution, anarchy, the collapse of everything. The more enduring republican danger still appeared to be the greater danger, much greater than the social danger as such; and it provided the major worry until around 1890. In fact it became more acute after 1878, leading Italians and foreigners to utter very pessimistic judgments on the short-term future of the monarchy between 1879 and 1881, something that had direct repercussions on Italy's international position.

But there was no need to wait until 1882 and the conclusion of the Triple Alliance to detect the pressure of conservative preoccupations on foreign policy. As early as the final months of 1870, the existence of the republic in France had as its corollaries the partisanship of the followers of Cavallotti for it, and conversely a certain cooling of the pro-French sympathies of the moderates, especially Bonghi.[234] Yet others shifted decidedly to positions of sympathy for Prussia.[235]

Nor was this taking place in the realm of journalism and public opinion alone. In the autumn of 1870, right at the outset of the historical phase with which we are concerned, the problems of domestic politics had intersected notably with

---

[233] Statements of Vittorio Emanuele to the French envoy, Choiseul (Choiseul, report, 21 April 1871, no. 95; AEP, *C.P., Italie*, t. 381, fol. 442r-v). And see as well statements he made to Fournier (below, ch. 20, n. 73).

[234] *La Perseveranza* for 6, 8, 11 September and 20 October 1870.

[235] In fact *La Nazione* of Florence changes its viewpoint radically: on 17 August 1870 ("La Storia") it is still asserting that Italy has bonds of gratitude and sympathy to Napoleon III and France. But on 7 September it declares that the proclamation of the republic imposes new duties on the Italians and warns them of new dangers. No Italian patriot, it says, can wish to see in Italy "the influence of republican and socialist France." It is a question of saving the nation and society from danger: from this day forth, we are a conservative people and, freed of our debt of gratitude to Napoleon III, "we do not have, nor wish to have, anything in common with committees of public safety, with universal republics, with the phalansteries and national factories that France is threatening us with" ("La Francia repubblicana"; and cf. 10, 13, 25, 29 September). In the wake of the Commune, the cry is: be anti-French in order to stay civilized ("Parigi," 26 May 1871). And cf. Civinini in *Nuova Antologia* 17 (May 1871): 48 ff.

foreign policy when the Duke of Aosta accepted the Spanish crown. Visconti Venosta had had much hesitation about agreeing to this, and the argument that had won him over had been the alarming prospect of seeing Spain topple into republicanism. In itself, a Spanish republic was not something to get upset about; but the general European situation had changed from the time when the duke had first refused the offer, and it had changed further since July, when the Italian government would already have been prepared to agree, in order to salvage peace in Europe by burying the Hohenzollern incident.[236] "[A] republic in Paris and a republic in Madrid create a situation which a prudent government has to worry about. Nor is it safe to assume that the French republic will be utterly ephemeral. The various fractions of the moderate parties in France are now prepared to unite around the republican form as being the one that least divides them, and therefore the one best suited to assume the responsibilities of peace and heal the wounds of war. If that happens the republic will last for a rather prolonged period in France. And if the republic falls entirely into the grip of the extreme party, then it will become propagandist, and if it does not actually create grave danger for us, it will certainly create embarrassment, and considerable difficulty."[237]

These then were the motives for the decision of Visconti Venosta,[238] who was not thinking, even remotely, of thus laying the foundation for a policy of Mediterranean expansion. He was concentrating entirely, especially after the Italian

---

[236] In July 1870, in fact, it had been decided to accept "to help Spain out of a difficult situation, and at the first announcement of the unfortunate demand for a guarantee against the return of the Hohenzollern candidacy, it appeared to Lanza and me that acceptance by the prince might be Italy's contribution to the preservation of European peace" (Visconti Venosta, personal letter to Nigra, 5 July 1893; Visconti Venosta archive). And cf. E. Mayor des Planches, "Re Vittorio Emanuele II alla vigilia della guerra del Settanta," *Nuova Antologia* 289 (16 April 1920): 344–45. The idea of serving the cause of Europe, the cause of liberty, order, and general security, which also meant the security of Italy as well, was the official justification to which Visconti Venosta held fast in parliament too (cf. his statement to the Chamber, 18 March 1873, *A.P., Camera*, p. 5379).

[237] Visconti Venosta, personal letter to de Launay, 18 October 1870, (Visconti Venosta archive; cited above at ch. 3, n. 2, and ch. 8, n. 28); the foreign minister charges de Launay with sounding out Wilhelm I and Bismarck. The Spanish government had let the Italian government "gather" that if the duke did not accept before the end of the year, a republic would be proclaimed in Spain (ibid., and Visconti Venosta to his brother Giovanni, 22–25 October 1870; Visconti Venosta archive). Massari, who was well informed about what the moderates were thinking, also speaks of the risks to which the monarchical cause was exposed after the changes that had taken place in France as the determining factor in the Italian decision (Massari, *La vita ed il regno di Vittorio Emanuele II* [new ed.; Milan, 1896], p. 525).

[238] Cf. too A. Stern, *Geschichte Europas seit den Verträgen von 1815 bis zum Frankfurter Frieden von 1871* 10:443 (Stuttgart-Berlin, 1924). This theme of the interest "of the dynastic principle in Europe, without which Spain would be republican," with added danger for Portugal as well, is emphasized by Oldoini, the Italian envoy at Lisbon. Oldoini adds that in this manner Italy protected itself against a French-Spanish alliance on the Roman question, which would have been a certain danger if Queen Isabella had remained on the throne (?). He further emphasizes that the motive of Vittorio Emanuele II had been to imitate the old policy of the Bourbons of France, applying it to Italy: to have sovereigns of the house of Savoy in Italy, Spain, and Portugal (?). Oldoini viewed this policy of Vittorio Emanuele as a lofty one (Oldoini's diary notes, entitled "Mio ritorno in Portogallo," AE, *carte Oldoini*, cart. 6, fasc. IX, cited above at n. 110). But these last are Oldoini's views, and although others in Italy certainly shared them, they were totally extraneous to Visconti Venosta's thinking. Oldoini, father of the more famous Countess of Castiglione, was no penetrating intellect: cf. Cavour's very disdainful opinion in *Carteggio Cavour-Salmour*, p. 115 and cf. p. 116.

entry into Rome, on not "leaving ourselves open to any reproach or accusation of restless uncontainable ambition,"[239] and was not even dreaming of conducting a policy of encirclement from the Alps to the Pyrenees so as to create difficulties for France. Indeed, he took care to obtain the assent of the French government to the candidacy of the Duke of Aosta before making up his mind.[240] So even then, considerations of a monarchical and conservative nature, backed up by the support of England,[241] had guided the decision. The result gave great pleasure to the duke himself, who very much desired the royal crown,[242] and satisfaction to the moderates, who considered it essential to prevent Spain from constituting itself as a republic.[243]

[239] Visconti Venosta, private letter to de Launay, cited at n. 237.

[240] Visconti Venosta, telegram to Cerruti in Madrid, 27 October 1870: "France, despite its actual distress, will always be the most powerful neighbor of Italy and Spain, and it is important, especially at present, to avoid seeming not to take its dispositions into account." And Visconti Venosta to Nigra, in Tours, 28 October 1870: "I place such importance on not committing myself officially in this affair without being sure of the dispositions of France, that I am asking you to take steps in confidence. . . . France, as the neighbor of Italy and Spain, could not be indifferent to the choice of a king for Spain. So we desire above all to be assured, and to be able to confirm when necessary, that the three Latin powers who rule the Mediterranean have proceeded in agreement on this occasion." And cf. his telegram of 29 October to Cerruti, in which he expresses satisfaction at France's consent. The government at Tours, in its response, clung to the same formula it had already used in treating with the government in Madrid, whose business it was to sound out the great powers officially: France leaves the decision to the will of the Spanish people; among all the candidacies, that of the Duke of Aosta "suits us the best" (AEP, *C.P., Italie*, t. 379, fols. 327v, 328, 329–30, 334).

[241] Visconti Venosta to his brother Giovanni, 22–25 October 1870 (Visconti Venosta archive; cited above at n. 237). And cf. his statements to De Cesare, in De Cesare, *Il conte Giuseppe Greppi e i suoi ricordi diplomatici (1842–1888)*, p. 202. But note that De Cesare must have made some mistake here, for it is out of the question that Germany [he means Prussia] was also pressing insistently, together with England and Austria, for the duke to accept.

[242] Visconti Venosta, letter cited in the previous note; and another to his brother on 1 November: "The Duke of Aosta, who strongly desires the crown of Spain—everyone to his own taste—has definitively accepted" (Visconti Venosta archive). But at first the duke had shown decided reluctance (Mayor des Planches, "Re Vittorio Emanuele II alla vigilia della guerra del Settanta"; Massari, *La vita ed il regno di Vittorio Emanuele II*, pp. 525 and 544).

[243] "Il duca d'Aosta Re di Spagna," in *La Perseveranza* for 18 October 1870. The article is by Bonghi.

IV. *The Present and the Future*

The Present and the Future

OLDER THEMES were thus interwoven with more recent ones in the moral and spiritual life of the Italians. Those that were more familiar formed a bond between the elders who had lived through 1848 and the younger men of 1870. Those that were novel foreshadowed new developments, and a different future. To be more precise: the old ideals continued to rule, with liberty and nationality together constituting the fulcrum of Italian life, but the manner in which they were interpreted hinted at the emergence of new problems and the advent of historical forces at least partially different from those of 1848 and 1859. With them there came the potential for ideological developments that would lead the nation far from the goals set for it at its birth.

Liberty was still the theme that gave the overall tone to the epoch. The fact that those who admired German power believed that their decision to express their admiration was a service to the cause of liberty, a cause on which the tyrant Napoleon III had trampled, was a strong proof of what the ideals of the Italians were around 1870. That they were deluding themselves detracts not at all from the seriousness of their conviction, nor does it have much importance that they were further mistaken in considering the *Kulturkampf* an affirmation of freedom of thought and freedom of the human will against Catholic obscurantism, and so to wish that a *Kulturkampf* might take place in Italy as well. In both cases they were reading their own sentiments and ideas into the conduct of the German chancellor, and this projection is strong evidence of the content of their spiritual life.

They believed in liberty and popular sovereignty, and in the case of popular sovereignty they still interpreted it in the old Rousseauesque sense. When democracy was under discussion, whether the attitude was favorable or hostile, it was direct, immediate action by the people that was meant. This is shown by the continuous appeal to plebiscites as the expression of the free national will. Gaetano Mosca had not yet appeared on the scene to undercut faith in these myths and concentrate instead on organized and capable minorities, on the political class as the only true actor in history.

They had faith in liberty, and those in government, the moderates, gave decisive proof of this during a particularly difficult phase for the Italian nation, refusing to engage in the use of force against the papacy at a time when Bismarck was urging them to do so, and the clericals themselves were agitating furiously against the state. In those two critical years between the spring of 1873 and the spring of 1875, the men of the Right kept faith with the creed of liberty, and in order to do so they did not hesitate to run the certain risk of turning the German chancellor against them, even though at that juncture he appeared to them Italy's only reliable and solid ally in Europe.

Analogously, they refused to have recourse to restrictive legislation against the followers of the International, though they considered it a monstrous and detestable thing. When dealing with the Catholic church and the papacy, the great majority of the moderates, who were Catholics themselves and believed that religious feeling had to be strong for society to be well ordered, took the view that they had to put up with a painful and inevitable period of conflict, but they never lost hope of a future free of conflict, with the two sides at peace and respectful of each other. But when dealing with the propaganda of the subversives, the future appeared to them even more disquieting than the present, for no agreement was possible now or ever, and there was no prospect but that of an unending struggle, without pity.

What resulted from this situation was the first evidence of sclerosis in liberal thought as it had been elaborated in the west in the nineteenth century. Here, said the liberals, are our columns of Hercules, and beyond them they refused to pass for several decades at least, though they were urged to do so. They gave up all forms of revolutionary ferment and adopted conservatism as a watchword; they began to have their first doubts about whether the ideals of 1789 should be considered ideals of absolute, eternal value, to be fought for everywhere and always, to be taken to their logical consequence, or whether principles less absolute, and a logic less consequential, were not now required, along with some sense of discretion, of measure and equilibrium, of the golden mean. This had been the message of the French liberals of the July monarchy, and the Italian moderates before 1848. Now that two decades of revolution were over, decades in which even the moderates had had to proceed faster than they had planned on doing, the liberals' old love for a middle way between revolution and reaction revived. The Paris Commune was there to warn them that they had to act quickly to put barriers in place. But new social forces that desired to do to the bourgeoisie what the bourgeoisie had done to the nobility in 1789 were growing.[1] The Commune was a much more serious event than June 1848, and Marx an opponent of a different order than the Saint-Simonians and Fourier. Under these pressures, the principle of the golden mean was interpreted in a more conservative fashion. The anxieties that liberalism had to digest were more drastic ones, and this tended to cause it to adopt harder, more rigid positions, though such stiffening was not consonant with its own essence, which was that of a flexible search for median solutions between the different extremes.

Something of the sort was happening in relation to the other great theme of the Risorgimento. In international questions the principle of nationality certainly re-

---

[1] "Among the people the notion is taking hold that there has to be another '89, in other words that they must to do to the bourgeoisie what the bourgeoisie did to the nobility. The bourgeoisie was certainly mistaken to think that its own ideal was somehow absolute in nature; but it is also certain that these new ideas, taken to their logical limit, would end with society falling apart" (Renan to Berthelot, 1 November 1869, in Renan and Berthelot, *Correspondance*, p. 355). These anxieties can be called the common property of many of the Italian moderates too.

mained the only one capable of rousing enthusiasm, of inflaming popular passion. It had been the theme to which the project of national redemption had appealed, in which it had found its justification; and like a beacon, it still shone forth.

The ancient flame was still alive, though its rays no longer lighted the way for all of the peoples, but only the Italian people. For the period of years examined here, this is documented by the phenomenon of irredentism, which from this point of view meant that the Italy of 1859 and 1866 lived on in the Italy of the end of the century, keeping the ideal of nationality alive even when it ran counter to the official policy of the government, and preparing the ground for the last great enterprise of the liberal and national Italy of the Risorgimento, which was the war against Austria-Hungary of 1915–1918.

But this ideal was also losing its original revolutionary thrust; the old dream of making a completely new Europe was renounced. Those who still held to the ideal of nationality jettisoned all extremism and embraced the philosophy of the golden mean, citing the need for European equilibrium, the general requirements of international life, the danger of ruining everything by being too rigid in applying principles. Marselli stated unequivocally that it was necessary to unite the principle of nationality with that of equilibrium, and many others echoed this. For the moderates, it was an utterly logical position: they wanted reformism to replace the revolution, and moral tension to slacken now that Italy had set its own house in order. For many on the Left, giving up the universal dreams of Mazzini and Cattaneo was not as logically coherent with their former beliefs: but this of course was the proof that the revolutionary spirit had come to an end. The principle of nationality had seemed to Cattaneo shining, pure, and everlasting.[2] Now, however, there was some doubt that it could always be taken as an absolute guide to political action, and purity and everlastingness were transformed into compromise and transience, into dealing with individual cases and coming to terms with European equilibrium and the international situation as it then stood.

The fact that in France Albert Sorel put the principle of nationality in the category of all the other tactics employed in politics to throw an idealistic cloak over very precise and concrete interests was not a great marvel. A large part of French thought and French public opinion had always been either indifferent or hostile to nationality; Michelet, Quinet, and the democrats had been bitterly contested on this basis, and fifteen years before Sorel the principle of nationality had been called *une grosse blague*, simply an instrument of war and revolution, a commonplace, by a man whose opinions were very different from his, Proudhon.[3] But Italy was different: here even the moderates had had to accept the message of Mazzini, transforming themselves from federalists into adherents of

---

[2] Cattaneo, *Dell'insurrezione di Milano*, p. 293.

[3] Cf. E. Dolléans, *Proudhon* (Paris, 1948), pp. 408–409. Evidently Sorel and Proudhon have different reasons. For Proudhon the reconstitution of the nationalities was only a diversionary movement by the reactionaries against the social revolution. In Italy, he thought, unity was desired by the bourgeoisie in order that they might attend to their own business and "get fat": cf. M. Amoudruz, *Proudhon et l'Europe* (Paris, 1945), p. 81.

the unitary state, and hoisting the banner of the nation's rights, until Rome was taken. In Italy, where the principle of nationality constituted the reason for the existence of the new common life, the skeptical words of Gaetano Mosca made a strange new sound in 1882 as he insisted on force, brutal force, as one of the major factors in the constitution of nations, and like his French predecessors drained the principle of nationality of its absolute ideal value, to make of it an instrument of war. Governments made use of it as it suited them. When one has to make war, one needs a reason, and in the absence of anything better the principle of nationality can always be interpreted in such a way as to furnish some reason: "this is how the world goes in the nineteenth century."[4]

The reasons lay, no doubt, in the novelty of European experience after 1870, especially in the all too visible play of great power interests around the Balkan nations, and the deal-making and compromises that went on at the Congress of Berlin in 1878. There was the fact that Italy had achieved its aims and wanted to hold on to what it had won without exposing it to risk. Whether the cause was the lesson of things as they are, or the natural desire to hold onto one's gains, faith in the principle waned and began to lose the absolute character that had made it, in Mazzini's case, a religion.

The lesson of reality led to the abandonment of general revolutionary messianism, it caused nations to look to themselves alone, to concentrate on their own power and force. The old principle of nationality led to the unfolding of a very different nationalism in the future, which found fierce supporters even in the countries that had actually been lukewarm for the rights of the nations, beginning with France and England.

This then was the flowing together of themes old and new. Exactly what concrete shape they were to take was still the secret of the future. By this I mean that fate had not yet decided that nationality should turn into nationalism, and the mission of Rome should turn from a mission of science to a mission of might; the way was not laid down from eternity, and above all the territory between the Alps and the Apennines was not a world unto itself. The various motifs could develop and interweave, one might dominate and the other decline, according to how matters developed north of the Alps. Ideals and forces had to gauge themselves not only against Italian life but also against European life; just as fear of the coming universal deluge was excited once again by an event outside Italy, the Paris Commune, likewise skepticism about great principles and the recognition of force as the supreme goddess were Italian manifestations of a general European attitude.

The motifs that have been separately analyzed here were nourished by the general experience of the west, not just by the Italian experience, and they intertwined, acting on each other within the general flow of the historical process, a process that had actually become what Renan had foretold in 1870, a kind of

---

[4] G. Mosca, "I fattori della nazionalità," in *Rivista europea*, anno 13, vol. 27, fasc. 4 (16 February 1882), pp. 708–709, 720.

oscillation between patriotic questions and democratic and social questions.[5] It could happen that certain tendencies, ideas, and sentiments that in 1870–71, and in the period immediately following, were almost the property of one political party, became in time the patrimony of the opposing party: that is, while those tendencies and ideas did not vary, they were abandoned by their earlier defenders and were seized upon by those who had once impugned them. This is what happened in the case of attitudes for Germany and against France, and vice versa.

In 1870 the proclamation of the republic in Paris had won the democrats allied with Cavallotti over to the French cause, but it had in some cases slightly diluted and in others washed entirely away the sympathy many moderates felt for France. Bonghi and *La Perseveranza* had merely deplored the instability and caprice of the French, but Civinini and *La Nazione* had passed resolutely over into the opposite camp. This was the first clear case of the influence of ideological currents on the attitudes of the parties to international relations, and the further course of events would accentuate much more this inevitable linkage between domestic problems and external problems. There were a few on either side who remained faithful to their old ideals: Bonghi and Visconti Venosta to the memory of Magenta and Solferino, and to a radical mistrust of Bismarckism,[6] Crispi to his old aversion for the French claim to superiority, and to the ancient conviction that Italy, in order to become great, would have to shake off its subjection to the politics and the civilization of France. But the majority, as usual, changed course as the times changed. The lively sympathies for Bismarck's Germany among groups on the Left at the time of the *Kulturkampf*, sympathies that were strengthened between 1871 and 1874 by the clerical and reactionary flavor of the French national assembly, withered rapidly as soon as the France of Gambetta, of free thought and democracy, replaced the France of the duc de Broglie, the France of "moral order." And in the end the Triple Alliance garnered its main support from the conservatives, who were driven by domestic concerns to look with fondness on the monarchies that stood for order, and with fearful repugnance on republican and radical France. Meanwhile, the democrats were raising a toast to Latin brotherhood, as the moderates had once done.[7]

---

[5] "Lettre à M. Strauss," in the *Journal des Débats* for 16 September 1870, reprinted in Renan, *La réforme*, p. 183.

[6] On Bonghi and his unfailing dislike of Germany and the Triple Alliance, cf. Maturi, "Ruggero Bonghi e i problemi di politica estera," and F. D'Ovidio, *L'avversione di Ruggiero Bonghi alla Triplice Alleanza* (Campobasso, 1915).

[7] The evolution of *Il Diritto* is typical. It strongly supported the German alliance between 1871 and 1876, but then changed its tune. As early as 15 September 1874 ("La politica del governo francese") it was saying: "we are no more enemies of France than we are friends of Germany. We have approved, and will always approve, of the anticlerical policy of Prince Bismarck." The writer goes on to say that the paper had opposed French policy because it was reactionary and clerical. "If . . . the German government should turn clerical, and . . . the French government should begin to oppose the ultramontanes, we too would change our tune." On 7 March 1876 ("Il discorso della Corona") the paper expresses its wonder at the fact that in the speech from the throne of the previous day Germany and Austria were mentioned and France was not, "now that this nation has definitely

Still others, who were preoccupied above all by the danger of clericalism and the Roman question, and feared that it was from that quarter that deadly peril might yet come for Italian unity, changed their stance more than once accordingly as France appeared to be more or less favorable to the Roman curia. In this they gave a practical demonstration of the truth of what Visconti Venosta had once asserted in a diplomatic context, that is that all Italian policy in foreign relations was dominated by the Roman question.[8] A case in point is Domenico Farini, who was hostile at first to "moral order," but then converted and sought to demonstrate the sympathies of liberal France for Italy. He assumed the role of intermediary between Gambetta, Depretis, and Cairoli, and sought to induce Umberto I to attend the universal exposition of Paris in 1878 because in this way the king would be convinced that the Italian monarchy had nothing to fear from the French republic or its expansion, indeed that the union of the two nations would guarantee the cause of liberty in Europe, defending and protecting the interests of the Mediterranean powers.[9] But then, after Tunis, and perhaps especially after the reconciliation between Leo XIII and the French republic, his *Diario* shows that his faith in the common "cause" changed into a distrustful, implacable aversion for France, which, like Crispi, he thought guilty of conspiring with the Vatican against the very unity of Italy.

But these are the secret ways of providence in history, through which ideas and aspirations sometimes find the bearer best suited to them, and like the torch of Marathon, are passed from hand to hand without changing their nature. What really was important in the controversies of 1870–71 for the future course of Italian history was the emergence of a fault line between political groups—a fault line created by differing preferences where foreign alliances were concerned. This divergence was not purely about concrete, specific cases, but was general and abstract, and appeared to be an a priori fact of political life. In this period the moderates in general were, in the jargon of the times, Francophiles, and the others Germanophiles. But contrary to Amari's mistaken belief that the Italians had lost their habit of projecting their yearnings and their hatred beyond the mountains and over the seas,[10] there remained a constant deep difference about what friendships to seek or to reject with this or that foreign state. It was an

---

adopted the republican constitution . . . [and] is showing that it desires to pursue a sincerely benevolent policy toward Italy, a policy entirely anticlerical." Finally, on 1 January 1878 ("L'on. Gambetta in Italia") *Il Diritto* salutes Gambetta, a loyal friend of Italy and a defender of liberty in all its forms, adding that "whatever may be the consequences of the development of the parties [in Italy], they are all unanimous in considering Italy as the natural friend of France." Italy as the "natural friend" of France: what a change from the language used between 1870 and 1874! On 13 September 1870 ("La pace") Germany had been, for *Il Diritto*, the "natural and permanent" ally of Italy.

[8] Visconti Venosta, personal letter to de Launay, 7 March 1871 (ACR, *Carte Visconti Venosta*, pacco 5, fasc. 2).

[9] Farini to Cairoli, 1 June 1878 (MRP, *Carte Cairoli*, pacco 31). The close of the letter is also revealing about how the Roman question biased all judgments: "if one day the struggle between Germany and the papacy should cease, and it might do so before long, I foresee one of the most important points of contact, affinity, and sympathy between us and the powerful empire dissolving."

[10] Amari, *Carteggio* 2:205.

unhappy circumstance, as Bonghi noted, "because a division between the parties that does not depend on the different ends they want to reach, or the means they want to use, but on an external alliance to which each is determined to remain faithful, is a corruption and a great danger. Alliances are tools that ought to appear neutral in themselves to any national party, and different alliances ought to be employed as the circumstances dictate."[11]

Italian public opinion truly was, then and later, divided in its sympathies for Germany and France. Among the elements that combined to range the Italians into these opposing parties were feelings that they took for granted, but also questions of principle, ideological reasons of domestic politics, and a priori determinations of the objectives of foreign policy: one side looked to the wide expanse of the Mediterranean, and the other looked only across the Alps.

France not only signified cultural ties of long standing, and the recollection of Magenta and Solferino, the Paris bourse and the Rothschilds; it also, and primarily, signified a similarity of domestic political development, and the continuing influence of the fortunes of the political parties in one country on the fortunes of those in the other. "It's all very well to rail at France," Nigra wrote to Minghetti. "Those who rail the loudest are still reacting, even unconsciously, to its ineluctable influence. The events of 18 March [1876] are in large part the result of the recent French elections, and the stabilization of the republic in France."[12] It was a little like what Tommaseo said of Manzoni, that France was always there before his eyes, an example to follow or to shun . . .[13]

Thus even though Italian foreign policy was pulled essentially into the orbit of Germany, domestic politics with its parties and ideologies continued to feel the tug of France. This was a strident disparity whose effects came fully to light in the period 1914–15.[14]

German political life lay at a much greater distance from the Italian experience, and the most it could offer was an example to be pondered, something to quicken the longings of conservatives unhappy with the parliamentary regime and eager for some kind of chancellorship in Italy. Even German culture, though it could and did cast a spell over the Italian university world, was never in a position to counteract the traditional and popular influence of French culture on the Italian elites in general. As for the German economy, it too only emerged as an important force in Italian life at a late stage,[15] and German finance gave

---

[11] Bonghi, *Nove anni* 2:357 (31 July 1870).

[12] 3 January 1877, from St. Petersburg (BCB, *Carte Minghetti*, cart. XX, fasc. 73).

[13] Tommaseo, *Colloqui col Manzoni* (Florence, 1929), p. 143.

[14] The Austrian ambassador, Haymerle, noted this in 1877: "The foreign policy [of Italy] is dominated by Germany, while the domestic situation of Italy undergoes the influence of France" (Haymerle, report, 22 December 1877, no. 76 A; SAW, *P.A.*, XI/86). And Artom wrote to Nigra on 23 November 1888: "Here we continue to have a radical domestic politics in the French style, and a Germanic foreign policy" (AE, *Carte Nigra*).

[15] Between 1870 and 1880, the volume of trade between Italy and Germany was very modest, far below the levels of trade with France, England, and Austria—or even with Switzerland and Russia (Corbino, *Annali dell'economia italiana* 2:163–64 [Città di Castello, 1931]). It grew considerably between 1881 and 1890, especially after 1887 (ibid., 3:188–89), thanks in part to the breaking off of

serious competition to the longer-established French finance only at century's end. But there was one thing that by itself was enough to counterbalance all these other factors together, and that was German military force, the myth, now widely believed, of German invincibility.

France and Germany were thus really the two poles on which depended peace and war for the Italian people. None of the other European powers was able to impinge so profoundly on Italian life.

Not England, certainly. The Franco-Prussian War was a harsh blow for British prestige. The government in London appeared to comport itself in a listless and impotent manner, and no one had a clear perception of the serious difficulty in which Britain found itself at the same time because of the dispute with the United States over the *Alabama*, which had provoked a strong campaign by the American papers in favor of Russia when the latter repudiated the clauses relative to the Black Sea, and even offers of support from the government in Washington to the government in St. Petersburg.[16] These European repercussions of Great Britain's world policy escaped notice, and what remained were the facts: England was taking a battering on all sides, it was unable to get Bismarck to budge an inch, and in substance it had to endorse Russia's gesture of force in the Orient. So the impression was that England was no longer at the helm of European politics: "and . . . one . . . of the effects of the recent war will be that the continental powers will no longer count on anyone except themselves, whether in acting or in preventing action." The old school "of those English statesmen who made it the glory of their country always to be on top of European events is dead, and in their place we have wary stewards who are stowing the maxim *rule Britannia* away in a bale of cotton."[17] These impressions evaporated when Gladstone was succeeded by Disraeli, and Gladstone's lack of interest in foreign policy by the imperial program of Disraeli. Gladstone himself, when he returned to power, changed his stance, and between 1880 and 1885 provided the most reliable, though not terribly resolute, support for Italian foreign policy. Then came Salisbury and the Italian-English accord of 12 February 1887. But even at times of the greatest diplomatic entente between the two governments, England never had a concrete influence in Italian life comparable to that of France or Germany. France and Germany intruded every day, even in the little commonplace affairs of individuals, with their fashions or their books, and the debates in their newspapers; England was far away. It remained as a sort of totem, an idol to which all turned with a bow of respect as being the homeland of liberty and parliamentary institutions, and at the same time, the dominating power on the seas. Incense swirled around it, but that only made it more remote. I am an English sort of chap,[18]

---

trade between Italy and France. Between 1891 and 1900 Germany rose to first place in volume of trade with Italy (ibid., 4:182), and this is even more true after 1900 (ibid., 5:210).

[16] Cf. Meine, *England und Deutschland*, p. 31; S. Goriaïnov, *Le Bosphore et les Dardanelles* (Paris, 1910), pp. 193–95; K. Rheindorf, *Die Schwarze Meer (Pontus) Frage, 1856–1871* (Berlin, 1925), pp. 100 and 107.

[17] "La politica inglese," in *La Perseveranza* for 21 February and 1 March 1871. The two articles are by Bonghi.

[18] Crispi, *Discorsi Parlamentari* 2:481 (a speech to the Chamber of 10 March 1881).

Crispi declared, and all who were faithful followers of the liberal idea could have said so too. But they were English in principle; and in practice, while doctrinaire thinkers continued to long for political rivalry between two parties on the British model, it was the French radicals and socialists who actually had an influence on the domestic struggle in Italy. Friendship with England and respect for England were dogmas that were given full expression in the ministerial statement of 22 May 1882, an appendix to the first treaty of the Triple Alliance, in which the Italian government declared that the stipulations of the treaty could "in no case" be considered as being directed against England. There might have been some cause for surprise in this state of affairs: England had been anything but helpful in 1859 and had never put itself directly on the line for Italy, whereas France had been the first and greatest collaborator toward the successful outcome of the Risorgimento, and Germany had evolved out of Prussia, whose alliance had allowed the Venetian state to be incorporated into Italy. Yet France and Germany were the objects of unconquerable love and unending hatred in Italy, while England received reverence pure and simple. The explanation lies partly in political and military considerations arising out of Italy's lengthy and undefended coastline, her maritime cities, and the omnipotent British navy. There was also the fact that for almost two centuries the temple of liberty for western thought had been the island from which, most recently, the message of Manchester had issued, and from which Gladstone, the political incarnation of liberalism as opposed to Bismarck, still spoke. The Italians could recall centuries of continuous interaction with the French and the Germans, centuries of love and hate, of conflict and war. They were bound up with a whole Italian tradition, ever since the age of Barbarossa, the communes, and the house of Anjou, a tradition that lived on in united Italy and gave a patina almost of antiquity to its modern history. This intensity of passion was missing in the case of England; it was an experience that the distant future still held in store for the Italians, on a day when the incense would dissipate and the totem would be seen for what it was, warts and all.

At the other extremity of Europe, there was Russia. Geographically it was remote, so that the two nations were unable to do each other "much good or much harm,"[19] as Nigra noted when he was ambassador to St. Petersburg. There had indeed been a rapprochement between 1876 and 1880, a period of friction between Italy and Austria, and this had even produced a certain amount of speculation in the Italian and foreign press about a secret accord, even an Italian-Russian alliance, supposedly fostered by Tornielli. But in the overview of our period, this was a parenthesis: in the subsequent phase the two governments were even more distant politically than they were geographically. This alienation reached a point between 1886 and 1895 where Crispi finally had to take steps to

---

[19] Nigra, personal letter to Mancini, 9 June 1881. Relations between Rome and St. Petersburg are "excellent and cordial," but lack any mutual commitment, which there is not now and never has been. In general there are no divergent interests; the two nations "are called to be friends, and they are" (De Vecchi archive). Nigra states again that no secret accord existed between Italy and Russia from 1876 to 1882–though there was a lot of talk about it in the press between 1877 and 1878—in a classified report of 1 February 1888 (AE, *Cas. Verdi*, 16, fasc. 1).

reduce it, turning to Nigra once again in the hope that his magic touch could bring back to life the friendly relations that had vanished.[20] Similarly, at the beginning of our period, the winter of 1870–71, the Italian government had clearly revealed that it saw Russia not as a possible friend and collaborator but as a gross threat in the Mediterranean, against which the barriers had to be erected.[21] The time of Salvatore Contarini and the idea of locating Italy at an equal distance from England and Russia as a way of safeguarding its Mediterranean interests[22] lay far in the future. Rather there was ongoing distrust of any Mediterranean policy at all on the part of the Russian empire, sustained not only by the view that England was Italy's traditional friend, with whom she must stand to eternity, but also by the recollection of the Crimea, and Cavour's words about the danger for Europe, for Italy, and for Piedmont, of Russian predominance in the Mediterranean. And now, at the end of October 1870, there came the unexpected Russian repudiation of the clauses concerning the Black Sea, to prove that the distant colossus was once again on the move, aiming at conquest and hegemony.[23]

Russia had to be kept out of the Mediterranean, especially now that the war of 1870 had brought to light the close rapport between the courts of Berlin and St. Petersburg, and Europe was facing the prospect of a Russian-German predominance which would mean the end of European liberty. Fifty years before, Alexander I had been greeted as a new messiah by the nations engaged in a struggle against the Napoleonic hegemony, and the flames of Moscow had seemed to be the aurora of liberty for the world.[24] He had defended in a laudable manner the independence of his country, and had stood up admirably for the independence of Europe, but when he returned to Russia he had been dragged down once more by this nation which was so much less civilized than he was personally.[25] From that time the empire of the tsar had been seen not as the defender of liberty, but as the new incarnation of the spirit of conquest, a new Napoleon in waiting. "My ambition is as vast as space, and as patient as time,"[26] Lamartine had made Russia say, and the words summarized the attitude of western public opinion, including Italian opinion, faced with the great Slavic state. The west had long feared the danger posed by Muscovite voracity for empire; it had trembled at the thought of Russia marching like Attila in the direction of Constantinople, and thence becoming the savage dictator of Europe. In Italy there were those who had thought the answer lay in "regaining the support of the Latin papacy," as the neo-Guelph

[20] Cf. ch. 16, n. 50 below.

[21] The attitude of the Italian government at the conference of London in 1871 will be treated in detail in the second volume of the present work. Cf. above, p. 101.

[22] Cf. "Legatus" (the pseudonym of R. Cantalupo), *Vita diplomatica di Salvatore Contarini* (Rome, 1947), passim.

[23] Note Engels's belief, in March 1871, that Russia was preparing for a war of conquest (which would also be a way of diverting attention from internal difficulties); Engels, *Notes sur la guerre de 1870–71*, pp. 300 ff. and cf. also p. 197.

[24] Constant, preface to the first edition of *De l'esprit de conquête et d'usurpation* in *Cours de politique constitutionnelle* 2:131.

[25] Balbo, *Delle speranze d'Italia*, ch. 9, pp. 93–94.

[26] In 1840, reported by Mickiewicz in *L'idea polacca e l'idea russa* (in *Gli Slavi*, p. 291).

Carlo Troya had put it in 1844,[27] while there were others who hailed with relief the creation of a united Germany, since its international mission was not that of violating the European nationalities, but on the contrary that of protecting them against Slavic invasion, of hurling Russia back into Asia.[28]

Russia was not only a gigantic political power, it was barbarism on the march: on 8 February 1855 Cesare Correnti portrayed the Crimean War as a war of ideologies, Europe against Russia, civilization against barbarity, liberty against the heroism of the enslaved.[29] His voice reechoed the opinions of many others, who had been proposing this scenario for some time. England versus Russia signified the clash of two opposing trends within the civilized world, it signified progress versus barbarism, the part of civilization that was moving forward versus the part that was moving backward, as Cesare Balbo had put it.[30] Cavour himself in 1848—long before the occasion on 6 February 1855 when he pointed out to the Piedmontese Parliament the mortal danger of a Russian victory bringing reactionary opposition to progress, constitutionalism, nationality, to everything that was the new lifeblood of Piedmont and Italy—had referred to the tsar as the acknowledged and potent enemy of the Italian Risorgimento. "Woe to us," he had said, if an insuperable barrier were not set up "against the barbaric torrent that threatens us from the north."[31] It is true that in 1859 and 1860 he had seen things differently, expressing appreciation for the considerable assistance the St. Petersburg government had undeniably given to the Italian cause, especially in the secret treaty of 3 March 1859 with Napoleon III.[32] In fact, one of his closest

[27] Cf. B. Croce, "Russia ed Europa," in *Pensiero politico e politica attuale* (Bari, 1946), p. 52.

[28] Thus Marselli, *Avvenimenti del 1870–71*, p. 90.

[29] Cf. Valsecchi, *Il Risorgimento e l'Europa*, pp. 450–51.

[30] Balbo, *Mémoire sur les derniers évènements de l'Orient* (1844), published as an appendix to *Delle speranze d'Italia*, p. 495). This *Mémoire*, which proposes an alliance between England, France, Austria, and Piedmont, presages Cavour's position. For Balbo's attitude to Russia, cf. ibid., p. 499, and *Delle speranze d'Italia*, ch. 9, pp. 102–103, where we find a strong similarity to Cavour's speech to the Chamber of 6 February 1855, a similarity apparent even in the imagery. On the thought of Gioberti, who also espoused the contrast between Russia and Europe as between serfdom and liberty, barbarism and polite society, cf. his *Il Primato morale e civile degli Italiani* 2:169 (Lausanne, 1846). And cf. in general E. Rota, "La partecipazione di Cavour alla guerra d'Oriente nei suoi precedenti ideali," in *Studi in onore di Gino Luzzatto* 3:149 ff.; and also D. Visconti, *La concezione unitaria dell'Europa nel Risorgimento* (Milan, 1948), pp. 127, 155.

[31] Cf. *Il Risorgimento* for 4 January, 28 March, 23 May 1848.

[32] On Cavour's appreciation of Russia's support, cf. Cavour, *Lettere* 6:337 and 339–40, and *Il Carteggio Cavour-Nigra dal 1858 al 1861* 1:174 ff., 201, 237–38 (Bologna, 1926), and 2:117. Visconti Venosta also acknowledged that "Russia favored rather than hindered our independence and unity: its hostility with Austria aided us and could aid us again" (in his instructions to Cadorna for the London conference, 28 December 1870; AE, *Missioni all'estero*, cart. 2). In his instructions to Barbolani, the new envoy to St. Petersburg, he states on 16 January 1875: "it is known that Russia contributed efficaciously, in accord with France, to the recognition of the kingdom of Italy on the part of the other great powers" (AE, reg. *Istruzioni* [1875–1882], no. 22).

On the encounter at Warsaw in 1860 between Alexander II and Franz Joseph, and its advantageous consequences for Italy, cf. L. Salvatorelli, *Prima e dopo il Quarantotto* (Turin, 1948), p. 153. And cf. especially the important article of P. Silva, "I rapporti fra il Piemonte e la Russia prima dello scoppio della guerra del 1859," *Nuova Antologia* (July 1945): 247 ff., which is based on unpublished Russian documents. In fact, later on during the grave crisis of Mentana, when many in Europe believed that Italian unity was likely to crumble, the Russian position was clearly friendly to Italy, certainly much more so than that of England: see Gorchakov's statements to Prince von Reuss

collaborators, Isacco Artom, had left among his papers a note to future historians advising them never to let the Italians forget the great service done to the cause of Italian independence by Russia's policy and by the entire Slavic family of nations.[33] It is also true that in his statements of 6 February 1855 Cavour's main intention was to back up with ringing proclamations the blank check he had signed by joining in the Crimean alliance. But the diplomatic advantage that Italy gained from the Russian position in 1859 was known to few, and the fact that to claim the public's attention Cavour had had to evoke the Russian peril was sufficient proof of what the public generally felt and thought about the Muscovite empire. His public statements were not forgotten, and continued to influence opinion, an influence that was reinforced from the other side of the political fence when Mazzini made similar declarations on the danger represented by the Cossacks and the knout for the cause of liberty and the nationalities.[34]

Russia was a huge, immense force, one that was both known and unknown, that seemed ever a compound of Europe and Asia, of Occident and Orient, of the civil and the barbarous, a body dressed in European clothing but animated with the spirit of the Tartars.[35] It was not yet a citizen of equal standing in the civil consortium of the other nations, the European cultural community to which Tolstoy, Dostoevsky, and Mussorgsky had not yet introduced Russian culture.[36] Russia was still Genghis Khan. The apocryphal political testament of Peter the Great was still taken at face value, and was cited every time there was alarm over some political move by the St. Petersburg government.[37] Even when it was no longer formally accepted as genuine, it was believed to express accurately the substance of the secret plans of the autocrats of St. Petersburg. "Se non è vero, è ben trovato," they had said in 1864, admitting that Russia was indeed showing

---

on the Russian interest in Italian unity, in seeing Italy strengthened rather than weakened, and on Italy's "warm" friendship (*Die auswärtige Politik Preussens, 1858–1871* 9:615–16; for the English attitude see ibid., 9:595–96). On the strong sympathy for Italy in Russian society, cf. Adelaide Ristori's letter to Cavour, 4 April 1861, published by C. Tumiati in *Il Ponte* 4 (1948): 1138.

[33] Artom, *L'opera politica*, p. 361. In Artom's view, the statements of Cavour on the necessity for Piedmont to take part in the Crimean expedition for the purpose of halting the Russian advance on Constantinople were made for public consumption: the real purpose was to shatter the alliance between Austria and Russia (ibid., pp. 347 ff.).

[34] Cattaneo also expressed aversion for the Russian autocrat and the "Asiatic principle of total military authority" (Cattaneo, *Epistolario* 1:356 and cf. p. 450). For Andrea Luigi Mazzini, Russia was "a power frontally hostile to the liberal mission of the European peoples" (cited in Morandi, *L'idea dell'unità politica d'Europa*, p. 51).

[35] Dostoevsky, *Diario di uno scrittore*, observes more than once (pp. 434, 642, 821) that in substance this was the view generally held of the Russians in Europe. Various testimony to this can be found in Rattazzi, *Rattazzi et son temps* 2:486; *D.D.F.*, 1st ser., 2:319; G. Boglietti, "L'autocrazia e il nihilismo russo," *Nuova Antologia* 57 (1881): 385. As late as 1898, Paul Cambon wrote: "The real Russian . . . is more distant from us than the Turk or the Chinese. We judge Russia on the basis of a tiny aristocracy of civilized aspect: what disappointments our infatuation holds in store for us!" (Cambon, *Correspondance* 1:446).

[36] Dostoevsky noted that *Anna Karenina* was perhaps the great proof that cultured Europe was asking Russia to supply (*Diario di uno scrittore*, p. 680).

[37] The demonstration that the testament was false, which Berkholz maintained in 1863, was furnished by Bresslau in 1879 ("Das Testament Peter's des Grossen," in *Historische Zeitschrift* 41 [1879]: 385 ff.).

patience and forcing itself to be civil, but adding that it was more formidable in this coiled state than it was when its policy was frankly one of expansion and provocation, more dangerous now that it was also playing at the game of revolution and of ideas, "stoking popular passions, speaking the language of emancipation to the people that it has selected as its victims. Before it proudly called itself Holy Russia, today it calls itself Slavic Russia; before it haughtily wrapped itself in the cloak of the barbarian and the Cossack, today it proclaims itself part of a great race, the redeemer of the entire Slavic race."[38]

Through the garish fantasies of the young Oriani the mounted Sarmatian warrior had galloped, the ultimate conqueror in European history. Ungainly like all titans, he had passed abruptly from infancy to manhood, from the cruelty of the wilderness to a ferocious form of civilization. Lacking all tradition and thus all ideals, raised on the confines of the real Europe, he was now the possessor of a handful of smuggled European ideas. Russian civilization was artificial, and the sun would have to warm the endless tundra for many centuries before it would bloom naturally there; indeed, the sun might never warm it enough.[39]

Yet Russia also began to make a few converts, who hoped to see the "decadent" west rejuvenated by the influx of fresh, virgin Slavic energies.[40] They turned an attentive ear to the voices rising from within the Slavic world in justification and praise of the Slavs. Thirty years before, this had been the message of Mickiewicz: the Slavs might be inferior from the point of view of mechanical progress, but they were superior from the moral vantage point. Their souls were greater, nowhere else were hearts so fervid, nowhere else was the future awaited so steadfastly. Their wait was solemn, for all anticipated the coming of a new idea.[41] Now the words of the Polish exile, who had contrasted the terrible spirit of Russia to the Christian spirit of his own nation, were picked up by the Russians themselves, and the great archimandrite of the Slav movement, Katkoff, had announced the imminent revelation of Russia under a new aspect. It would cease to be a dark Asiatic power and would become an indispensable moral force in Europe, achieving the realization of a Greek-Slavic civilization destined to complement Latin-German civilization, while the latter was fated in its absence to remain incomplete and inert in its sterile hauteur.[42] Dostoevsky pressed the

---

[38] This article, "Testamento di Pietro il Grande," published in *L'Italia* in 1864, was attributed by Ferrarelli to De Sanctis and published in De Sanctis, *Scritti politici*, pp. 3 ff. (I am assured by Benedetto Croce and Nino Cortese that De Sanctis was not the author, although since it was published in his journal it must be considered to conform to rather than contradict his ideas.) It states further that German unity will be a bulwark against Russia. *L'Osservatore Romano*, in the political review for 26 July 1872, states that Pan-Slavist propaganda is another element on which Russia can count, in addition to its army and its fleet, and that this element deserves more attention than it has received.

[39] Oriani, *Quartetto*, pp. 11–13.

[40] Cf. G. Boglietti, "Nihilisti e slavofili," *Nuova Antologia* 58 (1881): 255.

[41] Mickiewicz, *L'idea polacca e l'idea russa*, pp. 315 ff.

[42] In an article in the *Moscow Gazzette* on the eve of the Pan-Slavist congress of 1867 (Boglietti, "Nihilisti e slavofili," p. 242). On this, and on a work by Nikolai Danilewski entitled *Russia and Europe*, and referred to as the bible of Pan-Slavism, cf. K. Stählin, *Geschichte Russlands von den Anfängen bis zur Gegenwart* 4.1:264 ff. (Königsberg-Berlin, 1939); B. H. Sumner, *Russia and the Balcans, 1870–1880* (Oxford, 1937), pp. 56 ff., 76 ff.

point further, proclaiming that Russia was not the old Europe but a new, young, strong Europe striding forth, and that it fell to Russia to speak the new word, the final consecration of the fraternity of all men.[43]

But these words of emancipation were the same ones that appeared to westerners to be nothing more than a tenuous veil screening Russia's boundless political ambitions and its will to dominate. The call for a new civilization still masked the old spirit of Genghis Khan; Pan-Slavism was only the latest incarnation of the spirit of conquest. As such, it was a direct menace to Italy: toasts like the one that was offered during festivities at the Croat casino in Fiume at the beginning of 1871 to the emperor of Russia, whose dominion alone could ensure the prosperity of the Adriatic coast,[44] gave proof that Russophile propaganda was taking root among the Slavs, even along the Adriatic. So it was not simply a generic Russian-German supremacy over Europe that was feared, nor even, more specifically, Russia's ingress into the eastern Mediterranean: the danger was that of seeing Russia in the Adriatic. Thus ideological aversion to the Russia of the tsar, the Russia that sent deportees to Siberia, and distrust of the Tartar spirit, *le génie asiatique*, the semibarbarism of Russian life, all these general elements of western European thought assumed a precise political shape, becoming a vital and serious problem of international relations. An expanding Russia and an expanding Pan-Slavism gave little pleasure to the Italian politicians; Minghetti, Visconti Venosta, and Crispi were agreed on that.[45] Robilant spoke for their shared views when he said: "I bear Russia no ill will, but . . . I cannot look with indifference on its advance in the Balkan peninsula, because if it should take a single further step in that direction, that would have very heavy and perhaps irreparable consequences for us. Anyone who is not blind can see this."[46]

Balbo had made the observation that in Italy's interest, and in the interest of Christendom (that is, of the "community of peoples"), Austria was very much to be preferred as the master of eastern Europe to Russia.[47] The proposal made in his *Speranze d'Italia* to open up the way to the east for Austria and get it out of Italy had aligned the preoccupations of an Italian with the preoccupations of a European—the specific cause of independence in the peninsula and the general cause of Christendom. The latter was threatened with an enormous regression if Russia should gain preponderance in Europe because of the evident inferiority of Muscovite civilization, which would surely attempt to bring the other civilizations down to its level.[48] Italy's interest was identical with that of Europe: both required a barrier against Russia. The answer was to ease Austria out of Italy but

---

[43] Dostoevsky, *Diario di uno scrittore*, pp. 649 and 806.

[44] Report of Seyssel di Sommariva, the consul in Fiume, 10 February 1871.

[45] Minghetti, *Lettere fra la regina Margherita e Marco Minghetti*, p. 211. For Crispi, cf. his *Politica estera* 1:287, where for once Crispi makes an appeal to Cavour's authority (in relation to the Crimean alliance).

[46] Robilant, letter to Greppi, 29 December 1886 (in De Cesare, *Il conte Giuseppe Greppi*, p. 241).

[47] Balbo, *Delle speranze d'Italia*, ch. 9, pp. 103–104, and *Meditazioni storiche*, pp. 536–37.

[48] Balbo, *Meditazioni storiche*, pp. 518–19.

not sap its strength, so that it could function as a forward line of defense, protecting Europe from the Slavic tide in the Danube valley and the Balkans.

Now, with the spirit of revolution subsiding, while moderatism prevailed and the men of the Left were being attracted by moderate aims and methods, Balbo's ideas emerged triumphant. Austria's turn eastward, and its release of the Italian lands that were still unredeemed, were constantly linked from that time on.[49] This occurred notably in public speeches and press comment between 1876 and 1878, and also in article one of the separate Italian-Austrian treaty of 20 February 1887, negotiated by Robilant and destined to become article seven in the definitive edition of the Triple Alliance: with its formula of offsetting gains and losses, it was the diplomatic enactment of the old principles of the *Speranze d'Italia*. The necessity for Austria, the monster that Mazzini had so hated, the archenemy of the Risorgimento, to thrive became an axiom for all the Italian politicians, Crispi and Cavallotti included. Crispi followed in the steps of Balbo when he depicted Austria as the eastward-facing element of civilization.

The old fear that Russia might pour across Europe was now joined by alarm at the overwhelming power of Germany in the wake of the Franco-Prussian War. *La Perseveranza* began to make this an issue in 1871. Austria certainly represents the negation of the principle of nationality, the paper said, and we have never had much sympathy for it. But the situation today imposes on us a choice that has nothing to do with sympathy, since "the extraordinary events of the last ten months have in their evolution changed the face of the world and upset the equilibrium of the states, and we now view the eventual collapse of the Habsburg monarchy, or even its further debilitation, as a serious danger."[50]

If the Germans of Austria should be included with Germany proper, the latter, which already had too much weight, would acquire excessive force, while the Habsburg state, reduced to its Hungarian and Slavic parts, would sink to the rank of a second-class power, "and European equilibrium, already enormously unbalanced by the recent war, would be utterly convulsed. Italy would find itself side by side with a young and vigorous Germany in the Adriatic, with whom any form of peaceful competition, and likewise any eventual hostilities, would be much more arduous than they would be with Austria. This then is why, in the interest of all of Europe, and especially in our own interest, we cannot view without apprehension the progressive decadence of Austrian power."[51] In 1871 these were exclusively moderate ideas, but not many years would pass before even the fiercest enemies of Germany, with Crispi in the lead, would be convinced that it was better to be friends with the German empire, but not to abut it directly.

To the old anti-Slav role that the moderates of the Risorgimento had ascribed to the Habsburg empire there was now added the role, not anti-German exactly,

---

[49] The fact is that Cesare Balbo's ideas had already inspired efforts, tentative ones at any rate, on the part of official Italian policy: thus between 1863 and 1865 the solution of the Venetian question had been sought in the first place in accords with Austria, which was meant to take over the Danubian principates (cf. P. Silva, *Il sessantasei* [rpt.; Milan, 1919], pp. 220 and 32 ff.).

[50] "Le tribolazioni dell' Austria," in *La Perseveranza* for 14 June 1871.

[51] *La Perseveranza* for 17 June 1871.

of serving at any rate as a cushion between Italy and the too-vigorous empire of the Hohenzollerns.[52] Austria was a necessity. Perhaps not many people would have thought, as Robilant did, that there was no other question for which "Italy would be equally obliged to draw its sword and commit all its forces as it would be if the question should ever arise of defending the existence and the potency of Austria."[53] But almost all were convinced that the Habsburg empire still fulfilled one of the greatest needs of Europe and of Italy.[54]

Of course Austria was involved with the question of Trent and Trieste, a question that remained open even when it was not referred to. The ideal of nationality might be hedged round, attenuated, emptied of its general revolutionary import, but it was still the only idealistic principle that could be invoked in moral support of policy. Italy had not yet begun to dream of empire and of vital space, to feel that the sea must be its outlet; it still held to the idea of the nation, the national state, complete with all its lands and all its sons. And so, despite everything, the Italy of the Risorgimento lived on, the forefathers pointed the way to their sons and their grandsons. Like one of those—unredeemed—watercourses of the Carso that emerge and disappear but continue to flow underground,[55] the theme of the lands that had yet to be redeemed could break out in popular meetings, in the invocations and invectives of Carducci, in the propaganda of irredentist circles, or it might be hushed, sometimes even officially disowned by organs with government responsibility. No one could ignore irredentism, and no one renounced it in his heart, even those who held it folly to display it in the piazza, and put their trust in time to bring a solution that would satisfy Italy without causing Austria to collapse. At times this could even mean casting a friendly glance in Russia's direction, since it in turn acted as a check on the Habsburgs. It could mean anxiety at, and opposition to, the further expansion of Austria in the Balkans, and the spreading of its power down the opposite shore of the Adriatic, because expansion and increase of this kind might make the possibility of a final

---

[52] This idea was put forward by many at the beginning of 1878, for example (Haymerle, report, 19 January 1878, no. 8 A; SAW, *P.A.*, XI/87).

[53] Robilant said this in the course of conversations with his close friends (R. Cappelli, "Il conte Carlo Nicolis di Robilant," *Nuova Antologia* 171 [1 June 1900]: 392). Robilant was convinced that an Italian victory in a war against Austria "might be the ruin of that ancient monarchy, which I think I am not wrong in saying, bolstered as I am by the opinion repeatedly expressed by eminent Italian thinkers, that we have every interest in keeping alive, so that it may keep Pan-Germanism and Pan-Slavism at a distance from us; their contiguity would be very much more dangerous." Cession of the Trentino by Austria ought to be the consequence, and the price, of a solid and lasting Italian-Austrian alliance (Robilant, report, 3 October 1878, published in Rosi, *L'Italia odierna*, vol. 2, tome 2, p. 1767; cited below, ch. 20, n. 108).

[54] Even at the last, the firm opposition of Avarna and Bollati to Italy's entry into the war on the side of the Triple Entente was not motivated simply by their belief that the problems of the Mediterranean, not the "sentimental" question of Trent and Trieste, were paramount for Italy. It came from their conviction that the Habsburg empire was indispensable for European equilibrium, and their fear of a Slavic advance toward the west. Cf. the correspondence between the two ambassadors published by C. Avarna di Gualtieri, "Il carteggio Avarna-Bollati: Luglio 1914–maggio 1915," *Rivista Storica Italiana* 61 (1949): 249, 262–63, 389 ff., and vol. 62 (1950): 380, 391.

[55] The image is borrowed from Salvemini, "La politica estera della Destra" (1925), p. 209. Salvemini delineates perfectly the character of Italian policy to Austria and the persistence of projects similar to Balbo's (ibid., pp. 60 ff., 210).

compromise much more fortuitous. The best thing was to stick to the status quo, in expectation of the right moment at which to reconcile Austria's eastward expansion and the adjustment of its borders with Italy.

The difficulty was that this political line, though all in all it had its own logic and inner coherence, sought to harmonize two things: a sense of European equilibrium and the spirit of nationality, reason and passion. Political calculation repeatedly ran up against immediacy of feeling, and the government's task clashed with the cry of Italian passion for Trent and Trieste. Calculation required a strong Austria: an Austria that in given circumstances needed the friendship of Italy enough to cede territory in the Val d'Adige and beyond Isonzo, but was strong enough to impede a general cataclysm of the Danubian situation. Sentiment reminded the Italians not only that Trent and Trieste were unredeemed but also that Austria was the historical foe of their Risorgimento. Austria, in the popular imagination, was always the "Tedeschi" [Germans] of 1848 and 1859, the Five Days of Milan, Venice, Palestro and San Martino, and finally Lissa and Custoza. The phantasms of the past were alive, and close by, and their gaze was turned to the future. To get along with Austria meant getting along with the "hanging emperor," and it was something that political calculation was capable of, but never popular feeling. Minghetti was deluding himself when he asserted in the Chamber in 1872 that he could no longer understand feelings of hatred for Austria, since there was no longer any reason for them to exist, and that with the old rancor laid to rest, Austria should be seen as merely a sister nation, looked upon with benevolent affection, as our friend.[56] Only four years later, the commemoration at Milan of the seven-hundredth anniversary of the battle of Legnano, with the flags of Trent and Trieste wrapped in black bands at the head of the procession,[57] showed that the old hatred was still alive. It was a fatal contradiction, and with the Triple Alliance barely concluded, two Italian diplomats, and not junior ones, expressed private disapproval of the pact "because on the day we were required to march in the name of a treaty obligation, no one would budge."[58]

This then was the state of relations between Italy and Austria. Here there was no interference from ideological and party factors, there were no cultural influences, nor even particular financial ties. An evaluation could be made in terms of pure international politics, but it was complicated and indeed contradicted by passion, by a long-standing passion that in the end was stronger than all calculation. Neither in regard to Russia, nor in regard to England were emotions felt so strongly as they were in this case, but all this force of passion was concentrated on a single point, it did not embrace the entire life of the nation in all its forms, as happened with France and Germany. Italian foreign policy did not hinge on the city of Vienna.[59]

---

[56] Minghetti, *Discorsi Parlamentari* 5:260–61 (24 April 1872).

[57] Sandonà, *L'irredentismo nelle lotte politiche* 1:124–25.

[58] Tornielli and Pansa believed this (Pansa, *Diario*, under 31 December 1882).

[59] This is a concept repeatedly voiced by Visconti Venosta (Robilant, personal letter to Visconti Venosta, 28 April 1875; Visconti Venosta archive).

Italian public opinion moved between two poles, France and Germany, the two critical reference points both for calm analysis and for animosity. Setting aside Italy's friendship with England, everything else fit into this pattern. The manner in which the Italians took the side of one or the other of these two nations was what gave public debate its shape and its hue. Most people seemed to be aware that the essential problem of European politics after 1870 was that of relations between France and Germany, with everything else, like the Balkan question and colonial questions, clustered around it: so many sources of friction, but always that initial basis for the European dispute.

Italy claimed that it had inherited from the state of Savoy and the Piedmontese diplomatic tradition its policy of equilibrium between the forces battling for hegemony in Europe. A great power in name but not in fact, Italy was incapable on its own of bringing about any result on the continental scene, and the common view was that it had to find the key to success in a shrewd balancing act between the other powers. The equilibrium of Europe, said Visconti Venosta, was the necessary condition of Italy's prosperity, and nothing would do more to lessen it than the dominance of one part. In sum, this was the Savoyard tradition of balance between France and Spain, later between France and Austria. These were the calculations typical of so-called pure diplomacy, the rational, mathematical game, with each move thought out as if on a chess board.

But the Italians of the Kingdom of Italy also inherited from their ancestors something that was not the rational play of forces seeking equilibrium. They inherited passions that went far back in time, passions and a spirit of partisanship that, from the moment our history as a modern nation began, meant there was a deep split between the ideological tendencies, the feelings and aspirations of those who looked on one or the other of the two great continental powers as a guiding star. The Italian psyche was from that moment on torn between the French Zouave and the German Uhlan, as Carducci said. Giuseppe Verdi, it seemed, was right when he said that we were unable to go forward "without leaning on the arm of one or the other."[60] This meant that the pure diplomats had to take into account popular passions and party interests, and that the formidable weight of this a priori division of public opinion between opposition to France and oppostion to Germany weighed at every moment on Italian foreign policy.

This was the constant, perpetual theme of Italian politics. The others that have been examined, the idea of Rome and the anxieties of the conservatives, not only had not yet succeeded in suffocating the old ideals of liberty and nationality but were much less permanent, were tied more closely to the various twists and turns of events and so were more subject to adaptation and transformation, as the moment required.

The idea of Rome, though beneath the surface it was undergoing a process of fermentation, remained for a long time the idea of civic and secular Rome; its concrete repercussions on Italian foreign policy were always linked to the old problem of relations between the kingdom and the papacy, the struggle against

[60] Verdi, *Carteggi Verdiani* 3:98.

the Vatican and the black international. The Roman question was always there: it weighed profoundly on Italy's foreign policy and determined to a great extent Crispi's attitude to France, as much or more than his Mediterranean preoccupations did, for he believed France was weaving sinister plots with the Vatican to the detriment of Italian unity. This aggravated his natural propensity for dark suspicions and made him see, and often imagine, the Vatican and the Jesuits intent on instigating plots everywhere against Italy.[61] This was the reason for the firm refusal of the Italian government to let the Holy See take part in the first peace conference at the Hague in 1899.[62] This was the reason for Sonnino's veto, in article 15 of the pact of London, of the admission of the Holy See to any peace treaties. In comparison, the ghosts of Duilius and Scipio as yet had little power to fascinate, and for them to become a potent political force another generation would have to come to the fore, in a changed climate. The myth of Rome as *domina gentium* still lay in the future, though its roots were already there in these last decades of the nineteenth century.

Inversely, the preoccupations of the conservatives bore heavily on foreign policy after 1870 and did so above all between 1880 and 1896. Their influence then fell off steeply, until it vanished at the beginning of the new century with the policies of Giolitti, which embodied a new approach by the ruling class to the social question and the socialist movement. The latter for its part had also become a species of reformism, distancing itself from the perpetual revolution of the Bakuninian kind. But the inclination to champion France or Germany was a force that was always present.

On the other hand, the positions taken by men and parties in 1870–71 underwent mutation as the years passed, and that is no cause for surprise. It should be remembered that a political stance is a complex phenomenon produced by various factors. Thus for example the secularists of 1871–1875 saw in Bismarck's Germany the enemy of the papacy, whereas the secularists of the beginning of the twentieth century looked to the France of Waldeck Rousseau and Combes. Many things changed over time, men and events; but a few fundamental structures did not, and they were to guide future historical developments. Even the general European state of mind changed over time from what it had been in the spring of 1871.

Those were months of alarm and fearful prophecy. People asked themselves uneasily what new conquests Germany would undertake, what prey it was now eying.[63] Even in England there were fantasies about a possible German attack on

---

[61] A typical example occurred in 1890, when Crispi thought that the attitude of the government of Vienna regarding the *Pro Patria* of Trent and the *Dante Alighieri* might partly depend "on Vatican interference." In response Nigra begged him please "not to see Jesuits where there are none." It was not a question of clericalism but one of irredentism (Crispi, *Questioni Internazionali*, pp. 126–28 and 131).

[62] On this interesting episode, cf. the meticulous study of M. Toscano, "L'Italia e la prima conferenza per la pace dell'Aja del 1899," *La Comunità Internazionale* 4 (1949): 245 ff.

[63] H. von Sybel tried to counter these fears in an article published in the *Fortnightly Review* for 1 January 1871, and then, under the title "Das neue deutsche Reich," in *Vorträge und Aufsätze* (Berlin, 1874), p. 308.

the island, and a story about an imaginary battle of Dorking enjoyed immense success.[64] The Paris Commune produced consternation at the horrors threatened by the new barbarism coming from the bowels of society. Some saw the new Huns in Bismarck's Germans, some saw them in the incendiaries of Paris, and many saw them in both groups at once. In the aftermath, the calm conservative tenor of Bismarck's policy, the fact that there was no further vandalism like that inflicted on the column of the Place Vendôme, and the natural effect of time, all conduced to a substantial atmosphere of relaxation.

It had been feared that a new age of iron and flame was bursting upon humanity, and that there was no further purpose in talking of rights and international morality. But on 25 September 1871 the *Ligue Internationale de la paix et de la liberté* opened the fourth peace congress in Lausanne. Europe had appeared to be finished as a civil society; but eight days before the peace of Frankfurt, Garibaldi spoke to his friends in Nice of a European union with Nice as its capital,[65] and not long after, the work of Charles Lemonnier for a United States of Europe became known. European ideals in the tradition of Saint-Simon and Cattaneo resurfaced, and in time there were those who hoped that Italy would assume the great task of initiating a European federation, with Rome as the center of civilization once again and the Capitol welcoming the delegates of European unity.[66]

Much more important than all these congresses, speeches, and writings was the resolution through arbitration of the question of the *Alabama* in 1872. It was a great thing, truly novel and unexpected, that two powerful nations like England and the United States should agree to resolve peacefully a controversy that had become so threatening that at one point it seemed as if it might lead to war. It was also a great example for the continental states, though not an easy one to imitate readily, since Europe found itself in a phase of transition from the old states founded on force to the new states founded on the principle of nationality. If not immediately, then at the end of the journey on which Europe had embarked, there waited international arbitration and peace.[67] This great example was a welcome one to the Italians, for the president of the arbitration tribunal, Count Federico Sclopis, was an Italian. It was greeted with elation by the moderates like Bonghi, who, in perfect congruence with the whole eighteenth-century cast of their thought, believed in disarmament, in international arbitration, and in the organization of world peace.[68] The Left on the other hand, still haunted by the incubus of French clericalism, had no intention of sinking into such sugared reveries, and

---

[64] Meine, *England und Deutschland* , pp. 55–56 (200,000 copies of the story were sold between May and December).

[65] Garibaldi, *Scritti e discorsi politici e militari* 3:92–93.

[66] Novikov, *La missione dell'Italia*, pp. 288 ff.

[67] "Il tribunale di Ginevra," in *L'Opinione* for 19 September 1872. On the importance of the decision of the two states to go before an international tribunal, cf. as well the issues for 11 and 17 February ("La quistione dell'Alabama," and "La risposta dell'Inghilterra"). The paper also took a strong stand in favor of international arbitration on 20 July 1873 ("L'arbitrato internazionale"). For European debates on the problem, cf. Ter Meulen, *Der Gedanke der Internationalen Organisation* 2:89 ff.

[68] Maturi, "Ruggero Bonghi e i problemi di politica estera," pp. 416 ff.

though it considered the result felicitous, warned that there could be no illusions, that Italy had a special duty to prepare for the inevitable day when it would suffer an affront and would have to "rely on the reason of the scimitar."[69]

In England Henry Richard was soliciting the government to promote international arbitration. A petition with more than a million signatures was presented to parliament, and finally there came the victorious debate in the House of Commons on 8 July 1873.[70] And in Italy, on 24 November 1873, the Chamber of Deputies unanimously approved Mancini's proposal, which was accepted by Visconti Venosta, "that the king's government should work to render arbitration the accepted and normal method in foreign relations of resolving international controversies in matters susceptible of arbitration, in accord with justice; that when treaties are being stipulated, the government on suitable occasions should propose the insertion of a clause for the submission of any questions that may arise out of the interpretation and execution of the same treaties to arbitration; that it should persevere in the worthy initiative which it assumed some years hence of promoting agreements between Italy and the other civilized nations in order to render the essential rules of international private law uniform and obligatory, in the interest of the different peoples." But as the Neapolitan jurist himself said, this was no mirage of perpetual peace. The principle of arbitration was not made binding, even "in the life-and-death questions that may arise between two nations."[71] Yet these were notable steps, principally because they indicated that faith in the collective life of nations was returning. From his chair as prime minister, Marco Minghetti on that day had occasion to remember an opinion he had uttered fifteen years before: then he had called the hope of settling disputes between states by means of an arbitration tribunal utopian.[72] The incident of the *Alabama*, at least, had proved him wrong.

Humanity began to hope once more. As they shook off fear and dejection, men started to believe again in a better future, in a time to come when war, grief, and devastation might finally disappear. Europe came to terms with its new status quo. The "rosy dream" so dear to the men of the early nineteenth century, a dream dashed by the war of destruction between France and Germany, was resurrected: rapid economic development, wealth, enthusiasm for the conquests of technology, the pleasure of living an easier and more commodious life, all of these helped the average man to escape his anguish, and led him to bask in an expanded sense of security about himself and the future. The happy times en-

[69] "L'Italia all'arbitrato di Ginevra," in *Il Diritto* for 14 September 1872.

[70] Ter Meulen, *Der Gedanke der Internationalen Organisation* 2:45 ff. A banquet was held for Richard in Milan on 12 December 1873, and a few months later Lemonnier, the vice-president of the Peace League of Geneva, was also fêted (Mazzoleni, *L'XI Legislatura*, pp. 461 ff.).

[71] Mancini, *Discorsi Parlamentari* 4:233 ff. (*A.P., Camera*, pp. 33–36, as well for Visconti Venosta's speech and that of the rapporteur, Boselli). One of the most fervent proponents of arbitration at this time was Benedetto Castiglia (cf. his letters to Minghetti of 29 August and 19 October 1873; BCB, *Carte Minghetti*, cart. 39). The following year A. Turcotti published his *Introduzione al Nuovo Codice del diritto delle genti* (cf. Ter Meulen, *Der Gedanke der Internationalen Organisation* 2:113 ff.).

[72] Minghetti, *Della economia pubblica*, p. 494.

joyed by France in the July Monarchy returned for all of Europe. As the century waned, the continent lived out its last days of splendor, in that world of yesteryear that Stephan Zweig, in a time of desperation, would recall as a lost paradise. In sum, the atmosphere was greatly altered from what it had been in the winter of 1870–71. As the skies over Europe brightened, it was natural that tendencies, sentiments, and ideas in Italy should shift along the color spectrum as well.

But this optimism about progress, and satisfaction with the way life was lived, never succeeded completely in eradicating from the consciousness of those in government, and of Europe's more perspicacious politicians, the anxiety which the Franco-Prussian War had given rise to about the state of affairs. Projects for European federation and international arbitration did not in practice prevent the onset of an arms race of proportions never seen before. Despite the generic faith of the man in the street, the true character of the epoch was that of an armed peace, and political Europe was nervous, touchy, fundamentally much more ill at ease than it had been in the past—certainly much more than it had been between 1815 and 1848. Similarly, the changing attitudes of men and parties, and the rise and fall of various trends, could not conceal the fact that the underlying pattern of Italian life was still the one that had manifested itself at the moment when the Prussians had savored victory and the Italian forces had entered Rome.

Liberty and nationality, but with the faith they inspired sapped by anxieties arising from the advance of the masses and the requirements of European equilibrium, and attended in any case by a clear repudiation of all revolutionary enthusiasm; the idea of Rome, which was beginning to seethe in the collective psyche, though for the moment it signified only secular Rome against papal Rome; a much clearer demarcation between the supporters of France and the supporters of Germany: all these things constituted the burden of thought and feeling borne by the ruling class of united Italy as, from the new capital city of Rome, it set about its task of organizing the full-blown territorial state.

PART TWO

The Objective World

and The World of Men

I. *The Objective World*

Finance and the Army

THE TASK OF the Italian government was one of organization and consolidation, principally an internal task therefore. With the end of the Franco-Prussian War, even those who still wanted adventure could not at that moment have dreamed of new enterprises, and new glory.

The conditions that obtained in Italy compared to the other great powers were such as to block any dreams of this sort unless the dreamer were really deranged. Italy was the last in chronological order to join the European concert, for even before the creation of the German empire Prussia had been a great power for a long time, from the age of Frederick the Great. Italy was also the last in terms of demographic, economic, and military potential, so much so that it was a "great power" in name and form much more than it was in fact.

Its 26,801,154 inhabitants (this was the population of the kingdom on 31 December 1871)[1] left it at a notable distance behind Russia and Germany, with their 78 and 41 million inhabitants respectively, and even Great Britain with its 32 million. As for Italy's neighbors to the west and the east, France could still count 36,150,262 inhabitants despite the loss of Alsace-Lorraine,[2] and Austria-Hungary counted 35,000,000.

Passing from the field of demography to that of the economy, the distance between Italy and the others was even more noticeable, and the consequences profound. Here, notwithstanding the indubitable progress that was made from year to year, it was obvious at a glance how much this nation of ancient culture was a fledgling from the point of view of technical knowledge and production, and how backward the conditions of too many of its regions were, a fact that had slowed the progress of the whole.[3] Even the dullest must have been struck by the diversity of capacity and riches, not only in comparison to states with an older and stronger configuration like France and England but even in comparison to the German empire, though it had only recently been born politically. Whether from the point of view of moral and spiritual values or from that of wealth and material

---

[1] These and other data on Italian life are taken from the official publication of the statistical directorate of the Ministry of Agriculture, Industry, and Trade, *L'Italia economica nel 1873* (2d ed.; Rome, 1874).

[2] Hanotaux, *Histoire de la France contemporaine* 2:512, with other data there on French life.

[3] It is to be remembered that in the year 1860, 1,621 out of 1,848 communes in the Mezzogiorno had no paved roads, and almost none were supplied with drinking water (Nisco, *Storia civile del Regno d'Italia* 5:86 [Naples, 1890]). Further, the Mezzogiorno had only 125 km of rail lines, none of them on the islands, compared to the 850 km of the Piedmont-Liguria line, the 607 km of the Lombardy-Veneto line, 149 km in Parma and Modena, 323 km in Tuscany, and 132 km in the papal state (F. Tajani, *Storia delle ferrovie italiane* [Milan, 1939], p. 69). It is true that immediately after 1861 construction was begun on the great rail arteries of the Mezzogiorno: the Ancona-Brindisi, the Pescara-Sulmona, and the Naples-Foggia lines (ibid., pp. 70 ff.).

infrastructure, it was easy to see that, underneath the apparent similarity of their destinies, the two state creations of the nineteenth century, Germany and Italy, were far apart.

Clearly there was progress: in illustrating the financial situation to the Chamber on 12 December 1871,[4] Quintino Sella could point out with legitimate satisfaction how between 1861 and 1871 the railways had grown from 2,200 kilometers to 6,200, the telegraph from 16,000 to 50,000 kilometers of wire, the revenue from direct taxes from 175 million lire to 503 million, and the revenue from monopolies from 175 million to 296 million lire. These and similar data were sound evidence of the progressive and rapid strides made by Italian economic life after 1870,[5] toward a phase of much more intense and wider activity, of which large public works, and especially the improvement of the system of communications, finally creating a national market, were the necessary prerequisite. This improvement received recognition at the international level when the Cenisio (Fréjus) tunnel, the glory of Italian engineering, was inaugurated in September 1871, a few months after the approval by the Italian Chamber of Deputies of the convention for the Gotthard tunnel had opened up new prospects for trade between the Po Valley and central Europe. And further, the work on Italy's ports carried on since 1861, with a total outlay by 1870 of 68 million lire, the extension of the breakwaters at Genoa, Naples, Palermo, and Ancona, the refitting yard at Livorno, the dry dock at Messina, and the reactivation of the port of Brindisi (to mention only some of the projects completed),[6] also augured well for the future commercial development of the peninsula. This development was beginning to arrive, with a notable increase in import trade from 830 million lire in 1862 to 964 million in 1871, and in export trade from 577 million to 1,085 million. Overall, the annual total leapt from 1,407,000,000 lire to 2,049,000,000.[7]

But however encouraging these figures might be in relation to former conditions, and to the still very backward ones in some of the former states of the peninsula,[8] they made a very modest showing in comparison to the correspond-

---

[4] Sella, *Discorsi Parlamentari* 3:324–26. The growth of the provincial and national roads was less, from 22,493 km in 1863 to 27,217 km in 1870. For these and other data, cf. Corbino, *Annali dell'economia italiana* 1:180 and 193, and 2:222 and 239; further, E. Lémonon, *L'Italie économique et sociale (1861–1912)*, pp. 23 ff.; and the overview of the Italian railways from 1839 to 1884 in I. Sachs, *L'Italie: Ses finances et son développement économique depuis l'unification du royaume, 1859–1884*, p. 993.

[5] The period 1861–1870 was, however, a much more critical decade, and even in some ways a decade of blockage and crisis; cf. the acute analysis of G. Luzzatto, *Storia economica dell'età moderna e contemporanea* 2:350 ff. (Padua, 1948).

[6] Cf. Corbino, *Annali dell'economia italiana* 1:201 ff., and 2:222 ff.

[7] Sachs, *L'Italie: Ses finances et son développement économique*, p. 793. The data given by Sella in his speech on the finances on 12 December 1871, *Discorsi Parlamentari* 3:320–21, vary slightly; Lémonon, *L'Italie économique et sociale*, pp. 33–34; V. Porri, *L'evoluzione economica italiana nell'ultimo cinquantennio* (Rome, 1926; part of the work *I Cavalieri del Lavoro (1901–1926)*, p. 325. And cf. Corbino, *Annali dell'economia italiana* 1:121–23, and 2:149.

[8] The progress made was clearly acknowledged by foreign journalists and diplomats; for example, on 15 December 1871 the Austro-Hungarian chargé d'affaires to the Quirinal, Count Zaluski, said of the Italian budget for 1872: "though the treasury is far from presenting a very satisfactory

ing figures for the other great powers. Though beaten and bowed down, Italy's western neighbor, France, still maintained a crushing superiority over the new kingdom, with its 18,000 kilometers of rail lines and a total trade volume of more than 6 billion francs, three times as much as Italy.[9]

The 477 Italian public companies in 1871, with their 1,722 million lire of capital, though they represented a considerable increase compared with the 392 such corporations in the preceding year,[10] were still of little consequence compared to the number of similar corporations in France, England, and Germany, just as public savings in Italy were small compared to those abroad. The average income of the Italians, greatly inferior to that of the French, English, and Germans, was an eloquent symbol of the very different situation in which Italy found itself in comparison with the other great powers.[11]

If we examine the economic capacity of the kingdom from the aspect of public finance, the deficit in the state's budget, which was seemingly destined to become chronic, and the *corso forzoso* [the nonconvertibility of paper money into gold or silver] reveal that it was still scant. According to the data that Minghetti presented to the Chamber in the financial statement of 27 November 1873, the state had been 338 million in the red in 1868, 216 million in 1869, 307 million in 1870, 112 million in 1871, 113 million in 1872.[12] More recent and elaborate calculations also portray the deficit as ongoing and serious: 266 million in 1868, 195 million in 1869, 249 million in 1870, 79 million in 1871, 117 million in 1872, and 139 million in 1873.[13]

Nor was it only the state budget that suffered from the unending necessity to deal with emergencies. The budgets of the communes, the basic cells out of which the organic collective life was built, began to present similar characteris-

---

aspect, public wealth is increasing" (SAW, *P.A.*, XI/78, no. 79 B). In the *Journal des Economistes* for December 1872, L. Simonin praises highly the "marvelous" economic development of Italy (*L'Italie en 1872: Ses progrès et sa transformation*, pp. 9, 23, and 27 in the offprint seen [2d ed.; Paris, 1873]). And cf. the exact observations of Rosselli, "L'opera della Destra," in *Saggi sul Risorgimento*, pp. 217 ff.

[9] Hanotaux, *Histoire de la France contemporaine* 2:505–507.

[10] Sachs, *L'Italie: Ses finances et son développement économique*, p. 656.

[11] According to Pantaleoni, the wealth of the Italians amounted in 1884 to a little less than 48 billion, equal to roughly 1,660 lire per capita, while the wealth of the French fluctuated, according to different estimates, between 160–170 billion and 215–220 billion, more than three times as much in any case (M. Pantaleoni, "Dell'ammontare probabile della richezza privata in Italia," *Rassegna Italiana* 4 [1884]: 232–33 and 242). According to Coppola d'Anna, the average Italian income in 1870–1876 was 94 international units, while in France it was 235, in Germany 197, in Great Britain 295. In the period 1877–1885, average income in Italy rose to 117, compared to 256, 225, and 348 respectively (Coppola d'Anna, *Popolazione reddito e finanze pubbliche dell'Italia dal 1860 ad oggi*, pp. 49 and 67).

[12] Minghetti, *Discorsi Parlamentari* 5:349. Cf. A. Plebano, *Storia della finanza italiana* 1:423. The data for these years are known to be anything but homogeneous and reliable: hence the sometimes striking variations in the figures given by various scholars, for example by Sachs, Lémonon, and Corbino.

[13] F. A. Répaci, "Il bilancio dello Stato italiano dalla unificazione ad oggi (1862–1934/35)," *Rivista di Storia Economica* 2 (1937): 148 (table II). The figure is smaller in the statements of the accounts (ibid., p. 141, table I); and cf. *Il bilancio del regno d'Italia negli esercizi finanziari dal 1862 al 1907–08*, , pp. 134–35.

tics from 1868 onward, though on a smaller scale.[14] On 29 January 1871 *L'Opinione* raised a cry of alarm about this, emphasizing that in 1869 only 219 communes (9 urban and 210 rural) had closed their books in the black, whereas 432 (21 urban and 411 rural) had managed to balance them, and all the rest had closed them in the red. It is no surprise then, given this situation, if the 5 percent *rendita* was quoted, in August of 1871, at sixty lire in gold and sixty-four lire in paper money,[15] if the great scourge of the *aggio* grew every year,[16] and if in consequence the foreign exchange rate remained unfavorable to the lira.[17]

This was the great trial that united Italy had to pass in order really to convince all foreign observers, and many observers within the country itself, that it was a viable creature, capable of survival even when the patriotic excitement of the days of armed action had vanished. Other great and rich nations had had deficits in their state budgets before then, and were to have them again in the future, without causing anyone to predict their demise on that account. Italy too, once it had got through the initial phase and organized itself internally, would be able to permit itself the luxury, so to speak, of closing its annual financial accounts in the red without having it thought that the imminent end of the kingdom was being announced. A mere twenty years later, in the very serious financial crisis of 1890–1896, though the situation appeared grave, the prophets of doom and the expectant pallbearers were not on the scene any more, or else were negligible. But things were different in the years immediately following unification, and perhaps especially after 1870 and the capture of Rome. There was a new climate in Europe, one much less propitious for ideals in general, and in particular for the ideals of nationality and liberty.[18] It was certainly less propitious for Italy on account of the disappearance of the Napoleonic power, of which the Italians had often been suspicious and which had often been suspicious of Italy, but whose assistance at Magenta and Solferino the Italians basically never forgot. In this environment, politically less emotive, dominated by the clear, cold logic of the

---

[14] Corbino, *Annali dell'economia italiana* 1:272, and 2:327. But until 1868, total revenue for all the communes exceeded their expenditure: this gave rise to the conviction that the state skewed the budgets of the communes for the sake of balancing its own (ibid., 1:270). The budgets of the provinces were also moving gradually toward bankruptcy (ibid., 2:333).

[15] "Il ritorno della fiducia," in *L'Opinione* for 11 August 1871; and cf. the statistical picture in Corbino, *Annali dell'economia italiana* 2:323. [*Translator's note: rendita = rente*, a long-term government bond.]

[16] In 1867 the *aggio* averaged 7.81 percent. In 1873 it was 14.21 percent (Lémonon, *L'Italie économique et sociale*, p. 18). [*Translator's note: aggio =* the premium on gold and silver coin over paper money.]

[17] The average exchange rate in Paris in 1871 was 105.44. In 1873 it was 112.44 (Lémonon, *L'Italie économique et sociale*, p. 18 n. 1).

[18] With his usual perspicacity Bonghi took note of this change as early as 1871: "today certain ideal principles have lost their value, principles which in the past created a common bond of sympathy between one people and another, so that the dignity and the coherence of the liberal parties consisted in professing them even when they seemed to go against their own interests. It is no longer enough for a nation to state that it is laying claim to its right for it to receive practical assistance, or even expressions of good will; and liberty itself is adored in a less impartial fashion" ("Rassegna politica," for 1 November 1871 in *Nuova Antologia* 18 (1871): 679; and cf. Croce, *Storia d'Europa nel secolo decimonono*, pp. 254 ff.

German chancellor, alert to "facts" (including the facts of public finance), Italy was required to prove that it knew how to live, and to be a genuine and solid unity, not one confined to the noble souls of a handful of committed patriots, to the lofty and prophetic spirit of a few exceptional personalities. The country had to prove that it was viable not only amid the fervor of a bloody struggle, its hopes sustained by poetic anthems, but also when faced with the hard realities of the everyday life of an entire population, in the conduct of business and enterprises on which poetry had no influence, and in which everything depended on profit and calculation.

It had grown up too fast, this Italy, appearing on the scene out of nowhere, as though by a miracle: indeed, those who lived through the experience were not overburdened with historical consciousness and did not feel they had to go looking for the putative origins of the Risorgimento as far back as the first decades of the eighteenth century. For them it was enough to deal with the facts, the palpable reality, and what they saw was the sudden appearance of an Italian question after 1815. In this they perhaps revealed more historical and political intuition than many future professors of history, for they grasped the living essence of the revolutionary moment, the heart of the Risorgimento, and did not confuse it with the reforms and the reforming thought of the eighteenth century, which had been a necessary condition of the revolution, but were nevertheless a different thing from it.

Now the miracle of national unity was attributed in large measure to luck, since the military abilities of the Italians were certainly far from enjoying the same esteem as those of the Germans, the authors of the other contemporary miracle. The Italian miracle was therefore required to demonstrate that it rested on a solid foundation that would not crumble. Italy had to show that it knew how to get things done without poetic inspiration, in fact that it was capable of simple survival—which appeared rather doubtful for a number of years to many who thought that even after 1861, and especially after 1866, Italy was really regressing rather than progressing,[19] or at best was standing "fixed in the niches of its past."[20]

[19] For views of this kind, which were frequent in Europe, cf. Bernstorff's report to Bismarck of 6 January 1868 (skepticism in England about Italy's future, about the "strength and viability" and thus the "durability of united Italy"). Further, cf. Reuss's report to Bismarck of 17 January 1868 (the Russian desire that a dismemberment [*Zerstückelung*] of Italy be avoided). And cf. Bismarck to Usedom on 2 February 1868: the head of the Prussian government does not share the preoccupations and the opinions of the English and the Russians; he believes that their fears are exaggerated, that Italian unity is too well grounded in a deep and real need of the nation for it to be so easily lost again; but he also recognizes that the process of internal consolidation has not made the progress for which the friends of Italy were hoping, and that the primary interest of Italy is "above all to build up its own inner strength, consolidate its unity . . . and get its finances under control." Then again there is the dispatch to Usedom of 9 March 1868, which adopts a tone much less sympathetic to Italy (*Die auswärtige Politik Preussens, 1858–1871* 9:595–96, 615–16, 653–54, 771–74). It is true that this was in the aftermath of Mentana; but pessimism about Italy was not confined to that particular moment.

[20] Thus Francesco Ferrara, in January 1866 (cited in Luzzatto, *Storia economica dell'età moderna e contemporanea* 2:351).

There was no better test of whether it was viable or not than the question of its finances. This was a test that expressed the core values of a society like that of Europe after 1870, a society launched on a course of full-scale capitalist development, in which economic values increasingly outweighed spiritual ones, and even politics were increasingly connected, or even subordinated, to the economic realm. But it was a difficult test for a poor, economically backward country like Italy, in which the state's finances were based on a variety of previous state financial administrations, most of them crippled,[21] and were technically still in a very disorganized, indeed often chaotic, state, with the seven different systems of tax collection being unified only between 1872 and 1873, thanks to a "diabolical effort."[22]

This test was decisive: there were many skeptics and many who thought that the vessel of Italy was destined for shipwreck on the shoals of finance from the moment it was launched on its voyage. Many inside the country, clericals and reactionaries of every stripe, hoped that this would happen, that the edifice created with overweening violence by the wicked breed of patriots would break apart over the money problem. And even among the patriots themselves, many were nervous, frightened that what they had created politically could not withstand the trial of finance. An example was Michelangelo Caetani, the man who had brought the plebiscite of Rome to Vittorio Emanuele II, and who now feared "financial collapse" and dark days for his own country, not as a result of political and religious reaction, but as a result of the "curse" of its finances. Caetani foresaw "the demolition of the past and the ruin of the future,"[23] and, spurred by this anxiety, invested his capital in French securities, "despite losing a lot at the present rate of exchange, in order not to lose everything in the future."[24] In this he was following the example of the other Italians who, in 1872, had invested 620 million in shares of a French loan totaling three billion—in other words, a sum equal to approximately a tenth of what they had invested in shares of the public debt in their own country.[25]

Caetani, a Roman and a duke, was always a caustic spirit. The Roman curia

---

[21] Rosselli, "L'opera della Destra," in *Saggi sul Risorgimento*, p. 217; Luzzatto, *Storia economica dell'età moderna e contemporanea* 2:355.

[22] The expression is Giolitti's. He worked on this unification under Sella (Giolitti, *Memorie della mia vita* 1:17). For other failings of the administration, cf. as well Sella's letter to Perazzi in 1872 (in Sella, *Epistolario inedito*, p. 259). Until 1872 the tax was collected directly in some regions, while in others it was contracted out, and the consequences for the treasury were not beneficial. The criteria for the apportioning and collection of duties on consumption varied widely from one region to another (Corbino, *Annali dell'economia italiana* 1:225–26; and cf. in general Mazzoleni, *L'XI Legislatura*, pp. 289 ff.).

[23] Caetani, *Epistolario del duca Michelangelo Caetani di Sermoneta* 1:80, 107–108, 112, 118, 125, 128, 137–39, etc. (letters to Circourt of 1871, 1872, 1873, 1874).

[24] Ibid., 1:141 (22 November 1874).

[25] Cf. the polemics of *Il Diritto* in this regard: "Il patriottismo dei capitali italiani e l'imprestito francese" (22 July 1872); "L'aggio cresce . . ." (26 July); "L'imprestito francese in Italia: Avvertimento agli italiani" (28 July). On 1 August the paper expresses satisfaction that the amount of this offering subscribed in Italy is no more than 620 million.

had felt his sting, and now the new masters of Italy felt it in their turn.[26] He had the reputation of a great liberal, though his convictions were not strong enough to keep him from a deathbed retraction in which he made amends to his confessor for his patriotic past.[27] Tormented by physical pain, blindness, and moral anguish for the loss of his second wife, his was a restless and unquiet spirit, and too often his pessimism was a habit, a simple impulse to criticize everything;[28] but on the question of finance, his complaints were shared by many, who could only put their faith in God or in the "stellone" [Italy's lucky star].[29] The judgment Caetani formulated to his friend de Circourt on 2 August 1874 was trenchant and well founded: Italy as it then was could not hope "to carry out a violent act of conquest of itself," indeed it could not "continue to exist and grow in strength except through universal consensus, common welfare, and real improvement."[30] That was the nub: Italy could not carry out a violent conquest of itself, meaning that it could not act on its own economic and moral body as the Piedmontese divisions had acted against Austria, as the Thousand had acted against the Bourbon monarchy, with force. With unity achieved, the foreigner driven out, the local dynasties suppressed, weapons were no longer of any use, and unity had to be maintained by proceeding along the ways of peace, and with the tools and arts of peace.

The aims of politics changed completely, and the means had to change as well. Until 1870 the governing class had focused its will on making the kingdom complete by including in it first the Venetian state and then Rome. Now its energies still had to be keyed up to the same high pitch, or even higher, but the goals were different. Just as in Europe the political climate had changed totally with the fall of the Second Empire and the advent of German power, and in Italy a new and potent strain of ideas and sentiments was inoculated into the nation's life when Rome became the capital, likewise the themes and the motives of political participation changed. The questions in which men and parties had to show what they were worth became questions about internal affairs, administrative and economic in nature. They were no longer, as the principal organ of the Right in power noted,[31] the questions that had once had the power to fill the souls

---

[26] Pesci, *I primi anni di Roma capitale*, p. 161; Negro, *Seconda Roma*, pp. 131 and 140.

[27] This fact is categorically affirmed by Farini, who as president in the Chamber was asked by Minghetti to eschew a necrology of Caetani in parliament so that his retraction would not become known (Farini, *Diario* 1:282–83, and again pp. 669, 710, 712).

[28] It will be recalled that as a deputy he first resigned, then joined the Left out of dissatisfaction at the way things were going. Amari judged him one of the most learned, vivacious, and original men he knew, a delightful conversationalist, utterly courteous "but absolutely pessimistic in his beliefs about everything that touches him either directly or remotely" (Amari, *Carteggio* 3:347–48).

[29] Artom, general secretary at the foreign ministry, who in early 1874 was working to forge a cabinet that would include Sella, Visconti Venosta, and Minghetti, which he considered the only ministerial combination able to offer real guarantees of seriousness and stability, was dismayed by the "confusion of the parties" and their intrigues, and as he noted: "meanwhile the *aggio* is growing, the deficit is not shrinking, and revenue and public credit are feeling the effects. May God have mercy on us" (Artom to Nigra, 5 February 1874; AE, *Carte Nigra*).

[30] Caetani, *Epistolario* 1:139.

[31] "La nuova Roma," in *L'Opinione* for 4 July 1871.

of men so powerfully with passion; they were not questions that could be re-solved with emphatic speeches, nor even with audacious deeds. They required application, practical sense, the spirit of sacrifice. Only with practical sense could the new Rome be built, the Rome of modern civilization and liberty, in sum the Rome that Cavour had wished to see, not the Rome of the Caesars and of harangues by tribunes of the plebs.

And if the problem of finance constitutes a political problem, everywhere and always, spilling over from the strictly technical area of expertise into all aspects of the national life, in that particular moment of Italian history it became the political problem, the national problem par excellence, the one on whose resolu-tion depended the very being of the nation.[32] Everything led back to this and was reduced to this:[33] how to rescue the state's budget and succeed finally in balanc-ing the books, to prove with deeds to a world that still believed in the balanced public budget as an unshakable axiom, and was not yet accustomed to the colos-sal deficits of our own times, that Italy, having put the euphoria of the so-called radiant days behind her, was capable of living the everyday life, a life drab perhaps, hard and tiring at any rate, and offering none of the surface allure, the color and sound of military adventure. It was a trial that too many Italians, raised in a rhetorical culture and nursed on the "milk of eloquence," were liable to dismiss as prosaic, timid, and worthless, but which was in truth much more difficult to fight, and not less meritorious to win, than military battles. And it was a trial that sometimes disturbed the sleep of even an individual with his feet on the ground like Quintino Sella, making him see hundreds of millions of govern-ment bonds in his dreams, all dancing in a wild whirl . . .[34]

A financial collapse would have signified, at that historical juncture, the end of united Italy, and no prodigious figure in a red shirt, no Cavourian diplomatic ability, would have been able to put the pieces of the state back together again once it had revealed that it was incapable of looking after its own everyday financial livelihood. Many observers said so clearly and repeatedly in these years, politicians and foreign newspapers, friends and enemies of Italy. Glad-stone, unquestionably a friend, warned on one occasion when politicians and other personalities had gathered at Florence to honor him, that although he re-joiced to see things getting better, the Italians still had an enemy in their midst more terrible than a foreign army, and that was the enormous deficit weighing on the public finances.[35]

And if anyone had dismissed this as the warning of a man tarred with human-itarianism and ignorant of the world of power and force, he might have been answered by recalling that another great statesman, Bismarck, a man certainly

---

[32] This was perceived very clearly by Oriani, who justly praised Sella (Oriani, *La lotta politica in Italia* 3:243 ff.).

[33] Silvio Spaventa adverted to this in 1867: "Only one question in politics: finance" (Spaventa, *Lettere politiche (1861–1893)*, p. 108).

[34] Sella himself tells Lanza about this in a letter of 6 July 1871 (Lanza, *Le carte* 7:141).

[35] The anecdote is recorded by the hon. Pisanelli in an election speech given at Taranto on 8 October 1874 (see *L'Opinione* for 14 October 1874).

not tainted with pacifism, or to use the modern expression, a man above suspicion of preferring butter to guns, had included this warning in what he had to say to Minghetti and Visconti Venosta in September 1873 in Berlin: "You have only one enemy you must conquer at all costs, and that is the deficit." He insisted that the Italian government ought to turn all its attention to ridding itself of this foe, not to increasing its armaments, since the power of a nation resided above all in its credit rating.[36] And in the summer of 1874 he returned to this topic once more, repeating views he had voiced in 1868, evincing his surprise that the government in Rome, safe in the knowledge that it would have German support in case of French aggression, was not reducing its military expenditure in order to balance the budget.[37]

Thus the two leading statesmen of Europe, although so fundamentally diverse, agreed in their evaluation of the situation in Italy.[38] The organs of European opinion were united in counseling and admonishing the Italian politicians, sometimes even threatening them. Their evaluation of the financial situation of the new kingdom, in which foreign capital had a large stake,[39] did much to guide the attitude of the leading papers and journals: when in March 1874 the Chamber approved new funding of about 80 million for military expenditure, though the budget was not balanced, a united chorus made itself heard. According to the authoritative *Times*, which in those years often took a very cool attitude to Italy's finances,[40] no other country had less room for the luxury of spending public money in a useless and unproductive fashion. The *Standard*, another English paper of repute and the organ of the Conservative party, invited the Italians to

[36] "La quistione politica," in *L'Opinione* for 29 January 1874. Given the ties between *L'Opinione* and the foreign ministry, the report is believable; it is confirmed by *L'Opinione* again on 30 April, with the addition of the remark about armaments ("Le spese militari in Italia").

[37] Statements made by Bismarck to Keudell, the German envoy in Rome, and reported by the latter to de Launay (personal letter of de Launay to Visconti Venosta, 10 September 1874; ACR, *Carte Visconti Venosta*, pacco 8, fasc. 3).

[38] We can add Thiers, who in a conversation with General Ricci on 9 October 1872 said that he did not understand why the deficit had not yet been eliminated from the Italian budget ("Précis d'une conversation de M.r le Président de la République avec le général Ricci," ACR, *Carte Visconti Venosta*, pacco 5, fasc. 4).

[39] Between 1861 and 1870 the treasury paid out 848 million lire in interest (743 of them on the Paris market) on shares of the public debt held outside Italy. The interest paid out during the same period on shares held inside Italy was 1,748 million lire. At the end of 1870, shares of Italian government stock held abroad were worth two billion lire, out of the slightly more than eight billion lire which constituted the sum total of the kingdom's public debt. As for foreign capital invested in Italy at the end of 1870, principally in the railways, it amounted to slightly more than a billion lire (Corbino, *Annali dell'economia italiana* 1:165, 169, 255; and cf. also Luzzatto, *Storia economica dell'età moderna e contemporanea* 2:358 and 365). As Peruzzi noted, this brought a political advantage, which was that "in moments of political uncertainty, Italy bound the interests of capitalists large and small in the principal European states to its own fate" (Luzzatto, ibid., 2:358).

[40] The [London] *Times* in fact spoke for the businessmen of the City, holders of Italian government bonds who were irritated at having to pay tax on the interest they received (Cadorna, report, 4 December 1872, no. 369; Visconti Venosta, dispatch to Cadorna, 22 December 1872, no. 160; Cadorna, personal letter to Visconti Venosta, from Novara, 11 September 1874; ACR, *Carte Visconti Venosta*, 1874, pacco 8, fasc. 4). This did not prevent it from publishing from time to time articles in praise of Italy's economic progress, as on 12 September 1872. On the distrust and aversion of other English periodicals for Italian financial policy, cf. Maffei's report of 18 August 1872, no. 334.

cure themselves of the mania for military expenditure, and of the mania for place-hunting, which made every Italian dream of being a state employee with his salary safely inscribed in the budget; the *Standard* wanted the Italians to work more and spend less. The *Pall Mall Gazette* dwelt on the lack of courage shown by Cavour's successors in failing to deal vigorously with their financial situation, and on the impossibility for Italy of keeping a standing army of 360,000 men. In sum, the English press was unanimous and, what is more, U.S. politicians and papers joined the chorus with Senator Boutwell, who linked Italy to Spain, Greece, and other "dishonored" nations, in the lead.[41]

Similar sounds came from the direction of Germany, where public voices picked up and amplified the warning given by Bismarck in September of the preceding year. One paper that shouldered this task was the *Augsburger Allgemeine Zeitung*, the most important in southern Germany,[42] hostile to Italy by long tradition. Another, indeed the principal one, was the *Spenersche Zeitung*, whose record was also not one of unbroken approval for the Italian government.[43] From the columns of this organ of the German press there transpired rebukes much like those which the spokesmen of the City and of the Anglo-Saxon financial world in general had seen fit to impart: the Italians do not think of the fact that there is no military force where there is no monetary force, and that there is no monetary force where the finances are not in good shape. They ought to realize that, for now at least, they have no choice but to give up the idea of having an army equal to the army of one of the great powers; they ought to be trying instead to secure for themselves a reliable ally against every eventuality, which would allow them to reduce their military expenditure and stabilize their finances; and they should be thinking hard about these problems, though there are many in Italy who wish to arm the country even more, because a bankrupt state is never a strong ally.[44] In these statements a German disrespect for the Italian government of the day was undoubtedly present, just as the invitation, which could hardly have been more blatant, to an alliance with Germany betrayed Bismarck's old wish to bend Minghetti and Visconti Venosta to his own purposes in regard to politics in general, and the ecclesiastical variety in particular. But, disrespect apart, German opinion chimed with that of the Anglo-Saxon

---

[41] Cf. *L'Opinione* for 18 March, 8 April, 4 and 8 May 1874. Violent attacks on Italy for its financial condition occurred often in lesser organs of the British press in these years. One appeared in the *Examiner*, a weekly, on 1 April 1871. This attack was refuted by a British friend of Cadorna and an important businessman, Sir D. A. Lange, in *The Asiatic* for 18 July, making use of data initially furnished by the finance ministry to a member of the British cabinet to rebut many unjust accusations and remarks made by the *Examiner*. The latter, however, resumed its attack in August (Cadorna and Maffei, reports of 6 April, no. 204; 22 July, no. 229; and 1 September, no. 243).

[42] Cf. P. Wolframm, *Die deutsche Aussenpolitik und die grossen deutschen Tageszeitungen (1871–1890)* (Zeulenroda, 1936), p. 5.

[43] In January 1873 a report from Rome in this paper attacked Visconti Venosta for his attitude in the summer of 1870. This caused de Launay to make a friendly approach to the German foreign secretary, Balan (personal letters of de Launay to Visconti Venosta, 22, 23, 28 January, 10 February 1873; Visconti Venosta archive).

[44] Cf. *L'Opinione* for 30 April and 28 May 1874. The *Spenersche Zeitung* was an important paper, well regarded by the government (Treitschke, *Briefe* 3:310).

world, and also with that of the French, for whom Italy was synonymous with deficits.[45] Together they formed an unwelcome chorus of censure and warning that revealed, as well it might, even to the most committed supporters of a "great politics" regardless of the budget, what the importance of the financial problem was.

This was truly the political question par excellence, the vital question for the country—so vital that, if it were not somehow dealt with, Italy would either collapse or else would sink to the level of Egypt, a country under the financial control of others and thus a colony, not a free nation. There had been a clear foretaste of this on the day a diplomatic representative of a foreign government had come to see Sella and, stating brutally what others were thinking, had formally proposed that Italian finances be put under international control. This envoy was politely shown the door, but the problem remained, and from that day on Sella moved decisively to restore the public finances.[46]

He was right to aim for a balanced budget at any cost, even that of putting a heavy drag on the economy of a poor country, even that of rousing popular anger, discontent with the new state, and nostalgia for the old order of things. All the objectives normally valid, such as the necessity to develop economic activity and refrain from weighing it down with extra taxes,[47] were virtually nullified by the political imperative, which urgently demanded the attainment of the balanced budget in order to demonstrate to the world the vitality of the Italian state. It was the only really effective demonstration that could be used to meet the violent rhetoric, the accusations, and the maneuvers of the clerical and reactionary circles of Italy and Europe at this time.

The political imperative was categorical. Hence, at a time when the taxation

---

[45] *Voyage au Pays du déficit* is the self-explanatory title of a volume by Neukomm on Italy (Arcari, *Le elaborazioni della dottrina politica nazionale* 1:116 n. 28).

[46] This episode was related by Sella himself to a group of voters at Biella, on the evening on 30 October 1882. The story of the conversation was published in *Il Monte Rosa* of Varallo and reported in *L'Opinione* for 10 November. Sella did not specify who the foreign diplomat was, or the year in which the conversation occurred; probably it was in the very difficult autumn of 1864, when Sella took over the finance ministry for the second time (cf. Guiccioli, *Quintino Sella* 1:102, where there is a reference to the unacceptability, "from the point of view, too, of the country's honor," of the conditions demanded by foreign bankers for granting further credits; and also H. Fraenkel, *Storia di una nazione proletaria* [Florence, 1938], pp. 40–41).

[47] This is the reasoning, for example, of M. Bonfantini, "Per una storia d'Italia dal 1871 al 1915," *Società Nuova* 1, no. 1 (1945): 7–8. But Bonfantini reasons on the basis of theoretical premises, without grasping exactly what Italy's overall situation was at this time. See rather Corbino's eulogy of the policy of the balanced budget in *Annali dell'economia italiana* 1:15, and Luzzatto's in *Storia economica dell'età moderna e contemporanea* 2:372–73 and 377. Luzzatto observes that at that juncture, shoring up the state's budget was the necessary preliminary for the development of enterprise in the economy (ibid., 2:355), and that the advantage of the *corso forzoso* was to make people see how urgent the matter was (p. 372). Sereni remarks in *Il capitalismo nelle campagne (1860–1900)* (Turin, 1947), p. 82, that the financial policies of the Right were simply those of the bourgeois class, and that there was no mystical halo surrounding the effort to balance the budget; this observation is not cogent either, because even if we admit the premise, which in fact is open to some qualification (cf. n. 51 below), the fact remains that in the context of an entirely bourgeois Europe with an entirely bourgeois financial system, Italy could not embark on a revolutionary policy in this field all by itself. To balance the budget, using the methods of the time, signified the salvation of the unity of Italy in the Europe of the time: this, and nothing else, is the problem.

system was still unfinished, the controls very imperfect, and the methods of collection various and conflicting, the equitable and rational distribution of the public charge remained a dream, and taxes were piled on top of one another, all for the purpose of pulling in the quantity of money needed by the treasury.[48] Sella had to give up his idea of a global tax on aggregate income at progressive rates.[49] In result the tax burden fell especially heavily on the classes that possessed the least, for whom life was grim already, and who were hit the hardest by inequalities of the type produced by the tax on mobile wealth, which was imposed at a flat rate of 13.20 percent on all sources of income. This tax was rightly branded the tax on mobile poverty,[50] and the financial policies of the moderates had the appearance, and to some extent the reality, of being class-based, as they were so often accused of being then and later. Still, the accusation is offset by the fact that between 1871 and 1875 the levy on income and total wealth as a percentage of the overall tax revenue was the highest ever seen in the history of Italy, while the percentage derived from indirect taxes was the lowest, notwithstanding the grist tax.[51]

To have grasped this imperative, to have perceived its tremendous importance, is one of the Right's great claims to glory in its last years of government. In particular, it is indubitable proof of the statesmanlike qualities of Quintino Sella, the clear, hard head[52] that the times required, despite his unpopularity. Not a financial expert either by training or experience, he entered the domain of public finance out of necessity,[53] and he saw clearly and affirmed forcefully by word

[48] Plebano, *Storia della finanza italiana* 1:337.

[49] Cf. A. Garino Canina, "I principi finanziari di Quintino Sella," *Rendiconti del R. Istituto Lombardo di Scienze e Lettere* 73 (1939–1940): 565.

[50] Marselli, *La rivoluzione parlamentare*, p. 11; and cf. Morandi, *La sinistra al potere*, pp. 64–65.

[51] Respectively 49.67 percent for the levies on income and total wealth, and 44.37 percent for the levies on consumption. With the advent of the Left, the ratio became 47.40 percent and 46.62 percent between 1876 and 1880, and 45.45 and 48.34 percent between 1881 and 1885. From then on the levies on consumption were always heavier, except in the period 1896–1900 (Coppola d'Anna, *Popolazione reddito e finanze*, p. 102). Cf. as well E. Scalfari, "La politica finanziaria della Destra nel periodo delle origini (1860–1864)," *Nuova Antologia* (July 1947): 299, an article which cannot even be said to favor the Right's policies.

It is to be noted as well that over the entire period of the Right there was a progressive and constant increase in the percentage of direct taxation. In 1861–1865 direct taxes were 46.73 percent and taxes on consumption were 47.40 percent (the remaining 5.87 percent came from other charges and duties). In 1866–1870 the ratio was 47.13 to 46.90 percent. And in the period mentioned, 1871–1875, the ratio was 49.67 to 44.37 percent. In 1911–1915 the ratio was 38.46 to 54.94 percent. In 1936–1940 it was 37.97 to 56.68 percent (Coppola d'Anna, *Popolazione reddito e finanze*, loc. cit). Having said that, there is absolutely no doubt that levies on consumption weighed more heavily when the population was relatively poorer than they did, even at a higher rate, when the population grew richer; or that the tax burden was inequitably distributed. For example, landed property was very heavily taxed, much more heavily than mobile wealth was, partly as a result of the added taxes at the communal and provincial levels (cf. also Natale, *Giolitti e gli Italiani*, pp. 138 ff.). But the point remains the same: this was all part of the painful quest for methods that would produce immediate results, a quest that was unavoidable in the general circumstances.

[52] This apt description is Bacchelli's, in *Il Mulino del Po* 3:144.

[53] Garino Canina, "I principi finanziari di Quintino Sella," p. 562; cf. also Petruccelli della Gattina, *Storia d'Italia dal 1866 al 1880*, p. 158. Sella was criticized for being unacquainted with "the ingenious long-range expedients" used by the great experts in finance (*La terza Italia: Lettere di*

and deed that Italy's real political problem was that of its finances,[54] and that it was necessary to bear any brunt of unpopularity for the sake of saving the country from economic ruin and the dishonor[55] that would fatally have attended a political disaster. Sella carried the rest of the old Right along with him, including much less energetic men such as Marco Minghetti, who shared his conviction that the gaping hole in the public finances was of the sort "that let revolutions in, and the whole train of anarchy and despotism,"[56] and that although every day brought its own problems, Italy's main duty was to straighten out its finances, a more important and more worrying matter than even the ecclesiastical question.[57] Public opinion was right to see in Sella a political force far superior to that of an ordinary minister of finance, and politicians and parties, even when they did not love him, saw a leader in the man who was never prime minister, and always headed a ministry that was administrative and technical rather than political in the strict sense, as the more coveted interior and foreign ministries were. In a parliament that abounded in refined and learned orators, he was a plain and even labored speaker, as Cavour had been and Giolitti would be, though an effective one;[58] and yet, speaking in his spare fashion from his post as technical administrator, he exerted decisive political influence and was the most universally valued member of Lanza's cabinet.[59]

These then were the conditions of the times: as the *Saturday Review* noted in August 1872, benevolent for once despite its habitual sternness where the question of the public finances was concerned, Italy was called on to show "the sacrifices a new nation has to make in our time as it seeks to establish itself and rise to the level of an independent power,"[60] even when the armed struggle was over. It was finding to its cost that in the life of nations the test of living in peace is frequently a more painful one than the trials of war.

Thus it was that the cares of the men of the government remained focused on the problem of the state's finances. And the area most directly affected by this problem was that of the kingdom's military organization, the capacity to make war that in the history of international relations has always constituted the ulti-

---

un Yankee, translated with notes by F. Garlanda [3d ed.; Rome, no year], p. 302). Cf. as well Luzzatti, *Grandi Italiani: Grandi sacrifici per la Patria*, p. 47, who recognizes however that in the conditions of the time it was impossible for him to act differently. And this is the real point: whether or not the expedients of the experts in finance could have been applied in Italy then.

[54] Cf. Sella's speech at Biolio on 18 October 1874: "Suppose there were a mortal enemy of the unity and liberty of Italy. I do not know what line of conduct would better serve his ends than to get us to increase our expenditure, while keeping us from working harder and making more sacrifices by raising our taxes" (Sella, *Discorsi Parlamentari* 5:873).

[55] Cf. his speech to the Chamber on 27 March 1879 (Sella, *Discorsi Parlamentari* 5:833).

[56] In an election speech at Legnago on 4 October 1874 (in *L'Opinione* for 7 October).

[57] A speech to the Chamber on 7 May 1875 (Sella, *Discorsi Parlamentari* 6:538).

[58] The opinion is that of a knowledgeable observer, Martini, in *Confessioni e ricordi*, p. 130).

[59] He was well aware of it: "Sella feels his own importance, and wants to do everything; Lanza complains that Sella is too imprudent and intrudes in affairs that do not concern him," Dina to Castelli, 19 November 1870 (Castelli, *Carteggio politico* 2:492).

[60] Cf. "Un giudizio sull'Italia," in *L'Opinione* for 28 August 1872. Maffei, the chargé d'affaires in London, reports with satisfaction the comments of the *Saturday Review* on the general situation of Italy, and especially its relations with the papacy (Maffei, report, 18 August 1872).

mate and deciding factor of political and diplomatic action. If it was easy to play the role of ambassador with a Home Fleet like Britain's backing one up, as someone said, it was not so easy for those who could not count on a similar land or sea force. Inevitably this was the case for Italy, least among the great powers and so least in military force. Cuts in spending were absolutely necessary and could not be made from the budgets for public works or education, two areas that required increased and ongoing subsidy so that the nation's life could develop at a faster, more modern pace. So the ax fell mainly on the military budget, which underwent large reductions commencing in 1867.

Spending on Italy's war-making power between 1867 and 1870 shrank drastically in comparison to the years 1861–1865; and even following the alarm caused by the Franco-Prussian War, the beginning of European rearmament, and the reforms of General Ricotti, it never again exceeded 200 million annually until the budget was in balance. Spending on the navy diminished even more, almost by half, so that military spending sank to the lowest percentage of overall state expenditure ever seen in the history of the Italian state: 18.66 percent.[61] And as in other areas, a spending contraction of this type was particularly onerous for a country that, far from being able to build on a solid initial platform, was in a position of having to spend proportionately much more than the other great powers because it faced the problem of a complete overhaul of the armed forces. Starting with the effective introduction of compulsory military service for all—something that existed only on paper in 1870 given the many exemptions and substitutions available—the military system had to be rebuilt. It was not enough to say that the bare bones of the army of Piedmont were already in place, because the difficulty lay precisely here, in putting flesh on this skeleton and transforming it into a large and robust body. One of the first great problems was that of building fortifications on the frontiers, for the loss of Savoy had left the line of the western Alps from Cenisio onward exposed, and the acquisition of the Venetian state had extended Italy's frontier into zones hitherto lacking any provision for defense. It came to seem more pressing after the spectacle of the Germans pouring into France, a spectacle that brought to mind the epoch of the great invasions, the migrations of whole peoples,[62] and led Italy to look for a secure and unbro-

---

[61] Sachs, *L'Italie: Ses finances et son développement économique*, pp. 232 ff. and 274, offers the following data: effective spending, including ordinary and extraordinary expenditures, for the war ministry was 230, 289, 246, 262, 189 million lire for the years 1861–1865. It was 174, 178, 155, 162, 161, 162, 181, 192, 187, 192 for the years from 1867 to 1876 (1866 obviously cannot be calculated). For the navy, 79, 61, 59, 60 million (in round numbers) for 1862–1865; 46, 39, 32, 25, 29, 31, 35, 37, 38, 36 million in 1867–1876. In *Il bilancio del regno d'Italia*, pp. 118 ff., in which spending is analyzed starting with 1868, the figures are the following: war ministry, 167, 149, 183, 151, 166, 176, 183, 180, 186 million for the years from 1868 to 1876; navy, 35, 35, 32, 37, 31, 32, 34, 38, and 28 million. Coppola d'Anna, *Popolazione reddito e finanze*, gives the overall figures for military defense (p. 106), and the percentages (p. 108), from which it results that while military spending in the five-year period 1861–1865 counted for 34.76 percent of the total of effective state spending, in the five-year period 1866–1870 it fell, despite the war of 1866, to 25.75 percent, and in the period 1871–1875 to 18.66 percent. It then rose to 20.47 percent in 1876–1880, to 21.95 percent in 1881–1885, etc.

[62] Cf. for example G. B. Bruzzo, *Considerazioni sulla difesa generale dell'Italia* (2d ed.; Naples, 1871), p. 12.

ken defensive perimeter. "Open to offensive action" as they were, the Italians had better get busy, if not from true and deep patriotism, at least from the "presentiment of our material danger," Marselli warned,[63] urging that the problem of the defense of the country be tackled and, among other things, that Rome be fortified. Another expert, the major general of the corps of engineers, G. B. Bruzzo, followed with an opuscule on the necessity to study the question of the general defense of the state "in all its breadth, starting not from ideas cramped by current thinking, but large ideas that encompass the future."[64] He proposed a plan of his own to divide the country into three large sectors—Po Valley, central Italy, Mezzogiorno—structured in such a way that Italy would not be forced to surrender even if the capital itself were lost, and would be "like a great ship, which does not sink even if it takes water in some of its compartments."[65] What was new in this project was the assertion that Italy, exposed to invasion from the north, might also be invaded from the sea in the center or the south; that the old notion that Italy's fate depended on the Po Valley was out of date and should be mothballed;[66] and that the problem of national defense, along the Alpine frontier and the lengthy coastline, was now very much more formidable and complex.

Passing from the problems of recruitment and fortification to those of arming for war on land and sea, recruiting officers, dividing the kingdom into territorial sectors—in sum the problems of the structure of the armed forces—there was a sense everywhere of having to start virtually from zero, especially now that a different military organization, that of Prussia, was to be taken as a model instead of the French one admired for so many years. This was witnessed in the fierce debates on the project of Ricotti in the spring of 1871, the *Quattro Discorsi* of La Marmora, the newspaper polemics, and the great parliamentary debate from 15 to 21 June. These debates and polemics were to persist for the entire period of Lanza's government and then the entire period of Minghetti's, reaching a crescendo in 1873–74 when the increased fear of French aggression against Italy drove the Left to press the government to accelerate and expand the armaments program with the Nicotera proposal of 18 March 1873. Their anxiety was shared by many on the Right.

There was a drumbeat from the Left, especially *La Riforma*,[67] about the necessity to be ready, to be protected by a strong shield, to keep the powder dry, as Oliver Cromwell had advised.[68] As would later repeatedly happen, so now the policies of Sella were attacked by those who, protesting their own jealous love of

[63] Marselli, *Avvenimenti del 1870–71*, p. 72.

[64] Bruzzo, *Considerazioni sulla difesa generale dell'Italia*, p. 4.

[65] Ibid., p. 7.

[66] Ibid., pp. 6 and 24. For other relevant discussions, cf. A. Gandolfi, *Bologna e l'Appennino nella difesa d'Italia* (Bologna, 1871); and for the anxieties of Nino Bixio, G. Busetto, *Notizie del generale Nino Bixio* 2:88–89.

[67] 26 March 1873 ("La difesa non è offesa"); and cf. 20, 22, 23, 24 March ("La proposta Nicotera," "Confidate nel Ministero!" "Il trionfo del Ministero," "Riflessioni"). And note the earlier article of 25 July 1872 ("Si vis pacem, para bellum").

[68] The Cromwellian expression recurs more than once in the press of the Left: cf. *La Riforma* for 20 February 1871 ("Adolfo Thiers"); *Il Diritto* for 12 September 1872 ("Le esagerazioni del Diritto").

country while naturally accusing their opponents of having a tepid sense of national honor, demanded arms, arms, arms, even at the cost of a swollen budget deficit.[69] Two slogans served them egregiously as launch pads for attacks on the policy of paring expenditure to the bone: the first was that in the Europe of today the rights of nations needed to be made visible by means of force.[70] The other was that Europe was transforming itself into a gigantic barracks, with the devil waiting to take the hindmost.[71]

It was Crispi's minions on *La Riforma*, and Crispi himself, who cried that Italy must hasten, hasten, hasten to arm itself, that every day and every hour wasted constituted a grave danger for the institutions of the country and its liberty.[72] They were joined by professional soldiers like Cialdini, a rugged and acerbic individual despite his stiff formality,[73] who came close to driving a wedge into Lanza's cabinet in December 1869 with his opposition to the reduction in military spending.[74] Cialdini also blasted the policy of thrift in a very turbulent session of the Senate on 3 August 1870;[75] and on 4 June 1874 he warned his senatorial colleagues once more that financial prosperity is not enough for a state. It was not true, he said, that Italy had first to become rich so as to become strong—if anything it was more true that you needed strength to become rich.[76] This was to repeat the celebrated verdict of Machiavelli (already erroneous in its author's own lifetime and falser than ever in the modern world) that "soldiers and weapons find money and bread, but bread and money do not find soldiers and weapons."[77]

And there was Marselli, who lamented that the Italians would continue to live under an illusion, convinced "that humble deference can prevent a war that is bound to happen. The policy of weakness and superficiality inflicts its consequences on the war machinery: we do not have the keenness we ought to have, and which we would have if we really thought that war with France was inevitable, and might not be far off. No fortifications, no fleet, no solid organization of the army. Little money, little patriotism, little moral elevation. I do not despair of Italy, in fact I believe that time could remake it; but what if we do not have the time?"[78] Even Luigi Tosti, a mild Cassinese monk, became very alarmed at what

---

[69] In October 1870 Luzzatti himself, fearing the difficulties that might come with being in possession of Rome, wanted a "new and formidable ordering of the national defense . . . a strong army. . . . And the finances? It is clear that they will get worse; but today we must reverse the priorities of the present administration, and think first of defending ourselves and then of the financial situation" (Luzzatti, *Memorie* 1:310, and cf. 2:96). At other times Luzzatti vacillated between the two exigencies (ibid., 1:398).

[70] "L'organizzazione della forza," in *La Riforma* for 17 February 1871.

[71] Crispi in the Chamber, 4 February 1872: "the position in Europe has changed, and . . . to be strong and have peace, we have to arm ourselves, arm ourselves, continually arm ourselves" (Crispi, *Discorsi Parlamentari* 2:136–37).

[72] Crispi, in the speech cited in the previous note (ibid., 2:139).

[73] On Cialdini as a speaker, cf. *La Perseveranza* for 5 August 1870.

[74] Cf. the diary of General Govone, in Lanza, *Le carte* 6:375–76.

[75] *A.P., Senato*, pp. 987 ff.

[76] *A.P., Senato*, pp. 855–56.

[77] Machiavelli, *Arte della Guerra*, book 7, ed. Casella-Mazzoni, (Florence, 1929), p. 303.

[78] Marselli to Robilant, 8 January 1874 (AE, *Carte Robilant*). In another letter of 5 June 1874

he considered the high likelihood of a French armed action in favor of the pope, and so supported the Prussian alliance; he wanted serious attention to be paid to the army, for these were times for deeds, not debates.[79]

These and like arguments were employed by the paladins of rapid and total rearmament, in whose eyes the policy of Sella was a policy of renunciation. Nor can the element of truth in their affirmations be denied. In Europe post-1870, the Europe of armed peace, a country did need more than ever to be strong in order to make its voice heard, and, beginning with that new phenomenon in the history of the peoples, the arms race, the problems of military power and military organization were assuming, if possible, still greater importance in international relations. This much was true, and the Right did not deny it.[80] Bonghi especially touched again and again on the present and future perils of the European situation as it stood after the Franco-Prussian War. He warned that the experience of 1870 had demonstrated that the "body politic" of Europe did not exist, and that each nation had to trust only in its own strength and its own arms. Italy had especially to look to its arms, for since it had been unable to win a great battle during the process of state formation, it had been unable to acquire a proud, confident, dignified feeling of its own right, and so still had to gain full awareness of the abilities of its forces on land and sea.

So both sides were at one in seeing the age as an age of iron. They agreed with Cromwell that it was a time to "keep their powder dry,"[81] even if for the moderates there was pain and sorrow in recognizing that Europe was returning "to a time of arms and violence,"[82] transforming itself into a vast military camp, and that with the passing of the age of Cobden and his friends, they had lost any basis for their mode of reasoning among peaceful and reasonable men.[83] The age also inspired Crispi's group with a few shivers of apprehension, but at the same time they took an ill-concealed pleasure in the triumphant sense of force and power. "We believed in justice and liberty; today they believe in force and in number," wrote Marco Minghetti many years later, tired, embittered, and pessimistic at the

---

Marselli again expresses his fear that, with the rising tide of opinion in the country against any military spending, Italy will end up redoing the work of Govone on the eve of a war in Europe. Again in 1881, in the well-known article "Politica Estera e Difesa Nazionale" (in *Nuova Antologia* 58, p. 127), he expresses the same thought in contemptuous form: money is the only thing "that passive politics concentrates on providing in plenty; in fact it sacrifices everything else to that, including the dignity of the nation."

[79] Tosti, letter to Gabrio Casati, 25 May 1871 (in Quintavalle, *La Conciliazione fra l'Italia ed il Papato*, pp. 334–35 and cf. also p. 338).

[80] Cf. the editorial in *L'Opinione* for 13 March 1871: the "gilded dream" of universal peace is over, etc.; 29 March 1871 ("La difesa generale d'Italia"); 1 May 1871 ("Le spese militari," stating that in the new conditions of Europe, everyone understands that the moral force of a nation is in direct proportion to its military force); 15 May 1871 ("L'ordinamento dell'esercito"); 19 August 1871 ("La vera quistione," stating that although it is a peaceful nation, Italy must arm itself in order to deter anyone else from contemplating an aggression against it); 3 January 1872 ("La politica estera").

[81] With this expression Bonghi ended his first speech to the Chamber on the law of Guarantees, on 31 January 1871 (Bonghi, *Discorsi Parlamentari* 1:237). Nigra also makes use of it in a letter to Visconti Venosta of 6 March 1871 (Visconti Venosta archive).

[82] Thus Bonghi (*Nove anni* 2:451).

[83] "La questione militare," in *L'Opinione* for 17 January 1871.

close of his life.[84] But ever since 1871 *La Riforma* had been ready with its reply, exalting force, number, the vital élan of the young peoples with a future.

But it was even more true that at that moment the problem of salvation for Italy was a financial problem, with all the rest receding into the background, even the question of military force; and that, between continuing the deficit for the sake of a few more divisions and balancing the budget with a few divisions less, Italy's strength, even in relation to the other nations, lay in the balanced budget.[85]

Since it was Italy's fortune that Sella's line prevailed, the reorganization of the army and its rearmament were not given sufficient financial support. That this should be so was, to repeat, a necessity; but the fact remains that from the military point of view Italy fell even farther behind the other great powers,[86] and this situation of too great inferiority deeply influenced its foreign policy, because it was difficult to play the diplomatic game to the limit if one did not have the Home Fleet, or the Prussian Guard, at one's back.

In truth there were very few at that time who wanted Italy to engage in the game of foreign policy to the hilt. The nation was entirely caught up in its own serious domestic problems, and although the problem of the finances predominated, it did not exclude other aspects of the nation's life that gave serious cause for tribulation. One of these was the low level of public safety, which led many to share the dismay expressed by Bonghi and Dina at the shocking increase in criminality, the constant rise in crimes of violence, the limited efficiency of the police, or the state of constant danger that still obtained in more than one region, especially in Romagna and Sicily.[87] The blight of crime had serious effects on the nation and also provoked reverberations abroad. These turned particularly nasty

---

[84] Cf. above, ch. 2, n. 104.

[85] Lanza pointed this out with sound good sense to Cialdini in December 1869: "Take care, general, not to put the country in the dilemma of choosing between a reduction in the army and a reduction in revenue, because the army would become an object of hatred if it refused to cut back, even though it has earned the love of the country, and the country would say, rather than financial failure, let the army be destroyed first" (Lanza, *Le carte* 6:376).

[86] The expenditures on the armies of the other great European powers in 1874, for example, were the following (in Italian lire): Russia, 788,390,103; France, 719,929,753; Germany, 488,742,315; Great Britain, 378,418,040; Austria-Hungary, 254,983,593; Italy, 192,011,542. If relative proportions are looked at, Italy was the country that dedicated the smallest percentage of the overall state budget to spending on the army (L. Cisotti, "La pace armata e l'esercito italiano," *Nuova Antologia* 29 [1875]: 921–23).

[87] From 29,637 crimes involving bloodshed in the period 1863–64, there is a jump to 55,825 in the period 1869–70. Admittedly, in the second case the total is swollen by the addition of the Veneto (Rome does not yet figure in the statistics); but the increase is still striking. From January 1861 to May 1870, 75,000 arrest warrants had not been executed (Lanza, report on the bill for special provisions on Public Security; *Camera dei Deputati*, Collection of printed documents, XI Legislature, session of 1870–71, vol. 2, no. 83, and appendix A; cf. also no. 83 B, appendixes A and N). Hence, this verdict: "police that cannot universally guarantee the lives and the security of the citizens, punitive justice that in many provinces lacks the means to detect the crime" (Bonghi, *Nove anni* 2:462). Cf. *L'Opinione* for 5, 7, 12 January, and 26 February 1871 ("La sicurezza pubblica," "Polizia-Tribunali-Giurati," "Provvedimenti eccezionali," "L'amministrazione della giustizia"), and *La Perseveranza* for 5 and 25 January 1871, drawing attention to the seriousness of criminality in Romagna (the second article, "Cose serie," is by Bonghi). Cf. Minghetti, *Carteggio Minghetti-Pasolini* 4:203, 209, 213 ff.; Crispi in the Chamber on 10 June 1875 (Crispi, *Discorsi Parlamentari* 2:243 ff.); *L'Italia economica nel 1873*, pp. 348 ff.

in the British press, which was always quick to publish angry letters from subjects of Her Majesty Queen Victoria who, while traveling for pleasure in the peninsula, had been robbed by bandits, or more simply, had reacted with arrogant annoyance to the formalities of the police and the requests of the carabinieri.[88] Along with the financial mess, this was the issue that did Italy the most damage and made it a matter of urgency for the country "to scrub itself clean before the world of this opprobrious plague of extortionists, robbers, and assassins."[89] The low rate at which its government bonds were quoted on the European exchanges, and the stereotyped picture of Italy as a country of thieves and brigands (the picture that inspired De Amicis with the idea for the proud gesture of the little Paduan patriot), were the two great dangers for a country that wanted to organize itself as a modern state and be recognized and appreciated as such.

All this was more than enough to occupy the hearts and minds of the Italians. The facts spoke for themselves and constrained even the combative de Launay to acknowledge that Italy's domestic conditions were such that it could not afford any policy except the exclusive and peremptory one of defending the national territory.[90]

---

[88] For example, in the *Times* for 10 September 1872 there was published a letter from Naples that painted a grim picture of the recrudescence of brigandage in the Mezzogiorno. This letter was commented on in an editorial blaming the Italian government for not taking sufficiently energetic action (Maffei, report, 11 September, no. 348). But then in the *Times* for 3 December 1872 there appeared a letter denouncing the handcuffs used by the carabinieri as an instrument of torture (Cadorna, report, 4 December, no. 369, cited at n. 40 above). In sum, there were protests against the poor condition of public safety, and also against real or imagined abuses by the police forces.

[89] "X," in the "Rassegna politica," *Nuova Antologia* 27 (1874): 984.

[90] De Launay, report, 21 November 1870, no. 714; cf. as well his report of 14 November, no. 708; but especially his report of 17 November, no. 711: "the state of our finances, unless we want to march to total ruin, to bankruptcy, compels us not to get mixed up in any war as long as our territory is not threatened."

Political Apathy

BUT AS WELL AS FACTS there were impressions. Parallel to objective reality there was a subjective state of mind, and the last thing that it wanted at this moment was troublesome friction in Italy's relations with other countries. In a way this was a natural consequence of the relaxation of the extreme tension that, from 1859 until the taking of Rome, had continually unsettled the lives of many Italians. The members of the political elite who were then in their prime had lived for long years in a feverish atmosphere, and as one writer pointed out, the average forty-year-old Italian "may have heard of public tranquillity and the prosperity that comes about under its influence . . . but in reality he has never enjoyed this state of tranquillity. Isn't it natural to suppose that he might want to see for himself what it is like?"[1] More or less the same sentiment vibrated in the words of the foreign minister, Visconti Venosta, who since 1848 had grown used to the hazards of the battles fought, and also the conspiracies fomented, in the name of liberty, and he too was now convinced that the country wanted to rest and recover its strength after the prolonged turbulence that had bedeviled it for so many years.[2]

Beyond the personal desire for peace and quiet there was a conviction that it was finally time to put a stop to the restless passage from one desire to another, from one longing to another, in order not to consume all the nation's energies in this endless pursuit of ever-new aspirations. Rather, it was time once and for all to attend to the internal consolidation of the state, to preparing the Italians for their new role, to economic development.[3] This was repeated many years later by Michele Coppino, a member of the Left, in a commemoration of his friend Depretis: "in united Italy the question of raising the standard of living replaced the question of simply living."[4]

In its natural desire for quiet, it was as though the nation were drawing a great collective sigh of relief. A cycle had ended on the Capitol. In its heart Italy was eager for peace, however gray and monotonous, provided it brought calm, well-being, and serenity, with no more shocks.

But with this very natural desire there was mixed a less admirable sentiment, unfortunately a widespread one, and that was the notable indifference to public

---

[1] "La pacificazione interna," in *L'Opinione* for 23 September 1870. And also, by Bonghi, "Il Duca d'Aosta re di Spagna," in *La Perseveranza* for 18 October, stating that there is not a single Italian who does not long for quiet.

[2] In a speech of 9 November 1870 at a banquet given for him by the Patriotic Society of Milan (*La Perseveranza*, 11 November). Amari also thought that Italy had need "of political calm and administrative vigor" (Amari, *Carteggio* 3:314).

[3] "Roma Capitale," in *La Perseveranza* for 20 September 1870.

[4] Coppino, *Commemorazione di A. Depretis*, p. 27.

life shown by many, who were tired after having been plagued for so long by questions like the annexation of Venetia and Rome, by cries like "Rome or death," which were apt to disturb the world of one's family or one's town, threaten the conduct of business, and inject a sour note into the joy of living. There was an inclination, now that the hurricane had passed, to let national affairs take their course, and for each to occupy himself with his own "*particulare*" [private interest]. Only a few years earlier, when Venetia and Rome had still to be liberated, one foreigner was struck by the political passion of the Italians, by the way every conversation turned immediately to politics and never left the subject;[5] and fifteen years later, according to Jacini, everyone would be totally engrossed in foreign policy, ready to sort out the problems of Europe in the clubs and cafes.[6] But now, in these intervening years, many people had lost all desire to talk about politics, or to hear it talked about. Public controversies were left to those who had a taste for such things, and the number of these was small, to judge by the fact that the source of information with the widest circulation, the Milanese daily *Il Secolo*, printed barely 30,000 copies around 1880, and that among the organs of political opinion the figure for *Il Diritto* was less than 4,000, for *La Riforma* 2,500, for *L'Opinione* 7,000, for *La Perseveranza* 3,000, with *Il Popolo Romano* alone reaching 12,500.[7] What we have here is that attitude of knowing little and caring less about political debates and ideals that the "poet and historian" of the little people of Italy remarked as one of their distinctive traits[8]—except that here we are not really talking about the people of small means, who were understandably preoccupied by the hard and laborious problem of living from day to day, who were excluded from the moral and political life of the state by the harshness of their lives to the point where they were ready to trade their vote at the local elections for a glass of brandy,[9] and who were cut off perforce from the higher aspects of public life by the fact that they could not vote in national elections. Here we are dealing with the elite, with the middle class who had rights and who ought to have felt they had duties as well. One contemporary observer, who did not in fact draw pessimistic conclusions from the fact, called it a softness that went right to the marrow of their bones and cradled them gently, an intellectual and moral languor, a lassitude they could not shake off.[10]

---

[5] Taine, *Voyage en Italie* 1:355.

[6] Jacini, *Pensieri sulla politica italiana*, p. 60.

[7] D. Papa, *Il giornalismo* (Verona, 1880), pp. 265–66. The total circulation of 525 daily and weekly periodicals in 1874 was 797,590 copies. But here too, note the increase in the number of periodicals (dailies, weeklies, monthlies), which had risen rapidly from 185 in 1836 and 450 in 1864, to 723 in 1870, 765 in 1871, and 1,126 in 1874, of which 387 were dailies (P. Lioy, *Elettori e deputati*, pp. 53–55). For a comparison with the circulation of the principal foreign papers, cf. Papa, *Il giornalismo*, pp. 27 and 51–52: 30,000 copies of the *Times* and 170,000 copies of the *Daily Telegraph*; 72,000 copies of *Le Figaro* and half a million of the *Petit Journal*. The French chargé d'affaires, de Sayve, insisted on the slight importance of the press in Italy (report, 3 February 1872, no. 13; AEP, *C.P., Italie*, t. 384, fols. 106 ff.), as did the other chargé d'affaires, Tiby, in 1874 (report, 19 February 1874, no. 16; t. 389, fol. 112v).

[8] Bacchelli, *Il Mulino del Po* 2:334.

[9] Ferrario, *Qual'è la moralità de' campagnuoli*, pp. 31–32.

[10] Bonghi, in the "Rassegna Politica" for 1 December 1871 in *Nuova Antologia* 18, p. 912, and 30 November 1873, in *Nuova Antologia* 24, pp. 944–45.

The heroic era of the struggle for unity was over, and until the proletariat burst on the scene with the coming of the socialist movement and offered a great new challenge, giving a precise and concrete meaning to political life for the majority and rousing fresh emotion where before there had been indifference at best to the normal life of the state, it seemed that the Italians were without the will or the focus for an ardent political contest,[11] except where relations with the church were concerned. Here there was indeed a crisis, but it only fired the extremists, the clerical zealots and the free thinkers, not the mass of the people and the bourgeoisie, who felt the effects of the dissension and therefore wished to fan the flames as little as possible, and were reluctant to stage mass demonstrations. Another reason the will for political struggle sagged was that, having attained the goals at which the soul of the nation had been feverishly aiming for the last twelve years, many Italians were now left feeling disoriented, at a loss, unable to choose other new ideals right away. Now that they had what they wanted, the horizon seemed to shrink instead of expanding, as Villari said, leaving them somehow mistrustful and disillusioned, unable to decide what to do next, or what they wanted next.[12]

Even in Germany, the country that had won the greatest victories, a man like von Sybel was asking what ought to be done now,[13] so it was natural that the selection of new ideals should leave Italy, a country not nearly so triumphant, rather paralyzed. The result was that far too many people did not want to be bothered any more, or wanted to be bothered as little as possible, about national problems; they wanted to leave that worry to the category of professional politicians whose existence in a modern state they had already spontaneously accepted, since it left them free to forget about public affairs and attend solely to their own. In Bonghi's view the inclination to concentrate on what was tangible and not rack one's brains about the rest, to let things take their course, was spreading. People were more or less willing to put up with the present and hope for a better future.[14] And a foreigner observed that once the Italians no longer had their gaze fixed on the same common goal, meaning Rome, they each immersed themselves in their own personal concerns and individual passions.[15]

The phenomenon, much remarked on then and later, of the indifference of the voters to their responsibility, was a sign of this state of mind. And yet the body of voters, given the electoral system then in place, was already a select group: out of approximately 27 million Italians, of whom seven million were adult males, only 528,932 (in other words, 1.97 percent) enjoyed the right to vote in 1870.[16]

---

[11] Thus Bonghi, "Rassegna Politica" for 31 January 1872 in *Nuova Antologia* 19, p. 465; and cf. the "Rassegne" for 30 March 1872, vol. 19, p. 927, and 30 June 1872, vol. 20, p. 696; and the "Rassegna" for 2 November 1872, vol. 21, p. 746.

[12] "La scuola e la quistione sociale in Italia," in *Nuova Antologia* 21 (1872): 477–78.

[13] Meinecke, "Johann Gustav Droysen," p. 249.

[14] Bonghi in *Nuova Antologia* 19 (1872): 927.

[15] Tiby, the French chargé d'affaires, in his report no. 51 of [?] July 1874 (received in Paris on the 22nd); AEP, *C.P.*, *Italie*, t. 390, fol. 44.

[16] The data are in *L'Italia economica nel 1873*, pp. 727–28. On the divergences of the data in the *Manuale dei Senatori e Deputati*, cf. ibid.

They were an elite, a tiny "legal nation" compared to the "real" nation,[17] and what is more, a legal nation with severe structural imbalances, inasmuch as the right to the vote depended not only on the varying distribution of landed property but also on the different systems of land registry and taxation within Italy, and even on the reduction of the tax threshold, which meant that in Liguria thirty individuals out of every one thousand had the vote, while in Umbria the comparable figure was fifteen.[18]

This restricted elite showed that, with national unity achieved, participation in public life was no longer widely based, indeed was much narrower than it had been in the formative period of the struggles and the plebiscites. In all of Lombardy in 1870 there were 68,371 registered voters, but when in 1848 it had been a question of voting to join with Piedmont, 661,626 had been eligible to vote.[19] In Emilia the registered voters now amounted to no more than 42,248, but at the time of the plebiscite for annexation, 426,764 had voted; and so on. This drastic core contradiction is enough to explain the gap between the class that held power, a true oligarchy, and the rest of the country.

An electoral body as restricted as this could give the valid impression that the

---

[17] The expression [*paese legale, paese reale*] already appears in Jacini, *Sulle condizioni della cosa pubblica in Italia* (1870), p. 17.

[18] Cf. the statistical table in Lioy, *Elettori e deputati*, p. 188. The numbers of those having the vote per 1,000 inhabitants in 1870 were: Piedmont, 26.10; Liguria, 30.70; Lombardy, 19.70; Veneto, 15.10; Emilia, 19.90; Tuscany, 22.40; Marche, 15.10; Umbria, 15; Lazio, 15.20; Abruzzi and Molise, 16.70; Campania, 20.60; Puglia, 20; Basilicata, 17.20; Calabria, 16.40; Sicily, 16.10; Sardinia, 26.50. The average throughout the kingdom was 19.70. In 1876 it rose to 22.60, with continuing strong variations among the regions. (Cf. *La Statistica elettorale politica*, published by the Ministry of Agriculture, Industry, and Commerce [Rome, 1877], p. v.) In the single constituencies there were also strong variations; in 1865 only ten constituencies had from fifty to fifty-four registered voters per 1,000 inhabitants; twenty-five had from eight to ten; 129 had from ten to fifteen; 138 had from fifteen to twenty, etc. (Lioy, *Elettori e deputati*, p. 90). There was just as much imbalance in the formation of the constituencies, given that there were 1,848 voters per constituency in Sardinia and 1,589 in Liguria, as compared to 776 in Calabria, 775 in the Veneto (1866), 716 in Abruzzo, 694 in the Marche (ibid., pp. 89–90). But these last imbalances corrected, at least in part, the defects of the earlier ones, empirically and territorially, in the sense that to the higher ratio of voters in Liguria and Sardinia there did not correspond, as a result of the distribution of the constituencies, a larger number of representatives in parliament. In fact, Sardinia wound up having a smaller number of deputies than the Marche. I have used the contemporary statistical data. In the tables in the *Compendio delle statistiche elettorali italiane dal 1848 al 1934*, published by the Central Statistical Institute and the Ministry for the Constituent Assembly (Rome, 1946), vol. 1, tables 2 B and 6, pp. 9 ff., 36 ff., there are a few slight variations in the figures (cf. *L'Italia economica nel 1873*, p. 728). In any case there is no question that there were enormous disparities from region to region, both in the ratios of those having the right to vote and in the number of registered voters composing the constituencies. These disparities were denounced by Zanardelli in his celebrated report on the reform of national electoral law (*Compendio*, p. * 97).

By 1870 there are shifts with respect to 1865: according to the *Compendio* (table 6), the registered voters per constituency were 1,614 in Liguria, 1,540 in Sardinia, 1,352 in Piedmont, 1,201 in Tuscany, descending to 850 in the Veneto, 827 in Umbria, 805 in Abruzzo, 790 in Calabria, 775 in the Marche. The peak figures in Liguria and Sardinia are explained by the fact that in these two regions (as in the administrative districts of Bobbio and Novi), the tax threshold for acquiring voting rights was 20 rather than 40 lire (cf. Minghetti, *Discorsi Parlamentari* 8:118).

[19] The number of those voting had been 561,683 (cf. L. Marchetti, "I moti di Milano e il problema della fusione col Piemonte," in *Il 1848 nella storia italiana ed europea* 2:723, ed. E. Rota [Milan, 1948]).

two parties contending for power were really two brilliant general staffs, top-heavy with rival generals but short on troops.[20] No putative lack of preparation and maturity on the part of the masses could be claimed as an excuse, and yet in the elections of November 1870, only 238,448 of those registered, or 45.8 percent, took part in the first round of voting.[21] This was, and remained, the lowest level reached since the constitution of the kingdom of Italy, given that the preceding general elections, while not revealing a massive urge to get involved politically either, had at least shown higher percentages of voter participation: 57 percent in 1861, 54 percent in 1865–66, and 52 percent in 1867.[22]

In sum, there was a continuing decline in political involvement, all the more remarkable in that absenteeism was highest in the electoral districts of the leading urban centers, precisely where the political contest ought to have been keenest. At Milan 35.07 percent voted, at Genoa 39.12 percent, at Padua 32.63, at Bologna 28.26, at Florence 28.95, and at Livorno 16.21 percent.[23] Were it not for the provinces of the Mezzogiorno, in which unhappiness had driven the voters in larger numbers to the ballot boxes, from which they still expected some sort of remedy for their grievances, and where voter participation reached 61.15 percent in Sicily, the result of the elections would have been even more desolate.

Nor were the national elections the only ones that revealed a scarcity of interest in public affairs. Just as with public finance, where the deficit of the state's budget was augmented by the budget deficits of the communes and provinces, so too absenteeism at national elections came on top of absenteeism in communal and provincial elections. In the local elections of 1872, the percentage of those voting was barely 39 percent.[24] In the communal elections the percentage of voters was 10 percent in many places, and in some even 8 and 6 percent.[25] At Parma, in the last elections before 1870, out of 4,000 voters 108 showed up at the voting booth, and at Florence the number was 879 out of 8,200.[26] At Milan in June 1872 it was "not a pretty sight" when out of 9,366 voters, only 2,014 took part in the elections, or 21.5 percent.[27] And this was the city of the Five Days, the focal point of so much of the Risorgimento! In poor compensation for this

---

[20] G. Ferrero, *Potere* (Milan, 1947), p. 307.

[21] In the second round of voting, the percentage sank to 34.07 percent.

[22] In 1874 it began to climb again to 55.7 percent, and in 1876 to 59.2 percent (*Statistica delle elezioni generali politiche per la XXV Legislatura*, published by the Central Statistical Office [Rome, 1920], p. xxxviii). In France in 1876 the level was 74 percent; in England in 1874 it was 79 percent.

[23] *L'Opinione* complained that in the great cities barely one quarter of those registered bothered to vote. This phenomenon was to be constantly repeated: in 1919 still, abstention was much more noticeable in the great cities than in the countryside. At Palermo only 18.3 percent voted, at Catania 22 percent, at Naples 27.2, at Rome 29.7, even in Genoa only 44.7 percent. Meanwhile, in the constituencies of Ravenna and Forlì a level of 84.8 percent was reached, and in Cremona 83.6 percent (*Statistica delle elezioni generali politiche*, pp. xxxvi–xxxvii). And the objective causes adduced to explain the phenomenon only do so in part. Cf. ibid., and also *Compendio*, vol. 2, p. * 32 ff.

[24] *L'Italia economica nel 1873*, pp. 725–26. And cf. *L'Opinione* for 27 March 1873. Even in Spain the quota was higher (44 percent; Lioy, *Elettori e deputati*, p. 84). But Belgium had levels of abstention similar to those of Italy in municipal elections (*Compendio*, vol. 2, p. * 19 n. 1).

[25] *L'Opinione* for 27 March 1873; cf. as well L. Palma, "La riforma elettorale in Italia," in *Nuova Antologia* 36 (1877): 582.

[26] Serra Gropelli, *Le cinque piaghe del Regno d'Italia*, p. 157.

[27] *Il Diritto* for 28 June 1872.

indifference in the major cities, there was a more lively and militant involvement in the smaller centers, because, especially at this time, the contest in these was apt to revolve entirely around questions of purely local interest, not to speak of personal and family feuds.[28]

Really, it was as though the people had withdrawn to the Aventine,[29] and it was impossible to put a good face on things by claiming that the abstainers were clericals, faithful to the rule "neither elected nor electors" and harking back to the old order of things in revulsion at the present. Rather, the reactionaries could postulate that the small turnout at the ballot box proved that in 1870 groups committed to the nation were still a minority, and that the majority of the population would always be hostile to unity and the new regime.[30]

In any case the continual decrease from 1861 to 1870 in the number of those voting contradicted an explanation in terms of clerical influence, since hostility to the new order had generally been much stronger at the outset, and the passage of time had begun to dissipate prejudices and win over the reluctant. It might be the case that these prejudices were renewed by Italy's seizure of Rome, that in November 1870 it was not only enraged clericals, enemies of national unity, who could contemplate abstaining from voting as a sign of protest, but also Italian patriots whose Catholic sentiments were troubled by the open clash with the pontiff. The events of 20 September might well have provoked abstention by "honest men who fear God in their hearts."[31] But it is also true that Pius IX had not yet spoken, had not yet declared that it was not permitted "to take a seat in that hall," meaning Montecitorio.[32] The famous rule had certainly been pro-

---

[28] *L'Opinione* considers the dangers of this situation on 27 March 1873, stating that the smaller communes are the ones in which the extreme and subversive parties might make the most proselytes. This remark is aimed principally at clerical propaganda.

[29] Serra Gropelli, *Le cinque piaghe del Regno d'Italia*, p. 158.

[30] That groups committed to the nation were a minority is true. But they were an active and influential minority, whereas the others, the clerical-legitimists, were also a minority, and a fossilized one at that: cf. the acute analysis of Salvemini, "L'Italia politica nel secolo XIX," in *L'Europa nel secolo XIX*, pp. 372 ff.

[31] Giuseppe (read Giovanni) Fabrizi to Ricasoli, 15 November 1870 (Ricasoli, *Lettere e documenti* 10:164). Fabrizi, a deputy, opted not to run again.

[32] Until 1871 the response given by the Sacra Penitenzieria on 1 December 1866 remained valid, a response substantially favorable to Catholic participation in the electoral contest (the text in Eufrasio, "Il 'non expedit,'" *Nuova Antologia* 197 [1 September 1904]: 86). This reply was confirmed by the Penitenziere Maggiore to the bishop of Mondovì on 25 February 1867 (Montaldini, *Uno sguardo al passato, al presente, e all'avvenire dell'Europa*, pp. 156–57). In March of 1871 Montaldini himself sent a copy of the declaration of 1 December 1866 to the S. Penitenzieria, asking whether "in the present circumstances . . . it is *expedient* to participate in the national elections." The answer was *non expedire* (Montaldini, ibid., pp. 152 ff., which is the most detailed account of the affair; Eufrasio, in the article cited, goes astray here, referring to 1874 instead of to 1871). Still, the question was not seen as having been decided by this. In fact, on 5 July 1872 *La Voce della Verità*, the official organ of the Society for Catholic Interests, which was waging a battle against abstentionism (article "Le elezioni"), stated that to its knowledge the pope had not enjoined Catholics not to vote (and gave detailed references to Montaldini and the reply of the S. Penitenzieria of March 1871). In its reply of 6 July ("Le elezioni communali"), *L'Osservatore Romano*, which was strongly in favor of sticking to the rule "neither elected not electors"—in the national elections—was unable to adduce any formal pronouncement in this sense and confined itself to vague assertions (the rule was "evidently favored and approved by the highest authorities"), and to recalling the instructions of Pius VII at the time of the French invasion. The situation changed radically with the speech of Pius IX to the women of the Roman circle of Santa Melania on 11 October 1874, in which the pope affirmed that "it

nounced by Don Margotti, but agreement on this point was far from unanimous, even among zealous Catholics. Even after 1874, by which time *Roma locuta erat*, the debates continued, with some Catholics continuing publicly to maintain that it was important not to sever themselves from public life,[33] and the odd parish priest in Piedmont telling his flock explicitly to "go and vote, because "neither elected nor electors' is a load of rubbish!";[34] so logically abstention from voting was far from prevalent before 1874. In the elections held at Rome itself in January 1871 for two seats in parliament, there was a Catholic candidate representing groups opposed to abstention, an advocate named Pietro Venturi, in contention on the second ballot.[35]

The program of abstention was targeted, at all events, at the national elections. At the local elections, on the other hand, the clerical forces made a great showing in 1872, at Rome on 4 August, and notably at Naples on 1 September. On this occasion many, though not all, militant Catholics voted, officially authorized, indeed urged to do so by the ecclesiastical hierarchy, and led by priests and friars who showed up in considerable numbers at the voting booths,[36] waging a fierce battle against the liberal list and in favor of their own. In the capital, Pius IX

---

is not licit to take a seat in that hall" (Montecitorio; cf. "Ultime notizie," in *L'Osservatore Romano* for 13 October 1874, and the text of the pope's speech in the "Ultime notizie" on 14 October; also *La Voce della Verità* for 14 and 16 October). Thus *L'Osservatore Romano* for 28 October 1874 was able to state that the subject of the elections was now closed for Catholics ("no one can any longer be a Catholic who does not feel he must abstain totally"), with a reference this time not to Pius VII but to Pius IX and his speech to the circle of Santa Melania ("Gli elettori alla corte d'Assise"; and cf. in the issue for 18 November, "Le elezioni"). As for *La Voce della Verità*, it too declared on 17 November 1874: "in obedience to the inspired word . . . of the High Pontiff Pius IX, Italian Catholics have abstained." Pius IX returned to the subject with an even more clear-cut reply to the cardinals on 21 December 1874, speaking against the ministers of God who feel no shame in participating in the elections (*L'Osservatore Romano* for 25 December 1874). In sum, it can be stated that the first national election to be influenced by a definite stance on the part of the highest ecclesiastical authorities was that of November 1874. Cf. as well Jacini, *La crisi religiosa del Risorgimento*, p. 370 n. 1; Halperin, *Italy and the Vatican at War*, pp. 377–78.

[33] Thus A. Giuria, *I cattolici e le elezioni politiche* (Savona, 1876), is in favor of taking part in the voting. At Rome in 1879 there were meetings and projects to obtain the abolition of the *non expedit* (P. Campello della Spina, *Ricordi di 50 anni dal 1840 al 1890*, pp. 133 ff.; T. Tittoni, "Ricordi personali di politica interna," *Nuova Antologia* 342 [1 April 1929]: 308 ff.).

[34] An expression heard in 1886 at San Damiano, in favor of Giolitti (Giolitti, *Memorie* 1:41–42).

[35] The French chargé d'affaires at the Holy See, Lefebvre de Béhaine, reports on this (report, 25 January 1871, no. 15; AEP, *C.P., Rome*, t. 1049, fols. 121 ff.).

[36] Cf. G. Manfroni, *Sulla soglia del Vaticano* 1:101 (Bologna, 1920). In Rome the contest ended with a victory for the liberals (four-sevenths for the moderates, two-sevenths for the clericals, one-seventh for the democrats), giving rise to triumphant outbursts in the press of the Right and the Left, which exalted this new example of civic sensibility and strenuous patriotism which Rome had given to Italy (see for example *Il Secolo* for 7 August). But Tornielli, who at the time was chief of the political division at the foreign ministry, deprecated attempts to give a frankly political color to an election that ought to have remained on purely administrative territory, and observed: "Behind closed doors, we cannot help acknowledging that close to four thousand non-Romans are registered on the voter lists; three thousand alone are employees, doormen, guards, garrison soldiers, etc.," thus confirming the great accusation made by the clericals (Tornielli to Visconti Venosta, 6 August 1872, and cf. his letter of 3 August: ACR, *Carte Visconti Venosta*, 1872, pacco 5, fasc. 4). At Naples the clericals had a notable success. The chargé d'affaires to the Quirinal for Austria-Hungary, Herbert, and then the ambassador, Wimpffen, dwelt on the importance of clerical participation in the elections, in reports to Vienna of 10 August, 7 September, and 5 October 1872 (SAW, *P.A.*, XI/80). Cf. as well d'Ideville, *Les Piemontais à Rome*, p. 266.

himself had shown favor to Catholic participation,[37] and the editors of the Catholic papers, *L'Osservatore Romano*, *La Voce della Verità*, *La Stella*, had followed this august example, heatedly insisting that the faithful should vote in droves and thus resist the "invading torrent of impiety."[38] At Naples the election campaign had been supported by Riario Sforza, the cardinal archbishop, with the full approval of the pope and the Roman curia.[39] The contest had thus assumed an evident political color: the local elections gave the clericals a chance to show the political strength of their ranks; the outcome would be felt at the national level, with a victory for the Catholics signifying, in the eyes of many, a serious setback for the government[40] and, in general, for the Italian governing class. So it was the liberals versus the clericals, though as the French envoy to the Quirinal noted, it would be more correct to speak of the supporters and foes of Italian unity.[41] Crispi felt the same and called for solidarity among the *unitari* [meaning the former], regardless of their party, against the clericals.[42] And yet, even in these circumstances, the percentage of those coming out to vote barely scraped past 50 percent at Rome.[43]

The facile assumption that abstention can be explained as a "black" phenomenon is disproved by the fact that in the subsequent national elections, following

[37] Pius IX said: "Of course, of course, they didn't understand even though I repeated it many times, I am glad, I am glad if they take part in the local elections" (Campello della Spina, *Ricordi di 50 anni*, p. 121). In 1871 the Roman Union was founded to help in getting a "Christian element" into the municipal government on the Capitol (ibid., p. 119). In a speech to the former employees of the papal ministry of commerce and public works, the pontiff repeated "let everyone . . . do what he can, and follow the counsel of authoritative persons, and if we don't succeed it will be one more proof of the hypocrisy of the guarantees, and of liberty" (*L'Osservatore Romano*, 14 July 1872).

[38] For the propaganda of the Catholic papers, cf. *L'Osservatore Romano* for 5, 6, 12, 13, 16, 24 July; *La Voce della Verità*, especially in the appeal of 4 August, "Christians, let us go to the ballot box." On 6 August *La Voce della Verità* deplores the fact that more than half the Catholics have abstained; on 7 August it asserts that many priests did not vote. In fact, at Rome the black aristocracy had abstained almost completely from voting, having previously deplored the decision to support such action (Palomba, Austrian chargé d'affaires to the Holy See, reports of 13 July and 10 August 1872; SAW, *P.A.*, XI/229, nos. 4 A and 6 F). Manfroni also recognized that not all the clergy and not all the clericals came out to vote, since they feared trouble. But clearly, after the defeat the clerical circles and clerical papers would want to minimize as much as possible the degree of their participation in the election. Cf. Pesci, *I primi anni di Roma capitale*, pp. 511–12.

[39] This is stated by the French ambassador to the Holy See, Bourgoing (report of 3 July 1872, no. 17; AEP, *C.P.*, *Rome*, t. 1055, fols. 90 ff.). On Cardinal Riario Sforza and his actions at this time, cf. F. Di Domenico, *La vita del cardinale Sisto Riario Sforza* (2d ed.; Naples, 1905), pp. 232 ff.; E. Federici, *Sisto Riario Sforza cardinale di Santa Romana Chiesa arcivescovo di Napoli, 1810–1877* (Rome, 1945), pp. 300–301. The latter contains an absurd statement to the effect that the prefect of Naples had asked the cardinal in the name of the government [!] to get the Catholic vote out. On the actions of this prefect, d'Afflitto, cf. Lanza, *Le carte* 8:211–14; as for the government, we need only recall Lanza's circular to the prefects on 8 July, which was motivated by fears of a strong Catholic intervention in the electoral contest: cf. Vigo, *Annali d'Italia* 1:174 ff.

[40] This is stated by a source clearly not anti-Vatican or pro-Italian, the ambassador Bourgoing (in the report cited in the previous note).

[41] Fournier, report, 22 July 1872, no. 38; AEP, *C.P. Italie*, t. 385, fols. 239 ff.

[42] In a speech to a political meeting at the Argentina on 2 August (Crispi, *Scritti e discorsi politici*, p. 465).

[43] Out of 15,369 registered voters, 8,029 went to the polls, a little more than 52 percent. At Naples, out of 20,000 registered voters, 8,407 did so, or 42.03 percent (Naples, Archivio di Stato, gabinetto Prefettura; this information generously supplied by Dr. Giuliano Procacci). And these were record numbers!

the church's promulgation of the rule "neither elected nor electors," the percentage of those voting actually climbed rather than falling. Also there is the fact that in November 1870, the highest percentages of voter participation came from the provinces of the Mezzogiorno, in which the Catholics certainly could not be said to lack authority or numerical weight,[44] whereas a group of largely anticlerical provinces in Emilia-Romagna, including Piacenza, Parma, Modena, Reggio Emilia, Bologna, Ferrara, Forlì, and Ravenna, plus Livorno, the center of extremism in Tuscany, all thriving hotbeds of republicanism then and soon to be hotbeds of the International, of socialism, and even of anarchism in the future, were among those with the lowest percentages of voters.[45]

In truth the republicans figured largely among those who abstained, for their watchword had been to desert the ballot boxes and thus "strike a salutary terror into the monarchy, making it aware of its own isolation." They wanted to demonstrate their own indomitable hostility to the institution of monarchy by refraining from any act that might smack of consent, and thus depriving the constitutional regime of an indispensable pillar of its existence. The advice to abstain had come from the republican papers more than from the Catholic ones, and in the end the indifference and weariness of the voters supplied easy fodder not only for the venomous vaunting invectives of the blacks but also for those of the republicans. Praise in the *Osservatore Cattolico* for the faithful who had abstained was answered at the opposite extreme by the remarks of the *Gazzetta di Milano* to the effect that the abstentions had given voice to the will for radical change, and had demonstrated that the electoral law no longer reflected the mood of the nation.[46] Agostino Bertani thought the matter through, and since he did not believe that it was a profitable tactic, he was led to propose a "league of abstentionists," which

---

[44] Fonzi, "I 'cattolici transigenti' italiani," pp. 961–62, maintains, on the basis of voting data, that the *non expedit* was ignored in the Mezzogiorno, which may have been Catholic, and even legitimist and pro-Bourbon, but was also anticlerical and was still easily dominated by "liberal personalism" and by local clienteles. Thus the Mezzogiorno was not permeable by the "Opera dei Congressi," the great organization of the clericals. That Lombardy and the Veneto were the regions where the organized Catholic movement had its strongest bases results as well from the "petition" of 1887 (cf. Candeloro, *L'azione cattolica in Italia* [Rome, no year but 1949], p. 15).

[45] In the national elections in 1870, in the first round of voting, at Piacenza 33.04 percent voted; at Parma 33.69 percent; at Reggio 32.34; at Modena 36.38; at Bologna 28.26; at Ferrara 33.64; at Forlì 34.27; at Ravenna 31.69; at Florence 28.95; at Arezzo 32.48; at Lucca 32.27; at Pisa 34.61; and at Livorno 16.21, the lowest quota in the entire kingdom, in which the overall average was 45.8 percent. The averages in the regions were the following: Piedmont, 46.09 percent; Liguria, 40.76 percent; Lombardy, 40.34; Veneto, 41.37; Emilia, 32.42; Tuscany, 31.63; Marche, 37.97; Umbria, 30.77; Lazio, 43.27; Abruzzi and Molise, 56.99; Campania, 50.32; Puglie, 55.59; Basilicata, 57.97; Calabria, 58.59; Sicily, 61.15; and Sardinia 46.32 percent. In the second round the figures were much lower almost everywhere (*L'Italia economica nel 1873*, pp. 729–31). Livorno, though it was the city where the percentage of registered voters relative to the population was the highest in the entire kingdom (Lioy, *Elettori e deputati*, p. 84), had the lowest turnout in the elections of 1865 with 33 percent. On that occasion the provinces of Ravenna, Bologna, Forlì, Ferrara, Modena, and Parma had also been among the lowest, all falling below the national average. Note that until the elections of 1909 the Mezzogiorno and the islands always had the highest percentages of voter participation (*Compendio*, vol. 2, p. * 28; table 13 B, p. 9).

[46] Cf. the observations of *La Perseveranza* for 24 November 1870. On the different reasons for abstaining, cf. as well Rattazzi, *Rattazzi et son temps* 2:455.

would decide case by individual case whether or not to go to the ballot boxes.[47] Alberto Mario meanwhile compared the republicans, whom he considered too impractical, to the monks of Mount Athos, whose custom it was to gaze at their navels in the belief that from them they would behold the light of Mount Tabor shining forth.[48]

Just as the supposed passivity of the lower classes could not be adduced in mitigation, since it was irrelevant, so too the very low percentage of voter participation could not be imputed to the Catholics alone; and even if the republicans who wanted to isolate the monarchy were added to the total, the fact still was not satisfactorily explained. Indeed, the liberals of the time did not delude themselves about this. From both the Right and the Left, they openly blamed the apathy and the lack of solidarity among the liberals themselves,[49] the inertia of those who complained that others were not doing their duty, but then when the moment came to choose among the parties and the candidates, washed their hands of it all like Pontius Pilate.[50] In sum, the liberals blamed the indifference felt by a large part of the upper classes to the great problems of the nation's life;[51] and they were not off target.

It was a slackening of nervous tension, we might say, after a decade of turmoil like the one that had followed the formation of the national kingdom. The Austro-Hungarian envoy at Florence called it "blasé indifference following a state of overarousal,"[52] and Michelangelo Caetani noted that "after the enthusiasm and the heightened passion of great events we have arrived at this period, in which the achievement of so many aspirations and desires for liberty, independence, and unity has produced its natural effect: not satiety exactly, but the sense of detachment, of disillusion that comes from the peaceful possession of the good that had been desired, and that had been thought to be an inexhaustible fountain of complete felicity."[53]

As normally happens, ideals did not find an immediate and total correspondence in reality; hence on one hand the lassitude and exhaustion of many, and on

---

[47] The articles of Bertani on "Gli astensionisti" were published in *Il Lombardo* for 10, 17, and 29 January, 14 and 15 February, 6 and 7 March 1871. On Bertani's efforts to convince the republicans to vote, cf. J. White Mario, *Agostino Bertani e i suoi tempi* 2:357 and 361. On these internal differences among the republicans, cf. G. Spadolini, "I repubblicani dopo l'unità," in *Il Mondo* for 28 April 1951, pp. 9–10.

[48] Cited in Mazzoleni, *L'XI Legislatura*, p. 44. Mazzoleni was also opposed to abstention.

[49] "Le elezioni amministrative," in *L'Opinione* for 27 March 1873.

[50] "Agli elettori," in *L'Opinione* for 15 November 1870. On the "apathy" and "scandalous torpor" of the voters, cf. as well Bonghi in *La Perseveranza* for 15 November 1870, and *La Nazione* for 16 November 1870 and 15 January 1871. On 2 December Guido Borromeo informed Minghetti that at Milan Correnti would have to stand in a second ballot because none of his supporters had bothered to vote: "this indifference, or rather this repugnance is in my opinion the worst of our present ills" (BCB, *Carte Minghetti*, cart. XV, fasc. 69).

[51] *La Riforma* for 18 January and 6 August 1871.

[52] Kübeck, report, 13 January 1871 (SAW. *P.A.*, XI/77, no. 4 A). On 2 March (ibid., no 17 C), Kübeck is still emphasizing "the period of relative calm that has succeeded to the emotions of the previous year." The French chargé d'affaires, de Sayve, also speaks of political indifference, on the part of both parliamentary deputies and voters (report, 23 January 1872, no. 9; AEP, *C.P.*, *Italie*, t. 384, fol. 76).

[53] Castelli, *Ricordi*, p. 39.

the other the very harsh verdicts uttered then and later about the Italian state and its weakness and political enervation, verdicts in which two men as diverse as Mazzini and Ricasoli concurred, just as De Sanctis was shortly to do.[54] Condemnation of this kind was heard throughout the period of the Left and lasted until socialism appeared on the scene as an organized party.[55]

Italy wished for great things immediately, sweeping internal reforms, vast projects, a high standard of living; and since these things have to be built up slowly and with effort over decades, for the benefit of future generations and not of the present ones, dissatisfaction grew. To this there were added the disappointments and discontents inevitably caused by the drawbacks of the parliamentary regime: the too frequent changes of government, with phantasmagoric cabinets giving the impression that personal interests, passions, and ambitions were stifling any devotion to the public welfare; the long delays in the Chamber, the often seemingly fruitless debates, the fury of sterile and evanescent parties.[56] All of these made many reluctant to bathe in the "cloaca of political passions."[57]

And it is certainly true that ambitions and personal interests were at work, then as always, in the parties; that not everything was done for pure love of the public weal, that personal resentments, intrigues, and differences threatened the efficacy of the political process. Even within the Right, so renowned for the severity of its style and the general uprightness of its members there were problems enough to make an irascible soul like Ricasoli refuse the presidency of the parliamentary committee of the moderates, saying that he did not want to have to "lead people worse than eels for wriggling out of your grasp, who don't remember the day after what they said and promised the day before, who chatter too much and think too little, and are thus never firm in their intentions."[58]

As well, there was too much politics, which meant that every question became the subject of political contention involving parties and parliamentarians, and this had the effect of slowing down and impeding the functioning of the administration. There was a danger in transferring political competition onto a plane from which it ought to have been excluded, and it was to combat this corrupting practice that Stefano Jacini proposed to restrict the competence of parliament to the great national problems, leaving routine matters to be handled elsewhere.[59] Later Minghetti and Silvio Spaventa restated the importance of not allowing the

[54] Cf. esp. the letter of Ricasoli to Francesco Borgatti, 17 September 1870: "So what has the kingdom of Italy been able to do up to now? Nothing, nothing wise or historic or felicitous for itself and exemplary for others! What did it do? . . . It demolished!" (Ricasoli, *Lettere e documenti* 10:131–32). For De Sanctis, cf. the speech to the Chamber on 23 April 1874 (*La Critica* 11 [1913]: 331 ff.) and the articles of June 1877 in *Il Diritto* (*Scritti politici*, pp. 65 ff.). Cf. too the judgment of Crispi, in a letter to Primo Levi of 29 October 1882 (Crispi, *Carteggi politici inediti*, p. 393).

[55] Cf. for example the election speech of De Sanctis at Foggia on 11 May 1880 (*La Critica* 11, pp. 475–76).

[56] These are complaints already expressed by Jacini in *Sulle condizioni della cosa pubblica in Italia*, pp. 21 ff. Cf. as well the opinion of Ricasoli, *Lettere e documenti* 10:255, and the outburst of Lanza to Rattazzi in December 1871 (*Rattazzi et son temps* 2:487).

[57] The words of Ricasoli to Borgatti, 30 December 1871 (Ricasoli, *Lettere e documenti* 10:239).

[58] Ricasoli to Borgatti, 27 January 1872 (Ricasoli, *Lettere e documenti* 10:248).

[59] Jacini, *Sulle condizioni della cosa pubblica in Italia*, pp. 25 ff., 92 ff.

alternation of parties in government to imperil the institutions or prejudice the due process of law and legitimate interests, of making sure that local governments were free of the influence of political passions.[60]

All this helps to explain the creation of a general frame of mind combining distrust and reluctance to take part in public affairs with suspicion and even anger at the way things were going, and with a bleak pessimism of the kind that crept into the outlook of men as different as Carducci and Ricasoli. All those who were prone to anger or pessimism grasped the truth in many particulars, but they were no longer able to take in the whole and did not perceive that the ideal of Italy as a modern nation was, albeit slowly, coming into being in the modes and the forms that were possible. Sella was right to refute the generic charge of apathy with the observation that the Italians were working harder than they had ever done,[61] and the nonpolitical Lambruschini discerned the flow of events more accurately than did the politician Ricasoli (an uncivil fellow)[62] when, far from the petty everyday bickering of politics, he looked at the overall pattern and saw that there was a greatness in things, even when the men themselves were small: "men endeavor to steer the inevitable renewal of human affairs in the direction that suits them. But there is a hidden hand that breaks down and builds up invisibly, that prepares a moral order that may appear insignificant, yet which will be a marvelous thing in its effects. I do not know if we will see them, all of them at least; but some we will, and great and unexpected at that. I admire the divine wisdom that makes use of instruments which seem inadequate to the purpose to accomplish great changes. If Cavour were alive, and had done what Lanza has done, we would say: behold the hand of the master statesman. Instead we must say (and I am glad of it): behold the hand of God. These thoughts console me, and give me the courage to hope for the best for our country."[63]

More truly than in his epistolary diatribes or in his outbursts in familiar company, Ricasoli grasped the heart of the matter when a public speech compelled him to rise above trivial controversies, and he succeeded in formulating a judgment in which those controversies certainly do not vanish, but are reduced to noncritical proportions: "there will come a day when it will be acknowledged, and consecrated in the annals of Italian history, that it was the present cabinet that led the nation to Rome and has maintained it there during a very difficult phase. This will be a glorious period in contemporary history."[64]

The great weakness of the Italian state really lay not in the diatribes of the parties, the personal rivalries, and so on, but in the separation of the masses from public life. Sonnino pointed to this many years later in the Chamber in discussing electoral reform: "the great majority of the population, more than 90 per cent

---

[60] Thus Spaventa, in 1877 (Romano, *Silvio Spaventa*, pp. 230 ff.).

[61] "What do you mean apathy? Do you want there always to be some agitation in the piazze?" said Sella in a speech to the Chamber on 18 March 1872 (Sella, *Discorsi Parlamentari* 4:177).

[62] "Uomo selvatico" was Ricasoli's own description of himself (Ricasoli, *Lettere e documenti* 10:504).

[63] Lambruschini to Ricasoli, 26 December 1872 (Ricasoli, *Lettere e documenti* 10:271).

[64] Ricasoli, speech to the chamber, 17 May 1873 (Ricasoli, *Lettere e documenti* 10:500).

. . . feels itself entirely extraneous to our institutions; it sees itself subjected to the state and constrained to serve it with its blood and its money, but it does not feel that it constitutes a living and organic part of it, and takes no interest in its existence and its development."[65]

The other problems of Italian political life had nothing idiosyncratic about them. Analogous complaints about parliamentary intrigue, the decay in standards of behavior, the too-frequent cabinet crises, were being voiced in every continental country with a parliamentary regime and would go on being voiced. The pedantic moralizing of these tirades concealed the true, large political problem, the nature of which was quite different: it was to make all the Italians, not just a narrow circle of the privileged, full sharers in the rights and duties of public life, in the life of the state.

With this there is no intention of suggesting that the complaints were unfounded, or that there was not sometimes a risk that the inevitable element of corruption in public life would exceed the limit that has to be set, if the state, as Machiavelli said, is to remain well ordered.

And the line was crossed, not just by voters who ignored the ballot box, but also by a number of politicians, both deputies and senators, whose prolonged absences from the parliamentary sessions were the object of frequent criticism in the press of the Right and of the Left equally, admonitions which these journals were forced to repeat year after year.[66] It was poor consolation to recall that elsewhere too, even in England, the *alma parens* of liberty, the spectacle of half-empty parliamentary chambers was not infrequent, whether it was the heat that made the members long for the fresh breezes of the seaside and the mountains or, as Pitt thought, it was quail and fox that were the main lure for the honorable representatives of the nation.[67] Other, more conscientious politicians stood down at the general elections of November 1870, as though the moment signaled the close of a historical epoch which released those who had struggled only to forge the nation, and who now had the right to intone a *nunc dimitte*. This was the justification adopted by one of Italy's leading personalities in the Risorgimento, a man of lofty and unbending sentiments to whom no one could impute the sin of indolence or the lack of a sense of duty. But in Baron Bettino Ricasoli there was a tiredness, a disgust with political life, a desire to return to a serene existence and resume activities more consonant with the inclinations of his inner nature.[68] He

[65] 30 March 1881 (Sonnino, *Discorsi Parlamentari* 1:22 and cf. pp. 40–41).

[66] *La Riforma* especially sounds this note on 18 January, 7 and 10 June 1871, 21 and 24 January 1872, 11 and 16 March, 9 June, 20 November 1873. But also *Il Diritto* on 20 January and 17 April 1871, 7 November 1872; *L'Opinione* on 1 July 1872, 10 March 1873; *La Perseveranza* on 19 January 1871; Bonghi's "Rassegna Politica" for 31 January 1872 and 30 November 1873 in the *Nuova Antologia* 19, p. 465, and 24, p. 945. Rattazzi, in June 1871, found it painful to take part in sessions of a deserted Chamber (Castelli, *Carteggio politico* 2:503). In the session of the Chamber on 7 March 1873, there were public complaints by the president, the hon. La Porta, and Lanza, about the absenteeism of the deputies, which prevented the necessary voting quorum from being reached (*A.P., Camera*, pp. 5130–31). There were fresh protests on 22 and 28 April (ibid., pp. 5902–5903 and 5967).

[67] C. F., "Le riforme militari e la legge del 19 luglio 1871," *Nuova Antologia* 18 (1871): 115.

[68] These are words used by Ricasoli himself in his public letter of renunciation (*L'Opinione* for 14 November 1870; cf. Ricasoli, *Lettere e documenti* 10:144 and 166).

renounced his candidacy amid the sorrow and also amid a degree of anger on the part of the moderates,[69] who were already alarmed by other conspicuous defections, those of Peruzzi, Guido Borromeo, Carlo Alfieri di Sostegno. Though there were various reasons for this "noteworthy flight" by parliamentarians of the moderate party,[70] such a spectacle of desertion by men who had warned that liberty was a duty, the first of duties, had serious consequences. It was they who had said that the citizen "cannot refuse to take part in public service, cannot through indolence or egoism cut himself off . . . from the general and common interests of his homeland," and that if liberty had not yet done all that it promised in Italy, that was because too large a part of the nation was indifferent to the problems of the general welfare.[71] Though some of these refusals were withdrawn, as in the case of Ricasoli, who gave in to the stubborn desire of the voters to reelect their old representative and took his seat in parliament again, it remains true that this resumption of the accustomed routine was done out of jaded impotence, being dictated not by conviction but simply by a reluctance to appear discourteous to the voters; it was the sort of choice that leads a man to do his job as parliamentary deputy "as well as possible in the circumstances, or as ill."[72]

The old governing class thinned out, notable gaps appeared in its ranks not only through the natural destiny of mankind but also through the voluntary withdrawal of men whose physical powers were still intact, or almost. The result was governments composed in large part of men drawn from the public administration rather than of genuine politicians.[73]

For we who see them at a distance, and contemplate these years within the frame of Italy's whole history, such unforeseen retirements and defections represent nothing alarming: they are signs of the transformation of the governing class, of the shift in political direction, harbingers and indeed a necessary premise of the so-called parliamentary revolution of March 1876. We can descry the pending crisis of the moderate party and its decline as a governing class as we see the cadres of the Right shrinking into a close formation rather than expanding, losing men and energies instead of gaining them.[74] But even this is true only up

---

[69] Cf. the laments of *La Nazione* for 15 November 1870, and also 12 November; *L'Opinione* for 10 November; *La Perseveranza* for 10 November (Bonghi); letters of Massari and Ricasoli on 15 November in Ricasoli, *Lettere e documenti* 10:163. But one of the leading organs of the Left, *Il Diritto*, expresses the same complaint on 10 November.

[70] This is what *L'Opinione* calls it on 11 November 1870. Borromeo claimed reasons of health (ibid., 16 November; his letter also appeared in *La Perseveranza* for 17 November). Alfieri di Sostegno said that he could not assent to the transfer of the capital to Rome, and complained of the lack of any organization of the liberal party (ibid., 13 November). Another, Giovanni Fabrizi, refused to return to parliament because, offended by the manner of Italy's going to Rome, he did not intend to put his seal on the work of Sella and San Martino (Ricasoli, *Lettere e documenti* 10:165, where he is erroneously called "Giuseppe").

[71] Thus Alfieri di Sostegno in 1868, in "Del dovere di esercitare la libertà," in *L'Italia liberale*, pp. 428–29.

[72] Ricasoli, *Lettere e documenti* 10:143, 148, 150, 156, 161 ff., 172, 175, 176, 186, 194, 198, 240, 248. In 1874 Ricasoli once again made known his intention not to run for parliament; and once again he changed his mind (ibid., 10:317, 319–20, 323–24, and 328).

[73] *L'Opinione* for 11 and 13 July 1873 rues the fact that the cabinet of Minghetti is composed almost exclusively of men taken from the civil service.

[74] Cf. the shrewd observations of Morandi, *La sinistra al potere*, p. 63.

to a point, or more precisely it is not the whole truth: for deep down, beneath the contest of the two parties for the exercise of power, we can also make out a much greater danger, which was the remoteness of the great majority of the population from public life, and the reduction of the latter to a battle among generals.

At any rate, those defections and retirements seemed highly important at the time, for many took them to indicate not the passage from one governing group to another, but the decay pure and simple of the political class, and even the decay of liberal institutions, with parliament in the lead. They seemed to betray a lack of faith in the future of the country.[75] There was an antiparliamentary polemic, already vigorous and varied in those years, that fed on such displays of indifference among the voters and also among politicians, and on the consequent *longeurs* of parliamentary life.[76] It was a polemic that did not originate in an antiliberal attitude, as was to be the case fifty years later, but rather from disappointment that liberal institutions were not functioning well enough and were not sufficiently strong and respected.[77] Personal tedium, exhaustion from the long years of struggle, the desire for quiet, disdain for the attachment to private interests and for the indifference of many to the great questions facing the country, all flowed together and found a single outlet. There were men of worth who lost their taste for public life at this time: leaving aside Ricasoli, there was also De Sanctis, who at the sight of the spreading gangrene in public life, chose isolation for the time being at least and closeted himself with his literary studies.[78] Some of the moderates felt like saying, with Odilon Barrot, "give me back the enthusiasm of 1830," in their longing for a return to the enthusiasm of the past. It was not the ephemeral enthusiasm of street demonstrations that was missed, but the calm, frank, persevering kind without which Italy would not rise to the dignity of a cultivated and busy nation, and would not become, as it should, the providence of Latin civilization.[79] Even men of strong character and deep moral sentiment might grow melancholy and embittered because of "the mental sloth of others that depresses and unnerves you . . . the laziness of many of the so-called lib-

---

[75] So thought La Marmora: "it seems as well that many feel a lack of faith in the way things are going in Italy, to judge by the number and *quality* of those retiring from their role as deputies (Monale, Alfieri, Peruzzi, Ricasoli, etc.)" (in a letter to Lanza on 14 November 1870; Lanza, *Le carte* 6:248). Similar preoccupations are seen in D. Pantaleoni, "Delle probabili sorti del Regno d'Italia," *Nuova Antologia* 21 (1872): 624.

[76] It is enough to mention the writings of Jacini, *Sulle condizioni della cosa pubblica in Italia*, which appeared in 1870, and Sonnino, *Del governo rappresentativo in Italia*, which appeared in 1872. Cf. R. De Mattei, "La critica antiparlamentaristica in Italia dopo l'unificazione," *L'Educazione Fascista* (April 1928): 193–201, and *Il problema della democrazia dopo l'unità* (Rome, 1934), pp. 13 ff. and esp. 23 ff.

[77] This is also the view of C. Morandi, "Il pensiero politico di R. Bonghi," in *Annali di Scienze politiche* (Pavia), vol. 2 (1929), p. 233; M. Delle Piane, "Tendenze antiparlamentari in Italia ed accenni ad una risoluzione al di fuori del sistema dopo il 1880," *Studi Senesi* 52 (1938): 481–93, and "Il liberalismo di Ruggero Bonghi," *Rivista Storica Italiana*, 6th ser., 5 (1940): 19 ff. in the offprint seen (now in *Liberalismo e parlamentarismo*, pp. 15–28 and 52 ff.); Alatri, "Bonghi e la vita politica italiana," pp. 173–74.

[78] As he says in the letter of 31 May 1871 to Carlo Lozzi (F. De Sanctis, *Pagine sparse*, ed. B. Croce [Bari, 1934], p. 112; the letter is edited by C. Muscetta).

[79] The hon. Massari to the Chamber on 13 March 1872 (*A.P., Camera*, p. 1182).

erals, who are at bottom traditionalists . . . the lack of the kind of culture that makes men capable of debating things without being for or against them." Such a melancholy befell Antonio Labriola, who was led to question whether it was not the fate of the Italians, eaten as they were by the worm of Catholicism, to be laggard in thinking and sluggish in their progress, a people made to take pleasure in the vanity of classical memories and rhetorical commemoration, not to take part in the world's advance.[80] Such doubts assailed Marselli then, as he continued to mull over the question of whether the Italians were an aged people or a youthful one with a great future ahead, and who often enough felt little confidence in youth and future.[81] At this juncture it was possible to believe that the Italian people had taken for their motto *"chacun pour soi, Dieu pour tous."*[82]

The Italians felt that a historical period had ended, and they turned the page with regret, looking gloomily at the present.[83]

[80] Cited in L. Dal Pane, *Antonio Labriola: La vita e il pensiero* (Rome, 1935), pp. 293–94.

[81] Marselli to Robilant, 25 March 1873 (AE, *Carte Robilant*). In this letter he is inclined to see them as an aged people.

[82] Thus *Il Diritto* for 11 January 1875 ("L'apatia politica").

[83] On this state of mind, I can only refer to the pages of Croce, *Storia d'Italia dal 1871 al 1915*. pp. 1 ff.

High Politics or the Politics of Tranquillity?

THE FACTS OF the matter, the objective reality, and also the general mentality then current therefore meant that the period after 1870 was not the time for an active foreign policy on Italy's part. With unity achieved and Rome occupied, the country asked for nothing more than the peace and tranquillity needed to take care of its own business. How little foreign policy as such (meaning the web of relationships with the other great powers, and Italian action within the European concert) mattered to the post-1870 generation is shown by the fact that the leading personalities of the Italian political world were known for their concern for, and their cultural and practical training in, this or that sector of domestic politics—finance, administration, relations with the church—not for their diplomatic skill. They had other things to worry about than using smoke and mirrors to create a policy of greatness, for which there was lacking any basis. Sella became an expert in finance. Minghetti had a broader range, but in substance his energies were focused on problems of internal administration. Spaventa, who had the strongest theoretical vision of the liberalism of the Right, resembled Minghetti in having absolutely no practical interest in international problems, and being content, justly, to build Italy up from within.[1]

Attitudes among the leaders of the Left were no different, from Depretis, who saw foreign affairs as a bore and diplomats as the least welcome breed after professors,[2] to Cairoli, Zanardelli, Nicotera, Baccarini, and De Sanctis, who in essence committed their energies to administration, finance, the widening of the suffrage, relations between church and state, and similar domestic problems. Even Crispi was taken up, in that phase, mainly by problems of domestic politics; and it is not an accident that in debates in the Chamber on foreign policy, the Left did not send its captains into the fray, but figures of the second rank like Miceli, La Porta, Colonna di Cesarò.

It is telling that foreign policy remained the appanage of the Piedmontese diplomatic service, or of diplomats brought up under the direct influence of the Piedmontese diplomatic service. The foreign minister, Visconti Venosta, was a Lombard, it is true, but he was a product of the school of Cavour, and the course he steered followed unswervingly the guidelines laid down by the old subalpine diplomatic tradition. And he was surrounded by Piedmontese and a number of Savoyards,[3] from Artom, the general secretary, to the director of the political division, Tornielli, and the principal heads of mission abroad: Nigra in Paris, de Launay in Berlin, Cadorna and later Menabrea in London, de Barral at Madrid,

---

[1] Cf. Romano, *Silvio Spaventa*, p. 271.

[2] Martini, *Confessioni e ricordi*, p. 195.

[3] Many years later it was noted that this was still the case by Bülow, *Memorie* 4:658.

Blanc at Brussels, and Robilant, who went to Vienna within a few months. The exceptions were Caracciolo di Bella at St. Petersburg and Barbolani at Constantinople, but they were also among the least authoritative members of the team. This domination by Piedmontese was unique among the departments of the Italian government,[4] even the army which was tied so closely to the Savoy dynasty and Savoyard traditions, for there Pianell and Cosenz flanked Ricotti in senior positions. It was a state of affairs destined to last for a long time, being continued even after the fall of the Right, when two Piedmontese, Tornielli in the shadow of Depretis and Maffei di Boglio in the shadow of Cairoli, functioned as the *éminences grises* of Italy's foreign policy from 1876 to 1881. Only then did the advent of Mancini at the Palazzo della Consulta bring a mentality, a set of concerns, and a style that were not Piedmontese to the handling of affairs.

Continued Piedmontese domination was another clear sign that for the moment international relations did not hold the attention and the interest of most Italians. Italy wanted to be left in peace and to busy itself without having to worry too much about what was going on around it. Intent on its own domestic affairs, it was indifferent to the great events that were taking place beyond its borders— events, said one foreign observer, that produced no more than "a vague impression because of the insensitivity one finds in states whose own domestic preoccupations leave them unmoved by the troubles of others."[5]

Things would be different by 1889. Then, according to Jacini, all the forums and places of resort of the middle intelligentsia resounded with discussion of foreign policy, of alliances, diplomatic combinations, possible wars, frontier adjustments, and hardly at all with discussion of domestic questions.[6] But it is a certainty that in the years following the taking of Rome, conversations and debates in peoples' homes and in public gatherings all turned on quite different arguments, and that purely international problems (except for the very special problem that was the Roman question) left most people cold. What Italy wanted and needed, the government of the Right gave it, to the extent that human possibility allowed.

A few years later, Visconti Venosta, the man who had been directly responsible for the foreign policy of the country since 1869, affirmed that the aim of Italian foreign policy after 1870 had been that of "hastening the moment when the country would finally succeed in making itself little talked about. This meant giving Italy a period of time of which it had great need; a period in which, with a feeling of security, and without being distracted by other, more urgent preoccupations, our country could have the ease, the peace, and the time necessary to occupy itself with its domestic questions."[7]

---

[4] Count Guido Borromeo complained about this in a letter to Minghetti of 31 July 1871: "at the three principal courts we will be represented by Piedmontese. And then we laugh when the Pope still calls us the Subalpine Government" (BCB, *Carte Minghetti*, cart. XVI, fasc. 4).

[5] Kübeck, report, 2 March 1871, cited above at ch. 13, n. 52. The same opinion is found in his report of 13 January, cited in the same note.

[6] Jacini, *Pensieri sulla politica italiana*, p. 60.

[7] In an election speech at Tirano on 25 October 1874 (in *L'Opinione* for 30 October).

Incisively abridged, this was the same idea that Visconti Venosta had been constantly expressing ever since 1870, whether he was enunciating it as a guiding principle and fundamental directive in his personal letters to his most trusted colleagues abroad,[8] or making it the basis of formal declarations in the Chamber, when he had to defend himself against the slashing attacks of the likes of Miceli and La Porta.[9]

It was a program on which all the moderates were in substantial agreement. Some, like Minghetti, called it conservatism. Others less well known, like Guido Borromeo, used images almost identical to the ones used by Visconti Venosta in the speech at Tirano, and held out the need "to walk on tiptoe for now, in order not to make a lot of noise."[10] Others still, Spaventa for instance, warned that the acquisition of Rome, the city in which the government that had ruled a world empire had had its seat, "should not and cannot infuse any arrogance into our souls, or pretensions to dominion beyond our own borders," since "the logic and the possibility of exercising dominion outside one's own territory cannot be derived from the memory of a power that has not existed for centuries, and that no century will ever see again; it has to derive from actual needs and necessities, and from the living forces capable of satisfying them. Such is not our case."[11] Thus, all were in agreement that what was needed was "to surround Italy with peace,"[12] and for it to bear itself modestly for at least half a century, as it was put later.[13] The leading lights of the party disseminated this shared point of view using the vehicle of the press. They were led by Dina in *L'Opinione*, and it was he who first developed the notion, later picked up and repeated by Jacini in his celebrated notes on Italian politics,[14] that a historical period had now ended, a period in which the Italians had sought every occasion of unrest in Europe to exploit it for their own purposes. They had been feverishly anxious to reach their goal, which was national unity, and having attained that, they were entering upon a new phase in which agitation had to be replaced by calm, and the wish to see the waters

---

[8] Thus in a letter to Nigra on 27 February 1871: "Italy, in a word, has need of just one thing, security and peace" (Visconti Venosta archive).

[9] "Italy is satisfied to have achieved its destiny, it asks nothing more, it has no hostile designs on anyone. It has need above all of peace, of tranquillity, of security, to reorder itself and to develop the elements of its strength and its prosperity" (from a session of the Chamber on 14 May 1872, *A.P., Camera*, p. 2121); and again on 27 November of the same year, he said, "Italy wants above all to maintain what it has acquired, it wants to preserve at any cost what it has obtained with the aid, it is true, of fortune, but also with a great persistence in sacrifice, in will, and in faith. But though we are prepared for further trials, the great majority of the Italians would prefer to prevent them. Italy wants to have before it a long period of peace, security, and tranquillity during which it can develop its material and moral resources, can restore its forces, and attend to the great work of internal progress" (ibid., p. 3397). For all of this, see above, pp. 130–31.

[10] G. Borromeo to Minghetti, 3 March 1871 (BCB, *Carte Minghetti*, cart. XVI, fasc. 4).

[11] Spaventa, *La politica della Destra*, pp. 201–202.

[12] The expression is Bonghi's, in a speech delivered at Naples on 29 October 1874, in which he defended with vigor the foreign policy of the Right (published in the supplement of *L'Opinione* for 7 November, and in a separate opuscule [Rome, 1874], p. 9).

[13] "X," in the "Rassegna Politica" of the *Nuova Antologia* 51 (1880): 177.

[14] Jacini, *Pensieri sulla politica italiana*, pp. 15 ff., 66 ff. The only fundamental difference is that all these writers (correctly) put the break between the two periods in 1870, after the taking of Rome, while Jacini points to 1866 and begins the new period in that year (pp. 11–12).

turbid and roiled by the contrary desire to see everything tranquil and limpid, and the air still. Instead of continually looking beyond the Alps, scrutinizing even the slightest occurrences of European politics, the Italians must now concentrate on their own backyard, their domestic affairs. The time of "provocative" politics had ended: anyone who now dreamed of "a foreign policy of supremacy and primacy, a policy of tumult and disorder, would be out of his mind, and ought to be locked up. After the acquisition of Rome, our policy is to observe developments, and to gather our nation's strength."[15]

The theme developed in the press by the friends of the cabinet was thus shared by all the moderates; Visconti Venosta would later formulate it with great clarity (and in terms almost identical to the ones used by Dina) when he was no longer a minister and, speaking from the opposition benches, attacked the government of Depretis on its foreign policy on 23 April 1877. This is what he said on that day:

> When . . . our process of state formation was not yet complete Italy looked for a suitable opportunity in Europe's complications to crown the edifice of its independence and its unity, and found it.
>
> Now Italy has been made, Italy is a single constituted state, and I believe that the only fitting policy for us is a prudent, fair policy, free of any spirit of adventure, which will bring to the fore the advantage and the utility for European interests of the presence and the moral action of this young state in the concert of the great powers.
>
> I believe that this is the only way Italy can consolidate its international situation, making it secure in the present and the future, can obtain the benefit of faithful alliances and friendships, and can assure itself of that legitimate influence that every people has a right to wish for.[16]

This did not mean wrapping itself in seclusion, something more than ever to be deprecated; nor did it mean giving up all regular and continuous intervention in the great general questions of policy,[17] or abasing the national dignity. In fact it was *L'Opinione* that urged the Italians on one occasion to have a little more self-regard, so as not to be forever portrayed with napkins folded on their forearms at the entrance to a hostelry, awaiting the arrival of foreign tourists.[18]

What it did mean was that the government was resolute in defending at any cost the unity that had been achieved, and in particular the most recent addition to the kingdom, Rome. It had made up its mind not to take one step back from the position gained, not to retreat as Visconti Venosta wrote to Nigra on 27 February 1871.[19] The government would try in every way to prevent incidents, to accommodate itself to them when they occurred and were not of sufficient gravity to force Italy to abdicate its dignity or renounce its vital interests. Above

---

[15] "I partiti parlamentari," in *L'Opinione* for 20 July 1871.

[16] *A.P., Camera*, p. 2687. Here too a comparison with the analogous ideas later developed by Jacini shows that the moderates really did have a common program in foreign policy, in which there was hardly any room for individual differences; and it shows the especially strong links among the members of the Lombard group, Visconti Venosta, Jacini, Casati, etc.

[17] "La situazione politica," in *L'Opinione* for 28 July 1873.

[18] 9 January 1872.

[19] Letter cited above at n. 8 (Visconti Venosta archive).

all, the government would avoid any sort of adventure abroad. To use the suggestive phrase of the foreign minister, it would try not to get itself talked about. This was far from easy, in fact it was an extremely difficult course to follow given the circumstances: an outcry raised in Europe and even beyond Europe by the clerical party, loud wailing and violent protests against the "imprisonment" of the pope, and bellicose proposals cropping up in the parishes of France, Belgium, Spain, and Ireland, and in other places too—wherever there was an individual clothed in the priestly habit to exhort the faithful to a new crusade.

But according to the opposition, succeeding in going unnoticed was a task entirely insufficient, unequal to the dignity of the Italy that now looked out on the world from the Capitol. The watchword of the Right was "balance," and the Left replied that man does not live by bread alone, and a people does not live by balance alone.[20] The foreign minister said that the time had come to avoid getting talked about, and the opposition rose up as though this were an insult to the national dignity.[21] It had risen in a similar fashion two years before, in reaction to other words attributed to Visconti Venosta, who was reported to have said to his constituents at Tirano in the summer of 1872, "we are not rich, we are not strong."[22] The "more than Christian" humility of the man from the Valtellina stung the holy ire of the custodians of the national honor clustered round *La Riforma* and *Il Diritto* and all the other opposition journals. They aimed their fire beyond Visconti Venosta, at the government of the Right in its entirety, which they said was implementing a piteous policy, a policy degrading to united Italy, unworthy of the majesty of the Capitol.

This melody rose to a caterwauling pitch in the indignant verse and prose of Carducci, a man utterly fascinated by the heritage of the past, who was driven to call the Italy of his own day "vile." He flung the helmet of Scipio of the martyred saint, Goffredo Mameli, in the face of his contemporaries and taunted them with "those Livian fancies that were strong enough to push the conservatives as far as the Quirinal, and which perhaps may push them even farther."[23] Thanks to the irate Giosuè it is a melody that has become familiar to the generations of the twentieth century.

Carducci was not the only one driven to speak by the great phantasms of the past that came crowding into his mind and spirit. A much less eminent man, but

[20] Thus Depretis in a speech to the voters at Stradella on 10 October 1875 (in *Il Diritto* for 15 October).

[21] "La politica estera," in *Il Diritto* for 31 October 1874. And cf. the election speech given on 10 November 1874 at Aragona by Duke Gabriele Colonna di Cesarò, one of the protagonists of the Left where foreign policy was concerned (*Discorso*, p. 9).

[22] "Le condizioni d'Italia secondo il ministro degli esteri," in *La Riforma* for 8 September 1872. Cf. too "Ancora del discorso del ministro degli esteri," in the issue for 9 September. Visconti Venosta referred to this speech (the so-called program of Tirano) in his speech to the Chamber on 27 November 1872, saying first that he had spoken in an unscheduled meeting and could not vouch for the exactness of every account published in the papers; and second, that he was not accustomed to search out phrases that would render his thought in the least happy manner possible. In sum, he neither accepted nor denied responsibility (*A.P., Camera*, p. 3397).

[23] In the essay "Goffredo Mameli," dated 1872 (Carducci, *Opere* 18:398).

an active party politician, Michele Coppino, in commenting on the general sense of resignation and lack of faith, expressed his wonder that the Capitol had not infused the virtues of the ancient Romans into the Italians after 20 September.[24]

To have got to Rome was supposed to be the cure for all ills, the remedy for all the failings of the state's edifice, as though there dwelt in Rome the same fairy that transformed the rags of Cinderella into a splendid costume for the ball. People in this state of mind were ready to believe in miracles, and wiser and more prudent heads had already sounded a warning even before the troops came in through the Porta Pia.[25] But judicious warnings did not help, and belief in miracles still floated in the air, even turning the head of a man of intelligence and abundant European experience, though admittedly an eccentric, like Giuseppe Ferrari.[26]

No doubt these polemics were largely tactical, weapons in the contest between government and opposition. Many things were said that would soon be forgotten once the Left was in power, and among the protests directed at the cabinets of Lanza and Minghetti, those that dealt with foreign policy were, generally speaking, the sort that carried the least commitment for the majority of those on the Left.[27] In opposition, they raised a hue and cry against the lassitude of the government, claiming that it did not speak loudly enough in Europe against the insolence of France, a country of priests and reactionaries, and that it had forgotten the heroic deeds of 1859, and the Thousand, and the greatness of Italy, the helmet of Scipio and the red shirt, Vittorio Emanuele on horseback among the Zouaves at Palestro. But in government, they ended up pronouncing solemnly in the Chamber, on 23 April 1877, the same doctrine they had viewed as grave sacrilege years before when it was uttered by Visconti Venosta, Jacini, Dina, Bonghi, and their fellows. The speaker was Melegari, the foreign minister, a former Mazzinian who had long since become a moderate himself:[28]

---

[24] In a speech to the voters at Alba in September 1874 (cf. *L'Opinione* for 15 September).

[25] Cf. the article "Dopo Roma," in *La Perseveranza* for 10 September 1870. The gist is that not one of the present ills of Italy will be easier to cure after the acquisition of Rome: not the great moral debility of the citizens, not the great weakness of the government, not the persistent disorder of the finances. Let us go to Rome, then, but without cherishing any illusion that this fact alone will have the power to change everything.

[26] "But we are in Rome! Yes, it is true, we are, but with all the impediments and all the questions that tormented us in Turin and Florence. If a single problem had been solved, I would be delighted; but the most worrying details are still hanging over us as they were two or three years ago. I hear talk of the toll collector as though I were still in Florence; I hear the taxpayers screaming as though I were still at Turin. I am not speaking of the deficit, or the paper money. A military reform is urgently necessary to attain the same rate of progress as the other states, and I see the honorable ministers of war and the navy with their hands tied by the financial projections of the hon. Sella, whose plan peremptorily forbids them to introduce the necessary innovations for the space of five years" (speech to the Chamber on 14 May 1872, *A.P.*, *Camera*, p. 2107). Likewise, Nicotera in the session of 21 March (ibid., p. 1374).

[27] Bonghi is not entirely wrong to observe in *La Perseveranza* for 20 August 1870 ("L'opinione pubblica in Italia") that the opposition is endorsing any political orientation at all, provided it is different from the government's: as it is pro-Prussia today, and was pro-England yesterday, it might turn pro-Russia tomorrow, without there being "any precise concept" guiding any of these shifts.

[28] For Melegari's shift from Mazzinianism to moderatism (as with Visconti Venosta), cf. G.

The hon. Petruccelli asks why we have abandoned the policy that preceded the constitution of Italian unity. This is a very serious question, and I believe that the Chamber will be in accord with my opinion on this. Every state has a particular policy in the period of its formation, the policy we followed until the moment we came into possession of our capital. But in the judgment of the wisest and most expert men, this policy had to end when that period came to a close. Woe to anyone who should think of bringing it back! We would be face to face with all the dangers that could threaten our political existence.

In this regard then, we have followed the policy of our predecessors: that is, we have sought to reassure Europe, to make all the states realize that our foreign policy will be founded, henceforth, essentially on the conditions of peace and respect for all the legitimate interests and rights of the states that surround us.[29]

By an unintentional irony, these words were spoken shortly after Visconti Venosta, in the same session, had stated his own, perfectly identical, political credo as it had been elaborated and professed, in word and deed, by the entire Right after 1870.

The Left was doing no more than what any parliamentary opposition is supposed to do, so naturally its polemics were evanescent. This is shown by the fact that—for the sake of assailing the policies of the cabinet in general and Visconti Venosta in particular, policies which they generally accused of timidity, weakness, and servility vis-à-vis the church and France, in other words of fearfulness combined with ultramontane and reactionary intentions[30]—they did not hesitate on another occasion to do a volte-face and describe Visconti Venosta as domineering and avid to use force, "rashly eager to commit outrageously arrogant acts on weaker states."[31] This was the accusation made by a deputy, Englen, and also in substance by the "shadow foreign minister" of the Left,[32] Miceli, when in the session of 25 November 1872 there was a debate in the Chamber on the two disputes in which the Italian government was, or had been, involved: one was the dispute with Greece over the mines of the *Laurium*, and the challenge that arose because of them between the government of Athens and the Italo-French company, Roux-Serpieri; the other was the controversy with the Bey of Tunis in 1871, the so-called dispute of Gedeida.

It was easy to foresee that, once in government, this part of the opposition would shift its ground. The general ideas underlying its polemics against the indolence of the government were not very different, except for the question of

---

Ferretti, *Luigi Amedeo Melegari a Losanna* (Rome, 1942), and also *Melegari à l'Académie de Lausanne* (Lausanne, 1949).

[29] Session of 23 April 1877 (*A.P., Camera*, p. 2712). On the influence of the king on the government at this precise moment, see below ch. 20, n. 61.

[30] This is the accusation made by the hon. Miceli on 14 May 1872 in the Chamber (*A.P., Camera*, pp. 2109 ff.).

[31] *A.P., Camera*, p. 3328. And for Miceli's speech, pp. 3322–24.

[32] As Bonghi called him in a speech at Naples on 29 October 1874 (as cited at n. 12 above, p. 11; and in *L'Opinione* for 7 November).

relations with the papacy, where the divergence of views really was wide and substantial.

But Depretis, Zanardelli, Nicotera, Cairoli, and Rattazzi, the leader of the Left at that time and a man for whom, more than for any of his comrades, opposition to the government was a matter of parliamentary role-playing and personal authority, were not the whole opposition. There was also Crispi and his group. And outside the confines of the Left as a party, there were eminent men who, while opposing the Left on many questions, also dissented profoundly from the course the government was steering in foreign policy.

In these latter cases opposition was no longer a momentary feint, but took on the character of a true antithesis of principles and ideals. Depretis, Zanardelli, and Cairoli opposed the moderates mostly on questions of domestic politics. For one thing they stood for a more pronounced liberalism, or as they called it, democracy: in other words a widening of the suffrage and the advent of a governing class recruited on a broader basis; they stood for a much more pronounced anticlericalism; they had different views from the government on the financial problem and the taxation system as molded by Sella. But Crispi was different: it is not that in these years he was a leading parliamentary debater on international questions; indeed, like the other leaders of the Left, he was much more intent on domestic questions, was immersed in the struggle for liberty now that unity was a fact,[33] and in the struggle to strengthen the edifice of the state and make the Italians the Saxons of the Latin race, "founding parliamentary institutions and making them function in reality."[34] The difference was that for Crispi and his friends, opposition to the government was intimate and fundamental on foreign policy too, and it was not so much opposition to this or that specific action as it was an opposition of attitudes and mentalities.

It is not that the mind of Crispi was that of an imperialist, or even simply that of a twentieth-century nationalist. A spiritual son of the French Revolution, which he nevertheless detested, just as Mazzini and others did, because it had trampled on the Italian soul;[35] a Jacobin and a believer in the doctrines of natural law[36] who still could not throw off all humanitarian dreams despite the political realism he avowed (something that distinguished him from Bismarck, who had

---

[33] Cf. the program of *La Riforma* (Crispi, *Politica interna*, p. 32).

[34] "I doveri del Gabinetto del 25 marzo [1876]," in Crispi, *Scritti e discorsi politici*, p. 408; and his speech to the Chamber on 13 December 1871 (*A.P., Camera*, pp. 199 ff., not included in his *Discorsi Parlamentari*), which was the program for a whole party ("I nostri intendimenti," in *La Riforma* for 1 January 1872).

[35] Crispi, *Pensieri e profezie*, p. 130, and cf. p. 135. In this Crispi is linked to the anti-French current of ideas described above, and in a particular fashion to Mazzini (cf. above, p. 33).

[36] "I maintain that statutes do not create rights, that individual rights are innate, anterior to any written charter. Statutes can affirm them, guarantee them, sometime even offend against them, but it is not from statutes that man derives his rights," Crispi said in a speech to the Chamber on 5 December 1878 (*Discorsi Parlamentari* 2:315, and cf. 3:190). On the idea of the nation as understood in natural-law terms, cf. above pp. 53–54. Cf. as well Croce, *Storia d'Italia*, pp. 177–78; Volpe, *Italia moderna* 1:420–21, and *Francesco Crispi* (Venice, 1928), p. 32; F. Ercole, "La personalità storica e il pensiero politico di Francesco Crispi," in *Pensatori e uomini d'azione*, pp. 354–55.

always derided such fantasies), Crispi was always far from claiming that conquest was its own justification, from any conceptual nationalism. In domestic politics he continued to preach liberty, "our idol, our life," to deny the omnipotence of the state, to cite England as the best country to imitate, and to define himself as a liberal and a progressive, an enemy of all dictatorship and a man reluctant to call out the carabinieri when difficulties arose.[37] Only in his final phase, after 1894, did he begin to think that the parliamentary regime was not possible in Italy; but even then he protested that he would never do anything against parliament, leaving this task to those who should succeed him. In any case, there were a number of deputies and senators by then who were prattling about the drawbacks of parliamentary life, and his was certainly not an isolated voice.[38] The German-style constitutional regime that he worked for after 1896 was not really a shatteringly novel idea in contemporary debates, and was not the sole property of Sonnino.[39]

In foreign policy he remained doctrinally anchored to the ideal of nationality and sincerely protested his love for peace and distaste for war, even for war with France, which for him would have amounted to a civil war.[40] The age of totalitarianism, *Führer-prinzip*, and *Lebensraum* had not yet arrived. Crispi's thought always hinged on the great themes of the Risorgimento, such as unity, liberty, nationality, and in consequence he was far removed not only from fascistic doctrines but even from the nationalism of Corradini and the antihumanitarian and antidemocratic strains of an Oriani or a Turiello. He was an authoritarian in practice, but ideologically he never went so far as to renege on the principles that he had enunciated for the Left in 1876: "authoritarians often speak of the rights of the state. This is an error. The state has no rights and can have none. It is delegated by the people to carry out the functions that are attributed to it."[41] In practice Crispi's foreign policy was dominated by the mirage of the greatness of his own country; in theory he never dared to deny the ideal of the brotherhood of the peoples, and sometimes in the positions he took there was a curious amalgam of the naked appraisal of power and liberal ideology.[42]

---

[37] Cf. Crispi, *Discorsi Parlamentari* 2:149, 211, 313, and 3:214, 245, 459, 497, 500, 508, 548, 550–51, 576, 675, etc. For his frequent appeals to the English example see ibid., 3:14, 86, 194, 196, 199, 208, 286, 454, 508, 560, 594, 761. In the session of 26 May 1890, the hon. Luigi Ferrari interrupted one of his never-ending invitations to "go visit England, gentlemen," with the exclamation "he always comes out with England!" Crispi shot back, "England in these matters teaches us all a lesson" (ibid., 3:545). And cf. the acute observations of Jemolo concerning his legalistic spirit (Jemolo, *Crispi*, pp. 51 ff., 103 ff.). For Turiello, who belonged intellectually to the fin-de-siècle, Crispi was indeed the first who had begun to grasp what Italy should become, in Europe and beyond, "but his formation, which was doctrinaire and French, hinders him from doing so more fully" (Turiello, *Governo e governati in Italia* 2:214 [2d ed.]).

[38] Farini, *Diario* 1:607, 611, 625–26, 663.

[39] Cf. the meeting between Crispi and Queen Margherita on 2 January 1897 (Crispi, *Politica estera* 1:281 n. 1).

[40] Speeches to the Chamber on 3 February 1879, 7 April 1881, 4 May 1894 (Crispi, *Discorsi Parlamentari* 2:335, 494, and 3:743).

[41] Crispi, "I doveri del Gabinetto del 25 marzo," in *Scritti e discorsi politici*, p. 405.

[42] So for example in a letter to Cavallotti of 30 September 1882: on one hand he condemns those who in international politics live on illusions and defend wholesome theories of liberty in the abstract,

Conversely, the moderates did not in the least aim to create what was later to be called "Italietta"—a modest little country closed in its own parochial concerns. The reply of Minghetti to de Laveleye, the insistence on the expansive force of youth and the impossibility for a great country to contain all its activity within itself, were clear pointers to what the leaders of the moderates were thinking. Minghetti too wanted greatness for his country; speaking at the launch of the *Morosini*, he too recalled the ancient glories of Venice, and expressed the emotion he felt in his natural style, avoiding histrionics. Despite all Minghetti's sympathy for Gladstone, he deplored the latter's foreign policy as being too humanitarian. Minghetti asked himself what Italy was going to do, faced as she was with colonial expansion by other powers, and grew impatient in 1886 at the thought that Italy was standing by, a simple spectator, while the Balkan peninsula was carved up. It had already stood by while the French occupied Tunis: what was the Triple Alliance supposed to be for?[43]

Men like Minghetti and Visconti Venosta, though they did not waver in their drive to concentrate the country's resources for now on internal reconstruction, and to avoid any external complications, also dreamed of a time to come in which the nation, revitalized and cohesive, would be able to carry out radical actions beyond its borders as well, not so much in the form of conquests and military expeditions, for these things were in general extraneous to their way of thinking, but in the form of economic expansion and political and moral influence.

But one exception to their general aversion for conquests there was, and that exception was Tunis. Admittedly on 28 November 1880, summarizing in the Chamber the main outlines of the Right's foreign policy on the question of Tunis, Minghetti denied that he or his party colleagues had ever intended to achieve Italian domination over the regency; for them it was enough that the Bey remain independent, that the status quo be maintained. The latter, he said, they were indeed not prepared to see violated, for then the "legitimate influence" of Italy would have been diminished.[44] It is also true that in reviewing plans that had been made for an expedition in 1864,[45] he connected them, quite correctly, with the expectation "of the entry of other powers into Tunis . . . so that there could not be any permanent occupation, to the detriment of the independence of that country." But Minghetti was saying these things in public, at a time when the question of Tunis was already counted a policy failure, and when, far from ad-

---

contrasting them with Great Britain, which is assuring its own predominance in Egypt; on the other he defends the actions of the English government in Egypt thus: "On this occasion the cannon was not used to violate rights, and the foreigner did not bring slavery. Gladstone and Granville are a guarantee of liberty, and what happened to the Arabs of Tunisia will not happen to the Arabs of Egypt" (Crispi, *Carteggi politici inediti*, pp. 391–92).

[43] Minghetti, *Lettere fra la regina Margherita e M. Minghetti*, pp. 159, 175, 188–89, 195, 268.

[44] Minghetti, *Discorsi Parlamentari* 8:47.

[45] This is the meaning of his reference to the resolution to land our troops at Tunis "at a time when Italy had serious internal difficulties." On the plans for an expedition, cf. G. Cappello, "La spedizione francese in Tunisia," in *Memorie storiche-militari a cura del Comando del Corpo di Stato Maggiore*, fasc. 2 (1912), pp. 2–3, and in general G. de' Luigi, *Il Mediterraneo nella Politica Europea* (Naples, 1925), pp. 141 ff.; P. Silva, *Il Mediterraneo dall'unità di Roma all'impero italiano* (7th ed.; Milan, 1942), p. 329.

vancing demands for its own domination, Italy would have been glad merely to obtain the secure preservation of the status quo. There is room for reasonable doubt that his plans had always been so modest.

His close friend Visconti Venosta, with whom he had an intimate intellectual *rapport*, also minimized the importance of the episode of 1864, which he set in its true light in a letter to Nigra of 29 May 1894:

> You remember the events of Tunis in 1864, the dispatch of the squadron, our policy in the event of a landing by France or other powers. I have a clear memory of all this. I recall further that in the summer of 1864, in June I believe, at Fontainebleau, when the first negotiations for the September Convention took place, the emperor Napoleon, speaking of the question of Tunis among others, must have said something more or less as follows—that, without making any judgment on the interests that we might have there at that moment, if Italy should resolve to go to Tunis, he would not have offered opposition. About this incident, however, my recollection, as I say, is not clear. Many years later in a speech in the Senate, Pepoli read an extract from a report of his to Minghetti, in which there was recounted a similar reply made by the emperor to him in 1864. You can find Pepoli's exact words in Chiala's book *Pagine di storia contemporanea*—Fascicle II—Tunis, page 223. Blanc, in his speech to the Chamber a few days ago, referred to "agreement to a spontaneous occupation of Tunisia *of which we were officially notified by Napoleon III in 1867*." Here I do not know if he intends to refer to the period of Rattazzi's cabinet, which succeeded that of Ricasoli in 1867, or of the first months of Menabrea's cabinet, because nothing of the kind took place during the government of Ricasoli; or whether he said 1867 by mistake when he meant 1864. But if that is the case, it seems to me that Blanc and others before him have singularly exaggerated the import of what took place, viewing it as an occasion on which Tunisia was placed at Italy's disposition, and Italy refused to occupy it. The impression that has stayed with me, from that distant day to this, was always that if we had tried to pass from a few words spoken under the trees of Fontainebleau to actual deeds, the emperor's rather vague statement would have met sizable opposition from his own ministers, especially Drouyn de Lhuys, the guardian of the old traditions. Furthermore, the moment in itself was enough to make the whole subject meaningless. At the time we were trying to get a commitment from the emperor, if possible, to a French-English alliance on the Danish question, an alliance that would have led to the liberation of Venetia by Italy. And if no such combination could be formed, we were trying to conclude some important accord with the emperor that would decide the Roman question. In sum, either war with Austria or the September Convention. It seems to me a little hard to imagine the Italian government choosing at that juncture to head off to Africa instead, and substitute Tunis for Venice or Rome.[46]

But if Tunis was not thought of as a likely piece of territory for Italy in 1864, it certainly was later. Visconti Venosta himself had occasion to state in a meeting of the cabinet on 21 November 1870, referring to the supposed Turkish plans to

[46] Visconti Venosta archive.

occupy Tunisia, that it was in Italy's interest to oppose them, "since one day Tunis must fall to Italy."[47]

Clearly we cannot ask for too much precision here. These were aspirations, hopes for the future, and for that reason necessarily very elastic and vague, subject to changing circumstances, indeed to contradictory pressures,[48] and in any case closely tied to variations in the international situation. So it is that Visconti Venosta, around the end of 1870, could envision Tunis as an Italian city in the context of France's disaster and the pessimistic forecasts being made about its future, according to which it would no longer be able to exercise any influence in the Mediterranean or Africa.[49] Yet not long after, faced with the rapid, almost miraculous, resurgence of France, it was natural that he should change his tune and his outlook, as though coming into conflict with France over Tunis could never have entered his mind. At any rate, it is worth noting that even the cautious Visconti Venosta, so near in spirit not only to Minghetti but also to the Lombard conservatives typified by Jacini, who were fiercely opposed to any "megalomania," not only did not exclude but in fact looked forward to Italian influence in Tunis; he had already stated in 1864 that Italy could not consider anything that took place in Tunisia as "extraneous" to Italian interests,[50] and he expressed the hope that the "Turkish cake" would only be served up when Italy had exchanged its place at the "small table" for a place at the large table,[51] so that it would be in a position to get itself a good big slice.

Visconti Venosta held to the same vision that had already been held by Mazzini and Cattaneo,[52] though their political allegiance was so different from his. They too had fixed their gaze on that "great bastion and great watchtower over the Mediterranean" and had seen the danger it would pose for Italy in foreign hands: they believed that Tunis simply had to become an Italian center, and it was in fact this thought that had produced Mazzini's evocation of ancient Rome, which was destined to become the classic refrain accompanying every expansionistic effort by Italy from then on.

With Tunis went the east. For Minghetti, the future of Italy lay to a large extent

---

[47] Castagnola, *Da Firenze a Roma*, p. 96.

[48] So, in early April 1872, speaking with the French envoy, Visconti Venosta declared that Italy was not rich enough to permit itself the luxury of an Algeria, and that it had commercial interests in Tunis, while France's interests there were political. These statements were made to a French representative, but they were also very categorical (*D.D.F.*, 1st ser., 1:138). And in truth, he had already said much the same thing (no "luxury of an Algeria") in 1871 (personal letter to Cadorna, 23 March 1871; Visconti Venosta archive); and he said them again to Nigra on 25 January 1875: "We have no other end in view there [Tunis] than the maintenance of the status quo, with no *arrière pensée* of any kind" (Visconti Venosta archive).

[49] Many took this view at the time: cf. above p. 252 and below p. 464.

[50] *A.P., Camera*, p. 4286 (12 May 1864).

[51] So in a letter of 28 June 1864 to Emanuele d'Azeglio (cited in E. Passamonti, "Un colonialista del nostro Risorgimento," in *Atti del Primo Congresso di Studi Coloniali* [Florence, 1931], p. 4 in the offprint seen). Hence, when the eastern question was reopened in 1876–77, Visconti Venosta observed that it had broken too soon "for Italy to be able to get from it the advantages it might have hoped" (personal letter from Corti to Visconti Venosta, from Berlin, 9 July 1878; Visconti Venosta archive).

[52] Cf. Volpe, *Italia moderna* 1:98–99.

in the Orient, and for this reason he pointed to the danger of the Black Sea becoming a Russian lake.[53] And Giovanni Lanza repeated that Italy's legitimate expansion ought to be directed to the Orient: this made it a vital Italian interest that the other great powers should not lord it over the Mediterranean and the Levant.[54]

Crispi could claim that his Mediterranean ambitions were a heritage of Mazzini, who in 1871 had directed the Italians toward Asia. Minghetti, Visconti Venosta, and Lanza drew inspiration instead from the message of Cavour, which in turn descended from Balbo. But whatever the source, the mirage of the Orient also attracted the moderates, so that Visconti Venosta, complaining in 1878 that the policy of complete abstention endorsed by Corti practically amounted to an absence of any policy whatsoever, was also able with great finesse to lament the fact that the idea of Trent had driven the policy of the Left onto a detour during the eastern crisis, and to deplore the fact that the treaty of Berlin and its consequences were undermining Italy's position in the Orient.[55] So it was that in these grave questions, Crispi thought exactly like Minghetti and Visconti Venosta: Italy's failure to intervene in Egypt alongside England in 1882 was deplored by him and by them. Minghetti used to say that it had been the greatest error of foreign policy committed by the Italian government.[56]

On that occasion others had opposed an Italian intervention with all their strength, and continued to maintain unswervingly that the Italians ought to be well pleased not to have been dragged into the trap of Egypt: getting in would have been easy but getting out would have been hard, and Italy would have been stuck in a messy and unsavory situation that offered no advantage of any kind.[57] But even Robilant, who took this view, was far from believing that Italy should keep out of the Mediterranean; and at a time when he had yet to give the best and most constructive proof of what he purposed by securing the separate treaties between Italy and Austria and Italy and Germany which were conjoined in the Triple Alliance of 1887, and devising an understanding with England, measures that in combination created the first strong safeguard of Italy's Mediterranean interests, he maintained that Italy ought to lay hands on Tripoli without hesitation, seeing it not as a colonial matter but as a vital problem of Italy's Mediterranean, and hence European, position.[58]

---

[53] Minghetti in a letter to Visconti Venosta, 19 November 1870: "the future of Italy is in large measure in the east. Toward the Alps we have nothing to hope for except some frontier rectifications. Our trade flows eastward. It is necessary that the Black Sea not become a Russian lake" (Visconti Venosta archive).

[54] Lanza, *Le carte* 10:383–84 and 446.

[55] Visconti Venosta, letter to his brother Giovanni, 20 July 1878 (Visconti Venosta archive).

[56] Minghetti, *Discorsi Parlamentari* 8:216 ff.; Luzzatti, *Memorie* 2:150, and *Grandi Italiani*, p. 22.

[57] Robilant to Corti, 25 November 1883 and 1 March 1884 (AE, *Carte Robilant*). And to Minghetti he restated his profound conviction that the Italian government had done well to refuse; in fact, he reported the opinion of Kálnoky: "if M. Minghetti had been minister of foreign affairs in place of M. Mancini, he would not have agreed to go to Egypt either" (Robilant to Minghetti, 20 March 1883; BCB, *Carte Minghetti*, cart. XXIV, fasc. 48).

[58] Robilant to Corti, 21 July, 8 September, and 20 November 1884 (AE, *Carte Robilant*). At the

Analogously, just as it was Robilant's wish to see outbreaks of irredentism rigorously repressed in order to keep Italy from finding itself in a nasty situation, Crispi as prime minister adopted the views of his old adversary; indeed, of all the notions of which he was "cured," few were turned inside out so radically as his old revolutionary desire for a dissolution of the Habsburg empire, and in general for the construction of a new Europe in which the principle of nationality would be applied in a complete and total fashion.

In sum, what we do *not* have is blanket renunciation by one side while the other is embracing the programmatic nationalism of the twentieth century. The doctrinal lines are not clearly drawn. It is not a case of heroic impulses being pitted against those of the shopkeeper, imperial Italy versus Italy dressed as a waiter. There is no crude contrast of black and white.

And yet, between Crispi and the Right, especially Visconti Venosta, a difference there was, substantial, profound, and irreducible. The ideas and doctrines of each might not be totally at odds, indeed might flow from the same common spring, from the rights of man, liberty, and nationality. But the spirit, the mode of experiencing and acting, the style, were all at opposite poles from each other. And since they were political men and not philosophers, the only true measure is their actions, and the style of their actions. Crispi might make any number of speeches about his aversion to the spirit of conquest and his pacifism, but his soul was eaten by the anxious desire for Italy to become great overnight, and he was restless and excitable in action, nerves always at full stretch, impulsiveness alternating with brooding diffidence, so that in the end he was virtually a precursor of nationalism. He still lacked the conceptual clarity, but he already had the attitude.

It was the same in domestic politics, where his protestations of unlimited obeisance to the principle of liberty, to the law, to the final authority of parliament, were fine-sounding and orthodox, whereas liberal orthodoxy was not always nearly so palpable in his practice as head of government and interior minister. Once he was accused in the Chamber of passing Left laws while conducting Right politics,[59] and leaving aside those two designations, which have become so equivocal by now, one could say that his thought in the abstract was liberal, but his soul was authoritarian. His actions were guided much more by his soul than by his rational mind. The belief in reactive police measures, to which Zanardelli and Cairoli held, was set aside by Crispi in favor of anticipatory police measures; even in these, Crispi's approach was often somewhat brisk, and in practice he employed a narrow interpretation of "the government's best judgment as to whether or not on any given day, in a given city, permission to hold a public assembly might cause disorder."[60] He liked a tight grip on the reins, and liked to

---

century's close, Visconti Venosta told Wickham Steed "for Tripoli I too would put match to powder" (Wickham Steed, *Mes souvenirs* 1:135).

[59] Giovanni Bovio in 1890 (Crispi, *Discorsi Parlamentari* 3:499–500).

[60] Note for example the veto in 1889 of the commemoration of the martyrs of 6 February 1853 in Milan, the subsequent deployment of the troops, etc. (Crispi, *Discorsi Parlamentari* 3:277 ff.). Even in theory, for that matter, Crispi took the view that "the right of assembly . . . presents greater

hold them taut, not slack like Giolitti, though he was clever at knowing just how hard to tug in a dangerous curve. The frequent recourse in his parliamentary speeches to the themes of law and order and protecting the public are significant. Such themes are always used, and always ready for use, to justify wide police powers. Crispi tended to use expressions that were strikingly forceful and frank, but inappropriate and overbearing, as when, in the debate on the municipal guards, he warned the Chamber that he could get along without it if necessary and proceed by means of royal decrees.[61]

What characterized him was not his doctrines and theoretical schemes, but his conduct; and his conduct was, and appeared to all, friends and enemies, as the conduct of a potent personality, all too aware of his own dynamism and all too ready to dismiss others.[62] Crispi did things imperiously;[63] he was curt, easily irritated, and choleric; he never hesitated to bypass constitutional orthodoxy with sovereign ease, in effect putting authority before liberty. He grew ever more convinced that it was not a question of the constitutional regime so much as it was a question of individuals, and that "the regime, whatever it is, is an instrument that helps or harms according to the actions of the man in charge."[64] His

---

dangers than the right of association," after having declared that those two rights are "the ones most cherished by a free people" (ibid., 3:544).

[61] Crispi, *Discorsi Parlamentari* 3:443.

[62] On 10 June 1894 the faithful Abele Damiani wrote to Crispi: "I have realized for some time that it is useless talking to you unless one allows you to be in the right. Time has aggravated the idiosyncrasy of your character. By now the faithfulness of your friends is not enough, nor their age, nor their credit, nothing . . . you have to be right, especially when you are wrong—the advocate wearing the judge's robes; and you are the plaintiff too! . . . You blindly persist in following an adverse destiny, demonstrating even to those most faithful to you that you lack the energy of former times, while retaining your contempt for all advice. For me it only remains to close the book, because I have read enough" (MRR, *Carte Crispi*, b. 667, no. 32/19).

[63] For example, the brutal recall of Ressmann from the embassy in Paris on 5 January 1895 was decided by Crispi without the knowledge of any of the other ministers except Blanc, the foreign minister. When Umberto I told him of the "surprise" of Sonnino, Saracco, Boselli, and Barazzuoli, Crispi replied that they had been kept in the dark deliberately: "These matters are handled by the prime minister in conjunction with the foreign minister, and they report them to the king. . . . It was done this way from the time of Cavour to the time of Depretis. . . . These are not matters for the cabinet" (MRR, *Carte Crispi*, b. 667, no. 34/1. There is silence about this in Crispi, *Questioni internazionali*, pp. 174–75. Cf. Farini, *Diario* 1:631, which does record the protests of the ministers and the comment of Umberto I, who approves the substance of the measure, not the method). The method was certainly brusque, as with Corti (below, n. 84, and ch. 18, n. 43) and with Greppi (De Cesare, *Il conte Giuseppe Greppi*, p. 249). The minutes of the cabinet meetings are very summary (cf. E. Re, "I Verbali del Consiglio dei Ministri (1859–1903)," *Notizie degli Archivi di Stato* 2 [January–March 1942]). From them it does not appear, however, that such questions were always discussed collegially as a matter of course; cf. the deliberations for the nomination or transfer of diplomats, or the acceptance of resignations, of 16 November 1872, 4 January and 11 April 1875, 7 and 28 February, 17 March, 8 and 27 June, 23 November 1876, 7 October and 30 October 1879, 18 June 1880, 30 June 1881, 7 November and 13 December 1885, 28 December 1886. For the period of Crispi, cf. the deliberations of 16 and 24 December 1887 (the posting of Corti to the retirement list, etc.), 22 February 1888, 20 September 1894 (the posting of Tornielli on reserve and of Marochetti on temporary leave, etc.), and 30 October 1894. The placing of a consul general, Nicola Santasilia, on temporary leave, had been brought before the cabinet on 28 October 1894, shortly before Ressmann's case. The cabinet dealt with Ressmann on 16 January 1895, raising him to a higher grade, and on 2 September, when he was transferred from the reserve list to temporary leave (ACR, *Verbali delle deliberazioni del Consiglio dei Ministri*, vols. 2, 3, 4, and 5, under the date in each case).

[64] Crispi, *Pensieri e profezie*, p. 129.

dictatorial tendency expanded to the point of proroguing the Chamber in 1894, when it had to pronounce on the report of the Committee of Five concerning Crispi himself: his doing so was an emphatic negation of the very essence of the parliamentary regime and was certainly unprecedented.[65]

He also suffered from the continual fear of not being quick enough, of being overtaken by events. This was why he was so committed to anticipatory measures, and having the police take precautions, and so suspicious of the twin rights of assembly and association. In foreign policy, he suffered from the same urge to act and act fast, the fear of arriving too late, with Europe already launched on a full-scale race for power; so when Visconti Venosta, Lanza, Sella, and Spaventa were saying, let us put our own house in order before taking the international stage, Crispi was saying, we have to do so right away, even if the house is not yet tidy.

Indeed, their dissent here touched a deeper level, since it grew out of the global visions held by these men, the core of their feelings, and it went back once again to the fundamental heterogeneity of the forces of the Risorgimento. In Crispi's world outlook, Italy had become a nation on its own, by virtue of the potent breath of revolution—Mazzini and Garibaldi; and it would have done so, and done so even better, without Napoleon III. Italy was therefore a great country through innate virtue, powerfully inspired, already set to play a leading role in the consortium of peoples. If it did not do so immediately, the fault would be that of its government leaders alone, mediocre and tepid about unity yesterday, mediocre and pusillanimous today.[66] The greatness of the country, he said, was like "original sin for us . . . the original sin of all who, with Mazzini at their head, worked for the constitution of the entire *bel paese* into unity, into statehood. . . . [T]o be strong and powerful, it is enough to want to be, and know how."[67]

The others, the moderates, were convinced, sometimes to an excessive degree,[68] that the unification of Italy had been made concretely possible thanks principally, or even exclusively, to a very lucky combination of external circumstances, to a European situation in which the Second Empire and then Prussia had played their parts, and that the merit of the Italians had been to seize the right moment—Cavour and Vittorio Emanuele, the government rather than revolutionary initiative. But the gaining of that end did not imply that Italy was now so

[65] Cf. Jemolo, *Crispi*, pp. 100–101.

[66] "Certainly if those who have forgotten the traditions of the Italian revolution, its ends, and the greatness at which we aimed, continue to govern, not only will our domestic life grow more petty but we will increasingly humiliate ourselves abroad." Crispi to Primo Levi, 14 November 1891 (Crispi, *Carteggi politici inediti*, p. 462). Much earlier, on 27 July 1862, he had attacked in the Chamber the ministers "who, since they do not feel the force that representing a great nation gives them, act with the timidity of the small state that forms the nucleus of the kingdom of Italy" (Crispi, *Discorsi Parlamentari* 1:215). In this respect Crispi was constantly and totally coherent.

[67] In his speech for the inauguration of the monument to Garibaldi at Palermo, 27 May 1892 (Crispi, *Ultimi scritti*, pp. 163–64).

[68] A typical example is the following statement by Castelli, an intimate of Cavour and later of the leading moderates, a confidant of Vittorio Emanuele II, writing to Lanza on 1 August 1870: "Italy rose out of complications and *imbrogli*, foreign and domestic, more through negative than positive action. To crown the work we needed this war and I hope it will help us" (Lanza, *Le carte* 5:217).

empowered by innate virtue that it could pronounce its *adsum qui feci* before the older giants of European politics. We had been lucky, and now it was up to us to show that we were equal to our luck, in other words to do a good job of consolidating the state. The pedagogue d'Azeglio had summed up the moderate approach perfectly in his exclamation, "fare gli Italiani," meaning "[the task is] to make the Italians." Crispi's reply was, the Italians already exist, let us make a government worthy of them, and let us fling ourselves bravely forward into the future.

For him Italy was already a great power, in name and in fact, and so able to impose its will, provided there was a will to impose in those who governed it. For them, Italy was formally a great power, but not one yet in the effective reality of things, which is why they wished for a long spell of peace: it was the only environment in which Italy could grow firm and become a great power in actuality as well. A European war now, whatever the outcome, would be a disaster for the new Italy, Nigra once noted, well aware that he was expressing ideas that were shared by Visconti Venosta.[69] Why else would the latter have bemoaned the fact that the eastern crisis had burst too soon for Italy,[70] if not that he believed his country had not yet attained the capacity to present itself in the international arena with a strong hand to play? Had Robilant not also recognized, at the moment the eastern crisis broke out, that it would have suited Italy better if the question had been allowed to sleep undisturbed for another ten years?[71]

These were not uniquely the apprehensions of the moderates. The stubborn efforts of Italian diplomats in 1876, with the Left in government, to keep the flames from spreading in the Balkans, to get the great powers to proceed on the basis of a shared understanding, to have the European "concert" function, had been dictated by the same fundamental preoccupation with avoiding a great European crisis at a time when Italy would not have been able to deal with difficult situations. Or take Depretis, the same Depretis who is wrongly thought to have been indifferent to international problems, yet who, when the Egyptian crisis occurred in 1882, was anxious that it be considered by all the powers, including Germany and Austria, as an absolutely "European" question. He was driven by

---

[69] "I know, from intimate, and by now prolonged and well-tried, relations with you, your convictions about the grave matter of European peace, and I share them. So I know that for your part you will continue to work, to the extent that you can, to defer the eventuality of a war, which however it turned out, would be a disaster for the new Italy" (Nigra, personal letter to Visconti Venosta, 17 May 1875, concerning the "spring crisis"; Visconti Venosta archive). And indeed Visconti Venosta told Robilant on 1 July: "I *ardently* desire peace . . . peace is an absolute interest of our country. . . . It is absolutely in our interest that it be extended as long as possible, until Italy is able to act as a great power in a European crisis, and not appear to be dominated by that species of fatality that is the law of the weak" (cited in Salvemini, "La politica estera della Destra" (1925), pp. 193–94.

[70] Cf. above, n. 51. And see too Salvemini, "La politica estera della Destra" (1925), pp. 188 (2 March 1875).

[71] "I am in complete agreement with you that it would suit us perfectly if the eastern question were to slumber in peace for another ten years at least" (Robilant, personal letter to Visconti Venosta, 13 August 1875; Visconti Venosta archive).

the same fear that Italy, left alone this time to face England and France (as it had been isolated once previously facing Austria and Russia), would see its vital interests sacrificed in the Mediterranean.[72]

To state that no power in Europe had more need of peace than Italy, as the moderates did in unison after 1870, and as Depretis and Cairoli were later to repeat when they came to power, was not just an expression of sentimental reluctance to go to war, liberal faith in the peaceful development of humanity, a residuum of the optimism of Cobden about the pacific contest of commerce taking the place of the bloody clash of arms: it was also a firm conviction (with political realism receiving its full due) that Italy was not yet ready to protect its interests effectively, should the god of war take the destiny of Europe into his hands again.

The events of the period 1878–1881, first the Congress of Berlin, with Italy coming out of a great European crisis for the first time since 1856 without a single material or moral success to its credit (indeed with the burning sensation of failure) and then Tunis, with Italy having the door slammed in its face again, must have reinforced, even exaggerated, the feeling of many that Italy ought to weigh its chances in international politics with caution. The Russian ambassador, Uxkull, said so to Mancini one day with unaccustomed directness: Italy ought not to think of itself as a great power; if the great powers had admitted Italy to their councils, that had been done out of courtesy, not because they believed its consensus was indispensable.[73] Even when they did not speak out in this fashion, the other powers thought the same. Bismarck conveyed as much with sufficient clarity between 1879 and 1882.[74] Among the Italians themselves, there were many who often seemed not far from agreeing, though with gall and wormwood in their hearts: Blanc, the general secretary at the foreign ministry, stated on one occasion to the Austro-Hungarian chargé d'affaires, as well as his German counterpart, that Italy did not want the role of a great power for itself, a role for which it lacked the means.[75] On another occasion the king in person looked forward to

---

[72] Telegrams of Depretis to Mancini, 19 and 28 July 1882 (AE, *Telegrammi con il Presidente del Consiglio*, nos. 15 and 32); telegram of same to same, 25 June (MRR, *Carte Mancini*, b. 646, no. 13/6). On these efforts by the Italian government, cf. L. E. Roberts, "Italy and the Egyptian Question, 1878–1882," *Journal of Modern History* 18 (1946): 323. On the eastern question Depretis expressed the same desires as Visconti Venosta: "it is my opinion that Italy must make every effort to maintain peace, or to delay the solution of the eastern question" (Depretis, telegram to Vittorio Emanuele II; no date, but June 1876; ACR, *Carte Depretis*, 1st ser., b. 22, fasc. 69).

[73] Tavera, report, 30 September 1881 (SAW, *P.A.*, XI/91, no. 46 A). Mancini did not respond.

[74] Note, in fact, that Bismarck in January 1880 speaks of "five" great powers whose unstable equilibrium governs the world, whereas Italy "is of no account as a Great Power" (J. Y. Simpson, ed., *The Saburov Memoirs; or, Bismarck and Russia*, pp. 111 and 119). And cf. marginal annotation no. 12 of the emperor Wilhelm I to Bismarck's report of 24 September 1879: "Our support can only be directed toward one of the actual great powers, amongst which Italy and Turkey are not to be reckoned" (*G.P.* 3:99). The formal hexarchy of the European concert after 1870 was still, in substance, the pentarchy of the period before 1861.

[75] "As for Italy's posture in the future, the general secretary summed the matter up for me, saying that it does not wish to play the role of a great power, for which it does not possess the means, and that it intends to return to the conservative tradition of old Piedmont, and while maintaining the same

the day when the country should have gained sufficient internal strength to raise it to the rank of the great powers.[76]

Even in the public prints one met such affirmations as that "we entered the European concert as though being granted a favor, and had to go in with a modest demeanor, and claims,"[77] and that the achievement of heightened power was the natural and legitimate fruit of peaceful and enduring effort, in other words of the strengthening of the institutions and economic and intellectual development—the effort on which Italy was engaged.[78]

Always, when it was recommended that Italy behave in a subdued manner in the present, the underlying historical point of view was that the Risorgimento had been made possible by the favorable international conjuncture. An example is the journal *La Rassegna*, which did preach this modesty, and in which one could find a rapid historical digression recalling the "fortune" of the Risorgimento: "absorbed in the problem of our *being* . . . we made strides because our constituting ourselves as a nation, though it clashed with some interests, favored others, and we proved able to maneuver in the space between them. The collision between the interests of the French and Austrian empires gave us our first strong boost. Our second boost came from the collision of Prussian interests with those of Austria, the third from the collision between the Germans and the French. Both

---

good relations with all its neighbors, give its main attention to the level of material well-being of the country" (Tavera, report cited in n. 73). According to Tavera, these statements by Blanc are to be understood as the consequence of Uxkull's remarks to Mancini.

The analogous statements of Blanc to the German chargé d'affaires, von Derenthall, which were also made toward the end of September 1881, are in W. Windelband, *Bismarck und die europäischen Grossmächte, 1879–1885*, p. 313.

In part, his statements were certainly dictated by the anxious need to dissipate fears in Vienna and Berlin that an understanding with Italy, which is what Blanc was working at that time to obtain, might draw the two empires into colonial questions on Italy's side. The same need drove de Launay in January 1882 to state that Italy wanted only the maintenance of peace, "even renouncing any idea of increasing our influence in the Mediterranean sector" (in A. F. Pribram, *Les traités politiques secrets de l'Autriche-Hongrie, 1879–1914* 1:186 n. 30 [French translation: Paris, 1923]; cf. L. Salvatorelli, *La Triplice Alleanza: Storia diplomatica, 1877–1912*, p. 59). Blanc did indeed declare to von Derenthall that there would be no further Italian colonial policy of an adventurous sort. But Blanc's statements were also in part a reflection of the frame of mind of Italy's political elite after the defeat over Tunis: Italy really felt itself a country beaten in a diplomatic war (cf. the suggestive judgment of G. Salvemini, *La politica estera dell'Italia dal 1871 al 1915*, p. 59).

[76] Statements of King Umberto I to Count Ludolf, the Austro-Hungarian ambassador, on 24 November 1882: the king "professed that he is filled with the desire that Italy may have before it a period of domestic tranquillity, from which it may profit, and from which it will profit for the development of its resources, and to raise itself to the rank of the powers who constitute a solid guarantee for the continuation of peace" (Ludolf, report, 24 November 1882; SAW, *P.A.*, XI/92, no. 62 A). Naturally the leading consideration was the military inferiority of Italy, on which Umberto I had already dwelt in the first audience he granted Ludolf (Ludolf, report, 7 July 1882; ibid., XI/92, no. 26 A).

[77] From the article "La verità sulla nostra politica estera," published in *La Rassegna* for 26 August 1882. The Austro-Hungarian chargé d'affaires, Tavera, detected such a perfect correspondence between these statements and those of the general secretary at the foreign ministry, Blanc, that he attributed to Blanc the inspiration behind the article (Tavera, report, 26 August 1882; SAW, *P.A.*, XI/92, no. 41). The article in *La Rassegna* also contained an observation in the style of Visconti Venosta: "The question of Egypt arose at an awkward time, too soon for us, too soon for our alliances."

[78] "Italia e Francia," an article by Sen. C. Cadorna, in *L'Opinione* for 13 August 1881.

the prevailing liberalism in Europe, and the antipapal tendencies of the Protestant states saw in the victory of the Italian revolution, under a reliable and respectable monarchy, a civil interest to be helped rather than impeded. And so we came into existence."[79] Others who shared this analysis were led to refer to "our precipitous conquest of unity, liberty, and independence all at once,"[80] or to the luck that had smiled on Italy in a singular fashion for many years, in contrast to the present moment, in which reinforcing the inner bonds of the national edifice was turning out to be much more strenuous than the effort of raising it in the first place.[81]

From this historical view there necessarily followed a political stance, which therefore tended to become more pessimistic toward 1880; and the reaction to pessimism provided public justification for Crispi's appeals to greatness, and created the sense that greatness was on its way. But Depretis had certainly never been an adherent of revolution. Cairoli had been, but not in a deeply personal way, so that the great Italian heritage did not weigh on him as it did on Crispi.

It was precisely because a judgment about what the Risorgimento had meant was implicit in any political evaluation of Italy's role after 1870 that the breach between the moderates and Crispi was not resolvable. Crispi belonged with Garibaldi's thousand volunteers, and it would have been a waste of breath to lecture him on a Risorgimento that owed its existence to the favorable European conjuncture and to diplomacy. For him the Risorgimento was the Italian Revolution, an event that equaled the French Revolution,[82] and that had drawn all the Italians, willing or not, into a drama of passion and *virtù* [strength and resilience of character] displayed in conspiracy. Cavour might have been able to give it a veneer of diplomacy, but all the springs of its success lay deep within it. The Italy of Mazzini and Garibaldi had been potent already, and the country's forward march was fated: greatness lay ahead, provided only that the country's leaders did not lack courage.

Italy had to move. Crispi wanted it to prove immediately that it was alive and present on the European scene, he wanted to make the greatness he dreamed of come true right now. There was no other way to make up for the initial inferiority of Italy, to cancel the memory of its subjection to Bonapartist France, to keep faith with the ideals of the heroic days of the Risorgimento and evince its purely Italian grandeur, the *virtù* that lay at the heart of the Italian Revolution. The mission of Italy in the world was no longer a universal one in the tradition of Mazzini. The Europe of the moderates meant nothing to the soul of the Sicilian, and so, as we have seen, when universal ideologies, both revolutionary and conservative, began to melt away, the only goddess that remained was that of one's own nation, one's own homeland. But the goddess was great, and Crispi adored

---

[79] "La verità sulla nostra politica estera," in *La Rassegna* for 26 August 1882.

[80] "Auguri alla patria," in *La Rassegna settimanale* for 2 January 1881.

[81] "L'esercito e la marina," in *La Rassegna settimanale* for 22 May 1881.

[82] See Crispi's speech to the Chamber on 27 July 1862, with its reference to the first French republic, which "imposed itself, and did not ask to be accepted by the governments of Europe," while the "timidity" of the Italian government feels that it has reached the summit of fortune if a great power recognizes us (Crispi, *Discorsi Parlamentari* 1:215).

it. His adoration was voiced in Mazzinian tones still turgid with pathos, in a formal eloquence that was a far cry from the nude discourse of a Cavour or, later, of a Giolitti. The phantasms of eternal Rome spoke to his heart. Others might have had their fill of the struggle, and might think the time had come to labor in peace and quiet. Crispi, from the vantage point of unification achieved and Rome the capital of Italy, turned his gaze in the direction of European greatness, to be gained as soon as possible. And it was because the reality of things did not match his vision that a dark susceptibility overcame him, a constant readiness to see affronts to the national dignity in the words and deeds of others, a permanent inclination to believe that half the world was plotting against Italian unity.

In result, his opposition to the methods and intentions of the Right was thoroughgoing. Visconti Venosta's preference for letting time do its work, the *voir venir* typical of his diplomacy, seemed to Crispi mere incapacity, indolence, and servility. His own style, like his actions, was nervous and jerky, as though he were bounding on stage from the wings;[83] he could smile and seduce, but more often was brusque and overbearing, even discourteous in manner.[84] In substance, there was a permanent disquiet, for he never ceased to start at danger or to suspect a slight to Italian dignity, or to ignore the dictum of Cavour by making major questions of national prestige out of paltry affairs. There was a lack of measure and balance; his was a jarring politics of push and shove.[85]

He never sloughed off the frame of mind and the conduct of a conspirator. He used to say so when he was prime minister, he said it to Nigra: we are old conspirators.[86] Old conspirators! If one wishes, Nigra had been one after a fashion, along with Cavour. But he had been, so to speak, an official government conspirator who conspired for Italy in the uniform of a diplomat, and ever since his mental outlook and his style were those of a man of government. Visconti Venosta had indeed been a conspirator as a youth filled with Mazzinian enthusiasm. But from the Visconti Venosta of 1848 there had emerged the foreign minister of 1870, the consummate moderate among the moderates, a man made of nothing but equilibrium, discretion, finesse, an exponent of the art of chiaroscuro

---

[83] Thus Farini, *Diario* 1:577.

[84] Alberto Pansa, who was held in great esteem among French diplomats (Farini, *Diario* 1:130 n. 1), noted the following in his *Diario* under the date 16 August 1888: "Arrival in Rome. Visit to the Consulta. Rude reception by Crispi." The recall of Ressmann from Paris was also brutal in form: Crispi telegraphed to Ressmann on 5 January 1895, "Paris is no longer yours. Return to Italy, handing over your office to councillor Gallina, who will function in that capacity until the arrival there of a new ambassador" (MRR, *Carte Crispi*, b. 664, no. 18/6). For Crispi as *maître-charmeur*, on the other hand, cf. A. Billot, *La France et l'Italie: Histoire des années troubles, 1881–1899* 1:182 (Paris, 1905).

[85] "For the rest, with a coachman like Crispi in the box, we have to expect to feel bumps and jars at every moment," wrote Visconti Venosta to his brother Giovanni on 4 August 1888 (Visconti Venosta archive). He also refers to the lack of measure and balance in Crispi's policies in a letter to Rudiní, undated (but 1895; ibid.).

[86] Crispi liked to describe himself as an old conspirator: cf. his speech in Turin on 25 October 1887 (*Scritti e discorsi politici*, p. 709). And in a telegram to Nigra on 5 September 1887, accusing Cappelli of having leaked to *L'Opinione*, with Robilant's consent, the clauses of the Triple Alliance in February 1887, he writes "you will certainly not be surprised by these foibles of a few old diplomats, who do not have the habits of old conspirators" (AE, *Cas. Verdi*, I, fasc. B).

who retained not a trace of the conspiratorial habit. Crispi had remained, and remained to the last, an old conspirator. In youth he had outstripped all the rest as a conspirator, and it never left him in maturity, as prime minister and foreign minister. He cast off many conspiratorial ideas, including republicanism and the destruction of Austria, but he kept the soul and the instinct, the typical easy excitability and capacity to be swayed by every rumor. This made him accept alarmist statements without too much scrutiny whenever they touched certain tense and resonant strings inside him, such as the clerical peril and the French peril. He retained the conspirator's urgent drive to take action and make decisions, and the lack of balance and measure.

Another facet was his almost physical need to stay close to the piazza, to work on public opinion directly, to get reassurance and support there rather than in parliament. So there were the great speeches delivered at Turin and Palermo and Florence,[87] and the extended discourses on foreign policy delivered outside the halls of parliament. Indeed there were occasions when policy was announced in some theater before it was announced at Montecitorio, as when, in 1887, the secret agreement for peace made at Friedrichsruh between him and Bismarck was divulged to the citizens of Turin at the Teatro Regio.

Finally there was the individual man, with his strong consciousness of self and faith in his own genius; it made him anxious to act without delay, advanced in years as he was,[88] if he was to link his own name to the glory of Italy. The moderate leaders might well feel that they were indispensable to Italy as a group, as a governing class, not as individuals: it was the Right that was indispensable to Italy. Crispi in contrast had very little regard for his party comrades, and saw himself as the unique savior. It could have been said of him, as it was of Gioberti, that his thoughts ran thus: "Italy's troubles are caused by not having always followed the advice of Crispi. The remedy? Put yourselves in Crispi's hands."[89]

So it is that without actually arriving at the full-blown nationalism of the twentieth century (for he still lacked its determined clarity of principle), Crispi's attitude in foreign policy already had a nationalistic stamp. His nationalism was a state of mind, and it necessarily preceded the doctrinaire nationalism that came later. He believed in the greatness and prestige of his country; in the poetry of heroic deeds as opposed to the humble prose of housekeepers. As he said at the conclusion of a speech in the Chamber of 10 March 1881: "it is a fact that the more we recede from the days of our great revolution, the more our souls grow cold and mean, almost antipatriotic! Let us return to our origins, to those concepts and great ideas without which we would never have risen up, without which

---

[87] Still it has to be noted—and it is characteristic of Crispi's vacillation between liberal and authoritarian behavior—that he had informed the cabinet on 10 October of "the main points" of the speech given in Palermo on 14 October 1889; and that the speech delivered in Turin on 18 November 1890 was read by him to the cabinet on 15 November and approved by it (*Verbali delle deliberazioni del Consiglio dei Ministri*, as in n. 63, under these dates). In these cases liberal practice prevailed.

[88] Acutely noted by Volpe in *L'Italia moderna* 1:419.

[89] Said by Margherita Collegno about Gioberti in connection with *Il Rinnovamento* (Malvezzi, ed., *Il Risorgimento Italiano*, p. 481).

we would never have hurled down the seven princes nor demolished the papacy, without which we would not be here in Rome!"[90]

This was what his organ, *La Riforma*, had been saying from the first: poetry, as opposed to the "prose" of the moderates. In the field of politics, poetry meant enthusiasm and faith, élan and determination, lofty intentions and a lofty soul, the things that had made Italy; poetry "that audacious, but confidently, calculatingly, after the Italian campaign, rising from the fuming fields of Varese and San Martino, seated itself at the government of the adventurous fleet of Quarto, and with the famous words *quid times? Caesarem vehis* in its heart, if not on its lip, assured the perilous landing, and from Marsala to Calatafimi, from Palermo to Milazzo, and from Naples to Capua, from one marvel to another and from one prodigy to another, with a reality surpassing imagination, did not make a move in war that did not win the applause of the most meditated strategy, did not make a move in politics that was not superior to the most profound calculations of diplomacy," and that now, "almost the last effort of Italian genius, seemed to vanish or withdraw to its humble rock, where it wrapped up the flag that had inspired it," to make way for "a nude, stingy, gelid prose, like a cape of lead," that weighs on "the national instincts and inspirations."[91]

Prose was due above all to the lack of poetry in the moderates; and poetry had to be sought "in that creative enthusiasm, in that love of good and of progress, in that intuitive inspiration that is able to seize an epoch, a situation, as a whole, and direct it powerfully to the true end that is foreseen, infusing the activity and the energy that inflames it into all that surrounds it. We call *poetry* that which kept Themistocles from sleeping as he thought of the glory of Miltiades, which did not let Bolívar rest for thinking of the fame of Washington, which burned in the marrow of the first Bonaparte . . . *poetry*, in other words the happiest moments of Cavour, and the marvelous deeds accomplished by Garibaldi."

These words were perfectly adapted to express the attitude of Crispi's circle to Italy and its government. "Enthusiasm," "inspiration," "potency" in directing affairs: and at the same time the great personal ferment, ambition, which keeps a man awake thinking of the laurels of others. On the political level, what all this amounted to was action. If anyone objected that it was not perpetually a time for action, meaning febrile and turbulent action, and that after the tormented period of unity, after the twelve years from 1858 to 1870, peace and quiet were needed; or if anyone asked what the goals of this action ought to be, the first response from Crispi and his allies would have been that action had value in itself, generating energy, rousing strong thoughts, and inciting a people to magnanimous deeds—just the contrary of what was happening in Italy, where the ineptitude of its leaders and their exhaustion were creating lack of faith, skepticism, and sordid materialism.[92] Thus the spectacle offered by modern-day Italy was sad and depressing. As Carducci said, it was the spectacle of a country dominated by

---

[90] Crispi, *Discorsi Parlamentari* 2:486.

[91] "Il sentimento nazionale," in *La Riforma* for 25 June 1872.

[92] This reproof is found in the article cited in the previous note, and also in other articles from the same paper (cf. for example 24 January 1872 and also 1 February 1874).

Trissotino: "A profound skepticism, an indifference, a disdain for all that is beautiful, noble, and grand, a chasing after numbers alone, and after all that gratifies the senses and fills the purse, to the detriment of the heart and the intellect, all these are the distinctive characters of the present Italy."[93]

If, to descend from extraordinary men and epochs to a humble sphere, a good and vigorous administration also had the right to call itself "poetry," that was true only insofar as "it is able to give soul and life to all the latent forces of a nation, not only in the material order but also in moral development which must be its effect and complement." Instead, Italy had the administrators of the Right, "prudent men certainly, but prosaic; men who prefer the minutiae of analysis to the complex intuitions of synthesis; who study much but do little; who know how to create a commission to deal with every question, but nothing that might transmit their names to posterity; men who are petrifying the nation in the frigidity of their souls."[94]

In sum, again as always, action, action, action; and action of "synthesis," by intuition, not by analysis and study; action to create enthusiasm and arouse passions, even for the purposes of ordinary administration. This was activism at any cost, even without precise goals other than to move, to do, to create—or perhaps only to scream at the top of one's lungs, which was often the final outcome of the effort. This was the unquiet and disquieting state of mind of a section of Italian public opinion, a section numerically very modest at this time, but not negligible for the importance of its members. It was to constitute the first nucleus of what later became sizable platoons, swollen by the volunteers of enthusiasm and action.

In domestic politics, this state of mind would sooner or later create impatience with juridical limits, meaning impatience with the liberal tradition and everything that was most genuine and pure in it. It would open the way to an agitated state of mind, inclined at the limit to accept, at a certain moment, the "strong" state, in the form that Crispi wanted and tried to bring about, because it promised action and faith, and derided what it called the unimaginative skepticism of the wise, and exalted intuition and synthesis.

In foreign policy, such people were restlessly searching for a place to begin any action whatever, even if it was risky, for the risk made it beautiful. The inevitability of an imminent great event, an act of war naturally,[95] became fixed in their minds, and inspired by that belief they increased their disquiet and their confusion every day, which did much to create the very reasons for conflict. This was the turbid, unquiet atmosphere, tense and tumescent when even the slightest incident took place, that was created between 1871 and 1873 in Italy and France

---

[93] "Non in solo pane vivit homo," in *La Riforma* for 1 February 1874.

[94] "Il sentimento nazionale," in *La Riforma* for 25 June 1872.

[95] For example on 29 October 1882, at a moment when the international atmosphere had nothing particularly disquieting about it, when in fact there was an easing of tension between France and Germany, and good relations between Germany, Austria, and Russia, Crispi wrote to Primo Levi, "I tremble at the thought that if war broke out, something I believe is not far off, we would not be able to defend our position strongly" (Crispi, *Carteggi politici inediti*, p. 394).

by the nationalists, or as they were then called, the chauvinists of both sides. The French indeed were keyed up to an even more vociferous and disparaging mood than that of their opposite numbers south of the Alps, with many of them, including priests, nobles, and provincial bourgeois, dogmatically convinced of the fatal necessity of a conflict with Italy and trembling for it to begin.

For the Italians who identified with Crispi, their souls full of the painful memories of a distant past in which the peninsula had been politically dismembered, and recent memories, even more scorching, of a few inglorious military episodes during the recovery of nationhood, the urgent drive to act became something that was necessary if the Italians were to prove that they were not weak, that they were nobody's servants: it was like a patent of nobility that had to be won. And so it was bound up with a surly mistrust of other countries, an exaggerated susceptibility ready to see an offense to the national dignity in any gesture from abroad that was less than completely courteous. Visconti Venosta called this a sign of immaturity in a people.

All these things created an abyss between the Right and Crispi's coterie, who significantly had little use for Cavour.[96] They paid no homage to the Cavourian tradition, which was gospel to the moderates. Cavour had dared to risk all at the decisive moments and had not shrunk from the use of force, but his real genius showed in the timing of his actions, his sense of the right moment, his avoidance of programs that were too rigid and too long-term. He had been able to create a strong initial platform on which to build, and had then done so as fast as objective conditions permitted. But Cavour's great fault in Crispi's eyes was that of not having been committed to the unitary state from the outset.[97]

Here the rift was fundamental, and it explains why a government whose highest aim was a balanced budget was branded by Crispi as prosaic, frigid, and mean. When the Right said that military spending had to be contained for the time being because any state has to have its finances in order before anything else, *La Riforma* replied with the *ceterum censeo* of the elder Cato: it was absolutely necessary to arm, arm, arm, so as to be ready for the moment of supreme trial that was drawing near.

It was not just the love of action for action's sake that motivated those who wanted poetry and not prose, who called the policy of strict austerity unworthy of a great state. Amid all the travail over the coming, inevitable war with France, and the anxiety that Italy should display the bearing and the spirit and the force of a great power, in the midst of all the vague generic activism, the outline of a more precise objective began to emerge: this was the dream of Italian domination in the Mediterranean.

Mazzini had given birth to it,[98] and it had slowly insinuated its way into the minds of many. The restless spirit of Francesco Crispi was agitated to the core by this dream. *La Riforma* spoke of the Orient in August 1872, and of the individual

[96] Cf. above, p. 92.

[97] Well illustrated in Ercole, "La personalità storica e il pensiero politico di Francesco Crispi," p. 336.

[98] Cf. above, p. 159.

policy that Italy ought to have in regard to it, "more than any other power in Europe; because there is no other power whose geographical position and ancient traditions, and the sum of whose present interests, endow it with as many relations and contacts as Italy has with the populations that lie beyond the narrow sea that laps its coastline." The collapse or complete transformation of the Ottoman empire being inevitable, Italy ought to "exercise a decisive influence on events," provided only that there were men equal to the task in power.[99] The traditions of Venice and Genoa were trotted out.[100] History was summoned in aid of politics in a way that later nationalists would make familiar, and made the docile handmaid of the power claims of the great modern states, after having been throughout the Middle Ages the handmaid of theology and tool of the edification of Christian souls.

Cialdini provided a much clearer delineation, in diplomatic terms at any rate, of the dream of Italy as the arbiter of the Mediterranean basin. He was a man who diverged considerably on fundamental questions from the Crispi coterie: a believer in the alliance with France, and in a struggle together with France against Prussia as late as 3 August 1870, he found himself at the completely opposite pole from Crispi on this capital point of Italian foreign policy. But as an individual Cialdini was no less authoritarian and susceptible than Crispi, and suffered from the same military-style impatience with ordered civil life and the same scorn for the "accountants" who functioned as administrators of it. He too aspired to greatness, power, military force.

On the last point, he was a stubborn opponent in the Senate of the programs of Sella. A military man with all the usual disdain for financial problems, he called the program of "paring to the bone" intended to save the state a "monument to the inadequacy of our politicians," meanwhile launching emotional appeals to the government to cover "this poor Italy too" with iron, "to defend it from the arrogant of the earth and save it from the thunderbolts of heaven." He was not even above using an argument later destined to become trite and rancid in the mouths of the nationalists, which was to accuse civilians of scant affection for the armed forces, with admonitions to them to stop begrudging the soldiers the very bread on their plates, to stop portraying them as vampires who were devouring the contents of the treasury.[101] This is what he was saying in 1870; this is what he was still saying in 1874, when he once again attacked in the Senate the policies of a government that wanted to make the nation rich when it was just as necessary to make it strong[102]—with the difference, however, that in 1874 he too had become suspicious of France and the French.[103] For him too, though he was a Cavourian, just as for the anti-Cavourians who wrote for *La Riforma*, things were

---

[99] "La politica italiana in Oriente," in *La Riforma* for 22 August 1872.

[100] Cf. above, pp. 244 ff.

[101] Cialdini, speech to the Senate, 3 August 1870 (*A.P.*, *Senato*, pp. 987–92).

[102] *A.P.*, *Senato*, p. 856, 4 June.

[103] Cf. a letter of Cialdini to Nigra, 10 January 1874: the latter has a difficult task in Paris, "center of the intrigues and resentments, the political and religious hatreds that smolder against the kingdom of Italy" (De Vecchi archive).

felt to be going wrong, prose was triumphing over poetry. "We are far," he wrote to Castelli, "from that time of faith and enthusiasm represented by the genius of Cavour. Now we are swimming in doubt, coldness, prose, political cynicism."[104]

On the problems of expansion, greatness, potency then, the views of Cialdini and Crispi were the same: the Duke of Gaeta also dreamed of horizons of empire for his country, and said so in the clear and forceful manner that was one of his undoubted merits.

While on an extraordinary embassy to King Amedeo in Madrid,[105] Cialdini telegraphed on 28 February 1871 to Visconti Venosta that in a question that had arisen between Spain and Egypt over an interpreter at the Spanish consulate who had been mistreated by the Egyptian police, the English consul had intervened to mediate. He was displeased that the Italian consul had allowed this chance to be snatched from him by his British counterpart, a displeasure increased "all the more by the fact that I have reason to think that sooner or later Spain will do us some service in the Roman question, and in any case, after the fall of French power, Italy should aspire to diplomatic supremacy in the Mediterranean basin."

Here at least there were no shades of gray and the aim was clear: supremacy in the Mediterranean. The Mazzinian dream was shared now by many, even anti-Mazzinians. We have seen it embraced by Blanc, a pure Cavourian.[106] It was certainly hard to content oneself with the balanced budget and the tax schemes of Sella when one's head was full of mirages like that.

The government of the Right thus encountered opposition to its line even outside the parliamentary arena, in the devotion to poetry, which meant action: it might be action without a precise purpose, it might be vague and restless, but let there be action. Though the numerical weight of the lovers of "poetry" should not be overestimated, for they were few at that time, neither should their agitation be dismissed, for they were strengthened by a few adherents of unquestionable renown and caliber.

Luckily, the man at Italy's helm in the heaving seas of international politics in the years after 1870 was the right man for the circumstances, the man whom no accusation of prosiness would ever have perturbed: Emilio Visconti Venosta.

[104] 11 September 1870 (Castelli, *Carteggio politico* 2:481.

[105] Cialdini's embassy ended prematurely. He ought to have remained in Madrid as minister plenipotentiary at the termination of his extraordinary mission, but he returned to Italy in a fury against Visconti Venosta, who following the death of Prim took the view that the project was no longer feasible. Cialdini complained to the king about Visconti Venosta's way of proceeding (Cialdini to Vittorio Emanuele II, 6 February 1871; ACR, *Carte Visconti Venosta*, pacco 4, fasc. 1), and vented his anger at Visconti Venosta for—in his view—having made a fool of him, and also at Blanc, and Sonnino, whom he sent back to Italy for having failed him "in an unbefitting manner" (the entire correspondence about the matter, including telegrams and reports to Visconti Venosta, in Archivio della Casa Reale, *Carte Vittorio Emanuele II*, cart. V, ambasceria straordinaria a Madrid, 1870–1871, *Carte Cialdini*).

[106] Cf. above, p. 7.

II. *The World of Men*

Emilio Visconti Venosta

THE HANDSOME LAD with the blue eyes and long blond curly hair descending to his shoulders[1] had metamorphosed into a personage exuding gravity even in external appearance: he was tall and thin with long reddish side whiskers which he frequently stroked with an English gesture that accentuated the first impression he gave of calm and inner control, even of British phlegm.[2] The sensitive Emilio who cried easily, and seemed a sorrowing angel as he pleaded with his mother from behind a locked door, had become a statesman who appeared to many, including a young legation aide named Bernhard von Bülow, as one of the most calculating and cautious to be found.

Though he was now only a little over forty, he had already completed the entire arc of his moral and spiritual evolution: from the follower of Mazzini in 1848 had emerged the devotee of Cavour, and from the schoolboy who did not have "his head screwed on right," and thought more about revolution and conspiracy than he did about the philosophy of law, there had emerged a politician who always had his head screwed on right.

But if one looked more deeply, one saw that this man, whom Mazzini described as having been unfaithful to the dream of his youth and whom the Left always considered a renegade who merited particularly strong opposition,[3] had preserved his fundamental characteristics unchanged, though his outward aspect had altered in accordance with nature's decree, and he had changed political parties. It is not just that as a boy he was already dreaming of being a diplomat, for these were mere youthful reveries, despite the fact that they were to come true in the future. But the willingness to reason, the resort at critical moments to ratiocination rather than giving way to the flood of sentiment and the illusions of imagination, the ability to stay calm in all circumstances: these were the things in the youth of little more than twenty that impressed relatives, friends, and acquaintances, that gained him an ascendancy over fellow Lombards of the same age group not long after the great revolutionary furor of 1848 had passed,[4] and that still constituted the fundamental traits of the personality of the foreign minister of the kingdom of Italy.

[1] Visconti Venosta, *Ricordi di gioventù*, p. 7; other information at pp. 15, 64, 286, 518.

[2] Bülow, *Memorie* 4:335–36; F. Petruccelli della Gattina, *Storia d'Italia*, p. 157; E. De Laveleye, *Lettres d'Italie*, pp. 245–46; Cimbro [G. Faldella], *Salita a Montecitorio (1878–1882): Caporioni* (Turin, 1883), p. 102; G. Ricciardi, *Schizzi fotografici dei Deputati del 1, 2, e 3 Parlamento Italiano* (Naples, 1870), p. 40; Mazzoleni, *L'XI Legislatura*, p. 331.

[3] Cf. Mazzini's letter to him, 5 April 1853 (*Scritti* 49 = *Epistolario* 27:38 ff.). For the hostility of the Left see Rattazzi, *Rattazzi et son temps* 2:392; and "Nulla dies sine linea," in *La Riforma* for 5 August 1871: "Signor Visconti Venosta, this former Mazzinian, has become a calamity for Italy, like all renegades."

[4] Cf. Barbiera, *Il salotto della Contessa Maffei*, p. 213.

His soul was anything but icy, indeed he was capable of deep feeling, being sensitive and impressionable;[5] but he was also capable of total outward self-control. He was utterly dignified in appearance and diction, restrained in gesture; sparing and deliberate, but also measured and precise, in speech; firm and persevering even in stormy meetings, yet also very clever at conveying his meaning without stating it outright or compromising himself.[6] He was a slow and cautious judge, but also a sound judge, of men and things, and valued discretion far more than publicity.[7] He had a strong sense of his own limits and disliked being asked to transgress them—being asked, as he said, to transform himself from a flute player into a violin player.[8] He abhorred the easy ways of winning popularity,[9] and detested all rash gestures and all impatience, preferring instead to allow some leeway to his own natural indolence and irresolution, to let time do its work, to sit on an important decision for twenty-four hours in the certainty that nothing vital would be compromised and that the sky would not fall over that one issue; in the belief indeed that some difficulty might be smoothed out or some obstacle vanish during that interval.[10] He was always careful not to dash unthinkingly into a blind alley, and never let himself be put in a spot from which he

[5] He was such an affectionate father that he almost went out of his mind at the death of a baby daughter (Farini, *Diario*, MRR, under 12 March and also 24 April 1898); and cf. his moving note to Luzzatti in Luzzatti, *Memorie* 2:153, and a letter to him from Giovanni Morelli of 24 July 1886 that exhorts him to try to liberate himself from the melancholy that is oppressing him, while keeping sacred the memory of the lost child (Visconti Venosta archive).

[6] Thus *La Perseveranza* for 27 January 1871; and Bonghi in the same paper on 21 August 1870 on Visconti Venosta's speech in the difficult session of the Chamber on 19 August. He was among the slower orators; in his speeches he pronounced 80 words a minute, while Minghetti pronounced 100, Depretis 120, Sella 150 (Cimbro [G. Faldella], *Salita a Montecitorio (1878–1882): Il paese di Montecitorio*, p. 103.

[7] Among other things he had a horror of *post facta* revelations by excessively chatty diplomats and government insiders preoccupied with themselves and their own reputations. He once wrote to Nigra: "It is unpleasant to know at every moment that all the conversations in which one may have taken part fifteen or twenty years ago will be brought back to life in print. I agree that one should always be held to account for words that have had a positive and concrete effect, but not for those that came to one in the course of a distant conversation; for things one felt to be morally appropriate then are now beyond the reach of any competent judgment. For my part, I have always refrained from claiming merits in retrospect, but I am equally averse to polemics, corrections, posthumous defenses. In this too, my dear friend, we have always been in agreement" (3 December 1884; Visconti Venosta archive).

[8] When, despite his preference that a jurist be nominated, he was forced to accept the role of Italian arbiter in the question of fishing in the Bering Strait, he wrote to his brother that it gave him a most uncomfortable feeling: "I would not have hesitated . . . if it had been a political question. But here I am out of my depth. I am a man who knows how to play the flute, and they are forcing me to play the violin" (24 August 1892; Visconti Venosta archive).

[9] About the protracted and thorny question of the *Orénoque*, he told Nigra that he infinitely preferred the solution of a spontaneous withdrawal of the ship by the French to that of an official Italian request. The latter would have been popular domestically, "but that sort of popularity I take care not to earn" (Visconti Venosta, private letter to Nigra, 17 August 1874; Visconti Venosta archive).

[10] For this reason, too, Visconti Venosta, in the English manner, did not sacrifice his vacations even at turbulent periods, which gave rise to some comment among his subordinates. One of them, Pansa, wrote in his *Diario* on 7 September 1875: "It appears that even the minister has finally decided to return tomorrow; there is a man, for example, *qui ne se gêne pas* about taking his relaxation when it suits him." And cf. the attack in *La Riforma* for 19 August 1871 ("Il Ministro degli Esteri in vacanza").

could not backtrack or change his approach.[11] This meant that rather than try to dominate and constrain events with a strong hand, he was more disposed to let himself be borne (not towed) along by them as though riding a high wave, until the right moment arrived: then, smoothly and without duress, he could steer them in the direction he wanted.[12] He was reluctant to set out programs for the long term, to mortgage the future,[13] and preferred to advance step by step, from moment to moment, even letting events force his hand sometimes, adapting his proposals to the circumstances.

He was a man who at decisive moments needed not only the pressure of public opinion but also some stronger and more decisive personality among his cabinet colleagues to excite him to action, to serve as a spur, to create objective situations he could not resist while permitting him to cover what he was doing with a blanket of fleece, smudging the angles and rendering diplomatically acceptable to other states political decisions which at bottom were matters of force. He was not a man of rapid decisions, sudden flashes of intuition, or brisk snapping energy. A faithful Cavourian, he lacked, as did almost all the collaborators and successors of Cavour (who were deliberate rather than instinctual politicians, their choice of *métier* guided by human will and the power of reason and ideas rather than by a divine spark)[14] the boldness of the master, a boldness made of cold calculation certainly, but also of élan, shot through with that mysterious quality that allows a man to shift in an instant from the phase of pure cerebration in which the odds are weighed, to the phase of resolute action. But Visconti Venosta was a man admirably suited to situations that were already shaped by the

[11] He used to say that for a diplomat "it is very important to know how to quit when one is ahead of the game" (Bülow, *Memorie* 3:193).

[12] That the policy of letting time do its work may entail taking clear, decisive action at a certain point is stated by Visconti Venosta himself in a letter of 12 April 1878 to Robilant. "Neither do I observe with a tranquil mind the way things are going in our country. It may be that as we speak, the wisest course is to play for time. But the policy of deferring difficulties presupposes having the necessary energy and decision on the day when they can no longer be put off" (AE, *Carte Robilant*). In fact, at the most difficult period of relations with France, Visconti Venosta had indeed tried not to let himself be overcome by panic and lose his calm and his sureness of judgment, like the men of the Left; but he had also tried to be prepared in advance to deal with any surprise move: "We can only attempt to handle with bland delicacy a situation whose causes we cannot expunge overnight, trying not to compromise the future and hoping for the benefit of time. On our side I am trying to follow this policy, avoiding incidents, palliating them when necessary, giving proofs of a sincerely friendly and conciliatory disposition. . . . But you understand that this policy of dosing out calmatives cannot be the sum of our efforts. There is another aspect of policy that we also have a duty to attend to, which is to be ready for the worst cases, the ones we cannot control. As long as the situation holds an element of uncertainty and doubt, it is natural that we should make sure this is matched by an adequate degree of precaution" (Visconti Venosta, personal letter to Nigra, 2 February 1873; Visconti Venosta archive).

[13] Cf. his statements to the Chamber on 19 August 1870: "Gentlemen, I believe that it is dangerous to ask the government what precise line of conduct it intends to follow in present conditions, when our choices may be determined by circumstances that it is impossible to foresee and define. We cannot, gentlemen, usefully discuss uncertain eventualities, nor is there any government that can commit itself on the basis of hypotheses" (*A.P., Camera*, p. 4027).

[14] This has been noted acutely in the case of the "practicality" of Balbo by N. Valeri in *Problemi di storia del Risorgimento* (Milan, 1947), pp. 101–102 (cited by W. Maturi in "L'aspetto religioso del 1848 e la storiografia italiana," in *Convegno . . . 1848*, p. 267). But the observation fits the majority of the members of the post-Cavourian Right, Sella and perhaps Minghetti excepted.

logic of events and by the rapid will of some other individual who was more of a condottiere. Better than anyone else, he could translate choices into actuality on the diplomatic side precisely because of his temporizing, his delay, his step-by-step procedure, his concealment of plans of action already perceived and thought out by others, plans that personally he might not even accept in their entirety. He moved things along as though it were not the will of man but an inexorable fate that propelled them: a fate before which one could only bow one's head—he, his colleagues, the other governments of Europe.

If he had had to direct Italian policy in a period that required him to show daring and to play for high stakes, he would have been out of his depth. He was just the man to direct the foreign policy of a state that needed a calm and peaceful process of adjustment, a state whose only international requirement at the moment was to make the other states definitively accept the fait accompli.[15]

The man and the style were fully apparent in the stance he maintained during the summer of 1870, under the shadow of the formidable problems that the Franco-Prussian War posed for Italy, to which Visconti Venosta responded by playing for time and avoiding hurried decisions. Despite moments of hesitation[16] and moments in which he gave way to pressure from the king (whom he was less able to resist than Sella), in essence he continued to favor neutrality, at least until the conflict should have become generalized through the involvement of Austria and Russia. He was unwaveringly opposed to abandoning "moral means" and adopting forceful ones on the question of Rome.[17] Up to the eve of 20 September, he was the most reluctant to act of all the ministers, hoping until the last that Pius IX would take advantage of the very hesitation of the government in Florence and of its public statements, and agree to an accord with Italy, thus making possible the "middle" solution that would have profited Italy by avoiding the fatal

[15] In this sense the verdict passed on him by Guiccioli is not entirely mistaken: "He was a good enough minister when prudent abstention and shrewd inaction were wise courses. But on the day when the interests of our country, rightly understood, made necessary the choice of a clearly determined line of conduct, or, even more critically, made necessary a rapid and grave decision, I fear that V. would be unequal to his task" (Guiccioli, "Diario," in *Nuova Antologia* for 1 July 1935, p. 86). But instead of "good enough minister" [*discreto ministro*], Guiccioli ought to have written "superb minister" [*ottimo ministro*].

[16] Cf. Castagnola, *Da Firenze a Roma*, pp. 6–7 (concerning the cabinet meeting of 8 August 1870). On this evidence, F. Cataluccio, *La politica estera di E. Visconti Venosta*, p. 53, errs in stating that Visconti Venosta was a spokesman for those in Lanza's cabinet who wanted Italy to intervene on France's side (those who strongly favored this course on 8 August were Lanza, Castagnola, Gadda, and Acton). Visconti Venosta's position emerges from his exchange of views with de Launay (above, p. 9): we should stay neutral for now; if we were forced to abandon neutrality, we should side with France. Cf. Guiccioli, *Quintino Sella* 1:263–66, who has grasped the situation and depicted it well, especially in his summary at p. 265. And cf. below, n. 38.

[17] If cannon are required in order to get to Rome, he told the leaders of the Left, then you will be the ones to go there. As for me, I will not follow this course (Rattazzi, *Rattazzi et son temps* 2:348; this information effectively corresponds to the general attitude and convictions of Visconti Venosta, and so can be accepted, even if the source is Mme Rattazzi). On the conduct of the Italian government up to 20 September, which will be analyzed by Walter Maturi, and to which reference is made here only to the extent necessary to illuminate the figure of Visconti Venosta, see the ample and detailed examination in Halperin, *Italy and the Vatican at War*, pp. 28 ff. Less important is L. Parker Wallace, *The Papacy and European Diplomacy, 1869–1878* (Chapel Hill, 1948), pp. 116 ff.

radicalism of a unilateral Italian action.[18] In a meeting of the cabinet on 3 September he not only joined five colleagues in opposing the immediate occupation of Rome "whatever the hazard" desired by Sella and Castagnola, he stood alone in opposing such an occupation even if Prussian consent were guaranteed. The next day he spoke again, opposing any proposal to occupy Rome or even the papal state in general: he was on the far right, with Govone and Acton.[19]

When news arrived that a republic was born in France, then he too decided that the moment had come to "dare."[20] But his daring was always controlled: on 8 September he stated in another cabinet meeting that "at the present stage of developments, he would never agree to entering Rome by force."[21] Finally, after having absented himself from the meeting of 13 September, and opposing on the 15th the wording chosen for the plebiscite,[22] he made a supreme effort on 17 September, proposing as the ultimate act of appeasement that General Cadorna should declare that he would refrain from entering Rome if Count Arnim could obtain the immediate dismissal of the foreign troops in the pay of the pope and their departure from Rome without their weapons. This idea was naturally rejected by

---

[18] Visconti Venosta to Cadorna, 12 April 1871 (AE, *Ris.*, c. 51). The intermediate solution would have been the Leonine City (Rothan, *L'Allemagne et l'Italie* 2:280 and below, n. 40). In a letter to his brother Giovanni (undated but from early September 1870, for he says "today [in Paris] there was agitation in the boulevards, and cries of vive la République"), Visconti Venosta says: "I fear I cannot agree with my colleagues on Rome. I want to act as much as they do, but act rightly, and in such a way that I do not put myself in the wrong and compromise Italy" (Visconti Venosta archive).

[19] Castagnola, *Da Firenze a Roma*, pp. 30–31. There is no reference to this meeting of 3 September in the cabinet minutes, which were drawn up by Lanza and are in any case extremely terse (ACR, *Verbali delle deliberazioni del Consiglio dei Ministri*, vol. 2). Probably this meeting was the basis of the lurid account given in *Rattazzi et son temps* 2:351, by Mme Rattazzi, who with her usual chronological confusion lumps into a single day debates held and decisions taken in cabinet over several days—3, 4, and 5 September to be exact—and adds touches of fantasy, like the one about a mobilization in favor of Napoleon III (which belongs to 30 July if it belongs anywhere). We should interpret the meeting of 3 September not as an official session of the cabinet but as a semiofficial gathering which Lanza and his colleagues did not want on record, perhaps because there was still too much disagreement among them about what was to be done.

[20] Visconti Venosta, telegram to Minghetti in Vienna, 5 September: "The situation has changed with the advent of the republic. I believe that now is the time to dare. Telegraph me your advice, and the course that you would follow in the Roman question" (AE, *Ris.*, 51).

[21] Cabinet minutes for 8 September (ACR, *Verbali delle deliberazioni del Consiglio dei Ministri* 2:71–72; published in Crispi, *Politica interna*, p. 70, and in Lanza, *Le carte* 6:406). Castagnola, *Da Firenze a Roma* (pp. 36 ff.), errs in attributing this statement to the cabinet meeting of 7 September. It is to be noted that the instructions to General Cadorna approved by the cabinet said "that the troops will not proceed to occupy the city of Rome if it is necessary to take it with violence." These instructions belong to the phase, which lasted until 17 September, in which the Italian government was still under the illusion that the pope would not resist; or at least that there would be a popular uprising in Rome (cf. as well Blanc's personal letter to Minghetti, 12 September; BCB, *Carte Minghetti*, cart. XV, fasc. 66). It is worth noting that this is one of the rare cases in the very laconic cabinet minutes in which express mention is made of the views of an individual minister: a sign that Visconti Venosta wanted to mark his dissent strongly. He stated orally that if Rome were occupied with force he would resign (Castagnola, ibid., p. 39).

[22] Castagnola, *Da Firenze a Roma*, pp. 46–48. Ponza di San Martino, who returned from Rome on the evening of 11 September completely committed to an immediate occupation, had warned those in power not to put a spanner in the works—addressing Visconti Venosta directly (Blanc to Minghetti, in the private letter cited in the previous note).

his colleagues, and instead the telegram was sent ordering General Cadorna to take the city of Rome by force, leaving the Leonine City untouched.[23]

In sum, if Visconti Venosta had had his way, Italy would certainly not have gone to Rome in the manner it did. His position was like that of many others, and those not the least esteemed, among the moderates; Stefano Jacini, for instance, had deprecated the action of 20 September in very similar terms.[24] The conservatives of Lombardy, of whom the former Mazzinian Visconti Venosta was now a member in good standing, held to different positions than those of Quintino Sella. Visconti Venosta was conservative enough to present his resignation a few days later, though he withdrew it right away, because La Marmora had not been sent immediately to Rome as a guarantee to Italy and the world that a prudent and conciliatory policy would be adopted, and because, as he put it, the "subversive party" had got the upper hand.[25]

In the sequel, he exerted continuous pressure on his colleagues and clashed strongly with the most decided among them, especially with Sella, always seeking to put on the brakes, to attenuate, to postpone. He opposed the transfer of the capital to Rome, a transfer that he, like Jacini, did not accept at first.[26] He opposed, like Lanza and against Sella,[27] the immediate visit of the king to Rome, though when the flooding of the Tiber offered an occasion at the end of December he seized it immediately. He disapproved of the seizure of the Quirinal palace,[28] and dug in his heels against the Ruspoli amendment in February of 1871, again threatening to resign, and succeeding with the help of foreign pressure in getting the Senate to go back to a draft of the legislation that showed much more respect for the Holy See.[29]

---

[23] Minutes of the session of 17 September (ACR, *Verbali delle deliberazioni del Consiglio dei Ministri* 2:75; Crispi, *Politica interna*, p. 71; Lanza, *Le carte* 6:408; Castagnola, *Da Firenze a Roma*, pp. 52–53).

[24] Jacini, *Un conservatore rurale* 2:46.

[25] Visconti Venosta to Lanza, 25 September 1870 (the cabinet had decided instead, on the 24th, to send La Marmora to Rome only after the acceptance of the plebiscite). Lanza succeeded in convincing him to change his mind: Lanza to Visconti Venosta, 27 September (Visconti Venosta archive; cf. Castagnola, *Da Firenze a Roma*, pp. 68–69). The designation of La Marmora was in fact interpreted, domestically and abroad, in the sense that Visconti Venosta wished (Halperin, *Italy and the Vatican at War*, pp. 90 ff.). Note that in the session of 24 September Visconti Venosta had his dissent from his colleagues recorded in the minutes once again (ACR, *Verbali delle deliberazioni del Consiglio dei Ministri* 2:76; Lanza, *Le carte* 6:409).

[26] Cf. as well a letter of D. Pantaleoni to Minghetti in Vienna on 22 October 1870: "I esteem it urgent that you come back here and leave Vienna. . . . Visconti, with his typical honesty, has already told me that he was against moving the capital to Rome." Then Visconti Venosta changed his view, as Pantaleoni informed Minghetti on 4 November: "I am very glad that Visconti has receded from the opinion that he had stated to me. He is the best man we have in the cabinet, and certainly the most candid" (BCB, *Carte Minghetti*, cart. XV, fasc. 114).

[27] Lanza said to Castelli on 10 November that if the king were pushed (by Sella and company) to go to Rome before parliament had approved the plebiscite, he and La Marmora would resign. "If Sella still wants to win at any cost, I am convinced that this time he will live to regret it in Rome" (Castelli, *Carteggio politico* 2:489–90).

[28] Castagnola, *Da Firenze a Roma*, p. 86.

[29] Ibid., pp. 143–44. The Cencelli-Ruspoli amendment to the proposed law of Guarantees on 10 February (Jacini, *La crisi religiosa del Risorgimento*, p. 435) declared the Vatican museums and the Vatican library national property. In contrast, the text of article 5 of the bill as finally passed, after

Visconti Venosta's stance was thus far from revolutionary, and it earned him acid rebukes from the opposition then and later, as well as his reputation as a reactionary.[30] Politically he was the loser in this contest with the Left, whose actions had supplied the necessary premise for 20 September, and from his contest with Sella, who had succeeded in bringing the cabinet over to his point of view. And yet, diplomatically speaking, Visconti Venosta as foreign minister had rendered a notable service to his country in the eyes of Europe in this affair, precisely because of the way he had behaved.

As an open and frank defender of his views, he was able to try until the last minute to avoid the use of force in resolving the question of Rome, believing as he and others did that this great problem could only be resolved through the use of moral force. But once the event had taken place, rather than indulge in recriminations, he supported it with determination like so many other moderates, including Jacini and above all Massari, who was also opposed to the use of force, but who, once Italy had taken Rome, made a commitment to keeping it, and who took for his own the slogan, Rome or death.[31] It was Visconti Venosta's style to be irresolute while action was not yet imminent, to ruminate perhaps even too much. But when the action was under way, not only did he refuse to back off or blame others, he would not even permit any further fluctuation. Thus he also considered 20 September an irrevocable fact, and communicated to the Italian representatives abroad the official position that the Italian government would never retreat from Rome, that it was a *porro unum* that would be defended with every resource, including arms; and he busied himself in diplomatizing the revolutionary political deed. It had been desired by others, not him. Within the government Visconti Venosta had found the goad he needed in the "blockhead" Sella,[32] who was strongly backed from outside the cabinet by Minghetti,[33] just as

---

affirming that the supreme pontiff continued to be the master of the apostolic palaces of the Vatican and the Lateran, with all the adjoining and dependent edifices, gardens, and terrains etc., merely added: "the said palaces . . . and adjuncts, as also the museums, the library, and the art and archaeological collections within them, are inalienable, are exempt from any tax or burden, and are exempt from expropriation for reasons of public utility." On 11 February Visconti Venosta wrote to his brother Giovanni that he was losing patience and had decided to quit: "the best thing will be to leave these gentlemen [the parliamentary deputies] in midstream to teach them the need for a little discretion and a little discipline" (Visconti Venosta archive).

[30] He is called the leader of the reactionary tendency within the cabinet in the manifesto of a group of Roman liberals who were supporting the candidacy of Sella in November 1870 (*La Perseveranza* for 21 November 1870). Cf. further the accusations of the hon. Miceli in the Chamber on 25 November 1872 (*A.P., Camera*, p. 3324), and of the hon. Oliva on 16 May 1873 (p. 6418). Later, when the *Diario* of Castagnola appeared, Domenico Farini noted how the publication of this document disclosed "the pusillanimity of Visconti Venosta in 1870" (*Diario*, MRR, under 20 September 1895, referring to the extract printed in *Il Popolo Romano*).

[31] In the speech to the Chamber of 13 March 1872 (*A.P., Camera*, p. 1179).

[32] This is what Lanza called him (Lanza, *Le carte* 6:268). The identical expression is used in a note to Visconti Venosta of 15 November 1870 (Visconti Venosta archive). As for the prolonged debates (Tavallini, *La vita e i tempi di Giovanni Lanza* 2:178 ff., 453–54, 485, 489; Lanza, *Le carte* 9:68, 73, 79–80, 383 ff., and 10:376 ff., 429) on the roles of Lanza and Sella and their respective merits in the problem of Rome, it is clear that Sella's was, without any doubt, the stronger will. On 3 and 4 September he insisted that Rome should be occupied too, and Lanza was opposed, changing his mind only after the news of the proclamation of the republic in France on 5 September (Castagnola,

in 1864 he had accepted the initiative for the September Convention from Minghetti, then prime minister. Minghetti and Sella were both men of much greater intuitive quickness than Visconti Venosta, and Sella was untroubled by any reverential awe of the Roman curia, hence quicker to grasp the fated course of action and give their due to the baying Left, and to Mazzini and the republicans with their threats of revolution;[34] he was quicker to seize the occasion offered by events in Europe and the debacle in France. Again, we see that a context of revolutionary ferment was requisite for the government to be able to act; that it was necessary that a certain international situation come about for that revolutionary ferment to be translated by the government into concrete action.[35] But when faced with ineluctable events that he saw to be such because of the pressure the government was coming under from the Left in the Chamber, when forced into contact with a reality created by others, Visconti Venosta gave all he had to turning this reality into a lasting fact, accepted by the foreign nations; and his "softness" then played a precious role in consolidating that which the "hardness" of another member of the government had brought within reach.[36]

Diario, pp. 30–32, which is definitive on these matters; Guiccioli, *Quintino Sella* 1:300–301).

In Gadda's critique of Castagnola's *Diario* ("Roma capitale e il Ministero Lanza-Sella," *Nuova Antologia* 155 [16 September 1897]: 193 ff.), Gadda claims that Lanza and Visconti Venosta had settled on the occupation of Rome some time before, and that the only point of difference between them and Sella was about the moment at which to launch the enterprise. But the fact is that there was a much more important point of difference concerning the "mode" of the action. Sella embraced the policy of force, which was the one that they all had to embrace in the end. Lanza, and not Visconti Venosta alone (though it was the latter who defended his point of view to the last), was opposed to using force and also hoped that an accord with the pontiff could be reached, or at least that there would be an insurrection of the Romans which would relieve the Italian government of blame in the eyes of the Catholic world (cf. Halperin, *Italy and the Vatican at War*, pp. 35–36). This is the heart of the matter, not whether Lanza and Visconti Venosta also wanted Rome to be part of Italy or not, which of course they did.

[33] Sella to Minghetti, 21 September 1870: "I know that your counsel was decisive in bringing Emilio to overcome his hesitations, which in truth were not, and are not, minor ones. I thank you most warmly for the capital assistance you gave to those who, like me, see Rome as a case of *fata trahunt.*" And he urges him to encourage in the future (the plebiscite etc.) "our good Emilio, who has the advantage among so many contrasting opinions of an authoritative corroboration coming from you, than which none other is more efficacious" (BCB, *Carte Minghetti*, cart. XV, fasc. 127). Cf. as well Minghetti, *Carteggio Minghetti-Pasolini* 4:195; Luzzatti, *Memorie* 1:308; Crispi, *Scritti e discorsi politici*, p. 672; Farini, *Diario*, MRR, under 24 September 1895; Maioli, *Marco Minghetti*, p. 270).

[34] On 19 August 1870 Crispi had stated in the Chamber: "you can, by satisfying the national interest, prevent the outbreak of the revolution that you fear. . . . It is urgent to resolve the Roman question, first of all because the country's internal security requires it" (Crispi, *Discorsi Parlamentari* 2:78–79). Mancini said on the same day: "the initiative of private violence . . . would inevitably overtake the action of the government, if the country were to continue in its well-founded distrust of the efficacy of will and of the capacity of the leaders of the state" (Mancini, *Discorsi Parlamentari* 3:375). And Bertani stated on the following day: "If we do not act quickly we will find ourselves faced with the hard alternative of despotism or revolution" (Bertani, *Discorsi Parlamentari*, p. 141). And see the address of the Left to the government on 3 September in Crispi, *Politica interna*, p. 68.

[35] "Events have accomplished everything for us, and we have done little or nothing," Dina to Castelli, 17 October 1870 (Castelli, *Carteggio politico* 2:487, and *Ricordi*, p. 188).

[36] The difference between their two characters is well delineated by Sella himself in a letter to Minghetti of 5 October 1878: "Do not doubt that for my part I am doing, and will do, everything possible to come to agreement on all matters with Emilio [Visconti Venosta]. Every day I value him more highly for his elevation of character and nobility of sentiment. If there is excessive indecision,

In this phase his hesitations and denials, his conservatism and his concern as a Catholic, all served him and served his country; everything that hampered him as a politician helped him as a diplomat.[37] In accordance with the bent of his mind and his chosen style, he had proceeded step by careful step in his diplomatic circulars and in his discussions with the foreign envoys in Florence, never going too far, carefully giving the true impression that he did not hold exaggerated hopes and ambitions, that if anything he was being pulled along from moment to moment, was almost being overcome by events.[38] And if he, the complete moderate, was unable to withstand the flow of events, who else could be expected to do so? The official position of the Italian government—that it had entered the papal state and Rome to avert disorder, in fact to avert revolution—seemed true, was true, when pronounced by the foreign minister. He seemed to pose the alternative of accepting that solution, however repugnant, or else making another leap into the unknown. Visconti Venosta moved from the circular of 29 August, which speaks "of obtaining the moral adhesion of the Catholic governments which Italy has always seen as the most efficacious warrant of a good solution"[39] (openly acknowledging the international character of the accords with the papacy), and a memorandum of the same date which asserted that the Leonine City

---

or as you would say softness, *hinc* [on one side], there is too much hardness *inde* [on the other], and chemistry teaches me that the more opposition there is in the electrical charge of molecules, the stronger the molecular attraction is" (BCB, *Carte Minghetti*, cart. XXI, fasc. 54). But relations between the two men were not always amicable; in fact there was usually strong disagreement, as in 1870: cf. Lanza, *Le carte* 9:49; Castelli, *Carteggio politico* 2:501. In February 1874 Artom, who was busy trying to bring Minghetti, Sella, and Visconti Venosta together in the same cabinet, had to struggle hard to put an end to the personal friction between the two (Artom to Nigra, 6 February; AE, *Carte Nigra*).

[37] Minghetti perceived immediately and clearly how matters stood, writing to Luzzatti on 30 September 1870: "As for Rome . . . we could not fail to grasp the occasion. Visconti's attitude has, however, done a great deal to keep the powers sympathetic. If we had said right at the start that we intended to enter Rome by smashing through its walls, there would perhaps have been difficulties. When you face parliament, you have to take a firm, decided line; but in diplomacy, you need to have a softer, more fluid profile. Hence Sella and Visconti seem to me to be mutually necessary, and nothing would be worse than if they separated" (Luzzatti, *Memorie* 1:309).

[38] In 1906 he explained that he had proceeded as he did in the summer of 1870 because of the necessity not to compromise Italy, to temporize, on the eve of events whose outcome no one could foresee ("Le projet d'alliance franco-austro-italienne en 1869–70: Explications attribuées à E. Visconti-Venosta," *Revue d'Italie* [September 1906]: 605 ff.).

[39] *Libro Verde 17*, p. 11. Compare the more cautious official language of Visconti Venosta with that of Lanza, who is free to be much more declarative and specific in a confidential letter to a friend: "the definitive solution of the great question of the free exercise of the temporal power will result from a congress of the Catholic powers" (Lanza to Castelli, 8 September 1870). Castelli reacted by calling this "the most baneful of errors. Have no illusions: Rome occupied means Rome the capital" (Castelli, *Carteggio politico* 2:479–80 and cf. 482–83, and *Ricordi*, pp. 187–88). Foreign governments and their diplomats later frequently drew attention to the promises contained in the circular of 29 August and the other statements of Visconti Venosta when making representations to the Italian government, both generically and over particular issues, and complained about the wide gap between the legislation passed by Italy and what had been promised (Trauttmansdorff, reports to Beust, 20 and 24 December 1870, SAW, *P.A.*, XI/224, nos. 128 and 130 A; Beust, dispatch to Hoyos in Paris, 16 March 1871, ibid., XI/235; Lefebvre de Béhaine, reports of 11 and 20 February 1871, nos. 25 and 32, AEP, *C.P.*, *Rome*, t. 1049, fols. 190 ff., 252v). Monsignor Dupanloup likewise harks back to the circular of 29 August in 1874, in *Lettre de M. l'évêque d'Orléans à M. Minghetti . . . sur la spoliation de l'Église à Rome et en Italie* (Paris, 1874), pp. 7, 28, 54.

would be kept under papal sovereignty,[40] to a circular of 7 September which renewed Italy's guarantees concerning the arrangements with the powers for the protection of the spiritual independence of the pontiff,[41] and then to circulars of 11 and 14 October which merely refuted the claims of Pius IX that he was being denied freedom of communication and gave assurance that if necessary he would be perfectly free to leave Rome.[42] The culminating circular was issued on 18 October: in announcing the plebiscite and the annexation of Rome, it said nothing at all about the Leonine City, which by then had slipped from the grasp of the pope through the failure to reach an accord, through the fierce will of the inhabitants of the Borgo who had voted on 2 October, and through the surge of public opinion against the "territorial immunity" to which reference was still made in article 3 of the government decree of 9 October,[43] nor about any *adhésion*, even of the purely moral variety, offered by foreign governments. Instead it solemnly proclaimed that Italy assumed the burden of applying the notions of right and liberty to relations between church and state, and committed itself—alone—to guaranteeing the exercise of the high spiritual mission of the pontiff.[44]

In the sequel, the same attitude of prudence, calm, and dislike of rash steps prevailed. The government had quickly realized that there was little to be done for the moment about the pope, that those who were talking about reconciliation, accords, embraces between Pius IX and Vittorio Emanuele were indulging in

---

[40] The memorandum of 29 August, not published (*et pour cause!*) in the *Libro Verde* presented to parliament on 19 December 1870, is published in *Das Staatsarchiv* 20 (1871), no. 4290, pp. 219 ff., and on the Leonine City, pp. 226–27 (now in Bastgen, *Die römische Frage* 2:626 ff. [Freiburg-im-Breisgau, 1918]). Drafted by Blanc, it was not meant to be divulged; but as early as 17 October Cardinal Antonelli was referring to it in a circular to the nuncios drafted for the express purpose of rebutting it. The memorandum had been passed in confidence to the cardinal: "a manuscript copy came into my hand in consequence of an entirely casual circumstance" (*Staatsarchiv* 20 [1871], no. 4291, p. 227; Bastgen, *Die römische Frage* 2:635; and cf. Salata, *Per la storia diplomatica della questione romana* 1:12 and 44–45).

The memorandum was divulged, Visconti Venosta later declared, only as the result of an indiscretion (Rothan, report, 10 March 1871, no. 61; AEP, *C.P., Italie*, t. 381, fol. 133). "Inopportunely communicated to the English cabinet," says Artom in a letter of 26 March 1880 to Visconti Venosta (Visconti Venosta archive). The memorandum of 29 August was given by Blanc in confidence to Sir A. Paget, who sent it to London on 8 September 1870 (report no. 101; *F.O.*, 45/166). But at the end of August 1870 it expressed accurately the intentions of the Italian government! On the proposal to leave the Leonine City under papal sovereignty, which even Sella favored on the grounds that if the pope accepted he would be recognizing everything else done by Italy, see Castagnola, *Da Firenze a Roma*, p. 27; Guiccioli, *Quintino Sella* 1:304. Minghetti also approved the clause relinquishing the Leonine City to the pope (personal letters to Visconti Venosta from Vienna, 25 September and 4 October 1870; Visconti Venosta archive), if the pope would accept it. Cf. the statements of the hon. Oliva on 16 May 1873 concerning the memorandum and the attempt to cancel it from memory (*A.P., Camera*, p. 6418); and the statements of Sella to the Chamber on 16 March 1880, in his *Discorsi Parlamentari* 1:201–202.

[41] *Libro Verde 17*, p. 13.

[42] *Libro Verde 17*, pp. 59 and 64.

[43] On this, cf. Paladino, *Roma: Storia d'Italia dal 1866 al 1871*, p. 201; Halperin, *Italy and the Vatican at War*, pp. 109–10.

[44] *Libro Verde 17*, pp. 69 ff. On Italy's simply ceasing to refer any more to its former promises when it became evident that the European powers were focusing less on the loss of the temporal power than had been feared, see (as well as Halperin, pp. 111–12) Scaduto, *Guarentigie pontificie*, pp. 111 and 205.

wish-dreams. Therefore it abstained from even trying. "Europe would hold us to blame, and would also step in, if we offended the pope and his sentiments to no purpose by committing acts of imprudence, impatience, or violence after having obtained our main goal. What we need is a good deal of circumspection, forbearance, and tolerance."[45] For the moment no protests, dire warnings, or other difficulties were arriving from Europe;[46] in fact if anything Italy was receiving suggestions to speed things up.[47] On this point the Left had been correct in saying, through Mancini, that the hour could not be more propitious, given the isolation into which Pius IX had driven himself with his dogma of infallibility,[48] and that Italy had to act *fortiter in re*. It was the majesty of the Roman pontiff that kept the foreign minister from wanting to take any further steps, especially formal ones, that might have further direct and violent impact. The pontiff was still something more than a simple canon of the cathedral of Milan, and it was necessary at any cost to avoid uselessly exacerbating a conflict that was already too ferocious, perhaps setting in motion a train of consequences that might not be reversible, such as the departure of Pius IX from Rome, something that would certainly wound the Catholic sentiments of the population even more and heighten internal tensions. It was not only the effect on Europe that mattered, it was primarily the effect on the Catholic majority among the Italians. Thus Visconti Venosta had every reason to embrace a policy of *suaviter in modo*. This also applied to Europe of course, which before too long began to show signs of arousal: statements were made, and so were attempts to organize some action. A less delicate and more precipitate Italian policy would certainly have made it easier for outside nations to intervene. Less impulsive but of steadier purpose than Minghetti, who at one point had even imagined Vittorio Emanuele at the feet of Pius IX begging for his pardon, but had then insisted on transferring the capital immediately, Visconti Venosta did not want either outcome. He too was seized with awe and fear at what he and his colleagues had done, but for that very reason he held that this was the moment to put on kid gloves. So it was that while not only Sella and the Left but even his friends Minghetti and Nigra were arguing

---

[45] Visconti Venosta, letter to his brother Giovanni, 22–25 October 1870 (Visconti Venosta archive).

[46] Letter cited in the previous note.

[47] Minghetti, personal letter to Visconti Venosta, from Vienna, 21 September 1870: "Beust asked me very intently if it were possible to transfer the capital *immediately*. I answered that a certain amount of time would necessarily have to pass, in order to find out the will of the Romans, and for parliament to vote for the transfer and supply the necessary funds. . . . I conclude that in any case it is important to move with as much speed as is compatible with acting in a serious and dignified manner." He insists again on 25 September: "we have to shift the capital to Rome as quickly as possible while doing so in a serious and dignified manner"; and again on 9 October (Visconti Venosta archive). As for Sella, the motives that impel him to view an immediate visit by the king to Rome as necessary are expounded with extreme clarity in a letter of 26 October to La Marmora (Sella, *Epistolario inedito*, pp. 67–68 and cf. pp. 66 and 69–70).

[48] Mancini, speech to the Chamber on 19 August 1870 (*Discorsi Parlamentari* 3:374). This is also Salvatorelli's position, in *La Chiesa e il mondo* (Rome, 1948), pp. 149 ff. On the attitude of the powers, cf. Halperin, *Italy and the Vatican at War*, pp. 39 ff., 51 ff.; Salata, *Per la storia diplomatica della questione romana* 1:123, 129 ff.; Scaduto, *Guarentigie pontificie*, pp. 186 ff.; Jacini, *Il tramonto del potere temporale*, pp. 317 ff.

for a rapid transfer of the capital, so as to present Europe with a fait accompli before the Franco-Prussian War had ended,[49] Visconti Venosta in accord with Lanza postponed the formal and final conclusion of the affair. This tactic had its risks, for the future was unpredictable once peace was concluded, but it succeeded and obtained the great result that, with the war over, Europe was a collective spectator of the tranquil, confident, studied, and heralded (though unspectacular) entry of the king of Italy into Rome with the pope still enthroned in the Vatican.

Before 20 September it had been Minghetti who had urged on his reluctant friend that it was time to move on Rome. But after 20 September Visconti Venosta became the more decided of the two. Minghetti was worried about the fact that "we have been saying all over the place that the definitive solution of the question of the spiritual independence of the pontiff will be reserved for an accord with the powers," so he thought first of arranging an international convention. He then took the line that the government should at least make arrangements beforehand with the great powers in order to obtain their assent to the idea of a law of guarantees for the pope, in such wise that they would then be committed, and their future possibilities of diplomatic action on the question curtailed and hedged about.[50] For this reason the circular of 18 October appeared to Minghetti inadequate, since it communicated to the great powers the intentions of the Italian government, but contained no invitation, not even in veiled form, to discuss and to treat.[51] Visconti Venosta on the other hand, who had been so uncertain about, indeed hostile to, the entry into Rome by force, thought no more of asking Vittorio Emanuele II to genuflect before Pius IX,[52] and also took a line of greater independence vis-à-vis the powers than the one suggested by Minghetti. And so he began long months of endless hard work to avoid any foreign intervention in the domestic debate over relations with the pope and the church, and in the end he got results: the foreign legations were invited in June to move from Florence to Rome, and then at the last minute the official entry of the king into the Eternal City was announced on 2 July, clearly a surprise tactic to force the hand of foreign governments still reluctant to be represented in the Urbs.

---

[49] On 1 October 1870 from Tours, Nigra "strongly" counseled his minister that on the question of Rome it would be better to adopt as soon as possible "the total solution, in such a way that when the war is over and Europe returns to its normal state, it will find itself in the presence of a *fait*, or rather of a series of *faits*, irrevocably *accomplis*" (Visconti Venosta archive).

[50] On 1 October Minghetti telegraphed from Vienna to Visconti Venosta: "I cannot in any circumstances consent to your resignation. You have the duty and the right to insist on the execution . . . [blank space] of all that you have promised to Europe for the spiritual independence of the pope, accepting frankly the transfer of the capital as an inevitable necessity; all the rest you must impose on your colleagues. In the last resort I will appeal to the king rather than leave the government" (AE, *Ris.*, c. 51).

[51] Minghetti, personal letters to Visconti Venosta, 25 September, 22 and 27 October (Visconti Venosta archive). In a personal letter of Visconti Venosta to de Launay, 18 October, charging him to confer with Bismarck, Visconti Venosta says nothing about asking the German chancellor for his agreement, even in vague terms. In other words, Visconti Venosta played his hand rather well: he merely communicated the directives of the Italian government, leaving himself free to choose an appropriate response should there be grave protests.

[52] Cf. above, p. 178.

It was hard, and extremely delicate, work. By avoiding, at least until June, overly clear-cut formulations and overly precise commitments, Visconti Venosta gradually succeeded, as the European situation evolved, in protecting Italy's position even after the end of the Franco-Prussian War, in securing it against the chance of the other powers taking a firmly hostile position, in making Europe feel that, well, that is how things are, there is nothing more to be done; it was in the stars that Rome should be rejoined to Italy.[53]

What better proof could there be that fate was at work than the sight of a man like Visconti Venosta, so moderate, so aware of the responsibilities assumed by the Italian government in the face of Europe, so "put off" by the manner in which the Left went about, and by the weakness of some of his own colleagues, and above all so "put off" by the continuous connivance of Sella with the Left,[54] a man to whom alone (or virtually) the relative moderation of the various laws and provisions of the government was attributable,[55] accepting events that, as everyone knew, he had not wanted, but which in the end he was no longer able to block? No one could doubt that, within the cabinet, he was the champion of a policy of moderation: he was perhaps the only Italian politician to have a broad vision and precise ideas about the Roman question,[56] and his great speech of 30 January in the Chamber was truly worthy of the highest praise for the ability and the eloquence with which he had defended his point of view.[57] Undoubtedly he

---

[53] Paget, the English envoy at Florence, proffered this judgment of the course of events in a report to Lord Granville on 29 September 1870: "The Italian government started with very reasonable and moderate intentions when they invaded the Roman territory; Rome was not to be attacked, and the authority of the pope was to be preserved; the occupation was to be a purely military one confined to certain strategical points necessary for the preservation of order. . . . The government has not acted in bad faith, but it has been carried away by the force of circumstances, and by the popular current, resistance to which might have produced revolution." Halperin, *Italy and the Vatican at War*, p. 65, cites this passage, whose view he substantially shares. What it states is correct with regard to Visconti Venosta and Lanza, but not when applied to the government as a whole, since the government included Sella, a man who knew exactly what he was aiming at. In this connection there is a passage that seems to me noteworthy, in a letter written by Nino Bixio on 17 August 1870 to his wife, while on his way to Bologna; Bixio says that Sella has discussed very delicate matters with him, so delicate that they cannot be put into writing, "even though I am the man chosen by him to carry them out." Sella had something on his mind: it is probable that it was nothing less than the occupation of Rome (the text, first printed in Busetto, *Notizie del generale Nino Bixio*, p. 191, is now published in its entirety in E. Morelli, ed., *Epistolario di Nino Bixio* 3:496–97 [Rome, 1949]). Note too in this connection that Bixio was attached to the expeditionary force, in command of the second division, without the knowledge and against the express desire of General Cadorna (R. Cadorna, *La liberazione di Roma nell'anno 1870 ed il plebiscito*, pp. 61, 66, 531 ff.); and cf. C. Ricotti, *Osservazioni al libro di Raffaelle Cadorna: La liberazione di Rome nell'anno 1870* (Novara, 1889), pp. 29 ff.; Ricotti counters the hostile comments about Bixio made by Cadorna and fully acknowledges the ability Bixio showed in grasping "the very delicate concept of the mandate he received"—one almost hears the voice of Sella!

[54] Thus the Austro-Hungarian envoy to Florence, Baron Kübeck, in informing Beust of the resignation of Visconti Venosta over the Ruspoli amendment (report, 10 February 1871; SAW, *P.A.*, XI/77, no. 11 B).

[55] Kübeck, report, 14 February 1871, on the question of article 7 of the law of Guarantees (SAW, *P.A.*, XI/77, no. 13 A).

[56] Kübeck, report, 10 March 1871 (SAW, *P.A.*, XI/77, no. 19 A).

[57] Kübeck, report, 4 February 1871 (SAW, *P.A.*, XI/77, no. 9 B).

lacked energy;[58] and too often he was left contrite by faits accomplis or methods that ran counter to his own notions, by things now difficult or impossible to change.[59] Undoubtedly, as an Italian, he was also a "Machiavellian," and at times there might arise the suspicion that he was playing a scripted part in a well-choreographed production.[60] But withal he was the rock of order, the ivory tower of wisdom in a cabinet too often manipulated by that radical (for Vienna and Paris) Quintino Sella;[61] and the fact that he himself acknowledged that a less abrupt transition might have been conceivable, an intermediate solution to the Roman question found, his lament that the government had given way before popular pressure[62] made it all the harder to object to the concluding part of his reasoning, which was that the rapid march of external events (the Franco-Prussian War) had accelerated an extreme solution of the Roman question, that it was impossible now to turn back, and that any bargaining was unthinkable. All that could be done now was to surround the pope with honors and obedient attentions, give him the sense that he was entirely untrammeled on the spiritual plane, and avoid friction. On this point the Italian minister was ready to take into account the wishes of the other powers, to receive their opinions, even to anticipate their intentions by speaking first of the utility of an ongoing exchange of ideas among the various governments. It was the same where the transfer of the capital was concerned: since events had precipitated the solution, the only thing left was to live with the consequences, while proceeding with prudence and circumspection.[63]

In meetings he assumed that confidential and friendly tone so welcome to an interlocutor, who is easily persuaded in this fashion that he enjoys the minister's

---

[58] Kübeck, personal letter to Beust, 12 November 1870 (SAW, *P.A.*, XI/76). The same opinion is relayed by the French diplomats, especially Lefebvre de Béhaine, who actually says that both the weak king and his weaker ministers are no more than fronts for the radical element (report, 4 March 1871, no. 40; AEP, *C.P., Rome*, t. 1050, fol. 33. And cf. too the reports of Choiseul, 28 May and 20 June 1871, nos. 101, 106; ibid, *C.P., Italie*, t. 382, fols. 80 and 142).

[59] Kübeck, report, 18 March 1871 (SAW, *P.A.*, XI/77, no. 21 A).

[60] On 23 December Kübeck, in a personal letter to Beust, gave the following portrait: "Visconti is a true Italian, in the better sense. He is cooler, more discreet, and more dependable than most of his compatriots in official positions, but he instinctively practices Italian, meaning more or less Machiavellian, politics. He has a supple character that tends to find a way around large difficulties by means of expedients and negotiated compromises. He does not lack convictions or intelligent political schemes, but he does not always have the energy to see things through and, in the absence of initiatives of his own, he easily allows himself, even against his better intentions, to be influenced by his more or less radical colleagues. Though this may be only a role that he has accepted, he nevertheless carries it out well and thoroughly" (SAW, *P.A.*, XI/76).

[61] Kübeck, personal letter to Beust, 23 December 1870, cited in the previous note. Thiers also had "complete faith in the wisdom and fairness of Visconti Venosta," whom he too considered a guardian of order within the Italian government (Luzzatti, *Memorie* 1:339). Sella, in contrast, was rather deaf to counsels of moderation because of the anti-Catholicism he had picked up at university in Germany, and because of his links with the Left (Rothan, report, 6 April 1871, no. 87; AEP, *C.P., Italie*, t. 381, fols. 350v ff.); Rothan claims to have persuaded him to be more moderate.

[62] Statements of Visconti Venosta to Rothan (Rothan, *L'Allemagne et l'Italie* 2:280) and to Kübeck (cf. the following note).

[63] Statements of Visconti Venosta to Kübeck on 13 April 1871 (Kübeck, report, 14 April 1871; SAW, *P.A.*, XI/77, no. 28 A).

good graces and has free access to the *arcana imperii*.[64] Others' points of view were admitted, and he confessed that it might perhaps have been possible to avoid such and such an outcome, if only . . . the march of events were not so rapid and pressing. He would hint, sometimes in a veiled fashion, sometimes openly, at *les événements*, the force of things and circumstances, incumbent fate which overshadows individual men. "When a superior force dominates events, twist them as you will, they will always arrange themselves in the same pattern."[65] This was one of the trumps in the diplomatic game played by Visconti Venosta, and the best of it is that he believed in what he was saying.

It was a game, in sum, made all of finesse, chiaroscuro, implication, of calculated surrender to friendly confidentiality, as though his interlocutor, more than the representative of a foreign state, were a friend.[66] And the game was admirably kept afloat when necessary by another quality that Visconti Venosta had retained from his youth, when he had seemed a sorrowing angel: the precious ability "to be moved at the right time, but without committing himself to anything."[67]

Certain it is that between the autumn of 1870 and the spring of 1871, as the international situation fell into place, the game succeeded, and was precious for the country. It consisted in proceeding step by step

> along a way already laid out, shrewdly probing the terrain, almost refusing to trust in the written word anymore and preferring by far to influence foreign affairs through pieces of domestic legislation, or by insinuations of a personal and intimate character.

> Indeed one is forced to admit that this cabinet, so lackadaisical in the eyes of the impatient, proved very habile in exploiting circumstances whose concourse was singularly favorable to it. After having progressively drawn in the circle of its promises accordingly as the degree of compulsion it was under fell (the circulars of the chevalier Visconti Venosta and the parliamentary debates both testify to this), the government in the end used the transfer of its seat as a device to force the hands of the other states. Once assured of the adhesion of the other powers to his timid prospectus of 8 June last, the minister of foreign affairs naturally desired to profit from the occasion by having the king make his appearance at Rome surrounded by the diplomatic corps. If his goal was not entirely achieved, if the two great Catholic states did not choose to give the presence of their envoys the force of a gesture that could be

---

[64] Diplomats found Visconti Venosta very congenial; even Mme Rattazzi acknowledges this (*Rattazzi et son temps* 2:392). And for his ability to deal with journalists see Steed, *Mes souvenirs* 1:106–107

[65] Visconti Venosta to Nigra, 26 April 1885 (Visconti Venosta archive). In 1870 "the superior force was the immediate and absolute military prevalence of Prussia." In the case of Rome, events unfolded "following the logic of the fatality inherent in all institutions [i.e., the papacy] that are unable to change" (Visconti Venosta to Cadorna, 12 April 1871; AE, *Ris.*, c. 51).

[66] In dealing with Choiseul, which required the patience of Saint Anthony, Visconti Venosta attempted to cure him of his fixations (such as that Italy was hostile to France) by being "friendly and effusive" (Visconti Venosta, private letter to Nigra, 20 June 1871; Visconti Venosta archive).

[67] Rothan, *L'Allemagne et l'Italie* 2:90.

interpreted as the consecration of a principle, that was not for want of subtle maneu-vers, and even sudden surprises, both of which were part of the Italian approach.[68]

This rapid but telling sketch made by the Austro-Hungarian chargé d'affaires, Count Zaluski, on 22 July 1871, was truly an exact likeness and at the same time constituted well-warranted praise for the diplomatic style of Visconti Venosta and the approach he employed in the winter of 1870–71.

He was not, certainly, a great statesman,[69] but an able, expert, calm negotia-tor, a diplomat of the old school, a minister with an ample European range who knew how to render great services to his country. "The indolence that dominates him in everything he does"[70] was then transformed into an excellent tactical weapon. The motto with which his adversaries designated his policy, *inertia sapientia*,[71] became, contrary to what they intended, a political eulogy in these circumstances. Few knew as he did how to *voir venir*, to use an expression belonging to the language of the old diplomacy: to let things unfold according to their own internal drive, to give full play to the "salutary effect" of time, which he often liked to say he employed as a collaborator,[72] and wait until a favorable moment presented itself out of this unfolding and these salutary effects to step in with a helpful negotiation, a confidential accord, or at least a friendly exchange, by means of which things could be swung gently round to the desired end, and the torrent directed away from the precipice toward which it was rushing into a placid pool in which the last traces of foaming spume would subside.

His style of action and the tactical approach he adopted formed a bond be-tween Emilio Visconti Venosta and the classic tradition of European diplomacy, from the time of Kaunitz and Metternich. But even if we leave aside style and method in order to penetrate more deeply into his mental world, we are still struck at once by a number of substantial affinities with the high traditions of the Restoration and post-Restoration periods. To be precise, we are struck by his

---

[68] SAW, *P.A.*, XI/78, no. 53 A.

[69] Still, certain assessments that appear in Cataluccio, *La politica estera di E. Visconti Venosta* (pp. 7, 75–76, and another misguided statement on p. 111) about his lack of breadth, and especially about his cramped vision of Italy's position in European life, cannot be accepted. The exact opposite is true (cf. as well Maturi, "Un buon europeo: Emilio Visconti Venosta"). Other assessments made by Cataluccio are accurate (pp. 8–9, 113), and I agree with them. Cf. too the opinion of E. Serra, "Emilio Visconti Venosta e il 'colpo di timone' alla politica estera italiana," *Nuova Antologia* (January 1949): 42; but especially the high praise that came from a very superior journalist, Wickham Steed, *Mes souvenirs* 1:105 ff.

[70] Guido Borromeo to Minghetti, 29 March 1871 (BCB, *Carte Minghetti*, cart. XVI, fasc 4). Later, in 1896, Rudiní complained to Farini about the irresolution and fitfulness of Visconti Venosta: "If I had not stood in for him, if I had not composed his telegrams, we would never have concluded anything" (Farini, *Diario*, MRR, under 28 September 1896). This was an exaggeration, to say the least; but even Martini complained, in January 1901, that he had sent telegram after telegram to Visconti Venosta from Asmara about matters that required a prompt decision, without receiving the least reply (Martini, *Lettere*, p. 367).

[71] In addition to the parliamentary debates, cf. for example the election speech (*Discorso*) of Duke Gabriele Colonna di Cesarò (one of the systematic opponents in the Chamber of the govern-ment's foreign policy), delivered on 10 November 1874 at Aragona (pp. 6 and 9).

[72] Cf. for example this statement in the Chamber on 14 May 1872: "whether in certain questions it might be a good idea for us to employ time as our collaborator" (*A.P., Camera*, p. 2119).

"European" feeling for politics, the absolute and sincere conviction, first that there were no isolated problems in the modern world because they overlapped with one another in such a way that no part could be isolated and fixed without serious repercussions for the whole (and this was a fact that not even those determined to revolutionize the status quo, the lovers of novelty at any cost, would have been able to deny); and second and most important, that because of the inevitable concatenation of events, the freedom of action of every one of the powers had, at a certain point, to be limited by a sense of the general "expediency." The general expediency had been, and continued to be, expressed in the notions of European "equilibrium" and the "concert" of the great powers: these were really two elements of a single notion, for they had begun to converge in 1814, when Castlereagh and Metternich had sought a guarantee of equilibrium and found it in the accord among the great powers, the essential precondition for the liberty and security of Europe and the safeguarding of the peace.

In consequence, Visconti Venosta believed "that the nations do not live cut off from the world: the foreign policy and the domestic policy of a great state, as a result of their natural consequences and their natural relations, touch on the complex of interests and opinions that are interwoven in the European consortium." This after all was simply a statement of fact; he further believed, and this was both his hope and his aim, that to cut itself off from the others and to neglect solidarity was not in general "a good moral regime" for a nation.[73] Italy in particular, which could not separate its interests "from the general interests of Europe,"[74] ought to become, like England, "a peaceful and well-calibrated force within the consortium of nations," conducting itself in such a way that the government in Rome could take credit for protecting the interests "of the liberty and equilibrium of Europe."[75] These two terms were inseparable,[76] especially in the case of Italy, which was one of those countries "that cannot make a place for themselves and develop their own future except in a Europe where there exists a certain equilibrium of forces."[77]

And it was because liberty and equilibrium in Europe were inseparable that the hegemony of this or that nation was feared, that there was revulsion for the methods and goals of Napoleon I,[78] the evil genius of Europe, the Satan to whom

---

[73] Speech to the Chamber, 27 November 1872 (*A.P., Camera*, p. 3387).

[74] Speech to the Chamber, 19 August 1870 (*A.P., Camera*, p. 4027).

[75] Speech to the Senate, 24 August 1870 (*A.P., Senato*, p. 1230). The same notion appears in the debate in the Chamber on 19 August (*A.P., Camera*, p. 4029), and in his replies to Scialoja and Cialdini on 3 August: "Italy is called on to take its place within the great solidarity of the peaceful interests of Europe . . . the principal interest of Europe and of Italy . . . we . . . like all the other powers that cannot separate the interests of their own policy from the general conditions of European equilbrium" (ibid., pp. 997–98).

[76] Cf. as well his speech to the Chamber on 19 August 1870, about all the questions that involve the "equilibrium and liberty of Europe" (*A.P., Camera*, p. 4028).

[77] Visconti Venosta, private letter to Robilant, 1 July 1875 (published in Salvemini, "La politica estera della Destra" [1925], p. 194). These confidential statements fully confirm the sincerity of the ideas he expressed in public speeches, parliamentary debates, and elsewhere on various occasions.

[78] Cf. the letter to Robilant, 1 July 1875, cited in the previous note: "excessive and unnatural, hence ephemeral, combinations that call to mind those with which Napoleon I made and unmade his peace settlements."

one could only utter a vigorous *vade retro*. This revulsion was characteristic of the whole of European diplomacy from Metternich to Visconti Venosta, but not of Bismarck, with whom the methods of the French emperor, and to some extent his plans as well, were widely identified. This was the reason that mistrust of Bismarck's Germany was never entirely allayed, for to give it its head might entail the transformation of Europe into a fief of Germany and Russia.[79]

Even the principle of nationality Visconti Venosta now wished to see limited in its practical application, so that it did not become the spark of a general conflagration. The feeling for various interests, for the general expediency, the "European" feeling, arose to curb the love of country that had been the exclusive and overwhelming ideal of his youthful years as a conspirator, and which was certainly a living flame that still burned inside him.[80]

But those years were very distant now, for the Europeanism of Visconti Venosta the minister had become totally different from the Europeanism of Mazzini; it was one with the Europeanism of the Italian moderates, being very similar, for example, to that of Bon Compagni, and to the Europeanism of the politicians and diplomats of the Restoration and the July Monarchy. At bottom this very fact, as we have already had occasion to state, constituted a hidden bond between Visconti Venosta, a rebel in the flower of his student years against the Austria of Metternich, and Metternich himself. On the other hand, if respect for the formula of European equilibrium and the concert of the powers flowed down to Visconti Venosta from the world of the diplomats and politicians of 1814–15 and the Restoration, other fundamental strands of his thought, indeed its fundamental strand, which was that of liberty, led back to quite other sources.

Of course it was necessary to safeguard European equilibrium, not for the sake of suffocating with force the intimate aspirations of peoples and imposing authoritarian regimes, but because only by safeguarding equilibrium, and thus peace, was it possible to salvage the great ideal of the age, the ideal of liberty. Here the positions were reversed with respect to those of Metternich, for instance, and became instead very much like those of Gladstone: as with Gladstone, foreign policy itself was meant to express the sense of liberty, to be its fulfillment.[81]

This was a liberty that had, of course, practical bounds to its application, that was meant to find expression in the work of an intelligent conservative party, a liberty suited to "maintaining order, defending the honor, the morality, and the sincerity of liberal institutions," a liberty such that through it a program of liberal

---

[79] From the same letter, 1 July 1875: if Germany conquers France in a new war, "the probable result would be a Europe in which the west would belong to Germany and the east to Russia." And note too his fears about excessive German power and arrogance in 1877, at the moment of Crispi's voyage, fears which he expressed in a letter to Minghetti on 13 October 1877 (cited above, ch. 3, n. 23; published in Maturi, "Un buon europeo"). What he feared was "interpreting the policy of allying ourselves with Germany in such a way that we necessarily fall into absolute dependence on it, and become an element not of peace in Europe, but a source of fear and peril."

[80] On the "Europeanism" of Visconti Venosta, cf. the acute observations in Maturi, "Un buon europeo," which includes Visconti Venosta's emotional declarations to Minghetti about Italy.

[81] Cf. above, pp. 129 ff. On Gladstone and the other English liberals, cf. F. R. Flournoy, "British Liberal Theories of International Relations (1848–1898)," *Journal of the History of Ideas* 7, no. 2 (April 1946): 195 ff.

progress and social conservatism could be actuated. But within these limits his faith in liberty was untarnished and fearless: liberty "which is far from the spirit of intolerance or revolutionary violence, but which is inspired by respect for all rights."[82] He was indeed a conservative, and very much an opponent of the radicals, who apart from anything else were guilty, with their lack of measure and style, of transforming election meetings into contests of insult and outrage, fomenting in the masses "a deleterious sentiment of accusation and suspicion, not just against one or two individuals, but against all the classes that govern."[83] But he was not a reactionary; he did not wish to limit the sphere of parliamentary government and return to the Statuto, as Sonnino would by the end of the century—Sonnino, so much more avant-garde than Visconti Venosta around 1880, so much more conservative twenty years later. To those like Carlo Morini who deplored the substitution of the parliamentary regime for a constitutional one,[84] Visconti Venosta replied that Italy had been created through liberty and could be preserved only through liberty. If someone had asked Cavour

> through what regime he governed Piedmont so gloriously, he would have replied: through the parliamentary regime. . . . I do not know what the future holds for parliamentary government, I do not know into what political forms future societies will settle. But if parliamentary government is a difficult government, if it has many imperfections like all human creations, if it reflects the bad as well as the good qualities of the national character, up to the present it is still, within the framework of a constitutional monarchy at least, the system that best guarantees public freedoms, and renders a country that knows how to take advantage of it master of its own destiny. I believe that in Italy the parliamentary regime imparts to the government a force capable of protecting order and resolving conflicts threatening to national unity that it would not find in an Assembly endowed merely with limited representative privileges.[85]

Were there drawbacks? Of course there were. And like Minghetti and Jacini, Visconti Venosta also pointed to their origin in the coexistence of parliamentary government and administrative centralization, two institutions that could not be

---

[82] Visconti Venosta, speech to the Chamber of 14 May 1872 (*A.P., Camera*, p. 2119).

[83] Visconti Venosta, personal letter to Raffaelle De Cesare, undated but from the early months of 1895 (Visconti Venosta archive).

[84] Morini expressed these ideas in various writings, including *Corruzione elettorale* (Milan, 1894), *Corruzione parlamentare, Il potere regio in Italia* etc.; cf. as well *La decadenza del sentimento monarchico in Italia* (Florence, 1900).

[85] Visconti Venosta, letter to Morini, undated but 1895, concerning the volume *Corruzione elettorale* (Visconti Venosta archive). It is worth noting that after the events of May 1898, Visconti Venosta abandoned the Rudiní cabinet, causing a ministerial crisis. Giolitti even called him one of the "elements of the Left" in the cabinet, with Zanardelli and others (Giolitti, *Memorie* 1:140). This is going too far, especially since Visconti Venosta explained his resignation as a protest against Zanardelli's plan to take the government's *exequatur* away from the archbishop of Milan, which amounted to a violation of the principle of "a free church in a free state," the classic principle of the Cavourian moderates. Far from consensus, there was dissent between Visconti Venosta and Zanardelli (M. Rosi, *L'Italia odierna*, vol. 2, t. 3 [Turin, 1926], p. 1982; and esp. Steed, *Mes souvenirs* 1:116; L. Albertini, *Venti anni di vita politica* 1:15 [Bologna, 1950]. But it is certain in any case that on a fundamental principle of liberty, Visconti Venosta refused to budge on this occasion.

linked without reciprocally corrupting one another. "We have universal suffrage, the parliamentary regime, and administrative centralization. Out of the mixture of these three elements the race of hack politicians is born and prospers." But these evils he felt could be remedied with a thoroughgoing reform of the administrative structure, without altering in the least the parliamentary regime, the palladium of liberty. Without liberty, so much for Italy.

This faith was so strong, continual, and undisguised that it transfigured to a certain extent the image of Visconti Venosta, revealing beneath the veneer of the versatile and expert diplomat a firm conscience and unshakable solidity of conviction. So it was that he, whose style earned him the right to be raised to the hall of fame of the pure diplomats, gained a quite different and unforeseen prominence, and turned out to be, above all, a figure with a solid, sharp moral profile. We might put it this way: the content of the ideas of the minister of foreign affairs elevated his methods to loftier realms, gave a novel touch to his style. This man who was all finesse, shades of meaning, sense of limitations, all accommodation and accord, a man disposed to temper, conciliate, rise above factional resentment,[86] suddenly stiffened when it came to principles, became hard and stubborn, conceded nothing more,[87] with a firmness and irrevocability of purpose of which others would not perhaps have thought him capable. His moral world was a very firm one and was also permeated by a sentimental vein that did much to offset the aridity of pure reasoned calculation. Hence, just as he never forgot the France of Solferino, creating for himself a permanent reputation of being a Francophile, or as his adversaries put it, of being "tarred with French pitch,"[88] likewise on the most general level he never allowed the faith of his youth, which continued to be the faith of the mature man, to be blemished even remotely.

Liberty, peace, and civilization: for him these things were not "big high-sounding words" forged by the English for consumption by the stupidity of the continentals, as they were called by the most eminent of his colleagues, Bismarck,[89] nor was Europe simply the *notion géographique* of the iron chancellor. And it was with the hard and skeptical Prince Bismarck that the moral values and the sensibility of Visconti Venosta were destined to collide. At Berlin in September 1873 the German chancellor got on well with Minghetti while Visconti Venosta was much less to his liking.[90] This was not fortuitous: the antipathy was fully returned by the Italian, who confessed to a friend that Bismarck was "not a man I would want as the constant companion of my strolls."[91] Everything in the

[86] "An opposition can adapt itself to circumstances, it can suspend its activity, it can even cooperate patriotically"; what is needed is "a lofty political personality, conciliatory, faithful to principles, superior to the lesser ties of party" (Visconti Venosta, letter to Rudiní, undated but January–February 1895; Visconti Venosta archive).

[87] About Visconti Venosta's stubbornness in certain ideas, Codronchi speaks as well (Farini, *Diario*, MRR, under 12 March 1898).

[88] Farini, *Diario*, MRR, under 4 June 1898.

[89] Bismarck, *Erinnerung und Gedanke*, in *Die Gesammelten Werke* 15:317, 321, 323 (in the Italian translation [Turin, 1898], *Pensieri e ricordi* 2:98, 105, 108).

[90] About Bismarck's antipathy for Visconti Venosta, Radowitz, *Aufzeichnungen und Erinnerungen* 1:279, and Bülow, *Memorie* 4:343, are in agreement. Cf. as well the following note.

[91] Wimpffen, Austrian envoy at Rome, personal letter to Andrássy, 27 December 1873 (SAW,

two men was antithetical: from diplomatic style to ideas, from methods to purposes.

In 1870, when Bismarck's policy was in triumph thanks to the arms of Moltke, even then Visconti Venosta—and here especially the label of cautious calculator given him by Bülow appears singularly inadequate—had publicly reasserted at Milan his faith in the power of morality. Of course, he said, it was always possible to rupture "the bond of moral duress contained in European public opinion with an appeal pure and simple to force"; force simplifies many questions of foreign policy. But not the least of the many merits of Cavour was that of having imparted to our Risorgimento a sincerely liberal tradition: "our policy has always been to seek the support of the great moral forces of opinion."[92]

The polemical note here was explicitly directed against those Italians of the Left who believed that after 20 September they were free to treat the pope just like any parish priest or country chaplain, without regard to the sentiments of the Catholic world. But he was also aiming over the heads of Crispi, Oliva, and company, who admired and extolled Bismarckian methods of force; more than just the Roman question, his remarks embraced all the problems of Europe, including the Franco-Prussian War and the German claim to Alsace-Lorraine, claims that at that moment were being opposed in print by Visconti Venosta's spiritual comrades—Bonghi in *La Perseveranza* and the *Nuova Antologia*, Dina in *L'Opinione*. It was one of those admonitions "directed at daughter-in-law so that mother-in-law will comprehend," in other words intended not for the ostensible recipient alone; and in any case it was an admonition that expressed a way of understanding life and politics at the antipodes from the way they were understood by the German chancellor. Visconti Venosta was using indirect and veiled language; yet in his speech there emerged clearly, for those capable of understanding and drawing the parallel between what was taking place in Italy and what was taking place in France, a fundamental antithesis between the Italian national movement, with its liberalism, and the German national movement.

The moral power of public opinion imposed a bond. On no grounds, therefore, even during the gravest crises of national life, would there be any lapse, even momentarily, from liberal principles, or any resort to reactionary methods, he was later to say in a speech concerning relations with the papacy.[93] At the time he did so, Bismarck was preparing the *Kulturkampf* in Germany, preparing to use force in ecclesiastical and religious problems. What a contrast between Visconti Venosta's stance and that of the German chancellor, who was so much greater as a statesman but had such a narrower horizon of ideals!

The fact is that here Visconti Venosta was really, with Bonghi, the frankest and

---

P.A., XI/81; cited in Sandonà, *L'irredentismo nelle lotte politiche* 1:104). In the margin, Andrássy penciled a note: "Bismarck spoke to me about Visconti Venosta in virtually the same terms." The same information is found in a report of Tiby, the French chargé d'affaires, 21 January 1874, no. 7: "The Prussian, said M. Visconti Venosta, is a *compagnon de promenade* with whom it is not always very pleasant to stroll" (AEP, *C.P., Italie*, t. 389, fol. 49v).

[92] In his speech of 9 November 1870 at the banquet of the Patriotic Society.

[93] Speech to the Chamber, 14 May 1872 (*A.P., Camera*, p. 2118).

most direct spokesman for Italian moderatism, to which "Bismarckism" was so repugnant for the way it had brought European morality down "to the lowest level it has ever reached at any time." Well might the new system initiated by him have for its motto "iron and fire."[94] If it were not for the difference in stature, we might compare Visconti Venosta, on the spiritual plane, to Gladstone, who was, with Bismarck, the leading statesman of Europe at that time, but who stood in total and irrevocable opposition of ideas and principles to Bismarck: Gladstone, whom the Italian moderates so cherished for the depth and serenity of his liberal beliefs, his unspotted "virginity of soul,"[95] the profundity of his Christian feeling, a pure eternal spring from which there gurgled up continually an unruffled strength, a belief in justice; and whom they cherished for the love of liberty that was the cornerstone of British foreign policy. Gladstone too, in fact Gladstone above all, was inimical to Bismarck, who wound up hating him with a tenacious, angry, implacable hatred, and who let himself be steered blindly by this hatred between 1880 and 1885, even going against what the coldly calculating reason of state by which he was ordinarily guided would have enjoined. For his part the man from Hawarden felt no less antipathy for the iron chancellor, whom he called the "devil" (if we can believe the story told about the exclamation that escaped from the Briton as he stood before one of the canvases in which Lenbach had portrayed the gigantic and stern Prussian Junker[96]). Two worlds were in total antithesis, that of liberty and that of force, and Visconti Venosta belonged to the world of Gladstone. Bismarck, with his usual flair, intuited this immediately and placed the man from the Valtellina in the ranks of the reprobate.

This openly acknowledged antithesis never left Visconti Venosta's soul, and it inspired the mistrust of the government in Berlin which he never ceased to feel and which was fully returned, then and later.[97] It also permeated, sometimes unconsciously, the action of the Italian government, which never let go of, or backed off an inch from, its principles, and in their defense was willing to face the public cooling of its relations with Berlin in 1874–75. In just this case, there suddenly loomed a very different figure behind Visconti Venosta the diplomat and man of complete ductility: a Visconti Venosta who was as hard as Sella, hard as a rock, not to be shaken from the cult of his ideals.[98] Where these were involved, he was in fact stiffer and more intractable even than his good friend

---

[94] Thus Bonghi in his celebrated essay on Bismarckism, which dates from 1871; in Bonghi, *Ritratti e profili di contemporanei* 3:150 and 161 (= vol. 6 in *Opere*).

[95] Thus Bonghi in his essay on Gladstone (*Ritratti e profili di contemporanei* 2:302 (= vol. 5 in *Opere*), and cf. 304).

[96] Cf. H. Michael, *Bismarck England und Europa* (Munich, 1930), p. 326.

[97] So much so that in March and July 1896, Bülow, ambassador at Rome at that time, put pressure on Di Rudiní and on Umberto I himself to prevent Visconti Venosta from being given the foreign ministry, and clarifications with Berlin were necessary, so suspect was the "Francophilia" of Visconti Venosta in the German capital (Farini, *Diario*, MRR, under the dates 7 March, 20 July, and 30 October 1896; 6 April 1899). And cf. as well Bülow's report of 26 March 1895, in which Visconti Venosta is designated, along with Bonghi and Prinetti, as one of the most tenacious adversaries of the Triple Alliance (*G.P.* 7, no. 1462).

[98] Visconti Venosta's "loftiness" of character is praised by, among others, a severe judge of such things, Ricasoli (*Lettere e documenti* 10:124).

Minghetti, one of the great champions of Italian liberalism, and yet, despite all his liberalism, his theories and his writings, less hostile to Bismarck, indeed a man to whom the chancellor warmed.[99] Minghetti felt less mistrust of Bismarck not because he believed in liberty less, but because he was more malleable than the diplomat Visconti Venosta.

In truth, while Visconti Venosta always appealed to the example and the precepts of Cavour, and asserted that he was continuing, within his more modest limits, Cavour's policies,[100] in him and in many of his friends, especially those from Lombardy, there was something less and something more than pure Cavour: or to put it another way, there was a mixture of Cavour and d'Azeglio. What I mean is that while these men had fully absorbed a stringent liberalism from Cavour, there was in them nevertheless a desire, even a need, for morality in political life, a "household" morality similar to that of any private individual, which brought them closer to d'Azeglio. Cavour's stringent liberalism had not prevented him from being somewhat careless of the means he used, even to combat the Mazzinians.[101] A great statesman, Cavour had followed the practice of all the great statesmen: he had not paused too long over the question of means, or delayed taking action because of moral scruples or the considerations of pure right dear to the "parliamentary puritans."[102] But however lofty the end might be, d'Azeglio, a gentleman before all else,[103] would never have approved certain means, for he too was convinced, like Ricasoli, that an honest end does not purify the means if they are less than honest.[104]

Problems of morality and the formation of character caused d'Azeglio a tribu-

---

[99] Here too there are matching reports in Radowitz and Bülow that the German chancellor warms to Minghetti.

[100] There is much testimony; cf. the reference he made to Cavour in the stormy session of the Chamber on 19 August, and in the Senate on 24 August 1870 (*A.P.*, *Camera*, p. 4026, *Senato*, p. 1231); and the preface to W. de la Rive, *Il conte di Cavour* (Italian translation: Turin, 1911), p. ix.

[101] Salvatorelli, *Pensiero e azione del Risorgimento*, pp. 176, 188.

[102] To Bon Compagni, who hesitated to carry out Cavour's instructions to maintain contact with the Tuscan conspirators against the grand-ducal court to which he himself was the accredited envoy of the king of Sardinia, Cavour repeated "that this was no time for scruples" (Martini, *Confessioni e ricordi*, pp. 4–5). In 1860, when Cardinal Cosimo Corsi, the archbishop of Pisa, was brought to Turin to account for his openly unpatriotic and even antistate activities, and held there for more than a month and a half, Cavour wrote to Ricasoli: "this action perhaps verges on illegality, but it is so justifiable politically, that I flatter myself the action will be approved even by the parliamentary puritans" (Ricasoli, *Lettere e documenti* 5:81).

[103] Santangelo pronounces a trenchant verdict on d'Azeglio: "a vocation more moral than political made him a political personage of the first rank at a time when morality and politics coincided" (Santangelo, *Massimo d'Azeglio politico e moralista*, p. 280). On the other hand Cognasso has recently written of d'Azeglio's "habitual cynicism" (*Vittorio Emanuele II*, p. 96), a verdict followed by Padre Pirri, *Pio IX e Vittorio Emanuele II*, pp. 119* and also 196 n. 7. But the charge, which originates in the well-known letter of d'Azeglio to the king of 29 April 1855, has been exhaustively refuted by Ghisalberti, "L'intervento di Massimo d'Azeglio nella crisi politico-religiosa del 1855," *Ricerche Religiose* 18 (1947): 40 ff.

As to the opinions of Padre Pirri on the "very shallow relief" of d'Azeglio's spiritual and moral personality ("Massimo d'Azeglio e Pio IX al tempo del quaresimale della moderazione," *Rivista di Storia della Chiesa in Italia* 3 [1949]: 191), it will be enough to observe that it is amply refuted by the influence—which was primarily moral in nature—that d'Azeglio had on many of the moderates, influence that was slow to fade.

[104] Ricasoli, *Carteggi* 2:60.

lation to which he increasingly tended to submit, haunted by the qualms of a Piedmontese about the new Italy, and subject to twinges of irritation at ideas and sentiments that he was no longer capable of understanding; it was a tendency that often veered away from intensely felt morality toward a kind of petty moralizing.[105] When he still played a part in politics, he had created the myth of the "gentleman" king, inventing the requisite persona for Vittorio Emanuele II, a persona that was really more characteristic of his own sensibility. Later he took on the role of national pedagogue[106] and proclaimed that, having made Italy, it was now necessary to make the Italians.

In his pedagogism, he sometimes seemed to be turning the deep moral lessons of Manzoni into chapters in a school textbook. Manzoni was the remote source of the currents from which all the moderates drank, the exemplary model of sublime and pensive humanity who, from the depths of his religious feeling, drew the force of his convictions and the uprightness of his actions. Theirs was a sort of moral *manzonismo* not dissimilar to literary *manzonismo*, though more serious and valid in its underpinnings than the latter.

The compulsion to behave always as a gentleman, to act with candor in politics and even in foreign policy, an area where the devil finds the best and most frequent opportunities to tempt the consciences of men with exciting lures,[107] had flowed from the author of the *Ricordi* to many another moderate and, having inspired the honest (very honest indeed and very d'Azeglio-like) La Marmora,[108] it was now having its effect on Visconti Venosta too. This influence, the influence of d'Azeglio, was less patent and less avowed, less easy to discern also, than the radiant, solar influence of Cavour, and for the most part it went unremarked at the time, as it has gone unremarked by posterity. But it was not the less compelling for that, and the attitude of Jacini, Casati, Alfieri di Sostegno when it came to Rome as the capital would be enough to prove the point, for here their attitude was linked directly to the writings and discourses of d'Azeglio.

This was another distinguishing criterion between, on the one hand, classic

---

[105] *La Perseveranza* noted this on one occasion, in the course of a debate with Vidari, who did not accept the thesis of Bonghi (that with the fall of the Second Empire, the September Convention fell ipso facto, hence the Italians were free to go to Rome), and asserted that a d'Azeglio would never have said such things. The writer for the paper replied that d'Azeglio had certainly been honest and upright, "but also . . . a little too narrow-minded for the conduct of human affairs. The fact is that honesty and uprightness, as he understood them in certain moments of ill humor, would not even have got us as far as the treaty of Zurich; luckily these two virtues do not have such a short range: otherwise—so impatient and subtle are men—they would have been well and truly done for" ("La convenzione del settembre," in *La Perseveranza* for 10 September 1870).

[106] This happy expression is Ghisalberti's, in the article "Doppia verità di Massimo d'Azeglio," in *Il Giornale d'Italia*, 4 February 1948.

[107] Bonghi asserted in 1886 that "if there were a people entirely composed of foreign ministers, it would lose its soul" ("La politica estera dell'Italia," *Nuova Antologia* 89 [16 September 1886]: 305).

[108] Cf. his statements on fair-mindedness and sincerity as "the best sureties of a good and sound politics," and on the duty in politics to pay greater attention to the morality of actions than to their legality (La Marmora, *Un po' più di luce*, pp. 120 and 89). It is characteristic of La Marmora that he branded the proverb *à corsaire corsaire et demi*, which Bismarck liked to use, as a piece of wickedness: so great was the antithesis between the two men, whom fate had brought together for a moment in 1866.

moderatism, which united the group descending from d'Azeglio with the Tuscans of Ricasoli's stamp, men raised in an environment dominated by moral and religious fervor and hence resolutely prepared to make public morality coincide completely with private morality,[109] and, on the other, the left wing of the Right, which was immune to nostalgia for the spirit of d'Azeglio or Lambruschini. The split will be apparent if we compare men like Visconti Venosta and Ricasoli with Quintino Sella: Sella was the true heir of the Cavourian tradition in all its aspects, in liberal sentiment but also in the resolve, boldness, and versatility of his political action, though as an individual he was one of the loftiest and most rigid moral figures that Italian history has known.[110] It is very significant that between Visconti Venosta and Sella there frequently occurred intervals of the sort of bad relations that in the case of Cavour and d'Azeglio had been perpetual, and which it fell to their friends Dina and Artom to try to alleviate, just as it had once fallen to Castelli to act as mediator between Cavour and d'Azeglio, persuading Cavour to put up with things in d'Azeglio's nature that were too rigid at times, at others too flaccid; and persuading d'Azeglio to adapt to that in Cavour which was too uninhibited and nimble.[111] It is significant as well that the more stiff-backed members of the Right, alluding to Sella's role in the question of Rome, deplored this Piedmontese school with its loose and somewhat hypocritical morality as a decadent offshoot of the school of Cavour: "it spread in the moral domain, and it scorned noble moral examples like Balbo, Alfieri (Cesare), and d'Azeglio, men who loved Italy as much as anyone has."[112]

Thus, from beneath the diplomatic veneer, there transpired in Visconti Venosta the seriousness and the solidity of a man of moral preoccupations. Like La Marmora, he too would never have admitted, or even allowed the thought, that it is sometimes necessary to "perform evil actions, for if not, one succeeds in nothing in this rotten world; *à corsaire corsaire et demi*," and he would certainly never have dreamed of including among his collaborators persons able to carry out "dirty" jobs.[113] He would never have accepted the precept of Cardinal Richelieu that it is one thing to be *homme de bien selon Dieu* and another *selon les hommes*,[114] and he steadfastly denied that there were two gospels, two moralities, the public and the private,[115] not being disposed to lose his soul in order to be the foreign minister.

Not that he was an abstract moralist or visionary. Far from it; he looked reality in the face and did not dream of Utopian kingdoms, or imagine republics and

---

[109] Cf. Finali, *La vita politica di contemporanei illustri*, pp. 17–18.

[110] Jemolo gives a beautiful and faithful portrait of him in *Chiesa e Stato in Italia*, p. 317.

[111] A. Mauri, "Cenni biografici," a preface to Castelli, *Ricordi*, p. 12.

[112] Letter of Giuseppe [Giovanni] Fabrizi to Ricasoli, 15 November 1870 (Ricasoli, *Lettere e documenti* 10:164–65).

[113] According to Bülow (*Memorie* 4:389), Bismarck expressed himself thus to Bülow *père* in regard to Holstein; cf. Gooch, "Holstein: Oracle of the Wilhelmstrasse," in *Studies in German History*, p. 404.

[114] Cf. the discerning remarks of A. Huxley in *L'eminenza grigia* (Italian translation: Milan, 1946), p. 171.

[115] On d'Azeglio, cf. Vaccalluzzo, *Massimo d'Azeglio*, p. 249.

principates as they ought to be, but saw them rather for what they were. One day when De Laveleye was preaching to him about the inutility of armed struggle between states and expressing the hope that international justice would soon come to be, since the prosperity of one state was the necessary condition of the prosperity of another, Visconti Venosta responded yes, yes, you are speaking golden words, I seem to be hearing Cobden and Henry Richard, your words are reason incarnate, but please cast an eye on the situation of Europe, and you will see an armed camp. Your reasoning assumes peaceful and rational peoples; perhaps the world will be like that at the end of the twentieth century, but meanwhile we are trying not to be swallowed up by the nineteenth.[116]

But the realism of Visconti Venosta, like that of all the moderates, also included the moral forces and the great tenets of idealism, the principles without which the political struggle would have seemed a mechanical game of ephemeral importance. This made it a realism very different from that of the new realists who were singing hosannas to Bismarck. Visconti Venosta's realism paid close attention to public opinion, to the country's state of mind: his appeal to the moral forces was not a mere propaganda trick, but responded to a deeper conviction. His whole attitude on the question of Rome in the two decisive months of August and September 1870 flowed from his deep-rooted persuasion that it was necessary to resolve the problem but still avoid violence at any cost,[117] and likewise to make sure that Italian interests were not set against the general interests of Europe, that the country did not "act in isolation, with cunning and violence."[118] Perhaps he was ingenuous, and he would certainly have accomplished nothing without the indispensable input of force from the Left: but his attitude flowed from concerns of an elevated kind, and it would ensure that the government's action in the following period embodied continuity and dignity. His entire policy in regard to the papacy after 20 September continued to be inspired by the principle of using moral means and shunning force, even when he was being pushed to use force not only by the Left in parliament but also by Prince Bismarck, and he remained firm in his conviction that the struggle with the church could be brought to a conclusion only by holding fast to the same liberal attitude that moderates and nonmoderates, Right and Left, were agreed in wanting to see applied to all other domestic questions, but which the Left wished to throw over when it came to dealing with the papacy.[119] It was a great merit of Visconti Venosta and of the

[116] De Laveleye, *Nouvelles lettres d'Italie*, p. 145.

[117] Cf. what he has to say in his speech to the Chamber on 19 August 1870 about his policy: "our belief is . . . that . . . the Roman question must be placed on a footing such that it can make further progress toward a solution. . . . [I]t may be . . . that the course we are following in our policy is a long one; it remains to be seen whether there is a shorter one, or whether there are only ones that can be called shorter simply because after a short distance they lead to an abyss" (*A.P., Camera*, p. 4027; cited above at ch. 5, n. 19). And in the Senate on 24 August, replying to Senator Siotto-Pintor, he said: "and what does he want? Does he want to go [to Rome] with a violent and immediate invasion, does he want to resolve the question with a concrete action, whatever it may be, carry out a violent and bloody conquest? This policy would have two great drawbacks" (*A.P., Senato*, p. 1231).

[118] Visconti Venosta, speech of 19 August 1870 in the Chamber, *A.P., Camera*, p. 4027.

[119] A representative example is his speech of 14 May 1872 in the Chamber, replying to the violent attack of the hon. Miceli: "We know that in Italy we would not get any closer to reconcilia-

Italian government that they avoided an Italian *Kulturkampf*, something to which they were goaded for years with ever-increasing acrimony by the Left in Italy, and from abroad by the government leaders in Berlin.

This, then, was the man to whom the task of guiding Italian policy in its relations with other states was assigned, the task of continuing, as he himself said, the program of Cavour: "that liberal and conservative policy that intends to progress toward the future, but to progress with confidence, that aims to adapt the means to the end, and the end to the means."[120] And to progress with confidence meant, according to a superb dictate of Cavour which Visconti Venosta recalled in his speech at Tirano, "not making big questions out of little questions. Secondary questions certainly have to be handled in such a way as to maintain the nation's rights and dignity intact, because that is never a trivial issue, but they have to be handled calmly, not allowed to get out of hand, or exceed the measure of real national interest that is involved."[121] It meant following a policy that did not deviate from its path, nor lose sight of its goal, at which it arrived with moderation and calm, without exciting the national susceptibility unnecessarily, "or making people suppose that the political life of the Italians is woven of abuses submitted to and offenses suffered." It meant not suspecting at every turn that the national dignity had somehow been affronted: an attitude found only among peoples lacking in seriousness and in true greatness.[122] With Visconti Venosta, it was ragged clamor, disorderly tumult, shrill public lugubriousness that bruised his very vivid sense of national dignity. His aloofness from declamation and his restrained modesty were bound to a much deeper sense of national pride than that of many loud demonstrators.[123] Opposed to raising questions of national dignity unnecessarily, he maintained that, once raised, they had to be dealt with, accepting all the possible consequences of the action taken—up to

---

tion, that indeed we would be postponing it, if we sought reconciliation in reactionary methods, and the renunciation of liberal principles. . . . [W]e do not intend to create reconciliation by any other route than that of liberty; of that liberty . . . that springs from respect for all rights, and therefore from respect from the least coercible and most sacred among them, which is that of religious conscience" (*A.P., Camera*, pp. 2118–19).

[120] In his commemoration of Carlo d'Adda, cited in Cataluccio, *La politica estera di E. Visconti Venosta*, p. 22.

[121] This wise counsel recurs a number of times in the speeches of Visconti Venosta; thus on 14 May 1872 in the Chamber, replying to the hon. Miceli, he says: "we did not want to complicate the question, we did not want to create conflicts that could be avoided on account of interests much less important than what we saw as the highest interest of the country. We applied to politics and the handling of public affairs the same norms of everyday prudence that are followed with success in the handling of private affairs" (*A.P., Camera*, p. 2121). On Visconti Venosta's ability to ignore secondary questions in order to concentrate on what was essential, cf. as well J. Laroche, *Quinze ans à Rome avec Camille Barrère (1898–1913)* (Paris, 1948), pp. 29–30.

[122] Visconti Venosta, speech to the Chamber, 27 November 1872 (*A.P., Camera*, p. 3385).

[123] Visconti Venosta, letter to his brother Giovanni, 20 July 1878: "Yet it remains true that the treaty of Berlin and its consequences have diminished and compromised the position that Italy had in the Orient. Now we have *meetings*! Such agitation has serious risks, and is gradually making Italy's diplomatic situation weak, isolated, foolish and confused. But even more than by the risks, I am put off by the ridiculous aspect, and the offense to any true and delicate sense of national pride and seriousness. It is painful to view this sort of politics spilling out of the cafés into the country at large" (Visconti Venosta archive). [*Translator's note:* The English word "meetings" is in the original.]

and including war.[124] This was his characteristic mode of action, to reflect at length ahead of time, but then, when the die was cast, not to swerve on any account.

Visconti Venosta's policy was liberal and European, peaceful and grounded in moral force, a policy alert to the dignity of the nation yet moderate and conciliatory, treating the inevitable incidents with calm, "taking them at their true worth, not with passion and spite," and refusing to transform little incidents into great questions in order not to "create the sort of situation that imposes itself as though fated, so that it later becomes almost impossible to explain how it came about."[125] He always kept a tight rein on policy in the foreign ministry, without letting himself be swayed by the suggestions of one or another of his agents abroad, and especially without letting himself be snared and dragged off course by the *furor consularis*,[126] the mania of consuls who were forever ready to see the whole universe contained in the territories entrusted to their care, and the safety of the country dependent on an energetic response to something like a brawl in a tavern between Italians and foreigners. Finally, his was a policy on which the din of the press did not have the slightest influence: the journalists of the other parties raised loud cries of indignation, and the minister let them do so, persevering in his chosen direction. It would later be seen, with rue, how precious in the conduct of affairs this refusal to mix up little questions with great ones, to complicate questions that were serious enough already with superfluous pettiness and formal vanity, as when foreign ministers let themselves be influenced by overexcited consuls, really was: even before Crispi, in the case of Tunis.

The new general secretary of the foreign ministry, Isacco Artom, was in complete intellectual and moral accord with his chief. The cabinet had raised him to this position, replacing Blanc, on 30 November 1870, at the same time it made Luzzatti general secretary of the Ministry of Agriculture, Industry, and Commerce.[127]

---

[124] "[T]he question of the *Orénoque* is a small one, if you wish, but it is one of those questions that touch the national susceptibility, and because it is of this nature, it cannot be raised except to be resolved. This is an affair in which, once it is on the table, the Italian government simply could not accept a *fin de non recevoir* [a rebuff]. If we made a formal request, we would necessarily be stating that we were prepared to accept all possible consequences" (Visconti Venosta, personal letter to Nigra, 17 August 1874; Visconti Venosta archive).

[125] Visconti Venosta, speech to the Chamber on 27 November 1872. Similar ideas appear in his speech to the Chamber on 14 May 1872 (*A.P., Camera*, pp. 3398 and 2121).

[126] Cf. the verdict of Visconti Venosta on the Italian and French consuls at Tunis, on their way of pumping up the questions they dealt with in order to increase their own personal importance (conversation with the French envoy, Fournier, April 1872, *D.D.F.*, 1st ser., 1:138: the phenomenon he describes reached a crescendo with the rivalry of Macciò and Roustan in 1879–80). In general, note what he writes to Nigra on 30 May 1871 about the French envoy, Choiseul: "he is very new and a little moody; he doesn't know what consuls are like in general, and the French consuls in particular. . . . [W]e too had consuls in France who used to send me packets of French newspapers full of insults to the king and to Italy. I said to Choiseul [who was complaining about the attitude of the Italian newspapers to France], 'I confess that . . . I pay little attention to newspapers'" (Visconti Venosta archive).

[127] ACR, *Verbali delle deliberazioni del Consiglio dei Ministri* 2:85 (cf. Lanza, *Le carte* 6:415).

Artom too came from the very heart of the school of Cavour, having been the private secretary and trusted collaborator of the great count.[128] He too was a firm liberal, committed to preserving the Cavourian tradition against tendencies of the Bismarckian type.[129] He too had that strain of conservatism that Visconti Venosta had, and was averse to impatience, sudden moves, and disruptive policies. Bound by close personal friendship to his minister, so much so that he became an alter ego,[130] he was a rare example of the meaning of affinity between a general secretary and a minister, of two becoming as one.[131] He was an acute and subtle spirit, not brilliant but sound,[132] cultivated, and with a comprehensive grasp of Italy's ecclesiastical policy from 1860 on. In fact, he had previously been the author of draft instructions for negotiations with the Roman curia in February 1861,[133] and in 1875 he engaged personally in a polemic with Treitschke over the law of Guarantees.[134] The gaunt Artom[135] bore the brunt of the international debates on the Roman question: the memoranda and dispatches intended to justify the attitude of the Italian government abroad were his drafts, with a few changes by Visconti Venosta.[136] In sum, he was a personage of great importance, even though he was not known to the public at large, a man whose ideas and methods were perfectly in tune with those of Visconti Venosta.

[128] Cf. in general Artom, *L'opera politica*, vol. 1.

[129] On 21 May 1884 he writes to Minghetti: ". . . reasons which mean that Cavour's concept of liberty is now rivaled by a species of *statolatry* in the style of Bismarck, which appears at one moment as state socialism, at another as the tyranny of the state over the church" (BCB, *Carte Minghetti*, cart. XXIV, fasc. 65). His disapproval of authoritarian methods also transpires in his remarks about Crispi: "you already know what the state of things is here. It is a dictatorship; indeed, as Biancheri was saying to me, a real abdication of parliament. This may have considerable advantages, as well as drawbacks and dangers that you can imagine for yourself. There is only one star shining in the Italian political firmament. No one even thinks of mounting any opposition" (Visconti Venosta to Nigra, 21 December 1887; AE, *Carte Nigra*).

[130] Artom himself says so in a letter to Nigra of 8 March 1872: "although Visconti is for me a friend much more than a minister, and has given me and continues to give me the most complete liberty" (AE, *Carte Nigra*). When it came time for him to leave office in March 1876, he wrote to Nigra that he was giving up "with some regret these offices where I lived for six years in intimate communion of ideas with Visconti and you" (31 March 1876; AE, *Carte Nigra*).

[131] Farini desired this; *Diario*, MRR, under 26 March 1899.

[132] See the high praise that Cavour had for him (d'Ideville, *Journal d'un diplomate en Italie*, p. 239). The French diplomat recounts that Cavour placed Artom clearly higher than Nigra, and that his opinion of the latter was in substance not very favorable. This cannot be accepted: we know from utterly reliable sources of the high esteem that Cavour had for Nigra: cf. Luzio, *Garibaldi, Cavour, Verdi*; pp. 265 ff.; A. Luzio, *Aspromonte e Mentana*, p. 60). As for Visconti Venosta, he said of his collaborator: "when not too pessimistic, he is a man of good counsel" (to Minghetti, 8 July 1874; BCB, *Carte Minghetti*, cart. 35 a).

[133] Cf. Artom, *L'opera politica* 1:181 ff., and Cavour, *La questione romana* 1:308 n. 2 and pp. 320 ff.

[134] The letter from Artom to Treitschke is in Artom, *L'opera politica* 1:196 ff.

[135] He describes himself thus in a letter to Nigra of 30 April 1877 (AE, *Carte Nigra*).

[136] Salata, *Per la storia diplomatica della questione romana* 1:272 ff., observes that Artom is the drafter of Visconti Venosta's important letter to de Launay of 21 March 1875.

Costantino Nigra

COSTANTINO NIGRA was the third member of this triad of friends who were summoned by fate to work together and to share the same purpose;[1] men who were placed flank to flank by destiny and by choice, who stood near one another,[2] then and later, not only in mind but also in spirit, who were united in habits of sentiment, and also by affinity of ideas and a lofty sense of duty.[3]

The bold and handsome Nigra, of 1858–59, the thirty-year-old sent by Cavour to Paris to sustain the difficult role that the marchese Villamarina was not up to; the trusted aide who in March 1859 had urged the maestro to force the hand of French opinion by means of a pronouncement at Modena or Bologna, or in the legations at least, interrupting at any cost the baneful grind of diplomacy and setting the match to the fuse,[4] who again in 1866 had exerted pressure on La Marmora to force him to commit himself to action and war;[5] the tall, blond, and elegant Nigra, with his wide, gleaming eyes,[6] a subtle and fortunate seducer of female hearts, a man capable of bringing a touch of worldly glamour to politics by reciting to the Empress Eugénie, one evening in 1863 on the placid pond at

---

[1] Artom to Nigra, 29 September 1870: "the accord that in general exists among us on the most important questions is such as to make an exchange of phrases almost superfluous." And on 10 June 1872: "how often I wish I could ask you for your advice!" (AE, *Carte Nigra*). When in June 1871 Nigra wished to leave the Paris legation (see below), Visconti Venosta wrote him on the 20th: "By now we cannot leave things half done, and you and I and our friend Artom all have a common fate" (Visconti Venosta archive). Nigra responded on 24 June, recalling in turn the common friendship "of our good Artom, who esteems and loves both of us, as we love and esteem him."

[2] In 1898, for example, Visconti Venosta, who wished to leave the Rudiní cabinet, consulted Artom, who advised him to sound out Nigra, and Nigra answered that Visconti Venosta ought to remain at his post (Farini, *Diario*, MRR, under 22 March 1898).

[3] See Nigra's generous and frank declaration to Visconti Venosta, when the two men were discussing the former's leaving Paris: "Above all I must premise a consideration on which I do not doubt that you will be fully in agreement with me. In your relations with me and in my relations with you, we have always taken, and take, as a basis, the interest of our country in the first place, and our reciprocal and now long friendship in the second, with the latter naturally subordinate to the former" (Nigra to Visconti Venosta, 24 June 1871; Visconti Venosta archive). And earlier, on 20 November 1870, in writing to Artom that he did not accept for the moment the post in Vienna, which Visconti Venosta had offered him, Nigra said: "[W]hat I forgot to say to Visconti, and what I beg you to tell him in my name, is that now and always, I will never make an issue out of postings *with him*, and that when he believes that there is a true state interest, or a parliamentary necessity in favor of the great party to which he, you, and I have always belonged, not only can he freely dispose of the post that was entrusted to me, as is proper, but he will find me ready to accept any other, whatever it is, even though it might not suit me personally; this is something I probably would not do with another minister" (ibid.).

[4] Cavour, *Il Carteggio Cavour-Nigra* 2:87, 126, 133, 151.

[5] Cf. La Marmora, *Un po' più di luce*, pp. 119, 122, 170, 295, 303.

[6] He is so described, under the date 1864, by the Countess Savio in a *Giornale* sent by Raffaele De Cesare to Nigra (De Vecchi archive). Cf. as well Ch. zu Hohenlohe-Schillingsfürst, *Denkwürdigkeiten* 2:126; and F. Tommasini, "Erinnerungen an Wien (1900–1912)," *Berliner Monatshefte* 19 (July 1941): 470.

Fontainebleau, a Venetian barcarole;[7] Nigra, who was surrounded by an aura in which legend and story were melded, who was the object, as no other member of the Italian diplomatic corps was, of sympathy and antipathy, of high regard and harsh criticism;[8] Nigra, in our period, was a man whose style was very much like that of Visconti Venosta.

He had seemed to many, if not exactly a cynic of the stamp of Talleyrand, a man at any rate with a cold drive to succeed, both as politician and as lover, indifferent to the means he used. Instead he proved to be a man of fairness, bold perhaps but always fair,[9] able to be frank and straightforward while artfully employing shades of meaning and the charms of eloquence.[10] He was also capable of what Talleyrand would scornfully have called sentimentalism, as in his emotional attachment to the Napoleonic dynasty.[11] Ever since 1868 he had foreseen

[7] On this episode, narrated by Mérimée, cf. Nigra, *Poesie originali e tradotte*, ed. A. d'Ancona, p. 29. But Eugénie interrupted him brusquely (Salomon, *L'ambassade de Richard de Metternich à Paris*, p. 63; R. Sencourt, *L'imperatrice Eugenia* [Italian translation: Milan-Rome, 1932], p. 138). There is no need to touch here on the relationship between the empress and Nigra, because at this point history tends to vanish into legend. It will be enough to observe that one kind of exaggeration has recently been offset by the contrary exaggerations of Sencourt, according to whom Nigra inspired Eugénie not with tenderness but with hatred. He is contradicted not only by the memory that Nigra always held of the empress, who had made him a gift of a beautiful miniature of herself (R. De Cesare, "Gli ultimi anni di Costantino Nigra," in *Il Giornale d'Italia* for 4 December 1915), and by the visit that Eugénie paid to Nigra in Venice in the summer of 1905, but also the exact knowledge of well-informed men like Mérimée, General Fleury, and Prince Metternich, all of whom speak of Nigra as persona grata to the empress, notwithstanding her outbursts and her harangues about Italian questions, and especially about the pope (Salomon, ibid., pp. 60 ff.). Cf. now C. Richelmy, "Il silenzio di Costantino Nigra," in *Il Mondo* for 16 July 1949, p. 12, about a visit of Eugénie to Nigra, who was dying, in 1907).

[8] So for example Menabrea, according to an explicit statement he made to Pansa, had "a very low opinion of Nigra as a diplomatic agent" (Pansa, *Diario*, under 10 November 1875). In 1873 La Marmora publicly expressed his scant sympathy and esteem for Nigra (La Marmora, *Un po' più di luce*, passim, and esp. p. 334). Bonghi was spurred to defend Nigra in *Nuova Antologia* 25 (1874): 719. For Rattazzi's hostility, cf. Rattazzi, *Rattazzi et son temps* 2:176 and 407; and Luzio, *Aspromonte e Mentana*, pp. 61 and 397 ff. In France too there was a current of hostility: as well as d'Ideville, *Journal d'un diplomate en Italie . . . Turin 1859–1862* (cited above at ch. 15, n. 132), see M. Du Camp, *Souvenirs d'un demi-siècle*, vol. 1, *Au temps de Louis Philippe et de Napoléon III, 1830–1870* (Paris, 1949), p. 162, and vol. 2, *La chute du Second Empire . . . 1870–1882*, pp. 99, 104.

[9] Emile Ollivier testifies to this in a letter of 1 August 1905 to Nigra himself: "Few Italians have rendered more outstanding services than you to the work of national regeneration; and at the same time you were able, with your tact and your fairness, to gain the confidence and esteem of those whose interests and ideas were in contradiction to those you were charged with safeguarding." And immediately before this, he enumerates among Nigra's gifts a "strong sincerity" (De Vecchi archive). Cf. as well Luzio, *La Massoneria* 1:292.

[10] According to E. Ollivier, Nigra "combined a grace and a seductive flexibility with the most patent firmness of spirit. When you were negotiating with him, you might think at first that he was going to give way on all points, so preoccupied did he seem with not offending anyone. But when you came to the decisive point he suddenly assumed a grave demeanor and fixed a firm penetrating gaze on you, and instead of the weakness you had hoped to encounter, you met inflexibility" (*Il Giornale d'Italia*, 3 July 1907). De Moüy, who was attached to the foreign ministry of the government in Tours in the winter of 1870–71, recalls that in October 1870, Nigra, "who was accustomed to the nuances of society conversation, took care to cloak the calculated reserve of the Italian cabinet with his affable discourse" (de Moüy, *Souvenirs et causeries d'un diplomate*, p. 11).

[11] Nigra appreciated above all the "high" moral qualities of Napoleon III ("Il conte Costantino Nigra," a necrology by R. De Cesare in *Il Giornale d'Italia* for 2 July 1907).

the collapse of the Second Empire, and although he was treated with great benevolence at court and much sought after in Parisian high society, although he was tied to Paris by loves and deep friendships, he had wished to change his posting and go to London, or to Vienna. The fact is that although his own personal position was as satisfying as ever, "this life of continual uncertainty, and the Roman question, this tremendous sword of Damocles which will not be removed except on the day there is a radical and violent revolution in France, are making this residency extremely painful for me. You can add the accusations and the anger expressed in our press and by many of our members of parliament. You can add the antipathy of the king and the irritation of Rattazzi, who will not forgive me for having in some sense forced him to hand in his resignation with my telegrams.[12] And then, I have to confess to you that things in France are getting worse, and that it pains me to stand by as the great edifice of the French empire, with which the whole policy followed by us hitherto was linked, crumbles."[13]

His sympathy for Napoleon III and for France never distracted Nigra from his clear vision of Italian interests, or induced him to make a deal or cede a point when great questions were on the table. As in 1859–60, likewise now, he took pride in being the representative of Italy in Paris, not the spokesman for the French government to the Italian government. His deep sense of national dignity was married to a profound sense of personal dignity, and both were intransigent on essentials. Like Visconti Venosta, Nigra too was always guided by Cavour's great principle of giving way on little things in order to prevail on larger questions, of not transforming paltry incidents into serious issues while barring compromise and surrender on the really important issues.[14] Nigra made a sincere attempt to reconcile the interests of Italy with those of France; he was never less than upright in his dealings; he never shifted his ground on fundamentals; he never intrigued behind the back of one side or the other. This was how he comported himself in France, and later, as ambassador at Vienna, he aimed to bring the same fairness and candor to his conduct of affairs, and given that with Austria Italy could only be in an alliance or at war, and that since war was out of the question at the time, they were allies, he took the alliance seriously, and strongly disapproved, as Robilant had done previously, of anything that clashed with the spirit of the alliance, especially irredentist agitation and street demonstrations.[15] Nigra endorsed a policy of fair dealing, not only with France but with any other state. This was not an individual attitude dictated only by personal and sentimen-

---

[12] The statements of Mme Rattazzi about Nigra have to be read in light of this personal animosity of Rattazzi (Rattazzi, *Rattazzi et son temps* 2:176 and 407). But even before Mentana the relationship between the two men was not easy: "Rattazzi says about him [Nigra] what he says about Rattazzi. There is regard but not friendship—a difficult position for both" (M. Castelli to Vimercati, 15 August 1867; Archivio della Casa Reale, *Corrispondenza Vimercati*).

[13] Nigra to Artom, 19 January 1868 (AE, *Carte Nigra*), cited above at ch. 3, n. 37.

[14] Cf. W. Maturi, "Costantino Nigra secondo il carteggio col Cavour," *Il Risorgimento italiano* 22 (1929): 10, in the offprint seen.

[15] Cf. his strong personal letter to Crispi, 7 August 1890 (Crispi, *Questioni internazionali*, pp. 130 ff.; De Vecchi di Val Cismon, "Lo scioglimento della "Pro Patria' di Trento nel carteggio Crispi-Nigra," pp. 15 ff; cited above at ch. 6, n. 15). Cf. too De Cesare, "Gli ultimi anni di Costantino Nigra."

tal motives, it was a political method, a style of action that his close personal ties to the Napoleonic dynasty and to Paris might indeed reinforce, but could not create.

By remaining at Paris for another six years after the fall of the Napoleonic dynasty, he risked appearing to be a man ready to switch sides, changing his mind and his allegiance without inhibition. Indeed the Bonapartists did not forgive him for making the adjustment to the republic, and the ire of Prince Jérôme,[16] who involved his father-in-law, Vittorio Emanuele, cost Nigra a great deal of unpleasantness from his own king.[17] But the truth is that Nigra was not shifty: if he could have followed his own inclination, he would have changed his posting, but had not done so precisely because he did not want to create the impression with a sudden departure "that I was an agent of the emperor rather

---

[16] The dislike of Prince Jérôme for Nigra may have been based partly on rivalry over women; cf. Ressmann to Nigra, 31 December 1884, from Paris: "the ever beautiful but ever more *copious* Marchesa especially showed me a portrait of Nigra *hanging in her salon* in total disregard of highly placed jealousies" (MRT, *Carte Nigra*, 73/23). But the essential cause after 1870 was Nigra's straight dealing with the new French government. Nigra did not wish to make himself the tool of certain designs (evidently political ones) of the prince (Artom to Nigra, 29 April 1874; AE, *Carte Nigra*). The prince (your rival, Artom calls him) therefore launched a campaign against Nigra, even coming to Italy to confer with his father-in-law and advising Visconti Venosta to recall Nigra from Paris—this at a time when in Italy the papers of the Left were accusing Nigra of favoring Bonapartist intrigues in France (de Sayve, report, 5 March 1872, no. 27; AEP, *C.P., Italie*, t. 384, fols. 217v ff.). Once when Nigra, returning a visit previously paid to him, had gone with all his colleagues to one of the biweekly receptions of the count of Paris, Prince Jérôme hastened to inform Vittorio Emanuele, with who knows what additional comments of his own, and the king referred the matter to Vimercati, who was in Paris; Nigra concluded: "it weighs on me excessively, and I find it humiliating, that while both governments, and to some extent public opinion too, are showing themselves favorable to keeping me on in Paris, I am being exposed to the caprice of Prince Napoleon" (Nigra, personal letter to Visconti Venosta, 13 April 1874; Visconti Venosta archive). It should be stressed that just as Nigra refused then to assist the designs of Prince Napoleon, he likewise refused later to get involved in French domestic questions, as Melegari had instructed him to do; this gave him the opportunity to surrender his posting in Paris (cf. De Vecchi di Val Cismon, "L'episodio di Ems nel testo di C. Nigra," in *Nuova Antologia* for 1 September 1934, pp. 4–5 in the offprint seen). It should also be stressed that later Prince Jérôme was asking for money with which to start a major newspaper (Cialdini to Vittorio Emanuele II, 23 May 1877; Archivio della Casa Reale, *Carte Vittorio Emanuele II*, b. 40).

[17] If Vittorio Emanuele was already ill-disposed to him in 1868, perhaps because of the influence of Rattazzi, the situation later deteriorated yet further. In the autumn of 1873 the king personally asked Nigra, who was visiting Rome, to give up the Paris posting, and on 3 December he telegraphed to the faithful Vimercati, who was in the French capital: "I have had enough of Nigra in Paris. See that the Ministry of Foreign Affairs in France does not address any requests to him, and telegraph me" (Archivio della Casa Reale, *Corrispondenza Vimercati*). Nigra returned to Paris to remain there for only three more months. On 16 March 1874 he wrote to Visconti Venosta putting his posting at the minister's disposition and asking for the legation in Bern. (Not for the first time: an undated telegram [October 1873?] from the king to Artom records that Nigra desired to be transferred to Bern: "I am astonished, but if it is true, his demand is to be granted." The king proposed his favorite, Barral, for Paris; AE, *Ris.* 87.) Visconti Venosta stood fast, however, and persuaded Nigra to remain at his post; Nigra consented but asked the minister to tell the king that he had no desire to remain in Paris "against his wishes, all the less if I were to have to carry out a policy different to the one I have carried out to date, which is the policy of the king and of Italy, and not that of one or the other parties that are tearing apart this wretched France" (Nigra, personal letters to Visconti Venosta, 16 March and 13 April 1874; Visconti Venosta to Nigra, 24 March; Visconti Venosta archive). Note that Prince Napoleon had told Vimercati in Paris of "the resistance of the king" to Nigra's return to Paris (Vimercati to Minghetti, 29 November 1873; BCB, *Carte Minghetti*, cart. 39).

than the agent of Italy. . . . I was and am the representative of Italy, and not that of a foreign power."[18] And after some uncertainty between 1870 and 1872, Visconti Venosta kept him in Paris, rightly believing, in defiance of the ill humor of Vittorio Emanuele II, that there was no one else better able to represent Italy in the French capital, even after 4 September.[19]

Nigra was not a man who was ready to change internally and externally as the wind changed direction. He did not behave in this way with the foreign ministers in Rome, to whom he did not hesitate to express frankly and cogently his disagreement, when there was a difference about fundamental questions: thus, at the end of his career, he had an open clash with Prinetti.[20] Neither did he do so with others, continuing to assert his debt to Napoleon III publicly and vocally even after Sedan.[21] In him there was a strain of fidelity, friendship, attachment to persons once dear, in a word there was a sentimental disposition that can well be called romantic. The man who on 4 September 1870 had offered his arm to the Empress Eugénie to escort her out of reach of the howling, threatening crowd,[22] belonged to the generation of the young enthusiasts of 1848 and had fought for his ideal as a volunteer with the third company of *bersaglieri*, receiving a serious wound at Rivoli. His mind and intelligence, as a man and as a poet, were in origin those of a romantic, and in the romantic world he had remained, like a diplomatic herald of the principle of nationality, incarnating a generation that had turned away from the rational and mathematical mentality of the eighteenth century, but had not yet arrived at the positivistic mentality of the end of the nineteenth. His indulgence in a slight but decorous poetic vein, the sincerity and richness of his cultural interests, the loving cultivation of popular traditions were all factors that bound Nigra to the Romantic age.

Politically, like Visconti Venosta, he had an ample sense of the meaning of Europe which did not stifle, but did limit, his faith in the rights of nations, a sense that there was a measure imposed on the policy options of each individual state; in fact Nigra believed sincerely in the necessity of international peace.[23] The accord between them was not one of sentiments and ideas alone. At one time Nigra had served as a spur to action for no less a personage than Cavour, at a time

[18] Personal letter to Visconti Venosta, 26 March 1871 (Visconti Venosta archive).

[19] R. De Cesare, "Nigra a Parigi dopo l'Impero," in *Il Giornale d'Italia* for 30 October 1915. Nigra had an excellent relationship with Thiers and Rémusat. The Circourt salon, for one thing, had allowed him to have cordial relations, even under the Empire, with eminent members of the opposition (cf. Nigra's introduction to *Le comte de Cavour et la comtesse de Circourt: Lettres inédites . . .*, pp. 7 and 16). His friendship with the Rothschilds was also important.

[20] De Cesare in *Il Giornale d'Italia* for 4 December 1915; Tommasini, "Erinnerungen an Wien," p. 472.

[21] "I retain the most sincere gratitude to the emperor Napoleon and the imperial family, now in exile, for the special benevolence that both constantly showed me. I shall retain this sentiment faithfully, and I acknowledge it quite openly" (Nigra, personal letter to Visconti Venosta of 26 March 1871; Visconti Venosta archive).

[22] It was Nigra, not Prince Metternich, who gave his arm to the empress upon leaving the Tuileries (De Cesare in *Il Giornale d'Italia* for 30 October 1915).

[23] Note his efforts for the institution of a permanent arbitration tribunal during the Hague conference of May–July 1899 (Ruffini, *Scritti giuridici minori* 1:268; and esp. Toscano, "L'Italia e la prima conferenza per la pace dell'Aja del 1899," pp. 261 ff.

when the latter was already at the height of his creative daring, but now he was coming to resemble Visconti Venosta in method and style. This meant a preference for prudence and calm, for letting time do its work,[24] for not mortgaging the future in advance.[25] Nigra too became all finesse, skilled at playing the game, adept at modulating his tone,[26] reluctant to "slash at the water with his sword,"[27] a man of measure.

Measure was a key word for Nigra, so much so that one who knew him well from long experience of working together reminded him, years after their ways had parted, of these lines from Shakespeare's *Richard II*:

> . . . how sour sweet music is
> When time is broke and no proportion kept!
> So is it in the music of men's lives

which he felt expressed "gracefully a thought in which you customarily take enjoyment: it is the concept of "measure' in the actions of men."[28] His love of measure meant that in his writing, and in drafting official reports, Nigra was sparing of words and personal opinion, loath to flaunt predictions, disinclined above all to suggest plans and shape directives. Here too, his motto was *ne quid nimis*: concision and precision, no useless prolixity, no bloated compositions.[29] So spare and measured was he in his official prose that one may get the impression that his renowned qualities of sagacity and penetration were somehow becoming blurred, that a diplomat was turning into a bureaucrat. This is the impression that his official reports often leave, for they are clear and precise, but impersonal and much less idiosyncratic than those of the serious, alert, and sensible Robilant, or those of the loquacious de Launay. To find the real Nigra, who was an acute judge of men and affairs, a shrewd and exquisite intelligence, a profound observer not only of France but of European politics in general, to find all this we have to turn to his private letters. If the ones addressed by him to women (not his actual love letters, which are not extant), and by women to him, give off the gentle fragrance of a bygone era of courtesy, and if the abundant

---

[24] "Time, which restores calm and sound judgment of men and affairs to people, and the unfolding of circumstances, will gradually be able to modify this sentiment [the rancor of the French against Italy], and finally abolish it" (Nigra to Visconti Venosta, 6 March 1871; Visconti Venosta archive).

[25] Tracing a masterful sketch of the situation in France as regards Italy in the letter cited in the previous note, Nigra wrote: "I have sketched the situation as it seems to me to stand at the present moment and for a given period of time. If you were to ask me what might happen within one, two, or three years, I would hesitate to answer you, or rather I would answer you that I have no idea, and I would wait to reply in a more adequate manner after some time had passed. . . . In our attempted forecasts we simply have to leave a great deal to the unforeseen, though the measures we actually take should leave as little as possible to chance."

[26] "He was able to imply everything and infer everything," a French writer said of him (Tommasini, "Erinnerungen an Wien," p. 471).

[27] The expression is Nigra's in a letter to Crispi of 7 August 1890 (Crispi, *Questioni internazionali*, p. 132).

[28] T. Catalani to Nigra, 25 March 1891 (MRT, *Carte Nigra*, 69/16). Catalani had been with Nigra in London. The lines quoted are from *Richard II*, act 5, scene 5, 42–44.

[29] Thus to Mancini, from St. Petersburg, 12/24 February 1882 (AE, *Personale*, LVI).

correspondence between this celebrated diplomat and the leading scholars of Europe, especially the leading philologists,[30] takes us inside the extremely well-furnished mind of a scholar who was no mere dilettante,[31] his personal letters about political matters to Artom and Visconti Venosta, or later to Robilant, finally reveal Nigra to us in his full stature. No longer is he just a simple, though utterly precise and limpid, informant, but a political actor with a sure eye, a penetrating diagnostician with an unmistakable personality. But this is a Nigra who emerges almost nowhere else except in his personal, confidential correspondence: the sort of man who bares his soul, reveals what he really feels, only to a friend, while at work he wraps himself increasingly in the punctual but schematic, precise but impersonal, performance of the task assigned him. Does he fear to commit an indiscretion in official correspondence, is he being prudent? In part.[32] But the control and restraint of his official correspondence, which contrasts with the greater latitude given to personality in the correspondence of the other principal representatives of Italy abroad, also had another, perhaps more important, source than prudence and "measure." It was the disenchantment that befell Nigra, a species of moral fatigue verging on indifference and skepticism, an inner withdrawal from politics, as though he felt it no longer contained aught but bitterness, disillusionment, distress, and in the end, the vanity of all things.

It is this state of mind that is most striking in Nigra, and that differentiates him most clearly, as a man, from Visconti Venosta, who was so near him in style and political ideas. To those who knew him as an old man, at the end of the nineteenth century and the dawn of the twentieth, Nigra always appeared spiritually very much alive, but morally "tired, closed in on himself, and almost hopeless."[33] To another who had had daily contact with him at work, this man, once so disinterested[34] seemed actually to be sunk in egoism, no longer willing to put

---

[30] In the De Vecchi archive (and also in MRT), there are many letters to Nigra from Novati, Balzani, D'Ancona, D'Ovidio, Parodi, Rajna, Del Lungo, Meyer-Lübke, Gaston Paris, Schuchardt, Th. Sickel, etc., and especially from Graziadio Ascoli. When Nigra died, D'Ancona praised him highly in *Il Giornale d'Italia* (7 July 1907), as did Rajna in *Il Marzocco* for 14 July 1907 (reprinted as the preface to the edition cited of Nigra, *Poesie*).

[31] Münz had good reason to write to Nigra on one occasion: "I have continual admiration for your great learning, which would make you capable of holding a chair in any university" (MRT, *Carte Nigra*, 72/15; published by L. Collino, "Costantino Nigra nel pensiero dei suoi corrispondenti letterati ed artisti," in *Il Risorgimento Italiano* 22 [1929]: 655). And note the high praise of D'Ovidio in *Il Giornale d'Italia* for 1 January 1904.

[32] It is significant that in his last years in Venice, 1904 to 1907, he burned a large number of his papers and left others (like the fascicles of his *Ricordi diplomatici*) marked with the categorical instruction "to be burnt in case of death," or something similar. It was "a ferocious destruction" (De Cesare, "Gli ultimi anni di Costantino Nigra"; De Vecchi di Val Cismon, "Costantino Nigra: Un capitolo inedito dei *Ricordi diplomatici*," in *Nuova Antologia* for 16 January 1934, pp. 178–79; Richelmy, "Il silenzio di Costantino Nigra," p. 11).

[33] De Vecchi di Val Cismon, "Costantino Nigra," p. 177. Joël, the able chief of the Banca Commerciale, still admired the freshness of spirit of Nigra in 1905 (cf. Bogdan Graf von Hutten-Czapski, *Sechzig Jahre Politik und Gesellschaft* 1:448 [Berlin, 1936]). His memory was very lucid until the last; he was "a living archive," according to Luzio (*La Massoneria* 1:292; and cf. D. Orsi in *Nuova Antologia* for 16 November 1928, p. 138).

[34] In his letter to Visconti Venosta of 26 March 1871, cited above at nn. 18, 21, Nigra refused to change his posting and proposed to remain in France as long as "the present terrible crisis and danger" should last, and then to be relieved "of the enormous weight I have to carry" as soon as the situation

up with annoyance, and resentful of the scant recognition given him, so he said, by Italy.[35]

Certain it is that the man who appeared so sure of himself, so fortified with hope, when he went to Paris in Cavour's name, lost faith and hope along the bitter road of experience, and sought more and more to stay in the shadows, to avoid a leading role. Increasingly he lost his taste for politics. There surfaced in him a "lack of confidence that I can do any good, which holds me back to a great extent,"[36] he confessed in March 1871 to Visconti Venosta, who was proposing that he leave Paris for Vienna,[37] a move that even Nigra's friends recognized as opportune,[38] not to speak of his enemies, and the Left, which saw in him the incarnation of Italian Bonapartism.[39] It is surprising to find a man scarcely forty-two years old confessing that the years have diminished his confidence and augmented his sense of compunction, as though he were burdened with the weight of old age. But that is how Nigra felt: physically and morally jaded, more inclined

---

in France should have returned to normal. Then he added, rejecting the idea that he should request a posting to Madrid, "I would ask you to give me a discharge, or put me on reserve, or in a state of availability, or on leave of absence, accordingly as you judge to be in my best interest and in accord with the regulations. I am sure that you will do everything the rules permit you to do for me. If I retire without a pension, to which I have not yet earned the right, I will be left, to tell you the truth, in a very difficult position. But if I could keep my personal salary for a year or two, I will have time and leisure to sort myself out, and thus will not be a drain on the state treasury; I would be glad if in definitively taking leave of my career, I could say with some justice that I was not in debt to the government."

[35] This is how he is portrayed by Fasciotti, who had been with him at the embassy in Vienna, in a conversation with Tittoni (autograph notes by Tittoni, AE, *Ris.*, classified personal papers, Nigra envelope). A similar verdict appears in Richelmy, "La Triplice e gli ambasciatori italiani a Vienna," *Nuova Antologia* (November 1950): 304. So even in his last years, there were contrasting opinions on Nigra: because the criticisms of Fasciotti, and those gathered by Richelmy, are balanced by the admiration of Avarna, and the enthusiasm of Luzio (who knew him at Vienna) and of other scholars like Sorbelli (who spoke to me of this) for the affability with which he welcomed them etc.

[36] Nigra to Visconti Venosta, 10 March 1871 (Visconti Venosta archive). In the following letter of 26 March the same thought is expressed: "if I were a few years younger, if I were not so fatigued in spirit and body as I am, and if I had a little more faith in myself, I would not have hesitated to accept your offer."

[37] The legation in Vienna was offered him by Visconti Venosta on 17 November 1870; after a gap of two months the minister returned to the question on 26 February 1871 (Visconti Venosta archive). It was either Vienna or St. Petersburg.

[38] Artom to Nigra: "after the terrible changes that have taken place in France, there was a general opinion even among your closest friends that it was no longer a good idea for you to remain in Paris" (AE, *Carte Nigra*; 14 March 1871). The king was also worried (Nigra to Visconti Venosta, 24 June 1871; Visconti Venosta archive). The replacement of Nigra continued to be discussed, and not just in the press: the successor designated *in pectore* was Minghetti (Artom, personal letter to Robilant, 15 January 1872; AE, *Carte Robilant*), to whom Visconti Venosta turned as Nigra continued to insist that he wanted to leave Paris. Minghetti asked for time to think it over . . . and the matter ended there, certainly because Minghetti did not want to abandon the Italian political scene (statements of Visconti Venosta to Fournier in Fournier's report of 13 May 1872, no. 13; AEP, *C.P., Italie*, t. 385, fols. 51–52v; and cf. the report of de Sayve, 5 March, no. 27, ibid., t. 384, fol. 218r-v). Even *L'Opinione* for 26 November 1873, while praising him highly, held that it was necessary to replace him in Paris ("La diplomazia italiana").

[39] Among the ill-wishers was Guido Borromeo, who never let pass an occasion to complain about Nigra's remaining in Paris: cf. letters to Minghetti of 29 March, 31 July, and 16 September 1871 (BCB, *Carte Minghetti*, cart. XVI, fasc. 4). Marselli was also averse to Nigra (letter to Robilant, 17 November 1873; AE, *Carte Robilant*).

to hold back than to step in, preferring to contemplate than to decide.[40] "For some time I have been filled with scruples," he wrote to Visconti Venosta on 24 June 1871, at a time when it was he himself who wished to leave Paris, give up his career, and go into repose. "I no longer have the happy confidence of youth. If there occurred the least friction [between Italy and France] I fear that it would be ascribed to the good relations I had with the Empire. As well I feel very fatigued. Despondency, the belief that I am no longer equal to my task, often overwhelm my soul and leave me distraught."[41]

His decision to withdraw into private life was not put into effect, however, and Nigra remained in Paris for another five years, before going on to St. Petersburg, London, and Vienna. But that state of mind lasted, if not with the same acuity, at any rate as a persistent sense of disillusioned and bitter retreat into himself. Fifteen years later, at the beginning of the negotiations for the renewal of the Triple Alliance, Robilant informed him that the meetings would be taking place at Berlin with de Launay in charge, and that he, Nigra, would be playing an entirely secondary role, listening while others spoke without entering the debate or acting on his own; Nigra told the minister not to worry, since "my professional experience and my character incline me more to abstain than to encroach."[42]

The man was increasingly less disposed to act in the political arena, and increasingly driven to find refuge in poetry and study, in his *Reliquie celtiche* and *Canti popolari del Piemonte*. Not that he lacked the energy to do his duty, to take a strong position when it was necessary, even to state his own view without mincing words to an overbearing prime minister like Crispi.[43] He did not lose his capacity to make a strong impression anywhere, even in the difficult atmosphere of Vienna, with a personal prestige that made up, within certain limits, for the lack of prestige of the country he represented.[44] But the soul of the political actor

[40] To his physical tiredness and his "moral emotions" Nigra refers repeatedly in his letters to Visconti Venosta and Artom from November 1870 and March-April 1871.

[41] Visconti Venosta archive.

[42] Robilant, personal letter to Nigra, 15 October 1886 (De Vecchi archive); telegrams of Robilant to Nigra and Nigra to Robilant, 8 December 1886 (AE, *Cas. Verdi*, 1 b, *Triplice Alleanza*). This did not prevent Nigra from responding when he was asked, as was de Launay, by Robilant to propose a formula that seemed to him best to guarantee Italian interests in the Mediterranean (Africa and the Balkans). The formula he proposed was, in substance, that of article 1 of the separate Italo-Austrian treaty, and especially that of article 3 of the separate Italo-German treaty. Robilant thanked him and assured him that his formula would be used in preparing the draft of the treaty, which was later forwarded to de Launay and Nigra on 23 November 1886 (Robilant, telegram to Nigra, 27 October; Nigra, letter to Robilant, 1 November, and Robilant, personal letter to Nigra, 15 November; AE, *Cas. Verdi*, 1 b, *Triplice Alleanza*. On this invitation to Nigra and de Launay, cf. Crispi, *Politica estera*, p. 215).

[43] "In my position I can say what I think very freely to them [Kálnoky etc.], as to you and to anyone, even when what I think may be unwelcome" (Nigra, personal letter to Crispi, 7 August 1890; Crispi, *Questioni internazionali*, p. 132). Refusing on 8 August 1887 the offer of the foreign affairs portfolio, Nigra ended his telegram to Crispi thus: "I am addressing a man of resolve. I hope he will not do me the injustice of thinking that I speak with a will any less resolved" (AE, *riservatissimi Leg. Vienna*, fasc. C).

[44] At Vienna he succeeded in winning over even Kálnoky, who was notoriously not welcoming to diplomats. He and the ambassadors of Germany and Russia were the only ones to do so, and the other two were princes (an important attribute in Vienna!) and were backed up by the power of their empires, while Nigra was prized only because he was "such a remarkable spirit" ["geistig so bedeutend"] (*Erinnerungen und Gedanken des Botschafters Anton Graf Monts* [Berlin, 1932],

was growing inert, while the soul of the scholar and man of the world was quickening, as he passed entire evenings at the embassy with his collaborators in long readings of poetry and history,[45] and continued to charm men and women, even in old age, with the brio and elegance of his conversation.[46]

How little joy he reaped from political activity is shown by his refusal, on two occasions, to become foreign minister. The first was in June 1885, when Mancini, on the point of resigning, told Nigra that he was going to nominate him to take his place: Nigra responded immediately from London begging him "as a friend, and in all seriousness, to spare me the chagrin of turning down an eventual request from the king and from my friend Depretis."[47] The second occasion came, as is well known, on the death of Depretis in 1887, when Crispi and Umberto I personally and insistently[48] pressed him to assume responsibility for Italian foreign policy, and once again he refused without wavering.[49]

These are the two most significant cases of his shunning political activity at the highest level, but they were not isolated cases and were not due to passing spells of weariness. He likewise refused when asked by Crispi to go to Paris in 1894 and St. Petersburg in 1895,[50] to try to sort out situations that had turned difficult.

---

p. 121). On Nigra's personal prestige, cf. also J. M. von Radowitz, *Aufzeichnungen und Erinnerungen* 1:72; Waldersee, *Denkwürdigkeiten* 1:159 (Stuttgart-Berlin, 1922).

[45] Catalani, in another letter to Nigra of 17 July 1894, recalls the "long readings" and the evenings passed in company (MRT, *Carte Nigra*, 69/17).

[46] The worldly charm and the exceptional gifts as a conversationalist of Nigra, even in old age, are well known: cf. De Cesare, "Gli ultimi anni di Costantino Nigra." Nigra had received his apprenticeship in this respect in the salon Circourt in Paris and, as a classic diplomat, always believed in the great importance of social relations for diplomatic life (Nigra, introduction to *Le comte de Cavour et la comtesse de Circourt*, p. 7).

[47] Telegrams of Mancini to Nigra and Nigra to Mancini, 27 June 1885 (De Vecchi archive). The joke in this is that Mancini was saying exactly the same thing at the same time to Robilant, with the added remark: "I hope for and vividly desire your acceptance."

[48] The telegram of Umberto I, on 7 August, was in fact a very pressing appeal. Nigra answered on 8 August begging the king not to demand from him what he was unable to perform ("I have neither the qualities nor the temperament nor the position necessary to make a good minister of foreign affairs") and refusing the offer (AE, *riservatissimi Leg. Vienna*, fasc. C). The same thought is contained in his telegram to Crispi of 8 August: "do not request of me what I cannot perform" (ibid.).

[49] Crispi, *Politica interna*, p. 187, and cf. Crispi, *Carteggi politici inediti*, pp. 410–11. Again in February 1891, after his resignation, Crispi indicated that Nigra was the best choice as foreign minister; but "Nigra is another Farini; he doesn't wish to assume any responsibility" (Crispi, *Politica interna*, p. 267).

[50] King Umberto had telegraphed him on 30 July 1895 asking him to accept the difficult posting at St. Petersburg. Once again Nigra answered the king with a refusal, indeed a rather curt one, offering the government his posting at Vienna so that he could withdraw into retirement. It was a gesture of irritation from a man who suspected hidden ends in the proposal (AE, *Carte Nigra*; cf. ibid., telegrams between Nigra and Blanc, and Nigra and Crispi, in March 1894 concerning Paris; cf. Crispi, *Questioni internazionali*, pp. 162 ff.). Crispi sensed this and assured him that "in our mind there was not a thought less than respectful of you" (Crispi to Nigra, 12 August 1895; De Vecchi archive); and the king himself immediately took steps to reassure him (1 August) that no one was thinking of "removing" him from Vienna, where he was rendering excellent services (AE, *Carte Nigra*, and cf. Richelmy in *Nuova Antologia* for 16 November 1928, p. 155, and "Il silenzio di Costantino Nigra," p. 12). When he had regained his composure, Nigra wrote cordially to Crispi on 15 August explaining to him why he had been unable to accept: reasons of age and health; the need to spend fifty thousand lire annually, over and above his salary, in St. Petersburg; the fear of arousing once again, by going to the Russian capital, the "unjustified suspicions of the *Times*" (MRR, *Carte Crispi*, b. 662, no. 2/15).

I do not share Richelmy's view that Crispi wanted to remove Nigra from Vienna because he was

His fame grew, he seemed to be the man for critical junctures,[51] Crispi himself looked to him as a pilot in stormy weather—and he responded by retreating, by refusing to deal with squalls anymore. After 1870 Nigra's soul was marked by this absence of the joy of striving, as he himself said openly upon being transferred from St. Petersburg to London in 1882, a transfer which meant exchanging a post of only relative importance to Italy for one of fundamental importance; his lack of enthusiasm comes out in a letter of 11 December 1882 to his colleague Robilant:

> At the moment of my leaving St. Petersburg I feel a vivid and sincere regret. My position here was excellent, the welcome given me by this society exceedingly courteous and cordial. I had no problems of a political, or any other, kind at all; my relations, official and unofficial, were excellent. Now I have to begin a new life, adapt to new forms of usage, cultivate new relationships, and God knows with what result. I will have tedious problems that I did not have here, and a greater burden of work. Still, among the various posts to which I might have aspired, the one in London is certainly the most flattering. I will do the best that I can there. But though your friendship for me makes you say that I can render our country great services in London, my conscience warns me that I will have to be satisfied with rendering very modest ones. Huge mistakes I hope not to commit. I shall take care to live decorously, and shall certainly not bungle things. For the rest, you know from experience better than I do that our diplomatic activity, though it can be and sometimes is enhanced by the personal status of the ambassador, is worth no more in substance than the moral and material force that stands behind us, meaning the authority and might of the government and the country we represent.[52]

One is struck by the disillusioned tone, the skepticism about the possibilities of diplomacy (not unjustified, but still owned by a diplomat!), the revulsion at the tedium the future holds; one is struck above all by Nigra's reduction beforehand of his own role to that of living decorously and not bungling things . . . to very little, in truth. Had he really become so skeptical, so indifferent to any delight in novelty, so reluctant to move and change his life? Did he really cling so strongly

---

too much a partisan of the Triple Alliance (and Crispi?) and was acting as a brake toward Austria (Richelmy, "La Triplice e gli ambasciatori italiani a Vienna," p. 304). The fact is that Crispi was trying to get out of a difficult situation between Italy and Russia, and believed it necessary to send to St. Petersburg "a personage willing and able to renew relations of real friendship" between the two governments. Because Blanc, the foreign minister, had told him and the king that Nigra was a friend of the Russian foreign minister, Lobanov, they naturally thought of him.

[51] When in 1882 he was sent to London in connection with the transfer of Menabrea from London to Paris, Depretis and Mancini did this because in the British capital "we currently need exceptional ability [and] long experience of important negotiations" (Mancini, telegram to Umberto I, undated but 5 or 6 November 1882; MRR, *Carte Mancini*, b. 638, fasc. 5/6).

[52] AE, *Carte Robilant* (cf. also De Cesare, *Il conte Giuseppe Greppi*, pp. 218–19). Note that London was a posting "greatly desired" by Nigra, according to what he told Mancini (Mancini, telegram to Umberto I, [6] November 1882; MRR, *Carte Mancini*, b. 638, fasc. 5/10. And indeed, cf. Nigra's letter to Mancini, 5 November, ibid., 5/5). Three years later, at the moment of his leaving London for Vienna, he feels the same way: "I am sorry to leave the posting in London, where I have not a shadow of political, social, or other difficulty. I have no idea what awaits me in Vienna" (Nigra to Minghetti, 26 November 1885; BCB, *Carte Minghetti*, cart. XXV, fasc. 60).

to established personal routines? Was this the spirit that made his reports impersonal, precise and exact, but cold, as though he felt in his heart: what is the use?

It is singular, this retreat by a man who, twenty-five years earlier, had seemed utterly dedicated to politics, to struggle, to involvement in great decisions. Disenchantment, bitterness, physical and moral fatigue underlay his attitude. Nigra felt battered by the harshness of the political struggle and its inevitable ungenerosities, which it perhaps required a stronger, more disdainful character to shrug off than he possessed. He was wounded personally by the violent attacks on his professional conduct launched by the Left for years because of his friendship with Napoleon III and Eugénie, until their demand that he be transferred away from Paris was met in 1876.[53] The practice of diplomacy ingrained in him a certain skepticism about men and affairs, a distrust of any excess of passion that might cause a nervous outburst and wreck one's mission.[54] His family life brought him little consolation.[55]

But his fatigue and disillusionment were also a sign of the degree to which the living presence of Cavour, with its continual injection of stimulus, had had the capacity to transform his collaborators, making them into men of action, virtually inebriating them and filling them with audacity in the midst of the fray. With d'Azeglio, Nigra had been principally the author of the *Epitalamio* for the marriage of Alessandrina to the marchese Matteo Ricci; and he had shone under Manzoni's praise. But it had been the great Cavour who had shaped him into a diplomat, a politician, a man of action, leaving a lasting impression on the raw material, which was of a high grade to be sure, that he found to hand. In the glow of Cavour, Nigra, like others, had felt himself warmed in heart and mind: incontrovertible proof of the greatness of the minister of Vittorio Emanuele II, a man capable, like all true creators, of arousing and inflaming those around him. But now this living light, this flame, was gone, and in their hearts those who were not truly born for politics, not summoned by providence to feed on it and it alone, discovered that ultimately there was sadness and emptiness where before there had been animation and power.[56]

---

[53] Cf. articles in *La Riforma* for 11 January and 29 October 1872, and 7 December 1873. *Il Diritto* for 2, 3, and 5 April 1876 states openly that Nigra ought to change postings; and one of the first pieces of advice given by Cesare Correnti to Depretis was to remove Nigra (cf. the pro-memoria published by Morandi, *La sinistra al potere*, p. 134; and cf. Luzio, *Aspromonte e Mentana*, pp. 335 ff., for an attack on Nigra published by Petruccelli della Gattina in 1867). The posting to St. Petersburg was, however, requested from Melegari by Nigra himself, who, realizing immediately how matters stood, took the first step, cleverly using as his grounds Melegari's thoughtless instruction that he should intervene in French domestic politics to obtain the suppression of the French embassy to the Vatican (see the account of Nigra himself in De Vecchi di Val Cismon, "L'episodio di Ems nel testo di C. Nigra").

[54] This is the opinion of De Cesare in *Il Giornale d'Italia* for 30 October 1915.

[55] To Robilant, who in light of the international situation had denied him his annual holiday, Nigra wrote from Vienna on 1 November 1886: "You were here with your family, and had many relatives and friends you had made during a protracted stay. I on the other hand am here alone. If I fall ill, I am at the mercy of hired help. The older I get, the more I feel the need to see the few relatives and friends that remain, whom I cannot have here with me, at least once a year, because each year might be the last" (AE, *Carte Robilant*).

[56] Vimercati noted this as early as 1861: Nigra after the death of Cavour is no longer the Nigra of before. He needs the king to give him a little support (Luzio, *Aspromonte e Mentana*, p. 172).

To continue to function at the level attained in 1859–60 would have required of Nigra the complexion of a man of action that he did not have. Once he had written to Cavour: "I have done what I could. . . . I cannot give what I do not have,"[57] and what he did not have, or at any rate had in a measure unequal to the gifts of a lively, quick, and intelligent character, was the temperament of a fighter. That inner core of personality, idyllic and softly sentimental, that came to light in his *Idilli*,[58] transpired in other ways in politics. As a man he was alien to states of powerful passion. He was sincere and fair-minded, but with a sincerity and fair-mindedness that could never know the hard exclusive sway of great feelings. These qualities permitted him instead an adaptability to changing circumstances that was denied, for example, to Robilant. In Nigra even idealistic values did not have the rooted intractability they had in other men, so that whereas his friend Visconti Venosta always kept his distance from Bismarck and Crispi, Nigra admired Bismarck and felt a definite sympathy for Crispi.[59]

It was as though the inner life of Nigra grew tepid; and this was brought about not just by personal disillusionment. There was something worse: there was the fact that, with unity achieved, Italy did not correspond to the idealized vision of what it was meant to be. The resulting disappointment and dissatisfaction reached an extreme pitch in Mazzini, but they approached this level in a number of the moderates as well, including Nigra. Here again, though not in the same way as with Visconti Venosta, the humor was a little bit like that of d'Azeglio, the sour unhappy muttering d'Azeglio.[60] It galled them to feel the influence and prestige of their beloved native land, "most fair of all those warmed by the

---

[57] Cf. Maturi, "Costantino Nigra secondo il carteggio col Cavour," p. 11. He makes the identical affirmation to Crispi on 8 August 1887, in declining the nomination to the position of foreign secretary: "do not request of me what I cannot perform."

[58] Cf. Croce, *La letteratura della nuova Italia* 5:126 ff. (3d ed.; Bari, 1950); G. Petrocchi, *Scrittori piemontesi del secondo Ottocento* (Turin, 1948), pp. 3 ff.

[59] Proof of this is in various letters to Crispi: for example, on 5 September 1894, "I offer my prayers that you will decide to continue to sustain our Italy, which has such great need of you." In another of 15 August 1895 he says, "take courage, then, and persevere" (MRR, *Carte Crispi*, buste 666, no. 4/6, and 662, no. 2/15). Cf. as well De Cesare in *Il Giornale d'Italia* for 30 October 1915. It is true that Crispi treated Nigra with deference, something to which Nigra referred with satisfaction (De Cesare, *Il conte Giuseppe Greppi*, pp. 250–51). For example, at the moment of his departure for Germany to meet Bismarck, Crispi telegraphed Nigra that on all the delicate questions that were ongoing, he (Crispi) wanted him (Nigra) to telegraph him directly at his successive addresses in Milan, Frankfurt, and Hamburg (telegram, highly reserved, 27 September 1887; AE, *riservatissimi Leg. Vienna*, fasc. B). A little later, in expressing a personal opinion to Crispi, Nigra said: "take this opinion as that of a friend" (ibid., fasc C). The statement by G. Ardau, *Francesco Crispi* (Milan, 1939), p. 315 (followed by Richelmy, "La Triplice e gli ambasciatori italiani a Vienna," p. 304) that Nigra did not labor to advance the policies of Crispi has no foundation.

As for his admiration for Bismarck, cf. H. von Poschinger, *Fürst Bismarck und die Diplomaten, 1852–1890* (Hamburg, 1900), pp. 26 and 452; and also G. Cabasino-Renda, "Memorie e giudizi inediti di Costantino Nigra," in *Il Giornale d'Italia* for 22 December 1907.

[60] On this frame of mind in the elderly d'Azeglio, cf. Vaccalluzzo, *Massimo d'Azeglio*, pp. 285 ff.; Santangelo, *Massimo d'Azeglio politico e moralista*, pp. 266–67; P. Silva, *Figure e momenti di storia italiana* (Milan, 1939), pp. 170 ff.; A. M. Ghisalberti, "Come sono nati *I miei ricordi*," in *Rassegna Storica del Risorgimento* 34 (1947): 12 ff. in the offprint seen. But for its origins, which go back to the disappointments of 1848, cf. Omodeo, *L'opera politica del Conte di Cavour* 1:129.

sun,"[61] diminish day by day. Discontent and displeasure on numerous grounds accompanied the growth of the new Italy. To remain aloof and not be irritated at such spectacles as that "of scoundrels and crooks preening themselves as *Italianissimi*"[62] required the unsentimental carapace of the born politician,[63] or the remote serenity of the historian. But d'Azeglio and those like him were not politicians by instinct or temperament and could not yet be historians. They suffered the painful sensation of having been thrust aside, of having outlived their time, of being washed up on a lonely beach by the rolling waves of great events; such feelings came to d'Azeglio forcefully after 1852, and they came to Nigra in turn after 1870, even more after 1876.

Such a state of mind would have done little to promote comprehension and indulgence, and it must have had something to do with Nigra's disenchantment. Certainly it was common in many of his Piedmontese friends and acquaintances —though not in Visconti Venosta and Minghetti, who were made differently in this respect. One of those friends, Govean, openly identified with the pessimism of d'Azeglio in 1879, in a letter in which he complains to Nigra about the decadence of Italian political morality: "Once the great aims that guided the Italians in the past were no more, particular goals surfaced. And as d'Azeglio said, the new arrivals found the table set, and ate the food on it. Then there came along a bunch who made off with the plates and napkins. Now I say to you that there are others in the kitchen fighting over the pots and pans and kettles, with God only knows what hands."[64] Even from very high quarters, Nigra was receiving signals of discouragement, pessimism, and indignation, for Prince Eugenio di Savoia-Carignano, who passed for a man of capacity and openness of spirit, wrote him of the black pessimism to which he was prey.[65] Many years later it fell to Alfieri di Sostegno to convey to a foreigner the bitter feeling of having outlived their time that many of the men of 1859 were left with: he was asked by the viscount de Vogüé in 1896 why, at such a difficult moment for Italian political life, after Adua and the fall of Crispi, no one in Italy thought to summon the epigones of Cavour to take the helm, men hallowed by fame and known to all of Europe, just as France in difficult times had called on Thiers; the viscount expressed astonishment that no one was proposing to make use of Nigra's authority in Europe. Alfieri replied: "You are right, but time has marched on too fast; those men

---

[61] Cf. Nigra's paean in the verses for the d'Azeglio-Ricci wedding (Nigra, *Poesie originali e tradotte*, pp. 7–8).

[62] De Rubris, *Confidenze di Massimo d'Azeglio*, pp. 263 and 291.

[63] In 1833 Cavour observed "whatever the form of government, it is inevitable that the largest part of the individuals who hold power, and of those who aspire to it, should be corrupt" (Cavour, *Diario*, pp. 43–44).

[64] F. Govean to Nigra, 12 January 1879 (De Vecchi archive).

[65] "I do not speak to you of our country and of all the depressing developments there, for you must know of them as well as I; but you will recall *everything I had said to you about this*; was I mistaken?" (6 July 1875; De Vecchi archive). On 20 November 1874 Savoia-Carignano had written Nigra that when they next met, he would tell him "comment je juge les *affaristes* (passez moi le mot qui n'est pas français) de notre époque" (ibid.). [*Translator's note:* Writing in French, Savoia-Carignano asks Nigra to pardon his use of an Italianism (*affaristes* = *affaristi*) meaning, roughly, "sleazy traffickers."]

whose names still spring to your mind, the public and the politicians in Italy no longer think of, no longer know they exist. They are dead, embalmed in their great achievements."[66]

In 1871 Nigra did not yet think of himself as having died and been embalmed in this fashion, though he would later on.[67] But already he could tell that his environment was no longer the one in which he had earned his glory. The fall of the Napoleonic empire and the fiercely unjust attacks on him published by *La Riforma* and *Il Diritto*, the belief of his friends that it would be better for him to exchange Paris for another posting, were enough to burden a sensibility as keen as his and make him reflect on the lability of human affairs, above all politics and fame.[68]

So in the end, though so much like Visconti Venosta in general ideological orientation, and in the characteristic features of his diplomatic style, Nigra differed from his minister in his progressive disillusionment and skepticism, which were absent in Visconti Venosta. The parliamentary rough and tumble, the boredom and sometimes even the disgust engendered by polemics with adversaries, and even by having to get along with uncongenial colleagues whom circumstances imposed on him, never caused the foreign minister to shrink back into his inner self in the way that happened to Nigra.[69]

But these were differences of taste and sensibility, no less personal than their differences in appearance and bearing: Visconti Venosta dignified and a little solemn, Nigra scintillating and seductive. In the things that really counted for the history of Italy—that is, in their general approach and method of achieving things—the two men stood side by side, and with them stood Artom, a much less outstanding personality but a wise confidant and inspiring collaborator, a man moved by the same impulses as they.

[66] E. M. de Vogüé to Nigra, 5 September 1896 (MRT, Carte Nigra, 74/60).

[67] At the last, indeed, Nigra felt "that he had outlived his times politically" (De Cesare, "Gli ultimi anni di Costantino Nigra").

[68] Even later, he was grieved by the polemics aroused by the publication in 1895 of a fragment of his *Ricordi Diplomatici*: this is another significant clue to his nature (cf. De Vecchi di Val Cismon, "Costantino Nigra," pp. 178 and 180; D. Orsi in *Nuova Antologia* for 16 November 1928, p. 146.

[69] On 12 April 1871 Visconti Venosta wrote to Nigra: "Your letter seems to me to have been written in a moment of discouragement. I too experience such moments. The old will to carry on fails sometimes, and gives way to a feeling of tiredness, of disgust even. This, I fear, is unfortunately one of the first signs of the damage of advancing years. But at our age we have to fight back, and a little rest is enough to rebuild one's strength. . . . It will not be a matter of months, but a matter of a few years, at least, before we can intone a *nunc dimitte* and say to the generations that are pressing on us: the work is done, now you must preserve it" (Visconti Venosta archive).

Count de Launay

THE TWO OTHER major personalities of the Italian diplomatic world, de Launay, and from the summer of 1871 Robilant, were very different men. Aside from Nigra, de Launay, and Robilant, Italy's other representatives abroad, then and for a long time to come, were not outstanding individuals. This was true of those from the Mezzogiorno, Barbolani at Constantinople and Caracciolo di Bella at St. Petersburg, both of whom vanished from the scene in any case between 1875 and 1876. It was true of Barral, a favorite of the king who was publicly praised by La Marmora as a worthy product of the good old diplomacy of the kingdom of the house of Savoy,[1] the other side of the coin from Nigra, who represented a new and degenerate school; yet Barral was in fact nothing more than a diligent functionary.[2] It was true of Greppi, who became famous for living out a robust old age to the term of 103 years, an amiable man of the world, but certainly no Cavour, and no Talleyrand either.[3] Not even Cadorna, though he headed the legation in London until 1875 and was convinced of his own accomplishment,[4] had outstanding gifts as a diplomat; and as for Corti, he was then in Washington, a remote posting of little importance at that time. So it is that besides Nigra, only de Launay and Robilant stand out.

In the case of Count Edoardo de Launay, the weight his signature carried with the foreign minister derived in large measure from the importance of his posting. Berlin was, with Vienna and Paris, the most delicate and difficult of the Italian legations, and it is understandable that the man who headed it enjoyed notable prestige. In addition, de Launay was the dean of the Italian diplomatic corps, an old hand always ready to emphasize his experience in sounding a warning or giving advice,[5] assiduous, finicky, extremely touchy,[6] a jealous guardian of a

---

[1] La Marmora, *Un po' più di luce*, pp. 338–39.

[2] Artom to Nigra, 25 March 1871: "so we will be forced to name Barral to that post [Vienna]. He is a person acceptable to Vienna, but between us, he does not seem to me to be equal to the task" (AE, *Carte Nigra*). In fact, it was Robilant who went to Vienna, while Barral went to Madrid, accompanying King Amedeo; and it was Vittorio Emanuele II who wanted him in Madrid, beside his son (Visconti Venosta to Robilant, 10 May and 4 June 1871; AE, *Carte Robilant*).

[3] Bülow, *Memorie* 4:600.

[4] Artom to Nigra, 14 March 1871: "there is little chance of getting Cadorna out of there [London]. It seems that the climate agrees with him, and he believes he is doing excellently; he is a personal friend of Lanza: in sum, our wish to remove him from that posting has small probability of being granted" (AE, *Carte Nigra*). And cf. Minghetti to Visconti Venosta, 9 October 1870: "I confess that sometimes I am appalled at the incapacity of Cadorna for that job" (Visconti Venosta archive). Here, as in the case of Greppi, the documents confirm the verdict: diligent and meticulous, but nothing more.

[5] For example, on 23 February and 18 June 1872 he gives advice to Visconti Venosta and deplores the inadequacy of young diplomats, some of whom begin their careers in a state of ignorance, scarcely even knowing French, and with no seriousness of character. In nineteen years in

profession that he would have liked to keep from being contaminated by amateurs, meaning politicians who were sent out as diplomats with no technical
preparation.[7] Métier was everything for this vestal of the sacred flame, who was
completely immersed in his duty and was truly and honestly faithful to it.[8]

It would nevertheless be unjust to attribute the eminent position enjoyed by the
Savoyard in Italian diplomacy exclusively to the external circumstances that had
placed him in the midst of great events and in proximity to great men. Not that de
Launay can be said to have had superior gifts as a political actor, or particular
finesse as a diplomat: his intelligence was greatly inferior to that of Nigra, and he
was a much less solid and sensible man than Robilant; yet withal he had an
individual personality, he was not the usual pallid and uninteresting figure. His
reports were anything but typically bureaucratic, being prolix and often pointlessly verbose,[9] but expressing the ideas and feelings of their author resolutely
and impetuously. He had no hesitation in contradicting his minister and was
always prodigal with advice and warnings about the future. If the blueprint for an
average respectable diplomat is the figure sketched by the elder Bülow for the
benefit of his son at the beginning of his apprenticeship, a figure cautious in his
judgments, sparing with predictions, never harshly critical, always calm and
objective,[10] de Launay was very certainly not a diplomat, for he was driven to let
his minister know what he thought, and was forthright in expressing his own
opinion and his own personal preferences, his sympathies and antipathies. De
Launay had not the slightest inclination to play the part of the close-mouthed
diplomat, even when he was not officially authorized to speak for his govern-

---

St. Petersburg and Berlin only three young legation secretaries have satisfied him, he says; among
them was Sonnino (ACR, *Carte Visconti Venosta*, pacco 5, fasc. 2). Later he pressed Mancini to
make sure that young diplomats had the necessary "personal qualifications" (MRR, *Carte Mancini*,
b. 644, fasc. 8/10).

[6] In 1872 when there was a question of sending a military mission, headed by a general (Petitti di
Roreto) to be present at the maneuvers of the Prussian Guard, de Launay warned Visconti Venosta
that political questions had to remain entirely in his hands: "my *jeu* [game] must not be hampered by
currents over which I have no control. The position must be very clear" (12 August; ACR, *Carte
Visconti Venosta*, pacco 5, fasc. 2).

[7] On 1 October 1866 he was already writing to Greppi that the diplomatic service ought to be
reorganized and access to it barred to the outsiders who were now trying to leap in ahead of those who
had spent long years preparing for this career (Greppi, "Lettres du comte Ed. de Launay," p. 752).

[8] For instance, he refused a nomination to the Senate because, with the workload he had, he
would be unable to attend the sessions, and when he was free to do so, it would not be possible for
him "to participate in the debates with the absolute independence that alone makes a vote truly
conscientious in character" (in Rosi, *L'Italia odierna*, vol. 2, t. 2, pp. 1758 and 1761; and the
opinion of Rosi, p. 1702).

[9] De Launay certainly comes across as verbose in his correspondence, the most verbose of the
Italian representatives abroad. Even Greppi, who admired him, observes that he was one of those
who like to hear themselves talk (Greppi, "Lettres du comte Ed. de Launay," p. 739). He was also
prolix in conversation and debate (Hohenlohe-Schillingsfürst, *Denkwürdigkeiten* 2:296; de Moüy,
Souvenirs et causeries d'un diplomate, p. 106). Radowitz called him cloying and said that Bismarck
disliked him "for his copious and somewhat sugary chit-chat" (Radowitz, *Aufzeichnungen und
Erinnerungen* 2:30), while appreciating him as a sure friend of Germany. Bülow (*Memorie* 4:320–
21) was much more benevolent, referring to his sound political intelligence. In Cavour's circle he had
the reputation of being a "good diplomat," though Cavour had once called him a "whiner" (Cavour,
Carteggio Cavour-Salmour, pp. 142 and 170).

[10] Bülow, *Memorie* 4:295–96.

ment.[11] In sum his character was completely opposed to that of a typical representative abroad. He liked to be seen in the role of mentor; to be the Père Joseph to any Richelieu whatsoever would have been a dream come true. He had little desire actually to be a Richelieu, at any rate in the times in which he found himself, with those blessed parliamentarians to whom it was necessary to account for one's actions and procedures, and with whom it was necessary to discuss things about which good old-fashioned reason of state would have kept silent. So it was that he too made his own gallant refusal when, in 1876 and 1877, Depretis offered him the job of foreign minister.[12] But the motives of this refusal were as different as could be from those of Nigra, since they had nothing to do with lack of self-confidence, with disillusionment or skepticism. De Launay was always buoyed up by robust optimism where his own self was concerned, always cocksure, always quite certain that the light of reason shone before his eyes. He constantly and stubbornly endorsed the Italo-German understanding as the true panacea for all Italy's ills. He was unaffected by the *maladie du siècle*: pessimism, romanticism, melancholic withdrawal into one's inner self, all this would have made no sense to the solid Savoyard. He was *un homme à poigne*, a man of strength and energy, and the only thing necessary to make him feel completely at ease would have been greater authority at home for the state he represented abroad, a central power able to move more decisively, without all the hitches caused by assemblies, commissions, the publication of diplomatic papers, and similar pieces of liberal foolishness. He considered all of this a ham-fisted way of dealing with international relations, in which the only sound guidance still came from the precepts of the old, reviled, but ever so useful reason of state. De Launay believed in the *arcana imperii*; he believed in the conduct of state affairs as an exclusive academy, a temple reserved to a few elect, to the experts who had mastered the technique: for technique was something that could not be improvised. Horace's *odi profanum vulgus et arceo* could have been de Launay's motto as well, and in the mob he included parliamentarians and petulant party members,[13] diplomatic amateurs faking it as heads of legation, indiscreet journalists (another plague of the modern world), and even ministers who did not know how to make the importunate sit up on their hind legs and beg.

This was a realm of values quite opposed to that of Visconti Venosta. If we have to resort to pigeonholes, de Launay would be classified as the reactionary of Italian diplomacy after 1870, even more than the much-maligned Menabrea. Savoyard by birth, he was a continuator in this respect of the political tradition of

---

[11] "If what is wanted here is a representative who has not the faculty to give a personal opinion, at least until he receives specific orders, I would have to make a great effort to fit this role of silent personage vis-à-vis my colleagues" (de Launay, private letter to Visconti Venosta, 20 December 1870; AE, *Ris.* 10).

[12] De Launay, telegram to Vittorio Emanuele II, 18 [December] 1877 (ACR, *Carte Depretis*, 1st ser., b. 22, fasc. 69); and same to same, 24 March 1876 (Archivio della Casa Reale, *Carte Vittorio Emanuele II*, b. 32 and 41 for 1877).

[13] On 2 February 1871, irritated by a speech of Riccardo Sineo in the Chamber, he observed to Visconti Venosta that it was "really regrettable that whenever our Chamber sits, deputies with no competence in these matters permit themselves to criticize our diplomatic personnel, without anyone standing up to defend us" (report no. 775).

his native land, which had stood for the extreme right within the territories comprised by the state of the house of Savoy, and his diplomatic experience at the courts of St. Petersburg and Berlin had reinforced his innate authoritarian tendency. He set authority higher than liberty,[14] even if the ideological wind of Cavour's heritage sometimes blew him counter to the "utilitarianism" of Bismarck and within sight of the beaches held by the Italian liberals.[15]

It was just as natural that he should not be at one with Visconti Venosta. In regard to matters of substance, meaning the political direction to be followed and the ideals to be realized, and in regard to form, meaning diplomatic method, the two men were as different as possible. The moderate but firm liberalism of Visconti Venosta was set against the strong propensity for "authority" of de Launay, the former's political sympathies for France and fear of German expansionism against the hatred for France and admiration for Germany of the latter. De Launay believed that a victorious war against France was required to make of Italy a truly great nation and hoped it would take place,[16] while the very possibility made Visconti Venosta and Nigra quake.[17] The foreign minister's style was one of finesse and nuance, while the envoy to Berlin went ahead foursquare, his position always hard-edged and decisive.

None of this escaped de Launay, who shivered and stamped and trampled like a horse on whom the bit was drawn too tight: "I am often enraged by the fact that I am not listened to. Sometimes I write letters to the chevalier Visconti Venosta that cannot fail to sting him to the quick, but it is a pure waste of time. If they admit that I am right in principle, they still cannot find the resolve to act." With these words he confided his disappointment on 19 January 1874 to Count Robilant, then envoy to Vienna,[18] the colleague to whom he was most closely bound by ties of friendship.

[14] Cf. above, p. 371, and also his insistence, in February 1873, that "today it is necessary to counterbalance the excess of liberty by accentuating more the principles of order and authority" (personal letter to Visconti Venosta, 11 February 1873; Visconti Venosta archive).

[15] Thus he wrote in 1875: "The elevation of character of this great patriot [Cavour], his attachment to truly liberal doctrines, should inspire us with more confidence than the elastic principles of the utilitarian school to which Prince Bismarck belongs" (personal letter to Visconti Venosta, 31 March 1875; Visconti Venosta archive). De Launay wrote this in the context of relations with the Holy See, and Bismarck's effort to "enroll auxiliaries against the pope," Italy first among them. On this question de Launay took a very firm stance, advising the government to reject out of hand any attempt by the Germans to meddle in Italian policy toward the church, and to make Berlin understand that "charbonnier est maître chez soi [that everyone is master in his own house]" (personal letters to Visconti Venosta, 23 and 31 March 1875; Visconti Venosta archive).

[16] Cf. above, p. 16.

[17] Naturally there was little sympathy between de Launay and Nigra; cf. above, ch. 1, n. 56; and also de Launay, personal letter to Visconti Venosta, 21 February 1875: "it is completely abnormal that agents of our country . . . even in Paris during the festivities commemorating Petrarch . . . should manifest opinions that reveal all too clearly that they will die without recanting their extreme sympathies for France" (Visconti Venosta archive).

[18] AE, *Carte Robilant*; published in Salvemini, "La politica estera della Destra" (1925), p. 76. In a personal letter to Visconti Venosta on 11 June 1875, de Launay unburdens himself: "I do not speak to you of other subjects, my dear minister, since you have resolved not to respond to my private letters. . . . The responsibility is yours. The future will reveal which of us two was right. Before 1870 I preached in the desert for a long time. Events have proved me right in the end" (Visconti Venosta archive).

Count di Robilant

IN EFFECT, it would seem at first glance that there were numerous points of resemblance between de Launay and Robilant, whereas no substantial or formal affinity with Visconti Venosta or Nigra was apparent. Robilant, a brave soldier wounded at Novara who became a general and the commanding officer of the War College, and was then appointed envoy to Vienna, also lacked any trace of sentimental attachment to France.[1] Indeed he was very sure that there would arise "grave complications with France before too long," and therefore desired a close accord with Germany.[2] This made him disapprove of the policy of Visconti Venosta, which he judged to be too "conciliatory" to Paris,[3] so much so that de Launay, when he learned that his friend had been chosen for Vienna, hoped this would mean that the two of them would be able to take vigorous action together on their common program.[4] And like de Launay, Robilant employed a crisp, biting approach that was very different from the art of modulation employed by Visconti Venosta and Nigra.

But the analogies end there, for in substance Robilant, while certainly very different in style from his minister and his colleague in Paris, was also very different from his colleague in Berlin. He stood alone, a strongly marked personality.

Robilant issued from the high nobility of Piedmont and had right of entrée to

---

[1] On 4 January 1872, Armand Ruiz, a friend of Gambetta who later served as a contact between Gambetta and the leaders of the Italian Left (cf. below, ch. 20, n. 92), tells Robilant that he is writing to him from Paris with some trepidation, because "I have learned of all the ill you speak of us . . . your antipathy—I use the word antipathy to be polite—against my mad country" (AE, *Carte Robilant*). In 1875 Duke Decazes, the French foreign minister, likewise accused Robilant of not being a friend to France (Robilant, personal letter to Visconti Venosta, 7 July 1875; Visconti Venosta archive). On Ferdinando Ruiz, an officer from Naples who settled in France, where he became prefect of the Nièvre, cf. Pisacane, *Epistolario*, p. 463 n. X.

[2] Robilant, personal letter to Visconti Venosta, 7 February 1873; Visconti Venosta archive.

[3] De Launay to Robilant, 21 July 1871: "I fully agree with you about our minister of foreign affairs. Like you, I believe that he tends to be too conciliatory where France is concerned." After expounding his own views on Italian-French and Italian-German relations at length, he continues, "I know that you think as I do. We are perhaps the only ones in the diplomatic corps to be animated by these convictions. So let us work together to inspire more energy in our political masters" (AE, *Carte Robilant*; published in part—but not the part of interest here—in Salvemini, "La politica estera della Destra" [1924], p. 362).

[4] "[F]rom now on you and I will be two heads of mission who will certainly see eye to eye. I will go even further; I hope that the posting in Vienna will be a stepping stone for you to arrive one day at the position of minister of foreign affairs, so that you may carry out a policy of making Italy completely independent of foreign powers." De Launay adds that Robilant will certainly not lack the courage to state his own opinion "at the risk of displeasing Florence. For my part I often row against the current." De Launay also states that Robilant's nomination will be acceptable to Berlin, "for they know your point of view, and when necessary I will be there to elucidate" (De Launay to Robilant, 9 June 1871; AE, *Carte Robilant*).

the small closed world, everywhere present and often highly influential, that was the international aristocracy of the time. From this world his German mother, a Truchsess von Waldburg, had come, as well as his Austrian wife, a Clary-Aldringen, while he was related, in Russia, to the famous and uproarious general Ignatieff, whose wife was his cousin. A tall and elegant figure, his irregular features animated by an intensity of expression combining intelligence and moral uprightness,[5] he was lordly in origin and bearing, of impeccable courtesy, though with a certain underlying reserve that barred him from the facile expansiveness and the exuberance of the newly arrived; not a man for easy friendships, therefore, though he was not prickly or standoffish either and was capable of warm affection, was indeed a man with many distinguished friends, including Minghetti and Marselli. Dignified and commanding in presence despite the mutilation of his hand, Count di Robilant attracted notice even in a group of diplomats and men of the world. His inner character fully confirmed the first impression he made.

His spirit abhorred nuances: he was as clear-cut in speech as he was in character; his mental process was never confused or vague, always precise and concrete. Refusing to wrap the truth in flannel, he uttered it if necessary with brutal frankness;[6] even at difficult moments, it caused him no embarrassment to *mettre les pieds dans le plat*, even before the Austro-Hungarian foreign minister. It was a very different style from that of Nigra, and Robilant was certainly not an ambassador with whom it was easy to deal.[7] And yet, after spending years in this difficult posting, in an environment for the most part frankly hostile to the country he represented, he left the Austrian capital commanding a very high level of respect indeed.

But the energy displayed by Robilant was also different from the energy of de Launay, who was much more verbose and therefore less substantial. De Launay was often very vigorous in his confidential reports to his minister, but we may be allowed to wonder whether he was just as forthright, when necessary, with Jupiter himself in the shape of Prince von Bismarck, or even with the envoys of the master, Thile or Balan or Bülow.[8] Robilant was vigorous in his reports to Visconti Venosta, as to Depretis, Cairoli, or Mancini, but he was so as well in face-to-face meetings with Andrássy, Haymerle, and Kálnoky, and it was this that gained him the reputation of being an unaccommodating ambassador.[9]

---

[5] See the profile sketched by de Moüy, *Souvenirs et causeries d'un diplomate*, p. 224.

[6] "As you know I am accustomed to push frankness even to the point of brutality. So you can be sure that when I have spoken, I have said all I have to say" (Robilant to Corti, 29 December 1886; AE, *Carte Robilant*). He held the strong belief that "in politics there is nothing worse than illusions, than hiding from oneself the obstacles that lie in the way of achieving a result" (Robilant, report, 18 December 1883, no. 2020).

[7] So said Kálnoky: Robilant conducts himself with fairness and consistency as an ambassador, but is not an easy-going fellow (Cappelli, "Il conte Carlo Nicolis di Robilant," p. 392). The same expression is used in the semiofficial *Fremden-Blatt* for 17 October 1885, which in the lead editorial greets the appointment of Robilant as foreign minister with much praise.

[8] This might be the reason Radowitz called de Launay's language cloying (above, ch. 17, n. 9).

[9] Robilant enjoined Nigra to be energetic in dealing with the Ballhaus; and one day he observed, in connection with the large number of complaints that the Italian embassy had to make to the Austro-

Above all, Robilant's formal vigor corresponded to a much higher degree of energy and solidity of thought than de Launay possessed. Here, finally, we meet an individual not bent on success, disdainful indeed of vulgar approval, but born for action in general, and for political action in particular, even if he entered this field past his youth, after a long military career. Less learned than Nigra, less open to varied interests, of less brilliant intelligence, Robilant at times was also less perspicacious than Nigra in diagnosing a situation, for he was inclined to succumb to a recurring pessimism that made him exaggerate threats; this was evident in the early months of 1880, at the moment of greatest tension between Italy and Austria, when he suspected Bismarck of wickedly preparing to spur Austria into a war against Italy.[10] In this sort of situation, Nigra showed greater coolness of judgment. But Robilant, more blunt and robust, possessed the reflex to act that was beginning to fail Nigra. Like Sella, he was principally a character, a moral force, "an intelligence that inexorably *wished* for what it *saw*," and when he saw matters clearly, will and performance always followed.[11] When he was scarcely thirteen years old, at Vienna, and his maternal great-uncle, the marshal and Prince of Hohenzollern-Hechingen, had insisted that he should study in an Austrian military college and then join his regiment, he had romantically penned his reply in his own blood: "I will never serve other than my king and my country—signed in my blood—Charles Robilant."[12] Now, in full maturity, far from the romantic exaltation of youthful years, he still never flinched from his intended course.

He was by nature a man of action, with a breadth of conception and solid training, quick to grasp the essential element of a situation and not lose himself in what was peripheral,[13] decisive in taking initiative, and inflexible, when he had

---

Hungarian government: "I understand very well your annoyance at continually having to address complaints to the imperial and royal government. I know that nuisance all too well, having put up with it for over fourteen years. But it remains true that with the Austrian government nothing is gained by letting things pass. At Vienna they think of tolerance as *pusillanimity*, and if you let things pass, our government loses credit and the ambassador loses prestige. Of course one ought not to launch a complaint without reason, but when there is a reason one ought never to hesitate to back it up in the most forceful manner" (Robilant, personal letter to Nigra, 14 May 1886; De Vecchi archive and AE, *Carte Robilant*).

[10] Robilant, report, 9 February 1880, no. 1210 (AE, *Ris.*, c. 27). And cf. his personal letter to Corti, 21 February (AE, *Carte Robilant*); *D.D.F.*, 1st ser., 3:34. It is quite true that Bismarck was pressing Vienna to take a harder line (cf. Pribram, *Les traités politiques secrets de l'Autriche-Hongrie* 1:172–73; Simpson, ed., *The Saburov Memoirs*, p. 115; Salvatorelli, *La Triplice Alleanza*, pp. 53–56; W. Langer, *European Alliances and Alignments, 1871–1890* [New York, 1931], p. 201; E. Laloy, *La politique de Bismarck* [Paris, 1939], p. 420). But it is out of the question that he was thinking of staging a real crisis, with Italy as the intended victim. In order to live at peace with Italy, he maintained, "fear works better than love" (Windelband, *Bismarck und die europäischen Grossmächte*, pp. 111 ff.). There is an echo of the views of Robilant in Chiala, *Pagine di storia contemporanea* 2:49 (2d ed.; 1895), who also speaks of Bismarck as trying to rouse Austria to act.

[11] This judgment of Sella is found in Barzellotti, *Studi e ritratti* (2d ed.; Palermo, no date but 1917), p. 192.

[12] Cappelli, "Il conte Carlo Nicolis di Robilant," p. 388.

[13] De Moüy, who was French ambassador at Rome when Robilant was foreign minister, portrays him thus: "He directed foreign affairs from on high, being at the same time very firm, very well informed, and at bottom very reserved, beneath a cordial and vivacious surface" (de Moüy, *Souvenirs et causeries d'un diplomate*, pp. 224–25).

adopted a line of conduct, in following it through with resolution.[14] When he was appointed to a very challenging post, he threw himself body and soul into the work, and neither the ruggedness of the task nor the disappointments inflicted on him by the policies of his government succeeded in causing this hard, tenacious will to flag. He often wished for the repose of his "Tusculum" at Lingotto,[15] and sometimes expressed the hope that a foreign minister would send him back home,[16] or declared that before long he himself would set the matter right by leaving. Following "a wretched spell" of dealing with the Ballhaus, he disclosed his weariness and dismay to Nigra, who (paradoxically) had to exhort *him* not to lose heart.[17]

But these were temporary slumps, the kind that in a man of action vanish as soon as his labor restores him to himself. Their effect is like the effect upon Antaeus of being thrown to the ground: they produce a perpetual renewal of energy and combative will. Such a man re-creates himself out of pessimism and tiredness. Even after the ministerial crisis of February-April 1887 and the end of his period in government, the great bitterness that pervaded him[18] and the "real disgust for political life"[19] that he felt did not prevent him from agreeing a few months later to take charge of a new embassy, the one in London. This would have meant sitting down to the arduous handiwork of diplomacy once more: but soon he was absolved from all earthly cares and labors by his sudden, unfortu-

---

[14] Robilant's firm character, as well as his intelligence, made General Govone think of suggesting his name to Lanza as minister of war, or of the navy, in 1869 (Lanza, *Le carte* 6:364).

[15] He designates his villa thus in a letter to Corti of 1 March 1884 (AE, *Carte Robilant*).

[16] On 16 April 1884 he writes to Corti: "I am more fed up than ever with this Trappist existence, in which I am constantly forced to refill a bucket full of leaks. I continually invite Rome, indeed beseech them in every possible way, to send a successor more capable or fortunate than I. For now they pay me no heed, but the day will come when I will take it on myself to resolve the matter for once and for all—and that will be the day when the pentarchs triumph in Italy" (AE, *Carte Robilant*). And cf. his letters to Corti of 16 December 1882, and 1 March 1884: "there is talk that the pentarchs may come to power. That would be all we need. I have no wish to go crazy, and if some coalition is formed that makes my life here impossible, I will simply drop everything, and go off to settle in my Tusculum at Lingotto." Even when he was minister, he was looking forward to the moment of his "liberation" (letter to Corti, 30 May 1886; AE, *Carte Robilant*). In fact, at the end of 1882 Robilant had offered to resign over the question of the imperial visit to Umberto I: Mancini refused to accept (Mancini, personal letter to Robilant, 4 December 1882; Robilant to Mancini, 14 January 1883; Mancini archive).

[17] "If you could raise my morale somewhat . . . you would do me a real service, for I do not conceal from you that I see things in the blackest possible way," Robilant wrote to Nigra on 4 January 1882. And again on 4 December: "Since we parted I have once again had some very bad days. To tell the truth, these recur so frequently that I really feel tired and completely lacking in confidence" (De Vecchi archive, and also AE, *Carte Robilant*, where there is also a letter of Nigra to Robilant, 9 January 1882: "I beg you not to lose heart"). Robilant also wrote of his exhaustion to Minghetti on 6 January 1883 (BCB, *Carte Minghetti*, cart. XXIV, fasc. 48).

[18] Robilant to Corti, 26 April 1887: "I was treated the way I would have been if I had done nothing but damage to the country in my forty-three-year career. And that's all right with me, I make no complaint, I understand perfectly that in a parliamentary government it has to be so. But you will understand that it robs me of all desire to resume the struggle." Yet even then he adds: "Of course, if my efforts in any area were perchance still thought to be of some use, I would not hesitate to abandon my quiet life in order to serve the country with the same zeal and enterprise as in the past" (AE, *Carte Robilant*).

[19] Robilant to Corti, 10 July 1887; AE, *Carte Robilant*.

nate death. Truly, notwithstanding many intervals of pessimism about Italy and the Italians[20] that constituted a link between him and the old d'Azeglio too, he belonged to the legion of the strong.[21]

He was not filled with ambition, with desire for glory and power. These appetites, the natural endowment of the political man, were lacking in him. He would never, as the young Cavour did, have dreamed of being prime minister to the king of Italy; and perhaps it was this that was needed to make him a complete politician; it was certainly an obstacle to him as a minister in a parliamentary regime.

He himself professed to his friends that he did not believe he was cut out to be a minister: "that is not my affair, I feel, indeed I know; and I do not intend to put myself to the test. In my view one should not make a trial of such things, since it is Italy that would suffer! I am ready to do my country *all* the services it might ask, but to be a cabinet minister . . . there would have to be circumstances such that I believed I could not refuse, circumstances I hope Italy never has to face."[22] Not being a party man, he had no backing, "whereas to assume such a role successfully it is best to have a name and a personal political stature that inspire trust and respect in the country. In any case I feel no vocation to play the role of minister either with the Right or the Left, and hence if I were asked I would always refuse, unless the domestic situation were such that I were forced to remember that I am first of all a soldier. Let us hope there never comes a day when king and country need to use my breast as a shield, and that I am left in peace."[23] After actually making the experiment, he found in the political and parliamentary situation of February 1887 a "new confirmation of my complete ineptitude for parliamentary life, something which I have never hidden."[24]

And the truth is that in 1885, after first refusing in June-July at the moment of Mancini's leaving the cabinet,[25] he acquiesced in September only because he brought himself to believe that the hour had come at which king and country had need of him: the situation was tempestuous, with the Triple Alliance practically dead and dark clouds piling up on the European horizon. When he received a formal order from the king, the soldier obeyed and girded himself, resigned but courageous, to his new task.[26]

---

[20] "For the rest, what is taking place proves something else, which is that although we have made Italy, we have not yet made the Italians; that indeed the regime installed when the Left came to power has corrupted the Italians to the point where there is no more hope of making anything of them. My evaluation is harsh but accurate" (Robilant, letter to Corti, 28 February 1887; AE, *Carte Robilant*, previously published in F. Salata, "Il conte di Robilant," in *Il Corriere della Sera* for 7 August 1926).

[21] Nigra to Robilant, 11 December 1882: "I am perfectly well aware of what is going on in your mind, and I comprehend the waves of discouragement that must often sweep over you. But I urge you to resist. You have the temperament of the strong, and are one of the rare individuals on whom our country relies now, as in the past. Do not let yourself be discouraged by difficulties, and when they present themselves, think of the first word of your device, *pugna*" (AE, *Carte Robilant*).

[22] Robilant to Corti, 6 December 1877 (AE, *Carte Robilant*).

[23] Robilant to Corti, 18 December 1878 (AE, *Carte Robilant*).

[24] Robilant to Corti, 28 February 1887 (AE, *Carte Robilant*).

[25] Telegrams of Mancini to Robilant and Robilant to Mancini, 27 June (Mancini archive); Chiala, *Pagine di storia contemporanea* 3:399 (2d ed.; 1898).

[26] Chiala, *Pagine di storia contemporanea* 3:399–400. Robilant himself informed the marchese Cappelli, who was later his general secretary, of his acceptance on 28 September in these terms:

Robilant's indifference to the prospect of being a minister was not, however, purely the result of a lack of ambition, and of his feeling that he lacked experience as a parliamentarian. There was also a sort of instinctive distrust of the parliamentary struggle, a distrust that increased in the years between 1870 and 1887. It is not that he was an authoritarian in the manner of de Launay, though this belief was held even outside Italy[27] and was a charge often laid at his feet by his political enemies.[28] Here too, external resemblances conceal underlying differences. De Launay was an adamant admirer of the strong approach, which is why he admired Bismarck and Bismarckism, but Robilant did not hesitate to deplore unambiguously the antiliberal stance of the German chancellor. To his close friend Corti he wrote on 12 May 1884:

What to me is the most serious thing today is the war declared openly by Prince Bismarck on liberalism: it makes our intimate relations with the two empires to which we are allied ever more difficult, and without intimate contact there is no alliance that will hold, even if it is written on parchment and duly sealed. It must be added that only Joshua was privileged to make the sun stand still, so Bismarck deludes himself strangely if he thinks he can reverse the direction of the world: it is my belief that he is sowing the seeds of a tremendous whirlwind that will one day be harvested by a future emperor of Germany.[29] I do not, you understand, wish with that to imply that there is nothing to be done to stop the parliamentary regime from spreading here as it has in Italy, but I believe that a well-balanced country, as Prussia is, could give a very useful example of a just division of attributions between the

"After a desperate resistance I have had to give in to the insistence of Depretis, who was strongly supported by His Majesty. The king yesterday expressed to me his precise wishes in a manner equivalent to an order; and since an old soldier like me does not quibble about the orders of his sovereign, I telegraphed that I *would obey*! . . . I am resigned, as always when I have had to do my duty and sacrifice my own person for the service of the king and the inseparable good of the country. I have no illusions of any kind, but nonetheless I will fling myself courageously into the fray, and am ready to plunge from the Tarpeian rock, without even pausing at the Capitol first" (AE, *Carte Robilant*). And on 15 October he wrote to Visconti Venosta: "I do not delude myself in the slightest about my case. The country, sick of lawyers, applauded the choice of my poor person in the hope that I would be able to satisfy aspirations which it hides even from itself [*sue informolabili aspirazioni*]. Disillusionment will not be long in coming, and then we shall see what we shall see" (Visconti Venosta archive). And cf. telegram and letter of Robilant to Umberto I, and telegram of Umberto I to Robilant, 27 June–27 September 1885 (AE, *Carte Robilant*; Richelmy, "La Triplice e gli ambasciatori italiani a Vienna," pp. 299–301; the letter of 27 June is partially published in Salata, "Il conte di Robilant").

[27] Thus, in the view of the count of Saint Vallier, the French ambassador at Berlin, Robilant belonged, by birth and sympathies "to the purest right wing" (8 March 1880; *D.D.F.*, 1st ser., 3:51).

[28] As he himself said to Corti, "For the rest I would not be welcome [as foreign minister] for too many reasons, and also because, as I was told recently, I have a reputation for authoritarianism that is not consonant with the parliamentary setting" (8 September 1884; AE, *Carte Robilant*; and cf. his letter to Umberto I in Richelmy, "La Triplice e gli ambasciatori italiani a Vienna," p. 300). And in fact, when Robilant was nominated, Cairoli vented his feelings to his friend Napoli, criticizing Depretis for daring to do what the Right itself "though it had the ultraconservative Robilant at its core, would never have dared to do: make him foreign minister" (6 October 1885; MRP, *Carte Cairoli*, pacco 30).

[29] The same verdict is delivered in a letter of 4 December 1884 to Greppi: "it is certain that the arrogant chancellor is preparing dark days for his country when he disappears from the scene" (in De Cesare, *Il conte Giuseppe Greppi*, p. 234).

government and the organ of national representation, and this, I think, would be very desirable. It could be achieved in Italy too, by proceeding with fairness, intelligence, and firmness, since at bottom the country clearly shows that that is what it wants from us. Unfortunately the *Man* for the job is missing, and if Depretis should perish, I have no idea whose hands we would wind up in. For my part I continue to fear that we will have to call on Crispi, and in my view that would be the worst piece of luck that could befall us.[30]

In this letter we have the entire politics of Robilant, and also his deep distrust of the German chancellor and his lesser Italian emulator. Though ever since 1871 he had favored friendship with Germany, indeed had favored an understanding if it was to be a bond between equals and not one of lord and vassal, what he felt for Bismarck was respect for his undeniable qualities as a great statesman, but at the same time profound antipathy. Perhaps this antipathy had swelled as a result of a personal episode in September 1879 in Vienna, when Bismarck, who had come to the Habsburg capital to conclude the Austro-German alliance, purposely omitted to pay a visit to the Italian ambassador, while calling on the ambassadors of France and Turkey and the apostolic nuncio, in order to display ostentatiously what his humor was toward Italy at the moment.[31] But it was an antipathy based on much more serious and universal motives, including Bismarck's authoritarianism, his intolerance of everything that did not square with his point of view, his nervous fits and starts[32] and fierce rancors,[33] his bullying treatment of anyone the moment they were no longer his equal in power. Robilant also suspected further ambitious designs and feared that German hegemony was tending to become even more pronounced and overbearing; these suspicions and fears were exaggerated, it is true, but for all that were vividly felt by Robilant and many other contemporaries. All these things played a part in the dislike (which is the right name for it) of the Italian general for the iron chancellor. There is the additional fact that Robilant did not deceive himself about Bismarck's feelings for Italy, did not let himself be dazzled in the least by the effusions that poured out at friendly moments, by solemn declarations about the "natural alliance" between Italy and Germany. Instead he perceived with sure intuition that in the political game of the great Prussian, Italy counted for more or less according to the particular moment and the general situation, and that for Bismarck, as was only to be expected, the

---

[30] AE, *Carte Robilant.* It is only in light of his whole way of thinking, which we are trying to illustrate here, that the following words of Robilant can be properly understood: "Yes indeed, I suppose I am authoritarian, with my colleagues, with parliament, and with the country" (letter to Umberto I, 27 June 1885; AE, *Carte Robilant*; Salata, "Il conte di Robilant"; Richelmy, "La Triplice e gli ambasciatori italiani a Vienna," p. 300), for otherwise they might lead us to think (wrongly) that he was of the company of Bismarck and Crispi.

[31] This episode caused much comment (cf. Chiala, *Pagine di storia contemporanea* 2:43).

[32] "For the rest, as things stand the destiny of Europe is in the hands of the 'solitary of Varzin,' who manipulates men and things according to the daily rise and fall in his state of nervous excitation; hence the future is incalculable" (Robilant to Corti, 3 March 1880; AE, *Carte Robilant*).

[33] On 8 September 1884 Robilant writes to Corti: "Bismarck hates Gladstone as only he knows how to hate: even beyond the grave" (AE, *Carte Robilant*). This comment was utterly cogent: cf. Eyck, *Bismarck* 3:408, and on Bismarck as a "hater," ibid., 3:14.

sole consideration was German interest. In fact, if anything the feeling for Italy, at least after 1866, which Robilant thought—not wrongly—he detected in the chancellor, was one of condescension, not untainted by an underlying contempt. Indeed Robilant sometimes accentuated the chancellor's diabolical side and depicted his designs in the darkest hues, darker than they were in reality.[34]

Thus, when there was a phase of extreme Italian-German coolness in 1885, with the reported result that de Launay alone among all the Italian diplomatic representatives abroad was viewed in a dim light at Palazzo della Consulta [the Italian foreign ministry], Robilant confided to his friend Corti his own views, which were very different from those of the Italian admirers of the great chancellor. "So they are content with everybody except de Launay. They have no idea what it would take to find an ambassador capable of changing Bismarck's humor in regard to Italy. For the rest, you know my ideas about this: as long as it pleases God to preserve that scourge called Bismarck in the world, there is no hope of peace, for the present state of Europe certainly cannot be called peace."[35]

As minister, Robilant maintained this attitude of reserve to what he called the "*pro tempore* master of the world" with great firmness, dignity, and ability. He avoided personal visits, or as he called them, summonses *ad audiendum verbum*,[36] and shunned meetings,[37] being quite sure that only in this way would he gain respect from Bismarck for his person and his policies; and so indeed it was, with some help from the international situation.

The Italian took a different approach to the German even where international relations and the mode of conducting them were concerned. Bismarck was absolutely opposed to discussing major questions with anyone other than authorized diplomats and grew angry when he saw problems of international politics debated too fully in foreign parliaments, or analyzed too precisely in "green books" and "blue books." Bismarck revolutionized the outcomes of diplomacy, not its methods: despite the novelty of his cunning manipulation of public opinion by means of press campaigns,[38] which was the real innovation introduced by Napoleon III, by Cavour, and by him into diplomacy, he was still very much tied

[34] In his letter to Greppi of 4 December 1884, Robilant writes: "The end at which Bismarck aimed was to reduce us to impotence; no one wanted to understand this while there was still time, and now his end has been attained, and we are being treated like a squeezed lemon" (in De Cesare, *Il conte Giuseppe Greppi*, p. 234).

[35] 15 January 1885 (AE, *Carte Robilant*).

[36] Thus on 8 September 1884, on the eve of the meeting at Skiernevice, to which he did not wish "to give great importance," he said to Corti: "the capital fact for me was the summons of Kálnoky to Varzin to receive the *Word* and act accordingly. At that meeting a granite basis for European politics was laid for as long as Bismarck lasts; all the rest is merely accessory" (AE, *Carte Robilant*).

[37] On 2 September 1886 he writes to Corti: "I was glad to receive your congratulations on my absence from the various meetings at which the brilliant events that took place just recently [in Bulgaria] were more or less planned, events that will probably have an even worse sequel. As you can well imagine, it would have been an effort for me to do the slightest thing, even to listen politely; but I greatly laud myself on the reserve I maintained, and on the resistance I opposed to one [de Launay] who, on the strength of his own long experience, urged me not to let the occasion escape for an exchange of ideas with the temporary master of the world!" (AE, *Carte Robilant*). On de Launay's insistence that Robilant ought to meet Bismarck, cf. Chiala, *Pagine di storia contemporanea* 3:468 ff.; Crispi, *Politica estera*, p. 213; Salvemini, *La politica estera dell'Italia*, p. 72.

[38] On these press campaigns, cf. Bülow, *Memorie* 4:510–11 (in summer 1879, to overcome Wilhelm I's resistance to the Austro-Prussian alliance).

to the methods of classic diplomacy, which was conducted in secret exclusively by the "competent," those "technically adept" in the handling of international affairs. Only a very restricted group of initiates was worthy to discuss the *arcana imperii*, and before the vulgar mob one merely repeated Horace's *odi et arceo*. Robilant on the other hand, though he certainly did not possess a loose tongue or leak information easily, and though he believed as well that not everything is for public consumption, was nevertheless starting to give greater weight to the opinion of the peoples of Europe. For the German, this opinion was meant to serve the statesman as an arm of combat, a tactical resource to be used without regard to the sentiments of the multitude as such, but for the Italian it was something more. A liberal moderate in domestic politics, Robilant was on the road to applying liberal conceptions in foreign policy too, turning his back increasingly on the classic conception of the *arcana imperii*. When news got out prematurely about the signing of a treaty of alliance between Germany and Austria at the beginning of 1879, he commented to his friend Corti: "as regards the treaty, there is no one who believes that this is an isolated fact; for my part, I would like to be certain that Italy is not in the least involved. Certain it is that this conduct of policy by means of theatrical coups, with secret treaties etcetera, cannot in the long run bring good results. You will say that this is how it was always done, and I cannot deny it, but I would point out that times were different, and that today the peoples do not let themselves be fooled indefinitely in this manner."[39] Rare words indeed in the mouth of a diplomat, and certainly ones that never fell from the lips of Bismarck!

If that was Robilant's opinion of Bismarck, his verdict on Crispi was bound to be just as harsh. He did not deny the "great worth" of the man, from whom he had nevertheless had his share of unpleasantness and strong antagonism,[40] but he was offended, sometimes even shocked, by the way Crispi played to the crowd.[41] In the fiery Sicilian politician Robilant saw and feared the authoritarianism of a junior Bismarck, whose instincts and abilities all led him to dominate; he saw the vanity of the man,[42] and above all the propensity to let himself be carried away by a momentary impulse, the excitement of a new idea that had popped into his

[39] Robilant, personal letter to Corti, 8 February 1879 (AE, *Carte Robilant*).

[40] On 12 July 1887 Robilant writes to Greppi that Crispi "in the meantime has acquired absolute predominance, almost like the dictator of the country. In justice I have to say that up till now he has made very good use of this strong power, governing the state with an iron hand that had not been felt for a very long time" (in De Cesare, *Il conte Giuseppe Greppi*, p. 244).

[41] "I briefly feared the formation of a cabinet by Crispi, not for the consequences this development would have on me personally, but solely for the immense harm that would befall our country, which we are all struggling so hard to get back on the right track. But now that I have before me the text of the speech given by that tribune [at Palermo, 18 November 1883; Crispi, *Scritti e discorsi politici*, pp. 536 ff.], to the extent that it deals with foreign policy, I can no longer envision the king and the country allowing the person capable of expounding such deranged and senseless notions to seize power and spoil a work which it still sometimes seems to me impossible that we succeeded in accomplishing amid all the difficulties by which we found ourselves beset" (Robilant to Corti, 25 November 1883; AE, *Carte Robilant*).

[42] Robilant to Tosi, 3 August 1882: "That man [Crispi] wants to be the center of attention, and I greatly fear that if Depretis goes under when the Chamber sits again, and Crispi takes his place, it would be a fatal blow; there would be reason to despair of the lot of Italy" (AE, *Carte Robilant*).

head.[43] A dangerous man for the country, in sum, despite his undeniable gifts, faced with whom it was proper to pronounce a ritual *libera nos Domine*.[44]

It is hard to claim that the man who held these sentiments was an authoritarian in principle. Marselli, who had earlier served under him at the War College and was always his friend, a man of the Center Left, went much farther than he did. In 1873 Marselli was hoping to see "Bismarckian methods" applied in Italy to cure the ills of a country that had grown skeptical, numb to its most serious problems, a country that was sound asleep.[45]

Robilant was a military man by training and instinct and had been raised in a very different environment from the one in which men like Nigra, Visconti Venosta, Minghetti, and Sella had grown up. A single faith had been inculcated in Robilant: service to the king, which was exactly the same thing as service to the country. He had not had continuous direct contact with the liberal faith of Cavour,[46] which had been so influential for so many contemporaries, and had long been habituated instead to the environs of the barracks and the court, where liberal faith had made far fewer inroads. Yet despite all this he had fully and truly accepted the liberal state and the ideas of liberty. Because of the sincerity and honesty of his beliefs, Robilant, who was bound to de Launay by friendship of an

---

[43] Robilant to Corti, 10 July 1887: "It is certain that he [Crispi] is a man of great worth, and that there is no danger of him letting himself be guided by popular pressure. But when he is the absolute master, he might cause the ship of state to run serious risks, since sudden impulses [*colpi di testa*] are always a possibility with a man of his character." There are some who hope that Crispi and Robilant might join forces, "he to confront domestic squalls, and I to deal with foreign affairs as best I can." But Robilant says that this solution would entail two things that make it unlikely, indeed impossible: "the first is that Crispi would dare to throw his glove in the face of the radicals by seeking to enlist me." The second is "that I, if I were asked, would have to join forces with a man who knows how to do nothing, and is able to do nothing, except to dominate" (AE, *Carte Robilant*). Robilant writes again on 11 November to Corti: "It was a typical Crispian impulse [the brutally worded recall of Corti from London], and we will see more of them, since this man of undoubted intelligence was and always will be the victim of his sudden impulses" (ibid.). In a letter of 20 November, again to Corti, Robilant was kinder: "Italy is going through a very difficult period. Crispi is in a position of some peril, but is very strong at the same time, since no one can see any successor. Besides, men like him do not let themselves be thrown out easily; for that to happen, there would have to occur events that we must all hope that God does not visit on our country. His worst adversary is his own character, but there is reason to believe that he will succeed in overcoming it" (ibid.).

[44] Robilant to Corti, 8 April 1881 (AE, *Carte Robilant*). Crispi for his part disliked Robilant, as is well known. He once said, on the occasion of the dispute with Colombia, that Robilant (of all people!) had failed to stand up for Italian interests, had in fact compromised them "with unsatisfactory suggestions, and with an absence of dignity and energy" (Crispi to Alberto Pisani Dossi, 20 August 1886; ACR, Archivio Pisani Dossi, busta 1, fasc. 1).

[45] Marselli to Robilant, 7 January 1873 (AE, *Carte Robilant*). This extremely interesting letter is one long violent outburst against the "sleepiness" of everyone in Italy, at a time when "our possible adversaries are not standing around twiddling their thumbs." Marselli's presentiments are "dark, very dark." The same ideas occur in another letter of 25 March 1873: "I tremble at my own forebodings. I torment myself endlessly with the question whether we are an old people, or a young people with a great future ahead" (AE, *Carte Robilant*). Cf. above, ch. 1, n. 81.

[46] Not that Robilant had had no contact at all with Cavour: from him he received personal instructions both in the autumn of 1858, at the moment of the mission of d'Angrogna to Berlin, St. Petersburg, and Moscow, and in March 1861, before leaving for Naples. For Robilant, Cavour was the greatest man Italy had produced (cf. *Notizie storiche sulla famiglia Nicolis ed in particolare sul conte Carlo Felice Nicolis di Robilant, raccolte e pubblicate dal figlio conte Edmondo* [Venice, 1929], pp. 16 and 18; and also Salata, "Il conte di Robilant").

environmental and, so to speak, aboriginal, kind, was able to become a firm friend of Minghetti and Visconti Venosta too, forming ties that, if they did not amount to complete identification, certainly constituted affinity of ideas. Minghetti, who thought highly of him,[47] could say in writing to him about the *trasformismo* of Depretis that the opinions of the man from Stradella "on the course of events domestically and abroad are no different from those that you and I would hold";[48] and Minghetti later claimed that Robilant did not at all represent the Right in the Depretis cabinet—not because he was too reactionary but rather because he was willing to form an alliance with Nicotera.[49]

Robilant was impatient of the adversarial structure of parliament and the instability of cabinet formations; he distrusted democracy, which he now considered hegemonic in Italy, and which he thought would lead the country "where it has already led the other countries in which it prevailed."[50] Though they sprang from the old antidemocratic culture that was an essential part of Italian and French moderatism, this impatience and distrust were powerfully reinforced by a long series of experiences and reflections: discouragement at the seeming chaos of the political parties, the skittishness of parliamentary deputies, their indifference to the common good and exclusive devotion to private interests.[51] The same discouragement gripped Bonghi and elicited his work *Decadenza del regime parlamentare*, which came out in 1884, just as the ideas of Robilant were growing more somber.[52] Over the years it likewise fastened intermittently on many of the leaders of the Right, not just the irascible Ricasoli but also Lanza, Minghetti, Visconti Venosta, and even Sella.[53]

After the fall of the Right, Robilant with many others had hoped for the formation of a great center party, modeled on that of Cavour. This appeared once more to be the best instantiation of the parliamentary regime in Italy, where the systematic counterpoint of two parties on the English model did not seem possible; above all, it appeared to be the only way to form a stable and cohesive majority able to put a halt to the dangerous drift to the left and defend the established order with firmness.[54] Robilant thus supported the classic method, in Italian political

[47] Cf. the verdict on Robilant he gave to Queen Margherita (Minghetti, *Lettere fra la regina Margherita e Marco Minghetti*, p. 209).

[48] Minghetti to Robilant, 30 December 1882 (AE, *Carte Robilant*).

[49] Minghetti to Luzzatti, 12 August 1886 (Luzzatti, *Memorie* 2:263).

[50] Robilant to Corti, 24 August 1887 (AE, *Carte Robilant*).

[51] "In Italy everything is a personal question, the interest and the honor of the country count for nothing," Robilant writes to Corti on 11 April 1879 (AE, *Carte Robilant*). And again to Corti on 21 February 1880: "In Italy . . . everything else counts for naught compared to the *party*, which has to be kept in power at any cost, even despite a general collapse" (AE, *Carte Robilant*).

[52] Cf. as well E. Pesce, "Ruggero Bonghi," *Civiltà Moderna* 3 (1931): 280–81.

[53] For the discouragement of Sella (who was "so disgusted he felt sick"), of Lanza, who saw chaos increasing and a dark future ahead, and of Visconti Venosta, cf. Luzzatti, *Memorie* 2:89, 106, 176, 223. For Luzzatti himself see ibid., 2:98, 103. For Ricasoli see his *Lettere e documenti* 10:421. In 1882 Visconti Venosta stated to the Austrian ambassador, Wimpffen, that "because of the excess of parliamentarism, the government is nothing more than the executive committee of the Chamber" (Wimpffen, report, 17 February 1882; SAW, *P.A.*, XI/92, no. 10 B).

[54] Minghetti illustrated the *trasformismo* of Depretis thus in his letter to Robilant of 30 December 1882, cited above at n. 48.

history, of erecting a barrier against the extremisms of the left and the right, from Cavour to Depretis to Giolitti,[55] and like numerous others, he saw Sella as the man to head this coalition.[56] In the sequel he lost his illusions along with the rest about Sella,[57] when the latter came down off the pedestal he occupied as the only statesman able to save Italy,[58] and from then on the Italian parliamentary situation seemed increasingly uncertain to Robilant. He set store by Depretis initially,[59] but these hopes vanished in their turn, with disappointment following disappointment as Depretis revealed how old, tired, and physically incapable he was.[60] On top of all this there came his bitter personal experience as a diplomat: dissatisfaction with the actions of the government of his country in international questions,[61] ministerial crises at the least opportune moments,[62] uncertain and

---

[55] This fundamental aspect of Italian political history has been trenchantly described by Omodeo in *L'opera politica del Conte di Cavour* 1:144.

[56] Corti to Robilant, 20 March 1877: "For myself, I believe that what is most to be desired in the interests of the country is that a great center party should be formed under the aegis of Sella, which would be free of the worn-out elements of the Right, while openly refusing the ultrademocrats." Robilant replies on 25 March: "I too maintain that the remedy is the one you indicate, but at present I have little hope that it will be adopted" (AE, *Carte Robilant*).

[57] Robilant to Corti, 11 April 1879: "Sella, in whom I long placed my hopes, has shown himself for some time now unequal to the role he was meant to fill, and so I am searching in vain for the star on which to fix my gaze" (AE, *Carte Robilant*). And cf. Bonghi, *Programmi politici e partiti* (= vol. 1 of *Opere* [Florence, 1933]), p. 224. But following a discussion with Sella two years earlier, Corti had written to Robilant on 20 March 1877 that Sella "has very little belief in the future of the party he is supposed to lead, and the party lacks faith in him."

[58] Thus Luzzatti, *Memorie* 2:103.

[59] Robilant to Corti, 16 December 1882: ". . . the intentions of Depretis are excellent, God grant that he may have the power to translate them into deeds" (AE, *Carte Robilant*).

[60] Robilant to Corti, 30 May 1886: "we do indeed have a majority, but we are not strong. Depretis was always a master at finding expedients, tremendously habile, but never strong, and he is even less so today at his advanced age, with his infirmities." And on 16 March 1887, again to Corti: "the worst of it . . . is the very bad health, and also the advanced age, of Depretis!" (AE, *Carte Robilant*).

[61] "In any case, we do not conduct foreign policy, all we do is conduct domestic politics, or rather parliamentary alchemy" (Robilant to Corti, 16 October 1880). In another letter to Corti on 21 July 1884, he says: "parliamentary alchemy dominates everything else, and overrides every other consideration" (AE, *Carte Robilant*). And to Greppi on 5 September 1884, he writes that Italy is more isolated than ever, which was to be expected, "since with the parliamentarism that misgoverns Italy, it is impossible to conduct a . . . consistent foreign policy. For years I have tirelessly preached seriousness, but my voice is lost in the roar of Montecitorio" (in De Cesare, *Il conte Giuseppe Greppi*, p. 234 and cf. as well pp. 236 and 239).

[62] On 8 February 1877, informing Corti of rumored imminent changes in the composition of the cabinet, Robilant commented: "the skein is more tangled than ever, and we choose precisely such moments to permit ourselves the luxury of a crisis that might produce a radical shift in our foreign policy. Let me make it clear that I am speaking of Turkey and that I fear dreadful confrontations. Enough, may God have mercy on us" (AE, *Carte Robilant*). And on 27 December 1877, after Melegari had left the cabinet, he comments again to Corti: "there is more to cry about than to laugh at in all this: to be amusing ourselves with a ministerial crisis at a time like this, for no reason or idea whatsoever, for a question of personalities and cliques—yes, of political cliques" (AE, *Carte Robilant*). One thinks of the ironical comment of the *Times* in 1869 on Italian parliamentary life: "a parliamentary interpellation, a ministerial crisis, and a provisional government; then once again a ministerial crisis, a provisional government, and an interpellation!" (cited in Jacini, *Sulle condizioni della cosa pubblica in Italia*, p. 21). [*Translator's note:* In the absence of a precise reference to the issue of the *Times* in which this passage first appeared, I have retranslated it from Italian back into English.]

feeble directives, disparity of views, the center overridden by the tendencies of the various individual representatives abroad instead of giving leadership,[63] oscillations this way and that which continually undermined Italy's shrinking capital of prestige, the isolation, or as he called it, the moral *effacement* of Italy.[64] "[W]ithout a strong government no vigorous policy, of the sort which you and I are working at, can be conducted."[65]

In Robilant we observe the eternal reaction of the man charged with defending the interests and dignity of his country on foreign soil who becomes highly sensitive to every little slight, who feels it on his own skin, tormenting himself over everything that whittles away the force and international prestige of his homeland. Such a man, being convinced of the greater importance, indeed the primacy, of foreign policy over domestic politics, may be drawn to see the less helpful consequences of the clash of ideas in the domestic political arena, and unlike Machiavelli, to deny that the contest of the factions was the source of the greatness of Rome.

This state of mind was typical not just of Robilant and the other Italians who, though aloof from Crispi, were growing dejected at the way domestic political conditions were hindering the defense of the security and dignity of the country abroad.[66] Proof of this is the complaint of the French ambassador at Berlin, the Count of Saint Vallier, on 21 March 1881, about the deleterious influence of miserable electoral interests, the imbecility and inertia of a Chamber whose members thought only of getting reelected and were ready to sacrifice the greatness, security, and honor of the country to this base end, their absurd domestic politics causing disarray in foreign policy.[67] And yet at this time republican France was gaining strength and cohesion! Saint Valier was a partisan of the ancien régime, and the work of consolidation being carried out by men like Gambetta and Ferry

[63] Robilant to Nigra, 2 July 1881: "unfortunately, given our domestic situation, there is little hope of being able to conduct a sound foreign policy. Above all we ought to give it a uniform general direction, which we sorely lack. What use is it for me to attempt to bring the two countries closer together here, while . . . the representative of the Italian government at Bucharest [Tornielli] seems to have no other end in view than to set us at odds with Austria. I warn you, my dear colleague, that my patience has been severely tried for many years, and that if I had not been bolstered until now by my devotion to king and country, I would long ago have ceased to pursue a métier in which I have been punctured by so many thorns" (AE, *Carte Robilant*). And to Corti on 31 July 1885: "I am completely sick of the endless voyage without a compass that is becoming normal in Italy" (ibid.)

[64] Robilant to Corti on 17 August 1876: "no one pays us any attention in Europe, since circumstances have brought it about that the cabinet in Rome enjoys an *effacement* that could not be more total. Diplomatic relations require stability above all, and having one person, even a mediocre one, in charge of foreign affairs gives his country more of a voice in the council of Europe than a succession of outstandingly gifted individuals can" (AE, *Carte Robilant*). To Corti again, on 4 December 1878: "in the eyes of the other countries, Italy does not exist any more." And on 22 May 1879, to Corti: "one could say that we have lost all consideration in Europe, and that we haven't noticed it; we lurch about in the damnedest way, as though we were the masters of the situation" (ibid.).

[65] Robilant to Nigra, 11 February 1887 (De Vecchi archive; AE, *Carte Robilant*); previously published in Salata, "Il conte di Robilant."

[66] Cf., for example, Artom to Amari, 7 February 1882 (Amari, *Carteggio* 3:353).

[67] *D.D.F.*, 1st ser., 3:385–86. His later similar statements in September 1881, after France had prevailed in Tunis (ibid., 4:111) show that this was not just a passing mood caused by the fear of seeing France humiliated over Tunis.

was not perhaps to his taste. But another individual destined for great things in European diplomatic history, and who came from the ranks of those who built the republic in France, also deplored the present age, deplored the lapse into mediocrity that was democracy's law, and that necessarily entailed that the country should "slump" abroad. "We cut less of a figure all the time."[68]

The state of mind that afflicted Robilant was thus widespread; in it the antidemocratic tendencies of a Taine were reinforced by the lust for external prestige of a Sorel. But Robilant certainly lived it with a painful intensity, with the sustained force that was part of his nature. Robilant was not a nationalist, or to use the contemporary term, a chauvinist. His head was not turned by the phantasms of antique greatness, nor did he wish to fend the water aimlessly with sword strokes. But there were few, before him or subsequently, who had a haughty pride in their nation equal to his, a similar jealousy for Italy's dignity, inexorable in claiming its due,[69] such quickness to take offense, even against the omnipotent Bismarck, at the first hint of injury to Italian dignity.[70] This was the source of his irritation at the shilly-shallying and the mistakes of his government, which he imputed to the political struggle and party intrigues.

About the raw material, meaning the Italian people, his judgment oscillated. From time to time the scene seemed to darken, and he saw no more hope of a reawakening, imagining Italy reduced to the condition of a South American republic,[71] or likening it to an old woman covered in makeup, lacking youthful energy and élan.[72] At other moments he perceived that there was a great will to achieve in the air, a cultural and economic constructiveness which testified that the raw material was sound.[73] This vacillation of judgment, which derived from changes in circumstance and in his frame of mind, could be found in many other Italians; to remain within the ambit of the persons whom Robilant knew and esteemed, Marselli also passed from expressing faith in the Italian people[74] to venting the blackest pessimism that could possibly be imagined.[75]

[68] Cambon, *Correspondance* 1:131.

[69] Cappelli, "Il conte Carlo Nicolis di Robilant," p. 392.

[70] Haymerle speaks of the "well-known sensitivity" of Robilant (report, 13 October 1877, no. 61 B, conf.; SAW, *P.A.*, XI/86).

[71] "But all this matters little to our great contemporary patriots; their ideal is the system that flourishes in the republics of South America, and since we are well on our way, it won't be long before we reach the desired goal," Robilant wrote to Corti on 4 December 1878 (AE, *Carte Robilant*). He wrote again to Corti on 22 May 1879: "The worst of it is that the country does not appear to me capable of being roused. We have fallen into a state like that of the Spanish, with the detrimental difference that we do not enjoy the happy geographic situation of the Iberians, and also that our Spanish brothers of the Latin race possess virtues that unfortunately are missing in the majority of the Italians" (ibid.).

[72] The expression "vecchia imbellettata" was used by Antonio Scialoja in a letter to Luzzatti in 1873 (Luzzatti, *Memorie* 1:358).

[73] Robilant to Corti, 31 July 1885: "Unquestionably there is some rot in Italy, but there is also a lot of good; the country is on the move and at work, and asks for nothing better than to be well governed, which would not be utterly impossible. The launch of the *Morosini* yesterday was more splendid than I can tell, and even for those who, like me, are not very chauvinistic, there was reason to swell with pride" (AE, *Carte Robilant*).

[74] Marselli to Robilant, 13 January 1872: "What is happening in the country? Little, apparently; but underneath there is churning a degree of new economic and intellectual life. . . . A certain desire to study, to learn German, has awakened. A certain nausea with Arcadian politics is being felt. And

In any case, whereas opinions might differ on the raw material, the blame for the perceived weaknesses of Italy was increasingly directed at the institutional structure imposed on it. Observers pointed to what Bonghi called the blemishes that had become the inescapable concomitant of parliamentary government,[76] the absolute power of ministers, the arrogance of the parties and especially their excessive interference in the work of the civil service, their heterogeneity and lack of ideas, their corruption. Remedies were sought, and with the failure of the ideal of a great, homogeneous, strongly ruled, center party, a different antidote occurred to Robilant and others, an antidote that might be said to be innate in the Italian people: this was a race whose ancestral bent was to magnify the man who tramples down and contemn the man who strides forward;[77] a race that in the most splendid period of its civic history had given up on communal liberties and consequent faction struggles to entrust its lot instead to the *virtù* of condottieri of ancient or recent lineage; a race whose greatest political thinker had summed up the lesson of the events of his time by appealing for a prince to bring redemption.[78]

Like many another,[79] like his friend Marselli[80] and the young Vittorio Emanuele Orlando,[81] Robilant too believed that the remedy might come from the political capacity of an individual, a "Man" who would put things right and restore the correct apportionment of competence between the government and the national representative assembly that was the necessary condition for stable polit-

---

in the new generation there are forming . . . virile aspirations here and there, and a belief in great things is springing up" (AE, *Carte Robilant*).

[75] Cf. above, ch. 1, n. 81; and this chapter, n. 45.

[76] *Una questione grossa: La decadenza del regime parlamentare*, in Bonghi, *Opere* 1:310. And note as well the shafts of optimism in Zanichelli's prolusion of 1885, on "Le difficoltà del sistema rappresentativo-parlamentare" (in Zanichelli, *Studi politici e storici*, pp. 91 ff. and 106, and cf. as well "Il partito liberale storico in Italia," ibid., pp. 218 ff.).

[77] This apt expression is Bonghi's (in Alatri, "Bonghi e la vita politica italiana," p. 176).

[78] I take the liberty of referring here to my own book, *Del Principe di Niccolò Machiavelli* (Milan-Rome-Naples, 1926), passim.

[79] Volpe, *Italia moderna* 1:263; M. Delle Piane, "Il liberalismo di Ruggero Bonghi," in *Liberalismo e parlamentarismo*, pp. 22 ff. But I do not think it is possible to interpret the passage from the work of Bonghi (p. 324; cited at n. 76 above) as expressing the wait for a man of genius: in fact Bonghi speaks of the effect, which is usually "short lived," produced by the man of genius who has grasped the tiller of the ship of state. Bonghi was not in favor of the cult of personality; cf. rather Alatri, "Bonghi e la vita politica italiana."

[80] Marselli to Robilant, 6 December 1881: "Now as never before, Italy needs one of those men, of whom Piedmont had a plentiful supply, who at certain supreme moments have the courage to challenge any obstacle, because they have faith in the beneficent result of their effort. Instead, what have we got? An indifferent country, a tired and skeptical Chamber, a groping government that is getting ready to grind itself down over the scrutiny of the lists. Oh God!" (AE, *Carte Robilant*). The difference is that Marselli went much farther than Robilant, and desired Bismarckian methods.

[81] Delle Piane, "Il liberalismo di Ruggero Bonghi," in *Liberalismo e parlamentarismo*, p. 23. And cf. the outburst of Michele Amari to Hartwig, 7 July 1879: "I would be ready, at least in the bad mood I am in at the moment, to exchange your tyrant [Bismarck] for the crooks here, by which I mean our Chamber of Deputies and the idols it has created: it shatters one every six months, and then glues it back together and places it on the altar again. . . . They have lost any sense of shame, since they say openly in parliament that such and such a measure is necessary 'for our party,' as though this, and not the good of Italy, were at issue" (Amari, *Carteggio* 2:246, and cf. also 2:293 and 3:348).

ical development.[82] This nostalgic yearning for a miraculous individual was not a passing fancy: Robilant kept returning to it,[83] which shows that it was not a flash of lightning but a constant, deeply rooted, idea springing from the conviction that "the conditions in which Italy was created required a succession of men of the highest order to govern it, and now we are getting to the point where we are even running short of those of the second order."[84]

Italy awaited a strong man. In truth, Robilant did not desire that his coming should signify authoritarianism, dictatorship, or anything like them. The very fact that he looked to Sella, who was notoriously free of dictatorial tendencies, as the possible restorer of Italian political life, would be enough to show that, for Robilant, the strong man would have to move and act within the framework of liberal institutions, in a liberal spirit, without trying to stifle parliament despite all the abuse heaped on it.[85] He would limit himself to correcting its abuses, to imparting clarity of ideas and continuity of will to the action of the government; he would always be thinking of the interests and honor of the country, not little personal interests and party squabbles. Robilant's dislike of Bismarckism, his prophetic belief that the attempt by this new Joshua to halt the progress of liberal ideas was a mistake, confirm that the strong man, for him and for many others who wanted the same thing at this time,[86] was not to be a dictator, nor oppose liberal ideas; rather he was to permit them to develop to the full their beneficent effect, without the shortcomings that small men had introduced into political life.

And here we touch on the weak point of this mode of thinking: its ingenuousness, surprising in a man like Robilant who was anything but ingenuous. To put one's trust in a strong man while believing that one was preserving intact the essence of liberalism demanded by the times and the course of human history was in fact a piece of gross ingenuousness: as though the "strong" man would seriously be able to surrender all personal ambition and, once in authority, suppress the visions of mastery that take shape in the mind's eye of any human being who comes into possession of excessive power. It was inevitable that Sella, a liberal to the marrow and unwilling to pose as the strong man, should prove not to be the messiah and should disillusion the ambassador to Vienna, as well as

---

[82] Cf. above, pp. 520–21.

[83] Robilant to Corti, 11 April 1879, cited above at n. 51: "In Italy everything is a personal question; the interest and honor of the country count for nothing. One can only say that we completely lack men, or better say, *a* man." And on 3 July 1880, again to Corti: "there is no use thinking of the Right, the *Man* is lacking" (AE, *Carte Robilant*).

[84] Robilant to Corti, 3 March 1880 (AE, *Carte Robilant*).

[85] On 18 December 1878 he said to Corti, in discussing the formation of a new cabinet after the resignation of the Cairoli-Zanardelli ministry: "As regards an extraparliamentary formation, in the first place I do not see the necessity, or the suitability of it," even though he thought the situation very worrying (AE, *Carte Robilant*).

[86] In a letter in which he expresses his hope for "a great king and a great minister," able to dominate parliament and reform the moral development of the Italians (below, n. 101), Lanza observes that without this training, Italy "will not cure itself of the decay that is consuming it; it will remain a feeble, lightweight nation, buffeted by every wind that blows, by which I mean the violent passions of brazen or clever individuals" (Lanza, *Le carte* 10:392; Tavallini, *La vita e i tempi di Giovanni Lanza* 2:202). Lanza picks up the slogan of d'Azeglio, "[the task is] to make the Italians."

Bonghi and many others. Crispi was perhaps the strong man, but what his coming to power would mean, Robilant had long ago divined, with fear and loathing.

To hope to cure the undeniable ills of Italian political life as it then was by running to a great man; to believe in a panacea for the incontestable defects of parliamentary procedure through the sudden intervention of a *deus ex machina* able to straighten the situation out, cure the ulcers of the body politic as though by the touch of a magic wand, and steer foreign policy onto a wise and firm course, without altering in any way the spirit of liberty:[87] this was an illusion, a dangerous illusion that tended to prepare the ground for experiments in practical (though not yet conceptual) authoritarianism of the sort that in effect occurred within a short while. A setting favorable to Crispi was thus created.[88] Crispi for his own part had been declaring ever since 1865 that he was waiting for the man who would lift Italy up and give health and vigor to the "courageous invalid."[89] And among those who applauded him there were many who had earlier complained about the insipience of parliament and spoken of the need for a firm hand;[90] but even those who held that Crispi was a danger to the nation, including Robilant, unconsciously collaborated in his rise, with their prayers that a Man might come.

Robilant had a second antidote in mind as a corrective to the failings of the parliamentary regime, but it was fundamentally of the same nature as the first. This second antidote was likewise common property: Robilant endorsed it later than some,[91] but in unison with, or even ahead of others, contributing to the overall atmosphere, as he had to the feeling that the country was waiting for a strong man. Eight years before Bonghi startled Italy and irritated Umberto I with his *L'ufficio del principe in uno stato libero*,[92] Robilant was deploring the gaping political absence of the king.

"The constitutionalism *à outrance* of His Majesty," Robilant wrote on 15 January 1885 to his usual confidant, Corti, "is certainly very fine if considered from the theoretical aspect, but in my opinion it is utterly impractical. I maintain that even with the most scrupulous observance of constitutional principles, a considerable part of the direction of the state still remains to the king. I would say

[87] This rather contradictory frame of mind, with its belief in miracles, has been perfectly caught by Croce in *Storia d'Italia*, p. 176.

[88] See the acute analysis of Volpe, *Italia moderna* 1:262 ff.

[89] In a letter to Mazzini (Crispi, *Scritti e discorsi politici*, p. 352).

[90] For Marselli, cf. Crispi, *Carteggi politici inediti*, p. 429; for Amari, his *Carteggio* 2:305, 309.

[91] Cf. Turiello, *Governo e governati in Italia* 2:328 ff. (1st ed., 1882). There are clear hints as well in the commemoration of Lanza in April 1882 by Spaventa (*La politica della Destra*, pp. 125–26). Spaventa was certainly not one of those who longed for "strong men." But his criticism of the crown, which he openly blamed for the degeneration of politics, is perfectly in line with the criticism of Robilant and Bonghi (cf. Russo, *Francesco De Sanctis e la cultura napoletana*, pp. 269–70; and Romano, *Silvio Spaventa*, pp. 249 ff.). But Turiello's position is very different; he wishes for "the appearance of a frank, resolute, and authoritative man on the political scene, a man who understands spontaneously what the people expect from their government," and alludes openly to the two men whom Italy has given twice in this century to a neighboring nation, "two great men, of Italian name and blood, who twice in this century have set France back on its feet" (Turiello, ibid.). The reference to the two Napoleonic dictatorships is significant.

[92] Farini, *Diario* 1:218 and 222.

further that a prime minister who began getting the carriage of state back on track with some action in that area would be worthy of the highest praise, for it has been traveling close to the brink of the chasm for some time now."[93] This precedes, by quite a stretch, Bonghi's theory that the sovereign should maintain lofty, pure, and constant vigilance over the conduct of the organs of public power, that he ought to feel himself to be more—and should actually be more— than what extreme parliamentarians might wish. This is the demand for a more functional crown which Sonnino was to press even more pointedly at the beginning of 1897, voicing explicitly what was being said in many quarters about the failure of the royal power to carry out its functions.[94]

It is undeniable that the skeptical and at times cynical indifference of the king, at least in the first part of his reign,[95] the resigned fatalism which struck foreign ambassadors,[96] were a source of distress to faithful monarchists. They were stung at seeing Umberto I fail in courage and diminish his own stature, as though to escape notice.[97] But in appealing to their prince they were still only appealing to the capacities of an individual.

By invoking a strong man, they were searching for the *virtù* of a condottiere who would stand out from the common run of mortals; by invoking their prince, they were calling on a *virtù* consecrated by the regal crown and age-long tradition. In the first case, they were embarking on a course that might lead to the dictatorship of a "son of the people"; in the second on a course that might end in the prospect of a coup d'état by the crown. But in one case and the other, they felt the same blessed messianic sense of waiting for a Hero to redeem their native land from its many suppurating wounds. They were waiting for the Veltro of Dante and the prince of Machiavelli to descend to earth from the heroic summits of poetry and inspired political reverie, donning a tail coat and white shirt front,

[93] AE, *Carte Robilant*.

[94] Delle Piane, *Liberalismo e parlamentarismo*, pp. 64–65 and 90–91; Farini, *Diario 1898* (II), in *Nuova Antologia* (April 1950): 373.

[95] Wimpffen, the Austrian ambassador, reports the following statements made to him by Umberto I on 24 June 1881: "The king said to me that all questions can be reduced to matters of personal interest, especially to pecuniary motives. He makes no exception for the affair of Tunis, and the agitations it provoked. In his view they were no more than pretexts for individual passions, and at bottom no one thinks about it seriously any more, since the question was resolved by faits accomplis which one might regret, but which nothing can be done to change. The king expressed very little esteem for his ministers, in whom he places no confidence, but he was particularly hard on M. Depretis. 'M. Depretis,' His Majesty said to me, 'is habile, but he lives purely on compromise and concessions, and when I see him I never know what fresh untruths he is going to foist on me'" (Wimpffen, personal secret letter, 24 June 1881; SAW, *P.A.*, XI/91). Seven months before, however, the king had had high praise for Depretis, of whom he declared that he felt completely sure (Wimpffen, secret report, 26 November 1880; ibid., XI/90, no. 75 A).

[96] ". . . a preponderant fatalistic streak in the character of King Umberto" (Wimpffen, report, 1 April 1881, classified; SAW, *P.A.*, XI/91, no. 16 A). The queen, he says, displays "much more courage." And in the report of 26 November 1880 cited in the previous note, Wimpffen states that the king sees very clearly what the domestic situation is in Italy (republican agitation), but that, since he cannot find in himself or in the government the strength of will to remedy it, "he abandons himself to the current, and lets things take their course, while getting enjoyment from calling himself, as he did in speaking to me, a 'philosophe'."

[97] Cf. Bonghi, *L'ufficio del Principe in uno Stato libero*, in *Opere* 1:520. Visconti Venosta as well was complaining from 1882 about the passivity and the lack of faith in himself shown by the king (Wimpffen, report, 17 February 1882; SAW, *P.A.*, XI/92, no. 10 B).

or the uniform of a general traversed diagonally by the great red and blue ribbon of the military order of Savoy.

It would be pointless to object that they were appealing to the prince inasmuch as he was more than an individual man with his idiosyncrasy; that their appeal was to the institution, the function, the tradition of a sovereign principle of order in the state. Of course the appeal to the prince was different from the appeal to the man of genius, because the institution and the tradition were foremost; but it too was only made because the reigning prince was, or seemed to be, rather passive and of mediocre *virtù*, because doubts were raised about his capacities as a man. No one ever dreamed of asking Vittorio Emanuele II to take a more active role in the state; they prayed God not to let too many personal notions germinate in the fantasy of that monarch. After 1880 the office of the prince began to be discussed because the qualities of the new sovereign appeared to be extremely mediocre, and his interest in public affairs scant.[98] Nor was the firm, hard, more-than-feminine will of his blond queen sufficient to make up for these deficiencies. If the monarchy seemed to be turning into nothing more than a shadow, or a plaything, as Spaventa wrote in 1880,[99] that was due to the weaknesses of the sovereign, who was accused of protecting systematic corruption and injustice with his name.[100]

Thus the problem of an antidote was reduced to the problem of a man, whether born a prince or sprung from the people. Indeed, as Lanza had already said, the remedy we need would consist of a great king served by a great minister: such a combination would be a gift of providence to Italy.[101] And if the sense of waiting for a man of genius prepared the ground for Crispi, invocations of the prince would have ended by provoking, in those around him and finally in the prince himself, that veiled wish for a coup d'état that surfaced deleteriously in the repression of 1898.[102]

But in this Robilant thought like so many other leading liberals of his time, anxious to reach the unreachable perfection of political life, to have total liberty and total order, forgetting the warnings of Machiavelli and Rousseau about the inevitability of disagreement in a regime of liberty.[103] Aversion to democracy

[98] Even Farini found that the king ought to have been more active, visit the barracks more often, that he erred in one direction, whereas Vittorio Emanuele II had erred "in the opposite sense: he wanted to do too much" (Farini, *Diario*, MRR, under 14 February 1898). And Farini was one of those who subscribed to the precept *nihil de principe*.

[99] Romano, *Silvio Spaventa*, p. 251.

[100] In Spaventa's *Commemorazione* of Lanza, in *La politica della Destra* (above, n. 91).

[101] Tavallini, *La vita e i tempi di Giovanni Lanza* 2:202. In Lanza, *Le carte* 10:392, three dots are printed instead of the word "re" [king]. Cf. n. 86 above.

[102] After Mentana there had been whispers to the effect that it was necessary to save Italy by staging a coup d'état, abolishing the Statuto, and installing a royal dictatorship; Jacini had wisely dismissed them with contempt. He called this the remedy of a country blacksmith, "who can't do anything else except cut off an infected limb, because he doesn't know how to heal it and keep it whole" (Jacini, *Sulle condizioni della cosa pubblica in Italia*, pp. 79–80).

[103] "[Y]ou long for tranquillity. I believe it is very easy to obtain; but to maintain it along with liberty, that is what seems difficult to me. . . . Quiet and liberty appear to me incompatible; one must choose" (Rousseau, *Considerations sur le gouvernement de Pologne*, ch. 1, in *Oeuvres complètes*, p. 356).

was also an opinion commonly shared; Minghetti too felt that the France of Gambetta—radicalism, in other words—was a perilous example.[104] And so, to bring this long discourse to a close, there was nothing in the thought of Robilant that made him any more reactionary than many other moderates. Perhaps it was his customary way, so dry and clear-cut, even mordant, of expressing his ideas, or perhaps it was his characteristic touch of rigidity and aloofness, that made them seem more authoritarian than they were. Robilant's tone was certainly brisk, and his style declarative, haughty, and sometimes gruff, ill-suited to win him the sympathies of parliamentarians.[105] It was a far cry from the intelligent way of speaking employed by Visconti Venosta, who would never have made statements as terse and pithy as the ones made by Robilant in the Chamber on 23 January 1886,[106] or said "evidently I am withholding a part of what I think," or lost patience and let fall the scornful reference to "the four robbers we might have on our hands in Africa" on the eve of Dogali. Yet withal, how close Robilant was to the liberalism of Visconti Venosta, a liberalism with streaks of political and social conservatism which nevertheless abhorred Bismarckism! And as for Robilant's favorite maxim, *faire sans dire*, how close it was to Visconti Venosta's ideal!

Another factor was perhaps the memory, a grateful one to the moderates but less so to the democrats, of the vigor with which in 1870 Robilant had restored order in the turbulent province of Ravenna. Perhaps the fact that he was a soldier played a part (for he continued to be called general until the end of his days) in causing him to be seen as more conservative than he was.

He was certainly a distinctive personality, the strongest to be found in Italian diplomacy, Visconti Venosta and Nigra included. Among regular career diplomats he was an intruder,[107] and might have passed for one of those amateurs who usually set de Launay, the growling guardian of the temple, to barking. Artom had sought to oppose his nomination,[108] and *L'Opinione*, which was part of Artom's circle, had made critical comments about him.[109] But mistrust and mis-

---

[104] Minghetti to Robilant, 30 December 1882 (cited above at nn. 48, 54). And see the outright denunciation of the radicals by Zanichelli in *Studi politici e storici*, pp. 175 ff.).

[105] Cf. Chiala, *Pagine di storia contemporanea* 3:411; and also de Moüy, *Souvenirs et causeries d'un diplomate*, p. 225, who states that in Robilant one felt a certain lordly disdain that made him unpopular.

[106] "Gentlemen, I do not engage in sentimentalism of any kind in politics. I intend to follow a policy promoting the interests and the dignity of my country, but aside from that, I am not bound by prejudices or sentiments" (*A.P., Camera*, p. 16107). It was on the basis of these words that Baccarini accused Robilant of reactionary intent (which was a piece of real nonsense), saying: "if I am to take his expressions literally, I would have to say that he is raising a flag bearing the legend *Dieu et mon droit*." On this episode and its consequences, until the correction by Finali, cf. Chiala, *Pagine di storia contemporanea* 3:420–22.

[107] Marselli to Robilant, 17 November 1873: "Count Manzoni . . . was telling me that in the diplomatic service they always malign those they call 'intruders,' but that they make an exception for you" (AE, *Carte Robilant*).

[108] Artom to Nigra, 11 May 1871 (AE, *Carte Nigra*). Franz Joseph, on the other hand, had informed the Italian government that he would welcome the appointment of Robilant (Cappelli, "Il conte Carlo Nicolis di Robilant," p. 391). Lanza and Visconti Venosta both desired his appointment to Vienna.

[109] "La diplomazia italiana," in *L'Opinione* for 22 June 1871. The arguments adduced were two:

like had rapidly dissipated: within a short period of his nomination, he had already become what he would remain until 1885, a collaborator of the highest importance for the foreign minister, and for all in Italy who dealt with international problems, one of the great forces of Italian policy on the European stage.

---

there was no proof that Robilant had any aptitude for diplomacy, and to promote a major general to minister plenipotentiary of the first class instead of the second at one stroke would be to commit an injustice. The appointment, it was said, might rouse discontent in the diplomatic corps. This is one of the cases in which it is easy to spot the ties between Dina and Artom, for the latter, in another letter to Nigra on 19 June, observed that with the appointment of Robilant, there were no more places vacant on the diplomatic roll, so that it was impossible to grant several promotions that had been requested. In private, Dina called the appointment "a blunder" (Castelli, *Carteggio* 2:504).

Lanza and Minghetti

OVERALL THEN, this was a fine group of highly capable individuals, including as it did such men as Visconti Venosta, Nigra, and Robilant. These were persons to whom the responsibility for piloting the ship of Italy in the tempestuous and difficult European seas could safely be entrusted.

At the most important moments, and before the most agonizing decisions, the prime minister was naturally involved along with them. This happens to be less true of Lanza because occasions of such importance were rare in the period 1871–1873. The steadfast and very conscientious Lanza was the perfect type of the man of good sense,[1] and very different in style from Visconti Venosta because he was personally without nuances or half tones. He was rigid and intransigent, somewhat in the manner of Ricasoli, and thus had real qualities as a statesman, especially at delicate moments. He did not accommodate himself easily to the trivial skirmishes of parliamentary life and was sometimes a little too susceptible,[2] but basically his solidity and equanimity harmonized well with Visconti Venosta's disposition and program.[3] On the most difficult issue they faced, the Roman question, Lanza too was convinced that calm was the best course to follow,[4] and he also inclined to France, for he felt strongly the emotional impact of the memory of Magenta and Solferino, despite the seemingly hardy and rough face he presented to the world.

Minghetti was necessarily much more involved in foreign policy, for during his spell in office a number of difficult issues had to be decided, including the trip to Vienna and Berlin and the attitude to be taken to the *Kulturkampf*. The intel-

---

[1] It was Giolitti who characterized him thus (*Memorie* 1:20).

[2] On 31 May 1872 he sent his resignation to the king without warning and without informing his cabinet colleagues, because while he was answering Nicotera in the Chamber, the Right had not kept sufficiently quiet, and because he thought that the Right was showing him some malevolence. Pressed to withdraw it by Sella, he did so (cf. Lanza, *Le carte* 8:171–72.) Behind-the-scenes information about this was revealed to Fournier by Visconti Venosta, who gave a sketch of Lanza along the lines of the one given in the text above. Lanza was a prime minister "not very accommodating about the little things in life" (Fournier, report, 6 June 1872, confidential, no. 24; AEP, *C.P., Italie,* t. 385, fols. 131ff.).

[3] Cf. Spaventa, *La politica della Destra,* pp. 112–13, and 127–28; G. Massari, *Uomini di destra* (Bari, 1934), pp. 115 and 140; F. Fiorentino, *Ritratti storici e saggi critici* (Florence, 1935), pp. 277–79. Bonghi undoubtedly went too far in praising him as the most finished statesman of Italy after Cavour (though at a considerable distance behind Cavour), in *Ritratti e profili di contemporanei* 1:414 (= vol. 4 in *Opere* [Florence, 1935]).

[4] "It is necessary to choose our ground with care, establish ourselves in the role of good neighbor, and then if our neighbor does not wish to treat, so much the worse for him. We will keep the peace without molesting him, and wait until he calms down and regains the use of his reason. The main difficulty is to persuade the people of Rome and the majority in parliament that this is the political line to follow" (Lanza to Gabrio Casati, 27 October 1870, in Quintavalle, *La Conciliazione fra l'Italia ed il Papato,* p. 587).

ligent and cultivated Minghetti, with his European experience and his European friendships, was by this time the leading member of the moderate faction, much more than Sella, who stood alone for the most part and was always ready to overstep firmly drawn party lines.[5]

Minghetti was a close friend of Visconti Venosta, whom he had brought into the government for the first time in 1863. Visconti Venosta showed his attachment to Minghetti by remaining at the foreign ministry even after the fall of the Lanza cabinet; some people saw them as master and disciple.[6] Still, these two friends were not interchangeable. With his rapid intelligence and extraordinary facility of assimilation,[7] the supple and brilliant Minghetti was more flexible than Visconti Venosta, not so hard underneath, readier to yield on some points.[8] Sensitive and easily swayed by emotion, he was nevertheless more adaptable to changing times and circumstances, so much so that of all the leaders of the Right (Sella naturally excepted), he was the one most ready to forget about the Italian alliance with France and adapt himself to friendship with the rising star of Germany.[9] This required not only a quick and pliable character but also a certain capacity to detach himself from memories of the very recent past. So it was that this tall, blond, ruddy Bolognese, personable in appearance and elegant in spirit, a refined man of the world,[10] a great orator and a polished conversationalist,[11] highly cultivated, more a European than any of the politicians of the Risorgimento except Cavour,[12] a music lover[13] permeated with an aesthetic as well as a

---

[5] The moderates of Naples viewed Sella as a minister of the Left, pure and simple (*La Perseveranza*, 29 April 1871). Cf. too Petruccelli della Gattina, *Storia d'Italia*, p. 158. According to Giolitti, *Memorie* 1:35, in 1873 Perazzi had advised Sella to cross over to the Left, given that he represented ideas that were more advanced than those of the rest of the Right, etc.

[6] Minghetti as mentor and Visconti Venosta as his pupil: that is how the Austro-Hungarian envoy at Florence, Kübeck, portrayed them (Kübeck, personal letter to Beust, 23 December 1870; SAW, *P.A.*, XI/76; and earlier in his letter of 12 November, cited above at ch. 15, n. 58).

[7] An anecdote narrated by Giolitti will suffice: when Minghetti was prime minister and finance minister, Giolitti once waited in the gallery during a parliamentary debate, ready at a signal (a raised red sheet) from Minghetti to dash to the prime ministerial office. He returned with technical data that enabled Minghetti to go back into the Chamber and deliver an impressive speech off the cuff (Giolitti, *Memore* 1:21–22).

[8] Bacchelli delivered this verdict on Minghetti: "perhaps the least energetic, but the most sensitive, statesman of the Risorgimento" (*Il Diavolo al Pontelungo*, p. 265). The negative aspect of this judgment receives very authoritative, plus more blunt and graphic, support from no less a person than Cavour himself, for Ercole Oldofredi, who had been Cavour's intimate, wrote to Nigra on 14 June 1875: "Minghetti is a man of greater talent [than Farini], but he shifts his ground too much, and then, as Cavour used to say, 'he has no balls.' When it comes to words, he beats everybody with his glib talk; when it comes to deeds, his wrists tremble" (De Vecchi archive).

[9]A section of the French press branded him a "Prussophile" and was hostile when he formed his last cabinet in 1873 (Luzzatti, *Memorie* 1:361).

[10] Even in the Chamber he indulged in suave charm: cf. the episode narrated by Faldella, *Salita a Montecitorio, p. 234.*

[11] Cf. Petruccelli della Gattina, *Storia d'Italia*, pp. 177–78; Lipparini, *Minghetti* 1:254.

[12] Minghetti's cultural Europeanism, his similarity to the Italians whom Frederick the Great had admired, were what struck Ranke most when he met the Bolognese statesman on 26 September 1873 at Berlin (Ranke, *Tagebuchblätter*, in *Sämtliche Werke* 53/54 [Leipzig, 1890]: 599). Cf. L. Bianchi, "Una visita di Minghetti a Ranke," *L'Arduo* (January-December 1923): 156–57.

[13] Bonghi, *Ritratti e profili di contemporanei* 1:289–91.

moral sense of life, found it easy to sympathize with Bismarck,[14] whereas a wall of distrust separated the Valtellinese Visconti Venosta, a close friend of Minghetti, from the German statesman.

[14] On 22 October 1870, at a time of fierce internal division in the cabinet over the question of the transfer of the capital to Rome, Minghetti wrote to Visconti Venosta: "You must stay in the cabinet and impose your opinions on the others. I wish you would act a little more like Bismarck" (Visconti Venosta archive). This was exactly what Visconti Venosta would never do, and was incapable of doing!

Vittorio Emanuele II

ABOVE THE CURRENT holder of the office of prime minister there stood the supreme arbiter, the king. Yet the age of the *secret du roi** and of personal initiatives on the king's part, above and beyond those of his ministers, appeared to have ended. In this respect too the year 1870 had marked a shift that could no longer be reversed, for it had seen the failure of plans he had fomented in 1868 and 1869 and pursued down to the last moment with the mission of Vimercati to Metz. At the moment of truth Vittorio Emanuele II had had to recognize that the moral weight of public opinion had indeed become sufficiently powerful to bar the way even to the projects of a king. His caustic verbal exchanges with Sella were featured in popular mythology, as when he made a regally scornful reference to cloth merchants, and Sella replied proudly that cloth merchants had always honored their signature, whereas in this case the king would be signing a draft without being certain of being able to pay it.[1] They were appropriate symbols of a conflict, which had lasted from the time of Cavour, between the sovereign's desire to deal on his own with questions of foreign policy and the military, which were not meant for peaceful bourgeois to handle, and the new political reality of the liberal state, which was certainly happy to have a citizen king as a loved and respected head of state, a living symbol of the homeland, but which was no longer inclined to admit the existence of a mysterious sphere of special attributes reserved to the monarch and independent of government action. It was the ultimate conflict between the monarchical, diplomatic, and military tradition of the *arcana imperii* on one hand, and the insistent demands of the people's rights on the other. On one side, Lanza and Sella, both bourgeois; on the other,

---

* [*Translator's note: secret du roi* is a technical term denoting an organization used by the king of France in the eighteenth century to conduct diplomacy without the knowledge of his ministers. Generically it means the conduct of such diplomacy. In introducing the term here for the first time, Chabod gives it in French to make his meaning clear, then alternates between the French and the Italian equivalent, *il segreto del re*. I have kept it in French in all cases.]

[1] Guiccioli, *Quintino Sella* 1:267–68 (a variant account in Luzzatti, *Memorie* 1:306–307). It is worth pointing out that Guiccioli's work was revised in chapters 8 and 9 of vol. 1 (concerning the events of the summer of 1870). Guiccioli made the revision "taking account of conversations we had together, and new information supplied by Malvano about the negotiations of Witzthum" (Guiccioli to Visconti Venosta, 2 March 1885, sending him the revised manuscript; Visconti Venosta archive). On the methods used by the king to pressure Sella, which included "threats, flattery, scarcely credible promises, injuries," cf. the notes of Sella himself, published by P. Sella, *Quintino Sella nell'Agosto del 1870*, p. 3. From these notes it results as well that on 30 July the cabinet had decided to intervene on the side of France, with Sella and Govone alone voting against. Sella had resigned on the spot, which had caused the deliberation to be suspended, with no record being made of it; it was announced that there would be further discussion (p. 4). According to Guiccioli (ibid., 1:277), the intervention was to take the form of "armed mediation by Italy," not full-scale military operations alongside the French.

the king, Cialdini, and Menabrea, military men annoyed by the worries and fears of those bourgeois.

The king and his generals lost that match—for which Vittorio Emanuele later had good reason to be particularly thankful, when he realized what a pitfall he had nearly plunged into.[2] The king had to admit that, in forecasting the outcome of the war, the bourgeois Sella had been more perspicacious and accurate than the notional experts, who despite all their professional competence had got it badly wrong.[3]

But apart from the importance of the particular episode, the event sounded a warning for the sovereign that a secret Italian policy, differing from, and sometimes opposed to, official policy, had little or no utility any more. Hence, after showing Lanza his unconcealed distrust and displeasure about the "direction of the affairs of state," he was forced to backtrack when the honest and stubborn Piedmontese handed in his resignation on 7 September 1870, make peace with him, and allow him to take charge fully.[4] From that time on, no minister ever had to undergo a contest of this kind with the sovereign except for Minghetti, who in the summer of 1873 was forced to insist that the king must travel to Vienna and Berlin; and on that occasion the conflict was not nearly so sharp.

But it was not only the resistance of ministers disinclined to give in to the wishes of their sovereign that led Vittorio Emanuele to abandon most of his personal projects. The metamorphosis of the European situation in 1870 certainly played a much greater role. Where international relations were concerned, the king's education had been shaped by the Napoleonic age; he was bound by sentiment to the alliance with France, and also bound intellectually, in the sense that he was accustomed to ponder situations, calculate their outcomes, and decide what course to follow, on the premise that the European situation was dominated by the Second Empire. Since 1858, at any rate, that was how it had been: the fixed point of reference, the polar star to which the king directed his gaze to orient himself amid the tangled problems of Europe, was always his friend Napoleon III. Italian foreign policy in general had been based on the link with France, and the alliance with Prussia in 1866 figured as no more than a passing episode, absolutely incapable of changing the significance and the general guidelines of that policy; this general truth was true in particular for Vittorio Emanuele II.

[2] Rothan, *L'Allemagne et l'Italie* 2:80; E. Bourgeois and E. Clermont, *Rome et Napoléon III* (Paris, 1907), pp. 332 and 334; Cognasso, *Vittorio Emanuele II*, p. 367. Vittorio Emanuele said so again to de Launay in 1871: "We had a lucky escape" (de Launay, personal letter no. 2 to Visconti Venosta, 10 February 1873; Visconti Venosta archive).

[3] The king, Cialdini, Menabrea, and others were in fact certain until 6 August that France would win (Guiccioli, *Quintino Sella* 1:259 and 286). Very few observers foresaw the Prussian victory: Sella, Marselli, Bonfadini, and also, it seems, Luzzatti (Luzzatti, *Memorie* 1:307). After 20 September Vittorio Emanuele had the nerve to reprove Sella for not having persuaded him in time that the Prussians were really going to win, saying: "i avriô pôdú ranché quaich cosa! [we would have been able to grab something]." Sella was struck by this and said that only then did he realize what a difference there was between his conception of things and that of the king (Sella, *Quintino Sella nell'Agosto del 1870*, p. 6).

[4] Tavallini, *La vita e i tempi di Giovanni Lanza* 2:40–41; Castagnola, *Da Firenze a Roma*, p. 33; Cadorna, *La liberazione di Roma*, p. 37.

Now, suddenly, everything had changed. The Second Empire had crumbled. Prussian Germany had emerged in the forefront of Europe, a power for which the king felt little sentimental attraction—as he showed by his reluctance in 1873 to make the voyage to Berlin. There was an upheaval in values and attitudes that made the general panorama unrecognizable, and to find one's way one had to obliterate from memory twelve years of experience and trust to intuition and political instinct as one set about creating a new repertory of experience adapted to the new environment. Before the events of 1866 the great questions had been Venetia and Rome, while after 1866 Rome alone was the question. But that meant that it remained a constant factor, which implied a moral climate identical to that of 1859–60, combining the right of nationality, the consciousness of being Italian, and the urge to throw the foreign occupiers out of the peninsula, all of this accompanied by the same cast of characters: the revolutionaries, the party of action, Mazzini. But after 1870 Europe was suddenly Bismarckian, and the ideals to which one could appeal a decade before no longer served any purpose; Italy was now installed in Rome, and this meant that the program that had guided the country for a decade no longer had any function, military or international. Even Mazzini was old, worn out, disappointed, a man who had outlived his time.

From the point of view of the Italian sovereign, Napoleon III had been an ideal partner in a double game: ostensibly both sides had foreign ministers in place after the death of Cavour, but behind the scenes the trusted agents of the two sovereigns treated, unbeknownst to the ministers and indeed behind the backs of the ministers,[5] who, being faithful subjects, subsequently had to draw a curtain of ministerial responsibility and ministerial silence around the adventures of their sovereigns.[6] The "sphinx," the dark figure of 2 December, was just the man for

[5] "This mission of Vimercati [to Metz, August 1870] took place without the knowledge of myself or the ministers, and behind our backs" (Visconti Venosta, private letter to Nigra, 30 July 1893; Visconti Venosta archive). According to Visconti Venosta, Vittorio Emanuele wanted Rome in exchange for entering the war on France's side: "on the strength of a concession [from Napoleon III], the king guarantees to obtain the agreement of his ministers, and if he does not obtain it, to dismiss them, in which case he has an alternative cabinet ready, which would, I suppose, have been headed by Cialdini or Menabrea." As for Nigra, he did not see, nor wish to see, the draft for a treaty brought to Metz by Vimercati: "I was not involved at all in that negotiation, which I foresaw would come to nothing" (Nigra to Visconti Venosta, 30 April 1885, ibid.). And cf. the king's telegram of 14 July to Visconti Venosta: "in this grave question . . . I would prefer not to have obstacles thrown in my path by the cabinet" (in Mayor des Planches, "Re Vittorio Emanuele II alla vigilia della guerra del Settanta," p. 351).

On the other hand, Visconti Venosta had fully approved of the negotiations that took place while Menabrea was prime minister, in 1868–69, something that Vimercati pointed out in self-defense when accused by Visconti Venosta of "culpable irresponsibility" (Vimercati, private letter to Visconti Venosta, 29 August 1870; Archivio della Casa Reale, *Corrispondenza Vimercati*).

[6] Complaining to his brother Giovanni on 18 April 1878 about the indiscretions of Prince Napoleon and the duke of Gramont concerning the events of the summer of 1870, Visconti Venosta observed that they "place me, and my colleagues in the cabinet of 1870, in a rather unpleasant situation. The fact is that we could easily justify our conduct, but to do so we would have to reveal facts about King Vittorio Emanuele and the *imbrogli* [muddles, mischief] he created behind our backs, and which we were constrained, up to a point, to tolerate, and to try to remedy later through our own opposition and that of parliament. I would advise remaining silent as long as it is at all possible" (Visconti Venosta archive). Visconti Venosta referred to the same events in an undated letter to a Swiss (the year is 1895; the recipient is Chenevrière, of Geneva; Visconti Venosta archive),

Vittorio Emanuele. With these two as protagonists, friendship and marriage alliance had followed, making an excellent terrain on which to maneuver; Arese, Pepoli, and Vimercati on one side, and Prince Jérôme on the other, filled the supporting roles in an admirable manner.

Now, in contrast, there had emerged a different court, that of Prussia, with which Italy had a formally correct rapport, but no more; indeed, on the part of the Empress Augusta there was a strong dislike of Italy and its king,[7] which she ostentatiously displayed in 1873 by her absence from Berlin during Vittorio Emanuele's sojourn there. Nor was Wilhelm I the man to compensate with independent action of his own and thus repeat the situation in the Tuileries, where Eugénie had been hostile and Napoleon III had been determined to go ahead with his own plans. Above all, there was no chance of a secret court-centered policy, at variance with official policy, in Berlin. Such things were out of the question when the man at the helm of the government was the forceful Bismarck.

The general situation, then, was completely changed, and additionally it was very difficult for the king to find other players to join him in a game of secret dynastic policy. This is a fact of great importance, since *le secret du roi* depended on close personal relations between two heads of state, and also in light of the psychology of Vittorio Emanuele II, a strongly imaginative man and strongly desirous to act on his own, but also a creature of habit who found it difficult to form new relationships and adopt a fresh plan of action when his accustomed points of reference were shifted. He was getting old and increasingly felt that he lived in a rotten world.[8] Though he felt pride as he climbed the steps to the Capitol,[9] Rome also injected scruples into his conscience because of the offense to the Vatican. It was easy for others, especially Sella, to shout "viva Roma capitale!" but it was he, the devoutly Catholic sovereign, whose soul was at stake. Years before, on 25 May 1859, when he was with the army and engaged in lethal combat, he had written to Pius IX to ask for absolution, being "in peril of dying at any moment," and in the year preceding 20 September, when seriously ill at San Rossore, he had telegraphed to ask the pope for his pardon and his

---

in the context of the uproar caused in Switzerland by the publication of Nigra's *Ricordi diplomatici*. He said that he had kept silent in order not to aggravate the issue, "and because I would have been unable to portray events as they really were without touching on a delicate point by bringing the person of the king, and the relations between him and his ministers, into the picture. I believe that there are certain duties that survive the offices one has held."

[7] "The empress detests us, and this is another way for her to show it" (she had gone to Baden and so was absent from Berlin when Vittorio Emanuele arrived) (de Launay, personal letter, 3 September 1873; AE, *Ris.*, 10).

[8] When his son Amedeo renounced the Spanish throne, Vittorio Emanuele telegraphed to Visconti Venosta from Naples on 12 February 1873: "All this teaches me nothing new, but I am ever more persuaded that we live in a rotten world" (ACR, *Carte Visconti Venosta*, pacco 6, fasc. 10/C).

[9] There is no doubt that he was honestly proud of this. Cf. his letter to Erminia Ghisolfi of 21 September 1870: "the great work was accomplished, the dream of centuries came true. May the Italians continue to show themselves worthy of their glory and their fortune." He calls the day a "solemn one for our country"; and his spirit is calm, his mind serene (in Monti, *Vittorio Emanuele II*, p. 385, and cf. A. M. Ghisalberti, *Introduzione alla storia del Risorgimento* [Rome, 1942], p. 81 n. 1).

benediction.[10] Now all the old difficulties with the church came to a head as Porta Pia was breached: who knows whether the fears of his mother, who had believed that Carlo Alberto must be suffering the pains of purgatory "for having started this business," did not return to haunt the mind of the king?[11]

Pius IX thought of him as "poor Vittorio," and said so.[12] For all the thunder and lightning of his official protests there was an ever-present strain of paternal affection for the king which went back to the period before 1848: poor Vittorio, always surrounded by a band of swindlers, first d'Azeglio, Cavour, and Rattazzi, and now Lanza and Sella. But vice versa, King Vittorio also thought of the "poor pope" with a certain tenderness not unmixed with remorse, believing that he too was surrounded by the sort of "bad heads" that one always encounters, whatever the regime. Poor old man, he thought, we have already done enough to him;[13] and so he wished to show every form of regard "pour ce pauvre *diable* de Saint Père: il m'aime, je le lui rends."[14]

Tired and annoyed, Vittorio Emanuele tended increasingly to be locked into the orbit of his own habits, and became ever more reluctant to shoulder the outer burden of royal dignity.[15] Never a great traveler to begin with, he was even more

---

[10] [R. Ballerini], "Pio IX, Vittorio Emanuele II e Napoleone III: Ricordo storico del 1859–60," *La Civiltà Cattolica*, 14th ser., 3 (3 and 17 August 1889): 266 and 414.

[11] Cf. the letter of Vittorio Emanuele to Pius IX, 13 February 1852, in Pirri, *Pio IX e Vittorio Emanuele II* 1:95. This important volume documents well how the ecclesiastical policy of the d'Azeglio and Cavour cabinets was pursued against the king's will: cf. especially the king's letter to the pope of 9 February 1855, with a postscript that is particularly amazing (p. 157). For the king's superstitious Catholicism, and his fear at the thought of possible divine punishment, cf. H. d'Ideville, *Victor Emmanuel, sa vie, sa mort: Souvenirs personnels*, pp. 25, 27, 74, 77 n. 4; for his remorse, Rattazzi, *Rattazzi et son temps* 2:384. Note too the anecdote told to Farini by Queen Margherita (Farini, *Diario* 1:91). This is gossip: but the general attitude it depicts is confirmed by the documents, and the facts.

[12] Fournier, personal letter to Rémusat, 7 December 1872 (AEP, *C.P., Italie*, t. 386, unnumbered fol. between fols. 189 and 190): "The pope always refers to the king of Italy, to 'poor Vittorio,' in affectionate terms, and virtually declares that he was unable to act differently than he did. They correspond more frequently than is generally thought, and Commander Aghemo, the king's secretary, sees Cardinal Antonelli often." The Portuguese ambassador to the Holy See, Count Thomar, reported the same to Oldoini in the summer of 1871: "His Holiness always speaks with affection of the king personally" (Oldoini, confidential report, 25 July 1871, no. 145). Again in 1877, Aghemo, who had finally succeeded in obtaining a reception from the pontiff, stated to the Austrian ambassador that Pius IX "was not embittered against the king ('He is too Italian for that')" (Haymerle, confidential report, 3 March 1877, no. 12 C; SAW, *P.A.*, XI/85).

[13] Cf. above, ch. 8, n. 9.

[14] ". . . for that poor *devil* of a Holy Father: he loves me, and I return his love"; thus Vittorio Emanuele to the French envoy, Fournier, at the latter's first audience (Fournier, confidential report, 26 March 1872, no. 2; AEP, *C.P., Italie*, t. 384, fol. 273r-v. Ibid.: "'He [the pope] also has *des mauvaises têtes* [bad heads] about him; there are *mauvaises têtes* under every flag.'" The king forwarded a request to Pius IX to let him (the king) know if ever he (the pope) had a personal favor to ask of him, and in fact he did intervene more than once in affairs that mattered to Pius IX, even if they were not matters of political consequence (Haymerle, report, cited in n. 12; and Lumbroso, "Vittorio Emanuele II e Pio IX," in *La Tribuna* for 11 September 1911). Cf. Massari, *La vita ed il regno di Vittorio Emanuele II*, pp. 538 ff., and n. 23 below.

[15] In 1873, for example, he asked the foreign minister not to arrange a meeting between himself and the Shah of Persia, who had expressed a wish to greet him at Turin in the summer, for in that season he wished to dedicate himself to his favorite sport of hunting (telegraph of Aghemo, chief

loath now to voyage abroad, less willing to face the bother of meeting new faces and forming new ties: all the more reason for him not to feel at home in the new post-1870 world, in which, if he really wanted to start up a new network of personal policy, he would have had to begin by winning over the solitary of Varzin, Bismarck. So it was that the king participated in Italian foreign policy in a much less active and zealous manner than he had done in the period after the death of Cavour and before the taking of Rome.[16]

Reduced participation did not mean complete abstention, however. This would have been impossible for a man like Vittorio Emanuele II, even as he grew older and came to feel out of place in a changed world. Foreign and military affairs continued until the last to be the two sectors of national life to which he most willingly attended, as he had been taught to do by the long traditions of his and the other reigning houses, traditions whose origins went back to the age of monarchical absolutism, when, in the absence of internal political problems, with all authority concentrated in the prince and the main domestic task being the most efficient organization of finance, the life of the state was focused on the activity of its diplomats, which aimed to prevent or provoke war, and on that of its army, buttress of the throne and instrument of territorial aggrandizement.[17] For all that the myth created by d'Azeglio had consecrated him as the "Re Galantuomo" [Gentleman King], Vittorio Emanuele was always instinctively a soldier, and a monarch who wished to guide the warp and woof of diplomacy: he recruited his trusted aides and his most favored counselors from among his generals and diplomats, according them an esteem and friendship that no minister or member of parliament ever received. Until the last—and notwithstanding such men as d'Azeglio, Cavour, Ricasoli, Rattazzi, Minghetti, and Lanza; notwithstanding the personal manner, the jovial bonhomie with which he greeted them, the easy way he dispensed with formal etiquette, his affability, and even the coarseness he often flaunted, the vulgar crudity of his behavior that so enchanted the petit bourgeois and the peasant—until the last he remained a king by the grace of

---

royal secretary, to Visconti Venosta, 24 June 1873; ACR, *Carte Visconti Venosta*, pacco 6, fasc. 10/G). Even when faced with the much more serious matter of the voyage to Vienna and Berlin, he had temporized at first, claiming that he absolutely had to spend several weeks in the Alps (Minghetti to Prince Umberto, 5 August 1873; Visconti Venosta, telegram and dispatch to Robilant, 10 and 28 June 1873; BCB, *Carte Minghetti*, cart. 36 h).

[16] In July 1871 the principal intention of Vittorio Emanuele appears to have been, as he stated to Castelli, to watch over the affairs of the political parties, given that the transfer to Rome was meant to lead to efforts at transformation within them. In sum, he was concerned with domestic politics (Castelli, *Carteggio* 2:510–11).

[17] What is stated in Rattazzi, *Rattazzi et son temps* 2:408, is however entirely erroneous. Mme Rattazzi says, referring to February 1871, that the king also functioned indirectly as minister of war, since Govone had no authority or initiative. The truth is that Ricotti had succeeded Govone as war minister a number of months before, Govone having resigned on 6 September 1870 (Lanza, *Le carte* 6:71); and that the nomination of Ricotti on 7 September had angered Vittorio Emanuele, who would have preferred Gen. Bertolè Viale (Castagnola, *Da Firenze a Roma:*, p. 33). Mme Rattazzi has muddled the facts; she also speaks (Rattazzi, ibid., p. 407) of direct contacts in February 1871 between Vittorio Emanuele and Napoleon III!

God, a man placed at an infinite distance above any interlocutor whatsoever.[18] This authority he wanted to preserve, in a spirit not very different to that of his forebears pre-1848, by reducing to a minimum the will of the nation—which, in fact, in the formula hallowed by act of parliament was mentioned only in second place.[19] The cabinet ministers were "his" ministers: in this he certainly had the letter of article 65 of the Statuto on his side,[20] and also the spirit in which Carlo Alberto had conceded the constitution; but the interpretation of the Statuto had altered over time, and the new interpretation had prevailed in the Calabiana crisis.[21] In result, the king nourished in his heart a mistrust and, when there was personal antipathy, even a dislike, for his ministers, because of their belief that they were now the ministers of the country.[22]

This instinctive mistrust, which was practically innate, like his passion for women and hunting, had created a desire on his part to direct policy personally; when he got involved in problems of foreign policy even after 1870, it is not hard to see that the same mistrust was still there. Parliamentary deputies, he felt, often lacked wisdom, and ministers, even good ones, came and went, with no continuity in the directives they gave. Both deputies and ministers might be forced to surrender to popular pressure: the guarantor of continuity in foreign policy must be the sovereign. This was even truer when the situation was ticklish, and correct if not cordial relations had to be maintained with a foreign power despite profound and continuing sources of friction.

In actuality, though he intervened in relations with the Holy See by trying to smooth sharp corners when possible,[23] took charge of the question of Spain

[18] This was the view of Artom, who was in a position to know (Artom, *L'opera politica*, p. 222).

[19] Cf. on this Quilici's penetrating observations in *La borghesia italiana*, pp. 332 ff. The monarchy of the house of Savoy had to accept the parliamentary regime because it lost in 1848–49: H. McGaw Smyth, "Piedmont and Prussia: The Influence of the Campaigns of 1848–1849 on the Constitutional Development of Italy," *American Historical Review* 55 (April 1950): 479 ff.

[20] "The king nominates and revokes his ministers." Cf. Cognasso, *Vittorio Emanuele II*, p. 374. In this regard, there is precious testimony in a statement made by the king to Silvio Spaventa in December 1862: "You were mistaken in thinking that I wanted to form a government outside parliament; in any case, it would not have been such an unconstitutional step as it might seem at first glance" (Spaventa, *Lettere politiche*, p. 43).

[21] Omodeo, *L'opera politica del Conte di Cavour* 2:75.

[22] D'Ideville, *Victor Emmanuel, sa vie, sa mort* p. 86; Cognasso, *Vittorio Emanuele II*, pp. 80 ff., 370–71.

[23] Thiers addressed himself to the king, through Visconti Venosta, when there were complaints from the pope about the Italian government (Thiers, *Notes et souvenirs, 1870–1873* [Paris, 1903], p. 377). On his contacts with the pontiff see Monti, *Vittorio Emanuele II*, pp. 374 ff., 390 ff. There was an exchange of letters between the pope and the king in September 1871: Pius IX himself informed the French ambassador, d'Harcourt, of this (d'Harcourt, report, 27 September, no. 60; AEP, *C.P., Rome*, t. 1052, fol. 287. Pius IX wrote to Vittorio Emanuele that he had wanted to make Rome the capital of Italy, and had made it merely the capital of disorder and impiety; the king's reply was respectful and deferential). In the following year there was another letter of Pius IX to Vittorio Emanuele, and an evasive reply by the latter (Bourgoing, report, 22 September 1872, unnumbered; ibid., t. 1056, fol. 44v). Pius IX showed Count Campello della Spina another letter from the king to himself (Campello della Spina, *Ricordi di 50 anni*, p. 130). The third volume of the work of Padre Pirri, *Pio IX e Vittorio Emanuele II dal loro carteggio privato*, is awaited; meanwhile, cf. Lumbroso, "Vittorio Emanuele e Pio IX: Il loro carteggio inedito," in *La Tribuna* for 6 and 11 September 1911,

during the difficult reign of his son Amedeo,[24] kept an eye on Paris and on Nigra personally, and sometimes meddled in other matters,[25] the relationship that Vittorio Emanuele II tried to influence directly from 1875 to his death, throwing his own authority into the balance and pledging his personal word of honor, was that with Austria-Hungary.

This state was the old enemy of Italy. But after 1866, with the government in Vienna maintaining a favorable attitude overall on the Roman question, it was possible to forget the past, especially with the European situation so greatly altered. To the west, instead of an ally, Italy now had to reckon with the ill-concealed hostility of France, at least until 1875–76. It could not permit itself the luxury of hostility on its eastern flank as well: Austria had been the enemy when France had stood by Italy; Italy did not want both as enemies at the same time.[26] This was a paramount political motive, which made even Trent and Trieste recede in importance, a motive on which all those in the Italian government, then and for some time to come, were agreed, from Visconti Venosta and Robilant to Crispi.

But there was another motive inducing the sovereign to keep a close eye on relations between Rome and Vienna and rekindling something of his former ar-

---

but taking into account the critical remarks of Pirri, ibid., 1:vi. How attentively Vittorio Emanuele followed all developments relating to the Holy See also emerges from a letter of his chief secretary, Aghemo, to Visconti Venosta, of 21 January 1874: "now I must also inform you how fully satisfied his majesty was by, and how much he approved of, the tenor of the circular sent by you to the royal agents on the question of the conclave" (ACR, *Carte Visconti Venosta*, pacco 8, fasc. 5).

[24] Count de Barral communicated directly with him, orally and in writing, as well as with the government (Barral, personal letter to Visconti Venosta, 13 March 1872; ACR, *Carte Visconti Venosta*, pacco 5, fasc. 1; there and in fasc. 4, other personal letters of Barral to Visconti Venosta). Sometimes Vittorio Emanuele cautioned Visconti Venosta (thus, a telegram of 19 June 1872, from Florence: "I forewarn you that matters in Spain are going *to the devil*") and gave general directives himself: in August 1872, after the attempt on his son's life and faced with a grave situation, on which Barral briefed him personally, Vittorio Emanuele stated his belief "that we have to push the experiment to the limit," and consider abdication only "when we have exhausted all means of governing, and are faced with the absolute impossibility of going any farther" (Barral to Visconti Venosta, 18 August 1872; ibid., pacco 5, fasc. 4). When the moment of abdication came, on 12 February 1873, Vittorio Emanuele telegraphed to Vimercati in Paris: "everything happened so fast that it was impossible for me to halt the course of events" (Archivio della Casa Reale, *Corrispondenza Vimercati*, and see also in general *Carte Vittorio Emanuele II*, buste 32–35 and 37). On the telegram of 12 February, see also Massari, *La vita ed il regno di Vittorio Emanuele II*, p. 545.

[25] Thus the king sent telegrams to Visconti Venosta on 28 June 1872 and 20 April 1875 to solicit the reform of the justice system in Egypt "so as to assist Italian subjects in that country" (ACR, *Carte Visconti Venosta*, pacco 5, fasc. 10 q and pacco 9, fasc. 9 e). Naturally the nomination of Italian representatives abroad was subject to Vittorio Emanuele's approval: thus on 30 March 1875 Aghemo informed Visconti Venosta that the king approved the appointments of Greppi to Madrid and Corti to Constantinople, that he desired, immediately or as soon as possible, the nomination of Tornielli to an ambassadorial post abroad, and that Visconti Venosta was to find a way if possible not to harm the career of the marchese Migliorati (ACR, *Carte Visconti Venosta*, pacco 9, fasc. 4). The nomination of Greppi was approved by the cabinet on 11 April (that of Corti is not mentioned). But the promotion of Tornielli, along with that of Maffei, to minister plenipotentiary, took place only on 17 March 1876 (ACR, *Verbali delle deliberazioni del Consiglio dei Ministri* 2:215 and 252). This was also the practice with Umberto I: for the nomination of Menabrea to London and Nigra to Paris in 1882, cf. telegrams of Mancini to Umberto I, undated, and Umberto I to Mancini, 6 November (MRR, *Carte Mancini*, b. 638, fasc. 5/6 and 7).

[26] Cf. Salvemini, "La politica estera della Destra" (1924), p. 368.

dor. Of the old political system with which he had been thoroughly familiar, only the Habsburg empire was left in continental Europe following the collapse of the Napoleonic empire. What was more, the Habsburg court remained itself: a center with which *le secret du Roi* was still possible, since foreign policy and military questions remained very firmly in the hands of the emperor and his counselors, eluding the reach of the parliament and the pressure of public opinion. Of the two fellow players with whom Vittorio Emanuele had hoped to form the Triple Alliance of 1868–69, only Franz Joseph remained; but Franz Joseph was enough: with him Vittorio Emanuele could make personal contact over the heads of ministers. And with Franz Joseph there were old family ties that had never been broken.[27]

Both the objective state of affairs, and opportunities of a subjective kind (meaning the chance to take action in the manner to which he was already accustomed), drove Vittorio Emanuele to try to intervene, making himself personally and directly responsible for the peaceful, indeed friendly, conduct of his country vis-à-vis the double monarchy. In June 1874, when he was shown Andrássy's note to Wimpffen dated 24 May—the document that summed up Habsburg policy to Italy until 1915—he had openly stated that he approved categorically of the concepts set forth by the chief Austrian policymaker.[28] Now Andrássy's note included a blanket refusal ever to discuss handing over the lands that Italians called unredeemed, even in the guise of "*compensi*" [measures to redress the territorial balance], and nullified the old hopes first advanced by Balbo that Austria might turn to the east and release all Italian territory. Vittorio Emanuele had

---

[27] When, after much hesitation, he decided to visit Vienna and Berlin in September 1873, which meant presenting himself to a former enemy in the person of Franz Joseph, the king fell back on the blood relationship between the two dynasties (Castelli, *Ricordi*, p. 274).

[28] Sandonà, *L'irredentismo nelle lotte politiche* 1:113. Wimpffen could report that "the king shares your opinion on all points, and the arguments developed in that letter" (Wimpffen, personal letter, 7 June 1874; SAW, *P.A.*, XI/82). At Vienna there was of course much satisfaction (Robilant, personal letter to Visconti Venosta, 28 June 1874; Visconti Venosta archive). Cf. as well Salvemini, "La politica estera della Destra" (1925), p. 190 (and for the meeting in Venice, p. 189 as well). The king's words had been "almost the same" as those of Visconti Venosta (Robilant, letter cited; and Wimpffen, personal letter, 13 June, loc. cit.). In reality, the king—according to Aghemo, at least— had gone farther in his approval of the ideas of Andrássy.

Concerning this document, which is of fundamental importance for relations between Austria and Italy, it will not be amiss to point out that it was initially ignored, after the coming of the Left to power, both by Melegari, the foreign minister, and by Tornielli, the general secretary (though in 1874 he was director of the political division at the Palazzo della Consulta), whereas Wimpffen had immediately spoken to Melegari about it "as the basis on which the reconciliation between the two monarchies had been concluded." (And it was later repeatedly referred to by the Austrian side as having been approved as well by Vittorio Emanuele II; cf. Sandonà, *L'irredentismo nelle lotte politiche* 1:126; Gravenegg, for example, made a reference to it in speaking to Melegari in October 1876: Gravenegg, report, 14 October, no. 75 A; SAW, *P.A.*, XI/84.) A copy of the note was found by Tornielli "a few days after, upon opening a blotter that had been left on the work table of my predecessor [i.e., Artom]." Tornielli subsequently inquired of Robilant if Andrássy's letter, dated 24 May 1874, that turned up in this manner, and of which he forwarded a copy, were "the same thing as the note to which the cabinet of Vienna is now referring." This was the manner in which Melegari and Tornielli became acquainted with Andrássy's note, though there was nothing to tell them that the king and Visconti Venosta had endorsed it (Tornielli, personal letter to Robilant, 10 November 1876; AE, *Carte Robilant*).

subsequently stepped in to prevent a fresh outbreak of irredentist demonstrations and had gone on to offer profuse expressions of goodwill to Franz Joseph, to the point of creating embarrassment in Vienna for Robilant.[29]

But it was their meeting at Venice in April 1875 that decided the king to seek direct linkage with Vienna, bypassing even his own foreign minister. The king was moved, and not without reason, by the undoubtedly friendly and courteous gesture of Franz Joseph, who, to return the visit made to Vienna, had personally selected[30] the pearl of the Adriatic, which until nine years before had been in his possession.[31] And so, in that serene setting, Vittorio Emanuele virtually pledged himself, with his protests of faithful friendship, to bury all the territorial questions still open between Italy and Austria-Hungary, and also initiated his direct personal relationship with the government in Vienna. On 21 October 1879 Gen. Bertolè Viale, who had been the chief huntsman of Vittorio Emanuele II and now held the same office under Umberto I, recounted the scene in Venice to his friend Robilant in the following terms:

> [A]t the moment of parting, King Vittorio was speaking with Count Andrássy, and after restating his sentiments of strong friendship and his desire to preserve it, he added: "if something happens that it is important I should know of, address yourself to him" (pointing out Aghemo). "Ministers pass: but he is always by my side." I heard these words myself.[32]

---

[29] The fact that the emperor had not yet returned the visit paid him by Vittorio Emanuele created "a disagreeable situation for us," according to Robilant, who believed it necessary "to maintain a markedly cool stance not only toward Count Andrássy but also toward the emperor. But I confess to you that I very much fear this tactic may have served little purpose, since the king must have expressed himself to the Austrian military attaché in Rome in terms of such warm friendship for the emperor that the latter has most likely come to the conclusion that our august sovereign is not in the least resentful of the discourtesy that is being shown him" (Robilant, personal letter to Visconti Venosta, 4 March 1875; Visconti Venosta archive).

[30] Personal letters of Robilant to Visconti Venosta, 7 March 1875, and Visconti Venosta to his brother Giovanni, 14 March (Visconti Venosta archive). Andrássy confirms this to Károlyi, his ambassador to Berlin, in a personal letter of 21 March; SAW, *P.A.*, III/112. Cf. Massari, *La vita ed il regno di Vittorio Emanuele II*, p. 575.

[31] Haymerle, the new ambassador of Austria-Hungary, describes his reception on 6 February 1877 by Vittorio Emanuele: "upon seeing me enter, and without even giving me a chance to speak, he took my hand and spoke as follows (I am quoting practically verbatim): 'I am very pleased that the emperor has named you his ambassador; his friendship is very important to me; I love him; he was so good to me; I will never forget his generous gesture of Venice; I told the emperor that I would have been hard-pressed to do as much for him. I gave my word to the emperor that I am and will remain his friend; I will not fail to keep my word' (the last phrase was repeated throughout the interview)" (Haymerle, report, 6 February 1877; SAW, *P.A.*, XI/85, no. 9 A. Cf. Sandonà, *L'irredentismo nelle lotte politiche* 1:143). The king had made almost identical statements to the chargé d'affaires, Gravenegg, about his grateful memory of Venice, his faithful friendship for Franz Joseph, and his desire to remove all sources of perturbation in relations between the two nations (Gravenegg, report, 31 December 1876; SAW, *P.A.*, XI/84, no. 107).

[32] AE, *Carte Robilant*. Bertolè Viale's account accords fully with that given by Andrássy in his dispatch of 14 September 1879 to his chargé d'affaires in Rome, Prince Wrede: "King Vittorio Emanuele had knowledge of it [the note of 24 May 1874], and his majesty deigned to approve my view of matters by authorizing me to address myself directly to him in everything concerning these questions" (in Sandonà, *L'irredentismo nelle lotte politiche* 1:259). And indeed, cf. the communication of Wrede to Maffei, the general secretary at the foreign ministry, on 18 September: Maffei, telegram to Cairoli, 19 September 1879 (and another to Robilant in AE), in Rosi, *L'Italia odierna*,

Viale had reason to recall this moment, for a new and different version of the same scene had been played out a few weeks before between Umberto I and Haymerle. The latter, until then ambassador to the Quirinal, had just been appointed foreign minister for Austria-Hungary, and so took formal leave of the king of Italy on 2 October. On this occasion he sought to hand Umberto I a copy of Andrássy's famous note of May 1874, taking it from the pocket of his coat. Umberto I refused it, and this made Haymerle ask him, "for permission to communicate directly with him by letter if there should be some incident, without going through his ministers; this would be in conformity with what had been agreed between King Vittorio Emanuele and count Andrássy, and confirmed (according to Haymerle) by a telegram of Aghemo to the count." But this time the atmosphere was not that of Venice, and the cautious Umberto was not so ready to take an initiative as his father had been: Haymerle received the reply "that to do so would have implied a *distrust* between our two governments which was excluded by the statements made. He [the king] believed that, without having recourse to such channels, relations between the two governments would be good, as they had been in the past."[33]

This reply was much more proper constitutionally speaking, and politically meet, than the initiative taken by King Vittorio.[34] But because it came in the

---

vol. 2, t. 3, p. 1880, and also Rosi, *I Cairoli* 2:17–19. Sandonà, who had become aware from documents in Vienna of the existence of direct contacts between the king and the Austrian government through Aghemo (without, it is true, attaching much importance to the fact) expressed doubt about who was responsible for initiating this direct channel of communication (ibid., 1:259 n. 2). The doubt is now resolved.

[33] Cf. as well telegrams of Cairoli to Umberto I, 1 October, and Umberto I to Cairoli, 4 October 1879 (AE, *telegrammi a Sua Maestà*, nos. 204–205). Umberto states: "Haymerle . . . said to me exactly the same things he said in his talk with you. He referred to the letter of Andrássy to Wimpffen, adding that, since Maffei had not accepted a copy of it, he had brought it with him so that I might have exact knowledge of it. He insisted that I should keep this copy, and he asked me to pronounce explicitly in regard to the Wimpffen note, saying that since the personal feelings of Vittorio Emanuele were known, it was desirable that I should make a clear pronouncement that I felt the same way. I naturally stated that I was perfectly informed about the letter of Andrássy, and refused to read the document. In regard to the other note, I replied amicably that, without going into the reasons that caused it to be accepted at that time, I did not see why I was being requested to make a pronouncement in this sense, since in light of our good relations, I perceived a certain distrust in the request. From the general impression I got from Haymerle, I perceived sentiments of marked distrust." The Austrian documents to which Umberto I refers here in an extremely confused manner, are two: one is Andrássy's celebrated note to Wimpffen of 24 May 1874; the other is Andrássy's letter to the chargé d'affaires, Prince Wrede, concerning the incident provoked by the publication of the *Italicae res* of Colonel Haymerle. This is the communication made by Wrede to Maffei, and of which Maffei declared that he did not wish to be given a copy, in order not to prolong the incident further (cf. Rosi, *L'Italia odierna*, vol. 2, t. 3, pp. 1877 ff., and esp. p. 1880; Sandonà, *L'irredentismo nelle lotte politiche* 1:258–61).

In the meeting between Cairoli and Haymerle (on which see Cairoli's telegram to Umberto I, 1 October 1879; AE, *telegrammi a Sua Maestà*, no. 204), Cairoli had stated that he was unaware of Andrássy's note of May 1874: but this appears to have been merely a way of avoiding discussion of the issue; Cairoli must have known of the existence of the document (cf. Cairoli, telegram to Maffei, 20 September 1879, in Rosi, *L'Italia odierna*, vol. 2, t. 3, p. 1881).

[34] The joke is that Cairoli, then prime minister, appeared not to believe that such commitments were really made by Vittorio Emanuele II, "part of whose greatness lay in his scrupulous respect for constitutional forms [!] and for the manifestations of national sentiment" (Cairoli, telegram to Maffei, 20 September 1879, in Rosi, *L'Italia odierna*, vol. 2, t. 3, p. 1881; and forwarded to Robilant by

wake of a period of direct relations between the sovereign of Italy and the government of Vienna, it risked giving the impression, to those who were present, that there had been a change of mood on Italy's part. Starting from scratch, it was possible to be friends without being allies, but it was difficult, after the interruption of an alliance, to remain friends as before, even if friendship was explicitly affirmed, because there would always be something different—more in appearance than in reality perhaps, but still, things could never be quite the same, or so it would be felt: this was a warning sounded by Nigra on 9 August 1886 in writing to Robilant, who had informed him of his intention to take no steps for a renewal of the Triple Alliance as it stood.[35] The same observation could have been applied to the change in the behavior of the two sovereigns. The father had been wrong to resume the bad habit of maintaining personal relations with foreign governments without the knowledge of his ministers; the son, in order to disengage himself from this mechanism, within which he would not have been capable of handling himself with the aplomb of his father, was forced to make a refusal that could have seemed like a change of policy. It is no wonder that Haymerle departed in a state of suspicion and mistrust.

In any case, whatever the future attitude of King Umberto, at Venice Vittorio Emanuele had taken a new path, quite convinced of the great benefits it would have on good relations between his country and the Habsburg empire. Once again, events were to undeceive him, or ought to have done: despite all his protestations of friendship, and his regal guarantees that things would go in the manner ordained by him, whether his ministers willed it or no, those relations became more unsettled than ever in the last three years of his life. But the king, at least at the outset, was convinced that, once he was involved, it would all go smoothly. *Les ministres passent*; it was his mistrust of the discontinuous and varying parliamentary regime that inspired the sovereign, now as in the past, to take action personally. *Le Roi reste*: hence a royal word was a firm, unwavering guarantee. If necessary, the king would work on his ministers, for he was the "choir master" after all.[36] He did not emphasize this notion in 1875, when Minghetti and Visconti Venosta, two men he felt he could trust, were still in power; it was a theme he developed later, in his meetings with the Austrian ambassador, when the Left, of whom he was much more suspicious, were in power.

In fact, after the "parliamentary revolution" of March 1876, which makes us smile today when we hear it described as a revolution, but which to contempor-

---

Maffei, in AE). What a truly innocent soul Cairoli was! Crispi, too intelligent for that, acknowledged that intervention by the king in foreign affairs might be subject to censure, but he defended it on the basis that there must be continuity in foreign policy, overriding cabinet changes; it was his desire, however, that the king's will not be expressed without the intervention of the minister responsible— just the opposite of the practice of Vittorio Emanuele (Crispi, *Scritti e discorsi politici*, pp. 660–61).

[35] Nigra to Robilant, 9 August 1886 (AE, *Carte Robilant*; De Vecchi archive). Cf. Chiala, *Pagine di storia contemporanea* 3:475 n. 1, where Nigra's words are reported verbatim. Chiala calls him "the most illustrious of our diplomats."

[36] Responding to Melegari, who on 18 June 1877 had informed him of the outcome of a dispatch to Cialdini on the French crisis of 16 May, Vittorio Emanuele wrote curtly: "Not knowing, as I should have wished to, what instructions you gave to General Cialdini, I ask you to explain yourself more fully. Best regards" (19 June; AE, *telegrammi a Sua Maestà*, no. 35).

aries really appeared to be the end of an epoch and the beginning of another, Vittorio Emanuele tightened his grip on reins which had been loosely draped from 1870 to 1876, and began to order the Italian ambassadors, by means of the faithful Aghemo, to start writing directly to him once again.[37]

Before that his personal involvement had generally been confined to matters involving King Amedeo in Spain and Queen Maria Pia in Portugal, both countries with which there was an actual dynastic link; but now he corresponded with the duke of Magenta too, and in 1876, shortly after the advent of the Left, when ("unbeknownst to me," claimed the king), Cialdini was nominated as ambassador to Paris and MacMahon did not wish to have him there, it was Vittorio Emanuele who begged his former "comrade in arms" to give a proper welcome to the duke of Gaeta, and succeeded in getting the French president to accept him "resignedly."[38]

The king's intervention was not limited to foreign affairs only. Domestic politics were watched vigilantly by the sovereign, who sometimes confided to Depretis that his "mind was perturbed" by the situation, and urged the prime minister to use every means in his power to bring about a change in "this situation which for the moment does not seem very bright to me." The king wished to be relieved of "the state of grave preoccupation in which I find myself."[39] He was worried by the large question of the railway agreements, and "Zanardelli's obstinacy pains me," since it threatened to jeopardize the situation of the cabinet.[40]

---

[37] Archivio della Casa Reale, *Carte Vittorio Emanuele II*, b. 38. In fact, from this period there is a notable series of reports, principally from de Launay and Menabrea, but also from Robilant, to the king (ibid., buste 38, 39, 40, 41). A few of them are also to be found in AE, *Carte Robilant:* for example, the terse, but clear and perceptive, report that Robilant sent to Vittorio Emanuele on 26 January 1877 concerning the ensemble of Italo-Austrian relations (cited at length below, pp. 568–69). Through Aghemo, the king expressed strong satisfaction, inviting Robilant to "send more of these useful political bulletins" (Aghemo to Robilant, 8 February 1877). Another report from Robilant, briefer and less important, followed on 10 February. Finally, on 23 December, Robilant advised Aghemo by telegram—and simultaneously his minister—of the publication in the *Neue Freie Presse* of putative statements by Andrássy to the Austrian Delegation to the effect that if the irredentist movement continued in Italy, Austria would pass to the offensive and would take the Quadrilateral; there was a semiofficial denial in the *Wiener Zeitung* the following day: cf. Sandonà, *L'irredentismo nelle lotte politiche* 1:170–71. The king replied, again through Aghemo, with the following telegram from Turin on 24 December: "Try to see Andrássy and tell him that the king takes great offense at what has just been published in the *Neue Presse*, because it is an act of complete defiance of the word the king gave to the emperor. Tell him at the same time that if such articles are printed in Austria, he must not be surprised at the polemics that result" (for this telegram I follow the text in AE). [*Translator's note:* Chabod states this because the text, of which he provides a diplomatic transcription (in the philological sense) is telegraphic and contains jumbled grammar which he marks with a bracketed *sic!* My translation normalizes the syntax.] As for Menabrea, on 19 December 1877 he telegraphed to the king concerning the eastern question and announced that a report would follow (ACR, *Carte Depretis*, 1st ser., b. 22, fasc. 69).

[38] MacMahon's letter to the king, dated 29 June 1876, was brought by an officer acting under orders from the marshal (the French embassy was not informed of the move). Vittorio Emanuele telegraphed to MacMahon on 17 July and on 28 July also sent his palace prefect, Panissera, to Paris to speak with the marshal. The latter informed the king on the 18th that he accepted Cialdini "avec résignation" (Archivio della Casa Reale, *Carte Vittorio Emanuele II*, buste 38 and 39).

[39] Vittorio Emanuele, telegram (from Naples) to Depretis, 1 February 1877 (ACR, *Carte Depretis*, 1st ser., b. 24, fasc. 85).

[40] Vittorio Emanuele, telegram to Depretis, 4 November 1877; and cf. Aghemo's telegram, in

As the cabinet was being put back together in December 1877, the king reminded
Depretis of the suitability of Gen. Bertolè Viale for the war ministry and wanted
to know what he was doing about the portfolios of education and public works,
while for the finance ministry he suggested Agostino Magliani; and he also
wanted Depretis to consider the ministry of agriculture and commerce.[41] He
telegraphed Depretis that he should invite the minister of war to purchase horses
for the artillery and the cavalry,[42] and that he should immediately dispatch the
ministers of the interior and of war to Turin, where he wished to confer with
them.[43]

And it must be added that the active role taken by Vittorio Emanuele in the
political affairs of the country did not cause the ministers of the day to become
resentful or raise objections: they were more docile than many of their predecessors of the Right. Indeed, Depretis more than once begged the king to speed
his return to Rome, because he desired to speak with him and submit to him his
views of the situation and some measures he considered necessary; Depretis felt
that the presence of the king would have the effect of removing a number of
obstacles.[44] On other occasions it was Vittorio Emanuele who comforted the
prime minister to "have faith that the future will not be uncertain, and rely on my
strong support,"[45] who told him that the cabinet should not let any fear about the
future transpire, that it was the king's desire that "he show himself stronger than
ever."[46] Then Depretis would reply "that I will not lack either the courage or the
energy to merit the trust of Your Majesty."[47]

In truth, the Left found themselves in charge of the government in a very
difficult international context that was getting worse; domestically the situation
was certainly much better, but even here there were large issues to be dealt with,
and after the victory of March 1876 the parliamentary environment began to
deteriorate, as internal dissent sprang up among the different personalities and
groupings within the Left. To men in this position, almost all of whom had never
held power, it must have meant a great deal to be able to rely on the king as a
solid fixture, all the more in that this particular king, who was endowed with
political flair and a wealth of political experience, whose prestige was growing to
the point where it would soon pass over into legend,[48] was an affable, even

---

the king's name, to Depretis on 7 November, and the telegram of Depretis to Aghemo on 10
November (ibid., b. 24, fasc. 84). In fact, it was over the question of the railway agreements that
Zanardelli resigned from his post as minister of public works on 11 November, with Depretis taking
over temporarily.

[41] Telegrams of Aghemo, in the king's name, to Depretis, 22 and 23 December 1877 (ibid., b.
24, fasc. 85).

[42] Vittorio Emanuele, telegram to Depretis, 22 June 1877 (ibid., b. 24, fasc. 85).

[43] Vittorio Emanuele, telegram to Depretis, 21 June 1877 (ibid., b. 24, fasc. 85). On another
occasion, the interior minister had gone to Naples to confer (Vittorio Emanuele, telegram to Depretis,
3 February 1877; ibid., b. 24, fasc. 85).

[44] Depretis, telegrams to Vittorio Emanuele, 21 April 1876, and to Aghemo, 10 November 1877
(ibid., b. 24, fasc. 85 and 84).

[45] Vittorio Emanuele, telegram to Depretis, 3 February 1877 (ibid., b. 24, fasc. 85).

[46] Vittorio Emanuele, telegram to Depretis, 4 February 1877 (ibid., b. 24, fasc. 85).

[47] Depretis, telegrams to the king, undated (ibid., b. 24, fasc. 85).

[48] Castelli wrote to Vimercati on 29 April 1875 that "at this moment he [the king] can do

solicitous, man, who worried about the health and the ailments of poor Depretis, and sent him such telegrams as this: "I am uneasy knowing that you are not well; have the kindness to send me news of your health."[49] Though they could expect to hear him express disapproval and displeasure without mincing words,[50] he always used a communicative, human tone that added a distinct note of cordiality, even friendliness, to his moments of good humor. When the king concluded his telegrams with "best wishes," or even "friendly best wishes," he enveloped his dealings with his ministers in a certain atmosphere, made himself appear almost as a friend, one placed much higher than they certainly, but a living man for all that, sometimes bullish and arrogant, but a living being, not a protocol machine. Vittorio Emanuele's great secret was knowing how to handle men and win them over: it was a precious political tool in his hands, and he was careful to touch the resonant chords in the soul of each of his different interlocutors.[51] But this tool existed because of the fundamental nature of the king, who was well aware of the exalted dignity that separated him from the common run of mortals, yet who was continually drawn by a certain exuberance and facility, and also a primitive strain in his character, to put himself, in his dealings with men, on their plane, as though oblivious of his divine right. Here, in large measure, lay the secret of the fascination he undoubtedly exercised, and not only on petits bourgeois and peasants enthralled by his lack of stiffness and reserve but also on men in politics. It was one of his real assets as head of state, for he was able to act personally, and not just by fiat but through consensus, in cases where he did not have to deal with exceptional personalities like Cavour, or rigid and difficult men like Ricasoli and Lanza.

In his last years, he seems to have felt the old desire for direct command welling up in him once again. Certainly, when receiving Haymerle on 6 February

---

whatever he wishes, public opinion puts him above everything and everybody" (Archivio della Casa Reale, *Corrispondenza Vimercati*). And previously, on 11 May 1873, deprecating the lack of politicians, Castelli had written to Vimercati: "All is negative. The king alone rises in stature every day in general opinion" (ibid.). Minghetti quite rightly pointed out that one could not deal with Vittorio Emanuele as with any other prince who had inherited the crown of Italy, and impose all the constitutional forms on him like a straitjacket. It had to be remembered "that he was the prime author of the great undertaking of the liberation of the country" (M. Rosi, *Vittorio Emanuele II* 2:246 [Bologna, 1930]).

[49] Telegram, 30 January 1877 (ACR, *Carte Depretis*, 1st ser., b. 24, fasc. 85).

[50] So, when in February 1877, Vittorio Emanuele wanted to receive the new ambassador of Austria, Haymerle, without leaving Naples, saying that he had already received ambassadors and embassies at Naples and Turin, Depretis in turn said that he was sorry, but that he was unable to change his view, which was that the king was obliged to receive the ambassador of Austria at Rome. Vittorio Emanuele then had Aghemo telegraph him that "in order to satisfy your wishes, and to please you," he would leave for Rome immediately, though he was a little put out by having to do so (telegrams of Depretis to the king, undated, and of Aghemo to Depretis, 4 February, ibid., b. 24, fasc. 85).

[51] In 1872, replying to an allusion of Wimpffen "to his talent for manipulating the politicians of his country, his majesty responded 'About that you may be right. I know which string to pluck in every one of them'" (Wimpffen, report, 16 November 1872; SAW, *P.A.*, XI/235, no. 37 A). Castelli wrote to Vimercati on 11 May 1873 that there was no one who knew "his chickens" [i.e., those with whom he had to deal] better than Vittorio Emanuele (Archivio della Casa Reale, *Corrispondenza Vimercati*).

1877, he observed: "it is true, my ministers belong to a somewhat progressive party, but they sincerely desire to have good relations with your government, and if they balk, I will certainly make them do as I wish."[52] Many months later, he sent the trusty Aghemo[53] to assure Haymerle once again that he remained faithful to the memory of Vienna and Venice, despite the growing turbulence in the relations between the two countries, that he wanted to match the loyalty shown him by Franz Joseph with an equal loyalty in return, that his ministers knew that this was his wish and would not move a finger without his knowledge.[54] When he granted his last audience to Haymerle on 31 December, irritated by the purported revelations of the *Neue Freie Presse*, he insisted that it was a bad thing not to trust him when he had given his word that he was the emperor's friend; he insisted on the *moi*,[55] an old habit he had been wont to employ in the past in his relations with Pius IX.[56] This insistence put his interlocutor in an embarrassing position, for clearly he could not express the many doubts he felt, doubts not about the goodwill of Vittorio Emanuele, but about his real capacity to influence events.[57]

[52] Sandonà, *L'irredentismo nelle lotte politiche* 1:143–44, does not report these statements, though they are found in the report and also in the telegram of Haymerle: "though the Italian ministers were of the progressive party, nevertheless they had the best of feelings for Austria-Hungary, and if they should balk, the king would make them do as he wished." In the margin beside these expressions, Andrássy in fact penciled a sign and a question mark.

Still, Melegari certainly spoke as well, in his meetings with the Austrian representative, of the "lively" desire of the king to have the most friendly relations with Franz Joseph, a desire that was matched by the intentions of the government (Gravenegg, report, 14 October 1876, no. 75 A, cited above at n. 28; SAW, *P.A.*, XI/84).

[53] Aghemo, Haymerle observed, was related by marriage to the family of the countess of Mirafiori, and this relationship explained in large part the influence he enjoyed with his sovereign (report, 24 March 1877; SAW, *P.A.*, XI/85, no. 16 F). Haymerle, however, did not have a high opinion of him: "Aghemo is politically too uncultivated, too much an habitual deceiver, for one to be sure of his giving a faithful account of what one has said to him" (Haymerle, personal letter to Andrássy, 5 January 1878; SAW, *P.A.*, XI/88).

[54] "The ministers know that this is the king's wish, and Depretis especially will not move a finger without asking the king" (Haymerle, secret report, 24 November 1877; SAW, *P.A.*, XI/86, no. 69 A).

[55] "'You continue to distrust me,' the king said; 'I have given my word to the emperor that I am his friend; I recall it at every opportunity to prove that I do not wish to escape this obligation; it is a pity that you place so little value on my word. . . . Nothing will happen here without the permission of myself (*moi*) and parliament; and I myself (*moi*) have given my word'" (Haymerle, report, 5 January 1878; SAW, *P.A.*, XI/87, no. 1 A. There is a very summary reference in Sandonà, *L'irredentismo nelle lotte politiche* 1:177).

[56] See for example the declarations of Vittorio Emanuele to the nuncio Antonucci on 10 September 1849: "make sure His Holiness understands that when I have spoken, that is how it will be, and that I will never permit any wrong to be done to the Catholic church in my states," in Pirri, *Pio IX e Vittorio Emanuele II* 1:29 and cf. p. 157, in the king's letter of 9 February 1855 to Pius IX.

See further the king's reply in November 1876 to the question whether or not his ministers really were radical: "Suppose they are, what does it matter? Am I not still there? . . . If . . . it were a cabinet of cardinals, matters would not be proceeding differently," in Massari, *La vita ed il regno di Vittorio Emanuele II*, p. 585, and p. 586 for the expression "choir master."

To the French envoy, Fournier, Vittorio Emanuele made the following remarks at the conclusion of their first audience in March 1872: "Look here. . . . I know Italy well, and all the parties. When you need to get something done that you find difficult to arrange through my ministers, come and see me. We will try to sort it out by ourselves. I will do my best" (Fournier, report, 26 March 1872, no. 2, cited above at n. 14; AEP, *C.P., Italie*, t. 384, fol. 273v).

[57] Haymerle quite rightly observes in his report of 5 January 1878, cited above at n. 55: "Al-

Yet some capacity to influence events he still retained; he was a field still worth cultivating, thought the Austrian ambassador.[58] And in effect Vittorio Emanuele did succeed in doing a few things, at least in 1877, the most agitated year in the recent history of relations between Italy and Austria. He dispatched his emissary, Aghemo, to the new Austro-Hungarian ambassador, Haymerle, to repeat the assurance that the sovereign would see to it that no deviation from the course of rectitude in relations with Austria occurred, and to offer his (Aghemo's) services as intermediary for eventual confidential and direct communications with His Majesty.[59] He also tried to influence his own government concretely. In April, when the debate in the Chamber on the government's foreign policy was drawing near, Vittorio Emanuele even sent Aghemo to Rome from San Rossore,[60] to make sure that Depretis received clear instructions about the peaceful, anodyne tenor of the replies to be given to the various parliamentary questions.[61] These

---

though the king's frank and informal manner seems to make a conversation with him easy, the discussion can nevertheless be embarrassing for his interlocutor, because he always keeps coming back to his two favorite themes: 'have confidence in me,' and 'nothing will be done without me, or beyond me.' Now, how can one express doubt about either of these assertions? The details of foreign policy are difficult to follow; as to *domestic* affairs, recent weeks have not demonstrated that it is in his power to direct them as he pleases. A month ago, the king was firmly decided and convinced that he and Nicotera were moving together in the direction of a more conservative regime; today he has arrived at Crispi, and will perhaps finish up with Cairoli, despite all the aversion he professes to feel for this eventuality." And Haymerle repeats this in his personal letter of the same date, cited above at n. 53, to Andrássy: "The king continually demands that one trust in his word and in his power; but then in the end he just lets things happen."

Earlier, on 3 March 1877, Haymerle had noted: "I am entirely persuaded of the sincerity and loyalty of the assurances given by the king, but I do not place equal faith in his initiative, and the extent of his power. I must say that the phrase he uttered to me with such conviction: 'My ministers will do only what I wish,' left me at something of a loss; for it is clearly an illusion, which diminishes the value of the protestations made by the king" (Haymerle, report, 3 March 1877; SAW, *P.A.*, XI/85, no. 12 B). The question mark put by Andrássy in the margin beside certain expressions used in Haymerle's telegram of 6 February (above, n. 52) shows that at Vienna too there were serious doubts about the effective possibilities of action of Vittorio Emanuele.

[58] In his report of 3 March, after expressing his doubts about the king's effective power, Haymerle states further: "With this reservation, I believe that, provided that one acts in time, the present intentions of the king offer a favorable terrain to be exploited, if one wants to block the action of the Italian government, or push it in a certain direction." And when one needed to act in time, one turned of course to Aghemo! To the latter, in fact, Haymerle recommended vigilance, "because the king has little awareness of the course of events; the ministers give him only a very summary account; I am told that he almost never sees the dispatches sent to the embassies abroad; 'laisser-faire' has worked out so well for him that he will not easily abandon this pleasant habit."

[59] "M. Aghemo added that he knew that the king had pointed him [Aghemo] out to you [Andrássy] as a man in his confidence, and offered his services as an intermediary if I should ever want to communicate in confidence with his majesty" (Haymerle, report, 3 March 1877, cited above at nn. 12, 57, 58). Haymerle reported that he had replied to Aghemo with the advice to be vigilant reported in the previous note, and Andrássy expressed his thanks, saying that if necessary he would avail himself "with eagerness" of Aghemo's services (Andrássy, dispatch to Haymerle, 18 March; SAW, *P.A.*, XI/86; cf. Sandonà, *L'irredentismo nelle lotte politiche* 1:259 n. 2).

[60] Aghemo informed Haymerle of this (Haymerle, report, 28 April 1877; SAW, *P.A.*, XI/85, no. 25 C): "the king had sent him here expressly from Pisa to recommend strongly to the ministers that they use proper language when referring to neighboring powers."

[61] Vittorio Emanuele to Depretis (undated, but 19 April 1877): "I have learned of the questions put in the session of the Chamber the day before yesterday [17 April] about foreign policy, and I now inform you of how I want them replied to in the session on Monday, when these questions will be pursued. I desire that the government should limit itself to giving assurance that it will continue to

instructions were scrupulously carried out, for the speeches of Melegari, and of Depretis himself, in the Chamber on 23 April 1877, were in substance no more than a series of variations on the theme decided by the royal will, culminating in the statement of Depretis that Italy "has regulated its relations with all the powers in an honorable fashion, especially with those that are its nearest neighbors [meaning Austria-Hungary], whose prosperity it considers as its own prosperity, and as the main precondition of its own security."[62]

Haymerle, who was immediately informed of this royal intervention by Aghemo, had reason to be satisfied;[63] and he must have been just as gratified a few weeks later, when the subservient royal emissary told him, at the express bidding of Vittorio Emanuele, that upon the outbreak of the war between Russia and Turkey, the cabinet had seriously debated whether or not to go ahead with arms procurements and fortification works which, given the situation, would inevitably have been seen as aimed at Austria; but that Vittorio Emanuele had pronounced a firm veto on this, which his ministers had promptly obeyed.[64] The king wished his act of friendship for Austria to be made known to His Apostolic Majesty, and it naturally elicited thanks from Vienna and an attestation of Franz Joseph's trust in the sentiments of his royal Italian brother.[65]

Even when he did not go to the length of practical intervention, the words in which King Vittorio Emanuele voiced his friendship with the Habsburg empire were always unambiguous and heartfelt. Italy was in the grip of irredentist fever; but the king did not hesitate to disown it openly in his meetings with Vienna's envoy to the Quirinal. To Gravenegg he had stated, on the last day of 1876, that the furor in the press about the Trentino, which began with a notorious article in *L'Opinione* on 3 October 1876, had produced the most painful impression on

---

monitor very closely the course of events as they are unfolding in the Orient, and that any decisions it may take will always have as their aim the good of the nation, and will be inspired by the same independent attitude Italy has maintained until now. If in future serious measures have to be taken, the Chamber will be informed, and in the meantime the government will see to it that the interests of our nationals are properly protected. I would ask you to convey these wishes of mine to the foreign and interior ministers." Depretis replied (20 April): "I have informed the foreign and interior ministers of Your Majesty's telegram, and I take it upon myself to assure Your Majesty that in the forthcoming debate on the Green Book we will adhere to Your Majesty's wishes" (ACR, *Carte Depretis*, 1st ser., b. 24, fol. 85).

[62] *A.P., Camera*, pp. 2710 ff. (in this important session the well-known interrogation of Visconti Venosta, among other things, had occurred). Cf. esp. pp. 2712 and 2717 (the Chamber will be consulted if any grave matter is to be decided in light of "our honor" and "our vital, essential interests"; Europe has received assurances concerning Italian policy, relations with all the powers are excellent, etc.); and p. 2713 (protection of Italian nationals). All of this paraphrases the instructions given by the king.

[63] Haymerle did indeed express overall satisfaction to Andrássy, finding that on the whole there had been progress "toward the right outlook on the situation and on relations with us; . . . in my opinion the cabinet is presently on the right track," though he had some reservations and doubts about the future (Haymerle, report, 28 April 1877; SAW, *P.A.*, XI/85, no. 25 A).

[64] Haymerle, secret report, 12 May 1877 (SAW, *P.A.*, XI/85, no. 29 F). With this, doubts about Italy's unusual arms procurements, which as far as Haymerle was concerned had not been eliminated by the statements of Melegari and Depretis on 23 April, were removed.

[65] Andrássy, secret dispatch to Haymerle, 22 May 1877 (SAW, *P.A.*, XI/86). Vittorio Emanuele in turn offered his thanks, through Aghemo, who repeated his assurances that at need he would keep Haymerle informed (Aghemo to Haymerle, 25 June 1877; SAW, *P.A.*, XI/86).

him, but that it originated among a miserable lot of people[66] and sprang from animus against the cabinet of Depretis—in sum, that it had been inspired principally by reasons of domestic politics. When the new ambassador, Haymerle, resolutely brought up this thorny subject at his first audience, the king initially declared that he wanted nothing to do with all the polemics and demonstrations stirred up by the irredentists.[67] When Haymerle then asked that Italy state its view that, whatever might happen, it had no further accounts to settle with Austria, Vittorio Emanuele interrupted him with what Haymerle considered a highly significant "but of course!"[68]

In spite of all this the crisis grew ever more acute, the press furor ever more heated; it was of no avail for the king to let Haymerle know, first through Robilant during a brief visit of the latter to Rome, and then in November through Aghemo, of his firm desire to preserve good relations between the two states.[69] As December drew to a close, the *Neue Freie Presse* set off the scandal mentioned above when it revealed what it said were statements made by Andrássy before the Austrian Delegation, statements that were hostile, even threatening, to Italy. Aggravated, upset, and above all irked that Vienna did not take him at his word, Vittorio Emanuele let loose with one of those forceful and swaggering outbursts that were habitual with him: this was the man who in 1850 had proclaimed his scorn for the common rabble,[70] who in 1867 complained of having been unable to carry out a plan to allow the Garibaldians to enter Rome and when twenty or thirty thousand of them had gathered in the city, to march on them and stage a massacre, extirpating them from the surface of the earth,[71] who in 1877,

---

[66] "Von erbärmlichen Leuten . . ." (Gravenegg, report, 31 December 1876, cited above at n. 31).

[67] I reproduce here, with added emphasis, a passage from Haymerle's report of 6 February 1877, cited above at n. 31. It is not mentioned in Sandonà, *L'irredentismo nelle lotte politiche* 1:143, who follows the briefer telegram of the same date, rather than the report. "'We do indeed have some hotheads in Italy; *I want nothing to do with all these polemics and demonstrations*; but repression often merely makes matters worse. Still, if any really culpable act against Austria were to take place, it would be severely punished.'"

[68] Again I add the emphasis to this passage from Haymerle's report: "'but what we have the right to demand is that in Italy the view should be taken in all eventualities that accounts with Austria-Hungary are entirely closed—*But of course!' the king interjected*—'and that the cabinet should make a frank pronouncement in this sense, if doubts or contrary projects should come to light. As for myself, Sire, I dare to place my efforts to maintain the best of relations with your government under your protection.' 'You may count on it,' the king answered me; 'tell the emperor especially how much importance I place on his friendship.'" In the telegram too, Haymerle states: "The king greeted these words [about all accounts being closed] with a sign of agreement." Sandonà has nothing about this, and at *L'irredentismo nelle lotte politiche* 1:144 n. 1 he erroneously states that Haymerle's report is in German, not French. [*Translator's note:* The report is in French, the telegram is in German.]

[69] Haymerle, reports, 21 and 24 November 1877 (SAW, *P.A.*, XI/86, nn. 68 A and 69 A, secret).

[70] His statements to the Austrian envoy at Turin, Apponyi, at the end of June 1850, included the following: "There are some people who tremble at popular movements, but they make me laugh. Nothing is easier than to deal with them: one falls on the rabble and one crushes them like flies. Let them make a move and they will see; I will have them all hung!" And all this was spiced with exclamations and terms too expressive for Apponyi to repeat to Schwarzenberg (A. Monti, *La giovinezza di Vittorio Emanuele II (1820–1849)* [Milan, 1939], p. 513).

[71] Statements made by Vittorio Emanuele to Baron de Malaret, the French envoy (Malaret,

claiming that the Trentino and Albania meant nothing to him, told the Austrian ambassador that those who had designs on these territories were looked on in Italy as "dogs."[72] These were things that a sovereign ought not to have said in that manner, not even at that juncture, to an ambassador of Austria-Hungary. Though it may be true that in the mouth of a man like Vittorio Emanuele, who liked to use rough, vulgar, braggart talk, such affirmations meant less to an alert interlocutor than they would if uttered by someone else,[73] it is also true that the king himself was led to overshoot the mark by his own manner, by a superficiality that was often intentional and calculated to impress the other with the crudity of his expression, so that he denigrated in an unworthy fashion movements, ideas, and sentiments that were untimely and dangerous at that juncture, but that were held by men, not dogs.

And it was here that the danger lay in such personal interventions by the king, over the heads of his ministers and outside their control: the "mischief" he produced behind their backs could become a source of real trouble. As long as he took seriously the question of relations with Austria-Hungary, and tried to keep them friendly by opposing the mistimed clamor of demonstrations in the street, he gave proof of his seriousness and good sense, the good sense, or rather political intuition that had sent him down the right path on other occasions, against the views of his ministers, and even against the violent reaction of Cavour, as had happened at Monzambano in July 1859. It was not only legitimate from the constitutional point of view but politically very opportune for him to invite his ministers, when necessary, to consider very closely Italy's relations with the double monarchy, and to warn them that there was danger in letting policy oscil-

---

report, 29 November 1867, *Les origines diplomatiques de la guerre, 1870–1871*, 19 [Paris, 1926], p. 380; and cf. Luzio, *Aspromonte e Mentana*, pp. 431 ff.). The king was convinced that, with the ground cleared in this manner, it would then have been very easy for him to come to an agreement with the pope.

[72] " 'There is always talk of planned expeditions against the Trentino, of designs on the Trentino, and even on Albania. I do not even dream of such things. The individuals in Italy who advance these notions, we think of as dogs' (his exact words)" (Haymerle, report, 5 January 1878, cited above at n. 55). In the text of the telegram sent immediately after the audience, on 31 December 1877: "he [the king] is thinking neither of Trieste [*sic*!] nor of Albania. The people who raise these questions he calls riff-raff" (SAW, *P.A.*, XI/86, no. 93). *Triest* in the German text of the telegram is evidently a slip of the pen, or else an error of coding or decoding, which could easily happen given the similarity between *Trient* and *Triest* [i.e., Trent and Trieste].

[73] See, for example, how Malaret let the king talk on, without taking his outburst too seriously. That expressions of this kind ought not to be taken too literally is also shown by the fact that in March of 1872, receiving the new French envoy, Fournier, for the first time, Vittorio Emanuele again deplored the danger of the masses, the "*canaille . . .* our common enemy," and repeated almost verbatim what he had said five years before to Baron de Malaret: "If I had been allowed to do as I wished, I would have let 30,000 or 40,000 good-for-nothings, communards like those of Paris, seize control of Rome for several days and do there what communards usually do; but not one would have got out alive. It would have been an atrocity perhaps, but Italy would have been purged of this vermin for an entire generation. It would certainly have simplified things" (Fournier, report, 26 March 1872, no. 2, cited above at nn. 14 and 56; AEP, *C.P., Italie*, t. 384, fols. 272v–273r). This fantasy, in other words, became a cliché used by the king in meetings with foreign representatives. And Fournier indeed noted that, in general "there is in his words more passion, perhaps, than conviction" (ibid., fol. 275r). In the king there was "un singulier mélange de grosse bonhomie, de finesse, d'astuce même."

late with every gust that blew from the piazza. But it was an extremely serious matter when he embarked on personal ventures of which the ministers responsible were completely unaware, and which might have led him, and the country with him, into a situation in which the peril he had been trying to avoid would be heightened. There was nothing to object to politically if he arranged to be sent personal reports by Robilant or de Launay or Menabrea; but when he ordered Robilant, unbeknownst to the foreign minister, to make statements to the government in Vienna, he created a major political contretemps, quite apart from the constitutional irregularity.

Though his intentions were laudable, the way he set about achieving them was hazardous. Yet why should anyone be surprised? This was perfectly in character for Vittorio Emanuele II, a constitutional monarch and a gentleman, it was claimed, but who was convinced in his heart that bourgeois "laymen" would never be able to come to grips fully with the great affairs of state, foreign policy, and military questions; he made an exception for a man like Cavour—but even with him one had to watch out. His conception of the state was still entirely personal: *moi* continued to mean virtually the same thing when pronounced by him as it had when pronounced by Carlo Alberto, before the Statuto, and he still considered personal relations among sovereigns "the strongest link" among the different states.[74]

This last was a notion, for that matter, anything but unique and exclusive to Vittorio Emanuele, being the common property of the monarchs of continental Europe, including Wilhelm I of Germany, Tsar Alexander II, and naturally Franz Joseph. Even Victoria, Queen of England, was not immune to velleities of this kind, though she had had to bow to her ministers more than the others. The natural affection between uncle and nephew, Wilhelm I and Alexander II, the "age-old tradition," the "sacred legacy, which our fathers of august memory have handed down to us," could be appealed to in order to try to maintain good relations between Germany and Russia at the same time that Bismarck was struggling to impose an alliance with Austria, and against Russia, on his lord and master.[75]

Apart from the sovereigns themselves, most men who belonged to the court or had lived in intimacy with it for a long time, and military officers in general and often diplomats too, like de Launay and Robilant in our case, considered dynastic relationships and personal friendship among monarchs factors of great and sometimes decisive importance. Dynastic links were not yet an entirely negligible element in international relations: their era was drawing to a close, but had not yet vanished completely. That the personal surety of a monarch of a legiti-

---

[74] Thus Robilant in reporting personally to the king on 10 February 1877 (above, n. 37): "Various circumstances at the moment hinder relations between the two governments from being as close as would be desirable. But it is certain that by maintaining cordial contacts between the two sovereigns, the strongest link between the two states is preserved intact, and when circumstances change, contacts between the two governments will be able to become once more very cordial, as they were before."

[75] Cf. the typical expressions of Wilhelm I of Germany in the summer of 1879 (*G.P.* 2:21–22 and 66).

mate dynasty outweighed that of a transient minister[76] was not just a belief of Vittorio Emanuele II; that the person of the sovereign could alone offer the necessary guarantee of good relations between two countries, whereas the policy of one cabinet did not bind its successors, was a dictum repeated in October 1881 by Blanc, general secretary at the foreign ministry and a strong proponent of the voyage to Vienna by Umberto I.[77]

Vittorio Emanuele II was basically imperious and authoritarian underneath his pretense of being easy-going, and had a strong sense of himself as "the king," the supreme head through age-old tradition and divine right. No wonder that a king like that should believe that by giving his word he was ensuring the friendship of Italy and Austria; or that, as mistrust of Italy increased in Austria after he had given his word, he took personal offense and said so without beating around the bush.

His word of honor: Haymerle believed him,[78] but someone else might well have wondered how to reconcile declarations of his friendship for the Austrian emperor, of his attachment to his own word of honor, of his aversion for irredentist intrigues, with the mission of Crispi, which also took place in 1877, just when these royal testimonials were most profuse. Indeed, the question poses itself spontaneously when one turns to consider the letter that Crispi wrote Depretis from Turin on 27 August 1877, right after his meeting with the king and prior to his departure for Paris.

The king, who was in a good humor, writes Crispi, hopes for nothing from any combination arising out of the war in the Orient, because for us it is already late in the day; nonetheless he urged me to do everything possible to get in on the action and profit somehow. But about the real purpose of Crispi's voyage, an alliance with Germany, the king used different language. "The king feels the need to end his days with a victory, so as to give our army the force and the prestige that it lacks in the world's eyes. It is the language of a soldier and I understand it. . . . And unfortunately the king is right. If our generals had not let us down in 1866, and we had won in the Veneto and in the Adriatic, the Austrians would not dare to speak and write about us as they do."[79]

There might well be a blend of Vittorio Emanuele and Crispi himself in these words. The Sicilian politician was unquestionably not a faithful and precise reporter of things he had heard and seen, since his own personality always tended to overlay that of anyone else.[80] To say the least he had little aptitude for reckon-

---

[76] Cf. the expression of Wilhelm I in marginal note no. 1 to Bismarck's report of 24 September 1879 (*G.P.* 3:98).

[77] Statements of Blanc to the Austro-Hungarian chargé d'affaires, von Tavera (Tavera, report, 8 October 1881, highly secret, no. 78; SAW, *P.A.*, rot. 459. I use the manuscript copy of Senator Salata, since the fascicle could not be found in the archive in 1941).

[78] Cf. above, n. 57.

[79] Crispi, *Politica estera* 1:8–9.

[80] Crispi, in speaking to Farini in 1896 about his meetings with Bismarck and Lord Derby in 1877, reported that in making him the "offer" of Albania, Derby and Bismarck said to him: " 'This will . . . in any case be a pledged token [*Ce sera . . . toujours un gage*],' implying that it might later be possible to barter it to Austria in exchange for concessions to us on the eastern frontier" (Farini, *Diario*, MRR, under 26 October 1896. Crispi's own version of the meeting is in his *Questioni*

ing with the psychology of his interlocutors, and in particular had had little experience of Vittorio Emanuele; he probably took a couple of the boastful phrases that Vittorio Emanuele usually tossed out in the course of an interview at face value, expressions that needed to be taken with a grain of salt. But there is no more room for doubt when we review the secret instructions of Depretis to Crispi, which are also dated 27 August, because in these it is explicitly stated that it is the king's will, in accord with the prime minister, "to create friendly relations of the most intimate kind between Italy and Germany," arriving "at a complete and concrete accord by means of a treaty of alliance founded on our common interest and preparing for any eventuality. Italian interests might be harmed not only if the ultramontane party prevailed [in France] but also if Austria aggrandized itself by annexing several of the Ottoman provinces, which is a possible outcome of the war in the Orient. It is desirable that the two governments come to an agreement on this matter as well."[81]

The menace to Italian interests deriving from the eventual occupation of Bosnia Herzegovina by Austria: this was nothing less than the leit-motiv of the whole Italian press campaign that began with the celebrated article in *L'Opinione* on 3 October 1876, which had set off a burst of comment in Viennese circles, and which the king had condemned outright in his meetings with Gravenegg and Haymerle; this was the pretext used by the irredentists to demand that the balance be redressed in the Trentino, and on the Isonzo, to bring the old cogitations of Balbo up to date and force the government to defend Italian interests energetically! The alliance it sought with Germany was meant to serve Italy primarily against Austria, not against France: this was the "grave and most urgent question" that weighed on Depretis,[82] even though Crispi, when he saw how pointless

---

internazionali, pp. 237–38. It contains the same declaration—ascribed to Derby only—about the *gage,* and the same inexactitude in portraying Derby as having spoken first and Bismarck second). Farini annotates these statements by Crispi as follows: "one naturally has to make the due allowance here, because Crispi willingly forgets, or misrepresents." Now it is certain that in Crispi one finds at the very least a lack of precision in reporting events. His own account of his meetings with Bismarck and Derby is extant in two versions that are not exactly identical: the longer one related to Farini, and the more clipped one—with no mention of the *gage*—published in *Politica estera* 1:27, 34–35, 57. For his meeting with Bismarck, indeed, there is a third version, which de Launay immediately reported to Melegari on the basis of what Crispi told him. Bismarck is supposed to have said: "Why shouldn't you think about Albania?" (as he had already said to de Launay himself), which is somewhat less than saying "take Albania," and does not touch on the matter of the *gage*; the latter, however, reappears in Chiala, *Pagine di storia contemporanea* 1:275 (de Launay, report, 20 September 1877; AE, *Ris.,* c. 27; previously published by Salvemini, "Alla vigilia del Congresso di Berlino," *Nuova Rivista Storica* 9 [1925]: 86 ff.). Lack of precision accounts for evident incongruities in Crispi's accounts: typical is the mention of Fiume rather than Trieste in his interview with Andrássy on 20 October 1877 (Crispi, *Politica estera* 1:67; Salvemini, ibid., pp. 75 ff.). In other cases there is clearly and indubitably a willful alteration of the facts: an example is the assertion he made in 1892 to Chiala that he had not spoken with Bismarck of an alliance (even a purely defensive one initially) against France! (Salvemini, ibid., pp. 85–86); here, however, we have to take into account Crispi's position as he spoke, for in 1892 he was attempting to get back into government and so was forced not to compromise himself.

[81] Crispi, *Politica estera* 1:10.

[82] Crispi, *Politica estera* 1:38. Depretis to Crispi, 21 September: "You leave open a grave and most urgent question [that of Austria and eventual redress for Italy]. Be sure, if you can obtain nothing else, to leave some opening that will allow us to reopen the question and to insist. It seems to

it was to insist on the problem of Austria and of redress, insisted with rare lack of insight on an alliance against France alone, which would essentially have served Germany's ends.[83]

Now, the sovereign also wanted an alliance with Germany too: the meeting with Crispi at Turin before the latter's departure, and the second on 23 October upon his return,[84] the continuous telegrams and reports with which Crispi informed the sovereign step by step of the results of his voyage, the gratitude of Vittorio Emanuele, his preoccupation about the menace to Italian interests in the Orient—all these things convey a clear message. The conclusion is that Vittorio Emanuele, who in the spring of 1877 had repeatedly given his word to remain a faithful and loyal friend of the emperor of Austria, was willing to play a game in August and September of the same year that, if it had succeeded, would have left his friend Franz Joseph with his back to the wall. And then he was furious in December because at Vienna his word was discounted.

It has to be underlined that neither the king, nor (by any stretch of the imagination) Depretis, wanted to push this tactic to the point of taking up arms. In the bellicose trumpetings reported by Crispi, the words of the sovereign assumed a tone that, in practice, Vittorio Emanuele would certainly not have sustained; indeed, when the trip was over, he expressed to Crispi his regret that government and parliament had left him with a tiny army good for no more than the defense of the national territory and, with another of his braggart gestures, expressed his regret that he was unable to mobilize two hundred thousand men and resolve the eastern question all by himself. That his hands got itchy at the sight of all the turmoil in the Balkans was natural; and it was in character for him to hope for some "profit," a chance to grab something, *ranché quaich cosa* as he put it to Sella at the end of September 1870. Equally, it was natural that he should dream, like many other Italians, of a great military victory to make up for Lissa and Custoza: no sooner had he laid down his arms in 1866 than he was deprecating his incompetent ministers and beastly generals and dreaming of being given another chance to show what he could do.[85] When the eastern question was re-

---

me that it ought to be understood that in the eastern question we cannot remain indifferent to a solution that aggrandizes Austria." And cf. too Depretis's letter of 26 September where, in speaking of foreign affairs, the emphasis falls entirely on Austria (ibid., 1:53). Further, we see how in the meeting with Lord Derby the essential question is that of the eventual expansion of Austria to the east, and of Italy's right to have this redressed in the Alps—as Menabrea, for that matter, had already said (ibid., 1:57 and cf. pp. 28, 35; Menabrea, report, 5 October 1877, AE, *Ris.*, c. 27).

[83] Cf. Chiala, *Pagine di storia contemporanea* 1:280; G. Salvemini, *La politica estera di Francesco Crispi* (Rome, 1919), pp. 9–10; Salvatorelli, *La Triplice Alleanza*, p. 37.

[84] This meeting on 23 October is reported by Crispi in *Scritti e discorsi politici*, pp. 659 ff. The king—according to Crispi—spontaneously returns to the question of Austria: "You realize that it is in Italy's interest that no great power should aggrandize itself at Turkey's expense."

[85] Vittorio Emanuele to Prince Eugenio di Carignano, from Padua, 3 September 1866: "I have never had to suffer frustration equal to that of the last two months, and I am increasingly convinced that the human race is without faith. Emperors and kings are wicked oath-breakers, their peoples crazy and demented, ministers ignorant, incapable bastards; I was unable to guide the generals and they lost their bearings, committing one bestial error after another. I tell you I found myself in a pretty mess. But I had a famous lesson, and now I know how I must conduct myself in the future. That moment will yet come.

"How I got out of the situation I do not know. What I do know is that one way or another Venice is ours, and the Italians must be content. Like it or not, with the Quadrilateral in one's power one can

opened, he wished that Italy could be making the running, taking a leading role.[86] Though he regained his composure, he was intermittently revisited by aspirations and wish-dreams of glory as the international situation evolved. But we can quite safely assert that such desires and longing impulses would not have worked him up to the point where he was ready to use brute force.

A few months later, on the eve of his death, he managed to spread alarm one more time with his pronouncements at the New Year's reception at court: Italy, he said, must make itself feared; the skies of international politics were lowering; expenditures on the army were needed. It all savored of war: but when Depretis alluded to the interpretation that others were putting on his words, Vittorio Emanuele replied in astonishment that he had said the same things many times before (which was true), that they were not new and were not meant to alarm.[87] Big talk of this kind, he said, was merely intended to get the parliamentary deputies to spend more on the military.

Vittorio Emanuele probably thought that if he could introduce the specter of Bismarck with his brow furrowed like Jove on Olympus into the proceedings, Andrássy in Vienna would abandon his refusal to contemplate eventual redress. "Do everything possible to get in on the action and profit somehow." But even the king believed that the hour was late and that there was no more room for Italy, so a last-ditch gamble was tried. In his heart he was already half resigned to failure. It was as though Vittorio Emanuele were saying to himself: why not let Crispi have a go? Some good might come of it abroad, and at home there was a definite gain to be made by giving satisfaction to a man who had the power in parliament to threaten the government. There is a sign that some such notion was floating in the mind of the king, for more than once, when Crispi informed him about Decazes, Bismarck, and Derby, the king would reply by alluding explicitly to "ministerial aspirations,"[88] or expressing the wish "that his ministerial hopes would be realized."[89] It was as though the king wanted to steer the conversation away from foreign affairs and onto the parliamentary struggle, as though he were trying to stroke and soften up in advance the fiery politician whose imminent ascent to government he foresaw. Those hints, that manner of broaching argu-

---

say Hallelujah, and if the Baron de Broglie had let me take it earlier when it was offered to us, I would be in Vienna today with my triumphant army. Let us not think of it any more; the army is the only good thing that is still left to us, and I will demonstrate on another occasion what it can do. But I will have to get rid of certain generals. No one wants to listen to what I have to say, but unfortunately I am always right. Farewell dear Eugenio; I am preparing to go to Venice and I embrace you with all my heart" (Archivio della Casa Reale, *Carte Vittorio Emanuele II*, b. 24).

[86] According to Aghemo (Haymerle, report, 3 March 1877, no. 12 D; SAW, *P.A.*, XI/85).

[87] Depretis recounted this to the Austrian ambassador (Haymerle, report, 5 January 1878, no. 1 C, confidential; SAW, *P.A.*, XI/87). The view that the king's words were a tactic to pressure the parliamentary deputies also comes from Depretis and was the semiofficial line; Crispi adopted it too (cf. as well Haymerle, telegram, 2 January, no. 1; ibid., XI/87). Cf. Sandonà, *L'irredentismo nelle lotte politiche* 1:177.

[88] Telegram from the king, 17 September (Crispi, *Politica estera* 1:32).

[89] Telegram from the king, 7 October (Crispi, *Politica estera* 1:59). It will be remembered that at Rome the cabinet was in difficulty: Depretis himself telegraphed Crispi on 14 October: "be sure . . . to speed your return. Things are becoming serious, and your presence here is absolutely necessary" (ibid., 1:60). In fact, the crisis that led not long after to Zanardelli's, then Nicotera's and Melegari's, leaving the cabinet and Crispi's entering it, was developing.

ments, and those references to ministerial aspirations would seem very strange responses to a man who was depicting the danger of a war with France, or reporting that Bismarck and Derby were offering Albania to Italy, unless we assume that the king had consented to avail himself of Crispi as a kind of *missus dominicus* in order to have a little peace domestically, and dexterously bind to his person one of the leading politicians of Italy, dangerous but easy to seduce with the glamour of authority.[90]

For that matter the prime minister had acted no differently. Depretis tended to make use of men he trusted for confidential missions abroad,[91] since like most men of the Left he believed in a notional international solidarity deriving from party ideology[92] and distrusted professional diplomats, who were certainly not supporters of the left. Like the king he was tempted to try a little secret diplomacy, concocting useless muddles behind the ambassadors' backs and substituting *le secret du parti* for *le secret du roi*. The former was soon to be revealed as much more flimsy than the latter, for it crumbled over the affair of Tunis, amid

---

[90] Indeed, we see with what satisfaction Crispi reports to the king, and how easily praise of Vittorio Emanuele springs from his pen (Crispi, *Politica estera* 1:18–21); or how he can say to Depretis, "His Majesty the king was kinder than you" (ibid., 1:36).

[91] Between August and October 1876, Domenico Farini went to Paris and London (ACR, *Carte Depretis*, b. 23, fasc. 76, and b. 29, fasc. 111). In August 1877 Gen. Luigi Seismit-Doda went to Vienna and Graz with precise instructions from Depretis that Robilant was to be kept in the dark (ibid., b. 22, fasc. 69: Seismit-Doda to Depretis, 1 and 10 August 1877). He was meant to gather information and see how the overall situation stood. (On this figure, brother of the better known Federico, cf. L. G. Sanzin, *Federico Seismit-Doda nel Risorgimento* [Bologna, 1950], passim.) In February 1878 Domenico Farini went to Bucharest officially, causing Tornielli to protest at the too "manifestly political" color of his mission, which "will be equally displeasing to Vienna and St. Petersburg" (Tornielli to Depretis, 6 February 1878; ibid., b. 22, fasc. 71). Then too, Depretis received information frequently from Vienna, and also documents (obtained from an employee "of the known ministry"), from Sigismund Kaykowski. The go-between was often Cesare Correnti (who also forwarded information to the king: Archivio della Casa Reale, *Carte Vittorio Emanuele II*, busta 41); and other times, it was Count Ladislaus Kulczycki, who in 1870–71 had sent information to Visconti Venosta on the Vatican (AE, *Ris.*, c. 51; Visconti Venosta archive), and who lived in Rome at via dei Pontefici 64 (ACR, *Carte Depretis*, 1st ser., b. 22, fasc. 69 and 71).

[92] This was the case in relations with France, where, parallel to official diplomacy, contacts were made between Gambetta and men of the Left, often through Farini. In June and July 1877 Farini forwarded letters to Depretis from Paris (ACR, *Carte Depretis*, b. 22, fasc. 69). He was in constant contact with Armand Ruiz, who had access to Gambetta (letters of Gambetta to Ruiz, 14 March 1877, and Ruiz to Depretis, 17 March 1877, both ibid.; letters and telegrams between Ruiz and Farini in MRR, *Carte Farini*). In May-June 1878 there were close contacts among Cairoli, Farini, Ruiz, and Gambetta both over the commercial treaty between Italy and France, and concerning a visit by Umberto I to the universal exposition in Paris, to which the French attached great importance (Farini to Cairoli, 30 May and 1 June 1878; MRP, *Carte Cairoli*, p. 31; also a letter of Ruiz, 29 May, in ACR, *Carte Depretis*, 1st ser., b. 22, fasc. 69). Farini carried out another mission to Gambetta in October 1878, concerning the Egyptian question (Maffei, telegrams to Cairoli, 28, 29, 30, 31 October 1878; MRP, *Carte Cairoli*, register of telegrams to the prime minister, nos. 14, 16, 17, 21). In France these relations among Depretis, Cairoli, Farini, and Gambetta ("la politique occulte de M. Gambetta") were known (Waddington, statements to the Austrian ambassador, Wimpffen; personal secret letters, I and II, Wimpffen, 5 March 1880; SAW, *P.A.*, XI/90). And the Austrian ambassador, learning of them too, informed Vienna that Ruiz, a naturalized French citizen, knew Italy well and had served in the Piedmontese army, apparently in 1859; that he was a man trusted by Gambetta, whose secretary he was, and that he often came to Rome; and that Farini was the Italian political figure in whom Gambetta had most faith (Wimpffen, secret report, 25 June 1880, no. 44 C; SAW, *P.A.*, XI/90). On Ruiz, cf. Gambetta, *Lettres*, nos. 312, 314, 354, 562, 562 bis.

the disappointment on the part of Italian politicians on the left at the action of their friend Gambetta. *Le secret du roi* had had some importance in international relations; *le secret du parti* served only to generate false hopes and rude awakenings. Ever since the spring of 1877 Depretis had been thinking of sending quite another person, Domenico Farini, his usual diplomatic collaborator when it came to unofficial contacts, on a visit to Bismarck.[93] Then, pressed by events, and perhaps increasingly worried by the inadequacy of Melegari, the foreign minister,[94] he had decided to take the effective direction of foreign policy into his own hands, and had made up his mind by summer, spurred on in all probability by Tornielli, general secretary at the foreign ministry, who in international problems played the role of Egeria to the prime minister's Numa Pompilius.[95]

Tornielli had a long conversation with Keudell, the German ambassador, on 2 July, in which Keudell spoke of the danger posed by France, and even asked what Italy would do if Germany were ever attacked. When Tornielli adduced arguments against Austria and its territorial aggrandizement in the Balkans, Keudell responded with a warning that had no effect: "I fear . . . that if you try to create a linkage between the two things, meaning the shared position of Italy and Germany in the face of clerical conspiracy on one hand, and your own special position on the eastern question on the other, you might get a reply from Prince Bismarck that you would not care for."[96] A "cold shower"[97] like that ought to have warned the Italians against insisting further; instead it confirmed Depretis's notion that it would be useful to send "a reliable person" to Germany to try to discover, if possible, Bismarck's real intentions with regard to the eastern question, on which to date "it has not been possible to arrive at an exchange of ideas which might lead to a preventive accord."[98]

And so Depretis, the first and foremost author of the whole affair, had proposed Crispi as a person "about whose wisdom and discretion" the king could

[93] Farini, *Diario*, MRR, under 4 August 1898. "In 1877, in spring, I was preparing, at the invitation of Depretis, to leave for Berlin to see Bismarck. I had posted only one condition: someone would have to arrange for me to gain entrée. For whatever reason Depretis gave up on the idea; perhaps he substituted for my mission the mission undertaken by Crispi the following autumn." Farini was "the distinguished political man" to whom Chiala refers in *Pagine di storia contemporanea* 2:ix. Cf. too Farini, *Diario* 1:115.

[94] The view of Keudell, who relayed it to Haymerle. Keudell, it should be noted, was hostile to Melegari (Haymerle, report, 4 August 1877, no. 52 A, confidential; SAW, *P.A.*, XI/86).

[95] The great influence exerted on Italian foreign policy by the expert Tornielli, at a time when lack of experience (*Unerfahrenheit*) was rife in the government, Melegari included, is noted by the Austrian ambassador (Haymerle, personal letter to Andrássy, 12 May 1877; SAW, *P.A.*, XI/86).

[96] "Conversazione avuta col sig. de Keudell il 2 luglio 1877" (AE, *Ris.*, 10; papers found in the writing desk of Count de Launay). That the author of the memorandum is Tornielli results from the handwriting, and from the words "believe me, for since 1866 I have not surrendered for a single day the direction of our political division." Tornielli tried hard to persuade Keudell, who promised his personal cooperation in getting his government to see matters differently, but (as was his style) without challenging its prevailing tendencies head-on.

[97] The expression was used by Keudell himself in speaking with the Austrian ambassador Haymerle about his contacts with the Italian government (Haymerle, report, 4 August 1877, no. 52 A, cited above at n. 94; SAW, *P.A.*, XI/86).

[98] Depretis to the king, 9 August 1877 (ACR, *Carte Depretis*, 1st ser., b. 24, fasc. 85). Same to same, 19 August (Archivio della Casa Reale, *Carte Vittorio Emanuele II*, b. 40).

rest fully assured.[99] And he had made this choice because of pressure exerted by Crispi himself,[100] and also because he thought that in this way he could bind his dangerous friend to the government, making him partly responsible for foreign policy. The government's domestic situation was already worrying Depretis, who, among other things, was anything but happy with the profile his relationship with Zanardelli was assuming in the great question of the administration of the railways;[101] it may be that he already foresaw trouble looming in the cabinet and in parliament and wanted to keep Crispi happy.[102] A master of parliamentary strategy, Depretis always viewed problems of foreign policy partly, or even primarily, as a function of domestic politics.[103] By acceding to Crispi, what he really did was put handcuffs on a possible threat to his government, for Crispi was a much less subtle plotter of parliamentary maneuvers than he.[104] The king, who was also constantly alert to the domestic situation, must have been thinking along the same lines: it never hurts to try, and in any case, even if the voyage bore no fruit, Crispi, who was president [i.e., speaker] of the Chamber of Deputies after all, would be kept sweet, which could only help things domestically.

All these things can be, indeed must be, admitted. But in the end, it wound up being a double game of a not very attractive kind, and also, at that particular moment, a gross political error. For the fact is that, whatever the king's private feelings about the mission, however much or little faith he had in its outcome, by letting the president of the Italian Chamber of Deputies go off to make the rounds of Europe and treat of very delicate matters at a time when there was very little room in which to treat, he committed a blunder. Though some praise might be

---

[99] Depretis to the king, 9 August 1877, cited in the previous note. Depretis insists that Crispi should be allowed to leave as soon as possible, and asks Vittorio Emanuele to give him an audience, which the king had said he wished to postpone until 25 or 26 August (Vittorio Emanuele, telegram to Depretis, from Valsavaranche, 12 August; Depretis, telegram to the king, undated; ACR, as in previous note). Depretis persists: "I continue to hold that this voyage is not only useful but indispensable; no harm can come of it, since Your Majesty can fix the limits of the mission, which, in the hands of a wise and prudent individual, will be able to enlighten the government on the measures to be taken in the interests of the state."

[100] That Crispi put himself forward spontaneously is asserted by Chiala (*Pagine di storia contemporanea* 1:270 ff.) and is recognized also by Palamenghi-Crispi (Crispi, *Politica estera* 1:7, and *Politica interna*, p. 160). This contradicts the clarification sent on 16 February 1892 by Crispi to Chiala (*Pagine* 2:vii), in which the Sicilian statesman protested that the voyage "did not come about through my initiative, but on the proposal of the hon. Depretis, and with the king's agreement." Now it is perfectly true that Depretis had had the idea of sending a special emissary to Bismarck for some time. Still, it appears highly likely that Crispi put himself forward as the man for the job. The two versions, in other words, have to be combined (cf. Salvatorelli, *La Triplice Alleanza*, p. 34).

[101] In the telegram to the king of 9 August, cited above at nn. 98 and 99.

[102] That Depretis wanted to keep Crispi content was well known (cf. Seiller, report, 15 September 1877, no. 57 B; SAW, *P.A.*, XI/86).

[103] When a return visit by Franz Joseph was under consideration, Depretis telegraphed Umberto I on 19 July 1882: "In present circumstances, that is with national elections looming, a return visit which took place elsewhere than at Rome might have serious consequences for domestic politics" (ACR, *Carte Depretis*, 1st ser., b. 24, fasc. 85). Blanc mentioned this to the German chargé d'affaires (Tavera, secret report, 24 August 1882, no. 77; SAW, *P.A.*, XI/92).

[104] W. Schinner has rightly and perspicaciously called attention to these motives of domestic politics in Crispi's mission, in *Der österreichisch-italienische Gegensatz auf dem Balkan und an der Adria . . . 1875–1896* (Stuttgart, 1936), p. 18.

due, not for the method adopted but for the basic reasoning that had led him to speak and take action against irredentist disturbances, so much the more was he to blame for the fatuousness with which he allowed Bismarck to be approached, in the name of the Italian government, about an alliance against Austria, Italian rights to redress in the Alps, and similar ideas, which Bismarck and the other European governments had already wholly condemned.[105] The time was no longer right for "having a go," for doing everything possible to "get in on the action and profit somehow," because by behaving in this manner the Italian government continued the policy of making and retracting claims at the same time, of saying both yes and no, of creating continual uncertainty and confusion that was its great mistake between 1876 and 1878. By not curbing the public's anticipation of possible future "combinations" on the Adige and Isonzo rivers, by protesting in London and Berlin about Austria's plans to occupy Bosnia and Herzegovina while stating in Vienna that it wanted to maintain the best relations with the double monarchy and disavowing any desires for annexation,[106] the government ended up filling the Austrian government with quite justified suspicion and mistrust, and behind it, the governments in London and Berlin, while at the same time leaving the great hopes it had nourished at home profoundly dissatisfied, and opening the way to the violent crisis of the summer of 1878.

In accepting the Crispi mission (and the result would have been the same if someone else had gone in his place), the king also accepted this policy, going against his own better intentions of a few months previously. That the mirage of some territorial gain had the power from time to time to set his soul on fire, especially when the rumble of war in the Balkans and Armenia reawakened his soldierly impulses, making him (who knows?) remember fondly his brave charges against the enemy at Palestro and San Martino, was utterly natural. He was born and remained a soldier at heart, and it was only human that the dream of a splendid victory to crown his career should keep him awake nights. That he should hope to get some final advantage from the eastern crisis was more than logical; he was not the only one, nor were he and Crispi the only ones, to think

---

[105] Indeed Andrássy wrote to Haymerle on 13 August 1877 that "the cabinet in Berlin has advised the Royal Government not to irritate us. I know that your letter of the 4th current confirms it, and I believe I can expect, without fear of finding I was mistaken, that at the right moment it will renew with insistence these counsels of moderation at Rome" (SAW, *P.A.*, XI/86, secret. On this dispatch, cf. Sandonà, *L'irredentismo nelle lotte politiche* 1:169). Haymerle for his part informed Andrássy of the "cold shower" given by Keudell to the Italian government on the question of Austria, Bosnia, etc. (above, nn. 96, 97), and also that the English ambassador, Paget, had energetically advised the Italian government to keep quiet (Haymerle, personal letter, 4 August; SAW, *P.A.*, XI/86). It was logical that at the conclusion of Crispi's voyage Haymerle should observe to Depretis: "I imagine that M. Crispi brought back from his trip the conviction that our relations with Germany are on too solid a footing for Italy to be its friend without being on good terms with us, and without adhering frankly to the policy of the *two* powers." That is just what Andrássy said to Crispi, Depretis responded (Haymerle, report, 27 October 1877, no. 63 A; SAW, *P.A.*, XI/86).

[106] In summer 1877, Melegari stated to Haymerle that for Italy there did not exist a question of the Trentino (Haymerle, personal letter to Andrássy, 4 August 1877, cited in the previous note). And to Keudell, in their meeting of 2 July (n. 96 above), Tornielli stated that Italy was not asking Austria for one inch of territory; what it did want was that the military strength of each of the two states should remain the same in proportion to the other.

like that. But the moment had not yet arrived at which it would be possible to exploit the general situation to Italy's advantage. Above all, no advantage would ever be won as long as Italy continued to fix its gaze on Trent and look for it in a rectification of its frontier at the expense of Austria. This was to go down a blind alley, with no way out. The same Robilant who had first conceived the idea of linking the eastern question to that of the unredeemed lands,[107] and who later stated that the annexation of the Trentino ought to be "an objective of which our foreign policy never loses sight,"[108] but who also had the ability to see the developing situation in its true contours, had indicated how matters stood in his personal report to King Vittorio on 26 January of that year, the report that had given such pleasure to the sovereign. This is what the Italian ambassador to Vienna wrote:

> The arrival today at Rome of Baron Haymerle as ambassador of His Apostolic Majesty apparently puts an end at least to the tense state of relations between the two governments which had already begun to cause vivid preoccupation in Italian public opinion. I say "apparently" because at bottom the question that occasioned the dissension remains open until the question of the Orient is definitively settled, which does not appear to be on the point of happening. The current position is this: Your Majesty's government believes that it is counter to Italy's interests that Austria should augment its power in the Adriatic by annexing Bosnia and Herzegovina. The government of His Imperial Majesty for its part, while affirming that it has no desire to annex Turkish provinces, declares in a solemn, and also a threatening, way, that should this take place despite its intentions, it would refuse to cede so much as an inch of territory to Italy by way of redress. In my opinion we have reason on our side, but I maintain with equal firmness that it is pointless to be in the right if one lacks the means to make reason prevail. Fortified by its alliance with Germany, Austria does not fear us, and can therefore defy us with impunity. Since to my knowledge Italy does not have the sort of allies who, if need arose, would be disposed to support any claims it might make with armed force, it would very likely meet the fate that befell France at the hands of Germany in 1870.
>
> Of necessity therefore we must resign ourselves to seeing our neighbor perhaps increase its power, without risking our own prestige, and even perhaps our own existence, in pointless undertakings. What we ought to try to do is to acquire useful and efficacious alliances, while making an effort to maintain correct relations with Austria, avoiding for our part not only inopportune debates about the matter under discussion but also the sort of public demonstrations that give others formal grounds for complaint, faced with which, as always in the past, we are left with no way out

---

[107] On 7 August 1875, at the beginning of the new eastern crisis, he wrote Visconti Venosta that Austria might in the end be forced to annex Bosnia Herzegovina, something that at the moment perhaps no one desired. He thought that Italy ought to be very alert, because this might be a unique occasion to extend its frontier in the Val d'Adige or on the Isonzo (Robilant, personal letter to Visconti Venosta; Visconti Venosta archive).

[108] Cf. his report of 3 October 1878, published in Rosi, *L'Italia odierna*, vol. 2, t. 2, pp. 1765–67. He portrays the cession by Austria of the Trentino as the price of a solid and lasting alliance with Italy (cf. above, ch. 11, n. 53).

except to make rather undignified and ill-concealed excuses. If we do take this cautious approach, we shall perhaps be able to deal with the solution of the eastern question without peril, and in the end derive some advantage from it. The alliance of the three emperors, which suits Germany very well, holds firm at the moment of writing. But it will not last forever, and the day will come, not however in the very short term, in which it will dissolve, for German and Russian interests cannot proceed indefinitely in harmony. When this happens, we must be under no illusion: with things in Europe remaining as they are today, that is with France continuing to be weak (as we must hope) Austria will remain united to Germany in order to survive. Nor for my part would I wish it were different, since I would fear an alliance between a revived France and Austria, supported by Russia, much more. Our interest would be served if an alliance among Germany, Austria, and Italy could be established and maintained, and the interest of all of Europe would be exactly the same, for it would have no reason to fear war, the three powers united being strong enough to impose peace on the others. Meanwhile, there is greater anxiety at the moment concerning the mutually hostile attitude assumed by Germany and France in consequence of the stances adopted at the conference [of Constantinople] by their respective plenipotentiaries, and the statements in the press to which these gave rise in both countries, than there is concerning the Orient. And yet it is my opinion that the time is not yet ripe for a new Franco-German war; nonetheless we ought not to dismiss the symptoms that are currently manifesting themselves, inasmuch as they are precursors of a new struggle in the future between those two powerful nations.[109]

From this portrait, with its profound sense of reality, there clearly emerged the depth of the friendship between Austria and Germany, and hence the obvious consequence that it was pointless to go seeking the support of Berlin against Vienna.

If Vittorio Emanuele had pondered thoroughly the wise observations of his ambassador in Vienna, he might have been able, in the summer of 1877, to keep himself from breaking, in point of fact, his word, which he gave so freely and by which he set such store. And he might have spared his country experiments that in context were useless and in fact deleterious, such as the voyage round Europe of the president of the Chamber of Deputies.

Vittorio Emanuele has taken us far from our point of departure. In the first years after 1870 there was not yet any reason to fear his direct contacts with the government in Vienna, and foreign policy rested effectively in the hands of those who had full responsibility for it: Visconti Venosta and Lanza, Visconti Venosta and Minghetti, but primarily, in the normal discharge of affairs, Visconti Venosta and his immediate collaborators, Artom and the Italian envoys in the foreign capitals.

Among the envoys, as we have seen, there were certainly differing views, and in the case of de Launay divergences that were much more than subtle shades of disagreement. And yet the foreign policy of the kingdom of Italy was, and also

---

[109] AE, *Carte Robilant* (draft).

gave the appearance of being, one and unitary; and supreme control of it rested in fact with the minister, however hesitant, cautious, and uncertain he might seem to be. Visconti Venosta allowed those under him full freedom to debate and criticize, and they made ample and sometimes very lively use of it. He welcomed counsel, indeed required impetus from an external source at decisive moments. In 1873, on the question of the voyage to Vienna and Berlin, he received it from various parties, Robilant and de Launay abroad, and Minghetti (the deciding factor) at home. But counsel and impetus, his own intuition and his reaction to the stimulus of others, all fused together in the end, stamping his actions with a single uniform style.[110] So it was that in those years a fundamental unity and coherence marked the foreign policy of Italy, which, though it had been in existence for barely a decade, received from the calm and the dignity of sentiment of the foreign minister, and his abiding constancy of purpose, a patina, almost, of antiquity.[111]

[110] Justified homage was paid to the diplomacy of the Right in 1881 by "an ex-diplomat" (the Marchese d'Arcais), author of a notable article entitled "Le alleanze dell'Italia," in *Nuova Antologia* 59 (1881): 6–7.

[111] Thus, very aptly, Bonghi, in *Il Congresso di Berlino e la crisi d'Oriente* (Milan, 1878), p. 1.

• B I B L I O G R A P H Y •

CHABOD DID NOT compile a bibliography for *Storia della politica estera italiana dal 1870 al 1896*, although the very thorough index, the work of Rosario Romeo and Giuseppe Giarrizzo, included the names of authors cited. The following bibliography was compiled by the translator while the translation was being made, on the basis of references given by Chabod in the footnotes. In principle, it includes all published books and articles to which reference is made more than once. The aim has been to provide an instrument of purely indicative value for those using the book or wishing to locate items cited by Chabod, since only he himself could have provided an authoritative one.

Alatri, P. "Bonghi e la vita politica italiana." *Nuova Antologia* (October 1946).

———. See also P. Romano (pseudonym for P. Alatri).

Aleardi, Aleardo. *Canti di Aleardo Aleardi*. Florence, 1867.

———. *Epistolario di Aleardo Aleardi*. Verona-Padua, 1879.

Alfieri di Sostegno, Carlo. *L'Italia liberale*. Florence, 1872.

Amari, Michele. *Carteggio di Michele Amari*. Turin, 1896.

Antoni, C. *La lotta contro la ragione*. Florence, 1942.

Arcari, P. M. *Le elaborazioni della dottrina politica nazionale fra l'unità e l'intervento (1870–1914)*. Florence, 1934–1939.

———. *La Francia nell'opinione pubblica italiana dal '59 al '70*. Milan, 1938.

Arrò Carroccio, G. *Il cattolicismo ed il liberalismo*. Florence, 1872.

Artom, E. *L'opera politica del senatore I. Artom nel Risorgimento Italiano*. Bologna, 1906.

Augustine (Aurelius Augustinus). *De civitate Dei*. Edited by Dombart. Leipzig, 1863.

Azeglio, Massimo d'. *Scritti e discorsi politici*. Edited by M. De Rubris. Florence, 1931–1938.

Die auswärtige Politik Preussens, 1858–1871. Oldenburg i. O., 1936.

Bacchelli, Riccardo. *Il Diavolo al Pontelungo*. Fifth reprint.

———. *Il Mulino del Po*.

Balbo, C. *Della monarchia rappresentativa in Italia*. Florence, 1857.

———. *Delle speranze d'Italia*. Florence, 1855.

———. *Meditazioni storiche*. 3d ed. Florence, 1855.

———. *Pensieri ed esempi*. Florence, 1856.

———. *Pensieri sulla storia d'Italia*. Florence, 1858.

Barbèra, G. *Memorie di un editore*. Florence, 1883.

Barbiera, R. *Il salotto della Contessa Maffei*. 12th ed. Florence, 1918.

Battaglia, F. "Lettere di Angelo Camillo De Meis a Donato Jaia." *Memorie dell'Accademia delle Science di Bologna*, 4th ser., vol. 9 (1950).

Beau de Loménie, E. *Le responsabilità delle dinastie borghesi*. Italian translation: Milan, 1946.

Bellessort, A. *Les intellectuels et l'avènement de la troisième République*. Paris, 1931.

Bertani, Agostino. *Discorsi Parlamentari*. Rome, 1913.

Beust, Friedrich von. *Trois quarts de Siècle, Mémoires*. French translation: Paris, 1888.

Il bilancio del regno d'Italia negli esercizi finanziari dal 1862 al 1907–1908. Rome, 1909.

Binkley, R. C. *Realism and Nationalism, 1852–1871.* New York–London, 1935. Vol. 16 of *The Rise of Modern Europe*, ed. W. L. Langer.

Bismarck, Otto von. *Die Gesammelten Werke.* Berlin: Friedrichsruher Ausgabe, 1924–1933.

Boccardo, G. *Prediche di un laico.* Forlì, 1872.

Boglietti, G. "Nihilisti e slavofili." *Nuova Antologia* 58 (1881).

Bon Compagni, C. "Francia e Italia." *L'Opinione.* 27 November 1871.

Bonghi, Ruggero. *Opere.* Milan-Florence, 1933—. (See also Maturi, W.)

———. Vol. 1: *Programmi politici e partiti.*

———. Vol. 3: *Discorsi Parlamentari.*

———. Vols. 4–6: *Ritratti e Profili di contemporanei* (vols. 1–3). Florence, 1935.

———. Vol. 8: *Studi e discorsi intorno alla Pubblica Istruzione.* Florence, 1937.

———. Vols. 9–11: *Nove anni di storia di Europa nel commento di un italiano (1866–1874)* (vols. 1–3). Edited by M. Sandirocco. Milan, 1942.

———. Vol. 12: *Stato e Chiesa.* Milan, 1942.

Broglie, duc Jacques de. *Mémoires.* Paris, 1938–1941.

Bruzzo, G. B. *Considerazioni sulla difesa generale dell'Italia.* 2d ed. Naples, 1871.

Bulferetti, L. *Le ideologie socialistiche in Italia nell'età del positivismo evoluzionistico (1870–1892).* Florence, 1950.

———. *Socialismo risorgimentale.* Turin, 1949.

———. "Sul progressismo sociale della borghesia nel Risorgimento—Antonio Scialoja." In *Miscellanea del centenario*, published by the Institute for the History of the Italian Risorgimento, Turin committee. Turin, 1949.

Bülow, Bernhard von. *Memorie.* Italian translation: Milan, 1932.

Busetto, G. *Notizie del generale Nino Bixio.* Fano, 1876.

Cadorna, R. *La liberazione di Roma nell'anno 1870 ed il plebiscito.* Turin, 1889.

Caetani, Michelangelo. *Epistolario del duca Michelangelo Caetani di Sermoneta.* Florence, 1902.

Calcaterra, C. *Il nostro imminente Risorgimento.* Turin, 1935.

Calosso, U. *Colloqui col Manzoni.* 2d ed. Bari, 1948.

Cambon, P. *Correspondance.* Paris, 1940.

Campello della Spina, P. *Ricordi di 50 anni dal 1840 al 1890.* Spoleto, 1910.

Campo Fregoso, L. *Del primato italiano sul Mediterraneo.* Turin, 1872.

Cappelli, R. "Il conte Carlo Nicolis di Robilant." *Nuova Antologia* 171 (1 June 1900).

Capponi, Gino. *Lettere di Gino Capponi e di altri a lui.* Edited by Carraresi. Florence, 1885.

———. *Scritti editi e inediti di Gino Capponi.* Edited by M. Tabarrini. Florence, 1877.

Caracciolo di Bella, C. *Dieci anni di politica estera.* Città di Castello, 1888.

Carducci, Giosuè. *Lettere.* See following entry.

———. *Opere.* Bologna, 1935–1968.

Carré, J. M. *Les écrivains français et le mirage allemand.* Paris, 1947.

Castagnola, S. *Da Firenze a Roma: Diario storico-politico del 1870–71.* Turin, 1896.

Castelli, Michelangelo. *Carteggio politico di Michelangelo Castelli.* Rome-Turin-Naples, 1891.

———. *Ricordi di Michelangelo Castelli.* Turin, 1888.

Cataluccio, F. *La politica estera di E. Visconti Venosta.* Florence, 1940.

Cattaneo, Carlo. *La città considerata come principio ideale delle istorie italiane* (1858). Edited by Belloni. Florence, 1931.

———. *Dell'insurrezione di Milano nel 1848 e della successiva guerra.* Lugano, 1849.

————. *Epistolario.* Edited by Caddeo. Florence, 1949.

————. *Scritti politici ed epistolario.* Edited by G. Rosa and J. White Mario. Florence, 1892.

Caucino, A. "I frutti della legge sulle Guarentigie." *L'Unità Cattolica*, 23 July–4 August 1876. Offprint: Turin, 1876.

Cavallotti, Felice. *Discorsi Parlamentari di Felice Cavallotti.* Rome, 1914.

Cavour, Camillo Benso, count of. *Il Carteggio Cavour-Nigra dal 1858 al 1861.* Bologna, 1926–1929.

————. *Carteggio Cavour-Salmour.* Bologna, 1936.

————. *Cavour agricoltore: Lettere inedite . . . a G. Corio.* Edited by E. Visconti. Florence, 1913.

————. *Diario.* Edited by L. Salvatorelli. Milan-Rome, 1941.

————. *Discorsi Parlamentari raccolti e pubblicati per ordine della Camera dei Deputati.* Turin-Florence-Rome, 1863–1872.

————. *Discorsi Parlamentari.* Nuova edizione. Edited by A. Omodeo and L. Russo. Florence, 1932–.

————. *Lettere.* Edited by L. Chiala.

————. *La questione romana negli anni 1860–61: Carteggio del Conte di Cavour con D. Pantaleoni, C. Passaglia, O. Vimercati.* Bologna, 1929.

Cesare, R. De. *Le classi operaie in Italia.* Naples, 1868.

————. *Il conte Giuseppe Greppi e i suoi ricordi diplomatici (1842–1888).* Rome, 1919.

————. "Gli ultimi anni di Costantino Nigra." *Il Giornale d'Italia*, 4 December 1915.

Chiala, L. *Giacomo Dina e l'opera sua nelle vicende del Risorgimento italiano.* Turin-Rome, 1896–1903.

————. *Pagine di storia contemporanea.* Turin-Rome, 1892–1898.

Cione, E. *Francesco De Sanctis.* Messina-Milan, 1938.

Cognasso, Francesco. *Vittorio Emanuele II.* Turin, 1942.

Colonna di Cesarò, Gabriele. *Discorso.* Palermo, 1874.

Compendio delle statistiche elettorali italiane dal 1848 al 1934. Rome, 1946.

Congresso generale delle Società Operaie Italiane tenuto in Roma nell'aprile del 1872. Rome, 1873.

Constant, Benjamin. *Cours de politique constitutionnelle.* Edited by Laboulaye. Paris, 1861.

Conti, E. *Le origini del socialismo a Firenze (1860–1880).* Rome, 1950.

Convegno . . . 1848 = Convegno di scienze morali storiche e filologiche, 4–10 ottobre 1948: Il 1848 nella storia d'Europa. Rome: Accademia Nazionale dei Lincei, 1949.

Coppino, M. *Commemorazione di A. Depretis.* Turin, 1888.

Coppola d'Anna. *Popolazione reddito e finanze pubbliche dell'Italia dal 1860 ad oggi.* Rome, 1946.

Corbino, Epicarmo. *Annali dell'economia italiana.* Città di Castello, 1931–1934.

Corniani, R. *Il principio d'autorità in Italia ed il partito conservatore.* Turin, 1878.

Crispi, Francesco. *Carteggi politici inediti di Francesco Crispi (1860–1900).* Rome, 1912.

————. *Discorsi Parlamentari.* Rome, 1915.

————. *Pensieri e profezie.* Rome, 1920.

————. *Politica estera.* 2d ed. Milan, 1929.

————. *Politica interna.* Milan, 1924.

————. *Questioni internazionali.* Milan, 1927 (reprint).

————. *Scritti e discorsi politici di Francesco Crispi*. 2d ed. Turin-Rome, no year (but 1891).

————. *Ultimi scritti e discorsi extraparlamentari (1891–1901)*. Rome, 1913.

Croce, B. *Giosuè Carducci*. 4th ed. Bari, 1946.

————. *Storia della storiografia italiana nel secolo decimonono*. Bari, 1921.

————. *Storia d'Europa nel secolo decimonono*. 2d ed. Bari, 1932.

————. *Storia d'Italia dal 1871 al 1915*. 3d ed. Bari, 1928.

Della Torre, A. "Il cristianesimo in Italia dai filosofisti ai modernisti." Appendix to S. Reinach, *Orpheus*, vol. 2 (Italian translation: Palermo, 1912).

Delle Piane, M. *Liberalismo e parlamentarismo*. Città di Castello. 1946.

Depretis, A. *Discorsi Parlamentari di A. Depretis*. Rome, 1888–1892.

[Diamilla-Muller, E.]. *Politica segreta italiana, 1863–1870*. Turin, 1880.

Dostoevsky, Fyodor. *Diario di uno scrittore*. Italian translation: Milan, 1943.

Dreyfus, R. *M. Thiers contre l'empire, la guerre, la commune, 1869–1871*. Paris, 1928.

Droysen, Johann Gustav. *Historik*. Edited by Hübner. Munich-Berlin, 1937.

Durando, G. *Della nazionalità italiana*. Lausanne, 1846.

Engels, F. *Notes sur la guerre de 1870–71*. French translation: Paris, 1947.

Engels, F. and K. Marx. See under Marx.

Ercole, F. "La personalità storica e il pensiero politico di Francesco Crispi." In Ercole, *Pensatori e uomini d'azione*. Milan, 1935.

Eyck, E. *Bismarck*. Erlenbach-Zurich, 1941.

Falco, G. "Note e documenti intorno a Carlo Pisacane." *Rivista Storica Italiana* 44 (1927).

————. *La politica ecclesiastica della Destra*. Turin, 1914.

————. *Il riordinamento della proprietà ecclesiastica*. Turin, 1910.

————. "Spunti sociali nel pensiero e nell'opera di Cavour fino al '48." In *Convegno . . . 1848*.

Faldella, G. *Salita a Montecitorio (1878–1882): Il paese di Montecitorio*. Turin, 1882.

Farini, Domenico. *Diario*. Milan, 1942.

Favre, Jules. *Rome et la république française*. Paris, 1871.

Federici, F. *Der deutsche Liberalismus*. Zurich, 1946.

Ferrara, Francesco. "Il Germanismo economico in Italia." *Nuova Antologia* 26 (August 1874).

Ferrari, Giuseppe. *La disfatta della Francia*. Edited by U. Guanda. Modena, 1943.

————. *Scritti editi ed inediti*, vol. 1, *Carteggio inedito*. Edited by A. Monti. Milan, 1925.

Ferrario, E. *Qual'è la moralità de' campagnuoli e come possa migliorarsi*. Milan, 1875.

Finali, G. *La vita politica di contemporanei illustri*. Turin, 1895.

Fisher, H. "French Nationalism." In Fisher, *Studies in History and Politics*. Oxford, 1920.

Flaubert, Gustave. *Correspondance*. 4th ser. Paris, 1904.

Flori, E. "Massimo d'Azeglio e Roma capitale." *Nuova Antologia* (October 1950).

Fonterossi, G. "Garibaldi e l'Internazionale." *La Stirpe* 11 (1933).

Fonzi, F. "I 'cattolici transigenti' italiani dell'ultimo Ottocento." *Convivium* (1949).

Forni, E. *L'Internazionale e lo Stato*. Naples, 1878.

Fustel de Coulanges, Numa. *La guerra franco-prussiana*. Rome, 1945.

Galati, V. G. *Il concetto di nazionalità nel Risorgimento italiano*. Florence, 1931.

Gambaro, A. *Riforma religiosa nel carteggio inedito di Raffaello Lambruschini*. Turin, 1926.

Gambetta, Léon. *Lettres de Gambetta, 1868–82*. Edited by D. Halévy and É. Pillias. Paris, 1938.

Garibaldi, Giuseppe. *Scritti e discorsi politici e militari* (vols. 1–3). National Edition, vols. 4–6. Bologna, 1934–1937.

Garino Canina, A. "I principi finanziari di Quintino Sella." *Rendiconti del R. Istituto Lombardo di Scienze e Lettere* 73 (1939–1940).

Gavard, Charles. *Un diplomate à Londres: Lettres et notes, 1871–1877*. Paris, 1895.

Gentile, Giovanni. *L'eredità di Vittorio Alfieri*. Venice, 1928.

———. *Gino Capponi e la cultura toscana nel secolo decimonono*. 3d ed. Florence, 1942.

Gilbert, Felix. *Johann Gustav Droysen und die preussisch-deutsche Frage*. Munich-Berlin, 1931.

Giolitti, Giovanni. *Memorie della mia vita*. Milan, 1922.

Giordani, I., ed. *Le encicliche sociali dei Papi*. 2d ed. Rome, 1944.

Giraud, Victor. *Essai sur Taine, son oeuvre et son influence*. 2d ed. Paris, 1902.

Gobineau, Arthur de. See Tocqueville, Alexis de.

Goncourt, Edmond de. *Journal des Goncourt*. Paris, 1903.

Gooch, G. P. *Studies in German History*. London, 1948.

Greenfield, R. K. *Economia e liberalismo nel Risorgimento*. Italian translation: Bari, 1940.

Gregorovius, F. *Diari Romani*. Italian translation: Milan, 1895.

Greppi, G. "Lettres du comte Ed. de Launay . . . au comte J. Greppi." *Revue d'Italie* (December 1906).

Griffith, G. O. *Mazzini profeta di una nuova Europa*. Italian translation: Bari, 1935.

Guerrieri Gonzaga, C. "Cenni sulla tregua accordata al Vaticano." Preface to E. De Laveleye, *L'avvenire dei popoli cattolici* (1876).

———. *I parroci eletti e la questione ecclesiastica*. Florence, 1875.

Guiccioli, A. *Quintino Sella*. 2d ed. Rome, 1882.

Guillaume, J. *L'Internationale: Documents et souvenirs (1864–1878)*. Paris, 1907.

Halévy, D. *Le courrier de M. Thiers*. Paris, 1921.

———. *La fin des notables*. Paris, 1930.

Halperin, S. W. *Italy and the Vatican at War*. Chicago, 1939.

Hanotaux, G. *Histoire de la France contemporaine*. Paris (no year).

———. *Mon temps*. Paris, 1933 / 1938.

———. *Sur les chemins de l'histoire*. Paris, 1924.

Hohenlohe-Schillingsfürst, Ch. zu. *Denkwürdigkeiten*. Stuttgart-Leipzig, 1907.

Ideville, H. d'. *Journal d'un diplomate en Italie . . . Turin, 1859–1862*. 2d ed. Paris, 1872–73.

———. *Victor Emmanuel, sa vie, sa mort: Souvenirs personnels*. Paris-Brussels, 1878.

L'Italia economica nel 1873. 2d ed. Rome, 1874.

Jacini, Stefano. *Un conservatore rurale della nuova Italia*. Bari, 1926.

———. *La crisi religiosa del Risorgimento: La politica ecclesiastica italiana da Villafranca a Porta Pia*. Bari, 1938.

———. *Il tramonto del potere temporale nelle relazioni degli ambasciatori austriaci a Rome (1860–1870)*. Bari, 1931.

Jacini, Stefano Francesco. *Pensieri sulla politica italiana*. Florence, 1889.

———. *Sulle condizioni della cosa pubblica in Italia dopo il 1866*. Florence, 1870.

Jemolo, A. C. *Chiesa e Stato in Italia negli ultimi cento anni*. Turin, 1948.

———. *Crispi*. Florence, 1922.

Kaegi, Werner. *Historische Meditationen*. Zurich, 1942–1946.

Kohn, H. *Profeti e popoli*. Italian translation: Milan, 1949.

La Gorce, P. de. *Histoire de la seconde République française*. 9th ed. Paris, 1925.

La Marmora, A. *Un po' più di luce sugli eventi politici e militari dell'anno 1866*. 2d ed. Florence, 1873.

Lambruschini, Raffaello. *Scritti politici e di istruzione pubblica*. Edited by A. Gambaro. Florence, 1937.

———. *Scritti di varia filosofia e di religione*.

Langer, W. *La diplomazia dell'imperialismo*. Italian translation: Milan, 1942.

Lanza, Giovanni. *Le carte di Giovanni Lanza*. Turin, 1935—.

Launay, Edoardo de. See Greppi, G.

Laveleye, E. de. *L'avvenire dei popoli cattolici*. Italian translation: Rome, 1876.

———. *Lettres d'Italie*. Brussels, 1880.

———. *Nouvelles lettres d'Italie*. Milan-Brussels, 1884.

Leidner, F. *Die Aussenpolitik österreich-Ungarns vom deutsch-französischen Kriege bis zum deutsch-österreichischen Bündnis, 1870–1879*. Halle, 1936.

Lémonon, E. *L'Italie économique et sociale (1861–1912)*. Paris, 1913.

Lioy, P. *Elettori e deputati*. Milan, 1874.

Lipparini, L. *Minghetti*. Bologna, 1942.

Lopez de Oñate, F. See Mancini, P. S., *Saggi sulla nazionalità*.

———. *Carlo Cafiero*. Trani, 1947.

Luzio, A. *Aspromonte e Mentana*. Florence, 1935.

———. *Garibaldi, Cavour, Verdi*. Turin, 1924.

———. *I Martiri di Belfiore e il loro processo*. 4th ed. Milan, 1925.

———. *La Massoneria e il Risorgimento italiano*. Bologna, 1925.

———. *Profili biografici e bozzetti storici*. Milan, 1927.

Luzzatti, L. *Grandi Italiani: Grandi sacrifici per la Patria*. Bologna, 1924.

———. *Memorie*. Bologna, 1931–1935.

Luzzatto, Gino. *Storia economica dell'età moderna e contemporanea*. Padua, 1948.

———. *Studi in onore di Gino Luzzatto*. Milan, 1950.

Macchi, Mauro. *I dottrinarii d'Alemagna*. Milan, 1871.

Maenchen-Helfen, O. and B. Nicolajevski. *Karl Marx*. Italian translation: Turin, 1947.

Magliani, A. "L'azione economica dello stato." *Nuova Antologia* 28 (January 1875).

Maioli, G. *Marco Minghetti*. Bologna, 1926.

Maistre, Joseph De. *Considérations sur la France*. Lyon-Paris, 1860.

Malo, H. *Thiers*. Paris, 1932.

Malvezzi, A., ed. *Il Risorgimento Italiano in un carteggio di patrioti lombardi, 1821–1860*. Milan, 1924.

Mancini, P. S. *Diritto Internazionale: Prelezioni*. Naples, 1873.

———. *Discorsi Parlamentari di P. S. Mancini*. Rome, 1894.

———. *Saggi sulla nazionalità*. Preface by F. Lopez de Oñate. Rome, 1944.

Marcère, E. L. G. de. *L'assemblée nationale de 1871*. Vol. 2, *La présidence du maréchal de Mac-Mahon*. Paris, 1907.

Margherita, Queen. See Marco Minghetti.

Marselli, Nicola. *Gli avvenimenti del 1870–71*. Turin, 1871.

———. *La politica dello Stato italiano*. Naples, 1882.

———. *La rivoluzione parlamentare del marzo 1876*. Turin, 1876.

Martello, T. *Storia della Internazionale dalla sua origine al congresso dell'Aja*. Padua-Naples, 1873.

Martini, F. *Confessioni e ricordi, 1859–1892*. Milan, 1929.

———. *Lettere (1860–1928)*. Milan, 1934.

Marx, Karl and Friedrich Engels. "Carteggio da e per l'Italia (1871–1895)." *Movimento Operaio* 1, no. 1 (October 1949), no. 2 (November 1949); vol. 2, nos. 3–4 (December 1949–January 1950).

Massari, Giuseppe. *La vita ed il regno di Vittorio Emanuele II*. New ed. Milan, 1896.

Maturi, W. "Un buon europeo: Emilio Visconti Venosta." *La Nuova Europa* 2, no. 34 (1945).

———. "Costantino Nigra secondo il carteggio col Cavour." *Il Risorgimento Italiano* 22 (1929).

———. Preface to Bonghi, *Stato e Chiesa*, vol. 1 (= vol. 12 in *Opere*).

———. "Ruggero Bonghi e i problemi di politica estera." *Belfagor* 1 (July 1946).

Mayor des Planches, E. "Re Vittorio Emanuele II alla vigilia della guerra del Settanta." *Nuova Antologia* 289 (16 April 1920).

Mazzei, V. *Il socialismo nazionale di Carlo Pisacane*. Rome, 1943.

Mazzini, Giuseppe. *Scritti editi ed inediti*. National Edition: Imola, 1906–1943.

Mazzoleni, Angelo. *L'XI Legislatura: Memorie di un defunto*. Milan, 1875.

Meine, K. *England und Deutschland in der Zeit des Überganges vom Manchestertum zum Imperialismus, 1871 bis 1876*. Berlin. 1937.

Meinecke, F. *Cosmopolitismo e Stato nazionale*. Italian translation: Perugia-Venice, 1930.

———. "Johann Gustav Droysen: Sein Briefwechsel und seine Geschichtsschreibung." *Historische Zeitschrift* 141 (1929).

Metternich, Klemens von. *Mémoires*. Paris, 1880–1884 (Italian translation: Turin, 1943).

Meyer, A. O. *Bismarck*. Stuttgart, 1949.

La Mezzadria negli scritti dei Georgofili (1833–1872). Florence, 1934.

Michelet, Jules. *La France devant l'Europe*. Florence, 1871.

Mickiewicz, A. *Gli Slavi*. Turin, 1947.

Minghetti, Marco. *Carteggio tra M. Minghetti e G. Pasolini*. Turin, 1924–1930.

———. *Della economia pubblica e delle sue attinenze colla morale e col diritto*. 2d ed. Florence, 1881.

———. *Discorsi Parlamentari di Marco Minghetti*. Rome, 1888–1890.

———. *La legislazione sociale*. Milan, 1882.

———. *Lettere fra la regina Margherita e Marco Minghetti*. Edited by L. Lipparini. Milan, 1947.

———. *Ricordi*. 2d ed. Turin, 1888–1890.

———. *Stato e Chiesa*. Milan, 1878.

Mommsen, Theodor. *Agli italiani*. Florence, 1870.

Monod, G. *Jules Michelet*. Paris, 1905.

Montaldini, G. *Uno sguardo al passato, al presente, e all'avvenire dell'Europa*. Turin, 1872.

Monti, A. *Il conte Luigi Torelli, 1810–1887*. Milan, 1931.

———. *Vittorio Emanuele II*. Milan, 1941.

Morandi, C. *L'idea dell'unità politica d'Europa nel XIX e XX secolo*. Milan, 1948.

———. *La sinistra al potere*. Florence, 1944.

Moscati, R. *La diplomazia europea e il problema italiano nel 1848*. Florence, 1947.

Moüy, Charles de. *Souvenirs et causeries d'un diplomate*. Paris, 1909.

Namier, L. B. "1848: The Revolution of the Intellectuals." *Proceedings of the British Academy* 30 (1944).

Natale, G. *Giolitti e gli Italiani.* Milan, 1949.

Naujoks, E. *Die katholische Arbeiterbewegung und der Sozialismus in den ersten Jahren des Bismarckschen Reiches* (Giessen dissertation). *Neuen Deutschen Forschungen* 228. Berlin, 1939.

Negro, S. *Seconda Roma, 1850–1870.* Milan, 1943.

Nettlau, M. *Bakunin e l'Internazionale in Italia dal 1864 al 1872.* Geneva, 1928.

Nicolajevski, B. See Maenchen-Helfen, O.

Nigra, Costantino. Introduction to *Le comte de Cavour et la comtesse de Circourt: Lettres inédites* . . . Turin-Rome, 1894.

———. *Poesie originali e tradotte* . Edited by A. d'Ancona. Florence, 1914.

Nolde, B. *L'Alleanza franco-russa.* Italian translation: Milan, 1940.

Novikov, Yakov. *La missione dell'Italia.* Milan, 1902.

Omodeo, A. "Il conte di Cavour e la questione romana." *La Nuova Italia* 1, no. 10 (20 October 1930).

———. *La cultura francese nell'età della Restaurazione.* Milan, 1946.

———. *L'opera politica del Conte di Cavour.* 2d ed. Florence, 1941.

———. "Primato francese e iniziativa italiana." In Omodeo, *Figure e passioni del Risorgimento.* Palermo, 1932.

Oriani, Alfredo. *Fino a Dogali.* Bologna, 1912.

———. *La lotta politica in Italia.* 5th ed. Florence, 1921.

———. *Quartetto.* Milan, 1883.

Paladino, G. *Roma: Storia d'Italia dal 1866 al 1871 con particulare riguardo alla Questione Romana.* Milan, 1933.

Pasolini, G. See Marco Minghetti.

Perticone, G. *Gruppi e partiti politici nella vita pubblica italiana.* Modena, 1938.

Pesci, U. *I primi anni di Roma capitale, 1870–1878.* Florence, 1907.

Petrini, D. *Motivi del Risorgimento.* Rieti, 1929.

Petruccelli della Gattina, Ferdinando. *Storia d'Italia dal 1866 al 1880.* Naples, 1882.

Piccardi, Guido. "Un viaggetto a Roma uscente il novembre 1876." In *Le astensioni politiche dei 5 e 12 novembre 1876 celebrate in prosa ed in versi.* Florence, 1876.

Piola, Giuseppe. *La libertà della Chiesa.* Milan, 1874.

Pirri, P., S.J. *Pio IX e Vittorio Emanuele II dal loro carteggio privato.* Rome, 1944—.

Pisacane, Carlo. *Guerra combattuta in Italia negli anni 1848–1849.* Rome, 1906.

———. *Epistolario.* Edited by A. Romano. Milan, 1937.

———. *Saggio su la Rivoluzione.* 2 ed. Edited by G. Pintor. Turin, 1944.

Plebano, A. *Storia della finanza italiana.* Turin, 1899.

Poschinger, H. von, ed. *Aktenstücke zur Wirtschaftspolitik des Fürsten Bismarck.* Berlin, 1890–1891.

Prato, G. *Fatti e dottrine economiche alla vigilia del 1848: L'Associazione agraria subalpina e Camillo Cavour.* Turin, 1919.

Pribram, A. F. *Les traités politiques secrets de l'Autriche-Hongrie, 1879–1914.* French translation: Paris, 1923.

Quilici, N. *La borghesia italiana.* Milan, 1942.

Quintavalle, F. *La Conciliazione fra l'Italia ed il Papato nelle letter del p. Luigi Tosti e del sen. Gabrio Casati.* Milan, 1907.

Radowitz, J. M. von. *Aufzeichnungen und Erinnerungen.* Berlin-Leipzig, 1925.

Rattazzi, M. L. *Rattazzi et son temps.* Paris, 1881.

Reclus, M. *L'avènement de la 3 république.* Paris, 1930.

Renan, Ernest. *L'avenir de la science.* Paris, 1890.

———. *Correspondance, 1846–1871.* Paris, 1926.

———. *Correspondance, 1872–1892.* Paris, 1928.

———. *Mélanges religieux et historiques.* Paris, 1904.

———. *Oeuvres complètes.* Paris, 1947.

———. *La réforme intellectuelle et morale.* Paris, 1871.

Renan, Ernest and M. Berthelot. *Correspondance, 1847–1892.* Paris, 1929.

Rentsch, H. U. *Bismarck im Urteil der schweizerischen Presse, 1862–1898.* Basel, 1945.

Ricasoli, Bettino. *Carteggi di Bettino Ricasoli.* Edited by Nobili-Camerani. Bologna-Rome, 1939—.

———. *Lettere e documenti del barone Bettino Ricasoli.* Edited by Tabarrini-Gotti. Florence, 1887–1895.

Richelmy, C. "Il silenzio di Costantino Nigra." *Il Mondo,* 16 July 1949.

———. "La Triplice e gli ambasciatori italiani a Vienna." *Nuova Antologia* (November 1950).

Rinaldis, B. De. *Dei rapporti fra la Chiesa e lo Stato e del riordinamento dell'asse ecclesiastico a norma dell' art. 18 della Legge sulle guarentigie della S. Sede.* Naples, 1873.

Rohden, P. R. *Die klassische Diplomatie von Kaunitz bis Metternich.* 2d ed. Leipzig, 1939.

Romano, A. *Storia del movimento socialista in Italia.* Milan-Rome, 1954–1956.

Romano, P. (pseudonym of P. Alatri). *Silvio Spaventa.* Bari, 1942.

Rosi, M. *I Cairoli.* 2d ed. Bologna, 1929.

———. *L'Italia odierna.* Turin, 1918–1926.

Rosselli, N. *Carlo Pisacane nel Risorgimento italiano.* 2d ed. Genoa, 1936.

———. *Mazzini e Bakounine.* Turin, 1927.

———. *Saggi sul Risorgimento e altri scritti.* Turin, 1946.

Rossi, Alessandro. "Di una proposta di legge sul lavoro dei fanciulli e delle donne nelle fabbriche." *Nuova Antologia* 31 (1876).

Rothan, G. *L'Allemagne et l'Italie, 1870–71,* vol. 2, *L'Italie.* Paris, 1885.

Rousseau, Jean-Jacques. *Oeuvres complètes.* Paris, 1826.

Rubris, M. De. *Confidenze di Massimo d'Azeglio.* Milan, 1930.

Ruffini, F. *La giovinezza del conte di Cavour.* Turin, 1912.

———. *Scritti giuridici minori.* Milan, 1936.

———. *Ultimi studi sul Conte di Cavour.* Bari, 1936.

Russo, L. *Francesco De Sanctis e la cultura napoletana (1860–1885).* Venice, 1928.

Sachs, I. *L'Italie: Ses finances et son développement économique depuis l'unification du royaume, 1859–1884.* Paris, 1885.

Saint-Simon, Claude Henri de Rouvroy, comte de. *La riorganizzazione della società europea.* Italian translation: Rome, 1945.

Salata, F. "Il conte di Robilant." *Il Corriere della Sera,* 7 August 1926.

———. *Per la storia diplomatica della questione romana.* Milan, 1929.

Salomon, H. *L'ambassade de Richard de Metternich à Paris.* Paris, 1931.

Salvatorelli, L. *Pensiero e azione del Risorgimento.* 2d ed. Turin, 1944.

———. *Il pensiero politico italiano dal 1700 al 1870.* 3d ed. Turin, 1943.

———. *La Triplice Alleanza: Storia diplomatica, 1877–1912.* Milan, 1939.

Salvemini, Gaetano. *L'Europa nel secolo XIX.* Padua, 1925.

———. *Mazzini.* 4th ed. Florence, 1925.

———. "La politica estera della Destra (1871–1876)." *Rivista d'Italia* 27, no. 3 (1924) and 28, no. 1 (1925).

————. *La politica estera dell'Italia dal 1871 al 1915*. 2d ed. Florence, 1950.

Sanctis, F. De. *Scritti politici di Francesco De Sanctis*. Edited by Ferrarelli. Naples, 1889.

Sandonà, A. *L'irredentismo nelle lotte politiche e nelle contese diplomatiche italoaustriache*. Bologna, 1932.

Santangelo, P. E. *Massimo d'Azeglio politico e moralista*. Turin, 1937.

Scaduto, F. *Guarentigie pontificie e relazioni fra Stato e Chiesa*. Turin, 1889.

Sella, Quintino. *Discorso nel banchetto offertogli il 15 ottobre 1876 dagli elettori . . . di Cossato*. Rome, 1876.

————. *Discorsi Parlamentari di Quintino Sella*. Rome, 1887–1890.

————. *Epistolario inedito*. Turin, 1930.

Sella, P. *Quintino Sella nell'Agosto del 1870*. Milan, 1928.

Serra Gropelli, E. *Le cinque piaghe del Regno d'Italia*. Milan, 1870.

————. *Parrocchia e Diocesi: Piano di guerra contro la fazione episcopale*. Turin, 1864.

Sestan, E. *La Costituente di Francoforte (1848–1849)*. Florence, 1946.

Seton-Watson, R. W. *Die südslavische Frage im Habsburger Reiche*. German translation: Berlin, 1913.

Settembrini, Luigi. *Epistolario*. 2d ed. Naples, 1894.

Simone, G. De. *Del principio di nazionalità come fondamento delle nuove alleanze e dell'equilibrio europeo*. Naples, 1867.

Simpson, J. Y., ed. *The Saburov Memoirs; or, Bismarck and Russia*. Cambridge, 1929.

Sonnino, Sidney. *Discorsi Parlamentari di S. Sonnino*. Rome, 1925.

————. *Del governo rappresentativo in Italia*. Rome, 1872.

Sorel, G. "Germanesimo et storicismo di Ernesto Renan." *La Critica* 29 (1931).

Spaventa, Silvio. *Lettere politiche (1861–1893)*.

————. *La politica della Destra*. Edited by B. Croce. Bari, 1910.

Srbik, H. von. *Metternich*. Munich, 1925.

Steed, Wickham H. *Mes souvenirs, 1892–1914*. French translation: Paris, 1926.

Strauss, G. *La politique de Renan*. Paris, 1909.

Taine, Hippolyte. *Correspondance = Hippolyte Taine: Sa vie et sa correspondance*. Paris, 1906.

————. *Voyage en Italie*. 3d ed. Paris, 1876.

Tavallini, E. *La vita e i tempi di Giovanni Lanza*. Turin, 1887.

Taviani, P. E. *Problemi economici nei riformatori sociali del Risorgimento Italiano*. Genoa, 1940.

Ter Meulen, J. *Der Gedanke der Internationalen Organisation in seiner Entwicklung*. The Hague, 1917–1940.

Tocqueville, Alexis de [and Arthur de Gobineau]. *Correspondance entre Alexis de Tocqueville et Arthur de Gobineau, 1843–1859*. 2d ed. Paris, 1908.

Tommaseo, N. *Roma e l'Italia nel 1850 e nel 1870 e le nuove elezioni: Presagi di N. T. avverati, e perché più non si avverino*. Florence, 1870.

Tommasini, F. "Erinnerungen an Wien (1900–1912)." *Berliner Monatshefte* 19 (July 1941).

Toscanelli, Giuseppe. *Discorso alla Camera . . . 23 gennaio 1871 . . . contro il progetto de legge [sulle Guarentigie]*. Florence, 1871.

Toscano, M. "L'Italia e la prima conferenza per la pace dell'Aja del 1899." *La Comunità Internazionale* 4 (1949).

Treitschke, H. von. *Briefe*. Leipzig, 1920.

―――. "Libera Chiesa in libero Stato." *Preussische Jahrbücher* 36 (1875).

―――. *La Politica.* Italian translation: Bari, 1918.

Treves, R. *La dottrina sansimoniana nel pensiero italiano del Risorgimento.* Turin, 1931.

Turiello, P. *Governo e governati in Italia.* Bologna, 1882; 2d ed., 1890.

Vaccalluzzo, N. *Massimo d'Azeglio.* 2d ed. Rome, 1930.

Valsecchi, F. "Il 1859 in Germania: idee e problemi." *Archivio Storico Italiano* 93, no. 1 (1935).

―――. "Il 1859 in Germania: la stampa e i partiti." *Studi Germanici* 1 (1935).

―――. "La politica di Cavour e la Prussia nel 1859." *Archivio Storico Italiano* 94, no. 1 (1936).

―――. *Il Risorgimento e l'Europa: L'Alleanza di Crimea.* Milan, 1948.

Vecchi di Val Cismon, C. M. De. "Costantino Nigra: Un capitolo inedito dei *Ricordi diplomatici.*" *Nuova Antologia* (16 January 1934).

―――. "L'episodio di Ems nel testo di C. Nigra." *Nuova Antologia* (1 September 1934).

―――. "Lo scioglimento della "Pro Patria' di Trento nel carteggio Crispi-Nigra." *Rassegna Storica del Risorgimento* 21 (1934).

Verax. *Alfonso La Marmora: Commemorazione.* Florence, 1879.

Verdi, Giuseppe. *Carteggi Verdiani.* Rome, 1935–1947.

Vignoli, Tito. *Delle condizioni morali e civili d'Italia.* Milan, 1876.

Vigo, P. *Annali d'Italia: Storia degli ultimi trent'anni del secolo XIX.* Milan, 1908–1915.

Villetard, E. *Histoire de l'Internationale.* Paris, 1872.

Visconti Venosta, G. *Ricordi di gioventù.* Milan, 1904.

Volpe, G. *Italia moderna.* Vol. 1: *1815–1915* (Milan, 1943); vol. 2: *1898–1910* (Florence, 1949).

Voltaire. *Oeuvres complètes,* vol. 40. Paris, 1911.

Vorlaender, K. *Karl Marx* . Italian translation: Rome, 1946.

Vossler, O. *L'idea di nazione dal Rousseau al Ranke.* Italian translation: Florence, 1949.

Weill, G. *Histoire de l'enseignement secondaire en France (1802–1920).* Paris, 1921.

White Mario, J. *Agostino Bertani e i suoi tempi.* Florence, 1888.

Windelband, W. *Bismarck und die europäischen Grossmächte, 1879–1885.* Essen, 1940.

Zanichelli, Domenico. *Cavour.* Florence, 1926.

―――. *Monarchia e Papato in Italia.* Bologna, 1889.

―――. *Studi politici e storici.* Bologna, 1893.

Zerbi, Rocco. De. *Difendetevi!* Naples, 1881.

INDEX OF NAMES

About the Author

FEDERICO CHABOD was Professor of History at the University of Rome and Director of the Italian Institute for Historical Studies in Naples. WILLIAM McCUAIG teaches early modern European history at the University of Toronto and is the author of *Carlo Sigonio: The Changing World of the Late Renaissance* (Princeton).